KU-207-987

PRAISE FROM OUR READERS

Mastering Access 97

"**I read this book from cover to cover and found each page loaded with very practical information and explicit examples.** I commend the authors for their ability to communicate otherwise very technical detail in understandable 'user friendly' language. I highly recommend this book."
Jim Shannon, Montana

Mastering FrontPage 98

"**Best of the 9 FrontPage 98 books I own.** Sybex does it again! I have been reading computer books for the last 10 years and Sybex has been a great publisher—putting out excellent books. After reading 3/4 of the book so far, I know that the publisher and the authors take pride in their product. It's a wonderful book!"
Mike Perry, New Jersey

"**This is THE book for mastering FrontPage 98!** I skimmed through 4 other books before deciding to buy this one. Every other book seemed like a larger version of the weak documentation that comes with the software. This book provided the insight on advanced subjects necessary for administering a web. A must buy for FrontPage users."
Richard Hartsell, Utah

Mastering Windows 98

"**The first book I've read that does what it says it will do!** I learned more about Windows 98 in the first one hundred pages of this book than in all of the previous books I had read. My copy lies, dog-eared, beside my computer as a constantly ready source of easy to understand information. It really does show you how to Master Windows 98."
Steven Dean, Arizona

SYBEX
www.sybex.com

MASTERING

ACCESS 2000

PREMIUM EDITION

MASTERING™
ACCESS 2000
PREMIUM EDITION

Alan Simpson
Celeste Robinson

SYBEX®

San Francisco • Paris • Düsseldorf • Soest • London

Associate Publisher: Amy Romanoff
Contracts and Licensing Manager: Kristine
O'Callaghan
Developmental Editor: Melanie Spiller
Editor: Raquel Baker
Technical Editor: Dana Jones
Book Designers: Patrick Dintino, Catalin Dulfu
Graphic Illustrator: Tony Jonick
Electronic Publishing Specialists: Robin Kibby, Nila
Nichols
Project Team Leader: Leslie Higbee
Proofreaders: Susan Berge, Richard Ganis
Indexer: Ted Laux
Companion CD: Ginger Warner
Cover Designer: Design Site
Cover Illustrator: Jack D. Myers

Library of Congress Card Number: 99-62991
ISBN: 0-7821-2326-0

Manufactured in the United States of America

10 9 8 7 6 5 4 3 2 1

ACKNOWLEDGMENTS

This book was a massive undertaking. Many thanks to everyone on the team who stuck with it despite the brutal schedule.

Many thanks to Sybex's editorial and production teams for their much-appreciated support. Developmental Editor Melanie Spiller got us started on the right foot. Editor Raquel Baker kept things moving smoothly by managing the endless details skillfully. We also want to extend our gratitude to Electronic Publishing Specialist Nila Nichols, Production Team Leader Leslie Higbee, Proofreaders Susan Berge and Richard Ganis, Indexer Ted Laux, and to the many others on the Sybex team who made this book possible. A huge amount of thanks go to Technical Editor Dana Jones for her meticulous review of the book's new sections.

We're tremendously grateful to the Microsoft support team who kept us supplied with the latest test software as we raced to meet our deadlines.

And last, but not least, a million thanks to our families—Ashley, Susan, and Alec Simpson; and Ray, Ray, CoCo, D.D., Tal, and Zoe Robinson—for their patience and support through so many long bouts of frenzied book writing.

CONTENTS AT A GLANCE

TABLE OF CONTENTS

PART II • CREATING A DATABASE PROJECT

PART III • DATABASE TUNING AND ADMINISTRATION

PART IV • BUILDING A CUSTOM APPLICATION

PART V • REFINING A CUSTOM APPLICATION

PART VI • MACRO PROGRAMMING

INTRODUCTION

Welcome to *Mastering Access 2000 Premium Edition*, the book for new and intermediate Microsoft Access users and for aspiring application developers. Like Access, this book is geared toward experienced Windows users. You don't need to be a Windows genius to use Access, but if you're just making the transition from DOS to Windows, or just getting started with computers, you'll surely want to get your Windows "basic skills" down pat before you start using Access. (Our book, *Alan Simpson's Easy Guide to Windows 95*, can help you do that. It's also published by Sybex.)

Just in case you're wondering, we used Windows 95 exclusively while writing this book; however, Access 2000 also runs under Windows 98 and Windows NT, and we've sprinkled a few notes about Windows NT throughout the text. Readers who are using Windows NT should have little trouble following our instructions, although you may encounter some minor differences along the way.

New to Database Management?

You don't need to know anything about database management or programming to use this book. We start at square one in Chapter 1. As for programming—don't worry about it. Programming is definitely in the "not required" category when it comes to using Microsoft Access.

New to Access 2000 but an Old Hand at Access?

If you're an old hand at using Microsoft Access but are trying (or planning to try) Access 2000 for the first time, you can find out what's new by flipping to the "What's New in the Access Zoo?" sidebars at the end of most chapters. These brief sections highlight important new features that relate to the chapter you've selected.

If you have old Access databases that you'd like to use with Access 2000, be sure to check Appendix A of this book for an introduction to points you must consider *before* removing your old version of Access and for information about converting your existing databases.

Finally, you can view online details of what's new. After installing Access, simply use the Office Assistant to search for help with *What's New* and then explore the many subtopics that appear. Chapter 1 explains how to use the Access online help.

A Focus on Creating Applications

Microsoft Access is a huge product, and nearly every nook and cranny of it is already documented in the online help. In this book, rather than wasting paper repeating all of that information, we've opted to focus on two things: (1) general day-to-day use of Microsoft Access and (2) using Access to create custom Windows applications. To meet those goals, we've organized the book as follows:

Part I: An Overview of Access   This part is for experienced Windows users who are new to database management and/or Access. Here we cover basic skills and concepts and offer a hands-on guided tour.

Part II: Creating a Database   This second part of the book covers all of the basic Access objects you'll create to manage your data—tables, queries, forms, reports—and data access pages for publishing your data to the Web. The information presented here is vital to casual users, to more ambitious application developers, and to aspiring developers.

Part III: Database Tuning and Administration   Here you'll learn how to personalize Access, speed up databases for optimal performance, administer your databases and use database replication, and take advantage of networking and security features.

Part IV: Building a Custom Application   Most Access users eventually realize that, with just a little more effort, they can turn their databases into easy-to-use stand-alone Windows applications. Part IV of this book is all about that topic—creating applications.

Part V: Refining a Custom Application   We wrote this part of the book for application developers who aspire to learn Visual Basic programming and other more advanced application topics.

Part VI: Macro Programming   This part of the book has been excerpted from Susann Novalis' *Access 97 Macro & VBA Handbook* (Sybex, 1997). It goes into more detail than the basic macro information presented in Part IV, and teaches you advanced macro techniques that let you automate a database without having to learn about VBA programming.

Part VII: Appendices   You can't unleash the power of Access until you install the program. Part VII covers installation, CD-ROM information, and an in-depth discussion of one of the applications provided on the CD-ROM.

Features of This Book

This book offers several features that will help you learn Access and find the information you need, when you need it. Here are some examples:

Notes, Tips, and Warnings   These provide good ideas, shortcuts, references to related topics, and cautions that point out when you might want to think twice before clicking that mouse!

Sidebars   Sprinkled throughout the book, sidebars provide useful tidbits that will help you work smarter with Microsoft Access or Windows.

What's New in the Access Zoo?   Designed to help people upgrading to Access 2000, these end-of-chapter sections highlight new features discussed in the chapter.

Access in an Evening   Chapter 3 is a hands-on guided tour of Access, designed to give you a feel for working with the program in just a few short lessons.

About Access, Office, Windows, and the Internet   Chapter 4 highlights common features in Access, Office, and Windows so you can learn Access more quickly and take advantage of integration between Access and other programs in Microsoft Office. Learn to use the Hyperlink feature to link Access databases to the Web!

A Complete Macro Programming Guide in Part VI   The chapters in Part VI that are excerpted from Susann Novalis' *Access 97 Macro & VBA Handbook* (Sybex, 1997) are a complete guide to automating an Access database using macros.

CD-ROM   The CD-ROM in the back of this book contains demos of Access applications that you can purchase separately, as well as shareware, freeware, sample databases, and more. See Appendix B for more information.

Conventions Used in This Book

We use the standard terminology that just about everyone else uses to discuss Access. However, we do use a shortcut method to display a series of commands and/or options you follow to get a particular job done. We present the commands in the order you'll select them, separated with a ➤ symbol.

For example, the instruction Choose Help ➤ About Microsoft Access means "Choose *About Microsoft Access* from the *Help* menu" (using either the keyboard or the mouse). And the instruction Choose Start ➤ Programs ➤ Microsoft Access means "Click the *Start* button on the Windows Taskbar, choose the *Programs* option from the Start menu, and then choose the *Microsoft Access* option from the menu that appears" (again, using either the keyboard or the mouse). This approach lets you see, at a glance, the exact sequence of commands you must choose to get a job done. It also helps you remember command sequences that you use often.

We also use toolbar buttons and other symbols in the margin. The toolbars provide a convenient way to perform many common Access operations with a simple mouse click. For example, clicking the Print button shown at left prints the currently highlighted table, query, form, macro, or module. You'll often see a button in the margin the first time it's called for within a chapter.

Thank You

Our sincerest thanks go to you for choosing this book. We hope it serves you well. As usual, we welcome comments, criticism, and suggestions. You can reach us at:

Alan Simpson

Celeste Robinson

c/o Sybex, Inc.

1151 Marina Village Parkway

Alameda, CA 94501

Sybex Technical Support

If you have questions or comments about this book (or other Sybex books) you can also contact Sybex directly.

For the Fastest Reply

E-mail us or visit the Sybex Web site! You can contact Sybex through the Web by visiting http://www.sybex.com and clicking Support. You may find the answer you're looking for on this site in the FAQ (Frequently Asked Questions) file.

When you reach the support page, click support@sybex.com to send Sybex an e-mail. You can also e-mail Sybex directly at support@sybex.com.

Make sure you include the following information in your e-mail:

Name   The complete title of the book in question. For this book, it is *Mastering Access 2000 Premium Edition*.

ISBN number   The ISBN that appears on the bottom-right corner of the back cover of the book. This number looks like this:

0-7821-2326-0

Printing   The printing of the book. You can find this near the front of the book at the bottom of the copyright page. You should see a line of numbers as in the following:

10 9 8 7 6 5 4 3 2 1

Tell us what the lowest number is in the line of numbers. This is the printing number of the book. The example here indicates that the book is the first printing.

 NOTE   The ISBN number and printing are very important for Technical Support because it indicates the edition and reprint that you have in your hands. Many changes occur between printings. Don't forget to include this information!

Page number   Include the page number where you have a question.

For a Fast Reply

Call Sybex Technical Support and leave a message. Sybex guarantees that they will call you back within 24 hours, excluding weekends and holidays.

Technical Support can be reached at (510) 523-8233 ext. 563.

After you dial the extension, press 1 to leave a message. Sybex will call you back within 24 hours. Make sure you leave a phone number where you can be reached!

Other Ways To Reach Sybex

The slowest way to contact Sybex is through the mail. You can write Sybex a small note and send it to the following address:

SYBEX, Inc.

Attention: Technical Support

1151 Marina Village Parkway

Alameda, CA 94501

Again, it's important that you include all the following information to expedite a reply:

Name   The complete title of the book in question.

ISBN number   The ISBN that appears on the bottom-right corner of the back cover of the book and looks like this:

0-7821-2326-0

Printing   The printing of the book. You can find this near the front of the book at the bottom of the copyright page. You should see a line of numbers as in the following:

10 9 8 7 6 5 4 3 2 1

Tell us what the lowest number is in the line of numbers. This is the printing number of the book. The example here indicates that the book is the first printing.

 NOTE   The ISBN number and printing are very important for Technical Support because it indicates the edition and reprint that you have in your hands. Many changes occur between printings. Don't forget to include this information!

Page number   Include the page number where you have a question.

No matter how you contact Sybex, Technical Support will try to answer your question quickly and accurately.

PART I

An Overview of Access

LEARN TO:

- *Get around in Access*

- *Use Access in one short evening*

- *Open databases and projects*

- *Make the most of Access, Office, and Windows together*

CHAPTER 1

Getting Started and Getting Around

Microsoft Access is a database management system, or DBMS. As the name implies, a DBMS helps you to manage data that's stored in a computer database. The data you manage can be virtually anything, including:

- Names and addresses
- Business contacts, customers, and sales prospects
- Employee and personnel information
- Inventory
- Invoices, payments, and bookkeeping
- Libraries and collections
- Schedules, reservations, and projects

You may already know what kinds of data you plan to manage with Access, and you may already be familiar with other database programs and the basic concepts of database management. If not, you'll learn more about databases in the next chapter. But whether you're a seasoned veteran eager to start working in Access or a database newcomer wondering where to begin, the first step is to learn how to start Access and use its extensive Help system to coach you along as you work.

Access Isn't Just for Techies!

Don't worry if you know nothing about databases and don't want to become an expert on the topic. Access wizards can guide you through almost any step, and they can create databases for you automatically. So even if you need to set up something as complex as a system for managing orders, inventory, or assets—or something as simple as a list of contacts and birthdays—Access wizards can take care of the grunt work while you focus on getting useful information from your computer. You'll have a chance to try wizards during the hands-on tour in Chapter 3 and in many other chapters of this book.

If you're a technical type, never fear! Access has more than enough to make you happy. It's a full-featured application development system that includes the Visual Basic programming language and other tools for setting up sophisticated applications for yourself and your customers. You'll learn more about these features in Parts Four and Five.

Starting Access

To start Microsoft Access:

1. Start Windows in the usual manner.

 TIP If you're using Microsoft Office and have added Access to the Microsoft Office Shortcut Bar, you can start Access by clicking the appropriate button on the Office Shortcut Bar (see Chapter 4). Or if you've set up a shortcut icon for Access on the Windows Desktop, you can double-click that icon to start Access. Then skip to step 3 below.

2. Click the Start button on the Windows Taskbar and then choose Programs ➢ Microsoft Access.

After a short delay, you'll see the Microsoft Access startup dialog box shown in Figure 1.1. (If you've just installed Access, the list box below the Open an Existing File option is empty.)

FIGURE 1.1

The Microsoft Access startup dialog box. From here you can create a new database, a data access page, or a project. You can also open an existing file, or click Cancel to go to the main Access window.

Click here and then OK to create a new, blank database.

Click here and then OK to create a new database, page, or project.

Click this option to open an existing database. Then click a recently used database name or click More Files to search for and open a database. Finally, click OK.

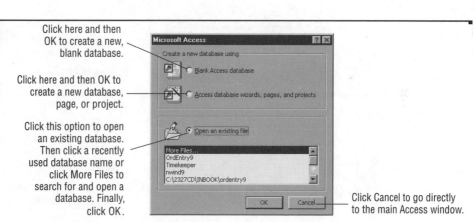

Click Cancel to go directly to the main Access window.

3. Do any of the following:

- **To create a new blank database**, choose Blank Access Database and then click OK.

- **To use the Database Wizard to create a new database**, choose Access Database Wizards, Pages, and Projects. Then click OK to open the New dialog box. (There's more about creating new databases in Chapter 5.)

- **To create a data access page or a project**, follow the preceding instructions for creating a new database. Then refer to Chapter 14 for details on working with data access pages, or Chapter 30 for projects. (You'll learn more about the difference between databases and projects later in this chapter.)

- **To open an existing database or project**, choose Open an Existing File. If a list of database names appears, choose a recently used database name in the list or click More Files so you can look for the database you want to use. Click OK. See "Opening an Existing Database or Project" later in this chapter for more details.

- **To go to the main Microsoft Access window** (shown in Figure 1.2) without creating or opening a database, click the Cancel button or press Esc.

FIGURE 1.2

The main Microsoft Access window that appears when you click Cancel in the startup dialog box and anytime you close an Access database. You'll also see this window if Access is set up to bypass the startup dialog box.

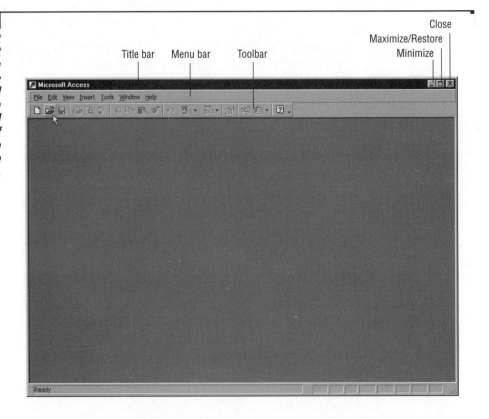

 NOTE If Access is customized to bypass the startup dialog box, you'll be taken to the main Access window as soon as you finish step 2, above. We explain how to bypass the startup dialog box later in this chapter.

Advanced users can learn about optional command-line startup switches for Access in Chapter 16 and by searching the Access Help index for *Startup Options, Command-Line Options*. We'll explain how to use Access Help in the "Getting Help" section, later in this chapter.

Organizing the Start ➤ Programs Menu Items

If your Start ➤ Programs menu has too many entries or isn't organized the way you like, you can rearrange it easily. Suppose you want to move Microsoft Access and other Microsoft Office programs from the main Start ➤ Programs menu into a Microsoft Office submenu that looks something like the image below.

All it takes is a little knowledge of Windows Explorer and these basic steps:

1. Right-click the Start button on the Taskbar and choose Explore.

2. Click the Programs folder in the left pane of the Exploring window. (It's below the Start Menu folder.) The right pane will show the contents of the Programs folder.

3. Right-click your mouse on an empty part of the right pane of the Exploring window and choose New ➤ Folder from the shortcut menu.

4. Type a new folder name, such as Microsoft Office, and press Enter.

Continued

CONTINUED

5. Click the + sign next to the Programs folder in the left pane; then use the vertical scroll bar to scroll the left pane until you can see the new folder you created and named in steps 3 and 4.

6. Drag the program (or folder) you want to move from the right pane to your new folder in the left pane.

7. Repeat step 6 as needed and then click the Close button in the Exploring window.

For more details on customizing the Start menu, choose Start ➢ Help and click the Index tab. Then type **Start Menu, Reorganizing** and press Enter. To learn more about Windows Explorer, look up topics below *Windows Explorer* on the Index tab in Help.

Creating a Desktop Shortcut

You can double-click a shortcut icon on the Windows Desktop to launch a program or open a file. To quickly add an icon that will launch the Access program from the Desktop, minimize or close any open windows and then follow these steps:

1. Use Windows Explorer to open the folder that contains Microsoft Access. For example, right-click the Start button on the Windows Taskbar, choose Explore, and navigate to the `Program Files\Microsoft Office\Office` folder. (It's usually on drive C.)

2. On the right side of the Explorer window, locate the Msaccess program icon. It will appear as a key next to the program name, `msaccess.exe`.

3. Hold down the right mouse button while you drag the icon to the Windows Desktop. Release the mouse button.

4. Choose Create Shortcut(s) Here from the shortcut menu.

In the future, you can start Access by double-clicking the Shortcut to Msaccess.exe icon on your Desktop. To discover other ways to create shortcuts for Access, look up the *Shortcuts* topics in the Access Help index or the Windows Help index. (To get Windows Help, click the Start button on the Taskbar and choose Help.)

Opening an Existing Database or Project

In word processing programs, you work with documents. In spreadsheet programs, you work with worksheets. In database management systems, such as Access, you work with *databases*. Chances are you'll want to create your own database. But you can get some practice now by exploring one of the sample databases that comes with Access.

 NOTE   In Access, you can also work with *projects* stored in .adp files. A project holds tools like forms and reports for working with SQL Server data. See "And What About Projects?" later in this chapter for more information on Access projects and how they are different from Access databases.

To open a database or a project:

1. Do one of the following, depending on whether you're starting from the startup dialog box, from the main Microsoft Access window, or from the Windows Desktop:

   - **From the startup dialog box** (refer to Figure 1.1), choose Open an Existing File. (This is the default choice.) Then if the name of the database or project you want to open is shown on the list, double-click that name and you're done. If the name isn't on the list, double-click More Files and continue with step 2. (If no list appears, click OK and continue with step 2.)

 TIP   As usual in Windows, you can choose an option from a list by clicking it and then clicking OK (or whatever button carries out the default command), or by clicking the option and pressing Enter. Or for quicker selection, try double-clicking the option you want.

    - **From the main Microsoft Access window** (refer to Figure 1.2), choose File ➢ Open, click the Open toolbar button (shown at left), or press Ctrl+O. You'll see an Open dialog box, similar to the example shown in Figure 1.3.

 TIP   If you recently used the file you want to work with, try this tip to open it quickly: Choose File from the menu bar, and look for the file name near the bottom of the File menu (just above the Exit option). Then click its name or type the number shown next to the name.

FIGURE 1.3

The Open dialog box.

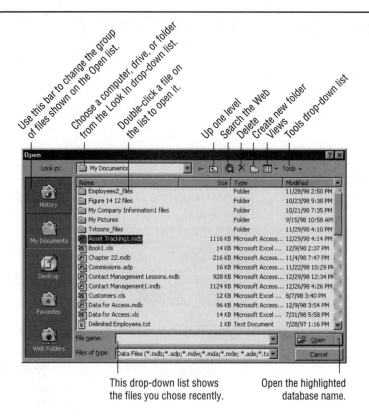

This drop-down list shows the files you chose recently.

Open the highlighted database name.

- **From the Windows Desktop**, locate the desired database or project using standard techniques in Windows Explorer, My Computer, or Network Neighborhood. When you find the file you want to use, double-click its name or icon (see the sample icon, shown at left). Or if you've used the file recently, click the Start button on the Windows Taskbar, choose Documents, and then click the name of your database in the list that appears. Access will start, and the database or project will open. You're done, so you can skip steps 2 through 4.

2. Use any of these methods to find the database or project you want to open:

- **To see the files you opened most recently**, click the button for History on the left side of the Open window.

- **To show the files in My Documents or on the Desktop** without having to navigate using the Look In drop-down list, click the My Documents or Desktop button.

An Overview of Access

- **To open an object shown in the list below Look In**, double-click the appropriate object icon or name.
- **To choose the computer, drive, or folder where the database is stored**, click the Look In drop-down list button and then click the appropriate item.
- **To open the folder that's just above the currently selected folder**, click the Up One Level button in the Open dialog box, or click anywhere in the list below Look In and then press Backspace.

 TIP To learn the purpose of any toolbar button in a window or dialog box, move your mouse pointer to that button and look for the ScreenTip near the mouse pointer. See "Using the Toolbars and Menu Bar" later in this chapter for more information.

- **To display a list of your favorite databases and folders**, click the Favorites toolbar button. The list below Look In will then show your favorite folders and databases only.
- **To add an item to your Favorites list**, make sure the appropriate item appears in the Look In text box or click an item name in the list below Look In. Then choose Add to Favorites from the Tools drop-down list.
- **To manually enter a drive, directory, and/or file name**, type the appropriate information into the File Name text box in the lower part of the Open dialog box or choose an item from the File Name drop-down list.
- **To change the appearance of the list below Look In**, click the Views button and select List, Details, Properties, or Preview.
- **To search for a database or project**, click the Tools drop-down list and select Find to open a dialog box you can use for searching.

 TIP You can delete, rename, and do other handy operations on items from the Open dialog box. To begin, right-click an item in the list below Look In. Then choose an option from the shortcut menu.

3. If you're choosing the database or project from the list below Look In, make sure its name is highlighted on the list. (Click the name if necessary.)

4. Click the Open button. (As a shortcut for steps 3 and 4, you can double-click a filename in the list below Look In.)

The database or project will open, and you'll see the database window or a form that either describes the database or lets you work with it.

TIP If the database or project you're planning to open usually displays a form, but you'd prefer to bypass that form and go directly to the database window, hold down the Shift key while you open the file. This action bypasses the form and any options that are set in the Startup dialog box (Tools ➤ Startup).

As Figure 1.3 shows, the Open dialog box contains many buttons and special features that we haven't mentioned here. If you've played with other Open dialog boxes in Microsoft Office or you've spent some time with Windows Explorer, you'll learn the fine points quickly. For more guidance, click the ? button in the upper-right corner of the Open dialog box and then click the part of the dialog box you're curious about. Feel free to experiment!

Opening the Sample Northwind Database

To use the Northwind database that comes with Access, you have to make sure it gets installed. By default, it gets installed on first use, which means the first time you try to use it, it will be copied from your Office CD to your computer. For this to work, you have to select Northwind.mdb from the File menu before it gets overwritten by other databases you open after you first install Access.

If you don't find Northwind.mdb on the bottom of your File menu, run Setup for Office again, and click Add or Remove Programs. In the window that lets you select the programs to install, click the Expand button for Microsoft Access for Windows. Then expand Sample Databases and change the setting for Northwind Database from Installed on First Use to Run from My Computer. Then click Update Now. Once the Northwind database is installed, you can open it this way:

1. Choose Open an Existing File from the Microsoft Access startup dialog box. Then highlight More Files (if it's available) and click OK.

   Or

   Choose File ➤ Open from the main Microsoft Access window.

2. Using the Look In drop-down list, navigate to the folder C:\Program Files\Microsoft Office\Office\Samples.

3. Double-click Northwind.mdb in the list below Look In.

4. Click OK to go to the database window if the Welcome form appears.

Maximizing Your On-Screen Real Estate

The Windows Taskbar can take up valuable on-screen real estate that you might prefer to make available to your database objects. Fortunately, hiding the Taskbar temporarily and bringing it into view only when you need to is easy. (Most screen shots in this book were taken with the Taskbar hidden.)

To hide the Taskbar temporarily, right-click any empty spot on the Taskbar, choose Properties, make sure the Always On Top and Auto Hide options in the Taskbar Properties dialog box are checked, and then click OK. In the future, the Taskbar will remain hidden until you move your mouse pointer to the edge of the screen where the Taskbar was lurking the last time you used it. (If you don't remember where the Taskbar was, move the mouse pointer to the bottom, top, left, and right edges of the screen until it pops into view.)

To display the Taskbar permanently again, return to the Taskbar Properties dialog box and deselect (clear) the Auto Hide option. (It's usually best to leave Always On Top checked.) Then click OK.

The *objects* (a term for database components, such as tables and forms) that are part of the Northwind database will appear in the *database window* (see Figure 1.4). You can move, size, maximize, minimize, and restore the database window using all the standard Windows techniques.

What Is a Database, Anyway?

A widely accepted definition of a database is "a collection of data related to a particular topic or purpose." If that sounds a bit stuffy, just think of a database as a general-purpose container for storing and managing information. The information can be anything from names and addresses to details about your business's inventory and orders.

There's more to a database than data. A database can also contain *objects* to help you manage that data, such as forms (for entering and editing data) and reports (for printing data in the format you want). All told, a database can contain any combination of the following types of objects:

Table   Tables are the fundamental structures in an Access database because they store the data you'll be managing (see Chapter 6). Within a table, data is organized into fields (columns) and records (rows). When you open a table, it is shown in a window called a *datasheet view*.

FIGURE 1.4

*The Northwind :
Database window with
Tables selected under
Objects.*

1. Under Objects, click the type of object you want to work with.

Database window

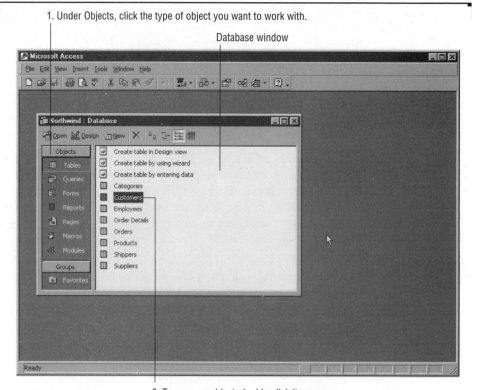

2. To open an object, double-click its name.

Query A query is a tool for asking questions about data in your tables and for performing actions on data (see Chapter 10). Queries can answer questions, such as: How many customers live in Connecticut, and what are their names and phone numbers? You can use queries to combine or join data from many separate but related tables. A query can, for example, join Customers, Orders, Order Details, and Products tables to answer the questions: Who ordered left-handed farkledorfers? and What is the value of those orders? Queries can also help you change, delete, or add large amounts of data in one fell swoop. Finally, you can use queries as the basis for your forms and reports.

Form Forms let you display and enter data in a convenient format that resembles fill-in-the-blank forms (see Chapters 11 and 13). Your forms can be plain and simple or quite elaborate with graphics, lines, and automatic lookup features that make data entry quick and easy. Forms can even include other forms (called *subforms*) that let you enter data into several tables at once.

Report   Reports let you print or preview data in a useful format (see Chapters 12 and 13). Like forms, reports can be plain or fancy. Examples include mailing labels, lists, envelopes, form letters, and invoices. Reports also can present query results in an easy-to-understand format. For instance, you can print sales by customer, receivables aging, and other management information for use in making business decisions.

Page   Data access pages are HTML files that display data in a format that can be browsed on the Web. Unlike other kinds of database objects, data access pages are stored in their own files instead of in an Access database or project file.

Macro   A macro is a set of instructions that automates a task you need to do often (see Chapter 21). When you run a macro, Access carries out the actions in the macro in the order in which the actions are listed. Without writing a single line of program code, you can define macros to automatically open forms, print mailing labels, process orders, and more. Macros enable you to assemble a collection of tables, queries, forms, and reports into turnkey *applications* that anyone can use, even if they know little or nothing about Access itself.

Module   Like macros, modules allow you to automate and customize Access (see Part Five). However, unlike macros, modules give you more precise control over the actions taken, and they require you to have Visual Basic programming expertise. You may never need to use modules, so don't worry if you're not a programmer.

During the hands-on lessons in Chapter 3, you'll have a chance to create a database complete with tables, forms, reports, a data access page, queries, and even a simple form module. You'll be astounded at how quickly you can do this job when you let the wizards do all the tough stuff for you.

And What about Projects?

An Access *project* is a set of database objects that can be used to work with data stored in tables on an SQL server. A project doesn't hold any tables or queries of its own. The only kind of Access objects it includes are forms, reports, macros, modules, and data access pages. A project can also include these kinds of SQL Server objects: views, database diagrams, and stored procedures.

A project can work with data stored on these servers:

- SQL Server 6.5
- SQL Server 7
- The Integrated Store that comes with Access

If you'd like to find out more about working with projects, take a look at Chapter 30.

Working in the Database Window

The database window is one of your main tools for using Access. When exploring the sample Northwind database and when creating databases or projects of your own, you'll use this simple three-step process to work with the objects listed in the database window:

1. Choose the *type* of object you want to create, use, or change using the buttons in the bar on the left side of the database window. That is, click Tables, Queries, Forms, Reports, Pages, Macros, or Modules.

2. If you want to use or change an existing object, click its name in the list of objects.

3. Do one of the following:

    *   **To create a new object of the type you selected in step 1**, click the New button along the top of the database window.

    *   **To use (or view or run) the object**, click the Open (or Preview or Run) button.

    *   **To change the object's appearance or structure**, click the Design button.

 TIP As a shortcut for opening (or previewing or running) an object, you can double-click its name in the database window.

What happens next depends on the type of object you selected and on the type of operation you chose in step 3. We'll say more about the various types of objects in upcoming chapters.

Closing an Object

Regardless of how you open an object, you can use any standard Windows technique to close it. Here are three sure-fire methods:

*   Click the Close (×) button in the upper-right corner of the window you want to close (*not* the Close button for the larger Microsoft Access program window).

- Choose File ➤ Close from the Access menu bar.
- Press Ctrl+W or Ctrl+F4.

Some Access windows also display a Close button on the toolbar.

If you've changed the object you were viewing, you may be asked if you want to save those changes. Respond to the prompt accordingly.

Uncovering a Hidden Database Window

Sometimes the database window will be invisible, even though you've opened a database. If that happens, you can return to the database window (assuming the database is open) by using any of these techniques:

- Press the F11 key.
- Choose Window ➤ *Name*: Database from the menu bar (where *Name* is replaced by the name of the open database, such as Northwind).

- Click the toolbar's Database Window button (shown at left).

If none of those methods works, close any other objects that are on the screen and try again. If you still can't get to the database window, you've probably closed the database. To reopen the database, choose File from the Access menu bar and then click the name of the database near the bottom of the menu. Or use File ➤ Open as discussed earlier in this chapter.

NOTE When you open some databases, a custom form window, rather than the database window, will appear. That's because whoever created that database has turned it into an *application*. Even so, pressing F11 usually will take you to the database window (unless the application designer has disabled this feature). Often you can bypass the initial form window and all the other startup options by holding down the Shift key as you open the database.

Changing Your View of Database Window Objects

You can use options on the View menu, or equivalent buttons on the database window toolbar, to change the size of objects and the amount of detail listed for them. Table 1.1 summarizes these options and buttons. In Figure 1.4, for example, we clicked the List button on the toolbar (alternatively, View ➤ List) to display database objects in a list.

TABLE 1.1: VIEW MENU OPTIONS AND EQUIVALENT TOOLBAR BUTTONS

VIEW MENU OPTION	BUTTON	DESCRIPTION
Large Icons		Shows each object as a large icon with the object name below the icon. Object names initially appear in rows; however, you can drag them as needed.
Small Icons		Shows each object as a small icon with the object name next to the icon. Object names initially appear in horizontal rows; however, you can drag them as needed.
List		Shows each object as a small icon with the object name next to the icon. Object names appear vertically, in one or more columns.
Details		Shows each object as a small icon with the object name next to the icon. Object names appear with one object to a line and five columns of detail about each object. The columns list the object's Name, Description, date/time Modified, date/time Created, and object Type.

- To resize a column, move your mouse pointer to the vertical divider that's just to the right of the column heading. When the pointer changes to a crosshair, drag the mouse to the left or right-click or double-click the divider for a snug fit.

- To sort a column in ascending order, click the appropriate column header button. To sort the column in descending order, click the column header button again.

- To add a Description to any object, right-click the object name in the database window, choose Properties, type a description, and then click OK.

Note: You can use the View ➤ Arrange Icons and View ➤ Line Up Icons commands on the menu bar (or right-click a blank area on the database window and choose the View ➤ Arrange Icons or View ➤ Line Up Icons options from the shortcut menus) to rearrange and align icons as needed. (If you don't see these choices on the View menu, click the arrows at the bottom of the menu to show more choices.)

Working with Groups of Objects

At the bottom of the bar on the left side of the database window under Groups is an item called Favorites. This is a place where you can add objects you use frequently, regardless of their type. Then, when you click the Favorites button, these objects appear in the database window together, instead of being separated by type.

Adding Objects to the Favorites Group

If you want to add an object to the Favorites list, first click the button on the Objects bar for the right type, to bring the object into view. Then right-click the object and select Add to Group ➤ 1 Favorites from the shortcut menu that appears. When you click the Favorites button under Groups, you'll see the object you added on the Favorites list.

Creating a New Group

If you're working with a complex database that includes many objects, you might want to group the objects into more than one category. For this reason, Access lets you create your own groups and add them to the database window Objects bar. Any group you add will appear under Groups, along with the Favorites button.

To create a new group, right-click any item under Objects or Groups and choose New Group from the shortcut menu that appears. Then enter a name in the New Group window and click OK.

TIP After you add new groups to the Objects bar, there won't be enough room to display all the object types. You can use the Show More button just above Groups to bring them into view. Or, resize the database window to make it longer, and drag Groups down to make more room for the Objects list.

Adding Objects to a New Group

To add an object to a new group, follow the instructions for adding an object to the Favorites list with this change: instead of choosing 1 Favorites, select the new group from the shortcut menu that appears after you select Add to Group.

Deleting a Group

If you don't need to use a group anymore, you can remove it from the Groups list on the Objects bar. Just right-click the group's name under Groups and choose Delete Group from the shortcut menu.

Managing Database Objects

The database window lets you do much more than just open objects. You also can use that window to manage the objects in a database—that is, to copy them, delete them, rename them, and so on. Here's how:

1. If the object you want to work with is currently open, close it, as described earlier under "Closing an Object."

2. If you haven't already done so, choose the type of object you want to work with (by clicking Tables, Queries, Forms, Reports, Pages, Macros, or Modules in the database window). Click the name of an object and then:

   - **To delete the object**, choose Edit ➤ Delete or press Delete; click Yes when prompted for confirmation. To delete the object and move it to the Windows Clipboard (without being asked for confirmation), hold down the Shift key while pressing Delete or press Ctrl+X. (Be careful, there's no undo for this operation; however, you can paste the object from the Clipboard by pressing Ctrl+V.)

   - **To rename the object**, click the object name again (or choose Edit ➤ Rename), type a new name (up to 64 characters, including blank spaces if you wish), and then press Enter.

   - **To copy the object** into this same database, choose Edit ➤ Copy or press Ctrl+C. Then choose Edit ➤ Paste or press Ctrl+V. Enter a valid object name (up to 64 characters), choose other options as appropriate, and then click OK. The copy will appear in the list of objects in its proper alphabetical position. (You may need to scroll through the object names to find the copy.) Copying can give you a head start on designing a table, form, report, or other object that is similar to the object you copied. You can then change the copied object without affecting the original.

   - **To create a shortcut icon on the Windows Desktop for the selected object**, choose Edit ➤ Create Shortcut, specify the Location (if you wish), and then click OK. In the future, you can double-click the shortcut icon on the Windows Desktop to start Access and open the object in one fell swoop.

 TIP Another way to create a shortcut to an Access object is to size the Access window so that you can see Access and the Windows Desktop at the same time. (One way to do this is to right-click an empty place on the Windows Taskbar and choose Cascade.) Then, if you want to put the shortcut in a folder, open that folder in Windows Explorer, My Computer, or Network Neighborhood. Finally, drag and drop the selected Access object to the Desktop or folder. You also can drag and drop tables and queries from the database window to Microsoft Excel, Microsoft Word, and other program windows (see Chapter 4).

- **To print the object**, choose File ➤ Print, press Ctrl+P, or click the Print toolbar button (shown at left). Then click OK from the Print dialog box to print the entire object.

- **To preview the object before printing**, choose File ➤ Print Preview or click the Print Preview toolbar button (shown at left). When you're done previewing the object, close it as described earlier under "Closing an Object."

- **To save the object with a new name in the same database**, choose File ➤ Save As.

- **To export the object to a Web Page, another Windows program, or to a different Microsoft Access database**, choose File ➤ Export. Complete the dialog box and click OK.

- **To import or link data from another program or database**, choose File ➤ Get External Data and then choose either Import or Link Tables. Complete the dialog box that appears and then click the Import or Link button.

TIP   Many of the operations described above also are available when you right-click an object or right-click any gray area on the database window. See "Opening Shortcut Menus" later in this chapter for details.

See Chapter 7 for more information about moving and copying objects between databases or about interacting with other programs. Or search the Access Help index for any of these topics: *Exporting Data*, *Importing Data*, and *Linking*.

Using the Toolbars and Menu Bar

Toolbars offer time-saving shortcuts to commonly used commands. To use the toolbars:

1. Move the mouse pointer to the toolbar button you want to choose.

2. Wait a moment, and a brief description (called a ScreenTip) will appear near the mouse pointer, as shown below.

3. Do one of the following, depending on the type of button you're pointing to (see Figure 1.5 for examples):

- **For a square (normal) button**, click the button.

- **For a drop-down button**, you have two choices. Either click the picture part of the button to take whatever action the picture shows, or click the drop-down arrow next to the picture and then choose an option from the menu or palette that appears.

- **For a drop-down list**, click the drop-down arrow next to the box and then choose an option from the list that appears, or click the drop-down arrow and then type your choice into the text box.

Examples of square (normal) buttons, drop-down buttons, and drop-down lists on toolbars.

Square (normal) button   Drop-down list

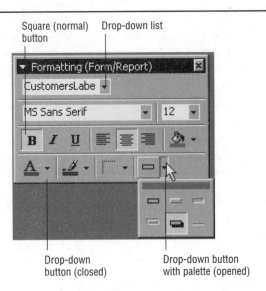

Drop-down button (closed)   Drop-down button with palette (opened)

 NOTE If you change your mind about choosing a drop-down button or drop-down list after you've clicked on its drop-down arrow, click the drop-down arrow again or click an empty area outside the toolbar.

 TIP If the drop-down button opened a palette, you can drag the palette anywhere on the screen. After you detach the palette from its button, the palette remains open and available until you click the Close button on the palette, click the arrow next to the drop-down button, or close the object you're working with.

Viewing Toolbars, ScreenTips, and the Status Bar

Toolbars, ScreenTips, the status bar, and other on-screen features are optional and customizable. If you don't see one of these features in Access, chances are it's just hidden (or turned off).

To display (or hide) the status bar or the startup dialog box (shown in Figure 1.1):

1. Open any database window. (The Tools ➣ Options and Tools ➣ Startup commands described below are available only when a database is open.)

2. Choose Tools ➣ Options from the Access menu bar and then click the View tab.

3. Select (check) an option to display (or turn on) the feature; deselect (clear) the option to hide (or turn off) the feature. For example, select Status Bar and Startup Dialog Box to display the status bar and startup dialog box described in Chapter 4. Click OK.

To display or hide ScreenTips (the descriptions that appear when you point to a toolbar button):

1. Choose View ➣ Toolbars ➣ Customize from the Access menu bar and then click the Options tab.

2. Select (check) Show ScreenTips on Toolbars to show a brief description of what a toolbar button does when you point to it.

3. Click Close.

You also can customize many startup features for the current database (including whether the database window, status bar, and built-in toolbars appear). To do so, choose Tools ➣ Startup. You'll see the Startup dialog box shown in Figure 1.6. As usual, you can select (check) options you want to turn on and deselect (clear) options you want to turn off. You also can type text into the text boxes and choose options from the drop-down lists. When you're finished making changes, click OK. See Chapter 16 for more about personalizing Access.

FIGURE 1.6

This sample Startup dialog box shows default options that work well for most people. Choose Tools ➣ Startup to get here.

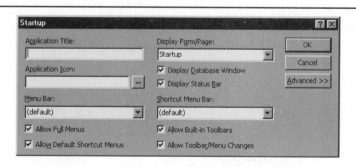

NOTE Pressing the Shift key when you open the database will bypass any Startup options that you've changed, giving you the default options shown in Figure 1.6.

Showing More of a Menu

Some of the drop-down lists for Access menu choices, such as Edit, come in two versions: a short list of the most commonly used commands and a longer list with extra commands. When you're viewing the short version of a drop-down list, it will have a Show More button like the one shown for the Edit menu here:

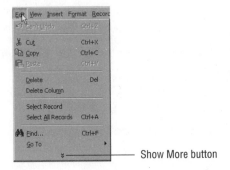

Show More button

To see the long version of a menu, click its Show More button. Or, just leave the menu open for a few seconds without making a choice. The short version will then transform into the longer list on its own, if there is one available. The long version of the Edit menu looks like this:

Positioning the Toolbar or Menu Bar

By default, the toolbar is *docked* just below the menu bar (refer to Figure 1.4). You can convert the toolbar to a free-floating element or dock it to some other edge of the screen. You can also move the menu bar or dock it in a new location. Follow these steps to move the menu bar or a toolbar:

1. Move the mouse pointer to the handle on the left side of the toolbar.

2. Drag the menu bar or toolbar toward the center of the screen, double-click to make it free-floating (see the example below), or drag it to some other edge of the screen to dock it there. To restore a floating menu bar or toolbar to its previous docked position, double-click its title bar.

When the toolbar is floating freely, you can drag it by its title bar to any place on the screen. Here are some other toolbar tips:

- **To close (hide) the floating toolbar**, click the Close button on the toolbar's upper-right corner or right-click any toolbar and click the toolbar's name in the shortcut menu that appears. (Shortcut menus are discussed in the next section.)

- **To redisplay a hidden toolbar**, choose View ➤ Toolbars, click the check box next to the toolbar you wish to view, and then click the Close button in the Toolbars dialog box.

- **To redisplay a default toolbar for the current view**, right-click any visible toolbar and then click the toolbar's name in the shortcut menu that appears.

If the redisplay procedures above don't work, choose Tools ➤ Startup, select (check) Allow Built-In Toolbars, and then click OK. Close and then open the database again. If necessary, choose View ➤ Toolbars to redisplay the toolbar.

 NOTE If you manually show a built-in toolbar, it will appear in every view. If you hide a built-in toolbar from within its default view, it will be hidden in every view (including its default view).

We discuss many other ways to use and customize the toolbars in Chapter 24. But for now, just knowing how to hide, display, and position the toolbar is enough. If you do need a quick reminder or more information on toolbars, use the Office Assistant to find help for *Toolbars*.

Opening Shortcut Menus

Access provides many *shortcut menus* to save you the trouble of looking for options on the menu bars and toolbars. Shortcut menus in the Open and Save dialog boxes also offer handy ways to manage your files and folders without leaving Access.

To open a shortcut menu that's tailored to whatever you want to work with, right-click the object or place you're interested in, or click the object and then press Shift+F10. For example, right-clicking a table name in the database window opens this menu:

 NOTE If the shortcut menus don't appear when you right-click, choose Tools ➤ Startup, select (check) Allow Default Shortcut Menus, and click OK. Then close and open the database again.

To select an option from the menu, do one of the following:

- Press Enter if you want to choose the boldfaced option on the menu.
- Click the option with either the left (primary) or right (secondary) mouse button.
- Type the option's underlined letter or highlight the option with your mouse, and then press Enter.

To close the menu without selecting an option, press Esc, Alt, or Shift+F10—or click outside the menu.

 TIP The term *right-click* means to point at something with your mouse pointer and then click the *right* (secondary) mouse button. (If your mouse is set up for lefties, you'll have to click the left mouse button instead.) This right-click trick is available throughout Access (and, indeed, throughout Windows). As you work with Windows and Access, be sure to experiment with right-clicking. It is a great way to discover some truly useful shortcuts.

Closing a Database or a Project

When you're done working with a database or a project, you should close it. Any of these methods will work:

- Click the Close button in the upper-right corner of the database window.
- Go to the database window and then choose File ➤ Close from the Access menu bar.
- Press Ctrl+W or Ctrl+F4.

As usual, you'll be prompted to save any unsaved work.

 NOTE You can have only one database open at a time. Access will automatically close the currently open database if you choose File ➤ Open or File ➤ New before closing the database or project that's open.

Getting Help

One thing we hope to teach you in this book is how to get answers to questions—even if *we* haven't provided those answers. You can achieve this goal easily if you learn how to use Access's plentiful built-in Help. We'll show you how to use this self-help tool next.

Summary of Self-Help Techniques

Table 1.2 summarizes many ways to get and use online Help in Access. Remember that you can use all of the standard Windows techniques while you're in the Help system to annotate Help, print a topic, change fonts, and so forth. For more information on those topics, see your Windows documentation or the Windows online Help. You can experiment by right-clicking in any Help text window and choosing options from the shortcut menu.

TABLE 1.2: MICROSOFT ACCESS 2000 ONLINE HELP OPTIONS AND TECHNIQUES	
TYPE OF HELP	**HOW TO GET IT**
Office Assistant	Choose Help ➤ Microsoft Access Help, or click the Office Assistant button on the toolbar.
Table of Contents	Choose Help ➤ Microsoft Office Help, click the Office Assistant's Search button, and click the Contents tab in the Help dialog box. If the Contents tab isn't visible, click the Show button first.
Search Help	Click the Index tab in the Help dialog box.
Find Help on the Web	Choose Help ➤ Office on the Web.
Display a Minimized Help Window	Click the ? Microsoft Access Help button on the Windows Taskbar.
What's This...?	Choose Help ➤ What's This?, press Shift+F1, or click the ? button on the toolbar or at the upper-right corner of a dialog box; then click the command or place you want help with.
Version Number, System Information, Technical Support	Choose Help ➤ About Microsoft Access.
Exit Help	Click the Close button at the upper-right corner of a Help screen.

Using the Help System and This Book

This book is designed to complement the Help system, not to replace it. Because the online documentation does such a good job of showing you the steps for practically any procedure you can perform in Access, and because many of those procedures won't interest everyone, we've taken a more conceptual approach here—one that should help you work more creatively. Instead of presenting hundreds of little step-by-step instructions (as the Help system does), this book deals with larger, more general concepts so that you can see how (as well as when, why, and sometimes whether) to apply the nitty-gritty details you'll find in the Help system.

Looking Up Information

Like a book, the Access Help system has a table of contents, which is a great way to learn how to do things. To get to the Help contents:

- Use the Office Assistant to open any Help topic, click the Show button if the left pane of the Help window is not visible, and then click the Contents tab in the Access Help dialog box.

  Or

- If you're already in a Help window and the Contents side of the Help window isn't visible, click the Show button on the left side of the Help toolbar to return to the Contents Answer Wizard or Index tab you selected most recently.

The Contents lists many options to explore. Figure 1.7 shows the Contents tab with the Data: Find book opened. To open or close a *book*, click the Expand or Collapse button before the book's name, or just double-click the book. To display a *topic* (preceded by a question mark icon, like this **?**), click that topic. In Figure 1.8, you see the Help window that opened after we expanded the Data: Find book and then clicked on the *About Using Wildcard Characters* topic.

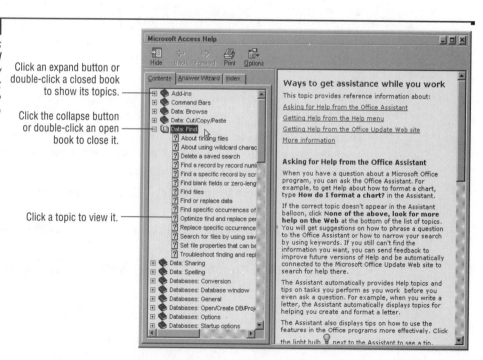

FIGURE 1.7

The Contents displays electronic books filled with help on many topics. Double-click books to open or close them. Click topics to display them.

Click an expand button or double-click a closed book to show its topics.

Click the collapse button or double-click an open book to close it.

Click a topic to view it.

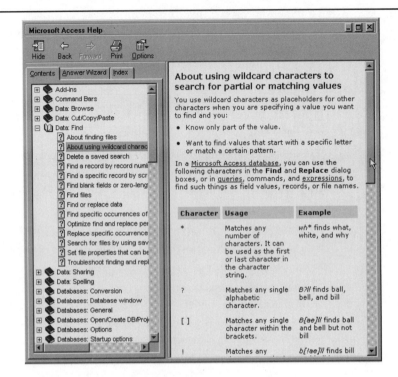

FIGURE 1.8

A Help window that shows information about using wildcard characters.

Here are some tips for using a Help window (see Figure 1.8):

- **To view Help text that's hidden at the moment**, use the vertical and horizontal scroll bars as needed, or resize the Help window.

- **To jump to a related topic**, click the small button next to that topic in the help text. The mouse pointer changes to a pointing hand when you point to a jump button.

- **To see the definition of a term or a button**, click any text that's underlined, or click a picture of a button. (Click anywhere inside or outside the definition, or press Esc to hide the definition again.)

- **To print the current Help window**, click the Print button on the Help window toolbar.

- **To return to the previous Help window**, click the Help window's Back button.

- **To show the Help Contents** if it's not visible, click the Show button on the Help window's toolbar.

- **To make the Help window reappear** if it's minimized or hidden, click the Microsoft Access Help button on the Windows Taskbar. (The button name is preceded by a small **?** icon.)

- **To close the Access Help window**, make sure it's the active window and then click its Close button.

Help with Whatever You're Doing

Even when you're not in a Help window, you should look at the status bar, preview areas, and any colored text on the screen for hints on what to do next. For example, you'll often see a hint box on the object and a description of available shortcut keys in the status bar, as shown in Figure 1.9. (Though that example won't appear until you design a table, as discussed in Chapter 6.)

FIGURE 1.9

Hint boxes and the status bar often provide further information about what to do next.

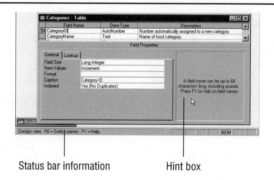

Status bar information   Hint box

Searching Help

Like any good book, the Help system also has its own index. You can search the index for help with just about any topic. Here's how:

1. Go to the Help window as explained earlier in this chapter and then click the Index tab. Figure 1.10 shows the Index tab's contents after we typed **wildcard** in the text box and clicked Search.

2. Type a word or select one from the list of topics. Search is not case sensitive. This step highlights the closest match to your entry in the list(s) below the text box.

3. Click Display (or double-click a topic).

FIGURE 1.10

The Index tab after we typed wildcard in the text box.

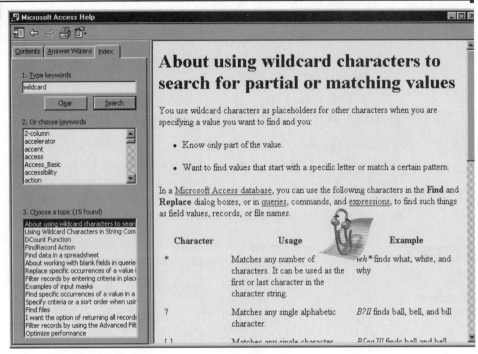

Once the Help topic is shown on the right side of the Help window, you can use any of the techniques described earlier to work with that information (see "Looking Up Information").

Asking the Office Assistant

The Office Assistant enables you to search for information by typing in a few words. The more specific your words are, the more on-topic the suggested topics will be. But you don't have to worry about matching a topic name exactly because the Office Assistant is pretty forgiving and even quite smart.

To use the Office Assistant, choose Help ➢ Microsoft Access Help from the Access menu bar, press F1, or click the Office Assistant button on the toolbar (see Figure 1.11). You can choose from several personalities for the assistant. Just click the Options button in the yellow bubble for the assistant and click the Gallery tab. Besides choosing the appearance of the assistant, you can change its behavior. Click the Options tab in the Office Assistant dialog box, make your selections, and click OK.

PART

I

An Overview of Access

FIGURE 1.11

The Office Assistant showing Help topics on customizing toolbars.

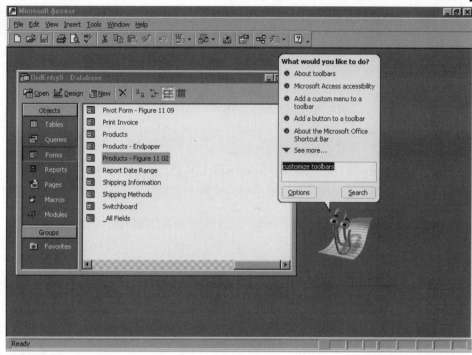

To get help from the Office Assistant, first open the assistant if it's not already visible on the Desktop. If you don't see a yellow bubble with a Search button, click anywhere on the assistant, and then type a few words describing what you want to do in the box under "What would you like to do?" and press Enter or click the Search button. When the list of related topics appears, click the topic you're interested in to open the corresponding Help entry.

In Figure 1.11, we typed **customize toolbars** and pressed Enter. The Office Assistant ignores extraneous words, such as *how do I fix*, and focuses on the important keywords, such as *toolbar* and *customize*. It then displays a list of topics that seem to answer your question.

Asking "What *Is* This Thing?"

Another way to get quick information is to use "What's This?" Help. This type of help explains the function of menu commands, buttons, or dialog box options.

1. Press Shift+F1 or choose Help ➤ What's This? from the Access menus. If you're in a dialog box, click the ? button in the upper-right corner of the dialog box. The mouse pointer changes to a combination arrow and question mark.

2. Click a button on the toolbar, select commands from the menus, or click a place in the dialog box to get help with that particular item.

If you change your mind about using What's This? Help before choosing a topic, press Esc or Shift+F1, or click the Help or ? button again, to return to the normal mouse pointer.

Here are some other ways to get What's This? Help:

- In a dialog box, right-click the option name or button you're curious about and choose What's This?
- In a dialog box, click or tab to the place you want help with and then press Shift+F1 or F1.
- In the menus, highlight the option you want help with and then press Shift+F1 or F1.

Version Number, System Information, Technical Support

Do you need to check the version of Access you're using to see how much memory and disk space are available or to find out how to get technical support? It's easy:

1. Choose Help ➤ About Microsoft Access to open the About Microsoft dialog box.

2. Click the System Info button (for information about your system resources) or click Tech Support (for details about getting help from humans).

3. Click the Close and OK buttons (or press Esc) as needed to return to Access.

Getting Out of Help

You can get out of Help in many ways, but the easiest is simply to make sure the Help window is active (Click the window or its Taskbar button if you need to.) and then click its Close button.

NOTE In addition to the online Help described in this chapter, Microsoft offers many other sources of help for Microsoft Access, Microsoft Office, and other Microsoft products. See Chapter 4 for information about these additional resources.

Exiting Microsoft Access

When you're done using Access, you should return to Windows before shutting down and turning off your computer. You can exit from Microsoft Access using the techniques you'd use with other Windows programs:

1. Go to the database window or to the main Microsoft Access window.

2. Choose File ➤ Exit, click the Close button in the upper-right corner of the Microsoft Access window, or press Alt+F4.

You'll be returned to Windows or to another open program window.

 TIP To exit Access when Access is minimized, right-click the Microsoft Access button on the Windows Taskbar and then choose Close.

Where to Go from Here

Where you go from here depends on your past database experience.

- **If you're new to Access and to databases**, continue with Chapters 2 and 3.
- **If you're new to Access but know something about databases**, try the hands-on guided tour in Chapter 3.
- **If you're familiar with Access**, flip to the "What's New in the Access Zoo" section at the end of most chapters in this book, including this chapter. For another view of what's new, open the Office Assistant, enter **What's New**, and then click a What's New topic.

What's New in the Access Zoo?

Some of the many features discussed in this chapter are new to Access 2000. New features include:

- Projects, special Access files that hold objects for working with SQL Server data
- Show More buttons on some of the Access menus
- A new Open dialog box with buttons for quickly showing the file lists for History, My Documents, the Desktop, and your Favorites
- A revised database window with buttons for optionally displaying objects by group instead of by type
- A revamped Help system that's easier to navigate
- New Office Assistant personalities

CHAPTER 2

Understanding Databases

Most people are accustomed to working with *information*, which is *data* that's organized into some meaningful form. You probably can recognize the information shown in Figure 2.1 as an invoice. You can find the customer's name and address, the products that person ordered, and just about any other information you might want simply by looking at the invoice. The invoice as a whole presents business information—namely, what happened in a transaction—by meaningfully drawing together various related items of data.

Invoice

E & K Sporting Goods
1337 West 47th Street
Fridley, NC 28228
USA
Phone: (704) 555-1555 Fax: (704) 555-1556

Invoice Date	8/31/95	**Contact Name**	Shirley Ujest	**Customer ID**	4
Order ID	16	**PO Number**	78	**Ship Date**	2/1/95
Order Date	2/1/95	**Terms**	Net 10 days.	**Shipping Method**	Federal Express

Ship To:
WorldWide Widgets
187 Suffolk Ln.
Boise, ID 83720
USA
(208) 555-8097

Bill To:
WorldWide Widgets
187 Suffolk Ln.
Boise, ID 83720
USA
(208) 555-8097

Product ID	Product Name	Quantity	Unit Price	Discount	Line Total
8	Billiard balls	2	$127.45	0.00%	$254.90
2	Football	1	$5.65	0.00%	$5.66

Subtotal	$260.56
Freight Charge	$2.00
Sales Tax	$0.00
Order Total	$262.56
Total Payments	$10.00
Total Due	$252.56

You'll never go wrong with our products along!

Suppose you want to store all of your invoices on the computer. You might consider buying a scanner and scanning each invoice into a computer file. Later, you could display a copy of the invoice on the screen and print it. You wouldn't even need a database management system; all you would need is a scanner and a simple graphics program.

Why Store Data?

The problem with the scanner approach is that all you can do is retrieve, view, and print the invoices. You can't analyze or reformat the data on the invoice. For instance, you can't print mailing labels, envelopes, or form letters for all your customers. You can't analyze your orders to view overall sales. Why not? Because the computer doesn't have the eyes or brains it takes to look into the invoice and pull out certain types of information. Only you can do that job because you do have eyes and a brain.

Flexibility Is the Goal

If you want the flexibility to display, print, and analyze your information in whatever format you wish, you first need to break down that information into small units of *data*. For example, a person's last name is one unit of data. That person's zip code is another. The name of a product the customer purchased is another unit of data, and so forth.

After breaking the information into discrete units of data, you can use a database management system, such as Access, to analyze and present that data any way you wish. If each person's surname is a discrete unit of data, for example, you can tell Access to alphabetize your customers by name or to find the order that Smith placed yesterday.

You can put the individual units of data into any format you wish—for example, mailing labels, envelopes, or invoices.

You Use Tables to Store Data

In Access, you must break all your information into data that's stored in tables. A table is just a collection of data that's organized into rows and columns. You can put any information that's available to you into a table.

Let's forget about invoices for a moment and focus on storing information about customers. Suppose you have a Rolodex or card file containing customer names and addresses, as shown below. For each customer, you maintain the same pieces of information—name, address, and so on.

How can you break down the information on this Rolodex into raw data that's neatly organized as a table? Easy. Just make a column for each data element, such as last name or state, and then list the corresponding data elements for each customer in rows, as shown in Figure 2.2.

FIGURE 2.2

Names and addresses, which might once have been on Rolodex cards, organized and typed into an Access table.

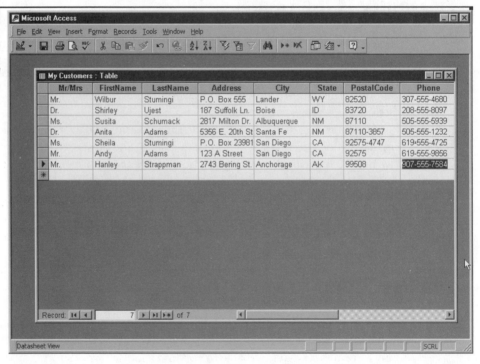

Terminology Time

Now is as good a time as any to get some terminology out of the way so that we can talk about tables and databases more precisely. Here are four terms you'll see often:

Table A collection of data organized into rows and columns.

Field A single unit (or column) of information in a table. The sample table in Figure 2.2 consists of fields named Mr/Mrs, FirstName, LastName, Address, City, State, PostalCode, and Phone, as you can see by looking across the top of the table.

Record The set of all data fields for one row of the table. The sample table in Figure 2.2 contains seven filled records: one for a customer named Wilbur Stumingi, another for Shirley Ujest, and so forth.

Database Contrary to what some people think, a database is not a table. A database is a collection of *all* the tables and other objects (such as forms and reports) that you use to manage data.

We'll tell you more about why a database might contain several tables later in this chapter.

The More Fields, the Better

Looking back at Figure 2.2, you may be wondering why we bothered to break the information into so many different fields. Isn't using the three fields Mr/Mrs, Last-Name, and FirstName a little excessive?

Not really, because organizing the data into separate fields now will make it easier to arrange the data in a meaningful form later. Here are some ways to arrange the data in the first record of the table shown in Figure 2.2:

Mr. Wilbur Stumingi

Mr. Stumingi

Stumingi, Wilbur

Dear Wilbur:

Wilbur Stumingi

Yo, Wilbur!

As you'll see in later chapters, you can rearrange the table columns in any order you wish, and you can use forms and reports to organize table data into any format.

Why Use Multiple Tables?

Earlier we said that a database can contain many tables. So now you may be wondering why you'd want to put more than one table into a database. The simple reason is that it's easier to manage data if all the information about a particular subject is in its own table. For example, if you're designing a database to track membership in an organization, you might create separate tables, such as these:

- All Members
- Committees
- Payments Made
- Your Company or Organization
- Membership Types and Dues
- Committee Members
- Payment Methods

If you're using Access to manage orders for your company's products, you might use these tables:

- Customers
- Order Details
- Payment Methods
- Products
- Employees
- Orders
- Payments
- Shipping Methods

Remember that these tables are suggestions only. Access really doesn't care *what* type of data you put into tables. All that matters is that you find a way to break the information you need to manage into the tabular fields-and-records format.

 TIP The Database Wizard and Table Wizard can create many types of tables for you automatically. These Wizards organize your database into tables and divide your tables into separate fields with only a small amount of guidance from you. The process is so fast and painless that you'll be creating complete databases in no time. You'll learn more about these Wizards in Chapters 3, 5, and 6.

When to Use One Table

Until you get the hang of how to structure a database, deciding whether data should go into one table or several tables is a bit difficult. But this general rule of thumb always applies: If a one-to-one correspondence exists between two fields, put those fields into the same table.

For example, it makes sense to put all of the My Customers information in one table because there's an exact one-to-one relationship between fields. That is, for every one customer, there's one customer name, one address, one city, and so forth.

When to Use More Than One Table

Just because you put all your customer information into a single table doesn't mean you should put all the information for an entire business in one table. After all, you wouldn't put all the information for your customers, orders, products, and so forth on one Rolodex card. Likewise, you wouldn't put all that information into a single table.

A better plan is to put customer data in one table, product data in another, and order data in yet another because no one-to-one correspondence exists among these categories of information. Any one customer might place many orders, and any order might be for many products. So here we have some natural one-to-many relationships among the subjects of your tables.

The One-to-Many Relationship

The *one-to-many relationship* describes a situation in which every record in a table may be related to many records in another table. For example, each one of your customers might place many orders (at least you hope so!). Therefore, it makes sense to put all of your customer data in one table and data about the orders they place in another table, as shown in Figure 2.3. (In the figure, only the first few fields from each table are shown. Additional information about customers and orders is scrolled off the screen.)

If we do use more than one table, however, we also need a way to determine exactly *which* customer goes with each order. And that's where the primary key field comes in.

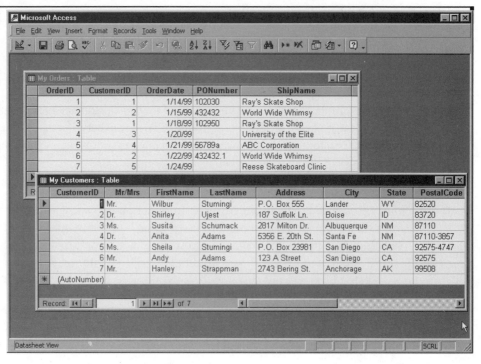

FIGURE 2.3

A one-to-many relationship between orders and customers. (Any one customer might place many orders.) The CustomerID field in the My Orders table identifies which customer placed each order.

The Primary Key Field

The *primary key field* in a table uniquely identifies each record in that table. In the My Customers table shown in Figure 2.3, only one customer has CustomerID 4. Even if that table has other people named Dr. Anita Adams from other cities, only one customer has the customerID 4. When we added the CustomerID field to the My Customers table, we made it the primary key so that Access would make sure that no two people were given the same CustomerID number.

TIP Your social security number is an example of a primary key field because it uniquely identifies you in the government's databases. Even though other people in the country may have the same first, last, and even middle names as you, *nobody* else in the country has the same social security number.

Notice, too, that the information in the My Orders table is compact. For example, the customer's honorific, first name, and last name aren't repeated in the My Orders table. All the My Orders table needs in order to get that information is the customer's unique ID number. Access can then dig up any information about that customer just by looking up the corresponding record in the My Customers table.

It's Easier Than It Looks

This business of breaking down information into data in separate tables confuses many beginners, and it has been known to end the careers of many budding database designers. But there's no need to throw in the towel if you're feeling uneasy. As you'll see in the following chapters, Access will help you figure out how to break your information into related tables, and it will help you define primary key fields for the tables. So all you really need to understand now is that:

- Your database is likely to contain several tables.
- Your tables will use a primary key field to uniquely identify each record in the table.

Where to Go from Here

Remember that the reason for breaking down information into raw data is to give you the flexibility to analyze and display data any way you wish. Once your data is organized into a database on disk, there's no limit to the type of *information* you can glean from that data. (Chapters 10 through 15 will explain more about analyzing and displaying data.)

Where should you go next in this book? Here are some suggestions:

- To learn the basics of Access in a hurry, try the hands-on practice in Chapter 3. In just minutes, you'll create a fully functional database—complete with data, forms, reports, a data access page, and a push-button menu for managing it.
- To get an idea about how Access and the other programs in the Microsoft Office suite can work together, check out Chapter 4.
- To find out how to create a database for storing your tables, proceed to Chapter 5.
- To find out how to create tables for data that's all on paper and not on any computer, see Chapter 6.
- To learn how to manage data that's already on the computer in some database format (such as Access, dBASE, Paradox, SQL, text, HTML, and so forth), jump to Chapter 7. You may be able to use that data without creating your own tables from scratch.
- To learn about projects, see Chapter 30.

CHAPTER 3

Access in an Evening

FEATURING:

This chapter is a hands-on guided tour of Access databases in eight quick lessons. These lessons probably won't make you an Access guru, but they'll give you both the big picture of what Access is all about and direct experience in using its most important features.

During these lessons, you'll use wizards to create an application for managing information about your contacts, complete with data, forms, reports, a data access page, and a push-button switchboard form that makes the database a cinch to use. You'll also learn how to enter data, sort it in alphabetical order, find specific information, customize forms and reports, isolate specific information by using queries, and tweak the descriptions that appear on the switchboard form.

 TIP Access offers many automated wizards to help you set up new databases, tables, forms, data access pages, reports, and queries in a flash. We strongly encourage you to use wizards, rather than from-scratch methods, to create most new objects, especially if you're new to Access or to database management. Once an object exists, you can tweak it as necessary. This "create it with a wizard and then refine it" approach is sure to save you time, and it will help you learn Access more quickly.

Before You Start These Lessons

Before you start these lessons, you already should have your basic Windows skills down pat—using a mouse; sizing, moving, opening, and closing windows; using dialog boxes, and so on. (If you haven't already done so, you should browse through Chapters 1 and 2 to get an idea of what you'll be doing here.)

For best results, give yourself 15 to 30 *uninterrupted* minutes to finish each lesson. If you need to pause after a lesson, see "Taking a Break" at the end of Lesson 1. To resume with the next lesson, see "Returning from a Break."

 NOTE If you will be using an Access project to work with SQL Server tables, instead of an Access database that holds its own tables, you can still benefit from going through the lessons in this chapter. The way you work with forms, data access pages, and reports is the same for databases and projects.

Lesson 1: Creating a Database and Tables Automatically

The first step to using Access is to start the program and go to the Microsoft Access startup dialog box or the main Microsoft Access window. If you don't know how, see Chapter 1 for help.

Creating an Instant Database

During these hands-on lessons, you'll create a new database (named Contact Management Lessons) that can help you manage information about your contacts. You'll use the Database Wizard to create this database. Here goes:

1. If you're starting from the Microsoft Access startup dialog box, choose Database Wizards, Pages, and Projects and then click OK.

   Or

   If you're starting from the main Microsoft Access window, choose File ➤ New from the menu bar.

2. Click the Databases tab in the New dialog box and then double-click the Contact Management icon.

3. Type **Contact Management Lessons** in the File Name text box of the File New Database dialog box and then click Create or press Enter.

 NOTE Access normally looks for and stores your databases in a folder named My Documents on the disk drive where Access is installed. To change this default location, open any database and choose Tools ➤ Options, click the General tab, and specify a folder name in the Default Database Folder text box. To return to the default setting, change the folder name in the Default Database Folder text box back to . (a period). See Chapter 16 for more details.

You'll see an empty database window titled Contact Management Lessons: Database. After a brief delay, the first Database Wizard dialog box will appear atop the database window, as shown in Figure 3.1. This dialog box tells you something about the database you're about to create.

FIGURE 3.1

The first Database Wizard dialog box appears on top of the Contact Management Lessons: Database window.

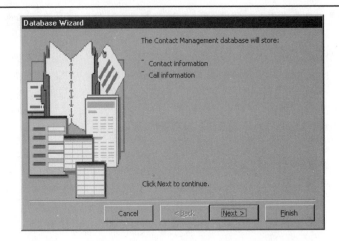

Understanding the Wizards

The Database Wizard will ask you a few questions and then use your answers to build tables, forms, and reports automatically. Read the first Database Wizard dialog box and then click Next. The second dialog box, shown in Figure 3.2, asks which fields to include in each table.

FIGURE 3.2

The second Database Wizard dialog box lets you choose optional fields for tables in the new database.

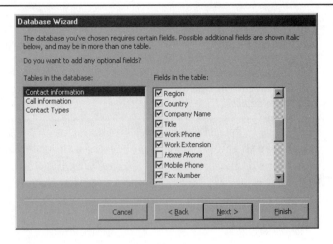

All the Access wizards work in similar ways, and they have the same buttons at the bottom of each dialog box (see Figure 3.2). Just follow the directions, answer questions, and use the buttons described below to navigate until you finish using the Wizard:

Cancel   Cancels the wizard and returns to wherever you were before you started the wizard.

Back   Returns you to the previous wizard dialog box.

Next   Continues to the next dialog box.

Finish   Goes straight to the last wizard dialog box. The wizard will use default settings for any dialog boxes that it skips. The Finish button is available only when the wizard has enough information to complete its job.

Choosing Optional Fields for Your Tables

A *field* is a single unit of information stored in a table; for example, a person's name, address, or phone number. When you use the Database Wizard to create a database, all the necessary tables and fields will be defined automatically and you don't have to make any changes. But if you do want to include optional fields, or omit fields, here are the steps to follow:

1. Scroll to and click the name of the table you want to work with in the tables list at the left side of the dialog box shown in Figure 3.2.

2. Look for the italicized field names on the list at the right side of the dialog box. These fields are optional. To include the field, check the box next to its name. To omit the field, clear the check mark from the box. As usual in Windows, clicking a checked box clears the checkmark; clicking an empty check box puts a checkmark in the box.

3. Repeat steps 1 and 2 as needed.

For these lessons, we'll assume you've chosen the fields that the Wizard suggested initially. That is, italicized fields are not checked, and non-italicized fields are checked.

Choosing a Style for Forms

The third Database Wizard dialog box lets you choose a background color and general style for database forms (called *screen displays* in the Database Wizard dialog box). In Figure 3.3, we've selected the Standard style. To choose a style, click it in the list of styles. The left side of the dialog box will show a sample form that reflects your current choice. Preview any styles you wish and then choose Standard, which is the style used throughout this chapter. When you're ready to continue, click the Next button.

FIGURE 3.3

The third Database Wizard dialog box with the Standard style selected for forms.

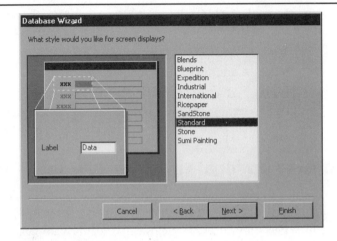

Choosing a Style for Printed Reports

In the fourth Database Wizard dialog box, you'll choose a general style for printed reports (see Figure 3.4). Again, you can click a style in the list and preview a sample until you find a style you like. Pick a style that appeals to you (or use the Formal style that we chose) and then click Next.

FIGURE 3.4

The fourth Database Wizard dialog box with the Formal report style selected.

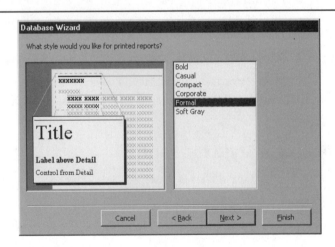

NOTE In Chapter 13, you'll learn how to set up your own form and report styles and add them to the list of predefined styles. You'll also find out how to reformat an existing form or report with a different style.

Choosing a Database Title and Adding a Picture

In the fifth Wizard dialog box (see Figure 3.5), you can choose a different title for your database. This title will appear on the Main Switchboard form (which you'll see soon) and on all reports. For now, Contact Management is fine, so leave the title unchanged.

FIGURE 3.5

The fifth Database Wizard dialog box lets you choose a title and a picture to use for your database. In this example, we've used the suggested title and chosen the Contacts.gif *picture from the* \Program Files\ Microsoft Office\Office\ Bitmaps\Dbwiz *folder.*

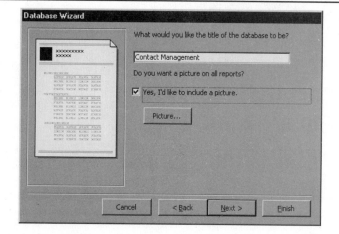

You also can include a picture on all reports. Just for grins, add a picture by following these steps:

1. Click Yes, I'd Like to Include a Picture to select that option and then click the Picture button.

2. Use the techniques discussed in Chapter 1 to locate the folder named \Program Files\Microsoft Office\Office\Bitmaps\Dbwiz in the Insert Picture dialog box (see Figure 3.6). Assuming you did a standard installation, you can just type \Program Files\Microsoft Office\Office\Bitmaps\Dbwiz in the File Name text box and press Enter.

3. Click a file name in the left side of the dialog box. Each time you click a file name, a preview of the picture it contains will appear in the preview area. The example in Figure 3.6 shows the `Contacts.gif` file name and preview selected.

4. Click OK when you're satisfied with the picture you've selected. The sample picture will appear in the Database Wizard text box, next to the Picture button.

5. Click Next to continue to the next dialog box.

FIGURE 3.6

After clicking the Picture button in the dialog box shown in Figure 3.5, you can search for and preview pictures. The list of graphics will depend on which software you've installed and which folder you've chosen to search.

Finishing Up

That's all the information the Wizard needs. In the final dialog box, you have two options:

Yes, Start the Database   Leave this option checked if you want to go to a switchboard form that lets you start working with your database immediately. Clear this option if you want to go directly to the database window, bypassing the switchboard. For now, leave this option checked.

Display Help on Using a Database   Checking this option will display online help about using a database. Leaving this option unchecked won't display any extra help. Leave this option unchecked for now.

To create the database with all the choices you made, click the Finish button now. (If you need to revisit any of the previous Database Wizard dialog boxes, click the Back button as needed.)

Wait patiently for a few moments while the Database Wizard conjures up an entire database of tables, forms, reports, and other objects. (On-screen bars will keep you informed of the Wizard's progress as it works.) When the Wizard finishes its job, you'll see the Main Switchboard form for your database (see Figure 3.7).

FIGURE 3.7

The Main Switchboard form gives you all the options you need to create and manage Contact Management data. Access creates a Main Switchboard form automatically any time you use the Database Wizard to create a non-blank database.

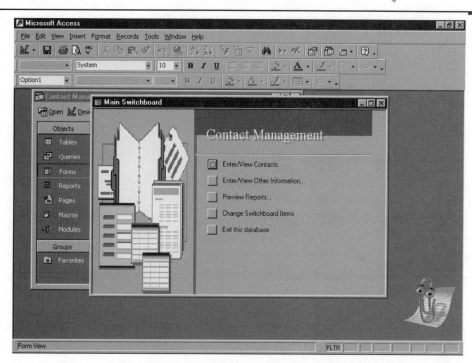

Congratulations! You've created your first Access database. Easy, isn't it? In the following lessons, you'll learn how to work with and customize your new database.

At Your Leisure

To learn more about databases and tables, see Chapters 5 through 7 of this book. Or go to the Access Help Contents, open the *Databases Open/Create DB/Project* book, and then peruse the subtopics. Or just skip all that and move on to Lesson 2.

If you want to take a break at the end of this or any other lesson, close your database as discussed next under "Taking a Break." Before you resume a lesson, reopen the Contact Management Lessons database (see "Returning from a Break").

Taking a Break

Any time you want to take a break at the end of a lesson, do one of these steps to save your work and close the database (*before* you turn off the computer!):

- **If you're viewing the Main Switchboard form**, shown in Figure 3.7, click the button next to the last option, Exit This Database.

- **If you're viewing the database window** (see Chapter 1), choose File ➤ Close from the menu bar, or press Ctrl+W, or click the Close button on the database window.

Then, if you're done using Access for a while, exit Access by choosing File ➤ Exit from the Access menu bar.

Returning from a Break

To resume with a new lesson after taking a break, use any of the techniques you learned in Chapter 1 to open the Contact Management Lessons database and its Main Switchboard form. Here's a summary of the steps:

- **If you're at the Microsoft Access startup dialog box and you see Contact Management Lessons in the list** under Open An Existing Database, double-click that name.

- **If you're at the Microsoft Access startup dialog box and Contact Management Lessons doesn't appear in the list**, make sure More Files is highlighted, click OK, and then double-click Contact Management Lessons in the list of file names.

- **If you're at the Microsoft Access main menu**, choose File from the Access menu bar. Then, if Contact Management Lessons appears near the bottom of the File menu, click its name. If it doesn't appear, choose Open Database and then double-click Contact Management Lessons in the list of file names.

- **If you're at the Windows Desktop** and you've used the Contact Management Lessons database recently, choose Start ➤ Documents ➤ Contact Management Lessons.

The Contact Management Lessons database will open, and the Main Switchboard form will appear (see Figure 3.7).

Some Important Switchboard and Database Window Tips

These tips are worth remembering as you work with the Contact Management Lessons database:

- **To open the Contact Management Lessons database window without opening the Main Switchboard first**, hold down the Shift key while you open the Contact Management Lessons database. You'll be taken directly to the database window.

- **To open the Main Switchboard form from the database window**, click the Forms tab on the database window and then double-click the form named Switchboard.

- **To open the database window without closing the switchboard form first**, press F11 or click the Database Window toolbar button or choose Window ➤ Contact Management Lessons: Database from the menu bar.

- **To open the database window when it's minimized on the Access desktop**, click the database window's Restore button, or double-click the window's title bar, or press F11.

Lesson 2: Exploring the Contact Management Lessons Database

Before you enter any data or print any reports, why not explore the Contact Management Lessons database and switchboard forms a little? You'll have plenty of places to investigate.

Exploring the Contact Management Form

Let's start with the first option on the Main Switchboard (refer to Figure 3.7):

1. Click the button next to Enter/View Contacts. You'll see the Contacts form, which lets you review or change information for each contact. Here's what you can do with the buttons at the bottom of this form:

   - **To log a call to the person whose record is shown on the form**, click the Calls button. (For now, click the Calls form Close toolbar button or press Ctrl+W to return to the Addresses form.)

- **To dial your contact's phone number** with your computer's modem, click the box that contains the phone number you want to dial and then click the Dial button. An easy-to-use AutoDialer box appears. (For now, click Cancel if you've opened that dialog box.)

- **To switch between page 1 and 2 of the Contacts form**, click the command buttons labeled 1 and 2—or click the Page Up and Page Down buttons.

2. Click the Contacts form's Close button or press Ctrl+W to return to the Main Switchboard form when you are finished exploring the Contacts form.

 NOTE In Lesson 4, you'll learn how to add and change data and how to use navigation buttons to move from record to record. For now, just take a look at what's available and don't worry too much about adding any data.

Exploring the Contact Management Reports

The Main Switchboard's Preview Reports option lets you preview and print a variety of reports about your contacts. Here are some steps to try:

1. Click the button next to Preview Reports. A new Reports Switchboard will appear (see Figure 3.8).

FIGURE 3.8

These options let you preview or print information about your contacts. The last option returns you to the Main Switchboard form.

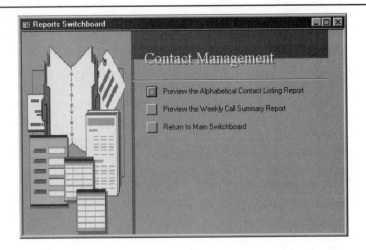

2. Click a button to preview one of the reports (the Alphabetical Contact Listing, for example). Lesson 5 will show you how to work with reports.

3. Return to the Reports Switchboard by clicking the Close button on the Preview window's toolbar or by pressing Ctrl+W.

4. Return to the Main Switchboard form by clicking the button next to Return to Main Switchboard.

Other Buttons on the Contact Management Main Switchboard

Figure 3.7 shows two more options on the Contact Management Main Switchboard.

Change Switchboard Items   Lets you add, change, and delete prompts on the switchboards and create new switchboards. We'll look briefly at ways to customize the switchboards in Lesson 8. Chapter 22 of this book explains how to create custom switchboards.

Exit this Database   Lets you close the Main Switchboard form and the Contact Management Lessons database window in one step and return directly to the main Microsoft Access menu.

Lesson 3: Creating and Customizing a Form

An Access form is like a fill-in-the-blanks paper form, except that you fill it in using the keyboard rather than pencil or pen. Our Contact Management Lessons database already has a nice form. But let's go ahead and create a new one for practice:

1. Close the Contact Management Main Switchboard form and return to the database window. To do so quickly, click the Close button in the upper-right corner of any Contact Management switchboard form, and then press F11 to restore the database window.

2. Click the Tables button in the database window, and then click the Contacts table name to highlight it.

WARNING   The Switchboard Items table contains entries that control the switchboard forms for your database. Do not change items in this table or your switchboards may stop working correctly. In Lesson 7, you'll learn how to use the Switchboard Manager to maintain this table in a safe manner.

---

3. Click the drop-down arrow next to the New Object toolbar button (shown at left, and second-to-last on the toolbar) and then choose Form from the menu that appears (or choose Insert ➤ Form). In the New Form dialog box, double-click AutoForm: Columnar. Wait a moment while Access creates an automatic form.

Access creates the form for entering and editing Contact Management data and names it Contacts (see Figure 3.9). The form contains one *control* for each field in your table. If you haven't added any data yet, the form will appear blank.

FIGURE 3.9

To create this form, choose the New Form option from the toolbar's New Object drop-down button and then double-click AutoForm: Columnar in the New Form dialog box.

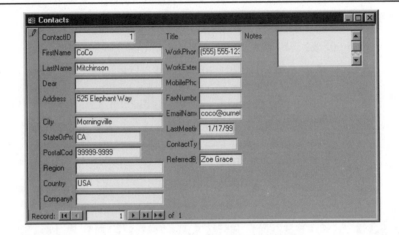

 NOTE A *control* is a graphical object that displays data, performs an action, or makes the form (or report) easier to read. You'll learn more about controls in Chapter 13.

Modifying and Saving the Form Design

The new form is fairly usable as-is. But chances are you'll want to tailor the Wizard's instant form to your own personal tastes. We'll show you some basic skills for designing fancier forms. When you finish the next set of steps, your form will resemble Figure 3.10.

FIGURE 3.10

The Contacts form
after changing some
field labels, dragging
fields to more conve-
nient places on the
form, and changing
the ContactID field.

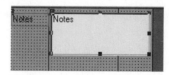

Whenever you want to change the look or behavior of something in Access, you must switch to design view. In design view, you'll see menu commands and toolbar buttons that help you make changes. You also may see a grid, which makes it easier for some people to size and align controls on the form. Let's switch to design view now and move some controls around on the Contacts form.

1. To switch from form view to design view, click the Form View toolbar button (shown at left), or choose View ➤ Design View from the menu bar.

2. To give yourself lots of room to work, maximize the design view window.

3. To hide or show the optional tools in design view (if they are covering your form or are missing), choose the appropriate options on the View menu. For example, if the toolbox is in your way, choose View ➤ Toolbox. For this exercise, select (check) the Ruler and Form Header/Footer options on the View menu. Leave the other options unchecked to hide those other tools.

4. Scroll down until you can see the Notes control and then click the Notes control (the empty box in the right corner of the form design view window). When selected, "move" and "size" handles appear on the control, as shown below:

5. Keep your finger *off* the mouse button and move the mouse pointer to any edge of the control until the mouse pointer changes to a "move" icon (a hand with all five fingers showing), as shown at left.

6. Press the mouse button (without moving the mouse) and drag the Notes control down and to the left until it's underneath the ReferredBy control, as shown below:

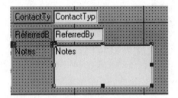

NOTE These mouse operations may take some practice. If you don't get them right the first time, repeat steps 5 and 6 until you do.

You've now moved the Notes control. You can use the same dragging technique to size controls and to move a label and/or text box independently. Always move the mouse pointer to an edge or corner of the control first until you see the mouse pointer change to the icon that best expresses what you want to do. The functions of the icons are summarized below:

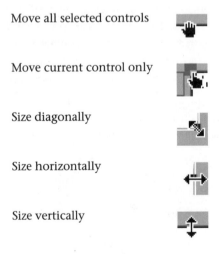

Move all selected controls

Move current control only

Size diagonally

Size horizontally

Size vertically

A Few Designer Tips

Here are some designer tips that might help you fine-tune the form. (You don't need to try them now.)

- **To select several controls at once**, hold down the Shift key as you select or drag a "lasso" around them. (To lasso those critters, start with no control selected and the mouse pointer on the grid or an empty part of the form, not on the control. Then drag a frame around all the controls you want to select.)

- **To select all the controls at once**, choose Edit ➢ Select All or press Ctrl+A.

- **To deselect one selected control or all selected controls**, click anywhere outside the selection area.

- **To deselect only one of several selected controls**, hold down the Shift key while clicking the control(s) you want to deselect.

- **To size and align the selected controls**, use the Format ➢ Align and Format ➢ Size commands from the menu bar (see Chapter 13).

- **To make a label fit its text exactly**, select the label, move your mouse pointer to any of the sizing handles, and then double-click the sizing handle. Or select the labels you want to resize and then choose Format ➢ Size ➢ To Fit from the menus.

- **To delete the selected control(s)**, press the Delete key.

- **To undo a change you're not happy with**, choose Edit ➢ Undo or press Ctrl+Z or click the Undo toolbar button.

To change the text in a label (the part that appears to the left of a control), follow these steps:

1. Click the label text so that selection handles appear around the label.

2. Click inside the selection. An insertion point will appear and the sizing handles will disappear temporarily.

3. Use normal Windows text-editing techniques, including these, to change the text:

   - **To highlight (select) text**, drag the mouse through that text or double-click a word.

   - **To position the blinking insertion point**, click the mouse or press the ← and → keys.

   - **To delete selected text or text at the insertion point**, press Delete or Backspace.

   - **To add new text at the insertion point**, simply type it.

4. Press Enter when you're done making changes. The selection handles will reappear around the label.

Try Some Hands-On Designing

Go ahead and try some more hands-on designing now. Don't worry if you don't get *exactly* the results we show—it's okay to make mistakes, and it's okay to experiment.

1. Change the label text for these controls, as follows:

   - Change the label for the StateOrProvince control from State/Province to **State/Prov**.

   - Change the label for the WorkExtension control from Work Extension to **Work Ext**.

   - Change the label for the EmailName control from EmailName to **Email**.

2. Resize all the labels on the form so they have a snug fit. The quickest way is to select all the controls (Ctrl+A) and then choose Format ➤ Size ➤ To Fit.

3. Click in an empty area of the form to deselect all the controls.

Next, resize the text controls that show field values on the right side of the form to make more room for their labels to be visible. First, hold down the Shift key and click on each text control in turn, without selecting their labels, too. (You should see a handle at the upper-left corner of each label control, but no others except those around the text controls.) Then point to the handle in the middle of the left side of any selected text box and drag to the right, leaving enough room for the longest labels to show. Then point to a handle in the middle of the right side of any selected text control and drag to make the text controls wider.

TIP To move a text control (one that shows a field value) closer to its label, make sure the text control is selected and then move the mouse pointer to the sizing handle at the upper-left corner of the text control (the pointer changes to a hand with one pointing finger). Drag to the left until the text control is closer to its label.

Preventing the Cursor from Landing in a Field

When you enter a new record, Access will assign a value to the ContactID field automatically. (You can't change this value.) The form will be more convenient to use if you prevent the cursor (also called the *insertion point* or *highlight*, depending on its shape) from landing in that field. To disable the ContactID control:

1. Click the ContactID control (the box to the right of the ContactID label) to select it.

 2. Click the Properties toolbar button (shown at left) or choose View ➤ Properties. You'll see the *property sheet* on the screen.

3. Click the Data tab at the top of the property sheet and then double-click the Enabled property to change its setting from Yes to No (see Figure 3.11). The ContactID control will be dimmed on the screen.

4. Click the Close button on the property sheet (or click the Properties button or choose View ➣ Properties) to hide the property sheet again.

FIGURE 3.11

FIGURE 3.11

The Enabled property for the ContactID control is set to No to prevent the cursor from landing on that control when you use the form for data entry.

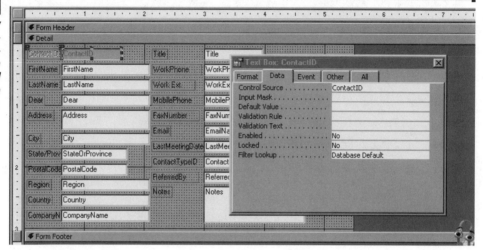

As you'll learn later in this book, *properties* are characteristics of elements in your database, and you can change them anytime. Don't worry too much about properties now.

Closing and Saving the Form

None of the design work you've done so far is saved yet, so saving is the next order of business. To save the form and close it:

1. Choose File ➣ Close or press Ctrl+W.

2. Click Yes when asked about saving the form.

3. Type **Contacts1** (or just accept the suggested form name) in the Save As dialog box and click OK.

4. (Optional) Click the Restore button on the database window to restore the window to its previous size.

That's all there is to it! The form name will appear in the database window whenever you're viewing form names (that is, after you've clicked on the Forms object tab on the database window). In the next lesson, you'll open the form and start using it.

At Your Leisure

To reinforce what you've learned and explore forms in more depth, look at Chapters 11 and 13. Or go to the Office Assistant, enter *Forms*, and then explore any subtopics that intrigue you. Or just move on to Lesson 4.

Lesson 4: Adding, Editing, Sorting, and Searching

Your database now contains several *objects*, including tables and forms. You can use either form to enter some data into the table.

Opening the Form

To open the Contacts1 form, follow these steps:

1. Start from the database window and click the Forms button.

2. Double-click the Contacts1 form name, or highlight (click) the name and then click Open. Your form will appear in form view (refer to Figure 3.10). Notice that the ContactID field is dimmed and the cursor is positioned in the FirstName field. The cursor skips the ContactID field because you changed the Enabled property for that field to No in the previous lesson.

 TIP If you prefer to use the Contacts form that the Database Wizard created for you automatically, either double-click the Contacts form name on the Forms tab of the database window or click the button next to the Enter/View Contacts option on the Main Switchboard form.

Entering Data

If you have a Rolodex or little black book of contact names, addresses, and other vital statistics, grab it now. Or if you don't want to bother with real names and addresses, use the fake one shown in Figure 3.12. Either way, follow these general steps to add some names and addresses to your Contacts table via the Contacts1 (or Contacts) form. (If the table is currently empty, you can skip to step 2 and begin entering data immediately.)

 1. Click the New Record button (shown at left) on the toolbar or the navigation bar (see Figure 3.12) to move to a new, blank record.

FIGURE 3.12

A new record added to the Contacts table via the Contacts1 form you created earlier.

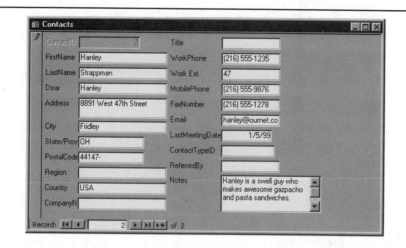

2. Type the person's first name into the First Name field; then press Tab or Enter or click anywhere within the Last Name field.

3. Type that person's surname into the Last Name field; then press Tab or Enter or click within the Dear field.

4. Fill in each of the remaining fields, as shown in Figure 3.12. Here are some tips to help you enter the remaining data:

- **To move forward from one field to the next**, press Tab or use the mouse. If the field doesn't display a vertical scroll bar and scroll arrows when the cursor lands in it, you also can press Enter to move to the next field. (The Address and Notes fields include vertical scroll bars and arrows.) If the field does display a vertical scroll bar and scroll arrows when the cursor lands in it, pressing Enter will end the current line of text and move the insertion point to the start of the next line *within* the field.

- **To leave a field empty**, press Tab to skip it or click the field you want to type in next.

- **To enter Postal Codes**, type the numbers only. The form automatically displays a hyphen after the first five digits. *Example:* When you type **441471234** in the Postal Code field, Access changes your entry to 44147-1234.

- **To enter telephone numbers**, type the numbers only. The form automatically displays parentheses around the area code and a hyphen after the exchange. *Example:* When you type **2165551225** in the WorkPhone field, Access changes your entry to (216) 555-1225 as you type.

- **To enter dates**, omit slashes between the numbers for the month and day if the numbers have two digits. If the numbers for the month and day have only one digit, type a slash to move to the next part of the date. Access will insert slashes in the field automatically. *Example:* When you type **121598** in the LastMeetingDate field, Access automatically changes your entry to 12/15/98 as you type. To enter the numbers for a January 5, 1999 meeting, type **1/5/99** or **010599**. (If you are entering dates where Access might not understand the century, for example, a birth date in 1925, enter 04071925 to make sure Access knows you are entering a date in the twentieth century. You will only be able to do this if the input mask on the field allows you to enter four digits for the year.)

NOTE You can enter the punctuation in the postal code, telephone number, and date fields, but doing so takes extra work. Data entry shortcuts, such as automatically inserting parentheses and hyphens in telephone numbers, are controlled by Input Mask properties in the table or form design. See Chapters 6 and 13 for more details.

5. Press Tab to move to the next blank record after filling in the last field (Notes).

6. Repeat steps 2 through 5 to fill in more names and addresses. For practice, make at least three entries. If possible, include some entries that have the same State/Province.

Making Changes and Corrections

If you're an experienced Windows user, you'll probably find that editing text in an Access form (or the datasheet view) is similar to typing and editing text in any other Windows program. But even if you're not experienced, these techniques can help you fix typing mistakes:

- **To delete text at the highlight or insertion point position**, use the Backspace and Delete keys.
- **To move to the next field**, press Tab. To move to the previous field, press Shift+Tab. To move to any field in the form, click that field.
- **To switch between navigation mode and edit mode**, press F2. You're in navigation mode when you use the keyboard (Tab, Shift+Tab, and Enter) to move to another field; in this mode, the field's contents will be selected, and anything you type will *replace* what's already in the field. When you switch to edit mode, you can *change* (rather than replace) what's already in the field; in this mode, the blinking insertion point replaces the selection highlight. You can press F2 any time you need to switch from one mode to the other.

- **To move to other records**, use the navigation bar at the bottom of the window (see Figure 3.13). Or press Page Up and Page Down to scroll up and down through existing records.

FIGURE 3.13

The navigation bar allows you to move through existing records and to add new records.

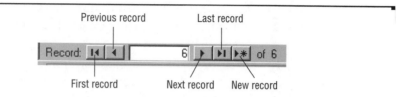

Previous record   Last record

First record   Next record   New record

 NOTE In the Contacts form created by the Database Wizard, Page Up and Page Down display the first or second page of the Contacts form, respectively. Pressing Page Down when you're on the second page of the form takes you to the second page of the next record. Pressing Page Up when you're on the first page of the form takes you to the first page of the previous record (if any).

 - **To switch to datasheet view**, where you can see all the data that you've entered so far, click the drop-down arrow next to the Form View toolbar button (shown at left, and the first button on the toolbar) and then choose Datasheet View; or choose View ➤ Datasheet View. You can make changes and corrections in datasheet view (shown in Figure 3.14), if you wish—it's not necessary to switch back to form view.

FIGURE 3.14

The sample table in datasheet view.

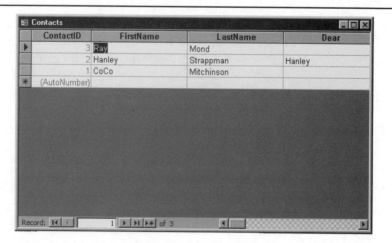

- **To resize columns in datasheet view**, move the mouse pointer to the vertical line at the right edge of the column header for the column you want to resize, and then drag the line to the left or right. For a snug fit, double-click the vertical line that's just to the right of the column name.

- **To move an entire column in datasheet view**, move the mouse pointer to the column name in the header, click the mouse, and then drag the column to the left or right.

- **To switch to form view**, click the drop-down arrow next to the Form View toolbar button and choose Form View; or choose View ➤ Form View.

 NOTE   If you click the Form View toolbar button (instead of clicking the drop-down arrow next to that button), you'll switch to the view that's shown on the button. For example, clicking the Form View button when you're in form view takes you to form design view and vice versa.

 TIP   You can't change the contents of the ContactID field, and there's no reason to. In fact, you can't even move the cursor into that field.

- **To move to a new, blank record**, click the New Record button on either the toolbar or the navigation bar (see Figures 3.12, 3.13, and 3.14).

 • **To delete a record**, click the record selector at the left side of the record and press Delete. Or click anywhere in the record you want to delete and then click the Delete Record toolbar button (shown at left). When prompted, click Yes if you're sure you want to delete the record or click No to retain the record. *Warning:* Once you click Yes to delete the record, it's gone for good!

Don't Save Each Record

 In case you're paranoid about losing your work (which certainly is understandable!), rest assured that as soon as you finish filling in (or changing) a record and move to another record, Access saves that record to disk. The only record that isn't saved is the one you're editing at the moment. (This unsaved record is marked at the left with a pencil icon.)

Sorting and Filtering

After you've put a few records into your table, you can unleash Access's real power. Let's begin by sorting (alphabetizing) the records:

1. Switch to datasheet view if necessary. To do so, choose View ➤ Datasheet View from the menu bar.

2. Click any person's surname to move the cursor into the Last Name column.

3. Click the Sort Ascending toolbar button (shown at left), or choose Records ➤ Sort ➤ Sort Ascending. Or right-click and then choose Sort Ascending from the shortcut menu.

Instantly your records are sorted (alphabetized) by surnames. You can follow steps 1 through 3 to sort on any field in your table. Try it and see.

Now suppose you want to see only contacts who live in Washington (or whichever state you want to look for). Here's a quick way to filter out those unwanted non-Washington contacts temporarily:

1. Put the cursor in any State/Prov field that contains WA—be sure not to highlight any text in the field.

2. Click the Filter by Selection toolbar button (shown at left) or choose Records ➤ Filter ➤ Filter by Selection. Or right-click the field and choose Filter by Selection from the shortcut menu. (If you prefer to see all records *except* those for your Washington contacts, right-click and choose Filter Excluding Selection instead.)

The non-Washington records will disappear temporarily (or, if you chose the exclude option, the Washington records will temporarily be hidden). To return the records to their original order and display the hidden records again, choose Records ➤ Remove Filter/Sort, right-click and choose Remove Filter/Sort from the shortcut menu, or click Remove Filter on the toolbar.

Filter by Input is another easy way to filter records. To see how Filter by Input works, point with your mouse anywhere in the State/Prov field (but not on the header!) and right-click. In the box after Filter For, enter WA and press Enter. As with Filter by Selection, to display the hidden records again, choose Records ➤ Remove Filter/Sort, right-click and choose Remove Filter/Sort from the shortcut menu, or click Remove Filter on the toolbar.

> ⚠ **TIP**   You can sort and filter records in form view or datasheet view. However, we suggest using datasheet view because the results are easier to see from there. See Chapter 9 for more about sorting and filtering.

Finding a Record

Suppose you've added hundreds, or even thousands, of names and addresses to your Addresses table, and now you want to look up a particular contact's address or phone number. Here's the easy way to do a lookup:

1. Switch to form view or datasheet view. (Choose View ➤ Form View or View ➤ Datasheet View.)

2. Click in the field you want to search. (In this example, click in any Last Name field.)

 3. Choose Edit ➤ Find, or press Ctrl+F, or click the Find toolbar button (shown at left). You'll see the Find and Replace dialog box.

4. Type *exactly* the last name you're looking for in the Find What text box. (Don't worry about upper- and lowercase, but do spell the name correctly.)

5. Click the Find Next button. The Last Name field of the first record that has the requested name will appear highlighted on the screen. (If Access didn't find a match, a message will appear; click OK to clear the message.)

 TIP If several people in your table have the same last name and you want to find each one in turn, continue to click the Find Next button as needed. When Access tells you it has finished searching, click OK.

6. Click the Cancel button in the Find and Replace dialog box when you're done searching.

Remember: Computers Are Dumb!

If your search doesn't find what you were expecting, remember that the computer isn't smart and it can't read your mind. You must click the field you want to search *before* starting the Find command and typing the text you want to search for. For example, if you click the Address field and search for *Strappman,* you'll get no match.

The exception to this rule is when you want to search all the fields in a table for a value. When this is the case, click the Find button with any field selected. Then, when the Find and Replace dialog box opens, change the setting for Look In to the table name.

The computer is also bad at guessing alternate spellings. If you type a first name such as Steven into your table and then search for Stephen, Access won't find the correct record. *Steven* and *Stephen* are similar enough for you to say "Yeah, that's a match." However, Access isn't smart enough to figure out that *Steven* and *Stephen* sound alike, and it certainly won't know if you want to match either name.

An Overview of Access

 NOTE Filter by Form, Advance Filter/Sort, and queries let you use wildcards to search for text that's similar to text that you enter. For example, you can tell Access to find a First Name *like* **St*en**. This statement will match records that contain Steven or Stephen in the First Name field. See Chapters 9 and 10 for details.

Closing the Form or Datasheet

When you're done playing with the data, close the form or datasheet view:

1. Choose File ➤ Close or press Ctrl+W. Access might ask you if you want to save your current work.

2. Click Yes if you want to save any filtering or other changes to the table or form; click No if you want to discard those changes.

Don't worry if you're not asked for permission to save your work—Access will ask only if you've altered the form or datasheet view. All the names and addresses you typed are stored safely on disk for future reference.

At Your Leisure

If you'd like to explore the topics described in this lesson on your own, skip to Chapter 9. To explore the topics online, go to the Help Contents, open the book *Finding and Sorting Data*, and then investigate the subtopics shown. Or move ahead to the next lesson now.

Lesson 5: Creating and Printing Reports

In this lesson you'll create, preview, and print a set of mailing labels. These mailing labels will be a nice addition to the reports that the Database Wizard created for you automatically.

Preparing Mailing Labels

Let's prepare a report that can print names and addresses on standard Avery mailing labels. Here are the steps:

1. Click the Tables button in the database window and then click the Contacts table name.

2. Click the drop-down arrow next to the New Object toolbar button (shown at left, and the second-to-last toolbar button) and then choose Report (or choose Insert ➤ Report from the menus).

3. Double-click Label Wizard in the New Report dialog box. In a moment the Label Wizard dialog box will ask, What Label Size Would You Like?

NOTE If you forget to choose a table (or query) in step 1, you'll need to choose one from the drop-down list in the New Report dialog box.

---

4. Choose Sheet Feed under Label Type if you are using a laser printer (or other sheet-fed printer) to print labels. Otherwise, choose Continuous (if you are using a dot-matrix printer to print labels).

5. Scroll to and click the appropriate Avery label size and then click Next.

TIP The Avery label number and label dimensions are printed on the package of labels. If you don't have labels already, just pick Avery number 5095 or some other two-across size.

---

6. Choose any font and color options you want to use. The Sample text at the left side of the dialog box will reflect your current choices. Click Next to continue.

7. Use these techniques to fill in the Prototype Label box, making it look like the example shown in Figure 3.15.

   - **To add a field to the label**, click in the Prototype Label box where you want the field to appear. Then double-click the field in the Available Fields list, or click the field and then click the > button. The field will appear in the Prototype Label box.

   - **To add a space, punctuation mark, or other text**, click where you want the space or text to appear (if the insertion point isn't there already) and then press the appropriate key(s) on your keyboard.

   - **To start a new line on the prototype label**, click the next line in the Prototype Label box or press ↓ or Enter.

   - **To delete a field or text**, position the insertion point in the Prototype Label box where you want to start deleting, and then press the Delete or Backspace key as needed. Or select text with your mouse or keyboard, and then press Delete or Backspace.

FIGURE 3.15

Fields from the Contacts table arranged for printing on a mailing label.

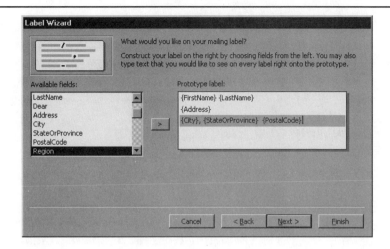

8. Click Next when you're done filling in the Prototype Label box. Access will ask you which fields you want to sort by.

9. Scroll down to PostalCode in the Available Fields list and double-click that field name. (If you prefer to sort by LastName and FirstName, double-click those field names instead.) Click Next to continue.

 TIP If you accidentally double-click the wrong field(s), click the << button to clear all the fields and then double-click the correct field(s). To clear just one field, click that field in the Sort By list, and then click the < button.

10. Click the Finish button in the last dialog box and wait a few seconds.

The Wizard will create a report with names and addresses formatted for the label size you specified. When the Wizard is done, you'll see a preview of the labels on the screen.

Closing and Saving the Report

You'll learn more about how to preview and print the report in a moment. But first, save the report and close the report preview window. To do so, choose File ➤ Close or press Ctrl+W. (If you click the Close toolbar button by accident, you'll be taken to design view. Just press Ctrl+W to return to the database window quickly.) Your report format is saved with the name Labels Contacts, as you can see by clicking the Reports button in the database window.

Don't Reinvent the Wheel!

Keep in mind that Access has saved the report format, not its contents. So even if you add, change, or delete addresses in the future, you do not need to re-create the reports to print the data. Whenever you print a report, Access automatically puts the table's current data into the report's format.

Previewing and Printing a Report

Previewing and printing a formatted report is a snap. Here are the steps:

1. Make sure your printer is ready. If you want to print on mailing labels, load the labels into the printer.

2. To see the list of available reports, do one of the following:

   - **If you're starting from the database window**, click the database window's Reports button. You should see the names of the reports the Database Wizard created, plus the one you created.

   - **If you're using the Main Switchboard form** in your Contact Management application, click the button next to the Preview Reports option. You'll see options for printing reports created by the Database Wizard. (Later in this chapter, we'll show you how to add your new Labels Contacts report to this list of options.)

3. To preview the report, do one of the following:

   - **If you're starting from the database window**, click the name of the report you want to print (for example, Labels Contacts) and then click the Preview button on the database window, or just double-click the report name. You also can choose File ➢ Print Preview from the menu bar.

   - **If you're starting from the list of reports** on the Reports Switchboard, click the button next to the report you want to view.

 TIP To print a report from the database window without previewing it first, right-click the report name you want to print, and choose Print from the shortcut menu that pops up.

---

4. The report will open in Print Preview mode with sample data shown. (Maximize the window if you wish.) Here are some tricks you can use to view your report:

- **To zoom in and out** between 100 percent magnification and a full-page view that fits on your screen, move the mouse pointer into the report area and click the mouse, or click the Zoom toolbar button (see Figure 3.16). Click the mouse on the Zoom button again to return to the previous size.

FIGURE 3.16

The Print Preview mode toolbar.

- **To zoom to various magnifications**, choose options from the toolbar's Zoom Control drop-down list. Or right-click in the report area, choose Zoom from the shortcut menu, and then choose a magnification. Or choose View ➢ Zoom Options from the menu bar.
- **To display multiple pages at once**, right-click in the report area, choose Pages, and then choose a page layout. Or choose View ➢ Pages Options from the menu bar. Or click the toolbar's One Page and Two Pages buttons.

5. Choose File ➢ Print (or press Ctrl+P) when you're ready to print the report, and then click OK in the Print dialog box that appears. Or to bypass the Print dialog box, click the Print toolbar button (shown at left).

NOTE The Print dialog box lets you choose a printer, print the report to a file, select a range of pages to print, and specify the number of copies and collation method. The Setup button in that dialog box lets you change the margins and layout for the report.

6. Click the Close toolbar button to return to the database window or the Reports Switchboard form.

At Your Leisure

If you want to learn more about reports before moving on to the next lesson, skip ahead to Chapters 12 and 13. Or go to the Access Help Contents, open the *Working with Reports* book, and then explore the subtopics shown.

Lesson 6: Creating a Data Access Page

Data access pages are a new feature of Access 2000. They are similar to forms, in that you can use them to view and sometimes edit data, but they are actually Web pages that can be opened from Access or Internet Explorer 5. Instead of being part of the database or project they belong to, data access pages are stored in their own HTML files, which makes them different from other types of Access objects you find in the database window.

You can start from scratch and create a data access page on your own, or you can get the Page Wizard to do all the hard work for you. In this lesson, you'll see how to use the Page Wizard to create a data access page for the Calls table, and then browse that data from Access or Internet Explorer.

Using the Page Wizard

Starting the Page Wizard is similar to using the Form Wizard and the Label Wizard:

1. In the database window, click the Tables button and highlight the Calls table.

2. Click the arrow for the New Object drop-down list on the toolbar and choose Page.

3. When the New Data Access page dialog box opens, double-click Page Wizard. The first step of the Page Wizard looks like this:

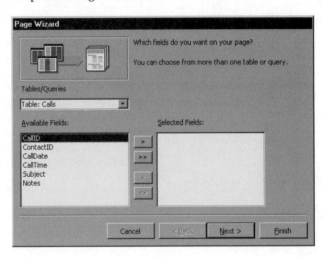

4. Make sure the Calls table is selected under Table/Queries. Then click the >> button to move all the fields in the Calls table to the Selected Fields list and click Next.

5. The next step lets you optionally group the records that are shown on the page. When you group records on a page, you can expand or collapse the detail records in each group. For this example, leave the grouping set to ContactID and click Next.

6. When the next step opens, optionally select up to four fields for sorting records and click Next.

7. Leave the title for the page unchanged.

8. Click the check box for Do You Want To Apply a Theme to Your Page? Then click Finish to have the Page Wizard do its work.

9. After a moment, a new Data Access Page window will open, along with a Theme dialog box. Select the theme you want to use (You can preview it on the right side of the window.) and click OK. The page will look something like the one below, depending on the theme you choose. This page has the Kids theme:

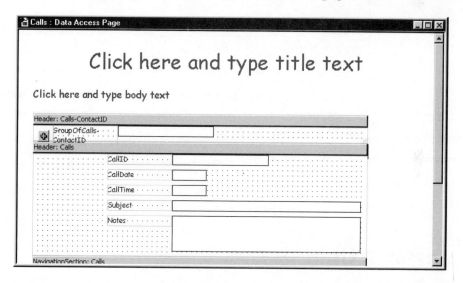

Unless you changed the setting for the open mode in the last step of the Page Wizard, the page will appear in design view. Next you'll see how to browse data by opening the page from Access or Internet Explorer 5.

Browsing Your New Page

To browse a data access page, use any of these techniques:

• **If the page is open in design view**, click the Page View button on the toolbar.

- **To open the page from the database window and view it with Access**, click the Pages button, right-click the page you want to view, and choose Open from the shortcut menu. The Calls page we just created looks like this when opened in Access with the detail records expanded:

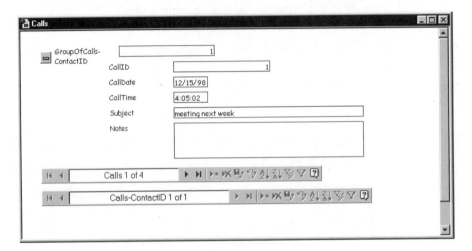

- **To open the page in Internet Explorer from the database window**, click the Page button, right-click the page you want to browse, and choose Web Page Preview from the shortcut menu.
- **To open the page from Internet Explorer**, enter the full name of the page, for example, C:\My Documents\Calls.htm, in the Address box.

For more information on data access pages, use the Office Assistant to look for topics about *data access pages*. Or, go directly to Chapter 14.

Lesson 7: Using Queries

You can use *queries* to isolate certain fields and records of data in a table, to sort data into alphabetical or numeric order, to combine data from several related tables, and to perform calculations on data in tables. In this lesson you'll use queries to set up a simple list that shows specific fields and specific records in the Addresses table in sorted order by last name. Then you'll change the query to show records for everyone in the table.

Creating a Query

To create a query from your Contacts table:

1. Click the Tables button in the database window, and then click the Contacts table name.

2. Click the drop-down arrow next to the New Object toolbar button (shown at left, and the second-to-last toolbar button) and then choose Query (or choose Insert ➤ Query from the menu bar).

3. Double-click Design View in the New Query dialog box. Figure 3.17 shows the query design window that appears.

FIGURE 3.17

The query design win-dow shows the field list for the Contacts table in the top pane and the design grid in the bottom pane.

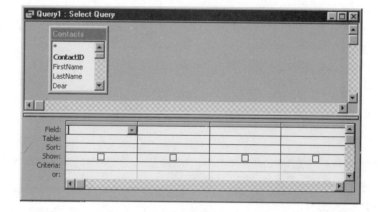

NOTE Using the Simple Query Wizard (and other query wizards) is often the easiest way to speed up the job of creating queries. However, for the query you'll be designing next, the from-scratch method is a little faster and it gives you practice using the query design window.

Choosing Fields to View

To fill in the design grid, you first choose the fields you want to work with in the order you want them to appear. Follow these steps now to add the LastName, First-Name, City, StateOrProvince, and WorkPhone fields to the grid:

1. Maximize the query design window so you can see more columns in the design grid at once.

2. Add the LastName field to the design grid by double-clicking that field in the Addresses field list near the top of the window. The LastName field will appear in the first blank column of the design grid. The Table row in that column will show the name of the table the field comes from, and the Show row will include a checkmark to tell Access to display that field when you run the query.

 TIP Here are two other ways to add a field to the query design grid: (1) drag the field name from the field list in the top of the query window to the appropriate column in the design grid; or (2) click the Field box in the appropriate column of the design grid, click the drop-down arrow that appears, and then choose the field name you want to use.

3. Add the FirstName field to the design grid by double-clicking that field in the Contacts field list. The field will appear in the next (second) column of the design grid.

4. Add the City field by scrolling down in the field list and double-clicking the City field name.

5. Use the same techniques described in step 3 to add the StateOrProvince and WorkPhone fields to the design grid.

 TIP If you add the wrong field to a column of the design grid, click in the Field box for that column, click the drop-down arrow, and then choose the correct field name from the list. To delete a column in the design grid, move the mouse pointer just above the field name in that column (until the pointer changes to a black ↓), click the mouse to highlight the entire column, and then press Delete.

Figure 3.18 shows the five fields in the query design grid.

Choosing Records to View

Suppose you want to view the list only for people who live in California. To do so, type **ca** (or **CA**) into the Criteria row under the StateOrProvince column. Here's how:

1. Click in the Criteria box in the StateOrProvince column.

2. Type **ca**, or any state that you've stored in the table (see Figure 3.19). Don't worry about typing exact uppercase and lowercase letters.

PART

I

An Overview of Access

FIGURE 3.18

Five fields—LastName, FirstName, City, StateOrProvince, and WorkPhone—added to the query design grid.

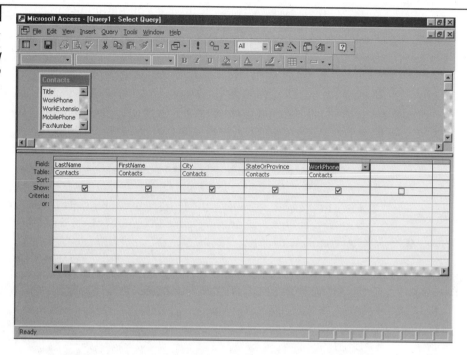

FIGURE 3.19

The query will display the LastName, FirstName, City, StateOrProvince, and WorkPhone fields of records that have California ("ca") in the StateOrProvince field.

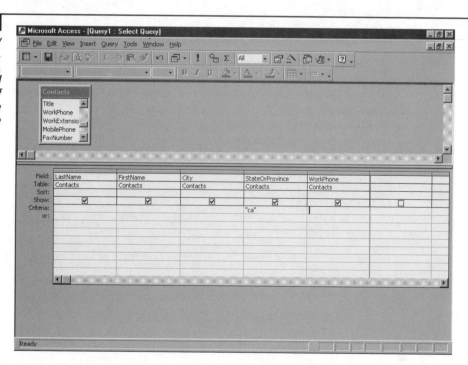

3. Press Enter. Access automatically adds quotation marks around the text you typed and moves the cursor to the next column.

Choosing the Sort Order

To sort the list by last name and then by first name within identical last names, tell Access which fields (columns) to sort by and whether you want to sort in ascending (A to Z) order or descending (Z to A) order. Here are the steps:

1. Use the horizontal scrollbar to scroll the design grid back to the LastName column, and click in the Sort box below the LastName column. Then click the drop-down arrow that appears and choose Ascending from the list.

2. Click in the Sort box below the FirstName column, click the drop-down arrow, and then choose Ascending. Figure 3.20 shows the query design window after you complete this step.

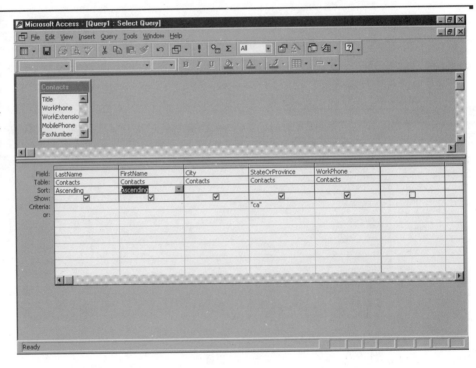

FIGURE 3.20

This query will sort the query results by last name and first name within identical last names. Because the StateOrProvince Criteria is set to "ca" (California), the query results will show data for people in California only.

TIP   If you chose the wrong column to sort by, click the Sort box below the appropriate column, click the drop-down arrow, and then choose Not Sorted.

Because the LastName column appears to the left of the FirstName column in the design grid, records will be alphabetized by people's last names. The FirstName field will act as a tie breaker, meaning that records with identical last names will be alphabetized by first name.

Running the Query

 Running the query is a snap. To try it, click the Run toolbar button (shown at left) or choose Query ➤ Run from the menu bar.

The query results will appear in datasheet view and will show only the Last Name, First Name, City, StateOrProvince, and WorkPhone columns, and only the people in California, alphabetized by last name and first name (see Figure 3.21). All the data is *live,* and you can change it the same way you change any data in datasheet view.

FIGURE 3.21

The query results appear in datasheet view.

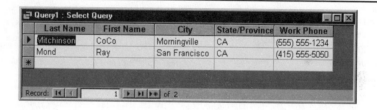

 NOTE   You might have noticed that the column headings (or captions) shown in Figures 3.14 and 3.21 don't exactly match the field names. For example, the field name for a person's surname is *LastName;* however, the column heading shows *Last Name* (with a blank space between words). These column headings are controlled by the *Caption* property in the table or query design. Chapter 6 explains how to change table properties, and Chapter 10 delves into changing properties in a query.

Changing the Query

Changing the query to display an alphabetized list of all the records in the table is easy. Try it now:

1. Click the Query View toolbar button (shown at left, and the first button on the toolbar) or choose View ➢ Design View to switch back to the query design window. Maximize the query design window if necessary.

2. Delete "ca" in the Criteria box below the StateOrProvince column. To do this quickly, select (drag your mouse through) "ca" and then press Delete.

3. Run the query again. (Click the Run toolbar button.)

Now the datasheet view resembles Figure 3.22. Because you removed the "ca" (California), the query results show all records in the table—not just the people from California.

FIGURE 3.22

The datasheet after removing "ca" from the StateOrProvince field of the query design, running the query again, and restoring and resizing the window.

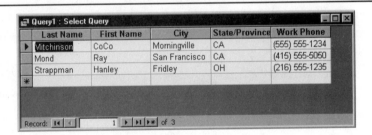

Just for grins, print a quick copy of this list now by choosing File ➢ Print ➢ OK or by clicking the Print toolbar button.

Saving and Reusing the Query

You'll probably want to see an updated list sometime later, perhaps after you've added, deleted, or changed some records. Rather than re-creating this query each time, you can save it and reuse it anytime. To save the query now:

1. Click the Save toolbar button or choose File ➢ Save.

2. Type a valid Access object name (such as **Contacts Phone List Query**) and then click OK.

3. Close the Select Query window (press Ctrl+W). The query design and datasheet will disappear, but your query will be saved.

TIP You can save the query design from the design window or the datasheet window—the steps are the same. You also can save the design when you close the window. If you're asked about saving changes, click the Yes button and enter a query name if prompted to do so.

To run a saved query, go to the database window (press F11 if necessary), click the Queries button, click the query you want to run (Contacts Phone List Query in this example), and then click the Open button on the database window. Or just double-click the query name. The query will run on the latest data in your table. (If you wish, close the datasheet window and return to the database window.)

 NOTE To change the query design instead of running the query, click the Queries tab on the database window, click the query you want to change, and then click the Design button on the database window.

At Your Leisure

To learn more about queries, see Chapter 10. Or use the Office Assistant to search for help topics on *queries*.

Lesson 8: Customizing an Application

Now you've created several database objects—a table, a form, a report, a data access page, and a query. But those objects aren't put together in a way that allows people who know nothing about those objects to use the database easily. To make your database extra easy to use, you can add these objects to the "turnkey" application that the Database Wizard created for you automatically. In this lesson, you'll learn some techniques for doing just that.

Adding a Hyperlink to a Form

Hyperlinks let you jump to other Access database objects or even to information on the Web. We'll step through a simple example here that shows you how to add a hyperlink to jump to the labels report from the Contacts1 form we created in Lesson 3. For more information on working with hyperlinks, check out Chapters 7 and 8.

1. Click the Forms button, click Contacts1, and then click the Design button in the database window. You'll see the form design window, where you can modify the form.

2. Click the Insert Hyperlink toolbar button to open the Insert Hyperlink dialog box.

3. On the left side of the Insert Hyperlink dialog box, click the button for Object in This Database. Under Select an Object in This Database, click the expand button for Reports. Then double-click the report called Labels Contacts.

4. A new underlined control will appear in the upper-left corner of the form design window. This control is the hyperlink. Drag the hyperlink to the place you want it to appear on the form.

5. To test the hyperlink, click the Form View toolbar button. Then click the hyperlink to open the report. When you close the report window, you'll return to the form window.

Adding Command Buttons to a Form

Let's begin by adding command buttons, like those shown in Figure 3.23, to the Contacts1 form you created in Lesson 3.

This Contacts1 form has four command buttons and a hyperlink in its form header. These buttons are similar to the Calls and Dial buttons on the Contacts form created by the Database Wizard.

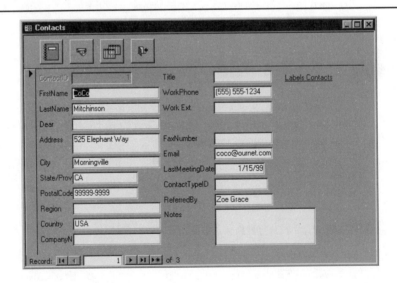

1. Go to the database window, click Forms, click Contacts1, and then click the Design button on the database window. You'll see the form design window where you can modify the form. Maximize the form design window to give yourself some room to work.

2. Move the mouse pointer to the bottom of the Form Header section until it changes to an up/down arrow crossed by a bar (shown at left). Then drag the horizontal line at the bottom of the section downward. This action increases the height of the Form Header section so that it is big enough to hold the command buttons. For this example, make the form header about .75 inches high. (Look at the vertical ruler, which is marked in .25-inch increments, as you resize the form header.)

3. Check to see if the *toolbox* (shown in Figure 3.24) is visible, because you will use it to create the command buttons. If the toolbox isn't visible, click the Toolbox toolbar button (shown at left) or choose View ➤ Toolbox.

FIGURE 3.24

The toolbox lets you create new objects on a form.

4. Make sure the Control Wizards button is selected (pushed in). You can drag the toolbox anywhere you want it on the design window.

NOTE If the property sheet or another tool is blocking your view in the form design window, hide that tool by choosing its name from the View menu.

5. Create a command button by clicking the Command Button tool in the toolbox and then clicking where you want the upper-left corner of the button to appear on your form. In this example, click the left edge of the Form Header (see Figure 3.23). The Command Button Wizard dialog box appears.

6. Click Report Operations in the Action Categories list (first column) and then click Preview Report in the Action list (second column).

7. Click the Next button to continue.

8. Click Alphabetical Contact Listing in the report names list in the next dialog box. (The Database Wizard built this report automatically when it created the Contact Management Lessons database.) Click the Next button to display another dialog box.

9. Click Next to accept the suggested button picture. Then the Database Wizard asks you to name your button.

10. Type **Alphabetical Contact List** and click Finish.

The button appears on the form as shown below. You can't test the button yet because it works only when you're in form view. (You're in design view now.) Before testing that button, you'll add three more buttons.

 TIP To move a button, drag it to a new location. If you want to bypass "grid snap" while moving or sizing an object, hold down the Ctrl key while you're dragging.

Creating the Button for Mailing Labels

Follow these steps to add a second button to your form:

1. Click the Command Button tool in the toolbox, and then click slightly to the right of the command button you just created.

2. Click Report Operations and Preview Report in the two columns in the next Wizard dialog box, and then click Next.

3. Click Labels Contacts in the list of available reports, and then click Next.

4. Select (check) Show All Pictures in the next Wizard dialog box. Then scroll up to Mailbox (The pictures are listed in alphabetical order, by picture name.) and click that picture name. This step will put a picture of an envelope going through a mail slot on the button.

5. Click Next.

6. Type **Labels Preview Button** and click Finish.

Creating the Query Button

Follow these steps to add a button that will run the query named Contacts Phone List Query:

1. Click the Command Button tool in the toolbox, and then click slightly to the right of the "mailbox" command button you just created.

2. Click Miscellaneous and Run Query in the two columns in the next Wizard dialog box, and then click Next.

3. Click Contacts Phone List Query in the list of available queries, and then click Next.

4. Click Next to choose the suggested picture in the next Wizard dialog box.

5. Type **Contacts Phone List Query** and click Finish.

Creating the Close Button

The final button will make it easy to close the form. To create it:

1. Click the Command Button tool on the toolbar and then click just to the right of the last button at the top of the form.

2. Click Form Operations in the first column, click Close Form in the second column, and then click the Next button.

3. Click Next to accept the default Exit picture in the next Wizard dialog box.

4. Type **Exit Button**, and click Finish in the next Wizard dialog box.

5. Save your work by clicking the Save button on the toolbar or by pressing Ctrl+S.

 TIP   To align buttons or other objects on the form, select the objects you want to align and then choose Format ➤ Align and an appropriate alignment option. To set equal horizontal spacing between objects, select the objects and choose Format ➤ Horizontal Spacing ➤ Make Equal. See Chapter 13 for more information.

Adding Visual Basic Code to a Form

Next you'll learn how to add some Visual Basic (VB) code to your form. Please don't think that programming is something you have to do in Access. You can create very powerful Access applications with no programming whatsoever. This little experiment with Visual Basic serves mainly as a way to get your hands dirty, so you can see how programming with VB works.

Follow these steps (carefully!) to add some programming code to your form now:

1. Click the Properties toolbar button or choose View ➤ Properties to open the property sheet.

2. Choose Edit ➤ Select Form. (Or just click the form selector, the box in the upper-left corner of the form window, where the rulers would intersect.) The property sheet displays the properties for the entire form.

3. Click the Event tab on the property sheet, and then scroll down to the OnOpen property. You'll add some code to maximize the Contacts1 form window any time you open the Contacts1 form.

4. Click in the OnOpen text box, click the Build (...) button that appears, and then double-click Code Builder. A module editing window will appear with the cursor positioned on the blank line between the Private Sub Form_Open and End Sub statements.

5. Press the Tab key and then type the following *exactly:*

```
DoCmd.Maximize
```

Be careful to type the text correctly—there's no margin for error when you're writing program code.

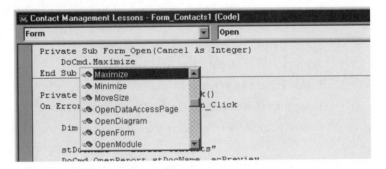

6. Click the Close button for the Microsoft Visual Basic window (the big window that holds the smaller Code window), or choose File ➤ Close and Return to Microsoft Access to return to the form design window. Notice that [Event Procedure] now appears as the OnOpen property.

7. Scroll down to the OnClose property of the property sheet. You'll add some code that restores the previously displayed window to its original size any time you close the Contacts form.

8. Click the OnClose text box, click the Build (...) button that appears, and then double-click Code Builder. A module editing window will appear with the cursor positioned on the blank line between the `Private Sub Form_Close` and `End Sub` statements.

9. Press the Tab key and then type *exactly:*

`DoCmd.Restore`

NOTE This `DoCmd.Restore` command restores a window to its previous size. For example, if you open the Contacts1 form from the database window, the database window will reappear at its previous size when you close Contacts1. Likewise, if you open Contacts1 from the Main Switchboard (as explained later), the Main Switchboard form will reappear at its previous size.

10. Click the Close button for the Microsoft Visual Basic window (the big window that holds the smaller Code window), or choose File ➣ Close and Return to Microsoft Access to return to the form design window.

11. Choose File ➣ Close ➣ Yes to save and close the modified form.

You'll return to the database window (press F11 if necessary).

NOTE When you're entering code in the Visual Basic window, the rules for editing are the same as when you're working with Word.

Customizing the Switchboard Form

The switchboard form that the Database Wizard created when you set up the Contact Management Lessons database provides buttons and options that make it easy to update and report on information about your contacts. Since you've gone to the trouble of setting up some new forms and reports, you'll probably want to add them to the switchboard. You also might want to change the names of options that appear on the switchboard.

To begin, open the Main Switchboard form and then click the button next to Change Switchboard Items. Or choose Tools ➢ Database Utilities ➢ Switchboard Manager from the menu bar. You'll see the Switchboard Manager dialog box shown in Figure 3.25.

FIGURE 3.25

The Switchboard Manager lets you create new switchboard pages, edit existing pages, delete pages, and choose a default switchboard page.

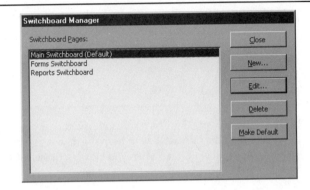

Adding the Addresses1 Form to the Main Switchboard

Follow these steps to add your new Contacts1 form to the Main Switchboard page:

1. Click Main Switchboard (Default) in the Switchboard Pages list and then click the Edit button in the Switchboard Manager dialog box. The Edit Switchboard Page dialog box will appear (see Figure 3.26 for a completed example).

FIGURE 3.26

The Edit Switchboard Page dialog box after adding a new item and moving it to the top of the list.

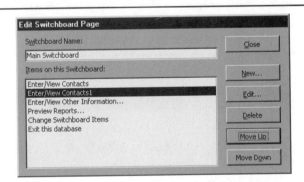

2. Click the New button to open the Edit Switchboard Item dialog box.

3. Type **Enter/View Contacts1** in the Text box.

4. Click the drop-down list button next to the Command box, and choose Open Form in Edit Mode. A Form box will appear.

5. Click the drop-down list button next to the Form box, and choose Contacts1. The completed Edit Switchboard Item dialog box looks like this:

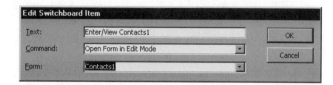

6. Click OK to return to the Edit Switchboard Page dialog box. Your new entry appears at the bottom of the Items on This Switchboard list.

7. Move your new item to the top of the list by clicking that item and then clicking the Move Up button four times. Figure 3.26 shows the completed Edit Switchboard Page dialog box.

 TIP   If you want to remove the old Enter/View Contacts option from the list, click that item in the Items on This Switchboard list, click the Delete button, and then click Yes to confirm the deletion.

8. Click the Close button to return to the Switchboard Manager dialog box.

Changing the Option Names on the Reports Switchboard

We think the options for printing reports on the Reports Switchboard are a bit verbose and maybe even somewhat wordy. If you agree, follow these steps:

1. Click Reports Switchboard in the Switchboard Pages list and then click the Edit button. Here's what you'll see:

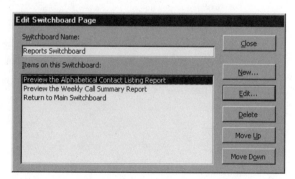

2. Click the first item in the Items on This Switchboard list, and then click the Edit button. The option name will be highlighted in the Text box.

3. Replace the selected text with **Alphabetical Contact List**. To do this task quickly, select "Preview the " (including the space after "the") and press Delete. Drag over the "ing Report" at the end of the name, and press Delete again. Then click OK.

4. Repeat steps 2 and 3 for the second item on the switchboard. Change the Text to **Weekly Call Summary**.

Now add the new Labels Contacts report to the list of items on the Reports Switchboard:

1. Click the New button to open the Edit Switchboard Item dialog box.

2. Type **Mailing Labels** in the Text box.

3. Click the drop-down list button next to the Command box and choose Open Report. A Report box will appear.

4. Click the drop-down list button next to the Report box and choose Labels Contacts.

5. Click OK to return to the Edit Switchboard Page dialog box. Your new entry appears at the bottom of the Items On This Switchboard list.

6. Click the Mailing Labels item, and then click the Move Up button once to move your new entry up a notch. The Edit Switchboard Dialog box will resemble the example shown below:

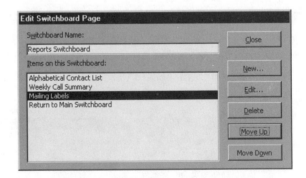

7. Click the Close button twice to return to the database window.

Putting It All Together with Startup Commands

When you open a database, Access looks for certain startup commands and executes them automatically. You can customize your database by choosing startup commands that hide the database window, go straight to a specific form, and more. The Database Wizard took care of setting up the essential startup commands for you automatically. But let's customize those startup commands just for practice:

1. Choose Tools ➤ Startup, or right-click any tab in the database window and choose Startup from the shortcut menu. You'll see the Startup dialog box (a completed example appears in Figure 3.27).

FIGURE 3.27

The Startup dialog box after we filled in the Application Title.

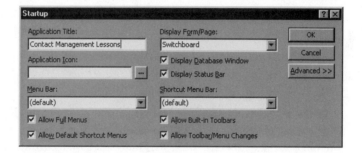

2. Type **Contact Management Lessons** in the Application Title box. (This title will appear on the Access title bar any time the database is open and on the Taskbar.)

3. Make sure Switchboard appears in the box below Display Form. (You can use the drop-down list below Display Form to choose any form that's available for the Contact Management Lessons database; however, using Switchboard gives you the most flexibility.)

4. Click OK. The new application title immediately replaces Microsoft Access in the window's title bar.

NOTE The Main Switchboard form automatically minimizes the database window when you open the form; therefore, you don't need to clear the Display Database Window check box in the Startup dialog box.

Testing the Application

Now you're ready to test the whole thing. Follow these steps to close and then reopen the database:

1. Choose File ➤ Close, or press Ctrl+W, until the Main Switchboard form and database window disappear.

2. Open the database you just closed by choosing File from the menu bar, then choosing Contact Management Lessons.

The Main Switchboard form will open, and you'll see the text Contact Management Lessons in the Access window's title bar. Now you can explore the Contact Management Switchboard form to your heart's content. When you're finished, do one of the following:

- **To close the Main Switchboard form and the database window**, click the button next to Exit This Database on the Main Switchboard form.

- **To close the Switchboard form but leave the database window open**, click the Close button on the Main Switchboard or Reports Switchboard form (or press Ctrl+W) and then press F11 to display the database window.

When you're done using Access, choose File ➤ Exit to return to Windows. Your database application will be stored safely on disk for future use. To use the application in the future, start Access and open the Contact Management Lessons database.

At Your Leisure

To learn more about creating applications, see Parts IV and V of this book.

There's More Than One Way to Create Turnkey Applications

As you've seen, there's more than one way to automate your work and to create turnkey applications with Access. For example, you can use a switchboard form, which Access sets up any time you use the Database Wizard, to create a database. You also can add hyperlinks, command buttons, and Visual Basic programming to forms as you did for your Contacts1 form. And you can use combinations of these and other techniques that you'll learn about in Parts IV and V of this book. Your application can be as simple or as sophisticated as you wish, depending on your requirements and your expertise. It's all up to you!

Where to Go from Here

Congratulations! You've just created your first Access database and your first custom Access application. The steps you followed to set up the Contact Management example also work for the other applications that Access can create automatically.

If you'd like to build a fancier application now, use the Database Wizard to create an Order Entry database. We'll use the Wizard-generated Order Entry database to illustrate key concepts throughout this book. Alternatively, you can copy our sample OrdEntry 9 database from the CD-ROM supplied with this book (see Appendix B for details). Having your own Order Entry database to experiment with as you read will make learning Access easier and more fun.

What's New in the Access Zoo?

You've just taken a look at many of the features that make it so easy for both beginners and experts to learn and use Access.

New features of Access 2000 shown in these lessons include the following:

- Data access pages, a new type of Access object for browsing data from Access or Internet Explorer.
- A new Visual Basic editing window.

CHAPTER 4

About Access, Office, Windows, and the Internet

FEATURING:

Microsoft Access is tightly integrated with Windows and Microsoft Office. In this chapter we highlight the most important integration features and point you to places where you can get more details. We'll also give you a brief overview of the features that let you share Access data via the Internet. If you're completely new to Access and Microsoft Office, you might want to skim through (or even skip) this chapter and come back to it when you find yourself asking questions such as, "How can I make the most of what I know about Windows and Microsoft Office?" and "How can I make the most of my Access data?"

Making the Most of Windows and Access

Microsoft Access is designed from the ground up to provide full support for all Windows features. Listed in alphabetical order below are some of the most important Windows-like features that you'll find in Access.

32-Bit Application   Microsoft Access 2000 is a 32-bit application, which means that it runs in its own protected computer memory area. Therefore, Access won't grind to a halt if some other program on your computer decides to misbehave. Access also takes advantage of the multithreading capabilities of Windows, something programmers will appreciate; the Jet database engine, Microsoft Access, and modules written for Visual Basic all run in separate threads. (On high-end Windows NT machines, multithreading allows several CPUs to cooperate on a single Access application at the same time.)

Briefcase Replication   Access takes advantage of the Windows Briefcase feature, which enables you to work remotely with replicas of your database and later merge the changes into your master databases. Any design changes made to the master databases also will be propagated to the replicas. Replication is ideal for managing remote changes to data and balancing the load over a network. See Chapter 18 for more details.

Database Explorer   The database window in Access looks and acts a lot like Windows Explorer, as well as windows that appear when you open My Computer or Network Neighborhood. To view database objects as large icons, small icons, a list, or a detailed list, choose options on the View menu, or click appropriate database toolbar buttons, or right-click an empty area inside the database window and choose View options from the shortcut menu. To arrange icons by name, type, creation date, or modification date, choose options on the View ➤ Arrange Icons menu, or right-click an empty area inside the database window and choose Arrange Icons options from the shortcut menu. Shortcut menu options are shown in Figure 4.1. See Chapter 1 for more on using the database window.

FIGURE 4.1

The Access database window lets you view object names and arrange icons, much as you do in Windows.

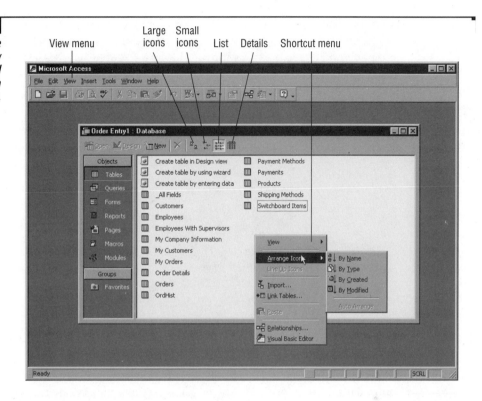

Long FileNames and UNC Paths   Like all programs designed for Windows, Microsoft Access supports long file names and Uniform Naming Convention (UNC) paths. UNC paths let you refer to files on a remote computer by supplying the computer name, rather than by permanently mapping a drive letter to the remote computer. For example, an Order Entry database file located in the My Documents folder on drive C of a computer named Hanley might have a tongue-twisting UNC name of \\Hanley\c\My Documents\Order Entry.mdb.

Plug-and-Play Screen Resolution   Plug-and-play screen resolution lets you change your screen resolution on the fly. To use it, minimize Microsoft Access and any other programs that are covering the Windows Desktop. Next, right-click any empty area of the Desktop and choose Properties. Finally, click the Settings tab in the Display Properties dialog box, use the slider control below the Desktop Area option to set the screen resolution you want to use, and then click OK. Respond to any prompts that appear, and then click the Microsoft Access Taskbar button to return to Access.

Shortcut Menus   Windows-style shortcut menus are available throughout Access. Simply right-click wherever you want to see a shortcut menu, and then click (or right-click) the shortcut menu option you want to use (refer to Figure 4.1).

Special Effects Access and its forms and reports can display the same sunken, raised, etched, chiseled, shadowed, and flat special effects you often see in Windows programs and dialog boxes, as shown in Figure 4.2. See Chapter 13 for more about using special effects.

FIGURE 4.2

An Access form that uses various Windows-style special effects.

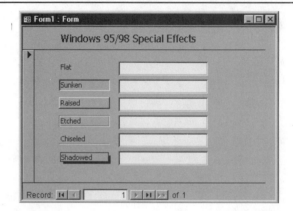

Windows Look and Feel Access uses all the standard Windows controls you've grown to love, including tabbed dialog boxes, option buttons, drop-down lists, command buttons, and checkmark-style (✓) check boxes. So once you've mastered Windows skills, working with Access will seem easy and natural. Figure 4.3 shows a typical Access dialog box.

FIGURE 4.3

Access uses all the familiar Windows conventions for quick learning and ease of use.

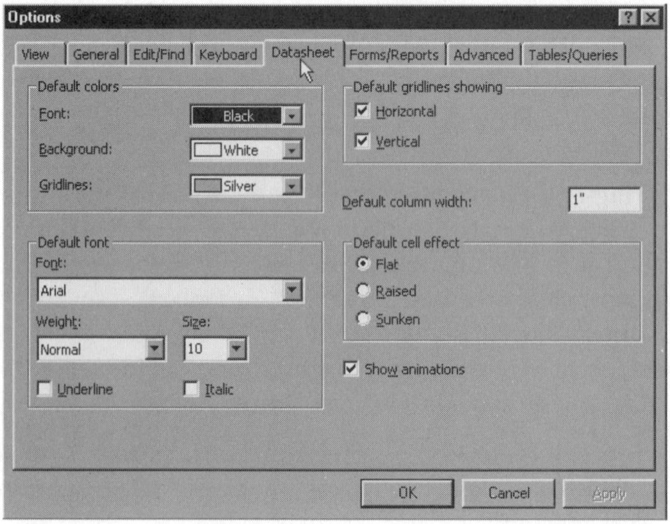

Windows Shortcuts Creating a Desktop shortcut to any Access object is similar to creating shortcuts in Windows. Simply drag and drop an object from the Access database window to your Desktop, and then use the dropped object as you would any shortcut. For example, double-click the shortcut to start Microsoft Access and open the associated object, or right-click the object to open a shortcut menu (see below) that offers a host of possibilities for working with the object. (See Chapter 1 for more on shortcut menus.)

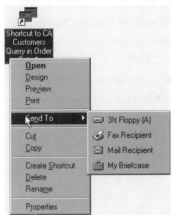

Making the Most of Microsoft Office and Access

Microsoft Access shares many common features with other programs in the Microsoft Office suite, especially Microsoft Excel and Microsoft Word. So if you've installed all or part of Microsoft Office, you can take advantage of these common features immediately. We'll take a look at some of these shared features next. Later in this chapter, we'll discuss convenient ways to share data across programs in Microsoft Office.

The Microsoft Office Shortcut Bar

The Microsoft Office Shortcut bar, shown below, lets you launch and switch between programs, open files, and more.

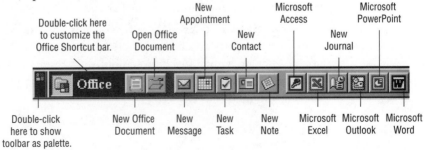

Displaying the Office Shortcut Bar

The Microsoft Office Shortcut bar usually appears along the right side of your Windows Desktop. If it doesn't appear, click the Start Taskbar button, and then choose Programs ➤ Office Tools ➤ Microsoft Office Shortcut Bar from the Start menu.

Handy Ways to Use the Office Shortcut Bar

Here are some things you can do when the Office Shortcut bar is visible:

- **To find out what an Office Shortcut bar button is for**, move your mouse pointer to the button. A ScreenTip will appear near the pointer to explain the button's purpose.

- **To choose a button on the Office Shortcut bar**, click the button.

- **To display the Office Shortcut bar as a floating palette of buttons**, move the mouse pointer to any empty area between buttons, and then drag the bar toward the middle of the screen.

- **To dock the floating Office Shortcut bar** along the right side of the Desktop, double-click the Office Shortcut bar's title bar.

- **To open the Control Menu for the Office Shortcut bar**, click or right-click the Office Shortcut bar's Control Menu icon, and then choose any of the options shown below:

- **To choose or hide bars on the Office Shortcut bar**, right-click an empty area between buttons on the bar, and select (check) or deselect (clear) the name of the bar you want to display or hide, respectively.

- **To switch to another bar on the Office Shortcut bar** when multiple bars are selected, click the button for the bar you want to use.

- **To customize the currently selected bar on the Office Shortcut bar**, right-click an empty area between buttons on the bar and choose Customize, or double-click an empty area between buttons. Then choose an appropriate tab from the Customize dialog box (see Figure 4.4), complete the dialog box as needed, and then click OK.

FIGURE 4.4

The Customize dialog box for the Office Shortcut bar after we clicked on the Buttons tab. (Don't worry if the Customize dialog box on your computer differs slightly from this example.)

Check items that should appear on the bar

Clear items that shouldn't appear

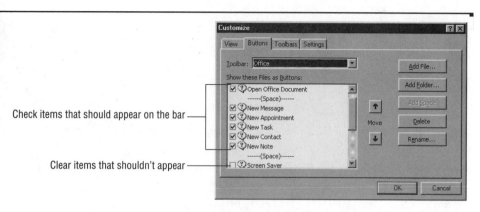

- **To add an Office Shortcut bar button that will launch a program** (including Microsoft Access) or open a document or folder, select the bar that should contain the new button. Next, use Start ➢ Find, or My Computer, or Windows Explorer to locate the program, document, or folder name you want to add as a button. Then drag the program, document, or folder name to any button on the Office Shortcut bar (when the mouse pointer displays a small + sign, you've hit the right spot on the Office Shortcut bar and can release the mouse button). Your new shortcut button will appear at the end of the Office Shortcut bar.

- **To remove a button from the Office Shortcut bar**, right-click the button and choose Hide Button.

- **To exit the Office Shortcut bar**, click or right-click the Control Menu icon at the top-left edge of the Office Shortcut Bar, and then choose Exit.

For more details on using the Microsoft Office Shortcut bar, see your Microsoft Office documentation, or click or right-click the Control Menu icon at the top-left edge of the Office Shortcut bar and then choose Contents and Index.

Common Bars

Common menu bars and toolbars appear throughout the Microsoft Office suite, so you won't have to waste time hunting for options you use often. Figure 4.5 shows the Microsoft Excel, Word, PowerPoint, and Access program windows opened on the Desktop. Notice the similarities among their menu bars and toolbars.

FIGURE 4.5

The Microsoft Office suite offers common menu bars and toolbars to speed your learning process.

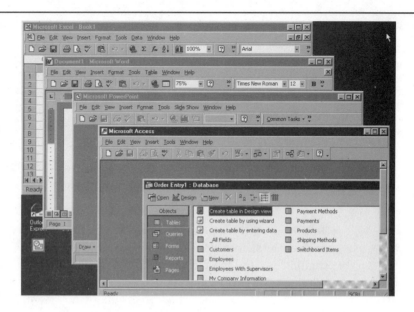

Common Dialog Boxes

Many dialog boxes—including New, Open/Import, Page Setup, Print, and Save—work the same way in all Microsoft Office programs. In Figure 4.6, for example, you see the Open dialog box for Microsoft Word. Figure 4.7 shows the very similar Import dialog box for Microsoft Access.

FIGURE 4.6

An Open dialog box in Microsoft Word.

3. Double-click a file name.   1. Choose the disk and folder to look in.

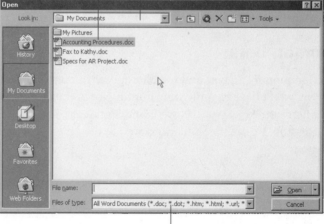

2. Choose the type of file to open.

FIGURE 4.7

An Import dialog box in Microsoft Access.

3. Double-click a file name.   1. Choose the disk and folder to look in.

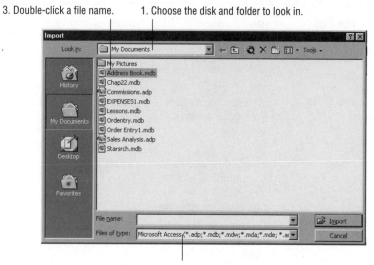

2. Choose the type of file to import.

Common Office Tools

You'll also find common tools that work in identical (or similar) ways throughout Microsoft Office. Table 4.1 briefly describes each tool and tells you which Microsoft Office programs offer it.

TABLE 4.1: COMMON MICROSOFT OFFICE TOOLS

FEATURE	WHAT IT DOES	MENU OPTION OR SHORTCUT	WHERE YOU'LL FIND IT
AutoCorrect	Corrects typing errors automatically	Tools ➢ AutoCorrect	Access, Excel, PowerPoint, Word (Chapter 9)
AutoFormat	Formats a document automatically	Format ➢ AutoFormat	Access, Excel, Word (Chapters 11, 12, and 13)
Save As	Saves objects with a new name	File ➢ Save As	Access, Excel, Exchange, PowerPoint, Outlook, Word (Chapter 7)
Export	Saves objects with a new format	File ➢ Export	Access, Excel, Exchange, PowerPoint, Outlook, Word (Chapter 7)

Continued ▶

TABLE 4.1: COMMON MICROSOFT OFFICE TOOLS (CONTINUED)

FEATURE	WHAT IT DOES	MENU OPTION OR SHORTCUT	WHERE YOU'LL FIND IT
Format Painter	Copies the appearance of one control or selection to another	Format Painter toolbar button	Access, Excel, PowerPoint, Word (Chapter 13)
Import/Link	Imports or links data from other programs and formats	File ➤ Get External Data ➤ Import; or File ➤ Get External Data ➤ Link Tables; or File ➤ Open	Access, Excel, Exchange, PowerPoint, Outlook, Word (Chapter 7)
Insert	Inserts date and time, page number, picture, object, and more (depends on program)	Insert menu options	Access, Excel, PowerPoint, Word (Chapters 8 and 13)
Options	Customizes default settings	Tools ➤ Options	Access, Excel, Exchange, PowerPoint, Outlook, Word (Chapter 16)
Print	Prints objects and documents (some programs also offer a preview feature)	File ➤ Print (Ctrl+P); or File ➤ Print Preview	Access, Excel, Exchange, PowerPoint, Outlook, Word (Chapter 9)
Properties	Displays and changes properties of the active document or database	File ➤ Database Properties; or File ➤ Properties	Access, Excel, Exchange, PowerPoint, Outlook, Word (Chapter 5)
Send	Sends the active document or object using electronic mail	File ➤ Send To	Access, Excel, Exchange, PowerPoint, Outlook, Word (Chapter 7)
Spell Check	Checks for and replaces spelling errors	Tools ➤ Spelling (F7)	Access, Excel, Exchange, PowerPoint, Word (Chapter 9)

Tapping the Microsoft Knowledge Base and More

Every Microsoft Office program offers many sources of help. For example, you can look in the *Getting Results* book, the Answer Wizard, the Help Index, the Help Contents, and the Readme file that come with most Microsoft Office programs. But that's not it by a long shot! You also can get in-depth technical help on a variety of Microsoft products from these resources:

Microsoft Office Update   This Web site has information on Access, along with all the other Office programs. To get to this site, make sure you are connected to the Internet. Then select Help ➤ Office on the Web from the Access menus.

Microsoft Download Service (MSDL)   The MSDL is a bulletin board service that contains Microsoft Software Library (MSL) articles and support files for you to download to your computer. Using your modem, dial (425) 936-6735 in the United States, or (905) 507-3022 in Canada.

Microsoft FastTips   This service offers recorded or faxed answers (in English) to common technical problems and lets you order catalogs, Application Notes, and popular articles from the Knowledge Base (KB) via fax or mail. Call (800) 936-4100 from any touch-tone telephone.

Microsoft Knowledge Base (KB)   The KB contains a comprehensive set of articles (updated daily) with detailed answers to how-to and technical support questions and lists of bugs and fixes. The KB is available on the World Wide Web. From the World Wide Web, you can do full-text searches of KB articles and download files automatically.

Microsoft Press publications   Microsoft Press offers development kits, resource kits, and a variety of books about Microsoft products and related technologies. Call (800) MSPRESS or (800) 677-7377.

Microsoft Software Library (MSL) on the World Wide Web   Here you'll find a collection of binary (nontext) files, including device drivers, utilities, Help files, and technical articles for all Microsoft products. You can also find this resource on the CD-ROMs for Microsoft TechNet and Microsoft Developer Network.

Microsoft TechNet and Microsoft Developer Network (MSDN) CD-ROMs   These subscription services offer KB, MSL, and other information on CD-ROM. To subscribe to these services, call (800) 344-2121 for Microsoft TechNet or (800) 759-5474 for MSDN.

Online support forums   Online support forums are frequented by end-users, third-party developers, and Microsoft support staff who can answer many of your questions quickly. You can find Microsoft forums on the Microsoft Network and other Internet services.

You can reach the KB and MSL at these Internet sites:

- Microsoft World Wide Web at www.microsoft.com
- Microsoft Gopher at gopher.microsoft.com
- Microsoft FTP at ftp.microsoft.com (supports anonymous logon)

You can reach the KB, MSL, or Microsoft forums from CompuServe by typing **GO MICROSOFT** at any ! prompt, or choose equivalent menu options. To reach the Microsoft Access forum directly, type **GO MSACCESS** or choose equivalent menu options.

For more information about all the resources mentioned above, use the Office Assistant to look up *Technical Information* from any Microsoft Office program. If you're connected to the Internet, you can access many of these resources by choosing Help ➤ Office on the Web from any Microsoft Office program's menu bar.

Sharing Access Information with Other Office Programs

Imagine having to retype all the names and addresses that you've painstakingly stored in your Access database—just to send form letters from Microsoft Word. And who in their right mind would want to retype data stored in Excel worksheets after deciding that a database table offers a more efficient way to store that information? None of that tedium and wasted effort is necessary when you use Windows technologies and the integrated Microsoft Office suite. In the next few sections, we'll summarize ways to transfer information to and from Access and point you to places in this book where you can get more details.

 NOTE If you get messages about difficulties in starting programs or establishing links between programs, chances are that your computer does not have enough memory to complete the job you're trying to do. To solve this problem, respond to any messages that appear, and restart your computer (Start ➤ Shutdown ➤ Yes). Then launch only the program or programs that absolutely must be in memory at the same time and try the operation again. If you still have problems, you may need to install more memory on your computer. (32MB is the minimum amount of memory that Microsoft recommends for the latest version of Office.)

Using Import and Export

You can use file *import* or *link* techniques to create an Access table from data stored in an external file, such as an Excel worksheet. To get started, go to the Access database window and choose File ➤ Get External Data ➤ Import or File ➤ Get External Data ➤ Link Tables.

To convert data in an Access table (or other object) for use in another program, such as Excel or Word, use the *export* feature. After exporting the Access data, you can start the other program, open the file you created, and use it normally. To start exporting data from Access to another format, go to the database window and click the table, query, form, or other object that contains the data you want to export. Then choose File ➤ Export.

Chapter 7 explains how to create Access tables from files stored in these formats: Access, Excel, Paradox, text files, Exchange(), dBASE, Lotus 1-2-3, ODBC databases, and HTML. There you'll also learn how to export data from Access to these formats: Access, Excel, Paradox, text, dBASE, Lotus 1-2-3, Rich Text Format, Microsoft IIS 1-2, Microsoft Active Server Pages, Microsoft Access Data Access Pages, Microsoft Word Merge, ODBC databases, and HTML. See Chapter 14 for information on how to use data access pages to browse Access data from the Internet.

 TIP Access 2000 has a new feature that lets you create a new database and import a file at the same time. In the Open dialog box, just open the data file of your choice. If it's a file that Access recognizes, like a spreadsheet or a text file, Access will create a new database and launch the appropriate import wizard to create a new table to hold the data.

Using OLE

Windows OLE technology offers many ways to share selected data or entire files between Microsoft Access, Microsoft Office, and other Windows programs. Chapter 8 provides step-by-step instructions for using these techniques to put data into Access tables, including OLE fields. But let's take a quick peek now at what's available.

Using the Clipboard

The cut-copy-and-paste technique offers a versatile way to exchange selected data between programs. If possible, the original formatting is preserved when you complete the paste operation. (When you paste rows from a Microsoft Access datasheet to another program, the field names also come along for the ride.)

In a nutshell, the cut-copy-and-paste procedure is as follows:

1. Select the object you want to move or copy using the standard selection methods for the program you're copying or moving from.

2. Choose Edit ➢ Copy (Ctrl+C) or Edit ➢ Cut (Ctrl+X), or click the Copy or Cut toolbar button if it's available. Your selection will be copied (if you chose Copy) or moved (if you chose Cut) to the Windows Clipboard.

 NOTE The Windows Clipboard is a scratchpad area in your computer's memory. Each time you copy or cut a selection to the Clipboard, the new selection replaces the previous contents of the Clipboard. Data on the Clipboard usually stay around until you exit Windows.

3. Start the target program and open the document, table, or other object where the copied or moved data should appear. Then put the cursor where the data should appear.

4. Paste the data from the Clipboard by following one of these steps, and then answer any prompts that appear.

- Choose Edit ➤ Paste (Ctrl+V) or click the Paste toolbar button.

- Choose Edit ➤ Paste Special (if available), complete the Paste Special dialog box, and then click OK.

- In Access only, choose Edit ➤ Paste Append to add records to the end of the table shown in the current datasheet or form.

5. The pasted material will appear on your screen.

Using the Insert Menu Commands

You also can use commands on the Insert menu to insert all or part of an object into the current document, presentation, OLE Object field, or other object. The steps for inserting and the appearance of the inserted data depend on which program you're using when you insert the data, which Insert command you choose, and which type of data you insert.

Here, for example, are the steps for inserting Access table data into a Microsoft Word document. The inserted data becomes a standard Word table that's independent of the original Access table.

1. Start Microsoft Word and open the document that should contain the Access table data.

2. Choose View ➤ Toolbars ➤ Database, and then click the Insert Database button. (You may have to add this button to your Database toolbar using the Customize dialog box.)

3. Click Get Data under Data Source in the Database dialog box.

4. Change the setting for Files of Type to MS Access Databases (*.mdb; *.mde) in the Open Data Source dialog box, and then locate the database you want to use. In the next dialog box, select the table you want to include in your document.

5. Click the Query Options button if you want to select fields and values to insert. Click the Table AutoFormat button to choose a format for the inserted data.

6. Click the Insert Data button, complete the Insert Data dialog box that appears, and then click OK.

Figure 4.8 shows the screen after we inserted the Employees table data from our sample Order Entry database into a Microsoft Word document.

In most Office programs, you can use the Insert ➤ Object command either to insert a new object that you create on the fly or to insert an existing object that's stored in a file. Chapter 8 takes you through the steps for inserting objects into OLE Object fields in Access, so we won't repeat them here. (The steps for inserting an object are similar whether you start from Access, Excel, Exchange, PowerPoint, or Word.)

FIGURE 4.8

Here we used the Insert Database button on the Database toolbar in Word to copy the Employees table data from our sample Order Entry database to a Microsoft Word document.

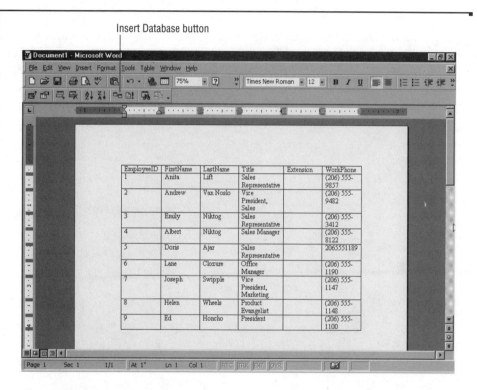

If the program can do so, it will show the inserted data with its "real" appearance; otherwise, the inserted data will appear as a "package" icon. (A *package icon* is simply an icon that represents the file the inserted data is part of.) In Figure 4.9, for example, we inserted the bitmap file named forest.bmp from the \Windows folder into the Word document from Figure 4.8. Next to the bitmap file, we inserted the Address Book Lessons sample database. Notice that the bitmap file appears as a picture, but the Address Book Lessons database object appears only as a package icon, because Word can't display an entire database at once.

To open an inserted object for viewing or editing, simply double-click the object's picture or icon. When you're done working with the inserted object, do one of the following:

- **If the object opened within the Access window**, click outside the object. The hash marks and sizing handles around the object will disappear, and the Access tools and menu bar will reappear.
- **If the object opened in a separate program window**, choose File ➤ Exit from the object's program window. You'll be returned to the Access window.

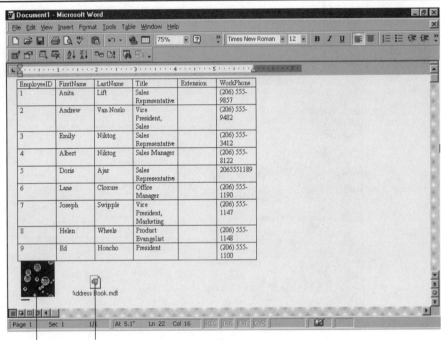

Inserted Access databases appear as "package" icons.

Inserted bitmap files have their "real" appearance.

Dragging and Dropping

The drag-and-drop technique is a convenient way to copy or move selected data from one open program to another. You can't drag and drop between all Windows programs, but a little experimentation should quickly reveal what's possible. Figure 4.10 shows the basic drag-and-drop procedure.

Here's how to reproduce the example in Figure 4.10:

1. Start Microsoft Word and Microsoft Access; then open a Word document that contains some text and an Access table that contains an OLE Object field. Next, tile the programs vertically on the screen by right-clicking an empty area of the Windows Taskbar and choosing Tile Vertically from the shortcut menu.

2. Select the text you want to copy in the Microsoft Word document.

3. Hold down the Ctrl key while dragging the selected text from the Microsoft Word window to the OLE Object field in the Microsoft Access window. When the mouse pointer reaches its destination, release the mouse button and Ctrl key.

These actions will *copy* the selected text to the OLE Object field. To *move* the selection, rather than copy it, do not hold down the Ctrl key while dragging.

FIGURE 4.10

We dragged and dropped selected text from a Word document to an OLE Object field in an Access table. In datasheet view, the copied text in the OLE Object field appears simply as Microsoft Word Document; in a form, however, the copied data will look much as it does in Microsoft Word.

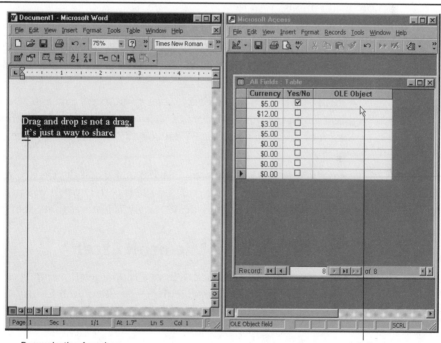

Drag selection from here. . .   to here.

Using OfficeLinks in Access

The OfficeLinks feature in Microsoft Access provides a nifty way to copy Access data to other Microsoft Office program formats and to immediately start the appropriate Office program. To use OfficeLinks, select a table, query, form, or report from the Access database window, and then choose options on the Tools ➤ OfficeLinks menu or on the OfficeLinks drop-down toolbar button (shown below).

Chapter 7 covers the OfficeLinks features in more detail, but in case you're curious now, your options are as follows:

Merge It with MS Word   Merges your Access data with a new or existing Microsoft Word document and starts Microsoft Word. This feature is especially handy for creating form letters and mailing labels from Access tables and queries.

Publish It with MS Word   Saves your Access data as a Microsoft Word Rich Text Format (RTF) file and starts Microsoft Word. Use this feature when you want to dress up your Access data or mix it with word processing text and pictures.

Analyze It with MS Excel   Saves your Access data as a Microsoft Excel file and starts Microsoft Excel. This feature is perfect when you need to examine Access data with the sophisticated analysis features that Excel offers.

Using Access Data from Microsoft Excel

Microsoft Excel and Microsoft Access have a special relationship because they both can interpret and display data in a tabular row-and-column format. Excel offers several ways to use Access data without ever leaving Excel itself.

 NOTE   Chapter 15 explains how to create PivotTables, which are special Excel objects that are embedded within an Access form. To create and use PivotTables that display Access data, you must start from Access, not from Excel.

Converting a Worksheet to an Access Table

You can import the current Excel worksheet to an Access table in a new or existing database. After you complete this procedure, the Excel worksheet and imported table will be independent of one another. (That is, changes to the worksheet in Excel won't affect the Access table, and vice versa.)

Open the worksheet you want to convert (in Excel, of course) and then:

1. If you have not previously installed the AccessLinks Add-In for Excel, select Tools ➢ Add-Ins. In the Add-Ins window, check the box for Access Links and click OK. Insert your Office CD when prompted, and click the Add or Remove Features button. In the next window, click the Expand button for Microsoft Excel for Windows and then for Add-Ins. Select Access Links, and then click the button for Update Now at the bottom of the window. Click OK when the update is complete.

2. Delete any blank rows in the worksheet. Then put the cursor into any cell within the worksheet.

3. Back in the Excel window, choose Data ➢ Convert to MS Access.

4. Choose whether to convert the data to a New Database or an Existing Database whose name you supply at the prompt, and then click OK.

After a brief delay, the Import Spreadsheet Wizard (described in Chapter 18) will guide you through the remaining steps, and your new table will appear in the Tables tab of the Access database window. You can then use the table as you would any normal Access table.

Creating an Access Form or Report from an Excel Worksheet

You also can create an Access form or report for use with the current Excel worksheet. The resulting form or report will reside in the Access database, and the Excel worksheet will be *linked* to a new Access table in that database. (That is, changes you make in Excel will update the linked table in Access, and vice versa.)

To create the form or report, start from Excel and follow these steps:

1. Open the worksheet you want to view with the form or report. If your worksheet contains any blank rows, delete those rows. Then put the cursor into any cell within the worksheet.

2. To create a form, choose Data ➢ MS Access Form.

   Or

   To create a report, choose Data ➢ MS Access Report.

3. If your worksheet isn't already linked to an Access database, you'll see a Create Microsoft Access Form or Create Microsoft Access Report dialog box. (An example appears below.) Choose whether to store the form or report in a New Database or an Existing Database whose name you supply, choose whether the worksheet has a Header Row or No Header Row, and then click OK. If you choose to create a new database, the new database will have the same name as your Excel file.

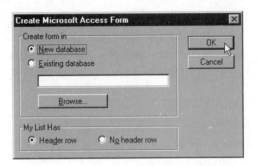

4. Follow the Form Wizard or Report Wizard instructions and complete the remaining steps.

Your Excel table will be linked to the Access database, and your new form or report will appear in the Forms or Reports tab of the Access database window and on the screen.

From Access, you can use the linked table and form or report normally. To use the form or report from Excel, click the View Access Form or View Access Report button that appears near the right edge of your worksheet (see Figure 4.11).

 NOTE From Access, you can add records to linked Excel worksheets and change records, but you cannot delete them. From Excel, you can add and delete worksheet rows and change cell data as you would in any normal worksheet.

To learn more about the AccessLinks add-in program that creates Access forms and reports (or to find out what to do if the Data ➢ MS Access Form and Data ➢ MS Access Report commands don't appear in Excel), look up *AccessLinks Forms and Reports* in the Excel Help Index. See Chapter 7 for more about linking and using Excel worksheets in Access. Chapter 11 explains how to use the Form Wizard, and Chapter 12 covers the Report Wizard.

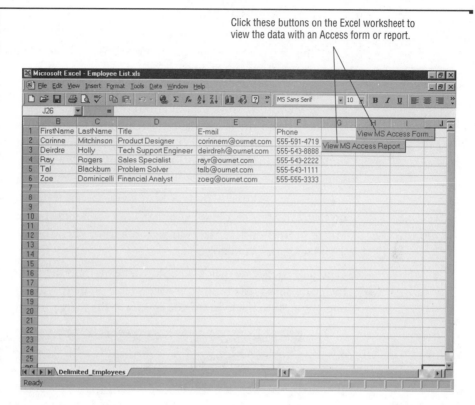

FIGURE 4.11

A sample Microsoft Excel spreadsheet named Employees, after we used the Data ➤ MS Access Form and Data ➤ MS Access Report commands in Excel. To view the Access form or report without leaving Excel, click the View MS Access Form or View MS Access Report buttons, respectively.

Click these buttons on the Excel worksheet to view the data with an Access form or report.

Using Access Data from Microsoft Word

As we mentioned earlier, you can start from Access and use the OfficeLinks feature to merge Access data with a new or existing Microsoft Word main document. You also can start from Microsoft Word and merge data from an Access table or query into a form letter, mailing label, envelope, or catalog main document. Here's one way to do the job, starting from a blank document window in Microsoft Word:

1. Choose Tools ➤ Mail Merge. The Mail Merge Helper dialog box will appear.

2. Click the Create button in the Mail Merge Helper dialog box and select the type of main document you want to create (Form Letters, Mailing Labels, Envelopes, or Catalog). When prompted, click the Active Window button.

3. Click the Get Data button in the Mail Merge Helper dialog box, and then choose Open Data Source.

4. Choose MS Access Databases from the Files of Type drop-down list in the Open Data Source dialog box. Then locate and double-click the database you want to use.

5. Click the Tables or Queries tab in the Microsoft Access dialog box, and then double-click the Access table or query that contains the data you want to use.

6. Respond to any prompts that appear. When you reach the main document window in Microsoft Word, use the Insert Merge Field button on the Mail Merge toolbar to insert the merge fields that contain the data you want to display, and type any text that should appear between fields; press Enter after inserting fields as needed. Figure 4.12 shows the document window after we added fields and some text to a form letter.

7. Start the merge: choose Tools ➣ Mail Merge (or click the Merge Helper button on the Mail Merge toolbar), and then click the Merge button; or click the Mail Merge button on the Mail Merge toolbar; or click the Merge button in the Mail Merge Helper dialog box.

8. Complete the Merge dialog box (shown below) and then click Merge. Word will merge the latest data from your Access table or query with your main document and output it to the location you specify in the Merge To drop-down list.

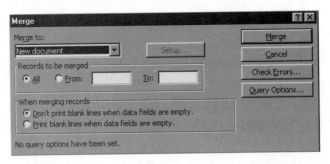

9. Print the results of the merge, and close the merged results file without saving it (if you merged to a new document).

10. Save your main document (File ➣ Save), and close it if you wish (File ➣ Close).

The next time you want to merge your main document with the latest Access data, just open the main document in Word (File ➣ Open) and repeat steps 7 through 10 above.

If you need help setting up merge fields on your main document, click the Help button on the Standard toolbar in Microsoft Word, and then click the Insert Merge Field button on the Mail Merge toolbar. Or look up *Mail Merge* and its subtopics in the Microsoft Word Help Index.

FIGURE 4.12

A sample form letter that uses fields from an Access table.

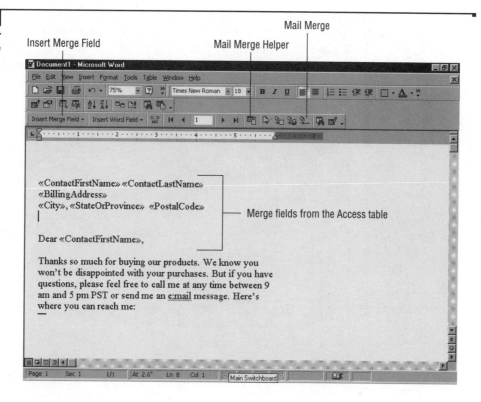

Merge fields from the Access table

Sharing Access Information via the Internet

Along with the other Microsoft Office programs, Access has great features for working with data through the Internet. You can:

- Create data access pages to present Access data on the Web.
- Import data that's already in HTML format.
- Export an Access table or query to HTML format.
- Use hyperlinks to jump to information on the Web or in other Office programs.

Creating Data Access Pages

Data access pages are a new feature of Access in Office 2000. They are HTML files, stored outside of an Access database, that work with Internet Explorer 5. While forms allow you to browse and edit data while you're working in an Access database or project, data access pages let you work with Access data from Internet Explorer 5. They can include browse buttons and other controls that are often seen on Web pages. Figure 4.13 shows an example of a data access page created with the Page Wizard. For instructions on how to use this wizard and customize data access pages, see Chapter 14.

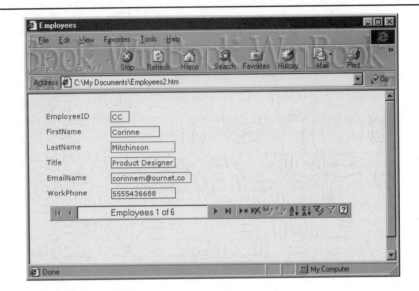

FIGURE 4.13

This data access page was created with the Page Wizard. It shows records from the Employee table and can be opened from Internet Explorer 5, as well as from Access.

Importing and Exporting HTML

HTML is the special formatting that's often used to prepare data for publication on the Internet. HTML controls the appearance of information as it's browsed and includes tags for characteristics such as bold and font size. Access lets you import data files that include HTML code. With a database open, choose File ➤ Get External Data ➤ Import and select HTML in the Files of Type drop-down list. Select the .htm or .html file you want to import, and click OK to start the HTML Import Wizard.

Exporting an Access table or query to an HTML file is just as easy. First highlight the table or query you want to export in the database window. Then choose File ➤ Export, and change the Save as Type option to HTML Documents. Access will let you select an HTML template (you can leave this blank) and ask you to name the new file. By default, the .htm file is created in \My Documents. To find out how to change the HTML template and other details about importing and exporting HTML data, see Chapter 7.

For Programmers and Techies Only

Two features in Microsoft Access, Microsoft Office, and other programs for Windows will dazzle and delight programmers and application developers. These features are *OLE Automation* and *Visual Basic for Applications*. For a brief look at what these features mean to you, please read on.

About Microsoft Visual Basic

Microsoft Visual Basic is a programming language for building programs across Microsoft Office. The beauty of Visual Basic is that you can reuse code written for Access in Microsoft Excel, Word, or Project with only minor changes.

Chapter 26 introduces you to Visual Basic. For online help with the language, look up *Visual Basic* and its subtopics in the Access Help Index. Or go to the Access Help Contents, double-click the *Microsoft Visual Basic* book, and then explore the additional books and subtopics that appear.

About OLE Automation

OLE Automation is a standard technology that programmers use to expose their OLE objects to development tools, macro languages, and other applications that support OLE Automation. From Access you can use Microsoft Visual Basic to manipulate OLE Automation objects. You also can use OLE Automation to manipulate Access objects from other programs, such as Microsoft Excel.

We'll introduce you to OLE Automation in Chapter 28 of this book. For more information on the topic, look up *OLE Automation* and its subtopics in the Access Help Index.

Where to Go from Here

This chapter has introduced you to the many ways that Microsoft Windows, Microsoft Access, and other programs in the Microsoft Office suite can work together to help you get the most from your Access data. It also gave you a bird's eye view of the Access features for working with data from the Internet. In the next chapter, you'll learn how to create instant databases and ready-to-use applications with just a few clicks of your mouse.

What's New in the Access Zoo?

Access has some new features that make it easier to import data and publish data for the Web:

- You can create a new database and import a file right from the Open dialog box. Just open a data file that Access recognizes, and it will create a database and launch an import wizard to create a table for the imported data.

- Access 2000 has a new type of object called data access pages. These objects are HTML files that can be used to browse Access data from Access or Internet Explorer 5.

PART II

Creating a Database

LEARN TO

- Create a database

- Create Access tables

- Link, import, and export data

- Add, edit, and view data

- Sort, search, filter, and print

- Query tables

- Create forms, reports, and data access pages with Wizards

CHAPTER 5

Creating a Database

I t's terminology time again! An *application* is a computer-based system that lets you perform useful tasks, such as managing orders, accounts receivable, product inventory, and other types of information. A *turnkey* application enables you to enter and use information with the turn of a key; that is, without worrying about how everything is put together behind the scenes. An Access *database* is a file that holds all the objects for a single application, including the tables, forms, reports, queries, modules, and macros. Finally, a *project* is a special purpose Access database that works with tables stored on an SQL Server. In this chapter you'll learn how to create databases and more than 20 different turnkey applications. If you want to find out about using projects, see Chapter 30.

If you haven't tried the hands-on lessons in Chapter 3, you should do so now. Those lessons take you through creating a database and turnkey application and give you practice using Access wizards.

 NOTE After creating your database, you can use the Database Splitter Wizard (Tools ➤ Add-Ins ➤ Database Splitter) to split it into one file that contains the tables and another that contains the queries, forms, pages, reports, macros, and modules. A split database can run faster than a single-file database over a network because only the table data is kept on the server. Form and report designs and other database objects reside on each user's local computer, so traffic over the network is minimized. See Chapter 19 for details.

A Database Is Not a Table

With some database management software, the term *database* is synonymous with the term *table*. However, Access follows the more formal database terminology in which *database* refers to all the data plus all the objects you use to manage that data. Remember that you don't need to create a new database each time you want to create a table or some other object. Instead, put all the tables and objects that make up a single application into one database. That way, objects that belong together will be stored in the same database.

Getting Started

The first step to creating any application is to set up a database file. If you plan to import or link most of your tables from data stored in other computer files (see Chapter 7) or if you're a developer who prefers to create most database objects from scratch, the best method is to start with a blank database.

 NOTE If you are using Access to work with SQL Server tables, you may want to use a project instead of a database. See Chapter 1 for information on the differences between databases and projects.

Beware! Starting with a blank database can be more work than starting with a wizard-created database of predefined objects. Taking the from-scratch route usually involves these general steps:

1. Create the blank database (see "Creating a Blank Database" in this chapter).

2. Create, import, or link the tables (see Chapters 6 and 7).

3. Create data entry forms (see Chapters 11 and 13).

4. Enter data using data entry forms or datasheet view (see Chapter 8).

5. Create additional forms, reports, data access pages, and queries as needed (see Chapters 10 through 14).

6. Use programming techniques, form buttons, macros, and other tricks to assemble the objects into a turnkey application (see Parts IV and V).

If you plan to let Access wizards create your database and application automatically, your work is done almost before you start. In fact, you often can get by with just three main steps:

1. Use the Database Wizard to create a database and a turnkey application (see "Creating a Database with the Database Wizard" in this chapter).

2. Enter data (see Chapter 8).

3. Print reports as needed (see Chapters 3 and 9).

Of course, you might need to tweak the turnkey application throughout its lifetime. The rest of this book will show you how.

TIP By studying the sample applications created by the Database Wizard, you can more quickly learn techniques for designing and customizing your own applications. For example, you can study database objects in design view to find out what makes those objects tick. You also can study the relationships among tables in the database using techniques discussed in Chapter 6.

Creating a Blank Database

To create a blank database:

1. Do one of the following:

- **If you're starting from the Microsoft Access main menu**, choose File ➤ New or press Ctrl+N or click the New toolbar button. You'll see the New dialog box, shown in Figure 5.1.

The New dialog box lets you create a blank database, a data access page, or a project (General tab). You can also create a database by choosing from several predefined turnkey applications (Databases tab).

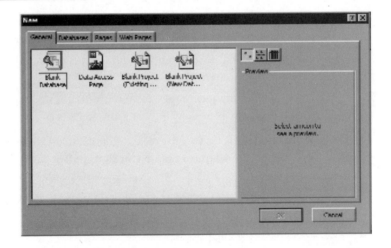

- **If you're at the Microsoft Access startup dialog box** (see Chapter 1), choose Blank Database and click OK. The File New Database dialog box, shown in Figure 5.2, will open. Skip to step 3.

FIGURE 5.2

Use the File New Database dialog box to choose a name and location for your new database. You also can create new folders and delete unwanted databases from this dialog box.

Choose a computer, drive, or folder from the Save In drop-down list.

Back to last Save In choice

Create New Folder

Search the Web

Tools drop-down list

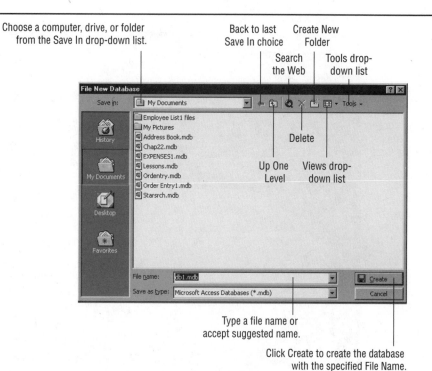

Delete

Up One Level

Views drop-down list

Type a file name or accept suggested name.

Click Create to create the database with the specified File Name.

Blank
Database

2. Click the General tab (if it's not selected already) in the New dialog box and then double-click the Blank Database icon (shown at left). The File New Database dialog box will open (see Figure 5.2).

3. Type the new database file name (or accept the suggested name) in the File Name text box. Your file name can be any length, and it can include spaces and most punctuation marks. Examples: Order Entry, My Videotape Collection, Mom's Database.

4. Select the folder you want the new database created in. Access usually suggests that you save the database in a folder named My Documents on drive C. To save the database to a different drive or folder, choose that drive or folder from the Save In drop-down list. For more details, see "Using the File New Database Dialog Box" later in this chapter.

5. Click the Create button.

Figure 5.3 shows the blank database window that appears next. From here you can start adding tables using any of the techniques explained in Chapter 6. Note that the database window in the figure is for a database created with the default name of db1. The name shown on the title bar of the database window will reflect whatever name you give your database or project file.

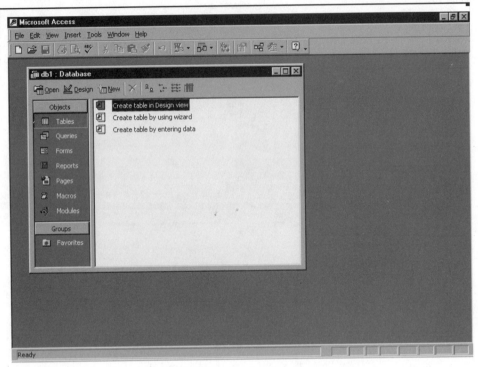

FIGURE 5.3

The empty database window that opens when you create a new blank database.

NOTE Access databases have the file extension .mdb and projects have the extension .adp. However, this extension—like that of most other files on your computer—usually is hidden from view. To show file extensions in dialog boxes that display file names, right-click the Start button on the Taskbar and choose Explore (or double-click My Computer on the Windows Desktop). When the Exploring or My Computer window opens, choose View ➢ Options, click the View tab in the Options dialog box, deselect (clear) Hide MS-DOS File Extensions For File Types That Are Registered, and click OK. Close the Exploring or My Computer window.

Using the File New Database Dialog Box

The File New Database dialog box (refer to Figure 5.2) is similar to the Open dialog box described in Chapter 1, and the easiest way to learn about this dialog box is to experiment with it. These tips will help you choose a location and file name for your database:

- **To choose the computer, drive, or folder where the database should be stored**, click the Save In drop-down list button, and then click the appropriate item.

- **To open objects shown in the list below Save In**, double-click the appropriate object icon or name.

- **To go to the last folder you entered in the Save In box**, click the arrow button at the right end of the Save In box.

- **To open the folder that's just above the currently selected folder**, click the Up One Level toolbar button in the dialog box, or click anywhere in the list below Save In and then press Backspace.

 TIP   To find out the purpose of any toolbar button in a window or dialog box, move your mouse pointer to that button and look for the ScreenTip near the mouse pointer.

- **To display a list of Favorite databases and folders**, click the Favorites button on the bar that runs along the left side of the File New Database window. The list below Save In will then show your favorite folders and databases only.

- **To create a new folder within the current folder**, click the Create New Folder toolbar button. In the New Folder dialog box that appears, type a folder name and then click OK. Open (double-click) the new folder if you wish.

- **To enter a drive, directory, and/or filename manually**, type the appropriate information into the File Name text box at the bottom of the File New Database dialog box or choose an item from the File Name drop-down list.

Here are some other things you can do in the File New Database dialog box:

- **To change the appearance of the list below Save In**, click the View button on the toolbar for the File New Database window. Then choose List, Details, Properties, Preview, or Arrange Icons as needed.

PART

II

Creating a Database

- **To explore the current folder (in Windows Explorer), display folder properties, and more**, right-click an empty area in the list below Save In, and then choose options from the shortcut menu.

- **To display or change properties for an item selected in the list below Save In**, right-click the item and choose Properties.

- **To manage an existing database file** (for example, cut, copy, delete, rename, or view its properties), right-click that file in the list below Save In, and choose an appropriate option from the shortcut menu.

When you're finished using the File New Database dialog box, click Create (to create the database shown in the File Name text box) or click Cancel (to return to Access without creating a database).

Creating a Database with the Database Wizard

Chapter 3 explains how to use the Database Wizard to create a turnkey application for managing address information. Here's the Cliffs Notes version of the steps to follow for creating any of the turnkey applications in Access:

1. Do one of the following:

    - **If you're at the Microsoft Access startup dialog box**, choose Database Wizards, Pages, and Projects. Then click OK.

    - **If you're at the main Microsoft Access window**, choose File ➢ New from the menu bar, or press Ctrl+N, or click the toolbar's New button.

2. Click the Databases tab (see Figure 5.4) in the New dialog box, and then scroll to the icon for the type of information you want to manage. When you've found the icon you want to use, double-click it and the File New Database dialog box will open (refer to Figure 5.2).

3. Type a database name (or accept the suggested name) in the File Name text box. If necessary, choose a drive and folder from the Save In drop-down list. Finally, click the Create button. When you complete step 3, an empty database window will appear briefly, followed by the first Database Wizard dialog box. Here's how to finish the job:

4. Read the description of the new database in the first Database Wizard dialog box, and then click Next to open the second Database Wizard dialog box (see Figure 5.5).

PART

II

Creating a Database

FIGURE 5.4

The New dialog box with the Databases tab selected.

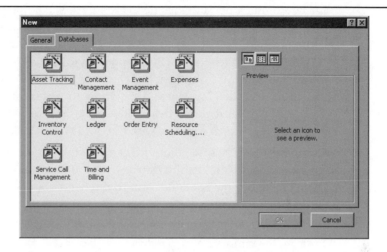

FIGURE 5.5

Use the second Database Wizard dialog box to choose which fields to include from each predefined table.

1. Click a table name.   2. Check/clear field names for the table.

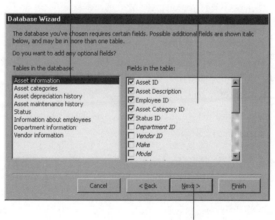

3. Click Next.

 TIP You'll find standard buttons at the bottom of each wizard dialog box. These include Cancel (cancels the wizard and returns to wherever you were before you started the wizard), Back (returns you to the previous wizard dialog box), Next (continues to the next wizard dialog box), and Finish (goes to the last wizard dialog box and assigns default settings for any dialog boxes you skip).

5. Choose which fields to include in each table and to tell the Wizard whether to include sample data. To choose a table to work with, click the table's name in the Tables in the Database list at the left. Then, in the Fields in the Table list at the right, select (check) the fields you want to include, and deselect (clear) fields you want to omit from the table. Optional fields are shown in italics. Required fields are checked initially and shown in normal (roman) type. (You won't be allowed to clear required fields.) Repeat this step as needed. When you're finished, click Next to continue with the third Wizard dialog box.

6. Choose a background color and general style for database forms (also called screen displays) in the third Database Wizard dialog box. The left side of the dialog box will show a sample form that reflects your current choices. Click the Next button to continue.

7. Choose a style for printed reports in the fourth Database Wizard dialog box. Again, the sample area will reflect your choice. Click Next to continue.

8. Specify a title for your database and pick a picture for use on reports in the fifth Wizard dialog box. (See Chapter 3 for pointers on choosing sample pictures.) After making your selections, click Next to go to the last dialog box.

9. Choose whether you want to start the database after the Wizard builds it in the last dialog box. If you check Yes, Start the Database, you'll be taken to a switchboard form that lets you work with your database immediately; if you clear this option, you'll go directly to the database window, bypassing the switchboard. You also can choose whether to display online help about using a database. Again, refer to Chapter 3 if you need more details.

10. Click the Finish button to create the database and its turnkey application form, named Switchboard.

That's all there is to it. Wait patiently for a few moments while the disk drive whirls and the Database Wizard creates an entire database of tables, forms, reports, and other objects. (You'll see progress bars as the Wizard completes its tasks.) When the Wizard finishes its job, you'll either see the main switchboard form for your database or the database window, depending on your choice in step 9. Figure 5.6 shows the sample Switchboard form for the Asset Tracking database, and Figure 5.7 shows the Tables tab on the database window for this same database.

FIGURE 5.6

The Switchboard for an Asset Tracking database created by the Database Wizard.

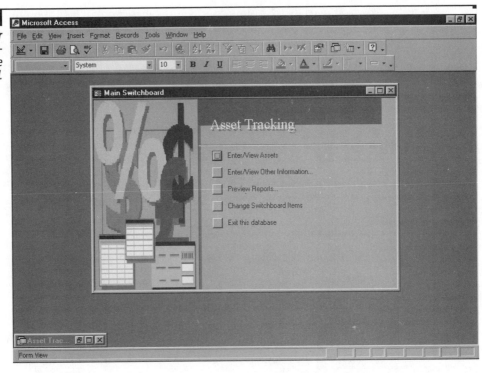

FIGURE 5.7

The Tables tab of the database window for the Asset Tracking database.

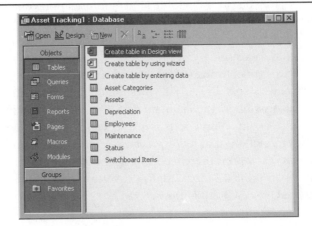

Now you're ready to explore your new database and fill it with useful information. The next section explains a little about each database that the Database Wizard can create automatically. For information on three other sample database applications that come with Access, look up *Sample Databases* with the Office Assistant. Not sure how to navigate the database window? See Chapter 1 for help. Finally, refer to Chapter 3 for pointers on creating a new turnkey application.

About the Sample Databases

If you already have an application in mind, Access can probably set it up for you automatically. The Database Wizard can create several different databases, including the following:

Address Book	Asset Tracking
Book Collection	Contact Management
Donations	Event Management
Expenses	Ledger
Music Collection	Order Entry
Service Call Management	Time and Billing
Wine List	

The following sections describe these databases and list key tables, forms, and reports in each database. (Pay special attention to the Key Reports in each list because they give you clues about the kind of information you can get out of the database.) The brief descriptions presented here can help you decide which databases you can use right out of the box and which you can use as a starting point for your own custom databases.

Rather than listing every table, form, and report in each database, we've described key objects only. In general, you should use the Switchboard forms—and not the database window—to maintain data, fill in forms, and print reports in these databases. Certain reports, such as invoices and purchase orders, aren't listed in the Key Reports sections that follow, because you must click a button on a form in order to preview and print those reports properly. You'll find an asterisk followed by the type of report printed—for example, (*Invoice)—next to the names of key forms that have special Preview/Print buttons.

Blank Database

Blank
Database

This database is for Access application developers and other people who want to create objects from scratch or to import or link objects from other computer databases (see Chapter 7).

Key Tables None

Key Forms None

Key Reports None

Address Book

Address Book

Use the Address Book database to keep track of names, addresses, phone numbers, and other vital statistics. Chapter 3 took you on a step-by-step tour of this database and showed you how to customize it.

Key Tables Addresses

Key Forms Addresses

Key Reports Addresses by Last Name, Birthdays This Month, Fact Sheet, Greeting Card List

Asset Tracking

Asset Tracking

Use the Asset Tracking database to track information about your company's assets. Great for businesses that own valuable stuff!

Key Tables Asset Categories, Assets, Depreciation, Employees, Maintenance, Status

Key Forms Asset Categories, Assets, Employees, Status

Key Reports Assets by Category, Assets by Date Acquired, Assets by Employee, Depreciation Summary, Maintenance History

Book Collection

Book
Collection

Bibliophiles, students, teachers, and librarians will love the Book Collection database, which lets you keep track of your favorite books, authors, and quotations.

Key Tables Authors, Books, Quotations, Topics

Key Forms Authors, Books, Quotations, Topics

Key Reports Quotes by Author, Titles by Author, Titles by Topic

Contact Management

Contact
Management

Everyone who hands you a business card or buys you lunch is a potentially valuable contact. Use the Contact Management database to record information about your contacts, track phone calls you make to them, and dial calls automatically using your computer's modem.

Key Tables   Calls, Contact Types, Contacts

Key Forms   Contact Types, Contacts

Key Reports   Alphabetical Contact Listing, Weekly Call Summary

Donations

Donations

Charitable organizations, nonprofit corporations, and starving book authors can use the Donations database to track contributions and fund-raising campaigns.

Key Tables   Contributors, Donation Campaign Setup, Pledges

Key Forms   Campaign Information, Contributors

Key Reports   Campaign Summary, Pledge Listing, Unpaid Pledges

Event Management

Event
Mangement

Managing administrative details for large events, such as seminars, training classes, meetings, and concerts, is a snap with the Event Management database.

Key Tables   Attendees, Employees, Event Types, Events, Fee Schedules, My Company Information, Payment Methods, Payments, Registration

Key Forms   Attendees (*Invoice), Employees, Event Types, Events, Fee Schedules, My Company Information, Payment Methods

Key Reports   Attendees Listing, Sales by Employee, Sales by Event

Expenses

Expenses

Filling out employee expense reports is easy when you use the Expenses database to do the job. Throw those tedious paper forms in the recycling bin and fill out those expense reports quickly on your computer.

Key Tables   Employees, Expense Categories, Expense Details, Expense Reports

Key Forms   Expense Reports by Employee (*Expense Report), Expense Categories

Key Reports   Expense Report, Expense Report Summary by Category, Expense Report Summary by Employee

Household Inventory

Household
Inventory

Perfect for insurance purposes, the Household Inventory database helps you keep a room-by-room inventory of every valuable item in your home. (Be sure to keep a backup copy of this database in your bank safety deposit box or some other place that will be secure in case a natural—or unnatural—disaster strikes.)

Key Tables   Categories, Household Inventory, Rooms

Key Forms   Categories, Household Inventory, Rooms

Key Reports   Inventory by Category, Inventory by Room, Inventory by Value, Inventory Details

Inventory Control

Inventory
Control

The Inventory Control database offers everything you'll need to manage your company's product inventory.

Key Tables   Categories, Employees, Inventory Transactions, My Company Information, Products, Purchase Orders, Shipping Methods, Suppliers

Key Forms   Categories, Employees, My Company Information, Products (*Purchase Order), Shipping Methods, Suppliers

Key Reports   Product Cost Comparisons, Product Purchases by Supplier, Product Summary, Product Transaction Detail

Ledger

Ledger

Use the Ledger database to maintain a chart of accounts and transactions against each account.

Key Tables   Account Types, Accounts, Transactions

Key Forms   Account Types, Accounts, Transactions

Key Reports   Account Summary, Summary by Account Type, Transaction Listing

Membership

Membership

The Membership database is perfect for organizations that must track information about members, committees, and dues payments.

Key Tables   Committees, Members, Member Types, My Organization Information, Payment Methods, Payments

Key Forms   Committees, Member Types, Members (*Invoice), My Organization's Information, Payment Methods

Key Reports   Alphabetical Member Listing, Committee Members, Invoice, Listing by Membership Type, Outstanding Balances

Music Collection

Music
Collection

If you're a music fan with many recordings in your library, you can use the Music Collection database to store information about your albums/CDs, favorite recording artists, and the locations of your best-liked music.

Key Tables   Music Categories, Recording Artists, Recordings, Tracks

Key Forms   Music Categories, Recording Artists, Recordings

Key Reports   Albums by Artist, Albums by Category, Albums by Format, Tracks by Album

Order Entry

Order Entry

If your business processes orders from customers, you'll want to try the Order Entry database, which has all the tools you need for managing customer, product, order, payment, and shipping information.

Key Tables   Customers, Employees, My Company Information, Order Details, Orders, Payment Methods, Payments, Products, Shipping Methods

Key Forms   Employees, My Company Information, Orders by Customer (*Invoice), Payment Methods, Products, Shipping Methods

Key Reports   Customer Listing, Receivables Aging, Sales by Customer, Sales by Employee, Sales by Product

Picture Library

Picture Library

Photography buffs can use the Picture Library database to list and describe pictures on each roll of film in your library. Great for tracking the thousands of shots you took at the Louvre!

Key Tables   Photo Locations, Photographs, Rolls of Film

Key Forms   Photo Locations, Rolls of Film

Key Reports   Photographs by Date Taken, Photographs by Film Roll, Photographs by Location, Photographs by Subject

Recipes

Recipes

If you use the Recipes database, you'll never have to wonder where you stashed your recipes for Cheez Whiz a la Orange and Twinkies Au Gratin. This database helps you plan, shop for, and whip up nourishing meals.

Key Tables   Food Categories, Ingredients, Recipes

Key Forms   Food Categories, Ingredients, Recipes

Key Reports   Recipe Details, Recipes (Sorted Alphabetically), Recipes by Category

Resource Scheduling

Resource
Scheduling

Use the Resource Scheduling database to schedule the use of company resources, such as meeting rooms, cars, overhead projectors, airplanes, and other equipment, and to assign each resource for use with a certain customer at a specific time.

Key Tables   Customers, Resource Types, Resources, Schedule, Schedule Details

Key Forms   Customers, Reservations, Resource Types, Resources.

Key Reports   Resource Schedule, Resources by Type

Service Call Management

Service Call
Management

Service companies that send technicians to customer sites can use the Service Call Management database to track customers, employees, work orders, invoices, payments, and more.

Key Tables   Customers, Employees, My Company Information, Parts, Payment Methods, Payments, Work-Order Labor, Work-Order Parts, Work Orders

Key Forms   Employees, My Company Information, Parts, Payment Methods, Work Orders by Customer (*Invoice)

Key Reports   Finished Work Orders in House, Revenue Entered by Employee, Sales by Month, Unfinished Work Orders, Work Order Summary

Students and Classes

Students and
Classes

Teachers and school administrators will like using the Students and Classes database to track students, classes, assignments, and grades.

Key Tables   Assignments, Classes, Departments, Instructors, Students

Key Forms   Classes, Departments, Instructors, Students

Key Reports   Class Listing by Department, Class Results Summary, Results by Assignment, Results by Student, Student Schedules, Students

Time and Billing

Time and
Billing

The Time and Billing database can help consultants, lawyers, and other professionals who bill their time by the hour, to manage their businesses more efficiently.

Key Tables   Clients, Employees, Expense Codes, My Company Information, Payment Methods, Payments, Projects, Time Card Expenses, Time Card Hours, Work Codes

Key Forms   Clients (*Invoice), Employees, Expense Codes, My Company Information, Payment Methods, Time Cards (*Time Sheet), Work Codes

Key Reports   Client Billings by Project, Client Listing, Employee Billings by Project, Project Billings by Work Code

Video Collection

Video
Collection

The Video Collection database can help film and television aficionados avoid being buried in the brown tape of a large video library. Use this database to store information about videotaped programs and movies.

Key Tables   Actors, Program Types, Video Programs, Videotapes

Key Forms   Actors, Program Types, Videotapes

Key Reports   Alphabetical Program Listing, Program Listing by Actor, Program Listing by Type

Wine List

Wine List

Oenophiles rejoice! The Wine List database can help you keep your wine cellar inventory under control. Never again will you confuse that mellow Muscat Canelli with a fine Fume Blanc, and you'll always know the vital statistics of each precious bottle.

Key Tables   Wine List, Wine Purchases, Wine Types

Key Forms   Wine List, Wine Types

Key Reports   Wine by Type, Wine by Vintage, Wine by Vintner

Workout

Workout

Tracking each activity in your exercise regimen and each day's progress toward physical perfection is no sweat with the Workout database.

Key Tables   Exercise Types, Exercises, Units, Workout Details, Workout History, Workouts

Key Forms   Exercise Types, Exercises, Units, Workout History, Workouts

Key Reports   Exercise Listing by Type, Workout History by Exercise, Workout Stats by Month

Changing the Database Properties

You can view, change, and define properties for your database by choosing File ➤ Database Properties from the menu bar, or by right-clicking the database window's title bar (or any gray area on the database window) and choosing Database Properties. Figure 5.8 shows the database properties for an Order Entry database that we created with the Database Wizard. Here's a description of the tabs in the dialog box:

FIGURE 5.8

The database properties for the sample Order Entry database with the Summary tab selected.

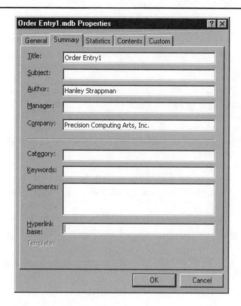

PART

II

Creating a Database

General   Displays general information about the database.

Summary   Displays and lets you change summary information, including a Hyperlink Base path (see Figure 5.8).

Statistics   Displays file statistics, including date created, modified, accessed, and printed.

Contents   Lists all the tables, queries, forms, reports, macros, and modules in the database.

Custom   Displays and lets you add and delete custom properties that can help you find a database quickly.

Click the appropriate tab in the Properties dialog box; then view and change the properties as needed. When you're finished, click OK to return to the database.

Why customize database properties? Because you can use them later to find a database if you've forgotten its filename or location. To look for and open a database based on its properties, choose the File ➢ Open commands in Microsoft Access, Word, or Excel. When the Open dialog box appears, click the Tools drop-down button, choose Find, specify the properties you want to look for in the Find dialog box, and then click the Find Now button.

To learn more about database properties, search for *Database Properties* using the Office Assistant. For details about searching for specific database properties in the Open dialog box, look up *Advanced Find Dialog Box* using the Office Assistant. Then click the *Find Files* topic and explore the option for finding a file using its properties.

Where to Go from Here

Once you've set up a database, you can start using it. For your next stop, go to the following chapters in this book:

- If you created a blank database and none of your data exists on a computer, continue with Chapter 6. You'll see how to create tables to enter your new data into.

- If you created a blank database, and some or all of your data exists on a computer, continue with Chapter 7. That chapter explains how to import or link data to your new database.

- If you used the Database Wizard to create a database, continue with Chapter 8 to find out how to enter end edit information in your data tables.

- If you want to work with an Access project, instead of a database, go to Chapter 30.

What's New in the Access Zoo?

In Access for Office 2000, you can now create projects, a special kind of Access database for working with tables on an SQL Server. A project can include forms, reports, data access pages, macros, and modules. It has no tables or queries, though. These objects are stored on an SQL Server instead of in the project file. See Chapter 30 for information on creating and working with projects.

CHAPTER <u>6</u>

Creating Access Tables

In order to manage data with Access, you must store the data in tables. If the data you want to work with is already stored in a computer database somewhere, you probably can use Access to get at it, as Chapter 7 explains. But if the data exists on paper only, or it isn't yet available, or it's in a format that Access can't import or link, your first step is to structure tables that will store the data. This chapter is all about creating tables.

If you used the Database Wizard to create a database, you can skip this chapter and continue with Chapter 8, to learn more about entering data into your tables. You can always return to this chapter later if you need to add, change, or delete table fields.

If you'd like to review or dive more deeply into topics covered in this chapter, go to the Access Contents Index; open the *Creating and Designing Tables* book, and then explore the subtopics. For hands-on practice with creating and opening a database and its tables, see Chapter 3.

Creating the Database

If you haven't done so already, you must create a database in which to store your tables, as explained in Chapter 5. If you have created a database already, be sure to open that database (see Chapter 1).

 NOTE Remember, a table is not the same as a database. A database can contain any number of tables. So don't create a new database each time you want to create a table. As long as your new tables are related to other tables in the current database in some way, you should continue to add those new tables to the current database.

Using the Table Wizard to Create Tables

Want a table in a hurry? Then follow these steps for using the Access Table Wizard:

1. Click the Tables tab in the database window and then click the New button. Or click the drop-down arrow on the New Object toolbar button (shown at left) and choose Table. Or choose Insert ➤ Table. You'll see this New Table dialog box next:

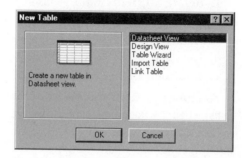

2. Double-click Table Wizard to open the Table Wizard dialog box, shown in Figure 6.1.

FIGURE 6.1

The Table Wizard dialog box will help you create a table.

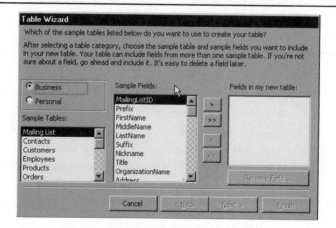

3. Choose either Business or Personal from the option buttons.

4. Scroll through the list of Sample Tables, and then click the sample table name that best describes the information you want to store (Mailing List, Contacts, Customers, or whatever).

5. Click a field name in the Sample Fields list for each field you want to include in the table, and then click the > button (or double-click a field name). Or click the >> button to copy all the sample fields to your table. The field names will be copied to the Fields in My New Table list in the order you specify. Here are some ways to manage the Fields in My New Table list:

- **To delete a field**, click that field in the Fields in My New Table list, and then click the < button.

- **To delete all fields** in the Fields in My New Table list, click the << button.

- **To move a field up or down on the list**, first delete that field from the Fields in My New Table list. Next, in the Fields in My New Table list, click the place where the field should appear. Finally, double-click the appropriate field name in the Sample Fields list.

- **To change a field's name**, click that field in the Fields in My New Table list, click the Rename Field button, type a new name for the field, and then click OK.

 TIP As with all the wizards, you can click the Back button to back up to a previous dialog box, Next to continue to the next dialog box, Finish to zip to the finish line, and Cancel to exit the wizard without creating the table. Always look at each wizard dialog box carefully for previews, tips, and other information that will help you decide what choices to make and what to do next.

6. Click the Next button when the Fields in My New Table list contains the fields you want to include in your table. The next dialog box suggests a name for the new table.

7. Leave the suggested name unchanged (if a table with this name doesn't already exist in the database) or type a new name. See the sidebar "Object Naming Rules" for details about how to name tables and other objects.

8. Assign a primary key. You have two options:

- **To have Access make the decision for you** (the easiest method), select Yes, Set a Primary Key For Me, and click Next.

- **To make your own decisions about the primary key**, select No, I'll Set the Primary Key, and click Next. In the next dialog box, choose from the drop-down list the field that will be unique for each record. You'll also need to tell Access which type of data the primary key field will contain (numbers that Access assigns, numbers that you enter when you add new records, or numbers and/or letters that you enter when you add new records). When you're done choosing primary key options, click Next.

 NOTE If you're not sure about how to handle primary key fields just now, don't worry about it. Select Yes, Set a Primary Key For Me in step 8, and click Next. You'll learn more about primary keys later in this chapter, under "Setting a Primary Key."

9. If your database already contains at least one table, you'll be asked to specify whether your new table is related to other tables in your database. Here's what you can do:

- **If you're not sure about the table relationships**, click Next to continue with the next dialog box for now. You can define relationships later, if necessary, when you understand more about them. "Defining Relationships Among Tables," later in the chapter, explains relationships and shows how to define them anytime.

- **If you do know which relationships you want to define** between the table you're creating and another table that already exists in the database, click the existing table in the list and then click the Relationships button. In the next dialog box, tell Access how your new table is related to the existing table and click OK. Repeat this step until you've defined all the relationships you want, and then click Next.

10. Follow the prompts in the final dialog box (which displays a checkered flag) to tell the Wizard what to do after creating the table. Then click the Finish button to create the table.

You'll be taken to the table design window or to the datasheet view or to a form, depending on your choice in step 10. To return to the database window now, choose File ➢ Close from the Access menu bar, or click the Close button on the window that appears, or press Ctrl+W. If you're prompted to save your changes, click Yes or No as appropriate.

 NOTE When you use the Table Wizard to create a table, Access automatically sets up input masks for certain fields (such as those that store telephone and fax numbers, postal codes, and dates). *Input masks* make data entry easier by controlling where data is entered, what kind of data is allowed, and how many characters you can enter. You'll find more about input masks later in this chapter.

PART

II

Creating a Database

We'll talk about the table design window and ways to change a table's structure later in this chapter. But first, let's look at ways to create a table without a wizard. The process begins with planning a table from scratch.

Object Naming Rules

Access gives you considerable freedom when you are assigning names to tables, table fields, forms, pages, reports, queries, macros, and modules. It will complain, though, if you don't follow the naming rules, which are as follows:

- The name cannot be the same as any other object of the same type within the database. For example, you can't have two tables named MailingList; however, it's okay to have one table named MailingList1 and another named MailingList2.
- You cannot give a table and a query the same name.
- When naming a field, control, or object, make sure your name isn't the same as the name of a property or other element that Access is already using. This rule is important if you're writing Visual Basic code.
- The name can be up to 64 characters, including spaces. However, the name cannot start with a space.
- The name can include punctuation characters *except* a period (.), an exclamation mark (!), an accent grave (À), or brackets ([ ]).
- If you plan to write programs for use with your database, avoid using spaces in object names. For example, use *CustomerInfo* instead of *Customer Info* (for a table name) or *LastName* instead of *Last Name* (for a field name). Programming is easier when the object names do not include spaces.
- The name cannot include control characters (ASCII 00 to ASCII 31).
- When naming fields, avoid choosing names that are the same as built-in Access function names or property names. Strange things may happen if you use those names.
- In a project, the names for tables, views, or stored procedures cannot include a double quotation mark (").

For more about naming rules, look up *Naming Rules* with the Office Assistant and click the topic *Guidelines for Naming Fields, Controls, and Objects*.

Planning a Table from Scratch

Instead of using the Table Wizard to create a table, you can plan and create a table from scratch. Your first step is to decide which fields to include in your table. If you're working from a fill-in-the-blank paper form, this task can be easy. Generally speaking, you can create one field for every "blank" on the form. An accountant, for example, might create a table that has a field for each blank on a Federal 1040 tax form. There's one catch to this one-blank, one-field approach: you generally should not include fields that contain the results of calculations. Why not? Read on.

Do Not Include Calculated Fields

Access can perform instant, accurate calculations on any data in your table and then display the results in queries, forms, and reports (which you'll learn about in upcoming chapters). So, for best results, do not create fields that store the results of a calculation. Here are the potential problems with storing calculation results in the table:

- You risk printing faulty totals or results that aren't based on up-to-the-minute data.
- You're wasting disk space. After all, there's no need to store what Access can calculate on-the-fly for you.
- You'll need to do the calculations yourself. Unless you're some kind of human calculator, doing the calculations yourself is a waste of time and can lead to errors.

In short, tables should contain raw data only—just the numbers you'll need to base calculations on later—and not the results of any calculations.

Creating a Table without Using a Wizard

Follow these steps to create the table from scratch, without using the Table Wizard:

1. Click the Tables tab on the database window and then click the New button. Or click the drop-down arrow on the New Object toolbar button and choose Table. Or choose Insert ➤ Table.
2. Double-click Design View in the New Table dialog box that appears next.

NOTE Chapter 8 explains how to define fields simply by entering data into a blank datasheet; it also explains how to add, rename, and delete fields from datasheet view.

You'll be taken to the table design window (see Figure 6.2) where you tell Access which fields will go into the table.

FIGURE 6.2

Use the table design window to define the name, data type, and properties of all fields in a table.

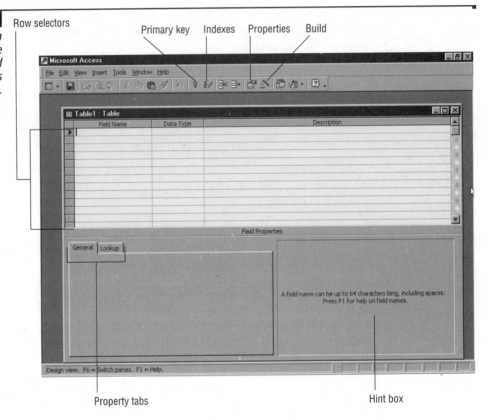

 TIP You might want to use the Table Wizard to set up a table that's almost like the one you want. Then, in the database window, right-click the table's name, choose Design, and use the techniques described in this chapter to tweak the table structure to perfection.

Defining a Table's Fields

Next you must define the fields in your table by following the steps that follow. As you define the fields, glance at the hint box in the table design window for guidance. (You also can press F1 for more information as you follow each step.)

1. Type a field name (up to 64 characters including blank spaces) in the Field Name column. Field names must follow the rules given earlier in this chapter (see the sidebar "Object Naming Rules").

2. Click the Data Type column next to the field name and select the appropriate data type from the drop-down list. (See "Choosing Appropriate Data Types," below, for more information.)

3. Click the Description column and type a description of the field (a description is optional, but very helpful). This description will appear on the status bar later, when you're entering data.

4. (Optional) Click the General or Lookup tab in the Field Properties area, and set properties for the field you're defining. See "Defining Field Properties" later in this chapter.

5. Repeat steps 1 through 4, putting each field definition on its own row, until you've defined all the fields in your table.

When you've finished defining the table's fields, save the table structure as discussed shortly under "Saving a Table Structure."

 TIP If you prefer to let a Wizard guide you through setting up a field, click in the Field Name column where you want the new field to appear. Then right-click and choose Build from the shortcut menu, or click the Build toolbar button (refer to Figure 6.2). The Field Builder will guide you through the remaining steps.

Choosing Appropriate Data Types

Access can store different types of information in different formats. So when you're defining a table without a wizard, you must think about what type of information will be stored in each field.

To define the data type of a field, click in the Data Type column next to the field name, and then click the drop-down list button that appears. You'll see the list shown below, and you can select a data type by clicking it. Table 6.1 summarizes the data types you can choose.

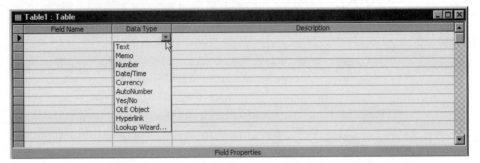

 TIP Be sure to assign the Text data type—rather than the Number data type—to fields such as telephone numbers, fax numbers, postal codes, and e-mail addresses. Unlike the Number data type, the Text data type lets you enter punctuation characters and letters, as in these examples: *(520)555-5947* for a telephone or fax number; *73444,2330* or *Hanley@RNAA47.com* for an e-mail address; *85711-1234* or *H3A3G2* for postal codes.

TABLE 6.1: ACCESS DATA TYPES

DATA TYPE	STORES
AutoNumber	A number that's assigned automatically and never changes again. *Tip*: Use the New Values property on the General tab to control whether numbers are assigned incrementally or randomly.
Currency	Dollar amounts.
Date/Time	Dates (e.g., 12/31/99) and times. *Tip*: Use the Format property on the General tab to control the appearance of the date.
Hyperlink	Hyperlink addresses.
Lookup	Values that come from another table, a query, or a list of values you supply. *Tip*: Use the Lookup tab properties to define a lookup field, or choose the Lookup Wizard data type to set up the lookup field automatically.
Memo	Large bodies of text up to 64,000 characters in length.
Number	True numbers such as quantities. *Tip*: Use the Field Size, Format, and Decimal Places field properties on the General tab to control the size and appearance of numbers.

Continued ▸

TABLE 6.1: ACCESS DATA TYPES (CONTINUED)	
DATA TYPE	**STORES**
OLE Object	Any OLE object, such as a picture, sound, or word processing document.
Text	Any written text up to 255 characters in length, numbers that you won't be using in arithmetic calculations, and certain numbers such as zip codes, phone numbers, or product codes that contain letters, hyphens, or other nonnumeric characters.
Yes/No	A True or False value only. *Tip*: Use the Format property on the General tab and the Display Control property on the Lookup tab to control the appearance of the field's contents.

To learn more about how to decide what data type to use for fields in a table, click in the Data Type column on the table design window and press F1. Or search for *Data Types* with the Office Assistant.

Defining Field Properties

You can change a field's properties (characteristics) using options on the General and Lookup tabs in the Field Properties pane in the table design window. Different data types offer different properties.

 WARNING The Field Properties area of the table design window shows the field properties for only one field at a time. Check to make sure the ➤ symbol on the row selector is pointing to the appropriate field name in the upper pane before you change properties in the lower pane.

To set a property for a field, follow these steps:

1. Select the appropriate field in the table design window's upper pane.

2. Click the appropriate tab (General or Lookup) in the Field Properties area in the table design window's lower pane.

3. Click in the box next to the property you want to set.

4. Do any of the following:

   • Type a value for the property.

   • Click the drop-down arrow (if one appears) next to the property, and click an option in the list that appears. For properties that offer a drop-down list, you also can double-click the appropriate property box to cycle through the available values for that property.

- Get help in setting the property by clicking the Build button (if one appears) or right-clicking the field and choosing Build.

You can get immediate help as you define field properties by pressing F1. You also can search for *Field Properties* with the Office Assistant.

Important General Field Properties

Here (in alphabetical order) are the most important field properties on the General tab. (We'll get to the Lookup properties later in this chapter.)

Allow Zero Length   If Yes, the field will accept an "empty string" as a valid entry, even if the Required property is set to Yes. That empty string will appear as two quotation marks with nothing in between ("") when first typed into the field; those quotation marks will disappear when you move the cursor to another field.

Caption   Lets you define an alternative name for the field that will be used in datasheet view and as labels when you create forms and reports. The caption offers a handy way to make your datasheet columns and labels more readable when field names do not contain spaces. *Example:* If you've named a field *Last-Name*, specify that field's Caption property as the more readable text *Last Name*.

Decimal Places   Lets you specify the number of digits to the right of the decimal separator in a numeric field. Choose "Auto" to have the Format property determine the number of decimal places automatically.

Default Value   Lets you define a value that's automatically inserted into the field; you can type a different value during data entry, if necessary. (See Table 6.2 for examples.) The default value for a Text field is the empty string; for a Number or Currency field, it's 0.

Field Size   Lets you specify the maximum length of text allowed into the field or the acceptable range of numbers. The default size for text is 50 and for numbers is Long Integer, although you can change these settings by choosing Tools ➤ Options, clicking the Tables/Queries tab, and changing values in the boxes under Default Field Sizes (see Chapter 15).

 NOTE   Access *doesn't* pad text that's shorter than its allotted width to fill out the rest of the field. Hence there's no disk consumption penalty for making the size of a Text field wider than it needs to be. However, a smaller maximum field size can conserve memory and speed up processing.

Format   Lets you define the appearance of data in the field. For example, you can show a date as 2/14/1999 or as February 14, 1999.

Indexed   Lets you choose whether to index this field and whether to allow duplicates in the index. See "Defining Indexes," later in this chapter, for more details.

Input Mask   Lets you define a pattern for entering data into the field. For help with creating the mask for a text or date/time field, click the Build button after selecting this property. The Input Mask Wizard will guide you through each step. You also can press F1 for help when the cursor is in the Input Mask property box.

Required   If set to Yes, the field cannot be left blank.

Validation Rule   Lets you create an *expression* that tests data as it comes into the field and rejects faulty entries. (See Table 6.3 for examples.)

 TIP   In addition to specifying a validation rule, you can limit the entry in a field to values from another table. To do so, you can (1) define relationships between tables; (2) define lookup fields; or (3) create a drop-down list in a form. We'll explain the first two methods later in this chapter and the third method in Chapter 13.

Validation Text   Defines the error message that will appear on the screen when faulty data is entered into the field. When writing the validation text, it's best to indicate which field is invalid so the user can more easily understand what's wrong during data entry. (See Table 6.3 for examples.)

TABLE 6.2: EXAMPLES OF DEFAULT VALUES YOU CAN ASSIGN TO A FIELD

DEFAULT VALUE	FILLS FIELD WITH
=Date( )	Today's date (use the Date/Time data type)*
=Now( )	Current date and time (use the Date/Time data type)*
0	The number zero (use with Number and Currency data types)
Yes	A "True" setting (use with Yes/No data type)
No	A "False" setting (use with Yes/No data type)
CA	The letters CA (for a Text field that defines the two-letter state abbreviation for California, used in the United States)

* Use the Format property on the General tab to determine the appearance of the field's contents.

PART

II

Creating a Database

TIP To test all your validation rules against existing data in the table, choose Edit ➤ Test Validation Rules ➤ Yes.

TABLE 6.3: EXAMPLES OF VALIDATION RULE EXPRESSIONS AND TEXT FOR ERRORS		
VALIDATION RULE	**POSSIBLE VALIDATION TEXT**	**HOW IT LIMITS ENTRY**
>0	The Unit Price must be greater than 0.	Disallows 0 or a negative number in a Number or Currency field.
<>0	A Rating of 0 is not acceptable.	Allows any negative or positive number, but not zero.
Between 1 and 100	The Rating must be between 1 and 100.	Accepts only numbers in the range of 1 to 100 (inclusive) in a Number or Currency field.
>=Date( )	Sorry, no Order Date backdating is allowed!	Allows only today's date or later dates in a Date/Time field.
>=#1/1/99#	Sorry, First Payment date must be January 1999 or later.	Prevents dates earlier than January 1, 1999, in a Date/Time field.

Setting a Primary Key

A *primary key* is a field (or group of fields) that uniquely identifies each record, much as a license plate uniquely identifies each car on the road. When you define a primary key, you tell Access to do three things:

- Make sure no two records in the table have the same value in the field (or group of fields) that defines the primary key
- Keep records sorted (ordered) by the entries in the primary key field
- Speed up processing

A primary key can be just one field, or it can consist of two or more fields. When two or more fields define a primary key, Access doesn't consider records to be duplicates unless the combined contents of all the fields in the primary key are identical.

 NOTE No field that is part of a primary key can ever be left blank during data entry.

To set a primary key in your table design, do the following:

1. Select the field you want to use as a primary key by clicking the row selector button to the left of the field name. Or, if you want to select multiple fields, hold down the Ctrl key and click the row selector for each field you want to define.

2. Click the Primary Key toolbar button (shown at left). Or choose Edit ➢ Primary Key from the menu bar. Or right-click the highlighted row selector and choose Primary Key.

The field(s) you've set as the primary key will have a key icon in the row selector, as shown below.

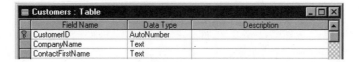

If you change your mind about assigning a field as a primary key, just repeat the two steps above. The key icon in the row selector will disappear, indicating that the field is no longer part of the primary key.

Defining Indexes

You can add an index to a field as a way to speed up sorting and searching on that field. Not all data types can be indexed, but any field that has a property named Indexed at the bottom of the General field properties tab is a candidate for indexing. Each table in your database can have up to 32 indexes.

NOTE   If the field's data type allows it, the field isn't a primary key, and the field name starts or ends with *ID, key, code,* or *num*, Access will create a Yes (No Duplicates) index automatically. To specify which field names will trigger an automatic index, choose Tools ➢ Options, click the Tables/Queries tab, and then edit or replace text in the AutoIndex On Import/Create box. See Chapter 16 for more details.

Be aware that indexes can slow down data entry and editing a little because Access must update the index whenever you add or change data. As a result, you should index only the field(s) that you're most likely to use for sorting and searching. (To save you time and trouble, the Database Wizard and Table Wizard set up indexes on appropriate table fields automatically.)

To add or remove an index on a field:

1. Click the name of the field you want to work with.

2. Click the General tab under Field Properties.

3. Click the Indexed property if it's available, click the drop-down arrow next to Indexed, and then click one of these options:

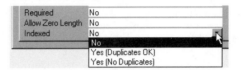

When defining a field as an index, be sure to choose Yes (Duplicates OK)—rather than Yes (No Duplicates)—unless you're absolutely sure that no two records in the table should have identical values in that field. To remove an index from a field, set the Indexed property to No. You'll see examples of indexed fields later in this chapter.

 WARNING   The primary key automatically gets an Indexed property of Yes (No Duplicates). You can't change that setting unless you remove the primary key on that field.

 TIP   You can view and change the index name, field name, sort order, and index properties for all the table's fields at once if you wish. To do so, choose View ➢ Indexes from the menu bar or click the Indexes toolbar button (refer to Figure 6.2).

Saving a Table Structure

Once you're (reasonably) satisfied with the fields in your table, you can close and save the table structure. Here's how:

1. Choose File ➢ Close from the menu bar, or press Ctrl+W, or click the Close button in the table design window. You'll probably see a dialog box similar to this one:

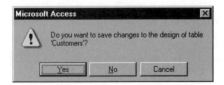

2. Click Yes.

3. Type the name you want to assign to the table (up to 64 characters, including blank spaces) if you're prompted for a table name, and then click OK. If you haven't defined a primary key, you'll see this dialog box:

4. If you're not sure how to answer, we suggest that you click Yes and let Access create a primary key for you. (Access will create a field named ID with the AutoNumber data type.) Your database usually runs faster if every table has a primary key.

You'll be returned to the database window, where you can see the new table name on the Tables tab.

TIP You can save the table structure without closing the table design window first. Just click the toolbar's Save button, or press Ctrl+S, or choose File ➤ Save any time you're in the table design window. Access will save the changes you've made so far, and you'll remain in the table design window.

WARNING When you save tables, forms, reports, queries, and other objects in your database, the database will increase in size. To make the current database smaller, you must compact the database. With the database open, choose Tools ➤ Database Utilities ➤ Compact and Repair Database. See Chapter 17 for more details.

Opening a Table

After you've created a table, you can open it anytime:

1. Click the Tables tab in the database window.

PART

II

Creating a Database

2. Click the name of the table you want to open.

- **To open the table for entering or editing *data*,** click the Open button or double-click the table name.
- **To view or change the table's *design* (structure),** click the Design button.

You also can open or design a table by right-clicking its name in the database window and then choosing Open or Design from the shortcut menu. The shortcut menu for tables also offers other handy options—Print, Print Preview, Cut, Copy, Save As, Export, Send To, Add to Group, Create Shortcut, Delete, Rename, and Properties. To find out the purpose of any option on the shortcut menu, point to that option with your mouse and look at the status bar for a brief description; then, if you need more details, press the F1 key.

Switching between Design and Datasheet Views

Once the table is open, you can switch quickly between datasheet view and design view. The differences between the two views are

- **In datasheet view** you typically work with the table's contents (data). However, you also can make some changes to the table's structure (more about this in Chapter 8).
- **In design view** you work with the table's structure only (field names, data types, properties), not with its contents.

To switch views while a table is open, click the View toolbar button:

   Switch from datasheet view to design view.

   Switch from design view to datasheet view.

You also can switch to design or datasheet view by choosing View ➤ Design View or View ➤ Datasheet View from the menu bar. Or click the drop-down arrow next to the View toolbar button, and then choose Design View or Datasheet View.

Why Two Views?

You will use datasheet view to add data to your table as explained in Chapter 8. Figure 6.3 shows some names and addresses typed into a table named Customers. In datasheet view, field names appear across the top of the table, and none of the underlying structural information (such as data types and properties) is visible. If some fields are scrolled off the right edge of the window, you can use the horizontal scroll bar at the bottom of the window to scroll left and right through the fields.

FIGURE 6.3

The Customers table in datasheet view.

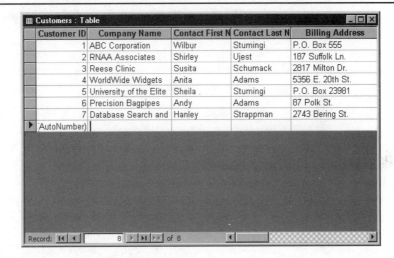

TIP When adding data to a table that includes an AutoNumber field (such as the CustomerID field shown in Figure 6.3), Access usually will number records sequentially starting with 1 (1, 2, 3, and so forth). You can use the trick described under "Changing the Starting Value of an AutoNumber Field," near the end of this chapter, to change the starting number for your table's records (1001, 1002, and so forth).

In design view you can see and change the underlying table structure. Field names are listed down the left column, and the data type, description, and field properties appear across the table. None of the table's data is visible in design view. Figure 6.4 shows the same Customers table in design view.

PART

II

Creating a Database

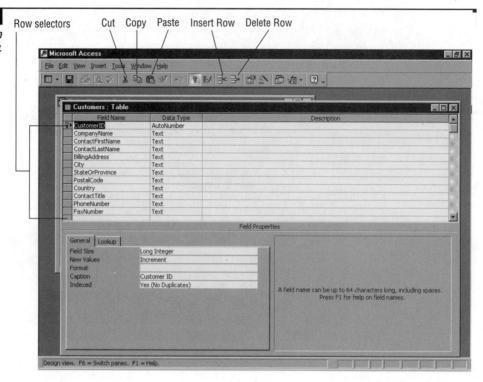

FIGURE 6.4

The Customers table in design view.

Modifying the Table Structure

Here are some techniques you can use to change a table's structure in design view. Open the table that you want to modify in design view (or switch to design view if you're in datasheet view).

- **To change a field's name, data type, description, or properties**, use the same techniques you used when creating the table structure.

- **To insert a new field into the structure**, move the cursor to the field below which you want the new field to appear, and then click the Insert Rows toolbar button (shown at left); or choose Insert ➤ Rows from the menu bar. You can also click the row selector for the field that will follow the new field, and press the Insert key.

- **To delete a field from the table structure**, move the cursor to the row that contains the field you want to delete, and then click the Delete Rows toolbar button. Or choose Edit ➢ Delete Rows from the menu bar. You can also click the field's row selector, and press the Delete key.

- **To undo an accidental insertion or deletion**, click the Undo toolbar button, or choose Edit ➢ Undo, or press Ctrl+Z.

 WARNING If you rename or delete fields, any queries, forms, reports, and other objects that rely on the presence of those fields won't work properly. You can bypass this potential problem by turning on the Name AutoCorrect feature before you make table structure changes. Choose Tools ➢ Options, click the General tab, and check the boxes for Track Name AutoCorrect Info and Perform Name AutoCorrect.

You can also make some changes to a table's structure in datasheet view. See Chapter 8 for more information on how this works.

Selecting Rows in Design View

While you're in table design view, you can select rows (that is, fields) to work with:

- **To select one row**, click the row selector to the left of the field you want to select. The row will be darkened (highlighted) as shown below:

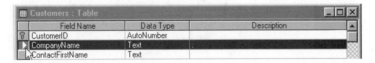

- **To select multiple adjacent rows**, drag the mouse pointer through the row selectors of all the rows you want to select. Or click the selector for the first row you want to select, and then Shift-click the selector for the last row you want to select.

- **To select multiple nonadjacent rows**, Ctrl-click the row selector for each row you want to select.

- **To deselect selected rows**, click any Field Name, Data Type, or Description box.

- **To deselect one selected row** in a group of selected rows, Ctrl-click the row you want to deselect.

PART

II

Creating a Database

After selecting one or more rows, use these techniques to manage them:

- **To move one selected row**, click its row selector again, but this time hold down the mouse button and drag the selection to its new location.

- **To copy the selection**, choose Edit ➢ Copy, or press Ctrl+C, or click the Copy toolbar button. Next, click the row selector for the empty row where you want to put the copy, and then choose Edit ➢ Paste or press Ctrl+V (or click the Paste toolbar button). Finally, rename the copied field, because *no two fields in a table can have the same name.*

- **To delete the selection**, press the Delete key.

- **To insert blank row(s) above the selection**, press the Insert key.

Saving Table Structure Changes

After changing the table structure, you can save those changes in any of these ways:

- Switch to datasheet view or close the table design window (File ➢ Close). If asked whether you want to save the new structure, click Yes if you want to save the changes or No if you don't want to save them.

- Choose File ➢ Save, or press Ctrl+S, or click the Save toolbar button. You'll remain in the table design window.

If the table already contains data, and your design changes will affect that data, a message will warn you of the change. Here's an example:

Read the warning carefully, and then click the appropriate command button.

Moving, Copying, Deleting, and Renaming Entire Tables

You can easily copy, delete, and rename entire tables from the database window. The techniques are explained in Chapter 1, under "Managing Database Objects."

Changing Properties of an Entire Table or Object

You can change the overall properties for a table or other Access object. For example, you can add a description that will appear in the database window. Here's how:

1. Go to the object's design view window or click the appropriate tab on the database window and then click the object's name. Different properties are available, depending on whether you start from the design window or the database window; however, you can change the Description property by starting from either window.

2. Choose View ➢ Properties from the menu bar, or click the Properties toolbar button (shown at left). Or if you're starting from the database window, right-click the object name and choose Properties.

3. Complete the Properties dialog box.

More Database Window Tricks

Viewing an object's Description from the database window is a simple process: choose View ➢ Details, or click the Details toolbar button, or right-click an empty area inside the database window and choose View ➢ Details.

You can sort objects in the database window by name, description, date created, date modified, or type. Any of these techniques will work:

- If you're viewing the database window in detail (View ➢ Details), click the column heading you want to use for sorting. For example, click the Name column heading to sort objects into ascending (A–Z) alphabetical order by object name. Click the column heading again to sort the objects in descending (Z–A) alphabetical order.

- Choose View ➢ Arrange Icons, or right-click an empty area in the database window and choose Arrange Icons. Then choose By Name, By Type, By Created, or By Modified.

Tables in the Order Entry Database

Throughout this book, we'll often refer to the OrdEntry9 database, which we created using the Order Entry Database Wizard described in Chapters 3 and 5. If you haven't created a sample Order Entry database yet, you might want to do so now. Having this database available on your own computer will make it easier for you to follow the examples in this book.

Figure 6.5 shows the tables that make up the completed Order Entry database and describes them briefly. We'll give you more details about these tables in the sections that follow.

FIGURE 6.5

The database window, showing all the tables in the Order Entry database. To explain the purpose of each table, we defined a Description property for some of the tables.

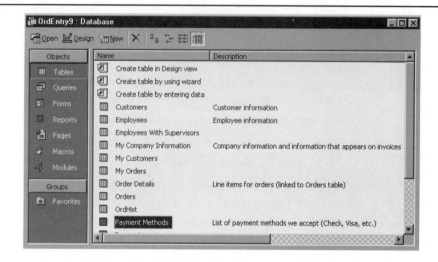

The Customers Table

The Customers table is an important table in the Order Entry database because it stores name and address data for customers. Figure 6.6 shows this table's field names and data types.

FIGURE 6.6

The Customers table structure in the Order Entry database.

Customers Primary Key and Index

The primary key in the Customers table is the CustomerID field. It's an AutoNumber field, which means that new entries are assigned an ID number automatically as they're added to the table. Furthermore, that number will never change (because the value in an AutoNumber field can't change), and no two entries ever have the same ID number. Like all primary key fields, CustomerID is indexed and duplicates aren't allowed.

NOTE   The New Values field property on the General tab offers you two ways to assign values to AutoNumber fields. The default choice, Increment, increases the field's value by 1 for each new record. To assign *random* long number values to new records, choose the Random option instead. Only one AutoNumber field is allowed in each table.

PART

II

Creating a Database

Changing Your Screen Display Size

Most figures in this book are shown with the Windows Desktop Area set to 800 by 600 pixels. However, a Desktop Area of 640 by 480 pixels was used for some examples. To change the Desktop Area on your own screen (if your monitor supports such changes and you're running Windows 95/98), minimize or close the Access program window (if it's open), right-click an empty area on the Windows Desktop (not the Access window), choose Properties, click the Settings tab, drag the Desktop Area slider to the appropriate setting, click OK, and then answer any prompts that appear.

About Validation and Input Masks

Many people assign input masks, the Required property, and other restrictions to certain fields. For example, if you explore the General properties of the Customers table, you'll notice that input masks are defined for the PostalCode, PhoneNumber, and FaxNumber fields, as described below:

> **PostalCode**   The input mask *00000\-9999* allows you to enter zip+4 codes without typing a hyphen. *Example:* You type **857114747**, and the input mask changes your entry to 85711-4747.

PhoneNumber The input mask *!\(999")"000\-0000* lets you enter phone numbers without having to type the parentheses around area codes or the hyphen after the exchange. *Example:* You type **6035551234**, and the input mask changes your entry to (603)555-1234.

FaxNumber The input mask *!\(999")"000\-0000* is the same one used for the phone number.

NOTE If you need to omit the area code when entering phone or fax numbers that have the *!\(999")"000\-0000* input mask, use the mouse or your keyboard to skip the area code portion of your entry.

You might want to remove these input masks if you want your own database to handle international names and addresses. Requiring a particular pattern, or requiring an entry at all, can prevent the entry of addresses in foreign lands. In fact, we don't even know the postal code or telephone number format used in Zimbabwe or Mongolia. Do you?

TIP Restrictive field properties can make data entry frustrating or downright impossible. When you're first designing a table, avoid making the field properties too restrictive. You can always make the table more restrictive after you've worked with it for a while.

NOTE The input masks listed above tell Access not to store constants like parentheses and dashes with the field values. This means that the phone number (505) 555-5332 would get stored as 5055555332. To find that number with the Find command or a query, you would have to remember to enter the number without the formatting characters. To have Access store the formatting characters along with the rest of the value the input mask is applied to, add *;0;* to the end of the mask.

The Products Table

The Products table stores information about products sold by the business that uses the database. Its structure appears in Figure 6.7. The ProductID field is the primary key in the Products table to ensure that each product the business sells has a unique identifying code.

FIGURE 6.7

The Products table structure in the Order Entry database.

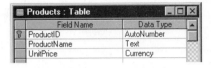

The Orders Table

The Orders table tracks all orders placed. Ordering information is divided into two tables (named Orders and Order Details) because a natural one-to-many relationship occurs between a given order and the number of details (or line items) that go with that order (see Figure 6.8).

FIGURE 6.8

A natural one-to-many relationship occurs between an order and the number of items ordered (sometimes called order details or line items).

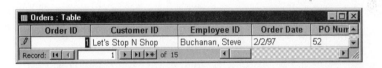

NOTE   The Order Entry database comes with an Orders by Customer form, which lets you enter and display data from several tables at once. You'll learn how to create similar data entry forms in Chapters 11 and 13.

Figure 6.9 shows the structure of the Orders table. The OrderID field is the primary key and is defined as the AutoNumber data type so that orders are numbered automatically as they're entered into the table. The fact that OrderID is an AutoNumber field will have implications for the Order Details table (as you'll learn shortly).

FIGURE 6.9

Structure of the Orders table in the Order Entry database.

The CustomerID field in the Orders table plays two important roles. First, it's an example of a field that uses Lookup properties. In this case the CustomerID field in the Orders table looks to the CustomerID field in the Customers table for a list of possible values. Lookup fields can make data entry quick and error free. (There's more about lookup fields later in this chapter.)

Second, the CustomerID field in the Orders table relates the Order to the CustomerID field in the Customers table, thereby ensuring that our database includes a valid customer record for each order placed. In the Customers table, CustomerID is an AutoNumber field. In the Orders table, the CustomerID field must have the Long Integer property for Access to match records correctly. A similar relationship exists between the OrderID field in the Orders table and the OrderID field in the Order Details table. (See "Defining a Relationship When One Field Is an AutoNumber" near the end of this chapter.)

Other interesting fields in this table include:

EmployeeID   A lookup field that lets you choose which employee sold the order.

ShippingMethodID   A lookup field that lets you choose a valid shipping method for the order.

SalesTaxRate   A number that's displayed in Percent format. A validation rule for this field requires entries to be less than 1 (<1) and displays an error message (validation text) if you enter a value greater than or equal to 1. *Example:* If you type **.065** into the SalesTaxRate field, Access displays a value of 6.5%. If you type **6.5** into this field, Access instead displays the validation text error message "This value must be less than 100%."

The Order Details Table

The Order Details table stores one record for each line item of an order. Its structure is shown in Figure 6.10. In this table the OrderDetailID field is defined as the AutoNumber field type and as the table's primary key.

Structure of the Order Details table in the Order Entry database.

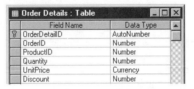

The OrderID field in the Order Details table relates each Order Details record to the appropriate record in the Orders table, which ensures that each line item belongs to a valid order. OrderID is the foreign key to the AutoNumber primary key field named OrderID in the Orders table. This field is indexed, with duplicates allowed, so that each order can have many line items.

 NOTE *Foreign key* is a fancy term for the table field(s) that refers to the primary key field(s) in another table. When the primary key has an AutoNumber data type, the foreign key field *must* be assigned the Number data type with the Long Integer field size. (See "Defining a Relationship When One Field Is an AutoNumber," near the end of this chapter, for more details about foreign keys.) For other data types, the foreign key and its related primary key must have *exactly* the same data type and size.

Other interesting fields in the Order Details table include these:

ProductID   A lookup field that lets you select a valid product from the Products table.

Discount   Like the SalesTaxRate field in the Orders table, this field is displayed in Percent format and must be less than 1.

The Employees Table

The Employees table stores employee information. Figure 6.11 shows this table's structure. Notice that the EmployeeID field is both an AutoNumber field and the table's primary key. The WorkPhone field is defined with the usual input mask for phone numbers.

PART

II

Creating a Database

FIGURE 6.11

*The structure for the
Employees table.*

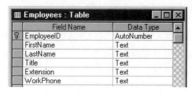

The Payments Table

The Order Entry application uses the Payments table to track which orders have been paid, how much of the order was paid, when the payment was made, and so forth. Figure 6.12 shows the structure for this table; the PaymentID is an AutoNumber field and the primary key for the table. Other interesting fields include the following:

OrderID   Ties the payment to an order in the Orders table, and it is indexed (with duplicates OK).

PaymentDate   A Date/Time field that has an input mask of *99/99/00*, which lets you enter dates such as *2/2/99* in any of these ways: **020299, 022/99, 2/2/99**.

CreditCardExpDate   A Date/Time field that has the same input mask as PaymentDate.

PaymentMethodID   A lookup field that lets you choose a valid payment method from the Payment Methods table.

FIGURE 6.12

*The structure for the
Payments table, which
keeps track of cus-
tomer payments.*

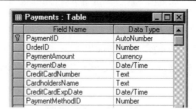

Other Tables in Order Entry

Order Entry uses two other small tables—Payment Methods (shown below) and Shipping Methods—which provide lookup information for the main tables already described.

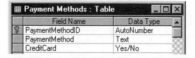

Finally, the table named My Company Information is used to define standard text and default settings for invoices. Its structure is shown below:

In the My Company Information table, several fields have input masks that we've already described. The SalesTaxRate field has a validation rule and text that will make Access reject entries greater than or equal to 1. The PostalCode field has a 00000\ -9999 input mask, and the PhoneNumber and FaxNumber fields have the !\(999")"000\ -0000 input mask.

We've mentioned lookup fields many times in this chapter. Now we'll explain how to set them up in Access tables.

About Lookup Fields

You can create *lookup fields* that speed up and simplify data entry in a table's datasheet or in a form. As the name implies, the lookup field *looks up* values from another place, and then automatically fills in the value you select. The source data can come from any of these places:

- A table that has a primary key field
- A query (or SQL statement) that displays specified columns and data from a table

- A fixed list of values that you enter when you create the field
- A list of all the field names in a table

For example, when entering data into the Order Details table, you can look up and fill in a ProductID field by selecting a value from a drop-down list. Figure 6.13 shows the ProductID field in the Orders form after we clicked on its drop-down arrow. To fill in (or change) the ProductID, we just click an entry in the list.

FIGURE 6.13

The ProductID lookup field (shown here on the sample Orders form) lets you look up and fill in the ProductID with a click of your mouse. The data for this lookup field comes from the Products table.

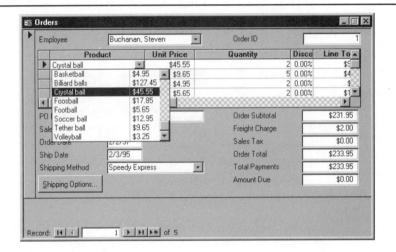

 NOTE In datasheet view, a lookup field always appears as a drop-down list, even if you've set its Display Control property to List Box in table design view. But when you add a lookup field to a form (such as the Orders form shown in Figure 6.13), Access automatically uses the Display Control property to decide whether to create the control as a drop-down list (which has a drop-down arrow that you must click to see the list) or as a list box (which shows the list itself, without a drop-down arrow).

How do you decide when to use a query, a table, a list of values, or a list of field names to display source data for your lookup field? The following sections offer some answers to this question.

Use a Query When...

You should use queries or SQL statements to display the list of values in a lookup field under the following conditions:

- You want columns in the lookup field's drop-down list to appear in a specific order (such as PersonID, LastName, FirstName).

- You want to display the results of calculations or to combine data from several fields into a single column. For example, a query or SQL statement makes it easy to display a customer or employee name as "Ajar, Doris" instead of showing the name in separate LastName and FirstName columns. (The EmployeeID field in the Orders table and Orders form displays employee names in LastName, First-Name format, as Figure 6.13 shows.)

- You want to restrict the lookup field's values to selected rows in a table. Suppose your Products table includes discontinued products that aren't available for sale. A query that filters out discontinued products offers a perfect way to display product names in the lookup field while preventing anyone from entering an order for discontinued products.

- You want changes to data in the query's source table(s) to be reflected in the drop-down list *and* in the lookup field that uses the query.

In a nutshell, queries and SQL statements are the best tools for making the lookup field display exactly what you want it to. They're also more efficient than using tables alone. You'll learn how to create queries in Chapter 10.

 NOTE An *SQL statement* is an expression that defines an SQL (Structured Query Language) command. Access uses SQL statements behind the scenes to interpret any queries you create in the query design window. SQL statements typically are used in queries and aggregate functions and as the record source for forms, reports, list boxes, and drop-down lists that Access Wizards create. For more about SQL, look up *SQL Statements* and its subtopics in the Access Help Index.

Use a Table When...

You can use tables to display the list of values in a lookup field under the following conditions:

- Columns in the table are arranged in the order you want them to appear in the lookup field's drop-down list during data entry.

PART

II

Creating a Database

- You want every record in the lookup table to be included on the drop-down list for the lookup field.
- You want changes to data in the source table to be reflected in the drop-down list and in the lookup field that uses the table.

Use a List of Values When...

Occasionally you might want to use a list of values when the list won't change often and it's fairly short. Such a list might be handy for honorifics or salutations. Keep in mind that changes to data in the value list will be reflected in the drop-down list but not in any records you added to the lookup field before you changed the list value.

Use a List of All Field Names in a Table When...

This method is useful mainly to application developers. Suppose you're designing a data entry form for a user who knows little about Access, and that user wants the option to sort the table's records by any field he or she chooses. You could add a drop-down list or list box lookup field that displays all the fields in the table, place a control for that new field on your form, and attach to the control's OnUpdate property a macro or event procedure that sorts the data by whatever field the user selects from the drop-down list or list box.

 NOTE If you want the user to sort by specific fields only, use a list of values that contains the sortable field names rather than a list of all field names in the table. The list of values method is preferable if the table you're planning to sort contains nonsortable field types, such as Memo or OLE Object fields.

If all this sounds like gobbledygook right now, don't worry about it. Access gives you plenty of ways to use lookup fields—even if you don't know about macros, event procedures, OnUpdate properties, and the like. If you're curious about using these techniques, see Chapters 21 and 26.

Setting Up a Lookup Field

You can use two methods to set up a lookup field in Access. First, you can use the Lookup Wizard, which guides you through the process step by step. Second, you can use the Lookup tab in the Field Properties area of the table design window to define the lookup field manually.

With the Lookup Wizard...

When you're first learning how to set up lookup fields, you might want to stick with the Lookup Wizard. Here's how to use it:

1. Switch to the design view for your table.

2. Move the cursor to the empty row that should contain your new lookup field. You can leave the field name blank because the Lookup Wizard will assign a field name for you.

3. Click the Data Type cell next to the blank field name, click the drop-down arrow, and then choose Lookup Wizard. The Lookup Wizard will take over, so follow the prompts in the dialog boxes.

4. Choose whether to get values from an existing table or query or whether to type the values you want. Click the Next button.

 TIP As usual, you can click the Next button to move to the next step, the Back button to back up to the previous step, and the Cancel button to bail out early while you're using the Lookup Wizard.

5. Complete the remaining dialog boxes, reading each one carefully and clicking the Next button to move ahead. Be sure to choose or define column names in the order you want to see them in the drop-down list during data entry. Keep these questions and answers in mind as you work through the Lookup Wizard dialog boxes:

   • **Which columns do you see in the drop-down list during data entry?** By default, the columns will appear in the order you chose them in the Lookup Wizard (though you may need to use the scroll bars to see them all); however, the primary key column usually will be hidden. You can change this default behavior in the Lookup Wizard dialog box that lets you adjust column widths. To do so, uncheck the Hide Key Column box, or hide any column by dragging (to the left) the vertical line next to the column name until the column disappears, or reposition any column by clicking its column name and then dragging the name to the left or right.

   • **What relationships are created behind the scenes?** If data for your new field comes from a table, the Lookup Wizard creates a relationship between the current table and the table whose data you're looking up. The field you're creating becomes the foreign key in that relationship. This behind-the-scenes action will ensure that you don't accidentally delete the lookup table or lookup fields without first deleting the relationship.

PART

II

Creating a Database

- **What values appear in the table after you choose an item from the drop-down list during data entry?** The *first* column you leave visible will appear in the table.

- **What values are actually stored in the new field when data comes from a related table?** If you've chosen to hide the related table's key column, the new field will store values from the *primary key field* of the related table. If you've chosen not to hide that table's key column, the field name you select in the second-to-last Lookup Wizard dialog box controls which data is stored in the new field. (This dialog box asks you to choose a field that uniquely identifies the row.)

- **What values are actually stored in the new field when data comes from a query or a list of values you type in?** The field name you select in the second-to-last Lookup Wizard dialog box controls which data is stored in the new field.

- **What name is assigned to the new field?** If data for your new field comes from a table or query, the Lookup Wizard gives the new field the same name as the primary key of the related table or the first field of the query. It sets the new field's Caption property to whatever name you choose in step 6, below. If data for your new field comes from a list of values you typed in, the Lookup Wizard uses the name you assign in step 6 for the field name and leaves the Caption property blank.

6. Type a label to use as the caption for your new field (if you wish) in the last dialog box, and then click the Finish button to finish the job. Respond to any prompts that appear.

In addition to handling all the details described in step 5, above, the Lookup Wizard also fills in the Lookup properties for you automatically. To see these properties for yourself, go to the table design window, click in the row that contains your lookup field, and then click the Lookup tab in the table design window's Field Properties area.

With the Lookup Properties Sheet...

Of course, you can define Lookup field properties without a Lookup Wizard, as follows:

1. Switch to the design view for the table.

2. Specify the Field Name and Data Type for your lookup field if you haven't done so already.

3. Click the Lookup tab in the table design window's Field Properties area.

4. Click in the Display Control property box, click the drop-down arrow that appears, and then choose either List Box or Combo Box.

5. Complete the remaining properties in the Lookup property sheet (see the next section for details).

Figure 6.14 shows the Lookup properties for the EmployeeID field of the Orders table. Figure 6.15 shows the query that's "behind" the SQL statement shown in the Row Source box of Figure 6.14. To display this query, we clicked in the Row Source box on the Lookup properties tab, clicked on the Build (...) button that appeared, and widened the second column in the query design grid. Figure 6.16 shows the results of running that query. (We ran this query so you can see the relationship between the query results and the Lookup properties.) See Chapters 3 and 10 for more about queries.

PART

II

Creating a Database

FIGURE 6.14

The Lookup properties for the EmployeeID field of the Orders table.

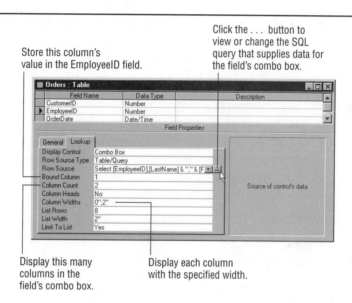

Store this column's value in the EmployeeID field.

Click the . . . button to view or change the SQL query that supplies data for the field's combo box.

Display this many columns in the field's combo box.

Display each column with the specified width.

FIGURE 6.15

The query behind the SQL statement for the Row Source property shown in Figure 6.14.

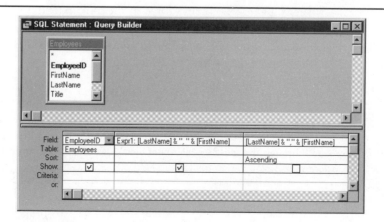

FIGURE 6.16

FIGURE 6.16

*The results of running
the query shown in
Figure 6.15.*

Important Facts about Lookup Fields

You'll have great success with setting up lookup fields if you remember these points:

- If you plan to use a table or query to supply values for the lookup field, that table or query must exist. (When using the Lookup tab, rather than the Lookup Wizard, you can create a query on the fly by clicking in the Row Source property box, and then clicking the Build button. See Chapter 10 for more about queries.)

- If you're using a table to supply values for the lookup field, that table must have a primary key.

- You can hide a column in your drop-down list by setting its width in the Column Widths property box to 0.

- The first column in the drop-down list is always the one you see in the lookup field (unless you've hidden the column by setting its column width to 0; in this case, the column you see is the first one that isn't hidden).

- The value that's actually stored in the lookup field is the one that's specified as the bound column (more about this shortly). The data type of the lookup field must be compatible with the bound column, regardless of what you see in the field during data entry.

NOTE The last two points, above, can be confusing. The easiest way to keep them straight is to remember that the first (unhidden) column controls *what you see* when you scroll through the table in datasheet view. The bound column controls *what actually is stored* (what you get) in the lookup field.

With these points in mind, let's take a closer look at the properties on the Lookup tab in the table design window.

Understanding the Lookup Properties

At first glance, the property sheet for the Lookup tab might seem rather daunting (refer to Figure 6.14). But it's not bad once you know more about it. Here's the scoop:

Display Control   Lets you choose the type of control used to display the field on the datasheet and forms. (For lookup fields, set the Display Control property to List Box or Combo Box.)

Row Source Type   Lets you choose the type of source for data in the field (Table/Query, Value List, or Field List). Generally, you'll want to choose Table/Query.

Row Source   Lets you choose the source of the control's data. In Figure 6.14 the row source is the SQL Select statement, which expands to the query shown in Figure 6.15.

Bound Column   Lets you specify which column in the row source contains the value to store in this lookup field. The data type for the field must be compatible with values in the bound column. For instance, if the bound column stores numeric values (such as EmployeeID values), the data type for the lookup field also must be numeric (Number, Currency); if the bound column stores Long Integer values, the data type for the lookup field must be either Long Integer or AutoNumber.

Column Count   Lets you specify how many columns to display. The example in Figure 6.14 tells Access to display two columns; however, the first column is hidden because its Column Widths setting is 0.

Column Heads   Lets you choose whether to show the column headings. By default, no column headings appear. To show column headings, change the setting to Yes.

Column Widths   Lets you specify the width of each column shown in the drop-down list. In Figure 6.14, the first column width is 0 (hidden), and the second column is 2 inches wide. When typing the column widths, use a semicolon (;) to separate each column's width specification; you can omit the unit of measurement ("). For example, if you type **0;2** in the Column Widths property box, Access will change your entry to **0";2"** when you move the cursor out of the Column Widths box.

PART

II

Creating a Database

List Rows   Lets you specify how many rows to display in the drop-down list at once (the default is 8).

List Width   Lets you specify the width of the entire combo box. (A List Width of Auto tells Access to calculate the width automatically.)

Limit to List   If set to Yes, only values shown in the drop-down list are allowed during data entry. If set to No, Access allows entries that aren't shown in the drop-down list.

For immediate help as you define Lookup properties, click in the appropriate property field and press F1.

Defining Relationships among Tables

You can define all the relationships among your tables at any time. There are several advantages to defining the relationships early on (before you add much data):

- When you open multiple related tables in a query (see Chapter 10), the related tables will be joined automatically, saving you a few extra steps.

- Access will create some needed indexes automatically to make your related tables perform more quickly.

- You can define *referential integrity* relationships between tables when joining them. Referential integrity ensures that the relationships between records in related tables remain valid and can prevent problems from occurring when you try to delete or change a record that's related to records in another table. *Example:* Referential integrity can ensure that every Orders record has a corresponding record in the Customers table (thus every order can be traced back to a customer). It also can prevent you from deleting a customer record if outstanding orders remain for that customer.

To define relationships among existing tables:

1. Close any open tables so that only the database window is visible.

2. Choose Tools ➤ Relationships from the menu bar, or click the Relationships toolbar button (shown at left), or right-click anywhere on the database window and choose Relationships. The Relationships window appears. (It will be empty unless you've previously defined relationships among your tables or used the Database Wizard to create the tables.)

3. Display tables for which you want to define relationships by clicking the Show Table toolbar button (shown at left), or right-clicking an empty part of the Relationships window and choosing Show Table, or choosing Relationships ➤ Show Table from the menu bar. You'll see a dialog box similar to this one:

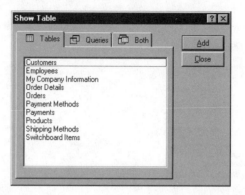

4. Add a table or query to the Relationships window by clicking an appropriate tab (Tables, Queries, or Both) in the Show Table dialog box. Then click the name of the table or query you want to add, and click Add; or double-click the table or query name. To add several tables at once, use the standard Shift-click and Ctrl-click techniques to select the tables, and then click the Add button.

5. Repeat step 4 until you've added all the tables and queries for which you want to define relationships. Then click the Close button.

6. Relate the tables as explained in the next section.

Figure 6.17 shows tables from the Order Entry database that are good candidates for relating. We've arranged and sized the tables, but haven't shown the relationships among them.

 TIP   To tidy up the Relationships window anytime, move the tables by dragging their title bars, and resize the tables by dragging their borders.

 NOTE   If you created the Order Entry database with the Database Wizard, all the relationships among the tables will be defined for you automatically, and the window will look more like Figure 6.18 than Figure 6.17 (although you'll certainly need to rearrange the tables to straighten out the spaghetti appearance of the lines between them).

PART

II

Creating a Database

FIGURE 6.17

*Tables from the Order
Entry database added
to the Relationships
window. The relation-
ships among the
tables haven't been
defined yet.*

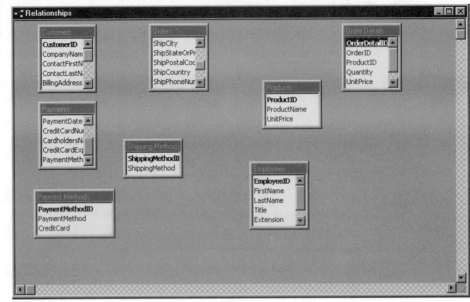

Relating Two Tables

To define the relationship between any two tables in the Relationships window:

1. Move the mouse pointer to the primary key field in the *primary table* (the table on the "one" side of a one-to-many relationship). That key is boldfaced in the list.

2. Drag that field name to the corresponding field in the related table (that is, drag it to the appropriate *foreign key*).

 TIP You can drag from the foreign key field in the related table to the primary key field in the primary table. The results will be the same.

3. Release the mouse button to display a dialog box similar to this one.

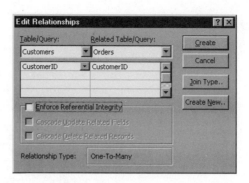

4. (Optional) Select (check) the Enforce Referential Integrity box to enforce refer- ential integrity between the two tables. Then you can tell Access how to handle changes and deletions in the primary table:

- If you want *changes* to the table on one side of the relation to automatically carry over to the related table, select (check) the Cascade Update Related Fields check box.

- If you want *deletions* in one table to carry over to the related table, select the Cascade Delete Related Records check box.

NOTE In order to define referential integrity between tables, the matching field from the primary table must be a primary key or have a unique index, the related fields must have the same data type (or be AutoNumber and Long Integer), and both tables must be stored in the same Access database. For more details about referential integrity rules, go to the Relationships dialog box and press the F1 key.

5. (Optional) Change the type of join between tables by clicking the Join Type but- ton, choosing the type of join you want to use, and then clicking OK. (If in doubt, don't make any change. You can always define the relationship in a query, as discussed in Chapter 10.)

NOTE *Join* is a database term that describes the correspondence between a field in one table and a field in another table. You can perform several types of joins, though the default join (called an *equi-join* or *inner join*) works fine for most situations. To learn more about joins, search for *Joins, Defining Types for Tables* in the Access Help Index.

6. Click the Create button to finish the job.

PART

II

Creating a Database

Access shows the relationship between the two tables as a join line connecting the related fields. The appearance of the line indicates the type of join you've chosen and whether you're enforcing referential integrity. In the example below, the thick, solid bars in the join line indicate that referential integrity is enforced between tables. The small *1* indicates the table on the one side of this relationship; the small infinity sign indicates the table on the many side of this relationship.

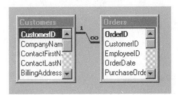

You can repeat steps 1 through 6, above, to define the relationships between as many pairs of tables as appropriate in your database. Figure 6.18 shows all the relationships between tables in the Order Entry database as the Database Wizard defined them.

FIGURE 6.18

The Order Entry Relationships window, showing all relationships the Database Wizard defined.

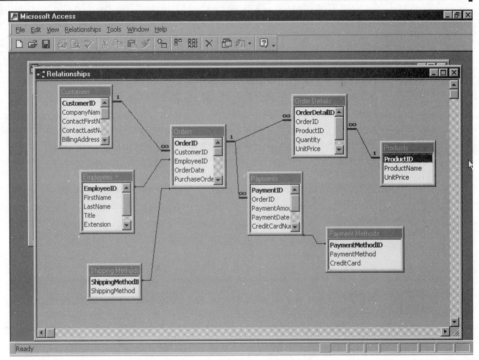

In the Order Entry database, referential integrity with cascaded updates and deletions is enforced between these tables: Customers and Orders, Orders and Payments, Orders and Order Details, and Products and Order Details. To make data entry more flexible, referential integrity is not enforced between these tables: Shipping Methods and Orders, Payment Methods and Payments, and Employees and Orders.

> **WARNING** When you're first designing a database, don't go hog wild with setting up relationships between tables. If the relationships between tables are too strict, data entry can be cumbersome. It's easy to add or remove relationships later if you need to, so don't worry too much about defining every possible relationship. Start conservatively, add a few sample records, and then decide whether the relationships should be more restrictive or less restrictive.

More Tips for Using the Relationships Window

Here are some other tips for using the Relationships window:

- **To show tables that are directly related to a selected table**, click the table and then click the Show Direct Relationships toolbar button (shown at left). Or right-click the table you're curious about, and choose Show Direct. Or click the table and choose Relationships ➤ Show Direct.

- **To show all tables and relationships that are currently defined for the database**, click the Show All Relationships toolbar button (shown at left). Or right-click an empty area in the relationships window and choose Show All. Or choose Relationships ➤ Show All from the menu bar.

- **To hide a table that you've added to the Relationships window**, click the table you want to hide. Then press Delete, or right-click and choose Hide Table, or choose Relationships ➤ Hide Table from the menu bar. This step does not delete the table from the database, and it doesn't delete any relationships defined for the table; it just hides the table from view. (To add the table to the view again, click the Show Table toolbar button, double-click the appropriate table name, and click Close.)

- **To clear all tables from the Relationships window**, choose Edit ➤ Clear Layout, or click the Clear Layout toolbar button (shown at left). When asked for confirmation, click Yes. The Relationships window will be empty. Again, no tables or relationships are deleted, but your work toward tidying up the Relationships window *will* be lost. To see all the tables and relationships again,

PART
II

Creating a Database

right-click any empty part in the Relationships window, choose Show All, and then tidy up the window as needed.

- **To change the design of any table shown in the Relationships window**, right-click that table and choose Table Design. When you're finished changing the table's design, click the design window's Close button or press Ctrl+W; you'll return to the Relationships window.

Printing the Relationships Window and other "Unprintable" Things

Alas, there's no way to print the Relationships window directly. Your best bet is to set up the window the way you want it and then press Alt+Print Screen to capture the screen to the Windows Clipboard. Then start the Paint applet (Start ➢ Programs ➢ Accessories ➢ Paint) and choose Edit ➢ Paste or press Ctrl+V. Finally, print the image from Paint by choosing File ➢ Print ➢ OK. You can also get printed information on relationships by running the Documenter. See Chapter 18.

Saving the Relationships Layout

When you use the Relationships window to add, change, or delete relationships, the relationships are saved automatically; however, changes to the window's layout are not. Therefore, any time you're happy with the appearance of the Relationships window, you should save the layout. There are many ways to save a layout: Choose File ➢ Save, press Ctrl+S, click the Save toolbar button, or right-click an empty part of the Relationships window and choose Save Layout. If you want to save the layout and close the Relationships window in one step, choose File ➢ Close, or press Ctrl+W, or click the window's Close button; then click Yes when asked about saving your changes.

After you've defined all the relationships among your tables, close the Relationships window (choose File ➢ Close). If you're asked about saving changes, click Yes.

Redefining (or Deleting) a Relationship

If you later discover that you've made a mistake while defining the relationships among your tables, you can follow the same steps presented under "Relating Two Tables" to return to the Relationships window and view existing relationships.

- **To change the relationship between two tables**, double-click the thin part of the join line, and then make your changes in the Relationships dialog box. Or right-click the thin part of the join line and choose Edit Relationship from the shortcut menu. Or click the thin part of the join line and choose Relationships ➤ Edit Relationship from the menu bar.

- **To delete the relationship between two tables**, right-click the thin part of the join line that you want to delete. Then choose Delete from the shortcut menu. Or click the thin part of the join line, and then press Delete or choose Edit ➤ Delete. When prompted, click Yes to confirm the deletion.

For more examples and information on defining relationships between tables, open the Microsoft Access Contents, open *Creating and Designing Tables*, open Defining Relationships and Setting Referential Integrity Options, and then explore the subtopics. You also can also use the Office Assistant to look for *Relationships* topics.

Important Tips for AutoNumber Fields

AutoNumber fields are great time-savers in Access. But you must understand how they work in order to use them effectively. To help you get the most from using AutoNumber fields, we'll first explain how to set a starting value for AutoNumber fields. Then we'll explain how to define a relationship between tables when one field's data type is AutoNumber.

 NOTE AutoNumber fields aren't always the best choice for assigning meaningful identifiers, such as customer numbers, because you can't delete or change AutoNumber field values. Furthermore, the autonumbering sequence will contain "holes" where you've deleted records. For example, if you've entered three customer records, the AutoNumber fields will have the values 1, 2, 3. If you then delete the customers whose AutoNumber fields are 2 and 3, the AutoNumber field for the next new customer will have the value 4. Sometimes this will be desirable, and sometimes it won't.

 WARNING If the table for which you're changing AutoNumber field values contains data, and that table is involved in a referential integrity relationship, you may lose records from related tables (if cascaded deletes are allowed)—or you may not be allowed to do step 13 below (if cascaded deletes are not allowed). Therefore, you should do the steps in the next section *only* if your related tables are empty (or contain only a few records that you don't care about).

Changing the Starting Value of an AutoNumber Field

Suppose you want to use an AutoNumber field to uniquely identify each customer in a table, bumping each new customer number up by 1. However, you want the numbering to start at some number other than 1, such as 1001 for four-digit ID numbers or 10001 for five-digit numbers. Here's how to change the starting value when you are in design view:

1. Open the table that contains the AutoNumber field in design view. (Make sure the AutoNumber field's New Values property on the General tab is set to Increment.)

2. Choose File ➤ Save As, enter a new name (such as _Temp) under Save Table … To, and then click OK.

3. Change the data type of the AutoNumber field from AutoNumber to Number (in design view for the new table); make sure its Field Size property is set to Long Integer.

4. Switch to datasheet view and click Yes when prompted for permission to save the table.

5. Type the starting number you want to use for the AutoNumber field, *minus 1*. (You also must enter a value in any required fields you've defined.) In the example below, we assigned the first customer an ID of 1000 so that our customer numbers for "real" data will begin at 1001.

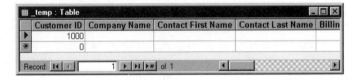

6. Close the temporary table (press Ctrl+W).

7. Highlight the name of that temporary table in the database window and choose Edit ➤ Copy.

8. Choose Edit ➤ Paste.

9. Type the name of the *original* table in the Table Name box (Customers in our example).

10. Click the Append Data to Existing Table option button.

11. Click OK to complete the copy.

12. Double-click the name of the original table in the database window (Customers in our example) to view its contents. You should see both the original record(s) (if any) and the newly numbered one(s), as shown below.

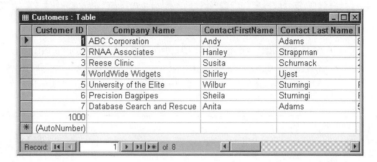

13. Skip to step 15 if the table doesn't contain old records. Otherwise, move the record(s) with the old numbers to the Windows Clipboard. To do this, drag the mouse pointer through all the record selectors *except* the selector for the new record you just added, choose Edit ➤ Cut (or press Ctrl+X), and then click Yes.

14. Paste the records back into the table by choosing Edit ➤ Paste Append ➤ Yes. The new records will start with the next available AutoNumber value (1001 in this example).

15. Click the record selector for the empty temporary record (1000 in this example), press Delete, and then click Yes to delete the record.

16. Add at least one new record to the table if the table was empty after you finished step 15 and you plan to compact the database that contains the table (see Chapter 18). Adding this new record will prevent the compacting operation from resetting the value for the next record added to one more than the previous value (effectively undoing your efforts in the above 15 steps).

17. Close the table and click No if asked about keeping the data on the Clipboard.

18. Highlight the name of the temporary table (_Temp), press Delete, and then click Yes as needed to delete it.

NOTE This procedure will work *only* if the temporary table's starting number (for example., 1000) is at least one higher than the highest AutoNumber field value that's currently stored in the table you're renumbering.

PART

II

Creating a Database

Any new record that you add to the table will be numbered starting at one more than the last record currently in that table.

Defining a Relationship When One Field Is an AutoNumber

When you define a relationship between two tables, and the primary key on the one side of the relationship is an increment AutoNumber field, the foreign key (that is, the corresponding field on the many side) must be the Number data type with its field size set to Long Integer. Figure 6.19 shows an example.

Primary key: The field that uniquely identifies each record on the one side of a one-to-many relationship.

When the primary key is the AutoNumber data type . . .

. . . the foreign key must be the Number data type with its Field Size property set to Long Integer.

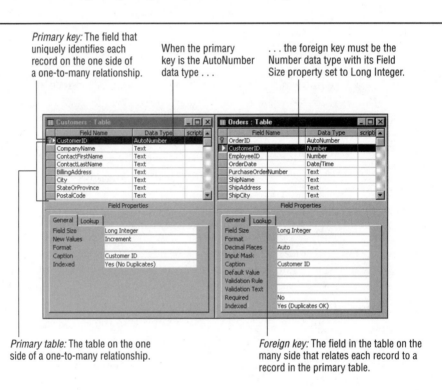

Primary table: The table on the one side of a one-to-many relationship.

Foreign key: The field in the table on the many side that relates each record to a record in the primary table.

 NOTE You also can match a Replication ID AutoNumber field with a Replication ID Number field. For information about replication, see Chapter 18 or look up Replication in the Access Answer Wizard.

The reason for this requirement is somewhat technical, but basically it's because Access stores AutoNumber field data as four-byte numbers. Only a foreign key that's exactly the same four-byte number will match the primary key. Setting the field size property of a number to Long Integer ensures that a four-byte number will be stored in the field.

If you forget to set the property of the foreign key to Long Integer, you won't be able to define a relationship between the tables. Or worse yet, if you add data to both tables without defining a relationship first and then try to access related records from both tables, the results will be incorrect and very confusing.

This requirement is just one of those picky little things you need to remember about Access. If you forget, and problems arise much later down the road, you might not think to check the field properties in the tables until you've spent 20 hours on hold with technical support and pulled out all your hair.

Documenting Your Tables and Database

Having a printed copy of information about your table structures can be very handy when you start developing other objects in your database. Chapter 18 covers these "database administration" tools in detail. But here's a quick preview of techniques for the curious:

- **To print design information about any database objects** (including tables or the entire database), choose Tools ➤ Analyze ➤ Documenter, or click the drop-down arrow next to the Analyze button on the Access toolbar and choose Documenter.

- **To view or change database properties**, choose File ➤ Database Properties, or right-click the database window's title bar or any gray area on the database window and choose Database Properties.

- **To print the table design window or the Relationships window**, use standard copy/cut-and-paste techniques to copy the screen to the Windows Clipboard, paste the Clipboard contents into Windows Paint, and then print the results. See the sidebar titled "Printing the Relationships Window and other 'Unprintable' Things" earlier in this chapter.

PART

II

Creating a Database

Analyzing Your Tables and Database Performance

Two Access Wizards can help you optimize your tables and improve database performance. You'll learn about both of these in Chapter 17. But for now, here's a summary of what's available:

> **Table Analyzer Wizard**   Analyzes any table you choose and lets you split it into related tables, if necessary. To get started, choose Tools ➤ Analyze ➤ Table, or click the drop-down arrow next to the Analyze button on the Access toolbar and choose Analyze Table.

> **Performance Analyzer Wizard**   Analyzes relationships, tables, queries, forms, reports, macros, modules, or all objects, and provides suggestions for making the selected objects work more efficiently. To use this Wizard, choose Tools ➤ Analyze ➤ Performance, or click the drop-down arrow next to the Analyze button on the Access toolbar and choose Analyze Performance.

Where to Go from Here

In this chapter, you've learned how to design tables using both the Table Wizard and various from-scratch methods. Where should you go from here?

- To learn how to import or link existing data into your tables, see Chapter 7.
- To learn more about entering data into your tables, see Chapter 8.

What's New in the Access Zoo?

The process of creating and managing tables with Access 2000 for Windows is the same as it was in earlier versions of Access. The main thing that's new when it comes to tables is projects. Projects are special databases that work with tables stored in an SQL Server database. See Chapter 30 for information on creating projects.

CHAPTER 7

Linking, Importing, and Exporting Data

You'll want to read this chapter if you already have data on your computer that you want to pull into an Access database, or if you want to export Access data to another program. Most procedures described in this chapter for linking, importing, and exporting data are quick and easy to use. However, a few fine points can be tricky, especially if you're working with open database connectivity (ODBC), Paradox, or dBASE database files. Luckily, lots of online Help is available. Search for *Import* or *Export* with the Office Assistant to get going quickly.

 NOTE See Chapter 4 for other ways to share data among Microsoft Office programs.

 NOTE If the data you want to work with is on an SQL Server, you can use an Access project, instead of a database, to access the data. Remember that a project can include forms, reports, data access pages, macros, and modules, but it cannot include any Access queries. You have to define and store views of the table data on the SQL Server. See Chapter 30 for more information on creating projects.

Link, Import, Export: What's the Difference?

Access gives you several ways to share data with other programs:

Link   Lets you directly access data in another computer database. Any changes you make via Access will affect the original database as well as the Access database. That is, you'll be working with *live data*. Note that you can link tables to an Access database, but not to a project.

 NOTE In some earlier versions of Access, linking was called *attaching*.

Import   Lets you make a separate copy of data from other programs or file formats and store it in an Access table. Changes you make via Access will not affect the original data.

Export   Lets you copy data from an Access table *to* some other program or file format, such as Microsoft Word or Excel, or even to a separate Access database. The exported data is an entirely separate copy that isn't linked to your original Access data in any way.

After importing or linking data from another program into Access, you can usually use that data as though you had created it in Access originally. For example, if you import or link a Paradox table into your Access database, you can open that table and use it as you would any Access table.

Similarly, you can use exported Access tables in other programs, just as though you had created the exported data in the other program originally. Thus you can export an Access table to Paradox format, fire up Paradox, and then open and use the table as you would any other "native" Paradox table.

NOTE   *OLE* is a technology that offers another way to combine information from separate programs. However, OLE lets you share *objects,* rather than *data.* We'll talk about OLE in Chapter 8.

Interacting with Other Databases

You can import or link data from any of these database formats:

- Microsoft Access
- Text files in delimited or fixed-length format
- dBASE III, IV, and 5
- Paradox
- ODBC databases, including Microsoft SQL Server (you'll need a properly installed and configured ODBC driver)
- Microsoft Excel
- HTML documents
- Exchange( ) and Outlook( ) files

In addition, Lotus 1-2-3 files can be imported, but not linked.

Before you bring data from one of these other formats into an Access database, you need to decide whether to link to that data or import your own copy of it. Table 7.1 lists some points that can help you decide.

TABLE 7.1: DIFFERENCES BETWEEN IMPORTED AND LINKED TABLES

IMPORTED TABLE	LINKED TABLE
Copied from the external table to your open database. (Requires extra disk storage.)	Linked to your open database. No copies are made. (Conserves disk storage.)
Use when you no longer need to have the original application update the table.	Use when you still need to have the original application update the table.
Converted to Access format and works exactly like a table you created from scratch.	Retains its original database format, but "acts like" an Access table.
You can change any properties, including the structure, of an imported table.	You can change some properties, but you can't change the structure of a linked table.
Access can work faster with imported tables.	Access may work more slowly with linked tables.
Deleting the table deletes the copy from your open database.	Deleting the table deletes the link only, not the external table.
Access translates certain data types of the original table to Access data types.	No data type translations are necessary.

Where You'll See Imported/Linked Tables

When you import or link data from another database, Access treats the data as it would one of its own tables. For linked tables, however, special icons in the database window indicate that the data is not stored in Access.

In Figure 7.1 we linked Access tables named Expense Categories, Expense Details, and Expense Reports (from another Access database); a Paradox table named Volumes; and a dBASE table named Monnames to an open Order Entry1 database. We also imported a table named Sales from a Microsoft Excel worksheet. Notice that the icons next to the linked tables include an arrow symbol to indicate a link to the external tables; however, the icon next to the Sales table looks like any other Access table icon.

FIGURE 7.1

Special link icons indicate linked tables.

Linked Access tables

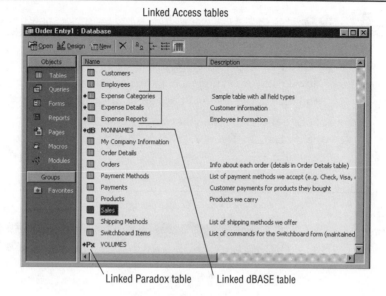

Linked Paradox table   Linked dBASE table

Importing or Linking a Table

Here are the general steps for importing or linking tables. The exact procedures will depend on the type of data you're importing or linking. Refer to the appropriate section below for more details.

1. Open (or create) the Access database you want to import or link the table to, and switch to the database window if it isn't visible.

2. Do one of the following, depending on whether you are importing or linking:

   • **To import**, choose File ➤ Get External Data ➤ Import, or right-click the database window (the shaded part, not a table name) and choose Import. Or click the Tables button in the database window, click the database window's New button, and then double-click Import Table in the New Table dialog box.

   • **To link**, choose File ➤ Get External Data ➤ Link Tables, or right-click the database window and choose Link Tables. Or click the Tables button in the database window, click the database window's New button, and then double-click Link Table in the New Table dialog box.

NOTE You cannot delete rows from linked Excel tables or text files.

3. Choose the type of data you want to import or link in the Files of Type drop-down list. For example, click the drop-down list button next to Files of Type, and then click Paradox to import or link a Paradox table.

4. Locate the file name you want to import or link, and then click it in the list below Look In. Figure 7.2 shows a typical Link dialog box; the Import dialog box is similar.

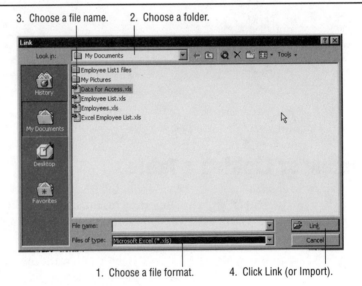

FIGURE 7.2

A Link dialog box for linking an Excel table.

3. Choose a file name.   2. Choose a folder.

1. Choose a file format.   4. Click Link (or Import).

 TIP The techniques for locating drives, folders, and files in the Link and Import dialog boxes are the same ones that work in the Open and File New Database dialog boxes (see Chapters 1 and 5, respectively).

5. Click the Import or Link button, or double-click the file name you want to import or link.

6. Respond to any additional prompts and dialog boxes that appear.

- If you're linking a dBASE table, you'll be prompted to choose one or more existing indexes to associate with the table. Choosing indexes will speed up access to the linked table.

- If you're importing or linking a table from Paradox or an SQL database, you may be prompted for a password. This password is set in the external program and is different from an Access user password.

NOTE Passwords of linked tables are stored in your database so that you can open the table later by double-clicking it in the Access database window. Be aware that the database password is stored in an unencrypted form. If you need to protect sensitive data in the linked table, you should implement user-level security rather than use a database password. (See Chapter 19 for instructions on using Access's security features to protect a database.)

7. Click OK if you see a message saying the operation is complete.

8. If the Import or Link dialog box remains on your screen, you can repeat steps 3 through 7 until you've imported or linked all the tables you want. When you're done, click the Close button as needed.

For more help on importing and linking tables, use the Office Assistant to look up *Import* or *Export* and then click an appropriate topic.

Importing or Linking Paradox Tables

Access can import or link tables (.db files) from Paradox versions 3, 4, 5, 7, and 8. Follow these steps:

1. Start from the Access database window and choose the Import or Link command. (Two easy starting points are to choose the File ➤ Get External Data commands on the menu bar, or right-click the database window and choose Import or Link Tables from the shortcut menu.)

2. Choose Paradox from the Files of Type drop-down list.

3. Locate the file you want to import or link, and then double-click it in the list below Look In. You may be prompted for a password.

4. Type the password that was assigned to the table in Paradox, and then click OK.

5. Click OK when you see the message saying the operation is complete.

6. Repeat steps 3 through 5 as needed. When you're done, click Close.

PART

II

Creating a Database

Having trouble? Perhaps the following tips will help:

- A linked Paradox table must have a primary key (.px) file if you intend to update it through Access. If that file is not available, Access won't be able to link the table. Without a primary key, you'll only be able to view the linked table, not to change it.

- In general, any ancillary file that Paradox maintains for a table (such as an .mb file for memo fields) should be available to Access.

- If you are importing or linking Paradox version 8 tables, you must have the Borland Database Engine (BDE), version 4.*x* or later, installed on your computer. Use the Office Assistant to look for help on *Import Paradox*, click the topic for *Import or Link Paradox Tables*, and check the notes in Access Help to get information on how you can get BDE on your computer if you don't have Paradox 8 installed on it already.

For more details about importing and linking Paradox tables, ask the Office Assistant to search for *Import Paradox*.

Importing or Linking dBASE Files

Access can import or link tables (.dbf files) from dBASE III, IV, and 5. Here are the basic steps for importing or linking a dBASE table:

1. Start from the Access database window and choose the Import or Link command.

2. Choose dBASE III, dBASE IV, or dBASE 5 from the Files of Type drop-down list.

3. Locate the file you want to import or link, and then double-click it in the list below Look In.

4. Double-click the index file you want to use if the Select Index Files dialog box appears. Repeat this step until you've specified all the index files associated with the .dbf file you chose in step 3, and respond to any other prompts that appear. When you're done, click the Close or Cancel button.

5. Click OK when you see the message that the operation is complete.

6. Repeat steps 3 through 5 as needed. When you're done, click Close.

When linking dBASE files, keep these points in mind:

- To improve performance later, you can have Access use one or more existing dBASE index files (.ndx or .mdx). The index files are tracked in a special information file (.inf) and are maintained automatically when you update the table through Access.

- If you use dBASE to update data in a linked .dbf file, you must manually update the associated indexes; otherwise, Access won't be able to use the linked table.

- If you move or remove any .ndx, .mdx, or .inf files that Access is using, then Access won't be able to open the linked table.

- To link tables on a read-only drive or CD-ROM drive, Access must store the .inf file on a writable directory. To specify this directory, you must specify the path for the .inf file in the Windows Registry.

For more about working with dBASE files, look up *Import dBASE* with the Office Assistant.

Importing or Linking ODBC Databases

 NOTE Even though you can use Access projects to work with SQL Server data, there may be occasions when you prefer to import or link the data instead. For example, if you want to be able to create Access queries for the SQL Server data instead of creating SQL Server views, link the data to an Access database via ODBC instead of using a project.

If everything is properly set up, you can use Access to open tables from other databases via ODBC drivers. Here are the basic steps for linking or importing tables this way:

1. Start from the Access database window and choose the Import or Link command.

2. Choose ODBC Databases from the Files of Type drop-down list.

3. Click the Machine Data Source tab in the Select Data Source dialog box if you want to work with data from another user or system. Double-click the data source you want to use. (If necessary, you can define a new data source for any installed ODBC driver by clicking the New button and following the instructions that appear. After creating the new data source, you can double-click it to continue. Alternatively, you can manage your ODBC data sources by double-clicking the 32-bit ODBC icon in Control Panel.)

4. Complete the remaining dialog boxes that appear, clicking OK as needed to proceed. (These dialog boxes depend on the data source you chose.) For example, you may be prompted for the following:

   - Your login ID and password

   - Whether you want to save the login ID and password (if you're linking)

- The tables you want to import or link
- The fields that uniquely identify each record

5. Click Close when you're finished importing or linking.

If you're having trouble with the importing or linking procedure, consider these points:

- Before connecting to an SQL database, you must install the proper ODBC driver for your network and SQL database. You can find information on this procedure by looking up *Installing Drivers* with the Office Assistant.
- Access includes the ODBC drivers for Access 97 and Access 2000, dBASE, FoxPro and Visual FoxPro, Excel, and Text. Before using any other ODBC driver, check with its vendor to verify that it will work properly.
- If you'll want to edit a linked SQL table, that table usually must contain a unique index. If no unique index exists, you can create one by executing a data-definition query within Access. For information on data-definition queries, use the Office Assistant to find help for *CREATE INDEX Statement*. Then click the topic *Work with Tables or Indexes by Using an SQL Data-Definition Query*.
- If the SQL table's structure changes after you link it, you'll need to use the Linked Table Manager to refresh your link to the table (see "Using the Linked Table Manager" later in the chapter) or delete and recreate the link.
- If an error occurs while you're importing, linking, or using an SQL table, the problem may be with your account on the SQL database server or the database itself. Please contact your SQL database administrator for assistance.

For more about the subtleties of importing and linking tables via ODBC, look up *Import an ODBC Table* with the Office Assistant.

Importing or Linking Other Access Databases

Normally you'll want to store all the tables, forms, reports, and other objects that make up a given application in a single Access database. But in a large company, different departments might create their own separate Access databases. Fortunately, it's easy to import objects (tables, queries, forms, reports, macros, and modules) or link tables from other unopened Access databases into your open database. Then you can use the objects as if they were part of your currently open Access database. This method is much easier than using copy and paste to copy several related objects at once. Also, linked tables allow many users to share a single copy of their data over a network.

NOTE You can import just the structure or both the structure and data of Access tables. If you intend to import objects (forms, reports, queries, and so forth) for use with tables in the open database, the name and structure of the tables in the open database must match the name and structure of the tables originally used to create the objects you're importing.

To import objects or link tables from an unopened Access database:

1. Choose the Import or Link command from the Access database window.

2. Choose Microsoft Access from the Files of Type list.

3. Locate the Access database you want to import or link, and then double-click it in the list below Look In.

4. Do one of the following:

- **To link**: you'll see the Link Tables dialog box shown in Figure 7.3; skip to step 6.

- **To import objects**: you'll see the Import Objects dialog box shown in Figure 7.4; continue with step 5.

PART

II

Creating a Database

FIGURE 7.3

The Link Tables dialog box.

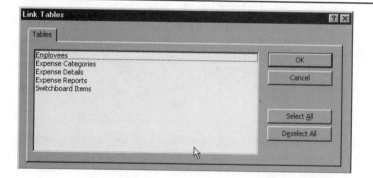

5. Click the tab for the type of object you want to import if you're importing objects. As Figure 7.4 shows, your options are Tables, Queries, Forms, Reports, Pages, Macros, and Modules. For additional import options, click the Options button (see Figure 7.4) and then choose any of the options shown. (For help with the options, click the ? button at the upper-right corner of the Import Objects dialog box, and then click the place you need help with.)

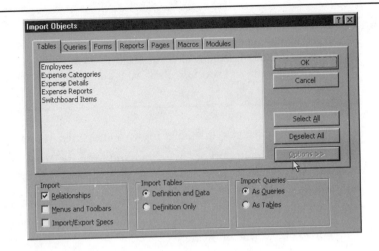

FIGURE 7.4

The Import Objects dialog box after clicking the Options button and the Tables tab.

6. Use any of the following techniques to select the object(s) you want to import or link, and then click OK to continue.

- **To select all the objects of a particular type** in one fell swoop, click the Select All button.

- **To deselect all the selected objects**, click the Deselect All button.

- **To select one object that isn't selected yet, or to deselect an object that is selected**, click its name.

Access will import or link all the objects you selected and return to the database window.

TIP The opposite of importing or linking a database is splitting it—a trick that can make your database run faster over networks. You can use the Database Splitter Wizard (Tools ➢ Database Utilities ➢ Database Splitter) to split a database into one file that contains the tables and another that contains the queries, forms, reports, pages, macros, and modules. See Chapter 19 for details.

PART

II

Creating a Database

Another Reason to Use Wizards

Objects created with Access wizards are perfect candidates for linking or importing into other Access databases that also contain objects created with those wizards. For instance, if you use the Database Wizard or Table Wizard (with default settings) to create Customers tables in two Access databases—Order Entry and Service Call Management, for example—those tables will have the same structure in both databases. If you then import into the Service Call Management database a report that was designed to print the Customers table in the Order Entry database, that report should work perfectly on the Customers table in the Service Call Management database.

Using Linked Tables

After linking a table from another database, you can use it almost like any other Access table. You can enter and update data, use existing queries, forms, and reports, or develop new ones. So even if the data resides in separate programs on separate computers, Access can use the external table almost as if you had created it from scratch in your open database. The only real restrictions are

- You can't change the structure of a linked table.

- You can't delete rows from a linked Excel table or text file.

 NOTE After *importing* a table from another database, you can use it exactly like any other Access table. Access will never know that your imported table wasn't originally one of its own.

Setting Properties of Linked Tables

Although you can't add, delete, or rearrange fields of a linked table, you can set some table properties, including the Format, Input Mask, Decimal Places, and Caption. You change these properties in the table design view (see Chapter 6). In the database window you can right-click the table name on the Tables tab, choose Properties, and change the Description property.

TIP Any time you click in a General or Lookup properties box in the Field Properties area of the table design window, the Hint box in the right side of the window will tell you if the selected property cannot be changed.

Renaming Linked or Imported Tables

Most objects will have their original file names when you import or link them to Access. After you've imported or linked such a file, however, you can give it a more descriptive name in your Access database window. For instance, you could rename an imported or linked dBASE table from CredCard to Credit Cards (From dBASE).

To rename an imported or linked table quickly, right-click its name in the database window, choose Rename from the shortcut menu, type a new name, and then press Enter.

Speeding Up Linked Tables

Although linked tables behave a lot like Access tables, they're not actually stored in your Access database. Each time you view linked data, Access must retrieve records from another file that may be on another computer in the network or in an ODBC database. You might grow some gray hairs waiting for this to happen.

These guidelines can help speed up performance in a linked table on a network or ODBC database:

- Avoid jumping to the last record of a large table unless you need to add new records.
- View only the data you absolutely need and don't scroll up and down unnecessarily.
- Create a form that has the Data Entry property on the Data tab set to Yes. That way, if you frequently add new records to a linked table, Access won't bother to display any existing records from the table when you enter data (see Chapter 13). This *data entry* mode (also called *add* mode) can be much faster than opening the form in edit mode and jumping to the last record. (If you need to see all the records again, choose Records ➤ Remove Filter/Sort.)

 NOTE Here are three more ways to open a form or table in data entry mode: (1) choose Records ➤ Data Entry after opening a table or form; (2) choose Open Form in Add Mode as the Command for a form you've added to a switchboard with the Switchboard Manager (see Chapters 3 and 22); or (3) in a macro design window use the OpenForm action to open a form and set the action's Data Mode action argument to Add (see Chapter 21).

- Use queries and filters to limit the number of records that you view in a form or datasheet.

- Avoid using functions, especially domain-aggregate functions, such as DSum( ), anywhere in your queries. These functions require Access to process all the data in the linked table. See Chapter 10 for more about these functions.

- Avoid locking records for longer than you need when sharing external tables with other users on a network. Hogging the locks will slow response time for others and make you unpopular in a hurry. See Chapter 19 for more about using Access on a network.

Using the Linked Table Manager

Access stores information about links to tables in your database. If you move the file that contains the linked table to another folder, Access won't be able to open the linked table. Fortunately, the Linked Table Manager can find the moved tables and fix things up quickly. Here's how to use it:

1. Open the database that you've linked the objects to.

2. Choose Tools ➤ Database Utilities ➤ Linked Table Manager to open the Linked Table Manager dialog box (see Figure 7.5). This dialog box shows the linked objects and the full path names of the associated source files.

FIGURE 7.5

The Linked Table Manager dialog box for a database with several linked files.

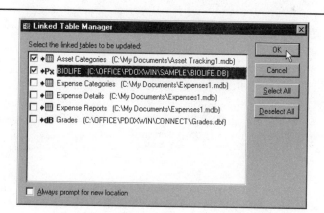

3. Click the appropriate check boxes to select the linked tables you want to update. If you select a table accidentally, click its check box again to deselect (clear) the box. Or click the Select All or Deselect All buttons to check or clear all the check boxes in one step.

4. Select (check) Always Prompt for New Location to force the Linked Table Manager to request the location for each table you checked in step 3.

5. Click OK.

6. Use the Select New Location Of dialog box that appears next to find the folder that contains the moved source table, and then double-click the file name that contains the linked table. Repeat this step as needed.

 TIP The Select New Location Of dialog box works the same way as the Open, File New Database, Import, and Link dialog boxes you already know and love. See Chapters 1 and 5 for techniques you can use in these dialog boxes.

7. Click OK when Access tells you that the links were refreshed successfully; then click Close in the Linked Table Manager dialog box.

What the Linked Table Manager Cannot Do

The Linked Table Manager is great for finding files that have wandered off to a different folder or disk drive or have been renamed. However, if anyone has renamed the linked table or changed its password, Access won't be able to find the table and the Linked Table Manager won't be able to fix the problem. In these cases, you must delete the link and then relink the table with the correct table name and/or password.

Also, don't expect the Linked Table Manager to move the database or table files for you. For that job, you'll need to use Windows Explorer or My Computer. Or go to any Access Open, File New Database, Link, Import, or Select New Location Of dialog box, right-click an empty area below the Look In list, choose Explore from the shortcut menu, and explore as you would with Windows Explorer.

Deleting the Link to a Linked Table

When you no longer need to use a linked table (or Access can't find it because someone has renamed it or changed its password), you can delete the link. To do this, open the database window that contains the linked table, and click the Tables tab. Then click the table whose link you want to delete, and press the Delete key. When asked if you're sure you want to delete the link, click Yes.

Remember that deleting a link deletes the information used to access the linked table, but it has absolutely no effect on the table itself. You can relink the table at any time.

Importing or Linking Spreadsheets and Text Files

You can import or link any of these spreadsheet and text formats into Access tables:

- Microsoft Excel.

- Lotus 1-2-3 or 1-2-3 for Windows (.wk1, .wk3, and .wk4 files). Lotus files can't be linked, only imported.

- Delimited text. (Values are separated by commas, tabs, or other characters.)

- Fixed-width text, including Microsoft Word Merge. (Each field value is a certain width.)

When importing from a text file, you can create a new table or append the data to an existing table. If your spreadsheet or text file contains field names in the first row, Access can use them as field names in the table.

Access looks at the first row of data and does its best to assign the appropriate data type for each field you import. For example, importing cells A1 through C10 from the spreadsheet at the top of Figure 7.6 creates the Access table at the bottom of the figure. Here we told Access to use the first row of the range (row 1) as field labels. Values in row 2 (the first row of "real" data) were then used to determine the data types for each field.

PART

II

Creating a Database

FIGURE 7.6

Importing a range of cells from an Excel spreadsheet into an Access table.

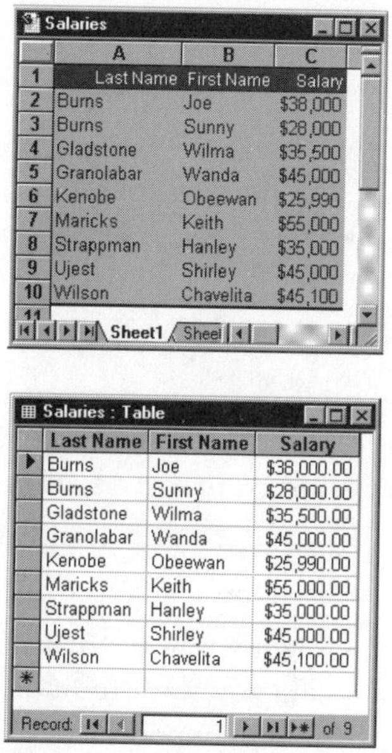

When you import cells A1 through C10 of this Excel spreadsheet . . .

	A	B	C
1	Last Name	First Name	Salary
2	Burns	Joe	$38,000
3	Burns	Sunny	$28,000
4	Gladstone	Wilma	$35,500
5	Granolabar	Wanda	$45,000
6	Kenobe	Obeewan	$25,990
7	Maricks	Keith	$55,000
8	Strappman	Hanley	$35,000
9	Ujest	Shirley	$45,000
10	Wilson	Chavelita	$45,100

Sheet1 / Sheet

. . . Access creates this table.

Salaries : Table

Last Name	First Name	Salary
Burns	Joe	$38,000.00
Burns	Sunny	$28,000.00
Gladstone	Wilma	$35,500.00
Granolabar	Wanda	$45,000.00
Kenobe	Obeewan	$25,990.00
Maricks	Keith	$55,000.00
Strappman	Hanley	$35,000.00
Ujest	Shirley	$45,000.00
Wilson	Chavelita	$45,100.00

Record: 1 of 9

You can change the field names and data types assigned to an imported table during the import procedure. Alternatively, you can create an empty table with the field names and data types you want, and then *append* an imported text file to the empty table. In Figure 7.7 we imported a delimited text file in which each field is separated by a comma and text fields are enclosed in quotes. Again we asked Access to use the first row as field labels. Access used the second row to determine each field's data type.

FIGURE 7.7

Importing from a delimited text file into an Access table.

When you import this delimited text file . . .

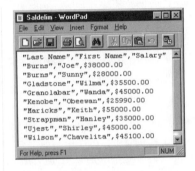

. . . Access creates this table.

Figure 7.8 shows the results of importing a fixed-width text file into an Access table. This time, we told Access the field name to use for each field. (Access correctly figured out the other details, such as field position and data type.)

Importing or Linking Spreadsheets

Importing or linking a spreadsheet into Access is a snap thanks to the Import Spreadsheet Wizard. But before you import or link, remember that the data in your spreadsheet must be arranged so that:

- Each value in a given field contains the same type of data.
- Each row contains the same fields.
- The first row in the spreadsheet contains either field names or the first actual data you want to import, or you've defined a named range for the data you want to import.

- If you are working with an Excel 4 or Lotus notebook that has multiple spreadsheets, you will have to save each spreadsheet in its own notebook before you can import it.

If the spreadsheet you intend to use doesn't fit these specifications, you'll need to fix it before importing or linking it into Access.

When you import this fixed-width text file . . .

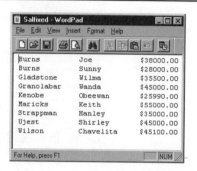

. . . Access creates this table.

To import or link a spreadsheet:

1. Start from the Access database window in which the table should appear, and choose the Import or Link command.

2. From the Files of Type drop-down list, choose the spreadsheet format you want to import. Your choices are Microsoft Excel (for importing or linking) and Lotus 1-2-3 (for importing only).

3. Locate the spreadsheet file you want to import or link, and then double-click it in the list below Look In. The Wizard will take over. If your worksheet contains a named range or multiple sheets, you'll see a dialog box similar to Figure 7.9. (The Import Spreadsheet Wizard and Link Spreadsheet Wizard dialog boxes are the same, except for their title bars.)

FIGURE 7.9

This Import Spreadsheet Wizard dialog box appears if your worksheet contains multiple sheets or named ranges. If you're linking an Excel worksheet, the Link Spreadsheet Wizard dialog box will be the same except for its title bar.

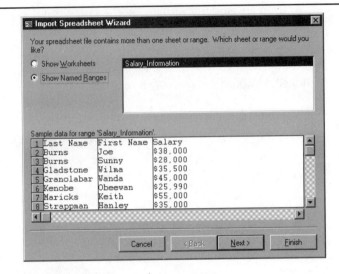

4. Choose whether to Show Worksheets or Show Named Ranges, click the worksheet or named range you want to use, and then click Next. Figure 7.10 shows the next dialog box you'll see.

FIGURE 7.10

This dialog box lets you specify whether the first imported or linked row contains field names. In this example, we're importing the spreadsheet shown at the top of Figure 7.6. Again, the Link Spreadsheet Wizard dialog box is similar.

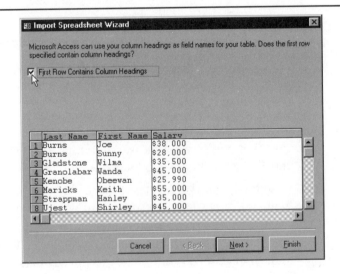

5. If the first row of the range you're importing or linking contains labels that you want to use as field names for the table, select (check) First Row Contains Column Headings. If you don't check this box, Access will start importing or linking data with the first row of the range and will assign the name Field followed by a sequential number as the field names (Field1, Field2, Field3,…). Click Next to continue to a dialog box that lets you choose whether to import the data into a new table or into an existing table.

6. Click your choice, and choose a table in the open database if you select In an Existing Table. Click Next.

7. If you're importing, you'll see the dialog box shown in Figure 7.11. From here you can specify information about each field you're importing. To tell the Wizard which field you want to define, click anywhere on the sample data for that field in the lower part of the dialog box. Then fill in the Field Name box, specify whether the field is indexed by choosing No, or Yes (Duplicates OK), or Yes (No Duplicates) from the Indexed drop-down list, and specify a data type by choosing an option from the Data Type drop-down list (if available). If you prefer to skip the field—that is, not to import it—select (check) Do Not Import Field (Skip). Repeat step 7 as needed, and then click Next.

PART

II

Creating a Database

FIGURE 7.11

This dialog box lets you specify the field name, indexing, and data type for each imported field, and it lets you skip fields as needed.

2. Choose options for the selected field.

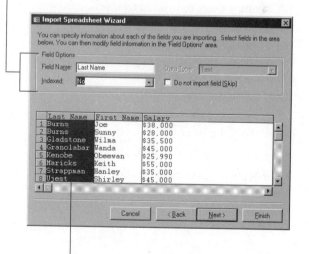

1. Click anywhere in the field you want to change.

8. If you're importing, the next dialog box will let you specify how Access should assign the primary key. You can let Access add the primary key, choose your own primary key from a drop-down list of available field names, or omit the primary key. After making your selection, click Next to continue.

9. The last dialog box lets you specify a table name if you chose to import data into a new table. If you're importing, you also can choose whether to analyze the new table's structure with the Table Analyzer Wizard. (Chapter 17 describes the Table Analyzer Wizard.) Complete this dialog box and then click Finish.

10. If you're asked for permission to overwrite an existing table, click Yes to overwrite the table and continue with step 10 or click No to return to step 8.

11. When Access tells you that it has finished importing or linking the table, click OK. You'll see the new table name in the database window.

Importing or Linking Text Files

A *delimited* text file is one in which fields are separated by a special character, such as a comma or tab, and each record ends with a carriage-return/linefeed combination. Typically, character data items are enclosed in quotation marks, as shown at the top of Figure 7.7.

A *fixed-width* text file is one in which each field is a specified width, and each record ends with a carriage-return/linefeed combination (see the top of Figure 7.8).

Before importing or linking a text file, make sure it's arranged so that each value in a given field contains the same type of data and the same fields appear in every row. The first row can contain the field names you want Access to use when creating the table.

The procedure for importing or linking text files is controlled by a Wizard that's fast and painless to use. In fact, reading these steps takes much longer than doing them:

1. Start from the Access database window in which the table should appear, and choose the Import or Link command.

2. Choose Text Files from the Files of Type drop-down list.

3. Locate the text file you want to import or link, and then double-click it in the list below Look In. The Wizard will take over (see Figure 7.12).

FIGURE 7.12

The first Text Import Wizard dialog box lets you choose a format for importing your data. If you're linking the text file, the Link Text Wizard dialog box will look the same, except for its title bar.

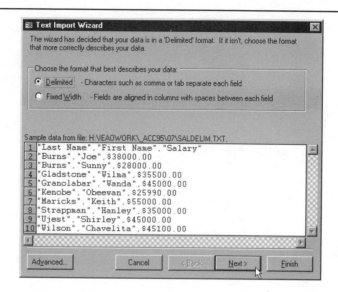

4. Choose the format that describes your data if Access didn't guess the correct format (either Delimited or Fixed Width), and then click Next.

NOTE The Advanced button in the Text Import Wizard and Link Text Wizard dialog boxes lets you define, save, load, and delete import specifications. You can use an import specification if you want more control over such things as the order of dates, date delimiters, time delimiters, and other details. In most cases, it's not necessary to use the Advanced button because the Wizard defines the specification for you. There's more about using import specifications later in this chapter.

5. What happens next depends on your choice in step 4:

- **If you chose Delimited**, you'll see the dialog box shown in Figure 7.13. Choose the delimiter that separates your fields, specify whether the first row of text contains field names, and specify the character that encloses text within fields (the Text Qualifier). As you make choices, the sample data in the dialog box will reflect your changes, so you can see immediately whether your choices make sense.

This Text Import Wizard dialog box lets you choose the delimiter and text qualifier (enclosing character for fields) for a delimited text file. You also can specify whether the first row of text contains field names. The Link Text Wizard dialog box is similar.

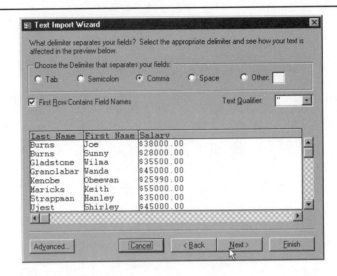

• **If you chose Fixed**, you'll see the dialog box shown in Figure 7.14. You might not need to change any of the settings, but if you do, the instructions in the dialog box explain how. (It's easy!) As you specify the field breaks and field widths, the sample data in the dialog box will reflect your changes.

This Text Import Wizard dialog box lets you specify the position and width of each field in your fixed-width file. The Link Text Wizard dialog box is similar.

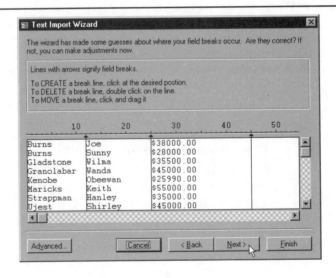

6. Complete the dialog box shown in Figure 7.13 or 7.14, and click Next.

7. Skip to step 8 if you're linking a text file.

Or

Use the next dialog box to choose whether to store your data in a new table or an existing table if you're importing a text file:

- **To save the data in a new table**, select In a New Table, click Next, and continue with step 8.

- **To add the imported data to the end of an existing table**, choose In an Existing Table, use the drop-down list to select the existing table, and then click Next. Skip to step 10.

WARNING When you add imported data to the end of an existing table, each field in the data file you're importing must have the same data type as the corresponding field in the destination table, each field must be in the same order, the data must not duplicate data in primary key fields, and the data must not violate any validation rules. If you're using the first row as field names, the field names in your data file must exactly match the names of your table fields. (Appropriate error messages appear if the data break any rules, and Access gives you a chance to continue importing data or to cancel the import procedure.)

8. If you're importing to a new table or linking, specify the field name, indexing, and data type for each field, and skip fields as needed. The procedures are the same ones given for step 6 of the earlier procedure "Importing or Linking Spreadsheets." Repeat this step as needed, and then click Next.

9. If you're importing to a new table, specify how Access should assign the primary key. You can let Access add the primary key, choose your own primary key from a drop-down list of available field names, or omit the primary key. Click Next to continue. The last dialog box lets you specify a table name.

10. If you're importing, you also can choose whether to analyze the table's structure with the Table Analyzer Wizard (see Chapter 17). Complete this dialog box, and then click Finish.

11. If you're asked for permission to overwrite an existing table, click Yes to overwrite the table and continue with step 12, or click No to return to step 10.

12. Click OK when Access tells you that it has finished importing or linking the table. You'll see the new table name in the database window.

PART

II

Creating a Database

Using an Import or Link Specification

You can ignore the Advanced button in the Text Import Wizard and Link Text Wizard dialog boxes and focus on only the main steps given in the previous section. But suppose dates in your text file aren't in the standard month/day/year order used in the United States. Perhaps your data uses a period instead of a slash as a date separator. Or maybe the text file was created with an MS-DOS or OS/2 program instead of a Windows program.

In situations such as these, you must use an *import specification* to provide extra details about your file's format. To load a previously saved specification or to define a new one, click the Advanced button in any Text Import Wizard or Link Text Wizard dialog box (refer to Figures 7.12, 7.13, and 7.14). Figure 7.15 shows the Import Specification dialog box for a delimited text file, and Figure 7.16 shows one for a fixed-width text file. As you'd expect, the Link Specification dialog boxes are the same, except for their title bars.

FIGURE 7.15

The Import Specification dialog box for a delimited text file. The Link Specification dialog box is similar.

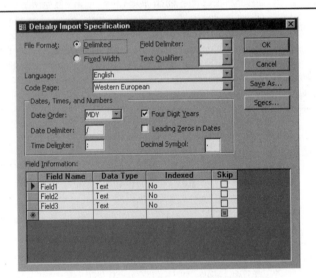

Filling in the Specification

At the top of the Import Specification or Link Specification dialog box, you can specify the File Format (either Delimited or Fixed Width). For delimited files, you also can specify:

Field Delimiter If the text file uses a character other than a comma (,) to separate fields, type the correct character, or open the drop-down list and select one. The drop-down list includes comma, semicolon, tab, and space options.

Text Qualifier   If the text file uses a delimiter other than double quotation marks (") to surround text fields, type the correct character, or open the drop-down list and select a character. Select {none} if your file doesn't use a text delimiter.

The Import Specification dialog box for a fixed-width text file. The Link Specification dialog box is similar.

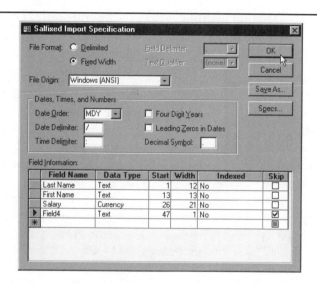

PART

II

Creating a Database

In the center portion of the dialog box, you can change these settings:

Language   If the language of the text file is English, you can leave this setting alone. Otherwise, use the drop-down list to change it to All.

Code Page   The drop-down list for this setting lets you select a different code page. The choices include various versions of Baltic, Cyrillic, Greek, Unicode, Western European, Vietnamese, and several others.

Date Order   If the text file has dates that aren't in the MDY (month, day, year) order commonly used in the United States, choose an option from the Date Order drop-down list. Foreign dates often appear in a different order, such as DMY (day, month, year) in France or YMD (year, month, day) in Sweden.

Date Delimiter   If the text file has dates that aren't separated by a slash (as in 11/9/53 for November 9, 1953), type the delimiter character in the Date Delimiter text box. Some countries use different delimiters, such as the period in France (09.11.53) and the hyphen in Sweden (53-11-09).

Time Delimiter   If hours, minutes, and seconds are delimited by a character other than a colon (:), specify the correct character in the Time Delimiter text box.

Four Digit Years If years in your text file include all four digits, as in 11/9/1953, select (check) Four Digit Years.

Leading Zeros in Dates If the dates in your text file include leading zeros, select (check) Leading Zeros in Dates. (United States dates normally appear without leading zeros.)

Decimal Symbol If a character other than a period (.) is used for the decimal point in numbers with fractions, specify the correct character in the Decimal Symbol text box.

In the Field Information area near the bottom of the dialog box, you can define the Field Name, Data Type, and Indexed options for each field, much as you do in table design view. To skip a field during the import, check the appropriate box in the Skip column. If you're working with a fixed-width file, you also can specify the Start and Width for each field. (However, it's often easier to drag the vertical lines in the dialog box shown in Figure 7.14.) If you do adjust the Start and Width values manually, make sure that no gaps exist between any two fields and that no fields overlap.

 TIP To calculate the Start value of a field, add the Start and Width values of the previous field. In Figure 7.16, for example, Field 1 starts at 1 and its width is 12. Thus Field 2 must start at 13 (1 + 12).

Managing Import and Link Specifications

You can save your specifications for later use when importing or exporting similar text files, and you can retrieve and delete import specifications as needed. Just use these two buttons in the Import Specification or Link Specification dialog box:

Save As Lets you save an import/export specification. Click Save As, type a descriptive name for your specification (or accept the suggested name), and then click OK. Access will save your specification and return you to the Import Specification dialog box.

Specs Lets you use or delete an existing import/export specification. Click the Specs button, and then click the specification you want to work with. To use the selected specification for the current file, click the Open button. To delete the specification, click the Delete button, click Yes, and then click Cancel.

Continuing with the Import or Link

When you're done changing the import or link specifications, click OK in the Import Specification or Link Specification dialog box. You'll return to the wizard dialog box you were using when you clicked the Advanced button.

Importing or Linking HTML Files

Access lets you import or link Hypertext Markup Language (HTML) files to an Access database. HTML is the special coding used for referencing graphic files and formatting in files that are published on the Internet. The files can be in .htm or .html format. Figure 7.17 shows Microsoft Internet Explorer being used to view the file C:\My Documents\Cajun Products.htm. Figure 7.18 shows the same file after it was imported as a new table into an Access database.

PART

II

Creating a Database

FIGURE 7.17

An HTML file being viewed with Microsoft Internet Explorer.

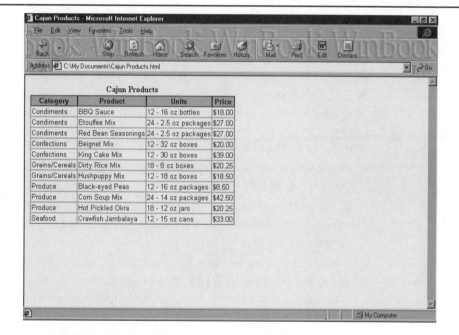

Cajun Products - Microsoft Internet Explorer

File   Edit   View   Favorites   Tools   Help

Back   Forward   Stop   Refresh   Home   Search   Favorites   History   Mail   Print   Edit   Discuss

Address C:\My Documents\Cajun Products.html

Cajun Products

Category	Product	Units	Price
Condiments	BBQ Sauce	12 - 16 oz bottles	$18.00
Condiments	Etouffee Mix	24 - 2.5 oz packages	$27.00
Condiments	Red Bean Seasonings	24 - 2.5 oz packages	$27.00
Confections	Beignet Mix	12 - 32 oz boxes	$20.00
Confections	King Cake Mix	12 - 30 oz boxes	$39.00
Grains/Cereals	Dirty Rice Mix	18 - 8 oz boxes	$20.25
Grains/Cereals	Hushpuppy Mix	12 - 18 oz boxes	$18.50
Produce	Black-eyed Peas	12 - 16 oz packages	$8.50
Produce	Corn Soup Mix	24 - 14 oz packages	$42.50
Produce	Hot Pickled Okra	18 - 12 oz jars	$20.25
Seafood	Crawfish Jambalaya	12 - 15 oz cans	$33.00

My Computer

To import or link an HTML file:

1. Right-click the background or title bar of the Access database window in which the imported or linked table should appear. Then choose Import or Link Tables from the shortcut menu that pops up.

2. Choose HTML Documents from the Files of Type drop-down list.

3. Locate the file you want to import or link, and then double-click it in the list below Look In to start the HTML Import Wizard. The first dialog box will show data as in Figure 7.10, where the Import Spreadsheet Wizard is shown. The only difference is the title of the dialog box.

4. Check First Row Contains Column Headings if Access can find the field names in the HTML file. Then click Next.

5. If you are importing, choose whether to create a new table or append the records to an existing table. If the latter, click In an Existing Table and select a table before you click Next.

6. If you're importing to a new table or linking, specify the field name, indexing, and data type for each field, and skip fields as needed. The procedures are the same ones given for step 6 of the earlier procedure "Importing or Linking Spreadsheets." Repeat this step as needed, and then click Next.

7. If you're importing to a new table, specify how Access should assign the primary key. You can let Access add the primary key, choose your own primary key from a drop-down list of available field names, or omit the primary key. Click Next to continue. The final dialog box lets you specify a table name.

8. If you're importing, you also can choose whether to analyze the table's structure with the Table Analyzer Wizard (see Chapter 15). Complete this dialog box and then click Finish.

9. If you're asked for permission to overwrite an existing table, click Yes to overwrite the table and continue with step 10, or click No to return to step 8.

10. Click OK when Access tells you that it has finished importing or linking the table. You'll see the new table name in the database window.

Refining an Imported Table's Design

After importing a table, you can improve its design in several ways. To get started, open the table and switch to design view. Then, as necessary...

- **Change field names or add descriptions**. This modification is especially helpful if you didn't import field names along with the data.
- **Change data types**. Access does its best to guess the correct data type for each field, based on the data you imported, and it gives you a chance to make adjustments. However, you can refine the initial choices as needed.
- **Set field properties**, such as Field Size, Format, and so forth.
- **Set a primary key** to uniquely identify each record in the table and to improve performance.

 NOTE See Chapter 6 for more information about changing and customizing tables.

Troubleshooting Import Problems

If Access has problems importing records into your table, the program will display a message similar to the one shown below. For each record that causes an error, Access adds a row to a table named *xxx*_ImportErrors (or *xxx*_ImportErrors1, *xxx*_ImportErrors2, ...) in your database, where *xxx* is the name of the imported table. You can open that ImportErrors table from the database window to view the error descriptions.

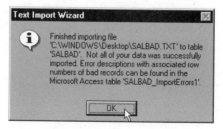

PART

II

Creating a Database

Figure 7.19 shows the ImportErrors table Access created when we tried to import the delimited text file shown at the top of the figure. Notice that the third line in `salbad.txt` contains a tilde (~), and the sixth line has an exclamation point (!) where the decimal point belongs. The SALBAD table at the bottom of the figure contains the records Access imported from the text file. Notice that the bad record in line 3 of the Salbad text file was imported into the table without the correct First Name or Salary, and none of the remaining records were imported at all.

FIGURE 7.19

The delimited text file at the top of this figure caused the error shown in the ImportErrors table. The first valid record from the text file was stored in the SALBAD table.

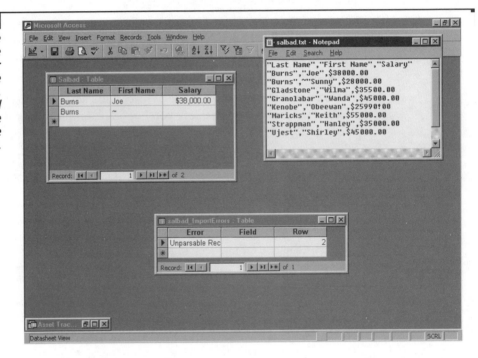

 TIP When importing a text file that might have bad data, do not assign any primary key. The resulting table records will appear in the same order as they appear in the text file, and blank table records and fields will be easier to trace to the corresponding lines in the text file. After cleaning up any problems with the imported data, you can assign a primary key to the table.231

Problems When Importing to New Tables

When importing records into a *new* table, Access may run into these problems:

- Access chose an erroneous data type for a field because the first row of data didn't properly reflect the type of data you were importing. This error can happen if you forget to check the First Row Contains Field Names option or if a field that contains mostly text values has a number in the first row.

- One or more rows in the file contain more fields than the first row.

- The data in the field doesn't match the data type Access chose for the field, or the data is blank. For example, a number may contain a bad character (as in the example of Figure 7.19), or a row may contain extraneous characters or summary information.

Problems When Importing to Existing Tables

When importing records to an *existing* table, Access may be tripped up if:

- The data in a numeric field is too large for the field size of a table field. For example, Access can't import a record if the table field has a Field Size property of Byte but the data contains a value greater than 255.

- One or more records in the imported data contains duplicate values for a primary key field in the table or for any field that has an Indexed property set to Yes (No Duplicates).

- One or more rows in the file contains more fields than the table contains.

- The data in a text file or spreadsheet field is the wrong type for the corresponding table field. For instance, the table field may be a Currency type, but the data might contain a person's name.

 TIP   Importing can take some time, but if the wait seems unreasonably long, it may be a sign that many errors are occurring. To cancel the import, press Ctrl+Break.

If Access reports errors or your imported table contains blank fields or records, open the ImportErrors table and try to figure out what went wrong. You may need to correct your data file, or you may need to change the structure of an existing table. After solving the problems, you can import the data again.

Be careful to avoid adding duplicate records when importing the data the next time. One way to prevent duplicate records is to copy your original data file and delete from the copy all records that were imported successfully into the table. Make any necessary corrections to your data or table, and then choose In an Existing Table when importing your data. Another way is to delete the table you imported the first time and then import again, or just let Access overwrite the first table you imported.

For more information about the ImportErrors table, look up *Import Errors Table Messages* with the Office Assistant and then click the *Import Errors Table Messages* topic.

Exporting Data from Access

You can export data from your Access tables to any of the HTML, text file, spreadsheet, or database formats already discussed; this procedure allows you to maintain your data in Access and use copies of it in many other programs. You also can export Access database objects to other Access databases and to your electronic mail program.

 NOTE   Many database programs do not allow table and field names to contain spaces or have up to 64 characters (as Access does). When you export a table, Access automatically adjusts names that aren't allowed in another program.

You can export data from your Access database using any of these options. (You'll learn more about them soon.)

Export   (On the File menu and the database window's shortcut menu) Converts an Access database object to a file in one of these formats: Microsoft Access, Microsoft Excel (3,4,5–7 and 97–2000), Text files (.txt, .csr, .tab, and .asc), Paradox (3,4,5, 7–8), Lotus 1-2-3 (.wk1, .wk3, and .wj2) HTML (.htm or .html), dBASE (III, IV, 5), Microsoft Word Merge, Rich Text Format, Microsoft IIS 1-2 (.htx or .idc), Microsoft Active Server Pages (.asp), and ODBC Databases. The type of file you can create depends on the type of object being exported. For example, pages, macros, and modules can only be exported to another Access database, while tables and queries can be sent to all the file formats listed above. Snapshot works with reports only.

OfficeLinks   (On the Tools menu and the OfficeLinks drop-down toolbar button) You can save data to a file and immediately start the appropriate Microsoft program. These options include Merge It with MS Word, Publish It with MS Word (as a Microsoft Word RTF file), and Analyze It with MS Excel.

Send To   (On the File menu) Sends an Access database object as a message or an attached file to someone else via electronic mail.

Exporting Objects

The basic steps for exporting objects are remarkably similar to those for importing objects:

1. Start from the database window that contains the object you want to export. If you want to export the entire object, click the object's name on the database window. If you want to export selected records from a table or query, open the table or run the query, and then select the records you want to export.

2. Choose File ➤ Export, or right-click a gray area in the database window and choose Export.

3. In the Export … To … dialog box, choose the export format for the data from the Save as Type drop-down list. For example, click the drop-down list button next to Save as Type, and then scroll down to and click Rich Text Format to copy the object to a Rich Text Format file.

4. Locate the folder that should contain your new file, and then type a filename in the File Name text box, or accept the suggested file name.

 TIP   The techniques for locating drives, folders, and files in the Export … To … dialog box are the same ones that work in the Open and File New Database dialog boxes (see Chapters 1 and 5, respectively).

---

5. If you chose Microsoft Excel 5–7, Text Files, or Rich Text Format, you also can choose one or more of these options:

   Save Formatted   Select (check) this option (if it's available) to save the exported data with as much formatting as possible; deselect (clear) this option to omit formatting in the exported data.

   Autostart   Select (check) this option to immediately open the exported file for viewing in the appropriate program.

6. Click the Save All button to export all records in the query or table you selected in step 1. To export just records that are selected, use the drop-down options for the Save All button and select Save Selection. If the file name you chose already exists, you'll be asked if you want to replace the existing file; click Yes to replace the file and continue with step 8, or click No to leave the file alone and return to step 5.

7. Respond to any additional prompts and dialog boxes that appear, or follow the prompts of the Export Wizard if one appears.

Access will copy your Access object to the format you requested and save the results in the file and folder you chose in step 5. If you chose Autostart in step 6, the file will open in the appropriate program. When you're ready to return to Access, click the program window's Close button, or choose File ➤ Exit.)

For more help on exporting objects, open the Office Assistant, enter *Export*, and explore one of the topics that comes up. The following sections show detailed procedures for exporting to different types of destination files.

Exporting to Text or Excel Files

You can export Access tables, queries, forms, and reports to text files that can be used with word processing programs and to Excel versions 3, 4, 5–7, and Excel 97–2000 worksheets. Here's how:

1. Follow steps 1 and 2 of the general "Exporting Objects" procedure, given in the previous section.

2. Choose one of these export formats for the data in the Save as Type drop-down list.

- **To export Access data for use with text-based word processors**, such as Windows Notepad or WordPerfect for DOS, choose Text Files.

- **To export Access data as a delimited Microsoft Word for Windows mail merge data file**, choose Microsoft Word Merge.

- **To export Access data as a formatted Rich Text Format file**, choose Rich Text Format. You can edit this type of file in Microsoft Word, WordPad, and other Windows word processors.

- **To export Access data to an Excel 4 worksheet**, choose Microsoft Excel 4. For Excel versions 5 through 7, select Microsoft Excel 5–7. For later versions of Excel, choose Microsoft Excel 97–2000. If you need to create an Excel 3 file, choose Microsoft Excel 3.

3. Locate the folder that should contain your new file, and then type a filename in the File Name text box (if necessary).

4. (Optional) Choose the Save Formatted or Autostart options described previously in the general procedure for exporting objects. Both these options may not be available, depending on the type of file you are exporting to.

5. Click Save All. Or, to export only whatever records may be selected, use the drop-down for the Save All button and select Save Selected.

NOTE If you chose Text Files and you did not choose Save Formatted, the Text Export Wizard will take over. The dialog boxes and options are similar to those described for the Text Import Wizard. See "Importing or Linking Text Files" and Figures 7.12 through 7.16, earlier in this chapter.

Access will save the data file in the format you chose. The first row of the spreadsheet or text file will contain the field names from the table or query. If you selected Autostart in step 4, the exported file will open in the appropriate program, and you can view or change it as needed. (Click the program window's Close button or choose File ➤ Exit to return to the Access database window.)

Exporting to Lotus 1-2-3, Paradox, or dBASE

Use the following procedure to export Access tables and queries to Lotus 1-2-3, Paradox, or dBASE files. Later sections explain how to export to other database formats.

1. Follow steps 1 and 2 of the general "Exporting Objects" procedure.

2. Choose one of the Paradox, Lotus 1-2-3, or dBASE export formats for the data in the Save as Type drop-down list.

3. Locate the folder that should contain your new file. If necessary, type a file name in the File Name text box.

4. Click Save All, or choose Save Selected from the drop-down list for the Save All button to save only selected records.

The resulting database or spreadsheet file will contain all the data from your table or query. For spreadsheets, the first row will contain the field names from the table or query.

Exporting to an ODBC Database

To export an Access table or query to an ODBC database:

1. Follow steps 1 and 2 of the general "Exporting Objects" procedure.

2. Choose ODBC Databases in the Save as Type drop-down list. The Export dialog box appears.

3. Specify a name for the table in the ODBC database, and then click OK.

4. When the Select Data Source dialog box opens, double-click the ODBC data source you want to export to. (If necessary, you can define a new data source for any installed ODBC driver by clicking the New button and following the

instructions that appear. After creating the new data source, you can double-click it to continue.)

5. Enter whatever information your ODBC data source requires, clicking OK as needed. As for importing ODBC data sources, you may need to enter a logon ID and password.

Access will connect to the ODBC data source and create the new table.

 NOTE When you export an Access table to an ODBC database, Access does not export the primary key and index information for the table. If you later link to your exported table without having modified its design in the ODBC database, Access will treat the table as read-only.

For more about exporting tables to ODBC data sources, look up *Export ODBC* with the Office Assistant.

Exporting to Another Access Database

Earlier in this chapter, you learned how to import or link objects from another Access database to the open database. You also can perform the inverse operation: copy a table, query, form, report, macro, or module from your open database to another existing Access database. Here's how:

1. Follow steps 1 and 2 of the general "Exporting Objects" procedure.

2. Choose Microsoft Access in the Save as Type drop-down list.

3. Locate the folder that contains the Access database you want to export to, and then click the database name in the list below Save In.

4. Click Save All, or select Save Selection from the drop-down list for this button to export whatever records are selected.

5. Specify the name for the object you're exporting in the Export dialog box, or accept the suggested name. If you're exporting a table, choose whether to export the table's Definition and Data or its Definition Only. Then click OK. If the database you're exporting to already has an object with the name you specified, you'll be asked whether to replace the existing database object with the one you are exporting.

6. Click Yes if you want to replace the existing object with the one you're exporting; click No if you don't want to replace the original object. (You'll be returned to step 5.)

Access will copy the object to the other database.

Exporting to HTML or HTX Files

HTML is the system of coding that's used to prepare files for publication on the Internet. Special codes are used to reference graphic files for logos or other pictures, and other codes, or formatting tags, are used to indicate how data should be presented (as headers and footers, font size, bolding, and so on). An HTX file is part of a publication that has dynamic links to a database. For an HTX export, Access creates two files: an .htx file that refers to an HTML template and an .idc file that includes information on how to connect to the ODBC data source that contains the data to be published.

The following steps can be used to export an Access table, query, or form to an HTML or HTX file. You can also send an Access report to an HTML file by going through this process:

1. Follow steps 1 and 2 of the general "Exporting Objects" procedure.

2. Choose HTML Documents or Microsoft IIS 1-2 in the Save as Type drop-down list.

3. Specify a folder and name for the new file in the Save As dialog box that appears.

4. Optionally click the check box for Save Formatting if you want to choose an HTML template for the new file.

5. Click Save All, or select Save Selection from the drop-down list for this button to export whatever records are selected.

6. If you are exporting to HTML and used the Save Formatting option, enter the name of the HTML template you want to use in the HTML Output Options window, and click OK. You can leave the HTML Template box empty if you want to use the default HTML settings.

7. If you chose HTX, Access will show you the HTX/IDC Output Options dialog box next. Use HTML Template to select a template file that may have specifications for a logo or certain types of headers and footers. The Data Source Name box is where you enter an ODBC connection used to get data for dynamic Web pages. User to Connect As is for the ODBC username, and Password for User is for the password needed to log on to the ODBC data source. Click OK to go ahead with the export after you make your entries.

Figure 7.20 shows the file Cajun Products.html created by exporting the table Cajun Products to an HTML file.

FIGURE 7.20

The file Cajun Products.html is being viewed with Microsoft Internet Explorer. This file was created by exporting the Access table Cajun Products to an HTML file using File ➤ Save As ➤ Export.

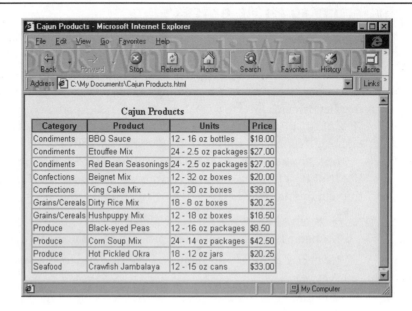

Using OfficeLinks

For some real razzle-dazzle, you can use OfficeLinks features to export Access data to a file and immediately start the appropriate Microsoft Office program. To use these features, choose the object or selection you want to export. Click the drop-down arrow on the OfficeLinks toolbar button and then choose an option, or choose options from the Tools ➤ OfficeLinks menu. Here's an example of the OfficeLinks toolbar button after we clicked its drop-down arrow:

Table 7.2 briefly describes the OfficeLinks drop-down toolbar button options and the Tools ➤ OfficeLinks menu options you can use. The OfficeLinks toolbar button is available on the database window's toolbar and the Print Preview toolbar.

TABLE 7.2: OFFICELINKS DROP-DOWN TOOLBAR BUTTON OPTIONS	
OPTION NAME	**PROGRAM NAME**
Merge It with MS Word	Microsoft Word for Windows (mail merge feature)
Publish It with MS Word	Microsoft Word for Windows
Analyze It with MS Excel	Microsoft Excel

To use OfficeLinks:

1. Go to the Access database window, click the button for the type of data you want to export (Tables, Queries, Forms, or Reports), and then select the object you want to export. Or open the table or run the query, and select the rows you want to export. Or open an object in print preview. (Choose File ➤ Print Preview.)

2. Choose Tools ➤ OfficeLinks and then choose the appropriate option. (The Merge It option is available for tables and queries only.)

3. Answer any prompts that appear.

Access will create the output file in the current folder and then open the file in the program you chose in step 2. When you're ready to return to Access, close the program by clicking its Close button or choosing File ➤ Exit.

 NOTE What you see in Access isn't necessarily what you get in the program opened by OfficeLinks. *Examples:* Data on Access forms and reports that you export to Excel will appear in rows and columns. Data on forms that you export to Word is stored in Word tables. Graphics and OLE objects will be blank because they can't be exported.

Mailing an Access Object

You can use the Send To feature to export Access objects to another person via e-mail. Rather than creating an ordinary file (as the Export and OfficeLinks features do), Send To attaches the object to an e-mail message, and then sends the message to your recipient list. The attachment can be sent as an HTML file, a Microsoft Active Server Page, a Microsoft Excel file, a Microsoft IIS file, MS-DOS Text, or a Rich Text Format file, depending on the type of object you are sending.

To use Send To:

1. Click the button in the Access database window for the type of object you want to send (Tables, Queries, Forms, Reports, Pages, or Modules), and then click the object you want to send. If you want to send selected records, open the object and select the records before you move to the next step.

2. Choose File ➤ Send To, and then select Mail Recipient or Mail Recipient (as Attachment). (If you're working in the database window, instead of with an open object, you can right-click the object and choose Send To from the shortcut menu.)

3. In the Send dialog box (shown in Figure 7.21), select the export format you want to use. If the Output option is available, click All or Selection, depending on whether you want to send all the records in the object, or just the ones that are selected. (This option will only be available if you have selected records in an open object.) Click OK.

FIGURE 7.21

In the Send dialog box, you can select the file format for an Access object you are sending to someone as an e-mail attachment.

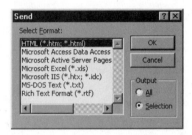

4. For HTML and HTX files, you will see an HTML Output Options dialog box. In this window, you can select a template file that may have specifications for a logo or certain types of headers and footers. For HTX files, the Data Source Name box is where you enter an ODBC connection to get data for the attached Web page. User to Connect As is for the ODBC username, and Password for User is for the password needed to log on to the ODBC data source. Fill in the required information (if you need to change the defaults) and click OK. If a Choose Profile dialog box appears, choose a profile and then click OK. Your electronic mail program will take over.

5. Respond to any prompts that appear, sign on (if necessary), and send the message as usual.

NOTE As in the case of the OfficeLinks features, what you see in Access isn't necessarily what you get in your e-mail messages. *Examples:* Data on Access forms and reports that you e-mail in Excel format will appear in rows and columns on a spreadsheet. Data on forms that you e-mail in Rich Text Format is stored in tables. Graphics and OLE objects will be blank.

 TIP In most e-mail programs, you can preview and even change the object before sending it to the recipient. When the e-mail message appears, just double-click the object's icon within the message. For example, if you're sending a Customers table in Microsoft Excel format, double-click the `Customers.xls` icon in your message to open the object in Excel. After viewing the object, close the program (File ➤ Exit), save your changes if necessary, and send the e-mail message normally.

PART

II

Creating a Database

To retrieve the file, the recipient must retrieve the e-mail message, open your message as usual, and double-click the object's icon in the message file. This action will start the program that's associated with the file you sent and let the recipient read the file. For example, if the recipient double-clicks on an `.xls` file icon in the message, the file will open in Microsoft Excel.

 NOTE The File ➤ Send To command is available only if your e-mail program is installed properly, and if it supports Messaging Application Programming Interface (MAPI). To use Access with an e-mail program that supports the Vendor Independent Mail (VIM) protocol, you must install and set up the dynamic-link library (named `Mapivim.dll`), which converts MAPI mail messages to the VIM protocol. You'll find information about installing and setting up VIM support in the Microsoft Office 2000 Resource Kit, available from Microsoft. To find out how to get this kit, search for *Microsoft Office Resource Kit* with the Office Assistant, and click the topic for *How to Obtain the Microsoft Office 2000 Resource Kit.*

Importing and Exporting from Nonsupported Programs

If you want to import data from, or export data to, a program other than one that Access supports directly, you can use some intermediate format that Access does support.

For instance, most programs let you import and export data in delimited text format. Thus you could export data to a delimited text file from one program, and then import that delimited text file into the other program.

Many programs also can use files that are in another program's format, either directly or after converting the file with some help from you. For example, Quattro Pro can open Lotus 1-2-3 .wk3 format files directly, and Access can create such files. Therefore, to export Access data to Quattro Pro, use the Export feature to export the Access table to Lotus 1-2-3 .wk3 format; then start Quattro Pro and open the exported .wk3 file normally. Similarly, both Microsoft Works and Microsoft Access can open and create dBASE files. So to export Access data to a Works database, use the Export feature in Access to export the Access table to dBASE format; then start Microsoft Works and open the existing dBASE file. No sweat!

For information on importing or exporting files in some other program, check that program's documentation. Be aware that delimited files often go by the name ASCII delimited file, ASCII text file, or simply DOS text file.

Where to Go from Here

If you took the hands-on lessons in Chapter 3, you already know the basic steps for adding, editing, and viewing data. In this case, you can skip Chapter 8 and move on to Chapter 9, where you'll learn how to sort, search, and print your data. But if you skipped those lessons, or you just want to know some extra tricks and tips for entering data more efficiently, continue with Chapter 8 now.

What's New in the Access Zoo?

Importing and exporting data with Access 2000 is pretty much the same as with Access 97. The main difference is that creating HTML and HTX files is simpler. You can create both these types of files with the Export command instead of going through the old File ➢ Save to HTML/Web Formats ➢ Publish to the Web commands. The new data access pages provide another easy way to create Web pages from Access data. For more information on data access pages, see Chapter 14.

CHAPTER <u>8</u>

Adding, Editing, and Viewing Data

I n Chapters 6 and 7, you learned how to open a database, create and open tables, and import or link to tables from other sources. In this chapter you'll learn how to view, add, change, and delete data in tables. We'll also introduce forms in this chapter, but you'll learn much more about forms in Chapters 11 and 13.

Datasheet View and Form View

You can work with Access data using either *datasheet view* or *form view* (both shown in Figure 8.1):

Datasheet View You can see many records on the screen in a tabular format. (Also called *table view*.)

Form View You can see one record at a time, in a format that resembles paper fill-in-the-blank forms.

Click an Expand button to show related records.   Datasheet view

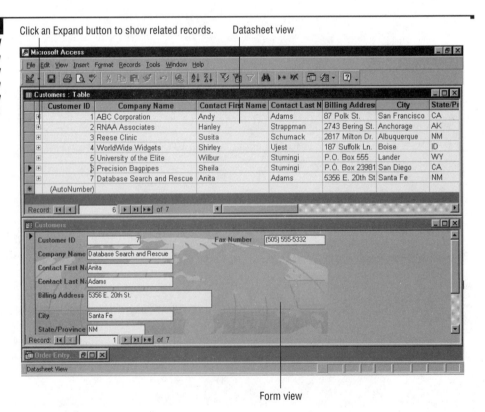

Form view

If you look at the datasheet view window in the top half of Figure 8.1, you can see Expand buttons for each record just to the right of the record selectors. Expand buttons are a new feature of Access 2000. They appear in a datasheet view when the table you are viewing is related to other tables. (See Chapter 6 if you'd like to brush up on table relationships.)

When you click an Expand button in a datasheet view, what happens next depends on how many tables the open table is related to. If the table is related to only one other table, Access opens a *subdatasheet view* to show any related records. If the table is part of more than one relationship, a dialog box opens where you can select the table with the related records you want to bring into view. You'll find out more about subdatasheet views later in this chapter.

Creating an Instant Form

Normally you'll be taken into datasheet view when you open a table. If you want to use form view, you must create a form or use an existing form. (Of course, you need to create the form only *once*, as long as you save it after you create it.) Chapters 11 and 13 cover forms in detail, but if you're itching to set up a quick-and-easy form right now, follow these steps:

1. Click the Tables or Queries button in the database window, and then click the name of an existing table or query.

2. Click the drop-down arrow on the New Object toolbar button (shown at left). Then choose AutoForm from the list that appears. Or choose Insert ➤ AutoForm from the database menu.

Access builds a simple form and displays it on your screen.

TIP If you don't mind doing a few extra mouse-clicks, you can get a nicer looking instant form than the one the simple AutoForm feature produces. In step 2 on the previous page, choose Form (instead of AutoForm) from the drop-down list on the New Object toolbar button. Then double-click AutoForm: Columnar in the New Form dialog box that appears.

Closing a Form

To close the form when you're done using it:

1. Make sure the form is in the active window. (If in doubt, click the form's title bar.)

PART

II

Creating a Database

2. Click the form's Close button, or choose File ➢ Close from the menu bar, or press Ctrl+W. If the form is new, or you made changes to an existing form, you'll be asked whether you want to save the form.

3. Click Yes to save the form. If you're prompted for a form name, type a form name (or accept the suggested name) and click OK. If you don't want to save changes to the form, click No.

You can click the Forms button in the database window to view the names of all saved forms.

Viewing Data in Datasheet or Form View

You can view table data anytime using either the datasheet view or the form you created:

- **To view data in datasheet view**, click the Tables or Queries button in the database window, and then double-click the table or query whose data you want to view. Or click the table or query name, and then click the Open button on the database window. Or right-click the table or query name and choose Open.

- **To view data in form view**, click the Forms button in the database window, and then double-click the form you want to open. Or click the form name, and then click the Open button on the database window. Or right-click the form name and choose Open.

NOTE Any time you open a form, you're also opening the underlying table or query automatically.

WARNING Some types of queries change data or create tables rather than display data, so be careful about opening any old query. You'll learn more about queries in Chapter 10.

Switching between Datasheet View and Form View

When you open a form, you can easily switch between views. To do so, click the drop-down arrow next to the View toolbar button (the first toolbar button), and then choose an option from the menu (Design View, Form View, or Datasheet View). Or choose appropriate options from the View menu (Design View, Form View, or Datasheet View).

The form view options won't appear if you open the table in datasheet view. So when you want maximum flexibility in switching between views, open the form rather than the table.

The Design View option is always available. How it acts depends on how you got to the current view:

- If you opened the current table in datasheet view, the Design View options will take you to the underlying table design (the table's structure).
- If you opened a form, the Design View option will take you to the form's underlying design (see Chapters 11 and 13).

Table 8.1 shows a summary of the Table View or Form View toolbar buttons you'll see from various views.

TABLE 8.1: TOOLBAR BUTTONS FOR SWITCHING AMONG VIEWS

IF YOU'RE IN THIS VIEW	THE VIEW BUTTON LOOKS LIKE THIS...
Form view or datasheet view	
Form design view	
Table design view	

 TIP To quickly switch to the view shown on the Form View or Table View toolbar button, click that button without clicking the button's drop-down arrow first.

Why Design View?

If you get confused, just remember that design view is for designing (creating and changing) objects—not for managing data. You cannot see or change data from design view. If you're in design view and want to return to your data, switch to datasheet view or form view.

If You Get Lost...

If you get lost, you can close all the objects until you see only the database window, or you can quickly bring the database window to the forefront by pressing F11. From there you can click the button for any type of object, click the name of any object, and then click the New, Open (or Preview or Run), or Design buttons, as explained under "Working in the Database Window" in Chapter 1. (Believe it or not, this procedure becomes second nature after you've done it a few times.)

Using Subdatasheets to View Related Records

Subdatasheet views are a nifty new feature of Access 2000 that let you view a table's related records from a datasheet view. With earlier versions of Access, you could only view related records for a table in a form view. Now you can take a quick look at related records without leaving datasheet view. For example, while the Customer table from the Order Entry1 database is open in a datasheet view, you can use subdatasheet views to see the records in the Orders table for each customer.

Opening a Subdatasheet View for One Record

When a table shown in a datasheet view is related to another table, Access automatically includes a column of Expand buttons just to the right of the record selectors. The Expand buttons for the Customer table, shown in both a datasheet view and a form view in Figure 8.1, are pointed out in that figure. To open the subdatasheet view for the current record, all you have to do is click the record's Expand button. A window of related records will open just below the record. Figure 8.2 shows a datasheet view for the Customer table with a subdatasheet view opened below the first record. The subdatasheet view shows the records from the Orders table for ABC Corporation, the first record in the Customer table.

Choosing a Table for a Subdatasheet View

Because the Customers table in the Order Entry1 database is related to the Orders table, and only that table, Access knows to look for related records in Orders when an Expand button in the Customer datasheet view is clicked. But what happens when the table open in the main datasheet view is related to more than one other table? In that case, the first time you click an Expand button in a datasheet view, Access opens an Insert Subdatasheet dialog box like the one in Figure 8.3.

FIGURE 8.2

The subdatasheet view opened here shows the records in the Orders table that are related to the first record in the Customer table.

Collapse button

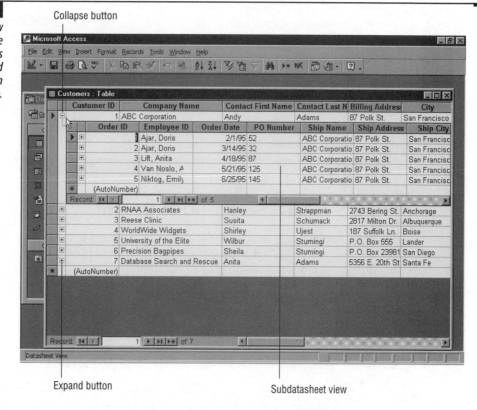

Expand button

Subdatasheet view

FIGURE 8.3

Use the Insert Subdatasheet dialog box to select the table for subdatasheet views when the master table is related to more than one other table.

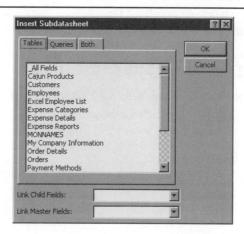

PART

II

Creating a Database

To use the Insert Subdatasheet dialog box, select the table or query with the related records you want to view. Then use the drop-down lists for Link Child Fields and Link Master Fields to select the fields that link the tables. (The child table is the table for the subdatasheet view, and the master table is the one open in the main datasheet view.) Then click OK to return to the datasheet view.

 NOTE If you want to change the table for a table's subdatasheet views, choose Insert ➤ Subdatasheet and select a new table and linking fields.

Closing a Subdatasheet for One Record

To close a subdatasheet view, click the Collapse button for the record the subdatasheet belongs to. This button is in the same spot as the Expand button you originally clicked. (Check Figure 8.2 if you're not sure where to look for this button; it's pointed out there.) The Expand button turns into a Collapse button as soon as the subdatasheet view opens. When you click the Collapse button, the subdatasheet view closes and the Expand button reappears.

Expanding All Subdatasheets for a Datasheet

Instead of opening and viewing one subdatasheet at a time, you can open all the sub-datasheet views for a table at once. To do this, choose Format ➤ Subdatasheet ➤ Expand All from the Access menus. You'll see a view similar to the one shown in Figure 8.4, where a subdatasheet of related records from the Orders table is shown below each record in the Customer table.

Collapsing All Open Subdatasheets

When all the subdatasheet views for a table are open, you are free to close them all individually by clicking their Collapse buttons, but it's quicker to choose Format ➤ Subdatasheet from the Access menus, and then select Collapse All.

PART

II

Creating a Database

FIGURE 8.4

In this datasheet view for the Customer table, all the subdatasheet views from the Orders table are shown at the same time.

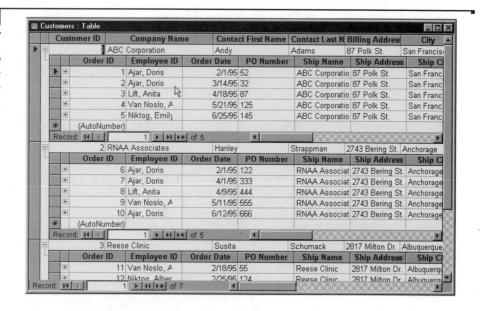

Removing a Subdatasheet

If you decide you want to remove the Expand buttons from a datasheet view, use Format ➤ Subdatasheet ➤ Remove. If you want to remove the subdatasheet view permanently, close the window for the main datasheet view and choose Yes when Access asks if you want to save your changes to the layout of the table. To add the subdatasheet back to the table, select Insert ➤ Subdatasheet and follow the instructions outlined in "Choosing a Table for a Subdatasheet View" above.

Inserting a Subdatasheet

The first time you open a datasheet view for a table, Access will automatically include Expand buttons to open subdatasheet views if the table is related to at least one other table in the database. If the table does not have a relationship to another table defined, Access can still show subdatasheet views, but you have to add them yourself. To do this, choose Insert ➤ Subdatasheet from the Access menu, and follow the instructions in "Choosing a Table for a Subdatasheet View" earlier in this section.

TIP   If you use Format ➤ Subdatasheet ➤ Expand All and Format ➤ Subdatasheet ➤ Collapse All frequently, you will probably want to add the buttons for these commands to the Table Datasheet or Formatting (Datasheet) toolbar. See Chapter 24 for instructions on customizing toolbars.

Customizing the Datasheet View

Customizing the datasheet view can be a quick and easy way to display and print an attractive list of data in a table. Figure 8.5 shows the original datasheet for a Products table, along with a customized version of that same datasheet. You can use a special Formatting (Datasheet) toolbar, menu commands, and right-clicking to change the appearance of datasheet view in a flash. The next few sections explain how.

 TIP   To print a tabular report that uses the same formatting shown in a datasheet view, customize the datasheet view and select records if you wish (as explained in this chapter). Then choose File ➤ Print (Ctrl+P), fill in the Print dialog box, and click OK. (To preview the records first, choose File ➤ Print Preview instead of File ➤ Print.)

FIGURE 8.5

A sample Products table in its original and customized datasheet views. We've removed the gridlines and changed the font to give the datasheet a custom look.

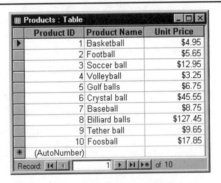

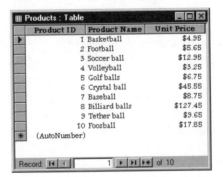

Using the Formatting Toolbar

The Formatting (Datasheet) toolbar, shown in Figure 8.6, enables you to change the appearance of text on the datasheet, to choose a color for the datasheet's background, foreground, and grid, and to control the appearance of gridlines.

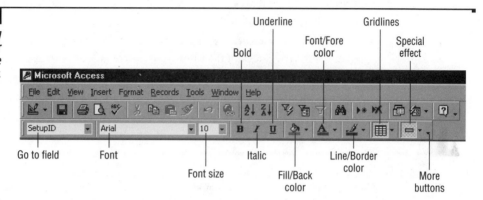

To use this toolbar, you first must display it on the screen (of course). Here's how:

- **If you are in datasheet view**, right-click the current toolbar, and then select (check) Formatting (Datasheet).

- **If no toolbar is visible**, choose View ➢ Toolbars. In the Toolbars dialog box, scroll down to and select (check) Formatting (Datasheet), and then click Close.

NOTE When you want to hide the Formatting (Datasheet) toolbar again, repeat one of the steps above, except *deselect* (clear) the Formatting (Datasheet) option.

Once the Formatting toolbar is visible, you can use it in many ways:

- **To jump to a particular column in the currently selected record**, choose a column (field) name from the Go to Field drop-down list.

- **To change the font for all text in the datasheet view**, choose a font name from the Font drop-down list.

- **To change the font size for all text in the datasheet view**, choose a font size from the Font Size drop-down list.

- **To boldface all text in the datasheet view**, click the Bold button. To turn off boldface, click the Bold button again. Use this same technique with the Italic and Underline buttons to turn italics and underline on or off.

PART

II

Creating a Database

- **To change the datasheet's background color**, click the drop-down arrow next to the Fill/Back Color button, and then click the color you want. Use this same technique with the Font/Fore Color and Line/Border Color buttons, respectively, to choose foreground (text) and gridline colors.

- **To change the appearance of gridlines (or to hide them)**, click the drop-down arrow next to the Gridlines button, and then click the picture that shows the type of gridlines you want.

- **To add a flat, raised, or sunken effect to the gridlines**, use the drop-down list for the Special Effect button to select an effect to apply.

- **To add or remove buttons from the Formatting (Datasheet) toolbar**, click the More Buttons button at the end of the toolbar, click Add or Remove Buttons, and click to select or deselect any button on the list.

 NOTE When you choose a sunken or raised effect for gridlines, Access always places horizontal and vertical lines on the grid. When you choose a flat effect for gridlines, Access can apply horizontal gridlines only, vertical gridlines only, both types of gridlines, or no gridlines.

Changing the Datasheet Appearances in One Fell Swoop

Instead of using the Formatting (Datasheet) toolbar to tweak appearances one at a time, you can use the Format ➢ Datasheet and Format ➢ Font commands on the menu bar to set several appearances at once.

- **To add cell effects, change the appearance of the gridlines, or choose a background color**, choose Format ➢ Datasheet.

- **To change the font, its style, size, color, and other effects**, choose Format ➢ Font.

- **To change the default appearance of datasheets for all databases that you open**, choose Tools ➢ Options, and then click the Datasheet tab. See Chapter 15 for more about personalizing Access.

When the Datasheet Formatting or Font dialog box appears, choose the settings you want. The sample area in the dialog box will reflect your current selections. When you're done, click OK to accept the changes, or click Cancel (or press Escape) to discard them.

Selecting and Arranging the Datasheet Rows and Columns

While in datasheet view, you can rearrange the datasheet columns, adjust the height of rows, change the column widths, and even hide columns.

Selecting Datasheet Columns

If you want to resize, move, or hide more than one adjacent column at a time, you first must select the columns you want to work with. Here are some techniques to use:

- **To select one column**, click the field selector at the top of the column.
- **To select multiple columns**, drag the mouse pointer through several field selectors. Or click the field selector for the first column you want to select. Then use the horizontal scroll bar if you need to, and Shift-click the field selector for the last column you want to select.
- **To deselect selected columns**, click in the data area of any column.

 NOTE When you move the mouse pointer to a field selector, the pointer changes to a thick, black ↓ shape.

Here's an example of a datasheet with one column selected:

Arranging Datasheet Rows and Columns

You can use the following tricks to adjust the height and width of rows and columns, to move columns, and to hide and redisplay columns:

 - **To change the height of all the rows**, drag the bottom edge of a row selector (shown at left) up or down. Or choose Format ➤ Row Height, or right-click a row selector and choose Row Height; then enter a height (in points), or select Standard Height to use Access's standard row height; and then click OK.

- **To change one column's width**, drag the vertical bar next to that column's field selector (shown at left) to the left or right. Or to quickly get the best possible fit for the column, double-click that vertical bar.

- **To change the width of one or several adjacent columns**, select the column(s) you want to resize. Next, choose Format ➤ Column Width, or right-click any data within the selection and choose Column Width. In the Column Width dialog box, enter a width (in number of characters), or select Standard Width and click OK, or click Best Fit. Alternatively, just drag the vertical bar next to a selected column's field selector to the left or right.

NOTE When right-clicking records after selecting multiple columns, be sure to right-click *data* within the selection. Do not right-click a field selector or you'll turn off the selection in adjacent columns.

- **To move columns**, select the column(s) you want to move. Then click one of the highlighted field selectors and drag the selection to the left or right. (The mouse pointer changes to the shape shown at left as you drag.)

- **To hide columns**, select the column(s) you want to hide. Next choose Format ➤ Hide Columns, or right-click any data within the selection and choose Hide Columns.

- **To hide or redisplay any columns you wish**, choose Format ➤ Unhide Columns. Select (check) the column names you want to show, deselect (clear) the ones you want to hide, and then click Close.

Freezing and Unfreezing Columns

When the table is wider than the screen, scrolling to the rightmost columns will force the leftmost columns off the edge of the window. Instead of scrolling back and forth to figure out which record the cursor is in at the moment, you can freeze one or more columns so they never scroll out of view.

In Figure 8.7 we froze the Company Name, Contact First Name, and Contact Last Name columns in the Customers table. Notice the heavy vertical line between the last frozen field (ContactLastName) and the first unfrozen one (PhoneNumber). This makes it easy to scroll to the Phone Number column and beyond without losing sight of the customers' names.

FIGURE 8.7

The first three columns are frozen so they don't move out of view when we scroll to the right.

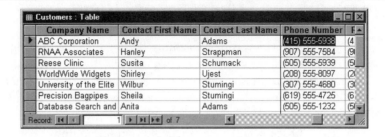

To freeze one or more columns:

1. Select the column or columns you want to freeze.

2. Choose Format ➤ Freeze Columns; or right-click any data within the selection, and then choose Freeze Columns from the shortcut menu.

The selected columns move to the leftmost positions in the datasheet automatically and remain visible as you scroll the datasheet columns to the right. A heavy vertical line separates the frozen columns from the unfrozen ones.

To unfreeze the columns, choose Format ➤ Unfreeze All Columns.

 NOTE   If the horizontal scroll bar disappears after you freeze columns, you won't be able to view the unfrozen columns or scroll to them. To solve this problem, either unfreeze all the columns or resize the frozen columns smaller. Then resize the datasheet window larger (if necessary) until the horizontal scroll bar reappears.

Saving or Canceling Your Datasheet Changes

If you've customized the datasheet view, you'll be asked if you want to save the layout changes when you close the table. To keep the customization settings for future sessions, click Yes. To discard the settings, click No.

You also can save your changes to the datasheet layout at any time. To do so, choose File ➤ Save, or press Ctrl+S, or click the Save button on the Table Datasheet toolbar.

Customizing the Subdatasheet View

A subdatasheet view can be customized using the same techniques described previously for datasheet views. First, open the subdatasheet view and click anywhere on it to select it. Then follow the commands outlined earlier for whatever type of change you'd like to make. The changes you make will be applied to all the subdatasheet views for the datasheet you are working with. If you remove a subdatasheet, though, and add it back, you'll have to reapply your formatting changes.

Now we'll switch gears and show you how to navigate forms and datasheets and how to enter data into your tables.

You can find more details about customizing the appearance of the datasheet view by searching for *Customize Datasheet View* topics with the Office Assistant.

Navigating Forms and Datasheets

You can use any of these techniques to *navigate* (move around in) a table. (Of course, you won't be able to scroll from record to record until you put some data in the table.)

- **To move through records**, use the navigation buttons at the bottom of the form or datasheet window. Or choose Edit ➤ Go To, and then choose the appropriate command from the pull-down menu. The Go To options are First, Last, Next, Previous, and New Record.

- **To scroll through records in datasheet view**, use the vertical scroll bar at the right edge of the window. As you drag the scroll box, the current record number and total records will appear next to the scroll bar, like this:

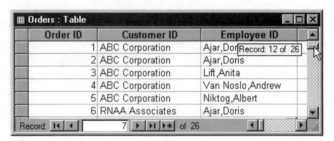

- **To scroll through columns in datasheet view**, use the horizontal scroll bar at the bottom edge of the window.

- **To scroll more fields into view in form view**, use the vertical scroll bar at the right edge of the window or the horizontal scroll bar at the bottom edge of the window.

 NOTE As usual, scroll bars appear only if the current window is too small to hold all the information at once. (If the window is very small, however, even scroll bars won't appear. Just resize the window larger as needed.)

- **To move from field to field and from record to record**, use the keys listed in Table 8.2.
- **To go to a particular record based on the contents of a field**, you can use Find. (For example, you can look up *Doe* or *Granolabar* in the LastName field of the Customers table). See Chapter 9 for more details.

 NOTE The rules for moving around a datasheet view also apply to subdatasheet views, with one exception. A subdatasheet view can have a horizontal scroll bar, but no vertical scroll bar. If some of the records in a subdatasheet view are obscured, you will have to use the vertical scrollbar of the master datasheet view to bring the extra records into view.

TABLE 8.2: SUMMARY OF KEYBOARD TECHNIQUES FOR NAVIGATING A TABLE

KEY(S)	DESCRIPTION
F2	Switches between navigation and editing modes.
F5	Selects the record number box (see Figure 8.8). Type a new record number and press Enter to go to that record.
↑, ↓	Moves to next or previous record (datasheet view), or next or previous field (form view).
Ctrl+↑, Ctrl+↓	Moves to first or last record in a table. (Highlight remains in current column or field.)
←, →	Moves to next or previous character (editing mode), next or previous field (navigation mode).

Continued ▮▶

PART

II

Creating a Database

TABLE 8.2: SUMMARY OF KEYBOARD TECHNIQUES FOR NAVIGATING A TABLE (CONTINUED)

KEY(S)	DESCRIPTION
Ctrl+←, Ctrl+→	Moves one word left or right in editing mode.
Tab, Shift+Tab	Moves to next or previous field.
Enter	In datasheet view, moves to next field. In form view, ends a short line or paragraph, or inserts a blank line in a memo field or text field that has Enter Key Behavior property set to New Line in Field.
Ctrl+Enter	Ends a short line or paragraph or inserts a blank line in a memo field or lengthy text field that has Enter Key Behavior set to Default.
PgUp, PgDn	In datasheet view, scrolls up or down one window full. In form view, scrolls to previous or next record. On a multipage form, scrolls to the previous or next page, or to the same page on the previous or next record.
Ctrl+PgUp, Ctrl+PgDn	In datasheet view, scrolls right or left one window full. In form view, scrolls to previous or next record.
Home, End	Moves to first or last field of record (navigation mode), or to start or end of text line (editing mode).
Ctrl+Home, Ctrl+End	Moves to first field of first record or last field of last record (navigation mode), or to start or end of text or memo field (editing mode).

For quick reminders about how to scroll through records, use the Office Assistant to search for help with *Shortcut Keys, Datasheet and Form View Keys, Navigating Datasheet View,* or *Navigating Form View.*

Adding Data to a Table

Adding new data to a table is just a matter of going to a new, blank record and typing the contents of each field. After filling one field, you can press Tab or Enter to move to the next field. Or click the next field you want to add data to—just as though you're filling in a Windows dialog box. Here are the steps:

1. Open the table in datasheet view, or open a form in form view. Then, if the cursor is not already in a blank record, use one of these techniques to go to a new, blank record:

- Click the New Record toolbar button (shown at left).
- Choose Edit ➤ Go To ➤ New Record from the menu bar.

- Click the New Record button on the navigation bar, near the bottom of the window (see Figure 8.8).
- Press Ctrl + T.

FIGURE 8.8

Navigation buttons on the navigation bar.

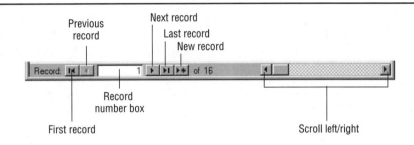

2. Type whatever you want to put into the current field (the field where the cursor is). Then press Tab or Enter to move to the next field, or click the next field you want to fill.

3. Repeat step 2 until you've finished entering data in the record.

Tips for Adding Records

Here are some pointers for adding records to a table:

(AutoNumber) If the table contains an AutoNumber field, that field will display just the word *(AutoNumber)* or a portion of that word. Don't worry about it, and don't try to change it. Access will fill that field automatically when you enter data into some other field in the record.

Empty To leave a field empty, don't type anything into that field. Just press Tab to move to the next field, or click the field you want to fill next. (You cannot move to another record if you leave a Required field blank.)

Date/Time You can press Ctrl+; to insert the current date. Or press Ctrl+Shift+; (that is, Ctrl+:) to insert the current time.

Ditto If you want to repeat the field entry from the previous record into a new record, press the Ditto key (Ctrl+" or Ctrl+').

Hyperlink Fields Use the techniques for filling in hyperlinks, discussed later in this chapter.

OLE/Memo Fields Use the special techniques for filling in OLE (pronounced "olay") object and memo fields, discussed later in this chapter.

PART

II

Creating a Database

After you fill in the last field of a record, you can press Tab or Enter to go to the next blank record. If you don't want to add another record, close the table or form (or go to a previous record). Don't worry about accidentally creating a blank record.

 NOTE   As you type into a text or memo field, Access will correct certain mistyped words, such as *hte* (changed to *the), THey* (changed to *They*), and *sunday* (changed to *Sunday*) as soon as you move the cursor out of the word. This magic is the work of Auto-Correct, which you'll learn about in Chapter 9. There you'll also learn how to check spelling in text and memo fields.

Saving a Record

Access saves the entire record to disk when you move to another record—you need not do anything special to save each record. However, if a record can't be saved because it fails validity checks, you'll see an error message describing the problem. See "Trouble-shooting Data Entry and Editing Problems" later in this chapter for help.

For quick reminders on how to add records to a table, use the Office Assistant to look for help topics related to *Adding Records*.

The Tiny Icons

While you're adding and editing table data, you'll see these icons at the left side of the datasheet or form window.

   Current record

   New, empty record

   Record is being edited; current changes not saved yet

How Do I Insert a Record?

You don't. This might seem odd, especially if you're a spreadsheet user. However, there's no reason to insert a new record between existing records in Access because you can sort the records in any order, at any time. So just continue to add new records to the bottom of the table and then use techniques described in Chapter 9 to alphabetize or sort the records later.

Changing Data in a Table

Changing the data in a table is easy. Just move the cursor to the data you want to change, and then use standard Windows text-editing techniques to make your changes. It's important, however, to check the screen to see whether the field contents are selected before you make a change. Figure 8.9 shows the difference.

- **If the current field contents are selected**, anything you type will instantly replace the current field contents. To deselect before typing, press F2 or click where you want to make a change within the field.

- **If the field contents are not selected**, anything you type will be inserted at the cursor position. You can use the ← and → keys to position the cursor within the field.

PART II
Creating a Database

FIGURE 8.9

Text selected indicates navigation mode; text not selected indicates editing mode.

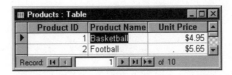

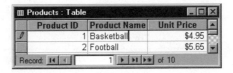

 TIP If you accidentally replace all the contents of a field when you meant to insert text, you can use any undo technique to immediately fix the error. That is, press Escape, click the Undo toolbar button, choose Edit ➤ Undo, or press Ctrl+Z.

Navigation Mode versus Editing Mode

Whether a field's contents are selected when you first get to that field depends on whether you're using *navigation mode* (keyboard) or *editing mode* (mouse) to move from field to field:

- If you enter a field using the keyboard (for example, by pressing →, ←, Tab, or Shift+Tab), that field's contents are selected instantly. This mode is called *navigation mode* because the arrow keys navigate you from one field to the next.

- If you move the cursor to a field by clicking with the mouse, the cursor moves to the exact mouse-pointer position, and text is not selected. This mode is called *editing mode* because the arrow keys position the cursor for editing the field's contents.

To switch quickly between navigation and editing modes, press the F2 key.

Keys for Editing Table Data

Table 8.3 summarizes keys you can use to edit data in datasheet view and form view. Remember that you also can use the mouse to select text within a field: simply drag the mouse pointer through text to select that text within a field.

TABLE 8.3: KEYS FOR EDITING DATA IN A TABLE

KEY	DESCRIPTION
F2	Switches between navigation mode (where pressing arrow keys selects a field) and editing mode (where pressing arrow keys moves the cursor within a field).
Backspace	Deletes selection or deletes character to left of cursor.
Delete	Deletes selection or deletes character to right of cursor.
Insert	Toggles between insert and overwrite modes.
Ctrl+' or Ctrl+"	Copies data from field above.
Escape	Undoes changes to field (first press), then remaining changes to record (second press).
Ctrl++	Adds new record.
Ctrl+-	Deletes current record.
Ctrl+;	Inserts the current date.
Ctrl+:	Inserts the current time.
Shift+Enter	Saves the current record, as long as data in that record passes all validity checks.
Ctrl+Alt+Spacebar	Inserts field's default value (if any).

If you ever need reminders on editing data, look up *Editing Data* with the Office Assistant.

Selecting Records and Fields

The row selector at the left of each record lets you select an entire record with a single mouse-click:

In datasheet view, you can select several adjoining records (as shown below) by dragging the mouse pointer through their record selectors. Or you can click the record selector of one record, and then Shift-click the selector of another record. Or you can select all the records in the table by clicking the table selector in the upper-left corner of the table, as pointed out here:

Table selector ——

Table 8.4 summarizes ways to select and deselect data in a table. The sections that follow explain how to delete, copy, and move the selected data.

TABLE 8.4: TECHNIQUES FOR SELECTING DATA IN A TABLE

TO SELECT...	DO THIS...
Part of field contents	Drag mouse pointer through a portion of the field, or use Shift+→, Shift+←, Shift+Home, or Shift+End.
Word to left or right	Press Shift+Ctrl+→ or Shift+Ctrl+←.
Full field contents	Move to the field with an arrow key, or press F2 to switch from cursor to selection, or click the field name (the label portion, not the field contents) in form view.
Entire record	Click the record indicator at the far left edge of the record or form, or choose Edit ➢ Select Record, or press Shift+Spacebar (navigation mode).
Multiple records	In datasheet view, drag the mouse pointer through appropriate record selectors, or extend the selection by Shift-clicking the last record you want to select, or hold down the Shift key while clicking adjacent record selectors, or extend the selection using Shift+↓ or Shift+↑.
Entire Column	In datasheet view, click field selector at top of column, or press Ctrl+Spacebar in navigation mode.
Multiple columns	Drag mouse pointer through field selectors, or Shift-click multiple field selectors, or press Ctrl+Spacebar to select column and then Shift+→ or Shift+← to extend selection.
Entire table (in datasheet view)	Choose Edit ➢ Select All Records, or press Ctrl+A or Ctrl+Shift+Spacebar, or click table selector (see preceding graphic).
Without using the mouse	Hold down the Shift key while moving the cursor with the arrow keys. Or press F8 to switch to "extend" mode (EXT appears in the status bar), and then use the cursor-positioning keys or mouse to extend the selection area. Or press F8 repeatedly to select the word, field, record, and then entire table. To turn off extended selection, press Escape (EXT disappears from the status bar).
Cancel selection	Press the F2 key, or click any data.

Deleting Data

Deleting data is simply a matter of selecting the data you want to get rid of, and then pressing the Delete key.

Deleting Data within a Field

Here are two ways to delete data within a field:

- Place the cursor where you want to start deleting data, and then press the Delete or Backspace key as needed to delete one character at a time.
- Select the data within the field, and then press Delete or Backspace to delete all the selected text at once.

If you change your mind and want to restore the deleted data, press Escape or click the Undo toolbar button. Or choose Edit ➢ Undo Delete from the menu bar, or press Ctrl+Z.

Deleting Records

To delete entire records:

1. Select the records you want to delete using the record selector at the left of each record.

2. Press Delete (or choose Edit ➢ Delete). You'll be asked if you're sure about deleting the record(s).

WARNING When you delete one or more records, there's no way to undo that deletion unless you re-enter those records from scratch. So think carefully before you proceed.

3. Click Yes to delete the selected records, or click No to avoid deleting the records.

If you want to delete the current record only, here's a shortcut. Make sure the cursor is in the record you want to delete, and then click the Delete Record toolbar button (shown at left), or choose Edit ➢ Delete Record. Answer Yes or No as appropriate when asked to confirm the deletion.

PART

II

Creating a Database

Other Ways to Delete Records

There are still other ways to delete records. For example, you can delete all the records that meet some criterion, such as all types of Billiard Balls in the Products table. How can you do this? One way is to create a filter (explained in Chapter 9) that isolates those records, select all those records (choose Edit ➤ Select All Records, or press Ctrl+A), and then press Delete. Another way is to construct a Delete query (see Chapter 10).

Copying and Moving Data

You can use all the standard Windows cut-and-paste techniques to move and copy selected data within a table, as well as between Access and other programs. Here is the general technique:

1. Select the data you want to move or copy.

- **If you want to copy (duplicate) the selected data**, click the Copy toolbar button, or choose Edit ➤ Copy, or press Ctrl+C.

- **If you want to move the selected data**, click the Cut toolbar button, or choose Edit ➤ Cut, or press Ctrl+X.

2. Move the cursor to where you want to put the data you copied or cut, and then click the Paste toolbar button, or choose Edit ➤ Paste, or press Ctrl+V.

 NOTE To add records to the end of an Access table, choose Edit ➤ Paste Append in step 2.

Access will try to complete your request, though it may need more information, depending on where you cut or copied *from* and where you pasted *to*. Read any messages that appear on the screen, and respond accordingly.

When Cut-and-Paste Won't Work

Access might not be able to paste selected data into a table for several reasons:

- Access cannot paste incoming data that is incompatible with the current data type(s). For example, you can't paste letters into a Number or Currency field.

- Access cannot paste incoming data that duplicates data in a primary key field or that duplicates data in an indexed field that doesn't allow duplicate entries.

- If the incoming data is too long for the field, data that doesn't fit will be truncated (chopped off). You can increase the amount of data that a field will hold by changing the field's Field Size property (see Chapter 6).

- If the incoming data fails a validation check that you've defined for the field, you can't paste the faulty data.

If Access can't complete a paste operation for any of these reasons, it will place problem data in a table named Paste Errors. You can open the Paste Errors table to view the data that wasn't pasted, and then perhaps paste data from that table into the original table on a field-by-field basis.

Using Hyperlinks in a Table

When you include a Hyperlink field in a table, you can use it to jump to almost any kind of information from a datasheet or a form. All you have to do is click the hyperlink address shown in the field to take off to another program or document somewhere. Here are some examples of the kinds of data a hyperlink address can point to:

- A Web page on the Internet
- An object like a form or a report in an Access database
- A word processing document, a spreadsheet, or a graphic

For example, we can add a hyperlink field to the Products database in the Order Entry1 database and use it to link to a page of product information stored locally or on the Internet. Once a hyperlink address that points to the page is entered, a single click on it opens the page with Microsoft Internet Explorer (or your default Web browser). Similarly, you could use a hyperlink field in the Employees table to jump to a résumé or photo for each person.

You can also include hyperlinks on forms and reports without including a hyperlink field in the underlying table. This method works when you don't need to store different hyperlinks for each record in a table (see Chapter 13). In this chapter, though, we'll focus on techniques for using hyperlinks that are stored in table fields.

These are the general steps for using hyperlinks in an Access table:

1. Select the table you want to add a hyperlink field to in the database window, and click Design.

2. Add a new field to the table and assign it the Hyperlink field type. Repeat this step for each hyperlink field you want to include in the table. For the example

mentioned above, you would add a field called Related Product Info to the Products table. (See Chapter 6 for details on adding fields to a table and making other structural changes.)

3. Click the View button on the toolbar to switch to Datasheet view. Select Yes when asked if you want to save your changes to the table's structure.

4. Move the cursor to the hyperlink field and click the Insert Hyperlink button on the toolbar to enter a hyperlink address in the table. Fill in the Edit Hyperlink dialog box as described next, and click OK. Or use one of the other methods outlined later in this section for entering a hyperlink address into a field.

To use the hyperlink, just click it. Figure 8.10 shows the Products table with a hyperlink entered in the Related Product Info for BBQ Sauce. The hyperlink points to the file C:\Program Files\Microsoft Office\Office\Samples\cajun.htm. After clicking the hyperlink, the Internet Explorer window opens to display cajun.htm as in Figure 8.11.

FIGURE 8.10

In the Products table, the record for BBQ Sauce has a hyperlink address entered in the Related Product Info field. When this hyperlink is clicked, the file cajun.htm *is opened.*

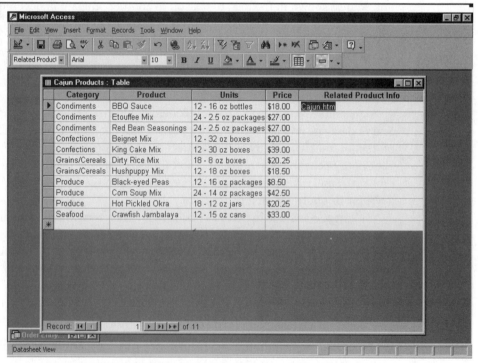

FIGURE 8.11

The HTML file
cajun.htm *was
opened by clicking a
hyperlink to it in the
Products table.*

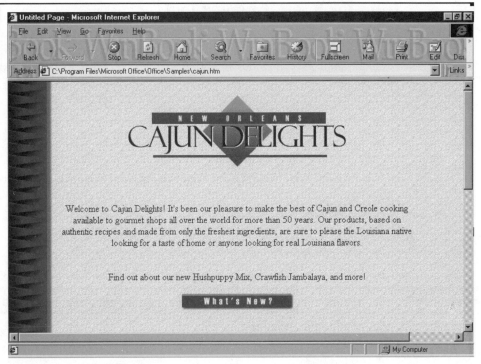

Entering Hyperlink Addresses

In the last example, we used the Insert Hyperlink button on the toolbar to enter an
address in a hyperlink field. You can also enter the same information in several
other ways:

- Use the Insert Hyperlink tool.
- Type in an address yourself.
- Copy and paste an address from a document into the hyperlink field.
- Copy and paste text from an Office document to create a hyperlink to that spot
  in the document.
- Drag and drop to create a hyperlink to an Office document, an icon, or a .url file.

All of the above techniques do not work for all situations. For example, you can't
drag and drop a hyperlink from one Access form to another form or a datasheet. So
you'll have to consider the nature of the hyperlink you are creating before you choose
the best way to enter the linking address.

Using the Insert Hyperlink Tool

The Insert Hyperlink tool opens a dialog box that lets you create hyperlinks to Internet addresses (.url files), documents on your computer or network, or an Access database. This dialog box includes an option that lets you jump to a specific spot. For example, you can move to a bookmark in a Word document, a named range in a spreadsheet, or an object in an Access database.

To use the Insert Hyperlink tool:

1. Open the datasheet or form with the hyperlink field you want to edit.

2. Click the hyperlink field, if it is empty, to activate the Insert Hyperlink button on the toolbar. If the field already contains a hyperlink address, don't click it. (You'll end up jumping to the address.) Instead, use the Enter key, Tab, or an arrow key to select the field.

3. Click Insert Hyperlink on the toolbar, or select Insert ➤ Hyperlink to open the Insert Hyperlink dialog box shown in Figure 8.12.

FIGURE 8.12

The Insert Hyperlink dialog box helps you enter hyperlink addresses. You can use a hyperlink to jump to an Internet address, a document on your computer or network, or an object in an Access database.

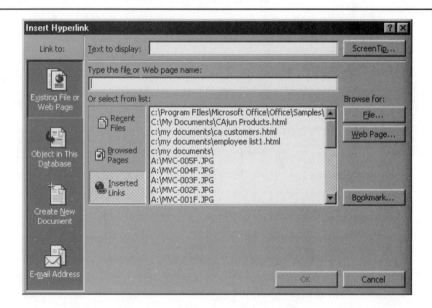

4. Under Type the File or Web Page Name, enter the location you want the hyperlink to jump to. Or use one of the many tools available in the window to select a location. Under Link To (at the left side of the dialog box), click the button for the kind of location you want to specify, or click one of the buttons to the left of

the location list to narrow down the entries. Then double-click a location on the list in the middle of the dialog box. If you click File under Browse For (on the right side of the dialog box), you can make your selection using a Link to File dialog box that works like other Open File dialog boxes. If you check the Files of Type drop-down menu in this dialog box, though, you'll find options for All Files, Office Files, Internet Files, Documents, Workbooks, Presentations, Binders, Databases, Projects, Shortcuts, HTML Files, Text Files, GIF Files, JPEG Files, VRML Files, and Templates. You can also browse for a location on the Web. Under Browse For, click Web Page to launch your default browser.

5. Click Bookmark if you want to jump to a specific spot in the file you entered in step 4. The appearance of the Select Place in Document dialog box depends on the type of document you are jumping to with the hyperlink. If you are linking to an Access database, you will see a window with a tree of database object types. You can use the Expand buttons in the window to bring lists of objects into view. Make your choice and click OK to return to the Insert Hyperlink dialog box.

6. After Text to Display, enter the name of the location as you want it to appear in the table. (You may not need to change this if the default is okay.)

7. Click the ScreenTip button if you want to enter a ScreenTip that will show when you point to the hyperlink field value without clicking it.

8. Click OK to accept the address you've entered in the hyperlink field.

 NOTE By default, a hyperlink address first appears in a hyperlink field as blue underlined text. Once you use the hyperlink, it changes to purple text. You can change these defaults with the Options dialog box. Choose Tools ➢ Options, click the General tab, and change the settings in the Hyperlinks section before you click OK.

Typing In Hyperlink Addresses

You don't have to go through the Insert Hyperlink dialog box to enter an address in a hyperlink field. If you prefer to type it in yourself, go right ahead. However, you must follow these rules:

• A hyperlink address can have up to four parts, separated by the pound sign (#): an optional display message that appears in the field instead of the address, the address, and an optional subaddress (pointing to a specific location). (Some

PART

II

Creating a Database

addresses for Word documents may have the fourth part, a subsubaddress, but this is filled in by Access.)

- If you are entering an address that begins with `http`, you don't need to enter the pound signs. For example, you can enter `http://www.microsoft.com` instead of `#http://www.microsoft.com##`.

- You can also leave off the pound signs if you are entering an address without an optional display message or a subaddress.

- To refer to an object in the open database, just enter the name of the object. If more than one object has that name, say both a table and a form called Products, precede the name with the object type, as in `Form Products`.

Table 8.5 shows a few examples of hyperlink addresses. For more examples and details on entering hyperlink addresses, use the Office Assistant to get help with *Entering a Hyperlink Address*.

TABLE 8.5: EXAMPLES OF HYPERLINK ADDRESSES

ENTER THIS ADDRESS	TO JUMP TO
`http://www.microsoft.com`	`http://www.microsoft.com`
Form Products	The form called Products in the open database.
Resume#C:\My Documents\Resume.doc##	The Word file called Resume in C:\My Documents; Resume will be shown in the hyperlink field instead of the complete address.
C:\My Documents\Resume.doc	The Word file called Resume in C:\My Documents.

 NOTE After you enter an address in a hyperlink field, it may look different in datasheet or form view. Access strips off the pound signs and subaddresses. To see the entire address, press F2. You can edit the address when it is displayed in this mode. Or right-click the address, and choose Hyperlink ➢ Edit Hyperlink to change the link using the Edit Hyperlink dialog box.

Copying and Pasting Hyperlink Addresses

If you have a hyperlink address somewhere in a document or on an Internet Explorer screen, you can copy and paste it into a hyperlink field:

1. Select the address you want to copy in the document or in the Internet Explorer window.

2. Click Copy on the toolbar.

3. Move to the hyperlink field you want to paste the address into. (Don't click the field if it already contains an address since we want to edit, rather than jump, at this point.)

4. Click Paste on the toolbar. If the address you selected was recognized as a defined hyperlink, you can instead use Paste as Hyperlink on the Edit menu.

Creating Hyperlink "Bookmarks"

To create a link to a specific location in a document:

1. Select the place you want to jump to in the document or other Office file.

2. Click Copy on the toolbar.

3. Move to the hyperlink field you want to paste the address into. (Don't click the field if it already contains an address since we want to edit, rather than jump, at this point.)

4. Choose Edit ➤ Paste as Hyperlink.

Dragging and Dropping Hyperlinks

There's yet another way to get a hyperlink address into a hyperlink field: dragging and dropping. This technique does have a limitation, though. You can't drag and drop from one Access form to another form or a datasheet. However, you can drag a hyperlink address in a document (defined or not), a selected portion of a document, an icon on the Windows Desktop, or a .url file.

1. Select the place in the document, the hyperlink address, or the icon you want to jump to.

2. Right-click and drag the selected item to the hyperlink field in form view or datasheet view.

3. Choose Paste Hyperlink when Access shows you a shortcut menu.

Editing a Hyperlink Address

To change a hyperlink address:

- Move the cursor to the address without clicking it, using Enter, Tab, or another cursor movement key. Then press F2 and make your changes. Press F2 again to select the entire field again.

    Or

- Right-click the address, choose Hyperlink ➢ Edit Hyperlink, and change the address using the Edit Hyperlink dialog box. Click OK to save your change.

Deleting a Hyperlink Address

To delete an address from a hyperlink field:

- Move the cursor to the address without clicking it. Then press Delete.

    Or

- Right-click the address and choose Cut from the shortcut menu that pops up.

Using OLE to Store Pictures, Sounds, and Other Objects

You can put pictures, sounds, charts, videos, and other objects into a field in a table using OLE. Of course, you can put such objects into a field only if you've defined that field's data type as OLE Object (see Chapter 6).

NOTE Do not confuse an *OLE object* (such as a chart, sound clip, or drawing) with an *Access database object* (such as a table, form, report, or macro). An OLE object is created in a program outside of Access. Once you've embedded or linked the OLE object into an Access table field, you usually can update the object without leaving Access.

Suppose you're creating a table to store information about employees and want to store a résumé in each record. Furthermore, you want to use WordPerfect, Microsoft Word, or Windows WordPad to create and edit those résumés. In those instances, you must define the field that should contain the résumé as the OLE Object data type—*not* the Text or Memo data type.

Figure 8.13 shows the structure of a table named Star Search Models (not part of the sample databases discussed in other chapters) that we'll refer to as we work through some examples here. Notice that we've defined several fields as the OLE Object data type.

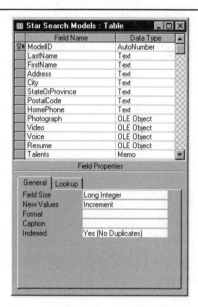

OLE has been around since the release of Windows 3.1. If you're already familiar with the concepts and jargon that go along with that technology, skip to "An Easy Way to Insert Objects" later in this chapter. But if you're new to OLE, you'll get a crash course next.

About OLE Servers and Clients

OLE lets you insert objects from one Windows program into another. The OLE world has two main types of programs, *servers* and *clients*.

Server An OLE server is a program that can "serve up" objects for use in other programs. Examples of OLE servers include the Windows Paint, Sound Recorder, and WordPad applets that come with Windows, the Microsoft Graph program that comes with Access, and the other programs in Microsoft Office (including Word, Excel, and PowerPoint).

Client An OLE client is a program that can accept the services (that is, the objects) provided by programs such as those named in the server program.

NOTE Access can act as a client or a server. Thus, you can embed or link an Excel spreadsheet into an OLE Object field in Access. (Here, Access is a client.) You also can embed or link an Access database into an Excel spreadsheet by choosing Insert ➢ Object from the Excel menu bar. (Here, Access is a server and the database appears in the spreadsheet as a "package.")

You rarely have to worry about whether a program is a server; all you really care about is the object. Let's say you scan a photograph and store that photo in a file named HelenPhoto.bmp. All you have to do is tell Access to stick HelenPhoto.bmp into any OLE object field, and you're done.

About the Source Program

Another buzzword that tags along with OLE is *source program*. In OLE the source program is the one that's used to create or edit the object. Suppose you use Microsoft Word to type a résumé and save that résumé as a file named HelenResume.doc. In this case, HelenResume.doc is the OLE object, which you can put into your Access table, and Word is the *source program* for that object.

Similarly, if you have a sound file named HelenVoice.wav on your disk, its source program probably is Windows Sound Recorder or some other sound-editing program.

Linking versus Embedding

The two ways to insert an OLE object into an Access table are called *embedding* and *linking*. Here's the difference in a nutshell:

Embed A separate copy of the object is put into your table. The copy in your table is completely independent of the original object.

Link Access maintains a connection to the original source object, so if one copy changes, the other copy changes as well.

Imagine that you created a document with Word and saved it with the filename HelenResume.doc. Then you inserted that document into an Access table. A week later, you fire up Word and change HelenResume.doc. If you originally *embedded* HelenResume.doc in your Access table, the copy in your Access table will not reflect the changes you made via Word. But if you *linked* HelenResume.doc into your Access table, the copy in your Access table will reflect those changes.

An Easy Way to Insert Objects

The easiest way to insert (link or embed) an object into your Access table is simply to pull in a completed copy of the object. A *completed copy* is an object, such as a sound, picture, or other document, that's already stored on disk. (You'll learn how to create OLE objects on the fly later in this chapter.) You need to know where that object is stored and what its name is. For example, a recorded sound might be stored as C:\Mymedia\HelenVoice.wav.

If you know the name and location of the object you want to insert into your file, here's how to insert that object:

1. Start Access and open the appropriate database and table. (You can open the table in either datasheet view or form view; it doesn't matter which. Just don't use design view!)

2. Move to the record and OLE Object field where you want to put the object.

3. Right-click the field and choose Insert Object, or choose Insert ➤ Object from the Access menu bar.

4. Click the Create from File option button in the Insert Object dialog box that appears. The dialog box will look something like this:

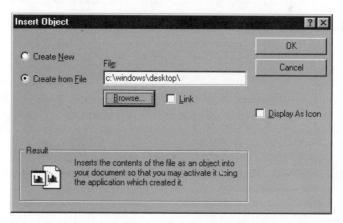

5. Type the exact location and name of the object you want to insert (for example, C:\Mymedia\HelenVoice.wav) into the File text box. If you don't know the exact location and name, you can use the Browse button to look for the object.

6. Do any of the following:

- **To establish a link** between the original object and the copy that's in your table, select (check) the Link check box.
- **To embed a copy** of the object in your table, leave the Link check box cleared.
- **To display the object as an icon only**, select (check) the Display as Icon check box.
- **To display the full object** (such as a photo), leave the Display as Icon check box cleared.

7. Click OK.

What the Object Looks Like

What you'll see once the object is in your table depends on several factors:

- In datasheet view, only a brief description of the object is visible, as shown below.

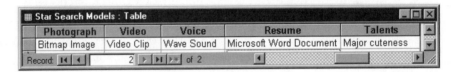

Photograph	Video	Voice	Resume	Talents
Bitmap Image	Video Clip	Wave Sound	Microsoft Word Document	Major cuteness

- In form view, the actual object appears if it's a picture, chart, or some other visual object (see Figure 8.14).
- If the object is a sound or another nonvisual item, or you selected Display as Icon when you inserted the object, an icon representing the object appears on the form, as they did for the Voice and Video fields in Figure 8.14.

NOTE We used techniques explained in Chapters 11 and 13 to create the form shown in Figure 8.14.

FIGURE 8.14

OLE objects from
the Star Search
Models table, shown
in form view.

Activating and Editing OLE Objects

Some objects that you put into a table, such as photos or charts, are meant to be looked at (though you also might need to edit them sometime). Other objects, such as sounds and animation clips, are meant to be activated. You can activate or edit an object by double-clicking it. What happens after you double-click depends on the type of object:

- **If you double-click a displayed object**, you'll open the *source program* for that object. The object will appear either in a separate program window or in a frame that allows in-place editing within the Access window. You can change that object if you wish. To return to Access, exit the source program by choosing its File ➢ Exit command or clicking its Close button (if a separate window opened), or clicking outside the editing frame (if the object appears within the Access window). Respond to any prompts that appear on the screen.

- **If you double-click a sound, video, or similar object**, Access will "play" the object.

PART

II

Creating a Database

TIP You can right-click an object to open an instant menu of commands relevant to that type of object.

Other Ways to Insert Objects

Access gives you several more ways to insert objects. You can use cut-and-paste techniques to insert all or part of an existing object. Or create an object right from your Access table. Or use drag-and-drop to embed an object from the server program into an Access OLE object field. The next few sections describe these tricks.

Using Cut-and-Paste to Insert (Part of) an Object

You can use the Windows Clipboard to cut and paste all of an object, or part of an object, into an Access table:

1. Open your Access data in datasheet view or form view.
2. Start the object's source program. For example, to start Paint, click the Start button on the Windows Taskbar, and then choose Programs ➤ Accessories ➤ Paint.
3. Create or open the object you want to insert into your Access table in the source program. If you want to link the object, the object must be saved in a named file on disk.

TIP To insert only part of the object, select that part using the program's techniques. For example, use the Select tool in Paint to select a portion of the picture.

4. Press Ctrl+C, or choose Edit ➤ Copy from the source program's menu bar.
5. Click the Microsoft Access button on the Windows Taskbar.
6. Put the cursor in your Access table in the appropriate field.
7. Do one of the following:
   - **To *embed* the object**, press Ctrl+V or choose Edit ➤ Paste from the Access menu bar. Then skip the rest of the steps below (you're done).
   - **To *link* the object or change its data type**, choose Edit ➤ Paste Special from the Access menu bar. (Pause a bit or click the More button on the

Edit menu to see this choice.) You'll see a Paste Special dialog box similar to this one:

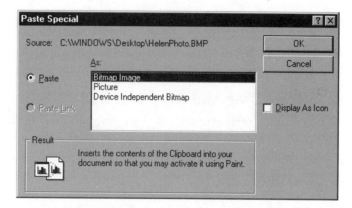

8. Choose options that reflect what you want to do. For example:

- Choose Paste to embed the object, or Paste Link to link it.

- Choose a different paste format from the As list. For example, choosing Picture embeds the object as a picture that cannot be modified or activated.

- Select (check) Display as Icon to display the object as an icon. The icon will appear along with a Change Icon button that lets you change the icon if you wish.

9. Click OK.

The form in Figure 8.14 shows a Paint picture that we selected and pasted into our Access table. Remember that only a brief description of the object will appear in datasheet view. (We'll explain how to make the picture fit better into its container soon.)

Creating an Object Just Before You Insert It

To create an OLE object before you place it in an Access field:

1. Start in datasheet view or form view, with the cursor resting in the OLE object field that will contain the object.

2. Choose Insert ➤ Object from the Access menu bar, or right-click the field and choose Insert Object.

3. Choose Create New in the Insert Object dialog box.

4. Double-click the type of object you want to create from the list of object types.

5. Create the object in the source program.

6. Choose File ➤ Exit from the source program's menu bar (if the program opened in a separate window), or click outside the OLE object field (if you're editing in place).

7. Click Yes or OK if asked about updating the embedded object.

That's it—you're done. You should be able to see the object in its field whenever you're in form view.

Using Drag-and-Drop and OLE

The latest version of OLE supports drag-and-drop and in-place editing. *Drag-and-drop* means that you can copy an object from any source to any destination just by dragging it across the screen. No need to go through any menus or the Windows Clipboard.

In-place editing means that when you double-click an OLE object in (say) your Access table, you won't be taken to the object's source program. Rather, the tools and capabilities of the source program will "come to you."

 NOTE The Microsoft Office 2000, Corel WordPerfect Suite 8, and Corel WordPerfect Suite 8 Professional suites are examples of Windows programs that support drag-and-drop and in-place editing via OLE. If you have Microsoft Word installed, try using it as the server as you follow the steps below.

Using drag-and-drop to embed an OLE object from a server document into your Access table is easy:

1. Open your Access table or form as usual, and scroll to the record that contains the OLE object field you want to update.

2. Start the OLE server program, and then open or create the object you want to embed into your Access table.

3. Select the object using normal selection techniques for the server program.

4. Make sure you can see the server program and your Access table or form. To do this quickly, open the two program windows you want to work with (and close or minimize others to reduce clutter); then right-click an empty part of the Windows Taskbar and choose Tile Horizontally or Tile Vertically.

5. Do one of the following to drag and drop the selected object:

   • **To copy the selected object** from the server program to the Access table field, hold down the Ctrl key while dragging the selection from the server program to the appropriate OLE Object field in your Access table or form.

- **To move the selected object** from the server program to the Access table field, drag the selection (without holding down the Ctrl key) from the server program to the appropriate OLE Object field in your Access table or form.

To conserve memory, close the server program.

Drag and Drop from Access to Other Programs

In addition to dragging and dropping from some program into Access OLE object fields, you also can drag and drop selected data from Access to other programs. Not all programs support such shenanigans, but WordPad, Word, and Excel certainly do. Suppose you want to drag and drop some data from Access into a Word table or an Excel spreadsheet. Here's how:

1. Select the rows in Access datasheet view.
2. Open a Microsoft Word document or a Microsoft Excel worksheet.
3. Make sure you can see the windows for both Access and the program you'll be dropping the data into. To do so, right-click an empty part of the Windows Taskbar and choose Tile Horizontally or Tile Vertically.
4. Move the mouse pointer just to the right of a row selector within the selected Access data. The mouse pointer changes to a hollow white arrow when it's positioned correctly.
5. Drag the selection to the Word document or Excel spreadsheet window, and then release the mouse button.

The selected data from Access will be copied to the Word document or Excel spreadsheet.

PART

II

Creating a Database

About Bound and Unbound Objects

In this chapter, we've discussed techniques that are specific to putting a "bound OLE object" into a table field. By *bound* we mean that the object is "tied to" a specific table.

As you'll see in later chapters (and various Help windows), however, Access can store an *unbound* OLE object, which is an OLE object that's attached to a form or report, rather than to a table. You'll learn how to put an unbound OLE object on a form in Chapter 13.

For more information about linking and embedding objects, look up *OLE Objects* and its subtopics using the Office Assistant.

Special Techniques for Memo Fields

If you need to type lots of text into a memo field, your best bet is to create a form for that table (see the "Talents" memo field back in Figure 8.14). Alternatively, you can press Shift+F2 to open a Zoom box. Either trick will give you more space to work in. As you'll soon discover, what happens when you press the Enter key in a memo field can vary, but here's what's most common:

- **If you're typing in a memo field on a *form***, pressing Enter ends a short line, starts a new paragraph, or inserts a blank line in the text, as it does in most word processing programs.

- **If you're typing in a memo field on a *table datasheet***, pressing Enter leaves the field and moves on to the next field or record.

- **If you're typing data in a *Zoom box***, pressing Enter (or clicking OK) closes the Zoom box. To insert a new line instead of leaving the field or closing the Zoom box, press Ctrl+Enter (instead of Enter) to end a short line or paragraph or to insert a blank line.

 TIP Try using the Zoom box (Shift+F2) any time you need to enter more text than will fit in the standard input area. The Zoom feature is available in property sheets, datasheet view, and grid cells in the design views for tables, queries, advanced filter/sort, and macros.

Controlling the Enter Key Behavior

A property named *Enter Key Behavior* controls the behavior of the Enter key within forms. To change this property, switch to the form's design view. Then click the control that has the property you want to change, open the property sheet (View ➤ Properties), click the Other tab on the property sheet, and then click the Enter Key Behavior box. Now change the property to either of these settings:

Default When selected, Access takes the action specified in the Move after Enter setting any time you press Enter in the field during data entry. For controls that display text fields, the Enter Key Behavior property usually is set to Default.

NOTE To change the default Move after Enter setting, choose Tools ➤ Options from the menu bar, click the Keyboard tab in the Options dialog box, and then choose one of the Move after Enter settings. Your options are Don't Move, Next Field (the default choice), or Next Record. Click OK. See Chapter 16 for more about personalizing Access.

New Line in Field When selected, Access inserts a new-line character any time you press Enter in the field during data entry. For controls that display memo fields, the Enter Key Behavior property usually is set to New Line in Field.

See Chapter 13 for more about changing properties on forms.

Special Techniques for Sizing Photographs

Photographs are tricky little devils to put into tables or onto forms, because any distortion or clipping is so immediately obvious. Suppose you scan a 3 × 5-inch photo and use the OLE techniques described earlier in this chapter to put a copy of that photo into a field in an Access table. In your form, you try various size modes—Clip, Stretch, and Zoom—as shown below. But nothing quite gives the fit you're looking for.

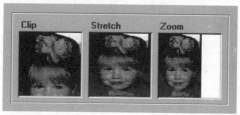

The problems for each size mode are as follows:

Clip The photo is larger than its frame in this case, so Clip shows only the upper-left corner of the photo.

Stretch The photo stretches (or shrinks) along both axes to fit the picture to the frame dimensions, which usually distorts the picture.

Zoom The photo stretches (or shrinks) equally along both axes so that the largest dimension fits in the frame, which minimizes distortion but usually leaves a chunk of white space within the frame.

The solution to the problem is straightforward—crop and size the photo *while you're scanning it* so that it will fit nicely into its container. Let's take it from the top so you can see how to measure the size of a container exactly.

TIP Another solution to the problem of ill-fitting photos is to size the container on the form to fit the photos. Of course, all the photos you intend to display on the form must be the same size.

Step 1: Create the Table and Field

First, if you plan to put a photo in each record of a table, you'll need a field in the table's structure to hold the photo. That is, you need to give that field a data type of OLE Object. For example, the Photograph field of the Star Search Models table (see Figure 8.15) is an OLE Object field that can store photos. After creating the table structure, close and save it in the usual manner.

FIGURE 8.15

The control that will display the photo in our sample form measures .9514 inches wide and 1.2431 inches tall.

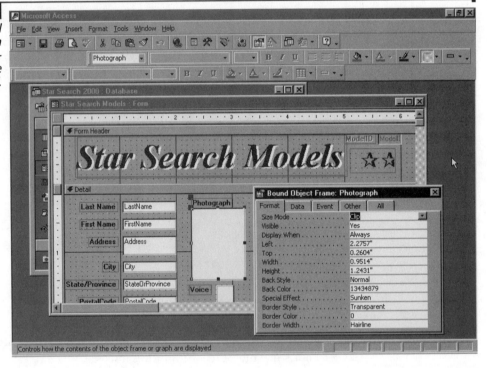

Step 2: Create the Form

Next, create a form that will display the photo and other data in the table. Use the techniques described in Chapters 11 and 13 to create the form and to size, position, and align its controls to your liking. The form in Figure 8.14, shown earlier, certainly will do the trick for displaying photos and other information. (If you just want to use a simple form, click your table name in the database window, and then choose Insert ➤ AutoForm, as described earlier in this chapter.)

Step 3: Measure the Photo's Container

When you're happy with the general appearance of the form, open it in (or switch to) design view. Click the control that will display the photo, open the property sheet (View ➤ Properties), and then click the Format tab. Locate the Width and Height properties and jot down those measurements. (You'll need them in a moment.) Figure 8.15 shows our Star Search form in design view. The control that displays the photo is selected and its property sheet is open. As you can see, the width of that control is .9514 inches, and its height is 1.2431 inches.

Step 4: Scan, Crop, and Size the Photo

Once you know the size of the container that will display the photo, you can scan the photo and also crop and size it to its container. Remember to do this while you're scanning so that you don't have to resize the photo after it has been stored on disk. Not surprisingly, most scanner software offers much more control and flexibility in this respect than a program such as Access, which is designed to do other things.

In Figure 8.16, we've scanned a photo using the scanning software (DeskScan II) that came with our aging HP ScanJet IIc (newer scanning programs offer similar, or superior, capabilities). We've scaled the image to 28 percent and framed a portion measuring 0.95 inches wide by 1.25 inches tall—pretty close to the size of the container in our Access form.

Be sure to size and crop, to the same size as the container, any other photos you'll be putting into the table.

Step 5: Link or Embed the Picture

Save the scanned image. Then return to your Access database, open your form, and put the picture in its container using the OLE techniques described earlier. If you sized the image carefully, it should fit perfectly into its frame without distortion, as shown earlier in Figure 8.14.

Troubleshooting Data Entry and Editing Problems

Next we'll look at solutions for some common problems that you might encounter when entering and editing data.

Duplicate Key Message

If the new record you entered into the table duplicates the contents of the primary key field in some other record, you'll see this error message when you try to move to another record:

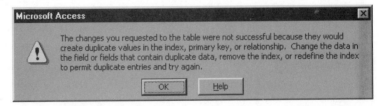

This message can be confusing because it doesn't appear until after you've filled in the record. Remember that it's referring to the field you defined as the primary key (or to an indexed field that doesn't allow duplicates) when you created the table's design.

To wiggle out of this jam, click OK. Then do one of the following:

- **To correct the duplicate**, move the cursor to the field that defines the primary key and enter a new, unique value in that field.
- **To avoid adding the record at all**, choose Edit ➤ Undo Current Field/ Record or press Escape to erase the entire new record.

If you really *do* need to put duplicate entries into the field, get out of the problem as described above. Then return to the table's design view and either remove the No Duplicates (or primary key property) from that field, or use two or more fields to define the primary key.

Can't Have Null Value in Index

If you see the message "Index or Primary Key Can't Contain a Null Value" when you attempt to leave a record, it means you've left the primary key field (or an indexed field with the Required property) in the current record empty. Click OK to return to the table. Then fill in the field that requires a value. Or to delete the entire new record, choose Edit ➤ Undo Current Field/Record, or press Escape.

Value Isn't Appropriate for This Field Type

If you enter the wrong type of data into a field, you'll see a message that the data you entered doesn't fit the Data Type or Field Size property setting for the field. For example, this message will appear if a field is defined as the Date/Time data type in the table design and you try to type a name, address, or dollar amount into that field.

Once again, click OK to clear the message, enter the correct type of data into the field, and then save the record again (by moving to some other record). Or press Escape to have Access undo your changes to the record.

New Records Seem to Disappear

If records seem to disappear after you enter them, don't panic. Simply close the table and open the table again. Remember that if the table has a primary key, Access maintains an ongoing sort order based on the field(s) that define the primary key. However, it doesn't re-sort the table until after you close it. (Waiting to re-sort the table makes data entry faster.)

PART

II

Creating a Database

So even though new records are at the bottom of the table when you enter them, they'll be in their proper sort-order position the next time you open the table. You can scroll around to find those records to verify that they're in the table.

Data Fails Validation Rule

If you've assigned a validation rule or the Required property to a field (see Chapter 6) and the new data in the field fails the validation rule, you'll see this message (or whatever custom message you defined for the field):

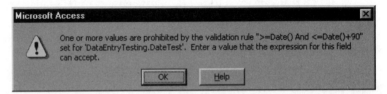

Click OK to clear the message. You must change the field value so it passes the validity check, or delete the entire record, before you can move on to another field.

If the data is indeed valid and your validity check is at fault, make the field pass the currently assigned validity check or delete the record. Then return to the table's design view and fix the Validation Rule property for that field. If necessary, fix fields that violate the newly assigned validation rule.

Access Won't Let You Add or Change Any Data

Several factors can prevent you from adding or changing data.

- **If you can't change any data in the table**, the Allow Edits property may be set to No for your form.

- **If you can't edit certain fields**, the Enabled and Locked properties for those fields on your form may be set to prevent editing. See Chapter 13 for more about forms and field properties.

- **If you're sharing data on a network**, you may be warned that a record you just changed has been changed by another user since you started editing it. You can then save the record and overwrite the changes the other user made (Click Save Record.), copy your changes to the Clipboard and display the other user's changes in the field (Click Copy to Clipboard.), or drop your changes. (Click Drop Changes.) If you chose Copy to Clipboard, you can then choose Edit ➤ Paste Append to add your record from the Clipboard to the table.

- **If you're working on a secured system**, the database administrator (the person in charge of keeping the database secure) can withhold the right to edit, and even view, certain data. If you can't get at some data you need to change, ask your database administrator to extend your rights as necessary.

- **If the current record contains an AutoNumber field that displays *(AutoNumber)* and you can't move the cursor to a new record**, try entering data into any field in the current record (except the AutoNumber field). Once some data exists, the AutoNumber field will be updated and you can move the cursor to a new record.

Changing the Table Design from Datasheet View

Earlier we said that datasheet view is just for entering data and that table design view is just for changing the table's structure. Actually, that statement was a teeny-tiny lie. The truth is that you can use datasheet view to:

- Change a field (column) name
- Insert a new text field, hyperlink field, or lookup field
- Delete a field
- Create a table from a blank datasheet

As you'd expect, the changes you make to the table's structure in datasheet view also will be reflected in design view and vice versa. So, if you'd like to change your table's design without leaving datasheet view, read on. (Sorry, you can't change the structure of linked tables.)

 WARNING Changing field names and deleting fields can have important consequences for objects in your database that expect those fields to be available. So don't make design changes in datasheet view unless you're sure they won't adversely affect other objects. Also, be aware that Access doesn't ask for permission to save the changes when you insert a column from datasheet view.

Renaming a Column

You can change a column name while you're in datasheet view. To tell Access which column you want to rename, use one of these techniques.

- Double-click the field selector at the top of the appropriate column. The column name will be selected, as shown below:

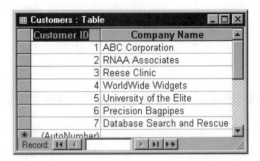

- Click the field selector at the top of the column whose name you want to change. Then right-click the selection and choose Rename Column. Again, the column name will be selected.

- Click anywhere in the column whose name you want to change and then choose Format ➢ Rename Column. You guessed it, the column name will be selected.

With the column name selected, type a new name, and then press Enter. Access will change the name in the field selector. If you switch to table design view, you'll see that the Field Name has changed there, as well.

Inserting a Text Column

To insert a new column (field) to the left of any existing column in the datasheet, open the table in datasheet view, and then:

1. Click in the column that will become the new, blank column and choose Insert ➢ Column. Or right-click the field selector at the top of the appropriate column and choose Insert Column. A new column will appear in the datasheet.

2. Rename the column as explained in "Renaming a Column," previously.

The new field will have a Text data type and a Field Size property of 50. If you don't like these settings, switch to table design view and change them.

Inserting a Hyperlink Column

To insert a new hyperlink column (field) in a datasheet:

1. Click in the column that will become the new, blank column and choose Insert ➢ Hyperlink Column. Or right-click the field selector at the top of the appropriate column and choose Insert Column. A new column will appear in the datasheet.

2. Rename the column as explained in "Renaming a Column," previously.

3. If you used the right-click method and chose Insert Column, enter a valid hyperlink address, such as `http://www.microsoft.com`, in any row of the new column. Access will recognize the address as a hyperlink and convert the field type from Text to Hyperlink.

Inserting a Lookup Column

Chapter 6 gave you the full scoop on defining lookup fields from table design view. Here's how to insert a new lookup column (field) from datasheet view:

1. Click in the column that will become the new, blank column and choose Insert ➢ Lookup Column. Or right-click the field selector at the top of the appropriate column and choose Insert Lookup Column. The Lookup Wizard will take over.

2. Respond to each Lookup Wizard dialog box (see Chapter 6), choosing options and clicking the Next button as usual. When you've filled in the last dialog box, click Finish to create the lookup column.

3. Rename the column (if necessary), as explained previously in "Renaming a Column."

The new field's data type and field properties will be set automatically. Of course, you can switch to table design view and change the Data Type and field properties if that is needed.

Deleting a Column

Deleting a column in datasheet view is easy, but be careful! When you delete a column, you're also deleting all the data in that column. What's more, you can't undo the column deletion. Here are the steps:

1. Do one of the following:

   - Right-click the field selector at the top of the column you want to delete (The column will be selected.) and choose Delete Column.

   - Click any data in the column, and then choose Edit ➢ Delete Column.

PART

II

Creating a Database

2. Decide if you want to permanently delete the selected field and data. If you're sure you want to delete the column, click Yes. If you've changed your mind, click No to leave the column alone.

If you chose Yes in step 2, the column will disappear from the datasheet (and from the list of fields in design view).

 NOTE If you try to delete a field that's part of a relationship, an error message will tell you to delete its relationships in the Relationships window first. Click OK to clear the error message, go to the Relationships window and delete the relationships (see Chapter 6), and then try deleting the field again.

Creating a Table from a Blank Datasheet

If you're more accustomed to using spreadsheets than databases, you might prefer to create tables from a blank datasheet, like this:

1. Open the database in which you want to create the new table.

2. Click the Tables button on the datasheet window and then click the New button.

3. Click Datasheet View in the New Table dialog box and then click OK (or double-click Datasheet View).

4. Type data into each column and row of the datasheet, as needed.

5. Use the techniques described earlier under "Renaming a Column" to name the columns. (Initially, they'll be named Field1, Field2, Field3,....)

6. Click the Save toolbar button or choose File ➢ Save to save your changes and name the table.

7. Type a table name (up to 64 characters) in the Save As dialog box, and then click OK.

8. Decide if you want to define a primary key. Click Yes to assign a primary key with a field name of ID, or click No to save the table without a primary key when asked.

Access will evaluate the data you've entered and automatically create appropriate field types and formats. To further customize the design of your new table, switch to design view and change the design as needed. When you're finished using the table, click its Close button or press Ctrl+W.

For more information about changing the table design from datasheet view, use the Office Assistant to look up *Datasheet View Adding Fields to Tables*.

Where to Go from Here

In this chapter, you've learned the basics of working with subdatasheet views, customizing datasheet view, entering data, and changing the table structure from datasheet view. Continue with Chapter 9 now to learn how to sort (or alphabetize) your data, search for particular records, filter out unwanted records temporarily, and print your data.

What's New in the Access Zoo?

If you've used an earlier version of Access, you'll be quite comfortable entering and editing data in Access 2000 tables and forms. All the basics remain the same. The big new addition is subdatasheet views. These new views let you view the records that are related to a table shown in datasheet view. With earlier versions of Access, you could only view related records together in a form.

CHAPTER 9

Sorting, Searching, Filtering, and Printing

FEATURING:

n this chapter we'll look at ways to sort (alphabetize), search for, replace, filter, and print data. These operations are available in both datasheet view and form view, although you may prefer to experiment with them from datasheet view where the effects are most obvious.

Sorting (Alphabetizing) Your Data

Sorting data simply means to put it into some meaningful order. For example, we often sort lists and address books alphabetically to make it easy to find information. When you're working with paper, sorting is a tedious and boring process. But with Access, all it takes is a few mouse clicks.

Quick and Easy Sorting

Here's how to do a quick, simple sort based on any field in your table (except a Hyperlink, Memo, or OLE Object field):

1. Open your table, query, or form in datasheet view or form view (as appropriate).

2. Click the field on which you want to base the sort. For example, to put employee names into alphabetical order, click the LastName column selector (in datasheet view) or the LastName field (in form view).

3. Do one of the following:

- **To sort records in ascending order** (smallest-to-largest or A to Z), click the Sort Ascending toolbar button (shown at left), or choose Records ➤ Sort ➤ Sort Ascending. Or right-click the column selector (in datasheet view) or the current field (in form view), and choose Sort Ascending from the shortcut menu.

- **To sort records in descending order** (largest-to-smallest or Z to A), click the Sort Descending toolbar button (shown at left), or choose Records ➤ Sort ➤ Sort Descending. Or right-click the column selector (in datasheet view) or the current field (in form view), and choose Sort Descending from the shortcut menu.

In datasheet view, you can easily verify the results by reading down the column that you based the sort on (see Figure 9.1). The results of the sort won't be so apparent in form view because you can see only one record at a time. But if you scroll through the records, you'll see that you're now scrolling though them in a sorted order. (If you're viewing a form, you can switch from form view to datasheet view to verify the sort.)

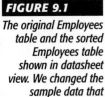

FIGURE 9.1

The original Employees table and the sorted Employees table shown in datasheet view. We changed the sample data that Access provides.

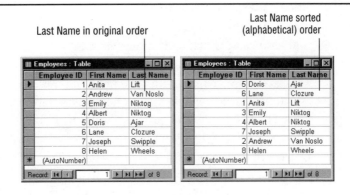

Last Name in original order

Last Name sorted (alphabetical) order

Sorts within Sorts

Sometimes you may need to sort on two or more fields. For example, if a table has many names, you might want to sort on the LastName and the FirstName fields. That way, surnames will be in alphabetical order, and within each name, they'll be sorted by the person's first name, as shown in Figure 9.2.

FIGURE 9.2

Sorting an Employees table on a single field and on two fields.

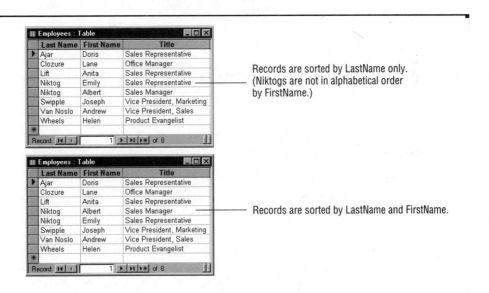

Records are sorted by LastName only. (Niktogs are not in alphabetical order by FirstName.)

Records are sorted by LastName and FirstName.

PART

II

Creating a Database

Sorting on two or more fields is easy:

1. Open the table or query in datasheet view. Or if you're currently viewing a form in form view, switch to datasheet view.

2. Move the fields that you want to sort on to the leftmost column positions if necessary (see Chapter 8). (The fields you're sorting on must be in adjacent columns.) Access will do the sort from left to right. Thus, to sort by surname and then by first name, arrange the columns with the LastName column just to the left of the FirstName column.

3. Select the column(s) you want to base the sort on. To do so, click the first column, and then Shift-click the additional sort column(s). In the example below, we moved the LastName and FirstName fields to the leftmost column positions and then selected those fields for sorting:

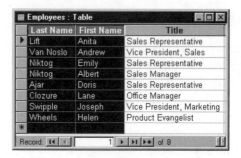

4. Click the Sort Ascending or Sort Descending toolbar button (depending on the order you want), or use the equivalent menu options or shortcut menu options given earlier.

Returning the Records to Their Original Order

When you're ready to return the records to their original, unsorted order, choose Records ➤ Remove Filter/Sort. Or right-click anywhere in the datasheet or form and choose Remove Filter/Sort.

NOTE Any time you close the table after using the sort feature (described above) or the filter feature (described later in this chapter), Access will ask if you want to save changes to the design of your table. If you choose Yes, Access stores the current sort and filter in the table's Filter and Order By properties.

To learn more about sorting, use the Office Assistant to find help. Then choose a sorting subtopic that interests you.

Finding Individual Records

Scrolling through records is fine for browsing. But when you're in a hurry, you'll probably want to use these search techniques to find specific data in your table:

1. Open the table, query, or form that contains the data you're looking for (if it isn't already open). You can use either datasheet view or form view—it doesn't matter which.

2. If you want to search only one specific field, click that field. The Find feature can search fields that have any data type except Yes/No, OLE Object, or Lookup.

3. Click the Find toolbar button (shown at left). Or choose Edit ➤ Find, or press Ctrl+F. If you're in datasheet view, you also have the option to right-click the column selector and choose Find from the shortcut menu. You'll see the Find and Replace dialog box shown below.

4. Type the text you want to look for in the Find What text box (for example, **Niktog**). To make the search more general, you can include the wildcard characters listed in Table 9.1.

TABLE 9.1: WILDCARD CHARACTERS YOU CAN USE IN THE FIND WHAT TEXT BOX

WILDCARD	STANDS FOR	EXAMPLE
?	Any single character	**Sm?th** matches Smith, Smyth, Smath, and so on.
*	Zero or more characters	**Sm*** matches Smith, Smithereens, Sm'ores, Sm.
#	Any numeric digit	**9## Oak St.** matches any addresses in the range of 900 Oak St. to 999 Oak St.
[ ]	Any characters in the brackets	**Sm[iy]th** matches Smith or Smyth, but not Smath.
-	Any characters within the range (must be within brackets)	**[N-Z]** matches any text starting with the letters N through Z, provided that you also select Match ➢ Start of Field.
!	Any character except the ones that follow (must be within brackets)	**[!N-Z]** matches any text that doesn't start with the letters N through Z, provided that you also select Match ➢ Start of Field.
"" (two double-quotes)	Zero-length strings	**""** matches zero-length strings, provided that you also select Match ➢ Whole Field.
Null or Is Null	An unformatted blank field	**Null** matches empty fields, provided that you also select Match ➢ Whole Field and have not selected (checked) Search Fields as Formatted.

5. To search all fields, instead of just the current field, change Look In to the table name. Choose a Match option (Whole Field, Any Part of Field, or Start of Field) from the Match drop-down list as needed. If you want to change some of the optional search settings, click the More button. Use the Search drop-down list to change the search direction from All to Up or Down, and select or deselect the Match Case and Search Fields as Formatted options. If you're searching in a lookup field and the Match box is set to Whole Field or Start of Field, be sure to select (check) Search Fields as Formatted; otherwise the search will fail.

NOTE By default, the Find and Replace features do a Fast Search, in which Access searches the current field and matches the whole field. To change the default setting, choose Tools ➤ Options, click the Edit/Find tab in the Options dialog box, and then choose an option under Default Find/Replace Behavior. For more details, see Chapter 16, or click the ? button in the Options dialog box and then click the Edit/Find option you're curious about.

6. Start the search by clicking the Find Next button.

Access will find the first record (if any) that matches your request. If the dialog box is covering data that Access has found, drag the box out of the way.

Repeat steps 4 through 6 (or click Find Next) until you've found the record you want. If Access tells you it can't find the search item, click OK to end the search. When you're done searching, click Cancel or press Esc to close the dialog box.

 TIP After closing the Find dialog box, you can press Shift+F4 to find the next occurrence of text you last searched for.

For more help on finding records, go to the Office Assistant and look for help on *Finding Records*.

Fixing Typos Automatically

If you're not such a hot typist, you'll be happy to know that Access can check and correct your spelling automatically as you type, or anytime you wish. You'll learn next about the AutoCorrect and Spelling features, which can search out typing mistakes and render them harmless.

 TIP The AutoCorrect and Spelling features in Access are almost identical to the ones you'll find in other Microsoft Office programs, including Word and Excel.

PART

II

Creating a Database

Correcting Mistakes as You Type

If you frequently find yourslef typng (oops, *yourself typing*) certain words incorrectly, or you often want to replace abbreviations (such as CEFGW) with their longer forms (Close Enough for Government Work), the AutoCorrect feature can help you. You simply teach AutoCorrect the word or abbreviation it should replace, and then provide its replacement word or phrase. In the future, Access will replace that typo or abbreviation with the correct word or phrase. AutoCorrect also can correct capitalization errors that occur when you type TWo INitial CApitals (instead of just one) in a word or when you forget to capitalize names of days.

 NOTE Adding new words to the list of automatic replacements has *no effect* on existing text.

Setting Up AutoCorrect Words and Settings

To teach AutoCorrect new words, or to change the AutoCorrect settings, open any database object or go to the database window.

1. Choose Tools ➤ AutoCorrect. (Pause a second or so after you choose Tools and wait for the AutoCorrect option to show up, or click the More button for the Tools menu to make it appear right away.) Figure 9.3 shows a sample Auto-Correct dialog box after we filled in the Replace and With boxes. (Notice that Access comes with an extensive list of commonly mistyped words that it can replace automatically.)

2. Use these techniques to turn AutoCorrect features on or off:

   - **To replace two initial capital letters** with just one initial capital letter, select (check) Correct Two Initial Capitals. Deselect this option to prevent automatic replacement when you type two initial capital letters.

   - **To capitalize the first letter of a sentence**, select (check) Capitalize First Letter of Sentence. Deselect this option to keep Access from capitalizing the first letter in each sentence.

   - **To capitalize names of days** if you forget to do so, select (check) Capitalize Names of Days. Deselect this option to prevent automatic capitalization when you type day names.

FIGURE 9.3

Use the AutoCorrect dialog box to customize the way Access replaces text automatically, as you type into text or memo fields. Choose Tools ➤ AutoCorrect to get here.

Replace these words...   with these words.

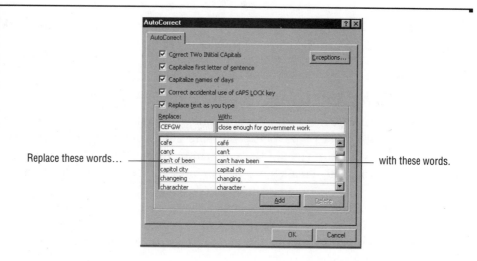

- **To have Access notice when you type with caps lock on** by mistake, select (check) Correct Accidental Use of Caps Lock Key.
- **To replace words shown in the left column of the AutoCorrect dialog box** with words shown in the right column, select (check) Replace Text as You Type. Deselect this option to prevent automatic replacements as you type.

3. Use these techniques to add, change, and delete words in the replacement list:

- **To add a new word to the replacement list**, type the misspelling or abbreviation into the Replace text box. Then type the correction or expanded form of the word into the With text box. Click Add to add the items to the list.
- **To change a word or its replacement**, scroll to and then click the appropriate word in the list below the Replace and With text boxes (the words are listed in alphabetical order). The Replace and With boxes will show the item you selected. Change the Replace or With text as needed, and then click the Add or Replace button (whichever is available) to update the list.
- **To delete a word and its replacement**, scroll to and click the appropriate word in the list. Then click the Delete button.

4. Repeat steps 2 and 3 as needed. When you're finished using the AutoCorrect dialog box, click OK.

NOTE You can add new words to the AutoCorrect list during a spell check. See "Checking Your Spelling," later in this section, for details.

Using AutoCorrect during Data Entry

As you type new text or paste a word or abbreviation into a text or memo field, Auto-Correct will fix typos or expand abbreviations automatically. (AutoCorrect has no effect on existing text.) The automatic correction takes place when you type a space or punctuation mark in the field or move the cursor to another field.

If you need to cancel an automatic replacement as you're typing, press Ctrl+Z (or choose Edit ➤ Undo AutoCorrect); the text will reappear as you typed it. To reinstate the automatic correction, press Ctrl+Z again (or choose Edit ➤ Undo).

Need more information? Go to the Office Assistant and look for help with *AutoCorrection*.

Checking Your Spelling

Access can check and correct the spelling in text or memo fields of a datasheet, or in selected text in a datasheet or form. The spell check ignores fields that don't have a Text or Memo data type.

Here's how to start a spell check:

1. Do one of the following, depending on how much text you want to spell check:

    • **To check your spelling in datasheet view**, select the records, columns, fields, or text within a field.

    • **To check your spelling in form view**, select the field or text within the field you want to check.

    • **To check all text and memo fields in a table**, go to the database window, click the Tables or Queries tab, and then click the table or query you want to check. Or open the table or query in datasheet view and select all the columns.

 2. Click the Spelling toolbar button (shown at left), or choose Tools ➤ Spelling, or press F7. Spell checking will start immediately.

3. Follow the screen prompts. Once spell checking begins, what you do next depends on what (if any) errors are found (see "Correcting or Ignoring a Word").

4. Click OK to clear the completion message when the spell check is complete.

Correcting or Ignoring a Word

When the spell checker finds a word that isn't in its dictionary, it will highlight the word in your datasheet or form, suggest a correction if it can, and pause so you can decide what to do next. Figure 9.4 shows the Spelling dialog box after it tripped over the word *Foosball,* which isn't in its dictionary.

FIGURE 9.4

The Spelling dialog box after Access found a word that wasn't in the dictionary.

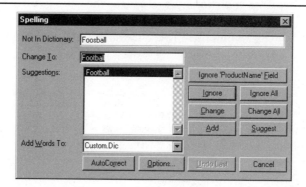

You can click any of these buttons (if they're available) when the spell checker is waiting for you to make a correction:

Ignore 'xxx' Field (where *xxx* is a field name) Click this button to ignore the named field during the current spell check. Spell checking will continue.

Ignore or **Ignore All** Click Ignore to ignore the current occurrence of the word shown in the Not in Dictionary box. Click Ignore All to ignore all occurrences of the word shown in the Not in Dictionary box. Spell checking will continue.

Suggest Click the Suggest button, or type a word into the Change To box and then click Suggest, to see alternatives to the word shown in the Change To box. To copy one of the suggested words into the Change To box, click the word you want to copy in the list next to Suggestions. You can repeat these steps as needed.

Change or **Change All** Lets you replace one occurrence (Change) or all occurrences (Change All) of the word shown in the Not in Dictionary box with the word shown in the Change To box. If necessary, use the Suggest button described previously, or type a word into the Change To box, or click a word in the Suggestions list to copy the word you want to use into the Change To box; then click the Change or Change All button, as appropriate. Spell checking will continue.

PART

II

Creating a Database

Add Lets you add the word shown in the Not in Dictionary box to the spelling dictionary that's shown in the Add Words To box. If necessary, choose a dictionary name from the Add Words To drop-down list before you click the Add button. (Do not add words that truly are misspelled to your dictionary! See the sidebar titled "Maintaining Custom Dictionaries" for more details.)

AutoCorrect Adds the word shown in the Not in Dictionary box to the Auto-Correct dictionary, and assigns the word in the Change To box as the replacement word. This button saves you the trouble of manually adding words that you commonly mistype to the AutoCorrect dictionary (as explained earlier in this chapter).

 TIP If you add a word to the AutoCorrect dictionary accidentally, complete the spell check (or cancel it). Then choose Tools ➢ AutoCorrect, highlight the incorrect word in the replacement list, and click the Delete button.

Options Takes you to the Spell Options dialog box (shown below). From here you can choose which language dictionary to use and choose whether to:

- **Always suggest** alternate spellings or suggest them only when you click the Suggest button.
- **Suggest words from main dictionary only**, or offer suggestions from both the main dictionary and the custom dictionary.
- **Ignore words in uppercase** (such as ASPCA), or include those words when spell checking.
- **Ignore words with numbers** (such as RNAA47), or include those words when spell checking.

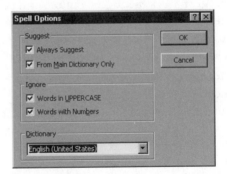

After choosing options in the Spell Options dialog box, click OK.

Undo Last Lets you undo the most recent change the spell checker made. Click this button as necessary to back out of changes one by one.

Cancel Ends the spell check and returns you to the datasheet or form.

Maintaining Custom Dictionaries

You can create a custom dictionary anytime you're using the Spelling dialog box. This trick can be handy if you want to set up a new custom dictionary for storing special-purpose terms. To create a custom dictionary:

1. In the Spelling dialog box, erase any dictionary name that appears in the Add Words To combo box.

2. Type a valid dictionary name and press Enter, or choose an existing custom dictionary from the combo box's drop-down list. The default dictionary name is custom.dic, but you can use any name for your dictionary as long as that name ends with a period and the letters *dic*. For example, mywords.dic and medical terms.dic are valid dictionary names.

3. If Access asks for permission to create the dictionary, click Yes.

The custom dictionary is a plain text file that lists one word per line in alphabetical order by word. Custom dictionaries are stored in the folder \Windows\Application Data\Microsoft\Proof on drive C (if you chose the default installation location). If you add a misspelled word to a custom dictionary by accident, you can use Windows Notepad or Windows WordPad (in text mode) to delete the incorrect words. Edit carefully!

For more details about spell checking, use the Office Assistant to find help topics for *Spelling*.

Replacing Data in Multiple Records

In addition to letting you fix spelling errors in some or all text and memo fields, Access lets you instantly change the contents of a field throughout all (or some) of the records in your table. But before you even think of experimenting with this Replace feature, please make sure you understand the following warning.

WARNING You can Undo only the last individual change that Replace makes. To play it safe, make a copy of the table before you replace data. That way, if you make a major mistake, you can close the table and then rename the unchanged copy of the table to replace the version that has unwanted changes. See Chapter 1 for help on copying and renaming database objects.

To replace data in a table:

1. Open the table, query, or form that contains the data you want to change.

2. (Optional) If you want to limit replacement to a single field, click that field. The Replace feature can replace text in fields that have any data type *except* OLE Object, AutoNumber, and Lookup.

3. Choose Edit ➤ Replace, or press Ctrl+H. (After you choose Edit, pause or click the More button to bring the Replace choice into view.) You'll see the Find and Replace dialog box shown below.

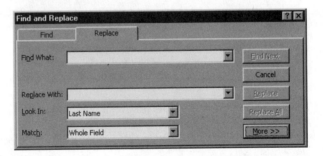

4. Type the value you want to search for and change in the Find What text box. You can use the wildcard characters listed in Table 9.1 if you wish.

5. Type the replacement text in the Replace With text box.

6. Change the setting for Look In to the table name, if you want to replace values in all fields, and use the Match drop-down list to select the type of match Access should look for. If you want to customize the search options further, click the More button and change the settings for Search, Match Case, and Search Fields as Formatted as needed. Then do one of the following:

   - **To make the change automatically** (so that Access won't ask you to verify each occurrence), click the Replace All button.

   - **To verify the changes in each record**, click the Find Next button. (If necessary, drag the dialog box out of the way so you can see the data Access is about to change.) Then if you do want to change the current record, click

Replace. If you don't want to change the current record, click Find Next. Repeat this step as needed.

7. Click Yes to continue with step 9, or click No to cancel the operation and return to steps 4, 5, or 6.

8. When Access cannot find any more matches, it will display a message. Click OK to clear the message.

9. Click the Cancel button when you're done replacing records.

Here are some tips you might want to know about:

- **To globally replace large amounts of data** more quickly, or to perform calculations on data (for example, raising certain product prices by 10 percent), use an *Update query* rather than Replace. See Chapter 10 for more about Update queries.

- **To change the default settings** for the Find and Replace features, choose Tools ➤ Options and click the Edit/Find tab. Change the settings under Default Find/Replace Behavior as needed, and then click OK. Chapter 16 explains more about personalizing Access.

A Search-and-Replace Example

Suppose that several people enter data into your table. Some of them spell names such as *Los Angeles* in full, while others use abbreviations such as *L.A.* This type of inconsistency is sure to cause problems down the road. Imagine that you want to send a form letter to all Los Angeles residents. If you isolate records that have Los Angeles in the City field, you'll miss all the ones that contain L.A. Why? Because computers aren't smart enough to know that Los Angeles and L.A. mean the same thing.

The cure for your dilemma is to change all the *L.A.* entries in the City field to *Los Angeles* (or vice versa). To do that, click the City field, choose Edit ➤ Replace, and then fill in the dialog box this way:

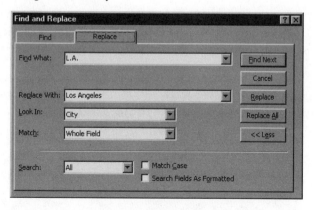

PART

II

Creating a Database

To start the replacement, click the Replace All button and bingo—you're done! (Just answer any questions that appear on the screen.)

 TIP To prevent the L.A. city names from creeping into your data in the future, you might want to add an AutoCorrect entry that changes "L.A." to "Los Angeles" automatically. See "Correcting Mistakes as You Type," earlier in this chapter.

If you ever need reminders or help while replacing data, go to the Office Assistant and look up *Replacing Values in Fields*.

Filtering Out Unwanted Records

You can use *filters* to temporarily isolate (or select) records you want to see and to hide unwanted records. For example, you can focus on your California customers while hiding information about customers located in other states. There are several ways to create a filter:

- **Filter by Input** lets you create a filter from a field's shortcut menu.
- **Filter by Selection** and **Filter Excluding Selection** let you create a filter by selecting text or clicking in a field that contains the text you want to filter.
- **Filter by Form** lets you create a filter by typing the values you're looking for into a fill-in-the-blanks form or datasheet.
- **Advanced Filter/Sort** lets you use a window that's similar to a query design window to create a filter. You can choose each field to search or sort by and specify the sort order and values you're looking for.

 NOTE You can filter fields that have any data type *except* Memo or OLE Object.

Table 9.2 compares the four filtering methods briefly, and the following sections explain how to use each one. If you still need more information, go to the Office Assistant and look for Help topics for *Filters*.

TIP To switch between designing a Filter by Form and designing an Advanced Filter/Sort, open the Filter menu in the design window for either type of filter, and then choose Filter by Form or Advanced Filter/Sort as appropriate.

TABLE 9.2: FILTERING METHODS COMPARED

IF THIS IS WHAT YOU WANT TO DO...	FILTER BY INPUT	FILTER BY (OR EXCLUDING) SELECTION	FILTER BY FORM	ADVANCED FILTER/SORT
Find records that meet one criterion *And* other criteria	Yes (if you specify the criteria one at a time)	Yes (if you specify the criteria one at a time)	Yes	Yes
Find records that meet one criterion *Or* other criteria	No	No	Yes	Yes
Find records that contain expressions as criteria	Yes	No	Yes	Yes
Find records and sort them in ascending or descending order at the same time	No	No	No	Yes

Filtering by Input

Filter by Input lets you use a field's shortcut menu to find records. You can use it for simple filters, such as finding all the records with "CA" in the State field. Filter by Input also works for more complicated filters that use comparison operators, wildcards, or functions. For example, you can use ">t" in a filter on the Last Name field to limit the records you view to those that begin with letters after *T*. Or you can use "D*" in the First Name field to see all records for people whose first name begins with *D*.

PART

II

Creating a Database

To use Filter by Input:

1. Open the table, form, or query you want to filter.

2. Right-click anywhere in the field you want to use for the filter, except in the field header.

3. Enter a value in the box after Filter For, and press Enter.

To see other examples of valid filter expressions, use the Office Assistant to search for *Examples of Expressions*.

Filtering by Selection or Exclusion

Let's suppose you've found a record that contains some data you're looking for—perhaps an order for tether balls in the Order Details table. Now you want to find all the other orders for that product, or all the orders for products *except* tether balls. Access makes jobs like these ridiculously easy:

1. Open the table, query, or form you want to filter (in either datasheet view or form view).

2. Locate the record and field that contains an instance of the data you want Access to filter for. For example, in the Order Details table, locate a record that displays the value *Tether ball* in the ProductID field.

3. Tell Access how much of the field to match:

• **To match the entire field**, select the entire field or click in the field without selecting anything. *Example:* To match *Tether ball* (the entire field), click in a field that displays a value of *Tether ball* as shown below.

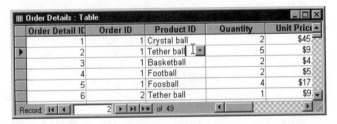

• **To match part of a field, starting with the first character** in the field, select text starting at the beginning of the field (see below). *Example:* To match fields that start with *Foo*, highlight *Foo* at the start of a field. Items such as *Football, Foosball,* and *Foot Powder* will match.

Order Detail ID	Order ID	Product ID	Quantity	Unit Price
1	1	Crystal ball	2	$45.
2	1	Tether ball	5	$9.
3	1	Basketball	2	$4.
4	1	Football	2	$5.
5	1	Foosball	4	$17.
6	2	Tether ball	1	$9.

Record: 4 of 49

- **To match part of a field, after the first character** in the field, select text within the field. *Example:* To match fields that contain *ball* (preceded by a space), highlight the word *ball* and the space that appears before ball, as shown below. Items such as *Crystal ball* and *Tether ball* will match, but *Football* and *Foosball* will not (because there's no space before *ball* in those item names).

Order Detail ID	Order ID	Product ID	Quantity	Unit Price
1	1	Crystal ball	2	$45.
2	1	Tether ball	5	$9.
3	1	Basketball	2	$4.
4	1	Football	2	$5.
5	1	Foosball	4	$17.
6	2	Tether ball	1	$9.

Record: 2 of 49

NOTE   In the preceding example, Access will not match *Golf balls* when you apply the filter, because the pattern "ball" doesn't fall exactly at the end of the field. To isolate *Golf balls* along with *Crystal ball* and *Tether ball*, select "ball" in a record that contains *Golf balls* in the ProductID field. This forces Access to use a more general pattern that says "Find the word *ball* preceded by a space *anywhere* in the field," rather than the less general pattern "Find the word *ball* preceded by a space at the end of the field."

4. Do one of the following to apply your filter:

- **To show only records that have matching values in the field**, click the Filter by Selection toolbar button (shown at left), or choose Records ➤ Filter ➤ Filter by Selection, or right-click the field and choose Filter by Selection.

PART

II

Creating a Database

- **To show only records that do not have matching values in the field**, right-click the field and choose Filter Excluding Selection. (Access will filter out records that contain null values in the field, as well as records that contain values that match the current field or selection.)

The datasheet view or form view will instantly reflect your filtering choices. The navigation bar at the bottom of the datasheet or form window displays *(Filtered)*, and the status bar shows *FLTR*, to remind you that you're looking at a filtered view of data.

To filter the remaining records even more, simply repeat steps 2 through 4 as needed. You also can use the sorting techniques discussed earlier in this chapter to sort or alphabetize the records.

NOTE When you apply a filter, you're actually setting the Filter property for the Table query or form. To view this property, switch to design view, and then choose View ➤ Properties or click the Properties toolbar button. If you're viewing form design properties, click the Data tab on the property sheet. If you're viewing query properties, click in the gray upper part of the query design window.

Removing or Reapplying a Filter

It's easy to remove a filter or reapply it at any time:

- **To remove (or reapply) the filter only**, click the Remove Filter toolbar button (shown at left). This button is a toggle—you click it to remove the filter (The button will appear pushed out.), and you click it again to reapply the filter. (The button will appear pushed in.) The ScreenTip under the button will flip-flop between Remove Filter and Apply Filter to reflect what action the button will take when you click it.
- **To remove both the filtering and sorting**, right-click any data field and choose Remove Filter/Sort. Or choose Records ➤ Remove Filter/Sort.

TIP The steps given above for reapplying and removing a filter work for *all* types of filters—Filter by Selection, Filter Excluding Selection, and Advanced Filter/Sort. You also can remove filters and sorting by clearing the Filter and Order By properties, respectively, on the property sheet in table design, query design, or form design view.

Saving Your Filter with the Datasheet or Form

You can save the filter so that Access will remember it the next time you open your table, query, or form. The following steps work for all types of filters—Filter by Selection, Filter Excluding Selection, and Advanced Filter/Sort:

1. Return to the datasheet window or form window.

2. Click the Save toolbar button, or press Ctrl+S, or choose File ➤ Save; or close the datasheet and click Yes when asked if you want to save changes to the design.

 NOTE Access automatically saves filters applied to a form when you close the form. Therefore, you don't have to explicitly save a form to use the filter the next time you open the form. Simply click the Apply Filter button (or its equivalent menu options and right-click shortcuts) to reapply the last filter you used.

The next time you open the datasheet or form, all the data will appear. To filter the data again, click the Apply Filter button.

 TIP To create a form or report that automatically inherits the filter you've saved with a datasheet, open the datasheet, apply the filter, and click the Save toolbar button. Then click the drop-down arrow next to the New Object toolbar button, and choose the Auto-Form, AutoReport, Form, or Report option. Note that for a report created this way, the filter is not saved when the report is closed. For a new form, the filter is saved, but you have to click the Filter button to activate it when the form is opened.

Filtering by Form

If you prefer a fill-in-the-blank method for designing your filters, try the Filter by Form feature. Here's how to use it:

1. Open the table, query, or form you want to filter (in either datasheet view or form view).

 2. Click the Filter by Form toolbar button (shown at left) or choose Records ➤ Filter ➤ Filter by Form. If you're in datasheet view, you'll see a blank, one-row datasheet, as shown in Figure 9.5. If you're in form view, you'll see a blank form instead (see Figure 9.6).

PART

II

Creating a Database

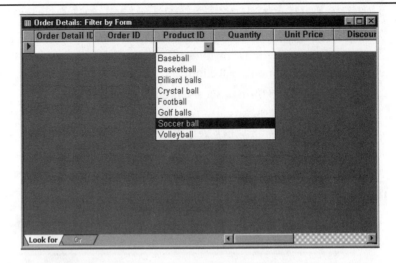

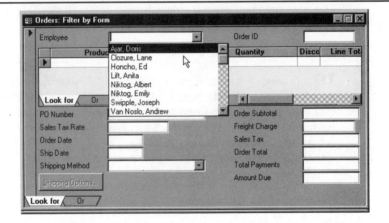

3. Click in the field you'll use to specify criteria that records must meet to be included in the filtered set of records.

NOTE A *criterion* is a set of limiting conditions, such as *tether ball* or *>47*, in a query or filter. One or more criteria are used to isolate a specific set of records.

4. Enter a criterion by selecting the value you're searching for from the drop-down list in the field (if the list includes values) or by typing a value or expression into the field. In a moment, we'll give you some tips and tricks for filling in the fields. You'll learn more about entering expressions in the later section on "Using Advanced Filter/Sort."

5. Repeat steps 3 and 4 as needed to specify additional criteria that must be true in any given record that makes it through the filter.

6. Click an Or tab at the bottom of the window if you want to specify alternative values that records can have in order to make it through the filter; then specify criteria for that tab by repeating steps 3 and 4 as needed. You can continue setting up more Or criteria, and you can flip to a different tab by clicking it.

TIP Think of the additional values shown on the same tab as meaning "And." For example, to include orders in which the product ordered is *tether ball* and the quantity ordered is *5*, specify **tether ball** in the ProductID field and **5** in the Quantity field. To also see orders for 2 of any item, click the Or tab and type **2** in the Quantity field.

7. Click the Apply Filter toolbar button when you're ready to apply the filter, or choose Filter ➤ Apply Filter/Sort from the menus.

Access will filter the records as you asked and display them in the datasheet or form. As with Filter by Selection, you can remove the filter and save the filter from datasheet view or form view as needed.

Filtering by Form—an Example

Let's look at an example that will show how easy it is to use Filter by Form. Suppose you want to isolate records in the Order Details table in which customers ordered five tether balls. You also want to see any order for basketballs, or any order for two or more crystal balls. Here are the steps:

1. Open the Order Details table in datasheet or form view (we'll use datasheet view for our example).

2. Click the Filter by Form toolbar button.

3. Type **tether ball** in the ProductID field (if you're using the sample data that Access provided, typing **t** is enough to display *tether ball* in the field).

PART

II

Creating a Database

NOTE Filters usually are not sensitive to uppercase and lowercase letters, so you don't have to worry about them. Thus, you can search for *tether ball* or *Tether Ball* or *TETHER BALL*, and so forth. Remember, however, that spaces *are* important, so a search within our sample data for *tetherball* will fail. (Filters on attached data might be case-sensitive. For example, SQL Server can be configured to be either case-sensitive or case-insensitive.)

4. Type **5** in the Quantity field. The Filter by Form window looks like this:

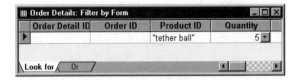

5. Click the Or tab at the bottom of the Filter by Form window, click in the ProductID field, and then type **basketball** (or just **bask**, given our sample data), as shown below:

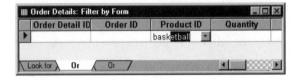

6. Click the next Or tab at the bottom of the window, click in the ProductID field, type **crystal ball** (or just **c**), click in the Quantity field, and then type **>=2** (which means greater than or equal to 2). Here's what you'll see:

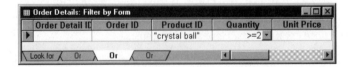

7. Click the Apply Filter toolbar button to see the results.

8. Select the ProductID and Quantity columns, and then click the Sort Ascending toolbar button as a finishing touch. This step sorts the results by ProductID and then by quantity within the same ProductID.

Figure 9.7 shows the Order Details datasheet after we completed the eight steps above. As you see, we've isolated all basketball orders, crystal ball orders of two or more, and tether ball orders of five.

FIGURE 9.7

Filtered records in the Order Details table.

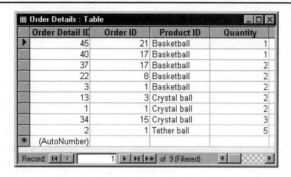

Tips and Tricks for Using the Filter by Form Window

These tips and tricks can help you use the Filter by Form window more efficiently:

- **To clear all fields in the Filter by Form window**, click the Clear Grid toolbar button (shown at left), or choose Edit ➤ Clear Grid.

- **To delete an Or tab at the bottom of the Filter by Form window**, click the tab you want to delete, and then choose Edit ➤ Delete Tab.

- **To get quick help with using the Look For or the Or tabs** on the Filter by Form window, click the Help toolbar button or press Shift+F1; then click the tab you need help with.

Speeding Up When Filtering by Form

Using Filter by Form will be fast on small tables, but it might be slow on very large ones. Fortunately, you can speed up overall performance for Filter by Form or optimize performance on individual forms.

If lists seem to display slowly while you're creating a Filter by Form filter, you can change some settings to speed things up. To speed up Filter by Form list performance for all tables, queries, and forms, choose Tools ➤ Options, and then click the Edit/Find tab. Check or clear options in the Show List of Values In group; then enter a maximum list size to display when you open a drop-down list for a field value. The more options you check and the more items you show in lists, the slower your filter will display the drop-down lists when you create the filter. Click OK when you're done making changes.

You also can speed up performance when displaying Filter by Form lists for text box controls on a specific form. To begin, open the design window for the form, choose View ➢ Properties, and then click the Data tab in the property sheet. For each text box control you want to optimize, click the text box control, and then choose an appropriate Filter Lookup property. Your options are as follows:

Database Default Use the settings shown on the Tools ➢ Options ➢ Edit/Find tab.

Never Never show available values in the drop-down list for this field; instead, show only Is Null and Is Not Null in the list.

Always Always show available values in the drop-down list for the field.

Perhaps an example can help you decide when to turn off Filter Lookup for a field on a form. Suppose you work for a huge company, and you often use Filter by Form to select employees who have a particular last name. Because you rarely use the FirstName field's drop-down list when filtering by form, you can speed things up by setting the FirstName field's Filter Lookup property to Never. With this setting, an accidental click the FirstName field's drop-down list won't bog you down while Access creates a long list of first names that you don't need to see anyway. (Of course, you can always click in the FirstName field and type a first name value if you occasionally want to filter by first name.)

 TIP If you often use the same nonindexed field to filter your data, consider adding an index to that field to speed things up, as explained in Chapter 6.

Using Advanced Filter/Sort

The Advanced Filter/Sort feature can be convenient to use if you need to create complex filters. With Advanced Filter/Sort you can sort fields and specify selection criteria all at once, without having to switch from tab to tab (as with Filter by Form). To use it:

1. Open the table, query, or form you want to filter, in datasheet view or form view.

2. Choose Records ➢ Filter ➢ Advanced Filter/Sort. The filter design window, shown in Figure 9.8, will appear.

FIGURE 9.8

The Filter window for the Order Details table. The first step generally is to copy or drag the field (or fields) you want to search from the field list into the QBE grid.

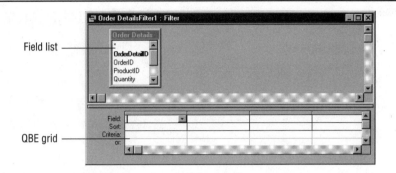

Field list

QBE grid

 NOTE   QBE is short for *query-by-example*, so named because you *query* (ask for) certain records by presenting *examples* of what you want. (The search criterion you enter is the "example.") The QBE grid for a filter is similar to the QBE grid for a query (see Chapters 3 and 10).

3. From the list in the upper pane of the window, drag the name of a field you want to search or sort by into the QBE grid in the lower pane of the window. Or double-click a field to copy it to the next available Field cell in the QBE grid.

4. Choose either Ascending or Descending from the Sort cell if you want to sort the records by the field you specified in step 3.

5. Type the value you're looking for into the Criteria cell under the field name.

 NOTE   Access may translate your criteria into syntax it understands by adding quotation marks or other punctuation marks to whatever you type into the Criteria cells. Usually you can enter criteria without the quotation marks or other punctuation marks, although it's perfectly fine to type them yourself. The examples in Table 9.3 (later in this chapter) show ways to enter equivalent criteria with and without punctuation marks.

6. Repeat steps 3 through 5 to specify as many criteria as you wish. (We'll explain more about how to enter criteria under "Creating Complex Filters" later in this chapter.) Figure 9.9 shows the QBE grid after we copied the ProductID and Quantity fields to the QBE grid, typed **9** (the ProductID for a tether ball) into the Criteria cell below the ProductID field, and chose Ascending from the Sort cell below the Quantity field.

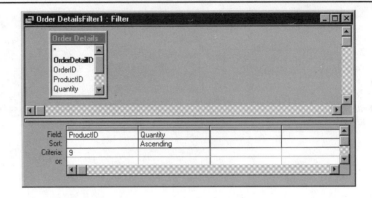

7. Click the Apply Filter/Sort toolbar button when you're ready to apply the filter, or choose Filter ➤ Apply Filter/Sort.

Any records that do not meet the criteria you specified will just disappear from view. But don't worry—they're only hidden, not gone. The navigation bar shows *(Filtered)* and the status bar includes a FLTR indicator to remind you that some records are hidden.

 TIP You can view and update the "advanced" filter that's behind a Filter by Selection, Filter Excluding Selection, or Filter by Form at any time. Just create one of those filters as explained earlier in the chapter, and then choose Records ➤ Filter ➤ Advanced Filter/Sort, or Filter ➤ Advanced Filter/Sort (depending on which options are available on the menu bar).

As with Filter by Form and Filter by Selection, you can remove the filter set up with Advanced Filter/Sort, (Click the Remove Filter toolbar button.) and you can save the filter with your datasheet or form. (Click the Save toolbar button in datasheet or form view.)

When you remove the filter, all the records in the table will be accessible again, and the *(Filtered)* and FLTR indicators will disappear. To reapply the filter, simply click the Apply Filter toolbar button.

Using Lookup Fields in Filters

Entering criteria values for a lookup field can be trickier in an Advanced Filter/Sort than it is in the simpler filters discussed earlier. That's because, in those simpler filters, Access creates an internal lookup query that joins lookup fields to their related tables and plugs in appropriate criteria values. To see this for yourself, create a Filter by Selection, Filter Excluding Selection, or a Filter by Form filter that selects values in a lookup field (such as ProductID), and apply the filter. Then choose Records ➢ Filter ➢ Advanced Filter/Sort to see the internal query that Access created automatically.

With the Advanced Filter/Sort feature, only one table (the table you're creating the filter for) usually appears in the filter window. Because you don't have the convenience of displaying values from the internal lookup query, you must enter (into the QBE grid's Criteria cell) the value that's actually stored in the lookup field, *not* the value shown when you're viewing the lookup field in a datasheet or form. In Figure 9.9, for example, we wanted to isolate orders for *tether balls*. To do that, we had to type **9** (the ProductID of a tether ball)—not the words *tether ball*—into the Criteria cell below ProductID.

See Chapter 17 for more about lookup fields, and Chapter 10 for more about automatic joins between tables.

Creating Complex Filters

When filtering your records, you're not limited to looking for one value in one field. The fact is, you can isolate records based on the contents of any combination of fields in the table. For example, you can select "all the orders that were placed within the last 60 days by companies in Bellevue, Washington or Jackson, Mississippi."

NOTE You can set up the same criteria with either Filter by Form or Advanced Filter/Sort. The main difference between these filtering methods is that Advanced Filter/ Sort lets you see all your criteria at once, whereas you must switch from tab to tab to see the Or conditions in a Filter by Form filter. Also, Filter by Form doesn't offer built-in sorting. (But, after applying the Filter by Form filter, you can arrange the columns you want to sort by from left-to-right, select them, and then click the Sort Ascending or Sort Descending toolbar buttons.)

Choosing Fields to Filter

When setting up an Advanced Filter/Sort, you first need to tell Access which fields to filter or sort, by copying field names from the field list into the QBE grid (see Figure 9.8). You've already learned two ways to copy field names, but here's the complete list of techniques for reference:

- **To locate a field name in the field list**, click in the field list and type (as many times as needed) the first letter of the field name you want to see, or use the vertical scroll bar.

- **To copy a field name into the QBE grid**, double-click the field name in the field list, or drag it from the field list to the first row (see Figure 9.9). Or click in an empty Field cell in the QBE grid, and then type the first few letters in the field name. Or click in the Field cell, click the drop-down arrow button that appears, and then scroll to and click the field you want to copy.

- **To copy several field names to the QBE grid**, Shift-click to select multiple adjacent field names in the field list, or Ctrl-click to select nonadjacent field names. Then drag any one of the selected field names into the QBE grid.

- **To copy all the field names from the field list into the QBE grid**, double-click the title at the top of the field list, and then drag any selected field name down to the QBE grid.

Specifying Selection Criteria

The selection criteria tell Access what you're looking for. To specify criteria, type an expression in the Criteria cell under a field name. The expression can be the exact thing you're looking for (such as Smith or 100 or 6/15/99), or it can use comparison operators such as > (greater than), < (less than), and so forth. Here are some rules about typing an expression:

- **In a number, currency, or autonumber field**, don't include a currency sign or thousands separator. For instance, type **10000** to search for the value $10,000.

- **In a date/time field**, the left-to-right order of the month, date, and year ultimately must match the order defined on the Date tab of the Regional Settings Properties dialog box in the Windows Control Panel. For instance, in the United States, you can enter **11/9/99**, or **9 November 1999**, or **9-Nov-99**, or **Nov 9 99**, and Access will replace the entry automatically with #11/9/99#.

- **In a text field**, you can type the text you're looking for in either uppercase or lowercase letters. Put quotation marks around text that includes spaces, punctuation, or Access operators such as the word Or.

- **In a memo field**, you'll probably want to use the * wildcard to search for text embedded within the field. See "Finding Part of a Field" later in this chapter for examples.

- **In a Yes/No field**, enter -1, Yes, True, or On for Yes; enter 0, No, False, or Off for No.

- **Operators are optional**. If you omit the operator, Access assumes you mean equals (=).

Using Operators and Wildcard Characters

When typing expressions in the QBE grid or the Filter by Form datasheet or form, you can use the operators and wildcards listed in Table 9.3 and the mathematical operators shown in Table 9.4.

TABLE 9.3: OPERATORS AND WILDCARD CHARACTERS			
OPERATOR	**OPERATOR MEANING**	**EXAMPLE**	**EXAMPLE MEANING**
		Comparison Operators	
=	Equals	=smith *or* ="smith"	Equals *smith*
>	Greater than	>5000	Greater than *5,000*
<	Less than	<1/1/99 *or* <#1/1/99#	Less (earlier) than *January 1, 1999*

Continued ▶

TABLE 9.3: OPERATORS AND WILDCARD CHARACTERS (CONTINUED)

OPERATOR	OPERATOR MEANING	EXAMPLE	EXAMPLE MEANING
		Comparison Operators	
>=	Greater than or equal to	>=M or >="M"	Greater than or equal to the letter M
<=	Less than or equal to	<=12/31/98 or <=#12/31/98#	Less (earlier) than or equal to December 31, 1998
<>	Not equal to	<>CA or <>"CA"	Does not equal CA
Between	Between two values (inclusive)	Between 15 and 25	A number from 15 to 25
In	Within a set or list of values	In(NY, AZ, NJ) or In("NY", "AZ", "NJ")	New York, Arizona, or New Jersey
Is Null	Field is empty	Is Null	Records that have no value in this field
Is Not Null	Field is not empty	Is Not Null	Records that do have a value in this field
Like	Matches a pattern	Like MO-* or Like "MO-*"	Records that start with MO- followed by any other characters (see Wildcard Characters in this table)
		Logical Operators	
And	Both are true	>=1 And <=10	Between 1 and 10, inclusive
Or	One or the other is true	UT or AZ or "UT" or "AZ"	Either Utah or Arizona
Not	Not true	Not Like MO-??? or Not Like "MO-???"	Records that don't start with *MO-* followed by exactly three characters.
		Wildcard Characters	
?	Any single character	P?-100 or "P?-100"	Values that start with *P* followed by any single character, followed by *-100*

Continued ▶

TABLE 9.3: OPERATORS AND WILDCARD CHARACTERS (CONTINUED)

OPERATOR	OPERATOR MEANING	EXAMPLE	EXAMPLE MEANING
	Wildcard Characters		
*	Any characters	(619)* *or* "(619)*"	Any text that starts with *(619)*, e.g., phone or fax numbers
[*field name*]	Some other field in the QBE grid	<[UnitPrice]	Records where this field's value is less than the value in the UnitPrice field

TABLE 9.4: MATHEMATICAL OPERATORS

OPERATOR	MEANING
+	Addition
-	Subtraction
*	Multiplication
/	Division
\	Integer division
^	Exponent
Mod	Remainder of division (modulo)
&	Join two text strings

You also can use the Date( ) function to search for records by date relative to the current date. Table 9.5 shows some examples. Another function, DateAdd( ), is handy for specifying a range of dates based on some interval other than days.

PART II

Creating a Database

TABLE 9.5: SAMPLE DATE( ) AND DATEADD( ) FUNCTIONS

EXAMPLE	EXAMPLE MATCHES
Date( )	The current date
<=Date( )	The current date and all dates before
>=Date( )	The current date and all dates after
<=Date( )-30	Dates earlier than or equal to 30 days ago
Between Date( ) And Date( )-30	Dates within the last 30 days
Between Date( ) And Date( )+30	Dates within the next 30 days
Between Date( )-60 And Date( )-30	Dates between 30 and 60 days ago
>DateAdd("m",1,Date( ))	Dates that are greater than 1 month ("m") from the current date
Between DateAdd ("m",-2,Date( )) And Date( )	Dates between two months ago and the current date
Between DateAdd("m",2,Date( )) And Date( )	Dates between the current date and two months from now
<DateAdd('yyyy",-1,Date( ))	Dates that are earlier than 1 year ("yyyy") ago

For more information on functions and how to use them, use the Office Assistant to look up the function you're interested in.

Specifying "And/Or" Criteria

Sometimes you'll want to show only those records that meet all of your criteria. For instance, to locate records in the Customers table for Wilbur Stumingi in San Diego, structure your criteria to match only records that have Wilbur in the ContactFirst-Name field *and* Stumingi in the ContactLastName field *and* San Diego in the City field.

At other times you'll want to show records that match *any* of the search criteria. For example, you might want to show products that have a unit price of $4.95 or $12.95.

Table 9.6 summarizes the techniques you use in the QBE grid to specify "And" and "Or" relationships among criteria.

TABLE 9.6: TECHNIQUES FOR SPECIFYING *AND* AND *OR* RELATIONSHIPS

TO SPECIFY THIS RELATIONSHIP...	IN...	DO THIS...
And	Multiple fields	Place the criteria in the same row of the QBE grid.
And	A single field	Use the And operator.

Continued ▶

TABLE 9.6: TECHNIQUES FOR SPECIFYING *AND* AND *OR* RELATIONSHIPS (CONTINUED)		
TO SPECIFY THIS RELATIONSHIP...	**IN...**	**DO THIS...**
Or	Multiple fields	Place the criteria in separate rows of the QBE grid.
Or	A single field	Use the Or operator, or use the In operator, or stack the criteria in the QBE grid.

Arranging the QBE Grid

If you're creating a really complex filter with lots of fields, you may want to rearrange the QBE grid. Roughly the same techniques that work for customizing the datasheet view also work with the QBE grid. For example:

- **To select a QBE column**, click the column selector at the top of the column. (The mouse pointer changes to a heavy black ↓ when it's positioned on a column selector.)
- **To select multiple columns**, drag the mouse pointer through several column selectors. Or click the column selector for the first column you want to select, and then Shift-click the column selector for the last column you want.
- **To select a criteria row**, click the row selector at the left edge of the row. (The mouse pointer changes to a heavy black → when it's positioned on a row selector.)
- **To select multiple criteria rows**, drag the mouse though the row selectors of several rows. Or click the row selector of the first row you want to select, and then Shift-click the row selector of the last row you want.
- **To delete the selected rows or columns**, press the Delete key, or choose Edit ➢ Delete Rows or Edit ➢ Delete Columns.
- **To insert as many blank rows or columns as you selected**, press the Insert key, or choose Insert ➢ Rows or Insert ➢ Columns.
- **To move the selected rows or columns**, click the row selector (for selected rows) or the column selector (for selected columns) inside the selected area. Then drag the selected rows or columns to a new position.

To adjust column widths in the QBE grid, drag or double-click the right boundary of the column selector at the top of the column(s).

Sample Filters

The various operators, functions, and And/Or logic in Access allow you to create a practically endless variety of filters. Following are some examples of filters that are meaningful in the context of our sample database; they should give you some food for thought (and useful guidelines) for creating your own filters.

Finding Part of a Field

Wildcards are useful for finding information that's embedded within a field. The filter below will isolate records for customers on the street named Polk in the city of San Francisco.

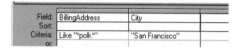

Initially, we typed the criterion into the BillingAddress field as simply *polk*. Access added the *Like* and quotation marks automatically.

The City criterion, San Francisco, is on the same row as the BillingAddress field criterion. So in order to pass through the filter, a record must have *Polk* somewhere within the BillingAddress field and also have *San Francisco* in the City field.

Wildcard characters work with all data types except OLE objects. Suppose you create a table of journal references, and the table structure includes a memo field named Abstract. To find all the records that have the phrase "vernal equinox" embedded somewhere in the Abstract field, set the field's filter criterion to **vernal equinox** or *Like "*vernal equinox*"*.

Wildcards are handy for isolating records with dates in a specific month. This criterion isolates records that have dates in March, 1999, stored in the OrderDate field (assuming the standard mm/dd/yy notation for dates in the United States):

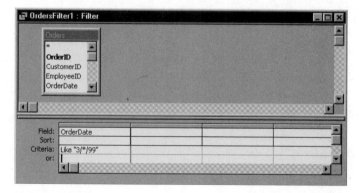

Finding Ranges of Values

You can use the various comparison operators to search for ranges of data values. For example, the filter below isolates customers whose last names begin with the letters *A* through *M* and sorts the names alphabetically by last name.

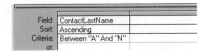

Field:	ContactLastName	
Sort:	Ascending	
Criteria:	Between "A" And "N"	
or:		

Notice that we used *N* at the high end of the range. That's because any name (or word) beginning with the letter *M*, even *mzzxxyxyx*, is "less than" *N*. But anything that comes after the letter *N* (in the dictionary) is considered to be "greater than" *N*. So even a simple last name like *Na* is excluded, because *Na* is greater than *N*.

Here's a filter that isolates and sorts (by PostalCode) customers located in the postal code range 92000 to 99999-0000:

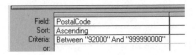

Field:	PostalCode	
Sort:	Ascending	
Criteria:	Between "92000" And "999990000"	
or:		

NOTE When entering criteria, be sure to specify only characters that are actually stored in the table. For example, the input masks for fields in Wizard-generated tables display punctuation characters (such as hyphens in a Zip code and parentheses in a phone number) in a datasheet or form, but they do not store those characters in the table. That's why we omitted the hyphen punctuation character in the Criteria cell shown above.

Here's a simple filter that isolates and sorts (by UnitPrice) records in the Products table that have a Unit Price value of $25.00 or less.

Field:	UnitPrice	
Sort:	Ascending	
Criteria:	<=25	
or:		

Filtering Dates

The filter below isolates records with dates from the first quarter of 2000 (January 1 through March 31, 2000). In this example, we didn't have to type the # symbols. Access adds them automatically when you type a date into the Criteria cell.

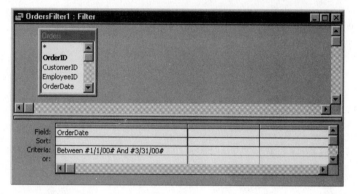

 TIP   You can use the Date( ) function in a filter to stand for the current date. See Table 9.5 earlier in this chapter.

Accepting Several Values from a Field

Suppose you want to isolate customers in the states of Alaska, California, and Wyoming. In this case, you want to accept records that have AK or CA or WY in the StateOrProvince field. There are three ways to set up the filter. Here's one:

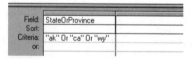

This "stacked" setup works just as well:

And so does this version, which uses the "In" operator to list acceptable entries:

Field:	StateOrProvince	
Sort:		
Criteria:	In ("ak","ca","wy")	
or:		

No particular method is better than another. So use whichever method seems most natural or convenient. Remember, too, that Access isn't picky about uppercase and lowercase letters in the Criteria cells; therefore, it's fine to enter the abbreviation for Alaska as **AK**, or **Ak**, or **ak**, or even **aK**.

Saving a Filter as a Query

Earlier in this chapter we showed you how to save a filter with the datasheet or form. Filters saved with the datasheet or form are available anytime you open the datasheet or form and apply the filter, and anytime you display a filtered datasheet or form and then create a new form or report from the filtered records.

You also can save a filter as a separate query object, which will be available anytime you need it. Here's how:

1. Return to the Advanced Filter/Sort filter design window. If you're viewing the datasheet or a form, choose Records ➤ Filter ➤ Advanced Filter/Sort. If you're in the Filter by Form window, choose Filter ➤ Advanced Filter/Sort.

2. Click the Save as Query toolbar button, or choose File ➤ Save as Query, or right-click in the upper pane of the window and choose Save as Query. (Save as Query is on the More part of the File menu, in case you don't see it right away.)

3. Type a name for the query, and click OK. As usual in Access, the name can be up to 64 characters, including blank spaces. Access will save the filter as a query.

When you want to reuse the query in the future:

1. Open the table to which you want to apply the filter. This must be the same table you used to create the filter originally.

2. Return to the filter window (see step 1 of the procedure for saving a filter as a query, just above).

3. Click the Load from Query toolbar button, choose File ➤ Load from Query, or right-click in the upper pane of the window and choose Load from Query.

4. Double-click the name of the filter you saved earlier. The filter will appear in the filter window. (The filter might look slightly different from the one you saved earlier, but it will work the same way.)

5. Click the Apply Filter toolbar button.

Troubleshooting Filters

Remember these points if your filtered results seem to have gone awry:

- If an Access operator (such as the word "And") happens to occur within text that you're searching for (such as the company name *Dewey Cheathem And Howe*), place the entire text in quotation marks:

```
"Dewey Cheathem And Howe"
```

Otherwise, Access will misinterpret your text as

```
"Dewey Cheathem" And "Howe"
```

- If you're searching for text that contains punctuation marks (that is, anything other than numbers or letters), put quotation marks around the text. You can use single quotation marks (') or double quotation marks ("").

- Avoid confusing *And* and *Or* logic. This logic doesn't always work the way you'd think of it in English. For instance, to find customers in Mississippi and Washington, you must use an *Or* criterion, such as *"MS" Or "WA"*. If you use an *And* criterion instead, Access never finds a match. That's because Access can't answer Yes when it asks the question "Does this record have *MS* in the StateOrProvince field and *WA* in the StateOrProvince field?"

- Remember that each Criteria row in the filter asks an entirely separate and independent question. If Access can answer Yes to any one of those questions, the record passes through the filter.

This last point is an important one and the cause of much confusion among neophyte database users. For example, look at this filter and see if you can figure out which Order Detail records will get through it.

Field:	ProductID	Quantity	
Sort:			
Criteria:	9	5	
or:		3	

At first you might say "It'll show all the orders for tether balls (ProductID 9) in which the Quantity ordered is 5 or 3." But that's not exactly correct. The filter will show all the tether balls in which the quantity ordered is 5 and all products (regardless of ProductID) for which the quantity ordered is 3. Why? Because two separate questions are being asked of each record:

Question 1 Does this record have 9 in the ProductID field and 5 in the Quantity field?

Question 2 Does this record have 3 in the Quantity field?

Any record that can pass either question comes through the filter. The second question above places no filter criterion on the ProductID field.

If you want to select all the tether ball orders that have a quantity ordered of 5 *And* all the tether ball orders that have a quantity ordered of 3, you must set up two complete questions, like this:

Field:	ProductID	Quantity	
Sort:			
Criteria:	9	5	
or:	9	3	

This second filter asks these two questions:

Question 1 Does this record have 9 in the ProductID field and 5 in the Quantity field?

Question 2 Does this record have 9 in the ProductID field and 3 in the Quantity field?

Only records that have the 9/5 combination or the 9/3 combination will pass through the filter.

As with most things in Access, you can get help as you create your own advanced filters. Go to the Office Assistant, search for *Filters*, and explore any topics of interest.

Quick Prints

 If you're looking at a datasheet or form on the screen and need a printed copy of that object, you can click the Print toolbar button (shown at left) to print the data without being prompted for further information. Of course, Access also gives you fancier ways to print things, as the next few sections will explain.

Previewing Your Printout

To get a sneak preview of how the data on the screen will look when printed:

1. Start from datasheet view or form view.

2. Click the Print Preview toolbar button (shown at left) or choose File ➢ Print Preview. A full-page image of the datasheet or form will appear.

3. Do any of the following:

- **To zoom in to or out of a portion of the image**, click the Zoom tool-bar button or click the image itself. Figure 9.10 shows our sample Products table after zooming in on the data.

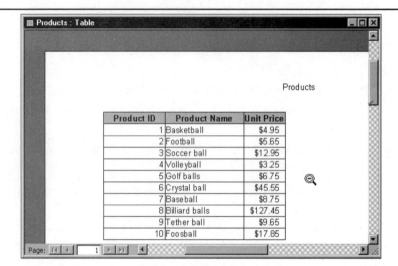

- **To zoom so that you can see two pages at a time**, click the Two Pages button on the Print Preview toolbar. To return to one-page view, click the One Page toolbar button, or click the Multiple Pages toolbar button and click 1 × 1.

- **To zoom so that you can see from 1 to 6 pages at a time**, click the Multiple Pages toolbar button and click your choice (1 × 1, 1 × 2, etc.).

- **To zoom to any magnification** between 10 and 200 percent or to the best fit, click the drop-down arrow next to the Zoom Control box on the toolbar, and then choose a magnification.

- **To output the data to another Microsoft program**, click the drop-down arrow next to the OfficeLinks toolbar button, and then choose Merge It with MS Word, Publish It with MS Word, or Analyze It with MS Excel (see Chapter 7).

- **To select options from a convenient shortcut menu**, right-click any-where in the image and choose an option from the menu, shown next. Zoom offers the same magnification options shown in the Zoom Control box, One Page shows one page at a time, Multiple Pages displays up to 6 "thumbnail" pages at a glance, Page Setup opens a dialog box where you can set margins and orientation for printing, Print opens the Print dialog box, Save As/Export saves the object being previewed to another object of the same type or exports data to another format (see Chapter 7), and Send sends the data as an e-mail message (see Chapter 7).

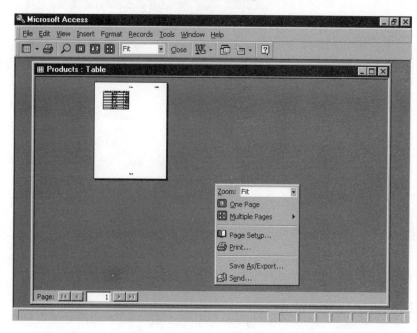

- **To immediately print** whatever is in the print preview window, click the Print toolbar button. Or choose File Print (or press Ctrl+P) and continue with step 3 of the procedure given in the next section.

- **To return to datasheet view or form view without printing**, click the Close toolbar button.

Printing Your Form or Datasheet

To print the current form view or datasheet view data without previewing it first:

1. Select the record(s) you want to print, if you want to print selected records.

2. Click the Print toolbar button (shown at left) if you want to use the default printing options and print immediately.

Or

If you want more control over printing, choose File ➢ Print or press Ctrl+P. You'll see the Print dialog box shown in Figure 9.11.

FIGURE 9.11

The Print dialog box.

Choose a printer.   Change printer properties.

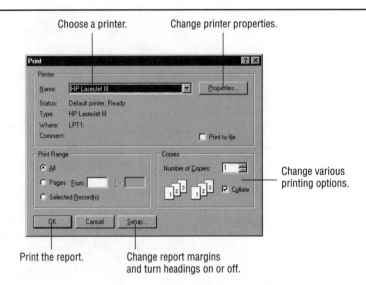

Print the report.   Change report margins
and turn headings on or off.

Change various
printing options.

3. Choose options in the Print dialog box as needed (more on these options in a moment).

4. Click OK when you're ready to start printing.

Most of the printing options are quite straightforward, but if you need more help, see "Changing the Page Setup" and "Changing Printer Properties," following, or click the ? button in the upper-right corner of the dialog box, and then click the option you're curious about. You also can explore Help topics for *Printing* with the Office Assistant.

Changing the Page Setup

The Setup button in the Print dialog box takes you to the Page Setup dialog box (see Figure 9.12). From there you can choose margin settings for your printed output and choose whether to print headings or whether to print the data only—without borders, gridlines, or layout graphics.

NOTE The options available depend on the type of object you're printing. For example, Figure 9.12 shows the Page Setup dialog box for a table that we opened in datasheet view. The Page Setup dialog box for a form or report also includes a Layout tab; the Print Data Only check box replaces the Print Headings check box on the Margins tab.

PART

II

Creating a Database

You can reach a more powerful Page Setup dialog box than the one shown in Figure 9.12 by choosing File ➢ Page Setup from the menu bar. When you use the menu bar options, you can change the page margin and header settings (from the Margins tab), and you can change various printer settings and properties (from the Page tab). If you're printing a form or report, you'll also find a Columns tab, which lets you control such things as the distance between rows of data on a report.

Changing Printer Properties

If you want to change the properties for the currently selected printer, click the Properties button in the Print dialog box. Or if you choose File ➢ Page Setup, click the Page tab, click the Use Specific Printer option, click the Printer button, select a printer (if necessary), and then click the Properties button.

Figure 9.13 shows the Properties dialog box for an HP DeskJet 660c printer. Other types of printers will have different property settings.

TIP For even more control over your printer's properties, click the Start button on the Windows Taskbar and choose Settings ➤ Printers (or use any equivalent techniques for opening the Printers window). Then right-click the printer you want to customize and choose Properties. Changes that you make by starting from the Printers window affect printer properties for *all* Windows programs, not just Access.

FIGURE 9.13

FIGURE 9.13

The Properties dialog box for an HP DeskJet 660C printer.

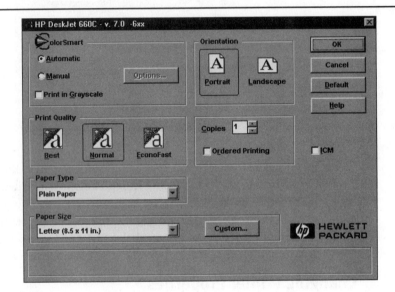

You use the Properties dialog box for a printer the same way you use properties dialog boxes for other objects in Windows:

1. Click the tab for the property you want to change, if there are tabs in the dialog box.

2. Set any options you want on the selected tab. If you're unsure about what to do, click the Help button.

3. Repeat steps 1 and 2 as needed.

4. Click OK when you're done choosing printer properties.

Making Your Print Settings Stick

At first glance, it's downright tricky trying to figure out which print settings will stick each time you print and which won't. These tips can help you:

- Changes made in the Print dialog box are always temporary; the next time you open the Print dialog box (File ➢ Print or Ctrl+P), the default settings reappear.

- Changes made from the Page Setup dialog box or printer Properties dialog box are stored with each form and report, and will take effect any time you open the form or report and print. (This is true whether you get to those dialog boxes from the Print dialog box or the File ➢ Page Setup menu options.)

- Print settings are always returned to the defaults after you print and close a table, query, or module. That is, changes you make in the Print, Page Setup, or printer Properties dialog boxes are discarded after you print and close the table or query.

Printing Tips

Here are some tips that should come in handy whenever you're printing from datasheet or form view:

- If you customize datasheet view before printing, your printout will show the custom datasheet.

- The Print Preview window will reflect any changes that you make via the Page Setup dialog box (File ➢ Page Setup).

- If you've created a shortcut to an Access object on the Windows Desktop or in a folder, you can quickly preview, print, or send the object via e-mail. First locate the shortcut, and then right-click it. Then choose Preview, Print, or Send To ➢ Mail Recipient from the shortcut menu.

- In Windows, you can print by dragging the shortcut icon for your Access object to a printer icon. To locate your printer icons, open My Computer and double-click the Printers folder; or click the Start button on the Windows Taskbar and choose Settings ➢ Printers. Or open Control Panel (Start ➢ Settings ➢ Control Panel), and double-click the Printers folder.

See Chapter 1 for information about creating shortcuts from Access objects.

Where to Go from Here

This chapter has presented a potpourri of procedures for sorting, searching, filtering, and printing data in datasheet view and form view. The next step is to learn about queries, which let you ask questions about data and change data automatically. If you feel comfortable using the Advanced Filter/Sort features described in this chapter, queries will seem easy.

What's New in the Access Zoo?

The Find and Replace functions in Access 2000 are now included in the same handy dialog box. Otherwise, the techniques you use to sort, search, filter, and print information are the same as in Access 97.

CHAPTER 10

Querying Your Tables

Queries allow you to answer questions about your data, to extract specific information from tables, and to change selected data in various ways. In fact, the ability to perform queries is a key reason for using database management programs—rather than spreadsheets or word processing programs—to manage large amounts of related data. In this chapter you'll learn how to use the query wizards and the graphical query by example (QBE) tools in Access to query your data with relative ease.

As you read through this chapter, keep in mind that many techniques for customizing datasheet view and creating filters apply to queries as well. So if you haven't worked through Chapter 9, you should do so before diving into queries. You also should understand the basic table design concepts (Chapter 6) and know how to edit in datasheet view (Chapter 8).

What Queries Let You Do

Queries let you see the data you want, in the order you want it. They also allow you to perform calculations on your data; to create sources of data for forms, reports, charts, and other queries; to make global changes to tables; and to create new tables.

 TIP If the main reason you're creating a query is to use it as a source of records for a multitable form or report, you may not need to set up a query at all. Often, the Form Wizard or Report Wizard offers a faster way to simultaneously design the form or report and create an SQL statement that defines the record source for you. Chapters 11 and 12 describe these versatile wizards in more detail. Of course, if you have many records, a form or report will operate faster if it uses a saved query (rather than an SQL statement) as its record source.

When you run most types of queries or apply a filter, Access collects the data you ask for in a *dynaset*. Although the dynaset looks and acts like a table, it's actually a dynamic or "live" view of one or more tables. Therefore, changes that you make after running a query usually will affect the underlying tables in the database itself.

 NOTE A dynaset is an updateable type of *recordset*, which is any collection of records that you can treat as an object. Some types of queries—such as those that create crosstabs and other summaries—generate recordsets in which some or all fields are not updateable.

Types of Queries

You can create several types of queries, as summarized below:

Select Query The most commonly used query type, a Select query lets you select records, create new calculated fields, and summarize your data. Select queries are similar to the filters discussed in Chapter 9.

However, unlike filters, Select queries also let you:

- Query more than one table.
- Create new calculated fields.
- Summarize and group your data.
- Choose which fields to show or hide.

Crosstab Query These queries group data into categories and display values in a spreadsheet-like format with summary totals. You can use Crosstab queries to compare values and see trends in your data, to view summary data, such as monthly, quarterly, or yearly sales figures, and to answer questions such as "Who has ordered how many of what?" Crosstabs are especially useful as the basis for reports and charts.

Make-Table Query These queries create a new table from a dynaset. Use Make-Table queries to create a backup copy of a table, save a history table of old records you'll be deleting from another table, select a subset of data to report on, or create a table for exporting to other applications.

Update Query Use these queries to make global changes to data in one or more tables. These queries offer a powerful, fast, and consistent way to change many records in one fell swoop. For example, you can use an Update query to increase the price of all tether ball items by 25 percent, or to empty out certain fields.

Append Query These queries add records from one or more tables to the end of an existing table. Append queries are especially useful for adding old records to the end of a history table. You can then convert the Append query to a Delete query (described next) and delete the old records from the original table.

Delete Query Use this type of query to delete a group of records from one or more tables. For instance, you can delete all customer records for people who haven't bought anything in five years or more. Or, after appending data to a history table, you can use a Delete query to remove the old records from the original table.

Pass-Through Query Strictly for SQL mavens, Pass-Through queries send commands directly to an SQL database server using the syntax required by that server. For information on this topic, search for help on *Pass-Through Queries* with the Office Assistant.

Data-Definition Query Also for SQL mavens, Data-Definition queries use SQL language statements to create or change database objects in the current database. To learn about this topic, search for help with *Data-Definition Queries* with the Office Assistant.

Union Query Another one for SQL mavens, Union queries use SQL language statements to combine corresponding fields from two or more tables or queries into one field. Use the Office Assistant to find help with *Union Queries*.

Access offers two ways to create queries: the query wizards and the "from scratch" methods. We'll look at the query wizards first.

Using Query Wizards

Query wizards offer a quick and easy way to perform the special-purpose queries listed below:

Simple Query Wizard Use this wizard to create a Select query for one or more tables. The resulting query can do simple selection, or it can calculate sums, averages, counts, and other types of totals.

Crosstab Query Wizard This wizard creates a crosstab for a single table or query.

Find Duplicates Query Wizard This wizard creates a query that can find duplicate records in a single table or query.

Find Unmatched Query Wizard Use this wizard to find records in one table that have no related records in another. For example, you can use this Wizard to create queries that find customers who haven't placed orders or to find employees who haven't sold orders to any customers.

Often the query wizards will be able to set up the perfect query for your needs. But even if the query that the wizard creates is only "almost good enough," using the wizards can save you time in the initial query design. You can always switch to design view (discussed soon) and tweak the wizard-generated query as needed.

To use the query wizards:

1. Click the drop-down arrow next to the New Object toolbar button (the second-to-last button on the toolbar) from any window in an open database, and then choose Query. If you're in the database window, you can click the Queries button, and then click New; or choose Insert ➢ Query.

2. Double-click one of the options described above (Simple Query Wizard, Crosstab Query Wizard, Find Duplicates Query Wizard, or Find Unmatched Query Wizard) in the New Query dialog box.

3. Follow the wizard's instructions and complete the dialog boxes that appear. (See Chapter 3 for information about basic techniques you can use with Access wizards.)

In a flash, you'll have a new query that you can either use as is or customize as needed.

Creating, Running, Saving, and Changing a Query

Now let's look at the basic steps for creating queries from scratch and for running, saving, and changing queries. Later in the chapter, you'll learn how to refine the basics to set up any query you want.

Creating a Query from Scratch

The query wizards can create the specialized queries discussed in the previous section. To create other types of queries, however, you'll need to start from scratch. Here are the steps to follow:

1. Click the drop-down arrow next to the New Object toolbar button (second-to-last button on the toolbar) from any window in an open database, and then choose Query. Or click the Queries button in the database window, and then click the New button; or choose Insert ➢ Query.

2. Double-click Design View in the New Query dialog box. A *query design window* named Query1 : Select Query opens, and the Show Table dialog box appears (see Figure 10.1).

 TIP If you already know which table you want to query, go to the database window, click the Tables tab, click the table you want to create the new query from, click the drop-down arrow next to the New Object toolbar button, click Query, and then double-click Design View. The Show Table dialog box won't appear when you follow these steps, but you can display it (if necessary) by choosing Query ➢ Show Table.

FIGURE 10.1

The Select Query window and Show Table dialog box appear when you create a new query from scratch.

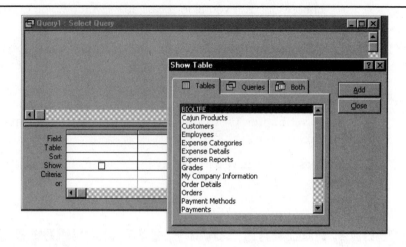

3. Use any of these techniques to add the tables you want to query:

   - **To choose which objects to list in the Show Table dialog box**, click the Tables, Queries, or Both tabs at the top of the Show Table dialog box.

   - **To add an object to the query design window**, double-click the object you want to add, or highlight the object and then click the Add button.

   - **To add multiple adjacent objects to the query design window**, click the first object you want to select; then Shift-click the last object you want (or drag your mouse through the object names). Click Add.

   - **To add multiple nonadjacent objects to the query design window**, click the first object you want to select; then hold down the Ctrl key and click each remaining object. Click Add.

4. Repeat step 3 as needed. When you're done, click Close. Join lines will appear automatically if you created relationships between tables (explained in Chapter 6) or if Access can figure out the relationships on its own. You also can join the tables manually, as described later in this chapter.

5. Click the drop-down list next to the Query Type toolbar button (shown below) to pick the type of query you want to set up, or choose options from the Query menu. Your options are Select (the default and most commonly used query type), Crosstab, Make-Table, Update, Append, and Delete. (See "About the

Query Design Window's Toolbar," later in this chapter, for details about the toolbar buttons.)

TIP To convert one type of query to another, simply choose the appropriate type from the Query Type toolbar button or the Query menu.

---

6. Double-click fields that you want to display in the dynaset or that you want to use with selection criteria in the tables area. Or drag the fields from the tables area to the QBE grid. Or select the fields from the drop-down list in the Field row of the QBE grid.

7. Specify any selection criteria that you want to use for isolating dynaset records in the Criteria rows under the appropriate column in the QBE grid. The techniques are similar to those for designing a filter (see Chapter 9).

8. Fill in other areas of the QBE grid as needed (see "Refining Your Query" later in the chapter).

9. (Optional) Specify properties for the query itself or for an individual field (see "Refining Your Query" later in this chapter).

The example in Figure 10.2 shows a complex Select query that's based on several related tables. This query will do the following:

- Select records in which the order was placed in February 1999 and the quantity times the unit price ([Quantity]*[Order Details]![Unit Price]) is greater than $75.

- Display the ContactLastName and ContactFirstName fields from the Customers table (see the Field and Table rows in Figure 10.2), the OrderDate from the Orders table, the Quantity and UnitPrice from the Order Details table, a calculated field named $, and the ProductName field from the Products table. In the dynaset, the $ field will have the column heading Total Price and will appear in Currency format (see the Field Properties sheet in the figure).

FIGURE 10.2

A Select query to find orders for a specified date and dollar amount of items.

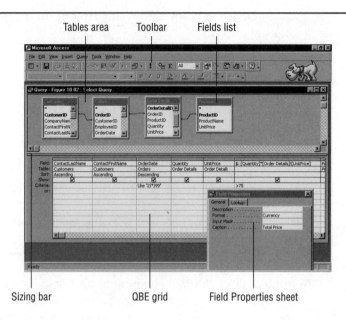

Sort the results by ContactLastName and ContactFirstName (in ascending order) and OrderDate (in descending order) for multiple orders from the same customer.

 NOTE Because both the Order Details and the Products tables have a UnitPrice field, we had to explicitly tell Access to use the UnitPrice field in the Order Details table when multiplying the Quantity times the Unit Price in the query. To specify the table name and field name, use the format [*TableName*]![*FieldName*], as in [Order Details]![UnitPrice].

Figure 10.3 shows the dynaset produced by this query.

FIGURE 10.3

The dynaset produced by the query in Figure 10.2.

Field properties shown in Figure 10.2 control this field's caption and format.

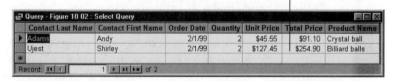

Tips for Using the Query Design Window

Here are some tips and shortcuts for designing a query:

- **To clear all the items from the QBE grid**, choose Edit ➤ Clear Grid. Be careful, though—you cannot undo Clear Grid.

- **To expand the editing area for an input cell in the QBE grid**, click in the cell you want to expand and then press Shift+F2. Or right-click the cell and choose Zoom. In the Zoom Box that appears, edit the text as needed, and then click OK to close the box.

 TIP The Zoom Box is available anywhere an expanded input area might be handy, including property sheets, a table's design or datasheet view, the QBE grid, the filter window, and the macro window.

- **To see which table each field in the QBE grid is from, or to hide that information**, choose View ➤ Table Names, or right-click the QBE grid and choose Table Names. When you select (check) the View ➤ Table Names option or the Table Names shortcut menu option, a Table row will appear in the QBE grid (see Figure 10.2). When you deselect the option, this row is hidden.

- **To change a field name in the QBE grid**, click to the left of the field name's first letter in the QBE grid and then enter the new name followed by a colon. We used this technique to change the original name of an expression field to $ in Figure 10.2. The new field name will be used in the dynaset unless you've specified a Caption in the Field Properties sheet (see Figures 10.2 and 10.3).

 - **To add tables to the query design window**, click the Show Table toolbar button (shown at left), or right-click an empty place in the tables area and choose Show Table, or choose Query ➤ Show Table. You can also open the database window (F11) and then choose Window ➤ Tile Vertically so that you can see the database and query design windows. Next, click the database window's Tables tab, and then drag the table name from the database window to the tables area of the query design window.

- **To remove a table from the query design window**, click the table and then press the Delete key. (This step doesn't remove the table from the database, only from the query design window.)

- **When a query gets too complicated**, consider using two queries. Create, test, and save the first query. Then, with the first query open in the query design or datasheet window, click the drop-down arrow next to the New Object toolbar button, choose Query, and then double-click Design View. Now design, test, and save your second query (which will be based on the first one). In the future, you can just run the second query to get the results you want.

For help with designing queries, look up any of the subtopics under *Queries* in the Access Help Index. Or go to the Office Assistant, enter *Create a Query*, and explore subtopics there.

Viewing the Dynaset

 You can view the dynaset that appears when you run a query, anytime: click the Query View toolbar button (shown at left), or choose View ➤ Datasheet View.

 TIP If you need to cancel a query while it's running, press Ctrl+Break. (This cancel procedure may not work for very large queries.)

The dynaset will appear in datasheet view (see Figure 10.3). From here you can do any of the following:

- **Edit records in the dynaset**. Your changes will update the underlying tables.
- **Customize the dynaset's appearance**. Use the same techniques you use to customize a datasheet (see Chapter 8). You can save your layout changes when you save the query.
- **Sort the dynaset**. Use the same techniques you use to sort a table (see Chapter 9).
- **Filter the dynaset**. Use the same techniques you use to filter a table (see Chapter 9).
- **Preview and print the dynaset as for any other table**. To preview the data, click the Print Preview toolbar button, or choose File ➤ Print Preview. When you're ready to print the data, click the Print toolbar button, or choose File ➤ Print. Chapter 9 offers more details on printing.
- **Return to the query design window**. To do so, click the Query View toolbar button (shown at left), or choose View ➤ Design View. Your query will reappear in the query design window exactly as you left it.

Viewing the SQL Statement behind a Query

If you're familiar with SQL (or you'd like to become better acquainted), you can view or edit your query in SQL view. To switch to SQL view, open the query in design or datasheet view. Then click the drop-down arrow next to the Query View toolbar button, and choose SQL View; or choose View ➤ SQL View. View or change the SQL statement as needed, and then click the Query View toolbar button to see the results in datasheet view.

 WARNING Structured Query Language (SQL) is used behind the scenes in queries and other Access objects. However, it's not for the faint of heart or the inexperienced database user. Be careful when changing SQL statements; if you make mistakes, your queries and other objects may not work properly. For more about SQL, look up *SQL StatementsIin Queries* with the Office Assistant.

Running an Action Query

If you've designed an action query (Make-Table, Update, Append, or Delete query), switching to datasheet view will let you see which records will be affected when you *run* the query. But no changes will be made to any tables, and no new tables will be created. Previewing in datasheet view gives you a chance to look before you leap.

When you're sure the dynaset correctly shows the records the action should affect, you can run the query this way:

1. Return to the query design window and click the Run toolbar button (shown at left), or choose Query ➤ Run.

2. Respond to any prompts from the action query to confirm your changes. (There's more about action queries later in the chapter.)

 TIP If the action query's confirmation messages annoy you, or if you're not getting confirmation messages, choose Tools ➤ Options and then click the Edit/Find tab. To make sure confirmation messages appear (the *safest* choice), check the Action Queries box under Confirm. To suppress those messages, clear the Action Queries box. Click OK to close the Options dialog box.

The action query will do its job, and you'll be returned to the query design window.

NOTE Running a Select query or Crosstab query is the same as viewing the query's datasheet.

For help with viewing and running action queries, look up *Action Queries* with the Office Assistant.

Saving Your Query

To save a new or changed query, use any of these techniques:

- **If you're in the query or datasheet window**, click the Save toolbar button (shown at left), or choose File ➤ Save, or press Ctrl+S.
- **If you're done with the query for now**, close the query design window or datasheet view (for example, choose File ➤ Close, or press Ctrl+W). When asked if you want to save your changes, click Yes.

If this query is new, you'll be prompted for a query name. Type a standard Access name (up to 64 characters including blank spaces), and then click OK. Note that Access won't let you save the query with the same name as an existing table or query.

When you save a query, Access saves *only* the query design, not the resulting record-set. That way, the query will operate on whatever data is in your tables at the time you run the query.

Opening a Saved Query

To reopen a saved query:

1. Start in the database window and click the Queries button.

2. Do one of the following:

- **To view the query's dynaset or run an action query**, double-click the query name, or highlight the query name and then click Open.
- **To open the query's design window**, highlight the query name and then click Design, or right-click the query name and choose Design from the shortcut menu.

After opening the query, you can switch between datasheet view and design view by clicking the View button on the Query Design or Query Datasheet toolbar.

About the Query Design Window's Toolbar

As you saw in Figure 10.2, the query design window's toolbar contains many buttons. Proceeding from left to right on the toolbar, Table 10.1 briefly describes what each one does. (In Table 10.1 we've omitted the standard Copy, Cut, and Paste buttons, which appear on most Access toolbars, and the Print, Print Preview, Spelling, and Format Painter buttons, which are dimmed and unavailable.)

TABLE 10.1: THE QUERY WINDOW'S MOST IMPORTANT TOOLBAR BUTTONS

BUTTON	BUTTON NAME	WHAT IT DOES
	Query View (Design View)	Switches to the query window, where you can design or change your query.
	Query View (Datasheet View)	Switches to datasheet view, where you can view the dynaset. If you're designing an action query, use this button to preview which records the query will affect.
SQL	Query View (SQL View)	Switches to SQL view, where you can use SQL statements to design or change your query.
	Save	Saves your latest changes to the query.
	Undo	Undoes your most recent change to a criterion entry (when you are still in that field).
	Query Type (Select Query)	Displays the QBE grid for a Select query.
	Query Type (Crosstab Query)	Displays the QBE grid for a Crosstab query.
	Query Type (Make-Table Query)	Displays the QBE grid for a Make-Table query.
	Query Type (Update Query)	Displays the QBE grid for an Update query.
	Query Type (Append Query)	Displays the QBE grid for an Append query.

Continued ▶

PART

II

Creating a Database

TABLE 10.1: THE QUERY WINDOW'S MOST IMPORTANT TOOLBAR BUTTONS (CONTINUED)

BUTTON	BUTTON NAME	WHAT IT DOES
	Query Type (Delete Query)	Displays the QBE grid for a Delete query.
	Run	Runs an action query. For Select and Crosstab queries, this button has the same effect as the Query View (Datasheet View) button.
	Show Table	Lets you add more tables to the tables area of the query window.
	Totals	Displays a Total row in the QBE grid. Use this row to specify how data will be grouped and summarized.
All	Top Values	Lets you choose whether to return a specified number of records, a percentage of records, or all values. Access uses the leftmost sorted field to choose which top values to display. You can choose a setting from the Top Values button's drop-down list, or type a number (e.g., 25) or a percentage (e.g., 47%) into the Top Values combo box.
	Properties	Opens the property sheet, where you can change field or query properties.
	Build	Opens the Expression Builder, which makes it easier to enter complicated expressions.
	Database Window	Opens the database window.
	New Object (AutoForm)	Creates a new automatic form that's based on the current query.
	New Object (AutoReport)	Creates a new automatic report that's based on the current query.
	New Object (Table)	Lets you create a new table. The table is not based on the current query.
	New Object (Query)	Lets you create a new query that's based on the current query.

Continued ▶

BUTTON	BUTTON NAME	WHAT IT DOES
	New Object (Form)	Lets you create a new form that's based on the current query.
	New Object (Report)	Lets you create a new report that's based on the current query.
	New Object (Page)	Lets you create a new data access page that's based on the current query.
	New Object (Macro)	Lets you create a new macro. The macro is not based on the current query.
	New Object (Module)	Lets you create a new module. The module is not based on the current query.
	New Object (Class Module)	Lets you create a new class module not based on a form or report.
	Office Assistant	Opens the Office Assistant.

TABLE 10.1: THE QUERY WINDOW'S MOST IMPORTANT TOOLBAR BUTTONS (CONTINUED)

Refining Your Query

In the next few sections, we'll explain how to refine your queries.

Filling In the QBE Grid

Filling in the QBE grid is perhaps the trickiest part of designing a query. Figure 10.2 showed a typical Select query and its QBE grid. The rows that appear in the grid depend on the type of query you're designing. For example, a Delete query will not have a Sort row.

Here are some techniques you can use to fill the rows in the QBE grid for a Select query. You'll find more examples in later sections.

- **In the Field row**, enter the fields you want to work with. Use double-clicking or dragging to add fields from the field list (see Chapter 9). Or to tell Access to display all fields even if the table structure changes, use the asterisk (*) field name (see "Using the Asterisk in a QBE Grid," following). Or double-click the table name to select all fields, and then drag any field to the Field row (all fields will come along for the ride). Or use the drop-down list in the Field row to select the field you want. You also can create new calculated fields in the Field row (see "Using Totals, Averages, and Other Calculations" later in this chapter).

- **In the Sort row**, choose the sort order you want for each field. Your options are Ascending, Descending, or Not Sorted. Like filters (Chapter 9), query fields are sorted in left-to-right order, so you may need to reposition columns in the grid.

Using the Asterisk in a QBE Grid

You can use the asterisk in a QBE grid to tell Access that you want all fields to appear in the dynaset. The resulting dynaset will *always* contain all the fields in the table, even if you add or delete fields in the table structure later.

To add the asterisk to a column in the QBE grid, double-click the asterisk (*) at the top of the appropriate fields list, or drag the asterisk to the grid. The Field row for the column will show the table name, followed by a period and the asterisk, like this:

Customers.*

If you use the asterisk, you still can sort on, select, group by, calculate with, and do other operations with a specific field. To do so, add the appropriate field to the QBE grid. Then to prevent that field from appearing twice in the dynaset, deselect the field's Show box.

 TIP   When you design Make-Table, Delete, or Append queries, consider using the asterisk so that the query always operates on the current structure of the underlying table, and the operation includes all the fields.

Changing Field Properties

Field properties govern the appearance of fields in the dynaset. By default, fields added to the QBE grid will inherit properties of the underlying table. However, calculated fields, such as the field `$:[Quantity] * [Order Details]![UnitPrice]` shown back in Figure 10.2, do not inherit properties. To assign or change field properties:

1. Click in the field you want to change. (If the Show box is checked, you won't be able to view or set field properties.)

2. Click the Properties toolbar button (shown at left) if the Field Properties sheet isn't visible. Or right-click the field and choose Properties. Or choose View ➤ Properties from the menus.

3. Click the tab that contains the properties you want to change, and then change the properties as needed.

To change field properties in another field, simply click in that field and change the properties as needed. When you're done using the Field Properties sheet, click the Properties button again or click the Close button at the upper-right corner of the Field Properties sheet.

Shown below is the Field Properties dialog box for the field that multiplies the quantity ordered field (`[Quantity]`) by the unit price field (`[Order Details]![Unit-Price]`) back in Figure 10.2. Here we've changed the format to Currency and set the caption to Total Price. When Access displays the dynaset, this calculated field's numbers will appear as dollar amounts (for example, $35.00) and the column heading will be Total Price (refer back to Figure 10.3).

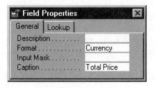

NOTE If you don't specify a field's Caption property, Access will use the field name that's assigned in the QBE grid as the column heading in the dynaset, unless the field has a caption in the underlying table.

To find out what a property does, click in a property box on the property sheet and then press F1, or press Shift+F1 (or click the Help toolbar button) and click the property you're interested in.

Changing Query Properties

You also can change the properties of the entire query. The steps are the same as for changing field properties, except that in step 1 you click an empty place in the tables area at the top of the query design window. The resulting Query Properties sheet looks like this for a Select query:

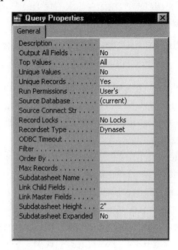

Viewing Unique Values

When you query a single table, Access normally shows all records that match what you're looking for. Sometimes, however, you'll want to eliminate duplicates by changing the Unique Values property in the Query Properties sheet from No to Yes.

Figure 10.4 illustrates this point. In order to see which credit card numbers are represented in the Payments table, we've queried to show nonempty CardHoldersName fields only. Notice that all records, including duplicate values, appear on the left side of the figure. To get rid of those duplicates (see right side of the figure), we changed the query's Unique Values property to Yes.

Here are some tips for working with unique values:

- Make sure the QBE grid includes only the field or combination of fields you want to view unique values in. For instance, to see unique credit card numbers, include only the CreditCardNumber field. To see unique combinations of credit card name and credit card number (for example, to show customers who paid with more than one credit card), include both the CardHoldersName and CreditCardNumber fields.

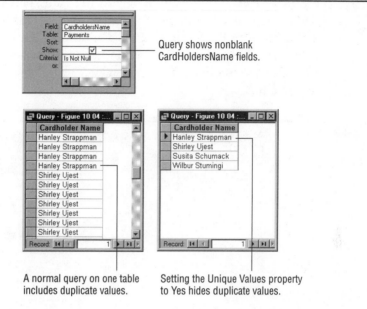

FIGURE 10.4

The Unique Values query property controls whether duplicate records appear in a single-table query.

Query shows nonblank CardHoldersName fields.

A normal query on one table includes duplicate values.

Setting the Unique Values property to Yes hides duplicate values.

- All property settings affect the current query design window. To see duplicate records again, change Unique Values back to No.

- Use a Totals query if you want to count duplicate values in your data. See "Using Totals, Averages, and Other Calculations" later in the chapter.

NOTE   When you query multiple related tables, Access normally returns the unique records (that is, the Unique Records property is Yes), but not the unique values. To see the duplicate records in a multitable query, change the query's Unique Records and Unique Values properties to No. To see only the unique records and values in a multitable query, change the Unique Values properties to Yes. (The Unique Records property changes to No automatically.)

Displaying Top Values

If you want Access to return only the top *n* records in the list, or the top *n* percent of the records (where *n* is whatever number you want), you can change the Top Values property in the Query Properties sheet or the Top Values combo box on the toolbar. Suppose you want to display the top 10 payments in the Payments table. The query

PART

II

Creating a Database

shown in Figure 10.5 will return the first 10 records, plus any records in which all the fields match the values in the 10th record. Note that the field used to display the top *n* values must be the leftmost Sort field in the QBE grid, and that you must sort that field in Descending order if you want to see the topmost values. (To see the bottom *n* values, change the Sort order to Ascending.) Figure 10.6 shows the results of the query in Figure 10.5.

FIGURE 10.5

A query for displaying the top 10 values.

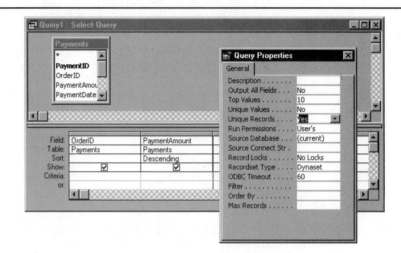

FIGURE 10.6

The results of showing the top 10 values.

TIP To return the highest or lowest values without displaying any duplicate records, set the Unique Values property in the Query Properties sheet to Yes.

Joining Tables

You can join tables to limit the records in your dynaset or to display data from several related tables at once. For example, if you join the Customers and Orders tables, the dynaset will show only related records (typically, customers who have unfilled orders in the Orders table). Similarly, if you join the Employees and Orders tables, the dynaset will show only the employees associated with orders in the Orders table.

Access will join tables for you automatically when you add them to the query design window:

- If you've established a relationship between those tables (see Chapter 6).

Or

- If the tables include fields with the same name and the same (or compatible) data type. For example, because the Customers and Orders tables both have a numeric field named CustomerID, Access can join them automatically.

Join lines appear between joined tables in the query design window to show you what kind of relationship the tables have, which fields are joined, and whether the relationship enforces referential integrity (refer back to Figure 10.2).

 TIP Sometimes you might not want Access to join tables automatically unless you've purposefully set up relationships between those tables via the Relationships window (Tools ➢ Relationships). To prevent automatic joins based on a "best guess" about which tables and fields are related, choose Tools ➢ Options and click the Tables/Queries tab in the Options dialog box. Then deselect (clear) the Enable AutoJoin check box and click OK. See Chapter 16 for more about personalizing Access.

You can join tables in three ways—inner join (also called equi-join), outer join, or self-join—as described in the following sections.

PART

II

Creating a Database

Inner Joins

In an *inner join*, records in the joined tables must have the same values for fields that are joined. This type of join answers questions such as, "Which customers have placed new orders?" You saw an inner join in Figures 10.2 and 10.3. When Access joins tables automatically on the basis of field names and data types, it always creates an inner join.

Outer Joins

In an *outer join*, all records from one table are added to the dynaset even if no matching values occur in the joined field from the other table. Records from the second table are combined with those from the first table *only* if matches occur in the joined field. The two types of outer joins are left outer joins and right outer joins.

Using the Employees and Orders example, a *left outer join* will show all employees and any orders they've sold (order information for some employees will be blank), as shown in Figure 10.7.

FIGURE 10.7

A left outer join of the Employees and Orders tables, along with the resulting dynaset.

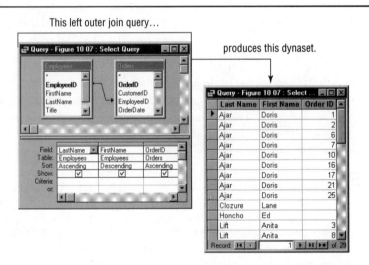

A *right outer join* will show all order numbers and the employees who sold them, (Employees who didn't sell orders won't appear in the dynaset.) as shown in Figure 10.8.

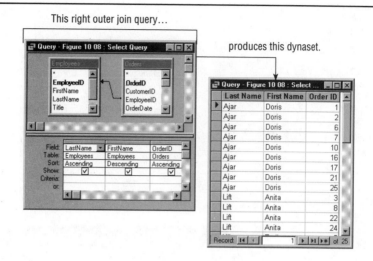

FIGURE 10.8

A right outer join of the Employees and Orders tables, along with the resulting dynaset.

This right outer join query...

produces this dynaset.

Self-Joins

In a *self-join*, the table is joined to itself. The self-join can be handy when one field within the table refers to another field within the same table. Consider, for example, the revised Employee table (named Employees With Supervisors) shown below.

Employee ID	First Name	Last Name	Title	SupervisorID	Wo
1	Anita	Lift	Sales Representative	4	(206)
2	Andrew	Van Noslo	Vice President, Sales	9	(206)
3	Emily	Niktog	Sales Representative	2	(206)
4	Albert	Niktog	Sales Manager	2	(206)
5	Doris	Ajar	Sales Representative	4	(206)
6	Lane	Clozure	Office Manager	9	(206)
7	Joseph	Swipple	Vice President, Marketing	9	(206)
8	Helen	Wheels	Product Evangelist	9	(206)
9	Ed	Honcho	President	9	(206)
(AutoNumber)				0	

Record: 7 of 9

Figure 10.9 shows a query that produces a list of supervisors and the employees they manage. To clarify the meaning of each column in the dynaset, we assigned captions to each field. Looking at the dynaset, it's easy to see this company's pecking order: President Ed Honcho manages Lane Clozure, Joseph Swipple, Andrew Van Noslo, and Helen Wheels; Sales Manager Albert Niktog manages Doris Ajar and Anita Lift; Vice President (Sales) Andrew Van Noslo manages Albert Niktog and Emily Niktog.

PART

II

Creating a Database

FIGURE 10.9

This self-join on an Employee table shows supervisors and their subordinates. Although not obvious from this example, the table on the left is named Employees with Supervisors; the self-join table on the right is named Employees with Supervisors_1.

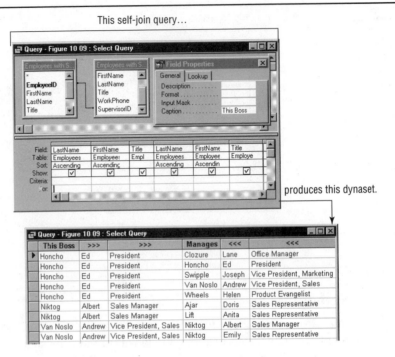

This self-join query…

produces this dynaset.

To create a self-join, add the same table to the query design window twice. (Access will add an underscore followed by a number to the second table name, as in Employees with Supervisors_1.) Then create an inner join between appropriate fields in the two tables (see the next section). In Figure 10.9, for example, we joined the EmployeeID field from the Employees with Supervisors table on the left to the SupervisorID field from the Employees with Supervisors_1 table on the right.

Defining an Inner Join

To define any type of join, you first define an inner join:

1. Start in the query design window and add any tables you want to join. If join lines appear automatically between the fields you want to join, you're done.

2. To join tables manually, drag the field name from one table onto a field name containing the same kind of data in another table. Usually you'll want to drag a primary key (which appears in bold).

3. Release the mouse button.

Inner join lines will connect the joined fields in each table, as shown here:

Changing the Join Type

To change the type of join between two tables:

1. Right-click the join line you want to change, and choose Join Properties. Or double-click the thin part of the join line. You'll see the Join Properties dialog box:

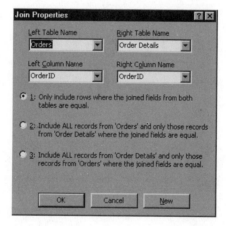

 NOTE If your mouse isn't on the thin part of the join line—or the join line isn't bold when you double-click it—the Query Properties sheet may appear instead of the Join Properties dialog box. If this happens to you, close the Query Properties sheet and try again.

2. Choose the option you want in the Join Properties dialog box. Option 1 produces an inner join. Option 2 creates a left outer join. Option 3 makes a right outer join.

3. If you want to change the properties of another join in the open query, select the tables involved using the Left Table Name and Right Table Name drop-down lists. Then repeat step 1.

4. Click OK. Access will update the appearance of the join line to reflect your choice in step 2.

Figures 10.7 and 10.8 show left and right outer join lines, respectively.

TIP If you find yourself creating the same manual joins often, you can establish a permanent relationship between the tables. To do so, return to the database window and choose Tools ➤ Relationships, or click the Relationships toolbar button; then define the type of join you want (see Chapter 6).

Deleting a Join

Deleting a join is easy:

1. Click the thin part of the join line you want to delete, so that it appears bold.

2. Press the Delete key.

WARNING If the join line isn't bold when you press Delete, you may delete a table from the query design window. If that happens, you'll need to add the table (Query ➤ Show Table) and its fields again.

For help with joining tables, look up *Joins* with the Office Assistant.

Showing an Entire Database Structure

As explained in Chapter 6, you can use the Relationships window to get "the big picture" of all the tables in your database and how they're related to one another. Here's a quick review of how to show the entire database structure:

1. Return to the database window and choose Tools ➤ Relationships, or click the Relationships toolbar button.

2. Choose Relationships ➤ Show All, or click the Show All Relationships toolbar button to show all the relationships.

3. If necessary, rearrange the tables on the screen so the join lines don't look like a pile of spaghetti (see Figure 10.10).

FIGURE 10.10

The Relationships window for the Order Entry database.

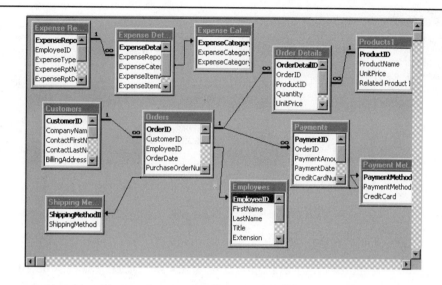

Creating AutoLookup Queries

Suppose a customer calls to place an order. Being a lazy typist, you don't want to reenter customer information that's already in the Customers table. To save your typing fingers, you can create a special Select query called an *AutoLookup query*. Then simply enter a valid CustomerID and Access will fill in the customer information automatically.

AutoLookup works in queries in which two tables have a one-to-many relationship and the join field on the one side of the relationship has a unique index. That is, the join field on the one side must either be a primary key or have its Indexed property set to Yes (No Duplicates).

NOTE Do not confuse a lookup field (Chapter 6) with an AutoLookup query. A lookup field displays a list of values that makes it easier to enter data into one specific field. An AutoLookup query automatically fills in corresponding data on the one side of a one-to-many query when you enter new data in the join field on the many side. As Figure 10.11 shows, you can use a lookup field (for example, CustomerID) in an AutoLookup query.

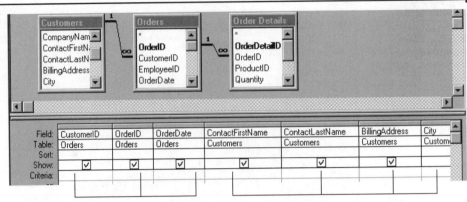

FIGURE 10.11

An AutoLookup query uses the join field from the many side of the relationship to look up and fill in information from the one side automatically.

These fields come from the many side.   These fields come from the one side.

In the classic example of Customers and Orders, the CustomerID field in the Customers table is a primary key on the one side of the relationship. The CustomerID field in the Orders table is on the many side of the relationship.

Here's the secret to designing an AutoLookup query: put the join field from the many side of the query into the QBE grid. This field is the *AutoLookup* field. For example, add the CustomerID field from the Orders table (not the Customers table) to the grid.

NOTE For an AutoLookup query to work, you must be able to update the AutoLookup field from the many side of the query. If you try to change a field that can't be updated, Access will display an explanatory message in the status bar.

Figure 10.11 shows an AutoLookup query in which CustomerID (from the Orders table) is the AutoLookup field for customer information. Figure 10.12 shows the dynaset after we chose RNAA Associates from the drop-down list for the CustomerID field in the empty row at the bottom of the datasheet. As soon as we selected a company name from the AutoLookup field, Access filled in the corresponding customer information automatically.

FIGURE 10.12

The dynaset created by the AutoLookup query in Figure 10.11. After we chose RNAA Associates from the CustomerID drop-down list, Access filled in the customer information automatically.

Customer ID	Order ID	Order Date	Contact F	Contact Las	Billing Address
WorldWide Widgets	17	2/11/99	Shirley	Ujest	187 Suffolk Ln.
WorldWide Widgets	17	2/11/99	Shirley	Ujest	187 Suffolk Ln.
WorldWide Widgets	18	2/28/99	Shirley	Ujest	187 Suffolk Ln.
WorldWide Widgets	19	3/15/99	Shirley	Ujest	187 Suffolk Ln.
WorldWide Widgets	19	3/15/99	Shirley	Ujest	187 Suffolk Ln.
WorldWide Widgets	20	4/1/99	Shirley	Ujest	187 Suffolk Ln.
University of the Elite	21	2/1/99	Wilbur	Stumingi	P.O. Box 555
University of the Elite	22	4/1/99	Wilbur	Stumingi	P.O. Box 555
University of the Elite	23	5/7/99	Wilbur	Stumingi	P.O. Box 555
University of the Elite	24	6/28/99	Wilbur	Stumingi	P.O. Box 555
University of the Elite	25	7/15/99	Wilbur	Stumingi	P.O. Box 555
RNAA Associates	26		Hanley	Strappman	2743 Bering St.

Query - Figure 10 11 : Select Query

Record: 50 of 50

When data is entered into the lookup field...   Access fills in these fields automatically.

WARNING When designing queries for data entry purposes, be sure to include required fields and validated fields, and be sure to check their Show boxes on the QBE grid. If the query doesn't include such fields, Access may display error messages about bad or missing data in those fields; unfortunately, the person entering the data won't be able to fix the problem because the fields aren't there. A catch-22 situation if there ever was one!

Prompting for Selection Criteria

If you find yourself changing the criteria each time you run a Select query, consider using *parameters* instead of specific values for the criteria. A parameter acts as a sort of placeholder that you can fill in when you run the query.

To define a parameter:

1. Create your query normally, but omit the criteria for now.

2. Click the Criteria cell of the field you want to search. In place of the data you're searching for, type a parameter in square brackets. The parameter can't be the same as an existing field name (though it can include the field name) and is best worded as a question or a prompt that tells the user what to do. Repeat this step for each field that you want to define as a parameter.

3. Choose Query ➤ Parameters, or right-click an empty place in the tables area of the query design window and choose Parameters. You'll see the Query Parameters dialog box (Figure 10.13 shows a completed example).

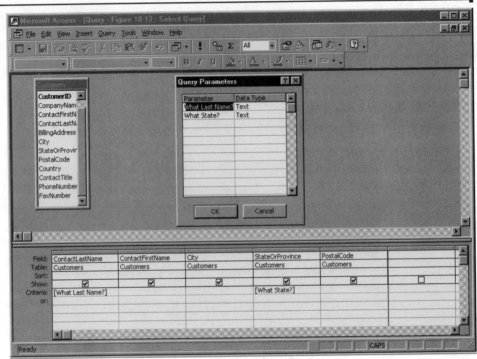

4. Type the first parameter you want Access to prompt for *exactly* as you typed it into the Criteria cell in the Parameter column, but without the square brackets. (If the spellings don't match exactly, Access will prompt for both spellings when you run the query, and you won't get the results you want.)

5. Choose a data type for the parameter in the Data Type column. This should match (or be compatible with) the data type of the field the parameter is in. (Access usually fills this in automatically when you tab to or click in the Data Type cell.)

6. Repeat steps 4 and 5 for each parameter. When you're done, click OK.

TIP As a shortcut, you often can skip steps 3 through 6 and not bother to define any parameters in the Query Parameters dialog box. When you run the query, it will display the prompts you entered in step 2 in order, from the leftmost prompt to the rightmost prompt. However, you *should not* skip these steps if (1) you're using parameters in a Crosstab query or in a parameter query that a Crosstab query or chart is based on, or (2) you're creating a parameter for a field with the Yes/No data type or for fields that come from a table in an external database. For Crosstab queries you also must set the ColumnHeadings property in the Query Properties sheet.

Figure 10.13 shows a query that uses parameters. Whenever you run this query, Access first displays this message:

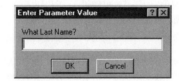

You can type any name you want, such as **Adams**, and click OK. Next you'll see the message "What State?" This time, type a state name, such as **CA**, and click OK. (Access always prompts for parameters in the order in which you list them in the Query Parameters dialog box. If you've left that dialog box blank, it prompts in order from leftmost parameter to rightmost parameter.) The resulting dynaset will show only California customers whose last names are Adams.

You also can use the parameter as part of a search criterion. For instance, you can replace the [What Last Name?] criterion in Figure 10.13 with Like [What Last Name?]&"*"

When you run the query, Access will show the same message. But your entry will be substituted with the more general "Like" expression. So if you enter Adams, Access will convert that entry to Like Adams* and display records that begin with the letters *adams* (Adams, Adamson, Adams and Lee, and so on).

 NOTE The & operator concatenates strings on either side of it. Thus, *Like "*"&[What Name?]&"*"* translates into *Like *Adams** if you enter *Adams* in the Enter Parameter Value dialog box. This example matches records such as McAdams, Adams, Adamson, and so on.

The bottom line is that you can use parameters anywhere you'd type normal text or a field name in a Criteria cell.

As usual, help is available for setting up parameter queries. In the Access Help, a good place to start is the *Working with Queries* book.

Using Totals, Averages, and Other Calculations

Access provides several ways to perform calculations on your data:

- You can perform calculations in Criteria cells, as discussed in Chapter 9.

- You can perform a calculation and display the results in a calculated field that isn't stored in the underlying tables. Back in Figure 10.2, for example, a calculated field named $ multiplied the [Quantity] field and the [Order Details]! [UnitPrice] field. The results appear in the Total Price column of Figure 10.3.

- You can group records according to certain fields, and display summary calculations for the grouped data. This lets you determine how many items were ordered on various dates, how many orders were placed by each customer, the dollar value of orders for each product, and so on.

You'll learn how to use calculated fields and data summaries in the following sections.

Using Calculated Fields

To create a calculated field, click in an empty Field cell in the QBE grid and type an expression that will do the calculation. When referring to other fields in the QBE grid, be sure to enclose their names in square brackets. If more than one table in your query has the same field name, you must specify both the table name and the field name, using the format [TableName]![FieldName]. For instance, to multiply the quantity field by the unit price field of the Order Details table, type [Quantity]* [Order Details]![UnitPrice] in an empty Field cell.

You can give the calculated field its own heading in the dynaset and use that heading as a field name in still other calculations. Just precede the calculation with the heading you want to use, followed by a colon, like this:

```
ExtPrice:[Quantity]*[Order Details]![UnitPrice]
```

Now you can use the ExtPrice calculated field in another calculated field. This example calculates the price with sales tax:

```
WithTax:[ExtPrice]*(1+[SalesTaxRate])
```

Here's the QBE grid for these calculations:

Field:	ProductName	SalesTaxRate	ExtPrice: [Quantity]*[Order Details]![UnitPrice]	WithTax: [ExtPrice]*(1+[SalesTaxRate])
Table:	Products	Orders		
Sort:	Ascending	Ascending		
Show:	☑	☑	☑	☑
Criteria:				

And here are the results:

Product Name	Sales Tax Rate	ExtPrice	WithTax
Baseball	6.00%	$8.75	$9.27
Baseball	7.25%	$17.50	$18.77
Basketball	0.00%	$4.95	$4.95
Basketball	5.00%	$9.90	$10.40
Basketball	6.00%	$9.90	$10.49
Basketball	7.25%	$9.90	$10.62
Basketball	7.25%	$4.95	$5.31
Billiard balls	0.00%	$127.45	$127.45
Billiard balls	0.00%	$254.90	$254.90
Billiard balls	5.25%	$127.45	$134.14
Crystal ball	0.00%	$45.55	$45.55
Crystal ball	0.00%	$45.55	$45.55
Crystal ball	0.00%	$45.55	$45.55
Crystal ball	0.00%	$45.55	$45.55
Crystal ball	0.00%	$136.65	$136.65

Query - Graphic 10 09 : Select Query

Record: 9 of 49

You can use the & operator to join text and fields into a single calculated field. When using this operator, be sure to enclose any text, including blank spaces, in quotation marks.

Let's look at some examples of calculated fields that use the & operator to display values from the Employee table's FirstName and LastName fields in a single column in the query result.

Assuming the FirstName is *Helen* and the LastName is *Wheels*, the calculated field shown below will display the result *Helen Wheels*:

```
[FirstName]&" "&[LastName]
```

To display the result as *Wheels, Helen* use this calculated field:

```
[LastName]&", "&[FirstName]
```

And if you're in an expansive mood, you can use this calculated field:

```
"Hey "&[FirstName]&" "&[LastName]&"! How are ya?"
```

to display this message:

```
Hey Helen Wheels! How are ya?
```

PART

II

Creating a Database

The following tips will help you make the most of calculated fields:

- **If you don't provide a name for a calculated field**, Access will assign a meaningless name, such as Expr1, Expr2, Expr3, and so on. You can change these to more useful names as needed.

- **If you misspell a field name within square brackets**, Access will treat the field as a parameter when you run the query. You'll need to click Cancel in the Enter Parameter Value dialog box and return to query design view to correct the faulty field name.

- **If you want to change the properties of the calculated field** (to control the caption and format displayed in the dynaset), right-click the field, choose Properties, and define the properties you want to use.

- **If you are typing lengthy calculations**, use Zoom (press Shift+F2) to expand the input area as described earlier in the chapter.

- **If you need to enter complicated calculations or criteria into a cell**, use the Expression Builder (see Figure 10.14) to help. To open the Expression Builder, click in the cell you want to edit and then click the Build toolbar button (shown at left), or right-click the cell and choose Build. You can then type in and change the expression directly in the editing panel at the top of the dialog box. Or to have the Expression Builder enter field names, operators, and expressions for you, position the cursor in the editing panel, and then click and double-click items in the three lower panels of the dialog box or click the operator buttons above the panels. (For more help with the Expression Builder, click the Help button in the dialog box.) When you're ready to leave the Expression Builder and save your expression, click OK.

FIGURE 10.14

The Expression Builder.

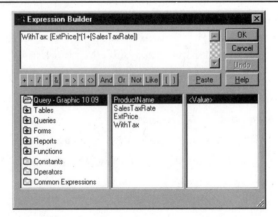

TIP You can't change the contents of a calculated field in a dynaset. But you *can* change other fields. The calculated field will be recalculated automatically.

Access provides literally dozens of functions that are useful in calculated fields. Some of the most useful are discussed under "Creating Your Own Calculation Expressions," later in this chapter. To find out about any Access function, use the Office Assistant to look up a specific function name, such as *Avg Function*.

Summarizing Your Data

Suppose you want to know the number of customers in Los Angeles or the average price of products purchased in February. For jobs like these, you need *summary calculations*. Summary calculations differ from calculated fields in that they compute some value, such as a sum or average, on *multiple records* within a table.

TIP For a truly easy way to summarize your data, use the Simple Query Wizard, described earlier in this chapter.

To perform a summary calculation:

1. Create a simple Select query as usual. Drag any fields you want to group by, or perform calculations on, to the QBE grid. Do not include the asterisk (*) field name in the QBE grid.

2. Click the Totals toolbar button (shown at left). Or choose View ➤ Totals. A new Total row will appear in the QBE grid, with Group By in each column.

3. Leave the Total row set to Group By for fields that you want to use for grouping (or categorizing, or subtotaling).

4. Choose one of the summary options in the Total cell (listed in Table 10.2) for the field you want to summarize.

5. Add calculated fields, sorting specifications, and selection criteria as needed. Then...

   • If you added selection criteria to columns that you don't want to group by, change the Total cell for those columns to Where.

   • If you created calculated fields in columns that you don't want to group by, change the Total cell for those columns to Expression.

6. Click the Query View toolbar button to see the results.

TABLE 10.2: SUMMARY OPERATORS USED IN QUERIES

SUMMARY OPERATOR	COMPUTES	WORKS WITH DATA TYPES
Avg	Average	AutoNumber, Currency, Date/Time, Number, Yes/No
Count	Number of non-blank values	All
First	Value in first record	All
Last	Value in last record	All
Max	Highest (largest) value	AutoNumber, Currency, Date/Time, Number, Text, Yes/No
Min	Lowest (smallest) value	AutoNumber, Currency, Date/Time, Number, Text, Yes/No
StdDev	Standard deviation	AutoNumber, Currency, Date/Time, Number, Yes/No
Sum	Total	AutoNumber, Currency, Date/Time, Number, Yes/No
Var	Variance	AutoNumber, Currency, Date/Time, Number, Yes/No

Remember these points as you design summary queries:

- Don't be concerned if Access changes your Totals queries slightly after you save, close, and reopen them. The queries will still work fine! For example, Access might change the summary operator in the Totals cell from *Avg* to *Expression* and transform the Field cell from an entry such as this:

```
Avg: [Order Details]![UnitPrice]
```

to an aggregate function such as this:

```
Avg: Avg([Order Details]![UnitPrice])
```

- You can't update the fields in the snapshot created by a Totals query.

 NOTE Unlike a Select query (which creates a *dynaset* that's usually updateable), a Totals query creates a *snapshot*. Although a snapshot looks the same as a dynaset on the screen, you cannot update any of the data in a snapshot.

- You can summarize as many fields as you wish, and you can include multiple copies of the same field in the QBE grid. Here's an example that displays the number of products and the average, minimum, and maximum price of products ordered by day in February 1999:

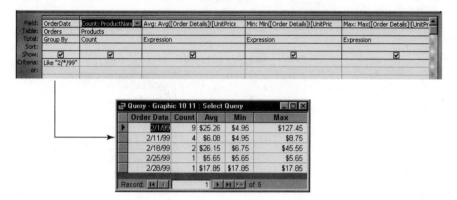

- To base calculations on all records in the table, do not use Group By in any column. For instance, to count the customers in the Customers table, put just the CustomerID field in the QBE grid and use the Count operator.

- To base calculations on groups of records (that is, to *subtotal* a group of records), use Group By in the Total cell for all fields that make up the group. This example counts the number of customers in each city and state/province:

Field:	City	StateOrProvince	CustomerID
Table:	Customers	Customers	Customers
Total:	Group By	Group By	Count
Sort:			
Show:	☑	☑	☑
Criteria:			

- You can sort on summarized fields to rank them. For instance, if you're calculating the average unit price for products sold each month, you can sort the Avg: [Order Details]![UnitPrice] field in descending order to rank products from highest average price to lowest, as shown in Figure 10.15. In the same figure, we used the Format ([OrderDate], "mmmm") function to extract the month name from the order date, in order to group the Unit Price values by month.

PART

II

Creating a Database

FIGURE 10.15

Average Price (descending) by month ordered. The function Format ([OrderDate], "mmmm") *extracts the month name from the order date.*

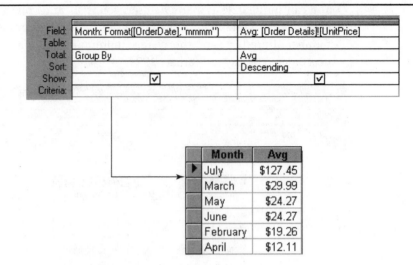

• You can specify search criteria for fields that you're grouping by, as you would in any query. This limits the display to the groups you chose in the Criteria cells of the Group By field or fields.

• To apply a search criterion *after* calculating the summary, enter that criterion in the field where you're doing the calculation. The following example calculates the average price of products sold in each month and displays (in descending order) only those with an average price greater than $15.

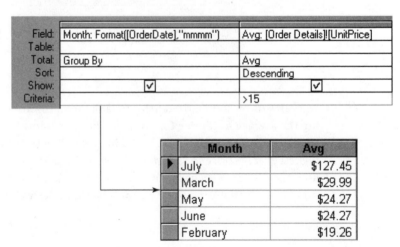

- To apply a search criterion *before* the calculation takes place, first use the Where operator in the Total cell for the field you want to select. You also must deselect the Show box for that field. The example below limits the average price calculations to products sold to customers outside the state of California. Compare the numbers shown below (which exclude the purchases by California customers) with the averages shown in Figure 10.15 (which include those purchases):

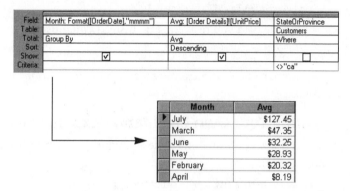

Field:	Month: Format([OrderDate],"mmmm")	Avg: [Order Details]![UnitPrice]	StateOrProvince
Table:			Customers
Total:	Group By	Avg	Where
Sort:		Descending	
Show:	✓	✓	
Criteria:			<>"ca"

Month	Avg
▶ July	$127.45
March	$47.35
June	$32.25
May	$28.93
February	$20.32
April	$8.19

- Summary calculations normally exclude blank records, but they will include zero values in a numeric field. If you need to count all records, including blanks, use Count(*) in the column's field cell, as shown below:

TIP Assuming you don't mind including records that contain null values, the calculation Count(*) runs much faster than Count([fieldname]).

- You can summarize calculated fields. However, the expression in each calculated field must refer to "real" fields, not to other calculated fields. For example, if you've defined the calculated field

  `ExtPrice:[Quantity]*[UnitPrice]`

  and want to calculate the average sales tax, you can't use the expression

  `AvgSalesTax:[ExtPrice]*1.05`

  for the field you're averaging. Instead you must repeat the calculation, like this:

  `AvgSalesTax:[Quantity]*[UnitPrice]*1.05`

For more help with calculating totals, look up *Totals in Queries* with the Office Assistant.

Creating Your Own Calculation Expressions

You can use Access functions to design your own summary expressions for analyzing data. Here's how:

1. Activate totaling in the query design window by clicking the Totals toolbar button.

2. Start in a blank column of the QBE grid. If you're using an *aggregate function* or *domain aggregate function* (described further on in this section), choose Expression in the column's Total cell. For *formatting functions*, set the Total cell to Group By.

3. Enter an expression that uses the function you want in the Field cell of the column. Some of the most useful functions are listed in Table 10.3.

 NOTE You can use Zoom (Shift+F2) when entering lengthy functions into the Field cell. Always type expressions on a single line (even if they don't appear on one line in this book).

4. Fill in other rows and columns in the QBE grid as needed.

5. Run the query as usual.

TABLE 10.3: USEFUL ACCESS FUNCTIONS

FUNCTIONS	WHAT THEY DO	EXAMPLE
Aggregate Functions		
Avg, Count, Max, Min, StDev, Sum, and Var	Perform statistical calculations on a group of records in the current table.	Avg([Quantity]*[UnitPrice]) averages the quantity times the unit price for a group of records.
Domain Aggregate Functions		
DAvg, DCount, DMax, DMin, DStDev, DStDevP, DSum, DVar, and DVarP	Perform statistical calculations on all records in any table or query, overriding Group By expressions.	DSum("[Quantity]*[UnitPrice]", "Order Details") shows the total quantity times the unit price for all records in the Order Details table.
Formatting Functions		
CCur, CDbl, CInt, CLng, CSng, CStr, and CVar	Convert expressions from one format to another. You can use these functions instead of changing a field's properties.	CCur(Avg([Quantity]*[UnitPrice])) converts to currency format the average quantity times the unit price for a group of records.
Format	Formats a number, date, time, or string.	Format([OrderDate],"mmmm") displays the month portion of the OrderDate field.
Left	Returns the leftmost n characters in a string.	Left([LastName],1) displays the first letter of the LastName field.
Mid	Returns a string that's part of another string.	Mid([PhoneNumber],1,3) displays the area code portion of a phone number field. This example assumes three-character North American area codes in which the parentheses aren't stored in the table.
Right	Returns the rightmost n characters in a string.	Right([Ship CSZ],5) displays the last five characters of a hypothetical Ship CSZ field (a combined City, State, and Zip Code field). This example assumes five-character United States zip codes.

PART

II

Creating a Database

You'll find that the following types of functions are especially useful for summarizing data:

Aggregate Functions Calculate statistics on a group of records in the current table. *Examples:* Count, Avg, Sum, Min, Max, and Var.

Domain Aggregate Functions Calculate statistics on an entire table or query, overriding any Group By expressions. *Examples:* DCount, DAvg, DSum, DMin, DMax, and DVar.

Formatting Functions Return specified parts of the data or format data in specific ways. *Examples:* Left, Right, Mid, and Format. These functions are useful with many types of calculated fields, not just summary calculations.

For a complete list of Access functions, search for *Functions, Reference Topics* in the Access Help Index. You also can use the Access Help Index to look up individual functions by name.

Sample Summary Calculation Expressions

For practice, let's look at some sample summary calculations. The example in Figure 10.16 groups and sorts records by Month, and it calculates both the value of orders in each month and each month's contribution to the whole, expressed as a percentage.

FIGURE 10.16

This example uses the Sum and DSum functions to calculate each month's contribution to total sales. It also uses the DatePart function to extract the month number from the OrderDate, so that we can present the results sorted chronologically by month, rather than alphabetically by month name.

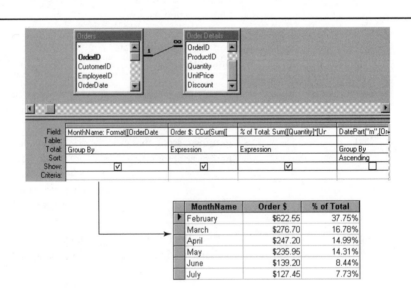

In Figure 10.16, we used the calculation shown below to isolate the month number portion of the order date; then we sorted this column in ascending order and hid it from view. (You can't see this calculation in Figure 10.16 because it has scrolled off the right edge of the screen.) This trick puts the months in chronological order (January, February, March, April, and so on), rather than displaying them in alphabetical order by month name (April, December, February, July, and so on). Here is that hidden calculation:

```
DatePart("m",OrderDate)
```

The calculation in the first column shows the month name portion of the order date:

```
MonthName: Format([OrderDate],"mmmm")
```

We used the following calculation in the second column of the QBE grid:

```
Order $:CCur(Sum([Quantity]*[UnitPrice]))
```

The calculation in the QBE grid's third column is as follows:

```
% of Total:Sum([Quantity]*[UnitPrice])/
     DSum("[Quantity]*[UnitPrice]","Order Details")
```

We used the Field Properties sheet to format the *% of Total* column as a percentage.

You can replace "mmmm" in the Format function to group by other time intervals. For example, "ww" groups by week of the year (1–54); "q" groups by quarter; "yyyy" groups by year; and "hh" groups by hour.

In Figure 10.17 we used the same summary calculations for the second and third columns. However, this time we added the Customers table to the query and grouped orders by CompanyName instead of month.

PART

II

Creating a Database

FIGURE 10.17

This example uses the Sum and DSum functions to calculate each company's total sales.

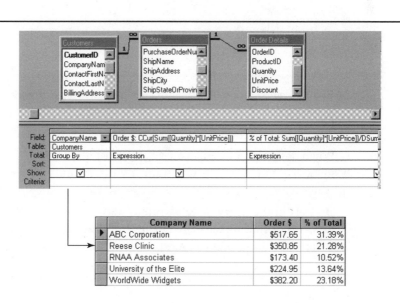

Company Name	Order $	% of Total
ABC Corporation	$517.65	31.39%
Reese Clinic	$350.85	21.28%
RNAA Associates	$173.40	10.52%
University of the Elite	$224.95	13.64%
WorldWide Widgets	$382.20	23.18%

With little effort, you can modify the example in Figure 10.17 to group orders by the first letter of the CompanyName (though there isn't an especially good reason to do so). Simply replace the expression in the first column's Field cell with this one:

```
FirstLetter:Left([CompanyName],1)
```

Creating Crosstab Queries

Crosstab queries let you cross-tabulate data in a row-by-column fashion. The example in Figure 10.18 answers the question "Who ordered how many of what?"

FIGURE 10.18

A Crosstab query makes it easy to see who ordered how many of what.

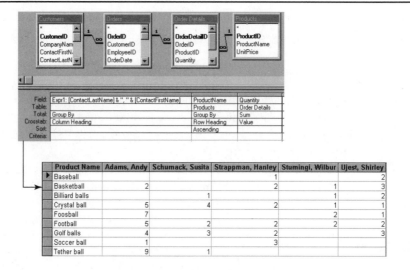

TIP To quickly create crosstabs of data in a single table, use the Crosstab Query Wizard described earlier in this chapter.

When designing a Crosstab query, you must decide which fields to use for row headings, column headings, and summary values, and how you want to summarize the values (for example, as sums or averages). Here are the steps to follow:

1. Start in the query design window and choose the tables you want to use. Put fields (including calculated fields) into the QBE grid. You can specify any search criteria and sorting you need.

2. Click the drop-down arrow next to the Query Type toolbar button, and then choose Crosstab. Or choose Query ➤ Crosstab.

3. Choose Row Heading in the Crosstab cell for the field you want to use for row headings. You can designate more than one field, but at least one field must have Group By in its Total cell. In place of a Field name, you can use expressions to group values together (see the next step for an example).

4. Choose Column Heading in the Crosstab cell for the field you want to use for column headings. Only one field is allowed, and it must contain Group By in its Total cell. In place of a Field name, you can use expressions to group values together. Figure 10.18 shows the expression `Expr1: [ContactLastName]&", "& [ContactFirstName]` used this way.

5. Choose Value in the Crosstab cell for the field you want to summarize. Then, in the Total cell for the field, choose the type of summary you want (usually Sum or Average). Don't choose Group By for this field.

6. Choose (Not Shown) in the Crosstab cell for those fields you want to group by without displaying them in the results.

7. Click the Query View toolbar button to view the results.

Access automatically determines crosstab column headings from the data in the table and then sorts the headings in left-to-right order across the columns. You can change this behavior with these steps:

1. Create and run the query as described above. Print the results or jot down the column headings, and then return to the query design window.

2. Open the Query Properties sheet. (Right-click an empty spot in the tables area and choose Properties, or click the Properties toolbar button.)

3. Type the headings you want to use (spelled exactly as they appear in the output) in the order you want them in the Column Headings box. Separate each heading with a semicolon (;) or new line (Ctrl+Enter). Or enclose the headings in double quotes and separate them with commas (see Figure 10.19). For example, type January;February;March; … (or "January","February", "March",…).

4. Run the query again to see the revised column headings.

PART

II

Creating a Database

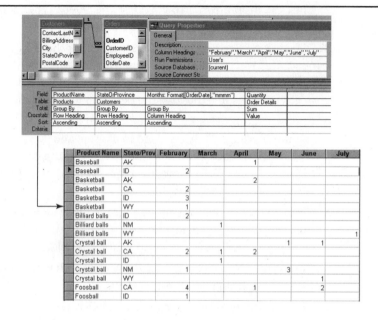

The Crosstab query shown in Figure 10.19 has two row heading fields (Product-Name and StateOrProvince). The column headings are taken from the month portion of the order date. We changed the Query Properties to list only the months February, March, April, May, June, and July. (There were no orders in the other months, so we omitted them.)

The online Help can guide you through Crosstab query setup. Just use the Office Assistant and look up any of the topics for *Crosstab Queries*. Or for fast setup, use the Crosstab Query Wizard to create a Crosstab query; then switch to the query design window and tweak the design as needed.

Creating Action Queries

Action queries differ from the queries discussed so far because they change or delete data in a table. The four types of action queries are as follows:

Update Queries Use these queries to change data in a group of records.

Append Queries These queries copy a group of records from one table to another.

Delete Queries Delete queries delete records from a table.

Make-Table Queries Use Make-Table queries to create a new table from a group of records in another table.

Action queries are very fast and can do a lot of damage if they aren't exactly right. So keep these data-saving tips in mind:

- **Always back up your database, or (at least) the tables you're going to change**. To copy a table, go to the database window and click the Tables tab. Then right-click the table you want to copy, choose Save As from the table's shortcut menu, type a name for the copy of the table, and then click OK.

- **For extra safety, you can design and test a Select query**. Then, when you're sure it will act on the proper records, convert it to an action query. To convert from one type of query to another, click the drop-down arrow next to the Query Type toolbar button, and then choose the appropriate option from the list, or choose equivalent options from the Query menu. (The steps in the sections below take a slightly more streamlined, yet still safe, approach to designing and running action queries.)

- **Double-clicking an action query in the database window runs the query** (as does highlighting the query and clicking Open). To warn you that this will happen, an exclamation point and descriptive icon appear beside the query name in the database window, as shown here:

      ♪ ! Query - Increase Price By 15%

To get help with action queries, go to the Office Assistant and enter *Action Queries*.

Update Queries

Update queries let you change all records or groups of records very quickly. To create an Update query:

1. Click the drop-down arrow next to the Query Type toolbar button in the query design window, and then choose Update Query. Or choose Query ➢ Update Query from the menus. The Query Type button changes, as shown at left.

2. Add the tables, include fields you want to update and fields you want to use for selection criteria, and set criteria to select the records you want to update, just as for a Select query.

3. Type a new value for the field in the Update To cell for each field you want to change, or type an expression that will calculate a new value. To empty out a field, type Null in the Update To cell for that field.

4. Click the Query View toolbar button (shown at left) to see which records will be updated before you update them, or choose View ➤ Datasheet View. Adjust the query criteria and preview the results until you select the records you want to update.

5. Return to the query design window and click the Run toolbar button (shown at left), or choose Query ➤ Run to run the Update query.

6. Click Yes if you want to proceed, when prompted with the number of rows that will be updated, or click No to cancel the operation.

NOTE You can't use an Update query to update Totals queries, calculated fields, or locked tables.

The left side of Figure 10.20 shows a Select query and the products it will find. The right side shows the Select query after we converted it to an Update query that raises prices for those items by 15 percent. After running the Update query, we converted it back to a Select query (by clicking the drop-down arrow next to the Query Type button and choosing Select) and displayed the revised records shown at the bottom right. Some items no longer appear, because their prices are now $20 or more.

FIGURE 10.20

A Select query to search for records with a current price less than $20, along with the Update query that raises prices of those products by 15 percent.

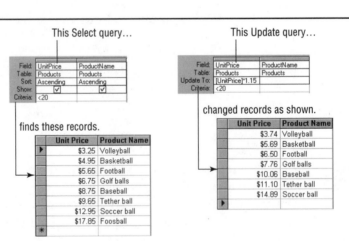

Understanding Cascaded Updates

Recall from Chapter 6 that you can use the Relationships window to define one-to-many relationships between tables, to enforce referential integrity between such tables, and to cascade updates to related fields automatically. If you use this method, Access will carry over updates to a field from the one side of the relationship to the related field on the many side, even if your Update query doesn't include tables on the many side.

Suppose we set up a one-to-many relationship and enforced referential integrity between Suppliers (a table that's not in our sample Order Entry database) and Products. Further, suppose we selected Cascade Update Related Records on the one side of each relationship. Therefore, if we use an Update query to change the SupplierID for a record in Suppliers, Access automatically updates the corresponding SupplierID in the Products table.

If you've defined Cascade Update Records for related tables, you don't need to create an Update query when you simply want a change made to the primary key on the one side to carry over to related records on the many side. Instead, go to form view or datasheet view for the table on the one side of the relationship, and change the data in the appropriate primary key field. Access will update the related field in the table on the many side of the relationship automatically.

 NOTE Values in AutoNumber fields can't be changed by editing in a table or form, or by running an update query. In the sample Order Entry database, all the IDs—including CustomerID, EmployeeID, OrderID, and ProductID—on the one side are defined as primary keys with the AutoNumber data type.

Append Queries

An *Append query* copies some or all records from one table (the *source table*) to the bottom of another table (the *target table)*. This query is handy when you use separate tables with similar structures to manage data.

For example, you might use a Products table to store current products and an Old-Products table to store discontinued products. Or you might store current, unfilled orders in an Orders table and filled orders in a history table named OrdHist.

TIP To quickly create a new table that has the same structure as an existing table, click the Tables tab on the database window, click the table that has the structure you want to copy, choose Edit ➢ Copy (Ctrl+C), and then choose Edit ➢ Paste (Ctrl+V). When the Paste Table As dialog box appears, type a new table name (for example, OldProducts), choose Structure Only, and click OK.

The example below will append records for shipped orders in the Orders table to the bottom of another table, called OrdHist, that has the same structure.

Field:	ShipDate	Orders.*
Table:	Orders	Orders
Sort:	Ascending	
Append To:		OrdHist.*
Criteria:	Is Not Null	

To create an Append query:

 1. Click the drop-down arrow for the Query Type toolbar button in the query design window, and choose Append Query. Or choose Query ➢ Append Query from the menu. (After you complete step 3, the Query Type button changes, as shown at left.) You'll see this dialog box:

2. Skip to step 3 if the table is in the same database. If the table you want to append to is in a different database, click Another Database, press Tab, and specify the drive, folder, and name of that database (for example, c:\My Documents\Mydata).

 TIP To look for the target database, right-click the Start button, choose Explore or Find, and then use standard Windows techniques to locate the database. When you find what you're looking for, close Explorer or Find, and then type the appropriate location into the File Name text box below Another Database.

3. Choose the target table from the Table Name drop-down list, and then click OK.

4. Add the table(s) with the records to be appended to another table to the query grid. Add fields to the query grid, (Include fields you want to copy and fields being used for selection criteria.) and set criteria to select the records you want to append in the query design window, just as for a Select query.

 NOTE If the field names in the source table match those in the target table, Access will fill in the appropriate Append To cells for the target table automatically. You can change this if necessary. If you're using the asterisk to copy all fields from the source table, delete field names from the Append To cells of columns that contain selection criteria.

5. Click the Query View toolbar button (or choose View ➤ Datasheet View) to preview your changes. Adjust the query and preview the results until you select the records you want to append.

6. Return to the query design window to run the Append query, and then click the Run toolbar button, or choose Query ➤ Run.

7. Click Yes if you want to proceed, when prompted with the number of records that will be appended, or click No to cancel the operation.

If an error message dialog box appears, respond to its prompts, as discussed later in "Troubleshooting Action Queries." (There's a Help button if you need it.)

Here are some important points about Append queries:

- When designing an Append query, you work with the source table. Records are *copied* (not moved) from the source table to the target table.

- The two tables must have similar structures and field names, but they needn't have identical structures.

- If the source table has more fields than the target table, extra fields are ignored.

- If the source table has fewer fields than the target table, fields with matching names are updated, and any additional fields are left blank.

- Access will copy only those fields that are included in the source table's QBE grid to the target table.

- If the two tables have identical structures, you can use the asterisk instead of field names in both the Field cell and the Append To cell. If the QBE grid also includes fields with selection criteria, leave the Append To cell for those fields blank.

- If the target table has a primary key, the results will appear in sorted order (by primary key) rather than with all the new records at the bottom.

- To have Access assign new AutoNumber values to records as they come into the target table, exclude the AutoNumber field (if any) from the source table's QBE grid.

- To retain AutoNumber values from the source table in the target table, include the AutoNumber field in the source table's QBE grid.

 WARNING If the AutoNumber field is a primary key in the target table, the incoming records must not contain values that generate key violations.

If you need to append only a few records to a table, you may prefer to use Paste Append (see Chapter 8). Chapter 7 explains how to append records to a non-Access database.

Delete Queries

Delete queries let you delete a group of records that meet specific search criteria in one fell swoop. This query, for example, will delete shipped orders from the Orders table:

Field:	ShipDate	Orders.*
Table:	Orders	Orders
Delete:	Where	From
Criteria:	Is Not Null	

The procedures for setting up a Delete query depend on whether you're deleting records from one table only (or from multiple tables involved in a one-to-one relationship) or from multiple tables that are involved in a one-to-many relationship.

 WARNING You can't undo Delete queries! Be sure to preview the records that will be deleted before you run the query.

Deleting Records from One Table

Let's take the simplest case first: deleting records from a single table or from multiple tables in a one-to-one relationship. Here are the steps to follow:

 1. Click the drop-down arrow next to the Query View toolbar button in the query design window, and then choose Delete Query. Or choose Query ➤ Delete Query from the menu. The Query Type button changes, as shown at left.

2. Add the necessary tables to the query, include fields you'll be using to select specific records, and set criteria to select the records you want to delete, just as for a Select query.

3. Double-click the asterisk (*) for each table you want to delete records from if you're querying multiple tables that have a one-to-one relationship.

4. Click the Query View toolbar button (or choose View ➤ Datasheet View) to preview your changes. Adjust the query and preview the results until you select the records you want to delete.

5. Return to the query design window to run the Delete query, and then click the Run toolbar button, or choose Query ➤ Run.

6. If you're prompted with the number of rows that will be deleted, click Yes if you want to proceed or click No to cancel the operation.

 TIP After running an Append query to append records from a "current" table to a "history" table, you can click the drop-down arrow next to the Query Type toolbar button and choose Delete to convert the Append query into a Delete query. Then click the Run toolbar button to delete the old records from the "current" table.

Understanding Cascaded Deletes

If you've defined referential integrity between tables involved in a one-to-many relationship and you've also selected Cascade Delete Related Records, Access will delete records on the many side of the relationship for you automatically, even if you haven't included the many side table in the query.

For example, the sample Order Entry database has a one-to-many relationship between Customers and Orders and between Orders and Order Details. The tables on the one side of the relationship have cascaded deletes selected. Therefore, if we create a single-table Delete query to delete a particular Orders record, Access will delete the requested Orders record and any corresponding Order Details records automatically.

Likewise, if we create a single-table Delete query to delete a particular Customer record, Access will delete that customer, along with any corresponding Orders and Order Details records for that customer—deleting, in effect, records in three related tables (which may or may not be what you want).

If you've defined Cascade Delete Related Records between related tables, you don't have to set up a Delete query when you want a deletion on the one side of the relationship to carry over to the many side. Simply go to form view or datasheet view for the table on the one side and delete the appropriate record or records. Access will delete the related records in the many side tables automatically!

WARNING The technique described above creates a delete cascade that will delete records in all related tables that have Cascade Delete Related Records selected in Relationships. Before you delete a record that in turn might delete records in other related table(s), make sure you know how the relationships between your tables are set up, and which tables will be affected. See Chapter 6 for information about creating relationships between tables.

Deleting Records from Multiple One-to-Many Tables

If you haven't set up cascaded deletes, and you want to delete records from multiple tables that are involved in a one-to-many relationship, you need to run two Delete queries, like this:

1. Click the drop-down arrow next to the Query Type toolbar button in the query design window, and then choose Delete Query. Or choose Query ➤ Delete Query.

2. Add the tables you want to use in the query.

3. Drag the field or fields you want to use for selection criteria, and define the criteria as usual from the table on the one side of the relationship (for example, Products).

4. Double-click the asterisk (*) in the table (or tables) on the many side of the relationship (for example, Orders).

5. Preview the query and run it as usual. This takes care of deleting records on the many side of the relationship.

6. Return to the query design window and delete from the window any tables on the many side of the relationship (for example, Order Details).

7. Preview the resulting query on the one side table, and run it again.

Make-Table Queries

A *Make-Table query* creates an entirely new table from the results of a query. Use Make-Table queries to:

- Work with a "frozen" copy of your data (perhaps for printing reports or charting).

- Create an editable copy of the record set that results from a summary, Crosstab, or unique values query.

- Export data to nonrelational applications, such as spreadsheets, word processors, and other programs that can't combine data from multiple tables.

To create a Make-Table query:

1. Click the drop-down arrow next to the Query View toolbar button in the query design window, and then choose Make-Table Query. Or choose Query ➤ Make-Table Query from the menu. (After you complete step 3, the Query Type button changes, as shown at left.) You'll see a dialog box that's similar to the one shown earlier for Append queries.

2. Skip to step 3 if the table you want to create is in the same database. If the table is in a different database, choose Another Database, press Tab, and specify the folder location and name of that database (for example, c:\My Documents\Mydata).

TIP As for Append queries, you can right-click the Start button, choose Explore or Find, and then use standard Windows techniques to locate the target database. When you find what you're looking for, close Explorer or Find, and then type the appropriate location into the File Name box below Another Database.

---

3. Type in or choose the name of the table you want to make in the Table Name drop-down list, and then click OK. If you choose the name of an existing table, Access will *overwrite* that table.

4. Add tables and fields, and set criteria to select the records and fields for the new table in the query design window, just as for a Select query.

5. Click the Query View toolbar button to preview your changes. Adjust the query and preview the results until you select the records you want to include in the new table.

6. Return to the query design window, and click the Run toolbar button to run the Make-Table query. If you chose an existing table in step 3, you'll be asked if you want to continue.

7. Click Yes if you want to delete the old table and continue or No to return to the query design window without deleting the table. (If necessary, you can click the drop-down arrow next to the Query Type toolbar button, choose Make-Table again, and specify a different table.)

8. Click Yes to proceed when prompted with the number of rows that will be copied or No to abandon the operation.

Troubleshooting Action Queries

Action queries must obey the same rules that apply when you're entering or editing data from the keyboard. If the action query is about to break a rule, you'll see a dialog box. At this point, the query hasn't really been executed (even though the dialog box message implies otherwise). Click No. Then return to the query or the original data, fix any problems, and rerun the query.

These are the most common causes of problems:

- An Append query or Update query is trying to enter data that isn't appropriate for the data type of the field. For Append queries, make sure the data types in the target table match the data types of the source table. For Update queries, make sure the update value is the correct data type for the field.

- An Append query or Update query is trying to add records that will cause key violations in a table that has a primary key. Remember, the primary key must have a unique value, and it can't contain null values. In an Append query, the "lost" records that violate the key won't be added to the target table (though, of course, they'll remain in the source table). In an Update query, no changes are made to records that will violate the key.

- Another user has locked records that your action query is trying to change. Your best bet is to cancel the query and wait until no one is using the table(s) involved in your query. Then try again.

- An action query is about to violate a referential integrity relationship between two tables. For instance, a Delete query can't delete records from the one side of a one-to-many relationship if the table on the many side contains related records. (It can, however, delete those records if the relationship allows cascaded deletes, as discussed in Chapter 6 and earlier in this chapter.)

Where to Go from Here

In this chapter, you've learned how to create many types of queries to ask questions about and perform calculations on your data, to update data, to delete data, and to add data from one table to another. In the next chapter, you'll learn how to use Form Wizards to generate forms instantly. As you'll discover, forms can display data from tables or queries.

What's New in the Access Zoo?

Most features of queries are the same in Access 2000 as they were in Access 97. However, a few things are new:

- Some of the query window menus and toolbar drop-downs now have expanded menus that only appear after you click the menu's More button or pause until the menu expands by itself. The Query menu and Query Type toolbar drop-down work like this. The Crosstab Query, Make-Table Query, and Delete Query choices appear on the expanded menu, but not on the first menu that appears.

- Five new query properties related to subdatasheets are available. To find them, right-click in the background area of a query window and select Properties. Then check the bottom of the Properties sheet. You'll see new lines for Subdatasheet Name, Link Child Fields, Link Master Fields, Subdatasheet Height, and Subdatasheet Expanded.

PART

II

Creating a Database

CHAPTER 11

Creating Forms
with Form Wizards

A form offers an alternative way to view and work with data in your tables. Unlike the datasheet view, which always displays data in rows and columns, a form can display data in just about any format. Perhaps the most common use of a form is to create a fill-in-the-blanks view of your data that resembles a paper form your company already uses.

With form wizards you can create great-looking data entry forms in about two seconds flat. You just pick the style you want, click your mouse a few times, and voilà, a form appears. You can use any wizard-created form, except a chart or Pivot-Table (described later in this chapter), to enter data into tables. This chapter explains how to use form wizards to create several types of predesigned forms. These designs (with a few tweaks here and there) probably can handle most of your data entry needs.

 TIP You can save lots of time by using form wizards to set up forms, even if you plan to customize those forms extensively. Chapter 3 explains how to work with wizards and gives you hands-on practice with them.

Just in case you're wondering whether Access has more form design tools to offer, the answer is a resounding Yes! If you need a more elaborate form than the form wizards can create, Chapter 13 explains how to design and customize forms and reports.

If you need extra help with designing a new form, double-click the *Working with Forms* book in the Access Help Contents, and then double-click books and topics that interest you.

What Kinds of Forms Can the Form Wizards Create?

The form wizards can create several types of forms showing fields from one or more tables and/or queries. To help you decide which type of wizard-designed form is best for your own data, we'll show some representative examples. Then we'll explain how to create forms with wizards, save those forms, and use them effectively.

Columnar Forms

In a columnar form, each field appears on a separate line with a label to its left; only one record is shown on each screen. The wizard fills the first column with as many fields as will fit on a single screen, then it fills the next column with as many fields as will fit, and so forth. Figure 11.1 shows a sample columnar form for the Customers table.

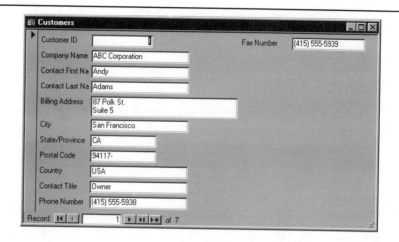

FIGURE 11.1

A columnar form for the Customers table, in the Standard style.

 TIP You can customize the styles available in form wizards. To get started, open any form in design view and choose Format ➤ AutoFormat, or click the AutoFormat button on the Form Design toolbar. Click the format you want to customize in the AutoFormat dialog box, and then click the Customize button. See Chapter 13 for more details.

Tabular Forms

Figure 11.2 shows a tabular form for the Products table. As you can see, tabular forms display fields in a horizontal row, with field labels at the top of the form. Each new row represents a new record.

FIGURE 11.2

A tabular form for the Products table in the International style. The tabular layout is best when you have just a few narrow fields to display, and you want to see several records on single screen.

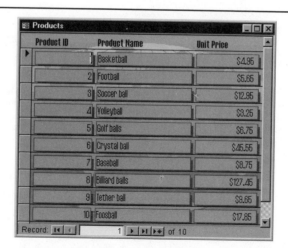

PART

II

Creating a Database

Tabular forms are best when you want to display just a few relatively narrow fields, and you want to see several records at once. To avoid spending most of your time scrolling back and forth in a tabular form, add just a few fields to the form.

Datasheet Forms

A datasheet form initially displays data in datasheet view, much as it appears when you open a table, or run a query, or when you use the Form View toolbar button to switch to datasheet view in any form. This type of form is often used as the basis for subforms, described in a moment. Figure 11.3 shows a datasheet form for the Employees table.

FIGURE 11.3

A datasheet form for the Employees table in datasheet view.

EmployeeID	FirstName	LastName	Title
1	Anita	Lift	Sales Representative
2	Andrew	Van Noslo	Vice President, Sale
3	Emily	Niktog	Sales Representative
4	Albert	Niktog	Sales Manager
5	Doris	Ajar	Sales Representative
6	Lane	Clozure	Office Manager
7	Joseph	Swipple	Vice President, Mark
8	Helen	Wheels	Product Evangelist
9	Ed	Honcho	President
(AutoNumber)			

Record: 1 of 9

You can switch from datasheet form to form view by choosing View ➤ Form View or by clicking the drop-down arrow next to the View toolbar button and then choosing Form View. In form view the fields appear in a tabular layout, but only one record is visible on each page of the form. Figure 11.4 shows the Employees form after we switched from datasheet form to form view; this example uses the International style.

FIGURE 11.4

The datasheet form, shown in form view. To resize the window to fit snugly, we chose Window ➤ Size to Fit Form.

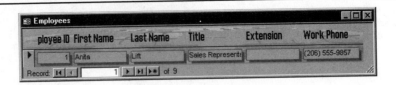

ployee ID	First Name	Last Name	Title	Extension	Work Phone
1	Anita	Lift	Sales Represent		(206) 555-9857

Record: 1 of 9

NOTE   The form wizards take their best guess when trying to fit labels and fields on your form. After creating the form, you may need to switch to design view and refine the design. In Figure 11.4, for example, the Employee ID label is cut off because the font is too large. To fix this problem, switch to design view and widen the label control or choose a smaller font for the labels.

Hierarchical Forms

Sometimes you'll want to work with related tables in your forms. For example, you might want to design an order form that includes customer and order information, along with details about the products ordered. A hierarchical form showing data from tables that have a one-to-many relationship is perfect for jobs like this.

The form wizards can create hierarchical forms in two basic flavors: a main form and subforms, or a main form and linked forms. (A *subform* is a separate form that's embedded in a main form.)

Figure 11.5 shows a main form with subforms and displays information from four tables: Customers, Orders, Order Details, and Products. The main form shows fields from the Customers table, arranged in columnar layout. The subforms for the Orders table and the Order Details and Products tables appear in datasheet layout.

PART

II

Creating a Database

FIGURE 11.5

This hierarchical main form shows fields from the Customers table, and its two datasheet subforms show fields from the Orders, Order Details, and Products tables. This example uses the Sandstone style.

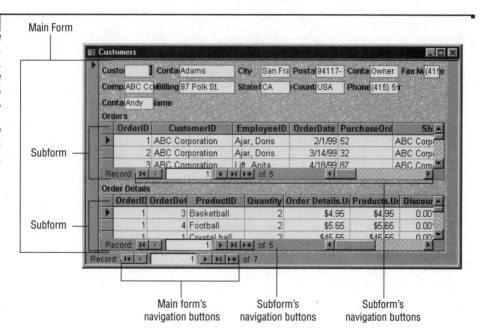

NOTE The main form and subform often go by the names *main/subform, form/subform*, or *master/detail form*.

Linked forms, such as those shown in Figures 11.6 and 11.7, also present multitable data hierarchically. But instead of showing all the fields from the main table crowded on the same page used for subforms, the main table's fields appear on a separate form. You can then click the command button near the top of the form to show records that are synchronized with the record on the first form. The linked form can be a main form or a main form with a subform.

Command button opens linked form.

Customer ID	**Contact Title** Owner
Company Name ABC Corporation	**Phone Number** (415) 555-5938
Contact First N Andy	**Fax Number** (415) 555-5939
Contact Last N Adams	
Billing Address 87 Polk St. Suite 5	
City San Francisco	
State/Province CA	
Postal Code 94117-	
Country USA	

Record: 1 of 7

Main form

To produce the forms shown in Figures 11.5, 11.6, and 11.7, we ran the Form Wizard and selected all fields from the Customers, Orders, and Order Details tables and just the Unit Price field from the Products table. While viewing the Order Details subform, we dragged the Unit Price field for the Products table next to the Unit Price field for the Order Details table; this arrangement lets us see the unit price from the Products table while we enter the actual selling price into the Unit Price field of the Order Details table. We also dragged the OrderID field in the Order Details subform to the left of the OrderDetailID field.

FIGURE 11.7

The linked form and subform appear when we click the Orders button shown in Figure 11.6. This form shows Orders, Order Details, and Product information for the customer whose name appears in Figure 11.6. To return to the main form, close the linked form.

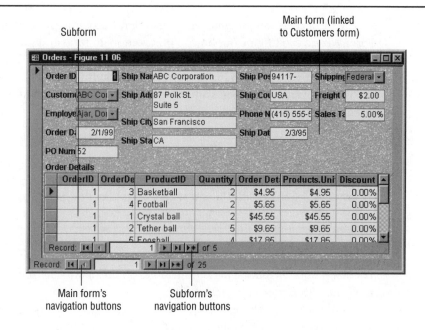

Subform

Main form (linked to Customers form)

Main form's navigation buttons

Subform's navigation buttons

 TIP If you've already created forms that include the necessary linking fields, you can quickly combine them into a main form with a subform. To do so, open the main form in design view, press F11 to bring the database window to the front, click the Forms tab on the database window, and choose Window ➢ Tile Vertically. Then drag the subform from the database window to an appropriate spot on the main form's design window and respond to any prompts that appear. See Chapter 13 for more details.

Making Hierarchical Forms Work Properly

To work properly, the main form and subform must be linked by a common field in a one-to-many relationship (or, less often, a one-to-one relationship).

- The table or query on the one side—for example, Customers—supplies data for the main form.

- The table or query on the many side—for example, Orders—supplies data for the subform.

- The forms are linked by a primary key field on the one side and a normal field (called the *foreign key*) on the many side. In the Customers and Orders example, CustomerID is the primary key field on the one side and a foreign key on the many side.

The most common problem with creating hierarchical forms occurs when the Form Wizard can't figure out how to link your main form and subform. This problem can occur, for example, if you haven't explicitly set up a relationship between the tables, either via the Relationships window or a multitable query. As you'll see shortly, the Form Wizard will let you know when this problem exists, and it will give you a chance to set up relationships.

NOTE Chapter 6 explains how to use the Relationships window to define relationships between tables in your database. Chapter 10 explains how to use queries to define relationships, select specific data, and perform calculations on data. Chapter 13 explains how to set properties that link main forms and subforms.

One way to get the most out of using the form wizards is to create hierarchical forms. For best results, include all fields from tables on the many side. You can always remove unwanted fields or rearrange them later.

In some cases involving multiple related tables that have lookup fields, Access may not connect the related tables and fields properly, and it might not tell you that it is unable to do so. For example, when we included all the Order Entry database fields from our sample Customers, Orders, Order Details, and Products tables on a form, the drop-down list for the ProductID field in the Order Details subform was empty, and the lookup values displayed incorrectly.

To work around this glitch, we opened the problem subform (Order Details Subform) in form design view, opened the property sheet (View ➢ Properties), and clicked on the OrderDetails.ProductID control. Then we changed its Row Source property to Products, its Column Count property to 2, and its Column Widths property to 0";1" and saved the subform. See Chapter 6 for information about lookup fields and Chapter 13 for details about working with properties.

You should also avoid renaming subforms or linked forms. Doing so can prevent Access from finding and opening those forms. If you do rename the forms, you'll need to open each main form and subform in design view, choose View ➢ Properties (if the property sheet isn't visible), and click the All tab on the property sheet. Then fix every reference to the old form name in the Name and Source Object properties and in all Event Procedures. (You can edit any event procedure, and then use the Edit ➢ Replace command to globally change references in the current module.) Be sure to fix these properties for the entire form and for any command buttons and subforms on the form.

For more details about creating hierarchical forms, look up *Creating Subforms* with the Office Assistant. Chapter 13 explains how to alter properties and select controls. See Parts IV and V for more about events and the Visual Basic program code that's used in Event Procedures.

Charts

Charts convert the numbers in your data to useful graphs that help to clarify the meaning of those numbers. The chart in Figure 11.8 shows the contribution of each customer's orders to the company's total sales. We used a Select query as the data source for the sample chart (refer to Figure 10.17 in Chapter 10). Chapter 15 explains how to create charts.

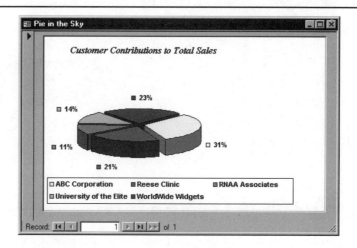

FIGURE 11.8

A pie chart showing the contribution of each customer's orders to total sales. We tweaked the appearance of this chart after the Chart Wizard created it.

PivotTables

A PivotTable lets you summarize large amounts of data, much as a Crosstab query does (see Chapter 10). But a PivotTable is more flexible than a Crosstab query because it lets you interactively switch the row labels, column labels, and summary calculations as needed. In Figure 11.9 you see a PivotTable opened in Excel from an Access form. Chapter 14 explains how to create and use PivotTables.

 NOTE   You must have Microsoft Excel installed to create and use PivotTables.

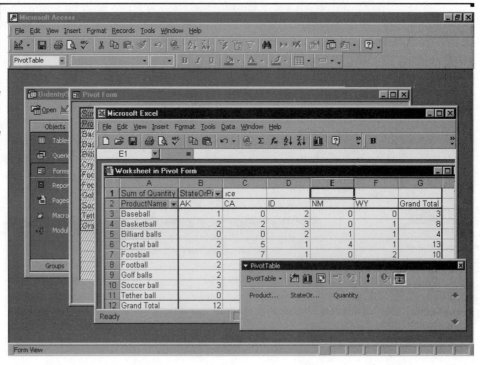

This PivotTable shows the number of each product sold, by state. After opening a form showing a PivotTable in Access, we clicked on the Edit Pivot Table button (not shown) to launch Microsoft Excel and customize the PivotTable as needed.

Using Wizards to Create a Form

Now that you've seen the many types of forms the form wizards can create, why not try the wizards? The steps are easy:

1. Start from any of these places:

- **To base your form on a specific table**, start from the database window, click the Tables button, and highlight the table name. Or open the table in datasheet view. If the table has a filter and sort order associated with it, the new form will inherit the filter and sort order automatically (see Chapter 9).

NOTE   You also can start your form from table design view. If you do, however, the form can be displayed in design view only; you'll get an error message that your table is exclusively locked (click OK to clear the message). To view the form in form view, pull down the Window menu and switch to the table design window. Then close the table design window (Ctrl+W), switch back to the form design window, and click the Form View toolbar button.

- **To base your form on a specific query (or saved filter)**, start from the database window, click the Queries button, and highlight the query name. Or open the query in datasheet or design view.

- **If you're not sure which table or query you want to base the form on**, start anywhere in Access (of course, a database must be open) or click the Forms button in the database window. If you know you want to use the Form Wizard (and not one of the AutoForm options), double-click Create a Form with the Wizard and skip to step 6 below.

2. Click the drop-down arrow next to the New Object toolbar button. You'll see this menu:

3. Choose one of these options:

   AutoForm Creates a one-column form using the template named in the Form Template box on the Forms/Reports tab of the Options dialog box (Tools ➢ Options ➢ Forms/Reports; see Chapter 16). Typically, this template is named Normal, and it resembles the Standard style shown in Figure 11.1. After choosing this option, skip to step 11—you're done! Using the Auto-Form option makes sense only if you selected a table or query in step 1.

   Form Opens the New Form dialog box, shown here:

TIP To open the New Form dialog box in fewer steps, click the Forms tab in step 1, and then click the New button in the database window. Or start from any place in the database window and choose Insert ➤ Form. To create an AutoForm quickly, highlight a table or query name on the Tables or Queries tab in the database window, and then choose Insert ➤ AutoForm.

4. Choose the table or query from the drop-down list (near the bottom of the New Form dialog box) on which you want to base the form. (This box may be filled in already.)

 NOTE You must select a table or query before choosing any of the AutoForm wizards or the Chart Wizard in step 5. If you plan to use the Form Wizard or PivotTable Wizard in step 5, you'll have another chance to choose tables and queries.

5. Click one of the following options (they appear in the list near the top of the New Form dialog box), and then click OK; or just double-click the appropriate option. When you click an option, the area in the left side of the dialog box will show an example and describe the form the selected option will create. Your options are as follows:

Design View Opens an empty form design window.

Form Wizard Opens the Form Wizard. From here you can select which tables, queries, and fields to include on the form, create subforms or linked forms (if appropriate), choose a style for the form, and specify a title and name for your form. Figures 11.1 through 11.7 show examples of forms that we created with the Form Wizard.

AutoForm: Columnar Creates a columnar form from all the fields in the selected table or query (see Figure 11.1) without asking any more questions.

AutoForm: Tabular Creates a tabular form (see Figure 11.2) without asking any more questions.

AutoForm: Datasheet Creates a datasheet form (see Figures 11.3 and 11.4) without asking any more questions.

NOTE When you choose AutoForm: Columnar, AutoForm: Tabular, or AutoForm: Datasheet, Access places fields in the order they're defined in the table design or query, puts the name of the table or query on the form's title bar, and uses the default style. The default style is the style you (or someone else) chose most recently. If necessary, the wizard will create a main form and subforms, even if you don't ask it to. After choosing an AutoForm option, skip to step 11 and then save your form.

Chart Wizard Creates a form that displays a free-standing chart of your table or query data (see Figure 11.8 and Chapter 15).

PivotTable Wizard Creates a form that can display a Microsoft Excel PivotTable (see Figure 11.9 and Chapter 15).

6. Assuming you chose Form Wizard in step 5, you'll see the first Form Wizard dialog box, shown in Figure 11.10. Use any of the techniques described below to add as many fields from as many tables or queries as you need, and then click Next.

PART

II

Creating a Database

FIGURE 11.10

Use this Form Wizard dialog box to specify which fields should appear on your form. You can select fields from as many tables and queries as you wish. Access will use your selections to decide how to lay out the form.

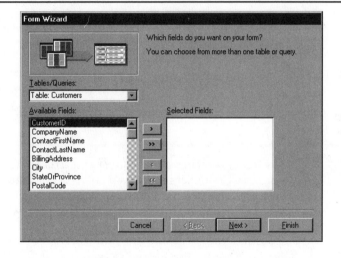

- **To select a table or query**, click the drop-down arrow button below Tables/Queries and then choose the table or query to use.

- **To add one field to the form**, click in the Selected Fields list where the new field should appear (optional). Then double-click the field in the Available Fields list, or click the field in the Available Fields list and then click the > button. The field you select will move to the Selected Fields list and will appear on the form in the order shown.

- **To copy all the Available Fields to the Selected Fields list**, click in the Selected Fields list where the new fields should appear and then click the >> button.

- **To remove a field from the Selected Fields list**, double-click that field, or click the field and then click the < button.

- **To remove all fields from the Selected Fields list**, click the << button. The fields will reappear in the Available Fields list.

7. If you chose fields from multiple tables, but haven't yet defined relationships between the tables, the Wizard will display the dialog box shown below. Click OK if you want to exit the Wizard and define relationships (see Chapter 6), or click Cancel to return to step 6 and remove some fields from your form.

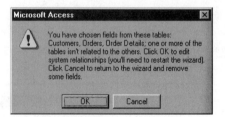

8. In the next dialog box or two, you'll be asked to choose a layout of Columnar, Tabular, Datasheet, Justified, Form with Subform(s), or Linked Forms, depending on which tables and fields you selected in step 6. Choose the options you want, and then click Next to continue to the next dialog box.

 TIP As you make choices in the dialog boxes described in steps 8 and 9, the Wizard will give you detailed instructions and show previews of your form as it takes shape. Just watch the screen carefully and you shouldn't have any trouble figuring out what to do.

---

9. Choose a style by clicking one of the available styles, and then click Next. For maximum readability, choose the Standard style. (As Chapter 13 explains, you can customize the styles and create new ones of your own. Later in this chapter we'll show you how to change a form's style instantly.)

10. Accept or change the suggested title(s) in the last Form Wizard dialog box (see Figure 11.11), choose the option that lets you view or enter information (because this option usually is most convenient), and then click Finish.

FIGURE 11.11

The final Form Wizard dialog box. It's often easiest to accept the default settings and click Finish. This example shows a final dialog box for a form with linked subforms; the final dialog box for a simple form without subforms is similar.

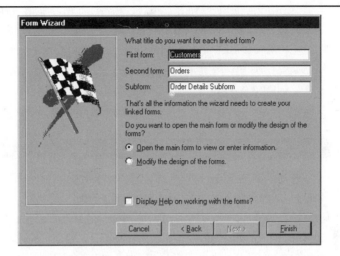

 WARNING The title you select in step 10 is used for the form name, the form's Caption property (which displays text on the form's title bar), the command button's Caption property (which displays text on the command button of a main form that has a linked form), and the Visual Basic code that Access creates behind the form. If a form with the same name already exists in the database, you'll have a chance to overwrite the existing form or choose a different title.

11. (Optional) Resize or maximize the form that Access created for you. As long as the form is not maximized, you can choose Window ➢ Size to Fit Form to get a nice snug fit of the form window around the form's fields.

After your form appears in form view, you can:

- Use your form to edit existing records or add new ones (see "Opening and Using a Form" later in this chapter).

- Edit or add records in datasheet view. To switch to datasheet view, choose View ➢ Datasheet View, or click the drop-down arrow button next to the Form View toolbar button and choose Datasheet View.

- Change the form's design in design view, as explained in Chapter 13. To switch to design view, click the Form View toolbar button, or choose View ➢ Design View, or click the drop-down arrow button next to the Form View button and choose Design View. Typically, you'll just need to rearrange or widen the fields and labels. You had a chance to rearrange and resize fields in the Chapter 3 hands-on lessons.

- Print or print preview the form (see Chapters 3 and 9).

- Sort or filter the records, or search for records that meet specific criteria (see Chapters 3 and 9).

- Save and close the form (see "Saving a Form" later in this chapter).

How the Wizards Build Your Form

The form wizards construct your forms from nothing more than your answers to a few questions. For their most important conjuring jobs, the wizards make sure data from multiple tables is synchronized properly, and they size and place fields and buttons on the form so that everything fits on the screen.

If the form is based on fields from multiple tables and/or queries, the wizard creates an SQL statement behind the form that specifies which tables, queries, and fields to use and sets up the necessary table relationships. All this happens automatically, so you don't have to worry about it, and you rarely need to set up multitable queries just to display fields from several tables at once.

When sizing each control, the wizard lays out all the necessary fields, regardless of the current page/form size. If the resulting form is too big for the screen, the wizard calculates the ratio of the total size of the too-big form to the desired page/form size; then it shrinks every control by that ratio to create a form of the maximum allowable size. Because the wizard uses a simple ratio method for sizing controls on forms—rather than trying millions of combinations to arrive at something that's esthetically pleasing—you may need to switch to design view and tweak the size, position, or font for controls that appear squashed. Chapter 13 explains how to do all that.

Saving a Form

If the wizard didn't save your form automatically, you should save the form if you want to use it later. Here's how:

1. Choose File ➢ Close, or press Ctrl+W, or click the Close button at the upper-right corner of the form to save and close the form; then click Yes. Or if you just want to save your latest changes, press Ctrl+S, or choose File ➤ Save, or click the Save toolbar button.

2. Type a name when prompted (up to 64 characters, including blanks) the first time you save a form that hasn't been saved before, and then click OK.

Opening and Using a Form

If you've closed a form, you can reopen it with these steps:

1. Start in the database window and click the Forms button.

2. Do one of the following:

- **To open the form in form view** (with data displayed), double-click the form name you want to open, or click it and then click the Open button.

- **To open the form in design view** (where you can change the form's design), click the form name and then click Design. Or right-click the form name and select Design.

Assuming you've opened the form in form view, you can use any technique discussed in Chapter 8 to edit data and add or delete records. Table 11.1 summarizes what you can do.

 TIP Copying offers a quick way to create a new form that's based on an existing form. To copy a form, click the Forms tab in the database window, highlight the form to copy, and press Ctrl+C. Next, press Ctrl+V, type a name for the new form, and click OK. If the Clipboard toolbar pops up during this process, click its Close button to hide it again.

TABLE 11.1: NAVIGATING AND EDITING IN FORMS

TO DO THIS...	PRESS, CLICK, OR CHOOSE THIS	TOOLBAR BUTTON
Switch from editing mode to navigation mode (cursor moves from field to field)	F2, or Tab, or Shift+Tab, or click the field name	

Continued ▐▶

TABLE 11.1: NAVIGATING AND EDITING IN FORMS (CONTINUED)

TO DO THIS...	PRESS, CLICK, OR CHOOSE THIS	TOOLBAR BUTTON
Switch from navigation mode to editing mode (cursor moves within a field)	F2 or click in a field	

Navigate in Editing Mode

End of field (multiline field)	Ctrl+End
End of line	End
One character to left	←
One character to right	→
One word to left	Ctrl+←
One word to right	Ctrl+→
Start of field (multiline field)	Ctrl+Home
Start of line	Home

Edit in a Field

Delete character to left of cursor	Backspace
Delete character to right of cursor	Delete
Delete selected text	Select text and then press Delete or Backspace
Delete to end of word	Ctrl+Delete
Delete to start of word	Ctrl+Backspace
Insert default value for a field	Ctrl+Alt+Spacebar
Insert new line	Ctrl+Enter
Insert system date	Ctrl+;
Insert system time	Ctrl+: (same as Ctrl+Shift+;)
Insert value from same field in previous record	Ctrl+' or Ctrl+" (same as Ctrl+Shift+')

Navigate in Navigation Mode

Current field (of the next record)	Ctrl+Page Down
Current field (of the previous record)	Ctrl+Page Up
Cycle forward or backward through header, detail section, and footer of form	F6 (forward) or Shift+F6 (backward)
Down one page or to next record if you're at end of a record	Page Down
First field (of the first record)	Ctrl+Home

Continued ▶

TABLE 11.1: NAVIGATING AND EDITING IN FORMS (CONTINUED)

TO DO THIS...	PRESS, CLICK, OR CHOOSE THIS	TOOLBAR BUTTON
Navigate in Navigation Mode		
First record	First Record navigation button or Edit ➢ Go To ➢ First	
Last field (current record)	End	
Last field (last record)	Ctrl+End	
Last record	Last Record navigation button or Edit ➢ Go To ➢ Last	
Next field (current record)	Tab or → or Enter	
Next record	Next Record navigation button or Edit ➢ Go To ➢ Next	
Previous field (current record)	Shift+Tab or ←	
Previous record	Previous Record navigation button or Edit ➢ Go To ➢ Previous	
Specific record	F5; then type record number and press Enter	1
Up one page or to previous record if you're at end of a record	Page Up	
Copy, Cut, and Paste Clipboard Contents		
Copy selected text to Clipboard	Ctrl+C, or Copy button, or Edit ➢ Copy	
Cut selected text to Clipboard	Ctrl+X, or Cut button, or Edit ➢ Cut	
Paste selected text from Clipboard	Position cursor and then press Ctrl+V or click Paste button, or Edit ➢ Paste	
Add, Delete, Select, and Save Records		
Add new record (shows all existing records; navigation buttons work normally)	Ctrl++ (plus sign), or New button, or New navigation button, or Edit ➢ Go To ➢ New Record	

Continued ▶

TABLE 11.1: NAVIGATING AND EDITING IN FORMS (CONTINUED)

TO DO THIS...	PRESS, CLICK, OR CHOOSE THIS	TOOLBAR BUTTON
Add, Delete, Select, and Save Records		
Add new record in Data Entry mode (hides all existing records)	Records ➤ Data Entry. To resume normal editing, choose Records ➤ Remove Filter/Sort or right-click form and choose Remove Filter/Sort.	
Delete current record	Ctrl+- (minus sign), or select current record and press Delete, or click Delete Record button	
Save changes to current record	Shift+Enter	
Select all records	Ctrl+A or Edit ➤ Select All Records	
Select current record	Click Record Selector bar at left edge of form, or Edit ➤ Select Record	
Undo all changes to current field or record	Esc, or Ctrl+Z, or Undo button, or Edit ➤ Undo repeatedly	
Undo most recent change	Esc, or Ctrl+Z, or Undo button, or Edit ➤ Undo once	
Miscellaneous Operations		
Datasheet view	Form View button's drop-down arrow and Datasheet View, or View ➤ Datasheet View	
Design view	Form View button's drop-down arrow and Design View, or View ➤ Design View	
Filter (apply)	Apply Filter button or Records ➤ Apply Filter/Sort, or right-click form and choose Apply Filter/Sort	
Filter by Input	Right-click in field; enter value after Filter For	
Filter by Form (create/edit)	Filter by Form button, or Records ➤ Filter ➤ Filter by Form, or right-click form and choose Filter by Form	

Continued ▶

TABLE 11.1: NAVIGATING AND EDITING IN FORMS (CONTINUED)

TO DO THIS...	PRESS, CLICK, OR CHOOSE THIS	TOOLBAR BUTTON
Miscellaneous Operations		
Filter Excluding Selection (create/edit)	Right-click field with value to exclude and choose Filter Excluding Selection, or Records ➤ Filter ➤ Filter Excluding Selection	
Filter by Selection (create/edit)	Filter by Selection button, or Records ➤ Filter ➤ Filter by Selection, or right-click field and choose Filter by Selection	
Filter (create/edit advanced)	Records ➤ Filter ➤ Advanced Filter/Sort	
Filter (remove)	Remove Filter button or Records ➤ Remove Filter/Sort, or right-click form and choose Remove Filter/Sort	
Find a record	Ctrl+F, or Find button, or Edit ➤ Find	
Form view	Form View button's drop-down arrow and Form View, or View ➤ Form View	
Print preview records	Print Preview button or File ➤ Print Preview	
Print records	Print button, Ctrl+P, or File ➤ Print	
Replace text in a record	Ctrl+H or Edit ➤ Replace	
Sort records (A–Z, 0–9 order)	Sort Ascending button, or Records ➤ Sort ➤ Sort Ascending, or right-click field and choose Sort Ascending	
Sort records (Z–A, 9–0 order)	Sort Descending button, or Records ➤ Sort ➤ Sort Descending, or right-click field and choose Sort Descending.	

PART

II

Creating a Database

Getting Around in Hierarchical Forms

Once you've created a main/subform (refer to Figures 11.5 and 11.7), using it is similar to using normal forms (see Table 11.1). However, you need to be aware of some crucial differences, which are described in Table 11.2.

TABLE 11.2: SPECIAL TECHNIQUES FOR USING MAIN/SUBFORMS

TO DO THIS...	PRESS OR CHOOSE THIS...
Using Navigation mode	
Exit last field of subform or move to next field if not in subform	Enter or Tab
Exit first field of subform or move to previous field if not in subform	Ctrl+Tab or click in main form
Move cursor from subform to main form	Ctrl+Shift+Tab or click in main form
Move cursor from record to record in main form	Page Up, or Page Down, or click main form's navigation buttons, or click in main form and choose appropriate options from Edit ➤ Go To menus
Move cursor from record to record in subform	Click subform's navigation buttons or click in subform and choose appropriate options from Edit ➤ Go To menus
Move cursor to first editable field in main form	Ctrl+Shift+Home or click in first editable field in main form
Toggle between subform datasheet view and subform form view	Click in subform and then choose View ➤ Datasheet View
Adding, Deleting, or Changing Records	
Add record to main form	Position cursor in main form, and then click New toolbar button or choose Edit ➤ Go To ➤ New Record
Add record to subform	Position cursor in subform, and then click New toolbar button or choose Edit ➤ Go To ➤ New Record
Change data in main form	Position cursor in appropriate field of main form and edit as usual

Continued ▐▶

TABLE 11.2: SPECIAL TECHNIQUES FOR USING MAIN/SUBFORMS (CONTINUED)	
TO DO THIS...	**PRESS OR CHOOSE THIS**...
Adding, Deleting, or Changing Records	
Change data in subform	Position cursor in appropriate field of subform and edit as usual
Delete record in main form	Click record selector in main form, press Delete, and then click Yes
Delete record in subform	Click record selector in subform, press Delete, and then click Yes

If you created a linked form, click the command button at the top of the main form, and then use the main form and subform as described in Table 11.2. When you're finished using the linked form, click its Close button or press Ctrl+W.

When using main/subforms, keep the following points in mind:

- You need to be especially careful to notice where the cursor is when you add or delete records in main/subforms. See Table 11.2 for details.

- You can adjust the row height, column width, and position of columns on a datasheet subform, just as you do in a table's datasheet view (see Chapter 8). For example, you can drag the rows or columns just as you would any grid in datasheet view. Access will save your changes automatically.

- You can set a filter for records in the main form or the subform(s).

- If you add a record to a subform and then change your mind while the cursor is still in the record, click the Undo toolbar button or press Esc.

Changing the Style of a Form

Suppose you used the form wizards to create a form that has the Ricepaper or International style, and now you decide that the Standard style would look better. You needn't re-create the form to change its style. Just follow these steps:

1. Open the form in design view. If you're starting from the database window, click the Forms button, click the form you want to change, and then click the Design button. Or if the form is currently open in form view, click the Design View toolbar button (shown at left) or choose View ➢ Design View.

2. Make sure the form itself is selected. (Click the box at the left side of the vertical ruler, if necessary.) Then choose Format ➢ AutoFormat, or click the AutoFormat button (shown at left) on the Form Design toolbar. You'll see the AutoFormat dialog box, shown in Figure 11.12.

FIGURE 11.12

Use the AutoFormat dialog box to instantly change the style for your form or to customize an existing style. Switch to form design view and choose Format ➢ AutoFormat to open this dialog box.

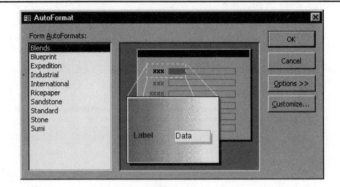

3. Click the format you want to use in the AutoFormat dialog box. The sample form in the dialog box will reflect your current choice.

4. Click OK to reformat the form, and respond to any prompts that appear.

5. Save your changes (Ctrl+S) and click the Form View toolbar button, or choose View ➢ Form View to switch back to form view.

See Chapter 13 for more about designing forms, using the AutoFormat feature, and creating custom styles. Or look up *AutoFormat* with the Office Assistant.

Where to Go from Here

This chapter introduced the many types of instant forms you can create with form wizards. From here you can continue with Chapter 12 to learn about designing instant reports with report wizards, or skip to Chapter 13 to learn about designing new forms and reports from scratch and customizing existing forms and reports.

What's New in the Access Zoo?

The Form Wizard in Access 2000 works the same as in Access 97, except for one difference. When you select the style for a form, there is now a new group of styles to choose from. Some old styles (Flax and Clouds among them) have been replaced with new styles like Sandstone and Ricepaper. Any old forms you created with the obsolete styles will still work. If you want to add the old styles to the new style list, see "Customizing AutoFormat Styles" in Chapter 13.

CHAPTER **12**

Creating Reports with Report Wizards

FEATURING:

For most of us, printing the data stored in tables or the information gathered from queries is an essential part of using a database. Access report wizards provide easy-to-use—yet powerful—tools for creating reports in several pre-defined formats. Even if you plan to customize the designs later (as we did in many examples shown in this chapter), you'll save time if you use the report wizards to set up reports.

 NOTE Chapter 3 explains how to work with wizards and gives you hands-on practice with report wizards. Chapter 9 covers printing. In Chapter 13, you'll learn how to design forms and reports from scratch, and how to customize existing designs.

If you need more help with designing a new report, use the Office Assistant to look for help on *Creating Reports* and explore the subtopics that appear.

What Kinds of Reports Can the Wizards Create?

The report wizards can create several types of reports showing fields from one or more tables and/or queries. To help you decide which type of wizard-designed report might be best for your own data, we'll show some examples. Then we'll explain how to create, save, and use wizard-generated reports.

Columnar (Vertical) Reports

In a columnar or vertical report, each field appears on a separate line with a label to its left. Figure 12.1 shows a sample columnar report for the Products table.

 TIP You can customize the styles available in report wizards. To get started, open any report in design view and choose Format ➤ AutoFormat or click the AutoFormat button on the Report Design toolbar. In the AutoFormat dialog box, click the format you want to customize and then click the Customize button.

A columnar report for
the Products table in
the Soft Gray style.

Products

Product ID	1
Product Name	Basketball
Unit Price	$4.95
Product ID	2
Product Name	Football
Unit Price	$5.65
Product ID	3
Product Name	Soccer ball
Unit Price	$12.95
Product ID	4
Product Name	Volleyball
Unit Price	$3.25
Product ID	5
Product Name	Golf balls
Unit Price	$6.75
Product ID	6
Product Name	Crystal ball
Unit Price	$45.55
Product ID	7
Product Name	Baseball
Unit Price	$8.75
Product ID	8
Product Name	Billiard balls
Unit Price	$127.45

PART

II

Creating a Database

Tabular Reports

Figure 12.2 shows a tabular report for the Products table. As you can see, tabular
reports display fields in a horizontal row with field labels at the top of the report.
Each new row represents a new record.

FIGURE 12.2

A tabular report for the Products table in the Bold style. The tabular layout is best used when you have just a few narrow fields to display and you want to see many records on a single page.

Products

Product ID	Product Name	Unit Price
1	Basketball	$4.95
2	Football	$5.65
3	Soccer ball	$12.95
4	Volleyball	$3.25
5	Golf balls	$6.75
6	Crystal ball	$45.55
7	Baseball	$8.75
8	Billiard balls	$127.45
9	Tether ball	$9.65
10	Foosball	$17.85

Wednesday, January 20, 1999   Page 1 of 1

Groups, Totals, and Summary Reports

Groups/totals reports, such as the one shown in Figure 12.3, organize your data into groups that appear in tabular format. At your request, the wizard will calculate sum, average, minimum, and maximum values for numeric and currency fields in each group and display sums as percentages of totals.

A Casual style groups/totals report that's grouped by Order Date and subtotaled on numeric and currency fields. This report is in Outline1 form. We tailored the appearance of this report after the Report Wizard created it.

Orders by Date

Order Date	2/1/99			
Product Name	**Quantity**	**Unit Price**	**Discount**	**$ Before Tax**
Basketball	1	$4.95	0.00%	$4.95
Basketball	2	$4.95	0.00%	$9.90
Billiard balls	2	$127.45	0.00%	$254.90
Crystal ball	2	$45.55	0.00%	$91.10
Foosball	4	$17.85	0.00%	$71.40
Football	1	$5.65	0.00%	$5.65
Football	2	$5.65	0.00%	$11.30
Football	1	$5.65	0.00%	$5.65
Tether ball	5	$9.65	0.00%	$48.25

Summary for 'OrderDate' = 2/1/99 (9 detail records)

Sum	20			$503.10
Avg	2.22	$25.26	0.00%	$55.90
Min	1	$4.95	0.00%	$4.95
Max	5	$127.45	0.00%	$254.90
Percent	25.97%			30.57%

Order Date	2/11/99			
Product Name	**Quantity**	**Unit Price**	**Discount**	**$ Before Tax**
Baseball	2	$8.75	0.00%	$17.50
Basketball	1	$4.95	0.00%	$4.95
Basketball	2	$4.95	0.00%	$9.90
Football	1	$5.65	0.00%	$5.65

Summary for 'OrderDate' = 2/11/99 (4 detail records)

Sum	6			$38.00
Avg	1.50	$6.08	0.00%	$9.50
Min	1	$4.95	0.00%	$4.95
Max	2	$8.75	0.00%	$17.50
Percent	7.79%			2.31%

PART

II

Creating a Database

When the Report Wizard Needs Your Help

Sometimes you'll need to add your own formatting refinements in report design view, especially for reports that present summary calculations and are based on queries that also involve calculations. Fortunately, making such refinements takes only a few minutes and is much faster than building a complicated report from scratch.

For example, after the Report Wizard created the first version of the report shown in Figure 12.3, the Quantity column heading was a bit too narrow, and formats for the Sum, Avg, Min, Max, and grand total calculations weren't quite right. To fix these problems, we switched to report design view, opened the property sheet (View ➤ Properties), and clicked on the property sheet's Format tab. Then we did the following:

- Widened the bold label for Quantity near the top of the report design.
- Selected all the controls that present summary calculations and changed their Text Align property to Right.
- Selected the control that displays average quantity (Avg in the Quantity column) and changed its Format property to Fixed and the number of decimal places to 2.
- Opened the Sorting and Grouping dialog box (View ➤ Sorting and Grouping), selected OrderDate in the Field/Expression column, and changed the Keep Together group property to Whole Group.

We also made similar changes to the first version of the report shown in Figure 12.5. See Chapter 13 for more about changing report formats.

The group/totals report shown in Figure 12.3 is based on the query shown in Figure 12.4.

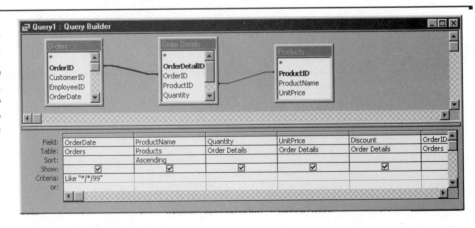

FIGURE 12.4

This multitable query supplies data for the report in Figure 12.3, showing orders placed in 1999. (See Chapter 10 for more about creating queries like this one.)

Summary reports are just like group/totals reports except that they omit the detail records between each group. Figure 12.5 shows a report that's almost the same as Figure 12.3, only designed as a summary report. (We omitted the Product Name field in Figure 12.5.) This report is also based on the query shown in Figure 12.4.

FIGURE 12.5

A summary report looks like a group/totals report, but without the detail records between each group. For variety, we've shown this report in the Corporate style, in Outline2 format. We tailored the appearance of this report after the Report Wizard created it.

Orders By Date (Summary)

Order Date		2/1/99		
	Quantity	**Unit Price**	**Discount**	**$ Before Tax**
				Summary for 'OrderDate' = 2/1/99 (9 detail records
Sum	20			$503.10
Avg	2.22	$25.26	0.00%	$55.90
Min	1	$4.95	0.00%	$4.95
Max	5	$127.45	0.00%	$254.90
Percent	25.97%			30.57%

Order Date		2/11/99		
	Quantity	**Unit Price**	**Discount**	**$ Before Tax**
				Summary for 'OrderDate' = 2/11/99 (4 detail records
Sum	6			$38.00
Avg	1.50	$6.08	0.00%	$9.50
Min	1	$4.95	0.00%	$4.95
Max	2	$8.75	0.00%	$17.50
Percent	7.79%			2.31%

Order Date		2/18/99		
	Quantity	**Unit Price**	**Discount**	**$ Before Tax**
				Summary for 'OrderDate' = 2/18/99 (2 detail records
Sum	2			$52.29
Avg	1.00	$26.15	0.05%	$26.15
Min	1	$6.75	0.00%	$6.74
Max	1	$45.55	0.10%	$45.55
Percent	2.60%			3.18%

Order Date		2/25/99		
	Quantity	**Unit Price**	**Discount**	**$ Before Tax**
				Summary for 'OrderDate' = 2/25/99 (1 detail record
Sum	2			$11.30
Avg	2.00	$5.65	0.00%	$11.30
Min	2	$5.65	0.00%	$11.30
Max	2	$5.65	0.00%	$11.30
Percent	2.60%			0.69%

PART

II

Creating a Database

Charts

Charts convert the numbers in your data to meaningful graphs. The chart in Figure 12.6 shows the contribution of each customer's orders to the company's total sales. We used a Select query as the data source for the sample chart (see Figure 10.17 in Chapter 10).

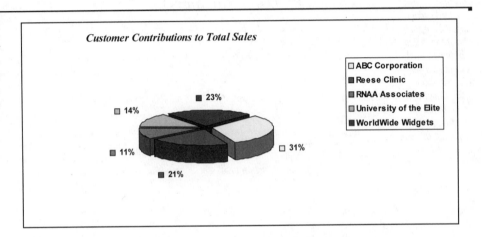

Charting is basically the same, whether you display the chart on a form or a report. So once you know how to create a form-based chart, you also know how to create a report-based chart. Chapter 15 explains how to create charts.

TIP If you've already saved a chart as a form, you can quickly convert it to a report. To do so, click the Forms button in the database window, right-click the chart you want to save as a report and choose Save As. In the Save As dialog box, type a name for the new report, change the setting for As to Report, and then click OK. The newly saved report will appear when you click the Reports button in the database window. You can also use this technique to save a form as a data access page.

Mailing Labels

You can design mailing labels that will print on standard Avery mailing label stock. Figure 12.7 shows some garden-variety mailing labels formatted for Avery 5196 (3.5" diskette) labels. See "Creating Mailing Labels," later in this chapter, to find out how to produce mailing labels from your Access data.

FIGURE 12.7

Mailing labels sorted in postal code, last name, and first name order. This example is formatted for Avery 5196 (3.5" diskette) labels. We used a Format function to display the postal codes with hyphens (for example, 92575-4747).

Wilbur Stumingi
University of the Elite
P.O. Box 555
Lander, WY 82520-
USA

Shirley Ujest
WorldWide Widgets
187 Suffolk Ln.
Boise, ID 83720-
USA

Susita Schumack
Reese Clinic
2817 Milton Dr.
Albuquerque, NM 87110-
USA

Anita Adams
Database Search and Rescue
5356 E. 20th St.
Santa Fe, NM 87110-3857
USA

Sheila Stumingi
Precision Bagpipes
P.O. Box 23981
San Diego, CA 92575-4747
USA

Andy Adams
ABC Corporation
87 Polk St.
Suite 5
San Francisco, CA 94117-
USA

Hanley Strappman
RNAA Associates
2743 Bering St.
Anchorage, AK 99508-
USA

Using Wizards to Create a Report

The procedures for creating a report with wizards depend on the type of report you choose, but these are the basic steps:

1. Start from any of these places:

- **To base your report on a specific table**, start from the database window, click the Tables button, and highlight the table name. Or open the table in datasheet view. If the table has a filter and sort order associated with it, the new report will inherit the filter and sort order automatically (see Chapter 9 and "Removing a Filter and Sort Order" later in this chapter for more details).

 NOTE You also can start from table design view. If you do, however, the report can be displayed in design view only, and you'll get an error message that your table is exclusively locked. (Click OK to clear the message.) To view the report in print preview, pull down the Window menu and switch to the table design window. Then close the table design window (Ctrl+W), switch back to the report design window, and click the Report View toolbar button.

- **To base your report on a specific query (or saved filter)**, start from the database window, click the Queries button, and highlight the query name. Or open the query in datasheet or design view.
- **If you're not sure which table or query you want to base the report on**, start anywhere in Access (of course, a database must be open). If you know you want to use the Report Wizard and not one of the AutoReport options, you can click the Reports button in the database window and double-click Create Report by Using Wizard. Then skip to step 6.

2. Click the drop-down arrow next to the New Object toolbar button. You'll see this menu:

3. Choose one of these options:

   AutoReport   Creates a one-column report using the template named in the Report Template box on the Forms/Reports tab of the Options dialog box (Tools ➤ Options ➤ Forms/Reports; see Chapter 14). Typically, this template is named Normal, and it is completely plain. After choosing this option, skip to step 11—you're done! Using the AutoReport option makes sense only if you selected a table or query in step 1.

Report   Opens the New Report dialog box, shown here:

 TIP   To open the New Report dialog box in fewer steps, click the Reports button in step 1, and then click the New button in the database window. Or start from any tab on the database window and choose Insert ➤ Report. To create an AutoReport quickly, highlight a table or query name on the Tables or Queries tab in the database window, and then choose Insert ➤ AutoReport.

4. Choose the table or query you want to base the report on from the drop-down list near the bottom of the New Report dialog box. (This text box may be filled in for you already.)

 NOTE   You must select a table or query before choosing any of the AutoReport Wizards, the Chart Wizard, or the Label Wizard in step 5. If you plan to use the Report Wizard in step 5, you'll have another chance to choose tables and queries.

5. Click one of the following options in the list near the top of the New Report dialog box, and then click OK (or just double-click the appropriate option). When you click an option, the area in the left side of the dialog box will show an example and describe the report the selected option will create. Your options are:

    Report Wizard   Opens the Report Wizard. From here, you can select which tables, queries, and fields to include on the report, choose how to group, total, and summarize your report, choose a style for the report, and specify a title and name for your report.

AutoReport: Columnar   Without asking any more questions, this option creates a columnar report from all the fields in the selected table or query (refer to Figure 12.1).

AutoReport: Tabular   Without asking any more questions, this option creates a tabular report (refer to Figure 12.2).

 NOTE   When you choose AutoReport: Columnar or AutoReport: Tabular, Access places fields in the order they're defined in the table design or query, puts the name of the table or query on the report's title and title bar, and uses the default style. The default style is the style you (or someone else) chose most recently when using the Report Wizard. After choosing an AutoReport option, skip to step 11 and then save your report.

Chart Wizard   Creates a report that displays a free-standing chart of your table or query data (see Figure 12.6 and Chapter 15).

Label Wizard   Creates mailing labels from your table or query (see Figure 12.7 and "Creating Mailing Labels," later in this chapter).

6. Assuming you chose Report Wizard in step 5, you'll see the first Report Wizard dialog box, shown in Figure 12.8. Use any of the following techniques to add as many fields from as many tables or queries as you need, and then click Next.

FIGURE 12.8

Use this Report Wizard dialog box to specify which fields should appear on your report. You can select fields from as many tables and queries as you wish. Access will use your selections to decide how to lay out the report.

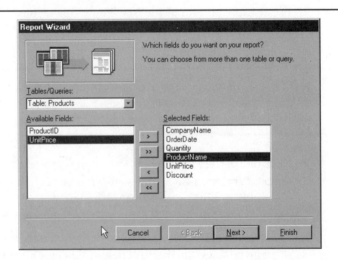

- **To select a table or query**, click the drop-down arrow button below Tables/Queries, and then choose the table or query to use.

- **To add one field to the report**, click in the Selected Fields list where the new field should appear. Then double-click the field in the Available Fields list, or click the field in the Available Fields list and then click the > button. The field you select will move to the Selected Fields list and appear on the report in the order shown.

- **To copy all the Available Fields to the Selected Fields list**, click in the Selected Fields list where the new fields should appear; then click the >> button.

- **To remove a field from the Selected Fields list**, double-click that field, or click the field and then click the < button.

- **To remove all fields from the Selected Fields list**, click the << button. The fields will reappear in the Available Fields list.

7. If you chose fields from multiple tables but haven't defined relationships between the tables yet, the Wizard will display the dialog box shown below. Click OK if you want to exit the Wizard and define relationships (see Chapter 6); or click Cancel to return to step 6 and remove some fields from your report. In the next few dialog boxes, you'll have a chance to customize your report. Your options will depend on which tables and fields you selected in step 6 and whether you choose to group your data.

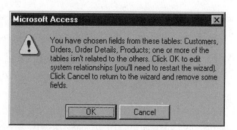

8. Pick the options you want in each dialog box, and then click Next to continue to the next dialog box. Here's a summary of the dialog boxes you'll see:

How to view your data The dialog box shown in Figure 12.9 appears if the report can be grouped in various ways. Choose the grouping option you want to use, and then click Next.

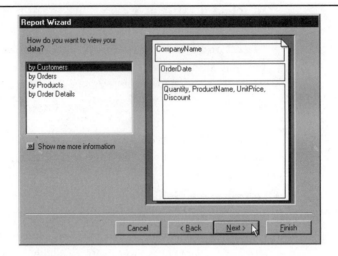

TIP As you make choices in the dialog boxes described in steps 8 and 9, the Report Wizard will give you detailed instructions and show previews of your report as it takes shape. Just watch the screen carefully and you shouldn't have any trouble figuring out what to do.

Grouping levels and grouping options The dialog box shown in Figure 12.10 appears if your report can be grouped by additional levels. To choose a grouping field, double-click it, or click the field name and then click the > button. To move it up a level, click the up arrow button in the dialog box; to move it down a level, click the down arrow button. To remove the bottom-most grouping field, click the < button. (Repeat as needed.) If you want to control the grouping interval for your additional fields, click the Grouping Options button in the dialog box, choose the interval you want from the appropriate Grouping Intervals drop-down lists, and then click OK. Click Next to continue.

Sort order for detail records and summary options The dialog box shown in Figure 12.11 appears if your report is grouped. From here, you can sort detail records by up to four fields, in ascending or descending order. To control various groups/totals and summary options, click the Summary Options button (if it's available); then select the options you want to use (see Figure 12.12) and click OK. Click Next to continue.

FIGURE 12.10

This Report Wizard dialog box lets you choose additional grouping fields and pick grouping intervals for those fields. This dialog box appears only if it's needed.

Click to group by the selected field.

Click to clear a grouping field.

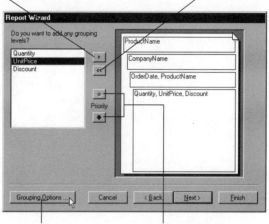

Click to group fields by intervals.

Click to change grouping priority.

FIGURE 12.11

Use this Report Wizard dialog box to choose the sort order for up to four detail fields, and to choose various summary options. This dialog box appears only if it's needed, and the Summary Options button appears only if your report includes numeric fields.

Choose up to four detail fields to sort by.

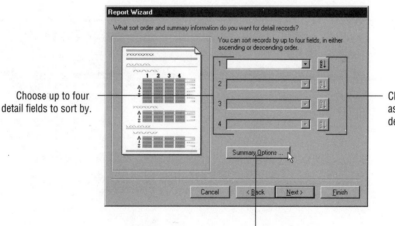

Click to choose ascending or descending sort.

Click to choose summary options (see Figure 12.12).

FIGURE 12.12

Clicking the Summary Options button in the dialog box shown in Figure 12.11 takes you to this Summary Options dialog box.

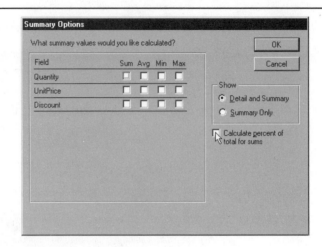

Report layout The appearance of this dialog box depends on whether your report is grouped. If it's grouped, it will resemble Figure 12.13; if it isn't grouped, it will resemble Figure 12.14.

FIGURE 12.13

Use this dialog box to choose a layout for a grouped report.

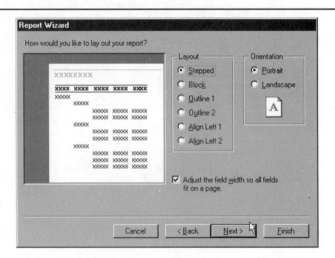

9. Click one of the available styles when asked to choose a style, and then click Next. (As Chapter 13 explains, you can customize the styles and create new ones of your own. Later in this chapter we'll show you how to change a report's style instantly.)

FIGURE 12.14

Use this dialog box to choose a layout for a report that isn't grouped. The term "Vertical" in the Layout group of this dialog box means the same as "Columnar."

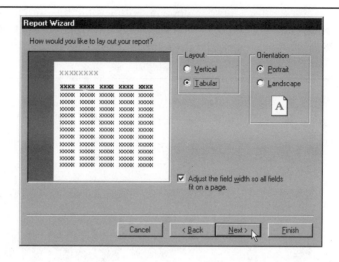

10. Accept the suggested title, or change it if you wish, in the last Report Wizard dialog box (see Figure 12.15). Make sure you've selected Preview the Report (because this option usually is most convenient), and then click Finish.

FIGURE 12.15

The last Report Wizard dialog box asks what title you want for the report, what you want to do next, and whether you want to display Help on working with the report. It's often easiest to accept the default settings and click Finish.

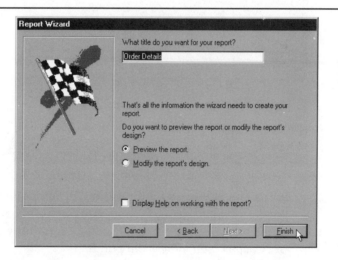

 WARNING The title you select in step 10 is used for the report name, the report's Caption property (which displays text on the report title bar), and the report title. If the report already exists in the database, you'll have a chance to overwrite the existing report or choose a different title.

PART

II

Creating a Database

Access will create your report and display it in the print preview window. Figure 12.16 shows a sample report in the print preview window. Any time your report appears in this window, you can do the following:

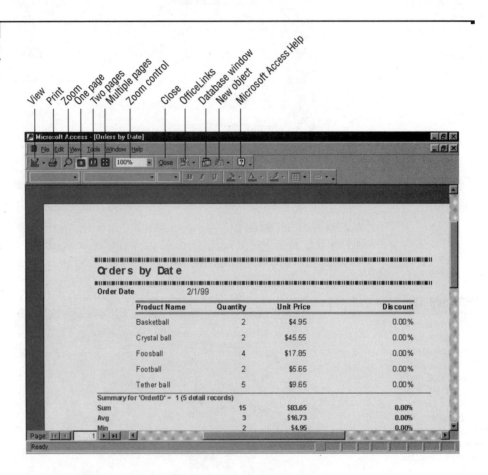

- **Print the report**. To print without opening the Print dialog box, click the Print toolbar button (see Figure 12.16). To print from the Print dialog box, press Ctrl+P or choose File ➤ Print, choose your printing options, and then click OK (see Chapter 9 for more about printing).

- **Zoom out or in on the report**. Click the Zoom toolbar button or click the magnifying glass mouse pointer on a spot in the report. You also can use the toolbar's Two Pages button and Zoom Control drop-down list, or right-click and choose the Zoom or Pages options as needed (see Chapter 9).

- **Send the report to a Microsoft Word file** and open it in Word. Click the drop-down arrow next to the OfficeLinks toolbar button, and then choose Publish It with MS Word.

- **Send the report to a Microsoft Excel spreadsheet** and open it in Excel. Click the drop-down arrow next to the OfficeLinks toolbar button, and then choose Analyze It with MS Excel.

- **Send the report to your network mail program**. Choose File ➤ Send To ➤ Mail Recipient (as Attachment), select the format you want for the message file, and click OK. When prompted, sign on to your mail system; then send the message as you would any network mail.

 NOTE Graphics and some complex formatting may not transfer to Microsoft Word or Microsoft Excel.

- **Close the print preview window and go to design view**, where you can change the report's design. Click the Close toolbar button or press Ctrl+W. Often you'll just need to rearrange or widen the fields and labels, as described in Chapter 13.

- **Save and close the report** (see "Saving a Report" later in this chapter).

 TIP You can use the File ➤ Export command to save a report as an HTML file, text file, Excel file, or a Rich Text Format file. See Chapter 7 for details.

How the Wizards Build Your Report

The report wizards go through the same steps that the form wizards do as they conjure up your automatic reports. That is, they make sure data from multiple tables is synchronized properly, and they size and place fields on the report so that everything fits on the page.

Continued

PART

II

Creating a Database

CONTINUED

If the report is based on fields from multiple tables and/or queries, the wizard creates an SQL statement behind the report that specifies which tables, queries, and fields to use and sets up the necessary table relationships. Because the wizard can do all this automatically, you'll rarely need to set up multitable queries just to display fields from several tables at once.

When sizing each control, the wizard lays out all the necessary fields, regardless of the current page size. If the resulting report is too big for the page, it calculates the ratio of the total size of the too-big report to the desired page size; then it shrinks every control by that ratio to create a report of the maximum allowable size. Because the wizard uses a simple ratio method for sizing controls on reports, you may need to switch to design view and tweak the size, position, or font for controls that appear squashed.

For more help with designing a new report with wizards, look up *Report Wizard* with the Office Assistant.

Creating Mailing Labels

You can design mailing labels that will print on standard Avery mailing label stock or other types of labels. Figure 12.7, earlier in this chapter, shows some standard mailing labels.

To create mailing labels using report wizards:

1. Start from the database window or from the datasheet view of a table or query as explained earlier.

2. Click the drop-down arrow next to the New Object toolbar button and choose Report.

Preparing for Dot-Matrix or Tractor-Fed Labels

If you want to print labels on a dot-matrix or tractor-feed printer, you may need to adjust the page size before you start the Mailing Label Wizard. To do so, click the Start button on the Windows Taskbar, and then choose Settings ➤ Printers. Right-click the icon for your dot-matrix printer, and choose Set as Default. Right-click the dot-matrix printer icon again, choose Properties, and then click the Paper tab. Set the Paper Size to Custom; specify the unit of measurement and the appropriate width and length. Click OK and then return to Access.

To learn more about creating labels for dot-matrix or tractor-feed printers, search for *Label Wizard* with the Office Assistant.

3. Click Label Wizard in the New Report dialog box. Next, use the drop-down list at the bottom of the dialog box to select the table or query you want to base the report on (if it's not selected for you already). Click OK.

4. In the dialog box shown in Figure 12.17, select a manufacturer from the Filter by Manufacturer drop-down list if you're using labels other than Avery. Then choose a label size, unit of measure, and label type as needed. If necessary, click the Customize button in the dialog box, create a custom label size, and then click Close. Or select (check) Show Custom Label Sizes and select a custom label. Click Next to continue.

PART

II

Creating a Database

FIGURE 12.17

This Label Wizard dialog box lets you choose a standard label or a custom size.

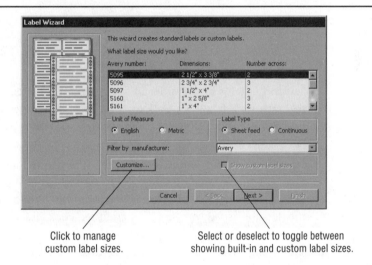

Click to manage
custom label sizes.

Select or deselect to toggle between
showing built-in and custom label sizes.

5. Choose font name, font size, font weight, and text color options when prompted. You also can select or deselect italics or underlining. Click Next to continue.

6. Choose the fields you want on the label from the dialog box shown in Figure 12.18. To add a field, position the cursor in the Prototype Label box, and then double-click a field in the Available Fields list. You also can type text or press Enter at the cursor position. To delete fields or text from the Prototype Label box, select the text with your mouse and press the Delete key. Click Next to continue.

NOTE   If the mailing label isn't large enough to hold all the lines and fields you specified, Access will explain the problem and let you know that some fields will be lost. You can return to the previous Label Wizard screens (by clicking the Back button as needed) and adjust your selections.

FIGURE 12.18

Use this dialog box to design your mailing labels. The Prototype Label box will reflect your latest changes, as shown in this example.

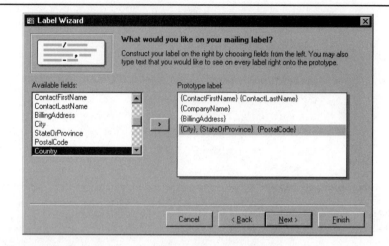

7. Select the fields in the order in which you want them sorted. For example, to sort customer labels for bulk mailing by zip/postal code and then by last and first name within zip/postal code, double-click PostalCode, double-click Contact-LastName, and then double-click ContactFirstName. Click Next to continue.

8. Specify a name for your report or accept the selected name from the final dialog box. The name must be unique because the Label Wizard won't let you over-write an existing mailing label report. Choose other options as needed (though the defaults usually are just fine) and then click Finish.

NOTE The title you select in step 8 is used for the report name and Caption property (which displays text on the report title bar).

Access will create the mailing label report and display it on the screen.

NOTE If you don't have enough horizontal space to display the entire label format, Access will let you know. You can go to design view and tweak the report design as needed (see Chapter 13). Or choose File ➢ Page Setup, click the Layout tab, and then reduce the number of columns or the size of the columns.

Formatting Postal Codes and Phone Numbers

If you use the Access wizards to create fields such as postal codes and phone numbers, the input masks cause values in those fields to be stored as text without punctuation characters. The same input masks cause the appropriate punctuation marks to appear for those fields in forms and datasheets. For example, Access uses this input mask for PostalCode fields:

```
00000\-9999
```

And this input mask for PhoneNumber fields:

```
!\(999") "000\-0000
```

Although most reports created by the wizards do take advantage of these input masks, the mailing labels don't. For example, a postal code might appear as either five numbers (85711) or nine numbers (857114747). A phone number might appear as 6195551234. To report those values in more readable formats, such as 85711-4747 for a postal code and (619)555-1234 for the phone number, you'll need to use the Format function in your reports.

For example, in design view for the mailing labels shown in Figure 12.7, we changed simple references to the postal code from [PostalCode] to:

```
Format ([PostalCode],"!@@@@@-@@@@")
```

To format a phone number field, such as [PhoneNumber], you could use this Format function:

```
Format ([PhoneNumber],"!(@@@) @@@-@@@@")
```

See Chapter 10 for more about formatting text (string) values. You can also open the *Visual Basic Language Reference* book in the Microsoft Access Help Contents and check the subtopics for *Functions*.

Saving a Report

If the wizard didn't save your report automatically, you should save the report if you want to use it later. Here's how:

- **To save and close the report**, return to design view by clicking the Close button on the print preview toolbar. Then choose File ➤ Close or press Ctrl+W, and click Yes.

• **To save your latest changes without closing the report**, press Ctrl+S, or choose File ➤ Save, or click the Save toolbar button.

 NOTE The first time you save a report that hasn't been saved before, you'll be prompted to enter a name for it. Type a name (up to 64 characters, including blanks) and then click OK.

Opening a Report

If you've closed a report, you can reopen it with these steps:

1. Start in the database window and click the Reports button.

2. Do one of the following:

   • **To open the report in print preview** (with data displayed), double-click the report name you want to open, or click it and then click the Preview button.

   • **To open the report in design view** (where you can change the report's design), click the report name and then click the Design button, or right-click the report name and select Design.

 TIP *Copying* is a quick way to create a new report that's based on an existing report. To copy a report, click the Reports button in the database window, highlight the report to copy, and press Ctrl+C. Next, press Ctrl+V, type a name for the new report, and click OK.

Removing a Filter and Sort Order

If your report is based on a table or query that you've filtered or sorted in datasheet view, the report will inherit the filter and sort order automatically and will be filtered or sorted the first time you preview or print it. You can remove the filter or sort from the report by following these steps:

1. Open the report in design view.

2. Choose View ➢ Properties if the property sheet isn't open. Click the Data tab on the property sheet.

3. Choose Edit ➢ Select Report to make sure you've selected the entire report.

4. Double-click the Filter On property in the property sheet to change that property from Yes to No. If necessary, double-click the Order On property to change it from Yes to No.

5. Save the report design (Ctrl+S).

The next time you preview or print the report, the records will not be filtered or sorted. If you later want to use the report with the filter and/or sorting, repeat the five steps above, except change the Filter On and/or Order On property from No to Yes in step 4.

Changing the Style of a Report

Just as you can change the overall style for forms, you also can change a report's style without re-creating the report from scratch. It's easy:

1. Open the report in design view. If you're starting from the database window, click the Reports tab, click the report you want to change, and then click the Design button. Or if you've switched to print preview from design view, click the Close toolbar button (shown at left) or choose View ➢ Design View.

2. Choose Format ➢ AutoFormat, or click the AutoFormat button (shown at left) on the Report Design toolbar. You'll see the AutoFormat dialog box, shown in Figure 12.19.

PART

II

Creating a Database

FIGURE 12.19

FIGURE 12.19

Use the AutoFormat dialog box to instantly change the style for your report or to customize an existing style. Switch to report design view and choose Format ➢ AutoFormat to open this dialog box.

3. Choose the format you want to use from the AutoFormat dialog box, and then click OK.

4. Save your changes (Ctrl+S) and click the Report View toolbar button; or choose View ➤ Print Preview to switch back to the print preview window.

Where to Go from Here

This chapter introduced the many types of instant reports you can create with the report wizards. From here, you can continue with Chapter 13 to learn how to design new reports and forms from scratch, and how to customize existing reports and forms.

What's New in the Access Zoo?

The Access 2000 database window has two new choices when the Report button is selected: Create Report in Design View, and Create Report by Using Wizard. These two new shortcuts bypass the New Report dialog box and bring you directly to the Report Design window or the first step of the Report Wizard. Once you're in the report design window, you'll see that it works the same in Access 2000 as it did in Access 97. In Chapter 13 you'll find out about some of the new controls you can add to reports.

Creating Custom Forms and Reports

FEATURING:

Access has some truly awesome tools for creating high-powered, good-looking forms and reports. If you've ever used a Windows drawing or painting package, you probably won't have any trouble learning to use the design tools. (If you've never used one of those programs, the mouse skills involved may take a little practice, but the overall process is still fairly simple.)

As you read this chapter, remember that you can customize the basic designs created by form wizards and report wizards (see Chapters 11 and 12), or you can create your own designs from scratch. If you're new to form and report design, you'll definitely want to start with a wizard-created design so you can experiment with the design tools right away.

TIP If you're planning to experiment extensively with Access form and report design tools, set up a new table—perhaps named All Field Types—that has one field for each data type that Access offers, and enter some records into it. Then use the form wizards and report wizards described in Chapters 11 and 12 to create a form or report that's based on fields in your All Field Types table.

Switching to Design View

To change the appearance of an existing form or report, you must switch to design view using any of these techniques:

- **To change a form or report that's not open**, go to the database window and click the Forms or Reports button (as appropriate) in the database window. Click the name of the form or report you want to change, and then click the Design button in the database window; or right-click the form or report name and choose Design.

 - **To change a form or report that's open** on your screen, click the Form View button on the Form Design toolbar, or choose View ➤ Design View if you're editing a form. Or click the Close Window (Close) button on the Print Preview toolbar, or choose View ➤ Design View if you're editing a report. Note that if you opened the report in print preview, clicking the Close Window button will close the report; you'll need to open it as described above.

NOTE The lessons in Chapter 3 gave you some hands-on practice with changing a form in form design view.

Remember that the tools for changing your form or report design are available in design view *only*. Therefore, except where the instructions specifically say to start from another view, be sure you're in design view before using any procedures described in this chapter.

When working with forms and reports, it's a good idea to hide the Taskbar temporarily. To do this, right-click an empty area on the Taskbar, choose Properties, and select (check) Always on Top, and Auto Hide. Then click OK. When you need to bring the Taskbar into view, just point to the bottom of your screen (or the side, depending on where the Taskbar is docked) and pause until it appears. See the sidebar titled "Maximizing Your On-Screen Real Estate" in Chapter 1 for more details.

Previewing and Saving Your Changes

As you work in design view, you'll want to preview your handiwork from time to time. To do so, click the Form View toolbar button (if you're designing a form) or the Print Preview button (if you're designing a report). Those buttons are on the left side of the Form Design and Report Design toolbars.

You also can preview your form or report by choosing options on the View menu:

- **To preview a form in form view**, choose View ➢ Form View.
- **To preview a form in datasheet view**, choose View ➢ Datasheet View.
- **To preview a report in print preview**, choose View ➢ Print Preview.
- **To preview a report in layout preview** (which presents just enough sample data to show you what the report will look like), choose View ➢ Layout Preview. You also can switch to layout preview by clicking the drop-down arrow on the Report View toolbar button and then choosing Layout Preview.

When you're ready to make more changes, go back to design view, as described in the previous section.

Another good idea is to save your changes whenever you're happy with them. Simply click the Save toolbar button or press Ctrl+S.

Creating a Form or Report from Scratch

Here's how to create an entirely new form or report without using the wizards.

1. Start from the database window and use one of these techniques:

- Click the Forms or Reports button in the database window, and then click the New button.

- Click the Tables or Queries tab, click the table or query you want to attach to your form or report, and then click the drop-down arrow next to the New Object toolbar button. Now choose either Form or Report, as appropriate. The New Form or New Report dialog box will open (see Figure 13.1 for an example of the New Form dialog box).

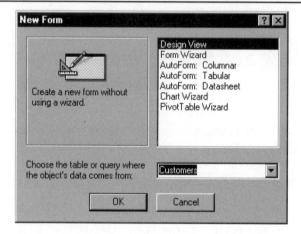

 TIP You can also double-click Create Form (or Report) in Design View, or Create Form (or Report) by Using Wizard, at this point to bypass the New Form or New Report dialog box and jump right to the design window or the wizard.

2. Choose form or report from the drop-down list in the dialog box to attach the form or report to a table or query. You don't need to choose a table or query if you're creating an unbound form, such as a dialog box or a switchboard (see Chapter 22).

3. Click the Design View option in the dialog box, and then click OK (or double-click Design View).

 NOTE If the datasheet for the table or query has a filter or sort associated with it, the new form or report will inherit the filter and sort order automatically. Chapter 9 explains how to add and apply filters and sorting in forms. "Removing a Filter and Sort Order" in Chapter 12 explains how to deactivate or activate the filter and sort for a report.

You'll be taken to a blank form or report window in design view. Think of this window as an empty canvas on which you're free to create anything you want. Of course, you do need to understand the available tools and techniques before you start creating anything. That's what the rest of this chapter is all about.

 TIP To undo a mistake you've made in design view, press Ctrl+Z, or click the Undo toolbar button, or choose Edit ➢ Undo immediately.

For online details about the design process, go to the Access Help Contents, open the *Working with Forms* or *Working with Reports* book; then open additional books and topics as needed.

Design Tools

Figures 13.2 and 13.3 show an empty form and report, respectively, in design view. In both figures, we've maximized the design window to increase the available work space. Let's take a quick look at the design tools shown in the figures.

FIGURE 13.2

An empty form (maximized) in design view.

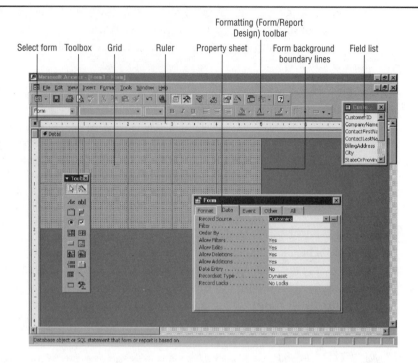

Labels (left to right): Select form · Toolbox · Grid · Ruler · Property sheet · Formatting (Form/Report Design) toolbar · Form background boundary lines · Field list

FIGURE 13.3

An empty report (maximized) in design view.

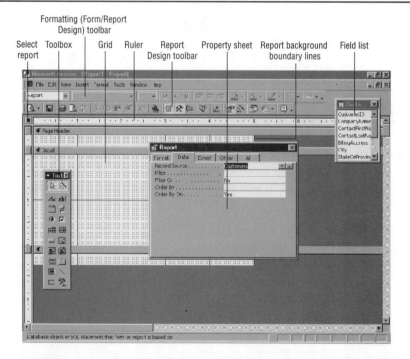

Labels: Formatting (Form/Report Design) toolbar · Select report · Toolbox · Grid · Ruler · Report Design toolbar · Report · Property sheet · Report background boundary lines · Field list

Choosing a Style for Your Design

Initially your form or report design will have a standard look, which works well for most people. However, Access comes with several predefined styles that you can use to change the appearance of a form design's background and the font, color, and border of controls on a form or report. As you'll learn later, you also can create your own custom styles.

 NOTE Control is Access lingo for any graphical object on a form or report that displays data, performs some action, or makes the form or report easier to read.

To choose a style for your design:

1. Select the controls you want your changes to apply to (see "Selecting Controls, Sections, Forms, and Reports" later in this chapter).

 NOTE If you don't select controls first, Access will apply the new style to the entire design.

 2. Choose Format ➤ AutoFormat, or click the AutoFormat button (shown at left) on the Form Design or Report Design toolbar. The AutoFormat dialog box will open (see Figure 13.4).

3. Select a style in the Form AutoFormats or Report AutoFormats list. The sample picture will change accordingly. The new style usually affects the design's background and the Font, Color, and Border of controls.

4. Click the Options button to change this behavior. Then select (check) the styles you want to apply, or deselect (clear) styles you want to leave unchanged (see Figure 13.4). Again, the sample picture will reflect your changes.

5. Click OK.

FIGURE 13.4

The AutoFormat dialog box for a form after we clicked the Options button. The AutoFormat dialog box for reports is similar. To preview a style in the AutoFormats list, click it and look at the sample picture.

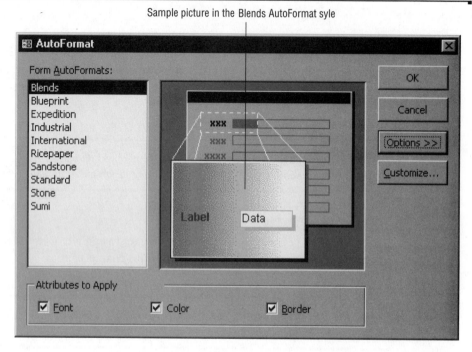

Sample picture in the Blends AutoFormat style

Access will apply the new style to the background of a form, to existing or selected controls, and to new controls. (Of course, you can change the style any time you want a different look, by repeating steps 1 to 5.) If you don't see a change, make sure the form or report is selected (and not some other object in the design window) before you click AutoFormat.

If your design contains a control whose appearance isn't defined for the AutoFormat style you chose, an Update AutoFormat dialog box similar to this one will appear:

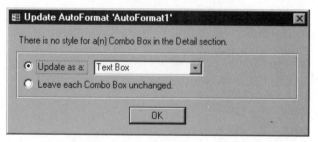

Choose one of these options, and then click OK:

- **To update the current control with the style for another type of control** in the AutoFormat style, click the drop-down arrow next to Update as A, and then choose the control that has the style you want to use.

- **To leave the current control's appearance unchanged**, choose Leave Each *xxx* Unchanged (where *xxx* is the type of control that doesn't have a predefined style—in the dialog box shown previously, the control is a combo box).

For more about creating your own AutoFormat styles, look up *AutoFormat* with the Office Assistant and click the topic for *Customize an Autoformat for a Form or Report*.

The Field List, Design View Toolbars, and Toolbox

The field list, design toolbars, and toolbox (see Figures 13.2 and 13.3) are optional tools that you'll learn more about later in this chapter. Here's a crash course on what they do:

Design View Toolbars   The design view toolbars—Form Design or Report Design, Toolbox, and Formatting (Form/Report)—offer a treasure trove of menu shortcuts, formatting features, and design tools. You'll probably want to keep all these toolbars handy as you work.

Field List   Lists all the fields in the underlying table or query. To place a field, simply drag it from the field list to your design.

Toolbox   Provides tools for adding controls to your design.

For now, just knowing how to hide and display those tools (and the property sheet) is sufficient.

- **To display or hide the design toolbars**, right-click any visible menu bar, toolbar, or the toolbox, and then choose the toolbar you want to display or hide. If no toolbars are visible, choose View ➢ Toolbars and select (check) or deselect (clear) the toolbars you want to show or hide.

 - **To display or hide the toolbox**, choose View ➢ Toolbox, or click the Toolbox button (shown at left) on the Form Design or Report Design toolbar.

 - **To display or hide the field list**, choose View ➢ Field List. Or click the Field List button (shown at left) on the Form Design or Report Design toolbar.

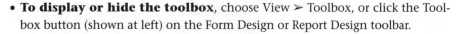

You can size and move the tools using these techniques:

- **To change a toolbar or toolbox to a floating palette of buttons**, double-click an empty area within the tool. Or drag an empty area within the tool away from the edge of the screen, and release the mouse button.
- **To move a floating toolbar or toolbox**, drag its title bar.
- **To size a floating toolbar or toolbox**, drag any border.
- **To display a floating toolbar or toolbox as a single row or column of buttons**, double-click an empty (nonbutton) area within the tool. Or drag the tool to an edge of the screen and, when the outline expands to the length of the edge you've dragged to, release the mouse button.

For details about working with toolbars, see "Using the Toolbars and Menu Bar" in Chapter 1. To find out what a toolbar or toolbox button is for, point to it with your mouse and then look at the ScreenTip below the mouse pointer and the status bar at the bottom of the screen. For online Help with toolbars, search for *Toolbars* with the Office Assistant.

The Property Sheet

You can use the *property sheet* (shown below) to view or change the properties of any controls that are selected in the report or form design window. The properties that appear on the property sheet depend on what part of the design you've selected.

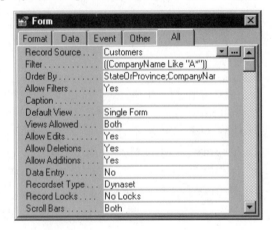

Like many tools in design view, the property sheet can be toggled on or off, displayed or hidden. To display or hide the property sheet, use any of the following methods:

- Click the Properties button (shown at left) on the Form Design or Report Design toolbar.
- Choose View ➤ Properties from the menu bar.
- Right-click any object and choose Properties.

 TIP If the property sheet isn't visible, you can open it by double-clicking an empty place on the design or by double-clicking any control.

Changing a Property

To change a property:

1. Select the object or objects you want to change. (See "Selecting Controls, Sections, Forms, and Reports" later in this chapter.)

2. Open the property sheet as described previously (View ➤ Properties).

3. Click the tab for the type of properties you want to change. (Properties that don't make sense for all selected objects won't appear on the property sheet.) From left to right, the property tabs are as follows:

   Format Lets you specify appearance properties. Format properties are changed automatically when you move or resize a control, and when you use the Formatting (Form/Report) toolbar buttons to customize a control.

   Data Lets you specify the source of the data and the data's display format. On forms, Data properties control such things as default values and allowable values. On reports, Data properties also control whether a text box shows a running sum.

   Event Lets you control what happens when certain events occur. For example, an OnClick event property defines what happens when you click a command button in form view. You'll learn more about event properties in Part Four of this book.

   Other This category is a catchall for things such as the name of a control when it's used in expressions, macros, and procedures; the text that appears on the status bar when you select the control in form view; how the Enter key behaves during data entry (see Chapter 8); whether the AutoCorrect feature is enabled (see Chapter 9); the custom shortcut menu that appears when you right-click a form or control; and the ControlTip text that pops up when you point to the control in form view.

All Displays all available properties for the control. When you're not sure which tab contains the property you're looking for, click the All tab.

4. Click in the text box next to the property you want to change. A drop-down list button and/or Build button may appear.

TIP When you select multiple controls and then change properties, your changes will affect all the selected controls. Thus, you can change the background color or font for an entire group of objects in one fell swoop. For another way to copy properties from one object to another, see "Copying Properties to Other Controls," later in this chapter.

5. Do one of the following:

- Type the property value you want. If you're entering lots of text into the box, you can press Shift+F2 (Zoom) to expand the box.

- Click the drop-down button if one is provided, and choose the property from the list.

- Click the Build button if one is provided, and build an expression with help from a "builder" dialog box.

- Double-click in the text box to choose the next available property from the drop-down list. Double-clicking is especially handy for quickly flipping Yes/No values.

TIP Take some time to explore the properties of controls on a form or report that you generate with a wizard. To avoid becoming overwhelmed by the sheer number of properties available, look at the properties on the Format, Data, Event, and Other properties tabs separately, rather than trying to wade through all properties on the All tab.

To learn more about what a property does, click in the appropriate property text box and look at the status bar at the bottom of the screen for a brief description. If you still need more details about the property, press F1.

The Ruler

The ruler is most helpful when you're sizing or moving objects by dragging. As you drag, a shadow on the ruler indicates the object's size and location. To hide or display the ruler, choose View ➢ Ruler.

The Grid

You can use the grid to align objects on the design. To hide or display the grid, choose View ➢ Grid.

 NOTE If you've turned on the grid but can't see the grid dots, set the grid density to 24 or less (as described in a moment).

Snapping to the Grid

As you move and size objects on the screen, they'll usually snap (align) to points on the grid, making it easier for you to keep objects aligned. This alignment will happen even if the grid isn't visible at the moment.

- **To activate or deactivate grid snap**, choose Format ➢ Snap to Grid.
- **To disable grid snap temporarily**, hold down the Ctrl key while moving or sizing an object.

Changing the Grid Density

The grid dots are visible only when the grid density is set to 24 or fewer dots per inch (and when Grid on the View menu is selected). To change the grid density:

1. Open the property sheet (View ➢ Properties) and click the Format tab.
2. Select the form or report. To do so, choose Edit ➢ Select Form (if you're designing a form) or choose Edit ➢ Select Report (if you're designing a report). (Select Form and Select Report are on the expanded portion of the Edit menu.) The property sheet shows properties for the form or report as a whole.
3. Scroll down to the Grid X and Grid Y properties, and set each to 24 or smaller. (The default setting is 24 for both properties.)
4. Close the property sheet if you wish.

PART

II

Creating a Database

Sizing Controls and Aligning Them to the Grid

To tidy up your design, you can size all the controls on the design, and you can align them to the current grid. Here's how:

1. To select all the controls, choose Edit ➤ Select All (or press Ctrl+A).

2. Do either (or both) of the following:

   - **To size all the controls** so they touch the nearest grid points, choose Format ➤ Size ➤ To Grid.

   - **To align all controls to the grid**, choose Format ➤ Align ➤ To Grid.

All the controls will size or align to their nearest grid mark. You can make additional changes using techniques described later under "Moving Controls," "Resizing Controls," and "Aligning Controls."

Changing the Size of the Form or Report

If the grid is on, the form or report background shows crosshair lines at 1-inch intervals. It also shows grid dots (if the grid density is 24 or less). Most important, the background shows the actual boundaries of the form or report (refer to Figures 13.2 and 13.3). If the form or report is too large or too small, you can change the size any time you wish:

- **To change the width**, drag the right boundary line of the background to the left or right.

- **To change the height**, drag the bottom boundary line of the background up or down.

- **To change both the width and the height**, drag the lower-right boundary corner diagonally.

Sizing the Background to Prevent Spillover Pages

If you want all your data to fit across a single page in a printed report, the background width *plus* the report margins must be less than (or equal to) the paper width.

To adjust the margins, choose File ➤ Page Setup from the design window's menu bar. Click the Margins tab, use the Margins options in the dialog box to set margin widths (see Figure 13.5), and then click OK.

FIGURE 13.5

The Margins tab in the
Page Setup dialog box.

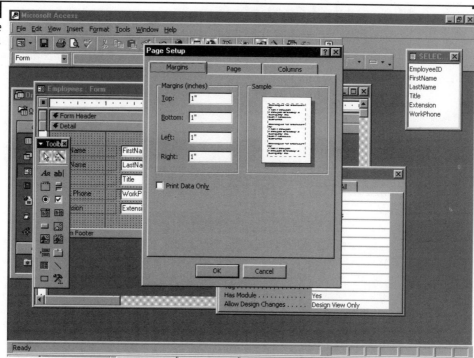

 NOTE If you try to change the margins to some small number and Access increases the width you specify, it's not a malfunction. Access is adjusting your entry to compensate for the printer's *dead zone*. The dead zone is the area at the outer edge of the page where the small wheels that pull the paper through the printer are located. The printer can't print in the dead zone.

Designer Skills

Becoming an Access designer is a three-step process. First you must learn what tools are available in design view, then you must learn how to use them, and finally you must play with them until you can create any form or report your imagination can conjure up. The rest of this chapter should help you achieve the first two steps; the last step you'll have to do on your own.

Adding Bound Controls (Fields)

When you want to show data from the underlying table or query in your form or report, you should add a *bound control* to your design. The most commonly used bound controls are text boxes. (Bound controls are created automatically when you use a form wizard or report wizard.)

 NOTE *Unbound controls* can include results of calculations and objects, such as informational text, graphics, lines, and boxes, that aren't connected to underlying data. Some wizards also add unbound controls to the designs they create.

To add a bound control to your design:

1. Display the field list if it's not visible (choose View ➤ Field List, or click the Field List button on the toolbar).

2. Use any of these techniques:

   - **To add one field to the form or report**, drag the field from the field list to the place where it should appear in the design.

   - **To copy all fields to your form or report at once**, double-click the title bar in the field list, and then drag the selected fields to the design.

   - **To copy several fields**, use standard Windows techniques (for example, Shift-click or Ctrl-click) to select multiple fields in the field list, and then drag the selected fields to the design.

Access will create a text box, list box, check box, combo box, or bound OLE object control, depending on the data type and the Display Control property defined for the field in the underlying table design or query design. (The Display Control property is on the Lookup tab of the table design view property sheet; see Chapter 6.)

The control will include a label that displays either the field's name or whatever text you assigned to the field's Caption property in table design view. If you want to change the label text, click inside the label until the insertion point appears, and then edit the text (or select the label text and type new text to replace it).

Of course, you also can use other tools in the toolbox to create a bound control, but doing so is not as easy as dragging fields from the field list.

About Inherited Properties

The bound controls will inherit all the Lookup properties from the underlying table fields, along with these General properties: Format, Input Mask, Caption, Default Value, Validation Rule, Validation Text, and Decimal Places.

Even though the Default Value, Validation Rule, and Validation Text properties are inherited, you won't see their settings on the Data tab of a new control's property sheet. You can add a Validation Rule, Validation Text, and Default Value property to the control on the form if you wish. If you do so, Access uses the form's Validation Rule and Validation Text in addition to the underlying table's Validation Rule for the associated field. The Default Value property assigned on the form will override the table's Default Value property.

Selecting Controls, Sections, Forms, and Reports

Before you can change, move, or delete objects in the design, you must select them. The first step is to click the Select Objects toolbox button (shown at left) so that it appears "pushed in." Then use any of these techniques:

- **To select one control**, click the control. Sizing and move handles will appear, as shown in Figure 13.6.

PART

II

Creating a Database

FIGURE 13.6

A selected control. This example shows the parts of a text box, which is a compound control that has both a label and a field.

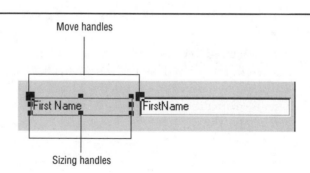

- **To select adjacent controls**, start at any point outside a control, and drag a rectangle over the controls you want to select.

TIP To control how precise you must be when dragging the selection rectangle over adjacent controls, choose Tools ➤ Options, and then click the Forms/Reports tab in the Options dialog box. Next, choose either Partially Enclosed (lets you drag the rectangle through only part of a control or group of controls) or Fully Enclosed (requires you to drag the rectangle completely around the control or group of controls). Click OK to save your changes.

- **To select nonadjacent controls**, parts of compound controls (such as a field and its label), or overlapping controls, hold down the Shift key and click each control you want to select. This standard Windows technique is called *Shift-clicking*.

- **To use the ruler to select controls**, move the mouse pointer to the horizontal or vertical ruler. (The pointer changes to a ↓ or ↑, respectively.) Then click the line that goes through all the controls you want to select. Or drag the mouse along the ruler until shading encloses the controls you want to select, and then release the mouse button.

- **To select a section in a form or report**, click the gray bar that shows the section name. You can also click any empty area in the background of a section. (You'll learn more about sections shortly.)

- **To select all controls on a form or report**, choose Edit ➤ Select All or press Ctrl+A.

- **To select the entire form or report**, choose Edit ➤ Select Form or Edit ➤ Select Report. Or, if the rulers are visible, click the box where the rulers intersect (below the File menu). Or click the Select Objects drop-down list (shown at left) on the Formatting (Form/Report) toolbar and choose Form or Report from the top of the list.

TIP If the property sheet "blanks out" suddenly when you click a control that's already selected, you can restore the property display in either of two ways: press Enter if you want to keep any changes you've typed into the control or press Escape if you don't mind discarding any changes you've typed in.

Here's how to deselect controls:

- **To deselect all selected controls**, click in an empty area of the design.

- **To deselect certain controls in a group of selected controls**, Shift-click the controls you want to deselect.

Working with Selected Controls

Once you've selected a control (or a group of controls), you can delete, move, resize, or align your selection and change spacing between selected controls.

Deleting Controls

To delete controls, select the controls you want to delete and press Delete. If you change your mind, immediately choose Edit ➢ Undo, press Ctrl+Z, or click the Undo button on the Form Design or Report Design toolbar.

To delete just the label portion of a compound control, click the label and press Delete.

 TIP To hide the label temporarily without deleting it, change the label's Visible property to No on the Format tab of the property sheet.

Moving Controls

You can position controls anywhere on the design. First, select the control or controls you want to move. Then choose one of the following options:

- **To move entire selected controls**, pass the mouse pointer over the controls until the pointer changes to an open hand, and then drag the selection to a new position. (To move controls to a different *section* of the report or form, make sure all selected controls are in the same section, and then drag them to the new location.)
- **To move part of a selected compound control**, pass the mouse pointer over the *move handle* in the upper-left corner of the control until it changes to an upward-pointing hand, and then drag the control to a new position.

 TIP You can hold down the Shift key while dragging, to move the control vertically or horizontally only.

- **To move a selected control by a very small amount**, press Ctrl+→, Ctrl+←, Ctrl+↑, or Ctrl+↓. The control will move in the direction of the arrow key you pressed while holding down the Ctrl key.

Resizing Controls

If a control is too large or too small, you can resize it in various ways. As always, you begin by selecting the control or controls you want to change. Then choose one of the following options:

- **To resize selected controls**, move the mouse pointer to a sizing handle (the pointer changes to a two-headed arrow), drag the sizing handle until the controls are the proper size, and then release the mouse button. If you've selected multiple controls, all controls will be resized by the same amount.

- **To size selected controls so that their data will fit the contents**, choose Format ➢ Size ➢ To Fit.

- **To size selected controls to the nearest grid mark**, choose Format ➢ Size ➢ To Grid.

- **To resize a label control to fit snugly around the label text**, double-click one of the label's sizing handles.

- **To make selected controls the same size**, choose Format ➢ Size, and then pick To Tallest, To Shortest, To Widest, or To Narrowest. Access will resize all selected controls according to the option you chose (for example, all selected controls will be as tall as the tallest control in the selection).

- **To size selected controls by a very small amount**, press Shift+→, Shift+←, Shift+↑, or Shift+↓.

 TIP If you frequently resize or align controls in the design window, you may want to use the Alignment and Sizing Tools toolbar. To bring this toolbar into view, right-click any toolbar and choose Customize. In the Customize dialog box, click the Toolbars tab, click the check box for Alignment and Sizing Tools to select it, and click Close.

Aligning Controls

Your forms and reports will look much nicer if text and data are neatly aligned. Here's how to align controls.

1. Select the controls you want to line up.

2. Choose Format ➤ Align from the menus, or right-click a selected control and choose Align. (Or, you can also open the Alignment and Sizing Tools toolbar, as described in the last tip, and use it instead of the Format ➤ Align commands.)

3. Choose Left, Right, Top, Bottom, or To Grid, as appropriate. For example, if you choose Format ➤ Align ➤ Left, all selected controls will align with the leftmost control in the selection.

 NOTE   If selected controls are overlapping when you align them, Access will place the controls in a staggered arrangement, which probably isn't what you want. It's best to make sure the controls don't overlap before you try to align them.

Adjusting the Horizontal and Vertical Spacing

You can further fine-tune your design by adjusting the horizontal and vertical spacing between two or more selected controls:

1. Select the controls you want to adjust. If you want to space the controls an equal distance apart, select three or more controls.

2. Choose Format ➤ Horizontal Spacing to adjust horizontal spacing between selected controls. Choose Format ➤ Vertical Spacing to adjust vertical spacing.

3. Choose one of these spacing options:

    Make Equal   Makes the horizontal or vertical distance between three or more selected controls equal. Access will space the selected controls evenly within the space that's available between the highest (or leftmost) and the lowest (or rightmost) selected control.

    Increase   Increases the horizontal or vertical space between selected controls by one grid point.

    Decrease   Decreases the horizontal or vertical space between selected controls by one grid point.

Duplicating Controls

The Duplicate feature offers a quick and easy way to create an evenly spaced and aligned copy of one or more selected controls. Simply select the control(s) you want to duplicate, and choose Edit ➤ Duplicate (or right-click the selection and choose Duplicate). You can then resize or move the copied control, or change its properties, as desired.

 TIP To create multiple copies of one or more controls with the same relative spacing and position for each copy, duplicate the control(s) once, adjust the spacing and position as needed (without making any other changes), and then make as many duplicates of the still-selected controls as you need.

Changing the Font, Color, Border, Appearance, and More

The Formatting (Form/Report) toolbar (see Figure 13.7) provides many great ways to beautify a control. You can change the text font and alignment; add foreground, background, and border colors; add special effects such as a raised, sunken, or etched border; and choose border width.

FIGURE 13.7

Use the Formatting (Form/Report) toolbar to choose fonts, text alignment, colors, borders, and special effects for a control. In this example, we've clicked the drop-down arrow next to the Line/Border Color button.

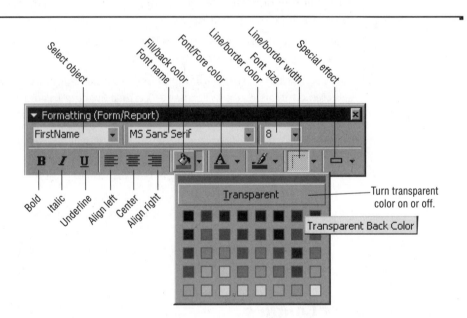

Follow these steps to work with this toolbar:

1. Do one of the following.

- **If the toolbar isn't visible**, right-click any toolbar that is visible and choose Formatting (Form/Report Design).

- **If no toolbar is visible**, choose View ➢ Toolbars, select (check) Formatting (Form/Report Design), and then click Close.

2. Select the control or controls you want to customize.

3. Click a button in the Formatting (Form/Report) toolbar, or click the drop-down arrow next to a button; then choose an option to apply the effect you want. (In the Fill/Back Color and Line/Border Color drop-down palettes, clicking the Transparent button makes the selected control transparent, so that the color shown in the control is the same as the color of the control, section, or form behind it.) As usual, you can find out what a button is for by moving the mouse pointer to the button and waiting a moment for a ScreenTip to appear.

 NOTE After pulling down the Fill/Back Color, Font/Fore Color, Line/Border Color, Line/Border Width, or Special Effect palettes on the toolbar, you can drag them off the toolbar to leave them open as you work. To return any palette to the toolbar, click the drop-down arrow for its toolbar button, or click the palette's Close button.

 NOTE Instead of using the toolbar, you can select the control(s) and change format properties in the property sheet; but that's doing it the hard way (unless the property sheet offers additional features that aren't available on the toolbar). For example, you can select from 16 million different colors by using the property sheet, instead of only the 56 different colors shown in the color palettes.

Controlling the Tab Order

The *tab order* controls the order in which the cursor moves through fields on a form when you press the Tab and Shift+Tab keys. After you've rearranged fields in a form, the current tab order may seem jumbled when you use the form in form view. To fix the tab order, follow these steps:

1. Choose View ➢ Tab Order in form design view. You'll see a Tab Order dialog box similar to the example shown in Figure 13.8.

PART

II

Creating a Database

FIGURE 13.8

The Tab Order
dialog box.

2. Under Section, select the section with the controls you want to reorder (for example, choose Detail).

3. Click the Auto Order button to have Access quickly set the tab order from left to right and top to bottom.

4. Click or drag through the row selector(s) for the rows you want to reposition (to assign the tab order manually). Then move the mouse pointer to one of the selected row selectors and drag the row or rows to a new position in the Custom Order list.

5. Repeat steps 3 and 4 as needed, and then click OK.

In form view, pressing Tab will now move the cursor forward in the new tab order. Pressing Shift+Tab will move the cursor backward in the new tab order.

 TIP To prevent the cursor from landing on a control when you press Tab or Shift+Tab in form view, return to form design view and set the Tab Stop property for that control to No. You'll find this property on the Other tab of the property sheet.

Copying Properties to Other Controls

Suppose you've formatted a control just the way you want it, and now you want other controls to have the same look. Making this happen is quick and easy:

1. Select the control that has the formatting you want to copy to another control.

2. Do one of the following:

- **To copy the format to one other control**, click the Format Painter button on the Form Design or Report Design toolbar.

- **To copy the format to several other controls**, double-click the Format Painter button.

3. Click the control that should have the new format. If you double-clicked the Format Painter button in step 2, continue clicking other controls that should have the new format.

4. Press Esc or click the Format Painter button again when you're done copying the format.

The format painter will copy any formatting properties that you can set via the Formatting (Form/Report) Toolbar, and almost every property that you can set via the Format tab on the property sheet. Pretty nifty!

Adding Help, Menus, and Prompts to Controls

By now, you've probably taken advantage of status bar prompts, shortcut menus, and ScreenTips to help you figure out what to do next, or to do something more quickly. Guess what? You can add these conveniences to any control on your form by updating properties on the Other tab of the property sheet.

NOTE When you drag names from the field list to your design, Access automatically fills in the Status Bar Text property with any text that appears in the Description column for that field in table design view. If the Description is blank, the Status Bar Text also will be blank.

To set up custom help text and shortcut menus that will appear in form view, select the control you want to customize (in form design view), open the property sheet (View ➤ Properties), and then click the property sheet's Other tab. Now assign values to any of these properties. Figure 13.9 shows a completed example.

PART

II

Creating a Database

FIGURE 13.9

A memo field, to which we've assigned Status Bar Text, Shortcut Menu Bar, and ControlTip Text properties.

Form design view

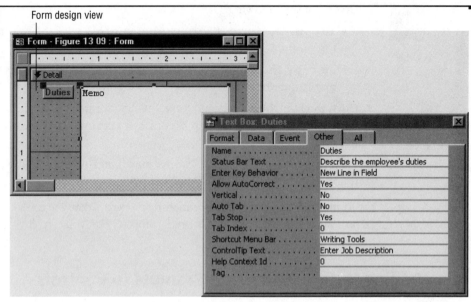

Status Bar Text   Displays a message on the status bar when the cursor lands in the control.

Shortcut Menu Bar   Displays a custom shortcut menu when you right-click the control. Chapter 25 explains how to create custom shortcut menus.

ControlTip Text   Displays a pop-up message when you point to the control with the mouse. ControlTips are similar to the ScreenTips that appear when you point to toolbar buttons.

Help Context ID   Displays information from a custom Help file that's named in the Help File property. (The Help File property appears on the Other tab when you select the entire form.) The custom Help will appear if you move the focus to (click) the control in form view and then press F1. You can create a custom Help file using Microsoft's Windows Help Compiler and a rich-text format text editor, such as Microsoft Word for Windows or the Windows Word-Pad. Many third-party companies also offer Help authoring tools.

NOTE Microsoft Office 2000 Developer is a package of tools that developers can use to create custom Office applications. One of these tools is the HTML Help Workshop Software Development Kit. Go to http://www.microsoft.com on the Web to find out more about this toolkit.

Figure 13.10 shows the form from Figure 13.9 after we switched to form view, clicked in the field, and let the mouse pointer rest in the field for a moment. Right-clicking the field would display a menu of options from our Writing Tools shortcut menu (not shown).

FIGURE 13.10

The field from Figure 13.9 in form view. Notice the status bar text at the bottom of the screen and the ControlTip text near the mouse pointer.

Form view

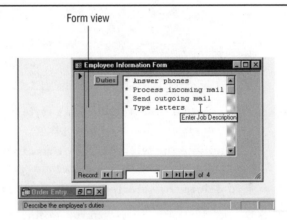

For more about any of these "helpful" properties, open the property sheet (View ➤ Properties), click the Other tab, click in the appropriate property box, and then press F1.

Customizing AutoFormat Styles

You can customize existing AutoFormat styles, add new styles, and delete unwanted styles in a flash. You can customize the font, color, and border controls in each section as needed. You also can set background colors for each section and choose a picture for the form background. (For more about displaying background pictures, see "Adding a Background Picture" later in this chapter.) Any new styles you add will be available to the form wizards and report wizards and in the AutoFormat dialog box, shown earlier in Figure 13.4.

PART

II

Creating a Database

To open the AutoFormat dialog box, click the AutoFormat button on the Form Design or Report Design toolbar, or choose Format ➤ AutoFormat. If you want to update or delete an existing AutoFormat, click that format in the Form AutoFormats or Report AutoFormats list.

When you click the Customize button in the dialog box, you'll see a Customize AutoFormat dialog box similar to this one:

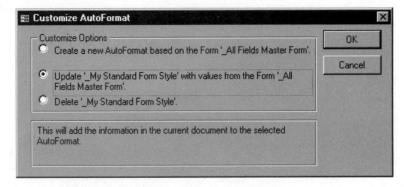

- **To create a new AutoFormat style** based on formats in your current form or report, choose the first option.

- **To update the selected AutoFormat style** with formats from your current form or report, choose the second option.

- **To delete the selected AutoFormat style**, choose the third option.

Click OK and then click Close when you are finished working in the AutoFormat dialog box.

Specifying the Record Source on the Fly

If you've accidentally chosen the wrong source for data in your report or form, or you wish to change it, here's what to do:

1. Open the property sheet (View ➤ Properties), and click the Data tab.

2. Select the entire form or report (Edit ➤ Select Form, or Edit ➤ Select Report).

3. Click the Record Source property box on the property sheet's Data tab. A drop-down list button and a Build button will appear.

4. Do one of the following:

- Type the table name or query name of the record source into the property box, or choose a table or query from the drop-down list.

- Build a query on-the-fly by clicking the Build button, and then clicking Yes if a message appears. Define a query that selects and displays the records you want, using techniques discussed in Chapter 10. Test and save the query if you wish. When you're done defining the query, choose File ➢ Close (or press Ctrl+W, or click the Close button in the SQL Statement dialog box) and answer Yes if prompted to save your changes. Press Enter to move the cursor to the next property box. An SQL statement will appear in the Record Source property box; this SQL code is just an equivalent way to express the query.

5. Preview the report or switch to form view.

If you see *#Name?* or *#Error?* in a control, that control has become undefined as a result of your efforts in step 4. Return to design view, delete the incorrect or extraneous control(s), and drag the appropriate field(s) from the field list to your design. Or open the property sheet in design view (View ➢ Properties), select the control you want to change, click the Control Source box on the property sheet's Data tab, and type in or select the appropriate field or expression.

For more information about troubleshooting #Name? and #Error? problems, look up *Troubleshooting Forms* with the Office Assistant, click *Troubleshoot Forms*, and then click the topic *#Error? or #Name? Appears in a Control*.

 TIP If you want to add one of the old styles from Access 97 to the AutoFormat list, open the old form in design view, click the AutoFormat button, and then click Customize. In the Customize AutoFormat window, click the first option, Create a New AutoFormat…. Then click OK and enter a name for the new (old!) style.

Sections, Headers, and Footers

All reports and forms are divided into sections, described next, to help you control what appears where on the finished form or report. We'll show some examples in a moment.

PART

II

Creating a Database

Form Sections

Forms are divided into as many as five sections:

Form Header   Always visible at the top of a form; printed only on the first page.

Page Header   Printed at the top of each page when you print forms (never visible in form view).

Detail   Generally used to show fields (data) from an underlying table or query.

Page Footer   Printed at the bottom of printed forms only. Never visible in form view.

Form Footer   Always visible on the bottom of the form window; printed only on the last page.

Figure 13.11 shows the design view for a completed form with a form header and footer, page header and footer, and detail section. Figure 13.12 shows the same form in form view. Remember that page headers and footers appear only on printed copies of the form and in print preview, so you'll never see them in form view. In Figure 13.13 you see the same form in print preview with its page header clearly visible. (To see the *Confidential! Secret!* page footer in print preview, click the form to make it fit on the page or use the vertical scroll bar to scroll to the bottom of the form.)

FIGURE 13.11

A sample form in design view, illustrating the various sections.

Form design view

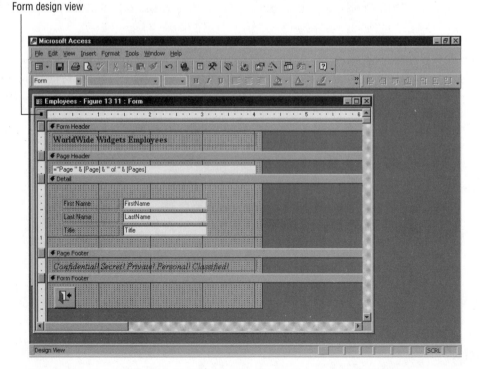

FIGURE 13.12

The design shown in Figure 13.11 looks like this in form view.

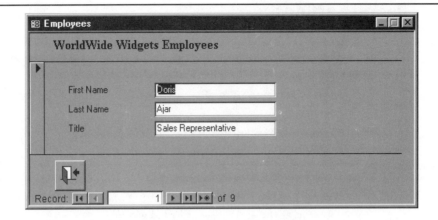

FIGURE 13.13

In print preview (and in printed copies of the form), the design shown in Figure 13.11 looks like this. Although it's cut off on this figure, the "Confidential! Secret! Private! Personal! Classified!" page footer also will appear at the bottom of each page in print preview and on the printed copies.

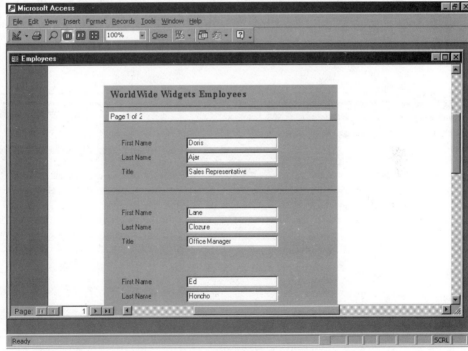

Report Sections

Reports can have sections similar to those in forms. But reports also can have grouping sections, which allow you to break data into separate groups. Each group can have its own header and footer. Here's a summary of the sections:

Report Header   Printed once at the beginning of the report (*Example:* a cover page).

Page Header   Printed at the top of each page.

Group Header   Printed at the top of each group.

Detail   Printed once for each record in the underlying table or query.

Group Footer   Printed at the bottom of each group (often used to place subtotals at the end of each printed group).

Page Footer   Printed at the bottom of each page.

Report Footer   Printed once at the end of the report. Often used to display grand totals at the end of a report that includes subtotals.

Figure 13.14 shows a report with multiple sections in design view, and Figure 13.15 shows the printed report.

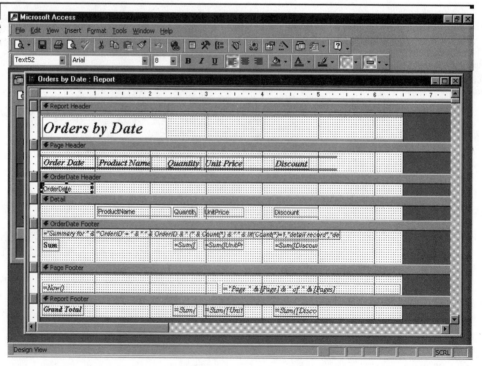

FIGURE 13.15

The report produced by the design in Figure 13.14. This report is sorted and grouped on the OrderDate and ProductName fields (although the ProductName group header and footer are empty).

Orders by Date

Order Date	Product Name	Quantity	Unit Price	Discount
2/1/99				
	Basketball	1	$4.95	0.00%
	Basketball	2	$4.95	0.00%
	Billiard balls	2	$127.45	0.00%
	Crystal ball	2	$45.55	0.00%
	Foosball	4	$17.85	0.00%
	Football	1	$5.65	0.00%
	Football	2	$5.65	0.00%
	Football	1	$5.65	0.00%
	Tether ball	5	$9.65	0.00%

Summary for 'OrderID' = 21 (9 detail records)

Sum		20	$227.35	0.00%
2/11/99				
	Baseball	2	$8.75	0.00%
	Basketball	1	$4.95	0.00%
	Basketball	2	$4.95	0.00%
	Football	1	$5.65	0.00%

Summary for 'OrderID' = 17 (4 detail records)

Sum		6	$24.30	0.00%
2/18/99				
	Crystal ball	1	$45.55	0.00%
	Golf balls	1	$6.75	0.10%

Summary for 'OrderID' = 11 (2 detail records)

Sum		2	$52.30	0.10%
2/25/99				
	Football	2	$5.65	0.00%

Summary for 'OrderID' = 12 (1 detail record)

Sum		2	$5.65	0.00%

Wednesday, January 20, 1999   Page 1 of 4

PART

II

Creating a Database

Adding or Removing Headers and Footers

The View menu provides commands for adding and removing report page headers and footers, and form page headers and footers. Adding a header or footer section is easy:

1. Choose View from the menu.

2. Choose the *unchecked* command for the section you want to add (Page Header/ Footer, Form Header/Footer, or Report Header/Footer).

Deleting a section is just as easy, but you should think carefully before deleting. If you delete a section that already contains controls, you'll lose all the controls in that section. Fortunately, Access will warn you if you're about to lose controls and will give you a chance to change your mind. (This operation has no "undo.")

NOTE It's a good idea to save your design (File ➢ Save or Ctrl+S) before you delete a section. That way, if you accidentally delete the wrong section, you can close your design without saving it (File ➢ Close ➢ No), and then reopen the previous copy in design view.

To delete a section, choose View and then choose the *checked* command for the section you want to delete. If Access asks for confirmation, click Yes only if you're sure you want to delete all the controls in that section.

NOTE You can move controls to another section of the form or report before deleting the section (see "Moving Controls" earlier in this chapter for details). You also can resize a section, as explained later in this chapter under "Sizing a Section."

Grouping Data in Reports

You can group data in reports (but not in forms) by creating sorting and grouping sections. These sections are handy for sorting data and printing subtotals, as shown earlier in Figure 13.15.

Sorting and grouping sections differ from the other sections described above in that:

- You can use sorting and grouping sections only in reports (not forms).

- You don't use the View menu to add or remove sorting and grouping headers or footers.

• A sorting and grouping header or footer is often based on some field from the underlying table or query or on some expression that involves a field.

The Easy Way to Create Groups/Subtotals

The easiest way to create a report with sorting and grouping sections is to start from the database window and use the Report Wizard to create the report (see Chapter 12). When the Wizard is done, your report design will include the sorting and grouping sections and controls needed to print subtotals, grand totals, and percentage totals. You can then switch to design view and tweak the report groupings to perfection.

Grouping without a Wizard

If you prefer to set up sorting and grouping sections without any help from a wizard, start in report design view and follow these steps:

1. Click the Sorting and Grouping button (shown at left) on the Report Design toolbar, or choose View ➤ Sorting and Grouping from the menus. You'll see the Sorting and Grouping dialog box. A completed example is shown in Figure 13.16.

2. Use the drop-down list under Field/Expression to select the field to group by, or type a custom expression of your own.

3. Change the Sort Order from Ascending to Descending to arrange groups from largest-to-smallest order (for example, from Z to A or from December to January).

PART

II

Creating a Database

The report from Figure 13.15, shown in design view, with the Sorting and Grouping dialog box open on the screen.

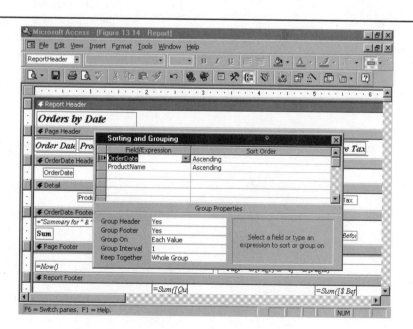

4. Change these properties in the lower pane of the dialog box, as needed:

Group Header   To create a header section for the group, change the Group Header property from No to Yes.

Group Footer   To create a footer section for the group, change the Group Footer property from No to Yes.

Group On   To choose how you want to form the groups, select options from the Group On drop-down list. The available options depend on the type of field you're grouping on, as summarized in Table 13.1.

TABLE 13.1: GROUP ON PROPERTIES FOR VARIOUS FIELD TYPES

CHOOSE THIS GROUP ON PROPERTY	TO GROUP RECORDS ON
Text Fields	
Each Value	Same value in the field or expression
Prefix Characters	Same first *n* number of characters in the field or expression (set *n* with the Group Interval property)
Date/Time Fields	
Each Value	Same value in the field or expression
Year	Dates in the same calendar year
Qtr	Dates in the same calendar quarter
Month	Dates in the same month
Week	Dates in the same week
Day	Dates on the same day
Hour	Dates in the same hour
Minute	Dates in the same minute
AutoNumber, Currency, or Number Fields	
Each Value	Same value in the field or expression
Interval	Values that fall in the interval you specify in the Group Interval property

Group Interval   To change the interval or number of characters to group on, type a number into the Group Interval box. For instance, to group records by the first three letters of a customer's last name, change Group On to Prefix Characters and set the Group Interval to 3.

Keep Together   To prevent a group that's less than a page in length from being split across two pages, change this property from No to Whole Group (keep the entire group together) or With First Detail (keep just the group header and first detail record together).

5. (Optional) Add any of the following to the header or footer section: fields from the field list, calculated controls (for subtotals and totals), horizontal lines, rectangles, and page breaks. See "Creating Calculated Controls" and "Adding Page Breaks" later in this chapter for more about those topics.

Creating More Than One Group

You can add more than one level of grouping. For instance, you might want to group orders first by OrderDate and then by ProductName within OrderDate, as shown in Figure 13.16.

To add another level, open the Sorting and Grouping dialog box. Click in the Field/ Expression column where you want the new group to appear in the grouping hierarchy. If you need to open up a new row in the dialog box, click the row selector where the blank row should appear, and then press Insert. Now fill in the Field/Expression, Sort Order, and Group Properties as described previously.

Deleting, Moving, or Changing a Group Header/Footer

You can hide, delete, or move a grouping section, and you can change the field or expression used for grouping, as follows:

- **To hide a group header or footer section (but keep the grouping)**, click in the appropriate row in the Sorting and Grouping dialog box. Then change the row's Group Header or Group Footer property (as appropriate) to No. Records will still be grouped and sorted as before, but the selected group header or footer for this section won't be printed.

- **To delete a grouping section**, click the appropriate row selector in the Sorting and Grouping dialog box, press the Delete key, and click Yes when asked for confirmation. Records will no longer be grouped or sorted by the field or expression, and any group headers and footers for this section will disappear from the report.

PART

II

Creating a Database

- **To move a grouping section**, click the appropriate row selector in the Sorting and Grouping dialog box and then drag the selected row up or down to a new position in the grouping hierarchy. Access will rearrange the group header and footer sections in the report design immediately.

- **To change the field or expression used for grouping**, click in the appropriate Field/Expression box in the Sorting and Grouping dialog box. Then select another field name from the Field/Expression drop-down list, or type in a different expression. To change the field displayed in the group header or footer section, delete the old field from the appropriate section in the report design, and then drag a new one from the field list. Or select the control and change its Control Source data property.

Hiding Duplicate Data in a Report

The sample report in Figure 13.15 and the corresponding report design in Figure 13.16 illustrate how the Sorting and Grouping feature can hide duplicate data. In those examples we placed the OrderDate control in the OrderDate Header section (*not* in the Detail section). That way, the order date information appears only when the order date changes, not on every detail line.

Another way to hide duplicate data in a report doesn't require the Sorting and Grouping feature. Here are the steps:

1. Base the report on a query or table datasheet that's sorted by the field you want to group on, or create the query on the fly, as discussed earlier in "Specifying the Record Source On the Fly."

2. Put the bound control for the group header in the detail section of the report. In Figure 13.17, for example, we put CompanyName in the detail section and used it as a sort field.

3. Open the property sheet (View ➢ Properties), click the control whose duplicate values you want to hide, and change the Hide Duplicates property on the Format tab to Yes. You also might want to change the Can Shrink property to Yes (to eliminate blank lines during printing) and the Can Grow property to Yes (to allow text, such as the company name, to expand as needed).

PART

II

Creating a Database

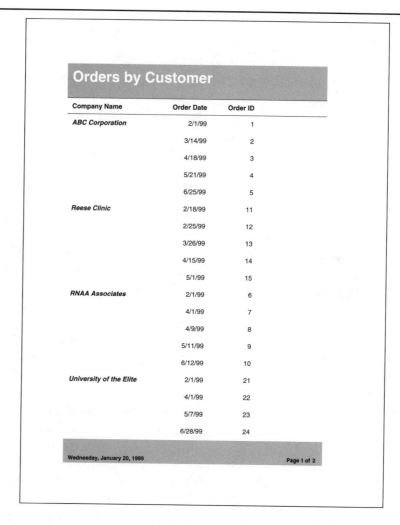

A report that's sorted by CompanyName, OrderDate, and OrderID, and that suppresses duplicate values in all three fields. We used the Report Wizard to create an ungrouped Tabular report on the Customers and Orders tables, and then changed the report's Record Source on the fly to sort each field in Ascending order.

Sizing a Section

Keep in mind that blank space in a form or report design always shows up as blank space in the final form or report. Suppose you leave a blank, two-inch-high page footer section at the bottom of a report design. Later, when you print the report, every page will have two extra inches of blank space at the bottom!

To fix the problem, change the height of the section as follows: Move the mouse pointer to the divider at the bottom of the section. When the pointer changes to a crosshair (shown below), drag the divider up or down and then release the mouse button.

A section can't be made smaller than the space required by the controls within that section. If you can't make a section as narrow as you'd like, first size or move the controls in the section so that they take up less height. Then resize the section again.

Summarizing Your Data by Hiding a Section

Suppose you've set up a report with detail lines, subtotals, and totals. Now you want to show *only* those subtotals and totals, without the detail lines. This type of report is called a *summary report* because it summarizes your data without providing unwanted details. That is, summary reports let you focus on the forest (your bottom line), while conserving the trees (paper).

In Chapter 12 you learned how to use the report wizards, which can produce summary reports quite easily. But you also can set up summary reports (or hide any section in a form or report) without using a wizard. The secret is simply to hide or delete information in the appropriate section, using either of these methods:

- Click the band at the top of the section you want to hide. (For example, click the Detail band to hide detail lines in a summary report.) Now open the property sheet (View ➤ Properties), click the Format tab, and change the section's Visible property to No. This method leaves all the controls in the section, but doesn't show the contents of the section in the finished form or report. If you change your mind about hiding the information in the section, just click the section's band again, open the property sheet, click the Format tab, and change the section's Visible property back to Yes.

- Delete all controls from the section; then size the section so that it has no height at all. Of course, this method is more drastic than the one above, and it doesn't allow you to redisplay the section later.

Adding Your Own Controls

You've already learned how to add controls to a report or form by dragging field names from the field list. But bound controls are only the tip of the object iceberg. In the sections that follow, you'll learn how to use the toolbox to create more than a dozen different types of controls.

Using the Toolbox

The toolbox (shown in Figure 13.18 and briefly described in Table 13.2) provides all the tools you'll need to create your own controls.

FIGURE 13.18

The Toolbox provides all the buttons you need to design controls of your own.

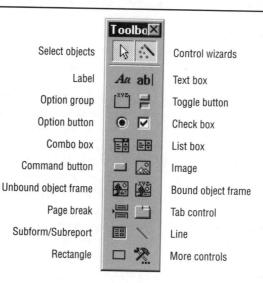

Select objects	Control wizards
Label	Text box
Option group	Toggle button
Option button	Check box
Combo box	List box
Command button	Image
Unbound object frame	Bound object frame
Page break	Tab control
Subform/Subreport	Line
Rectangle	More controls

PART

II

Creating a Database

TABLE 13.2: THE TOOLBOX BUTTONS SHOWN IN FIGURE 13.18

BUTTON NAME	WHAT IT DOES
Select Objects	Lets you select controls in the design window.
Label	Creates a control that displays descriptive text (e.g., title, caption, instructions).
Option Group*	Creates a control that frames a set of check boxes, option buttons, or toggle buttons. In form view, only one option in the group can be selected at a time.
Option Button	Creates a control that you can select or clear. (Sometimes called a radio button.)
Combo Box*	Creates a control also called a drop-down that's like a list box and text box combined. In form view, you can either type the text into the combo box or select an item from its drop-down list.

Continued ▶

TABLE 13.2: THE TOOLBOX BUTTONS SHOWN IN FIGURE 13.18 (CONTINUED)

BUTTON NAME	WHAT IT DOES
Command Button*	Creates a control that opens a linked form, runs a macro, calls a Visual Basic function, or runs a Visual Basic procedure.
Unbound Object Frame*	Creates a control that displays a picture, graph, or OLE object that isn't stored in the underlying table or query.
Page Break	Creates a control that starts a new page in a report or form or a new screen in a multiscreen form.
Subform/Subreport	Inserts a form or report within the form or report you're designing now.
Rectangle	Creates a control that appears as a rectangle or square. Used for decoration.
Control Wizards	Turns the control wizards on or off. In this chapter, we assume that the Control Wizards button is selected (pushed in), so that wizards are available to help you create option boxes, combo boxes, list boxes, charts, and command buttons.
Text Box	Creates a control that gives you a place to enter or view text in a form or report. Also used to display calculation results.
Toggle Button	Creates a control that acts as an on/off button. Toggle buttons can display text or a picture.
Check box	Creates a control that you can select (check) or clear (uncheck).
List Box*	Creates a control that gives you a list of choices.
Image	Creates a control that displays a picture. Image controls display faster and offer more image formats than Unbound Object controls, and they're recommended when you don't need to edit the object directly from the form or report.
Bound Object Frame	Creates a control that displays an OLE object (such as a picture) that is stored in the underlying table or query. (It's easiest to create bound controls by dragging fields from the field list.)
Tab Control	Creates a control with tabbed pages (like the ones you see in a Properties menu).
Line	Creates a control that appears as a straight line. Used for decoration.
More Controls	Displays a menu of ActiveX and other special purpose controls.

* A wizard will take you through the setup steps if the Control Wizards button is selected.

The Chart button, which creates a control that displays a chart, doesn't appear in the toolbox initially. Chapter 15 explains how to add this button and produce charts.

To create custom controls (such as the Calendar control provided with Access), choose Insert ➢ Custom Control.

Figure 13.19 shows a hodgepodge form, in form view, with many of the controls that Access offers. Figure 13.20 shows the same form in design view. Of course you'll probably never create a form as weird as this one, but it does illustrate the possibilities.

PART

II

Creating a Database

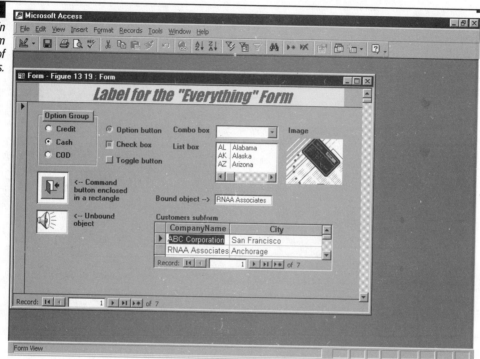

FIGURE 13.19

A hodgepodge form in form view. This form includes most types of Access controls.

To open the toolbox if it isn't visible, click the Form Design or Report Design toolbar's Toolbox button (shown at left), or choose View ➤ Toolbox.

Once you've opened the toolbox, using it is easy. The Select Objects and Control Wizards buttons are *toggle* buttons that you can click to activate or deactivate.

The steps for using the other buttons appear below:

1. Click the toolbox button you want to use. (If you want this button to remain selected until you choose another one, double-click the toolbox button.)

2. Click where you want the upper-left corner of the control to appear, or drag an outline to define the size and location of the control you're creating.

3. Respond to any prompts that appear (as described in the following sections).

4. Click the Select Objects toolbox button (if it's not selected already). Then select the control, if needed, (It may be selected already.) and adjust its size, position, colors, borders, lines, and other properties as needed.

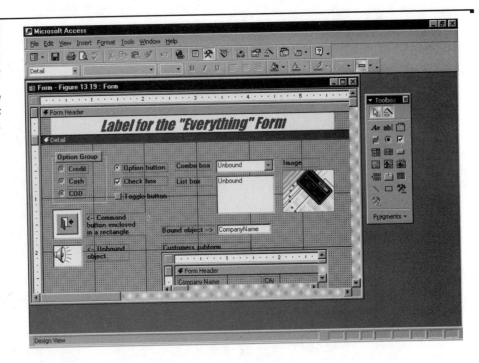

FIGURE 13.20

The hodgepodge form from Figure 13.19 in design view. We've hidden the toolbar, grid, and ruler so you can see the controls more easily.

To quickly learn how to use one of the toolbox buttons, click the button you're interested in and press F1. Or click the Help button on the Form Design or Report Design toolbar, and then click the toolbox button you want to know more about.

Changing Default Properties for Toolbox Tools

If you find yourself repeatedly changing the same old properties for a certain type of control, you can alter that control's default properties.

For the Current Form or Report Only

You can use either of two methods to change the default properties for newly created controls in the current form or report.

Here's one method:

1. Open the property sheet (View ➤ Properties) and click the All tab (or the tab for whichever group of properties you want to change).

2. Click the toolbox button for the object whose default properties you want to change. The title bar of the property sheet will reflect the name of the control you selected in step 1.

3. Change the properties as needed.

Here's the other method:

1. Set the properties for the controls that should serve as the model for other controls of the same type. For example, draw a rectangle and assign it properties that should be used for other rectangles in the design.

2. Select the control or controls that have the properties you want to copy.

3. Choose Format ➤ Set Control Defaults.

New controls placed in the design will have the new default properties you set.

 TIP To copy the properties from one control to other controls on your design, use the Format Painter. See "Copying Properties to Other Controls" earlier in this chapter.

For Future Form and Report Designs

Access also offers two ways to use your customized controls and other characteristics of the current design as defaults for new forms or reports.

The first way is to use your customized form or report design as a template for future designs. Access uses form and report templates to set up the initial appearance of a design:

- Any time you create a new design without a wizard.
- Any time you use the AutoForm Wizard (Insert ➤ AutoForm, or the equivalent New Object toolbar button) or AutoReport Wizard (Insert ➤ AutoReport, or the equivalent New Object toolbar button) to create a new design.

To specify your current form or report as a template:

1. Set the default controls for the form or report design, as described in the previous section, and then save the form or report (Ctrl+S).

2. Choose Tools ➤ Options and click the Forms/Reports tab in the Options dialog box.

3. Change the Form Template or Report Template option from Normal (the default template that comes with Access) to the name of the customized form or report you want to use for setting default characteristics in new designs.

4. Click OK.

Access will use the template named in the Forms/Reports tab of the Options dialog box for new designs that you create without wizards and for new designs created with AutoForm and AutoReport.

NOTE The Form Template and Report Template settings apply to any database you open or create. If the specified template isn't in the currently open database, Access will use the Normal template instead. To use your templates in other databases, import or export the templates as needed (see Chapter 7).

The second method is to create a new AutoFormat style or update an existing Auto-Format style with properties from the current design. You can then use the new or updated style to restyle the current form or report design or to set the initial appearance for any new ones you create. See "Customizing AutoFormat Styles" and "Choosing a Style for Your Design" earlier in this chapter.

Adding Labels

Labels display descriptive information, such as titles, captions, or instructions, on your form or report. The text in a label stays the same from record to record.

To create a label, click the Label toolbox button (shown at left), click where the upper-left corner of the label should appear or drag an outline to define the label's location and size, and then type the text for the label. Text will wrap automatically within the label. If you want to force text to a new line as you're typing, press Ctrl+Enter. Press Enter when you're finished typing the label text.

To customize the label, select the label and then use the property sheet or the Formatting (Form/Report) toolbar (refer to Figure 13.7) to change the text appearance, colors, borders, and so forth.

Adding Text Boxes

Text boxes provide a place for you to enter or view text. To create a text box, click the Text Box tool (shown at left). Then click where the upper-left corner of the text box should appear, or drag an outline to define the text box location and size. A field label and unbound text box will appear in your design.

TIP If you want your design to include a field from the underlying table or query, it's easiest to drag that field name from the field list.

- **To change the contents of the text box**, open the property sheet (View ➤ Properties), select the text box *control* (not the label), and then change the Control Source data property to a field name or expression.
- **To change the label text**, click in the label and edit the text normally. Or change the label's Caption property on the property sheet's Format tab.
- **To hide the label**, select the label and then change the Visible property on the property sheet's Format tab to No.

 TIP To prevent Access from creating labels when you add text boxes to the current form or report design, click the Text Box tool in the toolbox, and then change the Auto Label property on the property sheet's Format tab to No.

Adding Option Groups

An option group (shown below) contains a set of related buttons or check boxes from which you can select one button or check box in form view. (Option groups are rarely used on reports.) This control is especially useful when only one in a small list of options is valid and you don't need to let the user type a value.

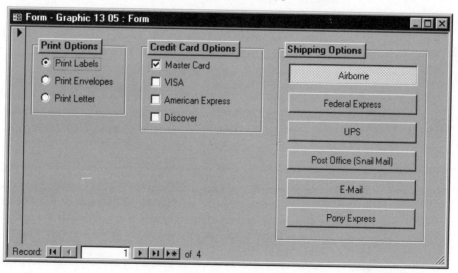

PART

II

Creating a Database

The selected option can be "remembered" so that the form can later decide what to do next (for example, print labels). Or the selection can be stored in a table field (for instance, the options could store 1 in the PaymentMethod field if you choose Master-Card in form view).

To create an option group:

1. Make sure the Control Wizards toolbox button (shown at left) is selected (pushed in).

2. Click the Option Group toolbox button (shown at left); then click in the design or drag an outline where the control should appear. The Option Group Wizard will take over.

3. Type the labels you want for each option when prompted, pressing Tab or ↓ after each entry. Each label must be unique. When you're done typing labels, click Next (or press Enter) to continue. You can choose whether to assign an option as the default selection in new records that you create.

4. Choose No, I Don't Want a Default, or select an option from the drop-down list next to Yes, the Default Choice Is. Click Next to continue.

5. Assign a numeric value to each option. Usually you can accept the suggested values. Each value must be unique. These values can either be stored in a table field or used in a macro or Visual Basic code to make decisions about what to do next. (For example, a value of 1 can mean "pay via Master Card.") Click Next.

6. Choose either of the options described just below when asked what you want Access to do when you select a value in your option group in form view.

   Save the Value For Later Use   Uses the value to make decisions in a macro or other procedure. The value is saved only as long as the form is open in form view.

   Store the Value in This Field   Stores the value in the table field you choose from the drop-down list.

7. Click Next.

8. Choose the options you want when asked what style and type of buttons you want for the group. The example in the Option Group Wizard dialog box will reflect your current choices. When you're done, click Next.

NOTE   It's customary in Windows programs to use the default style, Option Buttons, for buttons within an option group. This style makes it clear that only one option button in the group can be selected at a time. However, you also can display the option group buttons as check boxes (Only one box can be checked at a time.) or toggle buttons. (Only one button can be pushed in at a time.)

9. Type a label when the Wizard asks what kind of label you want for the group, and then click Finish.

The option group and its label will appear on the design. You can select the option group or its label and change their appearance with the usual techniques. If you'd like to change how an option group behaves, open the property sheet (View ➤ Properties), click the Data tab, and then do any of the following:

- **To control which field is updated** when you make a selection in form view, click the frame around the option group and change the field name listed in the Control Source property. To simply have Access remember the selected value (updating no fields), delete the field name in the Control Source property.

- **To change the option group's default selection**, click the frame around the option group and change the Default Value property.

- **To change the value assigned to a selection**, click the appropriate option button, check box button, or toggle button in the group; then change the Option Value property. Make sure all the values assigned to buttons in your option group are unique.

 NOTE Chapter 21 discusses how to create macros, and Chapter 26 introduces Visual Basic programming. In Chapter 23 you'll learn about using check boxes to make decisions.

Adding Toggle Buttons, Option Buttons, and Check Boxes

Toggle buttons, option buttons, and check boxes are simply different spots on the same leopard. That is, each control provides a button or check box that you can either select or deselect in form view.

Remember from the previous section that option groups are used to select just one item in a related group of items. By contrast, the individual controls discussed in this section typically are used to set any number of independent fields to Yes or No. For example, you can use a check box named Tax Exempt to indicate the tax exempt status of an order, another named Paid to indicate whether an order is paid, and still another named Filled to indicate whether an order has been filled. Most Windows programs use check boxes for these purposes, but Access also lets you use option buttons or toggle buttons.

NOTE You can use the Toggle Button, Option Button, or Check Box tools in the toolbox to add more options to an existing option group. Access automatically assigns an Option Value data property to new controls that you add, but you should check the value to make sure it's what you want.

To create one of these controls, click the appropriate tool in the toolbox, and then click in the design or drag an outline where the control should appear. The Option Button, Check Box, and Toggle Button tools are shown here:

You can change the Data properties for the button or check box as described previously for option group buttons.

Adding Combo Boxes and List Boxes

Combo boxes and list boxes (shown below) let you choose a field's value from a list.

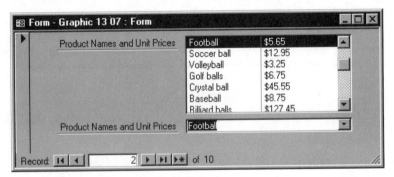

Combo boxes (shown above, at bottom), combine a text box with a drop-down list. The list stays hidden in form view until you click the drop-down button next to it. You can either type a value into the text box or select a value from the list. In list boxes (shown above, at top), the list is always visible, and the selected option is highlighted.

To create a combo box or list box:

 1. Make sure the Control Wizards toolbox button (shown at left) is selected (pushed in).

2. Click the Combo Box button (shown at left, top) or List Box button (shown at left, bottom) in the toolbox, as appropriate, and then click in the design or drag an outline where the control should appear. The Combo Box Wizard or List Box Wizard will take over.

3. Choose one of these options when asked how you want your box to get its values, and then click Next:

> **I Want the Box to Look Up the Values in a Table or Query**   Access displays the list from a table or query you select.

> **I Will Type In the Values That I Want**   Access displays the list from values that you type.

> **Find a Record on My Form Based on the Value I Selected in My Box**   Access displays the values from fields that are in the form's underlying table or query records.

4. Do one of the following, depending on your choice in step 3:

   - **If you chose to look up the values in a table or query**, select the table or query and click Next. Then select the fields you want to see in the combo box or list box and click Next. Continue with step 5.

   - **If you chose to type in the values**, type the number of columns to display, and press Tab. Now type in values for each column and row (pressing Tab to advance to the next column or row). When you're finished entering values, click Next. When prompted, choose the column in your combo box or list box that contains the value you want to either remember or store in the table, and then click Next. Skip to step 6.

   - **If you chose to display values from fields on the form**, choose the fields on your form that contain the values you want to see in the combo box or list box, and then click Next. (These fields will become columns in your combo box or list box.) Continue with step 5.

5. Adjust each column in your combo box or list box as instructed on the screen. If you chose to display values from fields on your form, you can select (check) Hide Key Column (Recommended) to hide the primary key field in the combo box or list box; or deselect (clear) this check box to show the primary key field. You also can rearrange columns as you would in datasheet view (see Chapter 8). Click Next.

6. If asked what you want Access to do when you select a value in your combo box or list box in form view, choose either of these options:

Remember the Value for Later Use Uses the value to make decisions in a macro or other procedure. The value is saved only as long as the form remains open in form view.

Store That Value in This Field Stores the value in the table field you select from the drop-down list.

7. Click Next.

8. (Optional) Type a label when asked what label you want for the combo box or list box.

9. Click Finish.

The combo box or list box (and its label) will appear. If you'd like to change the properties of a combo box or list box, open the property sheet (View ➤ Properties) and click the box portion of the control (not the label). Then customize the properties as explained next.

 TIP You can easily change a combo box to a list box, and vice versa, as explained later in the section "Presto Change Type."

The most important properties on the Data tab of the property sheet for a combo box or list box are as follows:

Control Source Specifies which field is updated when you select an item in the box. To simply have Access remember the selected value, delete the field name in the Control Source property box.

Row Source Type Specifies where the row data comes from (table or query, list of values, or list of field names).

Row Source Tells Access how to get data for each row. If you've selected Table/Query as the Row Source Type and have no idea about how to enter SQL statements for the Row Source, don't despair. Simply click in the Row Source box, and then click the Build button that appears. Now design (or modify) a query that will select and display the row data you want. When you're done, choose File ➤ Close ➤ Yes, or press Ctrl+W and then click Yes.

Bound Column Specifies which column number supplies data for the Control Source.

Limit To List   Specifies whether to let the user enter values that aren't shown in the combo box drop-down list.

Default Value   Specifies the default value assigned to the Control Source when you create a new record in form view.

The most important properties on the Format tab are:

Column Count   Specifies the number of columns to display in a combo box or list box.

Column Heads   Specifies whether column headings appear in a combo box or list box.

Column Widths   Specifies the width of each column shown in the box. Column widths are listed in column order from left to right and separated with a semicolon (;). Set the column width to 0 if you don't want to display the column.

List Rows   Specifies the number of rows to show in a combo box's drop-down list.

List Width   Specifies the width of the drop-down list in a combo box. For example, type 2 for a 2-inch-wide drop-down list. Or type Auto to make the drop-down list as wide as the text box.

Adding the Current Date and Time

It's easy to display the current date and time anywhere on a form or report. To do so:

1. Choose Insert ➤ Date and Time.

2. Fill in the Date and Time dialog box that appears (see below).

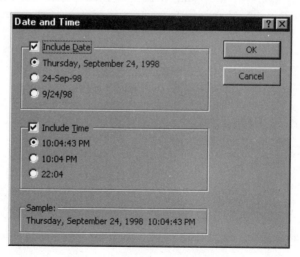

PART

II

Creating a Database

3. Click OK. A new text box will appear in the form header or report header (if one is visible), or in the detail section. It looks something like this:

=Format(Date(),"Long Date") & " " &

4. Drag the new text box to wherever it should appear in your design.

5. Switch to form view or print preview to see the results.

Presto Change Type

Access offers a time-saving *morphing* feature that lets you instantly convert one type of control into any other compatible type. For example, you can convert a list box to a combo box, or change a check box to a toggle button with just a couple of mouse clicks. Here's how:

1. Select the control you want to convert to another type.

2. Choose Format ➤ Change To, or right-click the control and choose Change To.

3. Choose any control type that's available in the menu that appears.

4. Change the control's properties as needed.

Adding Lines

You can draw a line anywhere within a section on a form or report design. Click the Line toolbox button (shown at left); then click in the design or drag an outline where the line should appear. To create a perfectly vertical or horizontal line, hold down the Shift key while you drag.

After creating a line, you can select it and move or resize it as needed. You also can use the Formatting (Form/Report) toolbar to change the line's color, thickness, or special effects.

Drawing Frames around Controls

The rectangle tool is especially nice for drawing neat frames around any control. To use it, click the Rectangle toolbox button (shown at left), and then click in the design or drag an outline where the rectangle should appear.

If the frame contains a background color, the frame may cover the controls behind it. That's easy to fix. Select the frame and then choose Format ➤ Send to Back. If you'd like to add a background color or other special effect to the frame, select the rectangle and choose the effects you want from the buttons and colors in the Formatting (Form/Report) toolbar. Raised, sunken, and etched effects and colored backgrounds look especially nice.

Adding Page Breaks

 You can add a page break to force a new page on a printed form or report. To do so, click the Page Break toolbox button (shown at left), and then click in the design where you want the page to break. (If you no longer want the page to break, select the page break control and press Delete. You also can drag the page break to a new place on the design.)

Here are some points to remember about page breaks:

- To avoid splitting data across pages, place the page break above or below other controls (not in the middle of a control).

- In a form the page break will appear in the printed copy only, not on the screen. (The next section explains how to break forms into multiple screens.)

- To print page breaks before or after a section in the printed form or report, click in the section where you want the page break, open the property sheet (View ➤ Properties), click the Format tab, and then change the Force New Page property from None to Before Section, After Section, or Before & After.

Creating a Multiscreen Form

If you want to create a form in which each page is the same size and each window shows only one page at a time, follow these steps:

1. Design your form normally.

2. Add a page break wherever you want the form to break, with each page break equidistant from the previous one. For example, if each detail area should be two inches high, put the first page break at 2 inches, the next one at 4 inches, and so on. You can use the vertical ruler's guidelines to help you adjust the page break position; or open the property sheet (View ➤ Properties), click the Format tab, and set the Top property for each page break to the measurement you want. (Access will move the page break automatically when you change the Top property.)

3. Size the Form Footer so that the top of the form footer section is at a multiple of the screen size you've chosen. Continuing with our 2-inch screen example, if you've placed page breaks at 2 inches and 4 inches and the last field is at 5.25 inches, place the form footer at the 6 inch mark on the ruler.

4. Select the form (Edit ➤ Select Form), open the property sheet (View ➤ Properties), and then click the Format tab. Now set Default View to Single Form; set Auto Resize to Yes; and set Auto Center to Yes.

5. Save and close the form.

To see the results, go to the database window and open the form. If the form is maximized, click the window's Restore button. Then choose Window ➤ Size to Fit Form.

Now, to view each screen of your form, press the Page Up and Page Down keys, or click above or below the scroll box in the vertical scroll bar. Pressing Page Up at the top of the form will take you to the previous record; pressing Page Down at the bottom of the form will take you to the next record.

TIP Navigating through a multiscreen form may feel somewhat clumsy if you are used to using Page Up and Page Down to move between records (instead of pages). You may prefer to use a tab control instead and place each screen of information on a separate tabbed page. See "Adding Tab Controls" later in this chapter for more information on this feature.

Adding Page Numbers to a Printed Form or Report

Access makes it easy to add page numbers to a printed form or report. Here's how:

1. Choose Insert ➤ Page Number. You'll see the Page Numbers dialog box shown below.

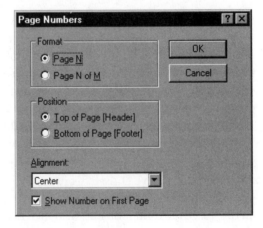

2. Select the format, position, and alignment, and choose whether to show the page number on the first page.

3. Click OK.

A text box control will appear at the top or bottom of the page (depending on your choice in step 2).

Adding Hyperlinks

In Chapter 8 we explained how to use hyperlink fields in a table to jump to other database objects or documents from a datasheet view or a form. With a hyperlink field in a table, you can jump to a different address from each record. For example, in the Employee table of the Order Entry database, you could store the address of each person's resume in a hyperlink field.

When you don't need to jump to a unique information source for each record in a table, you can use a hyperlink that's not tied to a hyperlink field. This type of hyperlink is placed on a form or a report in design view using the same basic techniques described in Chapter 8 for entering an address in a hyperlink field. In brief, you can do the following:

- **Use the Hyperlink toolbar button** to open the Insert Hyperlink dialog box

- **Copy and paste a hyperlink address** from a document or browser window onto a form or report design

- **Copy and paste selected text** to jump to a specific spot in a Microsoft Office file

- **Drag and drop a hyperlink address or text** from a Microsoft Office document

Figure 13.21 shows the Employees form from the Orders Entry database with a hyperlink address that jumps to the switchboard form in the same database. The hyperlink on the form was placed using the Hyperlink toolbar button. For details on using the Hyperlink tool or the other techniques listed above, check Chapter 8. The only difference is that you end up placing a label object on the form with a hyperlink address attached, instead of inserting an address into a field. If this process isn't clear, don't worry. We'll step through an example of using the Hyperlink toolbar button to place a hyperlink on a form a little later.

You can also use a few other techniques to include hyperlinks on a form or report. You can use an image object or command button with a hyperlink address attached. (Hyperlink Address and Hyperlink SubAddress properties are available for these kinds of controls.) When the image or button is clicked, the address specified by the hyperlink address properties is displayed.

If you're using a command button for a hyperlink, you don't have to set the hyperlink address properties yourself. The Command Button Wizard has an option that helps you create a hyperlink button. See the sidebar "Creating a Command Button Hyperlink" later in this chapter.

NOTE   If you place a hyperlink in a report, it will not be "hot." That is, nothing will happen when you click the hyperlink on the screen. But when you export the report to a spreadsheet or a document, the hyperlink will be active, enabling you to jump to the address the hyperlink points to.

Using the Hyperlink Toolbar Button

To add a hyperlink that's not attached to a field, follow these steps:

1. Open the form or report you want to add a hyperlink to in design view.

2. Click the Insert Hyperlink toolbar button (shown at left) to open the Insert Hyperlink dialog box.

3. On the left side of the Insert Hyperlink dialog box, click the button for the type of object or document you want the hyperlink to jump to. Then select, enter, or browse for the target of the hyperlink using the tools in the Insert Hyperlink window. Click OK to return to the design window. (See Chapter 8 for more information on valid hyperlink addresses, allowable shortcuts for addresses, and tips on using the Insert Hyperlink dialog box.)

4. The new hyperlink will appear in the upper-left corner of the form or report design. Drag it to the desired location.

A hyperlink object placed with the Insert Hyperlink tool is really just a glorified label object that has its Hyperlink Address property and/or Hyperlink SubAddress property defined. To check this for yourself (if you're interested!), right-click a selected hyperlink in the design window and choose Properties from the shortcut menu. Click the Format tab and look for the Hyperlink Address and Hyperlink SubAddress properties. The hyperlink shown in Figure 13.21 has Form Switchboard as its Hyperlink SubAddress property and nothing for the Hyperlink Address property. (If the hyperlink pointed to an object in a file other than the open database, that filename would appear as the Hyperlink Address property.)

Using an Image for a Hyperlink

Instead of using text such as http://www.microsoft.com or Form Switchboard to show a hyperlink on a form or report, you can use a picture:

1. Open the form or report to include the hyperlink in design view.

2. Place an image object on a form using the Image button in the toolbox. (See "Adding a Picture or Image," later in this chapter, for more detailed instructions on using this tool.)

3. Right-click the selected image, choose Properties from the shortcut menu, and click the Format tab.

4. Enter a URL address or filename for the Hyperlink Address property, or the name of an object in the current database for the Hyperlink SubAddress property. You can use the ... button at the end of either property line to open the Edit Hyperlink dialog box. (Chapter 8 explains the use of this dialog box.)

5. Test the image hyperlink by going into form view and clicking the picture. You should jump to the hyperlink address you entered in the Properties menu.

Adding Command Buttons

Command buttons perform some action when you click them in form view. For instance, you can add buttons that navigate through records, save or print records, open and close forms, print reports, run other programs, and so on. To create a command button:

1. Make sure the Control Wizards toolbox button (shown at left) is selected (pushed in).

2. Click the Command Button toolbox button (shown at left); then click in the design, or drag an outline where the button should appear. The Command Button Wizard will take over.

3. When asked what the button should do, click an action category (for example, Record Navigation) in the Categories list, and then click an action (for example, Go to Next Record) in the Actions list. Click Next to continue. If prompted for details about the action you chose, complete the dialog box, and then click Next.

4. When asked what the button should look like, either choose Text and enter the text that should appear on the button, or choose Picture and then select a picture. (To see all available pictures, select the Show all Pictures check box. To select a custom bitmap picture or icon from your hard drive, click the Browse button and then double-click the file you want to use.) Click Next to continue.

5. When asked what you want to name the button, type a meaningful name, and then click Finish.

The command button will appear in your design. To test the button's action, switch to form view and click the button.

TIP On command buttons that show pictures instead of text, it's a good idea to set the Status Bar Text and ControlTip Text properties on the Other tab of the command button's property sheet. Initially, the ControlTip Text will be set to the name of the action you chose. See "Adding Help, Menus, and Prompts to Controls" earlier in the chapter for details.

Creating a Command Button Hyperlink

At times you may prefer to use a command button, instead of the standard label-type hyperlink, to jump to a location in an Access database, somewhere else on your computer, or even on the Web. Create a command button without using the Command Button Wizard. Then:

1. Right-click the new command button and select Properties.

2. Click the Format tab.

3. Enter values in the Hyperlink Address and/or the Hyperlink SubAddress lines for the spot you want to jump to.

Adding Tab Controls

Access has a feature that lets you add your own tab controls to a form. A tab control is simply an object with multiple tabbed pages, like the Properties sheet you are now familiar with. This control makes it easy to organize a form with many objects into a less cluttered view of related information. For example, we could use a tab control to show review and salary data for an employee on its own page of the Employee form, instead of crowding it in with the basic details like name and address.

Here's one way to create the tab control shown in Figure 13.22:

FIGURE 13.22

This Employee form uses a tab control to show an employee's review and salary details on a separate page. This example shows the first page of the tab control.

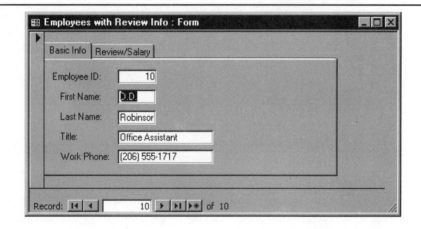

PART
II

Creating a Database

1. Add fields for Last Review Date and Salary to the Employees table in the Order Entry database called Resume.

2. Select the Forms tab, and click New from the database window.

3. Leave Design View highlighted, and select Employees as the table for the new form. Click OK.

 4. Choose View ➢ Toolbox to show the toolbox, if it's not visible. Click the Tab Control button in the toolbox. Then click and drag on the form to place a tab control. It will look like the graphic shown next.

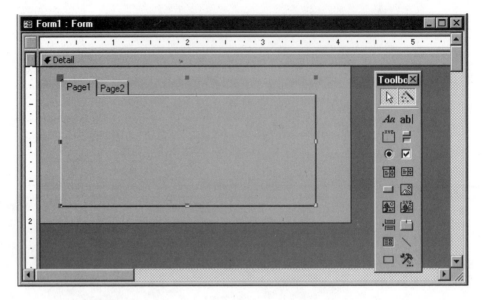

5. Change the caption for the first page of the tab control by right-clicking the page and choosing Properties from the shortcut menu. Enter **Basic Info** for the Caption property.

6. Place fields on the page by choosing View ➤ Field List. Then drag each field you want to show on the first page of the form from the field list to the tab control. For Figure 13.22, the Employee ID, First Name, Last Name, Title, and Work Phone fields were dragged onto the Basic Info page of the tab control. The fields were then aligned and spaced using the Format menu commands. The Left properties of the text objects (the areas that show the field values) were also adjusted to make more room for the field labels.

7. Right-click Page 2 of the tab control, and choose Properties from the shortcut menu. Enter **Review/Salary** for the Caption property.

8. Drag the Last Review Date and Salary fields from the field list to the second page of the tab control. Change the Left properties for the text objects to a larger number to make more room for the labels. Align the field with the Format menu command if you need to.

Switch to form view to test the action of the new tab control. Just click a tab to switch form pages. Figure 13.23 shows the finished form with the second tab control page visible.

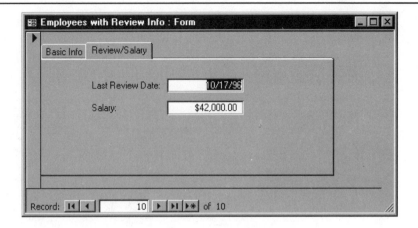

FIGURE 13.23

The Employees with Review Info form with the second page of the tab control visible.

Adding Pictures, Sounds, and Other Objects

Your forms and reports can include pictures, sounds, and other objects. These can be standalone *unbound* objects, such as a company logo, or they can be *bound* objects, stored in the underlying table or query.

Adding an Unbound Picture or Object

Unbound objects stay the same from record to record. Use them to display such things as a company logo on a report or form header, or to attach a sound file, containing instructions, to the form header.

To create an unbound object:

1. Click the Unbound Object Frame toolbox button (shown at left), and then click in the design or drag an outline where the control should appear. Or click in the section where you want to insert the object, and choose Insert ➤ Object. You'll see an Insert Object dialog box similar to the one shown in Figure 13.24.

2. (Optional) If you want to display the object as an icon, select (check) Display as Icon.

3. Do one of the following:

   - **To create the object from scratch**, choose Create New, select an object type from the Object Type list, and then click OK. Create the object in its source program, and then exit the program as appropriate. (For most programs, you can choose File ➤ Exit & Return, or click the program window's Close button, or press Alt+F4. Click Yes if asked whether you want to update the object.)

PART

II

Creating a Database

FIGURE 13.24

The Insert Object dialog box.

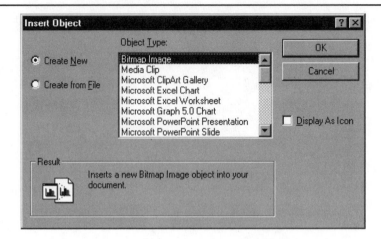

- **To create the object from an existing file**, choose Create from File. The Insert Object dialog box will change to include a Browse button and a Link check box. Type the filename in the File text box or use the Browse button to locate the file. If you want to link the object so that it changes whenever the original file changes, select (check) Link. If you want to display the object as an icon, select (check) Display as Icon. Click OK.

The object will appear in design view. If you want to be able to edit a picture or play a sound in form view, open the property sheet (View ➤ Properties), click the Data tab, and change the object's Enabled property to Yes.

 TIP Your form may scroll faster from record to record if you put the unbound object in the form header or footer section (*not* in the detail section).

If you want to edit the object while you're in design view, you can double-click the object; or right-click the object and choose ...Object ➤ Open from the shortcut menu that appears. Or select the object and choose Edit ➤ ...Object ➤ Edit from the design view menus. (The ... noted here before Object will appear on the menus as the name of the source program for the object.)

Here's an even quicker way to put an unbound OLE object into your design. Open the program you used to create the object (or use the program to create a new object). Select the object using the program's usual tools, and then copy the data to the Windows Clipboard. (Choose Edit ➤ Copy or press Ctrl+C to place fields on the page.) Close the program if you wish, and switch back to your form or report design. Now click in the section where the object should appear, and paste the object into your design (choose Edit ➤ Paste, or press Ctrl+V).

 TIP If the source program you're copying from supports OLE 2, try the drag-and-drop method. Right-click an empty part of the Windows Taskbar, and choose Tile Vertically so you can see both the Access window and the window that contains the object you want to copy. Then Ctrl-drag the selected object from the source program to your form or report design. The programs in the Microsoft Office and Corel WordPerfect suites support OLE 2, and so does the WordPad word processor (which comes with Windows).

Adding a Picture or Image

You also can use an image control to display unbound pictures and logos on your forms or reports. Image controls are faster than unbound object controls and are recommended if you don't need to change the picture after adding it to the design. To add an image to your design:

1. Click the Image toolbox button (shown at left); then click in the design or drag an outline where the control should appear. Or click in the section where you want to insert the object, and choose Insert ➤ Picture. You'll see an Insert Picture dialog box similar to the one shown in Figure 13.25.

FIGURE 13.25

The Insert Picture dialog box after we clicked the Preview button in the dialog box.

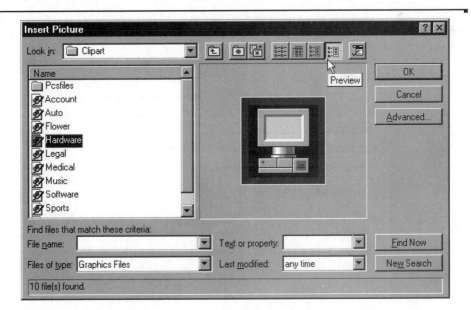

2. Locate and double-click the picture you want to insert. The image will appear on your design.

 TIP   If you want to display a different picture in an image control, right-click the control, choose Properties, click the Format tab in the property sheet, and then click in the Picture property box. Next, click the Build button; then locate and double-click a file name in the Insert Picture dialog box.

Adding a Background Picture

Suppose you want to add a background to your form or report, such as a picture of clouds, or a scanned image of a preprinted form or photograph. It's easy to do if you follow these steps:

1. Select the entire form or report. (Choose Edit ➤ Select Form, or Edit ➤ Select Report.)

2. Open the property sheet (View ➤ Properties) and click the Format tab.

3. Scroll down to and click in the box for the Picture property, and then click the Build button that appears.

4. When the Insert Picture dialog box appears (refer to Figure 13.25), locate and double-click the picture you want to use for the background design.

5. (Optional) Change the Picture Size Mode, Picture Alignment, and Picture Tiling properties as needed.

The picture you selected will appear as a background for the form or report design. To see the full effect of your new background, switch to form view or print preview. Later in this chapter, we'll give you some pointers on sizing pictures and setting up Access forms that look like the preprinted paper forms you may be using now.

To remove the picture background, repeat steps 1 and 2 above, scroll down to and click in the Picture property box, select and delete the filename text, and then press Enter. When prompted, click Yes to delete the picture from the background.

Using Non-Bitmap Pictures

Pictures come in many formats—bitmap (.bmp), Windows Metafile Format (.wmf), and Tagged Image File Format (.tif)—to name just a few. If you use the Image tool to place a graphic on a form or report, Access usually can display that image perfectly, because the Image tool can interpret many different picture formats.

However, if you use the Unbound Object Frame tool to put a non-bitmap image into a form or report design (or if you store the image in an OLE Object table field), you may get an object package, rather than the original artwork, when you try to view that image.

 TIP Use the Image tool or Picture property to place an image if you won't need to change the image later. Use the Unbound Object Frame tool if you will need to change the image. The Image tool and Picture property offer the widest variety of displayable image formats to choose from.

For example, suppose you use the Unbound Object Frame tool in form design view to place a Windows metafile object in the Form Header of a form. Instead of seeing the picture that was contained in the object you placed, you'll see a package icon that looks like this in form design view: (Its appearance in form view is similar.)

Acwiz.wmf

 NOTE In design view or datasheet view, you can double-click the package to view its contents if an association exists between the package type and a program on your computer.

If you prefer to see the actual picture (rather than the object package icon) on your form or report, you'll need to convert the image to a bitmap (`.bmp`) file or to some other graphics format that Access can display.

Once you've converted the object to a bitmap file, you can insert it via the Unbound Object Frame tool (or the Picture property or Image tool), as explained earlier in this chapter.

After placing the picture, open the property sheet (View ➢ Properties), click the Format tab, and then experiment with the Size Mode or Picture Size Mode property settings—Clip, Stretch, and Zoom—to see which option offers the best fit. See "Controlling the Size of Pictures," later in this chapter for more details on customizing the picture size.

If you don't have a fancy graphics conversion program, try this trick to convert the graphic to a `.bmp` file:

1. Place the graphic into a word processing program (such as Corel WordPerfect) using that program's tools.

2. Select the object in the word processing document (usually by clicking it), and copy it to the Windows Clipboard. (Press Ctrl+C.)

3. Exit your word processing program (if you wish).

4. Open Paint. Paste the graphic into Paint. (Press Ctrl+V.) Save the file as usual. Voilà! You've saved the graphic as a bitmap file.

Here are some other things you can do after copying a graphic to the Clipboard in your word processing program:

- Switch back to your Access form or report design. Click in the section where the image should appear, and then paste the image. (Press Ctrl+V or choose Edit ➤ Paste.) Again, the image will appear as a picture in your form or report (though it will be embedded as a word processing document, rather than a Paint picture). Double-clicking the image in design view will take you back to the word processing program.

- Store the picture in a table as a bound OLE object. Open the table in datasheet view or form view, click in the appropriate record and OLE Object field, and press Ctrl+V or choose Edit ➤ Paste to store the embedded picture.

Coloring the Picture Background

In some cases, the picture background will be white (or some other color). Setting the Back Color to Transparent won't help if the white background color is actually a part of the bitmap image. If you want the background color of the bitmap to match the background color of your form or report, you'll need to use the Windows Paint applet or some other graphics program to change the bitmap image's background color.

If the image is mostly white background, you'll need to crop the image. Use Paint, or a better graphics program if you have one. In Paint, select the area you want to crop, and choose Edit ➤ Copy To to copy just the selected area to a file. For more information on Microsoft Paint, start Paint (Start ➤ Programs ➤ Accessories ➤ Paint) and choose Help ➤ Help Topics or press F1.

Adding a Control for an OLE Object Field

Bound object controls are used to display a picture, chart, or any OLE object that's stored in the underlying table or query. Unlike unbound objects, bound objects will change from record to record. In form view, you can change the bound object by double-clicking it (see Chapter 8 for more information on entering data into OLE Object fields).

The easiest way to add an OLE object to your report or form is to drag it from the field list to your design. The field must be defined in the table as an OLE Object data type. (You also can use the Bound Object Frame tool to create the object, but it's not as easy.)

When you first add an OLE object to a form or report design, Access displays its actual size, clipping it to fit within the object frame if necessary.

Adding ActiveX Controls

Access comes with some special purpose tools called ActiveX controls. (In previous versions of Access, they were called custom controls or OLE controls.) These controls are typically used by programmers to add functionality to a form—functionality that's not available through Access itself. For example, the Microsoft WebBrowser control can be programmed to open a Web page in the control's own window. Some ActiveX controls also come with Microsoft Office 2000 Developer and are documented there; others are available from third-party companies or in other Microsoft products. Not all of these ActiveX controls will work well with Access, though. Check the Readme file for Access 2000 for a list of the controls that Microsoft has tested with Access.

To insert an ActiveX control into your design:

1. Click in the section where the new control should appear.

2. Click the More Tools button in the Toolbox (shown at left), or choose Insert ➢ ActiveX Control to show a menu of the ActiveX controls that come with Access.

3. Select a control from the menu.

4. Right-click the control, choose Properties, and set any properties you may need to adjust for the control.

For more information about ActiveX controls, look up *ActiveX Controls* with the Office Assistant.

Controlling the Size of Pictures

If you're not happy with the way Access sizes a picture or custom control, you can change the control's Size Mode (or Picture Size Mode) property:

1. Open the property sheet (View ➢ Properties), and then click the Format tab.

2. Select the object you want to change, or select the entire form (Edit ➢ Select Form) or report (Edit ➢ Select Report) if you want to change the background picture.

3. Choose one of these options from the Size Mode or Picture Size Mode property's drop-down list:

Clip   Displays the object at actual size. If the object is larger than the control frame, Access will clip the image at the borders. Clip is the fastest display method.

Stretch   Sizes the object to fill the control. Stretch may change the object's original proportions, especially in circles and photos. (Bar charts and line charts should look just fine.)

Zoom   Sizes the object's height or width to fill the frame without distortion, then shows the entire object without clipping.

 TIP   Remember that if you're working with a picture stored in a table field, the size mode affects the display of every picture in the table. For example, you can't assign the Clip size mode to one record, and the Zoom size mode to another. This is why it's so important to size and crop equally all the photos you'll be putting into a table.

The example below shows the same picture with different Size Mode properties assigned.

Changing the Front-to-Back Order of Controls

You can create some interesting effects by changing the front-to-back order of controls. That's how we added the drop-shadow gray rectangle around the computer example above. We also used the technique to place the white box first in front of the black one and then behind it in the example shown on the next page.

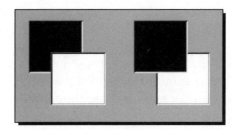

To change the front-to-back order of controls:

1. Select the control or controls you want to move in front of or behind another control.

2. Choose Format ➢ Bring to Front, or Format ➢ Send to Back, as appropriate.

To use this feature to uncover objects hidden by a newly drawn rectangle, select the rectangle and choose Format ➢ Send to Back.

Creating Calculated Controls

A *calculated control* uses an expression as its control source. Calculated controls let you display values calculated from data in one or more fields, or from other controls. For example, you can calculate the extended price of an item by multiplying the value in the quantity field by the value in the unit price field, like this:

```
=[Quantity]*[UnitPrice]
```

Access doesn't store the result of a calculated control in a table; instead, it recomputes the value each time the record is displayed. (In form view, calculated controls are read-only.)

To create a calculated control:

1. Create a control of any type that has a Control Source property on the Data tab of the property sheet. Typically, you'll use text boxes for this purpose, but combo boxes, list boxes, unbound and bound object frames, toggle buttons, option buttons, and check boxes also work.

2. Select the control and use one of these methods to enter the expression:

- Type an equal sign (=), followed by the calculation expression, directly into the box. Example: In a text box, type **=[Quantity]*[UnitPrice]** to multiply the value in the Quantity field by the value in the UnitPrice field.

- In the Control Source data property box, type the expression (preceded by an equal sign).

• In the Control Source data property box, click the Build button to open the Expression Builder (shown in Figure 13.26). The Expression Builder handles the messy details of Access expression syntax while you focus on what you want to do. Choose items in the dialog box by clicking and double-clicking entries in the three panels near the bottom of the dialog box and clicking operator buttons above the panels. As you do this, the Expression Builder automatically puts in the square brackets, dots, exclamation points, and other details required. When you're done using the Expression Builder, click OK.

FIGURE 13.26

A completed expression in Expression Builder.

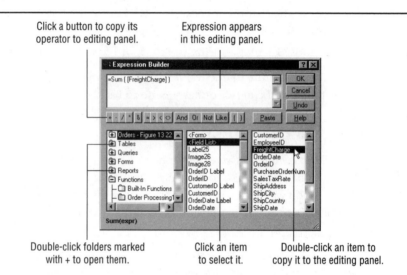

Click a button to copy its operator to editing panel.

Expression appears in this editing panel.

Double-click folders marked with + to open them.

Click an item to select it.

Double-click an item to copy it to the editing panel.

The top panel in Figure 13.26 shows a finished expression in the Expression Builder. Here are the steps we followed in the Expression Builder dialog box to create that expression:

1. In the bottom-left panel, we double-clicked the Functions folder (which is marked with a plus sign) and then clicked Built-In Functions.

2. In the bottom-center panel, we clicked <All>.

3. In the bottom-right panel, we scrolled down to the Sum function and double-clicked it to copy the function Sum (<expr>) to the editing panel at the top.

4. In the top panel, we clicked <expr> to select it.

5. In the bottom-left panel, we clicked Orders - Figure 13 22 (the name of the form we were designing).

6. In the bottom-center panel, we clicked <Field List>.

7. In the bottom-right panel, we double-clicked FreightCharge to copy that field name to the editing panel.

8. We clicked OK to close the Expression Builder dialog box and copy the expression into the Control Source property box. (If you don't type the initial equal sign (=) in the expression, Access will add it automatically when you click in another property box.)

9. We pressed Enter to complete the entry and move the cursor down to the next property box.

TIP   Instead of double-clicking an item in the bottom-right panel, you can highlight the item and then click the Paste button in the dialog box. Either way, Access will copy the item into the editing panel.

Keep the following points in mind as you enter calculated controls:

- For check boxes, option buttons, and option groups, you must change the Control Source data property. You can't simply type the expression into the control.

- Chapters 9 and 10 show examples of calculation expressions for filters and queries. To use those examples in a control, simply precede each example with an equal sign. Table 13.3 offers a few more examples.

WARNING   If you edit a control that was originally set up to show the contents of a regular field and include the regular field name in the new expression, be sure to change the control's Name property. Otherwise, you will get an error message when you switch to form view.

- The Expression Builder provides the easiest way to enter functions and to reference fields in tables, queries, forms, and reports. You also can use it to display page numbers and dates.

- You can use the Format property on the Format tab of the property sheet (or the Format function) to display calculated expressions in any format you wish.

For more information about entering expressions into calculated controls, search for *Expressions* with the Office Assistant, or click the Help button in the Expression Builder.

TABLE 13.3: SAMPLE EXPRESSIONS FOR CALCULATED CONTROLS

EXPRESSION	SAMPLE RESULT
=[ShippingMethodID] & ": " & [ShippingMethod]	*1: Federal Express* if ShippingMethodID is 1 and ShippingMethod is Federal Express.
=[Quantity]*[UnitPrice]	*350* if Quantity value is 10 and UnitPrice value is 35.
=[Products Subform].Form![UnitPrice] * 1.15	*46* if UnitPrice on a subform named Products Subform is 40.
="Page " & [Page] & " of "& [Pages]	*Page 3 of 5* on page three of a five-page printed report or form.
=Now( )	System date and time.
=DatePart("yyyy",Now( ))	*1999* (year portion of system date]and time).
=UCase([LastName] & ", "& [FirstName])	*STRAPPMAN, HANLEY* if LastName is Strappman (or strappman or STRAPP-MAN) and FirstName is Hanley (or hanley or HANLEY).

Note: All expressions must be entered on a single line.

Adding a Subform or Subreport

A subform or subreport is simply a form within a form or a report within a report. Figures 13.27 and 13.28 show a main form with a subform and a main report with a subreport, respectively.

In Chapters 11 and 12, you learned how the Form Wizard and Report Wizard can create main/subforms and main/subreports for you automatically. The same concepts described in those chapters also apply when you're creating a main/subform or main/subreport without a wizard. Here are the essential facts you need to know:

- Generally you use a subform or subreport when there's a one-to-many relationship between the data in the main form or report and the data in the subform or subreport. The main form or report is on the one side of the relationship, and the subform or subreport is on the many side. *Example:* A main form based on the Orders table and a subform based on the Order Details table will show each order and its related order details.

FIGURE 13.27

A main Orders form with an Order Details subform in form view.

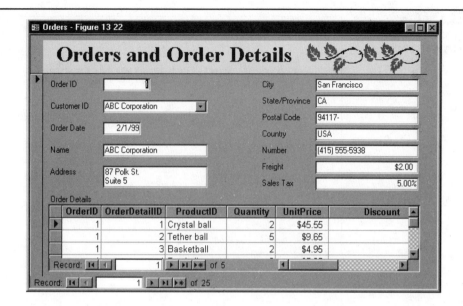

- You must create and save the subform or subreport before you can use it in a main form or report.

- Each main form or report can contain more than one subform or subreport, and you can have up to two nested subforms/subreports in a main form or report. (A nested subform/subreport is one that contains a subform/subreport of its own.)

- To display the subform as a datasheet, change the subform's Default View property on the Format tab to Datasheet. It's usually best to display a subform as a datasheet.

- In the main form or report, you can use expressions to refer to values in the subform or subreport. See "Creating Calculated Controls" above.

- Chapter 11 explains how to navigate through main forms and their subforms.

PART

II

Creating a Database

FIGURE 13.28

A main Orders report
with an Order Details
subreport.

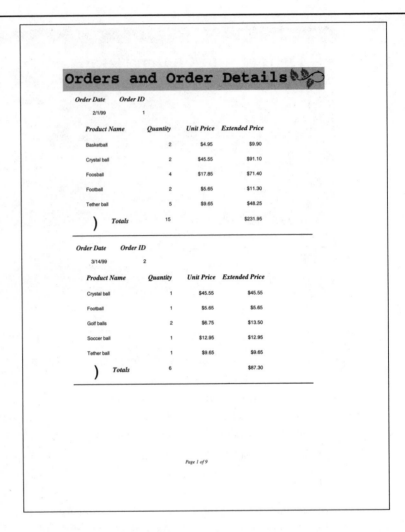

...Without a Wizard

To add a subform/subreport that already exists to a main form or report, without using wizards:

1. Open your main form or report in design view, and then press F11.

2. Choose Window ➤ Tile Vertically so that you can see both the database window and the form or report design.

3. Click the Reports or Forms button in the database window, as appropriate. (For example, click the Forms button if you're designing a main form.)

4. Drag the icon for the form or report you want to insert from the database window to your design. Usually, you'll want to put the subform/subreport into the detail section of your design.

To check or fix the subform/subreport link to the main form or report:

1. Open the property sheet (View ➤ Properties).

2. Click the Data tab.

3. Click the subform's or subreport's border (not the label).

- The Source Object property should show the subform or subreport name.
- The Link Child Fields property should refer to the linking field (or fields) in the subform or subreport.
- The Link Master Fields property should refer to the linking field (or fields) in the main form or report.

...With a Wizard

You also can use the Subform/Subreport Wizard to add the subform or subreport. This often is the easiest way to combine a subform or subreport with the main form or report. Here's how:

1. Start in the design view for the main form or report, and make sure the Control Wizards toolbox button is selected (pushed in).

2. Click the Subform/Subreport toolbox button (shown at left) and then click in the design, or drag an outline where the subform or subreport should appear. The Subform/Subreport Wizard will take over.

3. Do one of the following when asked how you want to create your subform or subreport:

- **To create a subform or subreport from existing tables and queries** and specify how to link them, choose Table/Query and then click Next. In the next dialog box, choose fields from as many tables and queries as you wish, and then click Next.

- **To create the subform or subreport from an existing report or form**, choose Forms (or Reports), choose the appropriate form or report from the drop-down list, and then click Next.

TIP As a shortcut, you can press F11 (if necessary) and choose Window ➤ Tile Vertically to show the form or report design and the database window side by side. Then click the Tables or Queries tab in the database window, and drag the table or query to the place on the design where you want the subform or subreport to appear. Continue with step 4 below.

4. When asked whether you want to choose fields from a list or to define which fields link your main form or report to the subform or report, fill in the dialog box according to the instructions shown, and then click Next.

5. When asked what name you want for your subform or subreport, type a name (or use the suggested name), and then click Finish.

6. Use the Data tab on the property sheet to check or fix the link between the main form/subform or main report/subreport if necessary, as described in the earlier procedure for creating subforms and subreports without wizards.

 TIP You might want to select the subform or subreport in the main form or main report and then change its Format properties. For example, change the Can Grow and Can Shrink properties to Yes, and change the Border Style property to Transparent.

Showing Fields from Another Table or Query

It's usually easiest to produce a form or report if the underlying query or table includes all the fields you want to display. However, you can still show data from other tables or queries even if they're not part of the underlying data. Here are some techniques to use:

- Add a subform or subreport, as described previously.
- In forms, base the form on a query that uses dynamic lookup (AutoLookup). See Chapter 10 for an AutoLookup query example.
- In forms and reports, create a combo box or list box as explained earlier in "Adding Combo Boxes and List Boxes." (If the field you place on a design is defined as a lookup field in the underlying table, a combo box or list box will appear automatically.)
- Use the DLookup function to display the value of a field that's not in the record source for your form or report. For details on this technique, look up *DLookup*

Function in the Access Help Index. Note that using DLookup usually isn't as efficient as creating a query that contains the records you want to use and then basing your form or report on the query.

 TIP If the fields you want to add to the form or report are in tables that can be linked to the record source for the document, follow the instructions in "Specifying the Record Source On the Fly," earlier in this chapter. After you open the query or SQL statement for the form or report, add the additional tables and/or fields you want to see. Then close the Query window and save your changes.

Putting a Preprinted Form on the Screen

If data to be entered into your tables will come from a preprinted form, such as a magazine subscription card, you can simplify the transcription process by scanning the printed form and using it as the background for your Access form so that the two will look exactly alike.

The whole trick to putting a preprinted form on your screen is to first scan the preprinted form to get an electronic bitmap image of it. Next use that bitmap image as the background picture for the form. Finally, align controls from the underlying table or query with prompts on the preprinted forms. The following sections explain each step in detail.

 NOTE See "Special Techniques for Sizing Photographs" in Chapter 8 for tips on sizing and storing photographs in OLE Object fields.

Step 1: Scan the Preprinted Form

You can scan the preprinted form into a file. If you don't have a scanner, contact a local print shop, desktop publishing office, or electronic prepress service bureau to see if they can scan the form for you. Be sure to size and crop the form to ensure that it will fit nicely on the screen. Figure 13.29 shows an example in which we've scanned a subscription form from a magazine, using the scanning software that came with an HP ScanJet IIc scanner.

FIGURE 13.29

A sample subscription form scanned and cropped in the scanning software for the HP ScanJet IIc scanner.

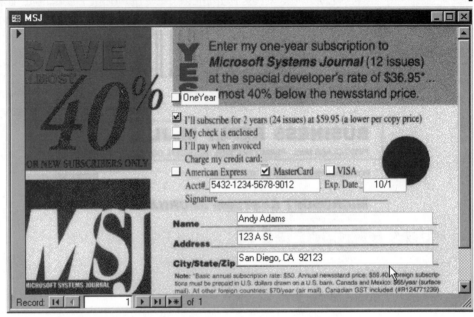

Save the scanned image to a bitmap file with a name that will be easy to remember later. We named ours MSJ.bmp. (Be sure to remember which folder contains the file so you'll know where to look for it later.)

Step 2: Create the Table

If you haven't already done so, create a table that will store data from the form. When creating the table, include at least one field per "blank" on the fill-in-the-blank form. Figure 13.30 shows the table we created to hold data from a preprinted subscription form. After creating the table structure, close and save the table normally.

TIP If you plan to query the data from the forms, or use the data to create form letters and other reports, be sure to break the name and address data into several fields (see Chapter 6).

FIGURE 13.30

The structure of a sample table named MSJ for holding data from a subscription form. This table structure reflects the structure of the original scanned form.

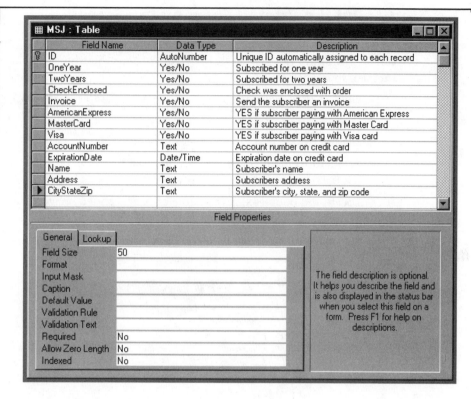

PART
II

Creating a Database

Step 3: Create a Simple Form

Create an instant form as the starting point for your custom form. Here's how:

1. Click the name of the table that will hold the data (MSJ in our example) in the Access database window.

2. Click the drop-down button next to the New Object toolbar button and then choose AutoForm, or choose Insert ➢ AutoForm. Access will create the form.

3. Choose File ➢ Close ➢ Yes, and save the form in the usual manner. (We named our form *MSJ Form*.)

Step 4: Put the Printed Form on the Screen

Next, put the scanned image of the printed form onto the AutoForm you created. You can use the form's various Picture properties to do so. Starting in design view, here are the steps to follow:

1. Open the AutoForm you created earlier (for example, MSJ Form).

2. Open the property sheet (View ➢ Properties), and then click the Format tab.

3. Choose Edit ➢ Select Form to select the entire form.

4. Scroll down to and click the Picture property in the property sheet; then click the Build button for that property.

5. Locate and double-click the name of your scanned image. In our example, we chose MSJ.bmp as the picture.

6. Set the Picture Size Mode, Picture Type, Picture Alignment, and Picture Tiling properties in the property sheet, as shown below:

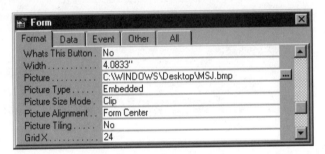

The original controls are still on your form, covering the background picture. To make the controls easier to see, choose Edit ➢ Select All from the menu bar to select all the controls, and then use the Back Color button on the Formatting (Form/Report) toolbar to make the control backgrounds opaque white, or some other color that's easy to see. Figure 13.31 shows an example.

PART

II

Creating a Database

FIGURE 13.31

The scanned image on a form in design view. Controls from the underlying table float above the background image, though in no particular order yet.

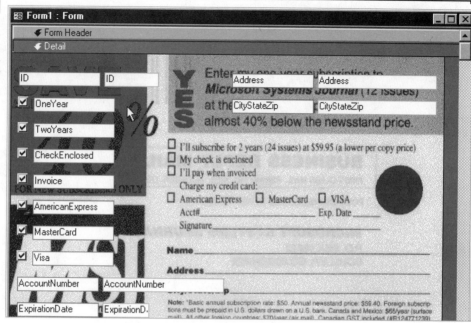

Step 5: Size and Position the Controls

The last step is to drag each control into position and delete the labels. Figure 13.32 shows an example in which we've positioned controls and removed their labels (except for the OneYear label). Then we switched to form view and typed some sample data.

FIGURE 13.32

Our sample MSJ Form with data for one record typed in. We need only delete the OneYear label on the form to make it look just like the preprinted form we scanned in originally.

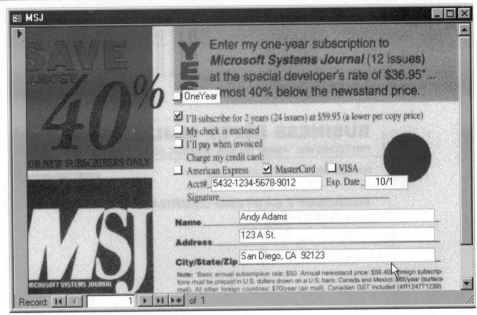

Printing a Report from the Form

If you want to print reports similar to the forms you use for data entry, follow these steps:

1. Open the form in form view or form design view. Or go to the database window, click the Forms button, and then click the form you want to print.

2. (Optional) If you want to view the report before printing it, choose File ➤ Print Preview, and preview to your heart's content.

3. Choose File ➤ Print, select any options you need from the Print dialog box, and then click OK. Access will print the form image along with the data from the table.

If you're printing on preprinted blank forms, rather than on blank paper, you may want to hide the image on the report background by printing the data only. To do so, go to the Print dialog box (step 3 above), click the Setup button, select (check) Print Data Only, and then click OK. Choose other options in the Print dialog box as needed, and then click OK again.

Saving the Form as a Report

You also can save the form as a report. To do so, return to the database window, click the Forms button, and then right-click the form you want to save as a report. From the shortcut menu, choose Save As, change the setting for As to Report, type a name for the report (for example, MSJ Report), and then click OK. You can then print the report or change the design as you would any normal report.

One Page per Form, Please

Here's an easy way to ensure that each report is printed on a new page:

1. Open the form or report in design view.
2. Click the band across the top of the Detail section.
3. Open the property sheet (View ➤ Properties), and then click the Format tab.
4. Change the Force New Page property to After Section.
5. Close and save the form or report (File ➤ Close ➤ Yes).

Then print the report normally, as convenient.

Form Letters, Mailing Labels, Etc.

Even though you're using a preprinted form to store and retrieve data, those data are stored in a plain old Access table. So feel free to design reports for form letters, envelopes, mailing labels, a customer directory—whatever—from that table. Or if you have Microsoft Word (either separately or as part of the Microsoft Office suite), you can export data to Word. Start in the database window:

1. Highlight the name of the table or query that will supply the data in the database window (MSJ in our example).
2. Click the drop-down list next to the OfficeLinks toolbar button, and then click the Merge It with MS Word button (or choose Tools ➤ OfficeLinks ➤ Merge It with MS Word from the menus). This activates the Microsoft Word Mail Merge Wizard.
3. Choose either Link Your Data to an Existing Microsoft Word Document or Create a New Document and Then Link the Data to It.
4. Click OK.
5. (Optional) If you chose to link to an existing Word document, select the document in the dialog box that appears and click Open.

6. Microsoft Word will start automatically and will display either an existing Word document or a new blank document, depending on your choice in step 3.

7. Insert merge fields from the table into your Word document (using the Insert Merge Field toolbar button), edit the document text, and use any other features offered in Word.

8. Prepare to merge the Word document with the data in your Access table by clicking the Mail Merge Helper toolbar button or choosing Tools ➢ Mail Merge. Then click Merge. Fill in the dialog box that appears, and click Merge once more.

9. Choose File ➢ Exit when you're done using Word. When asked whether to save your documents, save (at least) your mail merge main document. You'll be returned to Access.

After saving your mail merge main document in Word, you can return to Word at any time, open that document, and perform the merge again (starting with step 8 above). Any changes you've made to your Access data will be reflected in the merged output.

For help on using mail merge, look for help on *Mail Merge* with the Office Assistant. Chapters 4 and 7 of this book also provide information about using other Microsoft Office programs with your Access data.

First Aid for Designing Forms and Reports

Designing perfect forms and reports usually involves some trial and error. This section describes some common problems and how to solve them.

Grid dots are invisible   Turn on the grid (View ➢ Grid). If the dots are still invisible, select the report or form (choose Edit ➢ Select Form, or Edit ➢ Select Report, or click the square where the vertical and horizontal rulers intersect), open the property sheet (View ➢ Properties), click the Format tab, and change the Grid X and Grid Y properties to 24 or less.

The property sheet blanks out unexpectedly when you click a control that's already selected   Press Enter if you want to keep any changes that you've typed into the control, or press Esc if you don't mind losing the changes you've typed.

You can't size the form/report background properly   Some control or line probably is in the way. Try turning off the grid lines, setting the form or report background to white, and maximizing the window so you can see all the controls more easily. Move or resize controls as needed (be sure to look for controls at the edges of the report or form). Resize the background again.

The margins are too large   Choose File ➤ Page Setup, reduce the settings on the Margins tab, and click OK.

You need to put more on each page   Reduce the margins, increase the background dimensions, resize controls smaller, and move controls closer together to make room. You may also want to decrease the font size for labels and text boxes.

Blank pages appear in printed reports   This will happen if the width of the report plus the left and right margins exceeds the width of the page. Try some combination of the following: reduce the margins in page setup (File ➤ Page Setup), resize controls smaller and move them closer together, and reduce the report background width.

You don't want detail records in a subtotals/totals report   Open the property sheet, click the Format tab, click in the report's Detail section, and change the Visible property to No.

Report shows duplicate values   Use the Sorting and Grouping feature; or select the control that shouldn't show duplicate values, open the property sheet, click the Format tab, and change the Hide Duplicates property to Yes. See "Hiding Duplicate Data in a Report," earlier in this chapter.

Form or report shows duplicate records   Base the form on a query whose Unique Values property is set to Yes (see Chapter 10). Or create a "unique values" query for the record source on the fly as described earlier in "Specifying the Record Source On the Fly."

Your records aren't sorted the way you want them   Base the form or report on a table or query that's sorted the way you want it. Or create a query for the record source on the fly as described earlier in "Specifying the Record Source On the Fly." Or if you're designing a report, use the Sorting and Grouping features described earlier under "Grouping Data in Reports."

Your form or report is using the wrong table or query   Specify a new record source as described under "Specifying the Record Source On the Fly."

#Name? appears in a field in form view, print preview, or the printed report   You've probably changed the record source for your form or report, and now some controls are invalid. Either delete the bad controls or change their Control Source data property to a field or expression that reflects the current record source. This problem also can occur if the control source is misspelled or if the field in the underlying table or query no longer exists.

#Num! appears in a field in form view, print preview, or the printed report   This message appears in a control that contains a calculation expression in which the divisor evaluates to zero. (Computers hate it when you try to divide by zero.) For instance, #Num! will appear if [GrandTotal_Qty] in this expression evaluates to zero:

```
=[Total_Qty]/[GrandTotal_Qty]
```

To solve the problem, test for a zero divisor. For instance, change the simple expression above to the more robust expression shown here:

```
=IIf([GrandTotal_Qty]>0,[Total_Qty]/
  [GrandTotal_Qty],0)
```

The above IIF function translates to "If the grand total quantity is greater than zero, display the total quantity divided by the grand total quantity. Otherwise, display zero."

#Error appears in a field in form view, print preview, or the printed report   You've probably entered an incorrect expression into a calculated field, or you're using a circular reference to a control. (For example, in a control named MyCalc, you've entered an expression such as =[Num1]*[Num2]+[MyCalc].) Switch to design view and correct the expression or rename the control the expression belongs to.

You want to create or print a report from a form   This is easy. Right-click the form in the database window, and choose Save As. Then change the setting for As to Report, type a new name for the report, and click OK. If you just want to print the form as a report, open the form in design view or form view, and then choose File ➢ Print Preview.

You want to create a form from a report   This isn't so easy. Your best bet is to create the form from scratch or to use a form wizard that produces a form similar to the original report. You also can select controls from various sections of the report design, copy them to the Windows Clipboard, and then paste them into the form design.

For more troubleshooting advice, look up *Troubleshooting Forms* and *Troubleshooting Reports* with the Office Assistant.

Where to Go from Here

In this chapter, you've learned just about anything anyone could ever need to know about creating and customizing forms and reports. If you'd like to learn how to create data access pages next, continue with Chapter 14 now. Or if you are interested in learning how to set up charts and PivotTables, see Chapter 15. If none of these special purpose documents are your top priority, go ahead and explore topics in Part Three or Part Four.

What's New in the Access Zoo?

Access 2000 has some new ActiveX controls. To see what these controls are, open a form or report in design view, open the Toolbox, and click the More Controls button.

PART

II

Creating a Database

CHAPTER 14

Creating Data Access Pages

n the last three chapters, you learned how to create forms and reports. Now you'll find out how to work with *data access pages*, a new kind of Access 2000 object that lets you browse data with Internet Explorer 5, or right from Access itself.

 NOTE If you worked with Access 97, you may have used the Publish to the Web Wizard to create Web pages. This tool is not included with Access 2000. Instead, you can use the new Page Wizard, described later in this chapter, to create dynamic Web pages that show live Access data. Or, you can export data to an HTML file.

Data Access Page Basics

To see an example of a data access page, look at Figure 14.1. This page shows records from the Customer table in the Ordentry database. As you can see, the page is similar to an Access form, but has some visible differences. For one thing, the record navigation controls look slightly different and are part of a bar that includes buttons for tasks such as sorting and filtering records. These buttons are included on the page itself so they can be accessed from Internet Explorer 5, as well as from Access.

Types of Data Access Pages

The page in Figure 14.1 shows records from only one table. This is the simplest type of data access page. Pages can also show expandable groups of records, or objects like PivotTable lists that let you interactively analyze the data you are browsing. Whether you can edit or analyze data depends on the type of page you create:

Data entry page This type of page shows data from just one table and can be used to edit as well as view data.

Grouped page This type of page can show summary information for groups of records. Expand buttons on the page let you optionally show the detail records the summary information is drawn from. You can also filter and sort data on a grouped page. However, when you use a grouped page, you can only view data; you can't edit it.

Data analysis page A page can include objects like charts, spreadsheets, or PivotTable lists. When you use a spreadsheet on a page, you can use it to enter and edit data and perform calculations. With a PivotTable list, you can interactively change the way data is summarized by dragging and dropping row and column headers.

Later in this chapter, you'll see how to create all these types of data access pages.

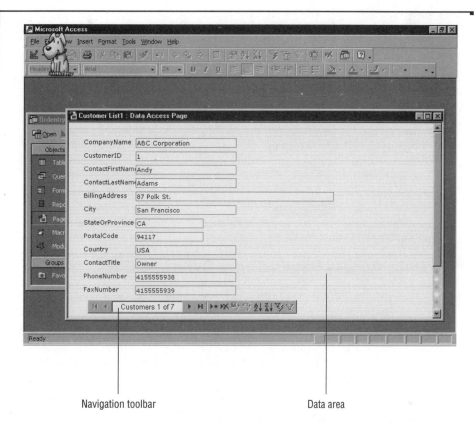

FIGURE 14.1

This data access page shows records from the Customer table in the Ordentry database.

Navigation toolbar   Data area

Where Data Access Pages Reside

The database window for Access 2000 has a new button for Pages along its left side. This is the button you click to see the data access pages that are part of whatever database or project you are working on. Figure 14.2 shows the database window for the Ordentry database when the Pages button has been clicked.

However, unlike other Access objects that are stored as part of the database or project they belong to, data access pages reside in their own HTML files. When you create a data access page, Access automatically adds a shortcut for the page to the Pages section of the database window. The page can then be opened from Access or Internet Explorer 5.

 NOTE To browse Access data from the Web using data access pages, you need to open the pages from Internet Explorer 5 and have a license for Office 2000. You also need to have an active Internet connection that allows you access to the Web server the data is stored on.

PART

II

Creating a Database

FIGURE 14.2

The new Pages button in the database window shows any data access pages that are part of the open database or project, even though pages are stored in HTML files that are separate from the .mdb *or* .adp *file.*

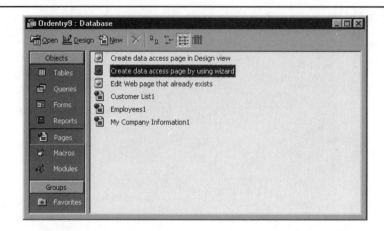

Data Access Pages Show Dynamic Data

Another important to thing to know about data access pages is that they are *dynamic*. That is, when you browse data using one of these special objects, you see the most up-to-date version of information that's available. This is different from Web pages that are created by exporting data to an HTML page. When you save data to an HTML file, you end up with a snapshot of the data as it was at the time the file was created. With a data access page, you get to see the data in its current state.

Ways to Create a Data Access Page

Access offers you several different ways to create data access pages. You can:

- Highlight the name of a table or query in the database window, and then choose AutoPage from the New Object drop-down list on the toolbar to create a simple columnar page.
- Use the Page Wizard.
- Start with a blank page and fill it with controls to show data, text, and other content.
- Open an existing Web page and add controls to display Access data.

You'll find out more about how to create pages using the last three techniques in this chapter.

NOTE The terms *data access page* and *page* are often used interchangeably in Access 2000. For example, the wizard that helps you create data access pages is called the Page Wizard. However, the design window where you work on data access pages is called the data access page design window.

Using the Page Wizard

Using the AutoPage feature is fine when all you need is a simple page that shows all the fields from a table or query in a columnar fashion. If you want to have more input in the design process, you can get help from the Page Wizard. The Page Wizard walks you through the process of designing a data access page so you don't have to go it alone in the data access page design window. When you work with the Page Wizard, you can:

- Select the fields that you want to show on a page. These fields can be from more than one table or query.
- Choose the master table for a page, if you select fields from more than one table.
- Group the records, if you like, using the values in one or more fields.
- Sort page records by up to four fields.
- Optionally include summary values, such as sums and averages.
- Apply a predefined theme to a page to give it a distinct look.

Starting the Page Wizard

The easiest way to start the Page Wizard is like this:

1. In the database window, click the Pages button.
2. Double-click Create Data Access Page by Using Wizard.

You'll see the first step of the Page Wizard:

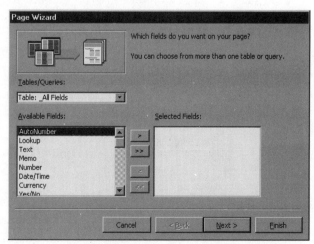

The table name that appears under Tables/Queries, and the list of Available Fields you see will depend on the tables that are part of the database or project you are working with. The rest of the dialog box will look like the one shown. At this point, all you have to do is proceed through the rest of the Page Wizard's steps and you'll end up with a fully functioning, dynamic Web page.

NOTE   If you don't need to publish a dynamic Web page that shows live data, export the data to an HTML file instead. In the database window, right-click the table or query you want to publish to the Web, and choose Export from the shortcut menu. Change the Save as Type to HTML Documents and click Save. Later, you can modify the page you create, as described at the end of this chapter.

Creating a Data Entry Page with the Page Wizard

Working with the Page Wizard doesn't require much explanation, especially if you're already familiar with the Form Wizard and the Report Wizard. The steps that the Page Wizard takes you through are much the same as the ones for those other wizards.

Here's an example of how to use the Page Wizard to create a page that lets you view and edit data in the Employees table:

1. In the first step of the Page Wizard, use the drop-down menu for Tables/Queries to select Employees. Under Available Fields, double-click any fields you want to include on the page, or click once on a field to select it and click the > button. The fields will appear on the Selected Fields list. To quickly select all the fields in the Available Fields list, click the >> button. To deselect any fields you accidentally selected, use the < and << buttons, which work the same way as the opposite arrow buttons work. Then click Next to go to the next step.

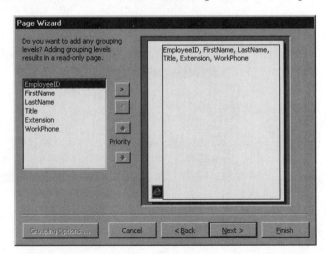

2. In this next dialog box, you can select fields to group the records that will appear on the page. For a data entry page, you can't include any groups, so just click Next.

3. The next step of the Page Wizard lets you optionally select sorting fields. If you want to sort the records that will appear on the page by LastName or some other fields, select those fields from the drop-down lists in the middle of the dialog box. Then click Next.

4. In the last step of the Page Wizard, enter a title for the new page. Then click Open the Page or Modify the Page's Design, depending on whether you want to make changes to the Wizard's work. If you want to change the page's look by applying one of the color/style themes that come with Access, check the box for Do You Want to Apply a Theme to Your Page? Then click Finish.

5. If you chose to apply a theme, you'll see this window:

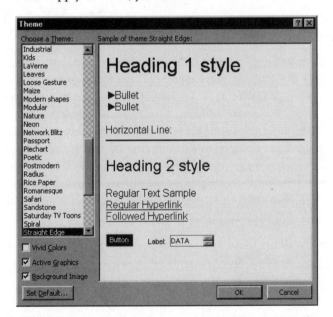

After the Page Wizard finishes its job, you'll see the new page opened in its own window. Figure 14.3 shows a page for the Employees table in the Ordentry database being viewed from Access. The fields on the page are arranged in a column, and one record is shown at a time. The data on a page can also be shown in a tabular fashion, as you'll see in the next section, "Starting with a Blank Page."

PART

II

Creating a Database

This page shows records from the Employees table. It was created using the Page Wizard.

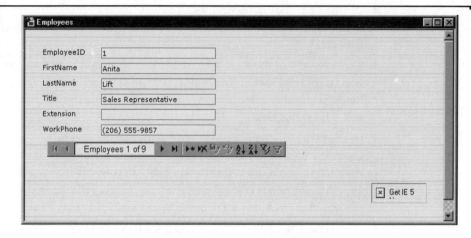

Creating a Grouped Page with the Page Wizard

As mentioned in step 1 of the previous instructions, you can place fields from more than one table or query on a page. The tables or queries should already be related, so the Page Wizard can get an idea of how to join the records from the multiple data sources. Figure 14.4 shows a data access page that lets you browse records from the Customers table in the Ordentry database, along with related records from the Orders table. As you change to a new master record, the related records shown on the page are automatically changed. The expand button for each customer record lets you bring the detail records into view or hide them as needed.

To create a grouped page with the Page Wizard, follow these steps:

1. Start the Page Wizard as described previously.

2. In the first step of the Page Wizard, use the drop-down menu for Tables/Queries to select the Customers table. Under Available Fields, double-click the Company-Name field.

NOTE   When you use the Page Wizard to create a grouped page from the master table for the page, select only the field from the master table that will be used to group the records. The Page Wizard will show any other fields you select from the master table in the detail records, rather than in the group header. You'll see how to add additional fields to the page's group header in the page design view window later.

FIGURE 14.4

The Page Wizard created this page that shows records from the Customers table along with related records from the Orders table.

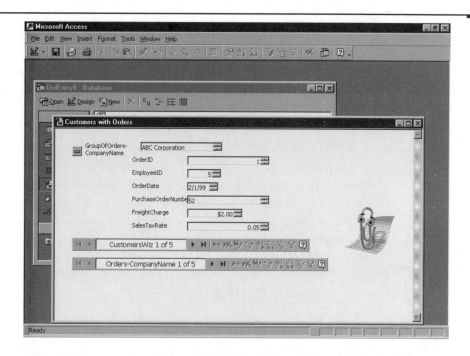

3. Before you click Next, change the setting for Tables/Queries to the Orders table. Add any of the Orders table fields you want to show in the page's detail records to the Selected Fields list. Then click Next to go to the next step of the Wizard.

4. The next dialog box is where you tell the Page Wizard to group the records by the CompanyName field in the Customer table. To do this, highlight the CompanyName field in the box on the left side of the dialog box. Click the > button to add a grouping level to the diagram shown in the right side of the window. The dialog box will look like the one shown below. Then click Next.

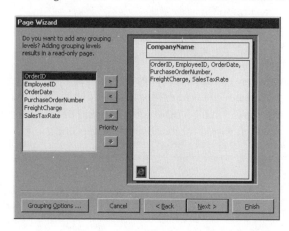

5. The next step of the Page Wizard lets you optionally select sorting fields. Select up to four fields to sort the records for the page's master table, if you want to. Then click Next.

6. In the last step, enter a title for the new page. Then click Open the Page or Modify the Page's Design, depending on whether you want to make changes to the Wizard's work. If you want to change the page's look by applying one of the color/style themes that come with Access, check the box for Do You Want to Apply a Theme to Your Page? Then click Finish.

Access will open the new page in a page view window or design view window, depending on the view option you selected in the last step of the Page Wizard. If you look at Figure 14.4, you can see that one record at a time from the Customers table appears in the data access page window. When the Expand button for the page's record is clicked, the related records in the Orders table for that customer are brought into view. The fields on the page are arranged in a column, and one record is shown at a time. The data on a page can also be shown in a tabular fashion, as you'll see in the next section, "Creating a Page Yourself."

Revising the Page Wizard's Work

Once you create a page with the Page Wizard, you are free to open the new page in the design window and make your own changes to the Wizard's work. See "Revising a Data Access Page" toward the end of this chapter for instructions on how to do this.

Creating a Page Yourself

If you're brave enough to face an empty data access page design window, you can try creating a new page on your own, without the help of AutoPage or the Page Wizard. If you want to do this:

1. In the database window, click the Pages button.

2. Double-click Create Data Access Page in Design View.

You'll see a data access page design window like the one shown in Figure 14.5. As you can see in the figure, the window includes a few default objects for titles, and an empty box labeled Section. After you add data to the page, you'll also find a Navigation section with a toolbar like the one pointed out in Figure 14.1.

NOTE Working in the data access page design window is similar to, but not the same as, working in the form or report design window. Look for notes further on in this chapter on the differences between form design and page design tools.

PART

II

Creating a Database

FIGURE 14.5

When you create a data access page yourself, you work in a window that looks like this.

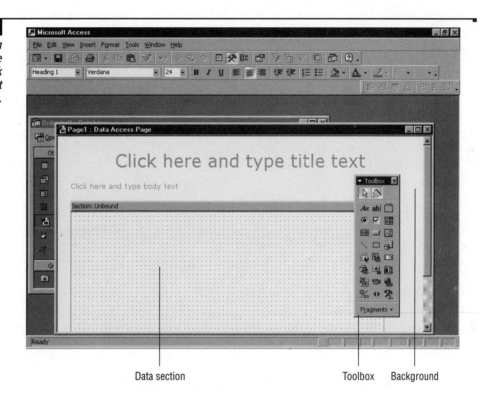

Data section   Toolbox   Background

The Sections of a Data Access Page

A new page has three sections:

- The background is where any titles appear; you can also place text, graphics, or other types of controls in this area.

- The area labeled Section: Unbound is where you place controls to show data. When you specify a record source for the page, the label for this area changes to Header: *tablename*, where *tablename* is the name of the master table for the data that will appear on the page.

- The navigation section (not visible in Figure 14.4) appears under the header section. Access places a bar of record navigation controls and other buttons in this area. Look at Figure 14.1 or Figure 14.3 to see what this bar looks like when a page is being viewed.

To work in a particular area of the data access page design window, just click it first to select it.

The Page Design Toolbar

When you're working in the page design view window, by default Access shows two toolbars: a Formatting (Page) toolbar and a Page Design toolbar. The Formatting (Page) toolbar has tools like those on the Formatting (Form/Report) toolbar for changing properties such as the colors and borders of objects. The Page Design toolbar is somewhat like the Form Design toolbar, but has some tools that are unique to page design. They are pointed out here:

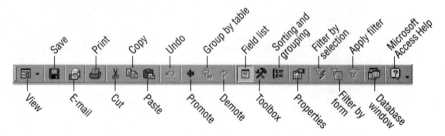

You'll see how to use the Promote and Demote tools in "Grouping Records on a Page" later in this chapter.

The Data Access Page Design Toolbox

If you look at Figure 14.4, you'll see a toolbox that looks similar to the one for the form and report design windows. The data access page design toolbox has several tools, though, that are not available while you're working on a form or a report. You'll find tools for adding Expand buttons and Record Navigation buttons to a page, as well as others for controls such as movies and hyperlinks.

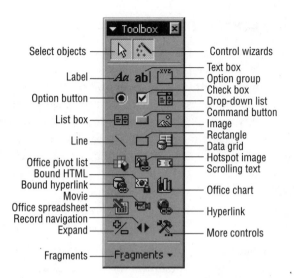

We won't give detailed instructions on how to use all these controls on a page, but we will cover the basics of working with data controls. For general instructions on adding other types of controls to a page, see "Including Other Controls on a Page," later in this chapter. Or search the Access Help index for the type of control you want to work with, and open the appropriate topic. You can also find more detailed information on controls such as hyperlinks and graphics in Chapter 13.

Notes on Working in the Data Access Page Design Window

Some things about working in the data access page design window are the same as when you're working in the form or report design window. For example, you can click an object to select it, or click a button in the toolbox and drag into the design window to add a new control. But there are some big differences, too:

- You cannot drag around a group of controls to select them as a group.
- You cannot use Shift-click to select multiple controls at the same time.
- Controls must be aligned and sized one at a time.
- Some changes, such as deleting a control, cannot be undone.
- You cannot size a control to fit its contents or the grid.
- The spacing between all objects in a group cannot be adjusted at once.
- When you add an object to the background of a page, it doesn't always show up where you click. It may appear at the last insertion point.

PART

II

Creating a Database

Aligning and Sizing Objects

In the form or report design view window, you can select a group of objects and align them to each other. For example, if you select three text objects and then choose Format ➤ Align ➤ Left from the menu, all three objects will be aligned along the left side of the leftmost object in the group. In the page design view window, there are no similar options available on the menu for aligning and sizing objects as a group.

There is an Alignment and Sizing toolbar, though, to help you align one object to another. This is not as quick as aligning a group of objects together, since you can only align one object at a time. But, it does guarantee good results when you need to align and size objects perfectly.

To use the Alignment and Sizing toolbar:

1. In page design view, choose Format from the menu.

2. Check the Alignment and Sizing option. The Alignment and Sizing toolbar, shown here, will appear. It may show up as a free-floating toolbar or docked under the bottom toolbar, depending on where it was last.

3. Click the object that is aligned or sized the way you want another object to appear.

4. On the Alignment and Sizing toolbar, click the button for the option you want to use: Align Left, Align Right, Align Top, Align Bottom, Size Height, Size Width, or Size Height/Width.

5. Click the object you want to align or size to match the one you selected in step 3.

Access will move or resize the last object you selected so it matches the first one you clicked.

Adding a Title to a Page

It would be hard to miss the large instruction at the top of the design window for a new page: *Click here and type title text* (see Figure 14.5). This text is visible in the design window, but not when you are viewing the page, unless you edit it. You can see this for yourself by switching from design view to page view.

If you want to add a title of your choice to the page:

1. Make sure you are in design view.

2. Click anywhere on the default text. It will disappear, and you'll see an insertion point.

3. Type the title you want.

4. If you want to change the title's properties, drag over the text to select it. Then right-click the selected text, choose Properties, and make your changes using the Properties dialog box. Or, use the tools on the Formatting (Page) toolbar.

The default page usually includes a left-justified subtitle (under the main title) that you are free to edit, or leave blank. As with the default title line, if you leave the subtitle unchanged, it will not appear when the page is browsed. To place additional titles or subtitles on the background of the page, use the Label tool in the toolbox. This tool works as it does in the form and report design window, except that you can't position a label wherever you want by clicking on the background. Instead, a new label will always show up at the current insertion point.

To add a label object to hold text, click the Label tool in the toolbox. Then click in the background of the top part of the page. The cursor will appear at the current insertion point on that area of the page. Then type the text you want to use. On the new page shown below, the title has been changed to *Customer List*, and the subtitle to *Internal Use Only*. The subtitle has also been italicized using the Italic button on the Formatting (Page) toolbar.

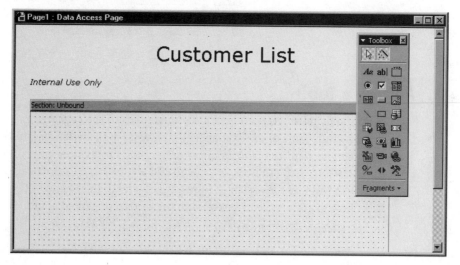

Adding Table Data to a Page

When you're ready to add data to a page, the best way to do it is with the field list. This tool, shown in Figure 14.6, is quite different from the field list you see when you work in the form or report design windows. If you check the figure, you'll see that instead of a single column list of the fields, the field list includes two tabs: Database and Page. The Database tab has Expand buttons for the tables and queries in the open database. Fields, or entire tables or queries, can be dragged from the field list to the data section of the page open in the data access page design window. The Page tab shows the tables, queries, and fields that are already part of the page you are working in.

FIGURE 14.6

Fields, or entire tables or queries, can be dragged from the field list in the data access page design window to the data section of the page being worked on.

Adding a Table

With the field list, you can drag individual fields to the page design view window, or drag an entire table or query at once. When you use the latter option, you get to choose whether you want the table or query presented as individual controls for each field or as a PivotTable list. (To find out how to add a PivotTable list to a page and work with it, look at "Adding a PivotTable List to a Page" later in this chapter.) The steps that follow show how to add a table to a page, with the fields represented as individual controls.

1. Click the Field List button on the toolbar, if the field list is not already open.

2. Click the Expand button for Tables. A list of the tables in the open database will appear.

3. Drag the icon for the table you want to display to the page design view window. Drop the icon at the place you want the upper left corner of the first text box to appear.

4. When you drop the table icon in the page design view window, a Layout Wizard dialog box will open. There are two options listed in this dialog box: Individual Controls and PivotTable List. Leave Individual Controls selected and click OK.

Figure 14.7 shows a data access page after the Customer table was dragged from the field list to the design view window. If you look at the label of the section containing the fields, you'll see that it has changed from Section: Unbound to Header: Customers. As soon as you drag a table, query, or field from the field list to the data section of the page, Access defines the RecordSource property for this area. If you want to check this:

1. Right-click the data area of the page.

2. Choose Properties from the shortcut menu.

3. Click the Data tab of the Properties sheet.

4. Check the value of the RecordSource property, near the bottom of the list.

 TIP To create a page that shows a master record with related records from another table, follow the instructions listed above for adding the master table to the page as individual controls. Next, in the field list, click the Expand button for the master table and then the Expand button for Related Tables that appears just under the master table name. Then drag the icon for the related table to the page and choose PivotTable List in the Layout Wizard dialog box.

PART

II

Creating a Database

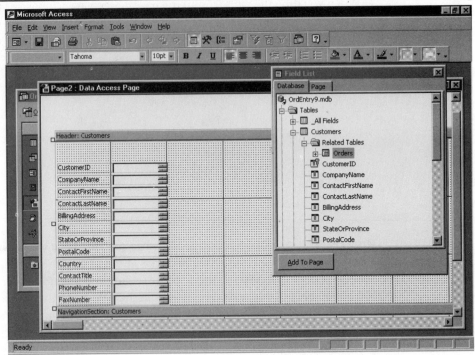

FIGURE 14.7

The Customer table, dragged from the field list to this page and placed as individual controls.

Adding a Field

If you want to add an individual field to a page, follow these simple steps:

1. Click the Field List button on the Page Design toolbar (shown at left).

2. In the Field List window, click the Expand button (+) for Tables or Queries, depending on whether the data you want to show is part of a table or query.

3. When the list of tables or queries appears, click the Expand button for the object containing the desired field.

4. Select the field you want to add to the page. In the field list shown next, Company-Name is selected on the list of fields for the Customers table.

5. Drag the selected field to the area of the page labeled Section or Header. Be sure to leave enough room to the left of the field for the field label.

The following graphic shows a page with three fields from the Customers table added to it: CustomerID, CompanyName, and PhoneNumber:

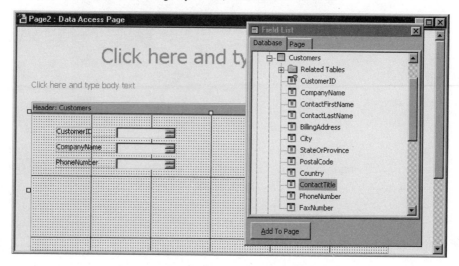

Next you'll see how to add related records from the Orders table to this page.

Adding Data from Related Tables

After you add fields from one table to a page, you are free to add fields from other related tables. For example, we can add fields from the Orders table to the page shown in the last example so that as each record in the Customers table is browsed, related information from the Orders table is also displayed.

Here's an example of how to do this:

1. Open the field list, if it's not already visible.

2. Click the Expand button for the master table for the page.

3. Click the Expand button for the Related Tables folder under the master table's name.

4. Click the Expand button for the related table containing the fields you want to show. For this example, the related table is Orders.

5. Drag the first related field, in this example OrderID, to the data area of the page. A Layout Wizard window like this will open:

6. In the Layout Wizard dialog box, select Individual Controls (to show each related record on its own page) or PivotTable List (to have the related records appear like a datasheet view). Then click OK.

7. If you chose Individual Controls in the Layout Wizard dialog box, drag any additional fields from the related table to the data area on the page.

If you chose the layout with individual controls, you'll end up with a page that looks something like the one in Figure 14.8. The same page is shown in Figure 14.9 in page view. As you can see, you have to browse through individual pages to see each order for a particular customer.

FIGURE 14.8

In this data access page design window, fields from the Orders table in the Related Tables folder for the Customer table have been added to the view. The Individual Controls layout was chosen.

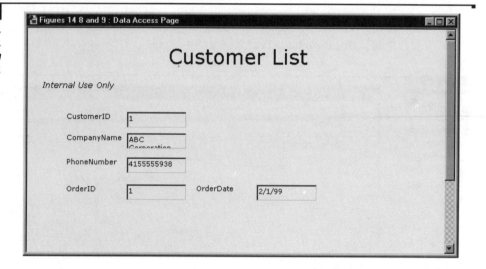

FIGURE 14.9

The data access page, shown in Figure 14.8, displayed in page view.

PART

II

Creating a Database

TIP If you try to add a related table to a page and Access opens a New Relationship dialog box, the table is already part of the page. If you really want to place the table again, perhaps as a PivotTable list instead of as individual controls, check the Page tab of the field list. If the related table is already on the list, delete it. Then go back to the Database tab and try to add the related field or table again.

Adding a PivotTable List to a Page

Figure 14.10 shows what the page in Figure 14.8 looks like when you select PivotTable List in the Layout Wizard dialog box. In a PivotTable list, related records are shown in a grid that resembles a datasheet view.

You can also add a PivotTable list that includes all the fields in a table or query to a page in one fell swoop. Just drag the icon for the table or query from the field list to the page design view window and choose PivotTable List when the Layout Wizard dialog box opens.

The OrderDate field in Figure 14.10 was added to the PivotTable list after it was created. After you place a PivotTable list on a page in design view, you can:

- Resize or move it
- Drag additional fields to the list
- Rearrange fields in the list
- Delete fields from the list

Next you'll see how to make these kinds of changes to a PivotTable list. If you want to find out how to use a PivotTable list to summarize data on the fly, see "Analyzing Data with a PivotTable List" later in this chapter.

FIGURE 14.10

For this page, the PivotTable list option was chosen in the Layout Wizard window that opens when you add a related field to a page.

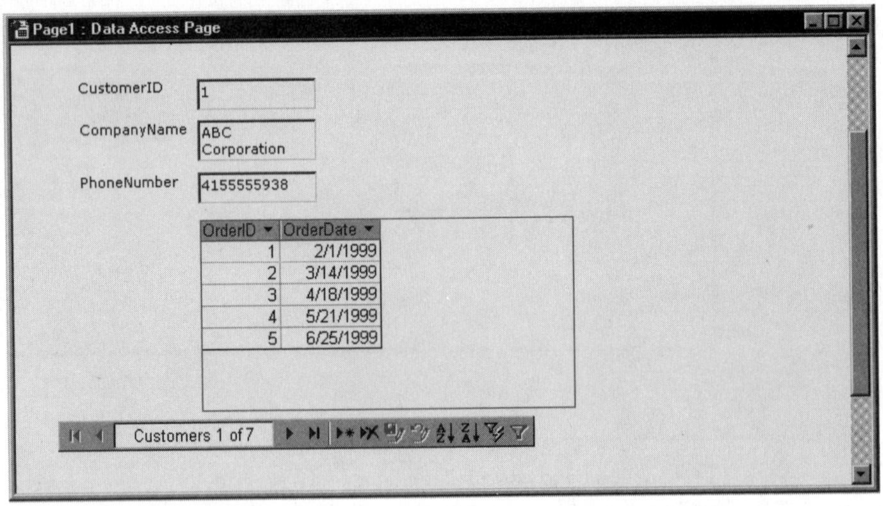

Resizing a PivotTable List

To resize a PivotTable list, select it first so it appears in the page design view window with handles like this:

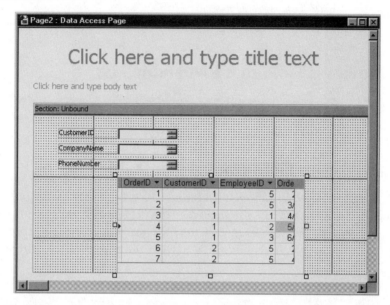

Then drag the handles of the PivotTable list to resize it. If you have problems selecting the PivotTable list, it may be that part of the PivotTable list is already selected. To get around this problem, click the background of the page. Then click once on the Pivot-Table list to select it so that its handles appear.

Moving a PivotTable List

A PivotTable list can be moved just like any other object in a design view window. Either drag the PivotTable list with your mouse, or select it and then use Ctrl and the arrow keys to slide it sideways or up and down.

Adding a Field to a PivotTable List

To add another field to a PivotTable list, simply open the field list and drag the desired field to the place you want it to appear. This is how the OrderDate field was added to the PivotTable list shown in Figure 14.10.

NOTE When you're dragging a field to a PivotTable list, drag into one of the existing columns. Access will not let you drop the field onto the background of the list. You'll know you are ready to drop when you see a bright blue border along the right side of the field that will precede the new field.

Moving a Field in a PivotTable List

To move a field to a different position in a PivotTable list, position your mouse pointer on the field's header. When the mouse pointer appears as a four-headed arrow, drag and drop the field into its new spot.

Deleting a Field from a PivotTable List

If you need to remove a field from a PivotTable list, just drag its header off the Pivot-Table list. You can also right-click the field header and select Remove Field from the shortcut menu. Or just click the field header to select the entire column and press Delete. (When a column is selected, it will appear with a light blue background.)

 WARNING Be careful when removing a field from a PivotTable list in design view; you can't undo your change. If you mistakenly remove a field that you really want to keep, you will have to drag it back onto the PivotTable list from the field list.

 NOTE If you remove a field from a PivotTable list in page view, your change isn't permanent. Next time you open the page, it will appear as it did the last time it was saved in the design view window.

Analyzing Data with a PivotTable List

A PivotTable list is much more than just a tabular display of records. Although it looks like a simple arrangement of rows and columns of data, in reality it is a sophisticated tool for analyzing and summarizing data on the fly. Next you'll see how to use a Pivot-Table list on a page to do the following:

- Filter the records that are shown on the list
- Add summary values to the list
- Group data using fields in the list

 NOTE   You can work with a PivotTable list to summarize data in design view or page view.

To illustrate the use of these PivotTable features, we'll use the PivotTable list shown in Figure 14.11. In the figure, the PivotTable list has the following fields from the Order Details table: OrderID, ProductID, Quantity, and UnitPrice. The ProductName field from the Products table is also part of the list. To create this PivotTable list, follow these steps:

1. Drag the Order Details table from the field list to the page design view window.
2. Remove the OrderDetailID and Discount fields from the PivotTable list by dragging them off the grid.
3. Drag the ProductName field of the Products table from the field list to the grid and drop it just after the ProductID field.

Filtering Records in a PivotTable List

If you look closely at the PivotTable list in Figure 14.11, you'll see that there are small drop-down buttons on the right-side of each field header. If you click one of these buttons, you'll see a list of the values in a field, along with check boxes for each value. These check boxes can be used to quickly filter the records in a PivotTable list:

- **To remove records with a certain value from the PivotTable list**, uncheck the box for that value on the drop-down list of field values.
- **To show records for a value**, make sure the check box for the value is checked.
- **To quickly filter for one value only**, uncheck the box for Show All at the top of the list; then check the box for the value you want to see.

After you check or uncheck the boxes on the value list, click the OK button at the bottom of the list to filter the PivotTable list records. When a field has a filter applied to it, its drop-down button will change from black to blue.

PART

II

Creating a Database

FIGURE 14.11

This PivotTable list shows fields from the Order Details and Products table in the OrdEntry9 database.

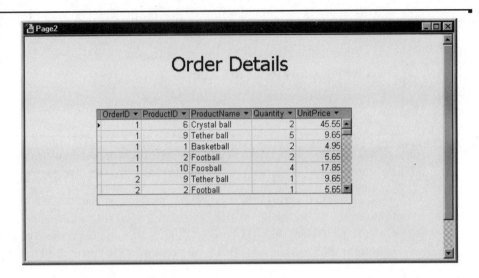

 TIP   If you want to use a field to filter records without showing it as part of the Pivot-Table list, right-click the field's header and choose Move to Filter Area from the shortcut menu. The field will be moved above the area of the PivotTable list where records appear. See Figure 14.12 to see a PivotTable where the ProductName field has been moved to the filter area. The current filter value is shown in the filter area, in this case, Tetherball.

Showing Summary Values in a PivotTable List

In a PivotTable list, you can show summaries of a field's values using the AutoCalc feature. When you use AutoCalc on a field, you get to show either the sum, average, minimum, or maximum of the values in the field. Access adds a line to the bottom of the PivotTable list and displays the summary value under the appropriate field.

Here's an example of how to use AutoCalc to show the total of the Quantity field shown on the PivotTable in Figure 14.12:

1. Right-click the header for the Quantity field.

2. Choose AutoCalc from the shortcut menu that appears.

3. Select Sum from the menu of AutoCalc options.

FIGURE 14.12

In this PivotTable list, the ProductName field has been moved to the filter area. It can then be used to create filters without appearing in the record area.

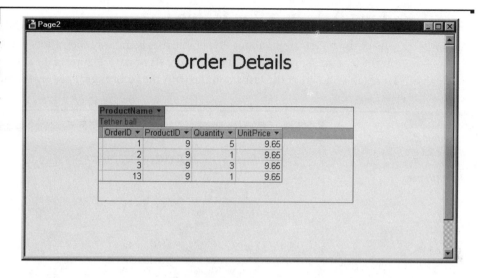

You'll see a line added to the bottom of the PivotTable list:

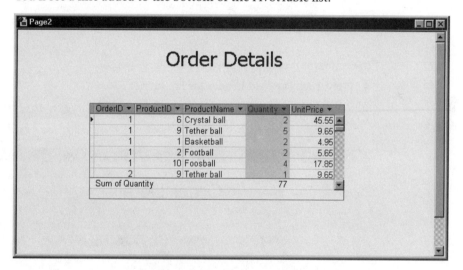

If you add additional summary values to a PivotTable list, they'll appear on the same line as the first value you placed. Unfortunately, their labels won't be visible, so you won't be able to tell what their values represent.

PART

II

Creating a Database

Grouping Data in a PivotTable List

One of the nicest things about PivotTable lists is the way they allow you to group data on the fly and see summary values for subsets of data. Figure 14.13 shows the same PivotTable shown in the last example, with the records grouped by ProductID.

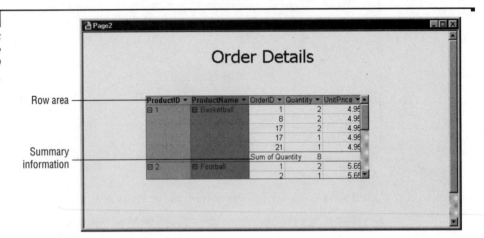

Row area

Summary information

To create this record grouping, follow these steps:

1. Right-click the field header for ProductID.

2. When the shortcut menu for the field pops up, choose Move to Row Area. The PivotTable list then looks like this:

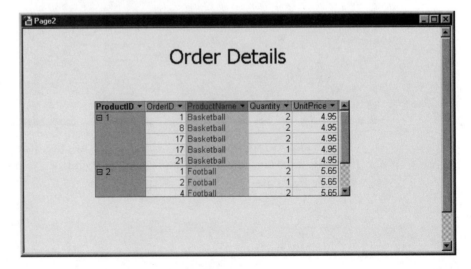

3. Right-click the field header for ProductName and choose Move to Row Area to show the product names along with the ProductIDs. The ProductName field should be moved to the second column in the PivotTable list. It will appear with a blue background, showing that it is being used as a record grouping.

4. The next step is to show the sum of the Quantity field. Right-click the Quantity field header and choose AutoCalc ➢ Sum from the shortcut menu. Total rows will appear for both the ProductID and ProductName. (Access assumes that ProductName is a subgrouping of ProductID.)

5. Since we don't need to show separate subtotals for each ProductName, right-click the ProductName header and uncheck Subtotal on the shortcut menu.

The final result looks like the PivotTable list in Figure 14.13. You can see that the grouping columns are shown in the left side of the list with colored backgrounds. The summary lines that show the total Quantity for each ProductID are shown after the last record in each group.

Removing a Group from a PivotTable List

If you change your mind about a group and you decide to remove it, right-click the group field header and choose Move to Detail from the shortcut menu.

Using Columns to Group Data

When records in a PivotTable list are grouped by moving fields to the row area, you end up with records that are arranged into groups vertically. You can also add fields to the column area of a PivotTable list. All you have to do is right-click the field you want to use for the column groupings and select Move to Column Area from the shortcut menu. When this is done in conjunction with row area groups, you end up with a crosstab where you can easily see records summarized by two or more categories.

Figure 14.14 shows a PivotTable list in which the OrderID values are used for the row groupings, and the ProductName field is used for column groupings. The ProductID and UnitPrice fields were dragged off the PivotTable list to make it easier to see just the number of each type of product sold for each order.

FIGURE 14.14

This PivotTable list has a row grouping by OrderID and a column grouping by ProductName. This makes it easy to see the number of each type of product in each order.

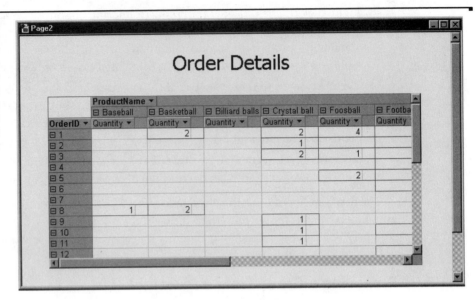

Order Details

OrderID	Baseball Quantity	Basketball Quantity	Billiard balls Quantity	Crystal ball Quantity	Foosball Quantity	Footba Quantity
1		2		2	4	
2				1		
3				2	1	
4						
5					2	
6						
7						
8	1	2				
9				1		
10				1		
11				1		
12						

Grouping Records on a Page

At the beginning of this chapter, we introduced *grouped data access pages* in the discussion of data access page types. To refresh your memory, this type of page lets you group records by field values to create a hierarchical display of records on the page. The master record for each group has an Expand/Collapse button that you can use to bring the detail records for the group into and out of view.

If you check back to Figure 14.4, you'll see an example of a data access page for the Orders table. This page is grouped on the Company Name field. At the top of the page, just to the left of the CompanyName field, there's a Collapse button. When this button is clicked, the order information just underneath the CompanyName field disappears from view, and the Collapse button is replaced with an Expand button. If you look towards the bottom of the page window, you'll see two navigation toolbars. The top bar is for moving through the Orders records for whatever company name is displayed at the top of the page. The bottom bar lets you change the customer whose name is shown in the CompanyName field.

The page in Figure 14.4 was created using the Page Wizard. Next you'll see how to create a grouped data access page on your own in the page design view window.

NOTE When you create a grouped data access page, it cannot be used for entering and editing data. This type of page only allows you to browse data.

Sections of a Grouped Data Access Page

Before we get into the details of working with groups on a page, let's take a quick look at the sections you'll see in the page design view window. Figure 14.15 shows the page created by the Page Wizard for Figure 14.4 in design view. The page design includes two group headers: one for the CompanyName field in the Orders table, and another called CustomersWiz that shows additional fields for each customer order. At the bottom of the window, you can see two record navigation sections—one for each group on the page.

PART

II

Creating a Database

FIGURE 14.15

The page from Figure 14.4 is shown here in design view. You can see two group headers and two record navigation sections.

Customers with Orders : Data Access Page

Click here and type title text

Click here and type body text

Header: Orders-CompanyName
GroupOfOrders-CompanyName
Header: CustomersWiz
OrderID:
EmployeeID:
OrderDate:
PurchaseOrderNumbe
FreightCharge:
SalesTaxRate:

NavigationSection: CustomersWiz
CustomersWiz |0-|1 of |2

NavigationSection: Orders-CompanyName
Orders-CompanyName |0-|1 of |2

In addition to group headers and record navigation sections, a page can include group footers and caption sections. The sections of a page serve these purposes:

Group header This section of a page shows data and may include controls to show summary data. Each page that shows data has at least one group header. The innermost group header on a grouped data access page is similar to the detail area in an Access report. This is where the controls for detail records appear.

Group footer This section comes after the group header and before the record navigation section. Group footers are usually used to hold controls that show summary values.

Caption A caption section holds the captions for columns of data. It appears above the group header it belongs to and is only visible when the group above it is expanded. This type of section cannot hold bound controls (ones that show data); only labels.

Record navigation The record navigation toolbar for a group resides in its own section. This section appears after the group footer, if there is one. Otherwise it follows the group header for a group. Like a caption section, a record navigation section cannot hold any bound controls that show data.

Grouping Records Using a Field

To create a group like the one on CompanyName in Figure 14.15, first open a new page in the design view window. Using the field list, drag the OrderID and whatever other fields from Orders you'd like to see on the page to the empty group header area of the design window. Then expand the Related Tables button under Orders in the field list, open the list of fields for Customers, and drag the CompanyName field to the group header, too. With this basic page in place, you can go through the instructions listed next:

1. Click the field you want to use for grouping records to select it. Make sure you select the data portion of the field's control and not its label.

2. Click the Promote button on the toolbar. A group header will be added to the page. The header will include the field that was promoted and an Expand button like this:

When you switch to page view, you can click the Expand button for the Company-Name field in the new group header to bring the related Orders records into view. The detail records, shown in their own group header, will have their own record navigation section so you can browse through the records, if there are more than one. When the Collapse button for the CompanyName field is clicked, the Orders information will disappear from view.

TIP On the page shown in Figure 14.4 and Figure 14.15, only one CompanyName record can be seen on the page at a time. If you want to view multiple CompanyName records in the page view window, make the innermost group header—the one that shows fields from the Orders table in these figures—smaller. To show multiple detail records at the same time without using a PivotTable list, arrange the controls for the detail records horizontally and resize the group header they belong to so there's no empty space beneath them.

Grouping Records Using a Table or Query

If you have fields from more than one table or query placed as individual controls on a page, you can quickly create a group that can hold all the fields for the master table or query. To see how this works, let's create a page grouped on the Orders table that can also show related records from the Order Details table:

1. Create a data access page in the page design view window that looks like the one shown in Figure 14.16. To do this, open a new page and use the field list to add the OrderID and OrderDate fields from the Orders table to the header area. Still working with the field list, click the Expand button for Related Tables under Orders, expand the Customers table, and drag the CompanyName field to the header area, too. Then, under Related Tables for the Orders table again, expand the Order Details table and move the ProductID, Quantity, and UnitPrice fields to the header area. Check Figure 14.16 for the placement of the fields.

2. In the header area of the page design view window, click the OrderID field to select it. Make sure you select the data portion of the field's control and not its label.

 3. Click the Group by Table button on the Page Design toolbar. A group header will be added to the page. The header will include the OrderID field that was promoted and the OrderDate and CompanyName fields that have a one-to-one relationship to the OrderID field. If there is extra space above the remaining fields in the header for Order Details, move the fields up. (Remember, you'll have to move them one by one since you can't select them as a group.) Then click the background of the Order Details group header to select it and drag its bottom border up to make it smaller. The page design view window will now look like Figure 14.17.

The header area of this page includes fields from the Orders, Customers, and Order Details tables.

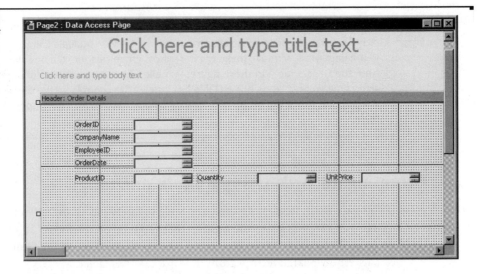

The page design view window seen in Figure 14.16 after the page was grouped on the Orders table.

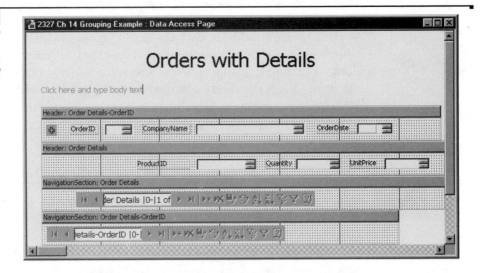

When you switch to page view after grouping the page on the Orders table, it will look like the data access page window shown in Figure 14.18. As you can see, there is a line with an Expand button for each OrderID. When the button for the first order on the page is clicked, the detail records for that order come into view with their own navigation tools.

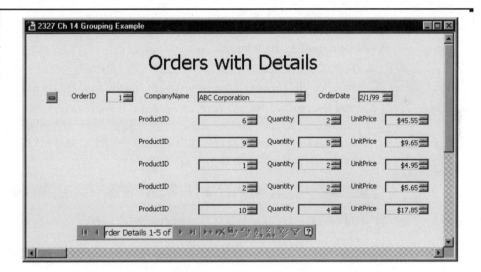

FIGURE 14.18

The page from Figure 14.17, shown in page view.

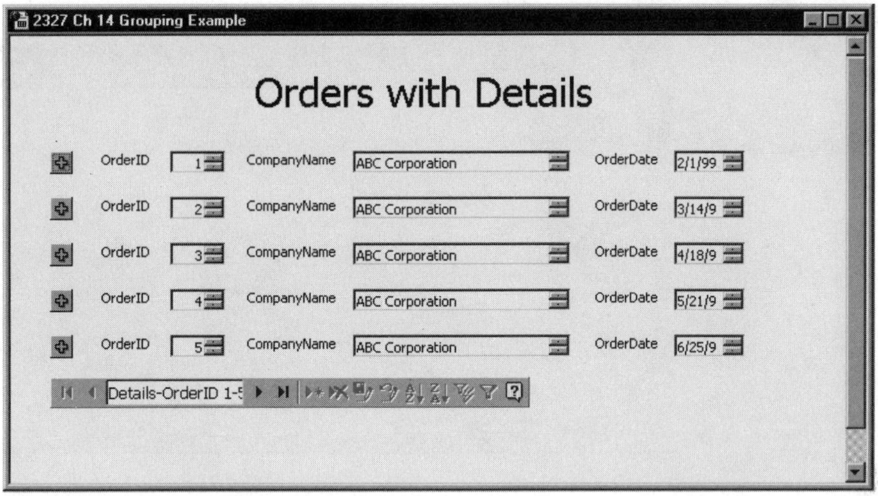

FIGURE 14.19

The page in Figure 14.18 after the Expand button was clicked for the first order.

Adding a Caption Section to a Group

The fields in the expanded detail area shown in Figure 14.19 have their own field labels that are repeated for each record. Instead of repeating labels this way, you can add a caption area to the page and use it to hold column headers for the fields. Here's how to create a caption area to hold field labels for the Order Details fields in Figure 14.19:

1. In the page design view window, click the background of the group you want to add a caption to. In this case, it is the Order Details header area.

2. Click the Sorting and Grouping button on the toolbar to open this window:

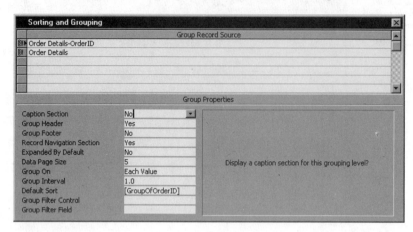

3. In the top half of the window under Group Record Source, click the line for Order Details. Then, in the bottom half of the Sorting and Grouping window, double-click the line for Caption Section to change it from No to Yes, and close the Sorting and Grouping window. You'll see a caption area added just above the group header for Order Details.

4. Drag the field labels for the ProductID, Quantity, and UnitPrice fields in the Order Details header to the new caption area just above them.

5. Drag the controls in the caption area and the Order Details header area up to remove extra space above them, if needed. Then click the background of each area to select it, and drag up on its bottom border to make it smaller. The resulting design will look like this:

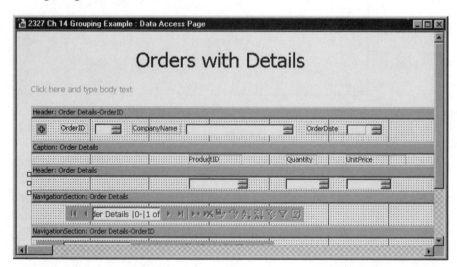

When this page is opened in the page view window, it will look just like the page in Figure 14.18. But, when you click the Expand button for the first order on the page, you'll see the fields from the Order Details table arranged as they appear in Figure 14.20. Compare this to Figure 14.19 to see the difference using a caption area can make.

FIGURE 14.20

The page in Figure 14.19 with a caption area added to show the field labels for the detail records.

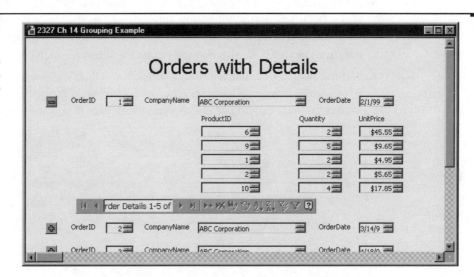

Adding a Summary Field to a Group Footer

When you have at least two groups on a page, as with the pages shown in Figures 14.17 through 14.20, you can include controls in the outer group's header or footer to show summary information for fields in the innermost group. For example, take the page in Figure 14.20. We can add a group footer for the Order Details-OrderID area and place a control there to show the total Quantity for each order. To do this, go through the following steps:

1. In page design view, click the background of the group header for Order Details-OrderID to select it.

2. Click the Sorting and Grouping button on the toolbar.

3. In the Sorting and Grouping dialog box, make sure the line for Order Details-OrderID is selected in the top part of the window. Double-click the line for Group Footer to change it to Yes. Then close the Sorting and Grouping window. If you look between the two navigation sections, you'll see an empty group footer for Order Details-OrderID added to the window.

4. Open the field list and, on the Database tab, expand Tables, then Orders, then Related Tables, and finally Order Details. Drag the Quantity field to the new group footer, positioning it so it appears under the control for Quantity in the Order Details group header.

5. Right-click the control for Quantity you just placed in the group footer for Order Details-OrderID and choose Properties from the shortcut menu. Click the Data tab and click the line for TotalType at the bottom of the properties list. Use the drop-down list for this line to change the setting from None to Sum.

6. Edit the label for the new summary control, if you like. You can click it twice to edit it, or open its Properties sheet and change the InnerText property on the Other tab. The control will look something like this in the page design view window:

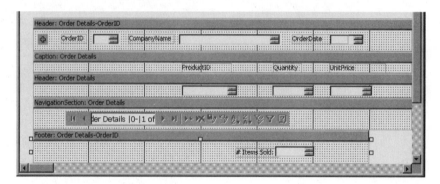

To see what the new summary control will look like when the page is opened, switch to page view. The summary control will be visible even when the detail records are not visible. When you expand a record to show the detail records grouped underneath it, the summary control will follow the detail records, as shown in Figure 14.21.

FIGURE 14.21

This page includes a summary control to show the total number of items sold for each order.

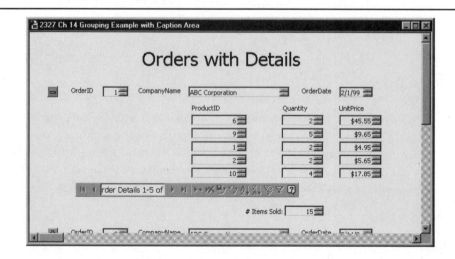

Removing a Group

To remove a group from a page, click a field in the group's header and click the Demote button on the toolbar. The fields in the group header will be moved one level down and the group header will be removed from the page's design.

 WARNING Be careful when you remove a group from a page; you can't undo your changes with the Undo button. And, although you can use the Promote button to create the group again, it may not include all the controls it originally held. Also, you will lose any work you did changing the spacing and alignment of the objects in the group.

Including Other Controls on a Page

Adding controls such as hyperlinks and images to a data access page is just like adding these objects to a form or report. See Chapter 13 for instructions and examples on how to do this.

Applying a Theme to a Page

With forms and reports, you can select a style using the wizard or the AutoFormat dialog box. For pages, Access lets you choose a *theme*. A theme is a group of style characteristics, such as font size, font style, and colors, that get applied to whatever objects are part of the page that is open in the data access page design window.

To select and apply a theme to a page:

1. Open the page in design view.

2. Choose Format ➤ Theme from the Access menu bar to open the Theme window, shown next.

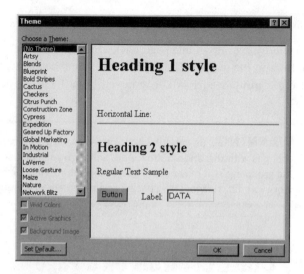

3. Under Choose a Theme, select a theme to preview. You may see a message that asks whether you want to install the theme, depending on the themes that are already set up on your computer. Figure 14.22 shows the Artsy theme previewed in the Theme window.

4. Check or uncheck Vivid Colors, Active Graphics, and Background Image as desired. (You can preview the effect of your choices on the right side of the window.)

5. Click OK.

If you look at Figure 14.23, you'll see the page that was shown in Figure 14.9 after the Blends theme was applied to it.

Setting a Default Theme

To set a theme as the default for new data access pages:

1. In the data access page design window, choose Format ➤ Theme from the menu bar.

2. When the Theme window opens, select the theme you want to use as the default look for new pages.

3. Click the Set Default button.

4. Click Yes.

5. When you return to the Theme window, click OK.

FIGURE 14.22

In the Theme window, you can select from about 30 themes that apply uniform looks to data access pages. The Artsy theme is being previewed here.

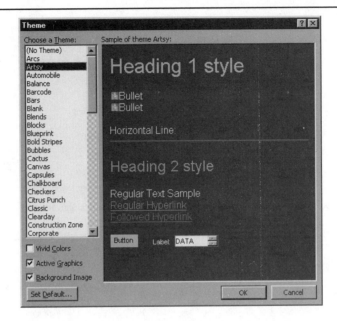

FIGURE 14.23

The data access page from Figure 14.9 after the Blends theme was applied to it.

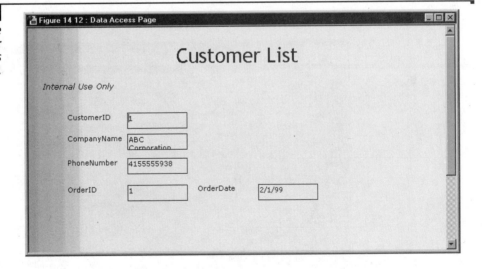

NOTE If you want to remove the default theme for new pages, follow the instructions above and select No Theme in step 2.

Removing a Theme from a Page

It's just as easy to remove a theme from a page. Open the Theme window as described in the last example, select No Theme in step 2, and click OK.

 NOTE Microsoft Script is a set of special commands that are used for adding special Web-related functionality to data access pages.

Saving a Data Access Page

 When you are at the point where you want to save your work on a data access page, click the Save button on the Page Design toolbar. You'll see a Save as Data Access Page window that looks similar to this:

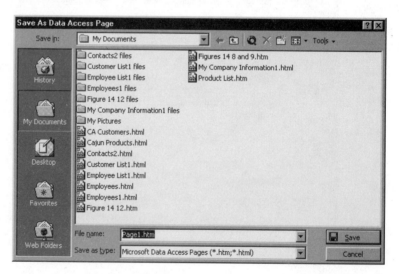

In the Save As window, navigate to the folder in which you want to save the page. Then enter a name in the box for File Name, and click Save.

Browsing a Data Access Page

Data access pages are unique in that they can be viewed using Access 2000 or Internet Explorer 5. The main difference is that when you are viewing a page with Access, you can switch easily to the data access page design window. If you are designing Web pages to be accessed on the Web, rather than through Access, you will, of course, be using Internet Explorer 5 rather than Access to open the pages.

Browsing a Page with Access

While you're working in the data access page design window, click the Page View button to see what the page will look like when it's opened in Access.

To view a page that's not currently open:

1. Go to the database window.
2. Click the Pages button.
3. Double-click the page you want to view, or select the page's name and click Open. You can also right-click the page and choose Open from its shortcut menu.

Access will open the page in page view, where you can use the navigation controls to browse through records.

Browsing a Page with Internet Explorer 5

Data access pages can be opened directly from Internet Explorer 5, as long as you know where they are located. Or, you can launch Internet Explorer 5 right from Access to see how a page will look from the browser by following these steps:

1. Go to the database window and click Pages.
2. Right-click the name of the page you want to browse.
3. Select Web Page Preview from the shortcut menu.
4. If you see a message that says Internet Explorer is not your default browser, and then asks whether you want to open the page with Internet Explorer 5, click Yes.

Access will then launch Internet Explorer 5 and show the data associated with the page in the browser window. In Figure 14.24, you can see the same Employees1 data access page that was shown in Figure 14.3. In the earlier figure, the page is being viewed directly from Access. In Figure 14.24, the page is being browsed with Internet

Explorer 5. As you can see, the first record from the Employees table is visible, and the navigation bar has buttons you can use to change the record that you see. You are free to edit the data right from Internet Explorer, or even filter your view to browse selected records. These tasks are performed the same way you do them from Access itself.

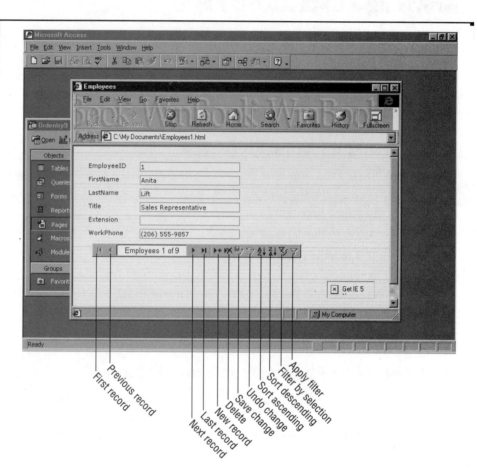

FIGURE 14.24

This data access page is being browsed with Internet Explorer 5 from Access.

Revising a Data Access Page

Access lets you revise pages you've created with the Page Wizard or on your own in the data access page design window. You can also revise Web pages created with other tools. This is handy because you can take a Web page that already exists somewhere and add Access to it in the data access page design window.

Revising an Access Data Access Page

If you need to revise a data access page that was created with Access:

1. Go to the database window.
2. Click the Pages button.
3. Right-click the page you want to work on, and choose Design from the shortcut menu. Or, select the page and click the Design button.

Access will open the selected page in a data access page design window, where you can add controls and make changes as described earlier in this chapter.

Revising Another Type of Web Page

When you create a page using Access, the page is automatically associated with the database or project it was created from. If you need to work on a Web page that was created outside of Access, follow these steps:

1. Start from the database window, and click the Pages button.
2. Double-click Edit Web Page that Already Exists. A Locate Web Page window will open:

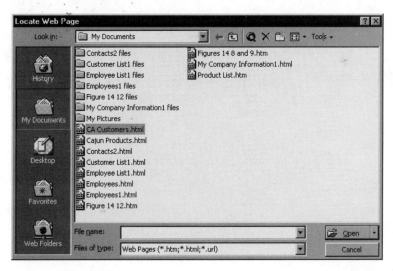

3. Navigate to the Web page you want to work on, and click it to select it.
4. Click Open.
5. Make your changes in the data access page design window.
6. Close the page and save your changes.

PART

II

Creating a Database

WARNING You may not be able to open some Web pages using this feature, depending on their format and how they were created.

Where to Go from Here

This chapter introduced you to data access pages, a new type of Access object for browsing data with Internet Explorer 5. You should now know how to create a data access page with or without the assistance of the Page Wizard. In Chapter 15, you'll find out how to present your Access data in charts and PivotTables.

What's New in the Access Zoo?

Access 2000 has a completely new feature called data access pages that you can use to browse your data using Internet Explorer 5. These new database objects are different from other Access databases because they are stored in their own HTML files, rather than as part of the database or project they belong to. You can design data access pages on your own, or use the Page Wizard to jump-start the process.

CHAPTER <u>15</u>

Creating Charts
and PivotTables

Access offers many ways to analyze and summarize your data graphically with *charts*: line charts, pie charts, bar charts, and other types of business charts. Charts can display numerical data in a compact, visual format that's easy to understand. They also can uncover trends and relationships that might otherwise go unnoticed.

PivotTables offer another way to summarize data. Instead of showing your data as a picture (the way charts do), PivotTables present the data in a tabular layout that you can change (pivot) dynamically.

In this chapter, we'll first show you how to create charts in forms and reports. Then we'll show you how to set up PivotTables. In no time, you'll be able to set up dazzling business charts and information-packed PivotTables with just a few mouse clicks.

Plenty of online help supplements the basic techniques presented in this chapter. For details on charting, look up *Charts* or *Graphs* with the Office Assistant, and then explore the related subtopics. You can also check the extensive help that's available from the Help menu while you're working in Microsoft Graph.

For help with PivotTables, look up *PivotTables* with the Office Assistant from Microsoft Access or Microsoft Excel.

 NOTE Before reading this chapter, you should know how to create, save, and use expressions in queries (Chapters 9 and 10), and you should know how to create forms and reports (Chapters 11 through 13).

Charting Your Data

Charting takes a bit of trial and error to bring out the best in your data. However, it will be easier if you know some basic charting terminology.

We can divide charts into two general categories: 2-D (two dimensional) and 3-D (three dimensional). To help you get your bearings, Figure 15.1 shows a typical 2-D column chart, and Figure 15.2 shows a sample 3-D column chart of the same data. Both figures are labeled to indicate the chart's many body parts. As you'll discover later in the chapter, you can use Microsoft Graph to customize any of the labeled areas to your heart's content.

FIGURE 15.1

A typical 2-D column chart labeled with the names of areas you can customize.

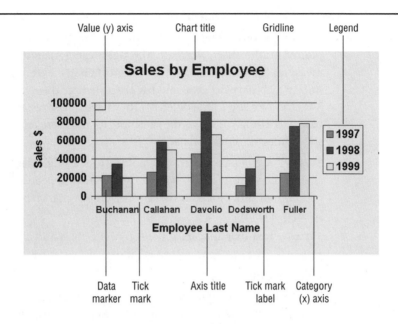

FIGURE 15.2

A typical 3-D chart labeled with the additional parts that won't appear on a 2-D chart.

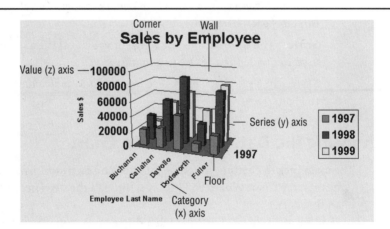

PART
II

Creating a Database

NOTE Throughout this chapter we've used data from the Northwind sample database that comes with Access. Chapter 1 of this book explains how to open this database. We changed some of the dates, so you may not see exactly the same charts if you try the examples.

The most important elements of a chart are described below:

Axes   The horizontal (x) and vertical (y) lines that establish the range of values plotted on the chart. Normally the x-axis categorizes the data and the y-axis measures the values. This is true for most charts, except pie charts and doughnuts (which have no axes) and bar charts (where the x- and y-axes are reversed). 3-D charts are also a little different. They have three axes: the z-axis is used as the *value* axis, the x-axis shows the categories for the chart, and the y-axis is used to show different series of data.

Series   A group of related data points from a single field that you plot, usually against the vertical axis. In charts, a data series appears as a line or a set of bars, columns, or other markers (depending on the chart type). You can plot several series in a chart.

Titles   Text that appears at the top of the chart and along the axes.

Gridlines   Lines that extend from the tick marks on an axis across the area you're plotting.

Tick marks   Small marks along an axis that divide it into segments of equal length. These make the chart easier to read and mark the scale.

Labels   These appear at each tick mark to identify values on the axis. You also can label each data value.

Scale   The scale defines the range of values on the axes and the increments used to divide the axes by tick marks.

Slice   In a pie chart, each slice represents a single charted value (glance ahead to Figure 15.4).

Choosing the Data You Want to Chart

The main trick to charting your data is to decide exactly *which* data to chart. Once you've done that, the Chart Wizard will lead you through the steps necessary to describe *how* to chart that data.

If all the fields to be charted are in a single table, you can just base the chart on that table. However, if you want to chart fields from two or more separate tables, or you want to chart the results of calculations on table fields, you'll need to create a query to join those tables or perform those calculations, and then base the chart on that query.

When designing the query, be sure to include the following fields in the QBE grid:

- Include at least one field for categorizing the data. Typically the category fields will appear on the chart's horizontal (x) axis. For instance, if you're charting sales by product category, include the CategoryName field. If you're charting salesperson performance, put EmployeeID or LastName in the QBE grid. You can include more than one category field if necessary. Thus, to chart sales by product category *and* by month, you'd include the CategoryName field and a date/time field (such as OrderDate) in the QBE grid.

- Include the field, or a calculated field, that you want to total, average, or count. This field usually appears on the chart's vertical axis. This field should be a numeric or currency value (such as extended price or quantity sold) that Access can total, average, or count and plot on the chart, or another type of field that Access can count. You can chart more than one field.

 NOTE Charts can be based on a table, Select query, Crosstab query, or Totals query. You can chart up to six fields of any data type except Memo or OLE Object. (In fact, the Chart Wizard won't even show Memo and OLE Object fields in dialog boxes that let you choose fields.)

When you've finished creating the query, you should save it (File ➤ Save) and close it (if you wish). Remember that only the design will be saved. This means that as the data changes in the table in the future, any charts that you've based on that query will change automatically to reflect the latest data in the table. (See "Freezing the Data in Your Chart," later in this chapter, for two ways to prevent this updating.)

Figure 15.3 shows an example in which we've joined several tables from the Northwind database in a query. (Note the join lines.) Here we've included only two fields in the QBE grid:

CategoryName   We want to chart total orders by product category, so we've included this column in the QBE grid.

ExtendedPrice   The second column contains an expression named ExtendedPrice, which calculates the numeric values (Quantity times UnitPrice) to be summed and charted.

FIGURE 15.3

The QBE grid in this query includes two fields, CategoryName and ExtendedPrice (a calculated field).

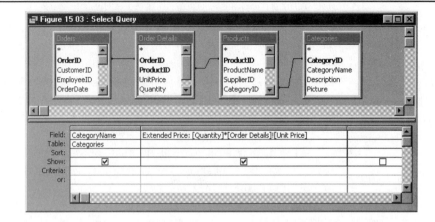

Figure 15.4 shows a pie chart that's based on the query shown in Figure 15.3. Each pie slice shows total sales within one product category.

FIGURE 15.4

A pie chart based on the query shown in Figure 15.3. Each slice of the pie represents the total sales in one product category. We used Microsoft Graph, described later, to customize this chart.

Now suppose you want to chart total sales by employees, and you want to break sales down by the order date. You could start with a QBE grid similar to the one shown in Figure 15.5.

FIGURE 15.5

The QBE grid contains the columns for the LastName, OrderDate, and the Sales (extended price). It also limits the selected employees to those whose last names start with the letters A through F.

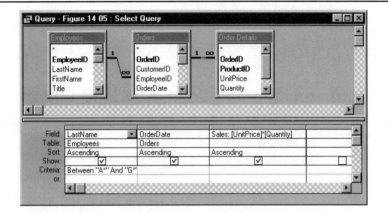

 TIP When the query or table being charted includes a date/time field, such as Order-Date, the Chart Wizard will let you group the date/time data. Therefore, you often don't need to group the data in the query. However, if your chart will contain too much data along the x-axis or in pie slices, and the Chart Wizard doesn't offer any way to group that data, it's best to specify criteria in your query. In Figure 15.5, for example, we used criteria in the query to limit employee names shown on the x-axis to last names that start with letters in the first part of the alphabet.

The sample chart back in Figure 15.1 shows one possible chart type and format for this data. In that example, the y-axis shows total sales amounts (labeled on the axis as Sales $). The x-axis shows employee last names (labeled as Employee Last Name). Each column (data marker) represents the total sales for a particular employee for one of the years 1997, 1998, and 1999. The legend explains which year each column represents.

To create the example back in Figure 15.2, we used the same query as for Figure 15.1, but we displayed it in a 3-D column chart. Notice how this chart shows the employee's LastName on the x-axis and the year (from the OrderDate field) on the y-axis; it uses a third z-axis for the values.

For both charts, we responded to questions from the Chart Wizard in the same way. That is, we chose to chart the OrderDate, LastName, and Sales fields; we grouped the OrderDate values by year; and we summed the Sales field. When the Chart Wizard asked what type of chart we wanted, we chose a 2-D column chart for Figure 15.1 and a 3-D column chart for Figure 15.2. The Chart Wizard figured out how to arrange the data on the chart automatically. Later, we used Microsoft Graph to customize each chart further.

PART

II

Creating a Database

Notice that in both Figures 15.1 and 15.2, we're charting just the extended price ([Quantity]*[UnitPrice]). To include discounts, shipping charges, and/or sales tax in the chart, we'd need to create the appropriate expressions and totaling queries (see Chapter 10 for examples).

About Freestanding and Embedded Charts

Once you've decided which fields to include on the chart, and you've created and saved the appropriate query, you must decide how you want to display the chart. You can display charts as either *freestanding* charts or *embedded* charts.

Freestanding Charts

Freestanding charts (refer to Figures 15.1, 15.2, and 15.4) are forms or reports that display only a chart. Like the proverbial cheese, the freestanding chart is meant to stand alone by showing overall results. For example, you can use a freestanding chart to sum total sales by category, to count customers in each state, or to show average sales by employee by month or year. Although a freestanding chart is still considered an "embedded" object, it isn't used as part of a larger report or form. To create a freestanding chart, you start from the database window, rather than from form or report design view. See "Creating a Freestanding Chart," later in this chapter, for more details.

Embedded Charts

Embedded charts are part of a larger form or report. Embedded charts can be linked to the underlying table or query, so they change to reflect values that relate to the currently displayed record (see Figures 15.7 and 15.8). Or they can be unlinked, so they do not change as you scroll from record to record (see Figure 15.6).

To embed a chart within a form or report, you start from the form design window or report design window and use the Chart toolbox button or the Insert ➤ Chart command. (The Chart command is on the expanded section of the Insert menu.) When creating an embedded chart, you can embed the chart in either of two ways:

- As an *unlinked* chart, which doesn't change from record to record
- As a *linked* chart, which does change from record to record

Use an *unlinked* embedded chart when you want to display multiple copies of the same chart. For instance, Figure 15.6 shows two forms, each for a different product category and each showing a copy of the same chart of 1999 sales in all product categories.

PART

II

Creating a Database

FIGURE 15.6

An unlinked embedded chart is the same in each record or printed report. Here the chart displays 1999 sales for every product category, regardless of the Category record that is being viewed.

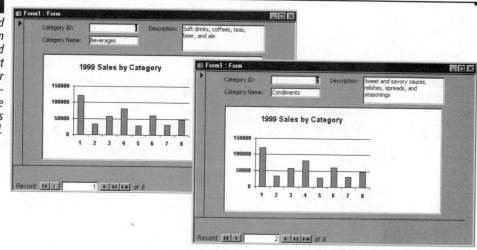

Use a *linked* embedded chart when you want the chart to change from record to record. For instance, by linking a chart of 1999 sales figures to a form that shows data from a Categories table, you can display sales results for just the category whose data you're viewing at the moment, as shown in Figure 15.7.

FIGURE 15.7

A chart that's linked to the CategoryID field of the Categories table shows the 1999 sales for one category at a time (Beverages in this example).

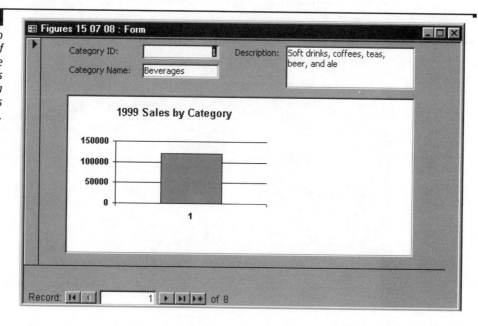

When you scroll to another record, the same chart shows the sales performance of *that* category only, as shown in Figure 15.8. If you look at the labels for the y-axis in Figure 15.8, you can see that they are different than the ones for the record in Figure 15.7.

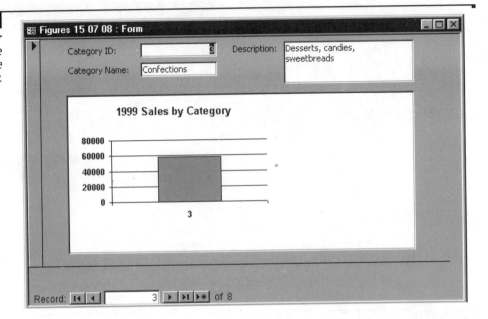

For the charts shown in Figures 15.6, 15.7, and 15.8, we used this query:

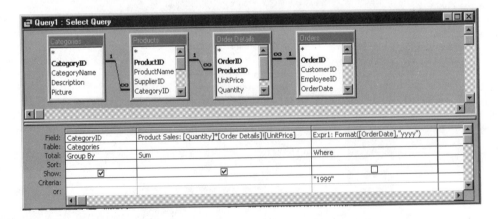

NOTE You may need to install Microsoft Graph before you can create charts from Access. To do this, insert your Office 2000 CD and click the Add or Remove Features button. In the window where you specify how you want features installed, expand the listing of options for Office Tools. Click the drop-down arrow for Microsoft Graph and select Run from My Computer. When you click Update Now, Microsoft Graph will be installed.

Creating a Freestanding Chart

Assuming you've already created and saved the query (or table) on which you want to base the chart, start in the database window and follow these steps to create a free-standing chart:

1. Click the drop-down list next to the New Object toolbar button (second-to-last item on the toolbar), and then choose either Form or Report. Or choose Insert ➢ Form or Insert ➢ Report from the toolbar. Or click the database window's Forms or Reports button, and then click the New button. The New Form or New Report dialog box appears.

2. Select the table or query on which you want to base the form from the drop-down list in the dialog box.

 TIP As a shortcut to steps 1 and 2 above, you can start from the database window, click the Tables or Queries button, and highlight the table or query you want to chart. Or start from an open table or query. Then use the New Object toolbar button or Insert menu options, as described in step 1.

3. Click the Chart Wizard option in the list and then click OK; or double-click Chart Wizard.

4. When asked which fields contain the data you want for your chart, choose up to six fields and then click Next to continue.

5. When asked what type of chart you'd like, click the button that represents the appropriate chart type. The Chart Wizard dialog box will describe the selected type in more detail (see Figure 15.9). Click Next to continue.

FIGURE 15.9

Use this Chart Wizard dialog box to choose a chart type.

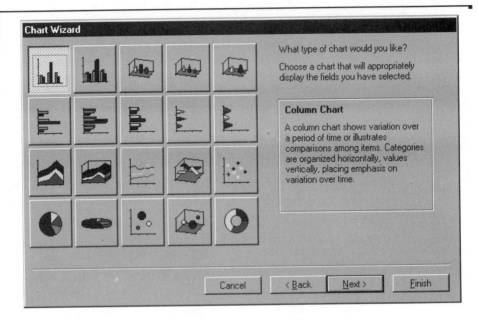

6. When asked how you want to lay out the data in your chart, follow the guide-lines listed next to place fields on the chart and to summarize and group the number and date/time fields as needed. As you make changes, the sample chart will reflect your current selections (see Figure 15.10). Click Next when you're ready to continue.

FIGURE 15.10

Use this Chart Wizard dialog box to place fields on the chart axes and to group or sum-marize date/time and number fields.

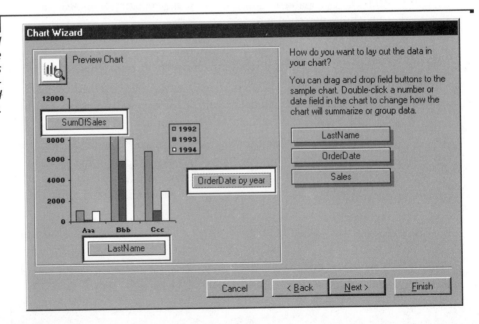

- **To put data on the chart**, drag and drop field buttons onto the appropriate places in the sample chart.
- **To summarize number data on the chart**, double-click a number field in the chart. A Summarize dialog box will open (see Figure 15.11). Click a Summarize option and then click OK.

FIGURE 15.11

Use the Summarize dialog box to choose how you want to summarize numeric data.

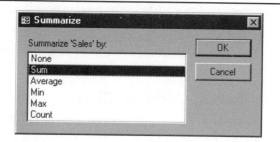

- **To group date/time data and limit it to a range**, double-click a date/time field in the chart. A Group dialog box will open (see Figure 15.12). Choose how you want to group the date/time field (by Year, Quarter, Month, Week, Day, Hour, or Minute). If you want to chart a limited range of date/time values, select (check) the Use Data Between option, and fill in the starting and ending values you want to include. Click OK when you're done choosing options.

FIGURE 15.12

Use the Group dialog box to choose how to group a date/time field and to specify the range of dates to include in the chart.

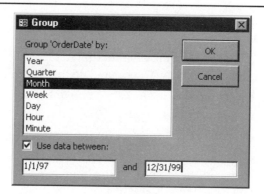

- **To remove fields from the chart**, drag the appropriate button off the chart. The word Series, Data, or Axis will appear in the empty spot.
- **To preview the chart in Microsoft Graph**, click the Preview Chart button near the upper-left corner of the dialog box. When you're done previewing, click the Close button in the Sample Preview dialog box that appears.

7. When the last Chart Wizard dialog box appears, specify a title for your chart, choose whether to display a legend, and select other options as needed. Then click Finish and wait for the Wizard to do its job.

The finished chart will appear in form view, print preview, or design view, depending on your choice in step 7.

Using the Freestanding Chart

Remember that any freestanding chart you create will be stored in a form or report. So when the chart is open in form view or print preview, you can switch back to design view as usual. When you're in form view or print preview, you can print the chart with File ➢ Print (or Ctrl+P). We'll explain how to customize the chart in design view later in this chapter.

You can close and save the chart with the usual File ➢ Close ➢ Yes commands. To reopen the chart, click the Forms or Reports button in the database window, and then double-click the name of the appropriate form or report. The chart will show current data (unless you based it on a "frozen" table or converted it to an image, as described later in this chapter).

Creating an Embedded Chart

To create an embedded chart of either type (linked or unlinked), follow this basic procedure:

1. (Optional) Add the Chart button to the form design or report design toolbox, as explained shortly. You need to do this only once.

2. Create and save the form or report you'll be placing the chart in. Be sure to leave enough room for the chart.

3. (Optional) Create a query for the chart if you need to base the chart on a query.

4. Open, in design view, the form or report you created in step 2 and use the Chart button in the toolbox, or the Insert ➢ Chart command on the menus, to create and embed the chart.

Let's look at each step more closely.

Adding the Chart Tool to the Toolbox

There are two ways to create embedded charts:

- Use the Insert ➤ Chart command on the form design or report design menus.
- Use the Chart button in the toolbox.

Although the Insert ➤ Chart command always appears on the design view menus, the Chart toolbox button isn't available initially. This button is easy enough to add:

1. Open any form or report in design view. For instance, click the Forms tab in the database window, click any form name, and then click the Design button.

2. Make sure the toolbox is visible (View ➤ Toolbox, or click the Toolbox button on the toolbar).

3. Display the toolbox as a floating palette (see Figure 15.13) for maximum flexibility. If the toolbox is docked at an edge of the design window, you can change the toolbox to a palette by moving the mouse pointer to an empty place near one of the toolbox buttons, and double-clicking that empty spot.

PART

II

Creating a Database

FIGURE 15.13

The form design window after we changed the toolbox to a floating palette, right-clicked the Toolbox, chose Customize, selected the Commands tab, and then clicked Toolbox in the Categories list.

Drag from here...   to here.

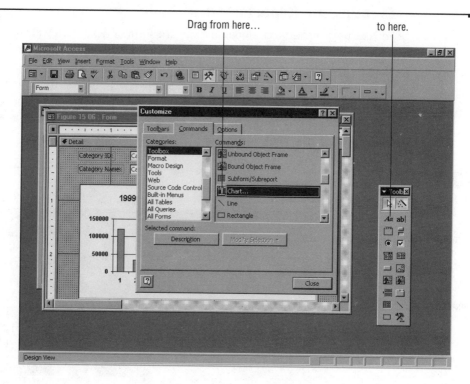

4. Right-click the toolbox, and choose Customize from the shortcut menu. The Customize dialog box appears.

5. Select the Commands tab and click Toolbox in the Categories list (see Figure 15.13).

6. Scroll down the list under Commands until the Chart button is visible. Then move your mouse pointer to the Chart button (see Figure 15.13) and drag that button to any button in the toolbox or to an empty spot in the toolbox.

7. Reposition the Chart button within the toolbox by dragging it to a new spot if you wish. (If you decide to remove the Chart button, simply drag it off the toolbox.)

8. Click the Close button in the Customize dialog box when you're finished customizing the toolbox.

The Chart button will be available in the toolbox anytime you design a form or report.

For more information about creating and customizing toolbars (and the toolbox), see Chapter 24. Or look up *Adding Toolbar Buttons* with the Office Assistant, and then click one of the subtopics that appears.

Creating the Report or Form

You can use standard techniques to create the form or report that will contain the chart, based on whatever table (or query) you wish. Just be sure to leave enough room for the chart that you'll be embedding later.

Figure 15.14 shows a sample form, in form view, that's based on the Employees table in the Northwind sample database. This form includes the EmployeeID, Hire-Date, FirstName, LastName, and Photo fields from the table. We've left empty space in the form for the embedded chart.

FIGURE 15.14

A sample form, in form view, based on the Employees table in the Northwind database that comes with Access. We've left empty space for the chart we'll be embedding later.

The EmployeeID field uniquely identifies each employee.

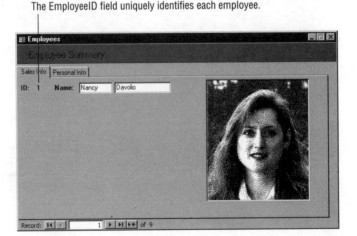

When you've finished designing the initial form or report, you should save it; then close or minimize the form or report to get it out of the way while you create the query for your chart.

Creating the Query for the Embedded Chart

When creating a query for an embedded chart, you can follow the guidelines described earlier under "Choosing the Data You Want to Chart." However, if you want the chart to change on a record-by-record basis, you also must include the field that links the chart to the report or form, since this field will tell the chart which data to display.

For instance, when creating a chart of total sales to embed on the form shown in Figure 15.14, you must include the field that links the data from that query to the Employees table. In this example, the EmployeeID field in the Orders table identifies which employee sold each order. Therefore, the underlying query must include that EmployeeID field, as shown in Figure 15.15.

PART

II

Creating a Database

FIGURE 15.15

When creating a linked chart that changes on a record-by-record basis, you must include the field that links the chart to the report or form.

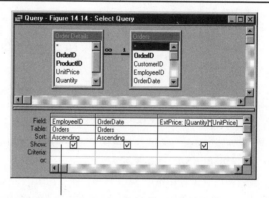

The EmployeeID field in the Orders table identifies which employee sold each order.

If you don't want the chart to change on a record-by-record basis, you won't need to provide a linking field. But you still must set up a query if the chart will plot the results of calculations on table fields, or if the chart is based on fields that come from more than one table.

Once you've created the query for the chart, you can close and save it (File ➢ Close ➢ Yes).

Embedding the Chart

Now that you've created a report or form to hold the chart, and a query upon which to base the chart, you can embed a chart into the report or form. The steps for creating an embedded chart are nearly identical to those for setting up a freestanding chart. The main differences are that you use the Chart toolbox button or the Insert ➤ Chart command to get started, and you must decide whether to link the chart to the form or report. Here are the steps:

1. Open the form or report you want to embed the chart into, in design view. If you plan to use the Chart toolbox button and the toolbox is hidden, choose View ➤ Toolbox or click the Toolbox toolbar button to display it.

2. Choose Insert ➤ Chart from the menu bar.

3. Click the place on the form or report design where the upper-left corner of the chart should appear, or drag to define the size of the chart. The Chart Wizard takes over at this point.

4. When asked where you want your chart to get its data, select Tables, Queries, or Both from the bottom of the dialog box. Then highlight the table or query that contains the data, and click Next; or just double-click the table or query you want to use.

5. When asked which fields contain the data you want for the chart, double-click those fields (or click the >> button to copy all the available fields). You can choose up to six fields. Click Next to continue.

6. When asked what type of chart you would like, click the chart type you want to use, and then click Next.

7. When asked how you want to lay out the data in your chart, follow the guidelines listed in step 6 of "Creating a Freestanding Chart," earlier in this chapter, to place fields on the chart and to summarize and group the number and date/time fields as needed. As you make changes, the sample chart will reflect your current selections (see Figure 15.10). To produce the finished example shown later in Figure 15.17, we chose not to show the EmployeeID, to show the OrderDate along the x-axis, to group orders by year, and to limit the chart to order dates between 1/1/97 and 12/31/99. Click Next when you're ready to continue.

The next Chart Wizard dialog box, shown in Figure 15.16, lets you choose whether the chart should change from record to record.

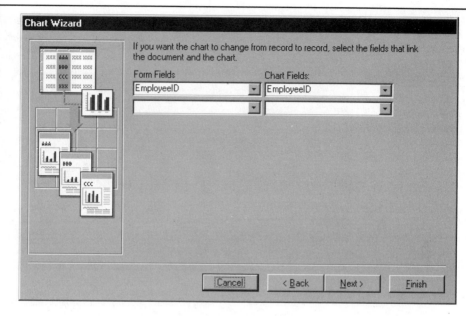

This Chart Wizard dialog box lets you choose whether the chart should change from record to record. To produce the example shown later in Figure 15.17, we chose EmployeeID for the linking fields, as suggested by the Chart Wizard.

8. Do one of the following, and then click the Next button to continue.

- **To link the chart and the form** so that the chart changes from record to record, choose the appropriate linking fields from the Form Fields and Chart Fields drop-down lists, or accept the suggested field names if they're correct. You can link up to three different fields.

- **To have the chart stay the same from record to record**, delete the field names or choose No Field from the top of the drop-down lists.

9. Specify a title for your chart when the last Chart Wizard dialog box appears, choose whether to display a legend, and select other options as needed. Then click Finish and let the Wizard to do its job.

An embedded object frame with a sample chart appears on the form or report. You can size and move that frame, or change its properties, using the standard techniques. You also can customize the chart as discussed shortly. To view the finished chart, switch to form view if you're working with a form or to print preview if you're working with a report.

Figure 15.17 shows (in form view) the finished Employee Summary form after we embedded a chart that's linked to the form's EmployeeID field.

FIGURE 15.17

The finished Employee Summary form (in form view) after embedding a column chart that's linked to the form's EmployeeID field. This chart is based on the query shown in Figure 15.15.

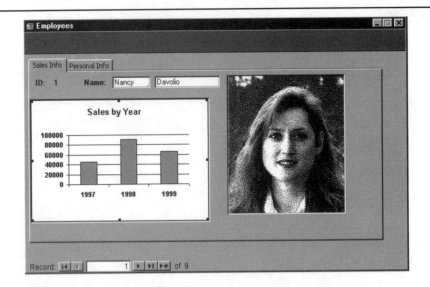

 TIP If you create a freestanding chart and later decide to convert it to a chart that's embedded in a form or report, you don't have to start again from scratch. Instead, select the entire form or report in design view (Edit ≻ Select Form, or Edit ≻ Select Report) and change the Record Source property on the Data tab of the property sheet to the name of the chart's underlying table or query. Then use the field list to add new controls to the form or report. If necessary, change the chart control's Link Child Fields and Link Master Fields properties so the chart will change as you scroll from record to record (see the next section).

Changing the Linking Fields

After creating an embedded chart, you may want to change the linking fields. This might be necessary, for example, if you chose the wrong linking fields while creating the chart, or if you decide to link a previously unlinked chart to your form or report. To change the linking fields:

1. Switch to design view and select the control that displays the chart. (Click it once, so it has sizing handles.)

2. Open the property sheet if it isn't already open. (Choose View ≻ Properties, or click the Properties toolbar button.)

3. Click the Data tab in the property sheet.

4. Change the Link Child Fields property to the appropriate linking field(s) in the chart's underlying table or query (for example, EmployeeID).

5. Change the Link Master Fields to the appropriate linking field(s) in the main form or report (for example, EmployeeID).

In the example below, the chart's Link Child Fields and Link Master Fields properties are each set to EmployeeID.

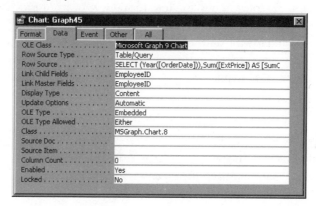

 NOTE The field names listed in the Link Master Fields and Link Child Fields do not have to be the same. For example, if the employee identifier field is named EmployeeID in one table and SalesPerson in the other table, that's okay. However, both fields must have the same kind of data and the same (or compatible) data type and size.

Changing the Chart's Query on the Fly

Let's suppose that after creating a freestanding or embedded chart, you realize that it doesn't present exactly the set of data you want. Perhaps you'd like to limit the data to a different time interval. Or maybe you'd rather present average values or plot the number of records instead of charting sums. Here are two ways to make a change:

- Delete the freestanding form from the database window, or delete the embedded chart in form design or report design view. Then, if necessary, change and save the query used to isolate the data. Finally, recreate the chart from scratch. This approach is rather drastic, but it might be quicker if you haven't spent any time changing the chart's appearance (as described shortly).

- Go to form design or report design view and customize the chart's data source using on-the-fly techniques discussed next. With these techniques, you change the underlying query that isolates the chart's data, rather than deleting the chart. On-the-fly changes are preferable if you've already spent some time customizing your chart, or you want to make a few quick changes without leaving design view.

You can easily create another form or report that contains a chart similar to one you've already designed. Just use normal copy and paste techniques in the database window to copy the original form or report, as discussed in Chapter 1. Or open the form or report in design view, form view, or print preview; then choose File ➤ Save As, type a new name, and click OK. Finally, open the copied form or report in design view and use the on-the-fly techniques described in this chapter to customize the chart.

If you opt for the on-the-fly method, start in form design or report design view and follow these steps:

1. Click the chart control to select it.

2. Open the property sheet if it's not already open (View ➤ Properties), and click the Data tab in the property sheet.

3. Click in the Row Source property box, and then click the Build button that appears. You'll be taken to an SQL Statement : Query Builder window like the one shown in Figure 15.18.

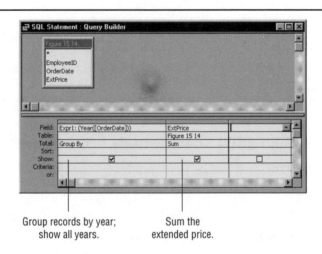

Group records by year;
show all years.

Sum the
extended price.

4. Modify the query using the standard techniques discussed in Chapter 10. In Figure 15.19, for example, we changed the sample query to calculate average sales instead of total sales and to limit the charted data to records in 1998 and 1999.

5. Preview the query results: click the Query View or Run toolbar button, or choose View ➤ Datasheet View, or Query ➤ Run. If necessary, return to the query

design window (by clicking the Query View toolbar button or choosing View ➤ Design View) and make any necessary changes. Repeat this step until the query returns the data you want.

FIGURE 15.19

In this example, we revised the query from Figure 15.18 to show average sales and to limit data to records in 1998 and 1999.

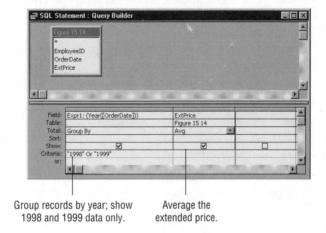

Group records by year; show 1998 and 1999 data only.

Average the extended price.

6. Click the query design window's Close button when you're done changing the query, or choose File ➤ Close, or press Ctrl+W. When asked about saving changes to the SQL statement, click Yes. You'll be returned to the form design or report design window.

7. Switch to form view or report print preview to see the effects of your on-the-fly changes.

Customizing a Chart

Your chart may need some final tweaking after you finish creating it. To customize the chart, you can change its properties in design view, use the design techniques described in Chapter 13, or refine it in Microsoft Graph as described in the sections that follow.

Changing the Chart's Size, Position, and Properties

You can make some changes to the size and appearance of the chart right in the report or form design window. Open the form or report that contains the chart (in

PART

II

Creating a Database

design view); then click the chart or its frame. Once the frame is selected, you can do any of the following:

- **Change its background (fill) color**, border color, and general appearance using the Formatting (Form/Report) toolbar. If that toolbar isn't visible, right-click any visible toolbar or the toolbox and choose Formatting (Form/Report); or choose View ➤ Toolbars, select (check) Formatting (Form/Report), and then click the Close button.

- **Move and size the frame** using the standard techniques for moving and sizing controls. (However, to change the size of the chart itself, you'll need to use Microsoft Graph, as described in the next section.)

- **Change other frame properties** using the property sheet. (If the property sheet isn't visible, click the Properties toolbar button or choose View ➤ Properties.)

To make changes directly to the chart, you need to go one step further than the properties sheet. Getting started is easy:

1. Open the form or report that contains the chart in design view.
2. Double-click the chart.

A hatched border will appear around the chart object, and your screen will resemble Figure 15.20. At this point, you are in chart editing mode using Microsoft Graph.

FIGURE 15.20

Double-clicking a chart in design view takes you to Microsoft Graph, where you can customize the chart.

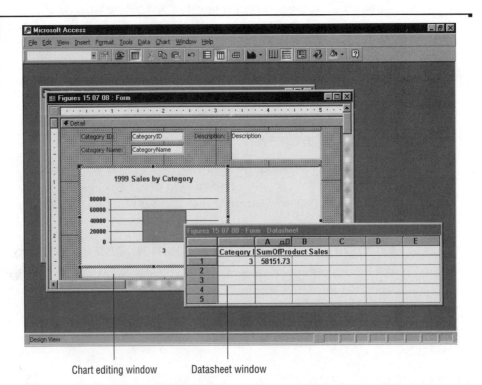

Chart editing window   Datasheet window

NOTE In previous versions of Access, a Microsoft Graph window opened after you double-clicked a chart object. With Access 2000, you don't see a separate Microsoft Graph window, but Microsoft Graph is activated when you switch to chart editing mode. Check the toolbar for Microsoft Graph buttons, such as Draw, By Row, and By Column.

You'll see an additional window open on the Access desktop, a datasheet window that shows the values being graphed.

 TIP To have the chart shown in the chart editing window reflect your actual data, switch to form view or print preview at least once after creating the chart and before changing it.

To customize the chart, first make sure the chart window is in front. (Click it if necessary.) To tailor an area of the chart, you can choose options from the menu bar, double-click an area, or right-click an area and choose options from the shortcut menu. For example, double-clicking a data axis on a bar chart opens the Format Axis dialog box shown in Figure 15.21. From here you can click the appropriate tab in the dialog box and then change the patterns, scale, font, number format, or alignment of data on the axis. (Click the Help button if you need more information about the dialog box.) When you're done making changes, click OK.

FIGURE 15.21

You can double-click an axis and use the Format Axis dialog box to change the patterns, scale, font, number format, or alignment of data on the axis.

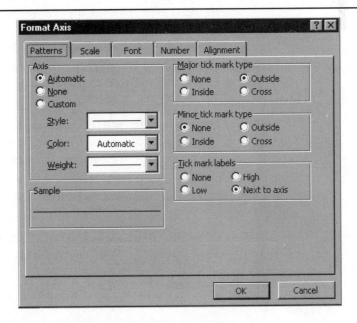

The best way to learn how to customize a chart is simply to experiment until you get the look you want. Each time you make a change, the Chart window will reflect your latest tweak. If you make a mistake and discover it immediately, you can choose Edit ➢ Undo or press Ctrl+Z (or click the Undo button on the Standard toolbar) to restore the chart to its most recent appearance.

The following guidelines will help you experiment more efficiently:

- **If no data appears on a chart that's linked to your form or report**, you're probably looking at a record that does not satisfy the query underlying the chart. Click off the chart object to get out of chart editing mode. Then switch to form view or report print preview and scroll to a record that does display a chart. Now return to design view and double-click the chart again.

- **To customize a particular area of the chart**, right-click that area and choose an option from the shortcut menu. Or double-click the area you want to change.

- **To resize the chart in your form or report design**, drag the borders of the chart window while you're in chart editing mode to reflect the chart size you want in your final design.

 TIP To fit the chart's frame to the resized chart, return to form design or report design view, and choose Format ➢ Size ➢ To Fit from the menus.

- **To change the chart type**, choose Chart ➢ Chart Type or right-click the chart and choose Chart Type from the shortcut menu; then select an option in the Chart Type dialog box that appears. You also can select a chart type from the Chart Type drop-down button on the Standard toolbar.

- **To associate the data series with the horizontal rows shown in the Datasheet window**, choose Data ➢ Series in Rows, or click the By Row button on the Standard toolbar.

- **To associate the data series with the vertical columns shown in the Microsoft Graph datasheet window**, choose Data ➢ Series in Columns, or click the By Column button on the Standard toolbar.

- **To change the color of a data series**, double-click the data series you want to change, click a color sample, and then click OK. Or click the data series and then choose a color from the Color drop-down button on the Standard toolbar.

- **To delete the chart's titles, data labels, legend, axes, grid-lines, or other anatomical parts**, select the object you want to delete, and then press Delete (or right-click the object and choose Clear).

- **To insert titles, data labels, a legend, axes, gridlines, or other anatomical parts**, choose Chart ➤ Chart Options, click the appropriate tab, make your changes, and click OK.

- **To customize any area of the chart**, double-click it, or right-click it and choose the Format option. You also can select certain objects (such as titles or axes) and click appropriate buttons in the Formatting toolbar.

- **To customize the spacing between tick labels**, double-click the axis to open the Format Axis dialog box (refer back to Figure 15.21). If the tick labels are too crowded or too far apart, click the Scale tab. Then, if the axis displays numbers, increase or decrease the Major Unit for scaling. For instance, if you double the major unit number, only half as many tick marks will appear on the axis. If the axis displays text, you can increase or decrease the number of categories between tick-mark labels and tick marks. You may need to adjust other options in the Scale dialog box to get the effect you want.

- **To change the alignment and orientation of tick labels**, double-click the axis, click the Alignment tab, and click one of the markers in the larger box.

- **To add arrows, shapes, and text annotations to your chart**, click the Drawing tool on the toolbar to open the Drawing toolbar. Click the button you want to use on the Drawing toolbar and then drag in the chart area to define the size of the object. If you're not sure how to use a Drawing toolbar button after selecting it, point to the button, pause, and wait for the floating tip to appear.

When you're done making changes, click off the chart object. This will bring you out of chart editing mode. Remember that if you changed the chart's size, you can return to Access (design view), select the chart control, and choose Format ➤ Size ➤ To Fit. This step will resize the frame for a better fit.

Building a Better Chart

Even after you've mastered the mechanics of creating charts, you still may need to experiment further in order to produce charts that are easy to understand. The tips offered below should help to make your charts more effective.

- Pick the chart type that most clearly represents your data. For example, line charts are good for illustrating trends. When you want to show how each element contributes to a total, try an area chart or stacked bar chart. If your goal is to compare values, column charts and bar charts are good choices. Pie charts are ideal for showing the relative contributions of different parts to the whole.

- Experiment until you find the best chart type for your data. This is easy: in chart editing mode, choose Chart ➤ Chart Type, and change the chart type.

- Avoid cluttering your charts with unnecessary data or labels that obscure the message you're trying to convey. For example, if you want to focus on first-quarter sales (January through March), there's no need to show sales for April through December. If necessary, use a query to filter out unwanted data.
- Make important information stand out in your charts. For example, explode the most important slice or slices in a pie chart, use bright colors or more noticeable patterns for key data items, or annotate important data points with the drawing tools. See the pie charts in Figure 15.22 for an example.

The annotation, percentage labels, and exploded pie slice in the sample chart at the bottom call attention to important details that may be less obvious in the chart at the top.

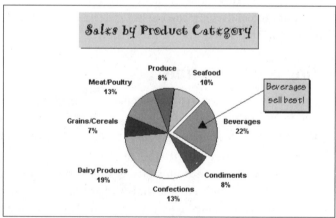

- Beware of 3-D charts. They give a more dramatic appearance, but can sometimes obscure important data points. 2-D charts often provide the clearest view of your data, as shown at the bottom of Figure 15.23. Sometimes, however, you can get a clearer view in a 3-D chart by changing its 3-D viewing angles in Microsoft Graph. To rotate a 3-D chart, right-click the plot area and choose 3-D View; then use the buttons in the Format 3-D View dialog box to adjust the elevation, rotation, and perspective (click the Help button in the Format 3-D View dialog box for details). Or click the edge of a wall of the chart, click one of the sizing handles, and then drag as needed to rotate the chart and change its perspective.

FIGURE 15.23

The 3-D chart in the sample chart at the top may look more dramatic, but the 2-D in the chart at the bottom presents the data more clearly.

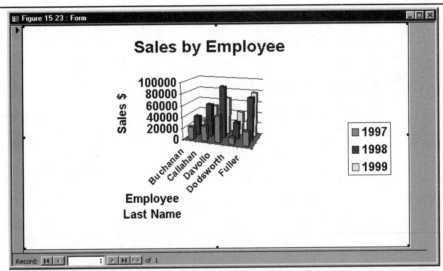

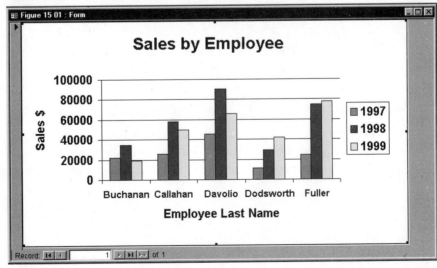

PART

II

Creating a Database

- Use a consistent scale to show charts that contain related data. This will make the data easier to compare.

For more help while you're in chart editing mode, click the Help button that appears in various dialog boxes, press F1, or choose options from the Help menu.

Freezing the Data in Your Chart

Recall that charts based on a query will always show up-to-date information. If you prefer, you can freeze the chart so that it shows data at a particular point in time and never changes. One way to freeze the chart is to convert it to an image, as described just below. Another way is to separate the chart from its underlying table or query by creating and running a Make Table query that places selected data in a separate table that never changes. Then you can base your chart on the frozen table, instead of the live data. (See Chapter 10 for more about Make Table queries.)

Changing the Chart to an Image

Normally your chart will display up-to-date information from the underlying table or query. If you prefer to freeze that chart's data so it never changes again, you can convert it to an image.

Only freestanding charts can be converted to images. Once you change the chart to an image, there's no way to undo that change, so use this technique with care!

1. Open the form or report that contains the freestanding chart in design view.

2. Click the chart to select it, and then choose Format ➢ Change To ➢ Image. Or right-click the chart and choose Change To ➢ Image. You'll be asked to confirm the change.

3. Click Yes if you're sure you want to freeze the chart into an image that cannot be changed. Or click No to leave the chart alone.

If you're sure the charted data will never change, convert the chart to an image to make your form or report open more quickly.

Charting Data from Other Programs

So far, we've focused on charts that display data from Microsoft Access tables and queries. However, your reports and forms also can chart data from other programs. Suppose your employee information is stored in an Access table, but your company's sales performance data is in a Microsoft Excel spreadsheet that's maintained by the Accounting department. You can use the embedding techniques described in the next section to send a memo (custom addressed to each employee) that graphically illustrates the company's sales performance.

Embedding Charts from Other Programs

Follow these steps to create a chart that uses data from another source, such as Microsoft Excel, Lotus 1-2-3, or data that you type directly into Microsoft Graph's datasheet window.

1. Open your form or report in design view.

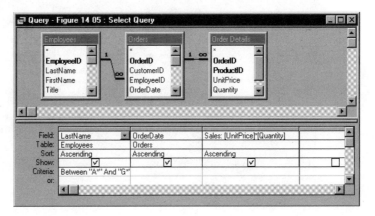

2. Click the Unbound Object Frame toolbox tool (shown at left).

3. Click the place in the form or report design where the upper-left corner of the chart should appear, or click and drag to define the chart's size. The Insert Object dialog box appears, listing all the OLE programs on your computer when Create New is selected.

4. Under Object Type in the Insert Object dialog box, click Microsoft Graph 2000 Chart, and then click OK.

As Figure 15.24 shows, Microsoft Graph opens with some sample data in the datasheet window and a sample chart for that data in the chart window. You can click in the datasheet window and change the existing data as needed. The results will be reflected instantly in the chart window.

FIGURE 15.24

Microsoft Graph opens with some sample data and a sample chart. The sample data is for reference only—it's not stored in any Access table. In this example, we clicked the datasheet window to bring its data to the front.

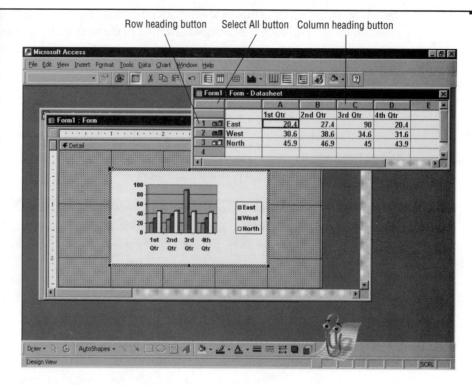

If you prefer to clear the existing data and type in data or import data from another program, click the Select All button (shown in Figure 15.24) and then press the Delete key. Now click in the cell where you want to start typing or importing data, and use the guidelines below to put data into Microsoft Graph's datasheet window:

- **To enter data into a cell**, select the cell you want to edit by clicking it or using the arrow and Tab keys to reach the desired cell, and then begin typing. Anything you type replaces the existing contents of the cell.

- **To import a text or spreadsheet file**, click where you want the first cell to appear. Choose Edit ➤ Import File, select the type of file you want to import from the List Files of Type drop-down list, and then double-click the file you want to import. Respond to any additional prompts that appear. For example, if you're importing a text file, a Text Import Wizard will ask you to provide more information about the file's format.

- **To import data from a Microsoft Excel chart**, choose Edit ➤ Import File, select Microsoft Excel Files from the List Files of Type drop-down list, and then double-click the chart you want to import. Respond to any additional prompts that appear.

 NOTE Text files generally have extensions of `.prn`, `.csv`, or `.txt`; spreadsheet files have `.wk*` and `.xl*` extensions; Microsoft Excel charts have `.xlc` or `.xls` extensions.

- **To import data that you've copied to the Clipboard**, choose Edit ➤ Paste or press Ctrl+V.

After importing or typing in your data, you can click the chart window to view and customize your chart as desired. When you're finished, click off the chart object to exit chart editing mode. The chart will appear in your Access form or report. If necessary, resize the chart in the design window, or return to Microsoft Graph and resize the chart window.

 NOTE You also can *link* charts developed in other programs that support OLE to unbound object frames in forms and reports, and to OLE Object fields in tables. See Chapters 8 and 13 for more information on using OLE to link and embed objects.

Creating PivotTables

PivotTables are powerful tools for gleaning management information from large amounts of data. Although they're similar to Crosstab queries (described in Chapter 10), PivotTables are much more powerful because they let you switch row and column headings dynamically and filter data on the fly, so you can focus on just the information you need to know at the moment.

 NOTE PivotTables aren't really native Microsoft Access objects at all. They're embedded Microsoft Excel objects that you create and modify by starting from an Access form. Of course, you must have Microsoft Excel installed, including its Access Links feature, in order to use PivotTables and the PivotTable Wizard that creates them.

Figure 15.25 shows a sample PivotTable after we created it within an Access form (using the PivotTable Wizard) and then clicked the form's Edit PivotTable button. This PivotTable answers the question: "What were the sales (by month) during the first half of 1999 for Produce sold to all companies by all employees?"

FIGURE 15.25

A PivotTable created from a query on the Northwind sample database that comes with Access.

Page axis   Column axis   Query and pivot toolbar

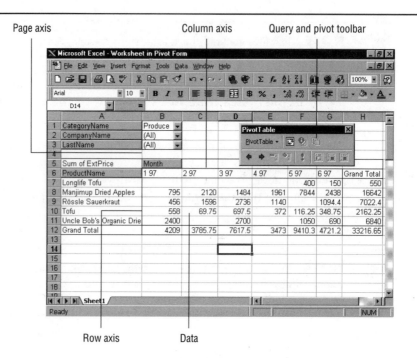

Row axis   Data

With just a few simple selections from the drop-down lists in the pages axis, this one PivotTable can answer many more questions:

- What were the sales (by month) during the first half of 1999 for Produce sold by the employee named Fuller to all customers?
- What were the sales (by month) during the first half of 1999 for Produce sold by the employee named Fuller to the company named La corne d'abondance?
- What were the sales (by month) during the first half of 1999 for all products sold by all employees to the company named La corne d'abondance?
- What were the sales (by month) during the first half of 1999 for all products sold by all employees to all customers?

You get the idea!

Now suppose you want to focus on employee sales performance rather than product sales performance. No sweat. Just drag the shaded LastName and ProductName controls to new positions on the PivotTable (see Figure 15.26), and the answers become clear instantly.

FIGURE 15.26

The PivotTable from Figure 15.25, after dragging the ProductName control to the page axis and the LastName control to the row axis.

Page axis   Column axis   Query and pivot toolbar

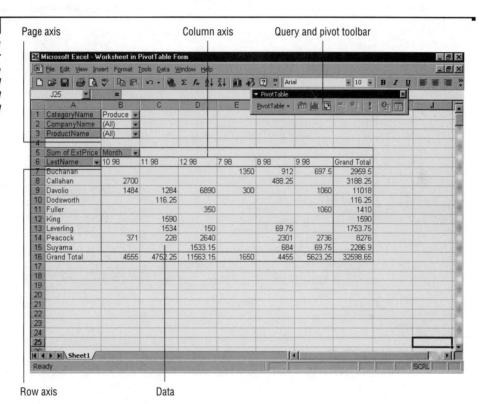

Row axis   Data

To summarize the sales by employee and product, move the ProductName control to the row axis (just below the LastName control), and the PivotTable will change once more (see Figure 15.27). As you can see, the possibilities for rearranging the PivotTable are practically endless and easily explored.

PART

II

Creating a Database

FIGURE 15.27

The PivotTable from Figure 15.26, after moving the ProductName control from the page axis to the row axis.

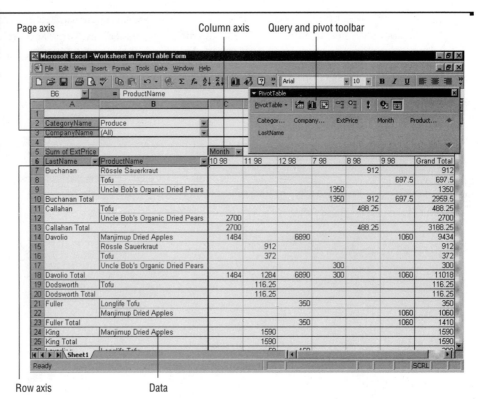

Page axis — Column axis — Query and pivot toolbar

Row axis — Data

Understanding PivotTable Buzzwords and Procedures

Before you create your first PivotTable, take a moment to understand the PivotTable buzzwords listed below. The labels on Figures 15.25, 15.26, and 15.27 show how each of these terms relates to areas on the sample PivotTables.

Row   The field or fields that contain values to use for row labels on the Pivot-Table's row axis. In Figure 15.25, the row field is ProductName; in Figure 15.26, the row field is LastName; and in Figure 15.27, the row fields are LastName and ProductName.

Column   The field or fields that contain values to use for column labels on the PivotTable's column axis. In Figures 15.25, 15,26, and 15.27, the column field is Month.

Data The field or fields that contain values to summarize in the body of the table. In Figures 15.25, 15.26, and 15.27, the data field is ExtPrice (extended price), and we've used the Sum function to summarize that field.

Page The field or fields that contain values to use for labels on the Pivot-Table's page axis. You can use these fields to filter data in the PivotTable. In Figure 15.25 the page fields allow filtering on CategoryName, CompanyName, and LastName. This filter lets us limit summarized values to sales in a specific category (such as Produce), or to a certain company (such as La corne d'abondance), or by a particular employee (such as Fuller). In Figure 15.26 the page fields are CategoryName, CompanyName, and ProductName; and in Figure 15.27 the page fields are CategoryName and CompanyName.

Creating a PivotTable requires just a few main steps:

1. Create and save a query for the PivotTable's underlying data (see Chapter 10) if necessary. Figure 15.28 shows the query we used to produce the PivotTables shown in Figures 15.25, 15.26, and 15.27. We used the following calculations for the ExtPrice (Extended Price), Month, and OrderDate fields, which are partially hidden in the Figure 15.28 QBE grid:

   - **ExtPrice**: [Quantity]*[Order Details]![UnitPrice]
   - **Month**: Format ([OrderDate],"m yy")
   - **OrderDate**: Between #1/1/99# And #6/30/99#

NOTE Because the PivotTable Wizard lets you choose fields from multiple tables, you might not need to create a query. However, you will need a query if you want to display calculation results (such as extended price, which multiplies quantity times unit price) or you want to limit the results to certain records (such as orders placed in 1999).

2. Use the PivotTable Wizard to create a form that contains an embedded Pivot-Table. See "Creating a PivotTable with the PivotTable Wizard," below, for details.

3. Open your form in form view, edit the PivotTable in Microsoft Excel as needed, and print the PivotTable if you wish. When you're finished editing, return to Access. All this is explained in "Editing a PivotTable" later in this chapter.

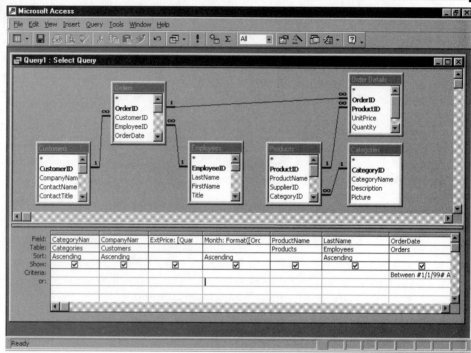

FIGURE 15.28

The query used to produce the data for the PivotTables shown in Figures 15.25, 15.26, and 15.27.

Creating a PivotTable with the PivotTable Wizard

Creating a PivotTable is easy, thanks to the PivotTable Wizard. Here's the quickest way to do the job:

1. Start at the database window, and click the Tables button (to create the PivotTable from a table) or the Queries button (to create the PivotTable from a query).

2. Click the name of the table or query that contains the data for your PivotTable.

3. Choose Insert ➢ Form; or click the drop-down arrow next to the New Object toolbar button, and then choose Form.

4. Double-click PivotTable Wizard in the New Form dialog box.

5. Read the first PivotTable Wizard dialog box, and then click Next.

6. Select the table or query that contains the fields you want to include in the PivotTable, if it's not already shown, and then select the fields. You can choose multiple fields and tables as needed. Click Next to continue. You'll see the last step of

the PivotTable Wizard, shown in Figure 15.29. You can skip the rest of the steps outlined here and click Finish if you want to edit the final result later. If you prefer to work out the details for the PivotTable's appearance now, use the Layout and Options buttons as shown next.

7. In the final PivotTable Wizard step, click the Layout button if you want to build your PivotTable now using the dialog box shown in Figure 15.30. Drag the desired fields to the page, row, column, and data areas. Here are some guidelines you can use when deciding what to drop where:

- **To show items in a field as row labels**, drag that field to the ROW area. You can use more than one field for row labels. For example, in Figure 15.27, both the LastName and ProductName fields are used for row labels.

- **To show items in a field as column labels**, drag that field to the COLUMN area. In Figures 15.25, 15.26, and 15.27, the Month field is used for column labels. You can use more than one field for column labels.

- **To summarize a field's values in the body of the PivotTable**, drag that field to the DATA area.

- **To be able to use certain fields for filtering the data shown in the PivotTable**, drag those fields to the PAGE area.

- **To delete a field from the PivotTable**, drag it off the white area of the sample PivotTable.

- **To customize a field**, double-click it to show a PivotTable Field dialog box like the one shown in Figure 15.31. This dialog box will vary depending on the type of field you are customizing.

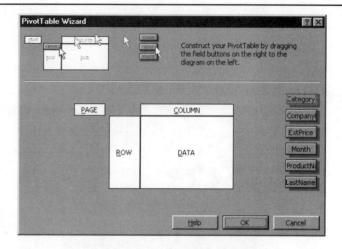

Figure 15.32 shows an example of the layout window after fields were dragged to the various PivotTable areas. Click OK when you're finished working with the PivotTable's layout.

FIGURE 15.32

The fields in this layout result in the PivotTable shown in Figure 15.34.

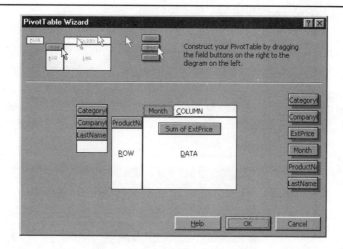

8. Back in the last step of the PivotTable Wizard, click the Options button if you want to change various formatting and data options for the PivotTable. Figure 15.33 shows the options you can change with this dialog box. When you're finished changing options, click OK to return to the last PivotTable Wizard step.

FIGURE 15.33

The PivotTable Options dialog box lets you turn various formatting and data options on or off.

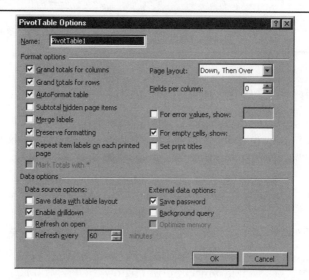

9. Click Finish to create the PivotTable.

10. Save the form when the PivotTable form appears on your screen. To do so, click the Save toolbar button, or choose File ➢ Save, or press Ctrl+S. Type a valid form name (up to 64 characters, including blank spaces), and then click OK.

Figure 15.34 shows a PivotTable embedded in an Access form in form view. Notice that the form doesn't show all the data in the PivotTable and that it doesn't offer any scroll bars. To see what's really in the PivotTable, you'll need to edit it, as explained next.

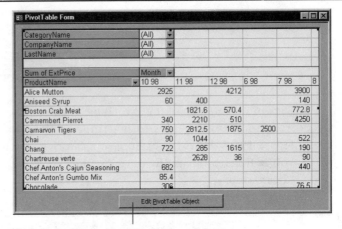

Click to edit the PivotTable in Microsoft Excel.

Editing a PivotTable

To view the details in a PivotTable or change the PivotTable in some way, you must edit the PivotTable in Microsoft Excel. As weird as it might seem, you must start the editing procedure from Access—not from Excel. Fear not, it's easy:

1. Open the form that contains your PivotTable in form view, if it isn't open already. That is, click the Forms tab in the database window, and then double-click the name of your PivotTable form.

2. Open the PivotTable in Microsoft Excel using one of these techniques:

- **To open the table in a separate Excel window**, click the Edit Pivot-Table Object button below the PivotTable, or double-click the embedded PivotTable.

- **To edit the PivotTable in-place (within the Microsoft Access window)**, right-click the PivotTable, and then choose Worksheet Object ➤ Edit. You probably won't use in-place editing very often because it's less flexible than editing in a separate Excel window.

 NOTE You cannot make changes to the PivotTable unless the underlying data is current (or already saved with the table). To refresh the data and make it current, choose Data ➤ Refresh Data from the Excel menus.

3. Change the PivotTable as needed. The next section offers some tips for changing PivotTables.

4. (Optional) If you want to print the PivotTable in Excel, try this shortcut (we'll assume here that you're editing in a separate Excel window). Choose File ➤ Page Setup from the Microsoft Excel menu bar. From the Page tab in the Page Setup dialog box, choose an Orientation (Portrait or Landscape), Scaling, and other options, as needed. You also can choose options from the Margins, Header/ Footer, and Sheet tabs. To preview the report, click the Print Preview button. To print the report, click the Print button in the print preview window or the Page Setup dialog box, fill in the Print dialog box, and then click OK.

5. Return to Access when you're finished viewing, changing, and printing your PivotTable, using one of these techniques:

- **If you're editing in a separate Microsoft Excel window**, choose File ➤ Close & Return to PivotTable Form from the Microsoft Excel menu bar, or press Alt+F4, or click the Excel window's Close button.

- **If you're editing in-place within the Microsoft Access window**, click outside the PivotTable (for example, on an empty area of the form, below the hash marks that appear at the bottom of the PivotTable).

6. Close the form if you're done working with it (Ctrl+W). Any changes you made to the PivotTable in Microsoft Excel are saved automatically.

Customizing Your PivotTable in Microsoft Excel

You can customize a PivotTable many ways once you've opened it in Microsoft Excel, and experimentation really is the best teacher when it comes to making PivotTables do what you want. These pointers should get you up and running quickly:

- **To pivot or reorder a field**, drag its shaded control button to a new page axis, row axis, column axis, or body position on the worksheet. We used this technique to rearrange the data in Figures 15.25, 15.26, and 15.27. Watch the status bar for tips about how to drag and drop a control once you've started to drag it.

- **To return to the PivotTable Field dialog box** (shown earlier), double-click a field control in the page, column, or row axis. Or right-click a field control or a value in the area you want to customize; then choose Field Settings from the shortcut menu that pops ups. From here you can change the field label, summarization method, number formats, and other attributes as needed.

- **To return to the PivotTable Wizard dialog box**, choose Data ➢ Pivot-Table and PivotChart Report from the Excel menu.

For more information about customizing PivotTables in Microsoft Excel, look up *PivotTables* with the Office Assistant.

But My PivotTable Data Isn't Current!

If you chose the default options in the last PivotTable Wizard dialog box, the underlying data that the PivotTable uses is not saved with the PivotTable or form. This is a safety measure to make sure you see the latest data any time you view the PivotTable. To see the most current data, you must open the PivotTable in Microsoft Excel, and then refresh the data (Data ➢ Refresh Data) each time you work with the PivotTable.

If you won't have access to the underlying Access table data and still want to edit the PivotTable later on, you'll need to save a copy of the data with the PivotTable. To do this, click Options in the final PivotTable Wizard dialog box, and select (check) Save Data with Table Layout—you can do this either when you first create the PivotTable in Access, or after you open it in Excel. (To start the PivotTable Wizard again from Excel, choose Data ➢ PivotTable and PivotChart Report.) Be aware that your PivotTable won't reflect changes to the original underlying data unless you refresh the data again.

Creating a Chart from a PivotTable

With just a few more keystrokes, you can create a chart from a PivotTable. Here's how:

1. Open the PivotTable in Microsoft Excel, as explained earlier in this chapter. Then customize the PivotTable fields as needed.

2. Select the PivotTable cells, *including* the column fields and row fields you want to chart, but *excluding* grand totals or page fields. To select cells, drag your mouse through them.

3. Choose Insert ➢ Chart to open the Chart Wizard.

4. Follow the instructions in the Chart Wizard dialog boxes.

5. View the chart (and print it if you wish). The chart always reflects your current selections in the page axis of the PivotTable. For example, if you select a category from the CategoryName page, the chart will show data for that category only.

6. Exit Microsoft Excel (Alt+F4) when you're finished viewing your chart.

For more details about charting PivotTables, look up *Plotting PivotTable Data* with the Office Assistant.

Troubleshooting PivotTable Problems

PivotTables are quite easy to use, but if you're having the troubles listed below, you might not agree. Fortunately, the fixes for most PivotTable troubles are straightforward:

Data field is using the Count function rather than Sum to summarize a numeric field   Your numeric data may contain blank values. To fix the problem, open the PivotTable in Microsoft Excel and click the cell that says "Count Of" followed by the field name. Next, click the PivotTable Field button in the PivotTable toolbar, and double-click the Sum option in the PivotTable Field dialog box.

Data in the PivotTable is cut off and you can't see any scroll bars   You're probably viewing the form in Microsoft Access form view. Starting in Access form view, click the Edit PivotTable Object button, or double-click the PivotTable. The PivotTable will open in Microsoft Excel and the scroll bars will appear.

Excel won't let you change your PivotTable   You've probably forgotten to refresh the data. Choose Data ➢ Refresh Data from the Excel menu.

Numbers aren't formatted properly (or at all) in the PivotTable   By default, numbers aren't formatted. To format numbers, right-click a cell in the unformatted data, and then choose Field Settings from the shortcut menu that appears. Next, click the Number button in the PivotTable Field dialog box, fill in the Format Cells dialog box that appears, and then click OK twice.

PART

II

Creating a Database

PivotTable toolbar is missing in Excel   From the Microsoft Excel menu bar, choose View ➤ Toolbars, select (check) PivotTable, and then click OK.

Starting from Microsoft Excel, you can't find the PivotTable   You can't get to the Access PivotTable from Excel. Start in Microsoft Access form view, and then click the Edit PivotTable button; or double-click the PivotTable. The PivotTable will open in Excel, and you can view and customize it as needed.

For more information about troubleshooting problems with PivotTables, look up *Troubleshooting PivotTables* with the Office Assistant.

Where to Go from Here

In this chapter, you've learned how to summarize data with charts and PivotTables. If you've been following this book in sequence, you now know all the basics for working with Microsoft Access. But don't stop here! The next chapter explains how to personalize Access to your own working style.

What's New in the Access Zoo?

The PivotTable Wizard in Access 2000 has been simplified. The third step of the Wizard, the one where you used to lay out the fields for a PivotTable, has been eliminated. Now you can go directly to the PivotTable window in Excel and lay out the fields there, or you can click the Layout button in the last PivotTable Wizard step if you want to change the layout the Wizard will choose for you.

PART III

Database Tuning and Administration

LEARN TO:

- *Personalize Access*

- *Speed up your database*

- *Administer your database*

- *Provide networking capability*

- *Add security to your database*

CHAPTER <u>16</u>

Personalizing Access

You can tailor your Access work environment to your own requirements and working style. If you're happy with the way Access is working now, there's no need to change the default settings, and you should feel free to skip this chapter. But if you'd like to learn how to tweak things a bit, read on.

Note that other chapters in this book explain how to customize the features described in Table 16.1, so we won't repeat those discussions here.

TABLE 16.1: OTHER PLACES TO LEARN ABOUT CUSTOMIZING ACCESS		
TO CUSTOMIZE THIS...	USE THESE OPTIONS...	AND SEE THIS CHAPTER OR HELP INDEX TOPIC
ActiveX Controls	Tools ➤ ActiveX Controls	Look up *ActiveX Controls* subtopics with the Office Assistant
Menus	View ➤ Toolbars ➤ Customize or Tools ➤ Customize	25
Security	Tools ➤ Security	19
Toolbars	View ➤ Toolbars ➤ Customize or Tools ➤ Customize	24
Switchboards	Tools ➤ Database Utilities ➤ Switchboard Manager	22

Personalizing Your Work Environment

You can personalize many aspects of your Access work environment by following these general steps:

1. Open a database (if one isn't open already), and choose Tools ➤ Options. You'll see the Options dialog box shown in Figure 16.1.

2. Click a tab to select a category. (For your convenience, we've arranged the following sections in alphabetical order according to the category of options that each tab controls.)

3. Change options, as described in the sections that follow. Depending on the option you're setting, you can type a value, select a value from a drop-down list,

select an option button, or select (check) or deselect (clear) a check box. Selecting a check box activates the associated option (that is, it says "Yes, I want this option"); deselecting the check box deactivates the option (that is, it says "No, I don't want this option").

4. Click OK when you're finished making changes.

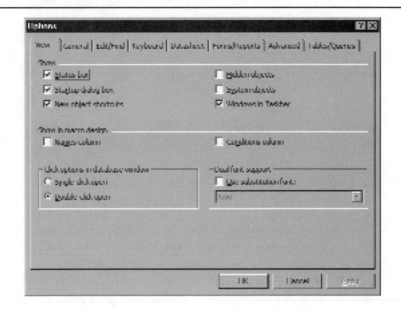

For more about the options discussed in the following sections, choose Tools ≻ Options, and click the appropriate category tab. Next, click the ? button at the upper-right corner of the Options dialog box, and then click the option you're interested in; or right-click the option name and choose What's This?; or click in a text box or combo box and press Shift+F1. You also can look up topics under *Default Settings* in the Access Help Index.

Changing Advanced Options

The Advanced options (see Figure 16.2) control how Access handles data in a multi-user environment and how it handles OLE and DDE operations.

PART

III

Database Tuning and Administration

FIGURE 16.2

The Advanced tab in the Options dialog box.

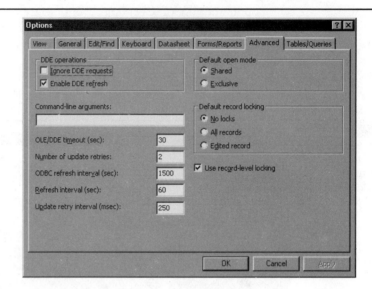

The OLE/DDE options are as follows:

DDE Operations   Select or clear options to choose whether to Ignore DDE Requests from other programs and whether to Enable DDE Refresh at the interval given by the OLE/DDE Timeout (Sec) setting.

OLE/DDE Timeout (Sec)   Specify the interval, in seconds (from 0 to 300), that Access will wait before retrying a failed OLE or DDE operation.

See Chapter 19 and the online Help for details about the following multiuser options on the Advanced tab: Default Record Locking, Default Open Mode, Number of Update Retries, ODBC Refresh Interval (Sec), Refresh Interval (Sec), and Update Retry Interval (Msec).

Changing Datasheet Options

The Datasheet options, shown in Figure 16.3, let you change the default appearance of the datasheet view when you first open a table or query. Most options are self-explanatory, so we won't trouble you with reading through the details about them. However, you might want to know about the Show Animations option. When Show Animation is checked, new columns that you add to a table in datasheet view appear to slide into place. Without Show Animation turned on, new columns appear instantly in a datasheet view.

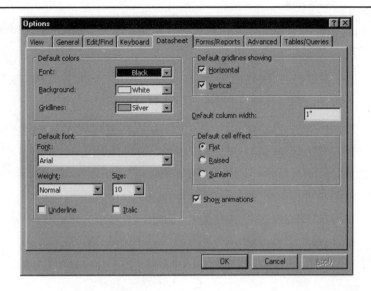

FIGURE 16.3

The Datasheet tab in the Options dialog box.

You can override the Default Colors, Default Gridlines Showing, Default Font, Default Column Width, and Default Cell Effect settings in datasheet view. To do so, choose the Font, Cells, and Column Width options on the Format menu, or use the Formatting (Datasheet) toolbar, as explained in Chapter 8.

Changing Edit/Find Options

Use the Edit/Find options, shown in Figure 16.4, to choose the default method for doing a Find or Replace operation, to control whether to confirm various types of changes, and to control the size of value lists when you use filter by form.

The Default Find/Replace options are listed below. You can override these settings in the Find and Replace (Edit ➤ Find) or (Edit ➤ Replace) dialog box, as explained in Chapter 9.

Fast Search   Searches the current field and matches the whole field.

General Search   Searches the current field and matches any part of the field.

Start of Field Search   Searches the current field and matches the beginning character or characters in the field.

The check box options in the Confirm pane let you control whether Access displays a confirmation message when you change a record (Record Changes), delete a database object (Document Deletions), or run an action query (Action Queries). It's a good idea to leave these options checked.

PART

III

Database Tuning and Administration

The Edit/Find tab in the Options dialog box.

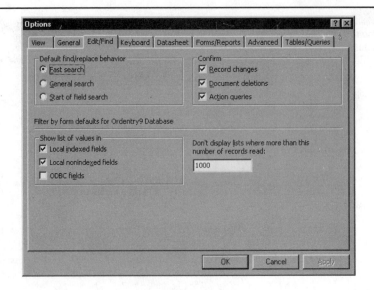

The options in the Filter by Form Defaults for Database control which fields supply values when you use the Filter by Form feature (see Chapter 9), and how many rows to display in a filter-by-form list. These options affect the current database only, and you can set different defaults for other databases. You can override the options for a given filter-by-form operation, as explained in Chapter 9. To speed up filter-by-form operations, limit the Filter by Form Defaults settings to local indexed fields, and reduce the number of records read.

Changing Forms/Reports Options

Use the Forms/Reports options, shown in Figure 16.5, to control the default templates used for form and report designs and to define the selection behavior when you drag the mouse pointer to select controls in form and report design view.

The Forms/Reports options are as follows:

Selection Behavior   Choose Partially Enclosed to have Access select controls that are even partially contained within the frame. Choose Fully Enclosed to have Access select only controls that are completely contained within the frame you draw while dragging the pointer.

FIGURE 16.5

The Forms/Reports tab in the Options dialog box.

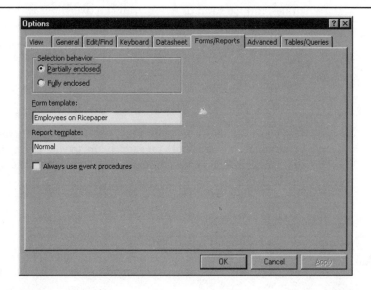

Form Template   The default is Normal, a built-in, general-purpose template that Access uses to create an AutoForm or blank form. You can specify any existing form in the database as the form template, if you wish. If you specify a form that doesn't exist in the database, Access will use the built-in Normal form template.

Report Template   As with forms, the default report template is Normal, but you can specify any existing report in the database as the report template. Access uses this template to create an AutoReport or blank report. If you specify a report that doesn't exist in the database, Access will use the built-in Normal report template.

Always Use Event Procedures   When this option is selected (checked), Access will bypass the Choose Builder dialog box and go directly to the Module window after the Build button is clicked on a property sheet.

NOTE   Form and report templates define whether to include a form or report header and footer, whether to include a page header and footer, the dimensions of each section, and the default properties for each control. A template does not create controls on a new form or report.

When designing a form or report, you can override the default settings in many ways. For example, you can change the default properties for new controls that you add to a form or report in design view, and you can use AutoFormat styles to format all or part of a design. See Chapter 13 for complete details about designing forms and reports.

TIP If you'd like to use custom control settings for all new forms or reports that you design, customize the properties for each control to your liking. Then save the design and define it as a template in the Form Template or Report Template option settings described previously.

Changing General Options

The General options (see Figure 16.6) let you change the following default settings.

FIGURE 16.6

The General tab in the Options dialog box.

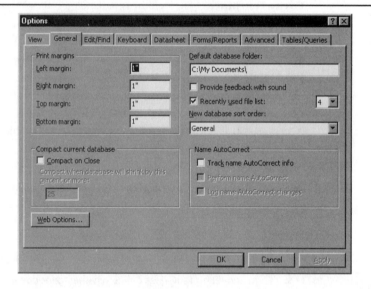

Print Margins Use the Print Margins options to assign default Left Margin, Right Margin, Top Margin, and Bottom Margin settings for new reports and forms. (The settings have no effect on existing forms and reports.) Initially all the margins are one inch wide.

> ⚠ **TIP**   To change the margin settings in an existing form or report, open the form or report in design view, choose File ➢ Page Setup, click the Margins tab, change the Top, Bottom, Left, and Right settings as needed, and then click OK (see Chapter 9).

Compact on Close   Check the box for Compact on Close to have Access remove dead space from the database when it is closed. If you check this option, you can change the percent in the box below to tell Access when it should compact. If the database would not shrink by at least the specified percent, Access will not bother to compact it.

Default Database Folder   Specify the folder in which Access will store or search for databases. The default is the dot (.) which stands for the default Access working directory, a folder named My Documents. (If you rename the My Documents folder in Windows, Windows will adjust the appropriate Registry settings to point to the renamed folder automatically.)

Provide Feedback with Sound   When this option is selected (checked), Access will play sounds when events, such as completion of printing, happen.

Recently Used File List   Check this option to have Access show the names of the last databases you opened at the bottom of the File menu. When this option is checked (the default setting), you can change the number of names that will appear on the list by changing the number in the box to the right.

New Database Sort Order   Choose the language used for alphabetic sorting of new databases. Options include General (for English), Traditional Spanish, Dutch, and several other languages. To change the sort method for an existing database, make the change here (in the New Database Sort Order text box), and then compact the existing database as discussed in Chapter 18.

Name AutoCorrect   This new option lets you tell Access to keep track of name changes to database objects. With this option turned on, Access will try to correct conflicts that arise after name changes.

Web Options   Click this button to open a window in which you can change the default appearance of hyperlinks. Access lets you choose the color for hyperlinks before and after they are followed, and whether they should be underlined.

NOTE In Access 97, hyperlinks were customized on their own tab: Hyperlinks/HTML. With Access 2000, use the Web Options button on the General tab to make these changes.

Changing Keyboard Options

The Keyboard options, shown in Figure 16.7, let you control how the Enter key, arrow keys, Tab key, and insertion point behave when you use the keyboard to move within or between fields in a form or datasheet.

FIGURE 16.7

The Keyboard options in the Options dialog box.

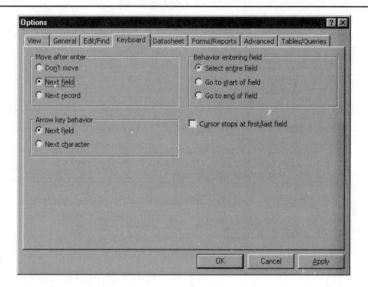

Move after Enter Determines what happens when you press Enter in a field. Your options are Don't Move (Enter has no effect.), Next Field (Enter moves the cursor to the next field.), or Next Record. (Enter moves the cursor to the first field in the next record.)

Arrow Key Behavior Choose Next Field if you want the cursor to move to another field when you press ← or →, or choose Next Character if you want the cursor to move within the field when you press those keys. If Next Field is selected, you can press F2 and then ← or → to move the cursor within a field.

Behavior Entering Field   Determines what happens when the cursor lands in a field. Your options are Select Entire Field, Go to Start of Field, or Go to End of Field.

Cursor Stops At First/Last Field   Determines what happens in a datasheet when you press the ← key in the first field of a row or the → key in the last field of a row. Select (check) this option to have the cursor stay in the current field, or deselect (clear) it to move the cursor to the previous or next record.

When designing a form, you can control the behavior of the Enter key in text boxes (that is, Text and Memo fields). To do this, open the form in design view, open the property sheet, and click the Other tab on the property sheet. Next, select the text box control, and then change the Enter Key Behavior property either to Default (so that it uses the Move after Enter setting discussed above) or to New Line in Field (so that pressing the Enter key moves the cursor to a new line in the field). To simplify entry of multiple text lines in a Memo field, the control's Enter Key Behavior is initially set to New Line in Field. If you choose Default instead, you typically must press Ctrl+Enter to enter a new line in the Memo field's text box.

Changing Tables/Queries Options

Use the Tables/Queries options (see Figure 16.8) to choose defaults for new table fields and indexes and to control default behavior in the query design window.

FIGURE 16.8

The Tables/Queries tab in the Options dialog box.

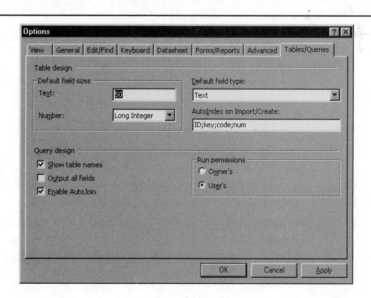

PART

III

Database Tuning and Administration

The Table Design options are as follows:

Default Field Sizes   Lets you specify the default field size for newly created text and number fields in table design view. Specify a Text field size from 0 to 255 characters; choose a default Number field size from the Number drop-down list.

Default Field Type   Lets you choose the default field type for newly created fields in table design view.

AutoIndex on Import/Create   Lets you specify fieldnames that are indexed automatically when you first create them in table design view or when you import them from an external file. The Indexed property on the General tab of the table design window will display Yes (Duplicates OK) for automatically indexed fields.

In the AutoIndex on Import/Create text box, enter the beginning characters or ending characters that the automatically indexed field names should contain, and separate each field name (or partial field name) with a semicolon (;). *Example:* the AutoIndex on Import/Create setting shown in Figure 16.8 will cause Access to automatically index field names such as ID, MyID, KeyField, Code1, and AutoNum.

WARNING   Each table can have up to 32 indexes. You're likely to bump up against that 32-index limit rather quickly if you include many field names in the AutoIndex on Import/Create option, or if many fields that you create or import include the field names listed in the AutoIndex on Import/Create text box.

The Query Design options are as follows:

Show Table Names   Lets you display or hide table names in the QBE grid. To override this setting, choose View ➢ Table Names in the query design window.

Output All Fields   When selected, all fields in a query's underlying tables or queries appear when the query is run; when deselected only the fields added to the QBE grid appear. To override this setting, change the query's Output All Fields property.

Enable AutoJoin   Lets you choose whether to create automatic inner joins between two tables that you add to the query design window. Access can create an inner join for tables if those tables are already joined in the Relationships window, or if the tables contain fields that have the same field name and the same or compatible data types in each table. Even if you disable automatic joins, you can create them manually in the query design window.

Run Permissions   Choose Owner's to run new queries with the owner's permissions, or choose User's to run new queries with the current user's permissions. These permissions are important on secured databases. To view or change a query's owner, choose Tools ➤ Security ➤ User and Group Permissions from the menus, and then click the Change Owner tab. To override the query's default run permissions, open the query in design view and change its Run Permissions property.

See Chapter 6 for details about designing tables, Chapter 7 for more information about importing tables, Chapter 10 for more about queries, and Chapter 19 for tips on networking and security.

Changing View Options

Use the View options, shown in Figure 16.9, to control the appearance of the database window and macro design windows and to choose whether the status bar and startup dialog box appear.

FIGURE 16.9

The View tab in the Options dialog box.

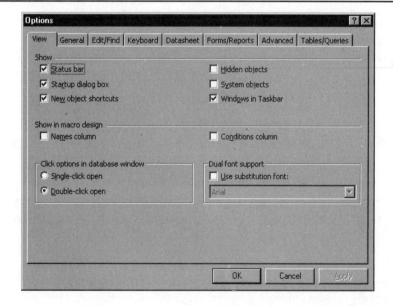

PART

III

Database Tuning and Administration

Status Bar Lets you display or hide the status bar. (Your life will be easier if you leave the status bar visible, so you can see the helpful hints Access displays there.)

Startup Dialog Box Controls whether the startup dialog box appears when you start Access. When this option is selected, Access displays the initial dialog box that lets you choose which database to open; when deselected, you're taken directly to the Access main menu, which has only the File, Tools, and Help menus.

NOTE If you turn off the startup dialog box, you must open a database (File ➢ Open) or create a database (File ➢ New) before you can choose Tools ➢ Options again.

New Object Shortcuts When checked, this option tells Access to show new object shortcuts like Create Form in Design View and Create Form by Using Wizard in the database window.

Hidden Objects Controls whether to display or hide objects in the database window if they have a property of Hidden. When you choose to display hidden objects, their icons will be dimmed in the database window. To hide an object, go to the database window, locate the object you want to hide, right-click the object's name, select (check) the Hidden property near the bottom of the dialog box, and then click OK.

System Objects Controls whether to display or hide the names of internal system objects that Access creates or system objects that you create. These system objects start with the letters Msys or Usys. If you select (check) the System Objects option, Access will show system objects along with other table names in the database window, though their icons will be dimmed. (It's best to leave these objects hidden to avoid confusion.)

WARNING Don't mess around with any of the system objects that Access creates if you aren't absolutely sure of what you're doing. The results can be disastrous.

Windows in Taskbar When checked, tells Access to show an icon on the Windows taskbar for each open database object or window. Otherwise, just one icon appears for Access itself.

Names Column   Controls whether to display or hide the Macro Name column in the macro design window. To override this setting, choose View ➤ Macro Names from the macro design menus.

Conditions Column   Controls whether to display or hide the Condition column. To override this setting, choose View ➤ Conditions from the macro design menus.

Click Options in Database Window   Lets you check Single-Click Open or Double-Click Open to specify how many clicks it takes to open an object from the database window.

Dual Font Support   When Use Substitution Font is checked, you can select a secondary font so you can show two kinds of text in the same document.

TIP   To change your screen's video resolution (if your screen supports adjustable resolutions and you're using Windows 95 or later), minimize Access and other programs you're running, so you can see the Windows Desktop. Then right-click any blank area on the Windows Desktop, choose Properties, click the Settings tab in the Display Properties dialog box, drag the slider control below the Desktop Area option, and then click OK. When prompted, click OK and then click Yes to accept the changes.

Personalizing a Database

You can personalize a database in several ways:

- Set *startup options* that take effect when you open the database. See "Changing Startup Options," next.

- Set *database properties* that document your database and make it easier to find the database later. See "Changing the Database Properties" in Chapter 5.

- Set *object properties* for objects that appear in the database window. See "Changing Properties of an Entire Table or Object" in Chapter 6.

Changing Startup Options

The startup options let you control options that take effect when you open a particular database. You can use the Startup dialog box instead of, or in addition to, an

AutoExec macro. The AutoExec macro will run after the Startup dialog box options take effect. (See Chapters 21 and 29 for more about macros.)

To set the startup options:

1. Open the database for which you want to set startup options.

2. Choose Tools ➤ Startup; or right-click any gray area on the database window and choose Startup. You'll see the Startup dialog box, shown in Figure 16.10.

FIGURE 16.10

The Startup dialog box after we clicked the Advanced button.

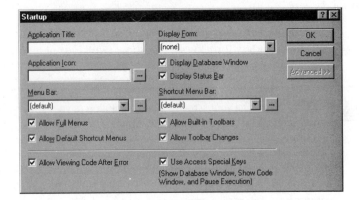

3. Change any of the options described just below.

4. Click OK to accept the new settings and close the Startup dialog box.

5. Close the database and open it again if necessary.

 TIP To bypass the startup settings and use the default options shown in Figure 16.10, hold down the Shift key while opening the database.

The Startup dialog box options are described below. Note that some options take effect as soon as you close the Startup dialog box; however, others don't take effect until the next time the database is opened (these "delayed" options are marked with an asterisk below).

Application Title Lets you display your own application title in the Access title bar. Type the title you want to display. To use the default application title of "Microsoft Access," leave the Application Title text box empty.

Application Icon   Lets you replace the standard Access "key" icon with an application icon of your own choosing. The icon appears in the Access title bar and on the application's Taskbar button. To specify an icon, type its name into the Application Icon text box; or click the Build button next to the Application Icon option, locate the icon (*.ico) or bitmap (*.bmp) file you want to display, and then double-click its file name. (On Windows NT, you can use icon files only, not bitmap files.) If you'll be distributing your application, it's best to put the icon or bitmap file in the same folder as your application. To use the default icon for Access, leave the Application Icon text box empty.

Menu Bar*   Lets you choose a global menu bar to display when you open the current database. Choose an existing menu bar from the drop-down list next to the Menu Bar option, or choose Default to use the Access default menu bar. Chapter 25 explains how to create custom menu bars. Until you create a custom menu bar, the only choice you'll see for this option is Default.

Allow Full Menus*   Lets you choose whether a full set, or a restricted set, of menus appears on the Access built-in menu bars. Select (check) this option to display a full set of built-in menus; deselect (clear) this option to display a restricted set of built-in menus that doesn't allow design changes to database objects.

Allow Default Shortcut Menus*   Lets you choose whether the Access default shortcut menus are available. Select (check) this option to display shortcut menus when you right-click a toolbar or other object; deselect (clear) this option to prevent shortcut menus from appearing when you right-click.

Allow Viewing Code after Error*   Lets you control whether to enable the Ctrl+Break key and allow code viewing in the Module window after a runtime error occurs in the application. (When you're finished developing your application, you may want to deselect this option to prevent users from viewing your code.)

Display Form*   Lets you choose which form to display when the database is opened. To avoid displaying any form, choose None from the Display Form drop-down list. The applications you create with the Database Wizard specify a form named Switchboard as the Display Form.

Display Database Window*   Lets you choose whether to display or hide the database window when you open the database. It's often handy to hide the database window if your database displays a form at startup. (Even if the database window doesn't appear at startup, you usually can display it anytime by pressing F11.)

PART

III

Database Tuning and Administration

Display Status Bar*   Lets you choose whether the status bar appears at the bottom of the Access window (usually it's best to leave this option checked so you can see the status bar). To turn off the status bar for all Access databases, choose Tools ➤ Options, click the View tab, and deselect (clear) Status Bar. The status bar won't appear in the current database if you've turned off the status bar for the current database, all databases, or both.

Shortcut Menu Bar*   Lets you choose a shortcut menu bar to display when you right-click a form or report in form view or print preview. Choose an existing shortcut menu bar from the drop-down list next to the Menu Bar option, or choose (Default) to use the Access default shortcut menu bar. See Chapter 25 for details on creating custom shortcut menus.

Allow Built-In Toolbars*   Lets you choose whether to allow users to display the Access built-in toolbars. This setting will not affect custom toolbars that you add. Normally you'll want to leave the toolbars available, unless you're developing an application that has its own custom toolbars and you don't want Access toolbars to appear.

Allow Toolbar Changes*   Lets you choose whether to allow users to change the built-in toolbars and custom toolbars. Select (check) this option to allow changes to the toolbars. Deselect (clear) this option to disable the View ➤ Toolbars ➤ Customize command and the right mouse button on toolbars.

Use Access Special Keys*   Lets you choose whether to enable or disable these special keys: F11 or Alt+F1 (displays the database window), Ctrl+G (displays the debug window), Ctrl+F11 (toggles between the custom menu bar and the built-in menu bar), Ctrl+Break (stops code from running and displays the current module in the Module window).

For details about any option in the Startup dialog box, right-click the option name and click What's This?, or click in an option's text box and then press Shift+F1. For information about important things to consider when you alter settings in the Startup dialog box, search for *Startup Dialog Box* with the Office Assistant, click See More, and then click the *Considerations When Setting Options in the Startup Dialog Box* topic.

Installing Wizards, Builders, and Menu Add-Ins

Access wizards, builders, and menu add-ins are contained in special library databases. You can use the Add-In Manager to install or uninstall existing libraries, and to add new library databases.

NOTE Library databases have the file extension .mda; otherwise, they are similar to standard databases (.mdb). Several libraries come with Access and are installed automatically by the Setup program (see Appendix A); however, these libraries do not appear in the Add-In Manager dialog box. You also can create your own libraries or purchase them from third-party suppliers.

To get started with the Add-In Manager, follow these steps:

1. Choose Tools ➤ Add-Ins ➤ Add-In Manager. The Add-In Manager dialog box, shown in Figure 16.11, will appear. Installed libraries are marked with an ×.

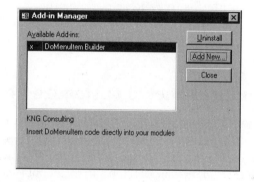

2. Do one of the following:

   • **To add an add-in to the list**, click the Add New button, locate and click the add-in's filename in the File Open dialog box, and then click OK (or double-click the file name). This procedure copies the library to the Access installation folder and installs it in the Available Add-Ins list.

   • **To install an available add-in**, click the add-in name in the Available Add-Ins list and then click the Install button.

   • **To uninstall a currently available add-in**, click the add-in name in the Available Add-Ins list and then click the Uninstall button. When the library is uninstalled, it's available on disk but won't be loaded into memory and can't be used. You can conserve memory and reduce the time it takes to load Access by uninstalling libraries that you aren't using.

   • **To quickly install or uninstall an add-in**, double-click the add-in name in the Available Add-Ins list (double-clicking will toggle the × on or off).

3. Click Close when you're done using the Add-In Manager. You'll be returned to the database window.

PART

III

Database Tuning and Administration

> **WARNING** Don't just experiment with installing and uninstalling add-ins. If you do, you might lose wizards and options on the Tools ➤ Add-Ins menus. To restore lost add-ins, reinstall Access and any third-party add-ins.

You can learn more about the Add-In Manager by searching for *Add-In Manager* with the Office Assistant.

Other Ways to Personalize Access

This chapter has discussed many ways to personalize Access. But there are more! You also can personalize the appearance and behavior of Access by changing options in Windows' Control Panel, by specifying startup options on the command line that starts Access, and by customizing the Registry file. The following sections briefly discuss these techniques.

Using Control Panel to Customize Access

Like most Windows programs, Access inherits many of its settings from options that you set in Windows' Control Panel. To get started with Control Panel, click the Start button on the Taskbar, and choose Settings ➤ Control Panel (or double-click the My Computer icon on your Desktop and then double-click the Control Panel folder). When the Control Panel window opens, double-click the icon for the settings you want to change (see Table 16.2). Remember that your changes in Control Panel will affect most other Windows programs.

TABLE 16.2: CONTROL PANEL SETTINGS FOR CUSTOMIZING ACCESS AND OTHER PROGRAMS		
ICON	**SETTINGS OPTION**	**WHAT IT DOES**
32bit ODBC	ODBC (32-bit)	Lets you add, delete, or configure data sources and install new 32-bit ODBC drivers on your computer. A data source includes the data source name, description, server, network address, network library, and other information used to identify and locate data on a network (see Chapter 18).

Continued ▶

TABLE 16.2: CONTROL PANEL SETTINGS FOR CUSTOMIZING ACCESS AND OTHER PROGRAMS

ICON	SETTINGS OPTION	WHAT IT DOES
Display	Display	Lets you choose the colors used for various parts of the screen and change the appearance of your Windows Desktop.
Fonts	Fonts	Lets you add and remove fonts and set TrueType options.
Network	Network	Lets you manage your network configuration, choose a primary network logon, enable or disable file and printer sharing, identify your computer to the network, and choose how to allow access to shared resources on your computer (see Chapter 19).
Passwords	Passwords	For networked computers, this option lets you change your Windows password and the password for other password-protected devices, allow remote administration of your computer, and choose personal preferences for users of your computer (see Chapter 19).
Printers	Printers	Lets you install and remove printers, change printing settings, and select the printer you want to use as the default printer.
Regional Settings	Regional Settings	Lets you specify international settings, including units of measurement, list separators, and formats for dates, times, currency, and numbers.
System	System	Lets you manage hardware devices on your computer, maintain hardware configuration profiles, and optimize various Windows settings for better performance. (Windows usually is optimized for better performance automatically.)

For more information about the options listed in Table 16.2, see your Windows documentation or use the Help ➢ Help Topics menus in Control Panel. You also can click any Control Panel icon and look at the status bar to find out what it does, and you can right-click options in the various Control Panel dialog boxes and choose What's This?

PART

III

Database Tuning and Administration

Using Command-Line Options When Starting Access

You can use *startup options* to open a database automatically, run a macro, supply a user account name or password, and more, simply by specifying options on the command line that starts Microsoft Access. Access gives you two ways to specify startup options:

On the Start ➤ Programs menu   Access always starts with any options you've specified in the Start ➤ Programs menu. Typically, only one Microsoft Access entry appears on this menu.

In a shortcut   Access starts with any options you've specified in the shortcut. You can set up as many shortcuts as you need (see Chapter 1), and you can place those shortcuts in a folder or directly on your Windows Desktop.

A standard Access startup command, without any command-line options, usually looks like this:

```
c:\msoffice\access\msaccess.exe
```

To specify command-line options, begin with the startup command shown above, then type a space, and then type additional options as needed (with each option separated by a space). The example below starts Access and opens the Order Entry1 database in the folder named My Documents on drive C (of course you must enter all the text on one line):

```
c:\Program Files\Microsoft Office\Office\msaccess.exe
   "c:\My Documents\Order Entry1"
```

WARNING   If the path to your database contains spaces, be sure to enclose the path in double quotation marks, as shown in the example above. If the path doesn't include spaces, you can omit the double quotation marks.

The following example starts Access and opens the Order Entry1 database in run-time mode:

```
c:\Program Files\Microsoft Office\Office\msaccess.exe
   "c:\My Documents\Order Entry1" /runtime
```

Table 16.3 shows the most commonly used Access command-line options. For a complete list and more information, go to the Office Assistant, search for Help topics on *Command Line Options*, and click *Startup Command-Line Options*.

TABLE 16.3: COMMONLY USED ACCESS COMMAND-LINE OPTIONS

OPTION*	EFFECT
database	** Opens the specified *database*.
source database / Compact target database	** Compacts the *source database* to the name specified as the *target database*, and then closes Access. Omit the *target database* name if you want to compact the database to the *source database* name.
/cmd	Can be used to return a value with the Command function. Must be the last option on the command line. Follow the /cmd with the value to be returned. A semicolon (;) can be used instead of /cmd.
database /Convert	Converts the specified *database* to an Access 2000 database and then closes Access.
database /Excl	Opens the specified *database* for exclusive access. Omit the /Excl option to open the database for shared access in a multiuser environment.
/Nostartup	Starts Access without displaying the startup dialog box. Same as choosing Tools ➢ Options, and deselecting Startup Dialog Box on the View tab of the Options dialog box.
/Profile user profile	Starts Access using the options in the specified *user profile* instead of the standard Windows Registry settings created when you installed Microsoft Access. The /Profile option replaces the /ini option used in previous versions of Access to specify an initialization file. See the Microsoft Access Developer's Toolkit for tools and information about creating user profiles.
/Pwd password	Starts Access using the specified *password* (see Chapter 19).
/Repair database	Repairs the specified *database*, and then closes Access (see Chapter 18). In Access 2000, works the same as /Compact.
database /RO	Opens the specified *database* for read-only access.
database /Runtime	Starts Access in runtime mode and opens the specified *database*. In runtime mode, users cannot access the database window or open database objects in design view. This option is useful for running turnkey applications, such as those the Database Wizard creates.
/User user name	Starts Access using the specified *user name* (see Chapter 19).
/Wrkgrp workgroup information file	** Starts Access using the specified *workgroup information file* (see Chapter 19).
/X macro	Starts Access and runs the specified *macro*. You also can run a macro when you open a database by using an AutoExec macro (see Chapters 21 and 29).

* To specify a forward slash (/) or semicolon (;) on the command line, type the character twice. For example, to specify the password ;eao/rnaa47 on the command line, type **;;eao//rnaa47** following the /Pwd command-line option.

** Specify a path name if necessary. If the path name contains any spaces, enclose the entire path name in double quotation marks. See the example earlier in the chapter.

PART

III

Database Tuning and Administration

Specifying Startup Options on the Start Menu

If you always want Access to use the same startup options, you can modify the Microsoft Access entry on the Start ➤ Programs menu:

1. Right-click the Start button on the Windows Taskbar and choose Explore. The Exploring - Start Menu window will open.

2. Double-click the Programs folder in the right pane of the window, and then double-click folders as needed until you locate the Microsoft Access shortcut icon.

3. Right-click the Microsoft Access shortcut icon and choose Properties. Or click the icon and press Alt+Enter.

4. Click the Shortcut tab in the Microsoft Access Properties dialog box.

5. Press the End key to move the insertion point to the right of the Access startup command in the Target text box.

6. Type a space, and enter the command-line settings you want to use.

7. (Optional) Set the Start In, Shortcut Key, and Run options in the dialog box. (To learn more about any of these options, right-click an option name and choose What's This?)

8. Click OK to return to the Exploring window.

9. Close the Exploring window.

The next time you use the Start ➤ Programs menu to start Access, your command-line options will take effect.

Specifying Startup Options in a Shortcut

Chapter 1 explained how to create shortcuts. Assuming you've already set up a short-cut for Microsoft Access, here's how to modify it to include startup options:

1. Locate the shortcut in a folder or on your Desktop.

2. Right-click the Microsoft Access shortcut icon and choose Properties, or click the icon and press Alt+Enter.

3. Fill in the Microsoft Access Properties dialog box, as explained in steps 4 through 7 of the previous section.

4. Click OK to accept the changes.

The next time you double-click an Access shortcut icon, Access will start with the command-line options you chose.

About the Registry File

When Access starts up, it reads various settings from the Windows *Registry file*. Many of these settings are defined when you install Access, and some are updated when you use certain Access utility options, such as the Workgroup Administrator discussed in Chapter 19. You'll rarely need to update the Registry file manually, but if you do so, *be very careful*—and back up the Registry first! Incorrect updates to the Registry can prevent Access and other Windows programs from working correctly.

If you do need to update the Registry, you must use the Registry Editor to make the changes. To get started, click the Start button on the Windows Taskbar, choose Run, type **regedit**, and press Enter. Your changes will take effect the next time you start Access.

To learn more about changing the Registry, search for *Registry* with the Office Assistant, and then explore subtopics as needed.

Where to Go from Here

In this chapter you've learned many ways to personalize Access to your own working style. The next chapter presents ways to analyze your databases and speed up their performance.

What's New in the Access Zoo?

The Options window that you use to customize Access 2000 has some new options. You'll find them on the View tab and the General tab. One of the more interesting options is the AutoCorrect feature. With this option turned on, Access tracks name changes to database objects and tries to make corrections when needed. Two Options window tabs that could be found in Access 97 are gone: Hyperlinks/HTML and Modules. Hyperlinks are now changed by clicking the Web Options button on the General tab, and Modules options are set in the Visual Basic Editor window.

PART

III

Database Tuning and Administration

CHAPTER **17**

Speeding Up Your Database

I f you're dreaming of a database that screams along at the speed of a Formula 1 Ferrari, but you're getting performance that's more like the plod, plod, plod of a desert tortoise, this chapter may be just what you're looking for. Here you'll find tips for tweaking that tired database engine so that it races swiftly along the information superhighway.

As you read this chapter, keep in mind that you can't make a Ferrari out of a Volkswagen Bug, or a Pentium out of an 80386. But you can squeeze the best possible performance out of the computer hardware you do have. If you're still hungry for speed after trying the suggestions in this chapter, you can always throw money at the problem and invest in faster, more expensive hardware.

For more tips on optimizing performance in a network environment, see Chapter 19.

So Where Do I Start?

For your convenience, we've divided this chapter into five performance areas:

- General performance
- The Performance Analyzer
- Tables
- Queries
- Forms, reports, and printing

Start with the suggestions in the General Performance category, and then work your way to the other categories if you notice sluggishness in those areas. Within each section that follows, we've arranged the tips in the general order that you should try them. So start at the top of each list of suggestions and work your way down to the bottom.

 NOTE The optimal settings in the categories that follow can vary with the type of computer hardware you're using to run Access. For best results, tweak one setting at a time, and monitor the performance after each change.

You can find out more about optimizing Access performance by searching for *Performance* with the help of the Office Assistant.

Speeding Up General Performance

Two basic methods are available to speed up general performance. First, you can make changes to general Windows settings, which may also speed up many Windows applications, not just Access. Second, you can make changes through Access that will speed up Access, but should have no effect on other Windows applications.

Tweaking Hardware and Windows Settings

For best overall performance in Access and Windows, you should maximize the amount of memory and disk available as discussed below:

- **Increase the memory (RAM) on your computer**. Microsoft recommends that you use Office 2000 on a machine with at least 32MB of RAM.

- **Optimize Windows**. Windows 95/98 can report any system optimization problems to you. You should check this report in the System Properties dialog box and take any action recommended. You should also check a couple of settings available to you from this dialog box. To see the system performance report and check these settings with Windows 95 or Windows 98, follow these steps:

  1. Open the Control Panel by selecting the Settings option on the Start menu and then selecting the Control Panel item.

  2. Double-click the System icon.

  3. In the System Properties dialog box, click the Performance tab and read the report within the Performance Status frame.

  4. Click the File System button and select the typical role for your machine using the drop-down list box on the Hard Drive tab in the File System Properties dialog box. Set read-ahead optimization to Full using the slider control. Click OK.

  5. Click the Graphics button in the System Properties dialog box. Make sure the slider control for Hardware Acceleration in the Advanced Graphics Settings dialog box is set to Full, unless you are having problems with your display. In that case, you may wish to back off this setting a notch or two. The on-screen help will guide you in deciding where to leave this setting. Click OK.

  6. Click OK in the System Properties dialog box to accept the settings. If you are prompted to restart Windows, click Yes to do so.

- **Optimize memory usage**. In most cases, letting Windows 95/98 manage memory for you is the best idea. However, in two situations, you may need to set your own virtual memory parameters. If you have only a little space on your default Windows 95/98 drive, or if a different hard disk drive has a faster access time, you should tell Windows 95/98 to use a different drive for virtual memory. Follow these steps for Windows 95 or Windows 98:

1. Open the Control Panel by selecting the Settings option on the Start menu and then selecting the Control Panel item.

2. Double-click the System icon.

3. Click the Performance tab in the System Properties dialog box, and then click the Virtual Memory button. The dialog box will appear as shown in Figure 17.1.

FIGURE 17.1

The Virtual Memory dialog box.

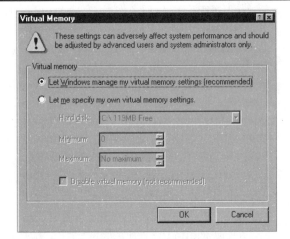

4. Select the Let Me Specify My Own Virtual Memory Settings option button. Then select the faster or less full drive using the Hard Disk drop-down list box. If you have a choice, opt for the fastest drive with at least 15MB of free space. Check with your hardware manufacturer on the optimum minimum swap file size for your system.

5. Click OK and then close the System Properties dialog box by clicking OK again.

6. Click Yes to restart Windows at the prompt. Restarting Windows makes the change in your swap file take effect.

• **Close unneeded applications and TSRs**. You can make more memory available by closing applications and terminate-and-stay-resident (TSR) programs that you aren't using. Using DOS-based TSR programs can slow system performance because of shifts from protected mode into real mode to allow the TSR to run. To prevent TSR programs from running automatically when you start up your computer, delete the appropriate lines in `autoexec.bat`, or convert them to comments by preceding the lines with a REM command, for example:

```
Rem DOSKEY
```

- **Defragment your hard disk and compact your databases**. To speed disk performance and maximize the amount of free space available, you should periodically delete unnecessary files from your hard disk, defragment your hard disk with a "defrag" utility, such as the Windows Disk Defragmenter, and then compact your Access databases (see Chapter 18). You should also take these steps before optimizing the size of your Windows swap file, as discussed next. If you are using the Microsoft Plus! Pack for Windows 95, have the System Agent run ScanDisk and Disk Defragmenter nightly to keep your disk performance top notch.

- **Peel off that wallpaper**. If you have a full-screen (Tile) wallpaper bitmap on your Windows Desktop, open Windows Control Panel and double-click the Desktop icon. Now replace the wallpaper with a solid color or pattern bitmap or no bitmap at all. Depending on your video display, eliminating wallpaper can free up between 256KB and 750KB of RAM.

Tweaking General Access Settings

You can do the following in Access to improve performance:

- **Open single-user databases exclusively**. When opening databases that won't be shared with other users, select the Exclusive check box on the Advanced tab of the Options dialog box. This setting tells Access not to spend time tracking multiuser record locking.

- **Store single-user databases and Access on the local hard disk**. Response will be faster if you install Access, and all databases that don't have to be shared, on your local hard disk drive, rather than on a network server.

- **Use indexes wisely**. Indexes can speed access to data, but they also can slow down record updating (see Chapter 6). For best results with indexes, you should

    - Create only as many indexes as necessary.

    - Create indexes on fields that you frequently sort by.

    - Create indexes on fields that you frequently search by.

    - Include only the fields that are absolutely necessary in a multiple-field index. You should consider a multiple-field index only when you search or sort on a combination of fields. For example, if you frequently search for customers with a particular last name in a particular zip code, then a multiple-field index on these two fields will help performance.

- **Put only tables on the server for multiuser databases**. Keep all other objects on the local machine's drive. You can use the Database Splitter Wizard to separate the tables for storage on the server.

- **Experiment with record-locking strategies**. You want a strategy that minimizes editing conflicts but allows appropriate access to the database. You must strike a balance between the performance penalties of multiple concurrent access and the inconvenience penalties of restrictive record locking. You can change the default record-locking setting on the Advanced tab of the Options dialog box.

- **Adjust parameters to avoid locking conflicts**. Experiment with the values of Refresh Interval, Update Retry Interval, Number of Update Retries, and ODBC Refresh Interval. To find these settings, open the Tools menu, select Options, and click the Advanced tab.

 NOTE For more information on record-locking strategies, see Chapter 19.

Using the Performance Analyzer

Access 2000 includes a Performance Analyzer. This tool examines your database objects and reports ways to improve their performance. The Performance Analyzer provides suggestions, recommendations, and ideas. The analyzer itself can perform suggestion and recommendation optimizations for you. Idea optimizations require that you work with Access's features yourself to perform the optimization.

 NOTE The Performance Analyzer can examine database objects only. It cannot provide information about how to speed up Access itself or the underlying operating system.

To show you what the Performance Analyzer can do, we've used it to analyze a database created to hold names, addresses, and similar information for a nonprofit corporation. Figure 17.2 shows the results. As you can tell, the Performance Analyzer has provided several tips for improving the speed even of this relatively simple database.

FIGURE 17.2

Using the Performance
Analyzer on a simple
database.

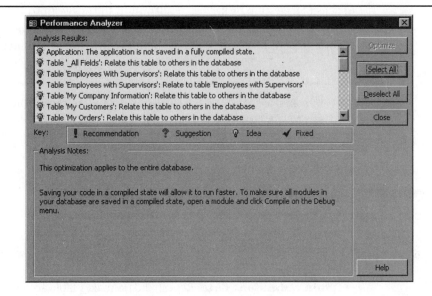

To use the Performance Analyzer, follow these steps:

1. Open the database you want to analyze.

 TIP Put a reasonable amount of data in your tables before running the Performance Analyzer. The query analysis step in particular takes into account the actual amount of data in each table.

2. Select Analyze from the Tools menu, and then select Performance from the cascading menu.

3. Click the tab in the Performance Analyzer dialog box for the type of object you would like to analyze. Then select each object you want to include in the analysis. You can either click the check box that precedes an object, or click the object's name and then click Select. Use Select All or Deselect All for quick ways to select or deselect the entire list of names on an individual tab.

4. Repeat step 3 until you have selected all the objects you want to optimize.

5. Click the OK button. The Performance Analyzer displays dialog boxes that tell you which objects it is analyzing. It then displays a list of Suggestions, Recommendations, and Ideas.

6. Select Suggestion or Recommendation in the Suggestions list box, and click the Optimize button. Or to implement an Idea, open the appropriate table, query, form, report, macro, or module and make the change recommended.

 TIP You can select the All tab to see a list of all database objects. Then use the Select All and Unselect All buttons to speed the process of selecting items.

Speeding Up Tables

If you follow these techniques, you can design tables that operate in the most efficient manner possible. Access even provides help for improving tables, in the form of the Table Analyzer Wizard.

- **Avoid redundant data**. Repeated data makes table access inefficient. Use the Table Analyzer Wizard to avoid common problems with tables. Select Analyze ➢ Table from the Tools menu and follow the directions provided by the Wizard.

- **Select appropriate data types for your fields**. Choosing text where a number would be better, for example, can increase the size of your tables and make join operations less efficient.

- **Build indexes for fields that will be searched, joined, or have criteria set**. Creating the indexes makes queries faster on the table.

Speeding Up Queries

Microsoft Access uses a special data-access technology to optimize queries automatically whenever possible. You can help Access do the job more efficiently by following the guidelines below. (See Chapter 10 for more about queries.)

- **Use and display only the fields you need**. Include only the fields you need in a query. Clear the Show box in fields used as selection criteria if you don't need to display those fields in the query result.

- **Use sorting wisely**. Sorting can slow down performance, especially when you sort on nonindexed fields.

- **Use Make Table queries for static data**. If you frequently need to base reports or analyses on data that doesn't change often, it's more efficient to run Make Table queries to create tables of selected (or calculated) data than it is to run Select queries. Then you can view or report on the new tables without running a query each time. If your data does change, you can run the Make Table queries again to re-create the static tables. Note that this technique does involve trade-offs: First, it uses extra disk space to hold the static tables. And second, if you forget to run the Make Table query after data changes, you won't get up-to-date information.

- **Use queries only when necessary**. Response will be faster if you base forms, reports, and other queries on tables (such as those created by Make Table queries), rather than on a query. Queries will, of course, be necessary if you need to pull information from several different tables that change often, or if you need to sort the data on a form or report.

- **Create queries that can be optimized**. For faster performance, avoid using restrictive query criteria (And, Or, and Not) on calculated and nonindexed columns. You can also speed up queries by using the Between … And, In, and = (equal) operators on indexed columns.

- **Avoid using domain aggregate functions**. Domain aggregate functions, such as DLookup, can slow down processing, because these functions must look up data in tables that aren't included in the query. If you need to include data from another table, it's best to add the table to the query or to create a subquery. (To learn about subqueries, search for *Subqueries* with the Office Assistant.)

- **Use fixed column headings in Crosstab queries**. Response will be quicker if you use fixed column headings in Crosstab queries whenever possible. To specify fixed column headings, go to query design view, choose View ➤ Properties, click an empty part of the tables area, and type the headings into the Column Headings property box (separated by commas), like this:

    ```
    "Qtr1","Qtr2","Qtr3","Qtr4"
    ```

For more information about optimizing queries, search for *Optimizing Queries* with the Office Assistant.

Speeding Up Forms, Reports, and Printing

The following tips can speed up your forms, reports, and printing. (See Chapters 11, 12, 13, and 15 for more about designing forms and reports and creating graphs.)

- **Use Data Entry mode to add records to large tables**. When adding new records in forms or datasheets that have many existing records, choose Records ➤ Data Entry to hide existing records while you add new ones. This is faster than moving to the blank record that follows the last record. To view all the records again, choose Records ➤ Remove Filter/Sort.

- **Use hyperlinks instead of command buttons** to perform tasks, such as opening forms. Database forms and reports are created without a VB module in Access 2000. (Objects created with older versions of Access, before Access 97, always included a VB module.) Forms and reports load more quickly when they don't have VB code attached. Since command buttons have VB code attached, you can increase system efficiency by using hyperlinks whenever you can.

- **Use pictures instead of OLE objects**. If you don't need to update OLE Paintbrush objects, graphs, and other embedded objects, convert them to pictures. To do this, go to form or report design view, right-click the object, and choose Object ➤ Convert. In the Convert dialog box, select Picture in the list box and click OK.

- **Be stingy with bitmaps and other graphics on forms**. Bitmap and other graphic objects (such as lines, bordered fields, and opaque fields) can slow the form's opening and printing time. Color bitmaps will be slower than black-and-white bitmaps. Of course, the very things that make forms more attractive and fun to use also slow down their performance. So you'll need to decide whether the trade-off of speed for aesthetics is worthwhile.

- **Close forms when you're not using them** to free up memory.

- **Avoid sorting and grouping on expressions**. Reports will be faster if you avoid unnecessary sorting and grouping on calculated expressions.

- **Avoid overlapping controls on forms and reports**. These controls take more time to display.

- **Use imported tables rather than attached tables**. If your forms include list boxes or drop-down lists based on unchanging tables in another database, import those tables rather than attaching them to your database (Chapter 7). Imported tables will take up more disk space than attached tables, but processing will be faster.

- **Use fast printing techniques**. For faster printing of reports and forms, try these tips:

  - If you plan to print a form or report with a laser printer, open the form or report in design view, and choose Edit ➢ Select Form, or Edit ➢ Select Report. Open the property sheet (View ➢ Properties), select Other Properties from the drop-down list, and set Fast Laser Printing to Yes. (Yes is the default setting for this property.)

 NOTE If you have an older laser printer, or need to print overlapping graphic items correctly, you'll need to leave Fast Laser Printing set to No.

  - Print in Portrait orientation where possible. Landscape printing can be slower, especially when printing many horizontal lines on nonlaser printers.

- **Convert a database application into an MDE file**. This feature (new in Access 97) lets you save a database in a compact format without its source code, which results in better performance when the database is used. However, users cannot view or edit source code. See Chapter 29 for details on creating an MDE file from a database, or search for *MDE* with the Office Assistant.

Where to Go from Here

Improving the performance of your database applications makes users happy. They receive a zippy response when they are working with the data. Once you have created a high-performance database application, however, you have to make it available to users. To do so, you have to know how to administer a database, which is the topic of the next chapter.

PART

III

Database Tuning and Administration

CHAPTER 18

Administering Your Database

This chapter covers the mundane, yet essential, housekeeping tasks that fall into the category of *database administration*. Topics include how to back up, compact and repair, convert, encrypt, decrypt, replicate, and document the structure of your databases.

Many database administration tasks are optional, and you should feel free to pick and choose those that interest you most. However, the following section, "Backing Up a Database," is a must for anyone using Access on a single-user computer and for database administrators.

 NOTE The *database administrator* is the person who is responsible for maintaining the integrity and security of a database on a multiuser network (for example, responsible for making backups, compacting and repairing databases, protecting data from prying eyes, and so on). Database administration tasks are discussed in this chapter and in Chapter 19.

Backing Up a Database

Backing up your database is the cheapest and most effective way to ensure your data against disasters. For example, if your database structure becomes damaged due to an unexpected power loss; or your hard disk fails due to old age, flood, fire, or other catastrophe, your data can become unreadable and may be irretrievably lost. This loss would be particularly disastrous with an Access database, since every object you create within a database is stored in one large database file! Up-to-date backups can save time, money, even your job—and they're easy to do. For maximum protection, store backups off-site, in a disaster-proof container.

 NOTE *Repairing* a damaged database is sometimes possible, as you'll learn later, in the section "Compacting and Repairing a Database." However, the best method of data protection is to make regular backups.

Exactly where you store your backups and how often you make them is up to you. If the database is small enough, you can back it up to a floppy. Or you can use a file compression program to create a compressed copy of the database, and back that up to a floppy. For larger databases, you'll need to back up to a tape drive, a Zip drive, or perhaps a hard drive with removable disks.

You may also want to keep a second backup copy of the database on your local hard disk. That way, if you make a change to the original database that somehow corrupts the original, you can quickly copy the local backup to the original filename without bothering with external drives or tape devices.

Backing up a database is basically a matter of copying two crucial files to the backup device:

> **The database file**   This file stores all your data and database objects and usually has the extension `.mdb`.
>
> **The `system.mdw` workgroup database file**   The Setup program creates `system.mdw` in the `C:\Program Files\Microsoft Office\Office` folder automatically. This file contains important information about each user's toolbar and option settings. It also stores workgroup security information. (A *workgroup* is a group of users who share data and the same system database file.)

 WARNING   If the `system.mdw` file is lost or damaged, you won't be able to start Access. If you can't restore this file from a backup copy, you'll need to reinstall Access (see Appendix A) and set up any toolbars, option settings, and security again.

To create a database backup, follow the steps below:

1. Close any open database by choosing File ➢ Close.

2. Make sure all other users also close the database, so that no open copies are on the system. (Database administrators: You may prefer to make backups in the wee hours of the morning so that network users don't have to spend time twiddling their thumbs while you churn out database backups.)

 TIP   You can also back up individual database objects by creating a database and then importing the objects from the original database to the copy (see Chapter 7). The advantage of this approach is that users do not have to close the database first.

---

3. Switch to whatever program you use to make backups. This can be the Windows Explorer, the Windows Backup program, a Zip drive, a tape drive system, or some other backup utility.

4. Copy the `.mdb` file to the backup destination of your choosing.

5. Copy the workgroup file to the backup destination. If you haven't set up a custom workgroup, this will be the system.mdw file from your Access directory. See Chapter 19 for information about setting up a custom workgroup file.

Restoring a Database from Backups

To restore the database from a backup copy, use your backup software to copy the .mdb file from your backup device to the appropriate database file in the database folder. If the file system.mdw was lost or damaged, copy that file from the backup device to the C:\Program Files\Microsoft Office\Office folder.

 WARNING   If the backup database and the original database have the same names, you'll be *replacing* the original file. If you want to keep the original file for some reason, rename the file before restoring the backup copy to your hard disk.

For more information about making backups, search for *Backup* and *System.mdw* with the Office Assistant. Also, consult the documentation that comes with your backup program.

Compacting and Repairing a Database

If you are responsible for maintaining a database, you will periodically have to compact it and, if necessary, repair it. In older versions of Access, there were separate utilities for these two chores. Now, in Access 2000, when you compact a database, Access automatically does any necessary repairs at the same time. Here's some information on why databases need to be compacted and how they can become damaged.

Why You Need to Compact a Database

As you add and delete records, macros, tables, and other objects in your database, the hard disk space formerly occupied by deleted objects can become fragmented into many small pieces that can't be used efficiently. This fragmentation, in turn, can slow down system performance to a sluggish pace and waste valuable disk space. The solution is to compact your databases periodically. *Compacting* reorganizes the space occupied by an Access database and can recover wasted space so that your system can perform better.

Before compacting a database, consider the following points:

- Because Access must copy the entire database during compacting, it will need as much available disk space as the database itself requires. You can check the size of the database and the available disk space with the Windows File Manager.

- To compact a database, you must have Modify Design permission for all tables in the database. Permissions are discussed in Chapter 19.

- If the database you need to compact is shared, make certain no one else is using it before you attempt to compact it. If anyone else has it open, the operation will fail.

- When you compact that table's database, if you've deleted records from the end of a table that has an AutoNumber field, Access will reset the next counter number to one more than the last undeleted counter number.

Compacting a Closed Database

To compact a database that is not open:

1. Choose Tools ➢ Database Utilities ➢ Compact and Repair Database.

2. In the Database to Compact From dialog box, choose the drive, folder, and file-name of the database that you want to compact; and then select the Compact button.

3. In the Compact Database Into dialog box, select the database to hold the compacted copy, or type a valid filename for the compacted database in the File Name text box.

4. Choose Save. Or if you want to compact into the same database, double-click the database name in the list box. If you use the same name in steps 3 and 4, Access will ask for permission to replace the original with the copy. (Choose Yes if you want to replace the existing file, or No if you want to specify a different name.)

Access will compact the database, displaying a progress message along the status bar as it does so.

 NOTE   To maintain optimum performance in your database, you must either compact it using its original name, or rename it with its original name after compacting.

PART

III

Database Tuning and
Administration

Compacting an Open Database

Access also lets you compact a database while you are working with it. It's a lot faster than going through the steps listed above for a closed database. All you have to do is choose Tools ➤ Database Utilities ➤ Compact and Repair Database. Access will compact the database and reopen it when it's finished with the job.

Compacting Other Areas of Your Hard Disk

As mentioned previously, a fragmented database can slow down Access performance. Likewise, a badly fragmented hard disk, or one that is low on free space, can slow down *all* the applications on your computer, including both Windows and Access. In addition to compacting your databases, as described here, you should also defragment your hard disk periodically and make sure that your hard disk has plenty of free space available.

To perform this task, you can use the Disk Defragmenter provided with Windows (Select Start ➤ Programs ➤ Accessories ➤ System Tools ➤ Disk Defragmenter.) or a defragmenter provided by another vendor. Most such tools work the same way. Select the drive you want to defragment, click OK, and then take a coffee break while the defragmenter does its work.

If you have the Microsoft Plus! Pack for Windows 95, you can use the System Agent to schedule the Disk Defragmenter to run on a periodic basis. We suggest scheduling it to run nightly to keep your disk working at top speed.

 WARNING You cannot use Disk Defragmenter to defragment a network disk, a CD, or a disk compressed with a compression program not supported by the version of Windows you are using.

For more information about compacting databases, search for *Compacting Databases* with the Office Assistant. For more about the Disk Defragmenter, search for *Defragmenter* in Windows Help.

Repairing a Damaged Database

Before turning off your computer, you should always exit Access properly by choosing File ➤ Exit. Proper shutdown ensures that all your database objects are saved to disk, and it prevents damage to your database.

If a power outage or some other mishap occurs, some data might not be saved, and your open database could be damaged. In most cases, Access can detect the damage automatically when you try to open, encrypt, or decrypt the damaged database, and it will ask for permission to repair it. Simply choose OK when asked if you want to begin the repair process.

Occasionally, however, Access might be unable to detect the problem, and the database may behave strangely. In such a case, you can use the Compact and Repair Database command to fix the corrupted database. The instructions are the same as those for compacting a database, except that we recommend that you make a backup copy of the damaged database before you start:

1. Close any open databases using File ➤ Close. As usual, any users on the network must also close the database.

2. Use the Explorer to make a backup copy of the database.

3. Choose Tools ➤ Database Utilities ➤ Compact and Repair Database.

4. Choose the drive, folder, and filename of the database you want to repair, and then click Repair.

Once the repair is done, click OK to clear the message that appears. You should now be able to open the database with the usual File ➤ Open commands.

If you were editing data when Access shut down unexpectedly, your last change may be lost after you repair the database. Return to the form or datasheet you were working with, and if necessary, reenter your changes. Also, check any other objects you were working on when the system shut down, and redo any changes that didn't make it into the database.

When Repair Doesn't Solve the Problem

Sometimes hard disk errors will prevent Access from repairing the database properly, or they may prevent Access from running at all. For these types of problems, you'll first need to run a hard disk repair utility (such as ScanDisk, which comes with Windows). Then try running Access and repairing the database again. If Access won't run at all, you'll need to reinstall it with the Setup program, as explained in Appendix A. If you can't repair the database satisfactorily, you must restore it from a backup copy.

You can find online information about repairing databases by searching for *Repair* with the Office Assistant. To learn about ScanDisk, search Windows Help for *ScanDisk*.

PART

III

Database Tuning and Administration

Converting from Other Access Formats

If you've upgraded to Access 2000, you can use the new version to work with databases created under Access 1, 2, 95, and 97 without going through any special conversions. However, before you can change the *structure* of any tables, modify the design of any objects, or add or remove database objects in an old database, you must convert that database to Access 2000 format.

 WARNING   You may not want to convert a database to Access 2000 format. You may need to share such databases with users who have not upgraded or cannot upgrade to Access 2000. If you convert, these users will not be able to access the data.

The first time you open a database that was created with a previous version of Access, you will see a Convert/Open Database dialog box. When this window appears, all you have to do is select Convert and then OK. This converts the database and leaves its name unchanged.

If you want to convert a database to Access 2000 without opening it, or you want to give the converted version its own name, follow these steps instead of opening the database directly:

1. Choose File ➢ Close if the database you want to convert is open. (Any users on the network must also close that database.)

2. If you are converting to the same database (instead of renaming the converted file), use the Explorer to make a backup copy of the database. Make certain that all linked tables are still located in the folder that the database refers to.

3. Choose Tools ➢ Database Utilities ➢ Convert Database ➢ To Current Access Database Version. If you are converting a secured database, you must have Open/Run, Open Exclusive, Modify Design, Administer, and Read Design permissions.

4. Choose the drive, folder, and filename of the database that you want to convert from the Database to Convert From dialog box, and then select the Convert button.

5. In the Convert Database Into dialog box, select the database that will hold the converted file, or type in a valid filename for the converted database in the File Name text box.

6. Choose Save. If you use the same name in steps 4 and 5, Access will ask for permission to replace the original with the converted copy. (Choose Yes if you want to replace the existing file; choose No if you want to specify a different name.)

TIP   Access 1.x objects that contain a back-quote character (') in their names will not convert. You must rename such objects using the version of Access in which they were created, before you can convert them.

When Access converts a database, it constructs a special table called the Convert-Errors table. This table contains information about any validation rules that would not convert to Access 2000. The ConvertErrors table contains fields describing the error, naming the field where it occurred, naming the table where it occurred, naming the table property containing the problem, and naming the value that would not convert. You can use this information to rewrite validation rules as necessary so that your database can function as it did before the conversion. In general, you will find yourself having to update user-defined functions; domain aggregate functions; totals functions; references to fields; and references to forms, queries, and tables.

TIP   If you need to convert a database to the previous version of Access, open the database and choose Tools ➢ Database Utilities ➢ Convert Database ➢ To Prior Access Database from the menus. Enter a name for the converted database in the Convert Database Into dialog box, and click Save.

Encrypting and Decrypting Your Database

You can *encrypt* a database to ensure that the database can be opened and viewed only in Access. Though encryption doesn't prevent another Access user from tampering with the database, it does prevent anyone from using another application (such as a word processor or utility) to inspect data in the database. Encryption is recommended if you plan to send a copy of a database to another Access user or to an off-site storage location.

TIP   You can use encryption/decryption in conjunction with the Access security features discussed in Chapter 19 and any security that your network software provides.

Decrypting reverses the encryption process. While you *can* open an encrypted database without decrypting it first, the database will be 10 to 15 percent slower in its encrypted state. Therefore, if you receive a copy of an encrypted database from another Access user, you probably should decrypt it before you start using it.

The following points apply to database encryption and decryption:

- When you open a database that has been encrypted, Access automatically determines whether the database is currently encrypted. If the database isn't encrypted, Access encrypts it. If the database is already encrypted, Access decrypts it.

- The hard disk must have enough space available to store both the original database and the temporary copy that Access creates during encryption/decryption.

- The database must be closed when you encrypt or decrypt it. If anyone has it open, the operation will fail.

To encrypt or decrypt a database:

1. Choose File ➤ Close if the database you want to encrypt or decrypt is currently open. In a multiuser environment, all other users must also close the database. You must have Modify Design permission to encrypt or decrypt a secure database, if user-level security is in force.

2. Choose Tools ➤ Security ➤ Encrypt/Decrypt Database.

3. Choose the name of the database you want to encrypt or decrypt from the Encrypt/Decrypt Database dialog box, and then click OK.

4. Type in a valid filename for the encrypted (or decrypted) database in the Encrypt Database As (or Decrypt Database As) dialog box, and click Save. Or if you want to encrypt/decrypt into the same database, double-click the database name in the list box. If you use the same name in steps 3 and 4, Access will ask for permission to replace the original with the copy. (Choose Yes if you want to replace the existing file, or No if you want to specify a different name.)

For more information about encrypting and decrypting databases, search for *Encrypt* or *Decrypt* with the Office Assistant.

 TIP Just as Access 1.*x* objects that contain a backquote character (') in their names will not convert, they will not encrypt. You must rename such objects, using the version of Access in which they were created, before you can encrypt them.

Viewing Information about Your Database

Once you have created a database of objects, you may want to review the attributes of those objects from time to time. Access provides you with two means of examining the properties associated with objects in a database. First, you can click any object in the database window and then select Properties from the View menu. This action opens a Properties dialog box like the one shown in Figure 18.1. This dialog box tells you what the object is, when it was created, when it was last modified, who owns it, and whether it has the hidden or replicated attributes. You can enter further documentation into the Description text box if you desire to do so. In this way, you can store a description of each object in the database.

FIGURE 18.1

The Properties dialog box for a table appears when you choose View ➤ Properties.

 TIP For tables, you can check off whether Access should perform Row Level Tracking in the Properties window. You may see other options for other types of objects in their Properties windows.

You can also view information about the database in general, as well as store additional information that documents the database and helps you to locate it. To view this information, select File ➤ Database Properties. The Properties dialog box shown in Figure 18.2 appears. The General tab displays the attributes of the database file. The Contents tab provides a list of all the objects in the database. The Statistics tab provides some summary information about how the database has been used.

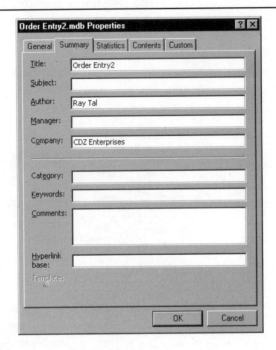

The most useful tabs, however, are the Summary and Custom tabs. The Summary tab allows you to record information about who created the database and who owns it. You can also enter a description on this tab, as well as keywords to aid in searching for the file.

The Custom tab allows you to define special properties for the database that help in searching for the file if you cannot remember its filename. Enter a name for a property in the Name text box, or choose one from the list box below. Select a type from the Type drop-down list box. Then enter a value for the property in the Value text box. To add to the list of custom properties for the database, select the Add button.

You can use the Summary and Custom tabs to record a lot of information that documents your database. You can also search for a database file using the summary information and custom properties called up by choosing the Advanced button in any file dialog box.

Documenting Your Database

When developing applications or sharing your database with other users, it is helpful to provide documentation about the various design elements in the database objects. Access makes it easy to produce database documentation for a single object, or for several objects at once. For instance, you can preview or print a report of the properties, code, and permissions associated with controls on a form or report, or all the objects a database includes.

To document an object or a set of objects, follow these steps:

1. Choose Tools ➤ Analyze ➤ Documenter. You'll see a Documenter dialog box, as in Figure 18.3.

The Documenter dialog box lets you choose which information to include in the object definition report.

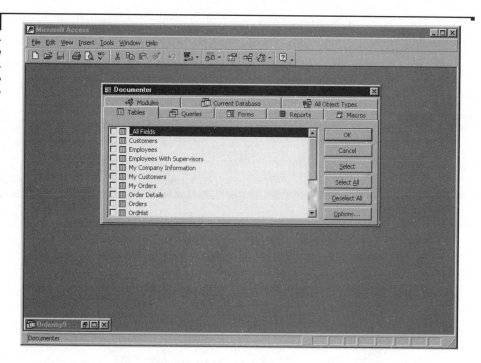

  TIP Depending on how you installed Access, you may have to install the Documenter using the Add/Remove Programs icon in the Control Panel.

2. Select the tab for the type of object you want to document. (Choose All Object Types to document the entire database.) Select the specific objects you want to document by clicking their check boxes. Use the Select All and Deselect All buttons to simplify this process.

3. (Optional) Click the Options button if you'd like to select which properties are documented for an object, and then select any properties you want by using the option buttons presented, and click OK.

4. Click OK to generate the object definition. After a few moments the Object Definition report appears in a print preview window.

5. Do any of the following:

   • **To view the report**, scroll through or zoom out or in as you would in any print preview window.

   • **To print the report**, click the Print toolbar button or choose File ➤ Print.

6. Click the Close Window toolbar button, or choose File ➤ Close.

Figure 18.4 illustrates the first page of an object definition report for the Customers table in an order entry database generated using the Database Wizard.

FIGURE 18.4

An object definition report's first page for the Customers table in an order entry database.

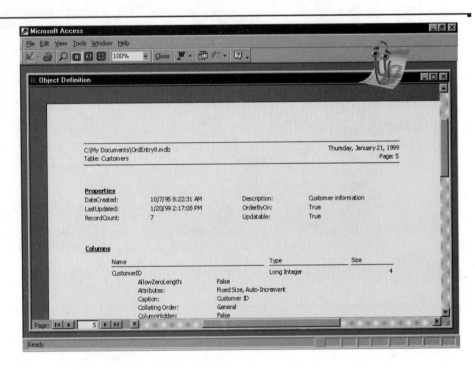

WARNING   The object definitions can take some time to generate, so be patient. Grab a cup of coffee, or turn on your favorite talk show to pass the time.

Replicating Your Database

These days almost everyone takes work with them on the road. What do you do when you want to take a copy of your database with you to work on? How do you manage changes you make while you are working away from the master copy? Access 2000 allows you to replicate your database in its entirety or a selected portion. When it is replicated, the database contains special tables and properties that enable Access to distinguish between the *design master*, the version that determines the overall structure of the database, and a *copy*. Changes in design take place only within the design master, and tools are available that allow you to synchronize all of the copies of the data.

NOTE   In previous versions of Access 2000, if the design master was a Microsoft SQL Server database, you could only update replica data with changes that were made to the master copy. Now, with Access 2000 and Microsoft SQL Server 7, changes made to data in a replica can be synchronized with the SQL Server database.

Creating a Replica

Replicas can be managed either through Access or the Windows Briefcase. You always have a choice of which you prefer to use to create and synchronize your replicas. Before creating a replica, you need to take three steps:

1. Remove the database password using Tools ➤ Security ➤ Unset Database Password.

2. Be certain the Briefcase is installed. (If it is not, use the Add/Remove Programs icon in Control Panel to install it.)

3. Be certain that Briefcase Replication was installed with Access. (If not, visit the Control Panel again.)

NOTE   If Briefcase Replication is not installed, Access will present a dialog box informing you of this fact when you try to create a replica the first time.

Then open the Explorer and drag the database to the Briefcase. When you drop the database file on the Briefcase, Access will begin to convert the database to a master file for replication. Answer the prompts as needed, and check the information in the last step for some Briefcase tips before you click Finish.

To create a replica using Access 2000, follow these steps:

1. Open the database you want to replicate, and make sure all users of the database on a network have closed the database.

2. Select Tools ➤ Replication ➤ Create Replica.

3. Click Yes in the dialog box to close the database.

4. Click either Yes or No in the next dialog box to make a backup of the database.

5. Use the file dialog box presented next to select a location and name for the replica. Optionally, check the box for Prevent Deletes, and then click OK.

 WARNING   Converting to a replicable database is a one-way process. The only way to make it nonreplicable is to create a new database and import the data from one of the replicas.

You can make as many replicas of your design master as you wish. In fact, you can even make replicas from a replica. The total group of replicas you make is known as the *replica set* for the database. You add to the replica set by creating a new replica as described above. You remove replicas from the replica set by deleting the database file for the replica you want to remove. Only members of a replica set and their design master can synchronize their data.

 TIP   If you move a design master or rename it, Access 2000 will not be able to synchronize it with any replicas that exist. To solve this problem, open any replica for the problem design master and choose Tools ➤ Replication ➤ Recover Design Master from the menus. Access will guide you through the process of getting links between the design master and the replica straight.

Creating a Partial Replica

 A partial replica includes a subset of the records in a database. For example, you might want to give a salesperson a replica of a database that includes records for their territory only. With Access 97, the only way to create a partial replica was with a VBA program. Now, with Access 2000, you can use the Partial Replica Wizard to get assistance with this task. The Wizard lets you choose a table and create a filter on one or more fields to select records for the replica.

To create a partial replica with the Wizard:

1. Open the design master that holds the records you want to replicate.

2. Choose Tools ➤ Replication ➤ Partial Replica Wizard.

3. In the first step of the Wizard, leave Create a New Partial Replica selected, and click Next.

4. Enter or browse for a name and location for the new replica. Then click Next.

5. In the next step, shown in Figure 18.5, select the table you want to filter. Then create a filter this way: First select the type of operator you want to use. (The default is =.) Then double-click the name of the field for the expression. When the field appears with the operator in the Filter expression box, replace *[Expression]* with the filter condition. For example, if you want the replica to include records from the Employees table for Nancy Davolio, double-click the LastName field and replace *[Expression]* with *Davolio*. You are free to add additional fields to the filter expression. First select And or Or. Then follow the instructions just described for adding text to the Filter Expression box. Click Next when your filter expression is complete.

FIGURE 18.5

With the Partial Replica Wizard, you can choose a table and create a multifield filter to select records for a replica.

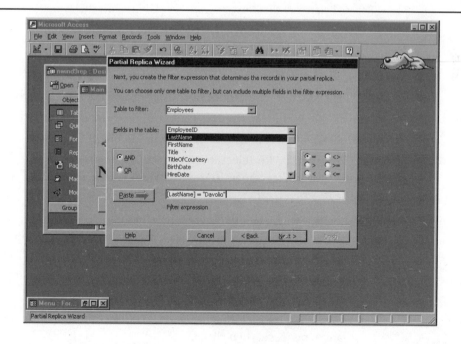

TIP If you're a hot shot, just type an expression directly into the Filter Expression box instead of clicking your way through the Partial Replica Wizard dialog box.

6. The next box lets you choose whether records from other tables in the database should be replicated. To include all the records in a table, leave its name selected (checked). Tables with bolded names are related to the table chosen for a filter in the last step. If you deselect one of these tables, only records that are related to the table chosen in step 5 will be included in the replica. If you uncheck one of the unrelated tables, none of its records will show up in the replica. Click Next when you are ready to move on to the next step.

7. In the final step, make your choice under Do You Want a Report? Then click Finish.

When the Partial Replica Wizard is finished its work, you'll see a report window open if you chose to create a report in the last step. This report will list the properties of the replica that determine the records it contains.

 TIP You can also use the Partial Replica Wizard to modify a partial replica. Start the Wizard as outlined above. In the first step of the Wizard, select Modify an Existing Partial Replica before you click Next.

Updating a Replica

How do you synchronize all of the changes made in your replica with the design master or with other replicas? The process is easy. Just follow these steps:

1. Open the Briefcase and select the database file.

2. Click the Update Selection button on the toolbar, or select Update Selection from the Briefcase menu. (You could also select Update All or click its button on the Briefcase toolbar.)

The Briefcase then automatically merges the changes with the copy of the database, either design master or replica, available on your desktop computer. If you would rather manage synchronization from Access, follow these steps instead:

1. Open the database you want to synchronize with the design master.

2. Select Tools ➤ Replication ➤ Synchronize Now.

3. In the Synchronize Database dialog box, select the type of synchronization you want to perform. Then click OK.

If members of a replica set develop synchronization conflicts, Access starts the Conflict Resolution Wizard and prompts you to resolve them when you open the replica that has the conflicts. Selecting Resolve in this dialog box causes Access to lead you step by step through the process of conflict resolution. You are offered the chance to copy fields or delete the conflicting record in order to resolve conflicts.

 TIP To check for conflicts at any time, choose Tools ➢ Replication ➢ Resolve Conflicts.

Converting a Replica Into a Design Master

You may encounter a situation in which you feel that a replica has been updated so significantly that you would rather have it as the design master. You can convert any member of a replica set into a design master using this procedure:

1. Open the replica that will become the new design master.
2. Select Tools ➢ Replication ➢ Synchronize Now.
3. In the Synchronize Database dialog box, check the Make Filename the Design Master check box before you click OK. (Access fills in Filename with the name of the file you opened in step 1.)
4. Choose OK to create the new design master.

You might also encounter a situation in which a well-meaning user has deleted the design master. In this case, choose the replica you want to use to replace the design master. Preferably this replica would be the most recently synchronized copy. Then synchronize this replica with as many others as you feel are necessary to build an accurate master copy of the data. Finally, open the replica that will replace the design master, and choose Tools ➢ Replication ➢ Recover Design Master. Click the Yes button when Access prompts you to confirm that you have synchronized this replica with all others.

Where to Go from Here

You have just learned quite a bit about administering a database in either a single-user or a multiuser environment. In discussing administration, we have covered topics that imply that your database resides on a network. The next chapter deals more fully with the issues of networking and security, and expands upon some of the issues dealt with briefly here.

PART

III

Database Tuning and Administration

What's New in the Access Zoo?

In the area of database administration, Access 2000 has some new features. They include:

- The ability to synchronize data on SQL Server 7 with changes made to a replica.
- A Conflict Resolution Wizard that helps you decide how to resolve conflicts that occur when changes are made to the same records in different replicas.
- A Partial Replica Wizard that helps you create replicas of selected datasets.

CHAPTER 19

Networking and Security

his chapter covers two issues that will be of interest to anyone responsible for an Access installation on a network. The first is the topic on most network administrators' minds: how to get peak performance from Access on a network. The second topic is setting up a security scheme to prevent unauthorized users from accidentally or deliberately harming objects within your Access applications.

Allowing Users to Share Data

In many organizations multiple users must have simultaneous access to the same data. Access is designed to support multiuser databases "out of the box," but you will need to consider a few factors carefully. The first is where to store the application itself. You can set up your database in either of two ways to allow multiple users to share data and other objects, as discussed in the sections that follow.

Option 1: Put the Entire Database on the Server

One way to give multiple users access to a database is simply to put the entire database (that is, the entire Access .mdb file) on the server, as shown in Figure 19.1. With this approach, there's no difference between a single-user database and a multiuser one; you just transfer the database to a shared drive and tell your users where to find it.

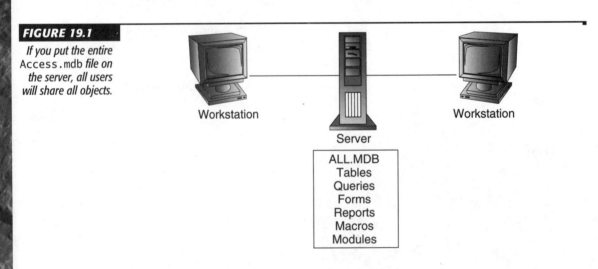

FIGURE 19.1

If you put the entire Access.mdb *file on the server, all users will share all objects.*

Workstation

Server

Workstation

ALL.MDB
Tables
Queries
Forms
Reports
Macros
Modules

The one advantage to this approach is that all users share all the same objects. Thus a change to any object, including a form, report, or macro, is instantly accessible to all users. Data changes—such as adding, editing, or deleting records from a table—are also immediately visible.

Option 2: Put Only Shared Data on the Server

The downside to putting the entire database on the server is that you end up with a lot of network traffic. Virtually every object that each user opens needs to come across the network. This includes forms and reports, which are normally static in an application in use, as well as the changeable tables. As an alternative, you can put just the shared tables on the server in a "data" database. Then set up a database that contains all objects except those shared tables, and put a copy of that "application" database on each workstation, as in the example shown in Figure 19.2. You can then use the File ➤ Get External Data ➤ Link Tables menu item to link the tables in the data database to those in the application database so that all users can see the shared data. (For more information on linked tables, see Chapter 7.)

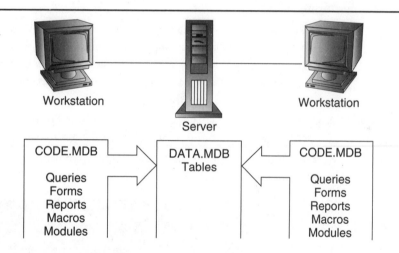

FIGURE 19.2

Splitting a database into a data database and an application database.

This approach has both an upside and a downside:

- It reduces network traffic because only shared table data is transmitted across the network. Forms, reports, and other objects are read from each user's local hard drive.

- The network administrator can more easily back up just the tables in the database, because the tables are stored independently of the other objects.

- If a user changes some other object (such as a form, report, or macro), that change affects only his or her workstation. Other users never see that change.

(The last item in the list can be either a curse or a blessing, depending on whether the user improves or destroys the modified object.)

 NOTE To prevent users from changing objects, you'll need to use Access security features to protect your database objects (see "Securing Your Database" later in this chapter).

Separating the Tables

Putting just the shared tables on the network is an easy job, thanks to the Database Splitter Wizard. Here we'll take you through an example using our Order Entry database generated using the Database Wizard.

To create the database of shared tables, you need to do the following (you should already know how to use the Windows Explorer or another utility to copy files and create directories):

1. Make a backup copy of the entire Order Entry database and give this copy a new name. (In the case of this example, the original database is named `Ordentry9.mdb`. We made a copy called `OrderEntryBackup.mdb`. Long filenames are useful.) This copy will provide a safety net in case you later decide that you didn't really want to split the database after all.

2. Open the database that you want to split. Hold down the Shift key when you open the database so the switchboard form won't open.

3. Select Tools ➤ Database Utilities ➤ Database Splitter. This action starts the Database Splitter Wizard, shown here.

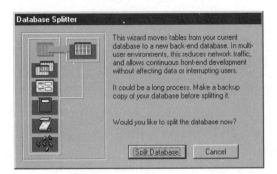

4. Read the information on the Wizard screen, and then click the Split Database button.

5. Enter a name for your back-end database (the one that will hold the tables) in the File Name text box of the Create Back-End Database dialog box. Make sure that the directory is the correct directory on the network drive. Then click the Split button.

WARNING   Be sure to close all open objects (tables, queries, forms, and reports) before splitting your database. Otherwise, the Database Splitter Wizard will not be able to properly export and reattach the tables.

6. Click the OK button when you see a dialog box announcing that the database was successfully split. You now have two versions of the database: the back-end version containing just the tables, and the original version containing all the rest of the objects and links to the tables in the back-end version.

7. Close the open version of the database.

At this point, the server holds a copy of the database tables (in their own .mdb file) that you want the users to share. By checking the Contents tab of the File ≻ Database Properties dialog box, you can see that this back-end database contains only the tables from the original database, as shown in Figure 19.3.

FIGURE 19.3

Ordentry9_be.mdb *contains only the tables from the original database.*

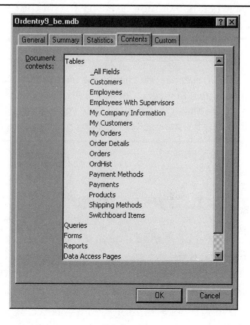

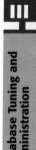

PART

III

Database Tuning and Administration

The original Ordentry9.mdb file contains all of the other database objects, plus links to the tables in the Ordentry9_be.mdb database. The names of linked tables are now marked with an icon in the local database, as shown in Figure 19.4.

FIGURE 19.4

The Ordentry9.mdb *database, after splitting, showing the tables linked to* Ordentry9_be.mdb.

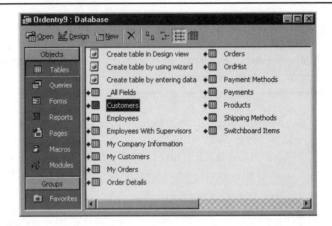

Now you can put a copy of the local database, the one with the forms and reports, on every user's workstation. When the user opens the local copy of the database, Access will automatically link to the shared tables on the server and handle any conflicts that arise when two or more users try to edit the same data. (See "Editing Data on a Network" later in this chapter.)

TIP If you ever need to change the links to the tables, select Tools ➣ Database Utilities ➣ Linked Table Manager. Check the Always Prompt for New Location check box in the Linked Table Manager dialog box, and you will have the opportunity to edit the link information using a standard file dialog box.

Preventing Exclusive Access

When users will be sharing data in an Access database, you need to make sure that no single user opens the database in Exclusive mode. Otherwise, no other users can open that database. The default values for most settings support shared access. To make certain that use of Exclusive mode is discouraged or prevented, you can take these steps:

• Choose Tools ➣ Options from the Access menu bar, select the Advanced tab, and make sure the Default Open Mode option is set to Shared, its default value.

- Set up a security system (discussed later in this chapter) that denies the Open Exclusive permissions to selected users. This is the strictest control, since it doesn't allow users to open the database exclusively.

Of course, you'll need to grant yourself and other administrative users the right to open the database in Exclusive mode so that you can perform operations that require exclusive use, such as backing up, compacting, and repairing the database.

For more information on compacting and repairing, see Chapter 18.

Creating Upgradeable Custom Applications

Separating the tables from the other objects in a database is not only good for reducing network traffic, but it is also a good strategy if you plan to market a custom application that you've created, or if you need to maintain a database that you've already distributed on a network to multiple users.

You can keep all the tables for an application in one database, and all the other objects in a separate database. To do this, create the tables and other objects in one database. Then use the Database Splitter Wizard, as in the example above, to split the tables into a separate database.

Be sure to distribute both databases to first-time buyers or users. When you release an upgraded version of your product, send the people upgrading only the database (.mdb) file that contains the objects, not the database containing tables. That way, you don't have to worry about users overwriting their existing data when they install your upgraded version. Instead, they'll just link the new front-end database to their existing tables.

 WARNING Avoid changing the structure of tables after the initial release of your application. Otherwise, you'll need to ship the revised tables, and you'll need to provide a convenient way for users to put their data into your newly structured tables. This procedure can be a nuisance for both you and the people upgrading.

Editing Data on a Network

Access uses a simple, common-sense strategy for handling conflicts that occur when two or more users edit the same data. The way Access handles such conflicts depends on the Record Locks property of the form your users are using to do the edits, as shown in Figure 19.5.

Choices for the Record Locks property.

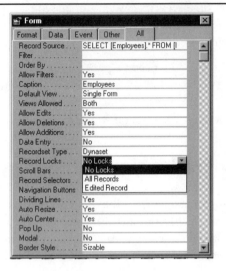

 NOTE We'll discuss conflict handling in datasheets a little later, since most often you'll have your network users working via forms.

If the Record Locks property is set to Edited Record, when one user is editing a record (so that the pencil symbol appears in that record's selector) and another user tries to edit that same record, the second user sees an international No symbol, indicating that the record is locked by another user.

 TIP Access may take up to 60 seconds to display the No symbol when another user is editing a record. You can change this interval on the Advanced tab of the Tools ➤ Options dialog box. Set the Refresh Interval to the maximum number of seconds you want Access to wait before updating a record's locking status. Be careful—if you set the Refresh Interval to a very small number, you will create unwanted, extra traffic on the network.

When the first user saves the changes, the No symbol disappears, Access updates the view of the record on both machines, and the second user can then view and change that same record. Figure 19.6 shows the situation where one user has "locked out" another user by editing a record.

PART

III

Database Tuning and
Administration

FIGURE 19.6

*With Edited Record
locking, only one user
can edit a record at a
time. Other users are
"locked out" of the
record.*

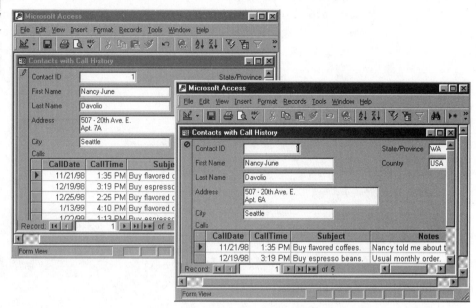

 NOTE Access saves the changes to a record whenever you move the cursor to another record, or choose Records ➤ Save Record, or press Shift+Enter.

If Record Locks is set to No Locks, both users will be allowed to edit the record. However, when the second user tries to save the changes after the first user has done so, Access offers the second user the chance to overwrite the first user's changes, copy the record to the Clipboard for pasting into the table later, or discard the changes, with the dialog box shown in Figure 19.7.

If you get this dialog box on your screen, it means you have tried to modify a record that another user has already changed. You have three choices for dealing with this situation:

- **Choose Save Record** to have your changes overwrite whatever the other user saved, without inspecting the records.

- **Choose Drop Changes** to leave the other user's record alone and discard any changes you have made.

- **Choose Copy to Clipboard** to leave the other user's record alone but place your own changes on the Windows Clipboard. When you do this, your form will be updated to show the other user's changes. If you decide you'd rather keep your version, simply click the form's record selector to select the whole record, and choose Edit ➤ Paste or press Ctrl+V to return your changes to the form. Then save your record again.

With No Locks, you'll get a Write Conflict warning when you try to change data that someone else has edited.

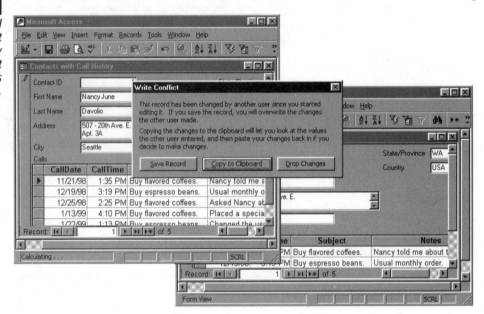

Refreshing Network Data

Access automatically refreshes each user's screen at regular intervals, to help ensure that each user is seeing current data. However, you can force Access to refresh your data at any time by choosing Records ➤ Refresh.

When Access refreshes the current form or datasheet, it updates changes and indicates deleted records. However, it does not reorder records, show new records, or update a dynaset to show or hide records that no longer meet the underlying query's selection criteria. To force Access to refresh a dynaset completely, press Shift+F9, the Requery button.

Tweaking Multiuser Settings

Access does not support a single network strategy that works perfectly for all situations. You may need to experiment with some of the default settings to achieve maximum performance with minimal conflicts on your own network. Here's how:

1. Choose Tools ≻ Options from the Access menu bar.

2. Click the Advanced tab to view the multiuser and ODBC settings, as below.

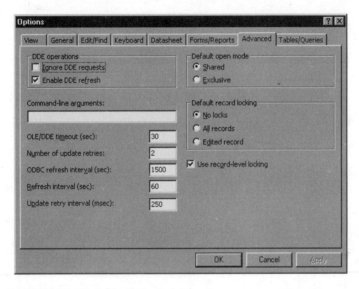

3. Use Table 19.1 (and the built-in help) to choose new settings.

4. Choose OK when you're done.

TABLE 19.1: MULTIUSER OPTIONS AND SETTINGS		
OPTION	**SETTING**	**RESULT**
Ignore DDE Requests	Default is No (unchecked)	Determines whether Access responds to DDE requests from other applications.
Enable DDE Refresh	Default is Yes (checked)	Determines whether DDE links are refreshed whenever the screen is updated.
OLE/DDE Timeout	0 to 300 seconds (default = 30)	Determines how long Access waits for an OLE or DDE operation to complete.

Continued ▐▶

TABLE 19.1: MULTIUSER OPTIONS AND SETTINGS (CONTINUED)

OPTION	SETTING	RESULT
Number of Update Retries	0 to 10 (default = 2)	Number of times Access will automatically try to save a change to a record that another user has locked.
ODBC Refresh Interval	1 to 3,600 seconds	Updates your screen at the specified interval when you're accessing a database using ODBC.
Refresh Interval	1 to 32,766 seconds (default = 60)	Updates your screen at the specified interval.
Update Retry Interval	0 to 1,000 milliseconds (default = 250)	Waits for the specified time before trying again to save a locked record. (See the section "Minimizing Locking Conflicts.")
Default Open Mode	Shared (default)	Database is open for shared use by default.
	Exclusive	Database is open for exclusive use.
Default Record Locking	No Locks (default)	Records are not locked during edits.
	All Records	All records underlying a particular object (e.g., a form) are locked when that object is open.
	Edited Records	Only the record being edited is locked.
Use Record-Level Locking	Default is Yes (checked)	Locks one record at a time instead of all those in the same page on your hard disk.

Record-Locking Strategies

The Record Locks property applies only to forms, reports, and queries. The Default Record Locking setting in the Advanced options tab applies to forms, datasheets, and Visual Basic code that loops through records in a recordset object. (The default record locking property does not apply when SQL statements are used to perform bulk operations.) The same rules for resolving write conflicts apply in all cases. If you encounter a record-locking conflict in a Visual Basic procedure, Access generates a custom error that you can trap and respond to.

For more information on dealing with errors in your Visual Basic code, see Chapter 26 or search for *Errors* with the Office Assistant.

Now that you know the various record-locking settings, how do you choose among them? It depends on how your users use the data and how much training you can give them. Let's look at the pros and cons of each strategy.

No Locks Strategy

As we explained previously, when you use the No Locks strategy (sometimes called *optimistic locking*), records are not locked while being edited. Two users can edit the record at the same time. When you try to save your changes to a record that somebody else has also changed, you'll be given the option to overwrite the other user's changes, copy your version of the record to the Clipboard, or discard your changes.

Although the No Locks strategy offers the most flexibility, it also creates two potentially unpleasant situations:

- After you make changes to a record, another user can easily overwrite those changes.

- Another user can lock a record that you're editing. You won't be able to save your changes until the other user unlocks the record.

An alternative to the No Locks strategy is to automatically lock whatever record is being edited.

Edited Record Strategy

When you choose the Edited Record locking strategy (sometimes called *pessimistic locking*), any record that's currently being edited by one user is locked and unavailable to all other users. No two people can edit the same record at the same time, which can be good and bad:

- On the upside, Access automatically ensures that no two users edit the same record at the same time. And you can be sure that once you start editing a record, you'll be able to save your changes.

- On the downside, other users may start getting irritated if you keep a particular record locked for too long. Also, if you don't have Use Record-Level Locking checked on the Advanced tab of the Options dialog box, a record lock in Access nearly always affects more than one record, since Access locks records in 4KB pages. This means that users can be locked out of records that no one else is editing.

PART

III

Database Tuning and Administration

NOTE When you're attached to an SQL database via ODBC, the rules of the SQL database govern locking. Access always acts as if you've selected the No Locks (optimistic locking) strategy.

The solution to the problem, of course, is to practice good network citizenship and make sure that you always save a record immediately after you've made your changes. That way, other users will have instant access to the modified record.

All Records Strategy

The most restrictive locking option is All Records. Once a user opens a form or datasheet, that user has a lock on all its records. No other users can change any records in the table as long as that person is using the table. Use this method only if you're absolutely sure that you want only one person at a time to be able to make changes to a table. The need for this option is generally limited to administrative table changes that have to be completed without interference from other users.

Choosing a Locking Strategy

Which locking strategy should you use? The answer depends on your data and your application, of course. But for almost all networked Access applications, we've found that the benefits of the No Locks strategy far outweigh its disadvantages. Although you'll have to train your users to deal with the occasional write conflict errors that may occur, the gain in performance more than balances this inconvenience.

In addition, in most workplaces you can use the natural workflow to reduce or eliminate record-locking conflicts. If Joe is responsible for customers whose last names start with A through M and Mary is responsible for those from N through Z, they won't even be trying to edit the same records at the same time.

Minimizing Locking Conflicts

When Access encounters a locking conflict, it will make several tries to save the record before giving up and showing an error message to the user. Access waits for whatever period of time is specified in the Update Retry Interval multiuser setting and then tries to save the record again. It repeats this process as many times as you've specified in the Number of Update Retries setting. If it can't resolve the conflict after that number of tries, then it displays a locking conflict error message.

You can minimize update conflicts and error messages by tweaking those two settings. For example, if users frequently get locking error messages, and you think it's because too many people are trying to save data at the same moment, then *increase* both settings. Access will wait longer, and try more times, before showing the error message. Of course, if many locking conflicts occur, this setting will make your application appear to be more sluggish as it makes multiple futile retries to save the data.

On the other hand, if you want Access to display a locking error message as soon as a conflict occurs, set the Number of Update Retries option to zero.

Securing Your Database

Access allows you to implement security on your database objects as you need it. By default, security is completely invisible to both the designers and the users of an Access database. As your needs require it, you can secure individual objects so that, for example, most users can't modify a particular form. If you are extremely concerned about security, you can use the Access security features to remove all but a few ways to retrieve data from your tables. In networked applications, a well-designed security system can help make the application more maintainable by eliminating many sources of potential disaster.

Security Concepts

To understand Access security, you'll need to grasp four basic security concepts: *users* and *groups* have *permissions* on *objects*.

- **An Access *user*** represents a single person who uses an Access application. Users are distinguished by their username, password, and a unique secret identifier called the Personal Identifier (PID). To use a secured Access application, a user has to type in her username and password to be able to get to any objects.

- **An Access *group*** is a collection of users. You can use groups to represent parts of your organization, such as Development and Accounting, or simply security levels, such as High and Low. Often you'll find that assigning users to groups, and permissions directly to those groups, makes a security system more maintainable.

- **An Access *permission*** is the right to perform a single operation on an object. For example, a user can be granted read data permission on a table, allowing that user to retrieve data from that table. Both users and groups can be assigned permissions.

- **An Access security *object*** is any one of the main database container objects (table, query, form, report, macro, or module) or a database itself.

WARNING Because both users and groups can have permissions, you may have to check several places to determine a user's actual permissions. The user's actual permissions are the *least restrictive* combination of the user's own permissions (called explicit permissions) and the permissions of all groups the user belongs to (called implicit permissions). So if Mary does not have permission to open the Accounting form, but she's a member of the Supervisors group that does have permission to open that form, she will be able to open the form.

Permissions Granted

Access includes a varied set of permissions that you can assign to groups and individuals on an object-by-object basis. You can grant any of the permissions listed in Table 19.2 to any group or to any individual user in a group.

TABLE 19.2: PERMISSIONS YOU CAN ASSIGN TO INDIVIDUAL USERS AND GROUPS OF USERS

PERMISSION	PERMITS USER TO:	CAN BE APPLIED TO:
Open/Run	Open a database, form, report, or run a macro	Databases, forms, reports, macros
Read Design	Look at an object in design view	All object types
Modify Design	View, change, and delete objects	All object types
Administer	Full access, including the right to assign permissions to users	All objects and the security system
Read Data	View, but not alter, data	Tables and queries
Update Data	View and change data, but not insert or delete	Tables and queries
Insert Data	View and add data, but not modify or delete	Tables and queries
Delete Data	View and delete data, but not add or modify	Tables and queries

Access Logons

Every single time you start Access, you must supply a valid username and password. Surprised? Think you've got a special copy of Access that doesn't require this step? That's because Access does its best to be helpful. When you launch Access, it automatically tries to log you on as a user named Admin with a blank password. If this process works—and you haven't activated your security system by assigning a password to the Admin user—Access suppresses the logon dialog box completely.

To be able to log on as any other user, you'll need to assign a password to the Admin user, as discussed below. The next time you start Access, you'll see this logon dialog box:

If for some reason you decide to deactivate security, you can suppress the logon dialog box by changing the Admin user's password back to a blank.

Workgroup Files

Access stores security information in a workgroup file, which is named system.mdw by default. Access includes a tool, called the Workgroup Administrator, to create new workgroup files. You can also use this tool to join a workgroup.

Creating a New Workgroup File

To create a new workgroup file, follow these steps:

1. Locate the Workgroup Administrator (wrkgadm.exe) item in Explorer and open it, as shown below.

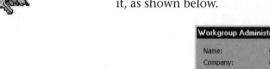

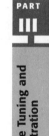

2. Click Create.

3. Enter a name, organization, and unique Workgroup ID (WID) and click OK. The WID is used by Access to make sure that your workgroup is unique. Store this information in a safe place—you'll need it if you ever need to re-create your original workgroup.

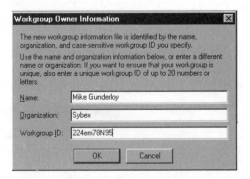

4. Supply a path and filename for the new workgroup file. You should use the .mdw extension for this file.

5. Click OK three times to create the new workgroup, confirm its information, and return to the main Workgroup Administrator screen.

6. Click Exit to close the Workgroup Administrator.

 WARNING The original workgroup file created when you install Access is *not secure* because Access creates it for you using the username and organization name you used for the Access install and a blank WID. Anyone who can get to your computer and use Help ➢ About in any Office application can recover this information and so re-create your original workgroup file. Armed with this file, an intruder can break any security scheme you design.

To learn more about workgroups and the workgroup information file, search for *Workgroup File* with the Office Assistant, and click *Create a New Microsoft Access Workgroup Information File*.

Joining a New Workgroup

You can also use Workgroup Administrator to switch from one workgroup file to another. You'll need to do this if you have secured databases from two different sources. To switch workgroups, follow these steps:

1. Locate the Workgroup Administrator (wrkgadm.exe) item in Explorer and open it.

2. Click the Join button.

3. Type in the name of the workgroup you want to join or use the Browse button to locate the file on your drive.

4. Click the OK button twice to join the new workgroup and confirm the information message.

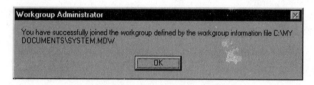

5. Click Exit to close the Workgroup Administrator.

Built-In User and Groups

Every Access workgroup comes with the built-in user and groups listed in Table 19.3 and Table 19.4. Access created this user and these groups to provide a bare-bones security system.

TABLE 19.3: DEFAULT ACCESS USER

USER	MEMBER OF	COMMENTS
Admin	Admins, Users	Default logon user

TABLE 19.4: DEFAULT ACCESS GROUPS		
GROUP	**CONTAINS**	**COMMENTS**
Admins	Admin	Any member has full permissions on all objects, regardless of security.
Users	Admin	Members by default have permissions on all objects.

The most important thing to realize about the built-in user and groups is that most of them are not secure and cannot be made secure. The Admin user and the Users group are identical in every single workgroup file ever created. If you assign permissions to Admin or Users, you are in effect making those permissions available to any Access user.

Since the Admin user has full permissions on all objects by default, and everyone is logged in as the Admin user unless they've activated their security (that is, placed a password on the database), this system ensures that all users can swap databases without worrying about security.

Ownership: The Super Permission

Another important security concept is the idea of *ownership*. Whoever creates an object in the first place, or imports it from another database, is the initial owner of the object. The owner can give ownership to another user or group, or any member of the Admins group can reassign the ownership of any object.

 TIP Assigning object ownership to a group such as Developers makes it easier for multiple developers to work with objects in a secured database.

The owner of an object always has Administer permission on that object, even if someone else tries to take it away—and in some cases, even if the interface erroneously reports that they don't have this permission. Therefore, an object's owner can do anything with that object, no matter how anyone else tries to limit the owner.

Working with Users and Groups

The first step for implementing a security system is to decide which users and groups you'll need. You'll need to keep at least one user—usually yourself—in the Admins group, since only members of the Admins group can create new users and perform other security tasks. Other users should be grouped by the tasks they need to perform, so that you can assign permissions to groups. A security scheme for a small database might look like the diagram in Figure 19.8.

FIGURE 19.8

Plan for security in an Access database.

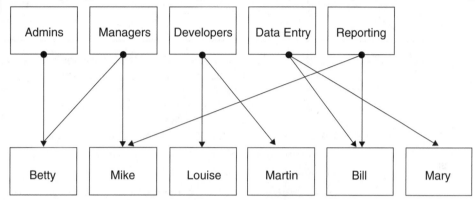

Select Tools ➤ Security ➤ User and Group Accounts from the Access menu to open the User and Group Accounts dialog box. From this dialog box you can create and delete users and groups, assign users to groups, and change your own password.

The Users Tab

The Users tab has a drop-down list at the top where you can select any user in the system. The Group Membership section shows which groups this user is a member of.

- **To create a new user**, click the New button. In the dialog box that appears, supply a unique name and Personal ID (PID) for the user. Click the OK button to create the user. Access uses the PID to uniquely identify the user you've just created.

 TIP The PID is *not* a password. New users are already created without a password. To assign a password to a user, close Access, reopen it, log on as the new user, and use the User and Group Accounts dialog box to set that user's password.

- **To delete a user**, select the user from the Name drop-down list and click the Delete button; then click the Yes button to confirm the delete. You can't delete any of the built-in users.
- **To clear the password of a user** who has forgotten his or her password, click the Clear Password button.
- **To add a user to a group**, select the group in the left list box and click the Add>> button.
- **To remove a user from a group**, select the group in the right-hand list box and click the <<Remove button.

 NOTE You can't remove any user from the Users group, and you can't remove the last member from the Admins group.

The Groups Tab

The Groups tab has a single drop-down list that shows you all of the existing groups in your database.

- **To create a new group**, click the New button, supply a name and Personal ID (PID) for the new group, and click the OK button. Access uses the PID to make this new group unique.

 TIP You should write down and save all of the PIDs you use for both users and groups, along with the WID for your workgroup file. If your workgroup file is ever lost or corrupted, you can use this information to re-create the information it contains.

- **To delete a group**, select the group in the combo box, click the Delete button, and click the Yes button to confirm the deletion.

The Change Logon Password Tab

To change your password, enter your current password and then enter the new password, typing it the same way twice. Access checks that you didn't accidentally mistype the new password.

Viewing Ownership and Permissions

To modify object permissions and ownership, select Tools ➢ Security ➢ User and Group Permissions from the Access menus.

PART

III

Database Tuning and
Administration

The Permissions Tab

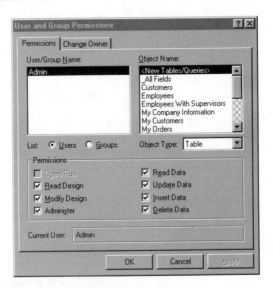

To check the permissions by user for individual database objects, click the Permissions tab. Then use the dialog box as follows:

- **To view a user's permissions on any object**, first choose the Users radio button. Then click the user whose permission you want to check in the User/Group Name list box. Select the type of object from the Object Type drop-down list. Select the object in the Object Name list box. The Permissions area will show the current explicit permissions for this user.

- **To view a group's permissions on any object**, first choose the Groups radio button. Then click the group whose permission you want to check in the User/Group Name list box. Select the type of object from the Object Type drop-down list. Select the object in the Object Name list box. The Permissions area will show the current permissions for this group.

- **To change permissions on an object**, first choose the user or group you want to change permissions for, as above. Select the type of object from the Object Type drop-down list. Select one or more objects in the Object Name list box. Click in the Permissions check boxes to select or deselect the various permissions. When the correct set of permissions is showing, click the Apply button to make the changes.

The Change Owner Tab

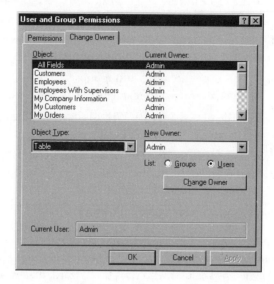

If you click the Change Owner tab, you can view the current owner of an object or change the owner.

- **To view the current owner of an object**, select the Object Type in the left combo box. Select one or more objects. The New Owner combo box will show you the current owner of these objects. (If you select objects owned by more than one user or group, the box will remain blank.)

- **To change ownership**, select the Object Type in the left combo box. Select one or more objects. Select the New Owner from the combo box and click Change Owner.

Securing Your Database

As you've seen so far, Access security can be a complex business. The interactions of users, groups, owners, objects, and permissions require careful study. However, following a few simple steps will help ensure the integrity of your security system.

1. (Optional) If you haven't done so already, use the Workgroup Administrator to create a new, unique Workgroup. Store the WID in a safe place.

2. Start Access and create a new user for yourself to use. Add this user to the Admins group.

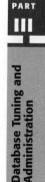

PART

III

Database Tuning and Administration

3. Change the Admin user password to any nonblank string. Store this password in a safe place in case you later decide to remove the security restrictions from the database.

4. Exit and restart Access. Log in as your new user. Change the password on your new user to something known only to you.

5. Create any other users and groups you require. Store the PIDs in a safe place in case you ever need to re-create one of these users or groups.

6. Run the Access Security Wizard (described below) to remove permissions from the database.

7. Assign permissions to those users and groups that you want to be able to work with objects.

The User-Level Security Wizard

Access includes a built-in User-Level Security Wizard to handle some of the tedium of securing a database. The User-Level Security Wizard makes a new copy of your database owned by the user who runs the Wizard, makes sure all objects in that database are owned by that user as well, and removes all permissions for the Admin user and the Users group from these objects. It also encrypts your database for protection from prying eyes armed with hex editors.

To use the User-Level Security Wizard, follow these steps:

1. Choose Tools ➤ Security ➤ User-Level Security Wizard from the menus. The Wizard starts by asking you whether you want to create a new workgroup information file, or use the current file. It will not allow you to use the default workgroup information file. If you are currently using the default workgroup, leave Create a New Workgroup... selected and click Next.

2. If you are creating a new workgroup, in the next window enter the File Name, a WID, and the other information needed for the new file. (You are free to use the defaults that are filled in already.) Then click the option to make the new file the default workgroup information file, or select the option to create a shortcut to the secured database. It's probably safest to opt for the shortcut method, unless you're sure you want to change the default workgroup information file. Click Next after you complete this step.

3. In the next step, you get to choose the database objects that are to be secured. You'll see a window like the one in Figure 19.9. If you don't want an object to be secured, uncheck the box to the left of its name. When you finish deselecting and selecting objects, click Next.

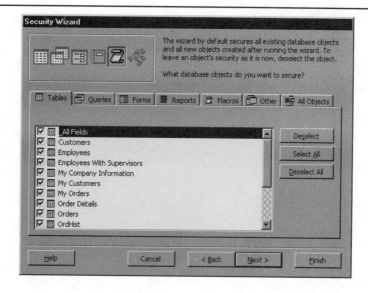

4. Enter a password to protect the VBA project that is part of the database (You can leave this blank if you like.) and click Next.

5. The next step lets you add optional security group accounts to the workgroup information file. These groups have already been defined by Access and have specific permissions associated with them. If you add one or more of these groups to the workgroup information file, you can then add users to them directly, instead of having to create your own groups first. To see the permissions that are part of each group, click the group and view the box on the right side of the dialog box. Select (check) each group you want to use and click Next.

6. By default, the Users group has no permissions set up. In the next step, the Wizard lets you optionally assign permissions to this group. To do this, check Yes, I Would Like to Grant Some Permissions... in the dialog box shown in Figure 19.10. In turn, click the tab for each type of object you want to assign permissions for, and check the box(es) for the permissions you want to allow. Then click OK. (Note that if you do assign permissions to the users group in this step, any Access user will have these permissions, since all users are part of the Users group for every database.)

PART

III

Database Tuning and Administration

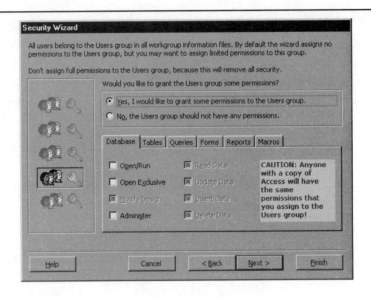

FIGURE 19.10

This step of the User-Level Security Wizard lets you optionally assign permissions to the Users group that every Access user is a part of.

7. Next you can add users to the workgroup information file, and assign passwords and Personal IDs. Either select a name from the list on the left, or click the Add a New User button. For each user you select or add, enter a password and optionally change the PID the Wizard assigns. Then click Next.

8. The Wizard also lets you assign users to groups or vice-versa. To do this in the next step, click Select a User... or Select a Group.... Then select a group or user from the drop-down list, and check the items you want to assign on the list below. Click Next when you're ready to move on.

9. In the last step, enter a name and location for the secured database and click Finish.

The Wizard will then create the new database and make secured copies of your objects in it. You'll see a report that lists information such as the workgroup ID and group names for the database you just secured. Here are some additional sources of information about security:

- In Help, open the *Securing a Database* topic. Then click any topic to view its information.

- For tips on planning database security, search for *Security* with the Office Assistant, and then click *Secure a Microsoft Access Database*.

- Clicking Help from the User-Level Security Wizard will provide you with an overview of using Access security.

Skating Past the Logon Dialog Box

Once you've activated the login procedure for Access (which you do by setting up a password for the Admin user), you'll always be faced with this dialog box as soon as you start Access:

If you get tired of filling out the dialog box, you can put your username and (optionally) your password into your startup command. That way, Access will fill in the dialog box automatically and take you right past it.

To set up a custom startup command, you can use any combination of these three custom startup switches:

database-name   If you want to create a shortcut to open a particular database when you start Access, follow the startup command with a blank space and the location and name of the database you want to open.

/User *username*   To supply a username at startup, follow the startup command with a space, followed by /User, followed by a space and your username.

/Pwd *password*   To supply your password at startup, follow the startup command with a space, followed by /Pwd, followed by another space and your password.

You can set up a custom startup command by using Windows Explorer. The procedure we'll explain here doesn't change the way your original copy of Access works at all. Rather, it creates a new icon on your Windows Desktop and associates it with your selected settings. Here are the exact steps for Windows 95 and Windows 98:

1. Launch the Windows Explorer, make sure it doesn't fill the whole screen, and navigate to the folder containing the msaccess.exe program (usually the C:\program files\Microsoft Office\Office folder).

2. Drag this program out of Explorer by holding down the *right* mouse button, and drop it on any blank area of your Windows Desktop. Select Create Shortcut(s) Here from the menu that appears when you drop the program.

3. Right-click the icon you just created. Select Properties from the menu and click the Shortcut tab in the Properties dialog box.

4. Enter the command-line switches in the Target text box, and choose OK.

Let's suppose that you've been assigned the username *Gondola* and the password *omnipotent*. Furthermore, you want to have this shortcut automatically open the database named ContactManagement1.mdb in the C:\contact folder. In that case you'd want to change the startup command in the Command Line text box to:

```
C:\Microsoft Office\Office\MSACCESS.EXE C:\contact\
    ContactManagement1.mdb /User Gondola /Pwd omnipotent
```

The one risk here, of course, is that anyone who has access to your computer, and a little knowledge of shortcuts, can look up your password in about two seconds flat. If that's a risk you cannot afford to take, then you can leave the password out of the startup command (in the example, remove /Pwd omnipotent). If you choose this option, you'll have to provide the password each time you start Access.

For more information on custom Access startup commands, search for *Startup* with the Office Assistant, and click *Startup Command-Line Options*.

Password Security

As you've seen in this chapter, the full Access security model can be quite complex to implement and maintain. If you're interested only in protecting your own database from prying eyes, you can use the Database Password feature, which is a simpler way to lock up your data. This feature isn't really suitable for networked, multiuser applications, since it doesn't let you distinguish among individual users. But it can be an easy way to add some security to single-user databases.

To set a password on your database:

1. Open the database, being sure to check the Exclusive box on the File Open dialog box, and choose Tools ➤ Security ➤ Set Database Password.

2. Choose a password and type it into both the Password and Verify boxes (typing it twice is a precaution to prevent you from making a mistake the first time).

3. Click the OK button.

When you attempt to open this database in the future, you'll see the dialog box below. Enter the same password you chose in step 2 to get into the database.

WARNING If you ever forget your database password, all of your data will be lost forever. There's nothing anyone, including Microsoft, can do to bypass this password once it has been set. Be sure to pick something you'll remember, and record the password in a safe place.

Where to Go from Here

In this chapter we've introduced two of the most complex issues in Access: multiuser record locking and security. Now that you've learned about all the basic pieces you need to create useful Access databases, we're going to turn our attention to the elements that distinguish a finished application from just another database. Part Four shows you how to enhance your project with macros, toolbars, menus, and other tools to make your users' lives easier.

What's New in the Access Zoo?

One of the new features in Access 2000 is record-level locking. Instead of locking an entire page of records when a single record needs to be locked, Access 2000 will now by default lock only the record being worked on. You are free to change this setting in the Options window.

The User-Level Security Wizard has been changed quite a bit. It now lets you create a new workgroup information file right from the Wizard. This Wizard prompts you through the entire process of setting up groups, adding users, and assigning permissions to the User group. This greatly simplifies the process of protecting a database.

PART

III

Database Tuning and Administration

PART IV

Building a Custom Application

LEARN TO:

- Create a custom application

- Use macros

- Create a custom switchboard

- Create custom dialog boxes

- Create custom toolbars

- Create custom menus

CHAPTER **20**

Creating a Custom Application

This chapter starts Part IV of this book, where we'll look at how to turn a database into an application (or *app*, for short). This chapter is also a transition for you, the reader, because you'll be going from the role of computer user to application developer. We'll explain what that's all about as we go along in this chapter.

What Is an Application?

An application is a database that's been automated, using menus, dialog boxes, and other familiar components of the Windows interface. The goal is to create a product that anyone—even people who know nothing about Microsoft Access—can use.

When you use the Database Wizard to design a database, the Wizard creates a simple application with forms, reports, and perhaps one or more switchboards. You can create much more elaborate applications than the ones the Database Wizard creates by creating every database object from scratch. Or you can create all the database objects—tables, queries, forms, and reports—using the Database Wizard. Then you can create your own switchboards and dialog boxes to tie those objects together in a smooth, easy-to-use application.

Who's Who in Application Development

Before we begin our foray into applications development, you'll need to understand the terms *developer* and *user*:

Developer   The person who creates the application—most likely yourself, since you're the one reading this book.

User   The person, or people, who will be using the completed application. This person might be a computer neophyte.

This chapter marks your initiation into the ranks of application developers. As a developer, your mission is to *create* applications that people with little or no computer experience or training can use.

How Much Programming Is Involved?

Historically, only people with advanced training and experience in computer programming were able to build custom programs (applications). But with Access, you can create very sophisticated custom applications with little or no programming.

Why? Because the tables, queries, forms, and reports that you create using techniques from the preceding chapters make up at least 90 percent of the overall application.

The other 10 percent of the application will consist of hyperlinks, macros, and/or Visual Basic procedures that determine how the application behaves as the user interacts with the program. We'll talk about macros and procedures in upcoming chapters. First you need to understand *events*, which are the triggers that launch your custom macros and procedures into action.

What Are Events?

The custom applications that you create with Microsoft Access are *event driven*. In English, that means that the application normally just sits there on the screen waiting for the user (the person using the mouse and keyboard) to do something. When the user does indeed do something, that action triggers an *event*, which the program then responds to.

Virtually every activity that occurs on the screen is an event. Here are some examples:

- Moving or clicking the mouse
- Pressing and releasing a key
- Moving the cursor to a control
- Changing the contents of a control
- Opening or closing a form
- Printing a report

For example, when you're using a form or switchboard and you click a command button, your action generates a "button click" event. The application *responds* to the event by carrying out whatever *action* the command button tells the program to do. The action is defined, by you, in the form of a macro or by Visual Basic code.

Microsoft Access can detect many kinds of events, and you can assign a custom action to any one of these events. Before we talk about how to create actions, let's look at how you go about finding the events to which you want to assign custom actions.

Finding Event Properties

You assign an action to an event by assigning a macro or procedure name to an *event property*. Every form, report, and control has its own set of events. To see the events, you need to open the form or report in design view, and open the property sheet. Then check the Event tab to see if any macros or procedures are associated with the events that are listed.

Here are the exact steps:

1. Open a database and open the database window; click the name of the form or report whose events you want to explore.

2. Click the Design button to open that object in design view.

   • **If you want to see events for the form as a whole**, choose Edit ➤ Select Form, or click in the square in the upper-left corner where the rulers meet.

   • **If you want to see events for the report as a whole**, choose Edit ➤ Select Report, or click in the square in the upper-left corner where the rulers meet.

   • **If you want to see events for a particular control**, click the specific control.

3. Open the property sheet. (Click the Properties button, or choose View ➤ Properties.)

4. Click the Event tab.

 TIP If you want to look at the events for a specific control, you can just right-click the control and choose Properties from the shortcut menu. Then click the Events tab.

The property sheet will show you all the events that you can assign actions to. The exact events that become available depend on which object is selected at the moment. For example, if you chose Edit ➤ Select Form under step 2, the property sheet would show event properties for the entire form, as in Figure 20.1.

FIGURE 20.1

Event properties for an entire form.

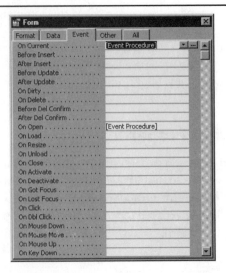

If you click a specific control before (or after) opening the property sheet, you'll see events for that particular control only. For example, Figure 20.2 shows the event properties for the currently selected command button, named Option1.

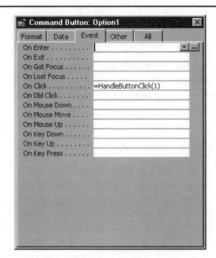

FIGURE 20.2

Event properties for a single control on a form.

In Figure 20.1, you can see that the On Current and On Open events have [Event Procedure] listed as their properties. Behind those event procedures is the Visual Basic code that determines what happens when the events occur. A little later in this chapter, we'll show you how to create a control and the action for that control using control wizards. But first, here's a quick overview of some of the many different types of events to which you can assign actions.

Sample Form Events

To see the event properties for a form as a whole, open the form in design view, choose Edit ➤ Select Form, and then open the property sheet and select the Events tab, as we did to display Figure 20.1. You can assign actions to many events, but let's start by focusing on the events that occur when the user first opens a form. Here they are, in the order in which they occur:

Open ➤ Load ➤ Resize ➤ Activate ➤ Current

You can assign an action to any one of these events using the On Open, On Load, On Resize, On Activate, and On Current properties. But why so many different events for the simple act of opening a form? Because having lots of events to assign actions to gives you great freedom in customizing how your custom application will behave when the user opens the form. For example, you can assign an action to the On Open property, and that action will play out first. You can assign a different action to the On Load event, and that action will play out second. You can assign custom actions to as many, or as few, event properties as you wish.

 TIP As always, you can get more information about an event by clicking on the event name in the property sheet, and then pressing the Help key (F1).

When the user closes a form, three events occur:

Unload ➤ Deactivate ➤ Close

To assign actions to these events, you use the On Unload, On Deactivate, and On Close event properties for the form.

To illustrate just how specific you can be when assigning actions to events, let's suppose you want some special action to occur when the user switches from one open form to another. The On Open and On Close events wouldn't do you any good in this case. However, the Activate and Deactivate events do occur when switching from one open form to another, like this:

Deactivate (first form) ➤ Activate (second form)

Sample Control Events

Every control on a form has its own set of event properties to which you can assign actions. The exact event properties that are available to you depend on the type of control you're working with at the moment. For example, the event properties for a text box are different from the event properties for a drop-down list.

But virtually all controls have some simple events that occur when the user enters the control (by clicking it or tabbing to it). Those event properties are

Enter ➤ GotFocus

To assign actions to these events, you first need to select a specific control (still in design view), open the property sheet, and click the Events tab, just as we did back in Figure 20.2.

When the user exits a control, these two events occur:

Exit ➤ LostFocus

Keep in mind that the events we've discussed here are just a few examples of the dozens of events that you can assign actions to. You'll see many more examples as we progress through this, and following, chapters. To get you started in creating your own controls and assigning actions to the events that those controls generate, we'll turn our attention now to the control wizards, the easiest way to create custom controls and actions.

Creating a Control and Action in One Step

The easiest way to create a control and to assign a custom action to it is via the control wizards, available in the form design screen. Here are the basic steps for creating a control and action using the control wizards:

1. Open the form to which you want to add a control in design view.

2. Make sure the toolbox is open. (If not, click the Toolbox toolbar button, or choose View ➤ Toolbox.)

3. Make sure the Control Wizards button in the toolbox is pushed in, as shown below.

4. Click the type of control you want to create. (The Command Button tool is a good one to cut your teeth on because it's easy to create and the wizard offers many options.)

 TIP Remember, if you forget what type of control the various buttons in the toolbox create, you can just point to a button and wait for the ScreenTip to appear.

---

5. Click the location in the form where you want to put the control you're about to create.

6. If the control you are creating is supported by the control wizards, you'll see the first wizard screen. Just follow the wizard's instructions, and make your selections as you would with any wizard.

When you've finished, you'll see the control on your form, already selected with sizing handles in case you want to move or resize the control.

To test the new control, switch to form view. In form view, use the control as you normally would. For example, if you created a command button, just click the command button. When you do, the action you chose while completing the wizard will be played out.

Note that when you add a control to a form, you change the form. When you try to close the form, you'll be asked if you want to save the change. Choose Yes if you're happy with your new control and want to save it.

Using Control Wizards

Let's take a look at a specific example of using the control wizards to create a fairly simple control. Suppose that you used the Database Wizard to create the Order Entry database. You open up the My Company Information form (Figure 20.3) and decide that perhaps you'd like to add a command button to that form that will allow the user to close the form without clicking on the built-in Close button.

FIGURE 20.3

We'll use the control wizards to add a Close button to this form.

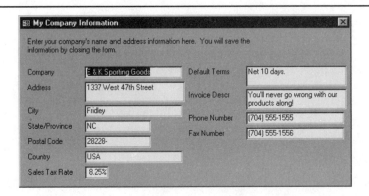

First, we need to close the form (Click its Close button.), get to the database window, and reopen the form in design view. In this example, we would click the Forms tab, click My Company Information as the name of the form to modify, and then click the Design button. You're taken to the form design window.

If the toolbox isn't open, click the Toolbox button, or choose View ➤ Toolbox. Then make sure the Control Wizards button in the toolbox is pushed in, as in Figure 20.4.

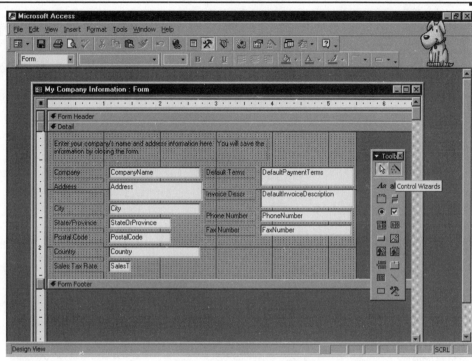

FIGURE 20.4

The My Company Information form in design view. The toolbox is open and the Control Wizards button is pushed in.

Now we can use the scroll bars surrounding the form to get down to the lower-right corner of the form, where we want to place the command button. We click the Command Button tool in the toolbox, and then click down near the lower-right corner of the form to place the button.

For a moment, we see an outline indicating where the button will appear. Then the Command Button Wizard kicks in automatically. The first Wizard window asks what we want this button to do. In this case, we choose Form Operations under Categories, and Close Form under Actions (since we want this button to close the form), as in Figure 20.5.

After making a selection, we click the Next button, and the second Wizard window asks how we want the button to look. It suggests using the Exit picture, which is a door with an arrow pointing the way out. But in this example, we decide we'd rather have the button just show the word *Close* (with the C underlined). So we click the Text option button and type **&Close** in the text box, as in Figure 20.6.

FIGURE 20.5

The first window of the Command Button Wizard asks what you want the button to do. The options are grouped in several categories.

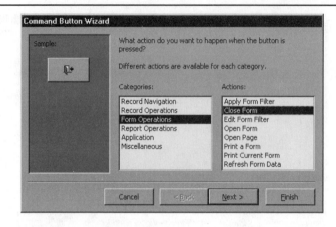

FIGURE 20.6

Here we've opted to put the word Close, rather than a picture, on the command button we're creating. An ampersand in front of a letter means "underline the next letter."

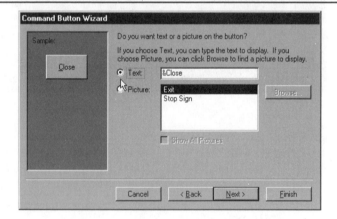

 TIP To underline a letter in a button's text, just put an ampersand in front of the letter you want underlined. As you'll see later in the book, the same technique applies to many controls, such as underlining hotkeys in your own custom menus. If you want to include an ampersand in the text on the button, just type two ampersands together, like this: &&.

We then press Next to open the final Wizard window, which asks what we want to name this button. The Wizard will suggest a generic name, like Command23, but we can use a more descriptive one. In Figure 20.7 we've opted to name this button CloseCompanyInfo. This name will help remind you of the button's purpose.

FIGURE 20.7

*Here we've opted to
name the button
CloseCompanyInfo.*

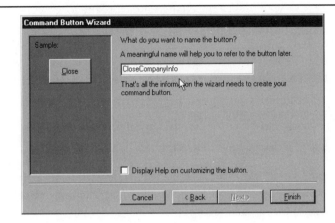

Finally, we choose Finish from the last Wizard window, and the Wizard disappears.
Now we can see the new command button on the form. You can size and move this
new button using the standard techniques. Figure 20.8 shows the new command button close to the lower-right corner of the form.

FIGURE 20.8

*The new Close com-
mand button appears
near the lower-right
corner of the form.*

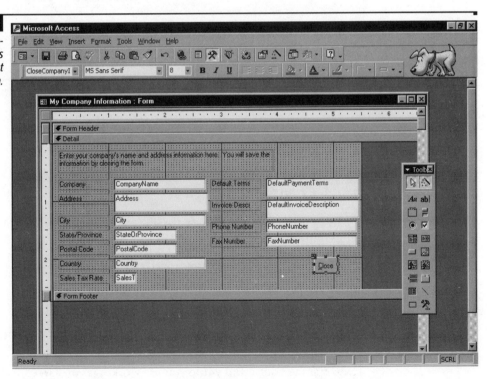

Now we can save the change and close the form. We can't use the new Close button to do that, though, because the controls you create work only in form view, not design view. So to close and save this form, you can choose File ➤ Close from the menu bar, or click the form's Close button. When asked if you want to save the changes to the design of the form, choose Yes. You'll be returned to the database window.

Testing the New Control

To test the new control, you first need to open the form in form view (not in design view). So in this example, we could just double-click My Company Information in the database window. The form appears looking pretty much the same as it did back in Figure 20.3, except that the form is wider, and now we can also see the new custom Close button, as in Figure 20.9.

To test the new command button, just click it. The form should close, which is all that we wanted this particular button to do.

More Wizard-Created Controls

The command button to close a form is just one example of a control that you can create using control wizards. The Option Group, Combo Box, List Box, Command Button, and Subform/Subreport tools in the toolbox also offer wizards to make creating those types of controls a bit easier. Your best bet is to simply experiment. Here are a few points to keep in mind as you do so:

- You can create controls only in design view.
- The control wizards will appear only if the Control Wizard button in the toolbox is pushed in before you start creating the control.
- If you change your mind while you are working, you can cancel the wizard.

- If you create a control and then change your mind and want to get rid of it, just click the control (in design view) and press Delete.

- The control wizards create the control and assign certain properties to it. To change the properties of a control that a wizard has created, make sure you are in design view. Then right-click the control and choose Properties from the shortcut menu that appears.

- The action that a control wizard creates is written in Visual Basic, a topic we'll introduce in Chapter 26. If you want to take a peek at the code that the wizard created, start from design view, right-click the control, and choose Build Event from the shortcut menu that appears.

- To test the new control, you must be in form view, not design view.

Whenever you need to add a custom command button, combo box, or option group on a form, try using a control wizard. If you can't get the control wizard to create the action that you want the control to perform, your next best bet is to create a macro—the topic of our next chapter.

Where to Go from Here

Creating custom Access applications is a complex subject. Here are some pointers for finding specific topics of interest:

- To try out some custom applications, see Appendix B and Appendix C.

- To learn about using hyperlinks to a form to perform actions, see Chapter 13.

- To learn about using macros to define custom actions, see Chapter 21.

- To learn about creating custom switchboards and dialog boxes for an application, see Chapters 22 and 23.

- To learn about creating custom menus and toolbars, see Chapters 23 and 24.

CHAPTER 21

Using Macros to Create Custom Actions

T he easiest way to create a control and a custom action for that control is to use the control wizards we discussed in Chapter 20. Adding a hyperlink to a form or report is another easy way to create a control that performs a simple action like opening a form or report. But as you develop more sophisticated applications, you'll probably want to define custom actions that are more complex than the actions you can set up with a hyperlink or the control wizards.

When you can't get a control wizard to create the exact action you want to perform, you can use either of these two alternative techniques to define a custom action:

- Create a macro.
- Write a Visual Basic procedure.

Visual Basic requires that you type long strings of commands very, very accurately. Macros, however, let you define actions using the simpler point-and-click approach. Unless you already happen to be a Visual Basic whiz, you'll probably find that macros are by far the quickest and easiest way to define custom actions in your application. In this chapter we'll focus on macros.

How to Create a Macro

The mechanics of creating a macro are fairly straightforward:

1. Click the Macros tab in the database window.
2. Click the New button. You're taken to a *macro sheet* that's tentatively named Macro1, as in Figure 21.1.
3. Click the drop-down list button in the Action column. You'll see a partial list of possible actions, as shown below. (You can use the scroll bar, the ↓ key, or type a letter to scroll down the list.)

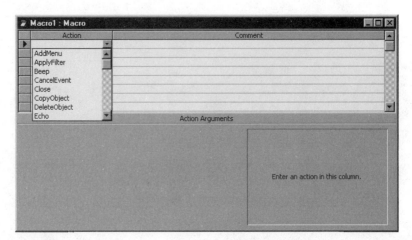

FIGURE 21.1

*A new, blank macro
sheet.*

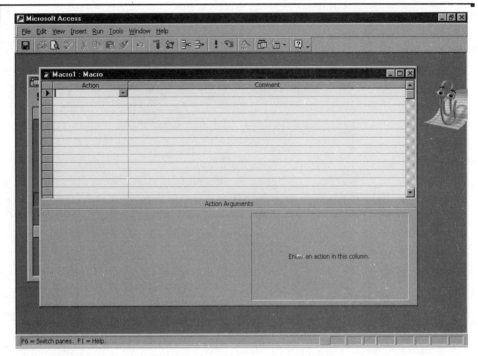

4. Choose whichever action best describes what you want the macro to do. For example, below we chose OpenReport (an action that will cause the macro to open up a report in this database). Notice that in addition to the word *OpenReport* appearing in the action column, the lower portion of the window shows some *action arguments* to be filled in, and the hint box tells us what the selected action will do.

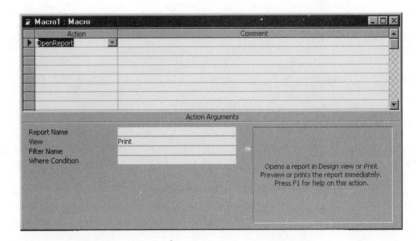

5. Fill in the selections under Action Arguments. For example, below we clicked next to Report Name and can now use the drop-down list to choose which report we want the macro to open. Note too that the hint box is now giving us information that's specific to the Report Name argument that we're filling in.

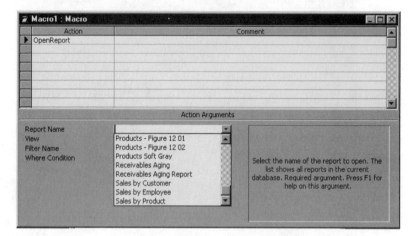

You need to fill in each *required argument* for your action. You can leave *optional arguments* blank if you wish. To determine whether an argument is required or optional, click the argument and read the hint box to the right.

6. (Optional) Click just to the right of the action you chose, and type in a plain-English description of what that action does. Note the comment next to our OpenReport action.

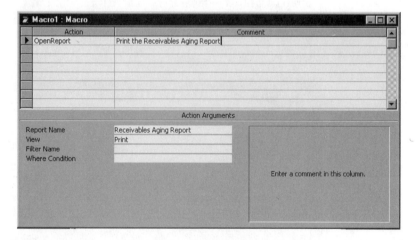

7. Click the cell just under the action you defined, and repeat steps 3 to 6 to define additional actions for this macro. When the macro is executed, it will perform every action in your macro, starting with the first and ending with the last. In Figure 21.2 we've added several actions and comments to our sample macro.

PART

IV

Building a Custom
Application

FIGURE 21.2

*A macro with several
actions defined.*

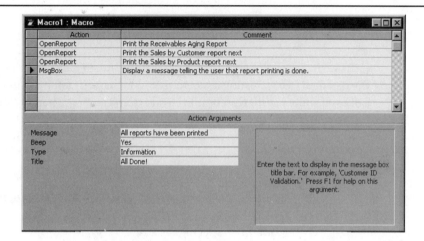

8. Close the macro when you are finished, and give it a name. (Choose File ➤ Close, or click the Close button in the upper-right corner of the macro sheet window.) You can choose Yes to save your changes and enter a new, more descriptive name for your macro.

The name you assigned to the macro appears in the database window whenever the Macros tab is active. For example, we named our macro PrintThreeReports when closing it, so now that name appears in the database window as you can see here.

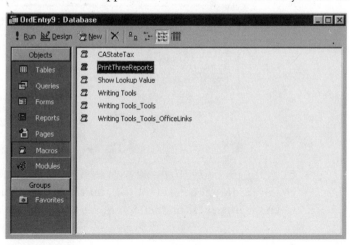

Determining When a Macro Plays

After you've created a macro, your next step is to determine *when* the macro will perform its actions. For example, you might want the macro to play:

- As soon as the user clicks on a particular command button on a form
- Right after the user changes the data in some control
- As soon as the user opens a particular form or report

As we'll discuss later, you can also have the macro play when the user first opens the database (see "Creating a Macro to Run at Startup" later in this chapter). Or you can assign the macro to an option in a custom toolbar (Chapter 24) or menu (Chapter 25) that you've created. Your options for *when* the macro is triggered are virtually limitless. For now, let's just take a look at how you'd assign a macro to a report, a form, or a particular control on a form:

1. In design view, open the form or report that you want to have trigger the macro.

- **If you want the form or report as a whole to trigger the macro** (for example, open/close the form, open/close the report), choose Edit ➢ Select Form, or Edit ➢ Select Report.

- **If you want a particular control in a form to trigger a macro**, select that control by clicking it once. (If you haven't created the control yet, you can do so right on the spot using the toolbox.)

- **If you want a particular section of a form or report to trigger the macro**, click the section bar in design view.

2. Open the property sheet and click the Event tab. All the possible events for the selected form, report, control, or section will appear, as in the example below.

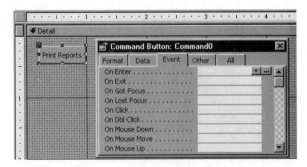

3. Click the property that you want to have trigger the macro. For example, if you're assigning the macro to a command button and want the macro to run when the user clicks on that button, click the On Click property.

4. Choose the name of the macro you want to execute from the drop-down list that appears. For example, below we're assigning the PrintThreeReports macro to the On Click property of a button we created earlier.

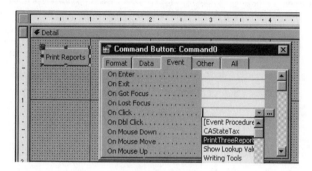

And now you're done. It's a good idea to save and close the form at this point, before you test the macro. Choose File ➤ Close and Yes when asked about saving your changes.

Running the Macro

To run the macro, you need to play the role of the user by triggering whatever event activates the macro. For example, if you assigned the macro to the On Click property of a command button, you need to open the form that holds the button (in form view), then click that button just as the user would. If you assigned the macro to the On Open property of a form, all you need to do is open the appropriate form.

TIP You can run a macro simply by clicking its name in the database window and then clicking the Run button. This technique is fine for testing a macro. But when creating a custom application, you want the user to have easier access to the macro, which is the reason that macros are typically attached to command buttons on forms.

All That in a Nutshell

Whether you're an absolute beginner or are accustomed to creating macros in other products, creating Access macros will probably take some getting used to. Here's a summary of the step-by-step instructions for creating a macro and assigning it to an event:

1. Click the Macros tab in the database window, and click New.

2. Choose an action from the Action column.

3. Fill in the required arguments for that action. You can create several actions within a single macro.

NOTE Remember that unlike some other products, such as Word or Excel, Access does not include a macro recorder to automate the process of defining macro actions.

4. Close and save the macro, giving it a name that will be easy to remember later.

5. Open in design view the form or report that you want to "trigger" the macro.

6. Select the control that will trigger the macro (or choose Edit ➢ Select Form, or Edit ➢ Select Report, if you want a form or report event to trigger the macro).

7. Open the property sheet and click the Event tab.

8. Click the specific event that you want to have trigger the macro, and then choose the macro name from the drop-down list that appears.

9. Close and save the form.

Once you've done all that, the macro will play every time you trigger the event to which you assigned the macro. The macro will not run (ever) in design view. You must open the form in form view or print the report, as a user would, in order to make the macro play its actions.

Summary of Macro Actions

Once you understand the mechanics of creating a macro and attaching it to some event, you still have to work through the mind-boggling stage of figuring out what you can and can't do with a macro. To help you sort through the overwhelming number of possibilities, here's a summary of every macro action that is available when you click the drop-down list in the Action column of the macro sheet.

AddMenu　Adds a menu to a custom menu bar (see Chapter 25).

ApplyFilter　Applies a filter, query, or SQL WHERE clause to a table, form, or report. Often used to filter records in the table underlying the form that launched the macro. You can use the ShowAllRecords action to clear the filter.

Beep　Just sounds a beep.

CancelEvent　Cancels the event that caused the macro to execute. For example, if a BeforeUpdate event calls a macro, that macro can test data and then execute a CancelEvent to prevent the form from accepting the new data.

Close　Closes the specified window. Typically used to close a form.

CopyObject　Copies the specified object to a different Access database, or to the same database but with a different name.

DeleteObject   Deletes the specified object, or the currently selected object in the database window if you don't specify an object.

Echo   Hides, or shows, on the screen, the results of each macro action as the macro is running.

FindNext   Repeats the previous FindRecord action to locate the next record that matches the same criterion.

FindRecord   Locates a record meeting the specified criterion in the current table (the table underlying the form that launched the macro).

GoToControl   Moves the focus (cursor) to the specified field or control on a form.

GoToPage   Moves the focus to the specified page in a multipage form.

GoToRecord   Moves the focus to a new record, in relation to the current record (for example, Next, Previous, First, Last, New).

Hourglass   Changes the mouse pointer to a "wait" hourglass (so the user knows to wait for the macro to finish its job).

Maximize   Expands the active (current) window to full-screen size.

Minimize   Shrinks the active (current) window to an icon.

MoveSize   Moves and/or sizes the active window to the position and measurement you specify in inches (or centimeters if you've defined that as your unit of measure in the Windows Control Panel).

MsgBox   Displays a message on the screen.

OpenDataAccessPage   Opens the data access page named in the macro arguments and moves to that page.

OpenDiagram   Opens an SQL diagram that's part of a project.

OpenForm   Opens the specified form and moves the focus to that form.

OpenModule   Opens, in design view, the specified Visual Basic module.

OpenQuery   Opens a Select, Crosstab, or action query. If you use this to run an action query, the screen will display the usual warning messages, unless you precede this action with a SetWarnings action.

OpenReport   Prints the specified report or opens it in print preview or design view. You can apply a filter condition with this action.

OpenTable   Opens the specified table in datasheet, design, or print preview view.

OpenView   Opens the specified SQL view in the open project.

OutputTo   Exports data in the specified object to HTML (.html), Microsoft Access Data Access Page (.htm), Microsoft ActiveX Server (.asp), Microsoft

Excel (.xls), Microsoft IIS (.htx; .idc), MS-DOS Text (.txt), or Rich Text (.rtf) format.

PrintOut   Prints the specified datasheet, form, report, or module.

Quit   Exits Microsoft Access.

Rename   Renames the specified or selected object.

RepaintObject   Performs any pending screen updates or calculations.

Requery   Forces the query underlying a specific control to be re-executed. If the specified control has no underlying query, this action will recalculate the control.

Restore   Restores a minimized or maximized window to its previous size.

RunApp   Starts another Windows or DOS program. That application then runs in the foreground, and the macro continues processing in the background.

RunCode   Runs the specified Visual Basic Function procedure. (To run a Sub procedure, create a function procedure that calls the Sub and have the macro run that function.)

RunCommand   Performs an Access menu command.

RunMacro   Runs a different macro. After that macro has finished its job, execution resumes in the original macro starting with the action following the RunMacro action.

RunSQL   Runs the specified SQL statement.

Save   Saves the specified object, or the active object if no other object is specified.

SelectObject   Selects the specified object. That is, this action mimics the act of clicking an object to select it.

SendKeys   Sends keystrokes to Access or another active program.

SendObject   Includes the specified database object in an e-mail message.

SetMenuItem   Sets the appearance of a command (for example, "grayed" or "checked" in a custom menu. See Chapter 25).

SetValue   Sets a value for a control, field, or property. Often used to automatically fill fields on a form, based on some existing data.

SetWarnings   Hides, or displays, all warning boxes such as those that appear when you run an action query.

ShowAllRecords   Removes an applied filter from the table, query, or form so that no records are hidden.

ShowToolBar   Shows or hides a built-in or custom toolbar (see Chapter 24).

StopAllMacros   Stops all running macros, turns Echo back on (if it was off), and reinstates warning messages.

StopMacro   Stops execution of the currently running macro.

TransferDatabase   Imports, exports, or links data in another database.

TransferSpreadsheet   Imports, exports, or links data from the specified spreadsheet.

TransferText   Imports, exports, or links data from a text file, and can also be used to export data to a Microsoft Word for Windows mail merge data file.

Keep in mind that you can get much more information about each action right on your screen. Just select the action and take a look at the hint box. If you need more information after reading the hint box, press Help (F1).

Executing a Macro Action "If..."

You can make any action, or series of actions, in a macro be conditional on some expressions. For example, suppose you want to create a macro that adds 7.75 percent sales tax to a total sale, but only if the sale is made in the state of California. That is, if the State field on the current form contains CA, then you want the macro to fill in another field, named SalesTaxRate, with 0.0775 and use that value in calculating the sales tax and total sale. To illustrate this concept, Figure 21.3 shows a sample form with the appropriate fields, named State, SubTotal, SalesTaxRate, SalesTax, and TotalSale.

FIGURE 21.3

A sample form containing fields named State, SubTotal, SalesTaxRate, SalesTax, and TotalSale.

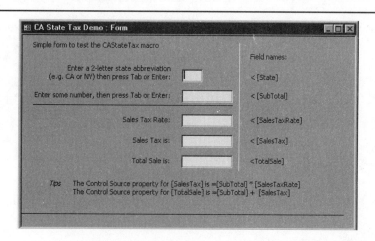

NOTE Remember that in order to name a field on a form, you need to open the form in design view. Then click the field you want to name, open the property sheet, and click the All tab. Then fill in the Name property with whatever name you want to give that field. While you're at it, you can use the Format property to assign a format, such as Currency or Percent, to fields that will contain numbers.

The last two fields on the form are calculated fields. The Control Source property for the SalesTax field contains the expression

    = [SalesTaxRate]*[SubTotal]

The Control Source property for the TotalSale field contains the expression

    = [SubTotal]+[SalesTax]

After you've created and saved the form, you can create the macro in the normal manner. But if you want to use conditions in the macro, you need to open the Condition column in the macro sheet. Just create (using New) or open (using Design) any macro sheet. Then click the Conditions button in the toolbar, or choose View ➤ Conditions from the menu bar. A new column titled Condition appears to the left of the existing columns, as in Figure 21.4.

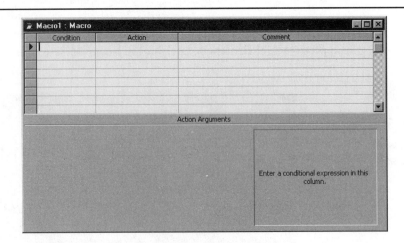

The condition you type in must be an expression that evaluates to either True or False, usually in the format *something = something*. For example, the expression

    [State] ="CA"

evaluates to True only if the field named State contains exactly the letters CA. If the field named State contains anything but CA (or is empty), the expression [State] ="CA" returns False.

NOTE As with other text comparisons in Access, macro conditions are not case-sensitive. So "ca" or "Ca" or "cA" would all match "CA" in this case.

An important point to remember is that the condition you specify affects only the action immediately to the right of the condition. If the expression proves True, the action is performed. If the expression proves False, the action is completely ignored. Either way, execution then resumes at the next action in the macro.

TIP You can repeat the condition in a row by typing three periods (...) into the condition cell immediately beneath the cell that contains the condition. The ... characters mean "apply the condition above to this action."

So let's create the CAStateTax macro now. For starters, we'll have the macro set the SalesTaxRate field to zero. Then, the next action will check to see if the State field contains CA. If that's True, that action will put 0.0775 into the SalesTaxRate field. The next actions will use the RepaintObject command to recalculate the calculated controls SalesTax and TotalSale. Figure 21.5 shows the completed macro.

FIGURE 21.5

The CAStateTax macro.

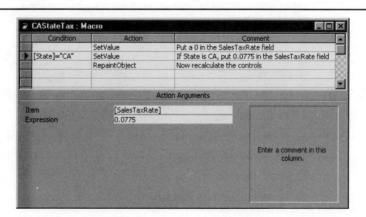

Since you can't see the action arguments for all three macro actions, we've listed them in Table 21.1 in the order in which they appear in the macro. (Leaving empty the action arguments for the RepaintObject action causes the entire object, the form in this example, to be recalculated.)

TABLE 21.1: CONDITION, ACTION, AND ACTION ARGUMENTS FOR CASTATETAX MACRO

CONDITION	ACTION	ACTION ARGUMENTS	
	SetValue	Item:	[SalesTaxRate]
		Expression:	0
[State]="CA"	SetValue	Item:	[SalesTaxRate]
		Expression:	0.0775
	RepaintObject		

After creating the macro, close and save it with whatever name you wish. In this example we've named the macro CAStateTax.

Finally, you need to decide *when* to call this macro into action. In this case we need the macro to recalculate the sales tax in two situations: after the user changes the value in the State field, and after the user changes the value in the SubTotal field.

So we open the form in design view, click the State field, open the property sheet, click the Event tab, and then assign the CAStateTax macro to the After Update property for that field, as below:

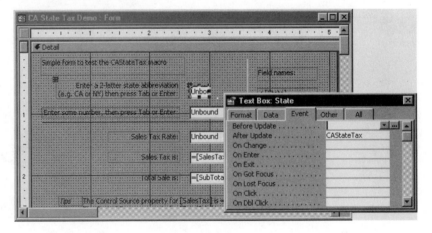

Then we click the SubTotal field and also set its After Update property to the CAStateTax macro.

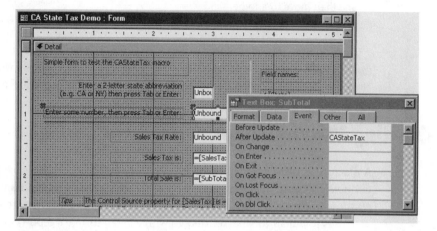

 TIP You can use Ctrl-click to select several controls, and then assign a macro to the same event on both controls at the same time.

Once those steps are complete, we can save the form and open it in form view. Then whenever we enter (or change) values in either the State or Subtotal fields (and press Tab or Enter to complete the entry), the SalesTaxRate, SalesTax, and TotalSale fields recalculate automatically. In the example shown in Figure 21.6, we entered CA in the State field and 100 in the Subtotal field. As you can see, the three fields beneath show the correct sales tax rate, sales tax amount, and total sale.

FIGURE 21.6

The macro and calculated controls automatically display the correct SalesTaxRate, SalesTax, and TotalSale.

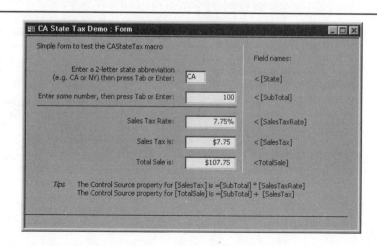

NOTE The After Update event is triggered only when you change the contents of a field and then move to another field.

Incidentally, the field names and tips that you see in Figure 21.6 are for your information only. They are just labels that have no effect on how the form functions. In "real life" you wouldn't have any reason to show that information to a user.

Creating Macro Groups

A macro sheet can actually contain several macros, each with its own macro name. Grouping several macros into a sheet can keep the list of macro names in the database window from becoming too lengthy and unwieldy. A good way to organize your macros is to put all the macros that go with a given form (or report) into a single macro sheet. That way, you can easily find all the macros that go with a particular form.

We often name our macro sheets for the form that triggers the macros in that sheet. For example, if we have a form named Customers, we might create a macro sheet named CustomerFormMacros that contains all the macros used by that form.

Creating a group of macros is a simple process. Just create or open a macro sheet in the usual manner. Then click the Macro Names button in the toolbar, or choose View ➤ Macro Names. A new column, titled Macro Name, appears to the left of the existing columns:

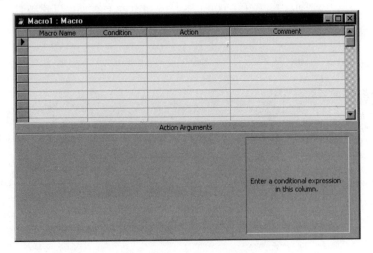

When adding a macro to the macro sheet, you need to type the macro name into the leftmost column. Then type in the first condition (if any), action, and comment in the usual manner. You can add as many actions to the macro as you wish.

Figure 21.7 shows an example of a macro sheet that contains five macros named AddNew, CalcTax, CloseAll, CloseForm, and PrintForm. Access stops running a macro when there are no more actions in the group or when it hits the name of another macro. We've added a blank line between each macro for readability.

FIGURE 21.7

A macro sheet containing five macros named AddNew, CalcTax, CloseAll, CloseForm, and PrintForm.

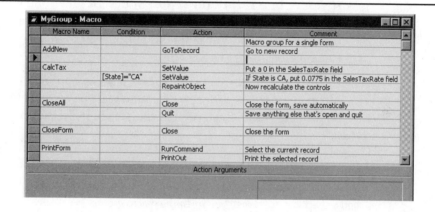

Close and save the macro sheet in the usual manner. For example, let's say you decide to name the entire macro sheet MyGroup. Then you can assign macros to events using the standard technique—that is, open the form or report that will trigger a macro in design view. Click the control that will trigger the macro (or choose Edit ➤ Select Form, or Edit ➤ Select Report). Open the property sheet, and click the drop-down list button for the event that you want to assign a macro to. The drop-down list now shows the names of all macros within all macro groups in the format MacroGroupName.MacroName.

For example, we're about to assign a macro to the On Click property of a control on a form. Notice that the drop-down list includes the names of all the macros within the macro group named MyGroup. To choose a specific macro to assign to this event, we just need to click the macro's name. The property sheet will show the macro group name and macro name in the MacroGroupName.MacroName format (for example, MyGroup.PrintForm).

Editing Macros

To edit an existing macro, you just need to reopen the macro sheet. Here's how:

- **If you're at the database window**, just click the Macros button, click the name of the macro (or macro group) you want to edit, and click the Design button. You can also right-click a macro's name and choose Design from the shortcut menu.

- **If you're in a form's (or report's) design view**, and want to edit a macro that you've already assigned to an event, just open the property sheet, click the Event tab, then click the Build (...) button next to the name of the macro that you want to edit.

When you use the latter method to open a macro group, you'll be taken to the macro group in general, not the specific macro that you assigned to the event. But once you're in the macro sheet, you can easily scroll to the macro that you want to edit.

 TIP   If you arrange macros in a macro group in alphabetical order by name, you can easily find a specific macro when you open the macro group.

Changing, Deleting, and Rearranging Macros

Once you're in the macro sheet, you can move, delete, and insert rows using techniques that are virtually identical to the techniques you use in a datasheet:

1. Select a row by clicking the row selector at the left edge of the row. Or select several rows by dragging the mouse pointer through row selectors, or by using Shift-click.

2. Do any of the following:

   - **To delete the selected row(s)**, press Delete, or right-click the selection and choose Delete Rows, or choose Edit ➤ Delete Rows from the menus.

   - **To insert a row**, press the Insert key, or right-click the selection and choose Insert Rows, or choose Insert ➤ Rows from the menu bar.

   - **To move the selected row(s)**, click the row selector again, hold down the mouse button, and drag the selection to its new position.

- **To copy the selection**, press Ctrl+C, click the Copy button, right-click the selection and choose Copy, or choose Edit ➤ Copy from the menu bar. The selection is copied to the Windows Clipboard. You can then use Edit ➤ Paste (Ctrl+V) to paste the copy into the same or another macro sheet.

- **To undo any of the above changes**, press Ctrl+Z, or click the Undo button, or choose Edit ➤ Undo.

Keep in mind that any changes you make to the macro are not saved until you save the entire macro. If you close the macro without saving it, be sure to choose Yes when asked about saving your changes.

Referring to Controls from Macros

One of the most common uses of macros is to use the SetValue action to fill in a field on a form. We used the SetValue action in an earlier example in this chapter to fill in a field named SalesTaxRate.

When you start to use macros in this way on multiple forms, you need to keep a couple of very important points in mind:

- When referring to a control on some form *other than the form that launched the macro*, you must use the full-identifier syntax of [Forms]![*FormName*]![*ControlName*] to refer to the control.

- Both forms must be open.

The way in which you refer to objects on forms can be one of the most confusing aspects of using macros, because if your macro opens a new form, you might think of that form as the "current form." But from Access's perspective, the form that *launched* the macro is the current form, even if that form does not have the focus at the moment. Let's look at a simple example to illustrate this situation.

Let's say you have a form named FormA. The form contains a text box control named OriginalText, as illustrated below.

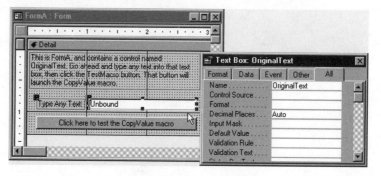

You also have a second form, named FormB, that contains a control named CopiedText, as shown below.

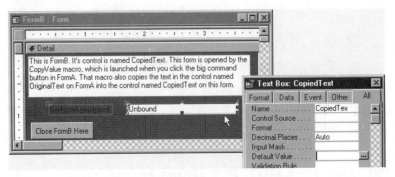

Let's say you want to create a macro that you'll launch from FormA. When you launch that macro, you want it to open FormB and take whatever text is in the OriginalText control on FormA and copy that text into the CopiedText control on FormB.

Figure 21.8 shows the appropriate macro (which we'll refer to as the CopyValue macro from here on out). Currently the cursor is in the SetValue action's cell, so you can see the action arguments for that action. Table 21.2 shows the action arguments for both actions (where we omit an action argument, we have left the argument blank in the macro sheet as well).

FIGURE 21.8

The CopyValue macro showing the action arguments for the SetValue action.

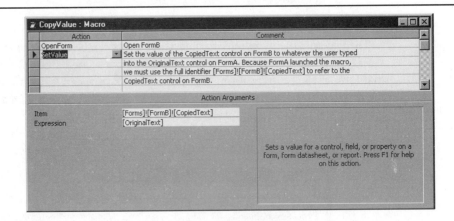

ACTION	ACTION ARGUMENTS	
OpenForm	Form Name:	FormB
	View:	Form
	Data Mode:	Edit
	Window Mode:	Normal
SetValue	Item:	[Forms]![FormB]![CopiedText]
	Expression:	[OriginalText]

TABLE 21.2: ACTION ARGUMENTS FOR THE COPYVALUE MACRO SHOWN IN FIGURE 21.8

Notice that we must refer to the CopiedText control using the full formal [Forms]![*FormName*]![*ControlName*], even though the OpenForm action has already opened FormB and FormB has the focus. We need to do so because FormA, not FormB, is the one that *launched* the macro. We can refer to the OriginalText control without all the formality because OriginalText is on the form that launched the macro.

On the other hand, you can always use the full, formal syntax. For example, we could have used these action arguments for the SetValue action, and the macro would still work just fine.

```
SetValue     Item:        [Forms]![FormB]![CopiedText]
             Expression:  [Forms]![FormA]![OriginalText]
```

Though a bit more cumbersome, this approach does have one advantage. Because we've referred to forms and controls specifically, we don't need to waste brain cells trying to keep track of which form opened the macro, which form has the focus at the moment, and so forth.

Typing Lengthy Identifiers

Typing those lengthy identifiers is a bit of a task, and they can be prone to typographical errors. But you need not type them by hand. You can use the expression builder instead. Just click the action argument you want to enter, and then click the Build (…) button that appears next to the control. For example, in Figure 21.9 we clicked the Item argument for the SetValue action and then clicked the Build button. Notice the Expression Builder.

FIGURE 21.9

The Expression Builder partially covering the macro sheet.

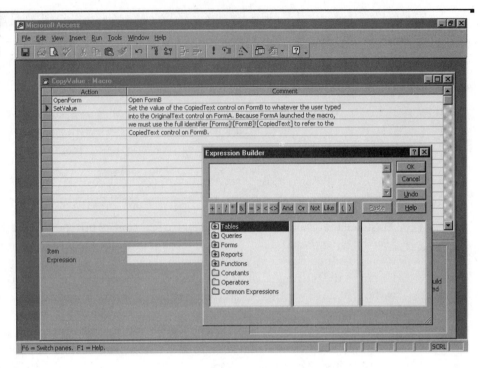

Now we can specify a control simply by working our way down to it. In this case we would double-click Forms (since the control is on a form) and then double-click All Forms. Then we would double-click FormB (since that's the one that contains the control we want to fill) and double-click CopiedText, the name of the control we want to fill. The top box in the Expression Builder now shows the proper expression for referring to the control (see Figure 21.10). When we click the OK button, that control is copied into the Item action argument.

FIGURE 21.10

Here we double-clicked Forms, All Forms, FormB, and CopiedText to build the expression Forms![FormB] !CopiedText].

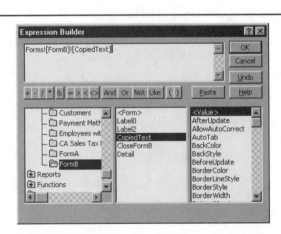

> **TIP** You can drag on the top or bottom border of the Expression Builder to increase the size of the boxes where it displays object names.

Assigning CopyValue to an Event

To get back to the macro shown in Figure 21.8, let's assume we save it with the name CopyValue and close it. Now we want that macro to play when the user clicks on the big command button on FormA.

To make that happen, we need to open FormA in design view, click the command button, open the property sheet, and click the Event tab. Then we can click the On Click property for that control and assign the CopyValue macro to that event, as shown below.

To test the macro, we then need to save FormA and close it (and close the FormB and CopyValue macros if they're open). Then open FormA, type in some text, and click the big command button. The macro will open FormB and copy whatever we typed into the FormA text box into the text box on FormB, as shown in Figure 21.11.

Making More "Generic" Macros

Here's another method for referring to forms and controls from within a macro. Rather than referring to a specific object, you can refer to "whatever object is current at the moment." The expressions you use are as follows:

```
[Screen].[ActiveForm]
[Screen].[ActiveReport]
[Screen].[ActiveControl]
[Screen].[ActiveDatasheet]
```

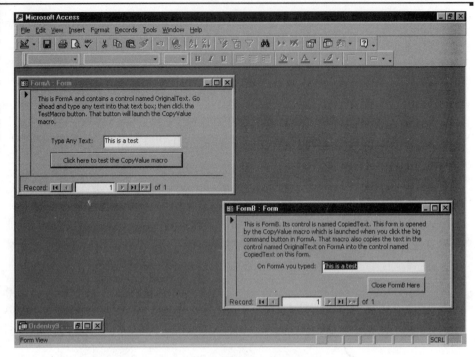

Let's look at another fairly simple example, using the [Screen].[ActiveControl] expression. First, let's say we have a form with three controls named FederalRate, StateRate, and CountyRate. The Format property of each control is set to Percent. (Below you can see the Format property for the FederalRate control.)

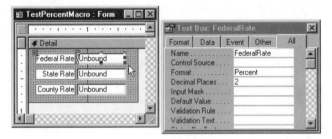

One of the problems with using the Percent format is that if the user types in a whole number, such as 30, the Percent format assumes 3000 percent rather than

30 percent. For example, you can see the results of typing in the values 30, 15, and 5 into this form in form view, below.

We decide to create a macro that says "If the user types in a number that's greater than or equal to one, divide that value by 100 to put it into percent format." To make things more interesting, we'll create a generic macro that will work with all three controls. That is, rather than create one macro for the FederalRate control, another for the StateRate control, and a third macro for the CountyRate control, we'll create a macro that refers to [Screen].[ActiveControl] that works with all three controls. Figure 21.12 shows such a macro, which we've named ConvertPercent. Notice that the macro has just one condition and one action.

FIGURE 21.12

The ConvertPercent macro uses [Screen].[ActiveControl] to refer to whatever control launched the macro.

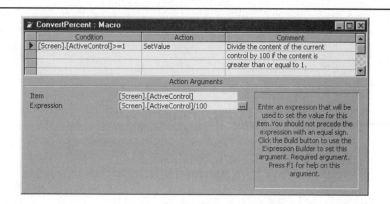

The condition

[Screen].[ActiveControl] > = 1

makes sure that the action is executed only if the content of the control is greater than or equal to one. The SetValue action arguments:

Item: [Screen].[ActiveControl]

Expression: [Screen].[ActiveControl]/100

take whatever number is currently in the value and replace it with that same value divided by 100.

Next we close and save the macro. Then we need to open the TestPercentMacro form in design view and set the BeforeUpdate event property of each control to the macro name, ConvertPercent in this example. Below, you can see we've set the `After Update` event for the FederalRate control to the macro name. We'd just need to do the same for the StateRate and CountyRate controls before closing this form.

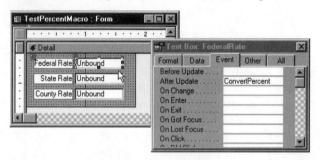

To actually test the macro, we need to go to form view. Nothing happens immediately because the `After Update` event occurs only after we type a new value into the control and move onto another control. In form view, let's say we again type **30** in the Federal Rate control, **15** into the State Rate control, and **5** into the County Rate control. The macro kicks in after each entry, giving the much better result shown below.

Dealing with Macro Errors

Everyone makes mistakes, especially when creating macros. As you know, when you run a macro, Access executes the first action in the macro, the second action (if any), the third, and so on, until it runs out of Action cells. However, if Access has a problem executing one of the actions in your macro, it stops the macro and displays an *error message* that suggests the nature of the problem. For example, while executing a macro, you might come up with a (somewhat obscure) message when Access hits a glitch.

After reading the message, you can click OK. You'll see the Action Failed dialog box showing you the specific action that caused the error, as in the example shown next.

This box provides the following information:

Macro Name   The name of the macro that contains the faulty action.

Condition   What the expression in the Condition column for the faulty line evaluated to (always True if the action has no condition).

Action Name   The specific action within this macro that caused the error.

Arguments   The arguments you assigned to this action.

To get rid of the error message box, you need to click the Halt button. If you then want to edit the offending macro, just open the macro's macro sheet in the usual manner. (That is, click the Macros button in the database window, click the name of the macro you want to edit, and click the Design button.) Once you get to the offending action of the appropriate macro, you're pretty much on your own in trying to figure out why the action didn't work. You may want to check the hint box or press F1 for more detailed information about the action so that you can determine the cause and come up with a solution.

TIP A common cause of macro errors is using faulty identifiers. For example, your macro might refer to a field named ZipCode that's not on the form that launched the macro. To fix this you might need to add the [Forms]![*FormName*]! prefix. Or perhaps your macro is referring to a control on a form that is no longer open when Access tries to execute the action.

 TIP Missing or extra spaces in field references are frequent causes of macro errors. Double-check your spaces if Access tells you an object cannot be found.

Single-Stepping through a Macro

When you run a macro, Access whizzes through all the actions in no time at all. If a particular macro is giving you a hard time, you can slow it down by running the macro in *single-step* mode, and watch the results of each action as Access performs them. To run a macro in single-step mode:

1. Open the macro's macro sheet. (Get to the database window, click the Macros button, click the name of the macro you want to run in single-step mode, and then click the Design button.)

 2. Click the Single Step button on the toolbar (shown at left), or choose Run ➤ Single-Step from the menu bar.

3. Close and save the macro normally.

4. Run the macro normally by causing whatever event triggers the macro.

This time, when you run the macro, Access will display the Macro Single Step window, shown below, just before it executes each action.

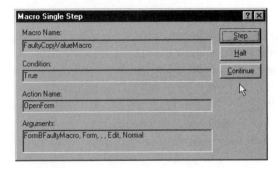

After observing the details of the action that's about to be played, you can use the command buttons to decide what you want to do next:

Step   Executes the action whose details are currently displayed in the Macro Single Step dialog box.

Halt   Stops the macro and closes the Macro Single Step dialog box.

Continue   Turns off the Single Step mode and runs the rest of the macro normally.

Creating a Macro to Run at Startup

As you may know, you can use the Tools ➢ Startup commands on Access's main menu to specify how you want your application to look when the user first opens the database. (Those menu commands are available whenever the database window is displayed.) In addition, you can also have a macro perform tasks automatically when the user first opens your database. All you need to do is create a normal macro and name it AutoExec.

The AutoExec macro runs after the options you defined in the Startup dialog box have been put into effect; you want to make sure to take that into consideration when creating your AutoExec macro. For example, if you've cleared the Display Database Window option in the Startup dialog, your AutoExec macro doesn't have to hide the database window, since it will already be hidden.

You can bypass the startup options and the AutoExec macro by holding down the Shift key as your database is opening. If you are developing applications, you should keep this technique in mind, because sometimes you might want to open your database from the user's perspective.

 TIP   You can also press the F11 key to make the database window appear on the screen, unless you've turned off the Use Access Special Keys option under Tools ➢ Startup or used the /runtime switch when launching Access.

At other times, you might want to go straight to the database window and standard toolbars so you can make changes to your application. To achieve the latter, just keep that Shift key depressed from the time you choose File ➢ Open until the database window appears on the screen.

Learning by Example

In this chapter, we've covered the mechanics of creating macros and assigning them to events. You'll find many practical real-world examples of macros in the chapters that follow. Exploring macros in other peoples' applications is also a good way to round out your knowledge of macros. For example, the sample Northwind database that comes with your Access programs, as well as some of the applications on the CD that comes with this book, contain several examples of macros.

To view the macros in an application, just open the database normally and get to the database window. In the database window, click the Macros button. Then click any macro name and click Design to explore the macro's contents.

In some applications, you might be surprised to see very few macros, or even no macros at all. A very sophisticated Access application might have very few macros associated with it for three reasons:

- The control wizards create Visual Basic code, not macros, to automate the controls you create.

- Many Access developers prefer Visual Basic code to macros because they are already familiar with Visual Basic.

- Many application developers will use the built-in macro converter to convert their macros to Visual Basic code, and then delete the original macro.

 MASTERING THE OPPORTUNITIES

Converting Macros to Visual Basic

Once you've created some macros and have them working properly, it's easy to convert them to Visual Basic code. To convert all the macros in a given form or report to code, first open the form or report in design view. Then choose Tools ➢ Macro ➢ Convert Form's Macros to Visual Basic (or Convert Report's Macros to Visual Basic if you're working with a report.)

If a particular set of macros isn't associated with a specific form (such as an AutoExec macro), you use a different technique to convert the macro. In design view, open the macro you want to convert. Then choose File ➢ Save As. When the Save As dialog box opens, change the As setting to Module, optionally change the name in the top box, and click OK. Then click the Convert button in the next window that opens, and click OK when the job is done. A Visual Basic window will open at this point. To return to the Macro window, click the Close button in the Visual Basic window.

You can find the Visual Basic version of the macro in the Modules tab of the database window. It will be named *Converted Macro–name* where *name* is the name of the original macro.

Where to Go from Here

From here you can focus on different aspects of creating a custom application or learning about Visual Basic:

- To learn about creating custom switchboards and dialog boxes for your application, see Chapters 22 and 23.

- To learn how to create custom toolbars and menus for your application, see Chapters 24 and 25.

- To learn about Visual Basic, that "other way" to create custom actions, turn to Chapter 26.

What's New in the Access Zoo?

Access 2000 has some new macro actions for working with data access pages and projects: OpenDataAccessPage, OpenDiagram, and OpenView. The OutputTo action has a new option for sending data to data access page format, and the text file options have been renamed.

CHAPTER <u>22</u>

Creating Custom Switchboards

A switchboard is a fancy term for a form that lets the user move around in your application. When you use the Access Database Wizard to create a database application, the Wizard creates a switchboard automatically. In this chapter we're going to look at techniques for customizing the switchboard that the Wizard creates. We'll also look at techniques for creating your own completely custom switchboards with whatever appearance you like.

Changing a Wizard-Created Switchboard

As you know, when you use a wizard to create a database, the wizard automatically creates a switchboard for that database. For example, when you use the Order Entry Wizard to create a database, that Wizard creates the switchboard shown in Figure 22.1.

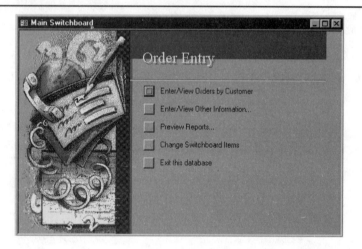

The switchboard appears automatically when you first open the database. If you happen to be at the database window, rather than at the switchboard, you can just click the Forms button, click the form called Switchboard, and then click the Open button to open the switchboard.

Changing Wizard-Created Switchboard Options

If you look at all the options on the Order Entry switchboard (see Figure 22.1), you'll see that one option actually lets you change the switchboard itself (the fourth option down in this example). When you choose that option, you're taken to the Switchboard Manager dialog box, which will look something like Figure 22.2 (depending on the database you're using at the moment).

FIGURE 22.2

The Switchboard Manager lets you make changes to any switchboard in the current database. This database contains three switchboards.

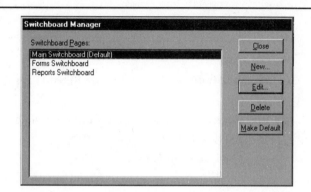

The command buttons on the Switchboard Manager are fairly self-explanatory.

Close   Click Close after you've finished exploring or modifying switchboards.

New   Creates a new, blank switchboard with whatever name you specify. To add options to that newly created switchboard, click its name and then click the Edit button. You'll be taken to the Edit Switchboard Page dialog box described in the next section.

Edit   To change an existing switchboard, click its name and then click the Edit button. You'll be taken to the Edit Switchboard Page dialog box described in the next section.

Delete   To delete a switchboard, click its name and then click the Delete button.

Make Default   Makes the currently selected switchboard the *default* switchboard (the one that appears automatically when the user first opens the database).

Defining and Changing Switchboard Items

When you choose the Edit button from the Switchboard Manager, you're taken to the Edit Switchboard Page dialog box. If you are working with a new switchboard, the list under Items on This Switchboard is blank. You can use the New button to create new items. When you edit an existing switchboard, the items on that switchboard are listed under Items on This Switchboard, as in Figure 22.3.

The Edit Switchboard Page dialog box lets you add, change, and delete individual options on the currently selected switchboard.

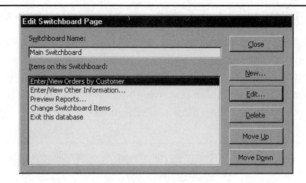

The command buttons in the Edit Switchboard Page dialog box are also self-explanatory.

Close   Click this button to return to the Switchboard Manager dialog box when you've finished making changes.

New   Add a new item to this switchboard.

Edit   Change the currently selected switchboard item.

Delete   Delete the currently selected switchboard item.

Move Up   Move the currently selected switchboard item up in the list.

Move Down   Move the currently selected switchboard item down in the list.

When you select a switchboard item and click Edit, you're taken to the small Edit Switchboard Item dialog box, as in the example shown below.

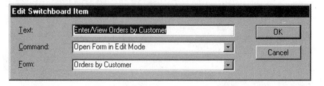

This dialog box is where you define how the item looks on the switchboard and what happens when the user selects that item. In the example shown, the Text that actually appears on the switchboard is "Enter/View Orders by Customer." To change that text, just click anywhere in the text and make your changes using standard editing techniques.

The Command box describes what will happen when the user selects the item. In the example, when the user chooses the Enter/View Orders by Customer switchboard option, the action that occurs is "Open Form in Edit Mode." But you can change that action, if you wish, simply by choosing a new option from the Command drop-down list. As you can see below, you have quite a few options for defining what happens when the user chooses the item.

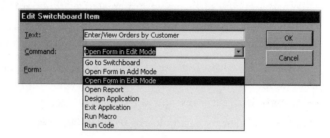

The last option in the Edit Switchboard Item dialog box lets you choose a specific object for the Command to act upon. For example, when the Command is Open Form in Edit Mode, the last option is titled Form, and you can select a specific form for the item to open, as shown below.

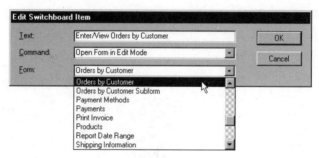

If, on the other hand, the Command box contained the action Open Report, the last option would be titled Report, and you could choose a specific report for the command to open.

After making changes to a wizard-created switchboard, you need to get back to form view to see and test the effects of your changes. Click OK and Close, as appropriate, to work your way back to the database window. If you really want to see how things will look to a person opening the database for the first time, you can close and then reopen the database. To do so, choose File ➢ Close from the Access menu bar, and from the File menu, select the name of the database you just closed.

Changing Wizard-Selected Art

When you use a database wizard to create a database, you're also given the option of adding a picture to the database's switchboards. You can change that picture after the fact, if you wish, using any bitmap image on your hard disk. You can use an existing clip art image, a bitmap image you created yourself, or an image you digitized using a scanner.

To change the picture on a wizard-created switchboard, follow these steps:

1. Open the database in the usual manner with Access's File ➤ Open menu commands.

2. Click the Close button in the upper-right corner of the switchboard, if the switchboard is currently open. Get to the database window (if it's hidden or minimized, just press the F11 key).

3. Click the Forms button in the database window.

4. Click the switchboard form name, and then click the Design button.

5. Click the picture that you want to change.

6. Open the property sheet if it is closed. (Click the Properties toolbar button, or choose View ➤ Properties.)

7. Click the All tab, and scroll to the top of the property sheet. You should see the control named Picture, as in Figure 22.4.

FIGURE 22.4

Properties for the control named Picture in a wizard-created switchboard.

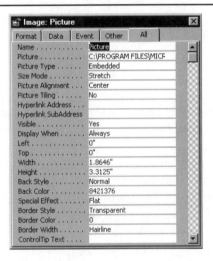

The second property in the property sheet is titled Picture, and it shows the location and name of the picture that's currently displayed in the switchboard.

8. Click Picture and then click the Build button. The Insert Picture dialog box appears, as in Figure 22.5 (though your Insert Picture dialog box might initially show the contents of some folder other than the one named Dbwiz).

9. Browse to the file that contains the picture that you want to display in your switchboard, and click OK.

The picture you chose will replace the one that's currently in your switchboard, and it will be stretched to fit the picture's container. You can use the Size Mode property to change the picture's sizing mode to Clip or Zoom and see which mode works best.

 TIP   You can borrow the graphics used by the Database Wizard for the switchboards it creates. You'll find them in `C:\Program Files\Microsoft Office\Office\Bitmaps\Dbwiz`.

10. Save the switchboard with the new picture and size mode: choose File ➢ Close, and click Yes when asked if you want to save your changes.

To see the results of the change, reopen the switchboard in form view. Or if you want to be sure to view the switchboard from the user's perspective, close the entire database (File ➤ Close). Then reopen the entire database by pulling down the File menu and selecting the name of the database you just closed.

Note that the picture you chose will appear on all the database's switchboards. The reason is that the database wizards actually create only one switchboard per database. When you're using that database, you might *think* you are going from one switchboard to another from time to time, but in fact, your database is just changing the title of, and items on, that one switchboard.

Creating a Switchboard from Scratch

As you know, using database wizards isn't the only way to create a database application. You can create all your tables, queries, forms, reports, and macros from scratch. Likewise, you can create custom switchboards for your application, completely from scratch.

To create a custom switchboard, first create a blank form that isn't bound to any table. To make it look like a switchboard rather than a bound form, you can hide the navigation buttons, record selectors, and other doodads that normally appear on bound forms. Then you can add hyperlinks, controls (such as command buttons), and macros to make the controls on the switchboard do whatever you want them to do. We'll take it step by step.

Creating the Blank Switchboard Form

The basic idea behind a switchboard is to provide a form that helps the user of your application do any of a variety of tasks, such as navigating from one form to another or printing reports. So typically you'd create tables, queries, forms, and reports for your application before you work on the custom switchboards. Then, within that same database, you'd follow these steps to create a new, blank switchboard form:

1. Click the Forms button in the database window.

2. Double-click Create Form in Design View. A new empty form opens in design view. The first thing you'll want to do is set some properties for it.

3. Click the Properties toolbar button (if the property sheet isn't open) or choose View ➤ Properties from the menu bar.

4. Choose Edit ➤ Select Form from the menu bar or click in the box where the rulers meet. You want to be sure the entire form is selected as the current object because you're about to set form properties.

5. Click the Format tab in the property sheet, and then set the first few Format properties as indicated below and shown in Figure 22.6. (Properties that are marked with an asterisk below are suggestions only. You might want to experiment with those properties when creating your own switchboards.)

FIGURE 22.6

Suggested Form properties for a custom switchboard.

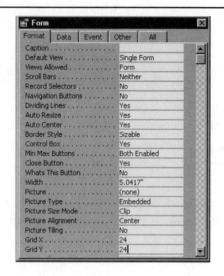

Default View:	Single Form
Views Allowed:	Form
Scroll Bars:	Neither*
Record Selectors:	No
Navigation Buttons:	No
Auto Resize:	Yes*
Auto Center:	Yes

TIP   Remember that you can get more information about a property right on your screen. Just click the property you're interested in and press Help (F1).

6. (Optional) Fill in the Caption property with whatever text you want to appear in the title bar of the custom form.

7. Click the Detail band within the form if you want to color the form. Then choose a color from the Fill/Back Color button on the Formatting toolbar. If that toolbar isn't visible, choose View ➤ Toolbars and click Formatting (Form/Report).

8. At this point you may want to size and shape the form to approximately the size you want the switchboard to be. Drag the lower-right corner of the shaded area within the form design window to size the switchboard.

9. You can save and name the form now. Choose File ➤ Close, choose Yes when asked about saving the form, enter the name you want to give the form (Main Switchboard, for example), and click OK.

The switchboard form is listed in the database window, in the Forms tab, just like all your other forms. You can treat it as you would any other form:

- **To see and use the form from the user's perspective**, click the form name and then click the Open button. (At this point, our sample form is completely blank.)

- **To make changes to the form**, open it in design view. (Click the form name in the database window and then click the Design button.)

 TIP Once the form is open, you can easily switch between form view and design view by clicking the appropriate View button in the toolbar or by choosing either Form View or Design View from the View menu in the menu bar.

Adding Controls to Your Custom Switchboard

Currently our switchboard is empty. We need to add some hyperlinks or controls to allow the user to choose actions. As with all types of forms, you create controls using the toolbox in form design view. You can create any control you wish, but chances are you'll want to create mostly hyperlinks and command buttons.

As you may recall from earlier chapters, you can use the Insert Hyperlink button on the toolbar to add a hyperlink to a form. If you need a control like a command button instead, use a control wizard to create a control and action in one fell swoop.

When creating controls on a switchboard, the decision on whether or not to use the control wizards centers around three factors:

- **If the control will perform a single action**, such as opening a form, and that form already exists, then you can use the Control Wizard. (You may prefer to use a hyperlink for opening a form or report for the performance reasons outlined in Chapter 16.)

- **If the control will open a form (or report) that you have not yet created**, you can create the control without using the Control Wizard. Later, after you've created the form or report that the control will act upon, you can go back to the switchboard and assign an action to the control.

- **If the control will perform two or more actions**, then you'll need to define the control's action using a macro (or Visual Basic code). You can create the control without the Control Wizard. Then later create the macro and assign that macro to the control on the switchboard.

The last alternative is perhaps the most common when creating switchboard controls because typically you want the control to perform two actions: open some other form or report, and then close the switchboard itself. Let's work through an example using that last approach.

 TIP Here's a quick way to create a command button and assign a macro to it. First create the macro, and then just drag and drop the macro name on to the form (in design view). You'll get a command button whose On Click property launches the dropped macro!

Let's say we want to create a command button on our switchboard that will open a form named AddressBook and then close the switchboard. For this example, we'll also assume that we previously created the form named AddressBook and that it exists in the current database.

1. Open the switchboard in design view.

2. Click the Toolbox toolbar button (if closed), or choose View ➤ Toolbox.

3. Make sure the Control Wizards button in the toolbox is *not* pushed in, because we don't want to use the Control Wizard in this example.

4. Click the Command Button button in the toolbox, and then click at the position where the button should appear in the switchboard. In Figure 22.7 you can see we've created a button, which is (tentatively) captioned Command0.

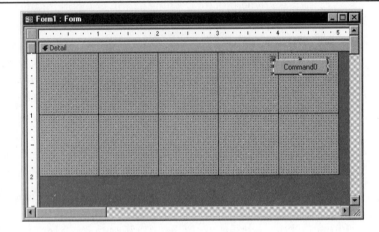

Though it's not absolutely necessary to do so, we could close the Main Switchboard form now, just to get it out of the way, by choosing File ➤ Close and then clicking Yes when asked to save changes.

Creating a Macro for the New Control

Next we need to create a macro that will open the AddressBook form and close the Main Switchboard form.

1. Click the Macros button in the database window.

2. Click the New button. A new blank macro sheet opens. We'll probably want to put all the macros for the Main Switchboard into this macro sheet.

3. Open the Macro Name column. (Click the Macro Names toolbar button.) Or choose View ➤ Macro Names from the menu bar.

4. Type a name for this macro, such as OpenAddressBook, in the Macro Name column.

5. Choose the OpenForm action in the Action column to the right.

6. Specify the name of the form you want to open in the Action Arguments (AddressBook in this example). Figure 22.8 shows how the macro sheet would look at this point.

FIGURE 22.8

*The first action for the
OpenAddressBook
macro defined in the
macro sheet.*

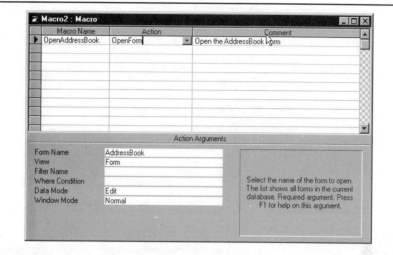

7. Create a second action to close the Main Switchboard by choosing the Close
action in the next Action cell down.

8. Complete the action arguments as shown in Figure 22.9.

FIGURE 22.9

*The second action in
the OpenAddressBook
macro closes the Main
Switchboard form.*

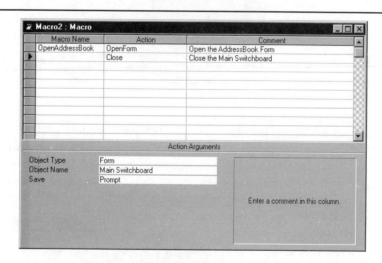

9. Close the macro sheet and give it a name. In this example we would choose File ➢
Close, click Yes when asked about saving the macro, give it a name such as
MainSwitchboardMacros, and then click OK.

Finally we need to assign that new macro to the On Click property of the button we created on the switchboard. While we're at it, we can change the caption on the button. Here are the steps:

1. Click the Forms button in the database window.

2. Click Main Switchboard, and then click the Design button.

3. Click the button to which we want to assign the macro (the button titled Command0 in this example).

4. Open the property sheet and click the Event tab.

5. Choose the On Click property, and choose the name of the macro you want this button to launch. In this example we want to choose the MainSwitchboard-Macros.OpenAddressBook macro (see Figure 22.10).

FIGURE 22.10

Assigning the MainSwitchboard-Macros.OpenAddress-Book macro to the On Click property of a button on the Main Switchboard form.

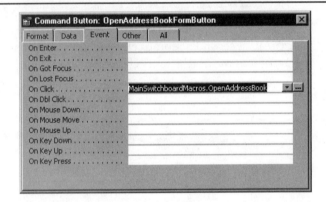

6. Change the caption on the command button: click the Format tab in the property sheet, and then type in a caption such as **&Address Book** (which will appear on the button as Address Book, with the *A* underlined as a shortcut key).

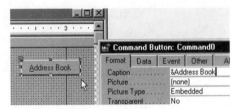

7. Close and save the Main Switchboard form.

To test your new control and action, open the Main Switchboard in form view. Then click the Address Book button. The macro will open the AddressBook form and close the switchboard, as in Figure 22.11.

PART

IV

Building a Custom Application

FIGURE 22.11

Clicking the Address Book button in the Main Switchboard opens this form and closes the switchboard.

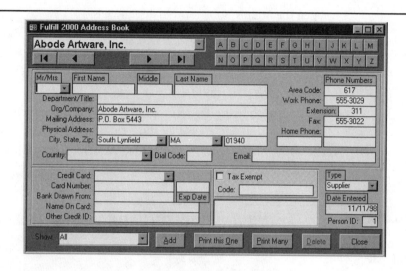

We realize we haven't mentioned anything about the AddressBook form prior to this chapter. But our goal here is to show you how to make a switchboard button open one form and close its own form. In Chapter 28 and in Appendix C, we'll talk more about the AddressBook form and the Fulfill application.

Making AddressBook Return to the Main Switchboard

In this particular application, clicking the Address Book button in the Main Switchboard sends users to a form named AddressBook. It stands to reason that, when users close the AddressBook form, they would expect to be returned to the Main Switchboard.

We could make a button on the AddressBook form that closes the AddressBook and then opens the Main Switchboard again. But there's just one problem. Suppose the user closes the AddressBook form by clicking the Close button in the top-right corner of the form's window or by choosing File ➤ Close from the menu bar. Neither task would trigger the action to open the Main Switchboard. So here's what we need to do:

- Create a Close button that, when clicked, closes the AddressBook form.

- Go to the property sheet for the AddressBook form as a whole, and create an action that opens the Main Switchboard form. If we attach that action to the On

Close property of the AddressBook form, it doesn't matter how the user exits the form—he or she will still be returned to the Main Switchboard form.

We'll create the Close button on the AddressBook form first. Since we want this button to do one simple act, we can use the Control Wizard to define the control and action in one fell swoop.

1. Open the AddressBook form in design view.

2. Open the toolbox if it isn't already open. (Click the Toolbox toolbar button, or choose View ➤ Toolbox.)

3. Make sure the Control Wizard button in the toolbox is pushed in, because we can use its help in this case.

4. Click the Command Button tool in the toolbox; then click the spot where the Close button should appear on the form (the lower-right corner in this example).

5. Choose Form Operations and Close Form when the Command Button Wizard appears, as shown in Figure 22.12.

FIGURE 22.12

The new button we're adding to the Address Book form will close the form.

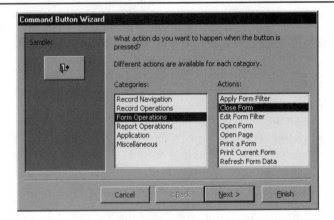

---

6. Click Next on the Command Button Wizard dialog box, and the next screen will ask about the appearance of the button. In this example we chose to have the button show the text &Close (see Figure 22.13; once again, the & symbol is used to specify the underlined hotkey).

FIGURE 22.13

The Close button on the AddressBook form will be captioned Close.

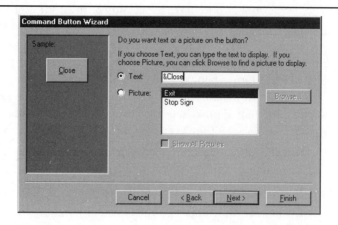

Clicking Next takes us to the Wizard window in which we can name the button. This is the name used within Access, not the text caption that appears on the button. We could name the button anything we want. In this example we named it Close-AddressBookForm and then clicked the Finish button.

When the Command Button Wizard is done, we're returned to our form, where we can see the new button. We can use the standard techniques for moving and sizing controls to position the button precisely. In the figure below, we've opted to put the button near the lower-right corner of the form.

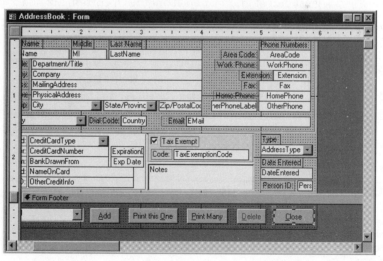

Now we still need to make the closing of the AddressBook form automatically reopen the Main Switchboard form. Keep in mind that the user will probably have several means of closing that form—not just our new Close button. So we need to find a way of saying, "No matter how the user closes this form, open the Main Switchboard form again."

We could create a macro that opens the Main Switchboard form, but let's try a slightly different approach, using a bit of Visual Basic. How do we write a Visual Basic procedure to open a form? Let's ask the Answer Wizard:

1. If the Office Assistant isn't visible, choose Help ➤ Microsoft Access Help from the menu.

2. Type **open form** in the Office Assistant text box and press Enter.

3. Click See More and then the OpenForm Action topic.

4. When the Help window for OpenForm Action opens, click See Also.

In the Topics Found window, select OpenForm Method and click Display.

 TIP An *action* generally refers to macros, whereas a *method* generally refers to Visual Basic code. We chose OpenForm Method in step 3 because we want to check out the Visual Basic approach to doing this.

A great deal of information about the OpenForm Method appears, but we mainly need to know the syntax. In this case the syntax is

```
DoCmd.OpenForm formname
```

followed by some optional arguments enclosed in square brackets. When we click the Example option, we see that the name of the form to open needs to be enclosed in quotation marks. To make life easy, we can just copy the example code from the Help screen right into our property sheet. To do that we just drag the cursor through the part we want to copy, as in Figure 22.14, and then press Ctrl+C to copy that selection to the Windows Clipboard.

FIGURE 22.14

An Example of using Visual Basic to open a form. We've selected the part we want to copy to our form.

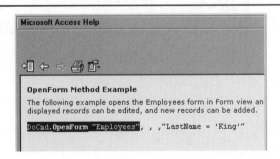

Now we can close the Help screens until we get back to the AddressBook form, which is still in design view. Now here's how we make the act of closing this form automatically open the Main Switchboard form. With the AddressBook form on the screen in design view:

1. Choose Edit ➤ Select Form, because we want to work with the form properties as a whole (not properties of individual controls).

2. Open the property sheet and click the Event tab.

3. Click the On Close property. When the Build(...) button appears at the end of the line, click it. A Choose Builder dialog box appears with these options:

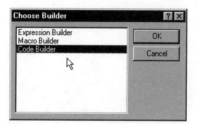

 TIP Remember, you can use either Visual Basic or macros to define many actions. Here we've used Visual Basic just because it's quick and easy to do so in this example. Chapter 26 introduces Visual Basic.

4. We're going to try our hand at some Visual Basic (VB) code, so click Code Builder and then click OK. The Microsoft Access window will disappear, and a Visual Basic window will appear in its place. Inside the VB window, a Code window pops up that already contains a couple of lines of Visual Basic code, `Private Sub Form_Close()` and `End Sub`. Any code we want to add must go between those two lines.

5. Put the cursor between the two existing lines of code, and then press Ctrl+V to add the line of code copied from the help window, earlier. Initially, the pasted text looks like the following.

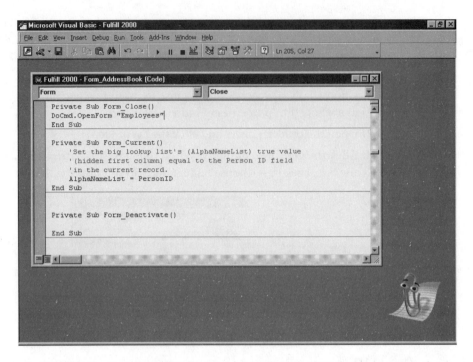

6. Change the form name in the code, as below, so that the code opens the form named Main Switchboard, not the form named Employees. (You can also press Home to move the cursor to the start of the line, and then press Tab to indent the line. Indenting the lines between the Private Sub and End Sub commands is a standard practice.)

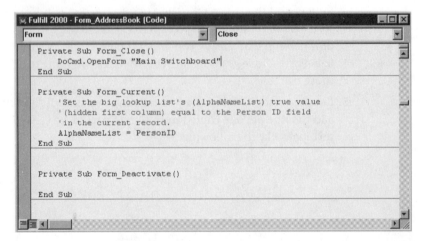

7. Choose Debug ➢ Compile to *compile* the code quickly and check for gross errors in the Visual Basic command. If you did everything correctly, you won't see any error messages.

8. Close the Visual Basic window by clicking its Close button, or by choosing File ➢ Close and Return to Microsoft Access from the Visual Basic menu bar. The property sheet now shows [Event Procedure] next to the On Close property, indicating that we've assigned a Visual Basic procedure to this event.

9. Close and save the AddressBook form.

To test the effects of all this, we can now open the Main Switchboard form in form view. When we click the Address Book button in that switchboard, the Address Book form should open and the Main Switchboard form should disappear. When we close the AddressBook form, that form should disappear and the Main Switchboard form should reopen.

Filling Out the Switchboard

We can continue work with the Main Switchboard form, adding whatever controls we think will be useful later down the road. We can also use the Label and Rectangle tools in the Toolbox to add some labels and boxes. The Back Color, Border Color, Border Width, and Special Effects buttons on the Formatting (Form/Report) toolbar can help make these embellishments even fancier.

 TIP If you create a rectangle around a group of buttons, and the rectangle ends up *covering* the buttons, don't panic. Just select (click) the rectangle and choose Format ➢ Send to Back from the form design screen's menu bar.

The Main Switchboard example we're showing you in this chapter was actually the starting point for a real application, named Fulfill 2000, that's on the CD-ROM that came with this book. As you'll see when you try that application, we've embellished the Main Switchboard.

For example, we added a light yellow rectangle behind the command buttons, and a label (Focus On) to the upper-left corner of that rectangle. We also added a large white rectangle as a placeholder for Fulfill's logo, which we'll create and add later. Figure 22.15 shows the Main Switchboard, in form view, at this stage of Fulfill's development.

FIGURE 22.15

The sample Fulfill
application's Main
Switchboard, in form
view, under
construction.

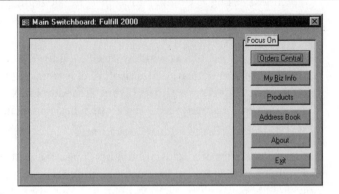

 NOTE When you explore the Fulfill application, you'll no doubt recognize that its Main Switchboard and other forms have evolved from what's shown here.

You can start exploring Fulfill at any time by copying it from the CD and opening it up in Access 2000. (If you get a message that the database cannot be opened because it is read-only, open the Explorer window. Navigate to Fulfill.mdb and select it. Then choose Properties from the File menu and uncheck the Read-Only attribute. Appendices B and C will help you.) Chapter 29 discusses ways of exploring Fulfill (and other custom Access applications) so you can start learning "by example" how all the pieces are put together in an Access custom database application.

Making a Switchboard Appear at Startup

If you create a custom switchboard for your application, and want it to appear automatically when the user first opens the database, set the Display Form option in Startup to the name of your switchboard. Here are the exact steps to follow:

1. Close any open forms to get to the database window.
2. Choose Tools ➢ Startup from the menu bar.
3. Choose the name of your main switchboard from the drop-down list box next to Display Form, as shown in Figure 22.16.

FIGURE 22.16

*The form named Main
Switchboard is the first
to appear when the
database opens.*

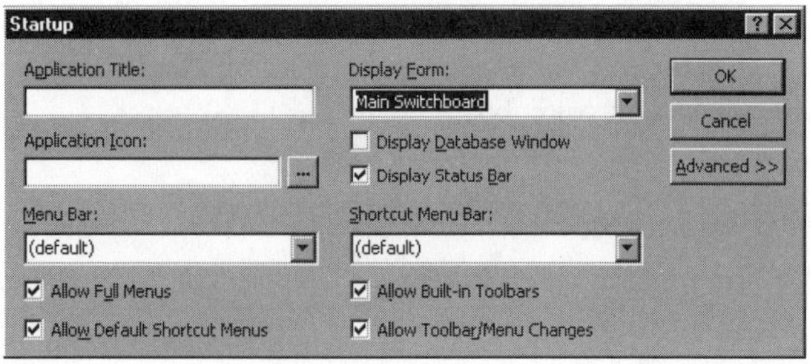

4. Click OK.

You can leave all the other settings as they appear in the Startup dialog box until you're further along in the development process. (We'll have more on those options in Chapter 29.) The next time you open the database, your custom switchboard will appear on the screen automatically.

Wizard-Created versus Custom Switchboards

If you've read this entire chapter, you may be confused by the vast differences between wizard-created switchboards and totally custom switchboards. Let's take a moment here to review the primary differences so you don't leave this chapter feeling confused on this topic.

Summary: Wizard-Created Switchboards

When you use a database wizard to create a database application, keep in mind the following points about the switchboard(s):

- To change items on a wizard-created switchboard, open the switchboard in *form view* and use the Change Switchboard Items option to make your changes.

- You can make design changes to the wizard-created switchboard by opening that switchboard in design view. However, any changes you make will affect all the switchboards in that database application.

- The reason that changes to one switchboard affect all switchboards in that database is that the Database Wizard really only creates one switchboard per database application. It just changes the items on that one switchboard, automatically, when you choose an item that takes you to a (seemingly) different switchboard.

- You can make a wizard-created database open with a different, custom switchboard of your own design. Just create your custom switchboard, and then choose Tools ➤ Startup. Under Display Form enter the form name of your new custom switchboard.

Summary: Custom Switchboards

When you don't use a database wizard to create a database, keep in mind the following points:

- Initially, your database application will have no switchboards at all.
- You create a switchboard by creating a new form that's not bound to any table or query.
- To ensure that the switchboard form doesn't look like a data-entry form, turn off the form's record selectors, navigation buttons, scroll bars, datasheet view, and so forth by selecting the entire form in form view, and making appropriate changes to the property sheet.
- You need to add your own controls (command buttons) to a custom switchboard, using the toolbox in form design view. You can also use hyperlinks for some simple actions, such as opening forms and reports.
- To make a switchboard appear automatically at startup, choose Tools ➤ Startup and set the Display Form option to the name of your switchboard.

Where to Go from Here

Next we'll look at ways of creating custom dialog boxes from scratch. As you'll see, the basic starting point is the same as it is for creating a custom switchboard. You create a form that's not bound to any table or query. Then you add appropriate controls and actions using the toolbox in the form design view.

If you prefer, you can explore other topics related to building custom applications:

- To view the Fulfill 2000 application's final custom switchboards, see Appendix C.
- To take a look at some custom switchboards in other sample applications, see Chapter 29 for some tips.
- To learn how to create custom toolbars and menus for your application, see Chapters 24 and 25.
- To learn about Visual Basic, see Chapter 26.

What's New in the Access Zoo?

Switchboards work the same in Access 2000 as they did in Access 97. Access will create switchboards for you when you use the Database Wizard to create an application. Or, you can start with an empty form that has no table or query bound to it and create a switchboard on your own.

CHAPTER 23

Creating Custom Dialog Boxes

As a Windows user, you've probably seen hundreds of dialog boxes. A dialog box is a window that pops up on the screen to give you information or to ask questions about what you want to do next. You make your selections from the box and then click OK to proceed. Or in some cases, you can click a Cancel button to back out of the dialog box gracefully without making any selections.

You can create your own custom dialog boxes in your Access applications. The procedure is similar to creating a switchboard: start off with a blank, unbound form, add some controls, and develop some macros or Visual Basic code to specify what happens when the user selects a control. You can also add some finishing touches, such as OK and Cancel buttons and a special border. In this chapter we'll look at all the factors involved by creating a sample dialog box for a sample database.

 NOTE The database used for the examples in this chapter, Chapter 23.mdb, is included on the CD in the back of the book.

Our Goal

We start with a database with a simple name and address table in it. We've also created a Mailing List form for entering and editing data in that table, as shown in Figure 23.1.

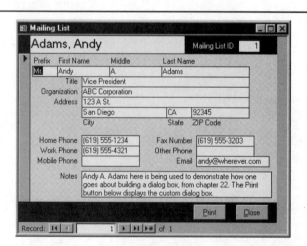

In addition, we've created four reports for this database. You can see their names in the database window in Figure 23.2.

FIGURE 23.2

Reports defined for the simple database.

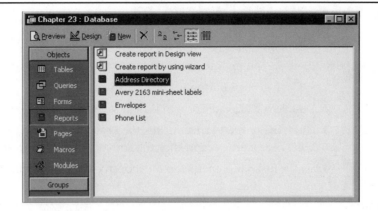

Now let's say our goal is to be able to hide the database window from users of this application. In order to print a report, we want the users to click the Print button at the bottom of the form. When they do so, a pop-up dialog box (see Figure 23.3) allows them to choose one or more reports to print or preview.

FIGURE 23.3

A custom dialog box appears when the user clicks on the Print button near the bottom of the form.

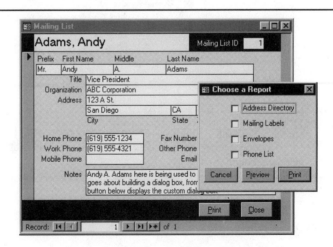

For the rest of this chapter, we'll look at the exact steps required to create such a dialog box. Remember, in this example we're assuming the table, form, and four reports have already been created. Our job here is simply to create the dialog box.

Step 1: Create the Dialog Box

Creating a blank dialog box is pretty much the same as creating a new, blank switchboard. Here are the steps to get started:

1. Click the Forms button in the database window.

2. Double-click Create Form in Design View.

3. Open the property sheet (Click the Properties button in the toolbar, or choose View ➤ Properties.) and click the Format tab in the property sheet.

4. Set the first few properties in the property sheet to the values shown in Figure 23.4.

FIGURE 23.4

An unbound form with Format properties set to make the form look like a dialog box.

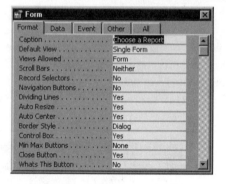

 NOTE Remember that the Caption property is the title that will appear in the title bar of your custom dialog box. So be sure to enter a caption that's suitable for the dialog box you're creating.

Add the Check Box Controls

Now that we have a blank form to work on, we need to add the controls that the user will select from. You can use any of the controls that the toolbox offers. In this example, we'll use check boxes and command buttons. Here are the steps for adding one check box:

1. Open the toolbox if it's closed. (Click the Toolbox toolbar button, or choose View ➤ Toolbox.)

2. Click the Check Box tool and then click in the form where you want the check box to appear. Access creates a check box with a generic name and caption (most likely Check0).

3. (Optional) Change the caption to something more descriptive, such as Address Directory. (Just click within the caption and type your change.)

4. Open the property sheet and click the check box (so it's selected). Use the All tab to give the check box a more descriptive name (DirectoryChosen, for example) and, optionally, set its default value to No.

 WARNING When assigning names to controls, be careful not to inadvertently assign the name to the control's label. Always click *directly on* the control you want to name before typing a control name into the property sheet. The top of the property sheet always shows the type and current name of the currently selected control.

Figure 23.5 shows our progress. The check box is on the form, and the name of that control in the property sheet is DirectoryChosen. The label (caption) for the control (on the form itself) is Address Directory.

FIGURE 23.5

The caption of the first check box control in the dialog box is Address Directory; its name is DirectoryChosen.

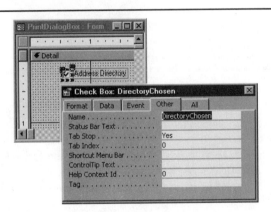

Next we follow those same steps to create three more check boxes, one for each possible report. Figure 23.6 shows all four check boxes in place. Table 23.1 lists the caption for each check box and the name we assigned to each check box. (You can't see the name of each check box because the property sheet shows properties for only one control at a time.)

FIGURE 23.6

Four check box controls added to our dialog box.

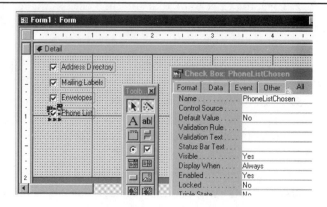

TABLE 23.1: LABELS AND NAMES OF THE CHECK BOXES SHOWN IN FIGURE 23.6

CAPTION	NAME
Address Directory	DirectoryChosen
Mailing Labels	LabelsChosen
Envelopes	EnvelopesChosen
Phone List	PhoneListChosen

 TIP Check boxes can be difficult to align and space evenly. Try using Edit ➤ Select All to select all the controls; then use Format ➤ Size ➤ To Grid, Format ➤ Align ➤ To Grid, and Format ➤ Vertical Spacing to get things in the ballpark. Then you can use other options under Format ➤ Align, as appropriate, to tidy up.

Add the Command Buttons

After the check boxes are in place, we need to add the command buttons. You probably know the routine by now, but let's go through the steps to create one of the command buttons. (The control wizards won't really help here because we haven't yet created the macros that will respond to the users' dialog box selections.)

1. Turn off the control wizards by clicking the button "out" as below.

2. Click the Command Button tool, and then click in the form where you want the command button to appear. A button with a generic name, such as Command0, appears.

3. Make sure the command button is selected, and then use the All tab in the property sheet to give the button a name and caption.

In Figure 23.7 we've created a command button, named it CancelButton, and assigned the caption Cancel.

Repeat steps 1 to 3 to create two additional command buttons, captioned P&review (which shows up as P̲review on the button face) and &Print (which shows up as P̲rint). You can then use dragging techniques and the options on the Format menu to size, position, and align the buttons to your liking. Figure 23.8 shows the finished dialog box. Table 23.2 lists the names and captions assigned to those buttons.

TABLE 23.2: NAMES AND CAPTIONS FOR THE COMMAND BUTTONS SHOWN IN FIGURE 23.8

NAME	CAPTION
CancelButton	Cancel
PreviewButton	P&review
PrintButton	&Print

FIGURE 23.8

*The custom dialog box
with three command
buttons.*

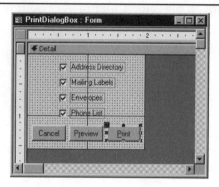

Print, Save, and Close the Form

With the controls in place, we can now name and close the form and optionally print
some "technical documentation" that will help us develop the macros in the next
step. Here are the steps to follow:

1. Choose File ➤ Close ➤ Yes, and enter a name such as PrintDialogBox. The new
dialog box name appears in the database window along with any other forms, as
in the example shown in Figure 23.9.

FIGURE 23.9

*Once closed and
saved, the new dialog
box is listed right
along with any other
forms in the database
window.*

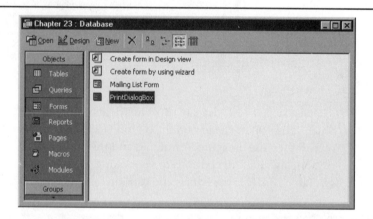

2. Choose Tools ➤ Analyze ➤ Documenter if you want to print the technical
documentation.

3. Choose Forms under Object Type, and click the name of the form that you want to document (PrintDialogBox in this example, as shown below):

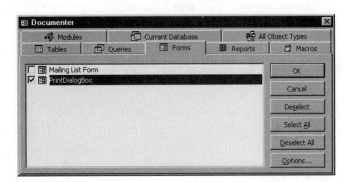

4. Click the Options button and limit the display to the options shown below.

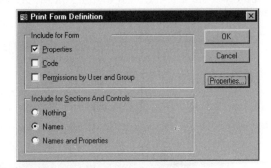

5. Choose OK (twice) and wait for the Object Definition window to appear.

You can then use the Print button in the toolbar to print the documentation. Then click the Close toolbar button to close the Object Definition window and return to the database window.

We'll use the printed documentation to help us remember the exact names we gave to the controls in the dialog box. The names of the controls appear near the end of the printout and will look something like this:

```
Command Button: CancelButton
Check Box: DirectoryChosen
Check Box: EnvelopesChosen
Label: Label1
Label: Label5
Label: Label7
Label: Label9
```

```
Check Box: LabelsChosen
Check Box: PhoneListChosen
Command Button: PreviewButton
Command Button: PrintButton
```

Step 2: Create the Macro Actions

Next we need some macros to define what will happen when the user makes selections from the dialog box. We need to start with a blank macro sheet:

1. Click the Macros button in the database window.

2. Click the New button to get to a new, blank macro sheet.

3. Open the Macro Name and Condition columns using the appropriate options on the toolbar or the View menu. You should see all four column headings listed across the top of the columns.

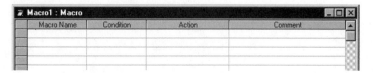

Now we're ready to start creating the individual macros. You can start off by typing just a comment into the first row(s) of the macro sheet.

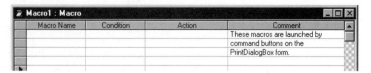

Cancel Printing Macro

One of the buttons on the PrintDialogBox form lets the user Cancel—that is, bail out without doing anything. The macro we assign to that button need only close the form. Follow these steps to create that macro:

1. Enter a name, such as CancelPrint, in the Macro Name column in a blank row beneath the comments you typed.

2. Leave the Condition column empty.

3. Choose Close in the Action column.

4. Fill out the Action Arguments as follows:

Object Type:	Form
Object Name:	PrintDialogBox
Save:	Yes

5. (Optional) Fill in the Comments column to describe what this macro does. Figure 23.10 shows the completed first macro.

FIGURE 23.10

The first macro typed into the new macro sheet.

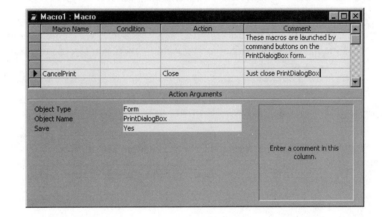

Preview Reports Macro

The next macro is a little trickier than the first because it needs to say, "If the DirectoryChosen check box is checked, preview the Address Directory report," and then "If the LabelsChosen check box is checked, preview the Avery 2163 minisheet labels report," and so on. So we need to explain one thing about the check boxes before we do that.

A check box is a control that can contain any one of two values, either True (checked) or False (unchecked). We don't actually use the check boxes to launch an action. Instead, we decide whether to perform some action based on whether a check box is checked or not. The "decision" part takes place in the Condition column of the macro. As you may recall from Chapter 21, the Condition column must contain an expression that evaluates to True or False. Since the value of a check box is inherently True or False, we only need to use the name of the check box in the Condition column of the macro. For example, if we put DirectoryChosen as the condition in a line, then DirectoryChosen proves True if the check box is checked and proves False if the check box is unchecked.

With that little tidbit in the back of your mind, let's go ahead and create the next macro in this sheet. We'll name this new macro PreviewReports. Here's how to proceed:

1. Leave one blank row beneath the CancelPrint macro. Type the name **Preview-Reports** into the Macro Name column of the new row.

2. Type **[DirectoryChosen]** in the Condition column.

 TIP The printed documentation for the form lets you easily look up the exact spelling of the check box controls on the form. That's how we "remembered" the DirectoryChosen name. In lieu of using printed documentation, you can use the Expression Builder to locate names of controls on forms.

3. Choose OpenReport in the Action column, and fill in the Action Arguments as follows:

   Report Name: Address Directory

   View: Print Preview

4. (Optional) Type a description into the Comment column.

At this point our macro sheet looks like Figure 23.11.

FIGURE 23.11

Starting the second macro, which we've named PreviewReports.

Macro Name	Condition	Action	Comment
			These macros are launched by command buttons on the PrintDialogBox form.
CancelPrint		Close	Just close PrintDialogBox
PreviewReports	[DirectoryChosen]	OpenReport	Preview the Address Directory report

Action Arguments

Report Name	Address Directory
View	Print Preview
Filter Name	
Where Condition	

Enter a comment in this column.

Next we need to repeat steps 2 to 4 to add three more rows to the macro. But we need to refer to different controls and report names. Figure 23.12 shows the complete macro.

FIGURE 23.12

The PreviewReports macro defined in our macro sheet.

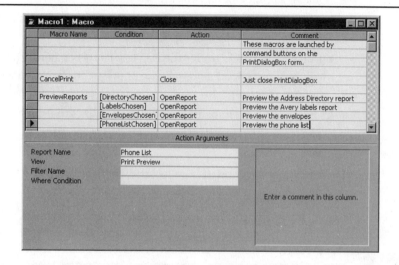

Table 23.3 shows the Condition, Action, and Action Arguments for the remaining three rows in the PreviewReports macro.

TABLE 23.3: CONDITIONS, ACTIONS, AND ARGUMENTS SHOWN IN FIGURE 23.12

CONDITION	ACTION	ACTION ARGUMENTS	
[LabelsChosen]	OpenReport	Report Name:	Avery 2163 mini-sheet labels
		View:	Print Preview
[EnvelopesChosen]	OpenReport	Report Name:	Envelopes
		View:	Print Preview
[PhoneListChosen]	OpenReport	Report Name:	Phone List
		View:	Print Preview

Print Reports Macro

Next we need a macro to print reports. This macro is virtually identical to the PreviewReports macro, except that the View Action Argument for each OpenReport action needs to be changed from Print Preview to Print. To create this macro quickly and easily, follow these steps:

1. Hold down the Ctrl key and click each of the four rows in the PreviewReports macro so that all four rows are selected.

2. Choose Edit ➤ Copy, or press Ctrl+C to copy those rows to the Clipboard (nothing happens on the screen).

3. Leave a blank row under the Preview Reports macro, click in the Macro Name column, and choose Edit ➤ Paste (or press Ctrl+V). An exact copy of the Preview-Reports macro appears.

4. Change the macro name from PreviewReports to PrintReports.

5. Change the View action argument in the first row of this new macro from Print Preview to Print.

6. Change the comment to reflect this change.

7. Repeat steps 5 and 6 for the remaining three rows in the PrintReports macro.

Figure 23.13 shows how the macro sheet looks at this point.

FIGURE 23.13

The PrintReports macro added to the macro sheet.

PrintDialogBoxMacros : Macro

Macro Name	Condition	Action	Comment
			These macros are launched by
			command buttons on the
			PrintDialogBox form.
CancelPrint		Close	Just close PrintDialogBox
PreviewReports	[DirectoryChosen]	OpenReport	Preview the Address Directory report
	[LabelsChosen]	OpenReport	Preview the Avery labels report
	[EnvelopesChosen]	OpenReport	Preview the envelopes
	[PhoneListChosen]	OpenReport	Preview the phone list
PrintReports	[DirectoryChosen]	OpenReport	Print the Address Directory report
	[LabelsChosen]	OpenReport	Print the Avery labels report
	[EnvelopesChosen]	OpenReport	Print the envelopes
	[PhoneListChosen]	OpenReport	Print the phone list

Action Arguments

Report Name	Phone List
View	Print
Filter Name	
Where Condition	

Enter a macro name in this column.

You may now save and close the macro in the usual manner. That is, choose File ➤ Close ➤ Yes, type in a name, such as PrintDialogBoxMacros, and click OK. The macro name appears in the database window whenever the Macros tab is selected.

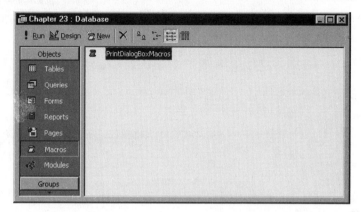

Step 3: Assign Macros to Dialog Box Buttons

Next we need to assign each of those macros to the three command buttons in the PrintDialogBox form. Here's how:

1. Click the Forms button in the database window, click the PrintDialogBox name, and then click the Design button to open that form in design view.

2. Open the property sheet and click the Events tab.

3. Click the Cancel button.

4. Click the On Click property in the property sheet, and then use the drop-down list button to choose PrintDialogBoxMacros.CancelPrint as the macro to run when the user clicks that button (Figure 23.14).

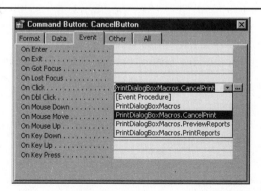

5. Click the button captioned Preview, and assign the macro named PrintDialog-BoxMacros.PreviewReports to that button.

6. Click the button captioned Print and assign the PrintDialogBoxMacros.PrintReports to the On Click property of that button.

7. Close and save the form (choose File ➤ Close ➤ Yes).

You're returned to the database window. The dialog box and its macros are complete. Assuming you had created the four reports mentioned at the start of this chapter, you could test the dialog box right now simply by opening it in form view and making selections.

As you may recall from earlier in this chapter (refer to Figure 23.3), we actually assigned this dialog box to the Print button on a form we had created earlier. The simple way to do this would be to open that form in design view, open the toolbox, and turn on the control wizards. Create the Print command button and, when the Control Wizard asks for actions, choose Form Operations ➤ Open Form ➤ PrintDialog-Box. The caption for the button would be &Print.

You could also use a hyperlink to open the PrintDialogBox form. Click the Insert Hyperlink dialog box, enter **PrintDialogBox** under Named Location in File, and click OK. Then move the hyperlink from the upper-left corner of the form to wherever you want it to appear. Click the caption and change it to **Print** (instead of showing the entire form name, PrintDialogBox). Figure 23.15 shows the Mailing List form with a hyperlink to the left of the Notes field that opens the PrintDialogBox form. Note that the Print command button, shown on the form in Figure 23.1, has been removed.

FIGURE 23.15

*The Mailing List form
with a Print hyperlink
instead of a Print com-
mand button.*

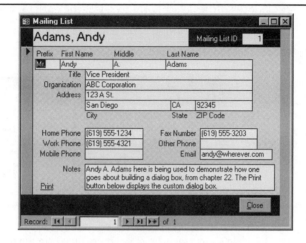

Finishing Touches

You can put a few finishing touches on your dialog box to refine its appearance and behavior, as we'll discuss in the remaining sections in this chapter. As always, these "features" are actually properties or specific controls that you assign to the form using the property sheet in the form design screen.

Modal and Pop-Up Properties

You may have noticed, in your day-to-day use of Windows, that most dialog boxes are "sticky"; that is, once the dialog box is on the screen, you can't just shoo it away by clicking some other window. You need to specifically complete the dialog box, close the dialog box, or choose the dialog box's Cancel key to get rid of the dialog box.

The technical term for "stickiness" is *modal*. That is to say, most dialog boxes are actually modal windows. By contrast, most "regular" application and document windows are *modeless*, meaning that you can do work outside the window even while the window is on the screen.

A second characteristic of dialog boxes is that they are *pop-up* forms. That is to say, once the window is on the screen, no other window can cover it. You might already be familiar with the Always on Top feature of Windows Help screens. When you activate that feature, you are, in essence, making the Windows Help window a pop-up window.

If you want to give your custom dialog boxes the modal and pop-up characteristics, follow these steps:

1. Open the custom dialog box in form design view.

2. Choose Edit ➤ Select Form to select the entire form.

3. Open the property sheet and click the Other tab.

4. Set the Modal and Pop Up properties to Yes.

 TIP To learn more about modal and pop-up properties and ways to combine them, press F1 while the cursor is on either property within the property sheet.

5. Close and save the form (File ➤ Close ➤ Yes).

To test your efforts, open the dialog box in the normal form view. When you click outside the dialog box, nothing will happen (except, maybe, you'll hear a beep). The only way to get rid of the dialog box is to specifically close it using one of its command buttons or the Close (×) button in its upper-right corner.

Dialog Box Border Style

Another characteristic of many dialog boxes that make them different from other windows is their border. Many dialog boxes have a thick, black border that cannot be sized. If you want to give your custom dialog box that kind of border, follow these simple steps:

1. Open the custom dialog box in form design view.

2. Choose Edit ➤ Select Form to select the entire form.

3. Open the property sheet and click the Format tab.

4. Set the Border Style property to Dialog.

PART

IV

Building a Custom
Application

 TIP   To learn more about border styles, press the Help key when the cursor is in the Border Style property box.

5. Close and save the form normally (File ➤ Close ➤ Yes).

To see the effects, open the dialog box in form view. Then try sizing the dialog box by dragging one of its edges or corners. Can't be done! If you try to "trick it" by using commands in the control menu (in the upper-left corner of the dialog box), no go. The menu will now offer only the Move and Close options, as illustrated below.

Default and Cancel Buttons

Two last features that many dialog boxes share are cancel and default buttons:

Cancel button   The button that gets pushed automatically when the user presses the Esc key.

Default button   The button that is automatically selected when the user presses Enter. This button will also have a darker border than other buttons on the same form.

You can make one (and only one) button in your dialog box the default button and any other single button the cancel button. Here's how:

1. Open your custom dialog box in design view.

2. Open the property sheet.

3. Click the Other tab.

4. If you want to make a button into the Cancel button, first click that button to select it. Then set its Cancel property to Yes, as below.

5. If you want to make some other button the default button, first click that button to select it. Then set its Default property to Yes, as below.

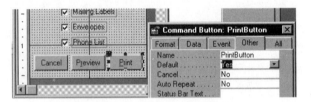

6. Close and save the form normally (File ➤ Close ➤ Yes).

When you reopen the dialog box in form view, the only visual difference you'll see is the darker border around the default button (the Print button in the example below). You can test the new properties by pressing the Escape or Enter key while the form is on the screen.

What we've learned here is the big secret to custom dialog boxes: they're really just forms that aren't bound to any particular table or query. You use the toolbox in form design to add controls, and maybe some hyperlinks, to that form. Then you create macros (or Visual Basic code) to define the actions that the dialog box will perform. You can even make your dialog box behave like the dialog boxes in bigger Windows applications by setting Modal, Pop Up, and Border Style properties to the form as a whole. You can also assign the Cancel and Default properties to any two command buttons on the form.

Where to Go from Here

In the next two chapters, we'll look at techniques for creating custom toolbars and menus. Those two features will add even more professional polish to your custom Access applications. Here are some other chapters you might want to explore:

- To get a refresher on the mechanics of creating macros, see Chapter 21.
- To see a custom application with lots of custom dialog boxes, try the Fulfill sample database on the CD (see Appendix C).
- To learn about exploring custom applications behind the scenes, see Chapter 29.

What's New in the Access Zoo?

Creating custom dialog boxes with Access 2000 is the same as it was with Access 97.

CHAPTER 24

Creating Custom Toolbars

anna-Barbera got it right in *The Jetsons*; most of us have ended up with push-button jobs. Microsoft's toolbars are a perfect example because they let you do virtually anything with the click of a button. With Access 2000, you can also add menu commands to toolbars to create "command bars" of all the tools and menus you use most.

Access's Toolbars

Microsoft Access comes with many built-in toolbars. Most of them are tied to specific views and are named accordingly:

Alignment and Sizing	Database
Filter/Sort	Form Design
Form View	Formatting (Datasheet)
Formatting (Form/Report)	Formatting (Page)
Macro Design	Menu Bar
Page Design	Page View
Print Preview	Query Datasheet
Query Design	Relationship
Report Design	Shortcut Menus
Source Code Control	Table Datasheet
Table Design	

Other built-in toolbars that aren't attached to a specific view include:

Utility 1 and Utility 2 toolbars   For creating your own custom toolbars.

Web   For browsing Web documents and searching the Web.

Toolbox   Offers buttons for creating controls in form design, report design, and page design. It's generally free-floating, but can be docked like any other toolbar (see the next section).

Hiding and Displaying the Built-In Toolbars

You can hide or display any number of toolbars at any time. Just follow these procedures:

- **To enable or display more than one toolbar**, choose View ➢ Toolbars ➢ Customize. Then, in the Customize dialog box, click the Toolbars tab and check each toolbar that you want displayed. Choose Close when you are finished.

- **To hide or display a specific toolbar**, right-click a toolbar and uncheck the name of the toolbar, or choose View ➤ Toolbars. Then check or uncheck the toolbar you want to hide or display.

- **To move a toolbar**, move the mouse pointer to any blank space in the toolbar and drag the toolbar to wherever you want to put it.

- **To dock a toolbar**, drag it to the edge of the screen until its outline expands to the width or height of the screen, and then release the mouse button. Or, double-click its title bar.

- **To undock a toolbar** so that it becomes free-floating, just move it away from the edge of the screen.

 TIP   You can quickly dock or undock a toolbar by double-clicking any blank space in the toolbar. To hide a floating toolbar, click the small Close button in the toolbar's upper-right corner.

Controlling the Size and Appearance of Toolbars

You can control the size of the buttons and the appearance of any toolbar by following these steps:

1. Right-click any toolbar and choose Customize, or choose View ➤ Toolbars ➤ Customize and click the Options tab.

2. Choose any combination of appearance features from the lower part of the dialog box:

    Large icons   Choose this option to make the buttons larger (handy on small laptop-size screens or on screens with resolutions higher than 800×600).

    List font names in their font   Leave this option checked to display font names in their own font, instead of in the system font.

    Show ScreenTips on toolbars   Clear this option if you don't want your toolbar to display ScreenTips.

    Show shortcut keys in ScreenTips   Check this option if you want to show a button's shortcut key with its ScreenTip when you point to it.

3. Choose Close after making your selection(s).

Modified versus Custom Toolbars

As an application developer, you need to be aware of the difference between a modified built-in toolbar and a custom toolbar:

Modified existing toolbar   If you modify an existing toolbar, that version of the toolbar will appear in *all* your databases.

Custom toolbar   When you create a new custom toolbar, it appears only in the database in which it was created.

 NOTE   The built-in Utility 1 and Utility 2 toolbars are initially blank. When you add buttons to those toolbars, that counts as modifying an existing toolbar—not as creating a new, custom toolbar. In other words, the Utility 1 and Utility 2 toolbars are accessible from all your databases.

Empowering or Limiting Your Users

You can use custom toolbars to determine what the users of your application can and can't do. For example, if you want users to be able to create and change objects, you can include design buttons on your toolbars. On the other hand, if you don't want the users to modify objects, you can keep them away from the design screens by excluding design buttons from your application's custom toolbars.

 NOTE   You'll need to create custom menus, discussed in the next chapter, to determine exactly how much freedom your user has.

Creating a Custom Toolbar

Here's how to create a new custom toolbar:

1. Make sure that the database you want to put the toolbar into is the currently open database.

2. Right-click an existing toolbar and choose Customize, or choose View ➢ Toolbars ➢ Customize. Then click New on the Toolbars page.

3. Enter a name (up to 64 characters) for your new toolbar, and then click OK.

A tiny (and sometimes hard to see) empty toolbar appears on the screen, as shown in Figure 24.1.

FIGURE 24.1

A new, blank toolbar
and the Toolbars tab
of the Customize
dialog box.

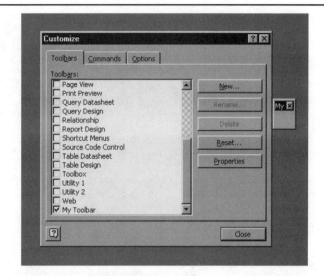

Adding and Deleting Buttons

To add buttons to your new toolbar, you can either use the Commands tab of the
Customize dialog box, or copy buttons from one toolbar to another.

Using the Commands Tab to Add Buttons

If you have the Customize dialog box open, follow these steps to add buttons to a
toolbar:

1. Click the Commands tab of the Customize dialog box. Choose a category of
button type from the Categories list. (Just click any category name.)

2. Click whichever Commands button you think you might want to add to your
toolbar. Click the Description button under Selected Command to check the
ScreenTip and description to make sure you know what the button will do.

3. Drag the button to your custom toolbar.

In Figure 24.2 we've already dragged a few buttons to the custom toolbar and are
now examining buttons in the View category.

Here we've just dragged two buttons to our custom toolbar and are browsing the Commands list in the Customize dialog box for more buttons to add.

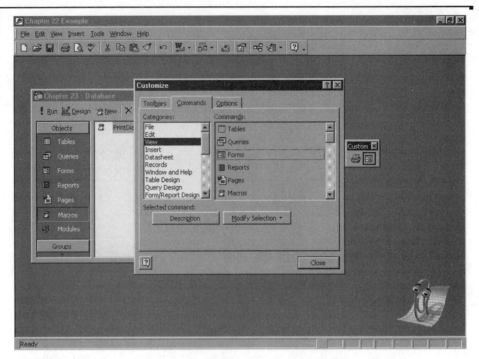

Copying or Moving Buttons between Toolbars

It is also possible to copy or move buttons from one toolbar to another. First make sure that both toolbars are visible.

What you do next depends on whether the Customize dialog box is already open. If it is, just drag a button from one toolbar to another to move it. To copy a button with the Customize dialog box open, press Ctrl while you drag it from one toolbar to another.

If the Customize dialog box is not open, press Alt while moving or copying.

Deleting Buttons

Deleting a button from a toolbar is also a simple task. First open the Customize dialog box. Next show the toolbar you want to change, if it's not already visible. (You may need to drag the Customize dialog box out of the way so you can see the button you want to delete.) Then just drag the button off the toolbar. You can also right-click the button you want to delete and choose Delete.

Refining a Toolbar

You can use any of these techniques to refine your custom toolbar while you're viewing the Customize dialog box:

- **To remove a button**, drag it off of your custom toolbar.
- **To move a button to a new location on the toolbar**, drag the button to its new location.
- **To add space between buttons**, drag the button slightly to the right (a distance a little less than half the width of the button). (Closing the dialog box and docking the toolbar allows you to have the space on the toolbar to undertake this operation.)
- **To delete space between two buttons**, drag the right button slightly to the left.

Saving and Modifying the Custom Toolbar

When you've finished adding buttons to your custom toolbar, choose Close from the Customize dialog box. You can then use any of these techniques, at any time, to view, hide, or change your custom toolbar (But don't forget, your custom toolbar will be available only in the current database.):

- **To hide or display a custom toolbar**, right-click any toolbar and then click the name of the custom toolbar that you want to hide or display. Currently displayed toolbars are indicated with a checkmark.

 TIP   If no toolbars are visible, choose View ➢ Toolbars and click a toolbar name.

- **To change a custom toolbar**, first display that toolbar, right-click it, and choose Customize to return to the Customize dialog box. There you can make changes using the same techniques that you used to create the custom toolbar.
- **To delete a custom toolbar**, choose View ➢ Toolbars ➢ Customize and click the Toolbars tab if it's not already active. Then scroll down to the name of the custom toolbar you want to delete, click it to highlight it, click the Delete button, and choose Yes.
- **To rename a custom toolbar**, choose View ➢ Toolbars ➢ Customize, scroll down to the name of the custom toolbar you want to rename, and click the Rename button. Type a new, unique name for your toolbar, and click OK.

NOTE The Delete and Rename buttons aren't visible in the Toolbars dialog box when the highlight is on a built-in toolbar because you can't delete or rename those toolbars.

- **To move/dock/undock a custom toolbar**, use the same techniques you'd use with a built-in toolbar, as described earlier in this chapter.

Creating Your Own Buttons

You're not limited to creating buttons that perform built-in Access tasks. You can create your own buttons to run macros, open tables, preview reports, and more. The general procedure is the same as for "regular" buttons. You just need to choose your buttons from the categories that start with the word *All*. Here are the steps:

1. Display the toolbar to which you want to assign a custom button.

2. Right-click that toolbar and choose Customize. Then click the Commands tab in the Customize dialog box.

3. Scroll down to and select one of the last few categories under Categories (beginning with the word *All*). The Commands list shows the names of all the objects in the current database that fall into that category (see below).

4. Drag the name of any object to your toolbar.

5. Repeat steps 3 and 4 to add as many buttons as you like, and then click Close.

A default button for that type of object appears on your toolbar. (You can change the button, as you'll see in the next section.)

When you move the mouse pointer to the custom button, the status bar and (in a couple of seconds) the ScreenTip describe what the button will do, as illustrated below.

 TIP You can also drag the name of any object from the database window into the toolbar to instantly create a button that displays that object.

Changing a Button's Face and Description

You can change the face of any button in any toolbar, and you can change the name or ScreenTip of any custom button you create. Here's how to make these types of changes to a button:

1. Right-click the toolbar that contains the button you want to change, and then click Customize.

2. Right-click the button in the toolbar that you want to change to show its shortcut menu. Do any of the following:

   - **To choose a different picture for a button**, select Change Button Image. You'll see a menu of images. Click the one you want to use.

   - **To change the name of a button**, type a new value in the box after Name.

   - **To change the ScreenTip**, choose Properties and, in the box after ScreenTip, enter the tip you want to see.

   - **To show text instead of a picture**, choose Text Only (Always). The text is taken from the Name property.

   - **To show text when the button is on a menu**, choose Text Only (in Menus). As you'll see later in this chapter, Access 2000 lets you add buttons to menus or add menu commands to toolbars. (You can also copy, paste, and reset button images using other items on a button's right-click menu.)

 NOTE Remember, you can change the Description only on custom buttons—not on the built-in buttons.

3. Repeat step 2 to choose a face and/or name and ScreenTip for as many buttons as you wish. Then click Close when you're done.

Resetting a Button Face

If you change a button face on a built-in button and then decide to go back to the original button face:

1. Right-click the button face you want to reset, and choose Customize from the shortcut menu (if the Customize dialog box is not already open).

2. Right-click the button again and choose Reset Button Image.

3. Click Close in the Customize dialog box.

Creating Your Own Button Face

So what do you do when you want to create your own button image? Once you have added a button to the toolbar, make sure the Customize dialog box is open, and then right-click the button. Select Edit Button Image from the context menu, and the Button Editor appears (see Figure 24.3). To create your own button image, follow these steps:

1. To change the color of a pixel, first click the color in the Colors frame, and then click the box on the Picture grid that represents the pixel. (Select the Erase color box to erase a pixel.)

2. To scroll the Picture grid (not all of it appears in the box), click the arrows below the grid.

3. To see what your new button image looks like, look in the Preview frame.

4. To clear the button face, click the Clear button.

5. To save the button image, click OK.

FIGURE 24.3

The Access Button Editor.

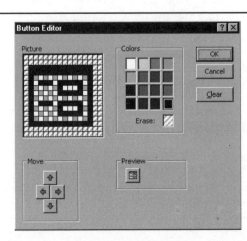

Adding Toolbars to Your Custom Application

As an application developer, you'll want to control exactly *which* toolbar appears *when*. First create a database with the Database Wizard, or open a database that you have already created, so that you can work through a couple of examples. (For the examples in this chapter, we will use the Northwind sample database included with Access.) Create a custom toolbar and add the buttons to it that you use most often when you work with a database.

The custom toolbar we created includes tools for jobs that we do frequently from Access. Its buttons switch to Excel, send a document to the Notepad, start an online meeting, open the Visual Basic Editor, and create a replica. Figure 24.4 shows this custom toolbar, which we creatively named My Applications.

FIGURE 24.4

The custom toolbar My Applications displayed in the Northwind database.

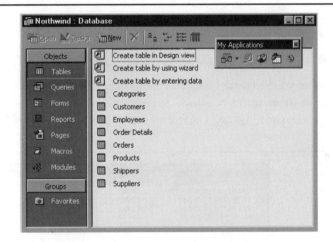

 TIP If Access doesn't provide a button for your application, you can use Visual Basic to launch it, and attach that code to a button on the toolbar.

We then created a second custom toolbar, named My Printing Preview, which contains icons for printing, print preview, and page setup (see Figure 24.5).

FIGURE 24.5

The custom My Printing Preview toolbar.

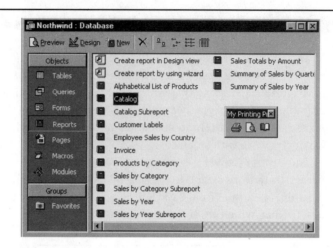

Creating Macros to Show or Hide Custom Toolbars

After you've created your custom toolbars, you need to create macros to show and hide them. In the Northwind application, we put all those macros into a single macro group named Global Macros, as shown in Figure 24.6.

FIGURE 24.6

The macro group named Global Macros contains the macros that show or hide the custom toolbars.

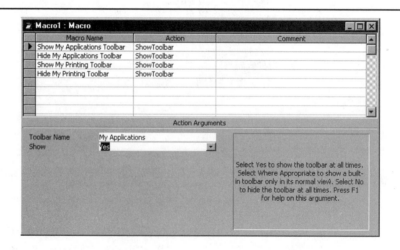

Table 24.1 shows the Macro Name, Action, and Action Arguments of each macro. (Notice that this macro group does not have a Condition column.) Basically, each macro uses a single ShowToolBar action. The Action Arguments for each Action name the toolbar to show or hide, and then use Yes to show the toolbar, or No to hide that toolbar.

TABLE 24.1: SAMPLE MACROS TO HIDE AND SHOW CUSTOM TOOLBARS

MACRO NAME	ACTION	ACTION ARGUMENTS	
Show My Applications Toolbar	ShowToolBar	Toolbar Name:	My Applications
		Show:	Yes
Hide My Applications Toolbar	ShowToolBar	Toolbar Name:	My Applications
		Show:	No
Show My Printing Toolbar	ShowToolBar	Toolbar Name:	My Printing Preview
		Show:	Yes
Hide My Printing Toolbar	ShowToolBar	Toolbar Name:	My Printing Preview
		Show:	No

Attaching Toolbars to Forms

In order to attach a toolbar to a particular form, you need to execute, from an event on the form, the macro that displays (or hides) the toolbar:

1. Open the form (in design view) that you want to display a custom toolbar.

2. Open the property sheet, select the Event tab, and choose Edit ➤ Select Form.

3. Assign the macro that *shows* the toolbar to the On Activate property.

4. Assign the macro that *hides* the toolbar to the On Deactivate property of that form.

Figure 24.7 shows an example using the Northwind application, in which we display the My Printing Preview toolbar when the form appears, and hide that toolbar when the user is done with the form. By using the On Activate and On Deactivate properties, we can make sure the toolbar is visible whenever the user is working with this form, and hidden whenever the user moves the focus to another form.

FIGURE 24.7

Form event properties
for the Northwind cus-
tomer phone list form.

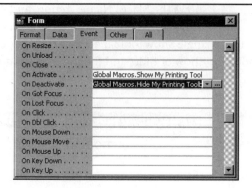

Attaching a Custom Toolbar to Print Preview

If you want your application to display a custom toolbar during print preview, you
need to open the report in design view, open its property sheet, and choose Edit ➤
Select Report. Assign the macro that shows the toolbar to the On Activate event properties. Assign the macro that hides the toolbar to the On Deactivate event properties.
The example in Figure 24.8 uses a report from the Northwind application.

FIGURE 24.8

Macros to hide and
display a custom tool-
bar when the user
looks at the report
named Alphabetical
List of Products in print
preview.

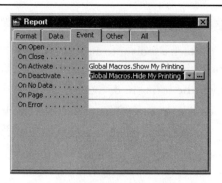

By the way, we know that all these form and report event properties can be confusing. For help while assigning macros to these properties, press F1 or search Help for
Order of Events.

Macro to Hide the Built-In Toolbars

When creating an application, you might decide to hide all the built-in toolbars from the user. As you know, you can turn off the built-in toolbars manually through the Startup dialog box. If you want your application to turn off those toolbars, have your AutoExec macro send the necessary keystrokes at startup. You can use a SendKeys action to have the macro press the appropriate keys, as in the following example.

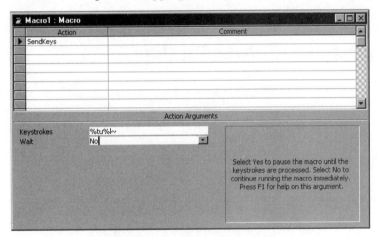

Notice the Keystrokes entries in the Action Arguments for the SendKeys action:

%t	Presses Alt+T to open the Tools menu
u	Types **u** to choose Startup
%l	Presses Alt+l (lower case L) to uncheck the Allow Built-In Toolbars check box
~	Presses Enter to choose OK

TIP When defining the arguments for a SendKeys action in a macro, press F1 for Help. Then click the green underlined *SendKeys* jump word, and scroll through that Help screen to find the codes you need to represent various keystrokes.

Redisplaying the Built-In Toolbars

If you want your application to redisplay the built-in menus when the user quits the application, have your "quit" macro execute a SendKeys action to restore the built-in toolbars. You might also want to have that macro redisplay the database window.

TIP The same macro that turns the built-in toolbars off will turn them back on.

If you ever need to turn on the built-in toolbars manually, go to the database window and choose Tools ➢ Startup from the menu bar. Then check the Allow Built-In Toolbars check box, and click OK. If no toolbar appears, choose View ➢ Toolbars and check Database.

Modifying a Built-In Toolbar

So far in this chapter, we've focused on creating custom toolbars for your custom applications. But you may also want to modify Access's built-in toolbars to better suit your own needs. As mentioned earlier, when you modify a built-in toolbar, that toolbar is accessible in all your databases.

 NOTE A custom toolbar is stored in the database it was created in and is available only in that database. Built-in toolbars (modified or not) are stored in the Access workgroup information file and are available to any database.

To modify a built-in toolbar:

1. Display the built-in toolbar that you want to modify.

2. Right-click that toolbar and choose Customize.

3. Make changes using the techniques described under "Adding and Deleting Buttons" earlier in this chapter.

4. Choose Close when you've finished.

That modified version of the built-in toolbar will appear in all your databases.

Combining Menus and Toolbars

Access 2000 lets you create *command bars* by adding menu commands to toolbars and buttons to menus. These hybrid bars can have virtually any combination of menu commands and toolbar buttons you can imagine.

You may have already noticed this feature while experimenting with the Customize dialog box. For example, if you select the File category on the Commands tab, you'll find commands, such as Save As, that are not represented by a button. You can drag these commands to a toolbar, and they show up as text. The custom toolbar below includes two buttons and the Save As command. When you click Save As, Access opens the Save As dialog box, as if you had chosen File ➤ Save As from the menu bar.

Once you add a menu command to a toolbar, you are free to show it as a picture instead of text:

1. Right-click the toolbar you want to change, and choose Customize. (If the toolbar isn't visible, choose View ➤ Customize and check the desired toolbar first.)

2. Right-click the command button you want to show as a picture on the toolbar. Choose Change Button Image and select an image:

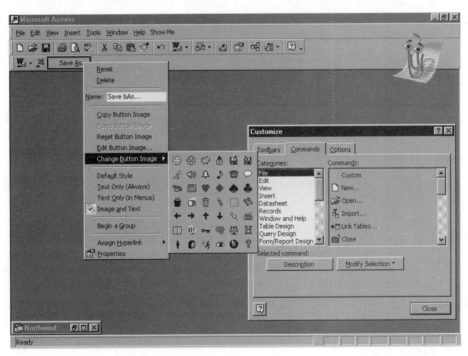

3. Right-click the button again and check Default Style if you want to show the button as a picture without text. Or leave Image and Text checked to show the button as a combination of an image and text. The Save As command on the toolbar below has this property checked.

Resetting a Built-In Toolbar

If you want to reset a built-in toolbar to its original state, right-click a toolbar and choose Customize. Make sure the Toolbars tab is selected in the Customize dialog box, and click the name of the built-in toolbar that you want to reset. Then click the Reset button, click OK, and click Close in the Customize dialog box.

Where to Go from Here

Adding custom toolbars can make your applications much more functional for users. They are truly a convenience feature in any application. However, toolbars usually need to be backed by menus. The next chapter explains how to create the custom menus that are necessary to support custom toolbars.

What's New in the Access Zoo?

Toolbars in Access 2000 work pretty much the same as in Access 97. One difference is that in the Customize dialog box, you'll find new toolbars, such as Formatting (Page), and buttons for new commands, such as Expand All and Collapse All.

CHAPTER 25

Creating Custom Menus

When developing an application, you'll probably want to give it some custom menus. As with custom toolbars, you can use custom menus to determine exactly what the user of your application can and can't do.

Displaying Custom Menus

You can display custom menus either with a particular form or globally within your application:

- If you attach a custom menu to a form, the menu bar is displayed only while that form is on the screen.
- A global menu is one that appears throughout your application, though it will be replaced by any custom menus that you attach to forms.

You can use the Customize dialog box, the same one we used in Chapter 24 to work with toolbars, to create either type of menu. We explain how to attach each type of menu to your application a little later in this chapter. For now, just keep in mind that you can use the Customize dialog box to create any number of custom menus for an application.

Creating Custom Menus

As you work through the examples in this chapter, you'll see that the steps for creating a custom menu are almost the same as those for creating a custom toolbar.

Follow these steps to create a new menu bar:

1. Open the database to which you want to add the custom menu bar.
2. Choose View ➤ Toolbars ➤ Customize.
3. Click the Toolbars tab (if it's not already active) and choose New.
4. Enter a name in the New Toolbar dialog box shown next, and click OK or press Enter. (Don't worry that it asks for a toolbar name instead of a menu bar name. With Access 2000, toolbars and menu bars can be combined and, in a sense, are interchangeable.) You'll see a new toolbar, usually floating within the Customize dialog box, like the one shown in Figure 25.1.

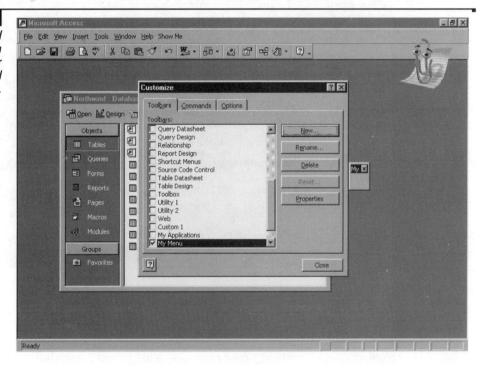

FIGURE 25.1

*A new menu bar called
My Menu is shown
without any buttons or
commands added
to it yet.*

5. Click Properties, select Menu Bar from the Type list, and click Close. If the new menu bar (which still looks like a toolbar) is no longer in sight, drag the Customize dialog box out of the way. Then drag the new menu bar and the Customize dialog box to new locations where you can see them at the same time.

At this point, you can add a built-in menu or a custom menu to the new menu bar. Leave the Customize dialog box open to continue your work.

Adding a Built-In Menu to a Menu Bar

To add a built-in menu, like File or Edit, click the Commands tab in the Customize dialog box and select Built-In Menus under Categories. Then drag your choice from the Commands list to the new menu bar. Figure 25.2 shows the My Menu menu bar after File and Edit menus have been added to it.

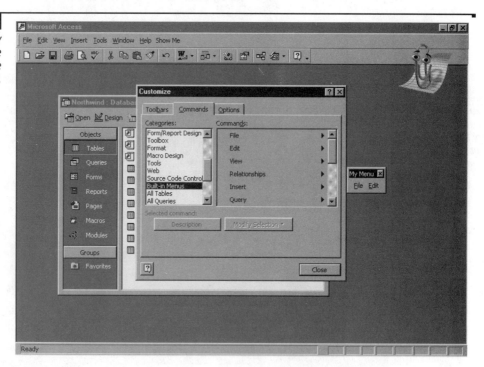

Adding a Custom Menu to a Menu Bar

To add a custom menu to a menu bar, click the Commands tab in the Customize dialog box and select New Menu under Categories. Then drag New Menu from the Command list to the menu bar you are customizing. To change the name of the command called New Menu, right-click the menu bar you just added New Menu to, and enter something in the Name box. The menu bar below, called My Menu, has a custom menu that has been renamed Report Menu:

The next step is to add commands to the custom menu. You can either use the Customize dialog box or drag commands from other menus. The trick is to click the custom menu first, before you start dragging buttons and commands to it.

Here's an example of how to add the Catalog report to the Report Menu on the My Menu menu bar:

1. On My Menu, click the Report Menu command. An empty box will appear below the name of your custom menu if no other commands have been added. Figure 25.3 shows how the screen will look. If other commands have already been added to the menu, you'll see them (instead of an empty box) with a line at the insertion point.

FIGURE 25.3

Adding commands to the custom menu.

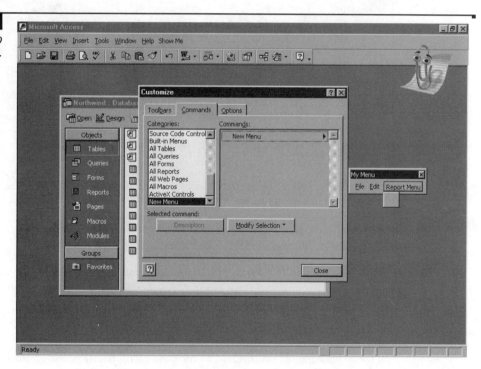

2. In the Customize dialog box under Catalog, click All Reports.

3. Drag Catalog (the name of a report) from the Commands list to the empty box under Report Menu. (If you have already added other choices to Report Menu, just drop the new choice on top of them.)

Repeat this process until you have added all the desired commands to the menu. Figure 25.4 shows the menu bar My Menu with three reports added to the Report Menu command.

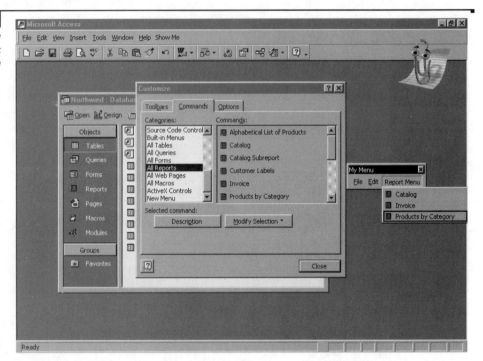

Copying Commands from a Menu

To copy a command to a menu bar or a menu command, first open the Customize dialog box. Make sure that both menu bars you want to work with are visible. Then select the command you want to copy. (To select a submenu command, click—don't drag—to get to the submenu. If you try to drag from the top level to the next command, Access will think you want to move the entire menu command.) Then press Ctrl while you drag the command to the new menu bar. If you are adding a submenu to a command, such as Report Menu in Figure 25.4, drag until you see an empty box or an insertion line on the submenu list, and then release your mouse button.

Customizing a Built-In Menu

You can use any of the techniques described in this chapter or in Chapter 24 to customize the built-in menus that are part of Access. Feel free to add toolbar buttons, built-in menu commands, or your own custom menus. You can also change the properties of any built-in menu:

1. Choose View ➤ Toolbars ➤ Customize to open the Customize dialog box.
2. Click the Toolbars tab if it's not already active.
3. Click the Properties button.
4. Select a toolbar from the Selected Toolbar drop-down list.
5. Change the properties as desired, and click Close to return to the Customize dialog box. Click Close again if you are finished changing menus and/or toolbars.

When the Customize dialog box is open, you can also right-click any toolbar button or menu command to get a shortcut menu. Many of the shortcut commands apply only to toolbar buttons and were described in Chapter 24. Here are a few shortcuts for menu commands:

Reset   Lets you return a built-in menu to its original state or restore a custom menu as it was the last time it was saved.

Delete   Removes a command from a menu bar.

Name   A place where you can enter your own names for menu commands, even the built-in ones.

Begin a Group   Makes the selected command the first one in a new group on the menu bar.

Properties   Opens a properties box where you can change the caption, ToolTip, and help information for menu items.

Saving a Custom Menu Bar

When you finish defining all the commands and actions on your custom menu, just click Close in the Customize dialog box.

If you change your mind about any changes you made to a toolbar or menu bar, you can always use the Reset button to restore a built-in command bar to its original state. If you reset a custom command bar, it will return to its last saved state.

Displaying a Global Menu Bar

If you want your custom menu to replace the built-in menus as soon as the user opens your database, you can change the Menu Bar setting in the Startup dialog box:

1. Open your database and choose Tools ➤ Startup from the menus.

2. Change the setting for Menu Bar to the name of your custom menu. (If you haven't created any custom menus, the only choice will be "default").

3. Click OK to close the Startup dialog box.

To test the new menu bar, close the entire database and reopen it. Your custom menu bar will appear instead of the built-in menu.

 TIP   If you have trouble returning to the normal built-in menus, close the database. Then hold down the Shift key and reopen the database. Holding down the Shift key tells Access to ignore the Startup Properties, so your custom menu won't appear. Use the Startup dialog box to return the Menu Bar setting to the default if you need to.

Attaching a Custom Menu to a Form or Report

If you want a custom menu bar to appear whenever the user opens a particular form or previews a particular report, follow these steps:

1. Open, in design view, the form or report you want to attach the custom menu bar to.

2. Open the property sheet (View ➤ Properties) and select the form (Choose Edit ➤ Select Form.) or report. (Choose Edit ➤ Select Report.) Select the Other tab in the property sheet.

3. Choose the Menu Bar property, and then select the name of your custom menu bar from the drop-down list.

4. Choose File ➤ Close ➤ Yes to close and save the form or report.

If you've assigned a menu bar to a form, the menu bar you specified will appear only when the form is open in form view. If you've assigned a menu bar to a report, the menu bar you specified will appear only when the report is open in print preview. If you've defined a global menu bar for your application, the menu bar you attached to the form or report will replace the global menu bar whenever the form or report is open. When the user closes the form or report, the application's global menu will reappear.

Editing a Custom Menu Bar

If you need to change a custom menu bar that you've created:

1. Choose View ➢ Toolbars ➢ Customize.
2. Click the Toolbars tab if it's not already active. Then make sure the name of your custom menu bar is checked (so the menu bar will be displayed).
3. Make your changes using the same techniques you used to create the menu bar.
4. Click Close when you're done.

Creating Shortcut Menus

A *shortcut menu* is a menu that appears when you right-click an object. The object can be a control on a form or a report. It can also be the form or report itself. In fact, any object that contains a Shortcut Menu Bar or Shortcut Menu property on its property sheet can have its own shortcut menu.

You can create either a global or a context-specific shortcut menu. The next two sections explain how. A prerequisite, however, is to have built a menu that can serve as the shortcut menu.

Building a Shortcut Menu

To create a custom shortcut menu, follow these steps:

1. Choose Views ➢ Toolbars ➢ Customize from the menus.
2. Click the Toolbars tab and select New.
3. Enter a name in the New Toolbar box and click OK.
4. Click Properties on the Toolbars tab, change the Type setting to Popup, and click Close.
5. Check Shortcut Menus on the Toolbars list to display the Shortcut Menu like this:

6. Click Custom on the Shortcut Menus. The names of any shortcut menus you have already created will appear on a submenu. Click the name of the new shortcut menu you just created in steps 1 through 4. An empty box appears, just to the left or right of the new shortcut menu name. Then drag a command from the Customize dialog box or another toolbar to the empty box, as described earlier in this chapter. To add additional commands, drag them to the shortcut command list that you are creating.

7. Click Close in the Customize dialog box when you are finished.

Setting a Global Shortcut Menu

To set a global shortcut menu that displays when a form or object does not display its own shortcut menu, set the Shortcut Menu Bar property in the Startup dialog box (shown in Figure 25.5). To set this property, take these steps:

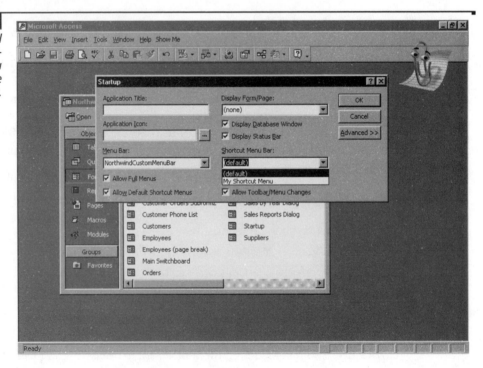

FIGURE 25.5

Creating a global shortcut menu by setting the Shortcut Menu Bar property in the Startup dialog box.

1. Select Tools ➤ Startup.

2. Use the Shortcut Menu Bar drop-down list box to select the shortcut menu you want to be global.

3. Click OK.

Setting a Contextual Shortcut Menu

To add a shortcut menu to a particular control on a form, or to a form itself, follow these steps:

1. Open, in design view, the form you want to attach the custom menu bar to.

2. Select the object you want to display the menu, or select the entire form.

3. Open the property sheet (View ➤ Properties). Select the Other tab in the property sheet.

4. Choose the Shortcut Menu Bar property, and then select the name of your custom menu bar macro from the drop-down list.

5. Choose File ➤ Close ➤ Yes to close and save the form.

Controlling Whether Shortcut Menus Appear

You determine whether a shortcut menu can appear for items on a form by setting the Shortcut Menu property for the form. To set this property, follow these steps:

1. Open, in design view, the form you want to display or not display shortcut menus.

2. Open the property sheet (View ➤ Properties) and select the form. (Choose Edit ➤ Select Form.) Select the Other tab in the property sheet.

3. Choose the Shortcut Menu property and then Yes or No from the drop-down list, depending on whether you want the menu to display or not.

4. Choose File ➤ Close ➤ Yes to close and save the form.

Converting Macro Menus to Access 2000 Menus

If you have menus created from macros or with the Menu Builder in older versions of Access, you can convert them to Access 2000 menus:

1. Open the database window for your database.

2. Click the Macros tab.

3. Select the macro that defines a top-level menu.

4. Choose Tools ➤ Macro ➤ Create Menu from Macro. (Use Create Shortcut Menu from Macro if you want to convert a shortcut menu.)

Access will create a menu with the same name as the macro. You can then customize the menu, if you need to, using the Customize dialog box.

PART

IV

Building a Custom
Application

Combining Menus and Toolbars

With Access you can freely combine menu commands and toolbar buttons to create hybrid command bars. With the Customize dialog box open, you can drag menu commands to toolbars, and toolbar buttons to menus. For an example, see "Combining Menus and Toolbars" in Chapter 24.

Where to Go from Here

Custom menus and toolbars (see Chapter 24) can make your database function like a stand-alone application. To begin building more complex applications, you need to use the more powerful programming features of Access. The next three chapters show you how to take advantage of Microsoft Visual Basic, Access's programming language.

What's New in the Access Zoo?

If you customized any menus or toolbars with Access 97, you'll find that the process is the same in Access 2000. The only difference is that there are new commands available, such as Diagram to support projects. You'll also find new buttons and commands for working with data access pages.

PART V

Refining a Custom Application

LEARN TO:

- *Use Visual Basic*

- *Create custom error messages*

- *Interact with other programs*

- *Pull it all together*

- *Work with projects*

CHAPTER 26

Introducing Visual Basic

I f you've experimented with hyperlinks and macros, you know that you can use them to automate lots of different database tasks. However, there are some cases where a macro or a hyperlink just isn't enough to do the task at hand. For example, if you want to prompt someone for the name of a file to import instead of using a macro to import a specific file, you need to don your propeller beanie and start programming.

The programming language for Access 2000 is Microsoft Visual Basic. This programming language is shared by Access and the other Microsoft Office applications.

Why Use Visual Basic?

Access provides macros that are easy to use and properties that can be set to run macros. Therefore, a legitimate question is why you would need to program in Visual Basic at all. In Chapters 21 through 25, for example, we showed you how to accomplish lots of tasks with macros. Can't you do everything you need with a macro?

The answer to that question is both yes and no. Yes, many Access users will never have to go beyond macros to accomplish what they need to do. However, no, you can't do everything with macros. Macros have some bad habits that prevent them from being ideal for every purpose. In general, you should use macros under the following conditions:

- When your focus is simplicity. Macros provide an extremely visual programming style. You do not have to learn syntax. You simply select from among the options provided, and the action you desire is automatically programmed.

- When you want to create a toolbar or menu. Visual Basic does not provide an alternative way of creating these objects.

- When you want to undertake an action at the time the database opens using the AutoExec macro. In this circumstance, you must use the macro.

- When the built-in error messages from Access are insufficient in case of trouble.

You should use Visual Basic when you have these goals in mind:

- When your focus is ease of maintenance. Unlike macros, Visual Basic procedures can be a part of the forms or reports that contain them. When you copy a form or report from one database to another, all of the Visual Basic procedures stored with the object are copied with it.

- When Access does not provide a function that you need. If no built-in function can perform a particular calculation, you can write your own function in Visual Basic.

- When you want to respond to error messages creatively. Using Visual Basic, you can create your own error messages or take an action that corrects the error without user intervention.

- When you need to check the state of the system. Macros will allow you to run another application, but they don't provide access to system level information. You cannot check, for instance, whether a file exists using a macro. Visual Basic, however, allows you access to system level information and actions.

- When you need to work with records one at a time. Macros perform actions on sets of records. Visual Basic allows you to step through records and perform actions on each single record while it is in focus.

- When you need to pass arguments between procedures. You can set the initial arguments for macros, but you can't change them while the macro runs. You can make such changes, or use variables for arguments, using Visual Basic.

What Is the Shape of Visual Basic?

So where does Visual Basic hide within the overall structure of Access? How do you use all of its wonderful features? To find Visual Basic, you need only look behind the Code button on the Form Design or Report Design toolbar. Clicking this button opens the code window for the form or report in focus (see Figure 26.1). Using this window, you write your custom procedures and functions.

FIGURE 26.1

The code window for the Contacts form in the Contact Management Lessons database generated by the Database Wizard.

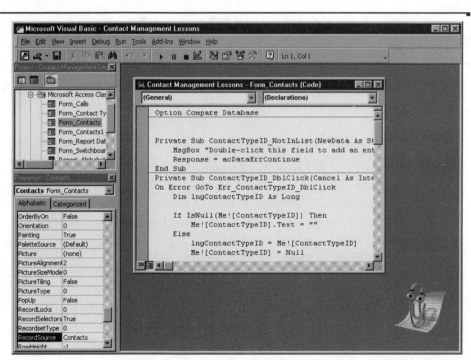

The code that you insert into a form or report applies only to that form or report, or to the objects contained within it. Although you can call these procedures from any other procedure included in your database, the code still applies only to the form or report and the objects contained therein. For code that needs to be accessible to any object in your database, create a module using the New button on the Modules tab in the database window. Place your global procedures and functions in this code window.

Visual Basic and Objects

Visual Basic is an object-oriented programming environment. This means that an *object* has a set of procedures and data associated with it. Some objects also have a visual representation, though others are available only in Visual Basic code. A good example of an object is a form. You draw the form on the screen, it is associated with a set of procedures, and data is displayed in the form.

Given this definition, reports are also objects, as are any of the controls that you use to build both forms and reports—objects can contain other objects. (Technically, tables and queries can also be considered objects.) Each object has *properties* associated with it, which govern the appearance and behavior of the object. Each object also has a set of *methods* defined for it, which are actions the object can take. Some objects, including forms, reports, and controls, also respond to a set of *events*.

You are already familiar with properties for objects. They are the same properties that you have been setting for forms, reports, and controls as you have worked with databases throughout this book. Methods should also be familiar, since you have used the methods (such as Recalc, GoToPage, and SetFocus) associated with forms. Events are very similar to event properties, into which you could insert a macro; however, you can write Visual Basic code that responds to each event, instead of relying on pre-defined macro actions.

Visual Basic and Events

Visual Basic uses event procedures to respond to events. By default, Visual Basic never does anything when an event occurs. If you want an object to respond to an event, say a button click or the activation of a form, you have to write the code for the procedure. Your code overrides the default action, allowing the action you define to take place in response to the event.

Each object defines the events to which it responds. If you look in the code window for the Contacts form in the Contact Management Lessons database, you can get a sense of how these events are made available to database developers (see Figure 26.2). The form contains several objects. The drop-down list box in the upper-left corner of the window lists all the objects associated with the form. The General object represents code that affects all the objects in the list. Each object, including the form itself, is designated by a name, which is one of an object's properties.

FIGURE 26.2

The list of objects in the code window for the Contacts form in the Contact Management database.

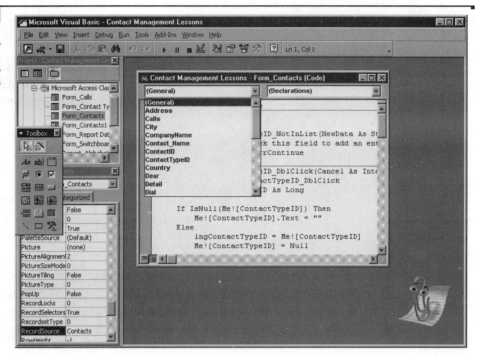

PART

V

Refining a Custom Application

The drop-down list box in the upper-right corner of the code window lists all the events to which an object responds, as shown in Figure 26.3. Each event is given a descriptive name, such as DblClick. When you select an event from the list, the code window displays the frame of the event procedure, consisting of a Private Sub statement and an End Sub statement. These two statements are required to frame the code responding to the event. They frame the block of code known as an *event procedure*, the set of statements that causes an action in response to an event.

Visual Basic and Statements

In order to build an event procedure, you have to use Visual Basic statements and functions. If you are not familiar with programming, you may feel overwhelmed by the number of statements available to you. Visual Basic provides flow control statements, such as If... Then... Else..., which govern the order in which other statements execute, and whether they are executed or skipped. (The two statements that frame an event procedure are, in fact, flow control statements.) Visual Basic also provides statements that cause an action to take place, such as Beep (which causes the system to send a beep to the speaker) or ChDir (which changes the current folder or directory). Visual Basic has dozens of such statements available. Help contains a complete reference for them.

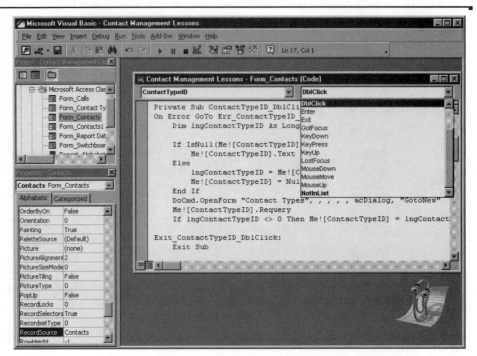

 TIP The next chapter covers Visual Basic flow control in more detail.

In addition, you can write statements that set an object property, assign a value to a variable, use a function, or use a method. To assign a value to an object property, you write a statement in the following form:

```
Set Object.Property = Value
```

To assign a value to a variable, you use a statement of this form:

```
Set Variable = Value
```

To use a function, first you select a function that calculates something or takes an action. Typically, functions return a value for your program to use—one that's calculated, or a code indicating the outcome of an operation. As a result, you often assign the value of a function to a variable for future use. The following statement, for example, uses the Date function to collect the system date and stores it in a variable named Today:

```
Today = Date
```

To use a method, you use the same kind of syntax that you use to set a property—but without an equal sign. You combine the name of the object with the method using dot notation to form the statement. One of the most useful object names is Me, which names the object currently in focus. The following statement causes the current object to redraw itself using the Refresh method associated with it:

```
Me.Refresh
```

Visual Basic and Variables

We mentioned variables just in passing. A *variable* is a name you give to Access, and Access then sets up an area of memory for storing an item and gives it that name. A variable is said to have a *type*, which describes the nature of the item that can be stored in it. By default, Visual Basic creates variables of the *variant* type, which means that anything can be stored in it. To create a variable and give it a name, you simply use it. Or you can explicitly name it in a statement called a *declaration* at the beginning of your procedure:

```
Dim strDialStr As String
```

This statement says to create, or "dimension" (hence the Dim statement), a variable named strDialStr as type String. The strDialStr variable can therefore contain only strings of characters. Attempting to assign data of some other type to it will cause an error. Visual Basic supports the following variable types:

Byte   Positive integers from 0 to 255

Boolean   Values that are either True or False

Integer   Whole numbers between –32,768 and 32,767

Long   Whole numbers between –2,147,483,648 and 2,147,483,647

String   Text up to approximately 65,500 characters in length

Currency   Numbers with up to four decimal places between –955,337,203,685.5808 and 955,337,203,685.5807

Single   Real numbers in the range $\pm 1.40 \times 10^{-45}$ to $\pm 3.40 \times 10^{38}$

Double   Real numbers in the range $\pm 4.94 \times 10^{-324}$ to $\pm 1.79 \times 10^{308}$

Date   Dates and times stored as real numbers

Object   Data that holds Object references

Variant   Can contain any of the preceding data types

When you name a variable, you should include the first three letters of its type in its name, as in the strDialStr variable shown above. The reason for including the type in the name is that you can always tell what can be stored in a variable by looking at its name. Late at night on a long project, or coming back to maintain code after two months away from it, you will appreciate this convention.

 NOTE To make a variable available to all procedures and functions in your application, place it in a global code module and precede it with the keyword `Public`.

Visual Basic and Procedures

Event procedures are not the only procedures you can write in Visual Basic. You can also write a procedure as a part of a global code module or at the General level of any form or report, and you can call that procedure any time you need to perform the action undertaken by the procedure.

The Contacts database uses this type of procedure to handle the button clicks in the switchboard. At the General level in the Switchboard form is the procedure `Handle-ButtonClick`. This procedure receives the button number as its argument, and takes action based on the button number received. One function can therefore service several buttons. The On Click property of each button is set equal to the name of this procedure. When a click takes place, the procedure is called to perform its task.

You need to remember two things about event procedures. First, event procedures cannot return values for the rest of the program to use. You cannot set a variable equal to the value of the event procedure. Second, when a procedure is a part of a form or report, it has reference only to that form or report. Place your procedures in global code modules if you want to be able to use them anywhere in your database application, and precede them with the keyword `Public`, rather than `Private`. If you would like to learn more about how to set up public procedures, go to the Office Assistant when the Visual Basic window is open. Type **public**, press Enter, and click *Public Statement* on the list of topics that appears. The Remarks section at the end of the Public Statement Help topic has lots of useful information.

Visual Basic and Functions

Functions are procedures that return a value for use by other statements in the program. The return value is set using the function name as a variable, as shown in the following function generated by the Database Wizard for the Contacts database:

```
Function IsLoaded(ByVal strFormName As String) As
   Integer
   ' Returns True if the specified form is open in
   ' Form view
```

```
' or Datasheet view.

Const conObjStateClosed = 0
Const conDesignView = 0

If SysCmd(acSysCmdGetObjectState, acForm,
   strFormName) <> conObjStateClosed Then
   If Forms(strFormName).CurrentView <> conDesignView _
     Then
     IsLoaded = ' Set the return value
                ' using
                ' the function name as a
                ' variable.
   End If
End If

End Function
```

NOTE Some of the statements that are split across lines above need to be entered on one line. To see how this function appears in the Visual Basic window, open the Contacts form in design view and click the Code button. Then click the Find button, enter Function as the Find What value, and change the setting for Search to Current Project. After a few clicks of Find Next, you should end up at the Function listed above.

Don't worry about the statements that seem like Greek in this function right now. Wait until you have some experience with Visual Basic before you try to start interpreting them. The main thing to remember about building a function is to set the return value and to use the Function and End Function statements to frame it.

NOTE Functions can take *arguments*, variables whose values are made available to the function for use. These variables are named in the parentheses following the function name. When you name them, you use the As keyword to name their type, just as you do when declaring a variable. If you do not want the function to modify the value stored in the variable, precede the name of the variable with ByVal.

Building a Sample Procedure

Speaking of getting some experience with Visual Basic, here's your chance. In this section, we build a real Visual Basic procedure! While this procedure will be simple, it will give you the basics. The next two chapters undertake some more complex actions. (Remember, we have three chapters to get you started programming with a language that people write whole books about. Be patient, give yourself some time, and study the Help files and sample code. You'll be an expert in no time!)

Having read the preceding sections, you have enough background to understand how a procedure is built. We have a surprise for you about how Access builds procedures. In many cases, you don't have a great deal of code to write because a wizard writes it for you. (Convenient, no?) As an example, we are going to add a command button that prints a copy of the form being viewed. You can practice on any database form that you want. Visual Basic works the same way in all forms.

To add the button, take these steps:

1. Open the form in design view.

2. Make sure the Control Wizards button is pressed in.

3. Select the toolbox button that draws the command button.

4. Drag with your mouse to draw the button on the form. After a brief pause, the Command Button Wizard appears (see Figure 26.4).

FIGURE 26.4

The first page of the Command Button Wizard allows you to select the type of action the event procedure performs.

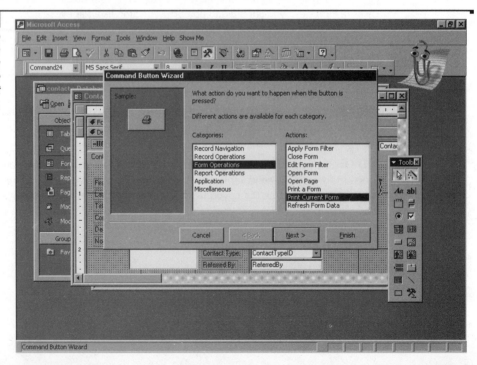

5. Select the class of action you want to take in the Categories list. Since we want to print a form, select Form Operations. Select the specific action in the Actions list, in this case, Print Current Form. Click the Next button.

6. Select whether you want a picture or text to appear on the button face by using the option buttons provided. If you choose text, enter the text as you want it to appear. If you choose a picture, you can use the browse button to select a graphic. Click the Next button.

7. Enter a meaningful name for your button in the text box on the last Wizard page. Make the name a mnemonic for the button's function. For the code example below, we used Print_Form. Then click the Finish button.

When the Wizard finishes, it has built the click event procedure for you. You can see the procedure by right-clicking the button and selecting Build Event from the menu that appears. The procedure created appears below:

```
Private Sub Print_Form_Click()
  On Error GoTo Err_Print_Form_Click


  DoCmd.PrintOut
  Exit_Print_Form_Click:
  Exit Sub


  Err_Print_Form_Click:
  MsgBox Err.Description
  Resume Exit_Print_Form_Click


End Sub
```

Congratulations! You've just programmed your first procedure, and using excellent programming form we might add. This procedure is very straightforward. The first statement turns on error handling (more about that in the next chapter). The second statement uses the PrintOut method of the DoCmd object to print the form. (The DoCmd object contains all the actions you can invoke using macros.) The next program line is a *label*, which is a string of text that carries out no action but can serve as a jump destination. Labels end in colons. The line following the colon causes the procedure to end. The remaining three lines are a label and error-handling code. (Again, more about that in the next chapter.)

The greatest thing about writing procedures for common objects in Access is that you have a wizard for each one. You do not have to be an expert programmer to get lots of work done in Visual Basic.

PART

V

Refining a Custom
Application

Converting Macros to Visual Basic

You can also convert macros you already have written into Visual Basic code. To convert macros associated with a form or report, open the object in design view and select Convert Macros to Visual Basic from the Macros submenu on the Tools menu.

To convert global macros, click the Macros tab in the Database dialog box. Then click the macro you want to convert. Open the File menu, select Save As, enter a name for the module (if you need to change the default name that's filled in for you), and change the setting for As to Module. Then click the OK button.

Learning More about Visual Basic

For more information about how to use the features of Visual Basic, take a look at these sources:

- Help on *Visual Basic* from the Office Assistant. You'll find several topics, including instructions on how to obtain the *Microsoft Office 2000/Visual Basic Programmer's Guide*.

- Any of the excellent books available on using Visual Basic in Access, including the *Access 2000 VBA Handbook* from Sybex.

- Use the Office Assistant to find help for *Office Developer*. Then click the topic for *Microsoft Office 2000 Developer Contents*. This topic outlines the many tools for Visual Basic programmers that are part of the Microsoft Office 2000 Developer package.

- The code that the Database Wizard generates whenever it creates a database of a specific type. You can learn a lot about how Microsoft programmers use Visual Basic by studying these examples.

- Two magazines, the *Visual Basic Programmer's Journal* and the *VB Tech Journal*, both of which bring you monthly discussions of how to use Visual Basic to accomplish specific tasks.

- The *Access/Visual Basic Advisor*, a newsletter from Advisor Publications, or Pinnacle Publication's *Smart Access* and *Visual Basic Developer*.

Where to Go from Here

Having introduced you to Visual Basic in this chapter, in the next two chapters we show you how to do some interesting work with this programming language. Chapter 27 explains how to create your own error messages, and Chapter 28 explains how to use OLE Automation to control other programs.

What's New in the Access Zoo?

In Access 97, Visual Basic procedures were edited in a Module window. Now, the Visual Basic Editor is available from Access. VB programmers working in Access will also find new commands that make it easier to work with SQL statements.

PART

V

Refining a Custom Application

CHAPTER 27

Creating Custom Error Messages

Even the best planned application occasionally screws up. When that happens in Access, an error is generated. You have two options for handling these errors: Let Access and Visual Basic do it for you or respond to the errors yourself. The first option is very convenient. You don't have to do anything. However, the result of an error is that your application stops executing. The user sees a dialog box and whatever was happening stops. Although using the cryptic error descriptions that Access provides by default for error handling is convenient for you, it is rather rude for users of your application.

The second option, handling errors yourself, is less convenient for you, but makes your application much more user-friendly. When you respond to the errors, you can interpret the error for your user and provide a suggestion about what to do. In many cases, you do not even have to inform the user that an error has occurred. You write code to correct the situation and restart the execution of your code.

This chapter teaches you how to handle errors yourself, and in the process shows you a couple of ways to go beyond the wizard-written code that you learned how to create in the last chapter. To learn how to handle errors, you need to learn about flow control in Visual Basic programs. But first, we need to focus on the two ways to create custom error messages: there's one way for macros, and one way for Visual Basic.

 WARNING There is one time when error trapping is absolutely necessary: when you use the Access Developer's Toolkit (ADT) to create a "runtime" version of your application. In this case, any untrapped error causes your application to quit completely.

Building Custom Error Messages with a Macro

When you are using macros, you can create a custom error message using the MsgBox action. To do so, create a new macro by clicking the New button in the Macros tab of the database window. On the macro sheet, select MsgBox as the action and fill in the properties. Figure 27.1 shows a completed error macro.

When you fill in the arguments, you can create a formatted message in the Message box using the @ character. Format your message in the following way:

```
Data Entry Form@This form does not support double-clicking. @Use the buttons
at the bottom of the form to scroll to the record you want.
```

The first third of the message, to the left of the first @ symbol, appears in boldface at the top of the message box window. The second third of the message, between the two @ symbols, appears on the next line. The remainder of your message appears just below, as shown in Figure 27.2.

FIGURE 27.1

A macro designed to notify users that double-clicking has no effect in this context.

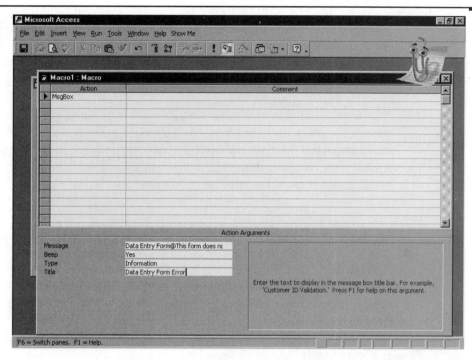

FIGURE 27.2

A custom message displayed using the MsgBox action.

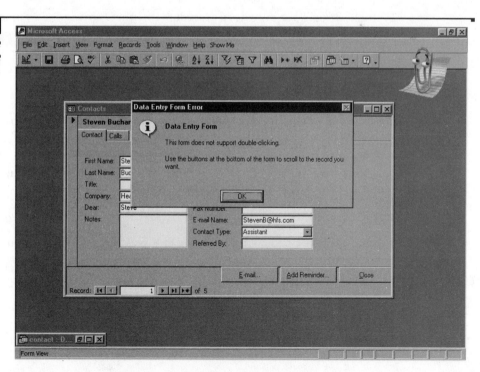

The remaining arguments for the MsgBox action govern additional features of the message box. The Beep argument determines whether a warning beep is played when the message box appears. The Type argument determines which icon is displayed in the message box: Information (as in the example in Figure 27.2), Critical, Warning?, Warning!, or none. The Title argument contains the text string displayed in the title bar of the message box window.

To display such a custom error message, you assign the macro to an appropriate event argument of the object to which it refers. In the case of a data entry form, we would assign this macro to the On Dbl Click event property for each object on the form. If your custom error message is intended to respond to an error generated by Access, assign it to the On Error event property.

Building Custom Error Messages in Visual Basic

To create a custom error message in Visual Basic, you need to learn a little more about Visual Basic programming. You need to learn how the flow of execution is controlled in a program, and you need to learn how to handle the flow of execution when an error occurs.

Flow Control in Visual Basic

Typically, Visual Basic executes a procedure by either copying the arguments into the variables made available to the procedure or (for ByVal arguments) giving the function access to the variable named in the argument. After arguments are made available, Visual Basic starts at the first statement in the procedure and executes each statement in sequence until it reaches the End Sub or End Function statement. If an error occurs, Visual Basic stops executing the code and displays an error message. It does not resume executing the code after the user dismisses the error message from the screen.

You can change the order in which statements are executed in several ways. For our purposes in explaining error handling, we will refer to these as using flow control statements and invoking flow control on error.

Flow Control Statements

To build effective custom error handling in Visual Basic procedures, you have to know how to control the flow of execution. We'll show you how to respond to several possible types of errors as this section progresses.

NOTE You can use flow control anywhere in your program. We are discussing it in relationship to errors because, given the way Access builds code for you, you are most likely to use flow control in building your own error handlers.

Conditionals Probably the most common way of controlling the flow of execution is a conditional statement. You set up a condition using an `If` statement. If the condition is true (and all conditions must evaluate to either true or false, logically), you execute the statement following the Then statement. If the condition is false, you execute the statement following the `Else` statement. You can express alternate conditions using an `ElseIf` statement. The whole conditional ends with an `End If` statement. Such a block of code looks like the following:

```
If ErrorNumber = 10 Then
  ' Code lines that execute if the ErrorNumber
  ' equals 10 go here.
ElseIf ErrorNumber = 100 Then
  ' Code lines that execute if the ErrorNumber
  ' equals 100 go here.
Else
  ' Code lines that execute if the ErrorNumber
  ' is equal to some other value go here.
End If
```

Loops Loops allow you to repeat a set of statements over and over again. In handling errors, you will find loops most useful when you are correcting an error condition. For example, in response to a File Not Found error, you might want to loop through the list of controls on a form to make certain that those used to represent the filename have valid values. When you find the control that needs correction, you could prompt the user to enter a valid value.

You have four different ways of looping available to you. A Do loop executes the statements that appear between the Do statement and the Loop statement until a condition, expressed in either the Do or Loop lines, is false or while a condition is true. (You determine whether the loop executes *until* or *while* by using the `Until` or `While` keywords.) You can exit such a loop at any time by using an `Exit Do` statement. Such loops look like the following:

```
Counter = 0
Do While Counter < Me.Controls.Count
  If Me.Controls(Counter).Text = "" Or _
    IsNull(Me.Controls(Counter).Text) Then
```

```
        Me.Controls(Counter).Text = InputBox("Enter _
            a proper filename")
    End If
    Counter = Counter + 1
Loop
```

NOTE   The space followed by an underscore (_) at the end of a line of code indicates that the line with the underscore is continued on the next line.

This example assumes that a form has several text controls on it, each holding a filename. The user has asked Access to open the files, and one of the controls is blank. An error occurs, and to handle it, you choose to check the text of each box to make certain none of them are blank. (You might also check for invalid characters as well.)

Every form has associated with it a collection of controls. Me is an Access keyword referring to the form to which the code is directly attached. You can access each control using the notation shown. The collection is named Controls, and each control can be identified by an index number. By using the variable Counter, you can start at the first control in the collection (Control(0)) and repeat the action for each control until the last one on the form (Control(9)). If we encounter a blank control, we use an InputBox statement; it displays the text in the argument and a text box in a dialog box, collects input from the user, and returns the text to be stored in the variable Me.Controls(Counter).Text, which is also the text property of the control. If you wanted to exit the loop when you found the first blank text control, you would place an Exit Do statement immediately before the End If statement.

TIP   You could accomplish the same task using the statement Do Until Counter = 10. The expression can also be placed on the last line, as in Loop Until Counter = 10.

You could accomplish the same error-handling task using a counted loop. These loops begin with the keyword For and execute a fixed number of iterations named in the first line. These loops have the following form:

```
For Counter = 0 To 9
  If Me.Controls(Counter).Text = "" Then
    Me.Controls(Counter).Text = InputBox("Enter _
        a proper filename")
  End If
Next Counter
```

In For loops, the counter is incremented for you automatically. In this case it starts at the value 0 and increments to 9 automatically. The Next statement marks the end of the loop code. Although the name of the counter variable is optional on the last line, it's a good idea to use it. If you have loops within loops, you can tell which Next goes with which For.

Visual Basic provides a loop to use with collections of objects that simplifies the task of looping. These loops have the following form:

```
For Each Control In Me
  If Control.Text = "" Or IsNull(Control.Text) Then
    Control.Text = InputBox("Enter _
      a proper filename")
  End If
Next
```

This form of the For loop allows you to avoid having to manage a counter. What if you aren't sure how many controls are on the form denoted by Me? Access knows, and this loop simply makes use of Access's internal count to increment a counter that is hidden from you.

 TIP You can exit a For loop at any point by using the Exit For statement.

The last type of loop executes a set of statements while a condition remains true. It has this form:

```
Counter = 0
While Counter < 10
  If Me.Controls(Counter).Text = "" Or _
    IsNull(Me.Controls(Counter).Text) Then
    Me.Controls(Counter).Text = InputBox("Enter _
      a proper filename")
  End If
  Counter = Counter + 1
Wend
```

This form of loop is very like a Do loop with some simplification of form. It is bounded by While and Wend statements, and once again you must increment your own counter.

PART

V

Refining a Custom
Application

NOTE To learn more about any statement used in Visual Basic, check the Visual Basic Help file. If you use the Help command while you're in the Visual Basic window, you'll end up in Microsoft Visual Basic Help.

Branches Branches are critical to error-handling code, as you will see in the next section. Understanding them is therefore essential to learning how to make Visual Basic handle errors elegantly.

The concept of branching goes back to the days when each line in your program was numbered. If you knew the flow of execution had to skip from one line to another distant line, you could use a GoTo statement to jump to the appropriate line number.

Although you can still use line numbers in Visual Basic, the practice is not recommended. (Eventually you have to renumber all the lines because of additions or changes to the program, and then all your line-number-based jumps have to be adjusted by hand.) Instead, you jump to labels, which are strings of text used as bookmarks in the code. A label is any string of text ending in a colon. Visual Basic keeps track of where they are and can move to them when you use a GoTo statement to request a jump.

The GoTo statement has the following form:

```
GoTo Label
```

And the label would appear in your program code in a line as

```
Label:
```

When Visual Basic encounters the GoTo Label statement, it moves to the text string Label: and resumes execution with the first line following.

A variant of the GoTo statement allows you to return the flow of execution to the line after the statement that caused the jump to take place. The variant form looks like this:

```
GoSub Label
'Other program lines go here
Label:
  If Me.Controls(Counter).Text = "" Then
    Me.Controls(Counter).Text = InputBox("Enter _
      a proper filename")
  End If
Return
```

The GoSub statement works exactly like GoTo in that the jump occurs to the text string Label: and the If statement is executed. However, when Visual Basic encounters the Return statement, execution returns to the line following the GoSub statement. You can jump out, execute some code, and return to where you were.

Another variation of both these statements begins with the keyword On, as in the following lines:

```
On ErrorCode GoTo Label1, Label2, Label3
On ErrorCode GoSub Label1, Label2, Label3
```

In each of these statements, ErrorCode can be a variable or an expression that evaluates to a value ranging from 0 to 255. If the value is 0, execution resumes with the next statement. If the value is 1, execution jumps to Label1. If the value is 2, control jumps to Label2. If the value exceeds the number of items on the list of labels, execution resumes with the next statement. If the value is negative or greater than 255, an error occurs. These variations are just ways to have a single jump statement branch to several labels.

 NOTE You must remember that Visual Basic ignores any label it encounters in the normal flow of execution. As a result, if you have several labels at the end of a procedure for handling errors, you need to have a means of stopping your program before it gets to those labels in the event no error occurred. We'll show you how in the next section.

The most effective branching statement, however, is the Select Case statement. It allows multiple branches, and it allows you to respond to discontinuous values of an expression or variable. As a result, you can collect an error number (Patience, that information is coming!) and branch to the statements that handle the error appropriately. You can even specify what to do in case there is no match for the values you specify. The Select Case statement looks like this:

```
Select Case ErrorNumber 'Evaluating the error number

Case 1, 2, 3 'Error numbers 1 through 3
  Debug.Print "I have mapped these error numbers _
    to the same message"
Case 5 To 8 'Error numbers 5, 6, 7, and 8
  Debug.Print "Error numbers 5, 6, 7, and 8 _
    receive this message through Debug.Print"
Case Is > 8 And ErrorNumber < 20 'Error numbers
                                 'between 8 and 20
  Debug.Print "I have demonstrated how to trap _
    error numbers within a range, specifically _
    between 8 and 20"
Case Else 'What to do when there is no match
  Debug.Print "All other error numbers get this
    message"
End Select
```

This example shows that you can use various expressions to form the matching statements. Each Case statement represents one possible match. The Case Else statement marks the code that will execute if no match is found. When a Case or Case Else statement executes, the code lines following it execute and the flow of execution jumps to the statement following the End Select statement.

Flow Control On Error

We're sure that seems like a lot about flow control, but error handling in Visual Basic depends on flow control. You use an On Error statement to determine the flow control when an error occurs. If you don't have an On Error statement in your procedure, execution stops when an error occurs. If you want the opportunity for your user to be able to correct the error or if you want execution to continue at all for any reason, you need to use one of these three variations of the statement:

> **On Error GoTo Label**   This version causes control to jump to the specified label when an error occurs. At the end of the error handler at that label, a Resume statement causes execution to resume with the line after the one that caused the error.

> **On Error Resume Next**   This version causes the error to be ignored and execution to continue normally.

> **On Error GoTo 0**   This version causes the current error handling to be canceled. You can then use another form of On Error to redirect flow control in a different way.

It's time to look again at the click event procedure you created for the Print button in the last chapter. Here is the procedure:

```
Sub Print_Form_Click()
  On Error GoTo Err_Print_Form_Click
  DoCmd.PrintOut
Exit_Print_Form_Click:
  Exit Sub
Err_Print_Form_Click:
  MsgBox Err.Description
  Resume Exit_Print_Form_Click
End Sub
```

Notice the On Error statement at the beginning of the procedure. When an error occurs anywhere in the procedure, it redirects execution to the label Err_Print_Form_Click. This label leads to code that handles the error. The Resume statement includes the label Exit_Print_Form_Click as an argument, which causes the resumption of execution at that label. The first statement following this label causes the event procedure to exit.

Notice the logic of building the procedure. If no error occurs, the statements execute sequentially until the Exit Sub statement causes the procedure to end. If an error occurs, execution jumps beyond the Exit Sub statement to the error-handling code. After the errors are handled, execution jumps back to the Exit Sub statement. This procedure provides an excellent template for developing error-handling routines.

You might recognize the MsgBox function in the error-handling code and guess that it performs the same function as the macro of the same name. It does. But what is that Err.Description argument? Visual Basic provides an Err object. When an error occurs, it makes the Err object, with its properties and methods, available to you. The Description property is the text string that describes the error. The MsgBox function builds a message box that announces that an error of this type has occurred.

The Err object also has a Number property. This property can be used with branching statements to allow you to handle any of several errors that might occur in your procedure. (The Select Case statement is especially useful for this purpose.)

For more information about the Err object, search Help for *Err*.

Building the Error Message

So, having been drilled in the basics of Visual Basic error handling, you might have guessed already how to provide a custom message to your users: use the MsgBox function and use your own text string rather than the one stored in Err.Description. Congratulations! You've mastered some of the mysteries of Visual Basic coding.

You might wonder why we say *MsgBox function* rather than *MsgBox statement*. The reason is that MsgBox returns a value. It has some subtleties, therefore, that you should know about.

First, MsgBox has three critical arguments, which must occur in the order specified. (Although you can omit the Buttons and Title arguments, you will almost always wish to supply them, since they provide information to your users.)

Prompt   The text string to display as the message.

Buttons   A number that determines which buttons are displayed in the message box. These numbers are represented by constant expressions maintained by Visual Basic for your use. As a result, you should use the constant names, as shown next.

Title   The text string to display in the title bar of the message box.

You can use the @ symbol to format the message string exactly as you do when you use the MsgBox macro to display a custom message.

TIP If you want to learn more about the arguments for MsgBox, search the Help file for the function name.

The Buttons argument can take the following values:

vbOKOnly   Show OK button only.

vbOKCancel   Show OK and Cancel buttons.

vbAbortRetryIgnore   Show Abort, Retry, and Ignore buttons.

vbYesNoCancel   Show Yes, No, and Cancel buttons.

vbYesNo   Show Yes and No buttons.

vbRetryCancel   Show Retry and Cancel buttons.

vbCritical   Show Critical Message icon.

vbQuestion   Show Warning Query icon.

vbExclamation   Show Warning Message icon.

vbInformation   Show Information Message icon.

vbDefaultButton1   First button is default.

vbDefaultButton2   Second button is default.

vbDefaultButton3   Third button is default.

vbApplicationModal   Only the Access application is suspended until the user responds to the message box.

vbSystemModal   Suspend all applications until the user responds.

vbMsgBoxHelpButton   Shows a Help button in the message box.

vbMsgBoxSetForeground   Puts the message box window in the foreground.

vbMsgBoxRight   Right-aligns text.

vbMsgBoxRtlReading   On Hebrew and Arabic systems, displays text right-to-left.

To combine any of these attributes to determine what is displayed and how, add these constants together using the plus sign.

The following code fragment shows how to build the same custom message that you built using the macro earlier in this chapter:

```
strMsg = "This form does not support " _
    & "double-clicking.@Use the buttons at the bottom of " _
    & "the form to scroll to the record you want." _
intResult = MsgBox (strMsg, vbOkOnly + _
    vbInformation, "Data Entry Form")
```

The variable `intResult` collects the return value of the function, which allows you to determine which button in the message box the user clicked. The possible return values are the following:

vbOK   The OK button was clicked.

vbCancel   The Cancel button was clicked.

vbAbort   The Abort button was clicked.

vbRetry   The Retry button was clicked.

vbIgnore   The Ignore button was clicked.

vbYes   The Yes button was clicked.

vbNo   The No button was clicked.

Obviously, you can use flow control statements to test the return value and take appropriate action in response to the user's click.

Where to Go from Here

Now that you have a grasp of flow control and error handling, in the next chapter we'll show you how to control other applications from inside your Access application. This is a slick trick, so be prepared to see some real magic.

Refining a Custom
Application

CHAPTER 28

Interacting with Other Programs

One of the greatest features of Access 2000 is its support for OLE automation, a technology that allows you to control one Windows program while you're working from another. This means that you can run a Visual Basic program from Access to perform a task, such as creating an Excel spreadsheet and entering data in it. To use this feature, you need to be able to program in Visual Basic. You also need to be aware of some quirks associated with OLE objects and their automation. In this chapter we will explain those quirks and provide you with a basic template for using automation in your own applications.

What Is OLE Automation?

By using OLE automation from Access, you can treat any application on your system as an object that belongs to Access. Imagine having Word or Excel behave exactly like a command button that you draw on a form. You could carry out any command in either application using the *object.method* notation. And you would have access to all of their commands. You could reliably start the application from within an Access application and direct the application to do exactly what you wanted it to do.

OLE automation gives you this kind of flexibility, but there are a couple of hitches:

- The application you want to control has to be an OLE automation server. In other words, it has to be designed to allow itself to be automated.

- When you automate an object, you get access only to the commands to which the designers allow you access. The set of commands available may change depending on whether the data object you intend to use is embedded in your database.

- You have to know something about the command structure of the program you are automating. In automating Word and Excel, for example, you use Visual Basic. However, you have to master program-specific extensions to Visual Basic.

You can work your way around most of the limitations you might encounter. Quite obviously, you would not try to automate a program that cannot be automated. And you can usually find your own ways to work around limited functionality. In addition, Access provides an object browser to allow you to see the automation objects available and the methods you can use. This chapter uses workarounds and the object browser.

Creating the Basic Object

To use automation, first you have to make an object out of the application you intend to automate. In this example, we will automate the creation of an Excel worksheet from Access. The worksheet will be based on a template we'll make ahead of time in Excel. The name and social security number from the Access record we are viewing will be filled into the worksheet, the worksheet will be saved, and Excel will be closed.

You must do two preliminary things to prepare to automate these actions. First, you must create an Excel template for the worksheet. Assume that the members of a nonprofit corporation want to build an Excel worksheet to track the fees their educational consultants earn. Open Excel, create a worksheet containing the boilerplate text, and save it as a template using File ➤ Save As. (Be sure to set the Save as Type to Template.) Figure 28.1 shows a simple worksheet of this sort.

FIGURE 28.1

A sample Excel template for tracking consultants' fees.

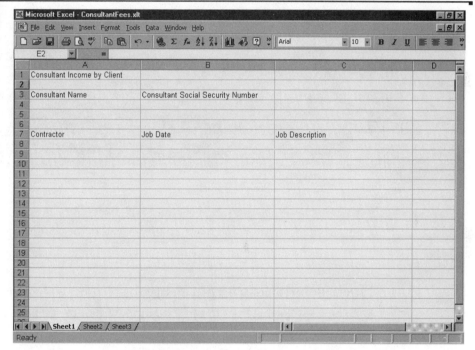

The second step is to open a data entry form that includes controls for LastName and SocialSecurityNumber in design view, and to add a button to the form. When you draw the button, select Application and Run MS Excel in the Command Button Wizard, as shown in Figure 28.2. Name the button AutomateExcel and finish the Wizard. You won't be using the actual code generated, but the Wizard will generate a useful event procedure template for you.

PART

V

Refining a Custom Application

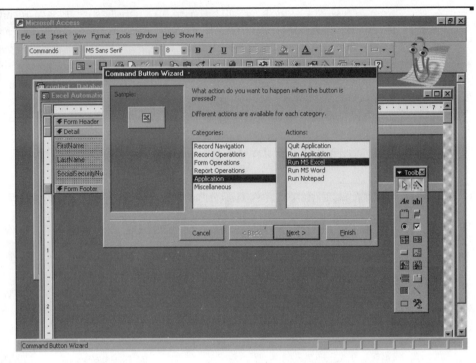

Now you are ready to create an object for Excel. Just follow these steps:

1. Right-click the button and select Build Event from the context menu.

2. Open the drop-down list in the upper-left corner in the code window and select General.

3. Open the drop-down list in the upper-right corner and select Declarations.

4. Enter the following lines in the code window after the Option Compare Database line:

```
Dim xlObject As Object ' Declare variable to
                       ' hold the
                       ' reference to the
                       ' Excel Object.
```

5. Open the Object drop-down list in the upper-left corner and select Automate-Excel. You will be taken to the Click event procedure that Access generated for you automatically.

6. Revise the lines of code after the On Error statement so they look like the following:

```
' Create an object for Excel
Set xlObject = CreateObject("excel.application")

' Make the Excel application visible
xlObject.Visible = True

On Error Resume Next
xlObject.UserControl = True
```

Your Click event procedure should look like Figure 28.3. At this point, close the code window, take the form to form view, and try out the button. Excel should start and become visible.

PART

V

Refining a Custom Application

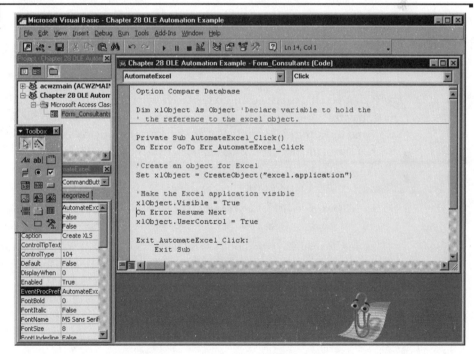

FIGURE 28.3

The click event so far.

What have you done so far? A pretty neat trick, actually. The Dim statement you added declared a variable that can hold a reference to an object. Whenever you want to use the object whose reference is stored there, you can use the variable name as the object name. You created the object variable at the form level so that it would remain available while the form was in use. If you created it in the event procedure itself, as soon as the event procedure terminated, Access would deallocate the variable's memory, effectively deleting it until the event procedure was run again. Then the variable would be recreated, but its original value would be lost.

The Set statement in the Click procedure sets the variable equal to the return value of the CreateObject function. The CreateObject function—you guessed it—creates objects out of whatever item you provide as its argument. In this case, we asked it to create an Excel application object. OLE automation–enabled applications provide strings that you can use as arguments to CreateObject to make objects out of them. CreateObject creates the object and returns a reference to the object. The reference is now stored in xlObject for later use.

Immediately after creating the object, we used it. Excel was started automatically because we created an object out of it. But Excel does not become visible until you decide to show it. The next line in the Click procedure sets the xlObject's Visible property to true, causing Excel to show itself on the screen.

Working with the Basic Object

Now that you have created an Excel object, you might like to do something with it. First, having started Excel, you need to create a workbook. Return the form to design view and open the code window. Place the cursor in the code window at the beginning of the blank line after xlObject.Visible = True and add the line below. (Be sure to substitute the correct path name for ConsultantFees.xlt if you stored it in a directory other than C:\Windows\Application Data\Microsoft\Templates.)

```
Set xlBook = xlObject.Workbooks.Add _
("C:\Windows\Application Data\Microsoft\Templates\ConsultantFees.xlt")
```

Having created the workbook using the last few lines of code, we want to insert the appropriate information from the database into the Excel worksheet. To do so, you have to activate the worksheet, select the cell using Excel's Range function, and activate the cell. To accomplish these actions, add these lines of code after the two lines listed above:

```
' Activate the worksheet, select the range, activate
' a cell in the range.
xlObject.Worksheets("Sheet1").Activate
xlObject.ActiveSheet.Range("A4").Select
xlObject.ActiveSheet.Range("A4").Activate
```

In these lines, you use the Worksheets object to activate the worksheet and the ActiveSheet object to work with the cells on the worksheet you activated.

 TIP You can use the Object Browser to add most of these lines. Press F2 to open the Object Browser. If you don't see Excel on the top drop-down list, choose Tools ➤ References, check off Microsoft Excel 8.0 Object Library, and click OK.

To actually insert information from Access into the Excel worksheet, you have to set the focus to the control containing the information on the Access form. You do so using the SetFocus method for the control. You can then set the value for the Active-Cell object in Excel. Insert these lines of code after the lines you just entered:

```
' Set the focus to the LastName control on the
' Access form.
LastName.SetFocus
' Place the last name in the active cell.
xlObject.ActiveCell.Value = LastName.Text
```

Next, you repeat the same process for the social security number cell using these lines of code:

```
' Repeat the process for the social security
' number cell.
xlObject.Worksheets("Sheet1").Activate
xlObject.ActiveSheet.Range("B4").Select
xlObject.ActiveSheet.Range("B4").Activate
SocialSecurityNumber.SetFocus
xlObject.ActiveCell.Value = SocialSecurityNumber.Text
```

To complete the operation of creating the spreadsheet, set the focus to the Last-Name control once again, since the last name of the consultant will be the filename for storing the workbook. Then use the Workbook's SaveAs method to save the spreadsheet:

```
' Set the focus to the Access Last_Name control
' and save the workbook.
LastName.SetFocus
xlBook.SaveAs (LastName.Text + ".xls")
```

Now take the form to Form View and click the button. Watch as Excel opens and builds the worksheet, completely under your control from Access.

Closing Your Automation Session

Having learned how to automate Excel and do some work with it, you might want to know how to stop Excel when you want to. Otherwise you could have multiple copies of Excel starting, and eventually your system would crash from lack of memory, even if you have a lot of memory. To automate the close routine, do two things: Use the Excel object's `Quit` method and set the value of any variables you used to store object references to the built-in value `Nothing`. The following lines of code, added after the lines you already entered, do the trick:

```
' Quit Excel and clear the object variables.
xlObject.Quit
Set xlBook = Nothing
Set xlObject = Nothing
```

Now when you click the button, Excel creates the spreadsheet and then closes itself, as shown in Figure 28.4. (The assumption is that you create these worksheets infrequently; otherwise, it would make more sense to keep the workbook open until you were finished, and to set the name of each sheet to the last name of the consultant.)

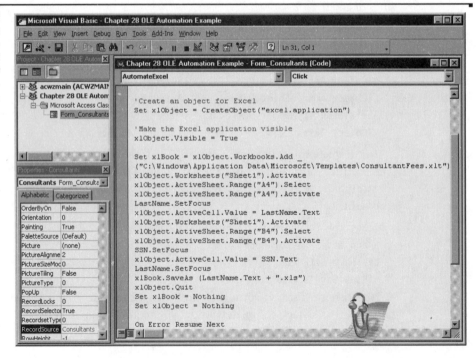

Where to Go from Here

OLE Automation offers you exceptional possibilities. You can conduct complete spreadsheet analyses, build documents, chart graphs, print presentations, and more, all from within Access. If you so desire, you can work from within Word or Excel as well.

The main question you might have is how you can learn more about using these Access features. Take these steps:

- Use the Object Browser to explore different applications to see which objects, properties, and methods are available to you.

- Check the documentation for each of your applications to learn the fundamentals of their macro languages. In Excel and Word, you can use Visual Basic, as well.

PART

V

Refining a Custom
Application

CHAPTER 29

Pulling It All Together

Chapters 1 through 28 have, for the most part, been about creating individual objects in Microsoft Access. Needless to say, many tools are available for creating tables, queries, forms, data access pages, reports, macros, and Visual Basic code.

But as with any endeavor, knowing how to create a finished product requires more than just knowing how to use the individual tools. For example, you might well know how to use a hammer, nails, saw, and drill, but do you know how to build a house? Likewise, perhaps you know every tool and technique your word processor has to offer. But then, how do you go about creating a novel?

You might think of this transition as going from "toolmaster" to "artist." And for most people that transition is sort of the second brick wall in the learning process. That is to say, there's the first brick wall of learning what tools are available and how to use them; then there's the second brick wall of learning how to apply those tools to actually create something useful.

Many people get past the second brick wall by doing some "reverse engineering" from other people's work. In the fine arts, we take this approach for granted, even though we use a different terminology. We talk about the artist's "influences." That is to say, the artist has mastered the tools of his trade, but in learning to apply those tools to create, the artist has no doubt observed and borrowed from other artists. The artist has reverse engineered the existing work to see what makes it tick.

We don't mean to imply that all works are plagiarism. To the contrary, anything the artist creates is uniquely his or her own creation. But in virtually every work of art or product that a human being creates, you can find some influences from the artists that preceded him or her.

So what does any of this have to do with Microsoft Access? Well, granted, Access is a tool for managing data. But it is also a tool for creativity. You can't create songs, novels, or houses from Access's tools, but you certainly can create Windows applications.

A good way to make the transition from being an Access toolmaster to an Access applications artist is to reverse engineer other people's applications to see what makes them tick—to see how more experienced Access developers have applied Access's tools to create their own unique applications. For the rest of this chapter (and book), we want to give you some tips on how to learn by example.

What's Available to You

Microsoft has provided three complete applications with Microsoft Access for you to explore. They are named Northwind.mdb, Contacts Sample Database.mdb, and Address Samples Database.mdb. You can typically find them in the C:\Program Files\Microsoft Office\Office\samples folder after you've installed Microsoft Access.

NOTE If any of the sample databases are missing from your Samples folder, you can install them from your original Office 2000 CD-ROM. From the Windows Desktop, click the Start button and choose Settings ➢ Control Panel ➢ Add/Remove programs. Click Microsoft Office 2000 or Access 2000, and then click Add/Remove. Follow the instructions on the screen to add just the Sample Databases.

We've also included a sample application named Fulfill 2000 on the CD-ROM that comes with this book, and we refer to that application throughout this chapter. To install and learn about Fulfill 2000, see Appendix C.

Opening and Using an Application

Keep in mind that an Access database application is an Access database (.mdb file) with macros and code to make it perform like a stand-alone product. This means that you can open any Access application by using the standard File ➢ Open Database commands within Access. You can also double-click the name of the .mdb file in the Windows Explorer, Find, or My Computer windows to launch Access and load the application.

To use the application, you just interact with the command buttons, menus, and toolbars that appear on the screen. If you want to go spelunking behind the scenes to see what makes the application tick, you need to get to the application's objects. The general term we use for all the behind-the-scenes stuff is *source code*. That term is a leftover from the days when the only thing you would find "behind the scenes" was program code. Nowadays, especially in an Access application, you'll see lots of objects—tables, queries, forms, data access pages, reports, and macros, as well as code—behind the scenes. But Access developers use the term *source code* anyway.

Getting to the Source Code

Before we describe how to get into source code, we need to tell you that it isn't always possible to get to the source code! If an Access developer sells his or her product for a fee, he or she might have secured the database to prevent you from getting to the source code, using the techniques we covered in Chapter 19. We respect a developer's right to do that and have no complaints about it. You might, however, be able to purchase the source code from the developer.

Many applications, like the four we mentioned earlier, are wide open to exploration. All you need to do is get past the forms and get to the database window. In the Fulfill 2000 application, the process is quite simple:

1. Choose Exit from Fulfill's main switchboard. You'll come to this dialog box:

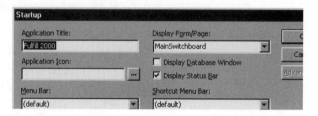

2. Choose To Fulfill's Database Window.

You're taken to the database window for all of Fulfill's objects. All the standard Access menus and toolbars are intact, so you can explore to your heart's content.

To go behind the scenes with the Northwind, Contacts, or Addresses sample databases, you may have to close any custom form that appears by clicking its Close button. If you don't see the database window, try pressing the F11 key to bring it into view.

If an application gives you access to its database window, chances are you can also modify its startup options. Doing so will allow you to get right to the application's database window, as well as the standard built-in menu bars and toolbars, as soon as you open the application. To change the startup options:

1. Choose Tools ➤ Startup with the application's database window showing.

2. Select (check) the various Display and Allow options from the Startup dialog box to give yourself access to all the normal Access tools, as shown in Figure 29.1.

3. Choose OK.

4. Reopen the database to activate the new settings. That is, choose File ➤ Close. Then choose File and click the database's name in the File menu to reopen with the new startup settings.

FIGURE 29.1

The Startup options determine how much access you'll have to built-in Access tools when first opening a database.

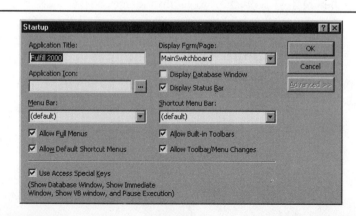

Finding Out What Makes It Tick

Once you get to an application's database window and have all the standard menus and toolbars in place, you're free to explore to your heart's content. Just click the type of object you want to explore (for example, Tables, Queries, Forms), click the name of the object you want to explore, and then click the Design button.

The bulk of the "meat" in most applications is in its forms. You can discover a lot about what makes an application tick by exploring its forms. Here's an example. Suppose you open, in design view, the form named AddressBook in Fulfill 2000. Your screen might initially look something like Figure 29.2.

PART

V

Refining a Custom
Application

FIGURE 29.2

Fulfill's AddressBook
form open in
design view.

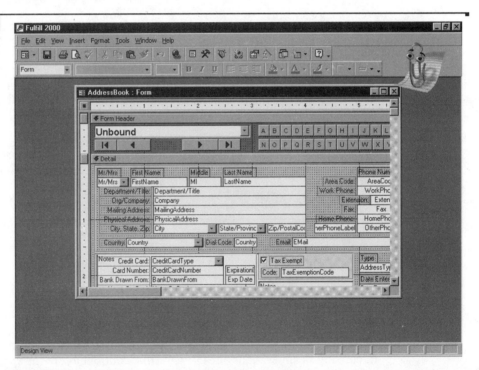

Why No Custom Menus in Fulfill 2000?

We've left custom menus and toolbars out of Fulfill 2000 on the CD-ROM because its main purpose in life is to act as an example for aspiring application developers to explore. If we were to turn Fulfill 2000 into a "real product," we'd have to do some more work.

Continued

CONTINUED

For starters, we would create all custom menus and toolbars. Then we would use the Access Developer's Toolkit (ADT) to round out the application even further. We'd use the ADT (or some other commercially available tool) to create a standard Windows 95/98 help system for Fulfill. And then we'd use the ADT to generate a runtime version of Fulfill 2000 so that we could distribute the application to people who don't own Microsoft Access. (The Microsoft Access Developer's Toolkit (ADT) is a separate product that must be purchased separately.)

Then we'd probably give away a few copies to interested parties to get some feedback and to find any weaknesses and bugs we didn't catch the first time through. We'd fix any remaining problems before actually selling the product.

To find out where this form gets its data, you need to look at the form's property sheet, so you choose Edit ➤ Select Form. Then you open the property sheet, click the All tab, and take a look at the Record Source property. There you'll see that the form is based on a query named AddressesAlphabetized, as below.

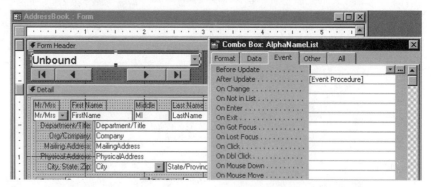

To see what makes that query tick, you just need to click the Build button next to the query's name.

In virtually all applications, the elements that control most of the application's behavior are the *event procedures* assigned to the form and individual controls. To see the events assigned to a form as a whole, choose Edit ➤ Select Form, open the property sheet, and click the Event tab. In this example, we've created four custom event procedures for the AddressBook form, as you can see in Figure 29.3.

FIGURE 29.3

The AddressBook form's behavior is controlled by four event procedures.

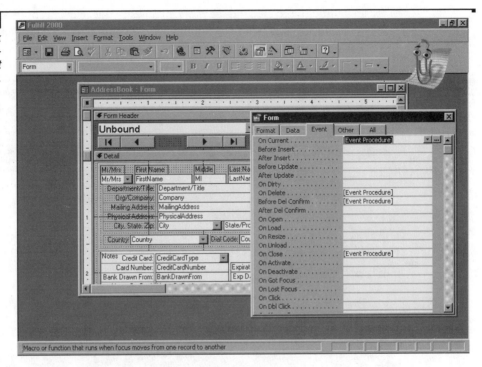

Many of the individual controls on a form will also have one or more custom event procedures assigned to them. To see a control's event procedure, click the control you're interested in and take a look at the Event tab in the property sheet.

In some cases, you may see the name of a macro in an event property. You can click that macro name and then click the Build button to explore the macro. In most cases, you'll probably see Event Procedure as an event's property. The Event Procedure is Visual Basic code that's stored right along with the form and is accessible only through the form's design view.

Let's take a "for instance." Suppose we click the big Unbound control in the Address-Book form. The property sheet informs us that (1) this control is a combo box, (2) its name is AlphaNameList, and (3) a custom event procedure is assigned to this control, as you can see below.

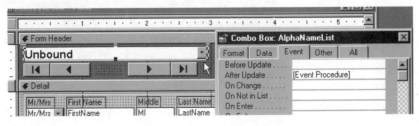

To go behind the scenes and see the Visual Basic code, click Event Procedure in the property sheet, and then click the Build button. The underlying code appears in a module window, as shown in Figure 29.4.

FIGURE 29.4

Visual Basic code attached to the After Update property of the AlphaNameList control in the AddressBook form.

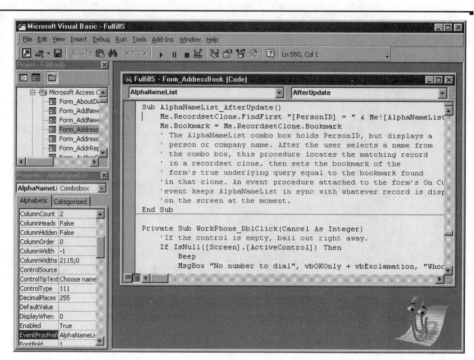

Unless you happen to be a Visual Basic expert, your reply to this finding might be, "Great, but I have no idea what any of that code means." One of the cool things about Microsoft Access is that the online Help is linked to keywords in the code. You can start learning what all the various Visual Basic commands do just by exploring Help right from this screen.

For example, to find out what *RecordsetClone* is all about, you could drag the cursor through that command to select it.

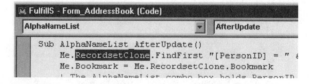

When you press Help (F1), a help screen appears, telling you about Recordset-Clone, as in Figure 29.5.

FIGURE 29.5

*Information about
RecordsetClone on the
screen.*

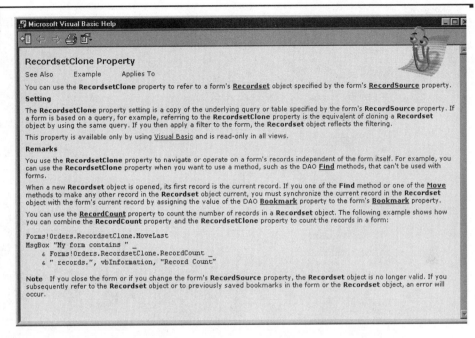

What Good Is This Information?

Now you might look at that so-called help screen in Figure 29.5 and think, "But it's so technical, it really doesn't help me at all." If that's the case, you're reading all of this much too early in your application-development apprenticeship.

The reason this information appears in Chapter 29 is that it won't do you any good until you know how to do all the stuff in Chapters 1 through 28! This kind of exploration is useful only when you're ready to go from toolmaster to artist. You have to know the "mechanics" of creating tables, queries, forms, data access pages, controls, reports, macros, and Visual Basic code before the nitty-gritty technical details of individual Visual Basic commands have any useful meaning to you.

Printing Technical Documentation

Pointing and clicking individual objects is just one way to explore existing Access applications. You can also print all the technical behind-the-scenes stuff. Here's how:

1. Open the application you want to explore, and get to its database window.

2. Choose Tools ➤ Analyze ➤ Documenter to get to the dialog box shown in Figure 29.6.

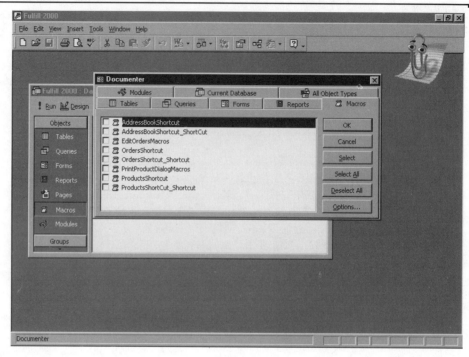

FIGURE 29.6

The Documenter dialog box lets you view and print technical behind-the-scenes information on any object in a database.

3. Click the tab for the type of object you want to explore, and then click the check boxes for the objects you want to document. Be aware that any given object can produce a lot of documentation, so you may want to document just one or two objects at a time.

4. (Optional) Click the Options button and specify exactly what you want to print. Then click OK after setting your options.

5. Click OK and give Access a few minutes to prepare the documentation. When the documentation is ready, you'll be taken to the report preview screen showing a window named Object Definition (Figure 29.7).

6. Click the Print button in the toolbar to print the documentation.

When you've finished, you can just click the Close button in the Object Definition window to return to the database window.

FIGURE 29.7

The Object Definition
window displays tech-
nical information
about one or more
objects in a database.

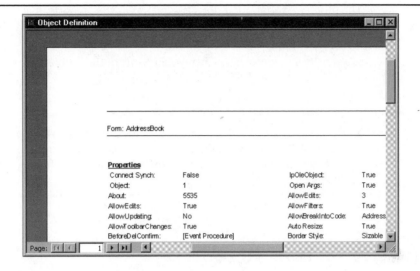

Modifying Existing Applications

Once you get to the source code (the database window) of an Access application, the temptation to start tweaking it to better meet your own needs will be strong. In fact, if you can get your hands on the source code for an application, the implication is that you want to modify the application. We have some advice to give you on modifying existing applications.

Modifying an existing application is a terrific way to help ease the transition from toolmaster to artist. However, if you try to customize an existing application before you've become an Access toolmaster, then you're very likely to find yourself in deep water very quickly. Just the simple act of deleting or renaming a single object—even one little field in a table—can wreak havoc throughout the rest of the application. Here's why.

Let's suppose we have a field named AddressLine2 in a table in an application. You decide you don't need that field, so you delete it from the table or you change its name to PhysicalAddress. You save the change and all seems fine.

But then as you start using the application, you keep coming across little *#Name?#* and *#Error#* messages, or you keep seeing a little window like this popping up on the screen:

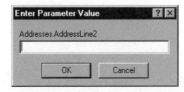

The problem is that other objects—queries, forms, reports, macros, and modules—might "expect" to find a field named AddressLine2 in that table. When you delete or rename that field in Access's table design view, *that change does not carry over to any other objects in the database.* So when you use one of those objects, it just flat-out doesn't work.

 TIP You can avoid some renaming problems by turning on the new AutoCorrect feature. Choose Tools ➢ Options from the menus, click the General tab, and check Track Name AutoCorrect Info under Name AutoCorrect. For more information on AutoCorrect, see Chapter 16.

Where to Go from Here

Exploring existing applications is just one way to make the transition from Access toolmaster to Access artist (or *application developer*). You can also find plenty of books that pick up where this one leaves off. An excellent book on macros is *Access 2000 VBA Handbook* by Susann Novalis, published by Sybex.

Another great resource for information, add-on products, training, and more is the *Access/Visual Basic Advisor* magazine. For information and pricing, contact:

Access/Visual Basic Advisor

P.O. Box 469030

Escondido, CA 92046-9918

Phone: (619) 483-6400

        or
        (800) 336-6060

Fax: (619) 483-9851

CHAPTER 30

Working with Projects

*P*rojects are a new feature of Access 2000 for creating client/server applications. With a project, you can create an application that works with data stored on an SQL Server database. We won't be able to teach you about creating client/server applications in this book because that topic could fill volumes on its own. Instead, this chapter will provide you with some basic information about projects. You'll also see how to work with the sample NorthwindCS project that comes with Access 2000 and find out how to create a new project yourself.

> **NOTE** If you want to work with data on an SQL Server, but don't need to create a client/server application, you can use an Access database (.mdb file) instead of a project (.adp file). See Chapter 7 for instructions on linking SQL Server tables to a database.

Project Basics

An Access project is stored in its own file with the .adp extension. (Access database files have the .mdb extension.) A project is organized similarly to a database in that it can include forms, reports, data access pages, macros, and modules. The main difference is that a project connects directly to data on an SQL Server instead of using tables that are stored in or linked to a database file.

A project can work with data on these SQL Servers:

- The integrated store that's part of Access 2000, Microsoft Data Engine (MSDE)
- SQL Server 6.5
- SQL Server 7 (SQL Server 7 Eval Edition available on the CD-ROM)

Elements of an Access Project

Many of the elements of an Access project are the same as those for an Access database. For example, a *project* can have forms, reports, pages, macros, and modules. These objects all work the same way for projects as they do for databases. However, a project has no queries. Instead, it has *views* and *stored procedures*. A project can also include *database diagrams*. The database window for a project has buttons on the Objects bar for all these objects:

Tables As with an Access database, tables hold data. For a project, tables are stored on an SQL Server.

Views Like queries in an Access database, views are used to show records from related tables, find selected information, and perform calculations. Views can be created using an SQL Server design tool that's similar to the Access query window.

Database diagrams These objects show the relationships between SQL Server tables as a diagram. The information you see in a database diagram is like the contents of the relationship window you can open for an Access database. However, the tools in the diagram window also let you make design changes to tables or delete tables from a database altogether.

Stored procedures Stored procedures are statements that are used to show data in related tables, find data, and do calculations.

Forms Forms are for viewing, entering, and editing data.

Reports These objects let you preview or print data.

Pages These HTML files are Web pages for browsing data with Internet Explorer 5.

Macros Macros are used to automate database tasks.

Modules These objects hold Visual Basic code.

If you'd like to see examples of views, stored procedures, database diagrams, and the SQL Server design tools that are available in a project for working with these objects, install the sample NorthwindCS project as described next.

The Sample NorthwindCS Project

Access 2000 includes a project called NorthwindCS that you can use to see how projects work, even if you don't have access to an SQL Server. The tables for the sample project are created and accessed using the Microsoft Data Engine (MSDE), which comes with Office 2000. The NorthwindCS project and MSDE are not installed automatically when you run the Office 2000 setup program, so you will need to follow the instructions outlined next.

Installing the Sample NorthwindCS Project

To install the NorthwindCS project, NorthwindCS.adp, follow these steps:

1. Place your Office 2000 CD in your CD-ROM drive.

2. When the Setup program starts, click the Add or Remove Features button.

3. In the Update Features dialog box, click the Expand button (+) for Microsoft Access for Windows.

4. Click the Expand button for Sample Databases.

5. Under Sample Databases, use the drop-down menu for Northwind SQL Project File to change its installation option to Run from My Computer. (By default, the setting for this file is Not Available.)

6. Click the Update Now button.

7. Click OK when the Setup program finishes adding the database to your computer.

After you install the Microsoft Data Engine, you'll find out where to find this project on your computer so you can open it.

Installing the Microsoft Data Engine

Before you can work with the NorthwindCS project, you will need to install Microsoft Data Engine (MSDE). You will also have to start the SQL Server Service Manager program that is part of MSDE. If you try to open the project without the Service Manager running, no tables will appear in the database window.

These steps show you how to install MSDE and start the SQL Server Service Manager:

1. Close any programs you have running on your computer.

2. Place your Office 2000 CD into your CD-ROM drive.

3. On your Windows Desktop, double-click My Computer.

4. Using the My Computer window, go to the folder for D:\Sql\X86\Setup.

5. Double-click the icon for Setupsql.exe.

6. Follow the prompts to complete the installation. You can accept the default settings in all the dialog boxes.

Starting the Microsoft Data Engine

After you install MSDE, you will have to start the SQL Server Service Manager that is part of MSDE before you can open the NorthwindCS project. If you forget to do this, you can open the NorthwindCS project, but the tables that are part of the project will not be available. When you click the Tables button in the database window, you will see an empty list instead of table names.

Start the Service Manager, as outlined next, before you open the NorthwindCS project to avoid this problem.

1. Click the Windows Start button and choose Programs ➣ MSDE ➣ Service Manager from the menu. An SQL Server Service Manager dialog box like this will open:

2. To start the Service Manager, click the Start/Continue button.

3. Minimize the SQL Server Service Manager window, if you want to clear it off the Windows Desktop while it's running.

Opening the NorthwindCS Project

After you install the NorthwindCS project and start the SQL Server Service Manager, you can open the project this way:

1. Start Access.

2. Click Open on the toolbar, choose File ➣ Open, or press Ctrl+O to show the Open dialog box.

3. In the Open dialog box, change the setting for the Look In box to C:\Program Files\Microsoft Office\Office\Samples.

4. Select the file called NorthwindCS.adp and click Open. You'll see a database window like the one shown in Figure 30.1.

Creating the Project Tables

The first time you open the NorthwindCS project (NorthwindCS.adp), you will have the option to create the SQL Server tables for the project using the Install Database dialog box. If you don't see this dialog box the first time you open the project, follow these steps:

1. In the NorthwindCS database window, click Tables.

2. An Install Database dialog box will open. Click Yes to create the tables for the NorthwindCS project.

PART

V

Refining a Custom
Application

3. When the Installation Successful dialog box opens, click OK.

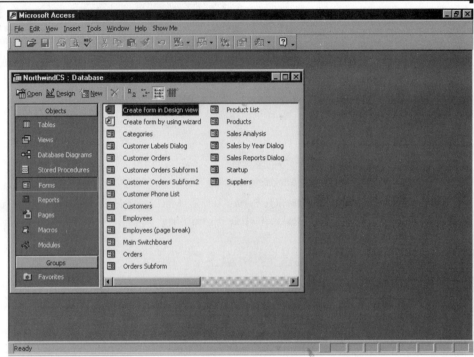

These tables will be created and added to the NorthwindCS database window: Categories, Customers, Employees, Order Details, Orders, Products, Shippers, and Suppliers.

Working with the NorthwindCS Project

Once the NorthwindCS project is opened, you can open its views, stored procedures, and database diagrams in design view to see what they look like. Of course, you are free to explore other types of objects as well, but they work the same for projects as for databases, so you won't find anything new.

 TIP The NorthwindCS project has its own custom Help system. Click Show Me on the toolbar to get to this help.

Views

Views, like the queries you find in an Access database, can be used to show records from one or more tables. They can include criteria to show selected records and expressions to show calculated fields. After you design a view, you can use it as the basis of a form or a report. Or, you can double-click a view in the database window to see its results.

The NorthwindCS project includes several predefined views. Figure 30.2 shows the view called Alphabetical List of Products open in a window that looks like a datasheet view. Any changes that you make to data shown in this window will be reflected in the data tables that underlie the view.

FIGURE 30.2

A view called Alphabetical List of Products from the NorthwindCS project.

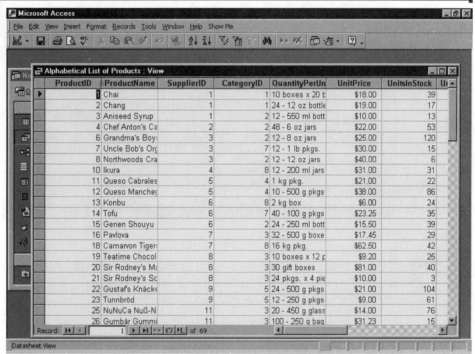

If you switch to design view for the Alphabetical List of Products view, you'll see a query designer window like the one in Figure 30.3. The query designer is somewhat like the query design window you see when you work with queries in an Access database. There are some big differences, though. The grid in the bottom half of the window is arranged with one field per row, instead of one field per column. Even with these differences, it should be easy for you to learn to design views if you are already comfortable working with Access database queries.

FIGURE 30.3

The Alphabetical List of Products view shown in design view.

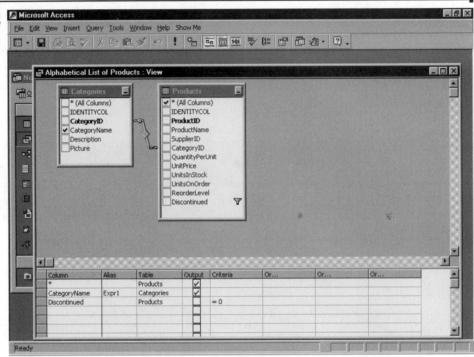

For more information on views, open the Office Assistant, enter *Views*, and click any of the topics that appear. You'll find help on creating views and working with them. The topic *Designing Queries* has several links to other help topics, such as *Query Designer Layout* and *Supported Query Types*.

Stored Procedures

Stored procedures are like views in that you use them to display records from one or more tables, filter records, and show summary information or calculated values. Stored procedures are formulated by entering SQL statements, though, instead of using the query designer. If you look at Figure 30.4, you can see the stored procedure called Ten Most Expensive Products that's part of the NorthwindCS project. In the figure, it is shown in design view. As you can see, the stored procedure is rather cryptic, unless you are familiar with SQL statements. This is not a tool for inexperienced project users. However, if you know what you're doing, you can use this tool to enter complex SQL statements.

FIGURE 30.4

A stored procedure
called Ten Most
Expensive Products.

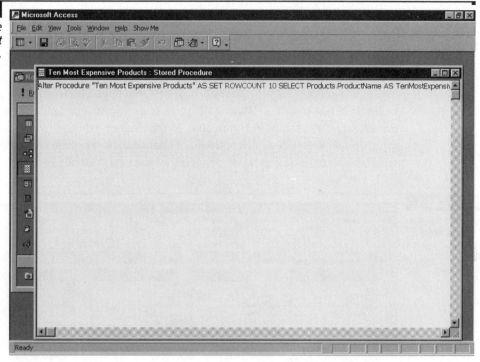

When you run the Ten Most Expensive Products stored procedure, Access opens a window like the one in Figure 30.5. You can see in the figure that the results are presented in a window like the datasheet view used to display tables.

FIGURE 30.5

The results of running
the Ten Most Expensive
Products stored
procedure.

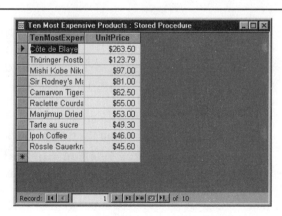

PART

V

Refining a Custom
Application

If you want to learn more about stored procedures, open the Office Assistant, enter *Stored Procedures*, and click any of the topics that appear. You'll find general information on stored procedures, and detailed instructions on how to create them.

Database Diagrams

Database diagrams show the relationships that you define between the SQL Server tables. When you open a database diagram, it appears in a diagram window like the one called Relationships in Figure 30.6. In the diagram window, you can define relationships between tables, delete them, or change their properties. You can also work with table designs, just as if you opened the tables individually in design view.

FIGURE 30.6

A database diagram called Relationships for the NorthwindCS project.

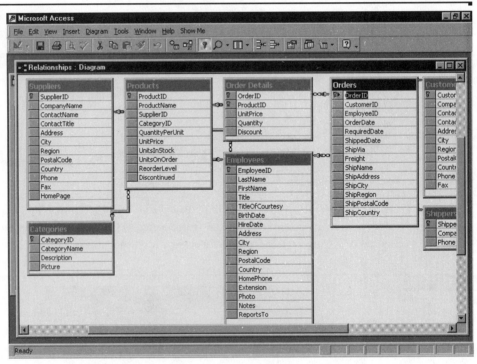

Here are a few quick tips on using the diagram window:

- **To see the name of the relationship that has been defined between tables**, point with your mouse to the symbols that join the tables in the window. (Table relationships are indicated by a graphical link made up of a key, a line, and a few chain links. If the tables are close together in the window, you may only see the key and a bit of chain.) The name of the relationship will appear on the Desktop in a yellow rectangle. For example, if you point to the link between the Orders and the Order Details tables, the name *Relationship 'FK_Order_Details_Orders' between 'Orders' and 'Order Details'* will be displayed.

- **To delete a relationship**, right-click the link between the tables and choose Delete Relationship from Database from the shortcut menu that appears.

- **To check or change the properties of a relationship**, right-click the link between tables and choose Properties. You'll see a Properties dialog box like the one in Figure 30.7.

The Properties dialog box for the relationship between the Orders table and the Customers table in the NorthwindCS project.

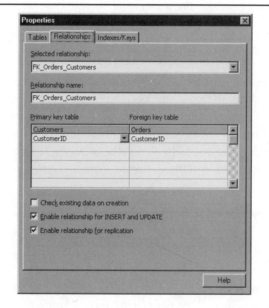

PART

V

Refining a Custom Application

- **To change the way a table appears in the window**, right-click the blue bar where the table name appears, and click one of the options at the top of the shortcut menu that pops up. Column Properties shows additional columns for each field for properties like Datatype and Default Value; Column Names shows all fields (the default display mode); Keys shows only the key fields (the primary key and foreign key fields used to link the table to other tables); Name Only shows the table name only; and Custom View displays only columns that you choose.

- **To add a field to a table**, right-click the field just below the place you want the new field to appear, and choose Insert Rows. In the blank row, enter the new field name. By default, the new field will have the Char data type. If you want to change the data type or change other properties of the field, right-click the table header and choose Column Properties. Then make your changes in the various property columns.

- **To delete a field**, click its row selector (the gray box to left of the field name) and press Delete.

 WARNING When you delete a field in the diagram window, you can't undo your change with the Undo command. You can close the diagram window and choose to cancel all your changes, but you will still have to redo any changes you made before you deleted the field and while the diagram window was open.

The Database Diagram Designer is a powerful tool with many more features than we have room to describe here. For example, you can use it to create subdiagrams and later merge them into one master diagram. To learn more about this feature and others, open the Office Assistant, enter *database diagrams*, and click any of the topics that appear. You'll find help on creating database diagrams, using the Database Diagram Designer, and working in the database diagram window.

Creating a New Project

Access lets you create a new project for existing SQL Server tables, or you can create a blank project for tables you'll create later. In either case, you start from the New dialog box. Make sure you have any information you need to connect to the SQL Server database. You will be prompted for this information so that the project can successfully connect to the SQL Server database when it is opened.

Creating a Project to Work with Existing Tables

To create a new project to work with existing SQL Server tables:

1. Click the New button on the Access toolbar.

2. In the New window, select the General tab.

3. Double-click the icon for Project (Existing Database) to open the File New Database window.

4. In the File New Database window, enter a name for the new project file. You can use the techniques outlined in "Using the File New Database Dialog Box" in Chapter 5 to enter a name. Don't bother to enter a file extension. Access will automatically add the .adp extension to the new project's name.

5. Click the Create button. Access will open a Data Link Properties window like the one in Figure 30.8.

FIGURE 30.8

When you create an Access project to work with SQL Server tables, the Data Link Properties window lets you choose the server and database where the tables reside.

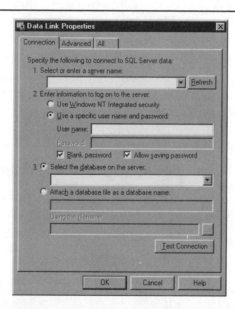

6. Under "1. Select or Enter a Server Name," enter the name of the server where the SQL Server database you want to use resides.

7. Under "2. Enter Information to Log on to the Server," enter your server logon information.

8. Click the radio button for Select the Database on the Server, and choose a database from the drop-down list; or you can click the button for "Attach a Database File as a Database Name and enter the names."

9. Click OK to attach the database you chose in step 8 to the new project.

Creating a Project for New Tables

You can start a new project even if you have not yet created the SQL Server tables the project will reference. As part of creating a project for new tables, Access starts the

Microsoft SQL Server Database Wizard. This Wizard guides you through the process of logging on to an SQL Server so you can make new tables. To create a project this way:

1. Click the New button on the Access toolbar.

2. In the New window, click the General tab.

3. Double-click the icon for Project (New Database) to open the File New Database window.

4. In the File New Database window, enter a name for the new project file. See "Using the File New Database Dialog Box" in Chapter 5 for tips on using this window. Access will add the .adp extension to the new project's name, so you can leave that part of the name off.

5. Click the Create button. Access will open a database window for the new project and then start the Microsoft SQL Server Database Wizard. The first step of this Wizard is shown in Figure 30.9.

FIGURE 30.9

When you start a project for new SQL Server tables, the Microsoft SQL Server Database Wizard gives you help creating a new database.

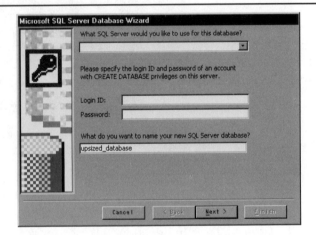

6. Under What SQL Server Would You Like to Use for This Database, use the drop-down list to select the server you want to log on to. Then enter your Login ID and Password, and a name for the new SQL Server database that will hold the tables for your Access project. Click Next when you're ready to go to the next step.

7. Follow the rest of the prompts to complete the process.

Once you're in the database window for the new project, you can use the table design view window to create new tables.

Where to Go from Here

We thank you for reading and wish you all the best in your endeavor to become a full-fledged Windows application developer. We know from experience that mastering this complex tool takes a heck of a lot of time, patience, and brain cells. But the creative prowess that mastery brings you is well worth the effort.

PART

V

Refining a Custom
Application

PART VI

Macro Programming

from Industry Expert Susann Novalis

LEARN TO:

- **Become an expert in using the macro Design window**

- **Create macros**

- **Design to avoid macro errors**

- **Analyze errors with troubleshooting tools**

- **Understand error codes**

CHAPTER **31**

Macro Basics

NOTE The material in Part VI is adapted for Access 2000 from Susann Novalis' *Access 97 Macro and VBA Handbook* (Sybex, 1997). For more information on using VBA with Access 2000, see the *Access 2000 VBA Handbook*, by Susann Novalis (Sybex, 1999).

icrosoft Access provides two sets of tools for automating your database: macro programming and Visual Basic for Applications (VBA) programming. Why two automation tools? Because Microsoft intends Access to be a database management system for the broadest possible spectrum of computer users. At one end of the spectrum, there are people who want to move beyond an interactive database application and pass more of the work to the computer but who have no programming background and are too busy to acquire one. Access macros are the solution for these people. At the other end of the spectrum, there are developers who need the additional power and the ability to deal with errors that VBA programming provides. In between, there are people with varying programming backgrounds and experience who may choose to use both tools.

In this part of this book, you'll learn about the essentials of macro programming. You'll see how to create macros for the three basic database operation categories: navigating through the application, maintaining data, and selecting groups of records for specific purposes. You'll also learn more about dealing with errors.

The fundamental goal of macro programming is to write programs that duplicate the steps you take when you work interactively with a database. You can design most macros by observing the interactive steps that you take to accomplish a task and then translating the steps into macro instructions. In this chapter, you learn how to control which sets of instructions are executed or skipped, how to design a macro that can make a choice between two alternatives, and how to design a macro that repeats actions.

The purpose of this chapter is to provide basic macro programming tools. Here, you will create only a few simple macros. In the remaining chapters of Part VI, you learn how to use the basic tools to write macros that display custom error messages; that automate navigation among forms, records, and controls; that maintain data; and that work with groups of records.

 NOTE Some of the macro basics presented in this chapter are a review of what you already learned in Chapter 21, "Using Macros to Create Custom Actions." You'll also find more detailed information on topics such as how to control macro program execution and how to manipulate form objects with macros.

The Macro Window

Macros are created in a specially designed Macro window. You can open a new Macro window from the Macro tab of the Database window by clicking the New button, or by clicking the down arrow of the New Object button on the toolbar and then choosing Macro. Access displays the macro sheet, shown in Figure 31.1.

In its default settings, Access displays only two of the four columns in the upper pane of the Macro window. You can change the default to display all four columns by checking the Names Column and the Conditions Column check boxes in the View pane of the Options dialog, as shown in Figure 31.2. (To see the Options dialog, select Tools ➢ Options.) If you change the defaults, new macro sheets display the four columns shown in Figure 31.3.

FIGURE 31.1

The Macro window, showing Action and Comment columns.

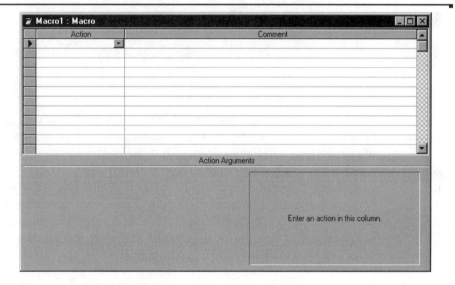

PART

VI

Macro Programming

FIGURE 31.2

Changing the Macro window defaults in the Options dialog box.

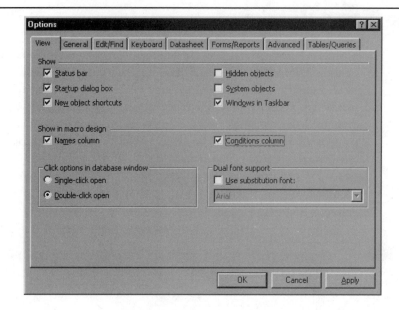

The upper pane of the Macro window contains specialized cells in four columns. Typically, you store several macros in a macro sheet and enter the names of individual macros in the Macro Name column. The Condition column is where you enter test conditions to control whether a part of the macro runs. The Action column is where you select macro actions by choosing from the combo box list displayed when you click the drop-down arrow. The Comments column is for recording the purpose or reason for the action and additional helpful comments. (Access ignores the Comments column.) The Comments column is a good place to describe what the macro accomplishes and when the macro should be run.

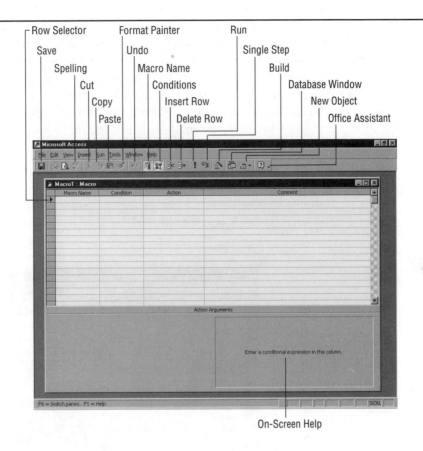

FIGURE 31.3

The Macro window, showing Macro Name, Condition, Action, and Comments columns..

The Macro Toolbar

The Macro toolbar, shown below, contains familiar editing tools for creating and editing macros, including the Save, Cut, Copy, Paste, Undo, Insert Row, and Delete Row buttons. Additionally, the toolbar contains buttons to show or hide the Macro Names and Condition columns, a Run button to run the first macro listed in the macro sheet, a Single Step button to help in troubleshooting macros, and a Build button to help in creating expressions. At the right end of the toolbar are buttons to display the Database window, to create a new object, and to obtain help from the Office Assistant.

The Run command in the Run menu and the Run button on the Macro Design toolbar run only the first macro listed in the macro sheet. Because a macro sheet normally holds several macros, you'll want convenient ways to select and run any macro in a macro sheet. While you are creating and testing new macros, it is often convenient to run them when the Database window or a Form is the active window as well as when the Macro window is the active window. You can customize the command bars for any view by adding a Run Macro command that allows you to run any macro stored in the macro sheet. We'll add a Run Macro button to the Macro Design, Form view, and Database toolbars. To do so, follow these steps:

1. Right-click the Macro Design menu bar or toolbar and select the Customize command from the shortcut menu. In the Toolbars tab, click the Database and Form View check boxes (see Figure 31.4).

2. Click the Commands tab in the Customize dialog. With Macro Design selected in the Categories list box on the left, scroll down the Commands list box on the right to display the Run Macro command. Click the Run Macro command, drag the command to each of the menu bars and drop it just to the left of the Office Assistant toolbar button (see Figure 31.5).

3. Click the Toolbars tab in the Customize dialog, clear the Form View and Database toolbar check boxes to hide the toolbars, and then click Close to close the dialog.

FIGURE 31.5

Adding the Run Macro command to the toolbars.

4. Click the new Run Macro button in the toolbar. The Run Macro dialog is displayed (see Figure 31.6). Type the name of any macro you want to run, or select it from the drop-down list.

FIGURE 31.6

You can type or select the name of any macro in the Run Macro dialog.

Macro Actions

In macro programming, you create a macro as a set of instructions. Each instruction is a row in the macro sheet. For each instruction you select the action you want to perform from a list of dozens of possible *macro actions*. Most of the macro actions duplicate the steps you take when you work interactively with Access by choosing a menu command, using the mouse to select and manipulate objects, or entering keystrokes as shortcut commands. Many of the macro actions are exactly equivalent to choosing menu commands, such as the ApplyFilter, Close, and Save actions. There is a RunCommand action that you can use to run almost any built-in command. Many of the actions mimic manual user interactions, such as the SelectObject action to select a specified database window object and the OpenForm action to open a specified form. The SendKeys action sends keystrokes as if you had typed them in. There are other actions that provide capabilities not available interactively, such as the Beep action to beep and the Echo action to turn off screen updating while the macro runs. To see a complete list of all the actions you can use in macros, see "Summary of Macro Actions" in Chapter 21.

Macro Arguments

Most macro actions require additional information before Access can carry them out. Each piece of additional information, called an *action argument,* varies with the action and may include, for example, the name of the object you take the action on, or the criteria for selecting records to take action on.

Before you can decide on the appropriate macro action, you need to be familiar with the capabilities of the macro actions. The Access Help provides in-depth information about macro actions and arguments. To get help on a particular macro action, choose Help ➤ Microsoft Access Help or click the Microsoft Access Help button on the toolbar to open the Office Assistant. Then enter the macro action you want to find out about and click Search (see Figure 31.7). When the Office Assistant displays a list of possible help topics for you to explore, click the one for *Name* Action, where *Name* is the name of action you entered.

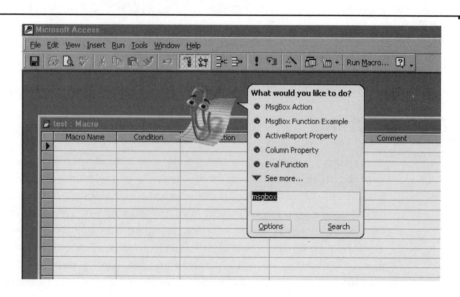

FIGURE 31.7

Getting help for the MsgBox action using the Office Assistant.

You can also get both on-screen and context-sensitive help while you are creating macros. When you select a macro action from the combo list in the Action column, the on-screen help box in the lower pane displays information about the action. To get additional help, press F1. Microsoft Access Help displays detailed information about the action and its arguments; for example, Figure 31.8 shows help for the OpenForm action.

The action arguments for the OpenForm action are:

- **Form Name** to specify the name of the form to be opened
- **View** to specify whether to open the form in Form, Design, Print Preview, or Datasheet view
- **Filter Name** or the **Where Condition** to specify whether you want to restrict the records that the form displays
- **Data Mode** to specify whether you want to allow adding new records without the ability to edit existing records, editing existing and new records, or viewing only
- **Window Mode** to specify whether the form is hidden or minimized, behaves like a dialog box, or has the mode set in its property sheet

After you enter a macro action in an Action cell by typing or selecting the name from the list, the lower pane of the macro sheet changes to display the action arguments for the selected macro action. When you click an argument box, the on-screen help box changes to display information for the selected argument. In many cases you can set the value for an argument by selecting from a combo box list. When an argument can be set to an expression, such as the `Where Condition` action argument for the OpenForm action, a Build button appears to the right of the argument box; clicking the Build button displays the Expression Builder. Access automatically fills in default values for some of the required action arguments; when a default value is not entered for an argument, the on-screen help box indicates whether the argument is required.

PART

VI

Macro Programming

FIGURE 31.8

Online Help for the
OpenForm action.

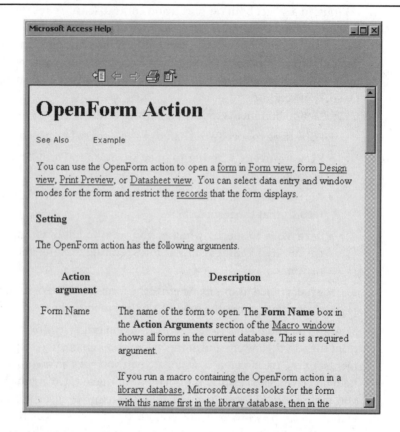

To explore these concepts, follow these steps:

1. Display a new macro sheet and select the OpenForm action in the first Action cell. Figure 31.9 shows the action arguments for the OpenForm action. Note that the View and Window Mode arguments are required and have default values.

2. Click the View, Data Mode, and Window Mode arguments and note the choices in the combo lists. The Form Name argument is also a required argument, although a default value is not displayed.

3. Click the Form Name argument. Click the down-arrow to display the list of all of the existing forms in the database. You can select a form from the list or enter the name of a new form you haven't created yet. If you enter the name of a new form, you must create and save the form before running the macro action.

4. Click the Where Condition argument. The Build button appears at the right of the argument box. Clicking the Build button displays the Expression Builder.

FIGURE 31.9

Action arguments for
the OpenForm action.

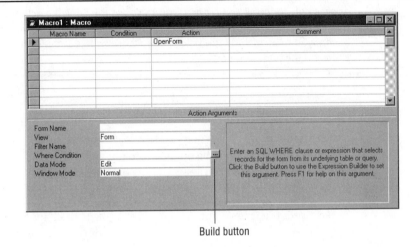

Build button

The rest of this section describes a few of the macro actions that are particularly important:

- **SetValue** action for performing calculations and for setting values and properties on forms and reports
- **RunCommand** action for running a built-in command
- **MsgBox** action for displaying a custom message box
- **SendKeys** action for sending keystrokes
- **RepaintObject** and **Requery** actions for displaying current data

Setting Values

A common task in macro programming is to change a value for a form or report. You may want to change the following:

- A data value in the underlying record source of the form or report
- A property setting for a form or report or one of its controls or sections
- A value that you want to calculate and store in an unbound control on a form (but not a calculated control)

You use the SetValue macro action to make these changes. The SetValue action has two arguments: Item (what you set) and Expression (what you set it to).

NOTE In macro programming, there are two ways you can change data stored in a table field: you can use the SetValue action to change a single data value, or you can use the OpenQuery or RunSQL macro actions to run an update query. The SetValue action applies only to forms and reports; you can't use the SetValue action to set the value of a field in a table or query directly. To change the value in a table field using the SetValue action, you must include the field in the record source for a form or report and run the action on the form or report.

The `Item` Argument

The `Item` argument is the reference to the field, control, or property that you want to set. The form or report must be open. Normally you use the fully qualified reference for the item you want to set. Here are some examples:

Item	Description
`Forms!Categories.Caption`	Sets or changes the Caption property of the Categories form.
`Forms!Categories!Description`	Sets or changes the data in the Description control on the form or the data in the Description field in the form's record source when there is no control bound to the field.
`Reports!Invoice.Section(3).Visible`	Sets or changes the Visible property of the page header section—Section(3) refers to a page header section—of the Invoice report.
`Forms!Customers!LastYearPurchases`	Sets the value of an unbound control on the Customers form that is not a calculated control; that is, the control has a blank ControlSource property setting.

 TIP When you type the reference in the `Item` argument, you don't need to enclose the object or property name in square brackets if the name includes no spaces or reserved symbols. When you tab out of the argument box, Access automatically encloses each part of the reference in square brackets. For example, Access changes `Forms!Categories.Caption` to `[Forms]![Categories].[Caption]`.

If the macro containing the SetValue action runs from the form or report with the field, control, or property you want to set, you can use the short, or unqualified reference. If the field, control, or property is on the form or report that is active when Access executes the SetValue action, you can use the properties of the Screen object to refer to the item. Here are some examples:

Item	Description
Description	Sets or changes the value of the Description control or field when the macro runs from the Categories form.
Caption	Sets or changes the Caption property of the Categories form when the macro runs from the Categories form.
Screen.ActiveControl	Sets or changes the value of the active control.
Screen.ActiveReport.Caption	Sets or changes the caption of the active report.

 NOTE   A macro *runs from a form or report* when the macro is assigned to an event recognized by the form, by a form control or section, by the report, or by a report section on the report.

Setting Data Values on a Form   You can use the SetValue action for a form to set the value of a bound control or the value of an unbound control that is not a calculated control. When you set the value of a control using the SetValue action, Access doesn't test the control's ValidationRule property. However, if the control is bound to a table field, Access does test the ValidationRule properties for the field and the table. Also, Access doesn't test the InputMask property you may have set for the field or the control. You can also set the value of a field in an underlying table, even if there is no control bound to the field; use the Forms!*formname*!*fieldname* syntax to refer to the field directly.

When you are working interactively with a form and you change data values or add new values or records, the controls and the form recognize all the data events listed on the Events tab of their property sheets. It's important to know that most of the data events that occur when you work interactively do not occur when you use the SetValue macro action to change data values or add new values. For example, when you use the SetValue macro action, the control does not recognize the BeforeUpdate, AfterUpdate, or the Change events; however, when you save the record, the form does recognize its BeforeUpdate and AfterUpdate events. When you use the SetValue action to set the values of a new record, the form does not recognize the BeforeInsert and AfterInsert events.

Setting Data Values on a Report   When you use the SetValue action for a report, the rules are a little different. You can use the SetValue action for a report to set the value of a control only if the ControlSource property is blank, that is, the control must be an unbound control that is not a calculated control.

The Expression Argument

The Expression argument is the expression that Access uses to calculate a value and then set the item to the result. The expression can include operators, constants, functions, and references to fields, controls, and properties on open forms and reports.

If the expression is a string value, enclose the string in double quotation marks. For example, for setting the LastName to Novalis, the Expression action argument is "Novalis". If the expression is a date value, enclose the date in number signs. For example, for setting the HireDate to 5/2/92, the Expression action argument is #5/2/92#. If the expression is a number value, no special symbols are required; for example, to set the UnitsInStock to 100, the Expression action argument is 100.

When you enter the Expression argument, note that Access assumes the value you enter is an expression (so you don't need an equal sign). For example, to set the Hire-Date to the current date, you set the Expression argument to Now(). If you do include an equal sign, Access evaluates the expression first and uses the result as the argument. Using an equal sign when it is not needed can cause the macro to fail. For example, if you want to set the value of a text box to "John Smith" and you type ="John Smith" in the Expression argument box, Access evaluates the expression and treats the result as the name of a control; when Access can't find the [John Smith] control, the SetValue action fails. Note that this is only true for the Expression argument of the SetValue action and the Repeat Expression argument of the RunMacro action. Other expression arguments need the = followed by the expression.

The expression may include references to fields, control, and properties on open forms and reports. You can refer to a field in the record source of a form whether or not the form has a control bound to the field, but you can reference the value of a field in the record source for a report only if the report has a control that is bound to the field or has a calculated control that refers to the field in the calculation. Normally, you use the fully qualified reference. However, if the macro containing the Set-Value action runs from the form or report with the field, control, or property you want to refer to, you can use the short, or unqualified, reference. If the field, control, or property you want to refer to is on the active form or report, you can use the properties of the Screen object. Here are some examples:

Expression	Description
Forms!Employees!LastName	Sets the item to the value in the LastName control or field on the Employees form.
LastName & ", " & FirstName	Sets an item to the concatenation of values in the LastName and FirstName controls or fields on the Employees form when the macro runs from the Employees form.
Screen.ActiveControl	Sets the item to the value in the active control.
Reports!Invoice!CompanyName	Sets the item to the value in the Company-Name control on the Invoice report.

When you want to use an aggregate function in the Expression argument to do calculations for a group of records, you must use the domain aggregate functions and not the SQL aggregate functions. For example, to calculate the sum of order subtotals, use DSum( ) instead of Sum( ).

NOTE   To perform a calculation on a group of records in a macro argument or in the Condition cell for a conditional macro, you must use the domain aggregate functions and not the SQL aggregate functions.

Using the SetValue Action to Hold Temporary Values on Forms

One difference between macro programming and VBA programming is that each handles temporary values differently. In VBA programming, you can create and name a variable as a specific location in memory that holds the value. In macro programming, you can't create a variable this way, but you can simulate a variable by storing a value temporarily in an unbound control on a form. To use a control as a variable, place an unbound control on a form and leave its ControlSource property blank. Often, you hide the control holding the variable by setting its Visible property to No. You use the SetValue action to store the value temporarily on the form. The value is available as long as the form is open; when the form closes, the value ceases to exist. Later in this chapter, we use an unbound control to hold the value of a counter that keeps track of repetitions of a macro loop; in Chapter 32, we use an unbound control to hold the primary key of a record so we can return to the record.

Using the SetValue Action to Push Values into Controls

There are two ways you can use a control on a form to hold the result of a calculation:

Calculated controls   You can enter the expression for the calculation as the ControlSource property of an unbound control; the expression "pulls" the result into the control. The calculated value is not stored and exists only while the form is open.

Programming   You can calculate a value as a programming instruction and "push" the result into either a bound or unbound control (but not into a calculated control). In macro programming, you use the SetValue macro action to calculate a value and push the calculated value into either a bound or unbound control. When the control is bound, the calculated value is stored permanently in the table field. When the control is unbound, the control simulates a variable holding its value only as long as the form is open.

Duplicating Built-in Commands

Access provides a large set of built-in commands. You run one of the built-in commands each time you choose a menu command from a built-in menu bar or a shortcut menu or each time you click a button on a built-in toolbar. In Access 2000, menu bars, shortcut menus, and toolbars are handled in similar ways and so they are all called command bars.

When you work interactively with the default command bars, you can observe that each view that you work with has a specific set of commands arranged in its command bars. For example, if a form in Form view is the active window, the Form view menu and the Form view toolbar are displayed; right-clicking in the form, in a form control, in a subform, or in a control on a subform displays the Form view shortcut menus. Figure 31.10 shows the default Form view menu bar, the default toolbar, and the default shortcut menu displayed when you right-click in a subform. The default command bars for a view include the built-in commands that are appropriate for the view.

FIGURE 31.10

The default Form view menu bar and toolbar with the shortcut menu for a subform displayed.

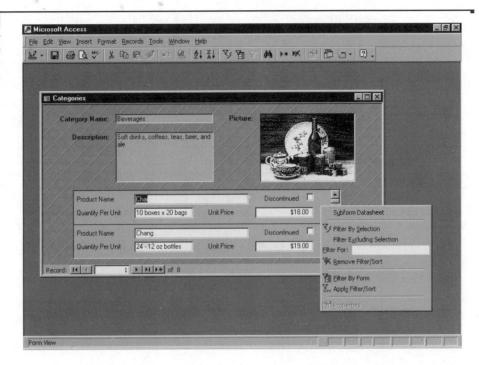

A specified built-in command may not be available for one of two reasons: The command may be appropriate for the view but may not be available at all times, or the command may be inappropriate to the view.

Appropriate but unavailable   Even if a command is included in a default command bar, the command may not always be available and may appear to be grayed out at different times as you work with the object. For example, in the Form view menu bar, the availability of the Undo commands in the Edit menu changes as you work with the form. When you first open a form in Form view, the command Edit ➤ Can't Undo is grayed out and unavailable. When you click a control and type a character, the command Edit ➤ Undo Typing is available. When you tab out of the control, the command Edit ➤ Undo Current Field/Record is available. When you save the record, the command Edit ➤ Undo Saved Record is available until you begin editing another record. When you begin editing another record, the cycle begins again and Edit ➤ Undo Typing is available.

Inappropriate   Access 2000 lets you modify the default command bars or create your own command bars for any view. In the customization process, you can add any built-in command to the command bars for a view, but the resulting command may not be appropriate for the view. For example, you can add the MacroNames command (to display the MacroNames column in the macro sheet) to the Form view toolbar, but when a form is active and you click the new Macro Names button, Access displays the error message shown in Figure 31.11 because the MacroNames command is inappropriate to Form view.

FIGURE 31.11

The error message that appears when you try to run an inappropriate command.

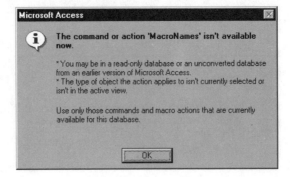

When you use the RunCommand macro action, you can specify any built-in command. Be careful to select only commands that are both appropriate to the view and available under the conditions that will be current when the macro runs. If you specify a menu command that isn't appropriate or available when the macro runs, Access can't execute the RunCommand action. For example, if you try to run a macro with the RunCommand action for the Undo command when you first open a form, Access can't execute the action; Access displays the error message (see Figure 31.12a) and then the *Action Failed* dialog (see Figure 31.12b).

FIGURE 31.12

The error message (a), and the Action Failed dialog (b).

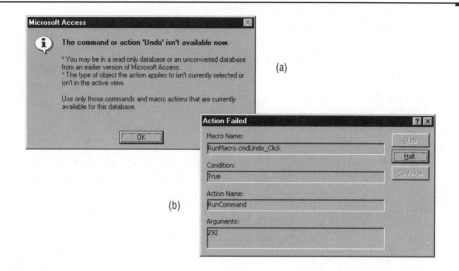

I always thought the best way to avoid failure in life is to become very familiar with hard work, honesty, and good friends. The best way to avoid failure with macros is to become very familiar with the commands that are appropriate for the Form and Print Preview views. It can be difficult to know if a particular command that may be appropriate for a view will also be available at the instant you plan to run the macro; testing your macros and seeing when they fail is the best way to learn.

Sending Messages

To display a message, use the MsgBox action. The result of the action is a *message box* that displays a custom message, a title, and the icon that you specify using the Msg-Box arguments. The message box has a single OK button that the user must press to close the message box and continue. Figure 31.13 shows a typical message box.

FIGURE 31.13

Use the MsgBox action to display a custom message.

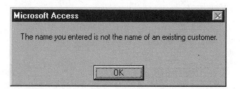

The arguments of the MsgBox action are as follows:

MsgBox Argument	Description
Message	You can enter up to 255 characters as the message. The message can be either a set of characters that you enter as the text message or the result of an expression that you enter as the Message argument preceded by an equal (=) sign.
Beep	You can sound a beep by setting the Beep argument to Yes.
Type	You can specify whether the message box displays no icon or an icon for the following types of messages: Critical, Warning?, Warning!, or Information.
Title	You can specify text to be displayed in the title bar of the message box.

 TIP You can also use built-in formatting to format the message in three sections. The first section is displayed in bold starting on the first line; the second section is displayed in plain text below the first section; and the third section is displayed in plain text beginning on the next line. Separate the three sections with the @ symbol.

Table 31.1 gives examples of custom messages.

TABLE 31.1: EXAMPLES OF CUSTOM MESSAGES

MESSAGE ARGUMENT	DESCRIPTION
The name you entered is not an existing customer	The text message is displayed in the message box.
="The name "&[LastName]&" is not the name of an existing customer"	Displays a message containing the value in the LastName control on the active form (see Figure 31.14a).
Unrecognized name@ The name you entered is not an existing customer.@ Press the New button to enter a new customer.	Displays the formatted message shown in Figure 31.14b.

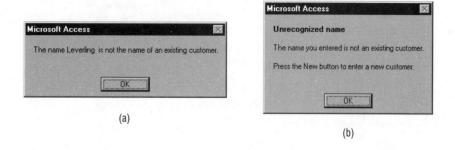

(a)

(b)

The MsgBox macro action displays only a single OK button. However, sometimes you need a message box that gives the user a choice. The Msgbox() function is a built-in function that displays a message box with a custom message and title and a set of buttons that the user can choose. The value returned by the function depends on which button was chosen, as shown in Figure 31.14. See the section "Using the Msg-Box Function as a Condition," later in the chapter for more information.

Sending Keystrokes

Use the SendKeys macro action to send keystrokes to Access or to another active Windows application.

SendKeys Arguments	Description
Keystrokes	Enter the characters (up to 255) that you want to send. If a key represents a character that is displayed when you press the key, then enter the character (for example, to send v, enter **v** as the Keystrokes argument). If a key represents a character that isn't displayed when you press the key, such as Tab, Enter, or a function key, you must enter a code in the Keystrokes argument.
Wait	Enter Yes to pause the macro until the keystrokes have been processed; otherwise, enter No.

Table 31.2 shows the special keystrokes you can send and their codes.

PART

VI

Macro Programming

TABLE 31.2: CODES FOR KEYS USED AS ARGUMENTS FOR THE SENDKEY ACTION

KEY	CODE
Backspace	{Backspace}, {BS}, or {BKSP}
Break	{Break}
Caps Lock	{CapsLock}
Del or Delete	{Delete} or {Del}
Down arrow	{Down}
End	{End}
Enter	{Enter} or ~
Esc	{Esc}
Help	{Help}
Home	{Home}
Insert or Ins	{Insert} or {Ins}
Left arrow	{Left}
Num Lock	{Numlock}
Page Down	{Pgdn}
Page Up	{Pgup}
Print Screen	{Prtsc}
Right Arrow	{Right}
Scroll Lock	{Scrolllock}
Tab	{Tab}
Up arrow	{Up}
F1	{F1}
F2	{F2}
F3	{F3}
F4	{F4}
F5	{F5}
F6	{F6}
F7	{F7}
F8	{F8}
F9	{F9}
F10	{F10}

Continued ▶

TABLE 31.2: CODES FOR KEYS USED AS ARGUMENTS FOR THE SENDKEY ACTION (CONTINUED)

KEY	CODE
F11	{F11}
F12	{F12}
F13	{F13}
F14	{F14}
F15	{F15}
F16	{F16}
Shift	+
Ctrl	^
Alt	%

You can use the SendKeys action together with the RunCommand action to automate a menu command that requires you to enter additional information before the command can be carried out. For example, the Save As command requires you to enter a new name if you are saving the object in the same database (see Figure 31.15).

When a command requires additional information (such as a new name), Access displays a dialog and suspends execution of the command until you enter the information and close the dialog. When you use the RunCommand macro action to run the command, Access suspends execution of the macro action until you enter the information and close the dialog. Because Access suspends execution when the dialog

PART

VI

Macro Programming

is displayed, the macro must send the information before displaying the dialog. You can duplicate the interactive steps as follows:

1. Use the SendKeys macro action a second time to send the characters {enter} or the ~ code for pressing the Enter key. Send the information and the keystroke to close the dialog before running the command that displays the dialog. Set the Wait argument of both SendKeys actions to No so that Access stores the keystrokes in a buffer and sends them to the dialog when the RunCommand action runs. When the RunCommand displays the dialog, Access inserts the information and carries out the command.

2. Use the RunCommand macro action to execute the command that displays the dialog.

As an example, suppose you want to use a macro to save a new form with the name frmExpenses. The mcrSaveAs macro, shown in Table 31.3, automates the procedure.

TABLE 31.3: A MACRO TO SAVE A FORM WITH A NEW NAME

ACTION	ACTION ARGUMENTS
SendKeys	Keystrokes: frmExpenses Wait: No
SendKeys	Keystrokes: {enter} Wait: No
RunCommand	Command: SaveAs

To test the macro, follow these steps:

1. Enter the macro shown in Table 31.3 in a new macro sheet and save the macro sheet as mcrSaveAs.

2. Open a new form in Design view.

3. With the form as the active window, choose the Macro command in the Tools menu and then choose the Run Macro command in the fly-out menu (or click the Run Macro button you added earlier to the toolbar). Select the mcrSaveAs macro in the Run Macro dialog and click OK. The macro runs and saves the form under the new name.

Displaying Current Data

There are several situations where controls on the active form do not display the most current data. One situation that requires you to update controls yourself occurs when two open forms display data from the same table. If you *change* data in one form, the second form updates automatically; however, if you *add* a new record to one form, the second form does not update automatically to show the new record. Use the sample Northwind database to explore the updating problem as follows:

1. Open the Customers and Customer Orders forms in Form view and arrange them side by side. The Customers and Customer Orders forms are based on data in the Customers table.

2. Modify the company name of the first record in the Customers form and press Shift+Enter to save the change. When you change a record in the Customers form, the Customer Orders form refreshes automatically. That is, the changes are displayed immediately in the Customer Orders form (see Figure 31.16).

FIGURE 31.16

When you change a record in one form, the second form updates automatically.

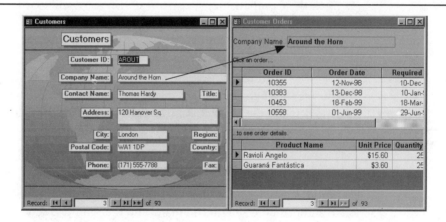

3. Add a new customer using the Customers form and save the new record. Note that the Customer Orders form does not include the new record (see Figure 31.17). When you add a new record in one form, the second form does not display the new record. To force the second form to display the current records, you must requery this form.

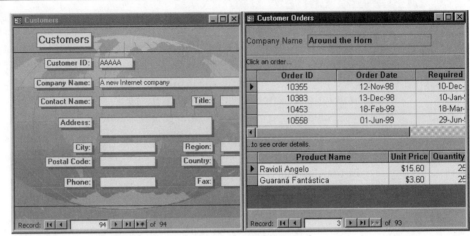

4. Click the CompanyName control on the Customer Orders form and press Shift+F9. Access retrieves the current records. (If the record you added has the AAAAA CustomerID, the new record becomes the first record in the Customers table and is displayed in the Customer Orders form.)

5. Click the Customers form and choose the Delete Record command from the Edit menu. Then click Yes in the confirmation dialog. The Customer Orders form displays the word *#Deleted* in each control for the deleted record (see Figure 31.18). To display the current records, you must requery the form.

6. Click the CompanyName control on the Customer Orders form and press Shift+F9. Access requeries the form and displays the current records.

You can use macros to automate these updates. You can use the RunCommand action to automate the Refresh command and the SendKeys action to send the F9 keystroke to recalculate calculated controls and the Shift+F9 keystrokes to requery the form's data source. You can also use the RepaintObject and the Requery actions.

The RepaintObject action completes any pending screen updates and pending recalculations of controls. For example, if you use the SetValue action to change the value in a control and a second calculated control depends on the value in the first control, you can use the RepaintObject action to update the second control. The Repaint Object action does not requery the object's data source and does not update the currently displayed records to reflect changes made to the data in the underlying tables.

PART

VI

Macro Programming

FIGURE 31.18

When you delete a record using one form, the second form does not update automatically.

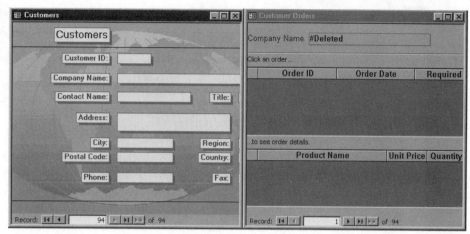

The Requery action can be used for a control on the active object or for any database object. The Requery action either reruns the query on which the control or object is based, or rereads the table on which the control or object is based. The Requery action displays the new or changed records or removes the deleted records. How it works depends on whether you are working with a form or in the database window when the Requery action is run:

Requery action for a control on the active form   To apply the action to a control, specify the name of the control as the Control Name argument using the short syntax. The Requery action updates the data in the specified control on the active object by requerying the source of the control. If the control is not based on a query or table, the Requery action recalculates the control.

Requery action for the active database window object   To apply the action to the active object, leave the Control Name argument blank. The Requery action has the same effect as selecting the database object and pressing Shift+F9. That is, the action requeries the underlying data source for the object that has the focus.

When a form contains controls that have separate data sources, such as combo boxes, list boxes, controls with aggregate functions, subform controls, and OLE controls, use separate Requery actions for the form and for each control that has a different data source.

NOTE You can use the Requery action only for an active database window object or a control on the active form. If the object you want to requery is not active, you must include a macro action that selects the object before you use the Requery action.

Creating Macros

Before you create a macro, you must decide which tasks you want Access to perform and when you want them performed. In Chapter 20, "Creating a Custom Application," you learned that programming in Access is *event driven*: an object recognizes special changes in its state that Access makes available to you as programming opportunities; Access automatically runs a program assigned to an event when the event occurs. Most of the macros you write are event macros. An *event macro* is a macro that runs in response to an event. You must decide which event is going to trigger the macro.

Because most macro actions duplicate interactive steps, often the best way to design a macro is to step through the task interactively and note the sequence of your actions. Normally there is a macro action corresponding to each step, so to create the macro, you simply translate your steps into macro actions. For more complicated tasks, it is often helpful to use a macro flow diagram to "document" your interactions.

Using Macro Flow Diagrams

A *macro flow diagram* is a diagram that represents the macro actions you want to run. The first operation box indicates the operation that causes the event and the small solid triangle attached to the operation box represents the event (see Figure 31.19).

FIGURE 31.19

Diagramming an operation that causes an event.

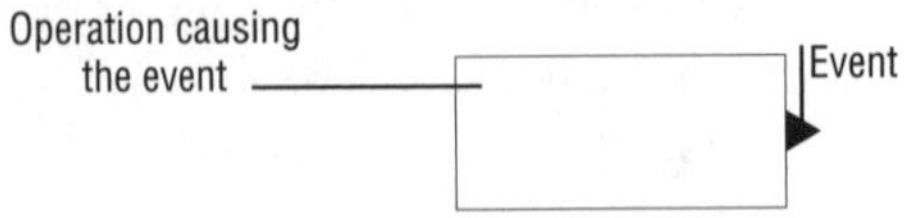

Operation causing the event ———— [ ] |Event

Your action can directly or indirectly cause an event. For example, when you click a command button, your action directly causes the button to recognize the Click event. When you open a form you cause a series of events: the form recognizes the Open, Load, Resize, and Activate events, the first record recognizes the Current event, and the first control recognizes the Enter and GotFocus events. While you directly cause the Open event, you cause the subsequent events only indirectly. When direct user action causes the event, we'll use an operation box with a shadow (see Figure 31.20).

 TIP If you'd like to learn more about events and how they are handled by Access, use the Office Assistant to search for help with *order of events*. Then explore the topics *Find out when events occur* and *Order of validation for controls and fields.*

FIGURE 31.20

Diagramming a user operation that directly causes an event.

User operation causing the event ——————— Event

Each subsequent operation box represents a macro action; each box includes an English phrase describing the action and the name of the macro action in italics. After the last macro action, you can include a termination box to indicate the end of execution; however, it is not necessary to include a macro action to terminate the macro. (A macro ends when it runs out of macro actions.)

Macro flow diagrams can be very useful for designing complex macros. Describing complex sequences of operations is easier through diagrams than text; a diagram is a precise and clear way to design and document your macros. Once you have drawn the macro flow diagram, you can generate the macro almost automatically. In this book, we'll use macro flow diagrams when the macro requires more than a few macro actions or when the sequence is complex.

Storing Macros in Macro Groups

There are two ways to store macros:

- Use a macro sheet to create a single macro with one or more macro actions and save the macro as a macro object that appears in the list of macros in the Database window.

- Use a macro sheet to define several individual macros. In this case, the set of macros stored in the macro sheet is called a *macro group*. Only the name of the macro group is displayed as a macro object in the Database window (not the names of the individual macros in the group).

PART

VI

Macro Programming

When you automate a database, you create tens if not hundreds of individual macros. Rather than creating macro objects for individual macros, it is more efficient to organize the various macros you create for a form or report into a single macro group called a *form macro group* or a *report macro group* and name the macro group to reflect the form or report as follows:

m[*formname*]   for a form macro group

m[*reportname*]   for a report macro group

As an example, you can store all of the macros for a switchboard form named frm-Switchboard in a form macro group named mfrmSwitchboard. Of course, these are just suggestions, and you are free to use whatever naming convention you like to keep your macros organized.

Naming Individual Macros

You use an individual macro to trap an event recognized by an object. You can name the event macro by combining the object name and the event name separated by an underscore, as follows:

objectname_eventname

As examples, the individual macro named

cmdCategories_Click

contains the actions you want to carry out when you click the command button named cmdCategories. The macro named

Form_Activate

contains the actions you want to take when the form becomes the active window.

Referring to a Macro in a Macro Group

To refer to an individual macro in a macro group, use the name of the macro group, followed by a dot (.), followed by the name of the macro:

macrogroupname.macroname

This reference is called the *full identifier* for the macro. As an example,

mfrmSwitchboard.cmdCategories_Click

is the full identifier for the macro in the group mfrmSwitchboard, assigned to the Click event of the cmdCategories button.

Editing in the Macro Sheet

Editing in the macro sheet is similar to editing in a datasheet. You can navigate around the macro sheet using the mouse or the normal Windows editing keys.

The rules for editing individual cells follow the normal Windows and Access editing rules. Tab into a cell to select its entire contents; when you tab to a cell, you are in *navigating mode*, and you can press F2 to switch to *editing mode* and then edit directly in the cell. For entering or editing longer expressions, press Shift+F2 to open the Zoom Box and display the entire contents in a separate edit window. The → keys allow you to move the insertion point; the Delete key lets you delete the character to the right of the insertion point, and the Backspace key lets you delete the character to the left of the insertion point.

You can copy individual characters or the entire contents of the cell to the clipboard by selecting what you want to copy, then pressing Ctrl+C, choosing Edit ➢ Copy, or clicking the Copy button on the toolbar. To paste the selection into another cell, click the Paste cell. (Place the insertion point where you want the contents to be pasted.) Then press Ctrl+V, choose Edit ➢ Paste, or click the Paste button on the toolbar. When you copy the contents of a macro action cell, only the action (not the action arguments) is copied to the clipboard.

You can change the height of rows and the widths of columns just as you do in a datasheet, but the rules for editing rows and columns in the macro sheet are somewhat different because you can select a row but not a column. You can select a row by clicking into the row selector; you can select several contiguous rows by clicking into the first row selector and dragging to the last row, or by pressing the Shift key and clicking into the last row selector. (You cannot select noncontiguous rows.) After selecting one or more rows, you can delete the selection by pressing the Delete key, or insert the same number of rows above the selection by pressing the Insert key, or copy the selection to the clipboard. When you copy a row, the entire macro action is copied, including the action arguments you set.

Additionally, you can move rows by first selecting the rows to move, then pressing the left mouse button while clicking the selection and dragging to the rows where you want to insert the selection; a bold horizontal line indicates the new boundary of the selection (the new upper boundary if you are moving the selection up and the new lower boundary if you are moving the selection down).

You can copy a macro to another macro sheet by copying the rows of the macro to the clipboard and then pasting the selection to a new location in the other macro sheet. You can use the clipboard to paste a macro into another Access database, but since you have to close the current database and open the other one in order to paste, it is usually more convenient to export the macro sheet to another database or import it from another database using the usual Access methods (File ➢ Export, or File ➢ Get External Data ➢ Import).

The Flow of Macro Execution

Access starts the execution of a simple macro with the first row containing the macro name, executes the action in this row if there is one, and ignores any comments in the row. Then Access looks for the next row that is not blank and moves to it. If there is an entry in the Macro Name cell, Access interprets this row as the beginning of another macro and stops execution. If the Macro Name cell is blank, Access moves to the Action cell to the right. If there is an entry in the Action cell, Access executes the action, ignores the comment, and moves to the next row that is not blank. If the Action cell is blank, Access moves to the next row that is not blank. Access continues to move down the rows of the macro sheet, examining one row at a time until it finds a row with an entry in the Macro Name cell, or until there are no more non-blank rows, or until it finds a StopMacro action. In either case, the macro ends. You don't have to end a macro with a specific end action. Since Access ignores blank rows, you can insert them between the macro actions of an individual macro and between the individual macros in a macro group to make them easier to read.

This execution pattern is called a *sequential* flow pattern: macro actions are executed sequentially as listed in the macro sheet. The section "Controlling Macro Program Execution," later in the chapter, describes two other flow patterns for conditional and repetitive execution.

 TIP When you create a macro, place only the macro name and a general comment in the first row and enter the first macro action in the second row. This macro design makes it easier to modify a macro later if you want to insert a new first action or copy the actions of the macro to another macro.

Running Macros

There are many ways to run a macro in addition to using an event to trigger it. This section describes nine ways to run a macro.

Running a Macro from the Macro Window

You can run the first macro in the active macro sheet by clicking the Run button in the toolbar or by choosing the Run command in the Run menu. You can run any macro in any macro sheet by clicking the Macro button in the (customized) toolbar or by choosing the Macro command in the (customized) Run menu to display the Run Macro dialog box. By default, the dialog box displays the name of the active macro sheet, and you must select the full identifier for the macro you want to run. For example, to run a macro named cmdCategories_Click macro that you have stored in the mfrmSwitchboard macro sheet, you select mfrmSwitchboard.cmdCategories_Click in the Run Macro dialog (see Figure 31.21a). When you click OK, Access runs the macro.

Running a Macro from Any Active Window

You can customize the menu bar and toolbar for any view to include the Macro command. With customized command bars, you can run a macro from any active window by choosing the Macro command and entering the macro's full identifier in the Run Macro dialog. As an exception, the Macro command is unavailable when the Module window is the active window.

When the Database window is the active window, you can also run the first macro in a macro group by selecting the macro group in the Macro pane and clicking the Run button.

Running a Macro from Another Macro

You can run a macro from a second macro using the RunMacro action. The second macro is referred to as the *calling macro*, and the macro you run is referred to as the *called macro*. Use the RunMacro action in the calling macro and enter the full identifier of the macro you want to call in the Macro Name argument. You must enter the full identifier even if both macros are in the same macro group. Figure 31.21b shows a macro group with a calling macro and a called macro. When Access executes the RunMacro action, control is transferred to the called macro; when the called macro is finished running, control returns to the calling macro at the row following the row with the RunMacro action. When you leave the two Repeat... arguments blank, Access runs the called macro once. You can use the Repeat... arguments to run the called macro in a repetitive loop. Macro loops are discussed later in this chapter.

PART

VI

Macro Programming

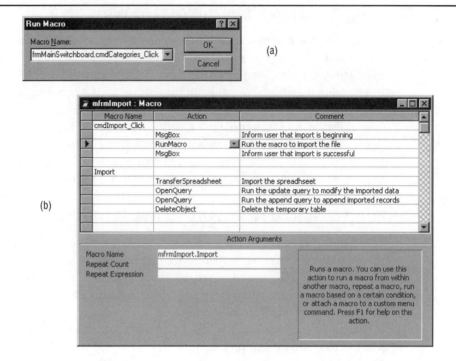

Use the Run Macro dialog to run any macro in a macro sheet (a). Use the RunMacro macro action to run another macro. Enter the full identifier for the called macro in the Macro Name argument (b).

Running a Macro from a Command Bar

You can create a custom toolbar button that runs a macro and place the button on any command bar. For example, to place a custom button on a toolbar, follow these steps:

1. Right-click the toolbar and choose the Customize command from the shortcut menu.

2. Click the Commands tab and select the All Macros category in the list box on the left. The Commands list box on the right displays all of the macros in the database (see Figure 31.22).

FIGURE 31.22

The All Macros cate-
gory lists the macros in
the database.

3. Select a macro and drag it to the toolbar. Access displays a custom toolbar button. When you close the Customize dialog and move the pointer to the new
   button, a tooltip indicates the name of the macro that runs when you click the
   button. You can customize the button image, the tooltip, and the status
   bar text.

4. With the Customize dialog open, right-click the new toolbar button and choose
   the Properties command on the shortcut menu. You can change the tooltip text
   in the ScreenTip text box in the Macro Design Control Properties dialog (see Figure 31.23a). Click the Close button to close the dialog.

5. Right-click the new toolbar button and choose the Change Button Image command to display the available button images (see Figure 31.23b).

PART

VI

Macro Programming

FIGURE 31.23

Customizing the tooltip text (a), and the button image of a toolbar button (b).

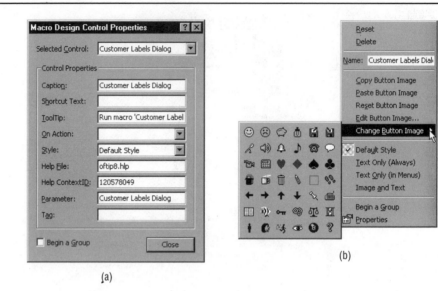

(a)

(b)

 NOTE When you add a custom command to run a macro to an application, the button appears in every database that you open. However, if you are in another database when you choose the command, the macro runs only if you have stored a copy of the macro in the current database.

Running a Macro from a Shortcut Key

You can run a macro from a custom key combination. For example, you can assign the key combination Ctrl+Z to open the Zoom box, a more convenient key combination than the default Shift+F2. (If you do this, you will be overriding the default action of Undo for Ctrl+Z.) You can assign custom key combinations using a special macro group that must be named AutoKeys. To assign a macro to a key combination, enter a code for the key combination in the Macro Name column, and then enter the actions for the macro or use the RunMacro action to call another macro. Not all key combinations are available for custom reassignment. To see a list of the available key combinations and the key codes, use the Office Assistant to find help for *autokeys* and click the topic *AutoKeys key combinations*.

The AutoKeys macro takes effect as soon as you save it. When you use an AutoKeys macro to reassign a key combination that Windows or Access normally uses, such as Ctrl+C for copy, your assignment takes precedence. To make your application easier to learn, do not reassign the common Windows and Access key combinations. Figure 31.24 shows an AutoKeys macro to open the Zoom box; this macro uses the SendKeys action to send the Shift+F2 key combination to Access.

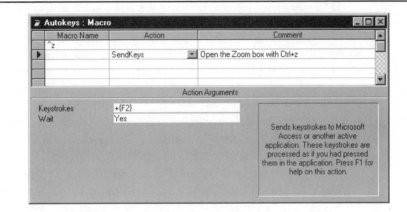

FIGURE 31.24

Using an AutoKeys macro to make custom key assignments.

Running a Macro at Startup

You can create a special macro and have Access run it automatically when you start up the database. You must create this macro in its own macro sheet and name the macro sheet AutoExec. (This is probably the only circumstance in which you must store a single macro in a macro sheet.) When you start up the database, Access uses the properties you set in the Startup dialog and then looks for an AutoExec macro. Access runs the AutoExec macro if there is one. While the Startup properties define most of the initial database settings, you can use an AutoExec macro for additional tasks you want to perform each time you start up the database. For example, you can open a hidden global variables form or arrange to download and import new data automatically.

Running a Macro from the Visual Basic Window

You can run an individual macro action in the Visual Basic window by typing **DoCmd** followed by a dot and the name of the macro action with the list of arguments. You must enclose all text arguments in quotation marks and use commas to separate multiple arguments. If you omit arguments, Access assumes the default values for the action; however, even if you omit an argument, you must still use a comma to hold the place of the omitted argument in the argument list unless you are omitting all arguments or you are omitting all arguments after the last one you want to specify.

NOTE When you run a macro action this way, you are actually running the corresponding Visual Basic *method*. Nearly all macro actions have equivalent Visual Basic methods. You can get help on the corresponding method by using the Office Assistant to search for the name of the action and choosing the corresponding method from the topics list.

For example,

1. Open the Visual Basic window by pressing Ctrl+G. The lower pane of the Visual Basic window, shown in Figure 31.25, is called the Immediate pane because statements you enter are evaluated immediately (see Chapter 32). Click the Immediate pane and type **DoCmd.** VBA displays a drop-down list of the macro actions you can run as VBA methods using the DoCmd (see Figure 31.25a). Choose the OpenForm action from the drop-down list and double-click to enter the action or type **OpenForm**.

2. Finish typing the expression **DoCmd.OpenForm "Categories"**. Notice that when you press the spacebar following the OpenForm method, VBA displays the syntax for the OpenForm method in a small box below the line you are entering as shown in Figure 31.25b; ignore the box for now and finish typing.

3. Press Enter. When you press Enter, Access executes the statement you typed and opens the Categories form.

The OpenForm macro action has six arguments. However, to open the form with all default values, you can specify the name of the form and omit the remaining arguments. (The corresponding VBA OpenForm method has the same six arguments plus an additional argument called OpenArgs, as shown in Figure 31.25b.)

You can run a macro in the Immediate pane of the Debug window by typing **DoCmd.RunMacro** followed by the full name of the macro enclosed in quotation marks. To run the macro once, use the following syntax:

```
DoCmd.RunMacro "macrogroupname.macroname"
```

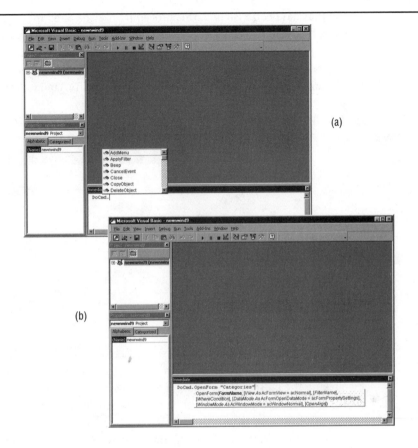

FIGURE 31.25

*The Immediate pane
of the Debug window
displays the methods
of the DoCmd object
(a), and the syntax for
the OpenForm
method (b).*

Running a Macro from a VBA Procedure

You can run an individual macro action or a macro in a VBA procedure using the
same syntax that you use to run the action or macro in the Visual Basic window.
(When you use the Visual Basic window you are writing VBA statements.)

Running a Macro by Trapping an Event on a Form or Report

Because Access uses the event-driven programming model discussed in Chapter 20,
the most important way to run a macro is by assigning the macro to an event property of an object. When the object recognizes the event, Access automatically runs the

macro that has been assigned; this procedure is also called *triggering* the macro. You can assign a macro to an event by entering the full identifier for the macro as the property setting for the event property, also called *trapping* an event. A macro that is assigned to an event is called an event macro or *event handler*. For example, Figure 31.26 shows an event macro assigned to the AfterUpdate event property of the Customers form.

FIGURE 31.26

Assigning event macros in the object's property sheet.

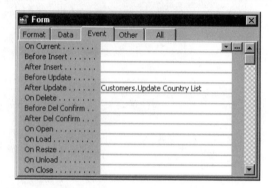

When you first start to program using macros, most of the macros you write are triggered by the Click event of command buttons. The user runs the macro explicitly by clicking the button. Before long, you are writing macros that are triggered by events that the user isn't aware of. For example, you can create a data validation macro to test a value when the user tabs out of a control, or a lookup macro that synchronizes a form to the value in a combo box when the user selects a value. When you use events other than the Click event to trigger macros, you minimize the need for the user to know when to run macros and you make your application easier to use.

Interrupting Default Processing

When you set an event trap by assigning a macro to an event, you affect the default processing that Access would normally carry out following the occurrence of the event. For example, when you change the value in a text box and take an action to save the change, the text box recognizes the BeforeUpdate event. The subsequent default behavior is that Access updates the control, and the control recognizes the AfterUpdate event. You can trap the BeforeUpdate event by assigning a macro for Access to determine if the edited value satisfies the validation rules for the control. The BeforeUpdate event is one of the events for which Access runs the macro before the default behavior takes place so the default behavior can be canceled. If the changed value in the text box fails to satisfy the validation rules, you can cancel the default behavior with the CancelEvent action. If the changed value satisfies the validation rules, the macro finishes, and then Access continues with the default behavior of updating the control.

Steps in Creating Event Macros

Here is a list of basic guidelines:

1. Determine which object and event you want to trigger the macro execution.

2. Design the macro. (Use a macro flow diagram if necessary.) Think through, or actually carry out, each step you take to accomplish the task. For more complex macros, you should draw the macro flow diagram to document the macro and to help with the design.

3. Determine the macro actions. If you are using a macro flow diagram, each operation box in the diagram translates into a separate macro action.

4. Create and save the macro. You must save a macro before you can run it.

5. Assign the macro to the corresponding event property.

Steps for Assigning a Macro to an Event

To assign the macro to an event, follow these steps:

1. Open the form or report in Design view and select the object that recognizes the event.

2. Display the property sheet (by clicking the Properties button in the toolbar or choosing View ➢ Properties) and click the Event tab.

3. On the line for the desired event, enter the full identifier for the macro by typing or by clicking the arrow and selecting the macro from the list. Use the syntax *macrogroupname.macroname*.

4. Save the form or report.

Continued

CONTINUED

Testing the Macro

You should always test the macro in context by causing the triggering event to occur (for example, by clicking the command button). Testing a macro in context allows you to observe how the macro interacts with other macros. Often the interaction of two or more macros gives unexpected results, requiring you to either redesign a macro or choose a different event to trigger an interacting macro.

You can also test a macro without triggering the event by choosing the Macro command to run the individual macro and see if it accomplishes the intended task. Some macros require that specific forms and reports be open and that a specific object is active when you run it—make sure these conditions are satisfied before you run the macro.

Documenting Macros

When you are working in a macro sheet, you can see the arguments for only one action at a time, and you have to click the row that contains the action to see its argument settings. This limitation makes understanding how the macro works more difficult. You can compensate for this limitation, at least partially, by using comments for every action that has arguments and including the most important information from the action arguments in your comments. While the effort required to comment nearly every action is substantial, you will find the rewards equally substantial. In this regard, Visual Basic code has the advantage of displaying all the details of your program as text so that you can see the entire program at a glance. Figure 31.27 shows the macro sheet for a dialog form named fdlgSales.

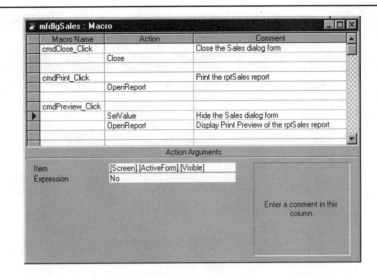

With macros, you can't see all the arguments for all the macros in a macro sheet on the screen, but you can print the macro's definition for reference. To print a macro sheet, choose File ➤ Print, and click OK in the Print Macro Definition dialog (see Figure 31.28). The printout shows all the conditions and arguments for all the macros in a macro sheet. You can also use File ➤ Print Preview to open an Object Definition report for the macro in a Print Preview window. Figure 31.29 shows a portion of the report for the macro sheet for the fdlgSales form.

Using flowcharts to document your macros is another way to document a macro and see its flow pattern at a glance.

FIGURE 31.28

You can print the macros in a macro sheet.

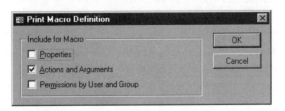

PART

VI

Macro Programming

FIGURE 31.29

Print Preview of a macro sheet.

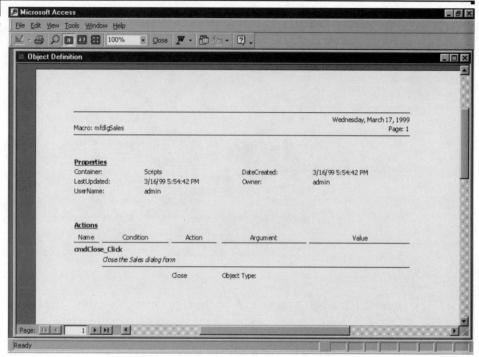

Manipulating Objects with Macros

In this section, we look at some simple examples of creating and running macros. We construct macros to automate simple navigation among forms.

NOTE In this chapter and the next few chapters, we'll be working with the Northwind database. Make a copy named NorthwindMacros.mdb of your original Northwind database.

It's a good idea to let users see the basic organization of the application at a glance. To do this, display a main menu form, or switchboard, with a list of the tasks that they can carry out with the application.

The Northwind database has a switchboard form called Main Switchboard that controls the navigation to the main tasks in the application (see Figure 31.30). There are command buttons to open the major task forms: Categories, Suppliers, Products, and Orders; a command button with the Print Sales Reports caption that opens the Sales Reports form as a secondary switchboard for selecting reports; a command button to close the Main Switchboard and display the Database window; and a command button to quit Access. The switchboard buttons are empowered with VBA procedures. For practice in creating macros, we'll replace the VBA procedures with event macros.

FIGURE 31.30

The Main Switchboard.

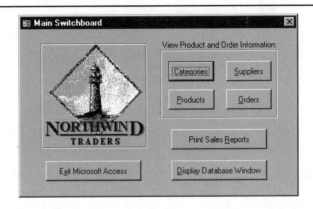

Forms Navigation

We'll create macros to automate navigation between forms by opening, hiding, or closing them.

A fundamental principle in forms navigation is that you allow users to work with only one form at a time.

Usually this principle means displaying only one form at a time; but, if two forms are displayed, this means preventing users from changing data using both forms. By controlling how users work with your forms, you can avoid data integrity problems.

There are many ways to apply this fundamental principle. The simplest way is to hide the Main Switchboard when a task form is opened. You hide an object by setting its Visible property to No.

Opening and Hiding Forms

For each of the five command buttons that opens a form, we create an event macro for the button's Click event that opens the form and hides the switchboard.

1. Open a new macro sheet and name it mMainSwitchboard. Resize and move the Macro window to display both the Database window and the Macro window.

2. Type **cmdCategories_Click** in the first Macro Name cell, click the Comment cell in the same row, and enter the comment **Open the form and hide the Main Switchboard**. The next step shows another way to define a macro action that opens a form: the drag and drop technique.

3. In the Database window, click the Forms button, then select Categories. Drag the icon and drop it in the Action cell in the second row; enter the comment **Open Categories**. Access automatically sets the action to OpenForm and sets the Form Name argument to Categories.

4. Click the next Action cell and choose the SetValue action. Set the Item argument to refer to the Visible property of the Main Switchboard and set the Expression argument to No, like this:

Item:	Forms![Main Switchboard].Visible
Expression:	No

Note that Access adds square brackets around the words *Forms* and *Visible* after you tab out of the argument text box. Click the Comment cell and enter the comment **Hide the main Switchboard**.

5. Save the macro. Table 31.4 shows the macro.

 NOTE When you drag a table, query, form, or report to the Macro window, Access inserts a row with an action to open the object and sets default arguments. When you drag a macro object, Access inserts a row with the RunMacro action.

TABLE 31.4: THE MACRO TO OPEN A TASK FORM AND HIDE A SWITCHBOARD

MACRO NAME	ACTION	ACTION ARGUMENTS
cmdCategories_Click		
	OpenForm	Form Name: Categories
	SetValue	Item: Forms![Main Switchboard].Visible
		Expression: No

 NOTE In this book, the comments and the default action arguments are not included explicitly in the tables that show the macros.

Testing the Macro

The next step is to test the macro to be sure it runs properly. When you test an event macro, you need to duplicate the conditions under which the macro will run when it has been assigned to an event. In this case, make sure the Main Switchboard is open. (If the Main Switchboard isn't open, Access won't be able to carry out the SetValue action and the macro will fail.) Since there is only a single macro, run it by clicking the Run button in the toolbar. If the macro runs as intended, the Categories form is open and the switchboard form is still open but is hidden.

Before assigning the cmdCategories_Click macro, create macros similar to the cmd-Categories macro in Table 31.4 for the command buttons that open the Suppliers, Products, Orders, and Sales Reports forms. Name the macro for opening the last form cmdSalesReports_Click. Since the SetValue action has identical arguments for all five macros, you can save time by copying the row with the SetValue action and pasting it to each macro. When you copy a row in the macro sheet, the argument settings are copied automatically. Save the macro sheet (see Figure 31.31a).

To assign the macros, follow these steps:

1. Unhide the switchboard by choosing the Unhide command from the Window menu and clicking the OK button in the Unhide Window dialog.

2. Switch to Design view and select the button with the Categories caption. Click the OnClick property on the Event tab of the property sheet. (The current property setting, =OpenForm("Categories"), is the VBA Function procedure.) A list of macro groups and the full identifiers of the individual macros is displayed.

3. Select mMainSwitchboard.cmdCategories_Click. The VBA Function procedure is now replaced by the macro (see Figure 31.31b).

4. In the same way, assign the other four macros to the OnClick property of their respective command buttons.

5. Save the form and switch to Form view.

PART

VI

Macro Programming

FIGURE 31.31

Replacing a VBA event procedure with an event macro.

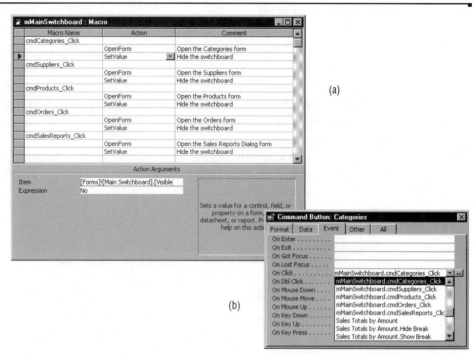

(a)

(b)

NOTE If you double-click within the double-click time limit of your computer, the control recognizes both the DblClick and the Click events; otherwise it recognizes two Click events. You can change the double-click time limit on the Buttons tab of the Mouse option of the Windows Control Panel.

Closing and Unhiding Forms

When you click one of the command buttons, a task form opens and the switchboard is hidden. After you are finished working with the task form, you need to close the form and unhide the switchboard.

Creating Reusable Objects Each of the main task forms needs a command button to close the form and unhide the switchboard. Since several forms need exactly the same command button, you can avoid having to recreate the button and its macro for each form by creating the button and its macro just once and reusing them on other forms. Create the command button on the Categories form.

1. Click the Categories button in the Main Switchboard. The Categories form opens and the switchboard is hidden.

2. Switch to Design view. If the Control Wizards tool button is pushed in, click the button to deactivate the wizards and then select the Command Button tool.

3. Click the form and create a button; set the Name property to cmdReturn and set the Caption property to &Return.

4. Save the form.

 NOTE You can provide an *access key* that can be used in place of clicking a command button. Assign a keyboard combination Alt+*letter* where *letter* can be any letter in the button's Caption property. Specify your choice by typing the ampersand (&) immediately before the letter in the Caption property. For example, set the Caption property to &Return to have the button's caption displayed as Return and to have the keyboard shortcut be Alt+R.

Creating a Global Macro   We'll create the macro for the Return button in a global macro sheet, taking care to avoid using names of specific objects that would prevent the macro from being reusable. A *global macro sheet* stores general macros that can be used on more than one form or report. Then, when you need the button, you can just copy it from the form to any other form.

1. Create a new macro sheet and save it as mcrGlobal. You can use this macro sheet to store global macros that can be assigned to objects on several forms and reports in your application.

2. Click the first cell of the Macro Name column and name the new macro cmdReturn_Click.

3. Click the Action cell of the next row and select the Close action. You can use the Close action to close a particular window by entering the type and name of the database object in the arguments; however, you can also use the action to close the active window by leaving the arguments blank. When you create a global macro, it should not refer to a specific form or report by name if the reference prevents the macro from being reusable.

4. Click the next action cell and select the SetValue action. Set the action arguments as shown next. Referring to the Main Switchboard form in this action

doesn't prevent the macro from being reused in this application because you want to unhide the switchboard whenever you close a main task form.

```
Item:              Forms![Main Switchboard].Visible
Expression:        Yes
```

5. Save the macro sheet. Table 31.5 shows the macro.

TABLE 31.5: THE MACRO TO CLOSE A FORM AND UNHIDE THE SWITCHBOARD

MACRO NAME	ACTION	ACTION ARGUMENTS
cmdReturn_Click		
	Close	
	SetValue	Item: Forms![Main Switchboard].Visible
		Expression: Yes

Assigning a Macro to a Button and Pasting a Reusable Control   After you assign the global macro to the Return button, the button is reusable. You can copy and paste the cmdReturn button to other forms in your database. When you paste a control, you paste its properties, too; this means that macros assigned to the control's event properties are also pasted.

1. Click the Categories form and select the Return button.

2. Click the OnClick event property and select the macro mcrGlobal.cmd Return_Click. The macro is assigned to the command button.

3. Select the cmdReturn button and copy to the clipboard. We'll paste this button and its macro to the other task forms.

4. Save the form, switch to Form view, and click the Return button. The Categories form closes and the switchboard is displayed.

5. One by one, click the other command buttons on the switchboard that open the Suppliers, Orders, and Products forms. Then switch to Design view, paste the cmdReturn button into the form, move the button to the lower-right corner, save the form, switch back to Form view, and click the form's new Return button.

6. Click the Print Sales Reports button, switch to Design view, and click the Cancel button. There is an event procedure assigned to the Click event that closes the form but does not unhide the switchboard. Click the OnClick property and select the mcrGlobal.cmdReturn_Click macro. Save the form, switch to Form view, and click the Cancel button.

Display the Database Window

When you click the command button with the Display Database Window caption on the Main Switchboard form, a VBA event procedure closes the switchboard and displays the Database window with the Categories table selected. Table 31.6 shows the equivalent macro that performs these operations. The macro closes the switchboard and uses the SelectObject action with the In Database Window argument set to Yes to select the table from the Tables pane in the Database window. The SelectObject action unhides the object if it is hidden and gives the object the focus. This means that if the Database window is hidden when you take the action, Access must unhide the Database window to display the object.

1. Enter the macro listed in Table 31.6 in the mMainSwitchboard macro sheet and save it.

2. Click the switchboard and switch to Design view. Select the DisplayDatabase-Window button, click the OnClick property, and select the macro mMainSwitchboard.cmdDisplayDatabaseWindow_Click.

3. Save the form, switch to Form view, and click the button. The switchboard closes and the Categories table is selected in the Database window.

TABLE 31.6: A MACRO TO SELECT AN OBJECT IN THE DATABASE WINDOW

MACRO NAME	ACTION	ACTION ARGUMENTS
CmdDisplayDatabaseWindow_Click		
	Close	
	SelectObject	Object Type: Table
		Object Name: Categories
		In Database Window: Yes

 NOTE Normally, you use the SelectObject macro action with the In Database Window argument set to No to duplicate the user action of clicking in a window to select it. As in the interactive situation, the object must be open before you can select it; but you can also use the SelectObject macro action to select and unhide an object.

PART

VI

Macro Programming

Closing the Database

When you click the Exit Microsoft Access button on the Main Switchboard form, the VBA event procedure quits Microsoft Access. However, if you intend to work on another database, it is preferable to close a database without quitting Access. When you work interactively, you close the database by clicking the Close button on the Database window, or by choosing the Close command on the File menu when the Database window is the active object. We'll create a macro to automate the process. We can use the SelectObject action to activate the Database window (and select the Categories table) and then use the Close action to close the database. Table 31.7 shows the macro.

1. Enter the macro shown in Table 31.7 into the mMainSwitchboard macro sheet and save the macro sheet.

2. Click the switchboard and switch to Design view. Select the Exit Microsoft Access button, change the Name property to cmdExitDatabase, change the Caption property to Exit Database, and change the ControlTipText to Close the Northwind database.

3. On the Event tab of the button's property sheet, click the OnClick property and assign the mMainSwitchboard.cmdExitDatabase_Click macro.

4. Save the form, switch to Form view, and click the button. The Northwind-Macros database closes.

TABLE 31.7: A MACRO TO CLOSE THE DATABASE

MACRO NAME	ACTION	ACTION ARGUMENTS
cmdExitDatabase_Click		
	SelectObject	Object Type: Table Object Name: Categories In Database Window: Yes
	Close	

Discarding the Form's Module

We have replaced all of the form's VBA procedures with macros, and the form no longer needs the form module stored with it. Whenever you load a form or report with a form or report module, Access must also take time to load the module. To avoid this delay, Access allows you to delete a form's module. A form without a form module is called a *lightweight form.*

1. Open the NorthwindMacros database.

2. Open the Main Switchboard in Design view and set the form's HasModule property to No. Click Yes in the confirmation dialog to confirm the deletion of the form's module. Then save the form.

Controlling Macro Program Execution

When you create a program, you can control the order in which Access executes the actions, also called the *flow of execution.* There are three basic flow patterns.

Sequential   In a sequential pattern, Access executes the program by running the macro actions one after another.

Conditional   In a conditional pattern, Access makes a decision by testing the value of a condition and carries out one set of actions if the condition is true and another set of actions if the condition is false.

Looping   In a looping pattern, Access repeats a set of actions either a specified number of times or until a condition is met.

A *condition* is a logical expression that is either true or false. Here are some examples of conditions:

```
UnitsInStock > 0
UnitsInStock < = ReorderLevel
Date() < 12/31/99
Category = "Beverages"
```

Suppose a customer wants to purchase an item. Before you can fill the order, you need to determine if the item is in stock. If the item is in stock, you can sell the item, but if the item is not in stock, you can't make an immediate sale and must place a backorder instead. A macro to automate the ordering process would test the value of the condition `UnitsInStock > 0` and then run different sets of actions to process the request.

PART

VI

Macro Programming

Conditional Macros

A *conditional macro* provides a way to test the value of a condition and take different actions depending on the value. A conditional macro contains a condition and two alternative sets of macro actions: one set of actions is carried out only when the condition is true; another set is carried out only when the condition is false. In a macro flow diagram, the condition is represented as a diamond-shaped decision box with two alternative paths, as shown in Figure 31.32.

If there isn't a separate set of actions that is carried out only when the condition is false, the conditional macro has one alternative, as shown in Figure 31.33.

FIGURE 31.32

The flow diagram for a conditional macro with two alternatives.

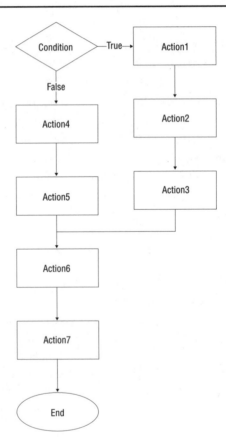

Controlling the Flow of a Macro with Conditions

Enter the condition you want to test in a Condition cell in the macro sheet. If the condition is true, Access executes the macro action that is in the same row and then moves to the next row. If the condition is false, Access skips the macro action that is in the same row and moves directly to the next row. If the next row has a condition, the testing procedure is repeated; if the next row doesn't have a condition, Access takes the action in that row.

The flow diagram for a conditional macro with one alternative.

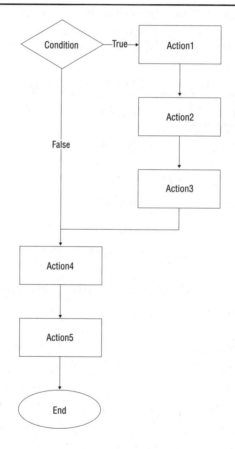

If you want to execute several consecutive actions when the condition is true, you can repeat the condition, or simply enter an ellipsis (...) in the Condition cell for each of the subsequent actions you want executed. The ellipsis acts like a ditto mark. When a consecutive subsequent row has an ellipsis in the Condition cell, Access executes

PART

VI

Macro Programming

the action if the condition is true, skips the action if the condition is false, and then moves to the next row.

The Conditional Macro with One Alternative

By design, the macro sheet easily handles a conditional macro that has only one alternative. Enter the condition you want to test into a Condition cell, and enter the action you want to take if the condition is true in the same row. If there is more than one action you want to take if the condition is true, enter the actions in consecutive rows, with an ellipsis in each Condition cell. Then enter the actions you want to take regardless of the value of the condition. Table 31.8 shows a conditional macro with one alternative. If the condition is true, Access runs all five actions one after another; if the condition is false, Access runs only the last two (Actions 4 and 5 in the Table 31.8).

TABLE 31.8: A CONDITIONAL MACRO WITH ONE ALTERNATIVE IN THE MACRO SHEET

CONDITION	ACTION
Condition	Action1
...	Action2
...	Action3
	Action4
	Action5

The Conditional Macro with Two Alternatives

When a conditional macro has two alternatives (as shown in Figure 31.32), you can convert the macro into an equivalent macro with a pair of one-alternative conditions, as shown in Figure 31.34, in which the second condition is the opposite of the first.

Here are some examples of conditions and their opposites:

Condition	Opposite Condition
[Amount] <=9	[Amount] > 9
[Name] = "Jones"	[Name] <> "Jones"
[EmployeeID] Is Null	[EmployeeID] Is Not Null
[Counter] < 4	Not [Counter] < 4
[Price] Between $.30 And $.50	Not [Price] Between $.30 And $.50

PART

VI

Macro Programming

FIGURE 31.34

The flow diagram for a macro with a pair of one-alternative conditions that is equivalent to a macro with a single two-alternative condition.

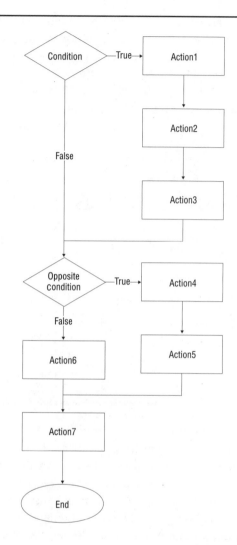

The Opposite Condition   To create the *opposite condition* of a condition, you can either change the operator in the condition or just place the *Not* operator to the left of the condition as in the last two examples. You can use the Not operator to test the opposite of a condition as follows:

> If *condition* is true then *Not condition* is false.

> If *condition* is false then *Not condition* is true.

When a condition is false, its opposite condition is true.

In the macro sheet, you enter the condition in a Condition cell and enter the set of actions you want to take if the condition is true in consecutive rows, with an ellipsis in the Condition cell of each subsequent row. In the next row, you enter the opposite condition and then enter the set of actions you want to take if the opposite condition is true in consecutive rows, with an ellipsis in the Condition cell of each subsequent row. Finally, enter the actions you want to take regardless of the value of the condition. Table 31.9 shows a conditional macro with two alternatives (in a macro sheet layout). If the condition is true, Action1, Action2, Action3, Action6, and Action7 are run; if the condition is false, Action4, Action5, Action6, and Action7 are run.

TABLE 31.9: A PAIR OF ONE-ALTERNATIVE CONDITIONS

CONDITION	ACTION
Condition	Action1
...	Action2
...	Action3
Opposite Condition	Action4
...	Action5
	Action6
	Action7

For example, suppose you are automating a catalog order business. When a customer calls to place an order for an item, the macro determines if the item is in stock. If UnitsInStock>0, the macro creates an invoice and decreases the inventory. If UnitsInStock<=0, the macro places a back order for the item. In either case, the macro places the customer on the mailing list.

If the conditional macro has two alternative sets of actions but no additional actions that you want to run regardless of the condition, you can use the StopMacro action to end the first alternative set. Table 31.10 shows a conditional macro: If the condition is true, Action1 and Action2 are run and the macro terminates with the StopMacro action. If the condition is false, Action3 and Action4 are run.

CONDITION	ACTION
TABLE 31.10: THE STOPMACRO ACTION	
Condition	Action1
...	Action2
...	StopMacro
	Action3
	Action4

Suppose you are automating a retail store that doesn't use a customer mailing list. In this case, there are no instructions to carry out regardless of the stock level. The macro determines if the item is in stock. If UnitsInStock>0, the macro creates the sales slip, decreases the inventory, and quits by using the StopMacro action. Otherwise, the macro places a back order and quits.

Using the MsgBox() Function as a Condition

You can also ask the user to decide which set of actions to execute by using the Msg-Box() function in the condition. The MsgBox() function displays a message box and a set of buttons that the user can choose. When the user clicks a button, the message box closes, and the function returns a value corresponding to the chosen button. When you use the MsgBox() function in the Condition cell of a macro, Access displays the message box and pauses execution until the user selects a button. When the user clicks a button, the function returns the corresponding value. Access then closes the message box, evaluates the condition using the returned value, and then continues to execute the macro.

As a simple example:

1. Open a new unbound form named frmMessage and create a command button named cmdMessage.

2. Click the OnClick property, click the Build button, select Macro Builder in the Choose Builder dialog (see Figure 31.35), and click OK. Save the macro sheet as mfrmMessage. By default, Access sets the event property to the name of the new macro sheet so you'll have to reassign the event property after you create an individual macro in the macro sheet.

PART

VI

Macro Programming

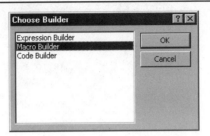

FIGURE 31.35

Click the Build button to the right of an event property to open the macro sheet containing the macro assigned to the event. If there is no macro assigned, a new macro sheet is displayed.

3. Enter the macro shown in Table 31.11 and save the macro sheet. The condition

```
Msgbox("Do you want to continue?", 4, "MsgBox Function and Macro
Action") = 6
```

is true if you choose the Yes button and false if you choose the No button. The first argument is the message, the second argument specifies the buttons, and the third argument specifies the title of the message box.

4. Click the OnClick property and assign the mfrmMessage.cmdMessage_Click macro.

TABLE 31.11: MACRO TO USE THE MSGBOX() FUNCTION IN A CONDITION

MACRO NAME	CONDITION	ACTION	ACTION ARGUMENTS
CmdMessage_Click			
	Msgbox("Do you want to continue?", 4,"MsgBox Function and Macro Action") = 6	MsgBox	Message: You clicked the Yes button
	...	StopMacro	
		MsgBox	Message: You clicked the No button

5. Save the form, switch to Form view, and test the command button (see Figure 31.36).

FIGURE 31.36

You can use the MsgBox() function as a macro condition to give the user a choice.

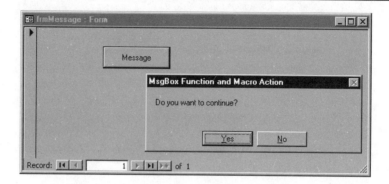

Using the Message Box Function to Collect User Input

The MsgBox() function is a built-in function that displays a dialog box containing a custom message and title and a set of buttons from which you can choose. You can display any of the following sets of buttons:

Button Sets			Button Set Type	VBA Constant
OK			0	VbOKOnly
OK	Cancel		1	VbOKCancel
Abort	Retry	Ignore	2	VbAbortRetryIgnore
Yes	No	Cancel	3	VbYesNoCancel
Yes	No		4	VbYesNo
Retry	Cancel		5	VbRetryCancel

Indicate the button set type by specifying the Button Set Type number or the built-in constant. When you use the MsgBox() function in macro programming, you must use the numbers and not the built-in constants. The MsgBox() function returns a value depending on which button the user selects, as follows:

MsgBox() Function Value	Button Chosen	VBA Constant
1	OK	vbOK
2	Cancel	vbCancel
3	Abort	vbAbort

Continued

Macro Programming

CONTINUED

MsgBox( )Function Value	Button Chosen	VBA Constant
4	Retry	vbRetry
5	Ignore	vbIgnore
6	Yes	vbYes
7	No	vbNo

The MsgBox() function has five arguments. The first three arguments are:

Prompt This is the string expression you want displayed as a message in the dialog box.

Buttons This is a numerical expression that allows you to customize the design of the dialog box by specifying four numerical codes as follows:

- The type and number of buttons you want to display (including one or more of the following: OK, Cancel, Yes, No, Abort, and Retry) by specifying the Button Set Type number
- The icon you want to display, if any (by specifying an Icon Type number)
- Which button is to be the default button if you display more than one (by specifying a Default Type number)
- The mode of the message box (by specifying a Modal Type number)

The Buttons argument is the sum of the four codes, which can be expressed using numbers or built-in constants:

Buttons = Button Set Type + Icon Type + Default Type + Modal Type

The Buttons argument is optional: if you omit this argument, an OK button is displayed and there is no icon.

Title This is the string expression you want displayed in the title bar of the dialog box. This argument is optional; if you omit this argument, the default title Microsoft Access is displayed. The fourth and fifth arguments allow you to identify context-sensitive help for the message box.

For reference, the Icon Type settings and their built-in constants are as follows:

Icon Displayed	Icon Type	VBA Constant
Critical Message	16	VbCritical
Warning Query	32	VbQuestion
Warning Message	48	VbExclamation
Information	64	VbInformation

Continued ▮▶

CONTINUED

The Default Type settings and their built-in constants are as follows:

Default Button	Default Type	VBA Constant
First button	0	VbDefaultButton1
Second button	256	VbDefaultButton2
Third button	512	VbDefaultButton3
Fourth button	768	VbDefaultButton4

And the Modal Type settings and built-in constants are as follows:

Mode	Modal Type	VBA Constant
Respond before continuing work in Microsoft Access	0	VbApplicationModal
Respond before continuing in any application	4096	VbSystemModal

The Built-in Decision Functions

Another way to make decisions is to use a *decision function*. Access provides three built-in decision functions you can use to make decisions: IIf() (the Immediate If function), Choose(), and Switch(). A decision function returns different values depending on the value of an expression. The first argument is the expression, and the remaining arguments are the possible values that the function can return. The three functions are closely related. Nevertheless, they allow you to make different kinds of decisions.

The Immediate If Function

The IIf() function lets you make decisions by testing a condition and returning one of two different values depending on whether the condition is true or false. The function has three arguments: the first is the condition, the second is the result you want if the condition is true, and the third is the result you want if the condition is false.

```
IIf(condition,true,false)
```

You can visualize the Immediate If function by using a diamond-shaped decision box to represent the condition and rectangular result boxes to represent the two possible results (see Figure 31.37).

PART

VI

Macro Programming

FIGURE 31.37

FIGURE 31.37

A flow diagram for the
IIf() function.

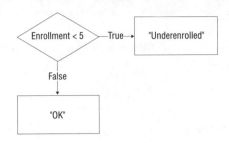

The Choose() Function

The Choose() function creates a lookup table that returns a value from a list depending on the position of the value in the list. The Choose() function takes several arguments. The first argument, called *indexnumber*, takes an integer value of 1 or greater. The remaining arguments make up the list of values the function can return.

> *Choose(indexnumber, value1, value2,...)*

If indexnumber = 1, value1 is returned; if indexnumber = 2, value2 is returned; and so on.

The returned value must be a number, date, or string, or a function that returns a number, date, or string. There can be at most 13 values in the list. You can visualize the Choose() function as a set of decision diamonds for testing the value of the index number, as shown in Figure 31.38.

FIGURE 31.38

A flow diagram for the
Choose() function.

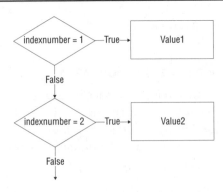

The *Switch()* Function

The Switch() function takes pairs of expressions as its arguments:

    Switch(condition1, value1, condition2, value2,…)

The first member of each pair of arguments is a condition that evaluates to true or false, and the second member of the pair is the value that is returned if the first member is true. The Switch() function evaluates the conditions, and for the first condition that is true, the Switch() function returns the corresponding value. If none of the conditions is true, the Switch() function returns a null value. You can visualize the Switch() function as a set of decision diamonds, as shown in Figure 31.39.

FIGURE 31.39

A flow diagram for the Switch() function.

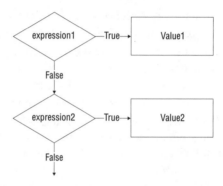

Table 31.12 shows examples of the decision functions.

TABLE 31.12: EXAMPLES OF BUILT-IN DECISION FUNCTIONS	
FUNCTION	**DESCRIPTION**
Iif(UnitsInStock<ReorderLevel, "Reorder Now","OK")	Returns Reorder Now or OK depending on the value of UnitsInStock.
IIf(UnitsInStock<ReorderLevel, "Reorder Now",Iif(UnitsInStock>100, "Overstock","OK"))	Uses a nested IIf function to display Reorder Now if the value of UnitsInStock is less than the reorder level, Overstock if the value is greater than 100, and OK otherwise.
IIf(IsNull(Units),0,Units)	Returns 0 (zero) if Units has the null value and returns the value in Units otherwise.

Continued ▌▶

PART

VI

Macro Programming

TABLE 31.12: EXAMPLES OF BUILT-IN DECISION FUNCTIONS (CONTINUED)	
FUNCTION	**DESCRIPTION**
IIf(IsNull(MiddleInitial), "",MiddleInitial)	Returns the zero-length string ("") if the MiddleInitial has the null value; otherwise, returns the value.
Choose(ShipVia, "Speedy", "United", "Federal")	Returns Speedy, United, or Federal if ShipVia is 1, 2, or 3.
Switch(Title="Ms.",1,Title= "Mr.",2,Title="Dr.",3)	Returns 1, 2, or 3 if Title is Ms., Mr., or Dr.

You can use the decision functions in calculated controls on forms and reports and in queries to create calculated fields, to define query criteria, and to create query update expressions. You can also use decision functions in macros to define action arguments and condition expressions, and in VBA procedures.

 NOTE Access carries out the decision functions in different ways. When you use the IIf( ) function on a form or on a report, Access evaluates the condition and then evaluates either the true or the false expression but not both. The Choose() and the Switch() functions work differently. The Choose() function evaluates every value in the list, even though it returns only one value. Likewise, the Switch() function evaluates every condition and every value, even though it returns only one value. Because Access is evaluating all of the expressions, these functions may be slow. Also, since all expressions are being evaluated, there can be undesirable results. For example, if one of the expressions that is not being returned results in a Division By Zero error, Access reports the error anyway.

Macro Loops

Using conditions in macros gives you a way to define different results depending on the value of an expression—this is referred to as a *decision structure*. A decision structure allows you to control which actions Access executes. Access provides another way to control the flow by providing the ability to run a macro repeatedly; the macro actions that are repeated are called a *loop*. The RunMacro action provides two ways to repeat actions:

- By running another macro for a specified number of times (a *counted loop*)
- By running another macro until a given condition becomes true or false (a *tested loop*)

You use the first action argument, Macro Name, to specify the name of the macro to be run and use either of the remaining arguments to repeat the macro. You use the second argument, Repeat Count, to enter the specific number of times you want the macro to run, and the third argument, Repeat Expression, to enter an expression that evaluates to true or false as a repetition condition. If you leave both repeat arguments blank, the macro runs only once.

Using either of the Repeat arguments to run a macro repeatedly is an example of a *loop structure*. A loop structure requires two macros: one macro (the calling macro) to call for the loop and another macro (the called macro) containing the actions you want to repeat. We'll look at a simple example of each kind of loop.

Create a Simple Loop to Run a Specific Number of Times

As an example of a counted loop, create a macro that calls another macro four times using the Repeat Count argument. The called macro displays a message box.

1. Open a new blank form in Design view. Save the form as frmLoop and set the Caption property to Loop Examples.

2. Place a command button on the form, set the Name property to cmdLoop-Count, and set the Caption property to Loop&Count.

3. Open a new macro sheet and save it as mfrmLoop.

4. Enter the macros shown in Table 31.13 and then save the macro sheet.

TABLE 31.13: MACROS FOR A COUNTED LOOP

MACRO NAME	ACTION	ACTION ARGUMENT
CmdLoopCount_Click		
	RunMacro	Macro Name: mfrmLoop.LoopCount Repeat Count: 4
LoopCount		
	MsgBox	Message: ="Loop"

5. Assign the cmdLoopCount_Click macro to the OnClick property of the cmd-LookCount button, save the form, and switch to Form view.

6. Click the button. A message box with the message Loop is displayed (see Figure 31.40).

7. Click OK. The message box is displayed again. Each time you click OK, the message box is displayed until it has been displayed four times.

FIGURE 31.40

The message displayed by the called macro.

When you enter a number in the Repeat Count argument, Access automatically sets up an *implicit counter* to keep track of the number of passes through the loop, and stops execution after completing the specified number of passes. You can represent these macros with the macro flow diagram shown in Figure 31.41.

FIGURE 31.41

The macro flow diagram for a loop to display a message four times. When you specify a number in the Repeat Count argument, Access sets up an implicit counter to keep track of the loops.

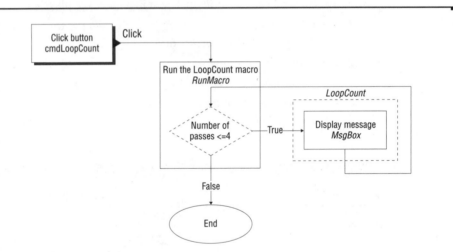

In the flow diagram, the operation box for the RunMacro action contains a dotted condition diamond to represent the testing of the implicit counter. Unless you keep track of how many message boxes have been displayed, you can't tell which pass Access is executing. You can have Access tell you which pass it is executing by defining an *explicit counter* and displaying the value of the counter as each pass is executed. Set the counter to 1 in the calling macro before the RunMacro action and modify the message to display the value of the counter. At the end of each pass, you increase the counter by 1 before returning to the calling macro. Hold the value of the counter in an unbound text box on the form. You can use either loop structure to specify that the macro is to run four times: by using a counted loop (with the Repeat Count argument set to 4), or by using a tested loop with the `Repeat Expression` argument set to the expression

    Counter <= 4

The result is the same: the macro runs for four circuits and displays identical sets of message boxes. Figure 31.42 shows the flow diagram for the tested loop.

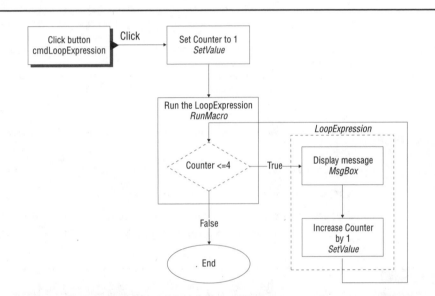

Creating a Tested Loop with a Counter

Create an unbound text box to hold the value of the counter and a macro that uses the counter to keep track of how many times the loop is run.

1. Switch back to Design view and place a second command button on the frLoop form. Then set the Name property to cmdLoopExpression, the Caption property to Loop&Expression, and the OnClick property to mfrmLoop.cmdLoop Expression_Click.

2. Select the Text Box tool, then click the form and place an unbound text box above the new command button. Next, set the Name property to Counter and set the Enabled property to No (but leave the Visible property setting as Yes so you can see the value of the counter variable). Select and delete the text box label.

3. Click the macro sheet and enter the macros shown in Table 31.14. The calling macro is cmdLoopExpression_Click, and LoopExpression is the called macro for the tested loop. The SetValue action in the LoopExpression macro increases the counter by 1 at the end of each circuit. Save the macro sheet.

MACRO NAME	ACTION	ACTION ARGUMENTS
TABLE 31.14: MACROS FOR A TESTED LOOP WITH A COUNTER		
cmdLoopExpression_Click		
	SetValue	Item: Counter
		Expression: 1
	RunMacro	Macro Name: mfrmLoop.LoopExpression
		Repeat Expression: Counter <= 4
LoopExpression		
	MsgBox	Message: ="Loop Counter ="&[Counter]
	SetValue	Item: Counter
		Expression: Counter + 1

Run the Loop

1. Click the form and switch to Form view.

2. Click the button. A message box displaying Loop Counter = 1 appears, and the value in the text box control is 1 (see Figure 31.43).

FIGURE 31.43

The message displayed by the tested loop with a counter.

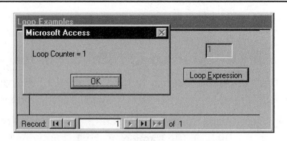

3. Click OK four times. When you click OK on the Loop Counter message box, the called macro increments the counter, and the first circuit is finished. Access returns to the calling macro, evaluates the Repeat Expression argument with the current value of the counter (Counter = 2), determines that the expression Counter <= 4 is true, and executes the next circuit. After two more repetitions, the message box displays the message Loop Counter = 4. When you click OK, the called macro increments the counter to 5, and the fourth circuit is now finished. Access returns to the calling macro, evaluates the Repeat Expression with the current value of the counter, determines that the expression Counter <= 4 is false, and terminates the calling macro. The value in the Counter text box is 5, and the loop terminates because the Repeat Expression is false.

4. Close frmLoop and mfrmLoop.

In this example, you used an explicit counter in the RepeatExpression argument to control the loop. However, the expression that you use for the argument can be based on a value in a control, a property of a control, or the value returned from a function.

Summary

The Access macro programming language is powerful yet surprisingly easy to learn. This chapter has introduced you to the basic components of the language. The main concepts are as follows:

- You can create macros using a structured macro sheet with specialized cells and combo lists of choices. The macro sheet design minimizes the need to learn programming syntax. Each instruction corresponds to a macro action with arguments to specify how the action is to be carried out.

- The macro actions duplicate the actions you take when you work interactively. In addition, there are macro actions that provide new capabilities.

- Typically, you store all of the macros for a form or a report in a form or report macro sheet. This book uses the naming standard *mformname*, or *mreportname* to document the association of the macro sheet with the form or report.

- Most macros are event macros that you assign to an event property of an object. Access runs the assigned macro automatically when the object recognizes the event. This book uses the naming standard *objectname_eventname* to document the association of the macro with the object and the event.

- Here are some especially important macro actions:

    The SetValue macro action   Is used to change values when you are working with a form or report. The SetValue action can change the value in the field in the underlying table or query, or the value of a control, form, or report property.

    The RunCommand action   Is used to run any built-in command that is appropriate for the view that is active and for the existing conditions when you run the action.

PART

VI

Macro Programming

The MsgBox action   Is used to display a custom message box and provides one-way communication with the user. You can also use the MsgBox function to provide a choice of buttons.

The SendKeys action   Is used to send key strokes as if you typed them using the keyboard.

- A goal in creating macros is to make them reusable. Normally, a reusable macro doesn't contain names of specific objects. A control with a reusable macro assigned to an event property can be copied and pasted to other forms.

- You can use unbound controls on forms to create variables that hold the temporary values that you need to refer to.

- Macro programming has three execution patterns: sequential, conditional, and looping. In a sequential macro, each macro action executes in the order listed in the macro sheet. In a conditional macro, you can provide alternative sets of instructions that you want carried out depending on the value of a condition. In a looping macro, the called macro executes repeatedly a specified number of times or until a condition is met.

In any kind of programming, the results aren't always what you intend. Mistakes may prevent a macro from running at all. If a macro does run to completion, you may get the wrong results. The next chapter describes the kinds of errors that will inevitably occur, gives examples of how you can troubleshoot errors, and shows how you can prevent some errors from occurring.

CHAPTER 32

Dealing with Errors in Macros

I n a broad sense, an *error* is anything that deviates from what you want in your application. Errors occur at every stage of application development: from the initial paper-and-pencil design of the database structure, to the creation of database objects and expressions, to the creation of macros and Visual Basic procedures that automate tasks and transform your interactive database into an application, to data entry and report printing, and so on. There is a good chance of error at each step. Errors can be large and obvious or small and subtle. You deal with the obvious errors right away. It's the subtle ones that cause the real headaches—the hidden errors that you aren't aware of until they spring out at unexpected moments. The best way to deal with errors is to avoid them in the first place. Learning about the kinds of errors that can—and will—occur is the best way to begin.

This chapter describes the troubleshooting tools available in macro programming. Macro programming provides very limited ability to deal with errors that occur when a macro is running—because you can't deal with an error that has already occurred, the best strategy is to design macros that avoid run-time errors. Visual Basic programming, by contrast, allows you to deal with errors that have already occurred. This chapter shows you how to create a simple Visual Basic error handler that you can use in an application that is automated with macros.

Kinds of Macro Errors

There are three kinds of macro errors:

Syntax errors   Occur when you violate the rules of Access syntax as you are creating macros.

Run-time errors   Occur when macros try to execute actions that are impossible to execute.

Logic errors   Occur when your macros are free of syntax errors, execute all of their actions, and yet fail to produce the results that you had intended.

Syntax Errors

Syntax errors occur while you are creating a macro in the macro sheet. These errors occur when you violate the rules of Access *syntax*, which is the set of rules governing the spelling of certain words and the arrangement of words, symbols, and operators that you enter into the blanks in the macro sheet. If you spell a macro action incorrectly, a syntax error occurs, and Access provides you with the following error message:

The text you entered isn't an item in the list.

If you omit a parenthesis in an action argument or a condition, you generate a syntax error, and Access displays an error message like the following:

Microsoft Access can't parse the expression: 'IsNull(Country'.

Access *parses* an expression when it separates the expression into its parts and recognizes the parts as known items that are correctly related according to a set of Access rules.

Access checks your syntax automatically and displays a default error message when it detects a syntax error. But some syntax errors aren't found until you run the macro. In this case, you may have entered an expression that Access can parse, using the wrong syntax for the situation. For example, if you use the wrong syntax to refer to a control in the GoToControl action, or if you forget to use an equal sign in the Find What argument of the FindRecord action, the macro won't run correctly.

Run-Time Errors

Run-time errors occur when some circumstance makes it impossible to execute your macro. For example, if you misspell the name of a control in a macro condition or action argument, syntax checking won't find the error—the error lurks until you try to run the macro. For example, if you have a control named grpTitle and you misspell it as grpTitl in a macro argument, when you try to run the macro, Access generates a run-time error and displays the following error message:

There is no field named 'grpTitl' in the current record.

This lets you know that an expression in your macro refers to a field that doesn't exist.

One way to avoid identifier errors like this one is to use the Expression Builder when you create expressions. With the Expression Builder, you create expressions by selecting object names from lists instead of by typing the names; thus you avoid all misspellings.

Here are some examples of situations that result in run-time errors in macros:

- Referring to a control on a form that isn't open

- Executing a built-in command that isn't available

- Moving the focus to a control using the control's full name instead of its short name

When it is not possible to execute a macro action, Access displays a default error message and stops the macro. For example, if you use the OpenForm action and misspell the form's name, Access displays the default error message shown in Figure 32.1.

PART

VI

Macro Programming

FIGURE 32.1

A typical default error message.

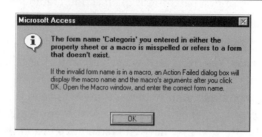

After you acknowledge the error message by clicking the OK button, Access displays the Action Failed dialog (see Figure 32.2).

FIGURE 32.2

The Action Failed dialog indicates the name of the macro and action that Access cannot execute.

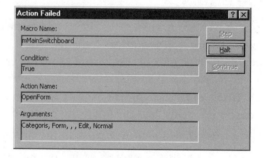

The Action Failed Dialog

The Action Failed dialog tells you exactly where the error occurred by providing the name of the macro, the action that caused the error, and the action's arguments. If there is a condition for the action, the dialog displays the condition and whether the condition has a value of True or False.

After you click the Halt button, you must determine what caused the error. (Often the default error message alerts you to the cause immediately and troubleshooting isn't necessary.) Take whatever steps are required to eliminate the problem. For example, for a simple misspelling error, you need to correct the spelling error in the macro argument.

Logic Errors

Logic errors occur when the macro action's arguments and conditions are correct and the macro executes without generating a run-time error, but the macro doesn't give you the result you intended. These errors are often the most difficult to understand and correct. Logic errors occur for a variety of reasons, such as:

- The macro actions are in the wrong sequence.
- Two macros are executed in the wrong order.
- An action has been omitted inadvertently.
- You misunderstood what a particular macro action does. (For example, you used the RepaintObject action when the correct action is Requery.)
- You specified the wrong field or control.
- You used the wrong operator. (For example, you used < when you should have used <=.)
- You attached the macro to the wrong event.

Because Access doesn't help you out by displaying a default error message or an Action Failed dialog when a logic error occurs, you have to develop a set of troubleshooting tools that you can use to isolate the cause of the error.

Troubleshooting

There are several troubleshooting tools available to help you analyze run-time and logic errors. To troubleshoot successfully, you must thoroughly understand two things: how your macro is supposed to work and how your macro actually does work.

Single Stepping Macros

You can use the Single Step feature to step through a macro one action at a time. Turn on the Single Step feature by choosing the Single Step command from the Run menu or by clicking the Single Step button in the toolbar.

TIP Add the Single Step button to the Form view toolbar so you can turn the feature on and off when you are in Form view.

With Single Step turned on, the Single Step dialog appears when you start to run a macro (see Figure 32.3).

PART

VI

Macro Programming

FIGURE 32.3

Use the Single Step dialog to troubleshoot a macro.

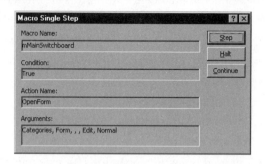

The dialog displays information about the action that is going to be executed next, including the name of the macro, the current value of the condition, the name of the action, and the settings of the action arguments. The Single Step dialog is similar to the Action Failed dialog, except that the Step and Continue buttons are available. You click the Step button to "step into" and execute the action displayed if the value of the condition is True. If the value of the condition is False, the action shown in the dialog is not executed; instead, Access steps into the next action and displays its Single Step dialog. Click the Continue button to step into the action and turn off the Single Step feature. If you don't click the Continue button, the Single Step feature remains on for the rest of the current macro and for all subsequent macros, until you turn it off. In between running macros, you can turn off the Single Step feature by clicking the Single Step button or by choosing (and unchecking) the Single Step command from the Run menu.

You can use the Single Step feature to watch the execution of each action that precedes an error; this information may help you to determine the error's cause. The Single Step feature can help you to observe the interaction of two macros that may have worked as intended when you ran them separately, but don't work correctly when they interact. Such observation can be useful in deciding that one or the other macro traps the wrong event.

Using Breakpoints

You can use a breakpoint when you want to stop a macro at a certain step and check the current values of controls and properties. You create a breakpoint by entering a dummy name, such as Break, in the Macro Name cell of the row where you want to stop.

You can use the Immediate pane of the Debug window (discussed later) to actually check current values.

TIP You can prevent execution of a specific action in a macro by entering **False** (or by entering **0**, which means the same thing) in the Condition cell in the same row. Use this technique when you want to run a macro without a particular action.

Printing Macros

You can use the Database Documenter to print out your macros; reviewing an entire macro in print is an excellent way to understand how the macro works.

1. Choose the Analyze command from the Tools menu and then choose the Documenter command from the fly-out menu to start the Documenter. The Documenter dialog has a tab for each object type and displays a list of your database objects for the selected tab (see Figure 32.4).

FIGURE 32.4

The Database Documenter.

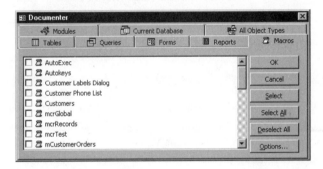

2. Click the Macros tab and then click the Options button. You can choose to include information about macro properties, actions, arguments, and security (see Figure 32.5). When you're finished changing any of these settings, click OK to close the Options dialog box.

FIGURE 32.5

The Documenter options.

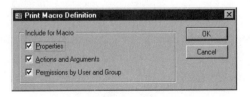

PART

VI

Macro Programming

3. Select the macro objects you want to document, then click OK. Access produces an Object Definition report, which you can print. Figure 32.6 shows a portion of the report for the mfrmSwitchboard macro group.

FIGURE 32.6

The Object Definition report for a macro.

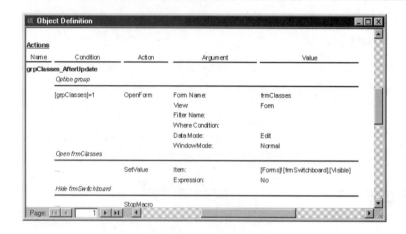

Using the MsgBox Action to Troubleshoot

Use the MsgBox action at critical points in a macro to tell yourself what the macro is doing. You can use a simple message like "Got to this point," or you can display the current value of a control or a property. When you want to display a message, enter it into the Message argument as either the message itself, for example:

    Got to here

Or you can enter it as the text expression:

    = "Got to here"

When you want to display the value of a control or property, you can enter an expression that concatenates the text message and the control or property name, for example:

    = "The value in the Address control is" & Forms!Customers!Address

A message box displaying this expression is shown in Figure 32.7.

FIGURE 32.7

Using the MsgBox *action to display a value.*

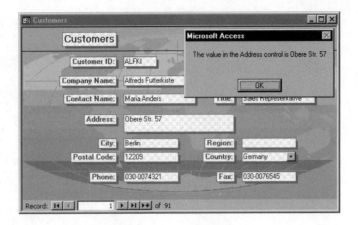

Using the Visual Basic Window to Troubleshoot

Another troubleshooting tool is the Visual Basic window (see Figure 32.8). To open this window from any other window, press Ctrl+G. You can use the Immediate pane of the Visual Basic window to display the value of a field, control, or property on a form or report, or to evaluate any valid expression. This information can help you to diagnose the error. You can also use the Immediate pane to assign values to controls and properties. In this way, you can change the values and run the macro again to see the result. You can even use the Immediate pane to run a macro action, a macro, or Visual Basic code.

FIGURE 32.8

*The Visual Basic win-
dow with the
Immediate pane
visible.*

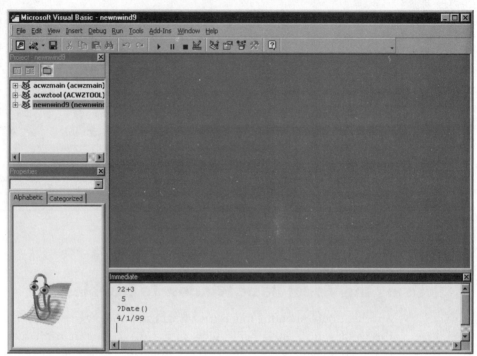

Using the Immediate Pane to Evaluate Expressions

You can display a value in the Immediate pane by typing a question mark followed by the expression you want Access to evaluate, and then pressing Enter.

1. Press Ctrl+G and click the Immediate pane if it's not active.

2. Enter **?2+3** and press Enter. The value of the expression is displayed in the next line.

3. Enter **?Date( )**. The next line displays the current date (see Figure 32.8).

4. Choose the Select All command in the Edit menu to select all of the text you entered, and then press Delete to delete the text.

Using the Immediate Pane to Display Values from Forms and Reports

You can display a value in the Immediate pane by typing a question mark followed by the name of the field, control, or property of a form or report. The form or report must be open, and you must use the fully qualified reference to the object or property. For example, with the Customers form open, do the following:

1. Type **?Forms!Customers!CompanyName** and press Enter. The next line of the Debug Immediate window displays the value in the CompanyName control for the current record.

2. Type **?Forms!Customers.RecordSource** and press Enter. The Debug Immediate window displays Customers as the name of the table that provides the records to the Customers form (see Figure 32.9).

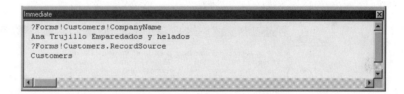

```
Immediate                                                                    [X]
?Forms!Customers!CompanyName
Ana Trujillo Emparedados y helados
?Forms!Customers.RecordSource
Customers
```

Using the Immediate Pane to Run a Macro Action or a Macro

You can run a macro action by typing **DoCmd** followed by a dot and the name of the macro action with the list of arguments. Enclose all text arguments in quotation marks and use commas to separate multiple arguments. If you omit arguments, Access assumes the default values for the action; you must still use commas to hold the place of the omitted arguments in the argument list unless you are either omitting all arguments or omitting all arguments after the last one you want to specify.

NOTE When you run a macro action this way, you are actually running the corresponding Visual Basic *method* of the DoCmd object. Nearly all macro actions have equivalent Visual Basic methods. You can get help on the corresponding method by searching online Help for the name of the action and choosing the corresponding method from the topics list.

To see how this works, type **DoCmd.OpenForm "Employees"** and press Enter. When you type DoCmd., a drop-down list appears, displaying the methods of the DoCmd object (see Figure 32.10a). You can double-click an item from the list to enter the item in the statement, or type the item yourself. When you press the space bar after entering the OpenForm method, Access displays a little window with the correct syntax for the method. (See Figure 32.10b). When you complete the statement and press Enter, Access opens the form. The OpenForm macro action has six arguments, and the corresponding Visual Basic OpenForm method has the same six plus an additional argument. To open the form with all default values, you can omit all arguments and specify only the name of the form.

FIGURE 32.10

Access helps you to create statements in the Immediate pane by displaying a list of choices (a), and syntax (b).

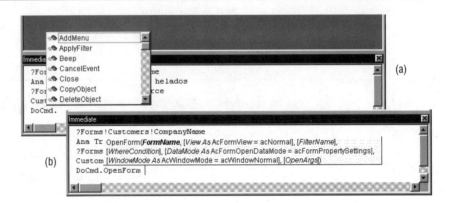

You can run a macro from the Immediate Pane by typing **DoCmd.RunMacro**, followed by the full name of the macro enclosed in quotation marks. For example, with the Main Switchboard open, enter **DoCmd.RunMacro "mMainSwitchboard.cmd Categories_Click"** and press Enter to run the macro you created in Chapter 31.

Using the Immediate Pane to Assign Values to Forms and Reports

You can assign a value using the Immediate pane by typing the full identifier reference of the object, followed by an equal sign, followed by the value. If the value is a text expression, you must enclose the expression in quotation marks. For example, with the Customers form open, enter the expression **Forms!Customers.Caption = "Hi there!"** and press Enter. Access immediately changes the Caption property of the Customers form to the expression you entered (see Figure 32.11).

FIGURE 32.11

Using the Debug Immediate window to evaluate expressions, run a macro action, and change a property, such as the caption for the form shown here.

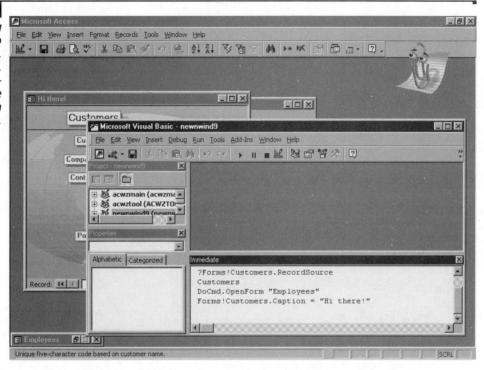

NOTE If the Customers form is in Form view when you assign the value, the changed caption is temporary; but if the Customers form is in Design view when you assign the value, the change is made in the form's property sheet, and you can save the changed value.

Handling Run-Time Errors: Macros versus Visual Basic

The result of successful troubleshooting is that you eliminate detectable run-time macro errors, and you correct logic errors. But even with the most thorough macro testing procedures, the application you develop will probably still have some run-time errors. As examples, standard unavoidable run-time errors occur in the following situations:

- If you enter a name in a combo box that is not in the list, and the LimitToList property has been set to Yes.

- If you enter a number that would result in an attempt to divide by zero.

- If you create or modify a record so that a required field is empty. (In this case, Access displays the default error message shown in Figure 32.12.)

FIGURE 32.12

A default error message that appears when you leave a required field empty.

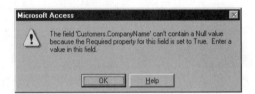

The Error Code for an Error

Each run-time error has an integer value, called an *error code*, that uniquely identifies it. Table 32.1 lists codes for some of the default error messages you may have seen.

TABLE 32.1: COMMON ERROR CODES AND MESSAGES

ERROR CODE	ERROR MESSAGE
3058	Index or primary key can't contain a null value.
3022	Duplicate value in index, primary key, or relationship. Changes were unsuccessful.
3200	Can't delete or change record. Since related records exist in '|', referential integrity rules would be violated.
3314	Field <name> can't contain a null value.
2427	Object has no value.
2237	The text you enter must match an entry in the list.
2079	Entry Required!
2105	Can't go to specified record.
2107	The value you entered is prohibited by the validation rule set for this field.

Continued ▶

TABLE 32.1: COMMON ERROR CODES AND MESSAGES (CONTINUED)	
ERROR CODE	**ERROR MESSAGE**
2110	Can't move to control <name>.
2169	The record being edited can't be saved. If you close the form, the changes you've made to the record will be lost. Close anyway?
3051	Couldn't open file '|'
7889	Couldn't find file '|'

When a run-time error occurs, Access displays the default error message and responds with default behavior. For example, when you try to save a new record without entering a value for the primary key, the run-time error with error code 3058 occurs, and Access displays the default error message and responds by canceling the save operation.

You can handle a run-time error by interrupting the default response, replacing the default message with a custom error message, and specifying the actions you want Access to take instead of the default behavior. Continuing with the same example, you can handle a 3058 error by displaying a custom message, moving the focus to the primary key control, suppressing the default message, and canceling the save operation. In order to handle a run-time error that has occurred, you must identify the error by its error code.

 WARNING A key difference between macros and Visual Basic is that you can't determine the error code with a macro—this means that you can't handle a run-time error that has already occurred using macro programming.

Using Macro Programming

You can't use a macro to determine the error code after a run-time error has occurred, so you can't prevent Access from executing its default response. When you can't prevent a particular run-time error from occurring,. you may be able to create a macro to display a custom message when the error does occur. For example, you can't prevent someone from entering a name that isn't in a combo list, so you can't prevent the run-time error (error code 2237) from occurring. But you can create a macro to display a custom message and trigger the macro with the NotInList event when such a

PART

VI

Macro Programming

name is entered. (The custom message this macro displays in response to the `NotInList` event is in addition to the default error message that Access displays in response to the 2237 error.)

If a run-time error causes a macro to fail, you can't stop Access from terminating the macro and displaying the Action Failed dialog. For example, if you run a macro to delete a record and a run-time error occurs because referential integrity prevents you from deleting the record (error code 3200), Access displays the default error message, and the action to delete the record fails. In Chapter 34, "Data Maintenance with Macros," you'll learn how to modify this macro to prevent the 3200 error from occurring.

Using Visual Basic Programming

An advantage of using Visual Basic programming is that you can create *error-handling code* to determine the error code when a run-time error occurs and then interrupt and modify the default response to the error. You can handle a run-time error in one of two ways, depending on which part of Access generated the error.

- If the run-time error is generated by the interface or the database engine, the run-time error triggers the `Error` event for the active form or report; you can handle the error by creating a Visual Basic event procedure for the `Error` event.

- If the run-time error is generated by a Visual Basic procedure, you can handle the error by adding error-handling code to the procedure itself.

Let's look at a simple error handler that you can use with your macro-automated application.

A Simple Visual Basic Error Handler for the `Error` Event

A form or report recognizes the `Error` event whenever the interface or the database engine generates a run-time error. You can use the `Error` event to set traps for specific run-time errors that may occur and tell Access what to do if one of them does. Create an event procedure for the `Error` event in the form or report module that is stored with the form or report.

Open the Form Module

As an example, we'll create an error handler for the Customers form.

1. Open the Customers form in Design view. Select the Country combo box and set the LimitToList property to Yes.

2. Click the form's OnError property, click the Build button to the right of the property box, select Code Builder, and click OK. The form module opens, displaying a *code template* or *stub* for the Error event consisting of the first and last lines for the procedure (see Figure 32.13). You may have to enlarge the Form_Customers (Code) window to make the code template visible.

NOTE You can also use the OnNotInList property to play a macro or run a Visual Basic procedure in the same circumstance, freeing the Error property for other macros.

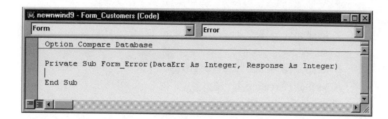

Words that Visual Basic uses as part of its language are called *keywords*. In the first line of the code template, the `Private` keyword indicates that the procedure applies only to the form or report with which it is stored, and the Sub keyword indicates that the procedure doesn't return a value. (Only Function procedures return values.) The End Sub keyword in the last line indicates the end of the procedure. Access names an event procedure for a form using the following syntax:

    Form_eventname

so the error handler for a form is Form_Error.

The Form_Error procedure has two arguments:

DataErr   Is the error code of the run-time error that occurred. Access passes the value of the error code to the Form_Error procedure.

Response   Is a response code that represents the way you want Access to respond to the run-time error. You set the value of this argument as one of the statements in the procedure. You can use built-in constants to specify the response. That is, to suppress the default error message, you set `Response` to the constant acDataErrContinue. To display the default error message, you set `Response` to the constant acDataErrDisplay.

You can enter Visual Basic code statements between the two lines of the code template. As an example, you can write a simple Visual Basic error handler that traps for two errors types:

Error code 3058   The error that occurs when you try to save a record without entering a value in a key field.

Error code 2237   The error that occurs when you enter a value in a combo box that isn't in the list, and the LimitToList property has been set to Yes. Listing 32.1 shows the code that traps for these errors.

Listing 32.1

```
Private Sub Form_Error (DataErr As Integer, Response As Integer)
If DataErr = 3058 Then
  MsgBox "You must enter a CustomerID, please enter it now."
  Response = acDataErrContinue
ElseIf DataErr = 2237 Then
  MsgBox "The country you entered isn't on the list"
  Response = acDataErrContinue
Else
  Response = acDataErrDisplay
  MsgBox DataErr
End If
End Sub
```

When the form recognizes the Error event, Access runs the Form_Error procedure and sets the DataErr argument to the error code of the error that occurred. The procedure compares DataErr to specific error codes as follows:

- The If clause compares DataErr to 3058. If there is a match, the procedure displays the custom message using the MsgBox function and sets the Response argument to acDataErrContinue to suppress the display of the default error message. The procedure jumps to the End Sub statement and terminates.

- If there is no match, the procedure jumps to the ElseIf statement, which compares DataErr to 2237. If there is a match, the procedure displays the custom message and jumps to the End Sub statement.

- If there is no match for the If or ElseIf clause, Visual Basic executes the Else clause, which sets the Response argument to acDataErrDisplay to display the default error message for the error that did occur. Then Visual Basic displays the error code and terminates.

Enter the Visual Basic Code

The title bar of the module in Figure 32.13 indicates that the module has been automatically named Form_Customers. Access automatically creates a form module to store the *event procedures* triggered by events recognized by the form and its controls. Form modules are analogous to the form macro groups we've been creating. In the same way that macro groups hold macros, form modules hold Visual Basic procedures.

Next you'll enter code in the Form_Customers module that will run when the OnError event is triggered.

1. Type in the code in Listing 32.1.

2. Choose Debug ➤ Compile.... When you *compile* a module, Access checks for errors and converts your code into a format that will execute faster. If there is an error in your code, Access stops compiling, displays a message, and highlights the line with the error.

3. Close the Visual Basic window. The Customers form Design view window will come back into view. Notice that the OnError property displays the expression [Event Procedure] to indicate that a procedure has been assigned.

4. Save the form.

5. In the Database window, click the Modules tab. The Modules tab contains only the Startup and the Utility Functions modules because the form module you just created is stored with the form and is not a separate database object.

Test the Visual Basic Error Handler

After you enter code for the OnError procedure, you can test it by following these steps:

1. Switch to Form view for the Customers form and click the New Record button in the toolbar (or at the bottom of the form).

2. Tab out of the CustomerID, enter a CompanyName, and press Shift+Enter to try to save the record. Your custom message appears.

3. Click OK. The default error message has been suppressed.

4. Click in Country combo box, type **Israel**, and press Enter. Your custom message appears after you click Enter to close the custom message, and the list of countries drops down.

5. Press Escape twice to undo the record. Close the form.

Designing to Avoid Macro Errors

Because you can't use macros to identify error codes after run-time errors have occurred, the best strategy for dealing with run-time errors that cause macros to fail is

PART

VI

Macro Programming

to avoid them whenever possible. The following is a list of ways to help you to create error-free macros:

Test preconditions in your macros.   Run-time errors occur when circumstances make your macro impossible to execute. Often you can avoid errors by creating and testing preconditions. A *precondition* is a condition for an action that you use to test whether running the action would cause a run-time error. For example:

- If a macro action refers to a control on another form, test to see if that form is open first.

- If a macro action requires the value of a control in a calculation, test to see if the value is null first.

- If a macro action tries to undo a change, test to see if the current record has been changed. (If you try to undo a record that hasn't been changed, the RunCommand action fails.)

- If a macro action saves a record, test to see if the primary key value is not null and is unique.

Test for errors and fix them as they appear.   When you create a macro, try to anticipate the different ways the user will try to interact with your application. Test your application by trying out different sequences of interactions. For example, click command buttons in different sequences to see if you can deliberately trigger an error.

Use macro flow diagrams.   A macro flow diagram is a valuable aid in understanding exactly what went wrong with your macro—for example, whether you are using the wrong event, the wrong macro action, or the wrong sequence of actions.

Use comments.   When you troubleshoot a macro, you must understand the purpose of each of its actions. Comments in the macro sheet are essential for seeing the purpose of a macro action at a glance without having to select the row to view the action arguments.

Use a consistent naming convention.   When you use a naming convention, such as the one used in this book, your objects are self-documenting: The object name includes information about the type of the object and its purpose. This information can help you to understand your macros more easily.

Create shorter macros.   Long macros are difficult to understand. It is often best to break a long macro into a set of short macros, each with a defined purpose. You can troubleshoot each short macro separately and isolate errors more quickly. This approach also helps you to create easily reusable macros.

Exceptional Macro Actions

When you issue an instruction as a macro action and Access is unable to carry out the action, the normal behavior is that a macro run-time error is generated, a default error message is displayed, the macro is terminated, and the Action Failed dialog is displayed. However, there are several macro actions with exceptional behavior that you need to know about. Figure 32.14 shows the different kinds of behavior.

FIGURE 32.14

The different behaviors that can occur when a macro action can't be executed.

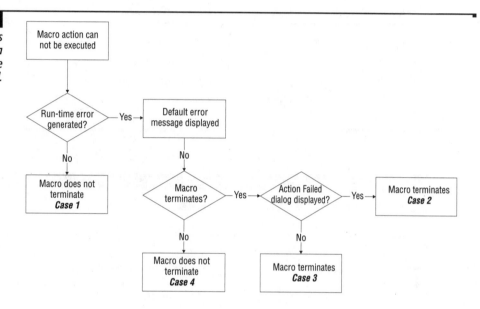

Case 1   The macro action can't be executed, yet a run-time error is not generated, and the macro doesn't terminate; examples are shown in Table 32.2.

Case 2   This is the normal behavior: A run-time error is generated, a default error message is displayed, the macro terminates, and the Action Failed dialog is displayed. A few examples of macro actions with normal behavior are shown in Table 32.3.

Case 3   A run-time error is generated, a default error message is displayed, the macro terminates, but the Action Failed dialog is not displayed. As an example, the DoMenuItem with the Save Record or Refresh command generates the run-time error (with code 3314) when you try to run the action and a required field has a null value. The macro terminates, but the Action Failed dialog is not displayed.

Case 4 A run-time error is generated, a default error message is displayed, but the macro does not terminate. Examples of case 4 are shown in Table 32.4.

TABLE 32.2: MACRO ACTIONS THAT DON'T GENERATE RUN-TIME ERRORS

MACRO ACTION	CAN'T BE EXECUTED WHEN
Close	The specified object isn't open or doesn't exist.
RunApp	The application isn't specified.
RunCode	The function name isn't specified.
SetValue	Either or both action arguments are blank.

TABLE 32.3: MACRO ACTIONS AND FATAL ERRORS RESULTING IN THE ACTION FAILED DIALOG

MACRO ACTION	FAILS WITH ERROR CODE	WHEN
GoToControl	2109	You use the full reference instead of the short name for the control. For example, using Forms!Customers!CustomerID instead of CustomerID gives the error.
RunCommand	2046	The specific menu command is not available when you try to run the action. For example, when you run the Undo menu command for a record that hasn't been changed.
RunCommand with the Save Record command	2046	The primary key is null or a duplicate of an existing primary key value.

TABLE 32.4: MACRO ACTIONS AND NON-FATAL ERRORS		
MACRO ACTION	**ERROR CODE**	**WHEN**
AddMenu	2502	The Menu Macro Name is blank.
ApplyFilter	3011	The filter name is specified but the filter doesn't exist.
TransferSpreadsheet	7889	The file to be imported can't be found.
TransferDatabase	3024	The database file to be imported can't be found.
TransferText	3011	The text file to be imported can't be found.

Whenever a run-time error is generated, you can create a Visual Basic Form_Error event procedure that traps for specific errors. You can use the event procedure to display an informative custom message, suppress the default error message, and take additional actions within the procedure; but you can't prevent a macro action from failing. When the event procedure ends, the subsequent behavior depends on the macro action and the specific error generated; in the normal case, the Action Failed dialog is displayed, and the macro terminates. In the exceptional Case 3, the macro terminates, but the Action Failed dialog is not displayed. While in Case 4, the macro continues with the next action.

Summary

This chapter has introduced you to dealing with errors in macro programming. The important points are:

- There are three kinds of errors: syntax errors, run-time errors, and logic errors.
- Access automatically provides syntax checking as you create the macro and displays an error message to indicate the error.
- When Access can't carry out a macro action (and a run-time error occurs), the Action Failed dialog is displayed, indicating the action that couldn't be executed.
- Access provides troubleshooting tools that you can use to analyze errors. These tools include executing a single macro action at a time, stopping a macro at a certain step, using the Immediate pane of the Visual Basic window to evaluate expressions when the macro is stopped, and using the MsgBox action to display values without stopping the macro.

PART

VI

Macro Programming

- Two fundamental differences between macro and Visual Basic programming are that with macros, you cannot determine the error code of an error that has occurred, and you can't prevent Access from terminating a macro. With Visual Basic programming, you can determine the error code and write error-handling code that replaces the default error handling.

- You can use a simple Visual Basic error handler to handle errors that occur when you are working in the Access interface.

- The best way to deal with macro errors is to avoid them in the design phase. A useful technique is to test for preconditions, running the macro action only if the precondition is met.

With troubleshooting tools in hand, you are ready to learn how to automate your Access database using macros. The next three chapters take you through the major automation techniques.

CHAPTER 33

Navigation with Macros

I n Chapter 31, "Macro Basics," you learned how to automate one type of navigation: basic form navigation. You learned how to open a form displaying all of its records, how to hide and unhide a form, and how to close a form when you are finished. There are other ways that you travel around in a database. When you work interactively, you use keystrokes, menu commands, default navigation buttons, and the mouse to move among controls, between records, and from one database window object to another. You can make your application easier to use by using macros to automate all types of navigation, including the following:

- Moving the focus to a specified control on a form or a subform
- Moving to a specified record using custom navigation buttons
- Finding a record that satisfies criteria and returning to a previous record
- Synchronizing two forms to display related records and keeping them synchronized

This chapter shows you macro techniques for automating these navigational methods. The chapter ends with a discussion of a special macro, called the AutoExec macro, that you can use to run actions automatically at startup.

 NOTE In this chapter, I assume that you have customized the Form view, Macro Design and Database menu bars and toolbars to include the Macro command that displays the Run Macro dialog. If you haven't customized the command bars you can do so now using the instructions found in Chapter 31. In this chapter, I will also assume that you've created the NorthwindMacros database as a copy of the Northwind database; if you didn't, create a copy now.

Navigation through Controls

You can create macros for moving to specific controls on forms and subforms and within records. This section shows you how to use macros to move in the following ways:

- To a specific control on the active form
- To a specific control on a subform of the active form
- To a specific control on another open form
- To a specific control on a subform of another open form
- From one control to another control in the same record

Moving to a Specific Control on the Active Form

When working interactively, you move to a specific control on the active form by using the mouse to click the control; you can use the GoToControl macro action to automate this mouse action.

Use the GoToControl action to move the focus to a control on the active form or to a field in the active table or query. By design, you can use the GoToControl action only when the datasheet or form already has the focus. In the Control Name argument, enter the name of the control or field (using the short syntax).

NOTE You must use the short syntax in the Control Name argument to refer to the field or control for the GoToControl action. If you use the full identifier syntax, Access displays an error message (see Figure 33.1), and the action fails.

FIGURE 33.1

Using the full identifier in the Control Name *argument of the GoToControl action leads to an error message.*

Create a macro to move the focus to a control on a form by following these steps:

1. Open the Orders form in the NorthwindMacros database.

2. Open a new macro sheet and save it as mcrTest. You'll use this macro sheet to store the example macros.

3. Enter the first macro in Table 33.1, named ToControl, and save the macro sheet.

4. Click in the Orders form, then click the Run Macro button on the toolbar (added in Chapter 31); select mcrTest.ToControl, and then click OK. The focus moves to the specified control, EmployeeID. (This control is labeled Salesperson on the Orders form.)

PART

VI

Macro Programming

TABLE 33.1: MACROS TO MOVE AMONG CONTROLS		
MACRO NAME	**ACTION**	**ACTION ARGUMENTS**
ToControl		
	GoToControl	Control Name: EmployeeID
ToControlOnSubform		
	GoToControl	Control Name: [Orders Subform]
	GoToControl	Control Name: Discount
ToOtherFormControl		
	SelectObject	Object Type: Form
		Object Name: Orders
	GoToControl	Control Name: EmployeeID
ToOtherFormControlOnSubform		
	SelectObject	Object Type: Form
		Object Name: Orders
	GoToControl	Control Name: [Orders Subform]
	GoToControl	Control Name: Discount
ToNextControl		
	SendKeys	Keystrokes: {tab}
		Wait: Yes

Moving to a Specific Control on a Subform of the Active Form

When working interactively, you move the focus to a specific control on a subform by clicking the control. Automating this single mouse action requires two macro actions: first, you must move the focus to the subform control (using a GoToControl action), and then you move the focus to the control (using a second GoToControl action).

1. Enter the second macro of Table 33.1, named ToControlOnSubform, and then save the macro sheet.

2. Click in the Orders form, click the Run Macro button on the toolbar, select mcrTest.ToControlOnSubform, and click OK. The focus moves to the specified control in the first record of the subform.

You can test the effect of trying to move to the control without moving to the subform control first by following these steps:

1. In the ToControlOnSubform macro, type **False** in the Condition cell of the first GoToControl action. When you enter the value **False** in a Condition cell, Access skips the macro action in the row and moves to the next row.

2. Click in a control on the main form and run the ToControlOnSubform macro. Access displays the error message, and the macro fails (see Figure 33.2). The macro fails because the focus is in a control on the main form, so Access looks for the control on the main form.

3. Delete the False condition and save the macro sheet.

FIGURE 33.2

The error message when you try to move to a control on a subform without first moving to the subform control (a), and the GoToControl macro action failure message (b).

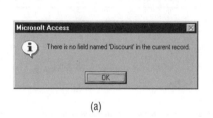

(a)

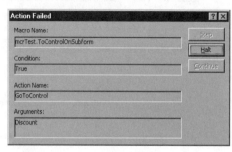

(b)

Moving to a Specific Control on Another Open Form

When working interactively, you can move to a specific control on an open form that isn't active in one step by clicking in the control. To automate this process, you must use two macro actions: First, use the SelectObject action to activate the open form. Then, use the GoToControl action to move to the control.

1. Enter the third macro of Table 33.1, named ToOtherFormControl, and then save the macro sheet.

2. Leave the Order form open, and click in the Main Switchboard form. Then click the Run Macro button on the toolbar, select mcrTest.ToOtherFormControl, and click OK. The focus moves from the switchboard to the form, then to the specified control.

Moving to a Control on a Subform of Another Form

Moving to a specific control on a subform that's on another open form requires three actions: the SelectObject action to activate the form, the GoToControl action to move to the subform control, and the GoToControl action to move to the control.

1. Enter the fourth macro of Table 33.1, ToOtherFormControlOnSubform, and then save the macro sheet.

2. Click in the switchboard and click the Run Macro button on the toolbar. Select mcrTest.ToOtherFormControlOnSubform, and click OK. The focus moves from the switchboard, to the form, and then to the specified control in the first record of the subform.

Moving within a Record

When you work interactively, you can use the keyboard instead of the mouse to move the focus among the controls of the active form. The Keystrokes argument for the SendKeys action for moving between controls are shown in Table 33.2.

TABLE 33.2: THE KEYSTROKES **ARGUMENT FOR MOVING BETWEEN CONTROLS**

TO MOVE THE FOCUS	KEYSTROKES	KEYSTROKES ARGUMENT
To the next control in the tab order	Tab	{tab}
To the previous control in the tab order	Shift+Tab	+{tab}
To the first control in current record	Home	{home}
To the last control in current record	End	{end}

You can use the SendKeys action to duplicate the keystrokes to move the focus among the controls of the active form. Set the Wait argument to Yes to pause the macro until the keystrokes are processed.

1. Enter the fifth macro of Table 33.1, named ToNextControl, and save the macro sheet.

2. Click the Orders form, click a control on the main form, and click the Run Macro button on the toolbar. Select mcrTest.ToNextControl and click OK. The focus moves to the next control in the tab order.

3. Click in a control on the subform and click the Run Macro button on the toolbar. Select mcrTest.ToNextControl and click OK. The focus moves to the next control in the subform's tab order.

Physical Navigation among Records

When you work interactively, you can navigate among records according to their physical location within the recordset; this is called *physical navigation*. The record you navigate to becomes the current record. The *current record* is the record you modify with subsequent mouse or keyboard actions.

You can use keystroke combinations, the default navigation buttons (in the lower-left corner of datasheets, forms, and reports), or the Go To command in the Edit menu to move to the first, previous, next, or last record in a set. Each of these physical navigation methods can be automated with macros.

Automating Keystroke Navigation

When you work interactively, you can use keystrokes for navigation among controls, provided you are in navigation mode and not editing mode. When you first open a form, you are in navigation mode. You can toggle between editing mode and navigation mode by pressing F2. You can duplicate the keystroke combinations for physical navigation among records by using the SendKeys action in a macro. Table 33.3 shows examples of the corresponding Keystrokes arguments.

TABLE 33.3: THE KEYSTROKES **ARGUMENT FOR MOVING AMONG RECORDS**

TO MOVE THE FOCUS	KEYSTROKES	KEYSTROKES ARGUMENT
To the first control of the first record	Ctrl+Home	^{home}
To the last control of the last record (or the first control in the last record of a subform)	Ctrl+End	^{end}
To the current control of the next record	Page Down	{pgdn}
To the current control of the previous record	Page Up	{pgup}

Moving to the Last Record in a Subform

As an example, create a new macro sheet named mcrRecord to hold macros to move among the records of the Orders form. The first macro in Table 33.4 moves the focus to the last control of the last record of the active form.

1. Enter the first macro of Table 33.4, named ToLastControlLastRecord, and save the macro sheet.

2. Click the main form of the Orders form. In navigation mode, click the Run Macro toolbar button, select the mcrRecord.ToLastControlLastRecord macro, and click OK. The focus moves to the last control of the last record.

3. Click the subform. In navigation mode (where the field value is highlighted), run the same macro as in the last step. The focus moves to the first control of the last record in the subform.

TABLE 33.4: MACROS TO NAVIGATE AMONG RECORDS		
MACRO NAME	**ACTION**	**ACTION ARGUMENTS**
ToLastControlLastRecord		
	SendKeys	Keystrokes: ^{end}
		Wait: Yes
ToLastRecord		
	GoToRecord	Record: Last
ToNextRecord		
	GoToRecord	Record: Next
ToLastSubformRecord		
	GoToControl	Control Name: [Orders Subform]
	GoToRecord	Record: Last
ToHiddenRecord		
	GoToRecord	Object Type: Form
		Object Name: Orders
		Record: First
	SetValue	Item: Forms!Orders!ShipName
		Expression: "hiddenname"

Automating the Default Navigation Buttons and Menu Commands

You can use the GoToRecord action to duplicate the effect of clicking a default navigation button in the lower-left corner of a form or choosing a subcommand in the flyout menu of the Go To command on the Edit menu.

Move to a Record on the Active Form

If the active form has a subform, there are two sets of records you can move around in: the records for the main form and the records for the subform. The result of the GoToRecord action depends on whether the focus is in the main form or in the subform control when you initiate the action.

1. Enter the Table 33.4 macros named ToLastRecord and ToNextRecord and save the macro sheet. When you leave the Object Type argument blank, the GoToRecord action makes the specified record in the active object the current record. If you want to make a record in another open object the current record, you can specify the Object Type and Object Name arguments as well.

2. Click in the Orders form and click in a control on the main form. Click the Run Macro button in the toolbar, select the mcrRecord.ToLastRecord macro, and click OK. The last record in the set of records underlying the main form becomes the current record.

3. Click the Run Macro button, select the mcrRecord.ToNextRecord macro, and click OK. Access displays a blank record at the end of any recordset to which you can add new records. When you run this macro again, there is no record to move to. Let's see what happens if we run the macro again.

4. Click the Run Macro button, select the mcrRecord.ToNextRecord macro, and click OK. The message box shown in Figure 33.3a is displayed followed by the Action Failed dialog shown in Figure 33.3b.

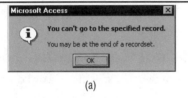

(a)

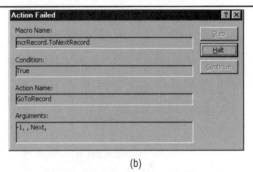

(b)

The ToNextRecord macro fails because there is no next record to move to when the blank record at the end of the recordset is the current record. You could prevent the failure by testing the form's NewRecord property. The NewRecord property has the value True if the current record is the new record, and False otherwise.

1. For the ToNextRecord macro, type **Not Screen.ActiveForm.NewRecord** in the Condition cell to the left of the GoToRecord action. If the current record is not the new record, this condition is true, and the GoToRecord action runs; otherwise, the action doesn't run.

2. Save the macro sheet.

3. Click the Run Macro button, select the mcrRecord.ToNextRecord macro, and click OK. Because the current record is the new record, Access takes no action, and the error has been avoided.

Unfortunately, testing the value of the NewRecord property doesn't always work. The Not Screen.ActiveForm.NewRecord condition is successful in detecting the end of the recordset only if you can add new records to the recordset. If you set the form's Allow Additions property to No, there is no blank record at the end of the recordset. In this situation, the ToNextRecord macro fails when the last record is the current record, and there is no other property you can test to avoid the failure. A similar situation arises when you use macros to move backwards through a recordset. If the current record is the first record and you try to use the GoToRecord action to move to the previous record, the action fails because there is no record to move to. At the beginning of the recordset, there is no property you can test using macros to determine if the current record is the first record.

The default navigation buttons and the built-in commands have internal code that detects the limits of a recordset. This code either disables the Next button and the Go To Next menu command automatically when the current record is the last record, or it disables the Previous button and the Go To Previous menu command when the current record is the first record. In VBA programming, you can test the EOF (End Of File) and BOF (Beginning Of File) properties to determine whether the current record is the end or beginning of a recordset, so you can create event procedures for physical navigation through a recordset. You can use the VBA procedures to create custom navigation buttons for a form. Unfortunately, the EOF and BOF properties are not available in macro programming.

Moving to a Record on a Subform of the Active Form

If the focus is in the subform, you can move to a specified record on the subform using the GoToRecord action. However, if the focus is in the main form of the active form and you want to move to a record on the subform, you must move the focus to the subform control first using the GoToControl action, and then move to the record using the GoToRecord action. The following steps show you how to create a two-step macro to do this.

1. Enter the second macro from Table 33.4, named ToLastSubformRecord, and save the macro sheet.

2. Click the Orders form and click a control on the main form. Click the Macro button in the toolbar, select the mcrRecord.ToLastSubformRecord macro, and click OK. The last subform record becomes the current record.

Moving to a Record on Another Open Form

Use the GoToRecord action to select a record on a different open form. Use the Object Type and Object Name arguments to specify the database object that contains the record that you want to select. The GoToRecord action does not activate the database object—you can even select a record on a hidden form as the current record.

As an example, let's hide a form, move to a record on the hidden form, and edit the record.

1. Enter the third macro, named ToHiddenRecord, of Table 33.4 and save the macro sheet.

2. Click in Orders form, then choose the Hide command in the Window menu.

3. Click the Run Macro toolbar button, select mcrRecord.ToHiddenRecord, and click OK.

4. Choose the Unhide command in the Window menu, select Orders, and click OK. Access displays the first record with the value hiddenname entered in the ShipName control.

5. Press Escape to undo the change.

Tabbing to the Next Record

By default, when you tab out of the last control of a record, you move to the first control of the next record. You can change the default behavior using the Cycle property. The Cycle property has three settings:

CurrentRecord　Use the CurrentRecord setting to prevent tabbing out of the record; then, if the focus is in the last control of the form's tab order when you press Tab, the focus moves to the first control in the same record.

CurrentPage　Use the CurrentPage setting to repeatedly cycle through the controls in a page for the same record.

AllRecords　Use the default AllRecords setting to allow tabbing to the next record or to the next page of the same record.

Logical Navigation among Records

Working interactively, you can move to a specific record (if you happen to know its position number in the recordset) by entering its number in the record number box at the bottom of the window and pressing Enter. Normally, you don't know the record's position number. This number changes each time you use a different sort order and may also change when you add a record to the recordset.

An easier way to navigate to a specific record is to use the data in the record instead of its physical location within a recordset. This approach is called *logical navigation*. You can find a specific record interactively by choosing the Find command in the Edit menu or by clicking the Find button on the toolbar, entering search criteria in the Find dialog box, and navigating directly to the first record that matches the criteria. If you want to search for a matching value in a particular control, click the control before displaying the Find dialog box.

Finding a Specific Record

Let's review the steps for finding a specific record interactively and then automate the search process.

Finding a Specific Record Interactively

As an example, we'll search for a specific customer in the Customers form in the NorthwindMacros application. The steps to find a specific customer are as follows:

1. Open the Customers form in Form view and click the CustomerID control. For the fastest search, select the search control and specify that you want to confine the search to the selected control.

2. Choose the Find command from the Edit menu or click the Find button on the toolbar. The Find and Replace dialog is displayed (see Figure 33.4). In this example, we'll find the record for the customer with company name Frankenversand with CustomerID FRANK.

FIGURE 33.4

Using the Find and Replace dialog to search for a specific record.

3. Enter **frank** in the Find What text box, check that Look In is set to Customer ID, and select Whole Field from the Match combo list.

4. Click the Find Next button. Access locates and displays the record.

Automating the Search Process

You can automate the search process by placing a lookup combo box on the form to display the CustomerID and CompanyName. Access uses the primary key to find the record, but the user normally prefers to specify a search value using other data, such as the CompanyName. Create a macro to find and display the record that corresponds to the CustomerID value you selected in the combo list. The macro synchronizes the form to the combo box.

Creating the Combo Box   The two purposes of the combo box are to display a list of customers and to hold the search value that the user selects from the list. The combo box acts like a variable by temporarily holding the search value on the form. To create the combo box, follow these steps:

1. Switch to Design view and create an unbound combo box in the form header. You can use the Combo Box Wizard to set some of the properties, or you can set all of the properties manually. Make sure the properties have the following values:

Property	Setting	Property	Setting
Name	CboFind	ColumnWidths	0.5, 1.75
ControlSource		BoundColumn	1
RowSource Type	Table/Query	ListWidth	2.5
RowSource	Customers	LimitToList	Yes
ColumnCount	2	Width	.75

2. Set the label's Caption property to Lookup.

3. Switch to Form view and click the arrow of the combo box, or place the cursor in the combo box control and press F4 or Alt+ ↓ to open the pick list (see Figure 33.5). When you select a value in the list, the value of the CustomerID is displayed in the combo box. The search value is held in the combo box.

FIGURE 33.5

Using a lookup combo box to select a search value.

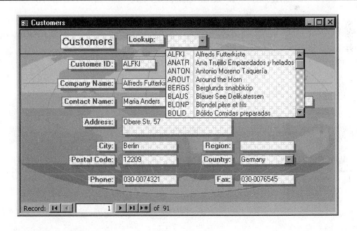

The important design features of the lookup combo box in this example are:

- When you search for a specific record, the search value is the primary key. To use the primary key as the value of the control, set the BoundColumn property to the primary key field. (This technique requires that the primary key be a single field.)

PART

VI

Macro Programming

- The combo box must be unbound. The combo box control acts like a variable to hold the search value.

- In creating the lookup combo box, you can use the Control Wizard or create the control manually. The final result is the same except that the Wizard creates an SQL statement for the RowSource property. You may see a slight performance gain by replacing the SQL statement with a stored query or a table.

Creating a Macro to Find a Record

You create a macro to find the record that matches the search value in the combo box. You'll want the macro to run when you select a different value for the combo box, and the combo box recognizes the AfterUpdate event.

Using the FindRecord Action   The simplest approach is to mimic the interactive steps:

1. Use the GoToControl action to move the focus to the control that you want to search (in this case the CustomerID control) and to limit the search to the values in that control. If you don't move the focus to a specific control, Access will search any of the controls on the form looking for the value you picked; when Access finds the value in the cboFind combo box itself, the search ends without finding the matching record.

2. Use the FindRecord action to find the first record that has a value in the CustomerID field that matches the value in the combo box.

3. Use the GoToControl action to return the focus to the combo box because that is where it was when you began the search and where you expect it to be after the search.

Table 33.5 shows the macro. This macro follows the *selection-centric approach* by selecting the control and then taking action on it.

TABLE 33.5: THE MACRO TO FIND A SPECIFIC RECORD USING THE FINDRECORD ACTION

MACRO NAME	ACTION	ACTION ARGUMENTS
cboFind_AfterUpdate		
	GoToControl	Control Name: CustomerID
	FindRecord	Find What: = cboFind
	GoToControl	Control Name: cboFind

NOTE The `Find What` argument of the `FindRecord` action can be text, a number, a date, or an expression. When you use an expression, you must precede the expression by an equal sign (=). You can also use wildcard characters; for example, to find a record with a control value starting with the letter M, set the `Find What` argument to M*.

Using the ApplyFilter Action A more efficient approach is to use a query to select the record directly from the form's recordset. The ApplyFilter macro action lets you apply a query to a table, form, or report to restrict or sort the records in the table or in the underlying recordset of the form or report. The ApplyFilter action has two arguments:

Action Argument	Description
`Filter Name`	The name of a query or a filter saved as a query that restricts or sorts the records
`Where Condition`	An expression that restricts the records in the form of a valid SQL WHERE clause without the word *WHERE* (The maximum length is 256 characters.)

You can apply the query directly as the `Filter Name` argument or you can enter the query's SQL WHERE clause (without the word *WHERE*) in the Where Condition argument. You must specify at least one of these arguments; whichever argument you specify for the query, the query's SQL WHERE clause must satisfy the maximum length requirement of 256 characters. If you specify both arguments, Access first applies the query and then applies the `Where Condition` to the result of the query.

WARNING If you specify the name of a query whose SQL WHERE clause exceeds 256 characters as the `Filter Name` argument, the ApplyFilter action doesn't select the specified records—the entire recordset is displayed instead. The action does not fail, and there is no default error message to indicate a problem.

The `Where Condition` argument for synchronizing the form to the value in the combo box is as follows:

```
[fieldname]=Forms![formname]![controlname]
```

In this expression, [fieldname] refers to the field in the underlying table or query of the form, and [controlname] refers to the control on the form that contains the value you want to match. For example, to synchronize the Customers form to the value displayed in the cboFind combo box, use the expression

```
[CustomerID]=Forms![Customers]![cboFind]
```

PART

VI

Macro Programming

or use the Screen object to refer to the active form as follows:

```
[CustomerID]=Screen.ActiveForm.cboFind
```

Notice that the full syntax is required on the right side of the expression, even though Customers is the active form when the macro executes the OpenForm action—this is an example of a case where you must use the full syntax to refer to a control on the active object. Notice also that the short syntax is required on the left-hand side of the expression.

Table 33.6 shows the macro. This macro follows the object-centric approach by taking action directly on the form's recordset. The macro performs better because Access doesn't have to take time to move the focus back and forth. Follow the next set of instructions to enter the macro and see it in action.

TABLE 33.6: A MACRO TO FIND A RECORD USING THE APPLYFILTER ACTION

MACRO NAME	ACTION	ACTION ARGUMENTS
cboFind_AfterUpdate		
	ApplyFilter	Where Condition:
		CustomerID=Screen.ActiveForm.cboFind

1. Create a new macro sheet named mCustomers, enter the macro in Table 33.6, and save the macro sheet.

2. Assign the mCustomers.cboFind_AfterUpdate macro to the AfterUpdate event of the cboFind combo box.

3. Save the form and switch to Form view.

4. Pick a customer from the combo list. Access selects and displays the record with the matching CustomerID. The message to the right of the default navigation buttons indicates that a filter has been applied (see Figure 33.6).

5. Click in the combo box and type **frank**; then select and delete the entire expression in the combo box and press Enter. Access displays a blank record.

6. Click in the combo box, type **zzz**, and press Enter. Access displays an error message. If you created the custom VBA error handler described in Chapter 32, the custom error message shown in Figure 33.7a is displayed—the message was intended for the Country combo box, and the VBA procedure we wrote in Chapter 32 isn't set up to distinguish between the two combo boxes. If you didn't create the VBA error handler, Access displays the default error message shown in Figure 33.7b.

FIGURE 33.6

Synchronizing a form to a lookup combo box using the ApplyFilter action.

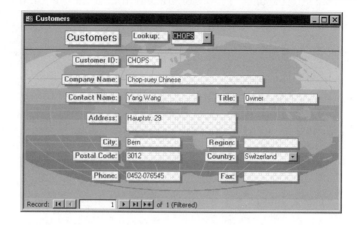

FIGURE 33.7

The custom VBA error message that is displayed when you enter a value not in the combo list (a), and the default error message (b).

(a)

(b)

When the Value Is Not in the Combo List

There is another way to handle the case when the typed value is not in the combo list that lets you display the typed value in a custom message box. When you type a value in the text box part of the combo list, the value is entered into a temporary control buffer. When the LimitToList property is set to Yes, Access compares the value in the buffer to the combo list. If the value is not in the list, the NotInList event occurs, and the run-time error is generated because Access cannot update the control. The typed value is in the buffer and is not available for you to display in a custom message box.

Instead of relying on Access to handle this situation, you can handle it yourself with macro programming. First, set the LimitToList property to No because you are going to create your own test. You can find out if the entered value is in the list by

PART

VI

Macro Programming

using the DCount( ) function to determine if there is another record in the combo box row source having a primary key value that matches the entered value. Use the syntax

```
DCount("*","[tablename]","[fieldname]=
Forms![formname]![controlname]")
```

Use the asterisk in the first argument to count all of the records. The second argument is the name of the table or query that provides the combo box rows. The third argument is the search condition for finding a combo box row matching the typed combo box value. In the search condition, the fieldname is the name of the matching field in the combo box row source and controlname is the name of the control on the open form that displays the value you want to match. Enclose each argument of the DCount( ) function in quotation marks. In this example, the condition

```
DCount("*","Customers","CustomerID=Screen.ActiveForm.cboFind") = 0
```

is true if there are no records in the Customers table whose CustomerID field has the same value as that displayed in the cboFind combo box on the active form. If the condition is true, the modified macro displays a custom message, sets the value in the combo box to null, and terminates. If the condition is false, the typed value is in the list, and the macro continues as before. Table 33.7 shows the modified version of the macro, which determines if the entered value is in the list before trying to find the record.

TABLE 33.7: THIS MACRO DETERMINES IF THE ENTERED VALUE IS IN THE LIST

MACRO NAME	CONDITION	ACTION	ACTION ARGUMENTS
cboFind_AfterUpdate			
	DCount("*","Customers","CustomerID=Screen.ActiveForm.cboFind") = 0	MsgBox	Message: ="The value you entered, " & [cboFind] & ", is not in the list of existing CustomerID's."
	...	SetValue	Item: cboFind Expression: Null
	...	StopMacro	
		ApplyFilter	Where Condition: CustomerID=Screen.ActiveForm.cboFind

The LimitToList property for the combo box must be set to No for this macro to work.

Returning to the Previous Record

After finding a particular record, you may want to undo the search and return to the previously displayed record. In order to undo the search, you need to know which record was displayed last. You can keep track of the previous record by holding the value of its primary key in a new, unbound, hidden text box (named PreviousID) in the form's header. Modify the cboFind_AfterUpdate macro to set the value of the PreviousID text box to the value of the primary key of the current record before running the ApplyFilter action (see Table 33.8).

TABLE 33.8: THIS MACRO STORES THE PRIMARY KEY OF THE CURRENT RECORD

MACRO NAME	CONDITION	ACTION	ACTION ARGUMENTS
cboFind_AfterUpdate			
	DCount("*","Customers", "CustomerID=Screen .Active-Form.cboFind") = 0	MsgBox	Message: ="The value you entered, " &[cboFind]& ", is not in the list of existing CustomerID's."
...	...	SetValue	Item: cboFind
			Expression: Null
	...	StopMacro	
		SetValue	Item: PreviousID
			Expression: CustomerID
		ApplyFilter	Where Condition: CustomerID=Screen.Active Form.cboFind

To return to the previous record, we'll place a command button (named cmdPrevious) in the form's header, and create a macro that uses the value held in the PreviousID text box to find and display the previous record (see Table 33.9). After displaying the previous record, the macro sets the value in the combo box to match the current record.

TABLE 33.9: THE MACRO TO RETURN TO THE PREVIOUS RECORD

MACRO NAME	ACTION	ACTION ARGUMENTS
cmdPrevious_Click		
	ApplyFilter	Where Condition: CustomerID=Screen.ActiveForm.PreviousID
	SetValue	Item: cboFind
		Expression: PreviousID

Here are the steps for undoing the search and returning to the previous record:

1. Click in the mCustomers macro sheet and modify the cboFind_AfterUpdate macro as shown in Table 33.8.

2. Enter the macro shown in Table 33.9 and save the macro sheet.

3. Click in the Customers form and switch to Design view. Place an unbound text box in the header section; set the Name property to PreviousID and the Visible property to No; delete the label.

4. Place a command button in the header section and set the Name property to cmdPrevious and the Caption property to Pre&vious (see Figure 33.8). Set the button's OnClick property to mCustomers.cmdPrevious_Click.

5. Save the form and switch to Form view.

FIGURE 33.8

Using a hidden unbound text box as a variable to hold the primary key value of the previous record.

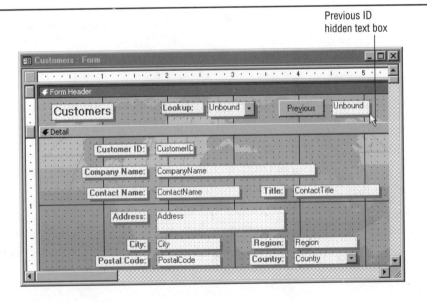

Previous ID hidden text box

Let's test the new logical navigation controls:

1. Use the combo box to select a customer. Note the customer you selected.

2. Use the combo box to select another customer and then click Previous. The previous customer is displayed.

3. Close the Customers form, then reopen the form in Form view. When you first open the Customers form, there is no value held in the PreviousID text box.

4. Without selecting a customer, click Previous. Access displays a blank record. When you click Previous and there is no value held in the PreviousID text box, Access displays the blank record at the end of the recordset.

Remove Navigation Buttons from a Form with Logical Navigation

The default navigation buttons at the bottom of the form allow you to move back and forth through the records and display a new record. Normally, in data entry operations, you don't need physical navigation; instead, you need to navigate in a logical manner: you locate and edit an existing record, locate and display another existing record, perhaps return to the previous record you just edited, and display a new blank record for data entry. Once you've provided for the logical navigation between records, the default navigation buttons for physical navigation are no longer necessary. (In Chapter 34, "Data Maintenance with Macros," you'll place a command button on the form to display a blank record.)

1. Switch to Design view, select the form, and set the NavigationButtons property to No.

2. Save the form and switch to Form view (see Figure 33.9).

PART

VI

Macro Programming

FIGURE 33.9

The Customers form with logical navigation controls. The default navigation buttons have been removed.

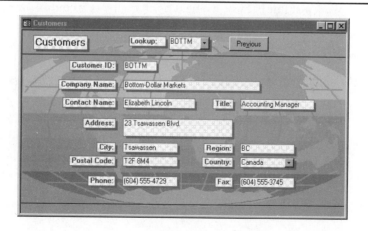

NOTE If you want to provide physical navigation as well as logical navigation, you have to create a custom set of command buttons that update the value held in the PreviousID text box, so clicking the Previous command button displays the previous record regardless of whether that record was selected logically or physically. The default navigation buttons do not update the PreviousID text box, so leaving them on a form with logical navigation gives inconsistent behavior.

Adding Logical Navigation to Another Form

The techniques for finding a record and then undoing the search depend on four controls and two macros:

Logical Navigation Controls	Macros
cboFind combo box	cboFind_AfterUpdate
combo box label	cmdPrevious_Click
cmdPrevious command button	
PreviousID text box	

We wrote the macros shown in Tables 33.8 and 33.9 to find customers by selecting a value for the CustomerID field of the Customers table. We can add logical navigation to any form that has the Customers table as an underlying table and find customer's records just by pasting these controls.

As examples, we'll add logical navigation to the Customer Phone List, Customer Orders, and Orders forms in the NorthwindMacros application. The record source for the first two forms is the Customers table, while the record source for the Orders form is an SQL statement that includes the Customers table as one of its tables. None of these forms has a control bound to the CustomerID field. Nevertheless, the macros work just fine because if a field is not bound to a control on a form, the fully qualified identifier (Forms!formname!fieldname) and the short syntax (*fieldname*) refer directly to the field in the underlying table.

To add logical navigation, follow these steps:

1. Switch to Design view, select the four logical navigation controls, and copy them to the clipboard.

2. Open the Customer Phone List form in Design view, increase the height of the header section, and paste the logical navigation controls to the header.

3. Save the form, switch to Form view, and select a customer from the list (see Figure 33.10a).

4. Open the Customer Orders form in Design view, choose Form Header/Footer from the View menu to display a header section, and paste the logical navigation controls in the header. Set the form's AllowEdits property to Yes—with the No value you can't change the value in the combo box and the search technique doesn't work.

5. Save the form, switch to Form view, and select a customer from the list (see Figure 33.10b).

6. Open the Orders form in Design view, choose Form Header/Footer from the View menu to display a header section, and paste the logical navigation controls to the header.

FIGURE 33.10

You can paste the logical navigation controls to any form that has Customers as an underlying table, including the Customer Phone List form (a), and the Customer Orders form (b).

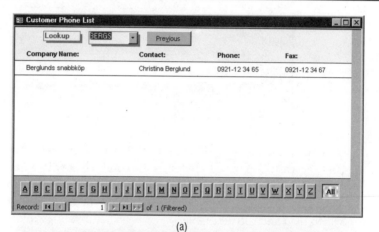

(a)

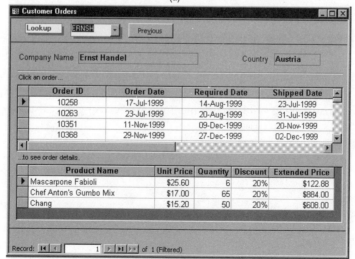

(b)

PART

VI

Macro Programming

7. Save the form, switch to Form view, and select a customer from the list (see Figure 33.11). When you select a customer, the macro selects all of the orders for the customer, and you can use the default physical navigation controls to browse through the selected records.

FIGURE 33.11

Use the logical navigation controls to select a customer in the Orders form, and then use the default physical navigation controls to browse the customer's orders.

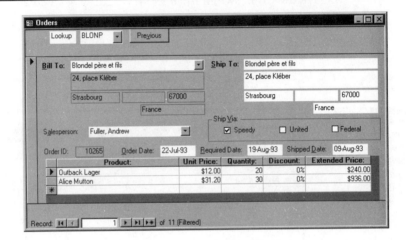

Adding logical navigation to select records based on another field in another table isn't this easy. You have to redesign the combo box with a new row source to display the new list, making sure to set the BoundColumn property to the column you are using for the search. You also have to modify the two macros to refer to the new search field and the new table.

Synchronizing Two Forms

Often when you are using a particular form for a task, you need to refer to information on another form. For example, while placing an order with the Orders form, you may need to edit the customer information using the Customers form (see Figure 33.12).

FIGURE 33.12

*While taking an order
using the Orders form
(a), you may need to
edit the information in
the Customers
form (b).*

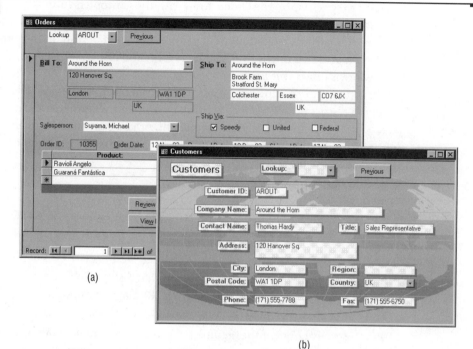

(a)

(b)

The Orders form in Northwind is designed for placing orders. The customer address information in the upper part of the main form is locked and disabled, so you can't edit customer information with this form.

TIP   One way to avoid data integrity problems in two tables that have a one-to-many relationship is to use separate forms for data entry into the tables. In the current example, Customers is the one table, and Order Details is the many table. The data entry form for the table on the many side (Orders) displays information from the table on the one side (Customers) in controls that are locked in order to impose a sequence for data entry. By requiring records for new customers to be entered and saved using a separate form, you easily avoid the problem of trying to place an order for a nonexistent (as far as Access is concerned) customer.

When you work interactively, in order to edit the customer's information, you open the Customers form and find the corresponding customer record (as shown in Figure 33.12b), so you can make changes to it. In this section you learn how to create

PART

VI

Macro Programming

macros to synchronize the Orders form with the Customers form after you finish updating a record there.

To automate this operation, we'll place a command button on the Orders form and create a macro that opens the Customers form and displays the relevant record. This procedure is called *synchronizing the forms*.

In addition to opening a form, the OpenForm macro action also lets you apply a query to restrict or sort the records displayed when the form opens. You can apply the query directly as the Filter Name argument, or you can enter the query's SQL WHERE clause (without the word *WHERE*) in the Where Condition argument of the Open-Form action as follows:

Action Argument	Description
Filter Name	The name of a query or a filter saved as a query that restricts or sorts the records. The query must include all of the fields in the form you are opening (or have the OutputAllFields query property set to Yes).
Where Condition	An expression that restricts the records in the form of a valid SQL WHERE clause without the word WHERE. (The maximum length is 256 characters.)

You can specify either of the arguments. Whichever argument you use, the query's SQL WHERE clause must satisfy the maximum length requirement of 256 characters. If you specify both arguments, Access first applies the query and then applies the Where Condition to the result of the query.

 WARNING If you specify the name of a query whose SQL WHERE clause exceeds 256 characters as the Filter Name argument, the OpenForm action doesn't select the specified records—the entire recordset is displayed instead. The action does not fail, and there is no default error message to indicate a problem.

Table 33.10 shows the macro that uses the Where Condition argument of the OpenForm action to synchronize the form being opened as follows:

```
[fieldname]=Forms![formname]![controlname]
```

In this expression, *fieldname* refers to the field in the underlying table or query of the form you want to open, and *controlname* refers to the control on the other form that contains the value you want to match. For example, to open the Customers form displaying a record synchronized to the record in the Orders form, use the expression

```
[CustomerID]=Forms![Orders]![CustomerID]
```

or use the Screen object to refer to the active form as follows:

```
[CustomerID]=Screen.ActiveForm.CustomerID
```

Notice that the full syntax is required on the right side of the expression, even though Orders is the active form when the macro executes the OpenForm action—this is an example of a case where you must use the full syntax to refer to a control on the active object. Notice also that the short syntax is required on the left-hand side of the expression.

TABLE 33.10: A MACRO TO OPEN AND SYNCHRONIZE A FORM TO ANOTHER FORM		
MACRO NAME	**ACTION**	**ACTION ARGUMENTS**
cmdReviewCustomer_Click		
	OpenForm	Form Name: Customers
		Where Condition: CustomerID= Screen.ActiveForm.CustomerID

To control which form the user can work with, you can require that the user work only with the Customers form and close the form before returning to work with the Orders form by setting the Modal and PopUp properties to Yes.

Here are the steps for automating the process:

1. Create a new macro sheet named mOrders, enter the macro shown in Table 33.10, and save the macro sheet.

2. Place a command button named cmdReviewCustomer on the Orders form and set the Caption property to Review &Customer. Click in the button's OnClick property and select the mOrders.cmdReviewCustomer_Click macro.

3. Save the form and switch to Form view.

4. Set the following form properties of the Customers form:

   PopUp   Yes

   Modal   Yes

5. Save and close the Customers form.

With these settings, when you click the Review Customers button on the Orders form, the synchronized Customers form opens as a dialog box. After you edit the customer information and close the Customers form, the Orders form immediately refreshes and displays the updated information.

A form with the Modal property set to Yes retains the focus until you close the form. You can't click in another window while the modal form is open; but you can click in menu commands and toolbar buttons. To prevent clicking in the menu commands and toolbars, set the PopUp property to Yes. A pop-up form stays on top of other open forms. A dialog is an example of a form with Modal and PopUp properties set to Yes.

Adding the Review Button to Another Form

An advantage of using the Screen object to refer to the active form is that the cmdReviewCustomer button and its macro can be copied from the Orders form to any other form that has the Customers table as one of its underlying tables, such as the Customer Phone List or the Customer Orders form without modification. As an example, we'll paste the button to the Customer Orders form.

1. Open the Orders form in Design view, select the cmdReviewCustomer button, and copy to the clipboard.

2. Open the Customer Orders form in Design view and paste the button to the form header.

3. Save the Customer Orders form and switch to Form view (see Figure 33.13).

4. Verify that the button works.

FIGURE 33.13

The Review Customer button and its macro can be pasted to the Customer Orders form (a), without modifying the macro because the macro uses the Screen object to refer to the active form. Clicking the button opens and synchronizes the Customers form (b).

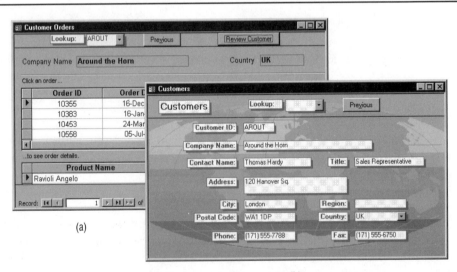

(a)

(b)

Keeping the Forms Synchronized

Sometimes you'll want to leave a related form open so you can view its information while you return to work in a different form. Each time you move to another record in the form, the related form should stay "in sync" by locating and displaying the correct related record. Suppose you want to view product information when you are taking an order using the Orders form. We'll place a command button on the Orders form and create a macro that opens and synchronizes a form displaying product information for the product currently selected in the Orders subform: As you click a different record in the Orders subform, the product information form needs to remain synchronized.

To avoid updating problems, we'll create a view-only copy of the Product List called frmViewProduct.

1. In the Database window, select the Product List form. Press Ctrl+C to copy the form, press Ctrl+V to paste it as a new form, and enter frmViewProduct as the name of the new form.

2. Open the frmViewProduct form in Design view and set the form properties as shown here. Set the form's PopUp property to Yes so the form remains on top but leave the Modal property set to No so the user can edit the Orders form while the frmViewProduct form is open.

Caption	View Product
DefaultView	Single Form
PopUp	Yes

3. Select the ProductName, QuantityPerUnit, Discontinued, and UnitPrice controls and set their Enabled property to No and their Locked property to Yes. We lock the data controls on the frmViewProduct form because the form is intended as a view-only form.

4. Save and close the form.

5. Open the mOrders macro sheet and enter the macro shown in Table 33.11. Save the macro sheet.

TABLE 33.11: A MACRO TO OPEN AND SYNCHRONIZE A FORM TO ANOTHER FORM

MACRO NAME	ACTION	ACTION ARGUMENTS
CmdProduct_Click		
	OpenForm	Form Name: frmViewProduct
		Where Condition: [ProductID] = [Forms]![Orders]![Orders Subform]![ProductID]

PART

VI

Macro Programming

6. Open the Orders form in Design view. Place a command button named cmdProduct near the bottom of the form and set the Caption property to Vie&w Product. Click the OnClick property and select the mOrders.cmdProduct_Click macro.

7. Save the form and switch to Form view.

8. Click a record in the subform and then click the View Product button. The View Product form opens and displays information for the selected product (see Figure 33.14).

9. Click the Orders form and select a different record in the subform. The View Product form continues to display the first product.

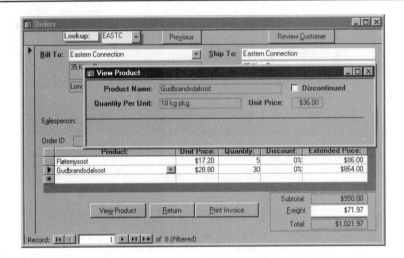

Create a Macro to Keep the Forms Synchronized

When you move to a different record in the Orders subform, it becomes the current record and the Orders Subform form recognizes the Current event. If frmViewProduct is open when you move to a different record, you can resynchronize frmViewProduct with a macro that uses the same OpenForm action. Because the form is already open, the OpenForm action just recalculates the Where Condition. If frmViewProduct isn't open when you move to a different order, don't take any action. Figure 33.15 shows the macro flow diagram.

FIGURE 33.15

*Resynchronizing a
form using the
Current event.*

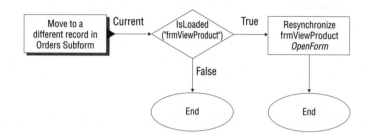

You can use the IsLoaded( ) function in the UtilityFunctions module in North-windMacros to determine if a form is open. Enter the name of the form enclosed in quotation marks as the argument of the IsLoaded( ) function. The IsLoaded( ) function returns the True value if the form is open and displays records, and returns the False value otherwise.

1. Open a new macro sheet named mOrdersSubform, enter the macro shown in Table 33.12, and save and close the macro sheet.

TABLE 33.12: A MACRO TO SYNCHRONIZE ANOTHER FORM

MACRO NAME	CONDITION	ACTION	ACTION ARGUMENTS
Form_Current			
	IsLoaded("frmViewProduct")	OpenForm	Form Name: frmViewProduct
			Where Condition: [ProductID]=[Forms]! [Orders]![Orders Subform]![ProductID]

2. Open the Orders Subform in Design view, click the form's OnCurrent property, and select the macro mOrdersSubform.Form_Current.

3. Save and close the subform.

4. Back in the Orders form, switch to Form view, click a row on the Orders sub-form, and then click the View Product button on the Orders form. The View Product form opens, synchronized to the selected product.

5. Click another row in the subform for the same order. The View Product form resynchronizes.

6. Close the View Product form. Click another row of the subform. The View Product form does not reopen.

PART

VI

Macro Programming

Create a Macro to Close the Related Form

When you close the Orders form, the View Product form should close also (if it is open). Create a new macro and run it when the Orders form closes and recognizes the Close event. This macro, called Form_Close, closes frmViewProduct if the form is open. Table 33.13 shows the macro.

TABLE 33.13: A MACRO TO CLOSE ANOTHER FORM		
MACRO NAME	**ACTION**	**ACTION ARGUMENTS**
Form_Close		
	Close	Object Type: Form
		Object Name: frmViewProduct

 NOTE The Close action does not fail and a run-time error does not occur if you specify the name of an object that isn't open or that doesn't exist. This means that it is not necessary to test to determine if a form is open before running the Close action.

1. Click the mOrders macro sheet, enter the macro shown in Table 33.13, and save the macro sheet.
2. Click the Orders form and switch to Design view. Click the form's OnClose property and select the mOrders.Form_Close macro.
3. Save the form and switch to Form view.
4. Click the Close button for the Orders form; the form closes.
5. Reopen the Orders form in Form view, click a row in the subform, and click the View Product button. The View Product form opens.
6. Click the Close button on the Orders form. Both forms close.

Synchronizing a Report to a Form

When you are finished taking the order, you can print out an invoice for the order. By default the Northwind application uses a VBA procedure to synchronize the Invoice report to the Orders form. We'll replace the procedure with a macro that uses the Filter Name argument to synchronize the report.

The record source for the Invoice report is the Invoices query. The Northwind database also has a query named Invoices Filter based on the Invoices query that you can use to select an invoice for an order. Figure 33.16 shows the Invoices Filter query in Design view. The Criteria cell below the OrderID Field cell indicates that the query selects the records corresponding to the order displayed in the Orders form. (The query uses Query By Form to get criteria from an open form.)

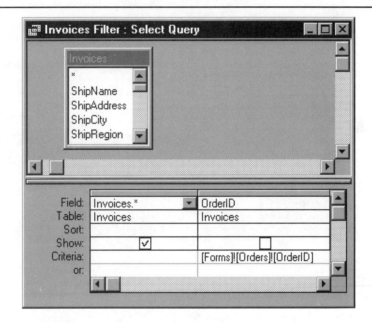

To see how the query works, follow these steps:

1. Open the Orders form and select an order.
2. Select the Invoices Filter query in the Database window and double-click to run the query. The query produces a record for each product in the selected order (see Figure 33.17).

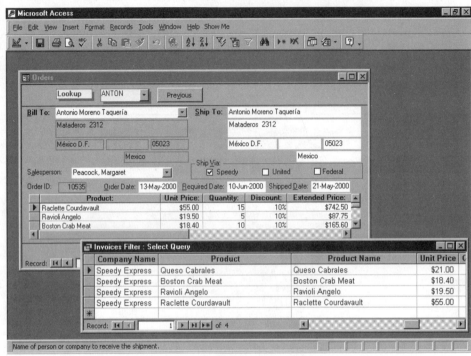

Testing for Report Data

We'll design the macro to determine if there really is an order before preparing the invoice. If an order contains no products, we don't want to print the report. A simple way to determine if there are products is by testing the value in the Total control on the Orders form. If this value is zero, nothing has been ordered, and the macro displays a message and stops. If this value is a number greater than zero, the macro opens the report, runs the filter query to select the invoice record for the order, and displays the synchronized Invoice in Print Preview. Table 33.14 shows the macro.

1. Click the mOrders macro sheet, enter the macro shown in Table 33.14, and save the macro sheet.

2. Click the Orders form and switch to Design view.

3. Select the PrintInvoice command button, click the OnClick property, and replace the VBA event procedure with the mOrders.PrintInvoice_Click macro.

4. Save the form and switch to Form view.

5. Select an order and click the Print Invoice button. The synchronized Invoice report is displayed.

TABLE 33.14: A MACRO TO SYNCHRONIZE A REPORT TO A FORM

MACRO NAME	CONDITION	ACTION	ACTION ARGUMENTS
PrintInvoice_Click			
	[Total] <= 0	MsgBox	Message: No products have been ordered. An Invoice won't be printed.
	...	StopMacro	
		OpenReport	Report Name: Invoice
			View: Print Preview
			Filter Name: Invoices Filter

Creating a Startup Macro

The Startup dialog allows you to customize the way your application starts. As an example:

1. Choose the Startup command from the Tools menu.

2. Enter the settings in Figure 33.18 to start the NorthwindMacros application. To do this, hide the Database window, display the Main Switchboard, and replace the default application title with Northwind Powered By Macros.

3. Click OK. The application title bar changes immediately.

PART

VI

Macro Programming

FIGURE 33.18

Setting startup properties using the Startup dialog.

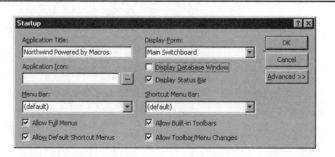

You can set additional startup conditions by creating a macro in a separate macro sheet and saving the macro sheet under the special name *AutoExec*. When the database starts up, Access first uses the startup properties in the Startup dialog and then runs the AutoExec macro (if there is one). As an example, we'll create a simple AutoExec macro that uses the MsgBox( ) function as a condition to ask if the user wants to import data. The second argument of the function specifies that the message box has Yes and No buttons and displays a question mark as an icon. Table 33.15 shows the macro.

TABLE 33.15: AN AUTOEXEC MACRO

CONDITION	ACTION	ACTION ARGUMENTS
MsgBox("Do you want to import data now? (Under construction)", 4+32,"Startup import") = 6	MsgBox	Message: Starting the Import process.
...	StopMacro	
	MsgBox	Message: Import will not take place now.

1. Open a new macro sheet and save it with the name *AutoExec*. Enter the macro shown in Table 33.15 and save the macro sheet.

2. Test the macro by choosing the Run command from the Run menu.

3. Close the database and reopen. Access opens the database using the startup properties set in Figure 33.18 and displays the custom message box (see Figure 33.19). Because the import process hasn't been developed, either choice leads to closing the message box(es) and returning to the Main Switchboard form.

FIGURE 33.19

Use an AutoExec macro to run macro actions on startup.

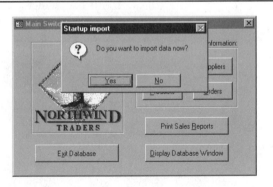

NOTE Bypass the Startup properties and the AutoExec macro by holding down the Shift key when you open the database.

Summary

This chapter has introduced you to using macro programming to automate navigation between controls, records, and forms. The important techniques are:

- You can use the GoToControl macro action to move the focus to a specified control on an active form or datasheet. Moving to a control may require other actions to select the form or datasheet first.

- You can automate navigation among records according to their physical location (physical navigation) by duplicating keyboard combinations using the SendKeys macro action or by using the GoToRecord macro action.

- In macro programming there is no way to test whether the current record is the first record in a recordset, and there is only a limited way to test whether the current record is the last record in a recordset.

- You can automate navigation to a specific record using data in the record (logical navigation) in two ways: you can duplicate the interactive search technique using the FindRecord macro action, and you can use the ApplyFilter action to apply a query to select the record. This second technique is normally more efficient.

- You can undo a search by creating macros that store the primary key of a record in a hidden text box and use the stored value to return to the record.

- In many cases you can create reusable macros by using properties of the Screen object to refer to the active form or control and avoid including the name of the object in the macro.

- You can use arguments of the OpenForm macro action to synchronize a second form to the first form. You can keep the second form synchronized as you browse records of the first form by using the form's Current event to repeat the OpenForm action each time you move to a different record.

- You can create a macro named AutoExec that Access runs automatically, immediately after setting the startup conditions you specified in the Startup dialog.

PART

VI

Macro Programming

CHAPTER **34**

Data Maintenance with Macros

I n this chapter, you'll learn how to automate data entry operations. For several of these tasks, you can create reusable controls, linked to reusable macros, that you can paste directly to other data entry forms. In order for the data entry macros to be reusable, the primary key control must have the same Name property on all data entry forms; that way the macro can always use the same reference for this control. You'll change the primary key control's Name property on each data entry form.

 NOTE Changing the Name property of a bound control does not affect the field name in the underlying table. You can refer to the field by using either `Forms!formname!control-name` to refer to the control or `Forms!formname!fieldname` to refer to the field.

In addition, whether the automated operation is reusable or not, use the properties of the Screen object to avoid referring to specific forms and controls (in order to minimize changes when you use the operation on another form).

In this chapter, you'll learn to automate operations that add new records; edit, enter, and validate data; reverse changes made during editing; save records; delete records; and work with two open data entry forms. When two data entry forms are based on the same underlying data, you can use macro programming to automate the updating of records to ensure that both forms display the most current data.

 NOTE This chapter assumes you have customized the Form view, Macro Design, and Database menu bars and toolbars to include the Macro command that displays the Run Macro dialog. If you haven't customized the command bars, you can do so now, as described in Chapter 31. This chapter also assumes that you've created the Northwind-Macros database as a copy of the Northwind database. Create a copy now, if necessary.

Using Macros to Validate Data

Typically, a data entry form is designed with combo boxes, list boxes, option groups, and check boxes to aid in fast and accurate data entry. In addition to using these special controls to improve accuracy, you can protect your data with validation rules that specify requirements for the data you enter.

Using ValidationRule Properties

Access provides opportunities to validate data by setting ValidationRule properties, and to display custom messages when the validation rules are not satisfied by setting the ValidationText properties. You can create validation rules and messages when you set field and table properties in table design and when you set control properties in form design, as follows:

- For an individual field, set the ValidationRule property in the field properties list in the table's Design view. Access tests a field's ValidationRule property when you try to tab out of the field. A field validation rule cannot contain references to other fields. If the validation rule is satisfied, Access updates the field value in the record buffer. If not, Access doesn't update the field, but displays the message you set in the ValidationText property (or a default message if you didn't set one). It prevents you from tabbing out of the field until you either undo the entry or enter a value that satisfies the rule.

- For a record in a table, set the ValidationRule property in the table's property sheet in table Design view. A record validation rule can refer to other fields in the same record. Access tests the ValidationRule property for the record when you try to save the record. Access also tests the referential integrity options you've elected when you try to save the record. If the validation rule for the record is satisfied, Access updates the record to the table. Otherwise, Access doesn't update the record, but displays your custom message (or a default message) and prevents you from saving the record until you either undo the record or enter values that satisfy the validation rule. Figure 34.1 shows the ValidationRule property in the field properties list and in the table properties sheet.

FIGURE 34.1

The ValidationRule property in the field properties list and in the table properties sheet.

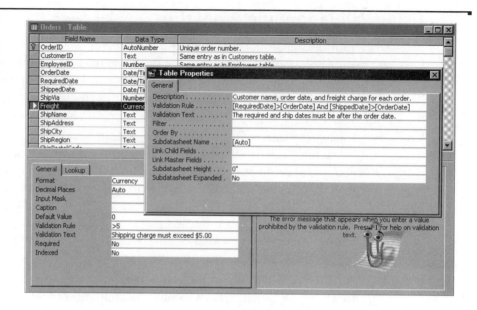

• For an individual control displayed in a form, set the ValidationRule property in the control's property sheet in form Design view. A control's validation rule can refer to other fields in the table, to fields and controls in other forms, or to the results of calculations with domain aggregate functions. Access tests the control's validation rule when you try to tab out of the control. If the control's validation rule is satisfied, Access updates the control to the record buffer. Otherwise, Access doesn't update the control, but displays your custom message (or a default message) and prevents you from tabbing out of the control until you undo the value or enter valid data. Figure 34.2 shows the ValidationRule property in a control's property sheet.

When you set validation rules in a form as well as in its underlying table, Access enforces both sets of rules. A validation rule that you set for a control at the form level overrides any validation rules you may have set at the table level. Validation rules for controls and fields are enforced in the following order:

1. The control's ValidationRule property as set in the control's property sheet

2. The field's ValidationRule property as set in the field's property sheet

3. The record's ValidationRule property as set in the table's property sheet

FIGURE 34.2

The ValidationRule property in a control's property sheet.

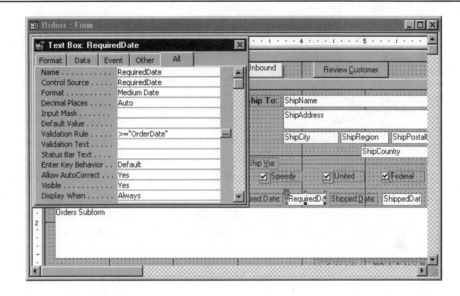

You can use macros and VBA procedures to set more complicated validation rules. For example, you can use programming when you want to do the following:

- Ask the user for input on whether to use a validation rule.
- Use more than one validation rule to validate a record.
- Change the timing of the validation.

The order of validation depends on which event triggers the validation macro or procedure. For example, a macro triggered by the BeforeUpdate event of a control is executed before the control's ValidationRule property is enforced.

NOTE This chapter assumes the primary key for a table is a single field. You'll have to modify the techniques when the primary key is more than one field.

Checking for Duplicate Primary Key Values

In this section, you'll use a macro to change the timing of the test for uniqueness of the primary key value. By default, Access tests for uniqueness when you try to save

PART

VI

Macro Programming

the record—you'll create a macro to perform the test as soon as you enter a value in the primary key control instead.

When you design a data table, you specify how the primary key is entered. You can do the following:

- Automatically assign sequential numbers by using an AutoNumber field as the primary key.
- Create your own expressions to assign unique values automatically.
- Permit the primary key to be entered as part of data entry.

No matter how the value is entered, Access checks for duplicate values when you try to save the record. Often, it is more convenient to test for uniqueness as soon as you leave the primary key control instead of waiting until you enter values in all of the data controls and try to save the record. You can create a macro to handle the uniqueness test yourself and run the macro as soon as you try to update the changed control.

Using DCount() to Test for Uniqueness

You can check for uniqueness by using the DCount( ) function to determine if there is another record in the table having a primary key value that matches the value entered in the control. Use the following syntax:

```
DCount("*", "tablename", "[fieldname]=Forms![formname]![controlname]")
```

The first argument is the name of the field you are using to count the records; you can use either the primary key field or the asterisk to count all of the records that satisfy the search condition. The second argument is the name of the table. The third argument is the search condition for including table records where fieldname is the name of the matching field in the table, and controlname is the name of the control on the open form that displays the value you want to match. Enclose each argument of the DCount( ) function in quotation marks.

As an example, we'll create a macro to validate the CustomerID for the Customers form in NorthwindMacros. In this case, the expression

```
DCount("*","Customers","CustomerID=Screen.ActiveForm.PrimaryID")
```

counts the number of records in the Customers table whose CustomerID field has the same value as that displayed in the PrimaryID control on the active form. If there is another record with the same primary key value, the DCount( ) function has the value 1; in this case, the macro displays a custom message and cancels the updating. If there isn't another record, the DCount( ) function has the value 0, the macro terminates, and Access updates the control. You run the macro after Access acknowledges that the data in the control has changed but before you update the control. That is, you run the macro when the control recognizes the BeforeUpdate event. Table 34.1 shows the macro to validate the uniqueness of the primary key value when you try to update the primary key control. The macro uses the CancelEvent action to cancel the updating of the control.

TABLE 34.1: A MACRO TO VALIDATE THE UNIQUENESS OF THE PRIMARY KEY			
MACRO NAME	**CONDITION**	**ACTION**	**ACTION ARGUMENTS**
PrimaryID_BeforeUpdate			
	DCount("*","Customers", "CustomerID=Screen .ActiveForm .PrimaryID")>0	MsgBox	Message: There is another record with this ID. You must enter a unique ID or press the Esc key to undo the record.
	...	CancelEvent	

1. Open the mCustomers macro sheet, enter the macro in Table 34.1, and save the macro sheet.

2. Open the Customers form in Design view and select the PrimaryID control. (If you haven't changed the name of the CustomerID control to PrimaryID, you can do so now by changing the control's Name property.)

3. Click in the BeforeUpdate property and select the macro mCustomers.Primary ID_BeforeUpdate. (Replace the Customer.ValidateID macro.)

4. Save the form and switch to Form view.

5. Choose the Go To command and then the New Record subcommand from the Edit menu. Enter **ALFKI** for the CustomerID and press Tab. Access displays the custom message (see Figure 34.3). (If the Edit menu is unavailable, make sure that the form's Modal and PopUp properties on the Other tab are set to No.)

FIGURE 34.3

Displaying a custom message before canceling the update.

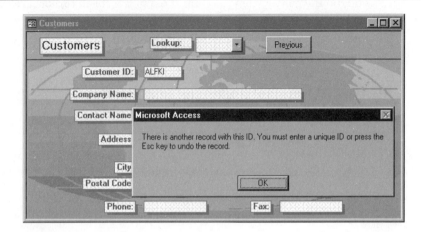

Display a Primary Key Violation Form instead of a Message

Instead of displaying a message that there is another record with the same primary key value entered previously in the table, it is often more helpful to display the previous record itself. With the previous record displayed, you can determine whether the record you are trying to enter duplicates a record already in the table or if the record only needs a different primary key value before it can be saved.

Create a Primary Key Violation Form

Create a copy of the Customers form to display the record with the duplicate primary key as follows:

1. Close the Customers form and select the form in the Database window. Press Ctrl+C to copy the form and then press Ctrl+V to open the Paste As dialog box. Enter **frmViewCustomer** for the new form name and click OK. We modify the new form in the next steps.

2. Open the new frmViewCustomer form in Design view, uncheck the Form Header/Footer command from the View menu to delete the header and footer sections. Click Yes in the confirmation dialog to delete the header and the header controls.

3. Select all of the data controls. Set their Enabled property to No and set their Locked property to Yes. Then rearrange the controls to minimize the size of the form.

4. Select the form and set the following form properties:

Caption	Primary Key Violation
BorderStyle	Dialog
PopUp	Yes
Picture	

5. Save and close the form. (Figure 34.4 shows the form.)

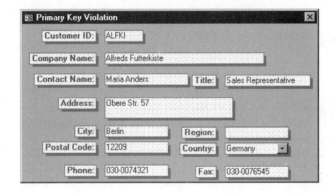

Modify the Macro

Next, we will modify the macro to open frmViewCustomer so that it will display the synchronized record. The modified macro is shown in Table 34.2.

TABLE 34.2: DISPLAYING A PRIMARY KEY VIOLATION FORM			
MACRO NAME	**CONDITION**	**ACTION**	**ACTION ARGUMENTS**
PrimaryID_BeforeUpdate			
	`DCount("*","Customers", "CustomerID=Screen .ActiveForm .PrimaryID")>0`	OpenForm	`Form Name: frmViewCustomer`
			`Where Condition: CustomerID = Screen.ActiveForm .PrimaryID`
	...	CancelEvent	

PART

VI

Macro Programming

1. Click in mCustomers macro sheet, modify the macro as shown in Table 34.2, and save the macro sheet.

2. Open the Customers form in Form view.

3. Choose the Go To command and then the New Record subcommand from the Edit menu. Enter **ALFKI** for the CustomerID and press Tab. Access displays the Primary Key Violation form for the CustomerID.

4. Close the Primary Key Violation form. Press Escape twice: first to undo the control and then to undo the record.

Adding New Records

 NOTE   You can automate a set of standard operations that all simple data entry forms need. You begin with operations for adding a new record, undoing changes, and saving a record.

In designing a command button to do a job, you analyze the interactive process, create a command button, and then create a macro to automate the process. In each case, you'll anticipate macro errors and standard run-time errors, and you'll include tests of preconditions in order to avoid those errors. By avoiding names of specific forms, you can make the control and macros reusable so you can copy them to other forms with little or no modification.

Creating Command Buttons for Data Entry Operations

Create a set of three command buttons for the data entry operations for the Customers form by following these steps:

1. Open the Customers form in Design view.

2. With the Control Wizards tool deselected, place three command buttons in the header section (Rearrange the controls to make room as in Figure 34.5.), and set a Name and Caption property for each as follows:

Name	Caption
cmdNew	&New
cmdUndo	&Undo
cmdSave	&Save

FIGURE 34.5

Place command buttons for adding a new record, undoing changes, and saving the record in the header section.

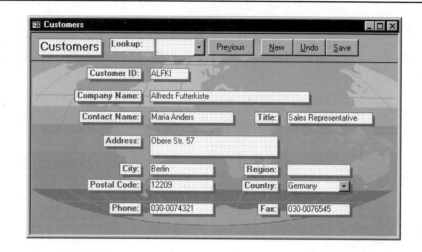

Analyze and Automate the Process

When you work interactively, you can add a new record by selecting the Go To command from the Edit menu and the New Record command from the fly-out menu, or by clicking the New button (either on the toolbar or grouped with the default navigation buttons on the form).

1. Select the Edit ➤ Go To ➤ New Record command. A new blank record is displayed.

2. Select the Edit ➤ Go To ➤ New Record command again. Because a new record is the current record, the New Record command is grayed out and unavailable.

You can use the GoToRecord macro action to move to a new record, duplicating the effect of the built-in command.

Create the Macro

You can create a macro that uses the GoToRecord action to go to a new record (see Table 34.3).

TABLE 34.3: A MACRO TO DISPLAY A NEW RECORD		
MACRO NAME	**ACTION**	**ACTION ARGUMENTS**
cmdNew_Click		
	GoToRecord	Record: New

1. Open the mcrGlobal macro sheet, enter the macro in Table 34.3, and save the macro sheet. We are creating reusable macros for the data entry operations, so we'll store them in the global macro sheet instead of in the form's macro sheet.

2. Select the New button in the form, click the OnClick property, and select mcrGlobal.cmdNew_Click.

3. Save the form and switch to Form view.

4. Click the form's New button. A new record is displayed.

5. Click the New button again. There is no response to additional clicks of the New button because the GoToRecord action doesn't fail when the current record is the new record.

Undoing Changes

 NOTE After you make changes to a control, you can undo the changes interactively either by selecting the Edit ≻ Undo Typing command (if the focus has not left the control), or by selecting the Edit ≻ Undo Current Field/Record command (if the focus has left the control, but you have not moved to another record). If you have not made any changes to the record, neither Undo command is available.

Take a look at how the Undo commands respond to changes in focus:

1. With the new record displayed, click the Edit menu. The Can't Undo command is grayed out and unavailable.

2. Using the Lookup combo box (or the default navigation buttons if you haven't hidden them), move to another record and click the Edit menu. The Can't Undo command is still grayed out.

3. Click in the Address control, change the address, then click the Edit menu. The Undo Typing command is available.

4. Tab to the next control and click the Edit menu. The UndoCurrentField command is available.

Design a Macro to Test the Dirty Property

You can create a macro to issue an Undo command with a RunCommand macro action. You must design the macro to run the Undo command only when the command is available, otherwise the macro action will fail. Because one of the Undo commands is available only when you have actually made a change to the record, you need a way to test whether the current record has been changed before issuing the command. To do so, you can use the form's Dirty property. (Yes, it is actually called the Dirty property.) The Dirty property has the value True if the current record has been modified since it was last saved, and the value False otherwise. The Dirty property is not listed in the form's property sheet because you can't set this property. Access controls the value of the Dirty property; you can only observe the value.

If the Dirty property is True, the record has been changed, and your macro reverses the change. If the Dirty property is False, the macro terminates. Table 34.4 shows the macro. This macro determines if the record has been changed before issuing the Undo command. It uses the Form property to refer to the active form.

TABLE 34.4: A MACRO TO UNDO A CHANGE

MACRO NAME	CONDITION	ACTION	ACTION ARGUMENTS
cmdUndo_Click			
	Screen.ActiveForm.Dirty	RunCommand	Command: Undo

1. Click in mcrGlobal, enter the macro shown in Table 34.4, and save the macro sheet.

2. Click in the form and switch to Design view. Click the Undo button, click in the OnClick property, and then select the mcrGlobal.cmdUndo_Click macro. Save the form.

3. Switch to Form view. Use the lookup combo box to select a customer, then click in the Address control and make a change.

4. Click the Undo button. The change is reversed.

5. Click in the Address control, make a change, and tab to the next control.

6. Click the Undo button. The change is reversed.

7. Select another existing record and click the Undo button. There is no response. The record has not been changed; the macro tests the precondition and terminates before trying to run the Undo command.

8. Click the New button and then click the Undo button. There is no response.

PART

VI

Macro Programming

Saving Changes

When you work interactively with a form, there are several ways you can save changes to a record. You can choose Records ➤ Save Record to save changes without moving the focus. You can choose File ➤ Close to close the active form. You can press Shift+Enter to save changes without moving the focus. You can press Ctrl+F4 to close the active form. Or you can move the focus to a different or new record.

You can also initiate saving a record by using the custom controls you've placed on the form, including clicking the Return button on the form, clicking the New button on the form, and selecting another record using the lookup combo box.

Create the Macro

You can create a macro with a RunCommand macro action to issue the Save Record command (see Table 34.5).

TABLE 34.5: A MACRO TO SAVE A RECORD

MACRO NAME	ACTION	ACTION	ACTION ARGUMENTS
cmdSave_Click			
	`Screen.ActiveForm.Dirty`	RunCommand	`Command: SaveRecord`

1. Click in mcrGlobal, enter the macro shown in Table 34.5, and save the macro sheet.

2. Click in the Customers form, make sure you are in Design view, select the Save button, click the OnClick property, and select the mcrGlobal.cmdSave_Click macro.

3. Save the form and switch to Form view.

4. Edit a record and click the form's Save button.

Date-Stamp a Changed Record

You can create a macro that saves the current date when you edit a record. Include a DateModified field with a Date/Time data type in each data table to keep track of the last edit date. It isn't necessary to place a control on the data entry form: you can use a macro to set the value of a field whether or not the form has a control bound to the field. Use the fully qualified identifier

`Forms!formname!fieldname`

or the short syntax when the macro runs from the active form

    fieldname

to refer directly to a field in the underlying table or query. If you do place a DateMod-ified control on a data entry form, set its Enabled property to No and its Locked prop-erty to Yes, set the TabStop property to No, and set the visual cues to indicate that the control can't be changed.

Add a DateModified Field and Control

As an example, let's add a DateModified field to the Customers table and a control to the Customers form.

1. Close the Customers form and open the Customers table in Design view.

2. Add a DateModified field, set the data type to Date/Time, and then save and close the table.

3. Open the Customers form in Design view. Drag the DateModified field from the field list to the upper-right corner of detail section of the form.

4. Set the control's properties as follows:

Property	Setting
BackStyle	Transparent
Special Effect	Flat
BorderStyle	Transparent
Enabled	No
Locked	Yes

5. Click the Format Painter button in the toolbar and click the label for the Date-Modified control.

You can create a macro that uses the built-in Now( ) function to set the value of the DateModified control to the current date and time (see Table 34.6). Run the macro after Access acknowledges that the record has been changed, but before the changes are updated to the table. (That is, run the macro when the form recognizes the BeforeUpdate event.)

PART

VI

Macro Programming

TABLE 34.6: A MACRO TO DATE STAMP A RECORD		
MACRO NAME	ACTION	ACTION ARGUMENTS
Form_BeforeUpdate		
	SetValue	Item: DateModified
		Expression: Now()

1. Click mcrGlobal, enter the macro shown in Table 34.6, and save the macro sheet.
2. Click the Customers form, click the form's BeforeUpdate event property, and select the mcrGlobal.Form_BeforeUpdate macro.
3. Save the form and switch to Form view.
4. Make a change in a control and click the form's Save button. The DateModified control displays the current date and time (see Figure 34.6).

FIGURE 34.6

Date-stamping a record.

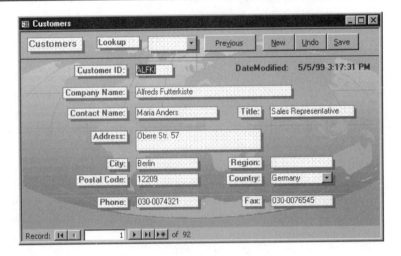

Saving a New Record

When you save a new record on a data entry form that has a lookup combo box, Access doesn't automatically run the query that provides the records for the combo box list. To illustrate this, we'll add a new customer using the Customers form.

1. Open the Customers form in Form view, click the New button, and add a new customer as follows:

| CustomerID | ARCHP |
| CompanyName | Archipelago Mercantile |

2. Click the Save button.

3. Click the down arrow of the Lookup combo box. The new record does not appear in the lookup combo list if you have used the combo box since you opened the form.

4. Update the combo box by choosing Records ➤ Refresh or by pressing the F9 key. Click the down arrow of the Lookup combo box. The new record is in the list.

You can automate the update by creating a macro that requeries the combo box using the Requery action and running the macro just after the new record is saved (that is, when the form recognizes the AfterInsert event). Table 34.7 shows the macro.

TABLE 34.7: A MACRO TO REQUERY THE LOOKUP COMBO BOX

MACRO NAME	ACTION	ACTION ARGUMENTS
Form_AfterInsert		
	Requery	Control Name: cboFind

1. Open the mcrGlobal macro sheet, enter the macro shown in Table 34.7, and save the macro sheet.

2. Click Customers and switch to Design view.

3. Click the form's AfterInsert property and select the mGlobal.Form_AfterInsert macro.

4. Save the form and switch to Form view. Find any existing customer using the Lookup combo box. (This ensures that the combo box list is created before you add a new record.)

5. Click the form's New button and enter the new customer:

| CustomerID | BOULD |
| CompanyName | Boulder Steamers |

6. Click the form's Save button and then click the arrow of the combo box. The new customer appears in the list.

PART

VI

Macro Programming

NOTE If you try this example and you still have the Customers.ValidateID macro attached to the AfterUpdate event for the form, you will see the message "There is another record with this ID." This is because cmdSave_Click macro, which is activated when you click the Save button, runs before the Customers.ValidateID macro.

Carrying Values Forward to a New Record

When you are creating a new record and the new record has fields with the same values as the previous record, you can speed data entry by having the fields in the new record filled in automatically. One way to carry values forward from the current record to the new record is to use the DefaultValue property. When you display the blank data entry record, Access automatically fills in any default values that you have set. This means that if you set the DefaultValue property of a control to the value it has in the current record, when you move to the new record, Access will carry the value to the new record.

You can create a macro to set the DefaultValue property for each control whose value you want to carry forward and run the macro when you take some action to save the changes in the current record. Use the form's BeforeUpdate event to trigger the macro so that the DefaultValue property settings that the macro makes are saved along with the data changes.

Setting the DefaultValue Property

The macro that we create to carry the values forward uses the SetValue action to set the DefaultValue property of a control; the only tricky part is the Expression argument.

If the control has a numeric value, you can use the control name as the Expression argument setting, as follows:

Action	Action Arguments
SetValue	Item: numcontrol.DefaultValue
	Expression: numcontrol

For example, the SupplierID is a number in the Northwind database, so you can set the DefaultValue of the SupplierID control as follows:

Action	Action Arguments
SetValue	Item: SupplierID.DefaultValue
	Expression: SupplierID

However, if the control has a string value, special handling of the Expression argument is required. For example, to set the DefaultValue property for a LastName control to a *specific* string value, such as Peacock, you must enclose the string in quotation marks as follows:

Action	Action Arguments
SetValue	Item:LastName.DefaultValue
	Expression: "Peacock"

But we want to set the property to a string *variable*, not to a specific value. To set a property to a string variable, Access needs to evaluate the variable and concatenate the result into a string. The final setting for the Expression argument is a string within a string. Access uses special syntax for indicating a string within a string. For example, to set the DefaultValue property for the LastName control to the current value in the LastName control, you can use the following syntax:

Action	Action Arguments
SetValue	Item:LastName.DefaultValue
	Expression: """"&LastName&""""

This syntax encloses the inner string "&LastName&" with pairs of double quotation marks. The pairs of double quotation marks simply mark the beginning and the end of the inner string. The result is the value in the LastName control, which must then be enclosed with double quotation marks because the result is a string. (The final result includes four sets of double quotation marks.)

PART

VI

Macro Programming

Strings within Strings

Use string delimiters to identify a string within a string. *A string delimiter* is a character or group of characters that marks the beginning or end of a string. You can use either single or double quotation marks to delimit the inner string. There are three ways to identify a string within a string:

Single quotation marks   Identify the inner string using single quotation marks as follows:

```
' "& controlname &" '
```

then enclose the inner string in double quotation marks for the final result:

```
" ' "& controlname &" ' "
```

Because the single quotation mark is an apostrophe, this syntax does not work properly if the value of the string variable also contains an apostrophe. In this case, Access can't distinguish between ' used as an apostrophe and ' used as a string delimiter, so Access generates a run-time error.

Double quotation marks   Identify the inner string using pairs of double quotation marks as follows:

```
"" "& controlname &" ""
```

then enclose the inner string in double quotation marks for the final result:

```
" "" "& controlname &" "" "
```

Use this syntax to avoid the run-time error generated if a value of the string variable contains an apostrophe.

VBA   In VBA there is a third way to identify a string within a string. You can use the ANSI representation for the double quotation marks, Chr$(34), or a string variable to represent the double quotation marks, such as strDouble. In this case, indicate the inner string by

```
strDouble & controlname & strDouble
```

then enclose the inner string in double quotation marks for the final result:

```
"strDouble & controlname & strDouble"
```

For example, when the Northwind company starts working with a new supplier, data entry for new products is required. During the data entry session for the supplier's products using the Products form, each new record has the same supplier name and, perhaps, the same category and even the same quantity per unit (see Figure 34.7a). In the Products form, the supplier and category controls are displayed as lookup fields. However the values in these controls are the numerical values of the SupplierID and CategoryID. The QuantityPerUnit control contains text values. The macro shown in Table 34.8 uses the double quotation syntax to delimit a string within a string for the QuantityPerUnit control. It carries values to a new record by setting the DefaultValue property.

TABLE 34.8: A MACRO TO CARRY VALUES TO A NEW RECORD

MACRO NAME	ACTION	ACTION ARGUMENTS
Form_BeforeUpdate		
	SetValue:	Item: SupplierID.DefaultValue Expression: SupplierID
	SetValue:	Item: CategoryID.DefaultValue Expression: CategoryID
	SetValue	Item: QuantityPerUnit.DefaultValue Expression: """" & QuantityPerUnit & """"

1. Create a new macro sheet named mProducts, enter the macro shown in Table 34.8, and save the macro sheet.

2. Assign the mProducts.Form_BeforeUpdate macro to the BeforeUpdate event of the Products form, save the form, and switch to Form view.

3. Change the value of the Units in Stock control and click the New button in the toolbar. The new record displays the values carried from the record you just edited (see Figure 34.7b).

PART

VI

Macro Programming

FIGURE 34.7

*Use a macro to set the
DefaultValue property
for controls whose val-
ues you want to carry
to a new record.*

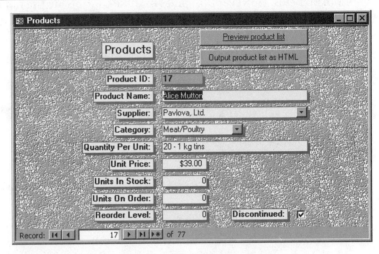

(a)

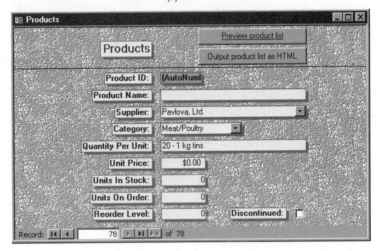

(b)

To Delete or Not to Delete?

When working interactively, you can delete a record by choosing Edit ➤ Delete
Record, or by selecting the record and pressing Delete. In designing the application,
you can decide whether you want to allow record deletions from a particular table.

WARNING   Once someone deletes a record, the information is gone. As you design your application, think carefully about whether or not to permit deletions. In many cases the database must provide a complete audit trail for all entries, and in that case you shouldn't permit any record deletions.

Not to Delete

In many applications, the choice is to prevent all deletions in order to maintain an audit trail of all transactions. To prevent deletions, you can use the form's AllowDeletions property. When you set the AllowDeletions property to No, the Delete Record command in the Edit menu is grayed out; if you select the record and press Delete, the system beeps, and the record is not deleted. You can prevent deletions of customers for the Customers form in NorthwindMacros as follows:

1. Open the Customers form in Design view and set the AllowDeletions property to No.

2. Save the form and switch to Form view. When you try to choose the Delete Record command in the Edit menu, the command is grayed out and unavailable.

To Delete

If you want to allow record deletion, you can automate the interactive process by creating a command button, named cmdDelete, and a macro that runs the RunCommand action to issue the DeleteRecord command. Table 34.9 shows the macro.

TABLE 34.9: A MACRO TO DELETE A RECORD		
MACRO NAME	**ACTION**	**ACTION ARGUMENTS**
cmdDelete_Click		
	RunCommand	Command: DeleteRecord

As an example, we'll allow deletions of a supplier using the Suppliers form.

1. Create a new macro sheet named mSuppliers, enter the macro shown in Table 34.9, and save the macro sheet.

PART

VI

Macro Programming

2. Open the Suppliers form in Design view and place a command button in the upper-right corner of the detail section; set the Name property to cmdDelete and the Caption property to &Delete.

3. Click in the OnClick property and choose the mSuppliers.cmdDelete_Click macro.

4. Save the form and switch to Form view.

5. Click the Delete button. Access displays the default error message shown in Figure 34.8. Click OK. Access displays the Action Failed dialog box. The macro action fails because Access is unable to delete the record.

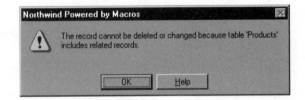

FIGURE 34.8

The default error message displayed when you try to delete a record that has related records in another table and the Cascade Delete Related Records option is not checked.

Access recognizes that the Suppliers table has related records in other tables. The Relationships layout, available by choosing the Relationships command from the Tools menu, shows that the Suppliers table is the "one" table in a one-to-many relationship with the Products table. Double-clicking the join line displays the Relationships dialog shown in Figure 34.9.

The Relationships dialog indicates that the Cascade Delete Related Records option is not selected; therefore you can delete a supplier only if the supplier isn't providing you with products. (Access permits you to delete a record from the "one" table only if there are no related records.) The default error message indicates that the supplier, Exotic Liquids, is providing Northwind with at least one product.

FIGURE 34.9

The Relationships dialog indicates that the Cascade Delete Related Records is not checked, so you can delete a supplier only if the supplier isn't providing any products.

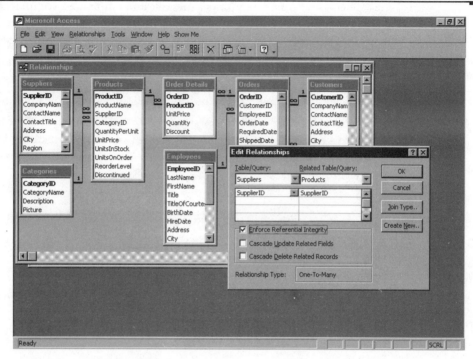

Handling the Macro Error When There Are Related Records

You can avoid macro failure by testing to determine if there are related records and running the action to delete only if there are no related records. You can use the DCount( ) function to count the number of related records. The syntax is

```
DCount("*","tblRelated", "fieldname=Forms!formname!controlname")
```

where *tblRelated* is the name of the related table, *fieldname* is the name of the matching field in the related table, and controlname is the name of the control on the open form that displays the value you want to match. In this example, you use the DCount( ) function to create the test condition:

```
DCount("*","Products","SupplierID=Screen.ActiveForm.SupplierID")=0
```

If the condition is true, the supplier is providing no products, and the macro deletes the supplier. If the condition is false, the supplier must be providing at least one product, so the macro displays a message and terminates. We'll include the count of the products in the message. Table 34.10 shows the modified macro.

1. Click in mSuppliers, modify the cmdDelete_Click macro as shown in Table 34.10, and save the macro sheet. This macro will delete a record if there are no related records.

2. Click in the Suppliers form and click the Delete button. Your custom message is displayed and the macro error is avoided (see Figure 34.10).

3. Add a new supplier with company name Golden Horizons. Save the record and then click the Delete button. The default confirmation message is displayed (see Figure 34.11). Click No.

TABLE 34.10: A MACRO TO DELETE A RECORD

MACRO NAME	CONDITION	ACTION	ACTION ARGUMENTS
cmdDelete_Click			
	DCount("*","Products", "SupplierID=Screen .ActiveForm .SupplierID")=0	RunCommand	Command: DeleteRecord
	...	StopMacro MsgBox Message: ="You can't delete this supplier because the supplier is providing "&Dcount ("*","Products", "SupplierID=Screen .ActiveForm .SupplierID")&" products."	

FIGURE 34.10.

The custom message displayed when you can't delete the record.

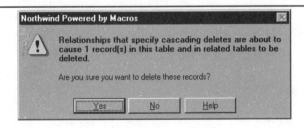

Northwind Powered by Macros

Relationships that specify cascading deletes are about to cause 1 record(s) in this table and in related tables to be deleted.

Are you sure you want to delete these records?

Yes   No   Help

FIGURE 34.11

The default confirmation message that appears when Access is about to delete a record.

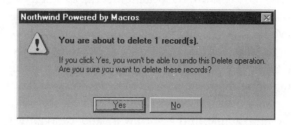

Modify the Macro to Suppress the Confirmation Box and Screen

Updates   You can choose to suppress the default confirmation box by starting the macro with the SetWarnings action. You can also include the Echo action to suppress screen updates while the macro runs.

1. Click in the macro sheet and insert two rows just after the row containing the macro name cmdDelete_Click.

2. In the first inserted row, select the Echo action and set the Echo On argument to No.

3. In the second inserted row, select the SetWarnings action.

4. Save the macro.

5. Click in the Suppliers form and click the Delete button on the form. The record is deleted without the confirmation box.

Cascading a Delete

Sometimes you want to allow a record that has related records to be deleted. If you select the Cascade Delete Related Records option, then when you try to delete the record, Access displays the message shown in Figure 34.12. You see this message in NorthwindMacros if you try to delete an order using the Orders form.

FIGURE 34.12

The default message displayed when you try to delete a record that has related records and the Cascade Delete Related Records option is checked.

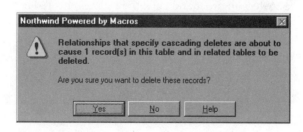

PART

VI

Macro Programming

The problem with the default message is that it doesn't give you very much information. You don't know how many records will be deleted if you continue. You also don't know how many tables are involved. You can replace this message with a custom message box that indicates the number of related records that will be deleted and the tables that will be affected if the operation continues. You can use the DCount( ) function to count the number of related records and the built-in MsgBox( ) function to create a message box with several buttons to provide a choice.

As an example, in the Northwind application, the Orders and Order Details tables are related. (Each record in the Order Details table corresponds to a product sold in an order.) You can verify that the Cascade Delete Related Records options is checked for the relationship. We'll place a command button named cmdDelete on the Orders form and create a macro that allows the deletion of records that have related records. Use the DCount( ) function to determine the number of Order Details records that would be deleted, as follows:

```
DCount("*","[Order Details]", "OrderID=Screen.ActiveForm.OrderID")
```

If there are no Order Details records for an order, the macro runs the menu command to delete the order. If there are Order Details records, the macro displays a custom message box to indicate the number of records that will be deleted and asks for confirmation; if the user confirms, the macro deletes the order, and the related Order Details records; otherwise, the macro terminates. Figure 34.13 shows the macro flow diagram for the macro and Table 34.11 shows the macro.

1. Open the mOrders macro sheet, enter the macro in Table 34.11, and save the macro sheet. This macro will delete a record when the Cascade Delete Related Records option is selected.

2. Place a command button in the header section of the Orders form, set the Name property to cmdDelete and the Caption property to &Delete.

3. Assign the mOrders.cmdDelete_Click macro to the OnClick property of the command button.

4. Save the form and switch to Form view.

5. Select an order and click the Delete button. Figure 34.14 shows the custom message box. Click No and close the form.

TABLE 34.11: A MACRO TO DELETE A RECORD			
MACRO NAME	**CONDITION**	**ACTION**	**ACTION ARGUMENTS**
cmdDelete_Click			
	DCount("*","[Order Details]", "OrderID= Screen.ActiveForm .OrderID")=0	RunCommand	Command: DeleteRecord
	...	StopMacro	
	MsgBox ("There are "&DCount ("*","[Order Details]", "OrderID=Screen .ActiveForm.Ord erID")&" Order Details records related to this order. Do you want to delete all?",4+64)=6	RunCommand	Command: DeleteRecord

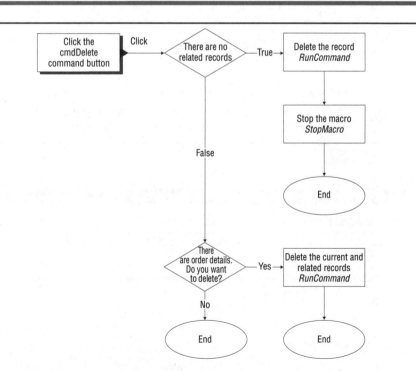

FIGURE 34.13

Macro flow diagram to determine the number of related records and allow the choice to delete.

PART

VI

Macro Programming

FIGURE 34.14

The custom message box to display the number of records in the related table that would be deleted.

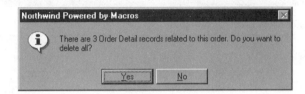

Other Ways to Delete a Record

The techniques we've created for deleting a record automate deletion using a custom command button. If you are working with a record that has related records in another table and you try to delete your record by choosing the Delete Record command in the Edit menu or by selecting the record and pressing Delete, Access displays either of the default error messages shown in Figure 34.8 and Figure 34.12. You can prevent the default error messages by eliminating the alternate ways to delete a record:

- You can customize the command bars to eliminate the Delete Record command. (See Chapter 24, "Creating Custom Toolbars," for information on customizing command bars.)

- You can disable the Delete key by adding a key assignment to the AutoKeys macro group (see Chapter 31). Table 34.12 shows the macro for reassigning the Delete key. To disable the key assignment, you can stop the macro without taking any other action.

 NOTE When you reassign a key using an AutoKeys macro, the reassignment is effective throughout the database, even when you are working in edit mode.

TABLE 34.12: A MACRO TO DISABLE THE DELETE KEY

MACRO NAME	ACTION
{Del}	StopMacro

Working with Data in Two Open Forms

There are times when you want to allow two data entry forms to be open at the same time. When two data entry forms are open, you need to make sure that both forms display the most current information. Access automatically updates the second form if you make changes to a record in the first form, but it doesn't update the second form when you add a new record or delete a record in the first form. In this next section, you'll learn how to use macro programming to update open forms.

Edit an Existing Record

While reviewing orders using the Customer Orders form, you may need to edit information in the customer's record; if the customer is new, you may also need to add a new customer record. In either case, you need to open the Customers form as a second open form.

Observing the Automatic Update of Edited Data

When you open the Customers form and edit an existing record, Access refreshes (automatically updates) the data in the active window. To observe the automatic refresh:

1. Open the Customer Orders form, select an existing customer using the lookup combo list, and click the Review Customer button.

2. Change the spelling of the company name and click the Save button on the Customer form. Notice that the changed spelling is displayed automatically in the Customer Orders form.

3. Locate the same customer in the combo box list. Notice that the changed spelling is also displayed in the combo box list.

When you change data using the Customers form, Access updates the data displayed in Customer Orders form as soon as the Customer Orders form becomes the active form.

Add a New Record

When a new customer calls, you need to display a new data entry record for the Customers form. You can automate the process by placing a command button named cmdNewCustomer on the Customer Orders form and creating a macro to open the Customers form and display a new blank record ready for data entry. Table 34.13 shows the macro.

PART

VI

Macro Programming

TABLE 34.13: A MACRO TO OPEN A NEW RECORD		
MACRO NAME	**ACTION**	**ACTION ARGUMENTS**
cmdNewCustomer_Click		
	OpenForm	FormName: Customers
		Data Mode: Add

1. Create a new macro sheet named mCustomerOrders, enter the macro in Table 34.13, and save the macro sheet.

2. Click in the Customer Orders form and switch to Design view.

3. Place a command button in the header section. Set the Name property to cmd-NewCustomer and the Caption property to &New Customer.

4. Click in the button's OnClick property and select mCustomerOrders.cmdNew Customer_Click.

5. Save the form and switch to Form view.

6. Click the New Customer button. Access opens a new record in the Customers form.

7. Enter a new customer:

   CustomerID: CAMDE

   CompanyName: Cameron Designs

8. Close the Customers form. The new customer is saved.

9. Click the arrow on the lookup combo box in the Customer Orders form. The new customer does not appear in the pick list if you have used the pick list since you opened the form.

Refresh Does Not Display New Records   When you edit an existing record, Access automatically refreshes (updates), but does not display *new* records. In order to display new records, you must requery the controls and the form. When working interactively, requery a control by pressing F9 and requery the form by pressing Shift+F9; separate actions are needed because Access can requery only one object at a time.

Requery the Combo Box and the Form Interactively   Let's go through the requery process interactively and then create a macro to automate it.

1. With the Customer Orders form active, press F9.

2. Click the arrow of the combo box. The new customer appears in the combo list.

3. Select the new customer from the list. The new customer's record is not displayed if you have used the pick list since you opened the form.

4. Press Shift+F9 and select the new customer again using the combo box. The new customer's record is displayed.

Creating a Macro to Requery a Form and Its Controls

You can create a macro that requeries the Customer Orders form and its cboFind combo box just after the new record is saved (that is, when the Customers form recognizes the AfterInsert event). If you display the property sheet for Customers, you can see that the form's AfterInsert event is already triggering the mcrGlobal.Form_AfterInsert macro, which requeries the lookup combo box on Customers as part of the logical navigation technique added in Chapter 33, "Navigation with Macros." You can modify this macro to requery the Customer Orders form and its combo box.

Of course, you only want to requery if the Customer Orders form is open. During the order review process, the Customer Orders form is open; however, if you've opened Customers directly to enter or edit customer information, the Customer Orders form isn't open. You can determine if Customer Orders is open by using the IsLoaded( ) function. If Customer Orders is not open, the macro terminates. If the Customer Orders form is open, the macro uses the SelectObject action to select the form before requerying (because the Requery action applies only to an active object). It then applies the Requery action to the combo box and to the form itself. Figure 34.15 shows the macro flow diagram. Table 34.14 shows this macro, which will select another form and requery the form and its control.

FIGURE 34.15

This is the macro flow diagram for the Form_AfterInsert macro. The macro determines if another form is open before taking action on it.

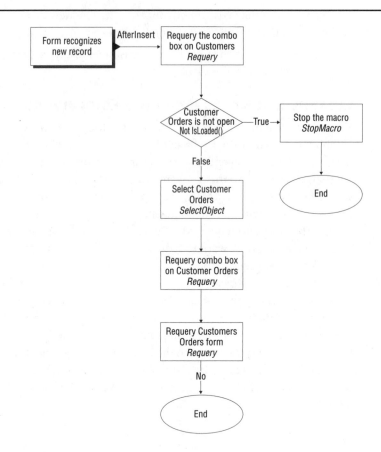

TABLE 34.14: A MACRO TO SELECT AND REQUERY

MACRO NAME	CONDITION	ACTION	ACTION ARGUMENTS
Form_AfterInsert			
		Requery	Control Name: cboFind
	Not IsLoaded ("Customer Orders")	StopMacro	
		SelectObject	Object Type: Form
			Object Name: Customer Orders
		Requery	Control Name: cboFind
		Requery	

1. Open the mCustomers macro sheet, enter the macro shown in Table 34.14 and save the macro sheet. The macro requeries the cboFind combo box on Customers and then takes action on Customer Orders. Leave the `Control Name` argument blank in the third Requery action; when no control is specified, Access requeries the active object.

2. Open the Customers form in Design view, click the AfterInsert property, and replace the mcrGlobal.Form_AfterInsert macro with the mCustomers.Form_ AfterInsert macro.

3. Save and close the form.

4. On the Customer Orders form, click the Review Customer button.

5. In the Customers form that opens, click the New button and enter a new customer:

   CustomerID: GREER

   CompanyName: Greer Gourmet

6. Click the Close button for the Customers form. Observe that when Customer Orders form is requeried, the form displays the first record in the default sort order.

7. Select the new customer's name from the lookup combo box. The new customer's record is displayed.

8. Close the Customer Orders form.

Summary

This chapter has introduced important macro techniques for automating routine data entry operation. You learned how to:

- Use macros to set complex rules for validating data. For example, you can change the timing of the validation test.
- Create reusable macros for command buttons to add a new record, undo changes, and save a record.
- Design a macro to test the Dirty property to determine if the Undo command is available before running it, since it is not always available.
- Date-stamp a record by using the form's `BeforeUpdate` event to run a macro that sets the current date.

PART

VI

Macro Programming

- Create a macro to set a control's DefaultValue property to carry values forward to a new record and use the special syntax required when the control contains string values.

- Create macros to delete records, test for related records, and offer the choice to delete a record and its related records (if the Cascade Delete Related Records option is set for the relationship).

- Create macros to update open forms because Access does not update a form automatically when you add or delete records in another form.

CHAPTER 35

Working with Groups of Records Using Macros

I n the previous two chapters, you've learned techniques for working with a single record, including navigating among controls, records, and forms; finding a specific record; and automating data entry operations.

This chapter focuses on working with groups of records. You'll learn how to automate two standard database operations: sorting and selecting groups of records. You'll learn how to sort records by using a macro to set a form's sorting properties. You'll learn how to use a form to collect your selection criteria, pass the values to a filter query (called Query By Form), and then use the filter query to retrieve the specific records. You'll also use the Query By Form technique to synchronize two combo boxes on a form.

This chapter will also show you how to create a custom dialog box to collect user input and pass the collected values to a filter query that selects records from a report's record source. The last section will show you a technique for carrying values in a data entry form forward to the next data entry session. This technique uses a data entry table to hold the new record and action queries to append the new record to the data storage table and update the data entry table to hold only the values you want to carry forward.

 NOTE This chapter assumes you have customized the Form view, Macro Design, and Database menu bars and toolbars to include the Macro command that displays the Run Macro dialog. If you haven't customized the command bars, you can do so now. This chapter also assumes that you've created the NorthwindMacros database as a copy of the Northwind database. Create a copy now if necessary.

We'll begin by creating a new form for the NorthwindMacros database that we'll use to illustrate the macros. You can create the new form, named frmOrderStatus, by using the Form Wizard and then modifying the results. Figure 35.1 shows the new frmOrderStatus form. Here are the steps:

1. Use the Form Wizard to create a new tabular form. Select OrderID, OrderDate, RequiredDate, and ShippedDate from the Orders table; CompanyName from the Shippers table, CompanyName from the Customers table; and LastName from the Employees table. Name the form frmOrderStatus.

2. Set the form's Caption property to Order Status and set the AllowAdditions property to No. The Order Status form is a review form and is not intended for

data entry; setting the AllowAdditions property to No hides the blank record at the end of the recordset.

3. Select all of the data controls, set their Locked property to Yes, and set their formatting properties as shown below. Because the form is not intended for data entry, lock the control to prevent inadvertent changes.

BackColor   12632256

SpecialEffect   Flat

BorderStyle   Transparent

 NOTE The reason you set the Locked property to individual controls rather than setting the form's AllowEdits property is as follows: if you set the form's AllowEdits property to No, you can't use a combo box on the form to choose records because you can't change (edit) the search value in the combo box.

4. Rearrange the controls, change the Caption properties for the labels as shown in Figure 35.1, and set the FontWeight property for the labels to Bold.

FIGURE 35.1

Create an Order Status form for sorting and selecting records.

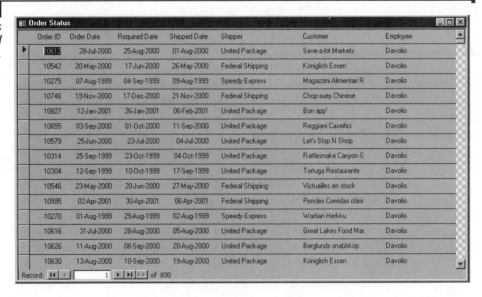

PART

VI

Macro Programming

Sorting Records

When working interactively, you can easily sort a group of records displayed in a form by the values in a single field. To sort by the values in a single field in ascending or descending order, right-click in the control and select the Sort Ascending or Sort Descending command in the shortcut menu. To remove the sort, right-click in a control and select Remove Filter/Sort in the shortcut menu.

Sorting Interactively

For practice, sort the frmOrderStatus form by any one of its columns:

1. Click a control in the Customer column and then click the Sort Descending button. The records are sorted in descending order by the values in the column.

2. Switch to Design view and observe that the form's OrderBy property is set to frmOrderStatus.Customers_CompanyName DESC.

3. Switch back to Form view, right-click in a control, and choose the Remove Filter/Sort command in the shortcut menu. The sort is removed and the records are displayed in their original order. If you switch to Design view, you will see that the OrderBy property is still set to frmOrderStatus.Customers_Company-Name DESC.

4. Switch back to Form view again. Choose the Apply Filter/Sort command in the Records menu. The sort is applied.

5. Save, close, and reopen the form. Access applies the OrderBy setting.

6. Remove the sort, then close and reopen the form. Access does not apply the OrderBy setting.

The OrderBy Property

You can use a form's OrderBy property to sort by a single field, or you can create a complex sort of several fields with some fields in ascending and others in descending order. The OrderBy property is a string expression that consists of the name of the field or fields you want to sort, arranged in the order of the sort and separated by commas; to sort a field in descending order, you type **DESC** after the name of the field. For example, to sort by customer and then by order date in descending order, you set the OrderBy property to

frmOrderStatus.Customers_CompanyName DESC, OrderDate DESC

You can set the OrderBy property in the form's property sheet; the setting is saved when you close the form. Interactively, you apply and remove the OrderBy setting using the ApplyFilter/Sort and RemoveFilter/Sort menu commands.

Automate the Sort Process

You can automate the sort process using the OrderBy and OrderByOn properties.

Using the OrderByOn Property

You use the OrderByOn property to apply or remove the sort specified in the OrderBy property by setting the OrderByOn property to Yes or No (or True or False in VBA). For a form, you can set the OrderBy property in the form's property sheet in a macro or VBA procedure and then use a macro or VBA procedure to apply and remove the sort using the OrderByOn property. For a report, you can also set the OrderByOn property in the report's property sheet.

Using a Triple-State Toggle Button

As an example, we'll create a button and a macro to sort the Order Status records by customer. We are going to use a toggle button instead of a command button because a toggle button has a value that can be used by the macro. Normally a toggle button has two values: True and False. Setting the TripleState property to Yes gives a third value: Null.

- When the toggle button has the value False, it looks like a command button.
- Clicking the button changes it to the Null state in which the button flattens but still appears raised.
- Clicking the button again changes it to the True state in which the flattened button appears sunken.

We'll create a macro to test the button's state and remove the sort if the button is in the False state, apply an ascending sort if the button is in the Null state, and apply a descending sort if the button is in the True state (see Table 35.1). Figure 35.2 shows the three states of the toggle button and the resulting sorts by customer.

FIGURE 35.2

Use a triple-state toggle button to remove a sort when the toggle button is False (a), apply an ascending sort when the button is Null (b), and apply a descending sort when the button is True (c).

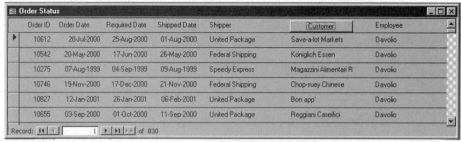

(a)

(b)

(c)

1. Switch to Design view. Select all of the controls in the detail section and set their Enabled properties to No. Then switch back to Form view. The controls don't need to be enabled when you use the OrderBy property for the sort.

2. Create a new macro sheet named mfrmOrderStatus, enter the macro shown in Table 35.1, and save the macro sheet. The macro uses Screen.ActiveControl to refer to the toggle button's value. When the toggle button has the value False, the Not Screen.ActiveControl is True and the macro sets the OrderBy property to "" (that is, the zero-length string) which is equivalent to removing the sort.

3. Delete the Customer label in the header section, replace it with a toggle button, and set the properties as follows:

Caption	Customer
TripleState property	Yes
Default Value	False
ControlTip Text	Click to toggle ascending, descending, and no sort

4. Assign the mfrmOrderStatus.tglCustomer_Click macro to the OnClick property of the toggle button.

5. Save the form, switch to Form view, and click the toggle button (see Figure 35.3). As you cycle through the states, the records are sorted by customer name in ascending order, and then in descending order, and then the sort is removed.

Although Access saves the OrderBy and OrderByOn settings that are in effect when you close the form, it does not save the state of the toggle button. As a result, the property settings and the toggle button can get out of synch with one another when you first open the form. We'll use the macro shown in Table 35.2 to initialize the OrderBy and OrderByOn settings when the form opens. You have to refer to the form explicitly in this macro and can't use the Screen object because the form is not the active object when the Open event occurs. (A form's Activate event occurs after the form's Open, Load, and Resize events.)

TABLE 35.1: A MACRO FOR THE THREE SORT ORDERS

MACRO NAME	CONDITION	ACTION	ACTION ARGUMENTS
TglCustomer_Click			
	Not Screen.ActiveControl	SetValue	Item: Screen.ActiveForm .OrderByExpression: ""
	IsNull(Screen .ActiveControl)	SetValue	Item: Screen.ActiveForm .OrderByExpression: "Customers.CompanyName"
	Screen.ActiveControl	SetValue	Item: Screen.ActiveForm .OrderByExpression: "Customers.CompanyName DESC"
		RunCommand	ApplyFilterSort

PART

VI

Macro Programming

TABLE 35.2: A MACRO TO INITIALIZE THE SORT SETTINGS		
MACRO NAME	**ACTION**	**ACTION ARGUMENTS**
Form_Open		
	SetValue	Item: Forms!frmOrderStatus.OrderByOn
		Expression: True
	SetValue	Item: Forms!frmOrderStatus.OrderBy
		Expression: ""

1. Click the mfrmOrderStatus macro sheet, enter the macro in Table 35.2, and save the macro sheet.

2. Assign the macro to the OnOpen event property of the form.

3. Save and close the form.

4. Open the form. The two sort property settings are initialized and in synch with the toggle button.

Sort by Any Column

When records are displayed in a tabular form, you can automate sorting the records by specific columns: replace the label of each column you want to sort by with a triple-state toggle button, and create a macro to sort the records by a field in the column, such as the one in Table 35.1. Using this technique, each of the sorts is independent, and the last button clicked determines the sort. This means that if you toggle the Customers button to sort ascending by customer, and then toggle the Employees button to sort ascending by employee, the result is that the records are sorted in ascending order by employee. Figure 35.3 shows the result; notice that the state of the Customers toggle button is out of synch because the toggle button is in the flattened raised state (to indicate an ascending sort by customer) while the records are sorted by employee.

The state of the Customer toggle button is out of synch: The button indicates an ascending sort by customer, but the records do not reflect the customer sort.

Macros for a Complex Sort

It is possible to write macros to keep the toggle buttons in synch with the current sort. Keeping the toggle buttons in synch with the current sort involves the same kind of macro programming that is required for a complex sort. In a complex sort, each subsequent sort on any field takes previous sorts into account. For example, in a complex sort, toggling a sort by customer and then a sort by employee would produce records sorted by customer, and then the records for each customer would be sorted by employee.

We'll do a complex sort for the Customer and Employee triple-state toggle buttons. When you click the Customer toggle button, the macro sets the sort depending on the current state of the Employee button. For example, if your click changes the Customer toggle button to Null (to sort ascending by customer), the macro determines the state of the Employee button and sets the form's OrderBy property as follows:

If the State of the Employee Button Is	The Macro Sets the OrderBy Property To
False (no sort by employee)	"Customers.CompanyName"
Null (ascending sort by employee)	"LastName, Customers.CompanyName"
True (descending sort by employee)	"LastName DESC, Customers.Company-Name"

Similarly, when you click the Customer Toggle button and change it to True (to sort descending by customer), there are three alternative sets of actions, and when you toggle the Customer button to False (for no sort by customer), there are three more alternatives, depending on the current state of the Employee button for each of the three states for the Customer button. The macro for the Customer toggle button has the nine alternatives, shown in Table 35.3.

TABLE 35.3: THE MACRO FOR THE CUSTOMER TOGGLE BUTTON HAS NINE ALTERNATIVES

MACRO NAME	CONDITION	ACTION	ACTION ARGUMENTS
TglCustomer_Click			
	Not tglEmployee And Not Screen .ActiveControl	SetValue	Item: Screen.Active-Form.OrderBy
			Expression: ""
	IsNull(tglEmployee) And Not Screen .ActiveControl	SetValue	Item: Screen.Active-Form.OrderBy
			Expression: "LastName"
	tglEmployee And Not Screen .ActiveControl	SetValue	Item: Screen.Active Form.OrderBy
			Expression: "LastName DESC"
	Not (tglEmployee) And IsNull(Screen .ActiveControl)	SetValue	Item: Screen.Active Form.OrderBy
			Expression: "Customers.CompanyName"
	IsNull(tglEmployee) And IsNull(Screen .ActiveControl)	SetValue	Item: Screen.Active Form.OrderBy
			Expression: "LastName, Customers_CompanyName"
	TglEmployee And IsNull(Screen .ActiveControl)	SetValue	Item: Screen.Active Form.OrderBy
			Expression: "LastName DESC,Customers .CompanyName"
	Not (tglEmployee) And (Screen .ActiveControl)	SetValue	Item: Screen.Active Form.OrderBy
			Expression: "Customers .CompanyName DESC"

Continued ▶|

TABLE 35.3: THE MACRO FOR THE CUSTOMER TOGGLE BUTTON (CONTINUED)

(CONTINUED)

MACRO NAME	CONDITION	ACTION	ACTION ARGUMENTS
	IsNull(tglEmployee) And (Screen .ActiveControl)	SetValue	Item: Screen.Active Form.OrderBy
			Expression: "LastName, Customers.CompanyName DESC"
	(tglEmployee) And (Screen .ActiveControl)	SetValue	Item: Screen .ActiveForm.OrderBy
			Expression: "LastName DESC, Customers .CompanyName DESC"

1. Open the frmOrderStatus form in Design view.

2. Following the steps for the Customer toggle button, replace the Employee label with an Employee toggle button named tglEmployee, and set the properties as described for the Customer toggle button.

3. In the mfrmOrderStatus macro sheet, create the tglEmployee_Click macro, modifying the macro in Table 35.1 to replace Customers.CompanyName with LastName. Save the macro sheet and assign the tglEmployee_Click macro to the OnClick property of the tglEmployee toggle button.

4. Click the mfrmOrderStatus macro sheet and modify the tglCustomer_Click macro, as shown in Table 35.3. Save the macro sheet.

5. Save the form and switch to Form view.

6. Click the Employee toggle button. The records are now sorted by Employee (see Figure 35.4a).

7. Click the Customer toggle button. The records are now sorted first by Employee and then by Customer (see Figure 35.4b).

PART

VI

Macro Programming

FIGURE 35.4

The records are sorted by employee (a), and then the records for each employee are sorted by customer (b).

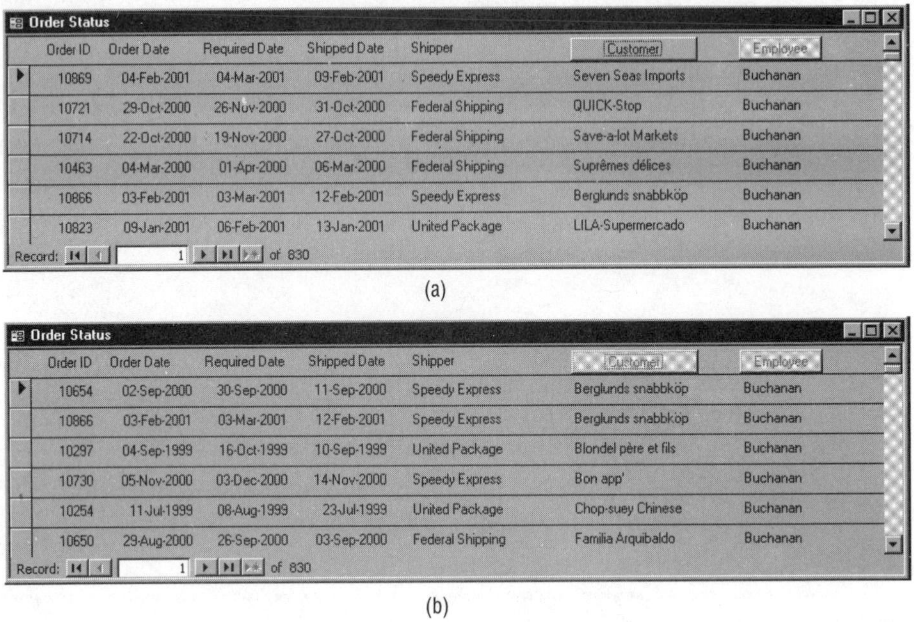

Order ID	Order Date	Required Date	Shipped Date	Shipper	Customer	Employee
10869	04-Feb-2001	04-Mar-2001	09-Feb-2001	Speedy Express	Seven Seas Imports	Buchanan
10721	29-Oct-2000	26-Nov-2000	31-Oct-2000	Federal Shipping	QUICK-Stop	Buchanan
10714	22-Oct-2000	19-Nov-2000	27-Oct-2000	Federal Shipping	Save-a-lot Markets	Buchanan
10463	04-Mar-2000	01-Apr-2000	06-Mar-2000	Federal Shipping	Suprêmes délices	Buchanan
10866	03-Feb-2001	03-Mar-2001	12-Feb-2001	Speedy Express	Berglunds snabbköp	Buchanan
10823	09-Jan-2001	06-Feb-2001	13-Jan-2001	United Package	LILA-Supermercado	Buchanan

Record: 1 of 830

(a)

Order ID	Order Date	Required Date	Shipped Date	Shipper	Customer	Employee
10654	02-Sep-2000	30-Sep-2000	11-Sep-2000	Speedy Express	Berglunds snabbköp	Buchanan
10866	03-Feb-2001	03-Mar-2001	12-Feb-2001	Speedy Express	Berglunds snabbköp	Buchanan
10297	04-Sep-1999	16-Oct-1999	10-Sep-1999	United Package	Blondel père et fils	Buchanan
10730	05-Nov-2000	03-Dec-2000	14-Nov-2000	Speedy Express	Bon app'	Buchanan
10254	11-Jul-1999	08-Aug-1999	23-Jul-1999	United Package	Chop-suey Chinese	Buchanan
10650	29-Aug-2000	26-Sep-2000	03-Sep-2000	Federal Shipping	Familia Arquibaldo	Buchanan

Record: 1 of 830

(b)

At this point, the macro for the Customer toggle button is able to detect the state of the Employee button before setting the sort order; however, to complete the complex sort, we would need to modify the macro for the Employee button to detect the state of the Customer button. The tglEmployee_Click button can be modified to include nine alternatives similar to those given in the macro in Table 35.3.

If there are three toggle buttons, there are three alternative states that need to be considered for each button, or a total twenty seven ($3 \times 3 \times 3 = 3^3$) for each button. While it is possible to use macro programming for three or more toggle buttons, a much better solution is to create on-the-fly a sort order that includes the sort fields in the order that the user selects them. This solution can be programmed much more efficiently using VBA, so we won't continue with the macro solution.

Using Query By Form to Find a Group of Records

An important database operation is selecting a group of records that meet one or more selection criteria. For example, in the Order Status form, you may want to display a list of orders for a particular customer, shipper, or employee; you may want to review all orders taken by an employee after a specific date; or you may want to see all orders to be shipped by a specific shipper before a certain required date.

When working interactively, you can select a specific group of records by creating and applying a filter. Microsoft Access provides several ways to create filters interactively, including Filter By Form and Filter By Selection. These techniques give the user powerful ad hoc querying abilities. You can also customize these techniques with programming. This section describes another technique called Query By Form that you can use to provide a simple interface for selecting a group of records.

Selecting a Group of Records Interactively

In this section, you'll select the orders for a specific customer. First, modify the record source to include the CustomerID from the Orders table, so the primary key can be used to select records.

1. Open the frmOrderStatus form in Design view. Click the form's RecordSource property and click the Build button at the right of the property box. The Query Builder opens (see Figure 35.5).

2. Select CustomerID, EmployeeID, and ShipVia from the Orders table and drag them to the grid. You'll be ready to sort by employee or shipper later by including their primary key fields now.

3. Choose File ➤ Save As and save the query as qryOrderStatus. Close the Query Builder window, click Yes to save the query, and click Yes in the next dialog to update the form's RecordSource property.

PART

VI

Macro Programming

FIGURE 35.5

The record source
for the frmOrder-
Status form.

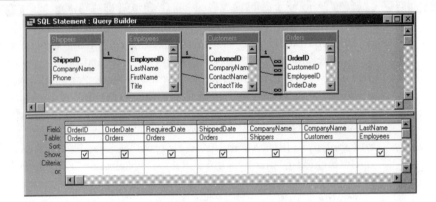

4. Switch to Form view and choose Records ➤ Filter ➤ Advanced Filter/Sort. The Filter design window opens.

5. From the field list, drag the CustomerID field to the first Field cell in the filter grid and type **alfki** in the Criteria cell (see Figure 35.6).

6. Click the Apply Filter button on the toolbar. The filter window closes and the selected records are displayed. Access indicates the number of filtered records in the lower-left corner of the form (see Figure 35.7).

7. Click the Remove Filter button on the toolbar to remove the filter.

FIGURE 35.6

Using the Filter design
window to create
a filter.

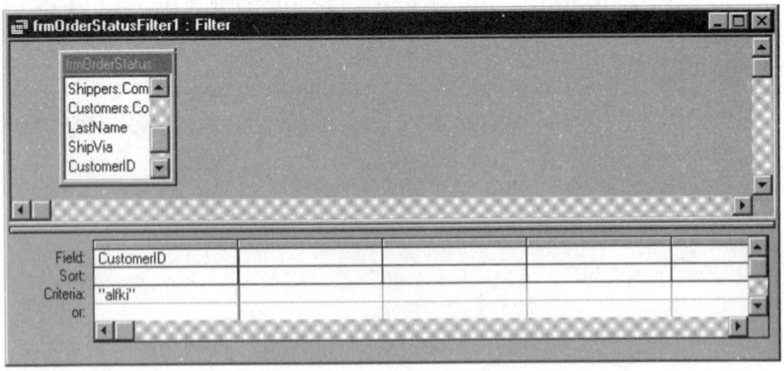

FIGURE 35.7

The filtered records.

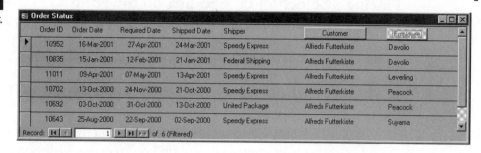

Creating a Filter Query

A filter is temporary and is destroyed when you close the form. Rather than use a filter, you can create a query and use it to select records. A *filter query* must be based on the same query that the form is based on and must include all the same fields.

1. In the Database window, select the qryOrderStatus query, then copy and paste the query as qfltOrderStatus.

2. Open the qfltOrderStatus query in Design view, right-click the upper pane, and choose the Properties command in the shortcut menu. Set the Output All Fields property to Yes. With this property setting, you can delete all fields from the query design grid except the fields you are using to select or sort records.

3. Delete all columns in the query design grid except the CustomerID column. In the next section, you enter selection criteria for the CustomerID field.

4. Save and close the query.

Automate the Selection Process

To automate the selection process, we'll use a search technique similar to the technique we used to find a single record in Chapter 33, "Navigation with Macros." The search technique uses a combo box variable to hold the search value and a macro triggered by the control's AfterUpdate event to apply a filter and select the records. Specifically, we'll do the following:

- Place a combo box named cboCustomer that displays a list of customer IDs and company names in the header of the form.

- Modify the qfltOrderStatus query to use the value selected in the combo box as the criteria for the CustomerID field.

- Create a macro that uses the ApplyFilter action to run the filter query and display the filtered records when the combo box recognizes the AfterUpdate event.

Placing a Selection Combo Box on the Form

Creating the combo box is easy because the CustomerID field in the Orders table is a lookup field. When you drag a lookup field created as a combo box (or list box) to a form, its lookup properties are copied, and the field is displayed as a combo box (or a list box) on the form. Although we do not want the search combo box to be a bound control, we can save the work of creating a combo box by dragging the lookup field to the form and changing the control's properties.

1. Switch to Design view and increase the height of the header section. Select all the labels and drag them down to the bottom of the header section. Select CustomerID from the field list and drag to the header section above the Customer toggle button. The field is displayed as a combo box.

2. Change the combo box Name property to cboCustomer and delete the setting for the ControlSource property. The ControlSource must be blank so that the combo box can be used to hold the search value as a variable. Note that the BoundColumn property is set to 1, so the combo box holds the value of the CustomerID for the combo box row that you select.

3. Change the label's Caption property to Select Customer and move the label above the combo box. (Point to the upper-left corner of the label box and wait for the mouse pointer to appear as a hand with a finger pointing. You can then drag the label without moving its text box at the same time.) Then use the Bold button to make the label appear in bold text so it is easier to see.

4. Save the form and switch to Form view (see Figure 35.8).

FIGURE 35.8

Create the Lookup combo box by dragging the Lookup field and deleting the ControlSource property. The Lookup combo box must be unbound in order to set a variable.

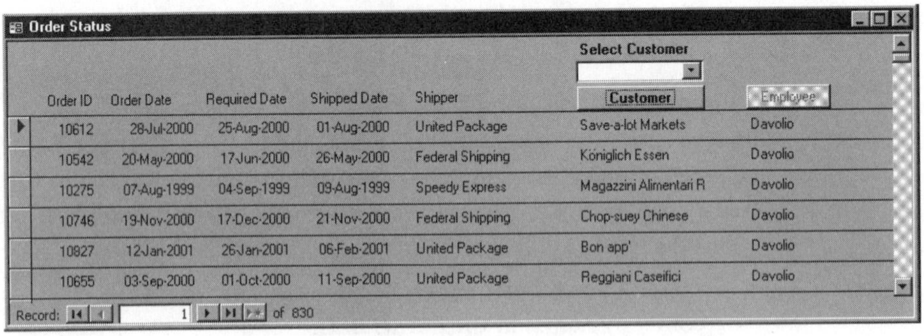

Order ID	Order Date	Required Date	Shipped Date	Shipper		Employee
10612	28-Jul-2000	25-Aug-2000	01-Aug-2000	United Package	Save-a-lot Markets	Davolio
10542	20-May-2000	17-Jun-2000	26-May-2000	Federal Shipping	Königlich Essen	Davolio
10275	07-Aug-1999	04-Sep-1999	09-Aug-1999	Speedy Express	Magazzini Alimentari R	Davolio
10746	19-Nov-2000	17-Dec-2000	21-Nov-2000	Federal Shipping	Chop-suey Chinese	Davolio
10827	12-Jan-2001	26-Jan-2001	06-Feb-2001	United Package	Bon app'	Davolio
10655	03-Sep-2000	01-Oct-2000	11-Sep-2000	United Package	Reggiani Caseifici	Davolio

Record: 1 of 830

Setting the Filter Query Criteria

Modify the filter query to use the value selected in the combo box as the criteria for the query's prefix field.

1. Open the qfltOrderStatus query in Design view.

2. Click the Criteria cell below CustomerID. In the next step, you will enter an expression in the Criteria cell so that the cell gets its value from the combo box on the form. When you design a parameter query to take its criteria values from a form, you are using *Query By Form* (also called *QBF*).

3. Press Shift+F2 (or Ctrl+Z, the custom key combination created in Chapter 31, "Macro Basics") to open the Zoom box and enter the full identifier of the combo box shown below (or click the toolbar Build button and use the Expression Builder to construct the expression). You don't have to type the square brackets yourself when the names don't include spaces or symbols; Access supplies the square brackets for you.

   [Forms]![frmOrderStatus]![cboCustomer]

4. Save the query. If you select a customer in the combo box and then click into the query and run it, the query selects the orders for the customer you chose.

Creating a Macro to Apply the Filter

Use the ApplyFilter action to restrict or sort the records in a table or in the record source of a form or report. Chapter 31 looked at examples of using the Filter Name and the Where Condition arguments to specify the filter. Here we use the ApplyFilter action to apply the qfltOrderStatus filter saved as a query. Table 35.4 shows the macro.

TABLE 35.4: A MACRO TO FILTER RECORDS

MACRO NAME	ACTION	ACTION ARGUMENTS
cboCustomer_AfterUpdate		
	ApplyFilter	Filter Name: qfltOrderStatus

1. Click the mfrmOrderStatus macro sheet, enter the macro in Table 35.4, and save the macro sheet.

2. Open the Order Status form in Design view and assign the mfrmOrderStatus.cboCustomer_AfterUpdate macro to the AfterUpdate event property of the cboCustomer combo box.

3. Save the form and switch to Form view.

4. Select a customer from the combo box. The records are filtered and displayed; Access displays the number of filtered records in the lower-left corner of the form (see Figure 35.9).

5. Click the Employee toggle button. The selection is sorted in ascending order by employee.

6. Choose the Remove Filter/Sort command in the Records menu, or right-click the form title bar, and select Remove Filter/Sort from the context menu. The filter and the sort are removed, and all records are displayed.

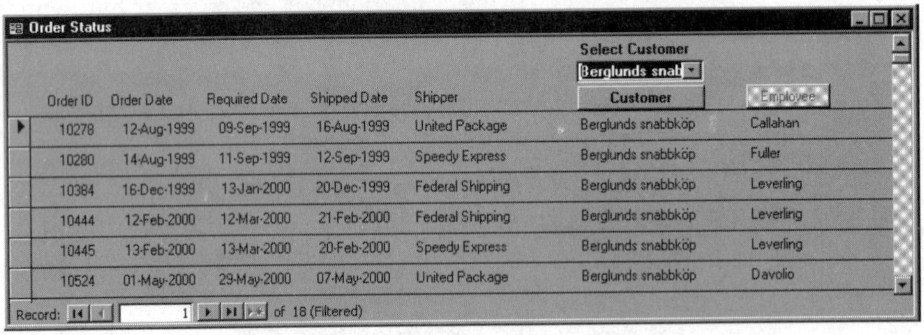

FIGURE 35.9

After you select a customer, the macro applies the filter query that uses the combo box value to select records (Query By Form).

Automate the Removal of the Filter

You can automate the removal of the filter by placing a command button in the form header and creating a macro to remove the filter.

1. Switch to Design view, place a command button in the header section, and set the Name property to cmdShowAll and the Caption property to &Show All.

2. Click in the window for the macro mfrmOrderStatus (or open the macro if it's not already on the desktop), then add a new macro at the end of the sheet called cmdShowAll_Click.

3. Click in the next row and select the ShowAllRecords action. The ShowAllRecords action removes the filter and sort and requeries the records.

4. Save the macro.

5. Assign the mfrmOrderStatus.cmdShowAll_Click macro to the command button.

6. Save the form and switch to Form view (see Figure 35.10).

7. Click the Show All button. The filter and sort are removed, but the combo box continues to display the value selected.

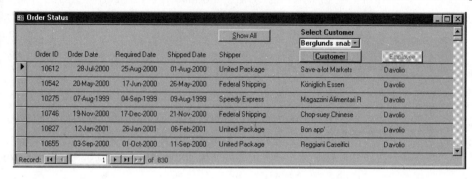

After you click the Show All button to remove the filter, the combo box should be null to indicate all records are displayed. Modify the macro that removes the filter so that it also sets the value of the combo box to Null. Table 35.5 shows the new macro.

TABLE 35.5: A MACRO TO REMOVE THE FILTER AND SORT AND INITIALIZE THE COMBO BOX

MACRO NAME	ACTION	ACTION ARGUMENTS
CmdShowAll_Click		
	ShowAllRecords	
	SetValue	Item: cboCustomer
		Expression: Null

1. Click the mfrmOrderStatus macro sheet, modify the cmdShowAll_Click macro as shown in Table 35.5, and save the macro sheet.

2. Click frmOrderStatus and click the Show All button. The combo box is null, and all the records are displayed.

Using Multiple Criteria to Select a Group of Records

Often you want to use more than one criterion for selecting records. For example, you may want to find all orders that are handled by a specific employee for a certain customer. You can place a selection combo box in the form header for each field you want to use in selecting records, modify the filter query to include the additional criteria, create a macro to apply the filter for each new combo box, and, finally, modify the macro that removes the filter so that it also sets the combo boxes to null.

Creating a Second Selection Combo Box

As an example, let's create a second process to select records for an employee.

1. Switch to Design view and drag the EmployeeID lookup field to the header section above the Employee toggle button.

2. Change the Name property to cboEmployee and delete the setting for the ControlSource property.

3. Change the label's Caption property to Select Employee and move the label above the combo box. The next step is to modify the filter query to include the value in the cboEmployee combo box as a selection criterion.

4. Open the query qfltOrderStatus in Design view, drag EmployeeID from the field list for the Employees table to the second Field cell, click the Criteria cell, and enter the expression **Forms!frmOrderStatus!cboEmployee**. (You can cut and paste the similar expression from the CustomerID Criteria cell and edit the field name.)

5. Save and close the query. The next step is to create the macro to apply the filter after the user selects an employee using the new combo box.

6. Click the mfrmOrderStatus macro sheet, select and copy the cboCustomer_AfterUpdate macro, and then click in a new row and paste the copied rows.

7. Change the name of the pasted macro to cboEmployee_AfterUpdate. The next step is to modify the macro that removes the filter and clears the combo boxes.

8. Insert a new empty row below the last row of the macro cmdShowAll_Click. Then select the SetValue action and set its arguments as follows:

   Item: cboEmployee

   Expression: Null

9. Save the macro sheet. The final step is to assign the new cboEmployee_AfterUpdate macro to the cboEmployee combo box on the Order Status form.

10. In Design view for the Order Status form, assign the new cboEmployee_AfterUpdate macro to the AfterUpdate event property of the cboEmployee combo box; save and close the form.

Testing the Multi-Criteria Selection Process

Let's test the process:

1. Open the frmOrderStatus form.

2. Click the Customer combo box and select Alfreds Futterkiste. Surprisingly, no records are displayed.

3. Click the Employee combo box and select the employee, Margaret Peacock. The two orders handled by Ms. Peacock for Alfreds Futterkiste are displayed.

Modify the Query Criteria to Return Records for All Values of an Empty Combo Box

As currently designed, the filter query requires that you make selections for both combo boxes (see Figure 35.11).

FIGURE 35.11

A filter query that returns records only when both combo boxes have a non-null value.

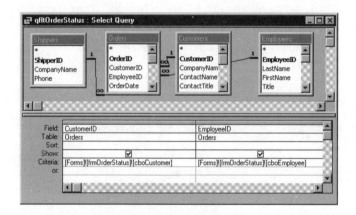

If the combo box for a field is null, the filter query looks for records with a null value in that field; finding no such records, the query displays none. Instead, the query returns records for all values in a field with a null combo box value. You can return all records for a combo box whose value is Null by changing the criteria to include a test for Null. For example, for the Customer combo box, use the expression

```
Forms!frmOrderStatus!cboCustomer Or Forms!frmOrderStatus!cboCustomer
Is Null
```

PART

VI

Macro Programming

If the value in cboCustomer is Null, this expression evaluates to True, and the query returns records with all values of CustomerID.

1. Go to Design view for the qfltOrderStatus query. In the Criteria cell for the CustomerID field, replace the criteria with the expression

> **Forms!frmOrderStatus!cboCustomer Or Forms!frmOrderStatus! cboCustomer Is Null**

2. In the Criteria cell for the EmployeeID field, replace the criteria with the expression

> **Forms!frmOrderStatus!cboEmployee Or Forms!frmOrderStatus! cboEmployee Is Null**

3. Save and close the query.

Retest the multi-criteria selection process as follows:

1. Click the Show All button. All records are displayed, and all combo boxes are blank.

2. Select Alfreds Futterkiste from the Customer combo box. The six orders for the customer are displayed (see Figure 35.12a).

3. Select Peacock, Margaret from the Employee combo box. The two orders for the customer that are handled by this employee are displayed (see Figure 35.12b).

FIGURE 35.12

You can select records using one combo box (a), and then narrow the selection with the second combo box (b).

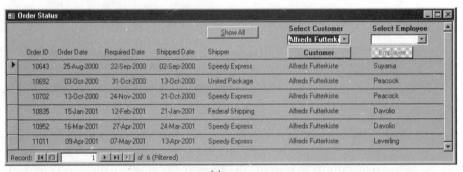

(a)

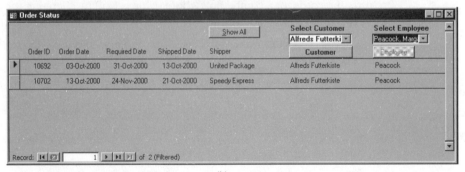

(b)

Adding a Null Row to a Selection Combo List

The multiple criteria selection process works, but there is an additional refinement you may want to make. After you select a value for one of the combo boxes, you should be able to reset the value of this combo box to null and remove part of the filter. For example, after you select orders for a specific customer and employee, you should be able either to view all of the orders for the customer by simply selecting a null row in the Employee combo box, or to view all the orders handled by an employee by selecting a null row in the Customer combo box.

Adding a Null Row by Using a Union Query

Displaying a null row in a combo box list is more difficult than you might expect. One solution is to create a second query consisting of rows with all null values and to then combine the two queries using a special query called a *union query*. You can use a union query to combine two select queries into a single recordset that contains the rows of both the first query and the second query and eliminates duplicate rows. A union query is an SQL specific query and must therefore be created in SQL view. In this example, we'll create each of the two select queries in query design view, paste their equivalent SQL statements together, and modify the result into a union query.

Union Queries

Use a union query when you want to create a single query that contains rows from two select queries. The two select queries must have the same number of fields, and the fields must be in the same order. Corresponding fields don't need to have the same names, but they must have compatible data types.

You can create a union query in SQL view by using the UNION operator to combine the SQL statements for each select query. The operator uses the field names from the first SELECT statement.

The UNION operator eliminates duplicate rows; use the UNION ALL operator if you want to return duplicate records. If you want to sort the rows, use a single ORDER BY at the end of the last SELECT statement; the field names that you use in the sort must come from the first SELECT statement.

You can learn more about creating SQL statements by searching for *SQL* or *SQL statements* with the Office Assistant.

PART

VI

Macro Programming

Here are the steps for adding a null row to the cboCustomers combo list:

1. Switch to Design view for the Order Status form, select the cboCustomer combo box, click into its RowSource property, and click the Build button at the right of the property box. Figure 35.13a shows the query in Design view and Figure 35.13b shows the equivalent SQL statement.

2. Choose View ➤ SQL View to show the SQL statement for the query. Make sure the entire SQL statement is selected. (It should already be selected for you.) Copy it to the clipboard. You'll need this statement later when you combine the two SQL statements.

3. Modify the SQL expression by removing the reference to the table name and the ORDER BY clause, as shown below. The modified SQL statement displays two null fields in each row (see Figure 35.14). (To see this yourself, click the View button while you're in the SQL Statement window.)

```
SELECT Null AS CustomerID, Null AS CompanyName FROM Customers;
```

FIGURE 35.13

The row source for the customers combo box in Design view (a), and in SQL view (b).

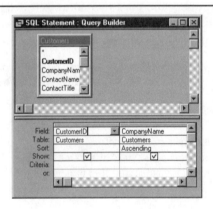

(a)

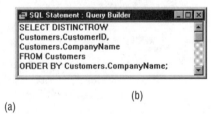

(b)

4. Close the SQL Statement window and save your changes. Then switch to Form view and click the arrow for the Customer combo box. An empty list is displayed (see Figure 35.15); if you select a row in the empty list, all customers are returned.

You now have two SQL statements: The first SQL statement (currently saved on the clipboard) produces a list with values in the CustomerID and CompanyName fields, while the second SQL statement produces a list with null values in these fields. You can combine the two lists into a single list and eliminate the duplicate null rows, so that the combined list has a single null row followed by the values.

FIGURE 35.14

The Design view for a
query that returns
null rows.

FIGURE 35.15

Using null values to
display an empty list.

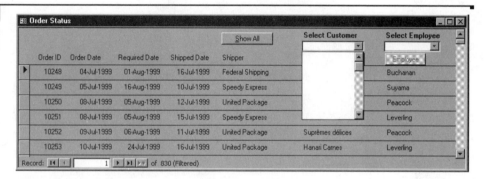

Creating the Combined List as a Union Query

You construct a union query by entering the expression for the SQL statement (without the final semicolon) that you want first in the combined list, then entering the UNION operator, and then entering the expression for the SQL statement that you want second in the combined list. The final statement must end with a semicolon.

1. Switch to Design view for the Order Status form and select the Customer combo box. Click in the RowSource property, and click the Build button, and choose View ➤ SQL View. To display the null row first in the list, use the displayed expression as the first SQL statement.

2. Delete the semicolon at the end of the SQL statement, type **UNION**, and press Ctrl+V to paste the SQL statement that you copied earlier. Delete the ORDER BY

clause (including the Customers.CompanyName that follows ORDER BY) because it is unnecessary. The final expression for the RowSource property is shown in Figure 35.16a. The datasheet view for this union query is shown in Figure 35.16b.

3. Close the SQL Statement window and save your changes.

4. Switch back to Form view and click the drop-down arrow for the Customer combo box. The first row is the null row.

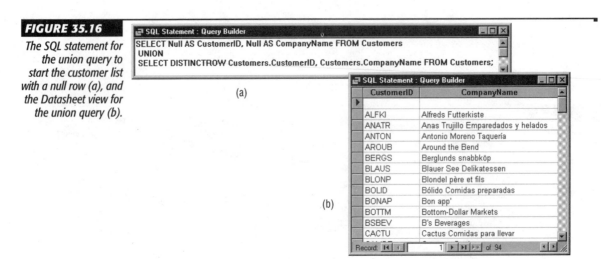

Adding a Null Row to Another Combo List

Use the same procedure to modify the SQL statement for the row source for the Employees combo box. This time the ORDER BY clause is needed to insure that the final list is in ascending order by name. Figure 35.17 shows the final result.

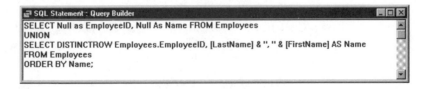

Testing the Modification

With each combo box displaying a null row, the multiple criteria selection process is much more powerful.

1. Select a customer from the Customer combo list. All orders for the customer are displayed.

2. Select an employee from the Employee combo list. Only orders for the customer that are handled by this employee are displayed.

3. Select the null row in the Customer combo list. All orders handled by the selected employee are displayed.

4. Select the null row in the Employee combo list. All orders are displayed.

You can continue to modify the frmOrderStatus form with combo boxes for each of the other fields you want to use to select records.

Finding Records to Print

The written reports you generate are important products of your application. In an order entry database, for example, you need to print invoices for individual orders, and the shipping department needs a printed order status for review.

This section shows you how to automate the selection of records for reports and the printing of reports. In Chapter 33, "Navigation with Macros," you learned how to generate a report for a single record. Now you'll learn how to generate a report for a group of records using two different methods to select the records:

- Select and display the records on a form and print a report synchronized to the form.

- Use a custom dialog to collect selection criteria from the user when the report isn't based on records displayed in a form.

Printing a Group of Records Based on the Current Form

After reviewing the status of orders using the frmOrderStatus form and selecting orders using the selection combo boxes, you can print out a report for the selected orders. First, create a simple tabular report, named rptOrderStatus, using the Report Wizard. We'll base the report on the same query that the frmOrderStatus form is based on so we can use the same filter query for both the form and the report.

1. Start the Report Wizard and, in the first screen, choose the qryOrderStatus query. Select the OrderID, OrderDate, RequiredDate, ShippedDate, Shippers_ CompanyName, Customers_CompanyName, and LastName fields. Click Next

to accept the defaults in the next four wizard screens, and then choose the Formal style. In the last screen, set the report title to rptOrderStatus, select the Modify the report's design option button, and click Finish.

2. Set the Caption property of both the report and the label in the report header to Order Status

3. Rearrange the controls and change the Caption properties for the labels as shown in Figure 35.18.

4. Save and close the report.

Even though the frmOrderStatus form and the Order Status report have the same record source, when you open each object, Access creates a separate recordset for each.

1. Open the frmOrderStatus form in Form view and select orders using the selection combo boxes.

2. In the Database window, double-click the rptOrderStatus report to open it in Print Preview. The report displays all of the orders, not just those selected using frmOrderStatus. (The form and the report have the save RecordSource property setting, but each object opens with its own independent recordset.)

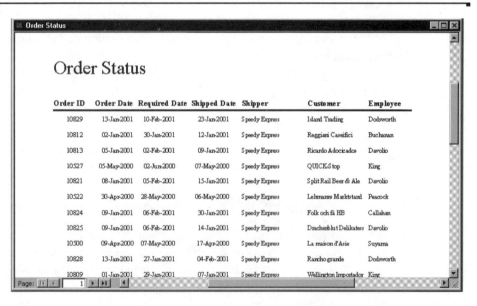

Order ID	Order Date	Required Date	Shipped Date	Shipper	Customer	Employee
10829	13-Jan-2001	10-Feb-2001	23-Jan-2001	Speedy Express	Island Trading	Dodsworth
10812	02-Jan-2001	30-Jan-2001	12-Jan-2001	Speedy Express	Reggiani Caseifici	Buchanan
10813	05-Jan-2001	02-Feb-2001	09-Jan-2001	Speedy Express	Ricardo Adocicados	Davolio
10527	05-May-2000	02-Jun-2000	07-May-2000	Speedy Express	QUICK-Stop	King
10821	08-Jan-2001	05-Feb-2001	15-Jan-2001	Speedy Express	Split Rail Beer & Ale	Davolio
10522	30-Apr-2000	28-May-2000	06-May-2000	Speedy Express	Lehmanns Marktstand	Peacock
10824	09-Jan-2001	06-Feb-2001	30-Jan-2001	Speedy Express	Folk och fä HB	Callahan
10825	09-Jan-2001	06-Feb-2001	14-Jan-2001	Speedy Express	Drachenblut Delikatess	Davolio
10500	09-Apr-2000	07-May-2000	17-Apr-2000	Speedy Express	La maison d'Asie	Suyama
10828	13-Jan-2001	27-Jan-2001	04-Feb-2001	Speedy Express	Rancho grande	Dodsworth
10809	01-Jan-2001	29-Jan-2001	07-Jan-2001	Speedy Express	Wellington Importador	King

Design the Macro to Synchronize the Report to the Form

Because the frmOrderStatus form and the rptOrderStatus report are based on the same record source, you can synchronize the report to the form by applying the same filter query to the report that you used to select records for the form qfltOrderStatus. You can automate the process by placing a command button named cmdPrint in the form header and creating a macro that applies the filter when the report is opened (see Table 35.6).

MACRO NAME	ACTION	ACTION ARGUMENTS
TABLE 35.6: A MACRO TO OPEN AND SYNCHRONIZE A REPORT		
cmdPrint_Click		
	OpenReport	Report Name: rptOrderStatus
		View: Print Preview
		Filter Name: qfltOrderStatus

Before printing a report, however, we want to determine if there are any records to print. There are a few ways to determine whether there are any records in the selection. One way is to use the report's NoData event to determine if there are any orders for the customer handled by the specified employee. The NoData event occurs when Access recognizes that the record source for the report has no records. If the recordset is empty, the report recognizes the NoData event immediately following its Open event and before its Activate event. You'll use the NoData event to trigger another macro, one that displays a message and then executes the CancelEvent action to cancel the subsequent steps that Access would take to format and print the report with no records. The macro determines whether one or both combo boxes have null values and displays different messages, depending on which combo box combination you've selected:

- Both a customer and an employee
- A customer but not an employee
- An employee but not a customer
- Neither a customer nor an employee

You can create messages that refer to the selected customer and employee by concatenating the combo box values with message text.

The flow diagram for the cmdPrint_Click macro (which runs when you click the Print button) and the Report_NoData macro (which is triggered when the recordset is empty) is shown in Figure 35.19. Table 35.7 shows the Report_NoData macro. The combo boxes on the frmOrderStatus form hold the values of the CustomerID and the EmployeeID and display the values of the CompanyName and the employee's name. We want the macro's messages to use the values displayed by the combo boxes. The displayed values are in the second column of each combo list, so we use the column property to specify the second column. Because the column property is zero-based, we use Column(1) to specify the second column.

FIGURE 35.19

A flow diagram for two macros: a macro that selects records for a report by applying a filter and a macro that stops the print process and displays separate messages when there are no orders for the selected customer or employee.

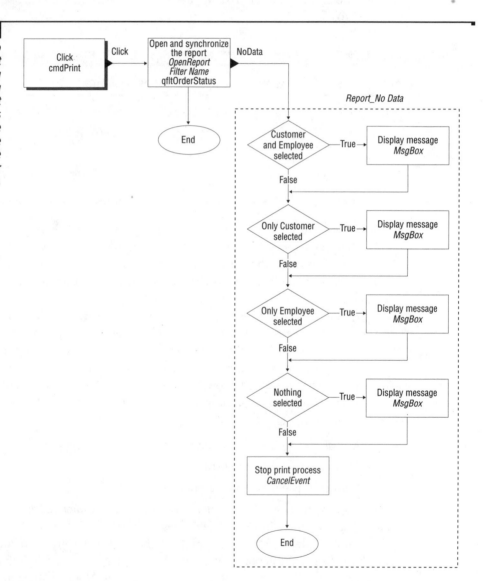

TABLE 35.7: THE MACRO TRIGGERED BY THE REPORT'S NODATA EVENT

MACRO NAME	CONDITION	ACTION	ACTION ARGUMENTS
Report_NoData			
	Not IsNull(Forms! frmOrderStatus!cbo- Customer) And Not IsNull(Forms!frmOrder Status!cboEmployee)	MsgBox	Message: ="There are no orders for the customer named " & Forms!frmOrder- Status!cboCustomer.Column(1) & " handled by the employee named " & Forms!frmOrderStatus! cboEmployee.Column(1)
	Not IsNull(Forms! frmOrderStatus!cbo- Customer) And IsNull (Forms!frmOrderStatus !cboEmployee)	MsgBox	Message: ="There are no orders for the customer named " & Forms!frmOrder- Status!cboCustomer.Column(1)
	IsNull(Forms!frmOrder Status!cboCustomer) And Not IsNull(Forms! frmOrderStatus! cboEmployee)	MsgBox	Message: ="There are no orders handled by the employee named " & Forms!frmOrderStatus! cboEmployee.Column(1)
	IsNull(Forms!frmOrder Status!cboCustomer) And IsNull(Forms! frmOrderStatus! cboEmployee)	MsgBox	Message: There are no orders.
		CancelEvent	

To place a Print button on frmOrderStatus and then create a macro to open and synchronize the Order Status report to the form by applying the form's filter to the report, follow these steps:

1. Click the mfrmOrderStatus macro sheet, enter the macro in Table 35.6, and save the macro sheet. Next, you'll create the macro from Table 35.7 that displays a message and then cancels the printing operation when there are no records.

2. Open a new macro sheet named mrptOrderStatus, enter the macro shown in Table 35.7, and save the macro sheet.

3. Open the frmOrderStatus form in Design view. Place a command button in the form's header section; set the Name property to cmdPrint and the Caption property to &Print.

4. Assign the mfrmOrderStatus.cmdPrint_Click macro to the OnClick event property of the command button. Save the form and switch to Form view.

5. Select the first customer and the employee named Margaret Peacock, then click the Print button. The report for these orders is displayed.

6. Switch to Design view of the report, click in the OnNoData event for the report, and then select the mrptOrderStatus.Report_NoData macro.

7. Save and close the report.

8. Select the customer named Bottom Dollar Market and the employee named Laura Callahan, then click the Print button. Access displays a message telling the user that there are no orders (see Figure 35.20). Click OK and make several other selections to display the messages.

9. Close the rptOrderStatus report.

10. Close the frmOrderStatus form.

FIGURE 35.20

The message displayed when there are no orders for the selected customers handled by the selected employee.

Using a Custom Dialog to Select Records

Instead of using a form to select and display the records that you want to print, you can create a custom dialog to collect selection criteria from the user and use these values as criteria for a filter query that selects the records for the report.

 TIP The custom dialog technique is useful for routine reports when there is no need to view the records in a form before printing the reports; the performance of your application improves because using the custom dialog eliminates the time used to display the form.

 TIP The Customer Labels dialog form lets you select customer labels for all countries or for one specific country (see Figure 35.21a). The form is powered by macros in the Customer Labels dialog macro sheet. These macros use the Where Condition argument of the OpenReport action to select records. The Customer Labels report can be opened independently to list labels for all customers.

The NorthwindMacros application uses customer dialog forms to collect user input as follows:

- The Sales by Year Dialog lets you specify a date range and whether the report should be a detail or summary report (see Figure 35.21b). The Sales by Year report is based on the Sales by Year query, which uses Query By Form to obtain its criteria from the Sales by Year Dialog form; this means that you can't run the Sales by Year report independently and must specify a date range using the Sales by Year Dialog. (The report is powered by VBA procedures which format the report depending on whether you checked the Show Details check box on the dialog form.)

- The Sales Reports dialog lets you specify any of three reports (see Figure 35.21c): the Employee Sales by Country report is based on a parameter query and displays default input boxes to collect user input for the date interval for the report, the Sales Totals by Amount report requires no user input, and the Sales by Category report uses the `Where Condition` argument of the `OpenReport` method to select records.

FIGURE 35.21

The NorthwindMacros database uses custom dialogs to select customer labels (a), to specify a date range for a sales report (b), and to specify one of three sales reports (c).

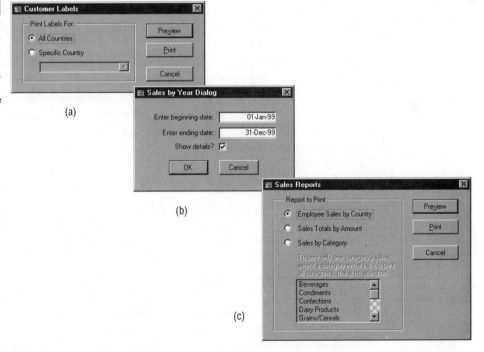

PART

VI

Macro Programming

These custom dialog forms use two basic techniques to select records:

Parameter query as the record source   In this technique the report's record source is a parameter query that requires input either from a default dialog or custom dialog. In this technique the report cannot be run without entering input into the dialog.

OpenReport macro action   In this technique the OpenReport macro action (or the OpenReport VBA method) uses the Where Condition argument to select records based on user input in the custom dialog. In this technique, the report can be run independently without displaying a dialog because the report's underlying record source is not used to specify selection criteria.

The second technique is more flexible because it allows the report to be used either with or without a custom dialog. Recall that there are two action arguments for the OpenReport action that you can use to restrict records: the Where Condition and the Filter Name arguments. When the selection criterion is based on a single expression, such as

```
Country = Screen.ActiveForm.[Select Country]
```

the Where Condition works well; however, when the selection criteria become more complicated, it is easier to create a filter query and use the Filter Name argument to apply the filter instead. The filter query obtains its selection criteria from the custom dialog form using Query By Form.

As an example, we'll create a custom dialog to select records for a new report that displays sales information by customer and by employee. The dialog provides choices for the customer and employee, and then prints only the orders corresponding to the selection. In this section, you'll create a custom dialog to select orders for all customers and a specific employee, one customer and all employees, one customer and one employee, and all customers and all employees.

Create the new report as follows:

1. Open the Sales by Category query in Design view and drag the CustomerID and EmployeeID fields from the Orders table to the design grid. CustomerID and EmployeeID are lookup fields; when included in the report, the CustomerID field looks up and displays the CompanyName, and the EmployeeID field looks up and displays the employee's LastName.

2. Check the criteria in the OrderDate column of the query to make sure that the date range there will pick up records in your copy of NorthwindMacros. (The Sales by Category query in the Northwind database that comes with Access looks for records in 1997. The database includes orders in that year. The same query in the NorthwindMacros database on the CD in the back of this book looks for dates in 1999. The dates for the order records in the CD database have been changed so the earliest records fall in 1999.)

3. Save the new query as qrySales.

4. Use the AutoReport: Tabular Wizard to create a new report based on the qrySales query and save the report as rptSales. Switch to Design view. Delete the CategoryID control and its label. Change the report's Caption property and the Caption property of the title label in the report header to Sales by Customer and Employee. Rearrange the controls as shown in Figure 35.22.

FIGURE 35.22

The rptSales report.

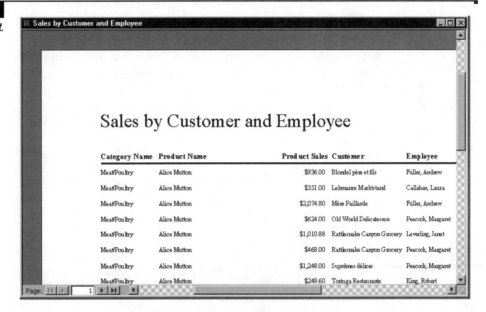

Create a Filter Query for the Report

When you are working with a form, you can create a filter while the form is in Form view, because the filter commands (Advanced Filter/Sort, Apply Filter/Sort, and Remove Filter/Sort) are available. However, the filter commands are not available for a report, so you work with the report's underlying record source to create the filter.

A filter query must include all of the tables that contain fields in the report or form that you are applying the filter to and all of the fields in the report or form. When you create the filter query, either drag all of the fields in the report's (or form's) field list to the design grid, or set the query's OutputAllFields property to Yes to show all of the fields in the query's data source. With the OutputAllFields property set to Yes, the only fields that must be shown in the filter query's design grid are the ones you are

PART

VI

Macro Programming

using to sort by or specify criteria for. (When you save a filter as a query, the OutputAllFields is automatically set to Yes.)

Create a Filter Query Based on the Report's Record Source

After determining the report's record source, you create a filter query to specify criteria for the Customer and Employee fields.

1. In the Database window, select the query qrySales, click the arrow on the New Object button in the toolbar, and then select the Query button and click OK. The query design window opens with the field list for qrySales in the upper pane.

2. Choose View ➤ Properties (or right-click in the upper pane and select the Properties command, or click the Properties button on the toolbar), click in the OutputAllFields property, and choose Yes. With the OutputAllFields property set to Yes, the datasheet includes all of the query fields (regardless of which fields are displayed in the design grid). In this example, you'll use the Customer and Employee fields to collect the user's choices.

3. Select the CustomerID and EmployeeID fields and drag them to the design grid. The selection criteria for these fields will come from the custom dialog that you create next.

4. Save the query as qfltSales (see Figure 35.23).

FIGURE 35.23

When you create a filter query, set the OutputAllFields property to display all the query fields.

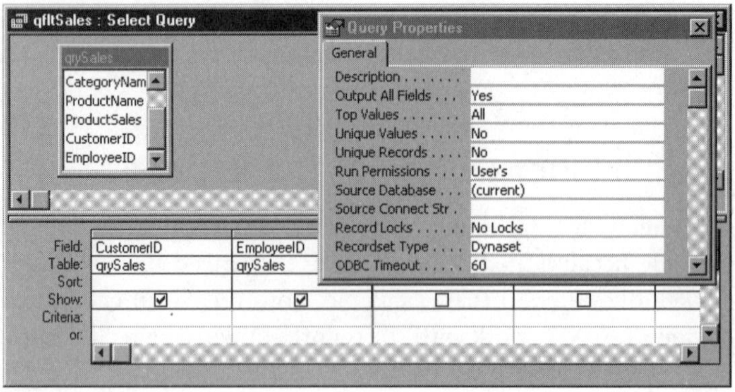

Creating a Custom Dialog

We'll create a custom dialog and set the form properties so that the form has the look and feel of a standard Windows dialog, with one exception: While you are developing the application, let the PopUp property remain at the default No value so you can switch between Design and Form view and use the menus and toolbars. When you are finished with the development stage, you can set the PopUp property to Yes to prevent access to the menus and toolbars.

1. Create a new blank form named fdlgSales and set the Caption property to Select Sales by Customer or Employee.

2. Set the following custom dialog form properties:

Property	Setting	Property	Setting
Default View	Single Form	Border Style	Dialog
Views Allowed	Form	Modal	Yes
Scroll Bars	Neither	Control Box	No
Record Selectors	No	Min Max Buttons	None
Navigation Buttons	No	Close Button	No
Auto Center	Yes	Shortcut Menu	No

You'll want to place unbound list boxes for customer and employee selection on the dialog. Design both list boxes to display an empty first row using the techniques you learned earlier, in the section, "Using Multiple Criteria to Select a Group of Records." When you choose the null value for a list box, the filter query returns records with all values for that list box. In fact, we can reuse the combo boxes for the frmOrderStatus form; we'll paste them to the dialog, change them from combo boxes to list boxes, and delete the macros that are pasted along with the combo boxes. (If you didn't create the combo boxes earlier, you can create them now.)

1. Open the frmOrderStatus form in Design view, select the Customer and Employee combo boxes and their labels, and copy them to the clipboard. Close the form.

2. Click into the dialog form and paste the clipboard contents.

3. Select the Customer combo box and choose Format ➤ Change To ➤ List Box. Change the Name property to lstCustomer and delete the AfterUpdate event property setting.

4. Similarly, change the Employee combo box to a list box, change the Name property to lstEmployee, and delete the AfterUpdate event property setting.

Placing Command Buttons on the Dialog

Place command buttons to display the report in Print Preview, print the report directly, and close the dialog.

1. Place three command buttons on the fdlgSales form and set the following properties for the two buttons:

Name	Caption
cmPreview	Print Pre&view
cmdPrint	&Print
cmdClose	&Close

2. Switch to Form view, choose Window ➤ Size to Fit Form, and then choose File ➤ Save (see Figure 35.24).

FIGURE 35.24

The custom dialog to select customers or employees.

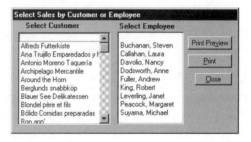

Setting Criteria for the Filter Query

The selection criteria expressions for the qfltSales filter query are based on the values you select in the list boxes. If you don't select a customer, or if you select the null value, the filter query returns sales for all customers. If you don't select an employee, or if you select the null value, the filter query returns sales for all employees. The criteria expressions are similar to those you created earlier to select records for the frmOrderStatus form depending on the values in the two combo boxes.

1. Open the qfltSales query in Design view, click the Criteria cell for CustomerID, and type the expression

   `Forms!fdlgSales!lstCustomer Or Forms!fdlgSales!lstCustomer Is Null`

2. Click in the Criteria cell for EmployeeID and type the expression

   `Forms!fdlgSales!lstEmployee Or Forms!fdlgSales!lstEmployee Is Null`

3. Save the query.

Creating the Macros for the Buttons on the Dialog

The fdlgSales dialog collects criteria for selecting one set of sales records to print. When you click the Print Preview button, a macro hides the dialog, opens the rptSales report, and applies the filter query to the report's underlying query. Because the dialog must remain open in order to provide the selection criteria to the filter query, you hide rather than close it. When you close the report window, another macro triggered by the report's Close event unhides the dialog. Table 35.8 shows the macro for the Print Preview button, which opens the report, and the macro for the report, which unhides the dialog.

TABLE 35.8: THE MACRO FOR THE PRINT PREVIEW BUTTON AND TO UNHIDE THE DIALOG

MACRO NAME	ACTION	ACTION ARGUMENTS
CmdPreview_Click		
	SetValue	Item: Screen.ActiveForm.Visible
		Expression: No
	OpenReport:	Report Name: rptSales
		View: Print Preview
		Filter Name: qfltSales
Report_Close		
	SetValue	Item: Forms!fdlgSales.Visible
		Expression: Yes

The macro for the Print button doesn't display the report, so the macro opens the rptSales report without hiding the dialog and then applies the filter query to the report's underlying query. The macro for the Close button uses the Close action to close the form. Table 35.9 shows the macros for the Print and Close buttons.

TABLE 35.9: THE MACRO TO PRINT THE REPORT WITHOUT DISPLAYING IT

MACRO NAME	ACTION	ACTION ARGUMENTS
cmdPrint_Click		
	OpenReport:	Report Name: rptSales
		View: Print
		Filter Name: qfltSales
CmdClose_Click		
	Close	

PART

VI

Macro Programming

1. Open a new macro sheet and save it as mrptSales. You store the macro triggered by the report's Close event in this macro sheet. Enter the Report_Close macro from Table 35.8.

2. Save and close the macro sheet.

3. Open a new macro sheet and save it as mfdlgSales. You store the macros for the cmdPreview and cmdPrint buttons in this macro sheet.

4. Enter the cmdPreview_Click macro from Table 35.8 and both macros from Table 35.9. Then save the macro sheet.

5. Assign the cmdPreview_Click, cmdPrint_Click, and cmdClose_Click macros to the OnClick event property of the cmdPreview, cmdPrint, and cmdClose command buttons respectively.

6. Save the dialog form and switch to Form view.

Attach and Test the Macros

1. Select a Customer from the first list box and click the Print Preview button. The report opens in Print Preview with the selected sales information.

2. When the Print Preview window opens, switch to Design view and set the report's OnClose property to mrptSales.Report_Close.

3. Save the report and switch to Report Preview.

4. Close the report. The fdlgSales dialog is unhidden.

5. Click the Print Preview button without making any list box selections. The report opens in Print Preview with all sales.

6. Close the report.

7. Select the Alfreds Futterkiste customer and the employee named Fuller, and then click the Print Preview button. There are no sales for this combination, so a report with no data is generated.

Creating a Macro for the NoData Event

You can use the NoData event, recognized by the rptSales report when there are no sales records, to trigger a macro that displays a message and cancels the printing process (see Table 35.10).

TABLE 35.10: A MACRO TO CANCEL THE OPENING OF A REPORT		
MACRO NAME	ACTION	ACTION ARGUMENTS
Report_NoData		
	MsgBox	Message: There are no sales records for this customer handled by the selected employee.
	CancelEvent	

1. Open the mrptSales macro sheet and enter the macro in Table 35.10. Close and save the macro sheet.

2. Click the rptSales report and switch to Design view. Click the NoData event and select the mrptSales.Report_NoData macro.

3. Save and close the report.

4. Select the Alfreds Futterkiste customer and the employee named Fuller, and then click the Print Preview button. Access displays the message (see Figure 35.25), cancels the printing process, and unhides the dialog.

FIGURE 35.25

The message displayed when the report has no data.

Modifying a Group of Records

You can automate the modification of groups of records in two ways:

Action Queries   You can create an action query to add, delete, or update groups of records; and you can then use the OpenQuery macro action to run the query.

SQL Statements   You can create an SQL statement to change a group of records, and you can use the RunSQL macro action to run the SQL statement.

Normally you get better performance by creating the action query in query Design view, storing the result as a saved action query and then using the OpenQuery macro action to run the query. When you save a query, Jet (the Microsoft Access database engine) analyzes the query and saves an optimized execution plan, along with the query; Jet can later use the execution plan to run the saved query. By contrast, when you use the RunSQL macro action to run an SQL statement, Jet must optimize the SQL statement on-the-fly each time you run the SQL statement.

Using the OpenQuery Action to Run an Action Query

When you are creating a new record and the new record has fields with the same values as the previous records, you can speed data entry by having the fields in the new record filled in automatically. In Chapter 34, "Data Maintenance with Macros," you used a macro to set the DefaultValue property for controls whose values you want to carry to the new record. Those settings are temporary and cease to exist when you close the form. Sometimes you want the most recent values entered in a data entry session to be saved when you close the form or the database, and then displayed in the data entry form the next time you open the form. In this case, the values that you want to carry to the new record must be stored in a table so they can be stored when you close the database.

Carrying Values Forward to the Next Data Entry Session

This section describes a technique for saving values between data entry sessions and carrying the values to the new record in the next data entry session. The technique is based on using a table that we'll call the *new record table* to hold the data values that you want to carry forward, and using a macro to run action queries.

Enter the new record into the new record table; when you save the new record, the macro runs an append query to add the record to the data table, and runs an update query to save only the values in the new record table that you want to carry forward and to set to null those fields that you don't want to carry forward.

As an example, we'll set up the technique for new products in the Northwind-Macros database. We'll plan to carry forward to the next data entry session only the values in the SupplierID, CategoryID, and QuantityPerUnit fields. We'll create a new form for data entry. (You could modify the Products form, but it is easier to create a new form.)

Creating the New Record Table

1. In the Database window, copy the Products table and paste it (structure only) as tblNewProduct. The new record table is designed to contain only a single record: either the new record you have entered but not yet saved, or a record with values you are carrying forward.

2. Open the table in Design view. Remove the primary key index for the ProductID field and change the field type to Number. Click the ProductName field and set the Required property to No. Save the table.

The tblNewProduct table stores only a single record and doesn't need a primary key. Because we don't want to carry the ProductName forward to the new record, the ProductName field in tblNewProduct will be null after the macro runs. This means that we must change the Required property to No so we can save the record to tblNewProduct table. We can make sure that the record that we save to the Products table has a non-null value for the ProductName field by validating the field using a macro instead of validating the field using the Required property.

Creating the Data Entry Form   Next, we'll create a new form for entering data into the tblNewProduct table.

1. In the Database window, copy the Products form and paste it as frmNewProduct. Open this new form in Design view, delete the BeforeUpdate property setting you added in Chapter 34, and set the following properties:

RecordSource	tblNewProduct
Caption	NewProduct
NavigationButtons	No

2. Place a command button in the header of frmNewProduct, set the Name property to cmdSave, and the Caption property to &Save.

3. Select and delete the ProductID control and its label. The macro takes care of setting the value of the ProductID control, so this control doesn't need to appear on the data entry form.

4. Save the form and switch to Form view (see Figure 35.26).

FIGURE 35.26

The new data entry form for products has the temporary table for its record source.

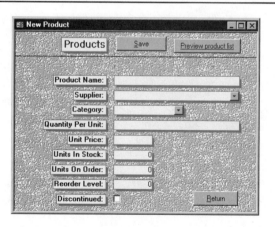

Creating the Action Queries   You create two queries: an append query to append the new data record to the Products table, and an update query that sets to null those data fields that you don't want to carry forward.

1. Create a new query based on tblNewProduct; use the asterisk method to select and drag all the fields to the first Field cell of the query. Click the Query type button in the toolbar and choose Append; enter Products as the name of the table to append the data to. Save the query as qappProduct (see Figure 35.27a).

2. Create a second query based on tblNewProduct. Drag all fields except SupplierID, CategoryID, and QuantityPerUnit to the design grid. (You should drag to the design grid all of the fields for which you are not carrying values to the new record.)

3. Click the Query type button in the toolbar and choose Update. Enter Null in the Update To cell of each field. Save the query as qupdProduct (see Figure 35.27b).

FIGURE 35.27

The append query appends data to the Products table (a), and the update query sets to Null the fields whose values are not carried forward (b).

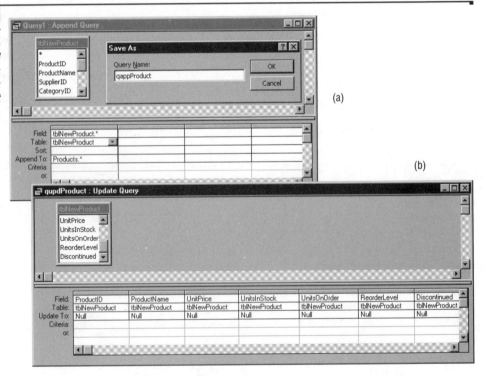

Creating the Macro   Next, you'll create a macro for the cmdSave button on the frmNewProduct form. The macro validates the data, sets the primary key value, saves the record to the tblNewProduct table, and then runs the action queries (see Table 35.11). The macro validates the data by testing for an entry in the ProductName field. If the field is null, the macro displays a message, places the insertion point in the ProductName control, and terminates. If the field is not null, the macro sets the ProductID value to a number that is one greater than the largest ProductID value in the Products table. (The SetValue action uses the DMax() domain aggregate function to determine the largest value in the table). The macro uses the SetWarnings action to turn off the default confirmation messages that Access displays before running an action query, and then runs the queries.

TABLE 35.11: A MACRO TO FILL A NEW RECORD WITH DATA FROM A PREVIOUS RECORD

MACRO NAME	CONDITION	ACTION	ACTION ARGUMENTS
cmdSave_Click			
	IsNull(ProductName)	MsgBox	Message: You must enter a product name before saving the record.
	...	GoToControl	ProductName
	...	StopMacro	
		SetValue	Item:ProductID
			Expression: DMax("Product ID","Products") + 1
		SetWarnings	Warnings On: No
		RunCommand	Command: SaveRecord
		OpenQuery	Query Name: qappProduct
		OpenQuery	Query name: qupdProduct

1. Open a new macro sheet named mfrmNewProduct and create the macro shown in Table 35.11.

2. Assign the macro to the Click event of the cmdSave button, save the frmNewProduct form, and switch to Form view.

Testing the Technique To test the technique:

1. Open the frmNewProduct form, enter data for a new product (see Figure 35.28a), and click the Save button. If you entered a value in the ProductName control, the record is saved to the Products table, and frmNewProduct displays a new record with the specified fields filled in with values from the previous record (see Figure 35.28b). If you didn't enter a value in the ProductName control, the custom message is displayed and the macro terminates (see Figure 35.29).

2. Open the Products table and verify that the new record has been added.

3. Open the tblNewProduct table and observe the single record storing the values that we want to carry forward.

FIGURE 35.28

Use the new data entry form to enter a new record into the temporary table (a). After you save the new record, the three values are carried forward (b).

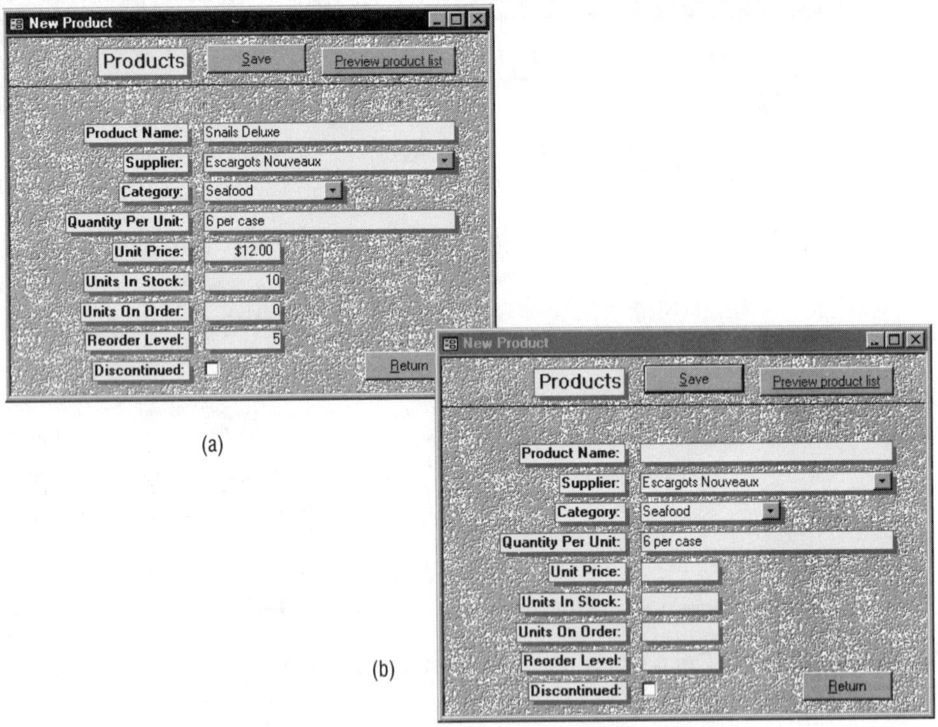

(a)

(b)

Summary

This chapter has introduced you to macro techniques for working with groups of records. You learned these important techniques:

- You can automate simple and complex sorts using macros to set the OrderBy and OrderByOn properties of a form.

- A simple way to find a group of records that satisfy a set of criteria is to use Query By Form. Use combo boxes or list boxes to provide choices and hold the selected values. Macros assigned to their AfterUpdate event properties run filter queries that use the values in the combo boxes or list boxes to select records.

- You can use a union query to display an empty row in a combo box or list box.

- You can use a form to select a group of records and base a report on the selected records; in the simplest method, the report has the same record source as the form.

- You can create a custom dialog form for collecting selection criteria for a report. A macro uses the input to filter the record source for the report. In this method, the report's record source is not modified.

- You can carry data values forward to another data entry session using a technique that enters data into a new record table and uses a macro to append the new data to the data table. The new record table stores the values until the next time you open the data entry form.

You have now completed the chapters that cover macro programming. These chapters have covered the most important macro techniques and have demonstrated the fundamental approach to macro programming:

You can design most macros by observing the interactive steps you take to accomplish a task and then translate your steps to macro instructions.

PART

VI

Macro Programming

You now have the skills to modify the techniques presented in this book and to create your own techniques. If you are new to programming, you should spend several weeks or months using macros to automate your databases. When you are thoroughly comfortable with macros and have a good understanding of the events that objects recognize, you'll be ready to continue on with VBA programming. See *Access 2000 VBA Handbook*, by Susann Novalis and Dana Jones (Sybex, 1999) to expand your knowledge in this area. Good luck with your Access programming endeavors!

PART VII

Appendices

LEARN TO

- *Install Microsoft Access*

- *Prepare Access databases*

- *Use the CD-ROM*

- *Install Fulfill 2000*

APPENDIX <u>A</u>

Installing Microsoft Access

You must install Microsoft Access 2000 before you can use it to manage your data. This appendix briefly explains how to install Access on a single-user computer.

 NOTE The single-user installation procedures might differ slightly, depending on whether you're installing Access as part of Microsoft Office Professional and whether you're installing it from its own CD-ROM.

Be sure to check the materials that come with your Access program for specific installation instructions, late-breaking news, and more details than we can provide in this appendix. For the most up-to-date information available, see the Readme file on your Office 2000 or Access CD-ROM. You can also find additional instructions for special types of installations in the Readme file for the Office Resource Kit.

Checking Your Hardware

Before you install Access, you need to find out if your hardware meets these requirements:

- A Pentium with at least 32MB of memory.
- About 200MB of hard disk space for a typical Office 2000 installation. Of course, you'll need extra space for your databases and/or projects.
- Windows 95, Windows 98, or Windows NT Workstation 4.0 with Service Pack 3.0. (Office 2000 does not work with Windows 3.*x* or Windows NT Workstation 3.5*x*.)
- A VGA or higher monitor. Super VGA with 256 colors is recommended.
- A Microsoft mouse, Microsoft IntelliMouse, or compatible pointing device.

 NOTE If you're installing Microsoft Access on Windows NT, you must be the Administrator or have Administrator privileges.

Preparing Your Access 1.*x*, 2.*x*, Access 95, and Access 97 Databases

Please read this section if you have old Access version 1.0 or 1.1 (1.*x*), version 2.0, version 7 (Access 95), or version 8 (Access 97) databases. If you're installing Access for the first time and do not have any old databases, feel free to skip ahead to the next section.

To use your old databases in Microsoft Access 2000, you can either convert them to the new format or use them in their original format.

- **Convert the old databases to the new format**. Doing so allows you to take full advantage of all the new features in Access. However, you should not convert your databases if others must use them with Access 1.*x*, 2.0, 7 (Access 95), or 8 (Access 97).

- **Use the old databases *without* converting them to the new format**. This method, called *enabling* the databases, allows people to view and update the databases with older versions of Access. However, it does not let you change database objects or create new ones in Microsoft Access 2000. In secure databases (see Chapter 19), you also can't change or add permissions unless you convert the old database to the new format.

 WARNING In general, databases will work more efficiently if you convert them to Microsoft Access 2000 format. Remember, however, that if you do convert your databases, they can't be used with Access 1.*x*, 2.0, 7, or 8. Of course, you can restore the old databases from backup copies you made before you converted. Or, you can use the new Convert to Previous feature to turn an Access 2000 database back into an Access 8 file.

Regardless of whether you decide to convert or enable your old databases, you must do these quick preparation steps *before* removing your previous version of Access.

1. Back up any databases you plan to convert. *Do not skip this step!*

2. If you're using Access 2.0, 7 (Access 95), or 8 (Access 97), skip to step 3. If you're using Access 1.*x*, you should be aware of and compensate for the following:

   - **Backquote character (') in object names**. Backquotes aren't allowed in Microsoft Access 2000 object names, and they'll prevent you from converting your database or opening the object in Access 2000. You must use Access 1.*x* to rename such objects before converting or using them in Access 2000.

- **Indexes and relationships**. Microsoft Access 2000 tables are limited to 32 indexes each. You won't be able to convert your databases if any tables exceed that limit. If necessary, delete some relationships or indexes in complex tables before converting the database.

- **Modules named ADO, DAO, VBA, or Access**. Modules with these names will prevent a database from converting because they are names of *type libraries* that Access references automatically. You'll need to change these module names before converting any databases that use them.

3. Use Access 1.*x*, 2.0, 7 (Access 95), or 8 (Access 97), as appropriate, to open your database and then open all of your forms and reports in design view. Click the Module tab of the database window.

4. Open any module in design view and then choose Run ➤ Compile Loaded Modules. If your database doesn't contain any modules, click the New button to create a blank module, and then choose Run ➤ Compile Loaded Modules. This step will ensure that all of your modules are fully compiled.

5. Close and save all of your forms, reports, and modules, and then close your database.

6. Repeat steps 2 through 5 for each database you want to convert.

7. Back up your databases again to preserve your work.

Now you're ready to install Microsoft Access 2000. After installing Access, you can convert or enable your databases, as explained later in this appendix under "Enabling and Converting Access Databases."

For more information about conversion issues, look up topics under *Conversion* in the Microsoft Access Answer Wizard. You also may want to search the Microsoft Knowledge Base for late-breaking information on conversion issues. The Knowledge Base is available on CompuServe (GO MSKB), the Microsoft Network (Use the Find tools to search for Knowledge Base.), and the Microsoft Internet servers at www.microsoft .com and ftp.microsoft.com. Chapter 4 offers more details about the Microsoft Knowledge Base and other sources of technical information about Access and other Microsoft products.

Installing Access on a Single-User Computer

Installing Access for use on a single computer is quite easy. Here are the basic steps:

1. Start your computer and make sure other programs are not running.

WARNING   When installing Access, be sure to do so on a "vanilla" system. Exit any nonstandard Windows shells or memory managers, any terminate-and-stay-resident (TSR) programs, and any virus-detection utilities. Check the Windows Taskbar and close any programs that are running. If any programs are started from your autoexec.bat file, restart your computer by choosing Start ➢ Shut Down ➢ Restart the Computer ➢ Yes. When you see the message *Starting Windows,* press F8 and choose Step-By-Step confirmation. You'll be asked whether to run each command in autoexec.bat. Press Y to run the command or N to bypass it.

2. Insert the Microsoft Office 2000 Premium Edition or your Access 2000 CD-ROM into your computer's CD-ROM drive.

3. If the Windows installer starts automatically, skip to step 6. Otherwise, click the Start button on the Windows Taskbar and then choose Run.

4. In the Command Line text box, type the name of the drive you put the setup CD-ROM in (for example, **d:**), followed by **setup** (or use the Browse button to search for the Setup program). For example, if you put Setup Disk 1 in drive D, type **d:setup**.

5. Click OK or press Enter.

 TIP   As an alternative to steps 2 through 5, you can choose Start ➢ Settings ➢ Control Panel, double-click Add/Remove Programs, and then click the Install button to start the Install Program from the Floppy Disk or CD-ROM Wizard. When the Wizard starts, follow the instructions on the screen.

6. When the Installation Wizard starts, follow the initial instructions that appear on the screen. In the first step, you'll be asked to supply your name, initials, organization, and CD Key. (The CD key should appear on a sticker on the back of your CD case.) After you make your entries, press Enter or click Next to go to the next dialog box.

7. Your Product ID will appear in the next window. Jot this number down in case you need to call Microsoft Tech Support in the future. Then review the license agreement, click I Accept the Terms in the License Agreement, and click Next.

8. In the next step, click Install Now for a typical installation. Or, click Customize if you want to select the Office components for your system. If you click the latter option, you'll get a chance to change the default folder for the Office files. To use the default folder, click Next. You'll see a window similar to the one in Figure A.1. (The window title may be different, depending on whether you've installed Access before.) Each Office component in the window has its own Expand button and drop-down list. The drop-down lists have these options:

Run from My Computer Installs the program files for the selected option on your computer.

Run all from My Computer Installs the files for all the components of the selected application onto your computer so you don't have to set this option for each individual component.

Run from CD Tells Setup to read the program files for the selected application from the CD when they are needed.

Run all from CD Runs all the components of the selected application from the CD. If you choose this option, you don't have to specify it individually for each component of the application.

Not Available Makes this option unavailable.

Installed on First Use Copies any necessary files from the CD to your computer the first time you use the selected feature.

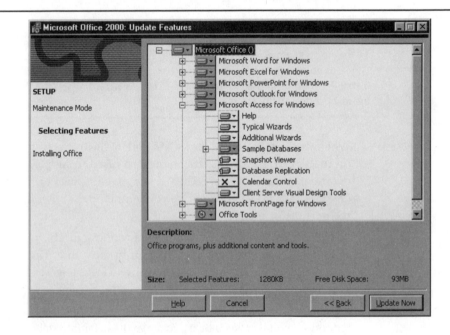

TABLE A.1: MICROSOFT ACCESS COMPONENTS THAT YOU CAN INSTALL	
COMPONENT	**DESCRIPTION**
Microsoft Access	The Access program and minimum utilities needed to run it. This option is required for an initial installation of Access.
Help	Online Help and language reference files.
Typical Wizards	The easy to use question-and-answer tools that help you create tables, forms, reports, queries, and so on. Use the Add-In Manager (described in Chapter 16) to install or uninstall wizards that you've purchased separately from Access.
Additional Wizards	Tools that let you perform advanced tasks like converting macros to Visual Basic code and documenting databases.
Sample Databases	The sample databases and applications that Microsoft supplies with Access, including Northwind and Solutions.
Snapshot Viewer	A tool that lets you view, print, and mail Access reports as report snapshots.
Database Replication	The feature that lets you keep different copies of databases in sync (see Chapter 18).
Calendar Control	The OLE custom control and associated Help files that let you create fully programmable calendars in your forms and reports (see Chapter 13).
Client Server Visual Design Tools	These tools let you design tables, database diagrams, and queries for SQL Server databases from Access.

9. Use the drop-down lists to adjust the installation settings for any components you want to change. Then click Install Now.

10. Depending on how many options you chose to install on your computer, Setup will take anywhere from a few minutes to several minutes to update your system. Wait patiently for this task to finish and *don't* restart your computer in the middle of the process. (The computer isn't really dead, it's just thinking.) When Setup is finished, you'll see a message indicating that you must restart your computer. At this point click Yes.

11. After your computer restarts, a window will appear with the title Finishing Microsoft Office 2000 Setup. Once the setup is complete, the window will disappear.

After installing all the files you need, Setup will create a Microsoft Access option on the Start ➤ Programs menu. When you've completed the installation, go to Chapter 1 of this book, where you'll learn how to start Microsoft Access and get around in it.

Running Setup to Add or Remove Components

If necessary, you can run the Setup program again to add Microsoft Access components that you chose not to install initially or to delete components that you no longer need. To add or remove components, follow these steps:

1. Start the Setup program from the Microsoft Access CD-ROM or the Microsoft Office 2000 Premium Edition CD-ROM, as explained earlier.

2. Click one of these buttons in the next dialog box:

   Repair Office   Reinstalls Office to its original state.

   Add/Remove   Takes you to a screen similar to the one shown earlier in Figure A.1. From here you can change the installation settings for components you want to add or remove. (Use the Not Available option on a component's drop-down list to remove it from your system.)

   Remove Office   Removes all previously installed Office components from your hard disk.

3. Follow any instructions that appear on your screen to complete the installation or removal of components.

Enabling and Converting Old Access Databases

As mentioned earlier, you can convert your old Access 1.*x*, 2.0, 7 (Access 95), or 8 (Access 97) databases to the new Access 2000 database format, or you can just *enable* the databases for use with Access 2000 without converting them.

Enabling a Database

To enable a database that was created in an older version of Access, start Microsoft Access 2000 and open the database (see Chapter 1 if you need details). You'll see a Convert/Open Database dialog box that explains your options, as shown in Figure A.2.

FIGURE A.2

The Convert/Open Database dialog box lets you choose whether to convert a database to the new Access format or open (enable) it in its old format.

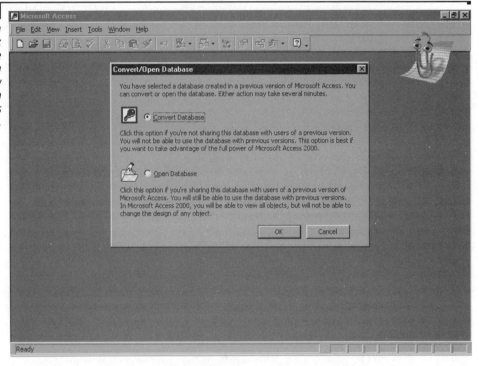

1. Choose Convert Database to convert the database to the new format, or choose Open Database to enable the database (leaving it in the old format).

2. Click OK and follow any instructions that appear.

Your database will be either converted or enabled, depending on your choice in step 1.

Converting a Database

To convert a database, you can either open it and choose the Convert Database option described above, or follow these steps:

1. Close all open databases. If you're using a network, make sure that no one else has opened the database you want to convert.

2. Choose Tools ➤ Database Utilities ➤ Convert Database ➤ To Current Database Version.

3. Locate and click the database you want to convert in the Database to Convert From dialog box. Click the Convert button.

4. Type a new name for the database in the Convert Database Into dialog box, or just select a different directory location if you want to keep the same name. Click Save.

5. Respond to any prompts that appear while Access converts your database. When conversion is complete, you can open the new database and use it normally.

After converting (or enabling) your old database, you may discover some changes in the way database objects behave; you may need to tweak your applications to make them work more smoothly.

WARNING   Once you convert a 1.*x*, 2.0, 7 (Access 95), or 8 (Access 97) database to Access 2000 format, you can't open that database in its original version. You can convert an Access 2000 database back to Access 97, if the need arises, by opening it and choosing Tools ➢ Convert Database ➢ To Prior Access Database Version.

TIP   If your database is very large, the conversion steps given above may fail. (It's rare but possible.) If that happens, create a new blank database and then try using the Import procedures discussed in Chapter 7 to import just a few objects (about 20 to 30) at a time. The Import process will convert the objects as needed.

The steps given above apply to the simple case of converting an unsecured database without linked tables on a single-user computer. For more information about conversion issues, look up *Conversion* with the Office Assistant and select the *Conversion and Compatibility Issues* topic.

APPENDIX B

About the CD-ROM

The CD-ROM that comes with this book contains sample databases, shareware, freeware, and demos for you to enjoy. To see the contents of the CD-ROM, follow these steps:

1. Put the CD in your CD-ROM drive.
2. Close any open applications so that you're just at the Windows Desktop.
3. Double-click your My Computer icon.
4. Double-click the icon for your CD-ROM drive (typically D:).

The contents of the CD are displayed in a My Computer window, looking something like Figure B.1.

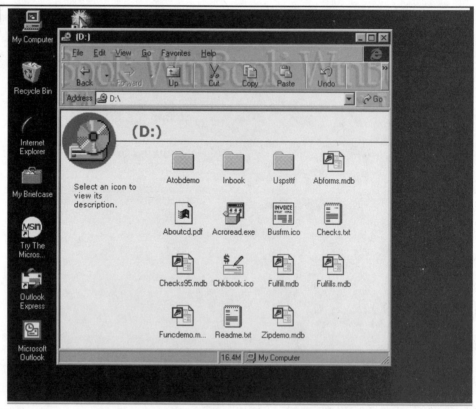

FIGURE B.1

The contents of the CD-ROM disk displayed in a My Computer window with Large Icons view.

TIP If you don't see the Large Icons view, you can just choose View ➤ Large Icons from the menu bar in the D: window. To show or hide file name extensions, choose View ➤ Options (or Folder Options), click the View tab, then either clear or check the Hide File Extensions For Known File Types option.

Opening an Access Database

Most of the files on the CD-ROM are Microsoft Access 2000 databases, as indicated by the Access icon, shown here.

If you try to open a database directly from the CD, you'll get a read-only error message. You will have to copy the databases to your hard drive and take off the read-only attribute before you can use them. Step-by-step instructions for making the copy and changing the read-only attribute follow.

Copying a Database to Your Hard Disk

If you want to be able to add, change, and delete data in one of the sample databases, you must copy the database to your hard disk, change its read-only attribute, and then run it from the hard disk. Here's how:

1. Exit to the Windows Desktop if you're in Microsoft Access.

2. Open (double-click) your My Computer icon.

3. Double-click the icon for your hard disk (typically C).

4. Double-click your My Computer icon again. Then double-click the icon for your CD-ROM drive.

5. Size and position the windows for the hard drive and CD-ROM so that you can see both the destination folder (the folder you want to copy *to*) and the object you want to copy. For example, in Figure B.2, you can see the folder named My Document on drive C (where you want to copy to) and several databases from the CD-ROM.

FIGURE B.2

The destination (My Documents in drive C: in this example) and databases from the CD-ROM visible on the Windows Desktop.

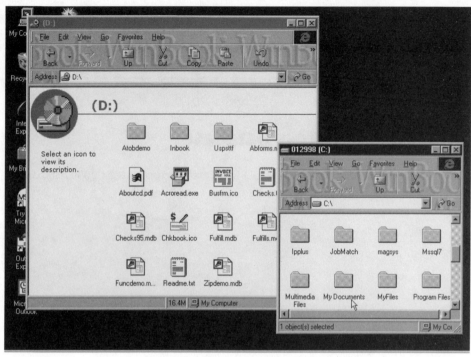

6. Drag and drop the icon for the database you want to copy from the CD-ROM drive's window over to the destination folder's icon.

7. Double-click the destination folder's icon to open a window for it. Right-click the name of the copied database and choose Properties. Then uncheck the read-only attribute, and click OK.

That's all there is to it. To run the database from your hard disk:

1. Open (double-click) the folder on your hard drive that contains the database (My Documents in this example).

2. Double-click the icon for the database you want to open.

You won't get the read-only message this time because you've opened the database on a "normal" read-write disk.

NOTE Remember that the ROM in CD-ROM stands for "read-only memory." You cannot change anything that you open directly from the CD-ROM. You can only change items that you copy to, and run from, your hard disk.

In the sections that follow, we'll describe the contents of each database.

Fulfill and FulfillS

The databases named Fulfill and FulfillS contain a sample data-entry database application that you're free to use, abuse, ignore, explore, and tinker with at will. The difference between the two is as follows:

FulfillS (or FulfillS.mdb)   The Fulfill database application with some fake data already entered. Explore from the CD or copy it to your hard disk if you want to add, change, or delete data.

Fulfill (or Fulfill.mdb)   Same as FulfillS but without the fake names and addresses, products, and orders. To use this version, first copy it to your hard disk.

Appendix C contains more information about using Fulfill 2000 with its many special bells and whistles. Chapter 29 explains how to explore Fulfill 2000 "behind the scenes" to see what makes it tick and to learn some tricks for your own custom applications.

ZipDemo and FuncDemo

The ZipDemo (or ZipDemo.mdb) database illustrates a Microsoft Access *event procedure* that does something very useful: after you type in a zip code, it autofills the city, state, and area code fields on the same form. The Fulfill databases use the same technique to do the same job.

The FuncDemo (or FuncDemo.mdb) database illustrates sample *function procedures* (also called *user-defined functions*) written in Visual Basic:

NumWord( )   Converts a number, such as *123.45*, to words, such as *One hundred twenty three and 45/100*. Cary Prague's Check Writer application uses this function to print checks.

Proper( )   A function that Access forgot. Converts any case (for example, *alan simpson, ALAN SIMPSON, aLaN SiMpsOn*) to proper noun case (*Alan Simpson*).

You can open and explore the ZipDemo and FuncDemo databases right from the CD; there's no need to copy either to the hard disk.

The Inbook Folder

The Inbook folder contains some sample databases used in examples throughout the book:

- Contact Management Lessons (or Contact Management Lessons.mdb) used in the hands-on lessons at the start of this book.
- OrdEntry9 (or OrdEntry9.mdb) is used heavily throughout the first few chapters.
- Star Search 2000 (or Star Search 2000.mdb) illustrates the use of photos in a database as described in Chapter 8.
- Chapter 21 (or Chapter 21.mdb) includes sample forms and macros.
- Chapter 23 (or Chapter 23.mdb) shows a custom dialog box for selecting print options.
- Chapter 28 OLE Automation Example (or Chapter 28 OLE Automation Example.mdb) includes Visual Basic code for creating an Excel spreadsheet from Access.
- NorthwindMacros (or NorthwindMacros.mdb) is the database used in chapters 31–35 on macro programming.

Database Creations, Inc.

Database Creations, Inc. is another valuable resource for Access users, and the company has graciously given us the rights to distribute several of its products and demonstration databases free of charge.

The Database Creations products and demos you'll find on the CD include:

- Check Writer 2000
- EZ File Manager Sampler
- EZ Search Manager Sampler
- Business Forms Library Sampler
- Cool Combo Box Techniques
- Yes! I Can Run My Business Demo
- EZ Access Developer Suite Demo

Most of the following material on these programs is from Database Creations.

Check Writer 2000 (Microsoft Network Award for Best Access Application)

Check Writer 2000 is a fully functional Check Writer, including Check Register and Check Reconciliation modules. You can pay your bills, print checks, and balance your checkbook using an incredible Access 2000 application. This application won the Microsoft Network Access Product of the Year award and is part of the full accounting system Yes! I Can Run My Business, which won the Readers Choice award given by the readers of the Microsoft Access Advisor magazine in 1998. A complete user guide is also included in the directory.

To install Check Writer 2000 and its documentation in Word format on your computer, run the file `D:\DatabaseCreations\FreeAccessSoftware\Check Writer(Award Winning)\CK2000.exe` and follow the prompts. To run the program after it's installed, choose Start ➢ Programs ➢ Database Creations Products ➢ CheckWriter2000. Use Start ➢ Programs ➢ Database Creations Products ➢ CheckWriterDoc to view the documentation for this program.

From the Check Writer Read Me File

Check Writer for Microsoft Access 2000 © 1999 Database Creations, Inc.

The main Check Writer switchboard contains four basic functions:

Check Writer/Register   Add, change, delete, or print checks, deposits, and adjustments, or display the check register.

Check Reconciliation   Display the Check Reconciliation system.

Bank Accounts   Add, change, or delete Bank Account information.

Setup   Enter your company information, recurring payees, and default bank account number.

The Check Writer comes with two sample bank accounts and a selection of transactions to get you started. You can practice with those and then create your own accounts.

You start by creating your own bank account (Bank Accounts icon), and then make that bank account the default bank account (Setup icon). Once you have done that, you can open up the Check Writer and enter transactions.

Use the buttons at the bottom of the form to navigate from record to record or between functions. Click the Register icon to display the Check Register. In the Register, click the Check icon to return to the Check Writer form to enter or edit checks.

You can change the account being viewed at any time using the combo box at the top of the Check Writer form. You can only change the transaction type for new checks and can choose between checks, deposits, and a number of adjustments that you can add to by using the Setup icon.

You can enter the payee for a check or select from the combo box in the payee line of the check. You can add more recurring payees in the Setup screen.

When you mark a check as void, a void stamp will appear on the check and it will not be counted in the Check Register or Check Reconciliation.

The area below the check is the voucher stub and anything you enter is printed when you select certain types of checks.

Click the Find button to display a dialog box showing five ways to find a check, deposit, or adjustment.

Click the Print button to display a dialog box allowing you to print the current check/deposit/adjustment, marked checks, a range of checks by date, or a range of checks by check number. You can modify the reports that print the checks for custom paper.

The Check Writer is normally $179.95. Mention *Mastering Microsoft Access 2000*, and you can buy the full product, including the mini general ledger, for only $99.95. To order this product, call Database Creations at (860) 644-5891, fax us at (860) 648-0710, or e-mail us at info@databasecreations.com. You can also look for our newest products at our Web site at www.databasecreations.com. If you want to trade up to the full Yes! I Can Run My Business accounting product, we will take up to $200 off the retail product price for the Royalty Free Developers Edition.

EZ File Manager™ Sampler

The EZ File Manager is one of eight products in the new EZ Access Developers Suite. The complete File Utilities tool, which helps you compile, compact, repair, and back up attached databases is included, along with the entire documentation set from the EZ Access File Manager to give you a complete overview of the product.

Install the sampler and then copy the form and module to your own application to add file-management capabilities to your application. Run the file D:\DatabaseCreations\FreeAccessSoftware\EZFileManagerSampler\EZ File Manager.exe to install the EZ File Manager Sampler and documentation on your computer. Then choose Start ➢ Programs ➢ Database Creations Products ➢ EZ File Manager Sampler to run the program. You can open the documentation for this program by choosing Start ➢ Programs ➢ Database Creations Products ➢ EZ File Manager Sampler Doc.

EZ Search Manager™ Sampler

The EZ Search Manager is one of eight products in the new EZ Access Developers Suite. The complete SmartSearch tool is included, along with the entire documentation set from the EZ Access Search Manager to give you a complete overview of the product.

Install the sampler and then copy the forms to your own application to add an incredibly flexible search interface to your application. Run the file `D:\DatabaseCreations\FreeAccessSoftware\EZSearchManagerSampler\EZ Search Manager.exe` to install the EZ Search Manager Sampler and documentation on your computer. Then choose Start ➤ Programs ➤ Database Creations Products ➤ EZ Search Manager Sampler to run the program. To open the documentation for this program, choose Start ➤ Programs ➤ Database Creations Products ➤ EZ Search Manager Sampler Doc.

Business Forms Library Sampler

The Access Business Forms Library Sampler is a sample of the Business Forms Library collection of 35 forms and reports. These contain some really innovative techniques that have never been seen anywhere else. The entire library contains tables, forms, reports, and macros for each of the forms and reports. You can integrate them into your own applications, saving yourself hundreds of hours of work. Microsoft liked these forms so much that they distributed this sampler in the Microsoft Access Welcome Kit with Microsoft Access 2.0. The forms have been updated for Access 2000 and come with a complete user guide.

Run the file `D:\DatabaseCreations\FreeAccessSoftware\BusinessFormsLibrarySampler\BusFrm2000.exe` to install the Business Forms Library Sampler and documentation in Word format on your computer. Then choose Start ➤ Programs ➤ Database Creations Products ➤ Business Forms Sampler 2000 to run the program.

Cool Combo Box Techniques

This is a demonstration database of 25 of the coolest combo and list box techniques. Full documentation is included in the CD directory. This comes from a highly acclaimed paper given by Cary Prague at the Microsoft Access conferences.

Run the file `D:\DatabaseCreations\FreeAccessSoftware\CoolComboBoxTechniques\Coolcombo.exe` to install the Cool Combo Box Techniques examples and documentation in Word format on your computer. To use the Cool Combo Boxes program, choose Start ➤ Programs ➤ Database Creations Products ➤ Cool Combo

Boxes 2000. If you want to view the documentation, select Start ≻ Programs ≻ Database Creations Products ≻ Cool Combo Boxes Doc.

Yes! I Can Run My Business™ Demo

Yes! I Can Run My Business is the most popular accounting software available for Microsoft Access users today. The product is fully customizable and includes all source code. It includes all typical accounting functions, including sales, customers, A/R, purchases, suppliers, A/P, inventory, banking, general ledger, fixed assets, and it features multicompany accounting for any size business. Priced at under $1,000 for a LAN version, it is one of the best values for small businesses. For developers, a version is available with royalty-free distribution rights for around $2,000.

The full product includes over 1,500 pages of professionally written documentation. Yes! I Can Run My Business won the Microsoft Access Advisor magazine Reader's Choice award for best accounting system last year.

To install the demo, run `D:\DatabaseCreations\Demos\Yes! I Can Accounting\Yes4demo.exe`. Then choose Start ≻ Programs ≻ Yes! I Can Run My Business Version 4 Plus Demo ≻ Yes! I Can Run My Business v4 Demo to run the demo.

You can copy the `D:\Database Creations\Demos\ Yes!ICanAccounting\Yes! I Can Run My Business Brochure.pdf` file to your hard drive to review the online color brochure using Adobe Acrobat. The free reader is included on this CD. The entire Yes! I Can Run My Business product retails for $599.95 for the end-user version and just $2,295 for the developer's version. Mention the code MASTCD and purchase the developer version for just $2,095.95. View additional samples at `http://www.databasecreations.com`.

EZ Access Developer Suite™ Demo

The EZ Access Developers Suite is a new product specifically designed for Access 2000 and Access 97 developers to help them create great Access applications. The suite consists of eight separate products. Each can be easily integrated into your application to provide new functions in a fraction of the time it would take you to create them yourself. These products are guaranteed to save you hundreds of hours of development time. Think of them as a library of over 100 predesigned, preprogrammed interfaces that you can legally steal and use with your application.

The eight EZ Access Suite pieces include:

- EZ Report Manager
- EZ Support Manager
- EZ Search Manager

- EZ Security Manager
- EZ File Manager
- EZ Extensions
- EZ Application Manager
- EZ Controls

See the demo and read each of the embedded reviewers' guides in the demo for a complete overview of each product. To install the demo on your computer, run `D:\DatabaseCreations\Demos\EZAccessSuite\EZ Access Suite Demo.exe`. This program will appear on your hard drive under EZ Demos, and you can best access it through Explorer rather than via the Start button. The entire EZ Access Developer Suite retails for $799.95, and individual products are $199.95. Mention the code MASTCD and purchase the entire suite for just $599.95. View additional samples at `http://www.databasecreations.com`.

Specials from Database Creations, Inc.

You can purchase our fully customizable business accounting product named *Yes! I Can Run My Business* at $50 to $200 off our regular prices:

- Single User Edition: $495.95, only $449.95
- Unlimited Multiuser: $599.95, only $499.95
- Royalty Free Developer: $2,299.95, only $2,095.95

You can purchase our complete EZ Access Developer Suite for $200 off our regular prices:

- Complete EZ Access Developer Suite: $799.95, only $599.95

You can also request a free catalog of all our products and services, including books, videos, and add-on software for Microsoft Access 2000 and 97, Visual FoxPro, and Visual Basic 6.0.

> Database Creations, Inc.
> 475 Buckland Road
> S. Windsor, CT 06074, USA
> Telephone: (860) 644-5891
> Fax: (860) 648-0710
> E-mail: info@databasecreations.com
> Web: http://www.databasecreations.com

NOTE If you have problems running any of the Database Creations programs or demos included on this book's CD, try downloading a new copy from the Database Creations Web site at http://www.databasecreations.com.

United States Postal Service Barcodes

TAZ Information Services has generously donated their shareware TrueType font for printing PostNet and PLANET barcodes. (POSTNET: United States Postal Service Barcodes and FIM Patterns TrueType™ Font Copyright © 1998 TAZ Information Services, Inc. All Rights Reserved. PLANET: United States Postal Service PLANET Barcode TrueType™ Font Copyright © 1998 TAZ Information Services, Inc. All Rights Reserved.)

Installing the PostNet Font

The shareware TrueType font for printing PostNet barcodes is contained in the file Pnbccass.ttf. This font must be installed using the Windows Control Panel. To install the font:

1. Insert the CD-ROM that comes with this book into your CD-ROM drive.

2. Click the Start button at the Windows Desktop and point to Settings.

3. Click Control Panel.

4. Double-click the Fonts folder.

5. Choose File ➤ Install New Font from the Font window's menu bar.

6. Make sure the Copy fonts to Font Folder check box is selected.

7. Choose the drive letter for your CD-ROM drive from Drives.

8. Double-click the TAZInfo folder.

9. Click the PNBARS (TrueType) font.

10. Choose OK and follow the instructions on the screen.

Once it is installed, you can use the font as you would any other TrueType font. For example, when creating a report in Microsoft Access's design view, you can choose any control on the report. Then use the Formatting (Form/Report Design) toolbar to choose the PNBARS font for that control.

Installing the PLANET Font

The shareware TrueType font for printing PLANET barcodes is contained in the file Planet.ttf. This font is basically the inverse of the PostNet font. The tall bars of the PLANET code are the short bars of the PostNet code and vice-versa.

 WARNING   The PLANET code has been developed and tested by the USPS for possible tracking of mail. Do not use this code until a formal announcement from the USPS has been made stating that the code has been implemented as a mail-tracking option.

To install the PLANET font:

1. Insert the CD-ROM that comes with this book into your CD-ROM drive.

2. Click the Start button at the Windows Desktop and point to Settings.

3. Click Control Panel.

4. Double-click the Fonts folder.

5. Choose File ➤ Install New Font from the Font window's menu bar.

6. Make sure the Copy fonts to Font Folder check box is selected.

7. Choose the drive letter for your CD-ROM drive from Drives.

8. Double-click the TAZInfo folder.

9. Click the PLANET (TrueType) font.

10. Choose OK and follow the instructions on the screen.

Once it is installed, you can use the font as you would any other TrueType font. For example, when creating a report in Microsoft Access's design view, you can choose any control on the report. Then use the Formatting (Form/Report Design) toolbar to choose the PLANET font for that control.

From TAZ Information Services

The remainder of this section was supplied by TAZ Information Services. If you have any questions about their products, please contact them directly at

TAZ Information Services, Inc.
PO Box 452
Linthicum, MD 21090-0452, USA
Telephone: (800) 279-7579
America Online: TAZINFO

Specifications

To meet the U.S. Postal Service (USPS) specifications, the barcodes must be set in 16 point, and the FIM pattern must be set in 72 point.

The frame bar that begins and terminates the POSTNET is generated by the keyboard character "s" or "S." The bar coding of the Zip Code itself follows USPS formats for 5-, 9-, or 11-digit Zip Code information by simply typing the numbers. The FIM patterns are obtained by typing the character of the desired pattern (either "a" "A," "b" "B," or "c" "C" for FIM A, FIM B, or FIM C, respectively).

Following are the three formats defined and an example of the keyboard input necessary to generate the proper POSTNET. In these examples, the address P.O. Box 452 and Zip Code 21090-0452 are used.

Five-Digit Zip Code (A Field)

Frame Bar	5-digit ZipCode	Correction Character	Frame Bar
S	21090	8	S

Keyboard = s210908s

Zip + 4 Code (C Field)

Frame Bar	5-digit ZipCode	+4 Code	Correction Character	Frame Bar
S	21090	0452	7	S

Keyboard = s2109004527s

Delivery Point Barcode (DPBC) (C Prime Field)

Frame Bar	5-digit ZipCode	+4 Code	Delivery Point	Correction Character	Frame Bar
S	21090	0452	52	0	S

Keyboard = s210900452520s

The generation of the Correction Character is accomplished by adding the digits in the Zip Code to be used (either 5, 9, or 11 digits). The correction character is the number that must be added to this sum to produce a total that is a multiple of 10. In other words,

Correction Character = $10 - (X(\mathrm{mod}\ 10))$

where X is the sum of the digits.

For example, $2 + 1 + 0 + 9 + 0 + 0 + 4 + 5 + 2 = 23$. The next highest multiple of 10 is 30. Thus, the Correction Character is 7; $30 - 23 = 7$.

The generation of a Delivery Point is, generally, to append the last two digits of the address line (street address, P.O. Box, rural route, etc.) to the zip +4 zip code number. The Correction Character is then generated on this number, that is, on the sum of digits (21090045252) = 30. Thus the Correction Character is zero (0).

However, because of the wide variation of address line numbers, such as fractional streets, letter suffix, and so on, no complete rule can be given here. A publication titled *Letter Mail Barcode Update*, dated May 1992, is available through your postmaster and contains all the rules for the generation of the delivery point.

CASS Certification

Preprinting the POSTNET barcode on your mail can improve delivery through the USPS. By obtaining a CASS Certification of your mailing list, you can substantially reduce your postage costs. TAZ can perform the CASS Certification of your mailing list required for reduced postage rates via disk or online file transfer. See the file Cass.txt in the USPSTTF folder for further information.

Disclaimer

TAZ Information Services, Inc. makes no warranties on these trial copies of the USPS Barcodes and FIM Patterns TrueType font and the PLANET: United States Postal Service PLANET Barcode TrueType™ Font. In no event shall TAZ Information Services, Inc. be liable for any damages whatsoever arising out of the use of or inability to use this sample product.

Registering Your Fonts

Thank you for trying the USPS Barcodes and FIM Patterns TrueType Font and the PLANET: United States Postal Service PLANET Barcode TrueType™ Font. If you have any questions about these fonts, please contact TAZ Information Services, Inc. TAZ will attempt to answer all questions; however, support is guaranteed only for registered users.

To register your fonts, please print and complete the form titled REGISTER.TXT in the USPSTTF folder on the CD-ROM that came with this book.

To check with Better Business Bureau of Greater Maryland, call (900) 225-5222.

SQL Server 7 Evaluation Edition

Microsoft SQL Server 7 Evaluation Edition is a program that you can experiment with to learn more about SQL Server databases. SQL Server 7 is the leading Microsoft Windows® database, which brings you business solutions, powerful data warehousing capabilities, and integration with Microsoft Office 2000.

At some point during NT installation, you may be asked for a 10-digit CD key code. We entered all 3s and it worked.

The remainder of this section is from Microsoft. If you have any questions about this product, or to get the latest information on SQL Server 7, please check out the SQL Server Web site at www.microsoft.com.

SQL Server 7 Features

SQL Server 7 is flexible enough to be used on laptop databases and small business servers all the way up to large databases. It works well with existing applications, and has customization capabilities that allow you to build new applications that meet your specific requirements. Some of the new features include:

Query processor   SQL Server 7 comes with a redesigned query processor that provides powerful support for large databases and complex queries.

Full-text search   SQL Server 7 can handle complex, full-text database searches. This new release supports linguistic search, which allows you to create special indexes of pertinent words and phrases in selected columns of selected tables.

Web Assistant   A wizard and formatting option in this release enhances the SQL Server Web Assistant, making it easy for you to generate HTML files from SQL Server data.

Microsoft English Query   This feature allows you to create applications that accept natural language queries (queries written in plain English) instead of complex SQL queries.

Integration with Microsoft Office 2000   SQL Server 7 is fully integrated with Microsoft Office 2000, as well as Windows NT Server, BackOffice, and Microsoft Office 97. This integration makes it easy for you, your customers, or your employees to access data from any location, using familiar desktop applications. This also allows you to share reports and easily view and analyze data over the Internet using Office Web Components. Web Components are new in Office 2000, and they offer online, dynamic views of data through spreadsheet, chart, and PivotTable® features.

APPENDIX C

Installing and Using Fulfill 2000

Fulfill 2000 is a sample order-entry database application that you can use and explore freely. It's especially designed for "SHMOOP" users (where SHMOOP stands for small office, home office, mobile office, and home PC), who are, as you may know, the same users that Windows itself is geared to. You can use Fulfill to manage any kind of business (for example, a mail-order business) that takes orders over the phone.

Fulfill 2000 is a completely custom Access application. We didn't use database wizards to create it. Fulfill offers many more bells and whistles than the wizard-generated order-entry application and is, in our opinion, much easier to use. Even if you don't need an order-entry database, you might still want to try Fulfill. You'll probably discover some neat tricks that you can incorporate into your own custom Access databases.

The CD-ROM that comes with this book contains two versions of Fulfill 2000:

FulfillS.mdb   This version of Fulfill already contains some hypothetical data to show you how Fulfill works.

Fulfill.mdb   This version comes with most of Fulfill's tables empty so that you can add your own data from scratch.

We suggest that you try the FulfillS version first. If you then decide you can use Fulfill in your "real work," you're welcome to copy and use the Fulfill.mdb version. Just be sure to read this disclaimer first.

 WARNING   Although every effort has been made to prevent bugs and errors, Fulfill 2000 has never actually been tested in the field. If you plan to use Fulfill 2000 to manage "real data," we strongly suggest that you run it in parallel with your existing manual or automated order-entry system for a while to see if it performs as you expect. Address any problems or errors to the author, whose address appears in Fulfill's Help ➤ About ➤ Author screen.

The focus in this appendix is on how to *use* Fulfill 2000. If tinkering with Fulfill makes you curious about what makes it tick, you're more than welcome to peek under the hood. Chapter 29 discusses techniques for exploring Fulfill 2000 and similar open applications behind the scenes.

Copying Fulfill 2000 to Your Hard Disk

Fulfill 2000 is an Access database and therefore will work only on a computer that has Microsoft Access 2000 installed. All you need to do is copy FulfillS.mdb (or Fulfill.mdb) from the CD-ROM onto your hard disk. You can use any copying technique you want. Then make sure its read-only attribute is not checked. You can copy Fulfill to any folder you want. Here are some step-by-step instructions to copy FulfillS.mdb to the My Documents folder on drive C:

1. Close any open applications to get to the Windows Desktop.

2. Insert the CD-ROM that came with this book into your CD-ROM drive.

3. Double-click the My Computer icon at the Windows Desktop.

4. Double-click the drive C icon, and then move and size the window so you can see the icon for the destination folder (the folder you'll be copying *to*), My Documents in this example.

5. Go back to My Computer and double-click the icon for your CD-ROM drive (typically drive D).

6. Size and position the window so you can see both the destination folder and the FulfillS.mdb file, as in Figure C.1.

FIGURE C.1

Ready to drag FulfillS.mdb from the CD-ROM to the My Documents folder on drive C.

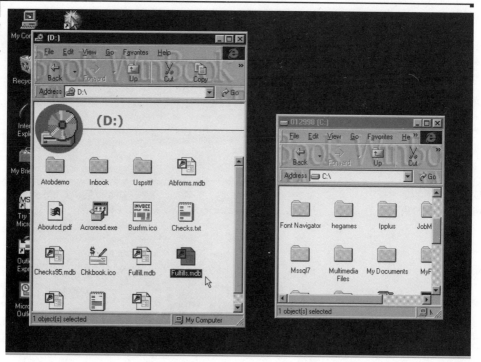

7. Drag the `FulfillS.mdb` file (or `Fulfill.mdb` file) from the CD-ROM drive to the My Documents folder, and then release the mouse button.

8. Double-click the My Documents folder and right-click the icon for `FulfillS.mdb` (or `Fulfill.mdb`). Select Properties, and make sure the read-only setting is unchecked. Click OK.

You can close the windows for My Documents drive C and your CD-ROM drive.

Starting Fulfill 2000

Once you've copied `FulfillS.mdb` (or `Fulfill.mdb`) to your hard disk, you can use either of these techniques to start Access and load the Fulfill 2000 database:

- Open the folder in which you've stored the database and double-click the `FulfillS.mdb` file icon, as below.

Or

- Start Microsoft Access and use the File ➤ Open Database commands to browse to and open `FulfillS.mdb` (or `Fulfill.mdb`).

Microsoft Access 2000 will start up with the main switchboard for Fulfill 2000 displayed, as in Figure C.2.

FIGURE C.2

The main switchboard for Fulfill 2000.

NOTE When Fulfill 2000 starts, you will have access to the standard Access menus and toolbars. Normally, we would have created custom menus and toolbars for an application such as this. But we want you to be able to explore "behind the scenes" easily, so we left all the standard Access tools in place.

Entering Information about Your Business

The first time you use Fulfill 2000, you need to tell it about your business. You need to provide this information only once, not every time you start Fulfill. To enter information about your business:

1. Click the My Biz Info button in the main switchboard.

2. Fill in the blanks as instructed on the screen, and then click the Click Here When Done button. You're returned to Fulfill's main switchboard.

If you're using FulfillS 2000, you'll see some data already filled in, as in Figure C.3. You can leave the information as it appears or change it if you prefer.

FIGURE C.3

The form for filling in information about your own business in Fulfill 2000.

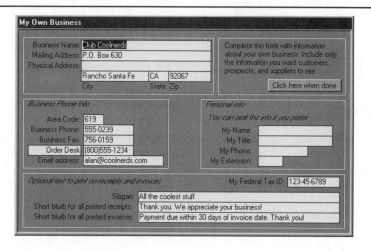

Using Fulfill's Address Book

An important part of any order-entry system is the ability to manage the names and addresses of customers, prospects, and suppliers. Fulfill 2000 comes with a handy address book that makes list management very easy. To get to Fulfill's Address Book (see Figure C.4), just click the Address Book button on Fulfill's main switchboard. If you're using FulfillS, you'll see the address for a hypothetical company on the screen.

FIGURE C.4

Fulfill's Address Book form with a sample company address displayed.

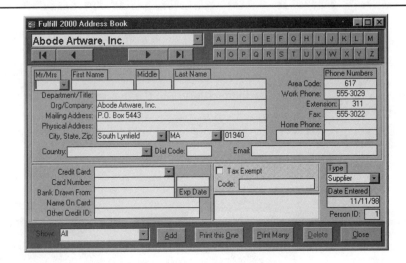

Adding a Name and Address

Adding a new name and address to Fulfill's address book is simply a matter of clicking a button and filling in the blanks. (If you don't read the sections that follow, though, you might miss lots of little time-savers and shortcuts.) To get started, click the Add button near the bottom of the Address Book form.

Entering the Name and Company

The first few blanks in the Address book are for typing a person's name and affiliation. If you don't have the name of a particular person for this address (just a business name), you can leave these fields blank and skip right down to Department/Title or Org/Company. If you do have a person's name,

- Type an honorific (Ms., Mr., etc.) or choose one from the drop-down list under Mr/Mrs as shown below. You can leave this field blank if you want.

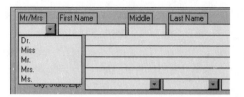

 TIP   If you want to open a drop-down list without taking your hands off the keyboard, just press Alt+↓. Then you can use the ↑ and ↓ keys to point to a selection, and press Enter to select it. Also, if you want to change the Mr/Mrs drop-down list, double-click the Mr/Mrs blank and follow the instructions on the screen.

- Press Tab to move to the next field, or just click the next field you want to fill.
- Type a middle name or initial. If you enter a single character, such as *C*, Fulfill will automatically add the period for you (*C*.).
- Type a Last Name.

 TIP   If you're not sure how to fill in a blank on a form, try right-clicking and choosing Info from the shortcut menu that appears.

- Type any information for department, title, organization, or company name affiliated with the address you're entering into the Department/Title and Org/Company blanks. You may also leave either or both fields empty.

 TIP   Tips for aspiring developers: The custom shortcut menu is assigned to the Address Book form's Shortcut Menu Bar property. Macros named AddressBookShortcut and AddressBookShortcut_Shortcut display the menu. The Info help is handled by a module named ShortcutMenuInfo.

Entering the Street Address

Now you need to enter the mailing address:

- If the blinking cursor isn't in the Mailing Address field yet, click the field or press Tab until the cursor gets there.

- Type in the mailing address (required), and then press Tab or Enter. The cursor jumps to the Zip Code field, for reasons we'll describe in a moment.

- If you need to type in a second address line, do so in the Physical Address line. You can just backtrack to that field at any time by clicking it or by pressing Shift+Tab.

NOTE Pressing Tab or Enter *always* moves the blinking cursor forward to the next field in the form. Pressing Shift+Tab always moves the cursor back to the previous field. You can move the cursor to any field on the form simply by clicking that field.

Entering the City, State, Zip, and Area Code

After typing in the mailing address and pressing Tab or Enter, the cursor lands in the Zip Code field. Fulfill will try to fill in the City, State, and Area Code fields automatically after you enter a zip code. Note that when entering a U.S. zip+4 code, you can omit the hyphen and Fulfill will add it for you. For example, if you type 920671234 as a zip code, Fulfill will automatically change that to 92067-1234. Type a zip code and press Tab or Enter to see how Fulfill works:

- If you *don't* hear a beep, Fulfill has made a "best guess" on the City, State, and Area Code and filled in those fields. *But you still need to check, and perhaps correct, Fulfill's guess because Fulfill doesn't always get it right!* The cursor lands on the Work Phone field.

- If you *do* hear a beep, Fulfill doesn't know that zip code. You'll have to fill in the City, State, and Area Code fields yourself.

Fulfill will not change the City, State, or Area Code fields if you've already filled them in. Fulfill assumes that if you've already filled in the field with some information, it shouldn't try to second-guess you with its own information!

Fulfill is pretty accurate when filling in the City, State, and Area Code fields for a particular zip code. But it's not 100 percent accurate because some zip codes cover multiple townships and area codes. (Not to mention the fact that zip and area codes get reconfigured all the time!)

⚠ **TIP** Tips for aspiring application developers: The zip codes are stored in a table named ZipLookup. The event procedure that looks up the zip code and fills in the City, State, and Area Code fields is attached to the After Update property of the Zip/PostalCode field in the AddressBook form.

Making Fulfill 100 percent accurate on filling in the city, state, and area code from the zip code would require storing a huge collection of data that would eat up disk space and slow down your work. As it stands, Fulfill contains a list of about 44,000 zip, city, state, and area code combinations that make it accurate enough to be worth including.

If Fulfill doesn't find a zip code you type in often, you can add that zip code to the list. Just double-click the field where you type in the zip code, and then follow the instructions on the screen.

Optionally, you can add the city, state, zip, and area code combination to the City drop-down list, as we'll discuss next.

Using the City Drop-Down List If most of the addresses that you type in are within your own vicinity, you can pre-enter the city, state, zip, and area code so that you don't have to type in *any* of that information in the future. To do so, double-click the City field, and you'll see the dialog box shown in Figure C.5. (If you're using Fulfill5 you'll see some examples already typed in.)

FIGURE C.5

Double-clicking the City field takes you to a dialog box for modifying the City drop-down list.

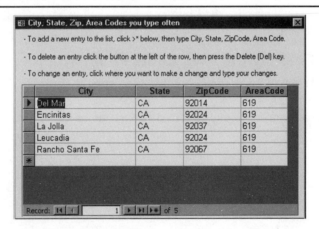

Follow the on-screen instructions to add, change, or delete any city, state, area code, and zip code combination(s) that you would otherwise need to type in often. Click OK to return to the Address Book form.

In the future you'll be able to choose any city, state, zip, area code from your custom drop-down list. After typing in the mailing address for an address in your own vicinity, click the drop-down list button in the City field. Your custom list will appear, as in the example below. Just click the one you want, and Fulfill will fill in the City, State, Zip, and Area Code fields for you.

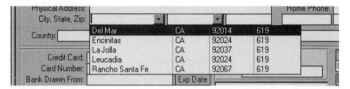

Note that Fulfill also has a drop-down list button for the State field, which you can use to fill in the two-letter abbreviation for any state in the United States.

Entering the Country

If you are entering an address that's within the United States, leave the Country and Dial Code fields empty. Blanks in those fields mean USA. If you are entering an address from a foreign country, you can type in the country name and dialing code or choose a country from the Country field's drop-down list. You can also customize the Country drop-down list to better suit your own needs, using the standard Fulfill technique: just double-click the Country field and follow the instructions that appear on the screen.

Entering the Area Code, Phone Numbers, and E-mail Address

When filling in the phone numbers, enter the area code only once at the top of the list, unless one of the phone numbers uses a different area code, such as 800, in which case you *do* want to type in the area code, as shown in the Toll Free example below:

You can leave any field blank if you don't have the appropriate information. Also, note that you can add a label and phone number for the last number in the list. For example, we typed in a "Toll Free:" label next to the phone number in the example shown.

When typing the phone number, you can omit the hyphen. For example, if you type 5551323, Fulfill will convert that to 555-1323 after you move to another field. If you do need to type in an area code with a particular phone number, you can omit the parentheses. For example, if you type 8005553323, Fulfill will convert your entry to (800)555-3323. (This formatting is handled by a Visual Basic procedure that's tied to the After Update event for the HomePhone field. If you need to enter phone numbers in a different format, you will have to remove the event procedure from that field.)

There are no shortcuts for the E-mail field. If the name you're entering has an e-mail address, just go ahead and type it into the E-mail field.

Entering Credit Card Information

If you're entering the name and address for a customer who regularly pays by credit card, you can record that credit card information in the Address Book. Choose a credit card from the Credit Card drop-down list. If you accept a credit card that isn't in the list, you can add it to the list. Just double-click the Credit Card field and follow the on-screen instructions.

WARNING   Fulfill 2000 does not have any built-in security features to prevent unauthorized users from seeing credit card information. If security is a concern, you should either omit the credit card information or, at the least, omit the expiration date.

You can leave any of the Credit Card fields blank if you prefer. When typing in the expiration date, you should use the standard mm/yy format. But you can omit the slash and leading zero. Fulfill will assume that the first number you enter is for the month and the second two numbers are for the year. For example, if you type 1299 Fulfill will convert your entry to 12/99. If you type 199 Fulfill will convert that to 01/99 (after you move to another field). Be careful, though, when entering years from 2000 to 2009. Fulfill always assumes that you will be entering the last two numbers of the expiration year. Because of this, an entry of 121 will be converted to 01/21, not 12/01. If you want to show an expiration date of 12/01, you need to enter 1201.

TIP More tips for application developers: Most of the underlying fields in the Address-Book table are of the text data type, which makes it easier to create these little custom conversion routines. The conversion routines themselves are attached to the After Update properties of the various Phone fields and the ExpirationDate field.

Entering Tax Exempt Information

The Tax Exempt fields are for those rare customers who reside in a state where you normally charge sales tax, but who are, for whatever reason, exempt from sales tax. If you acquire such a customer, you can select (check) the Tax Exempt option. Optionally, you can record the account number or whatever information that customer offers to justify their tax-exempt status. When you enter orders for this customer later, Fulfill will not charge sales tax.

 NOTE Fulfill charges sales tax only to customers in areas where you are required to charge sales tax. If a particular customer is in a region where you don't charge sales tax, you don't have to mark that person as tax exempt. Fulfill won't charge them sales tax anyway. You set up your sales tax rates in the Orders form, as we'll discuss later in this appendix. You don't need to concern yourself with that problem right now.

Entering Customer Notes

The empty white space under the Tax Exempt fields is for entering optional notes. The notes can be as long as you want them to be. Now you might be thinking, "Yeah, but the box is so small." Here's a little trick for you:

- Double-click the Notes field to make it larger, as below.
- Double-click it again to shrink it back down to size.

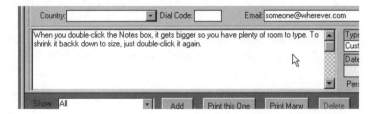

> ⚠️ **TIP** Tip for aspiring application developers: The AddressBook form contains two controls bound to the Notes field—one named Notes, and an invisible one named BigNotes. The event procedures that make BigNotes visible/invisible are attached to the On Dbl Click property of the Notes and BigNotes controls.

Address Type, Date Entered, and Person ID

The final step in entering a person's name and address is to identify the addressee as a customer, prospect, or supplier. You can use the drop-down list button under Type to do so:

You can't change the Type drop-down list, so double-clicking it does nothing. Fulfill uses the information in the Type field when printing information about customers and *must* be able to identify the address as belonging to either a customer, prospect, or supplier.

The Date Entered and Person ID fields in Fulfill's Address Book are filled in automatically and cannot be changed. (In general, a yellow-tinted field on a form is for information only and cannot be changed.)

When you've finished typing in all the information for one name and address, click the Add button to enter another address or click Close to return to the Main Switchboard.

It's not necessary to enter every name and address through the Address Book form. As you'll discover, you can enter customer, prospect, and supplier addresses on the fly while entering orders and information about your products. But if you're not using FulfillS and you want to try out some of the navigation and printing techniques discussed in the sections that follow, you should add at least a few names and addresses so you have some data to work with.

Navigating with the Address Book

The tools across the top of the address book are for *navigation*—finding a particular address to change or print. The address book is automatically kept in alphabetical order, based on the following rules:

- If an entry appears in the Last Name field, then the address is listed in alphabetical order by name.

- If a particular address has no entry in its Last Name field, then the entry is listed in alphabetical order by Company name.

So for example, suppose you have the addresses in three records of the Address Book, as shown in Table C.1.

FIRST NAME	LAST NAME	COMPANY
		Sybex, Inc.
Sylvia	Levanthal	A & B Furniture
Andy	Adams	

TABLE C.1: SAMPLE DATA IN FIRSTNAME, LASTNAME, AND COMPANY FIELDS

Because the last two rows have Last Name entries, they are listed in alphabetical order by name. Since the first entry has no Last Name contents, it will always be listed in alphabetical order by company. Thus, the three entries would be alphabetized as follows:

Adams, Andy

Levanthal, Sylvia

Sybex, Inc.

TIP Tip for aspiring developers: The tricky alphabetization scheme is handled by a calculated field in the query named AddressesAlphabetized.

Navigating Fulfill's Address Book is pretty easy once you understand those rules. You just use the tools at the top of the form to zero in on the name you're looking for. Here are the exact steps:

1. Click one of the letters in the Rolodex button area to jump to that part of the alphabet. (If nothing in the alphabetical list starts with the letter you clicked, you'll just hear a beep and nothing will change.)

2. The drop-down list box to the left of the Rolodex buttons shows the first address entry that starts with that letter.

3. Use the drop-down list button to view nearby names, as shown below. To jump to one of those names, just click it in the drop-down list.

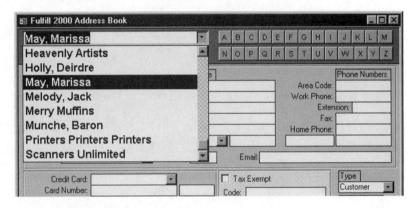

You can also use the navigation buttons that surround the A...Z to move from record to record. To see where one of those buttons will take you, rest the mouse pointer on the button for a couple of seconds and wait for the ScreenTip to appear:

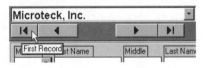

Searching the Address Book

If you're sure you've entered a particular name and address, but can't seem to find it using the navigation buttons, perhaps you've just forgotten the exact spelling of the person's last name or the company name. You can search for any text in any part of an address.

NOTE If you use the Show option to limit the display of addresses to Customers, Prospects, or Suppliers, and you want to include *all* addresses in your search, set the Show option back to All before you begin the search.

1. Right-click the specific field you want to search.

Or

Right-click any field on the form if you want to search all the fields in all the records.

2. Choose Find from the shortcut menu to display the Find and Replace dialog box:

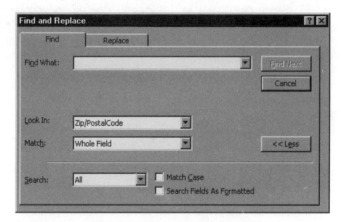

3. Type the text you're looking for in the Find What box.

4. Set other options in the Find dialog box as follows:

Look In The field you right-clicked will appear in this box. This is the field that will be searched. To broaden the search to all fields on the form, use the drop-down for this box and select Fulfill 2000 Address Book.

Match Choose Whole Field, Start of Field, or Any Part of Field. The last option provides the broadest search and has the best chance of finding a match.

Search Choose Up to search up from your current position, Down to search down from your current position, or All to search the whole address book. The last option provides the broadest search, and is most likely to find a match.

Match Case   Select this option only if you want to locate an exact upper-case/lowercase match to the text you typed. Leaving this option cleared provides a better chance of finding a match.

Search Fields as Formatted   Looks for a specific format match rather than just an informational match. Leave this option cleared to increase your chances of finding a match.

More/Less   Click More to expand the Find and Replace dialog box and bring the options for Search, Match Case, and Search Fields as Formatted into view. Click Less to hide these options.

5. Click the Find Next button to begin the search.

If Fulfill finds a match, the first matching record will be displayed. If you can't see the information behind the Find and Replace dialog box, just drag the dialog box out of the way (by its title bar). If the found record is not the one you're looking for, you can click the Find Next button to locate the next record that matches your request. When you find the record you're looking for (or are ready to give up), close the Find and Replace dialog box. (Click its Close button.)

If you can't find the record you're looking for, perhaps you misspelled something in the entry. You might want to print a directory of all the names and addresses you've entered to see how everything is spelled. We'll talk about printing in a moment.

Limiting the Address Book Display

If you have lots of addresses in your address book and want to limit the display to Customers, Prospects, or Suppliers, choose an option from the Show drop-down list near the bottom of the form (see below).

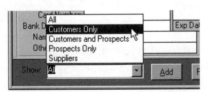

Any addresses that aren't of the type(s) you specified will be virtually invisible until you reset the Show option to All.

Printing from the Address Book

You can print information from the Address Book in a variety of formats at any time. If you want to print only the address currently showing on your screen, click the Print This One button to open the Quick Print One Address dialog box shown in Figure C.6.

FIGURE C.6

*Options for printing
one name and address
from Fulfill's
Address Book.*

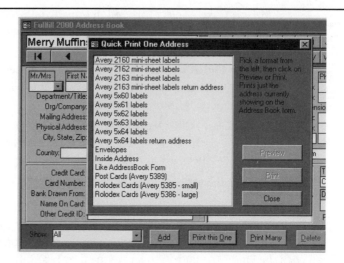

Click the format you want to print. Then click the Preview button if you want to see how the address will look when printed. To actually print the address, prepare the printer and click the Print button. When you've finished printing, click the Close button in the Quick Print One Address dialog box to return to the Address Book form.

NOTE The various label and card formats available in the Print dialog boxes are standard Avery labels for laser and ink-jet printers. You can purchase those labels at most office-supply and computer stores. The mini-labels (Avery 2x6x) are for very small print runs (usually one or two labels) and work properly only with certain printers.

If you want to print several addresses, click the Print Many button to open the standard Print Names and Addresses dialog box shown in Figure C.7.

To use the Print Names and Addresses dialog box, select a format from the drop-down list box. Depending on the format you select, the dialog box will display additional options. For example, suppose you choose the Address Directory format, as in Figure C.8.

FIGURE C.7

Options for printing several names and addresses from Fulfill's Address Book.

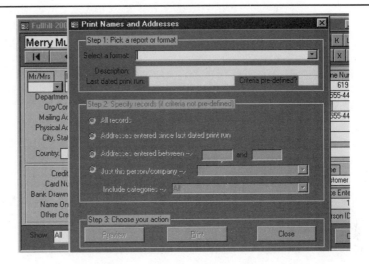

FIGURE C.8

Print Names and Addresses dialog box with the Address Directory report format selected.

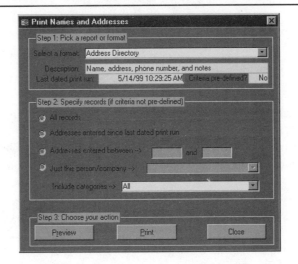

The yellow-tinted fields tell you some things about the format you've selected:

Description   Describes the format you've selected.

Last Dated Print Run   The date and time you last printed in this format using the second option under step 2 (described in a moment).

Criteria Pre-defined? If it is set to Yes, you cannot choose Criteria under step 2 because the criteria are already defined for this format. (The Categorized Address Summary and Possible Duplicates reports are the only two with predefined criteria.)

After selecting a format that allows you to specify your own criteria, you can choose options under step 2 in the Print Names and Addresses dialog box to specify which records you want to include in the printout:

All Records All names and addresses within the selected category will be printed.

Addresses Entered Since Last Dated Print Run Only new entries— those addresses entered since the date and time shown in the yellow Last Dated Print Run box will be printed. For example, if you want to print Rolodex cards only for addresses that you've never printed before, you would choose this option.

Addresses Entered Between If you choose this option, you can specify a range of dates to include. Initially the option will suggest "today" by setting both the start date and end date to today's date, but you can type in any range of dates you wish.

Just This Person/Company You can pick a single person or company to include in the printout.

The Include Categories option lets you limit the printout even further. For example, if you choose Customers and Prospects from the Include Categories drop-down list, only addresses for those two categories will be printed. Suppliers will not be included in the print run. If you select All next to Include Categories, then all types of addresses—Customers, Prospects, and Suppliers—will be included in the print run.

 TIP Tips for aspiring developers: The Print dialog boxes are forms named AddressPrint-One and AddrRepPrintDialog in Fulfill. Visual Basic code attached to the Print and Preview buttons handles much of the work of setting up an appropriate query and previewing/ printing the reports.

Once you've made your selections, you can click the Preview button to see how the printed report will look. Once you're in the Preview mode, you can click the document or use the various Zoom tools on the toolbar to change magnification. When you're done previewing, click the Close button in the toolbar.

To print the addresses, click the Print button. If you requested labels or cards, you'll hear a beep and see a message reminding you to load the proper stock into the printer. Load the paper and then click OK to start printing.

Managing Your Product List

Before you start filling orders, you should type in information about some (or all) of the products you sell. You can add products on the fly while entering orders, but you need at least a few products in the list to get the benefits of Fulfill's order form.

If you're using FulfillS, several products and product categories are already entered for you. You may want to follow along in the sections that follow, though, to get a feel for the Products component of Fulfill.

Adding New Products

When you want to add a product to the list of products that you sell, follow these steps:

1. Click the Products button in Fulfill 2000's Main Switchboard. You'll come to the form shown in Figure C.9.

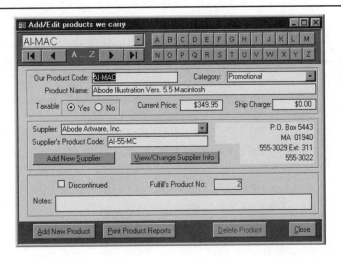

2. Click the Add New Product button near the bottom of the form.

3. Fill in the blanks for a single product, using techniques summarized in the sections that follow.

Entering Product Information

You can assign whatever code or abbreviation you like to each product you carry. However, each product must have its own unique identifying code. (That is, no two products can have the same ID code.) Later, when you're entering orders, Fulfill will present products in alphabetical order by code. Therefore, you should try to come up with a code that will be easy to remember.

You also need to assign the product to a product category. Choose a category from the Category drop-down list, or if you need to create a new category, double-click the Category field. You'll come to a screen like the one in Figure C.10. Follow the on-screen instructions to add, change, or delete a product category, and then choose OK to return to the Products form.

FIGURE C.10

Double-clicking the Category drop-down list in the Products form takes you to the Change the Product Categories dialog box.

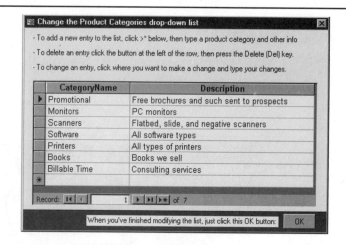

Type in the rest of the information as follows:

Product Name   Enter a name or description that specifically identifies this product.

Taxable   Choose Yes if this product is taxable in the region(s) in which you charge sales tax. If the product is not taxable, choose No.

Current Price   Type the current selling price of the product.

Ship Charge   If this product carries its own special shipping charge, type in that amount. Otherwise, leave it at $0.00. (For example, you might add an extra shipping charge to especially large or heavy products that are costly to ship.)

Entering Product Supplier and Other Info

If the product you're describing here is one you purchase wholesale from a supplier, then use the drop-down list button to choose that supplier. If you haven't already

PART

VII

Appendices

entered the supplier's name and address into Fulfill's Address Book, click the Add New Supplier button and follow the instructions on the screen to fill in the new supplier's name and address.

The yellow-tinted supplier information comes from Fulfill's Address Book and cannot be changed on this form. You may, however, click the View/Change Supplier Info button if you need to make a quick change to the supplier's information while in the Products form.

Use the Supplier's Product Code field to store the product code that the supplier uses to identify this product.

 TIP   If you are the supplier as well as the seller, enter your own name and address into Fulfill's Address Book as a Supplier. Then choose your own business as the Supplier when entering information about the product.

Finally, you can use the Notes field to record any other descriptive information about this product. The yellow-tinted Fulfill's Product No code is assigned automatically. You can select (check) the Discontinued box should you stop carrying this product at some time in the future.

 NOTE   Once you start entering product information, you should complete the whole form. Otherwise, Fulfill might not save the entry when you close the form. Or you might get stuck, at which point you'll need to either complete the form or choose Edit ➢ Undo from the menu bar to cancel out the entry.

Navigating in the Products Form

You can also use the Products form to look up and change existing information. Your product list is kept in alphabetical order by your Product ID, so to quickly locate a product in your product list:

- Use the Rolodex-style buttons to click a part of the alphabet (where you're looking to match the first letter of a product's ID code).

    Or

- Use the VCR-style buttons to move from product to product.

If on your first try, you don't land on the appropriate product, select a nearby product ID from the drop-down list, as shown below.

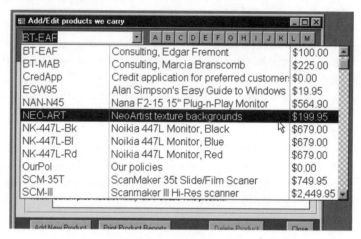

Printing Product Information

To print your product list:

1. Click the Print Product Reports button near the bottom of the Products form to display the Product Reports dialog box.

2. Select (check) the report(s) you want to print.

3. Click the Preview button to preview the reports.

4. Click the Print button to print the report(s).

Entering Orders

After you've entered some data into the My Biz Info, Address Book, and Products portions of Fulfill (or have copied FulfillS, which contains the sample data), most of your work with Fulfill will center around the Order Forms.

To add, view, change, or print orders, you start by clicking the Orders Central button in Fulfill's Main Switchboard, which opens to the Orders Central switchboard shown in Figure C.11.

FIGURE C.11

The Orders Central switchboard is where you'll do all your work with orders.

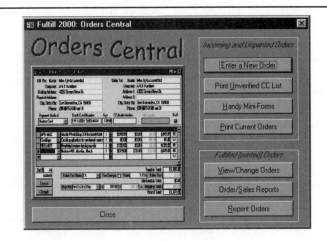

Entering a New Order

When you are ready to take an order, open a blank order form by clicking the Enter a New Order button in the Orders Central switchboard. The first step in taking an order is to identify the customer (or prospect), as shown in Figure C.12.

FIGURE C.12

Identify the customer or prospect.

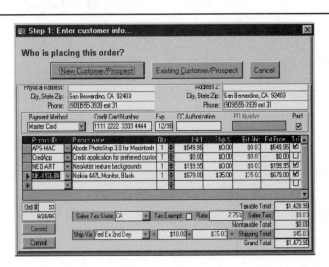

If a new customer or prospect (one whose name isn't already in Fulfill's Address book) is placing the order, click the New Customer/Prospect button. Then see "Adding a New Customer or Prospect On the Fly," below.

If an existing customer or prospect (one whose name is already in Fulfill's address book) is placing the Order, click the Existing Customer/Prospect button.

After you choose Existing Customer/Prospect, you're taken to the dialog box shown in Figure C.13. The navigation tools at the top of this dialog box work exactly as they do in the Address Book form discussed earlier in this appendix. All you need to do is locate the Customer/Prospect who is placing the order, and then click the To New Order Form button.

FIGURE C.13

Use the navigation tools at the top of this form to locate the customer or prospect who is placing the order. Then click the To New Order Form button.

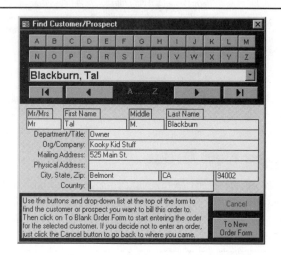

At this point, you can skip down to the section titled "Filling In the Rest of the Order Form."

Adding a New Customer or Prospect On the Fly

If you choose New Customer/Prospect in response to the question "Who is placing this order?" you'll be asked to enter information about the new customer or prospect (see Figure C.14).

FIGURE C.14

Use this form to enter a new customer (or prospect's) name and address before moving on to the order form.

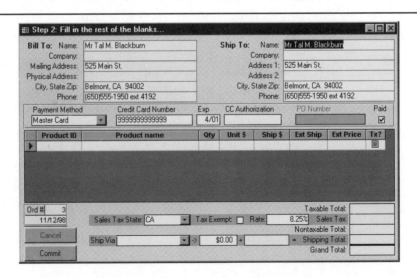

When entering the customer's (or prospect's) name and address, you can use some handy shortcuts and techniques that the Address Book offers to speed your data entry. (If you skipped all that, see "Adding a Name and Address" earlier in this appendix.) After you've filled in as many blanks as you can, click the To New Order Form button to move to the order form.

Filling In the Rest of the Order Form

The actual order form is shown in Figure C.15. Notice that much of the order form is already filled in for you:

FIGURE C.15

After you click the To New Order Form button, you're taken to the actual order form with many of the blanks already filled in for you.

The Bill To name and address is already filled in with the customer's name and address. These yellow-tinted boxes cannot be changed here on the order form.

The Ship To name and address are, initially, the same as those in Bill To. You can change any of that information simply by clicking where you want to make a change, and then typing in the new information.

If you've stored credit card information for this customer, the Payment Method is set to that credit card, and the credit card number and expiration date are filled in automatically.

Filling In the Payment Information

When filling in the payment method section of the form, you can use these handy techniques and shortcuts:

Payment Method   Choose any payment method from the Payment Method drop-down list shown below. If you need to add a new payment method to the list, just double-click the Payment Method field and follow the instructions on the screen.

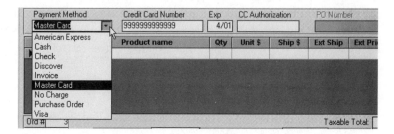

Credit Card Number and Expiration Date   Fill in the Credit Card Number box only if the customer is paying by credit card. If you choose the credit card that you entered into the Address Book for this person, the card number and expiration date will be filled in automatically.

CC Authorization   If you have some means of verifying a credit card purchase while entering an order, you can fill in the authorization number in the CC Authorization box. Optionally, you can leave this field blank and fill it in at any time in the future, as we'll discuss a little later in this section.

PO Number   If you chose Purchase Order as the Payment Method for this order, you can type the customer's Purchase Order number into the PO Number field.

Paid   If you select (check) the Paid box, the order is marked Paid, and Fulfill will print a receipt. If you leave the Paid check box empty, Fulfill will print an invoice.

Filling In the Order Details

When you get to the Order Details section (line items) of the form, here's how to proceed:

Product ID   Click the Product ID field and then click the drop-down list button that appears to see your list of products (as shown below). You can type the first letter of the Product ID you're looking for to quickly jump to that section of the list. When you see the Product ID you're looking for, click it to select it. The Product Name appears, and the cursor jumps to the Qty (quantity) field.

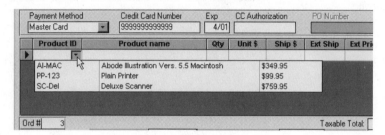

 NOTE   To add a new product to your product list on the fly, double-click the Product ID or Product Name field. Then choose Add a New Product. Fill in the blanks and choose Close. When you get back to the order form, use the Product ID drop-down list button to select the new product.

Qty   The default quantity is one (1). If you need to enter a different value, just type it in. You can type in fractional numbers, such as 2.5 (for 2.5 hours of billable time, for instance).

Unit $ and Ship $ The values entered in the unit price and per-unit shipping charge fields are "suggestions" based on the contents of the Products field. However, you can change either value for the current order. Fulfill automatically calculates the extended shipping charge (Ext Ship) and extended price (Ext Price).

Tx   By default, this box is checked to indicate that an item is taxable. You can click the box to remove the checkmark if an item should not be taxed.

You can add as many line items as necessary.

Sales Tax and Ship Via

The sales tax rate for an order is based on the values that you put into the drop-down list. To change the sales tax you charge in any given state, double-click the Sales Tax State field. You'll come to the Change the Sales Tax dialog box shown in Figure C.16. Change the values that need to be changed, following the instructions in the dialog box, and click OK to return to the order entry window.

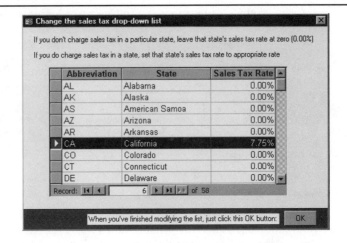

You should check the Sales Tax State entry to make sure that Fulfill has entered the correct state, tax exempt status, and rate for you. If any one of those is incorrect, type in the corrected value. Fulfill automatically calculates the sales tax amount from your entry.

You can also choose a shipping method from the Ship Via drop-down list. If you need to add a shipping method or change its dollar amount, double-click the Ship Via field and follow the instructions on the screen.

Note that the Shipping Total is based on the shipping charge of your Ship Via selection, plus the total per-unit ship charge from the Ext Ship column of the line items.

Cancel or Commit

Once you've completed one order, take a look at the form to check for any errors (it's always easier to correct errors *before* you save your work). Figure C.17 shows a sample completed order on the screen.

FIGURE C.17

A new order entered using Fulfill 2000.

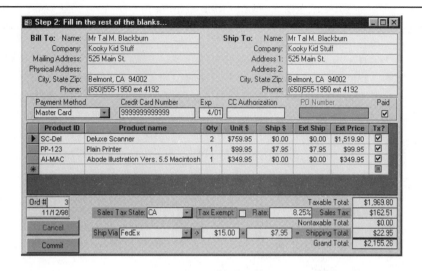

When you're finished, click the Commit button to save the order. If you don't want to save this order, click the Cancel button. You'll be returned to Orders Central (see Figure C.11). From there, you can either enter another new order (by clicking Enter a New Order again), return to the Main Switchboard (by clicking the Close button), or start printing information about the current order(s) by using the buttons beneath the Enter a New Order button (described in the next section).

Tools for Managing Current (Unprinted) Orders

Several buttons in Orders Central provide quick tools for managing current orders (*current orders* being orders that have been typed into Fulfill, but not yet printed as invoices, receipts, and so forth). Those buttons are

Print Unverified CC List   Prints a list of credit card orders and expiration dates, to make it easier for you to call in for verification on those cards.

Handy Mini-Forms   Offers three small forms that make it easy to (1) fill in credit card verification numbers (after you've called in for authorization using whatever means you have available), (2) mark unpaid orders as Paid (after you've received payment), and (3) change any addresses currently marked as Prospect to Customer (after the prospect has actually made a purchase).

Print Current Orders   Prints packing slips, invoices, receipts, and labels for current orders.

You can print current orders at any time. For example, you might want to take in orders for the entire day, verify the credit card purchases, and fill in the verification numbers using the Handy Forms described previously. Then at the end of the day, use the Print Current Orders button to print the day's invoices, receipts, packing slips, mailing labels, and shipping labels.

Once you have printed current orders, they are no longer considered "current." Rather, they're considered "printed" (or "fulfilled") orders. If you need to review, change, or reprint those printed orders, you can use the last three buttons in Orders Central, as discussed next.

Tools for Managing Printed Orders

The lower three buttons in Orders Central let you work with all orders in Fulfill. That is, you're not limited to current (unprinted) orders. We'll discuss these buttons in the sections that follow.

View/Change Orders

The View/Change Orders button takes you to an order form that's used strictly for viewing, changing, and printing orders. When you click the View/Change Orders button, you come to an order form that has navigation tools. You can turn those navigation tools on or off simply by clicking the Navigation Tools On/Off button in the toolbar. Figure C.18 shows the View/Edit Orders form with the navigation tools turned on.

FIGURE C.18

The View/Edit Orders form with the navigation tools turned on.

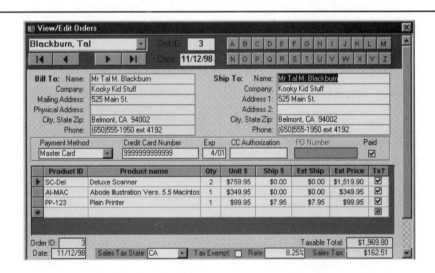

To locate a specific order, you can use the same basic techniques you use to navigate the Address Book. That is, orders are organized in alphabetical order by Bill To name. To look up a specific order, you first look up the name of the person or company that placed the order. The following three techniques will help you find your orders:

- Click one of the Rolodex-style buttons to jump to a section of the alphabet (where you're looking for the name of the person or company that placed the order).

- Click the drop-down list button just to the left to see nearby orders. There may be more than one order for any customer, but the drop-down list also shows the Order ID and Order Date (see below). You should be able to zero in on a specific order easily.

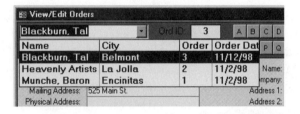

- You can use the VCR-style navigation buttons to scroll through orders as well.

On a 640 × 480 monitor, the navigation buttons make it hard to see the bottom of the order form. So, once you find the order you want to work with, click the Navigation Tools On/Off button in the toolbar to hide those tools and see the entire order form. Or, drag the border of the window to make it larger.

 WARNING Canceled orders do show in View/Change Orders with a checkmark in the Canceled box. Canceled orders are never printed and are never used in calculating sales, sales tax, or any of the other reports available from the Order/Sales Reports button.

If you change an order and need to reprint it, you can just click the Print This Order Now button in the toolbar. (It's the one that looks like the Print button on the standard Access toolbars.) When you've finished viewing and changing orders, click the Close button to return to Orders Central.

Order/Sales Reports

The Order/Sales Reports button lets you print information about all orders or a range of orders you specify. When you click the Order/Sales Reports button, you're taken to the Reports Based on Orders dialog box:

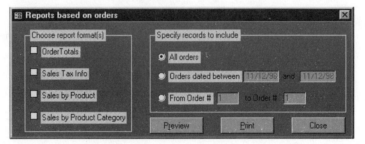

You can select any combination of reports simply by clicking their check boxes. You can also include all orders, orders within a certain range of dates, or a range of orders by Order ID. Then click the Preview button to preview the reports on the screen or click Print to actually print the reports. When you've finished with this dialog box, click the Close button to return to Orders Central.

Reprint Orders

If you need to reprint any invoices, receipts, or labels for orders that you've previously printed using the Print Current Orders button, click the Reprint Orders button. You'll be taken to the Reprint Orders dialog box:

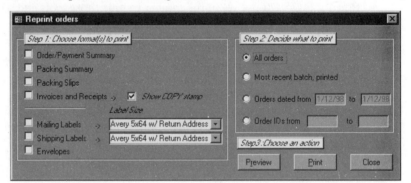

As instructed on the screen, select a format (or formats) to print. Then decide what to print, and click the Preview or Print button. Click the Close button to return to Orders Central.

Exiting Fulfill 2000

To exit Fulfill 2000, get back to the main switchboard and click the Exit button. Choose any one of the following options in the Where to? dialog box:

- **To Windows 95/98/NT**   Closes Fulfill and Microsoft Access and takes you back to Windows.
- **To Fulfill's Database Window**   Keeps Fulfill and Access open and takes you to Fulfill's database window, where you can explore behind the scenes (see Chapter 29).
- **Cancel**   Neither of the above; takes you back to Fulfill's main switchboard.

Questions, Comments, Snide Remarks

As mentioned earlier in this appendix, we've made every effort to make Fulfill 2000 bug free and accurate. However, a freeware product such as this does not have the benefit of beta testing (testing in the field), so bugs and mistakes can slip by. If you plan to use Fulfill for real work, you *are*, in a sense, the beta tester!

We will try to keep up with Fulfill and release additional versions with bug fixes and improvements, but we need your feedback to improve the product. If you find a problem or have a suggestion, feel free to contact the author, Alan Simpson, whose addresses are listed in the Help ≻ About ≻ Author box in Fulfill, as well as in the introduction to this book.

To check for any new versions of Fulfill or to see a list of FAQs (Frequently Asked Questions), check out Alan's Web site at http://www.coolnerds.com/coolnerds. TIA (Thanks in advance) for taking the time to do that. :-)

Master's Reference

A

Access Window

When you start Access and open a database, Access displays the main window. A status bar spans the bottom of the window with seven small fields. The status bar displays the following status indicators:

CAPS   Caps Lock is on.

EXT   Extend mode is on (as when selecting one or more fields or records).

FLTR   A filter is applied to the displayed data; click the Remove Filter button or select Records ➤ Remove Filter/Sort to display all records.

MOV   The Move mode is activated (as when moving columns in a datasheet or query grid); press the Esc key to end Move mode.

NUM   Num Lock is on; press the Num Lock key to turn Num Lock off.

OVR   Overtype mode is on (Text you enter will replace existing text.); press Ins to toggle between Overtype and Insert modes.

SCRL   Scroll Lock is on; press the Scroll Lock key to turn Scroll Lock off.

Action Queries

By default, Access queries are Select queries, which means they display information but do not modify it. Unlike Select queries, action queries let you change data in existing Access tables. Access has four types of action queries:

Append query   Adds a group of records from one table to another.

Delete query   Deletes a group of records.

Make-Table query   Creates a new table based on another table.

Update query   Changes data in a table.

To create an action query, open an existing query in design view or create a new query; then click the Query Type button and choose Make Table, Update, Append, or Delete.

To ensure that you modify the proper records, run a Select query and examine the results before running an action query.

To Create an Append Query

An Append query selects data from existing tables and adds new records at the end of another table (the receiving table).

1. Open a new query.

2. Select the tables that contain the data you want to append to the receiving table, and select Add. Select Close when you have selected all needed tables.

3. Create or update the query's Query by Example (QBE) grid. Select all the fields you want to append to the receiving table, including the field that contains the data for the primary key in the receiving table.

4. Include in the QBE grid columns all the fields used for limiting record selection, and include the criteria as appropriate.

5. Choose Query ➤ Select Query from the main menu and click the Datasheet View button to verify your query. Switch to design view to return to the query definition.

6. Select Query ➤ Append Query. Select Current Database to add records to a

table in the database you are using. Select the table to contain the records. Select OK.

7. Enter the field in the receiving table for each field in the QBE grid in the Append To row.

8. Click the Run button.

To Create a Delete Query

To define a new Delete query:

1. Create a new query in design view.

2. Select the tables that contain the data you want to delete from the Show Table dialog box and then select Close.

   You must include an asterisk field from each table in the QBE grid to delete records in the table.

3. Enter criteria, if any, in the QBE grid.

4. Select Query ➢ Select Query from the main menu, and switch to datasheet view to verify your query. Switch to design view to return to the query definition.

5. Select Query ➢ Delete Query.

   The QBE grid changes; the Delete row is added and the Sort and Show rows go away. The grid now shows From in all columns containing table names (and asterisks) and Where in all columns containing criteria.

6. Click the Run button.

To Create a Make-Table Query

Create a new table following the steps in "To Create an Append Query" with one difference: In step 6, select Query ➢ Make-Table Query and enter the name of the new table.

To Create an Update Query

To define a new update query:

1. Create a new query in design view.

2. Select the table that contains the data you want to change, and then select Close.

   The columns in the QBE grid must contain the fields that will be updated and any fields used for criteria.

3. Enter criteria, if any, in the QBE grid.

4. Choose Query ➢ Select Query from the main menu, and switch to datasheet view to verify your query. Switch to design view to return to the query definition.

5. Select Query ➢ Update Query.

6. Enter the new value for each field to be changed from the Update To row in the QBE grid.

7. Click the Run button.

Add-Ins

Access includes some add-in programs, like the wizards, that provide additional functionality. You can also create your own add-ins using Visual Basic or buy third-party add-ins, which can then be added to a database using the Add-In Manager. To open this tool, make sure the database you want to work with is open. Then select Tools ➢ Add-Ins ➢ Add-In Manager.

Installing an Add-In

To install an add-in, start the Add-In Manager as described previously. Then click the Add New button. In the Open dialog box that appears, select the .mda or .mde for the add-in you are installing and click Open. The add-in will appear on the list in the Add-In Manager dialog box. Click Close when you are finished with the Add-In Manager.

Removing an Add-In

To remove an add-in from a database, start the Add-In Manager. On the list of Available Add-Ins, select the add-in you want to remove and click Uninstall. Then click Close.

Analyzing Flat-File Tables

Access can look at your flat-file database table, split it into two or more tables, and set up the relationship between the new tables. To run the Table Analyzer Wizard:

1. Choose Tools ➤ Analyze ➤ Table from the database window.

2. Select Next until you have passed the introductory pages, if necessary. Access will ask if you want the Wizard to decide what fields go in the new tables.

3. Choose Yes or No, and then press Next.

4. Continue responding to the Wizard.

If the Wizard cannot find fields to suggest that you move to another table, it allows you to perform the split yourself.

AutoCorrect

Access can automatically correct an error or expand an abbreviation with an AutoCorrect dictionary that you define for it. This dictionary is also shared with other applications in the Microsoft Office suite, so if you have already loaded applications from the suite (such as Excel or Word), you don't have to reenter the AutoCorrect terms.

To enable AutoCorrect (which is set to "on" by default when you install Access):

1. Select Tools ➤ AutoCorrect.

2. Check the Replace Text as You Type option.

3. Select OK.

To add terms to the AutoCorrect list:

1. Select Tools ➤ AutoCorrect.

2. Enter the value in the Replace text box that, when typed, will be changed. Enter the new value (what Access will replace the text you enter with) in the Withtext box.

3. Click the Add button.

4. Repeat steps 2 and 3 until all terms have been entered. Then select OK.

To remove a term, highlight the term in the list and click the Delete key. Select OK when all terms you wish to delete have been removed.

AutoForm

To create a basic data entry form quickly, select a table or query from the database window, or display the table or query in datasheet view. Click the New Object button and then choose AutoForm; Access creates a data-entry form that displays one field per line. This form can be edited using the standard Access design tools—just like any other form.

AutoReport

To create a basic report showing all fields from a table or query, select a table or query from the database window, or display the table or query in datasheet view. Click the New Object button and then choose Auto-Report; Access creates a columnar report. This report can be edited using the standard Access design tools—just like any other form.

B

Borders

Borders provide a visual guide to objects on the screen. For example, you might use dark, wide borders to highlight fields.

To Change the Border of a Control

To change the thickness and style of a control's border on a form or report:

1. Open the form or report in design view. Then select the control(s) you want to change.

   - To select a single control, click it.

   - To select more than one control, press and hold down Shift while you select the controls.

   - If the controls are in a rectangular area, click the arrow in the toolbox and drag a rectangle around the area.

2. Click the drop-down menu for the Line/Border Color button on the toolbar, or select View ➤ Properties from the main menu and select the Border Color property. Click the ... at the end of the line.

3. Click the color you want to use.

4. Click OK if you are working with the Property dialog box.

To Change the Border Line Size of a Control

To change the thickness of a control's border on a form or report:

1. Select the control(s) you want to change.

2. Select the drop-down menu for the Line/Border Width button on the toolbar, or select View ➤ Properties from the main menu and select the Border Width property.

3. Click the desired width.

Buttons

Buttons are a common feature of a graphical user interface (GUI). When you click a button, Access performs a predefined task, such as displaying the next record.

To Create a Button on a Form or Data Access Page

To create a new button on a form or data access page:

1. Open the form or page in design view.

2. Select the button tool in the toolbox and then point and drag over the location where you want a button. Click Cancel from the Command Button Wizard if you want to assign a macro to the button yourself.

3. To assign a macro to the button, click the button to select it; then click the Properties button in the toolbar or select View ➤ Properties from the main menu. Click the Event tab, or right-click and select Properties. Use Tab to move to the right of On Click (or click directly in the cell) and enter the name of the macro.

   - If the macro is part of a macro group, enter the group name, a period, and the macro name in the On Click property.

   - Alternatively, click at the end of the cell and select the macro you want to assign to the button from the list of available macros that Access displays.

   - You can use the Macro Builder by clicking the ellipsis (the button with ... on it) at the end of the cell, selecting Macro Builder, and clicking OK.

You can also create a button and assign a macro to it directly by using the drag-and-drop feature:

1. Open the form or page in design view.

2. Open the database window by pressing F11.

3. Click the Macro button in the database window. Select the macro you want to assign to the new button.

4. Drag the macro name to the form or page and release the mouse button. Access creates the button and assigns the macro name to the On Click property.

5. Click the Properties button in the toolbar or select View ➤ Properties from the main menu to change the text on the button's face. Change the button's Caption property.

To Place a Picture on a Button

To replace the face of a button with a bitmap:

1. Open the form or page in design view.

2. Select the button on which you want to place the bitmap. If no picture has been assigned to the button, the Picture property for the button appears as *(none)*.

3. On the Format tab of the Properties sheet, for the Picture property enter the complete filename of the bitmap, including drive, directory, and filename. Bitmap files have the file extension .bmp. You can also click the button following the text box and select a predefined bitmap image.

When set, the property value changes to *(bitmap)*, and the bitmap image replaces the face of the button.

To Delete a Bitmap from a Button's Face

To delete a bitmapped image:

1. Open the form in design view.

2. Select the button whose bitmap you want to delete.

3. Select the entire text in the Picture property from the Format tab of the Properties window. The Picture property should display *(bitmap)*.

4. Press Delete.

5. Press Tab or click outside the property cell. Access will ask if you want to delete the graphic from the button. Select OK.

C

Calculations

A calculated control contains the result of an arithmetic operation (such as addition or multiplication) using existing fields (such as Payment Amount), functions (such as Average), and constants (such as 1.23). The calculation is stored in an expression that is assigned to the Control Source property of a control on a form or report. Calculated fields are for display only—they cannot be edited in form view.

To Add a Calculated Control to a Form, Data Access Page, or Report

To add a control that performs calculations to a form or report:

1. Open the form or report in design view.

2. Add a control, such as a text box, to the form or report.

3. Be sure the control is selected; the mouse pointer appears as a vertical bar when it is over the selected control.

- If the object is not a check box, option button, or option group, enter the expression in the control. (You can also enter the expression directly in the Control Source property, which is on the Data tab of the Properties box.)

- If the object is a check box, option button, or option group, enter the expression directly in the Control Source property.

4. To view or change the Properties box, select View ➢ Properties from the main menu, or click the Properties button in the toolbar and choose the Data tab. You must use this technique if the control is a check box, option button, or option group.

Check Boxes

A check box control indicates whether a value is on or off, true or false, selected or not selected. An *X* appears in the box when the value is on, true, or selected; the box is empty when the value of the field it represents is off, false, or not selected.

To Add a Check Box to a Form, Data Access Page, or Report

To add a check box to represent the value of a field:

1. Open the form, page, or report in design view.

2. Choose the Check Box button from the toolbox.

3. Select the field name from the Field List. (If the Field List is not displayed, select View ➢ Field List.) The field type of the selected field should be Yes/No.

4. Drag the field to the form. Access includes a default label to the right of the check box.

To Add an Unbound Check Box to a Form, Data Access Page, or Report

You can create an *unbound* check box (one that is not tied to a field). Unbound check boxes can represent the value of an expression—for example, whether the total amount of an order is over a specified limit and therefore must be verified.

To add an unbound check box:

1. Open the form, page, or report in design view.

2. Choose the Check Box button from the toolbox.

3. Click the area to contain the control.

4. Enter the expression in the Control Source property of the Data tab of the Property window. If the Property window is not visible, click the Properties button or select View ➢ Properties from the main menu.

If the field represented by a check box has a Numeric data type, the value -1 is the same as true (or yes) and 0 is the same as false (or no).

Colors

You can set the color of objects, such as text on a report or input fields on a form, using the color palette. You can use color to draw attention to special information or sections of a report or form.

To Set the Color(s) of an Object

To set the text, fill, and border color(s) of an object:

1. Select the object(s) you want to change. Access calls these objects controls. To select multiple controls, select the first control and then hold down Shift while you select the remaining controls.

2. Select the drop-down button on the toolbar that corresponds to the change you want to make. Each button has a block of color representing the current value. To choose that color, click the icon itself. To change the color, click the down-pointing arrow to the right of the icon.

Here's how to make other color changes:

- To change the background color, select the icon that looks like a tipped paint can.

- To change text color, select the Font/Fore Color (A) button.

- To change the border color, choose the icon that has a line slanting up and to the right.

- To change the border width, choose the icon with the upside-down L.

- To add special effects, click the Special Effect icon. The icon picture varies based on the last effect chosen.

You can also change these properties from the Properties box. Select the control(s), right-click, and choose Properties. Alternatively, choose View ➤ Properties from the main menu. Use the Format tab and move to the Back Color, Special Effect, Border Style, Border Color, or Border Width property. Once selected, each of these properties will display a pop-up box or a pull-down list with options appropriate to the selected property. Select the option you want and, if you are selecting from a pop-up box, click OK.

Columns

Datasheets and query grids are arranged in columns. Access lets you adjust all columns in the same way.

To Change the Width of a Column

To make a column wider or narrower:

1. Click the border separating the column from the column to its right. The pointer changes to a double-headed arrow with a vertical line down the middle.

2. Drag the double-headed arrow to the new location for the column border and release the mouse button.

To Change the Width of a Column Using the Keyboard

1. Select Format ➤ Column Width and then enter the new width in the Column Width text box.

2. To select the default width, check the Standard Width.

3. To have Access set the column width so that all values in the column are displayed, select Best Fit. Otherwise, select OK.

To Hide or Display a Column

To hide a column:

1. Select the column header of the column or columns you want to hide.

2. Select Format ➤ Hide Columns.

To display (unhide) a column:

1. Select Format ➤ Unhide Columns.

2. Select the columns you want to unhide (display). Visible columns are displayed with a check in the list.

3. Select Close.

To Freeze or Unfreeze Columns

When you move to the left or right of a datasheet, columns will normally disappear to make room to display new columns. Keeping a column visible when you scroll horizontally can help you keep track of which record you're viewing. Here's how to keep a column visible:

1. Select the column or columns you want to keep on the left side of the display by clicking the column's heading.

2. Select Format ➤ Freeze Columns.

To return to normal view (with no columns frozen), select Format ➤ Unfreeze All Columns.

To Rearrange Columns

To change the order of columns using the mouse:

1. Move the mouse pointer to the top of the columns you want to move so that it changes to a solid, down-pointing arrow.

2. Click the column headings. The columns appear in reverse video.

3. Click and drag the column heading to the column heading of the new location. For example, to move the column one column to the left, drag the selected column's heading to the heading of the column one column to the left.

4. The pointer displays a small box attached to an arrow. When the small box is positioned inside the column heading of the new location, release the mouse button. The existing columns are shifted to the right.

To change the order of columns using the keyboard:

1. Click the headings of the columns you want to move.

2. Press Ctrl+F8. MOV appears in the status bar at the bottom of the datasheet.

3. Press the right arrow to move the column to the right. Press the left arrow to move the column to the left.

4. Press Esc to leave Move mode.

To Save Layout Changes

To save changes to the column layout from within a table's datasheet view or form view, select File ➤ Save or press Ctrl+S.

Combo Boxes

A combo box allows you to enter a field value into a text box or select a value from a list that drops down from the box itself. Combo boxes are useful data-entry shortcuts that you can use on forms.

To Create a Combo Box with Predefined Values

To define a combo box and define the valid values:

1. Open the form in design view.

2. Select the combo box tool from the toolbox.

3. To create a combo box bound to a field, open the field list; then select the field from the Field window and drag it to the form. This will set the Control Source property of the option group to the field name. Go to step 5.

4. To create a combo box in an unbound option group, click the form where you want the combo box to appear. You must manually set the expression within the Control Source property for the option group.

5. Select the combo box.

6. Open the Properties window by clicking the Properties button in the toolbar or selecting View ➤ Properties from the main menu. Choose the Data tab.

7. Select the Row Source Type property and set it to Value List.

8. Select the Row Source property and enter the values directly, separated by a semicolon to display a single-column drop-down list. For example: **Cash;Check;Charge**.

- To display a multicolumn drop-down list, enter the number of columns in the Column Count property on the Format tab. Select the Row Source property on the Data tab and enter the values directly, each separated by a semicolon. The number of values must be divisible by the number of columns. For example, in a two-column table that contains a payment method and payment code, enter: **Cash;100;Check;200;Charge;300**.

- In a multicolumn combo box, the Bound Column property refers to the column that contains the value to be stored in the combo box when a selection is made. Thus in the payment example, set the Bound Column property to 1 to store the text of the payment method; set the Bound Column property to 2 to store the payment code.

Creating Combo Boxes That Look Up Values in Other Queries or Tables

You can have Access look up the values in a table or query when you click the combo box. The pull-down list displays the first field in the table or query you use. If you want to display a field other than the first field, you must create a custom query.

To Create a Combo Box with Lookup Values

To define a combo box that displays values from a table or query:

1. Open the form in design view.

2. Select the combo box tool from the tool box.

3. Open the field list; then select the field from the Field window and drag the field name to the form to create a combo box bound to a field. This sets the Control Source property of the option group to the field name.

4. Click the form where you want the combo box to appear to create a combo box in an unbound option group. You must manually set the expression within the Control Source property for the option group.

5. Select the combo box.

6. Open the Properties window by clicking the Properties button in the toolbar or selecting View ➤ Properties from the main menu. Choose the Data tab.

7. Select the Row Source Type property and set it to Table/Query. Select the Row Source property and select the table or query that contains the values to be displayed in the pull-down list. The pull-down list will display the first field from the table or query.

You can use *structured query language* (SQL) statements instead of a query as the lookup source. SQL statements execute somewhat faster than queries.

To Use SQL Statements in Combo Boxes

To use SQL statements as the expression for combo boxes:

1. Create a query to select the records with the values you want to use. In design view, select View ➤ SQL View from the main menu.

2. Select the SQL statement displayed in the SQL text window and copy it to the Windows Clipboard.

3. Open the form containing the combo box in design view. Select the Row Source property and press Ctrl+V to paste the contents of the Clipboard into the property value. This tells Access what information is requested.

4. Set the Row Source Type property to Table/Query. This tells Access to display values from a table or query rather than from a predefined list.

To Create Combo Boxes That Display a List of Field Names

To create a combo box that displays a list of a table's or query's field names:

1. Follow steps 1 through 6 in "To Create a Combo Box with Lookup Values" earlier.

2. Select the Row Source Type property, and set it to Field List.

3. Set the Row Source property to the query or table containing the field names.

Compacting and Repairing a Database

As you use a database, fragmentation occurs, which means that data gets spread over the disk where it is stored and searches take longer.

Compacting a database defragments it. When you compact a database, you can either replace the current version or save the compacted database to a new file. To defragment a database:

1. Go to the File Manager (or a third-party utility) and make a copy of the database to be compacted in another directory, in case compacting fails.

2. Return to Access and select Tools ➤ Database Utilities ➤ Compact and Repair Database. If you have a database open, Access will compact the open database and reopen it for you. You can skip the rest of the steps unless you want to compact another database. If this is the case, close the open database.

3. Select the filename of the database you want to compact, and click the Compact button. Database files have the extension .mdb. Access suggests a new filename. Accept this name or type another in the File Name text box. Click Save.

4. If you enter the filename of the existing file, Access will warn you that the file already exists and ask you if you wish to replace it. Select Yes to overwrite the file or No to enter a different file Name.

Access displays a progress indicator in the status bar at the bottom of the window. The program displays a dialog box indicating success or failure upon completion of the task.

Control Messages on the Status Bar

When adding a control to a form, set the control's Status Bar Text property to the text you want to display when the control is edited during data entry. The property defaults to the field's name.

Controls

Controls are objects added to a form, data access page, or report: a graph, picture (such as a logo), field from a table, or text used as a label for a field or a heading of a report. Although all these objects are called controls, only button controls actually control any action. Controls are used to do things like display data from a record, provide a heading on a report, or display a bitmap of a logo on a form.

Controls are the building blocks of forms and reports. For example, you must have one control for each field in a table you want to display on a form, data access page, or report.

Bound and Unbound Controls

A bound control is one that is linked to a field in a table—it displays data from a table. An unbound control is one that is not linked to a field. On a form, for example, data entered by a user as a parameter to a query is an example of an unbound control. A label on a form is another example of an unbound control.

To Add, Move, or Delete Controls

Everything on a form, page, or report is a control. Fields (bound or unbound to a table or query), graphs, text, and control buttons are all controls.

The following steps show you how to manipulate controls on an Access form, page, or report:

1. Open a form, page, or report in design view.

2. Select the type of control you want to add from the toolbox. For example, select a text box, command button, or label. If you select a text box tool or

bound object frame tool, you can click a field from the field list.

3. Move the mouse to the form. Click where you want the upper-left corner of the control to appear and drag to the bottom-right corner. Release the mouse.

Access may ask you further questions about your control, depending on which type of control you selected. For example, if you insert an object (using the unbound object frame button in the toolbox), Access will ask you to identify the object type and the filename.

If you want to add a field with an OLE data type (a field that can store documents, sounds, and other objects), select the bound object frame tool in step 2. In design view, the object appears as an empty box—no image is displayed. The image is retrieved from the individual record and displayed in the control when you are in form or report view. Furthermore, in form or report view, double-clicking the object launches the OLE server application and lets you modify the object.

To Add a Control

With the Duplicate command, you can add a control that is the same size and shape and is evenly spaced on a form, page, or report. This command is useful for evenly spacing buttons and check boxes.

1. Open the form, page, or report in design view.

2. Select an existing control by clicking it in the toolbox.

3. Open the Properties window by clicking the Properties button in the toolbar or selecting View ➤ Properties from the main menu. Choose the All tab.

4. Set a control's properties by entering the desired value in the cell to the right of the property's name, as appropriate.

5. Select Edit ➤ Duplicate.

If the control is not in an option group, Access creates a copy of the control and places it on top of the original control. Move the new control to its new location and select Edit ➤ Duplicate. If the control is in an action group, Access displays the new control underneath the original control. Access also displays a third control aligned with the first two controls.

To Add a Label to a Control

After you position the label, the mouse pointer turns into an I-beam. Type the text for the label. When you are done, click anywhere outside the label. Access automatically wraps text to fit the size of the control.

If you want the label to have more than one line of text, press Ctrl+Enter to begin a new line.

To Move a Control

1. Click the control. Black-dot handles surround the control, and a dark, open-hand icon appears over the control.

2. Drag the button to move the control, and release the mouse when the control is in the desired location.

To Resize a Control

To change the size of a control:

1. Click the control.

2. Move the pointer to one of the handles that surround the selected control. Click and drag the outline to a new size when the pointer changes to a two-headed or four-headed arrow.

To change selected controls on a form or report to a common size, select Format ➤ Size. Select To Tallest, To Shortest, To Widest, or To Narrowest to change the size of the selected controls. (You can't use these techniques when working with a data access page.)

If you change the content formatting within a control on a form or report, such as increasing the font size, you can automatically resize the control to fit the new property. Select Format ➤ Size and then choose To Fit.

To Change the Space between Controls

To change the horizontal or vertical spacing between controls on a form or report:

1. Select the controls.

2. To change the horizontal spacing, select Format ➤ Horizontal Spacing, and then select Make Equal, Increase, or Decrease.

3. To change the vertical spacing, select Format ➤ Vertical Spacing, and then select Make Equal, Increase, or Decrease.

4. Repeat steps 2 and/or 3 until the desired spacing is achieved.

To Delete a Control

To remove a control from a form, page, or report:

1. Click the control to select it.

2. Press Delete or select Edit ➤ Delete from the main menu.

To Select Multiple Controls on a Form or Report

To select more than one control at a time while working on a form or report, select the first one

MASTER'S REFERENCE

and then, while pressing and holding the Shift key, select the remaining controls.

To select the controls within a vertical or horizontal range, click the horizontal or vertical ruler and then drag the mouse to the end of the range. All controls within the bounds you set are automatically selected.

To Change the Appearance and Behavior of a Control

You can modify controls in several ways. For example, you can change the color and 3-D effect of a control by selecting the Palette button in the toolbar and clicking the options you want. Likewise, you can change the text within a label control by changing its Caption property.

To Combine Text and a Function in a Control on a Form or Report

You can combine text and the result of a function in a single control to give a function value the appearance of a label. For example, instead of displaying only the current date in the page header section, you can combine text and the results of the Now( ) function, or you can change the field in the page header section to read *Report Date and Time:* followed by the date and time. To do so, you work with the control's Control Source property.

1. Be sure the report or form is in design view. If you are in report preview mode, click the Close button on the toolbar.

2. Click the control you want to change, or add a new text box control and click it.

3. Open the Properties window by clicking the Properties button, or select View ➤ Properties from the main menu.

The Control Source box in the Data tab provides space for you to enter the new value of the Control Source property. Control Source refers to the location or contents of the text box. For example, the Control Source of a report date control is set at =Now( ) by the Report Wizard.

4. Click the box to the right of Control Source. Press Shift+F2 to open the Zoom window, which provides a larger window in which to enter the Control Source value.

5. Enter the expression. For example, enter an = sign, your text (surrounded in quotes), the & symbol, and a function for the date as: =`"Report Date: "` & `Now()`.

Access reads the expression as follows:

- The = sign means that the contents of the control will be replaced by what follows.

- `"Report Date: "` is text that will appear in the field when it is printed or displayed.

- The & tells Access to concatenate `"Report Date: "` with the current date and time, which is supplied by `Now()`.

6. Select OK. The Control Source property cell is replaced by the contents of the Zoom window.

To Modify a Control's Label

By default, Access includes a bound control's label when you add the control to a form, page, or report. Access considers the control and its label as a group; when you click the control, you select both the field and its label.

To modify a control's label, click the label to select it. You can now modify the label or click the control itself to work with it.

To Align Controls on a Form, Data Access Page, or Report to a Grid

To align controls to predefined grid lines:

1. Open the form, page, or report in design view.

2. Select View ➤ Grid from the main menu if the grid is not displayed.

3. Select Format ➤ Snap to Grid from the main menu if you are adding a new control.

4. In a former report, align existing objects to the grids by selecting the control(s) and then selecting Format ➤ Align ➤ To Grid from the main menu. This step may cause the controls to change their size slightly.

To Use a Control as a Model for Other Controls

If you add several controls of the same type to a form or report, you can set the characteristics (size, shape, and font, for example) of one of the controls and use it as the model for existing or new controls of the same type.

To apply the control's characteristics to *new* controls:

1. Select the control.

2. Select Format ➤ Set Control Defaults from the main menu.

Converting Access Databases from Earlier Versions

You can use data from previous versions of Microsoft Access, but you cannot change objects within that database (reports or forms, for example) unless the database is converted. To convert a database created in a previous version of Access, do the following:

1. Close the database if it is open.

2. Select Tools ➤ Database Utilities ➤ Convert Database ➤ To Current Access Database Version from the Access menu. Access displays the Database to Convert From dialog box.

3. Enter the filename of your old database in the File Name text box and click OK. Access displays the Convert into Database dialog box.

4. Enter the new name for the converted database and click OK. Access performs the conversion and creates your new file.

Converting a Database to the Prior Access Version

If you need to use a database with the prior version of Access, there's a new feature in Access 2000 that can help you out. To convert a database to the prior version of Access, do the following:

1. Close the database if open.

2. Select Tools ➤ Database Utilities ➤ Convert Database ➤ To Prior Access Database Version from the main Access menu. Access displays the Database to Convert From dialog box.

3. Enter the filename of your old database in the File Name text box and click OK. Access displays the Convert into Database dialog box.

4. Enter the new name for the converted database and click OK. Access performs the conversion and creates your new file.

Copy a Database Object to Another Database

To save design time, you can copy a table, query, form, etc., to another database. To copy one Access database object (table, query, etc.) to another Access database:

1. Open the database window by pressing F11. Select the object you want to copy.

2. Select File ➤ Export from the main menu.

3. Enter the name of the database you are copying to in the Export dialog box and click Save.

4. Enter a new name for the object that will be copied to another database when Access displays the Export dialog box.

5. Click OK.

Counting Records

To display a count of the number of records in a table (or subset as defined by a query):

1. Open the query in design view.

2. Select View ➤ Totals in the main menu, or click the Totals icon in the toolbar if the Total row is not displayed in the QBE grid at the bottom of the window.

3. Click in the box in the Field column and select Count from the Total row.

4. Run the query by clicking the Run button (the one with the exclamation point on it) in the toolbar or by selecting Query ➤ Run from the main menu.

Criteria

Criteria are used to select records in queries and filters. Criteria set the conditions that must be matched in order for a record to be included in a dynaset.

To Create Criteria

To add criteria:

1. Do one of the following:

   • Open a query in design view.

   • Open a table in datasheet view or open a form in form view. Then select Records ➤ Filter ➤ Advanced Filter/Sort from the main menu.

2. If the field used for comparison has not been included in the grid at the bottom of the query window, drag it from the field list to a new column in the Field row.

3. Select the cell in the Criteria row underneath the field heading of the field used for comparing values. For example, to select parts with prices less than $1.00, select the cell in the Criteria row in the Price column.

4. Enter the criteria expression. For example, to find customers that live in California, enter "CA" (including the quotation marks) in the Criteria row of the State column.

5. If you want to enter one of several criteria a field must meet in order to include the record in the filter or query, enter the "or" condition in the cell beneath the first criteria expression. For example, to select all customers who are doctors or lawyers, enter "doctor" (including the quotation marks) in the Profession field's Criteria box, and enter "lawyer" in the

cell immediately underneath "doctor." "Lawyer" appears in the Or row.

6. Fields used in criteria expressions are displayed in the dynaset. (A dynaset is a subset of fields and records that you can edit as though you were working with an entire table or group of related tables.)

7. To use the field in such expressions but exclude it from the dynaset, open the query in design view and click the Show box so it is not selected (the check box is empty). Do one of the following:

   • If you are designing a query, click the Run icon or select Query ➤ Run.

   • If you started from a datasheet or a form, choose the Apply Filter button or select Filter ➤ Apply Filter/Sort.

Access may display your criteria expression in a format slightly different from that used when the data was entered. For example, if you enter the expression <7/1/99 as the criterion for a field of data type Date/Time, Access translates it to <#7/1/99#, since dates in expressions must be surrounded by the # character. Similarly, text strings will be surrounded by quotes when values include embedded blanks, such as "New Jersey" or "Price Per Unit".

To set criteria that meet the opposite of a value, use the NOT operator. For example, to find customers that are not doctors, enter Not "doctors" in the Criteria row of the Profession field.

To Use Criteria in Totals Calculations

Your criteria can specify which records to include in calculations that compute totals.

To limit the groupings, enter the criteria fields in columns that use Group By in the Total row. If you enter > **1000** in the Order field's Criteria cell, Access selects all records in which the Order field's value is $1000 or more. Thus, all records in which an order was greater than $1000 are included in the dynaset.

To set the criteria on the total value of a field, enter the criteria field in columns that use an aggregate function (such as Sum) in the Total row. If you enter > **1000** in the Order field's Criteria cell, Access adds up the total value of all orders for a customer; if the total amount of all the orders for the customer in the table is over $1000, the customer records are included in the dynaset.

To set the criteria of the records that should be included in the total value for a field, set the Total row to Where and enter the criteria in the Criteria Row. If you enter > **1000** in the Order field's Criteria cell in this case, Access sums up only those records in which an individual order is over $1000 and includes the total for orders over $1000 in the dynaset.

To set the Totals value:

1. Open a query in design view.

2. Click the Totals button on the toolbar, or select View ➤ Totals from the main menu.

3. Select the Total option you want (such as Sum).

Crosstabs

Crosstabs can be used with aggregate functions to display a field value (sum, count, average, etc.) in row and column format. Crosstabs are generally used to summarize data, not show each record. Given the proper data in a table, crosstabs can show the total number of parts sold by state by quarter or the average rainfall by state by month.

To Create a Crosstab

The easiest way to create a crosstab is with the Crosstab Wizard. Select the Query button in the database window and select New. Then select Crosstab Query Wizard and click OK. Follow the Wizard's direction.

To Run a Crosstab from the Database Window

To execute a Crosstab while the database window is displayed:

1. Move to the database window by pressing F11.

2. Click the Query tab. Access lists all queries, including Crosstab queries, in the same list.

3. Highlight the Crosstab query you want to run.

4. Double-click the query name or select the Open button.

5. Access displays the results of the Crosstab query in a datasheet.

Calculation Types

Access can perform a variety of calculations either automatically (by selecting a type in a Crosstab) or by explicitly setting a calculation in a property box.

Avg   Computes the average value.

Count   Counts the number of records a query selects.

Expression   Evaluates an expression for this field.

First   Displays the value in the first record (using the current sort order).

Group By   Performs no calculation (the default).

Last   Displays the value in the last record (using the current sort order).

Max   Finds the largest (maximum) value.

Min   Finds the smallest (minimum) value.

StDev   Computes the standard deviation.

Sum   Adds all values.

Var   Computes the variance of all values.

Where   Specifies a limiting expression; fields that use the Where value are not displayed; Where values are used to restrict records in a Crosstab.

To Set Column Order

By default, Crosstabs display columns in ascending order (A–Z). Although this option works well for most Date/Time and Text fields, it arranges data alphabetically rather than by month when monthly summaries are requested (April, August, December, etc.).

To fix the order of the columns based on their value:

1. Select the columns whose order you want to control with the query in design view.

2. Click anywhere in the top of the query window (but not on a table), and then open the Properties window.

3. Click in the Column Headings box.

4. Enter the column names in the order in which you want them to appear, separated by semicolons. Alternatively, enter one column name per line by entering a column name and then pressing Ctrl+Enter to begin a new line. If a column name is more than one word, surround the name in quotation marks.

5. Close the Properties windows or click anywhere else on the screen.

To Use Crosstab Queries in Reports

To use a Crosstab query in a report:

1. Set fixed columns headings with the Crosstab in design view.

2. Click the New Object button and select Report from the drop-down list on the toolbar. Select Design View in the New Report dialog box.

3. Click the Field List button in the toolbar or select View ➢ Field List.

4. Drag the fields from the query to the report on the blank report.

5. Add the fields you want such as page number and report title).

6. Save and/or run the report.

Customizing Access

You can customize the way Access displays data, prints forms and reports, and the defaults it uses throughout the system.

To Customize Access Options

To set the options that work throughout all modules in Access:

1. Select Tools ➢ Options from the main menu. The Options dialog box appears.

2. Click the tab for the category of options you want to change. Make your changes to the selected page.

3. Repeat step 2 for all the options you want to change.

4. Select OK.

D

Data Access Pages

Data access pages are HTML files that you can use to browse data from Access or Internet Explorer 5. References to these objects appear in the database window for a database or a project, but they are stored in their own HTML files separate from the database or project file they are associated with. Data access pages are also referred to as *pages*.

To Create a Data Access Page

To create a new page:

1. Move to the database window by pressing F11.

2. Click the Pages button and select New. At the bottom of the dialog box, Access asks you for the name of the table or query to use for the page.

3. Type the name of the table or query, or click the down-pointing arrow to display the list of available tables and queries and select one.

4. Double-click Design View to set up the page yourself. Or double-click Page Wizard to have Access lead you through the basic page design steps.

To Save a Page

To save a page for future use, select File ➢ Save or press Ctrl+S.

To Save a Page as a New Page

To save a page to a new file with a different name, select File ➢ Save As from the menu. In the Save As window, enter the name for the new file and click OK.

To Delete a Page from a Database

To delete a data access page from a database:

1. Highlight the page you want to delete in the database window.

2. Press Delete. Select Yes to remove the page from the database and delete the page file itself, or click No to remove the page from the database but leave the HTML file for the page alone.

3. Select Edit ➤ Undo Delete from the main menu to undelete a page deleted by mistake. You can only undelete the most recently deleted object.

To Apply a Theme to a Page

Access has several predefined themes you can choose from, in order to apply a uniform look to a page. To select a theme and apply it to a page:

1. Open the page in design view.

2. Choose Format ➤ Theme from the menu.

3. Select a theme under Choose a Theme.

4. Check any options you want to use in the lower-left corner of the window.

5. Click OK.

To Change the Size of a Page or Page Section

Here's how to change the size of a page or page section:

1. Open the page in design view.

2. Click the section you want to resize to select it.

3. Move the pointer to one of the handles on the border of the section you want to

change. The cursor turns into a double-headed arrow.

4. Click and drag up or down until the section is the size you want. Similarly, change the width by moving the mouse to the left or right border and dragging the double-headed arrow so the section is the size you desire.

To Browse a Page

To browse a page that you're working on from Access, click the View button. A Page View window will open where you can see how the form will appear with data.

To browse a page using Internet Explorer 5:

1. In the database window, right-click the page you want to browse.

2. Choose Web Page Preview from the shortcut menu.

Data Types

Each field in a table contains a different type of data: text, dates, or numbers, for example. When creating or modifying a field in a table, select from one of these types.

AutoNumber   Can contain numbers automatically assigned by Access to the next higher value in the table. The value is limited at 2,147,483,647.

Currency   Can contain numbers representing money, up to 15 digits to the left of the decimal point and 4 digits to the right.

Date/Time   Can contain dates and times. Only valid dates and times are allowed.

Hyperlink Can contain hyperlink addresses: valid URLs or references to database objects, Office documents, etc.

Memo Can contain numbers and letters up to 32,000 characters (including spaces).

Number Can contain numbers, including those with decimals.

OLE Object Can contain any object that provides an embeddable or linkable object, such as a graphic, document, spreadsheet, or sound file. The object must be smaller than 128MB.

Text Can contain numbers and letters up to 255 characters (including spaces).

Yes/No Can contain Boolean values (true/false, yes/no, on/off). The field may contain only one of two values.

If a field is used to look up data in a table or list, select Lookup Wizard for the field type.

The currency data type should be used in calculations in which you want to keep the number of digits fixed and where precise calculations are required.

Databases

A database is a collection of tables, queries, forms, data access pages, reports, macros, and modules (program code).

To Create a Database

1. Select File ➢ New from the main menu or press Ctrl+N.

2. Click the General tab and select Database. Click OK. Enter the name of the new database in the File Name box. Database names must be legal filenames: they are limited to 255 characters and numbers. Access supplies the .mdb file extension.

3. Click OK in the File New Database window.

To Open a Database

1. Select File ➢ Open from the main menu, press Ctrl+O, or choose the open icon in the toolbar.

2. Select the drive, directory, and filename of the database you want to open.

3. Select OK. Access displays the database window.

To Copy, Rename, or Delete a Database

To copy, rename, or delete a database within Access:

1. Close the database file. In a multiuser environment, all users must close the database.

2. Choose File ➢ Open from the menu, right-click the name of the database you want to work with, and choose Copy, Delete, or Rename from the shortcut menu.

You can also delete a database using the Windows Explorer or a third-party file utility.

To Copy a Table to Another Database

To copy an existing table to another Access database:

1. Open the source database.

2. Highlight the table in the database window.

3. Select Edit ➢ Copy.

4. Open the destination database.

5. Select Edit ➢ Paste from the main menu.

6. Enter the table's name in the Paste Table As dialog box.

7. Select whether you want to paste only the table's structure or whether you want to copy the structure and the data. You can also choose to append data to an existing database.

8. Select OK.

Damaged Database

If an Access database becomes corrupted because of a hardware problem, such as an interruption in power or a problem with a hard disk, you may be able to recover the data. Use the instructions listed earlier for "Compacting and Repairing a Database."

Database Documenter

The Database Documenter lets you print information about an entire table or specific elements within a database. To run the Database Documenter:

1. Select Tools ➤ Analyze ➤ Documenter.

2. Click the tab for the type of object (Tables, Reports, etc.) you want to document. (You can select more than one object and more than one object type.) Select the objects to document.

3. Repeat step 2 until all objects you want to document are selected.

4. To set specific options for printing information about tables, fields, and indexes, select Options. Set the options and select OK.

5. Select OK. Access builds the report and opens the report preview window, from which you can browse or print the report.

Database Utilities

Access includes database utilities you can use to split a database, manage link tables, and work with switchboards.

Database Splitter

The Database Splitter lets you split a database into two databases: one with data that can be placed on a server for sharing and another with forms, reports, etc. To open it, select Tools ➤ Database Utilities ➤ Database Splitter.

Linked Table Manager

The Linked Table Manager lets you manage the paths to any tables you have linked to the open database. To open it, select Tools ➤ Database Utilities ➤ Linked Table Manager.

Switchboard Manager

The Switchboard Manager is for customizing switchboard forms. To open it, select Tools ➤ Database Utilities ➤ Switchboard Manager.

Database Window

The database window is the main window that Access displays when you open a database.

Datasheets

Datasheets display data from tables and queries. To open a datasheet, click the table or query that you want to run in the database window and click Open.

To switch between datasheet view and design view, click the Datasheet and Design buttons in the toolbar, or select View ➤ Datasheet View or View ➤ Design View from the main menu.

To Navigate within a Datasheet

The quick buttons for record access are in the bottom-left corner of the datasheet window.

In the middle of the navigation buttons is the record counter of the current record. Press F5 or click in the box; then enter the record number you want to display and press Enter.

To handle more information than fits on a single screen, Access displays scroll bars. Use the scroll bars to navigate around the datasheet.

You can move directly to the column of your choice by selecting the field from the Field list on the toolbar.

To limit the records displayed by a query's datasheet, specify a filter.

Subdatasheets

If the table shown in a datasheet window is related to another table, you can view the related records using subdatasheets. Depending on the relationship between tables, Access may automatically include a subdatasheet as part of a datasheet view.

Adding a Subdatasheet to a Datasheet View

To add a subdatasheet to a datasheet:

1. Open the database datasheet view.

2. Choose Insert ➢ Subdatasheet from the menu.

3. Select the table for the subdatasheet view.

4. Click OK.

Opening or Closing a Subdatasheet

If the table shown in a datasheet has a subdatasheet defined, you will see an expand button (+) to the left of each record in the datasheet window. To expand a subdatasheet for a record, click the record's expand button. To close a subdatasheet, click the collapse button (-) for the record it belongs to.

Opening or Closing all the Subdatasheets for a Datasheet

Use Format ➢ Subdatasheet ➢ Expand All to open the subdatasheets for all the records in a datasheet view. To close all open subdatasheets, use Format ➢ Subdatasheet ➢ Collapse All.

Removing a Subdatasheet from a Datasheet

If you need to remove a subdatasheet, choose Format ➢ Subdatasheet ➢ Remove from the menu.

To Close a Datasheet

When you have finished working with a datasheet and want to return to the database window, select File ➢ Close or press Ctrl+W.

You can also leave a datasheet by selecting another view using the toolbar—for example, select the Design button from the toolbar.

Editing Data and Records

Tables consist of records, which contain the actual data you want to keep.

To Add a Record Using a Datasheet

You can add data to a datasheet in two ways:

- Move to the bottom of the datasheet to the record marked with an asterisk (*). You can move to this row by using the scroll bars or by selecting Edit ➢ Go To ➢ New Record from the main menu. This row is reserved for new data. When you begin to enter data in this row, Access inserts another row immediately below. You can also select Insert ➢ New Record from the main menu.

- Select Records ➤ Data Entry from the main menu or press Ctrl++. Access displays a blank row. When you begin to enter data in this row, Access inserts another row immediately below.

If a default value has been defined for the field, press Ctrl+Alt+Spacebar and the value is displayed. When you want to insert the value from the previous record into the current field, press Ctrl+'.

To Find a Value in a Datasheet

To find a text string in one or more fields in a datasheet:

1. Click the heading of the column containing the field you want to search. The entire column changes to reverse video.

2. Click the Find button in the toolbar. (It looks like a pair of binoculars.)

3. Enter the value you want to find in the Find What box of the Find and Replace dialog box.

4. Press Tab and choose the Look In type.

5. Press Tab to move to the Match box. Click the down-pointing arrow key or press Alt+↓. Select Any Part of Field. This search will find the value anywhere in the field, not just at the beginning of the field.

6. Select Find Next. Access displays the result of the search in reverse video.

7. Select the Find Next button to find the next occurrence of the value.

8. Select the Cancel button when you are done searching the field.

To Select Data in a Datasheet

To cut, copy, or paste fields or records, you must first select the data. Use these keyboard and mouse techniques to select data:

Select a field   Press F2, or click at the beginning of the selection and drag the mouse to highlight the data, or click the left edge of the cell.

Select adjacent fields   Select the value within the first field; hold the Shift key and press the appropriate arrow key. Or click the left edge of the field (mouse cursor points down), and then drag the mouse to extend the selection.

Select text within a field   Move the insertion point to the beginning of the field, and then hold down Shift and move to the end of the selection. Or click at the beginning of the selection and drag the mouse to highlight the data; or click at the beginning of the selection, hold down Shift, and click at the end of the selection.

Select the current record   Press Shift+Spacebar. Or click the record selector (the small box at the leftmost edge of the window).

Select a word within a field   Move the insertion point to the beginning of the word, hold down Shift, and move to the end of the word. Or double-click anywhere in the word.

Select more than one record   Press Shift+Spacebar, hold down Shift, and press ↑ or ↓ until all desired records are highlighted. Or click the record selector and drag the mouse pointer to the last record.

Select all records   Select Edit ➤ Select All Records from the main menu or press Ctrl+A. Or click the small record selector above all rows and to the left of all column headings.

Select the current column   Press Ctrl+Spacebar. Or click the column heading.

Select adjacent columns   Press Ctrl+Spacebar; then press Shift and ← or →. Or click the first column heading and then drag the mouse to the left or right.

To Copy or Move Data within a Datasheet

To copy or move data within the same datasheet:

1. Select the data you want to copy or move.

2. Do one of the following:

   - **To copy the data**, press Ctrl+C or select Edit ➢ Copy from the main menu.

   - **To move the data**, press Ctrl+X or select Edit ➢ Cut from the main menu.

3. Move the insertion point to the new location for the data.

4. Press Ctrl+V or select Edit ➢ Paste from the main menu.

To Copy or Move Records between Datasheets

You can copy or move records from one datasheet to another datasheet (including datasheets in other databases) as long as the fields are in the same order. If the selection you copy has more columns than the destination datasheet, the extra columns are not copied. If the selection you copy has fewer columns, null values are used for the missing columns.

To copy or move records:

1. Select the records you want to copy or move with the datasheet in datasheet view.

2. Do one of the following:

   - **To copy the records**, press Ctrl+C or select Edit ➢ Copy from the main menu.

   - **To move the records**, press Ctrl+X or select Edit ➢ Cut from the main menu.

3. Open the datasheet to receive the records. (If the columns are not in exactly the same order as the source columns, rearrange them now.)

4. Select Edit ➢ Paste Append from the main menu to append records to the end of the datasheet. If you want to replace records in this datasheet, select the records first and then press Ctrl+V, or select Edit ➢ Paste from the main menu.

To Copy Data to the Clipboard

Select any field(s) and/or record(s) and then select Edit ➢ Copy. The data is copied to the Windows Clipboard.

To Delete Data in a Datasheet

After selecting the data, press Delete or select Edit ➢ Delete from the menu.

To Delete Records in a Datasheet

To remove records from a datasheet:

1. Select the records you want to delete with the datasheet in datasheet view.

2. Press Ctrl+X or select Edit ➢ Delete Record from the main menu. Access asks you to confirm the delete.

3. Select OK to delete the records or Cancel to keep them.

Displaying Records in a Datasheet

This section describes how to change the way your data appears on the screen.

To Display the Most Current Information in a Datasheet

If you are making frequent updates to a table or working in a multiuser environment, the data displayed in a datasheet may not be current. You have two options for updating the datasheet display:

- **Refreshing the records** shows the most recent status, including which records were deleted, but does not show new records, change the order of the records, or change which record is current.

- **Requery** displays new records and removes deleted records, so the order of records and the current record may change.

If you change a record's value so that it no longer meets the criteria of a query, specify Requery to remove it from the display.

To refresh the display, select Records ➤ Refresh from the main menu.

To requery the database, press Shift+F9.

To Change Row Height

You can change the height of each row in a datasheet by using the mouse or the menus.

To change the row height using the mouse:

1. Move the pointer to the border of any row so that the pointer changes to a two-headed arrow with a bar through it.

2. Click and drag so that the row expands or contracts to the desired height, and then release the mouse button.

To change the row height using the menu:

1. Select Format ➤ Row Height from the main menu.

2. Enter the desired row height in the Row Height box, or click Standard Height to use the default height.

3. Select OK.

To Change Column Width

To change the width of a column of data, select the right border of the column heading and drag it to the desired position. Drag to the left to make the column narrower or to the right to widen the column.

To Remove Gridlines

By default, datasheets are displayed with horizontal and vertical lines separating each row and column. To remove these gridlines, select Format ➤ Cells and select the gridline options. Check or uncheck Horizontal and Vertical to view or remove these gridlines.

Dates

Access tables can store date information. This section describes how you can enter and display dates in Access.

To Add the Current Date and Time

To add the current date and time to a form or report:

1. Open the form or report in design view.

2. Add a text box to the appropriate area (section) of the form or report.

3. Click the Properties button in the toolbar or select View ➤ Properties.

4. Enter **=Date()** (for the current date) or **=Now()** (for the date and current time) in the Control Source property on the Data tab.

5. Set the Format property with a standard or custom format.

Date Functions

Access uses the following date functions:

CVDate *(expression)*   Converts a date expression (for example, "July 25, 1999") to a serial date; serial dates are between -657434 (January 1, 100 AD) and 2958465 (December 31, 9999 AD).

Date   Returns date with date stored as a double.

DatePart *(period, date)*   Returns the part of the *date* specified by *period*. *Date* can be a string expression that contains a date, or it can be a Date/Time field. For period parameters, see the list below.

DateSerial *(year, month, day)*   Returns the serial date for the given *year* (0 through 9999), *month* (1 through 12), and *day* (1 through 31). *Year*, *month*, and *day* are numbers or numeric expressions.

DateValue *(string)* Returns a date based on *string*. *String* holds the date in the format specified in the International portion of the `Win.ini` file.

Date$ Returns date in the form mm-dd-yyyy (for example, 07-22-1999).

Day *(serial date)* Returns the day number (from 01 to 31) of the *serial date*.

IsDate *(argument)* Returns true if the *argument* is a valid serial date or date expression.

Weekday *(number)* Returns an integer representing the day of the week, from 1 (Sunday) through 7 (Saturday); *number* is a serial date or numeric expression.

Use the following strings for the DatePart *period* parameter:

d	day
h	hour
m	month
n	minute
q	quarter
s	second
w	weekday (01 is Sunday, 07 is Saturday)
ww	week number (01–52)
y	day of the year (01–366)
yyyy	year

Default Property

The default property is assigned to a command button on a form. It determines which button in a group will be pressed when the user presses the Enter key. The button with the default property appears emphasized.

Default Values

Setting a default value for fields speeds up data entry. During data entry, you can have Access fill in the default value for fields by pressing Ctrl+Alt+Spacebar.

To Set a Default Value for a Field

To set the default value for a field so that Access fills in the value when a new record is created:

1. Open the table in design view.
2. Select the field you want to change by clicking it.
3. Select the Default Value property in the General tab in the Field Properties window at the bottom of the screen.
4. Enter the default value (an explicit value or expression) in the Default Value box. Enter **=Yes** or **=No** in Yes/No fields.

If you change a field's default value, existing data for the field is not changed.

Design View

When you design an Access object, such as a form, page, report, or query, you define the object's layout or properties. When your design is ready to be tested, you can switch to run mode and test the object. For example, you can design a form in design view and then switch to form view, which displays the first record in the table or query using the form you have designed.

To Switch between Design View and Form View

You can switch between design view or form view and run mode, which displays the result of your design, by using buttons on the toolbar or by using the menu.

Toolbar Click the down-pointing arrow button to the right of the View button, and then choose Design View to switch to Design mode. Click the Run button (the one with the large exclamation point). This button's face changes depending on the object you are working on: for example, when you are working with a query, it shows a datasheet because the datasheet is the object used to display the results of a query.

Menus Select View from the main menu. The pull-down list of menu options corresponds to the type of object you are working on. For example, if you are working with a query, the pull-down options are Design View or Datasheet View. Select Design View to return to design view, and select Datasheet View to execute the query. Similarly, if you are working with a form, you can select View ➢ Design View to move to design view, View ➢ Form View to see the data filled in on the form, or View ➢ Datasheet View to view the data in a datasheet.

To Modify an Object in Design View

To modify an object's design in design view:

1. Open the database window by pressing F11.

2. Select the button for the type of object you want to modify: select the Table, Query, Form, Page, Report, or Macro button. Access displays a list of the objects of the type you selected. For example, if you selected Table, Access displays a list of all the existing tables.

3. Select the name of the object you want by pressing ↑ or ↓ until the name is highlighted; then select Design by clicking the Design button (or by pressing Alt+D). Access displays the object you selected in the appropriate design window. For

example, if you selected a table, Access opens the Table Design window for that table.

Drawing Tools

Lines and rectangles add visual clues to your form, helping you to group related elements, draw attention to important fields, or add interest to the form. Rectangles can surround existing form and report elements (fields).

To Draw Lines

To draw a line on a form or report:

1. Open the form or report in design view.

2. Display the toolbox (select View ➢ Toolbox if the toolbox is not visible).

3. Select the line tool.

4. Click the mouse to display the first endpoint, drag to the other endpoint, and release the mouse button.

5. Click the line button in the toolbar to change the line thickness or color.

Alternatively, change the border color and border width properties.

To Draw Rectangles

To draw a rectangle on a form or report:

1. Open the form or report in design view.

2. Display the toolbox. (Select View ➢ Toolbox if the toolbox is not visible.)

3. Select the rectangle tool from the toolbox.

4. Click to display the first corner and drag to the opposite corner; then release the mouse button.

5. Select Format ➤ Send to Back from the main menu if the rectangle is drawn over existing controls. The existing controls appear on top of the rectangle you have drawn.

6. To change the line thickness, color, or 3-D appearance of the rectangle, click the appropriate button in the toolbar; alternatively, open the Properties window, select the Format tab, and change the desired property.

To Modify Existing Objects

To delete an object, click it. When the black squares that mark the corners of the object appear, press Delete or select Edit ➤ Delete from the main menu.

To move an object, click it and hold down the mouse button. When the black squares (handles) marking the corners appear, move the mouse until a solid black hand appears. Drag the object to its new location.

To change the size of an object, click it. To stretch or shrink the drawing's size and shape, click and drag any of the black boxes that appear.

Drop-Down Lists

Drop-down lists are similar to combo boxes. They let you enter a value in a control by making a selection from a list. The difference is that combo boxes are for forms and you can set them up so they allow you to enter values that don't appear on the combo box list. Drop-down lists are for pages and they don't allow you to enter values that don't appear on the list.

To add a drop-down list to a data access page:

1. Open the page in design view.

2. Open the toolbox, if it's not already showing.

3. Click the Drop-Down List tool.

4. Click the spot on the page where you want the drop-down list to appear.

5. When the Combo Box Wizard starts, follow the instructions to create the list.

Dynaset

A dynaset is a set of records resulting from a query or filter. When you edit records in a dynaset, you are actually editing the records in the original tables. Unlike some database programs that create a separate table as the result of a query or filter, Access's dynasets are simply a subset of the actual, live records in the original table, so you must be careful when editing data—you are working with the actual data. Changes you make in the dynaset are made to the original record, not a copy.

E

Editing Data

Once you have entered data in Access, you'll need to update it. This section gives you directions for doing so.

To Change a Cell Value

The following options work in the grids Access uses throughout the system. For example, you can change a cell value in the Property window, a datasheet view, or query grid.

You can change a value in a cell in one of three ways.

- Enter the value you want directly in the cell. For example, enter some text or Yes/No.

- Click the down-pointing arrow or press Alt+↓ to display a list of options. Use ↑ and ↓ to highlight the option you want, and then press Enter.

Many cells are restricted to a set of values, such as Yes/No. Click the down-pointing arrow or press Alt+↓ to display a list of options. Click directly on the option name.

Embedding and Linking Objects

You can store other documents (word-processing documents, bitmaps, graphics, spreadsheets, and even sounds) in a field in a table if the field has an OLE Object data type. The objects themselves (the spreadsheets or graphics, for example) are created in other Windows applications that support object linking and embedding (OLE).

With OLE, when you display a record containing a field of the OLE Object data type and double-click the field, Windows automatically launches the application that created the object. Furthermore, you can edit the object in the application that created it. You can then save and update the object in the field in the Access table.

To Embed Objects in Forms and Reports

The following instructions are used to create new unbound objects on forms and reports. These objects are constant; they do not change when a different record is displayed, for example. If the object is a Windows

Paintbrush file, the unbound control will display the same image on each form and page of the report.

Objects, such as the Windows Paintbrush image, can be embedded into an unbound control on the form or report or linked into an unbound control on a form or report.

- If the source is embedded, the object is stored within the Access database.

- If the object source is linked, changes to the object can be made in another program (such as Windows Paintbrush); when changes are made, Access will use the newest version.

Since linked files are saved outside of Access (that is, the linked objects are kept in a separate file), they can be used in more than one Windows application. Changes to the object will be reflected in all Windows applications linked to the object.

To Add and Embed an Unbound Object in a Form or Report

These instructions will create a new object on a form or report, launch the application you specify, let you create the object, return you to the form or report, and embed the newly created object. You can also insert a graphic image from an existing file.

1. Select the form or report you want to modify and open it in design view.

2. Select the unbound object frame button from the toolbox.

3. Move the mouse to the form. Click the upper-left corner of the control and drag to the bottom-right corner. Release the mouse button. Access displays the Insert Object dialog box. The list of object types will depend on the OLE-compatible applications you've installed.

4. Do one of the following:

- **To insert a graphic image from an existing file**, select Create from File. Select the file you want; then select OK.

- **To create a new graphic image** using an OLE-compatible application, select the type of object you want to embed. When you select OK, Windows launches that application (the OLE server). When you have finished creating the image, select File ➤ Exit or File ➤ Exit and Return (or a similar File menu option). The OLE server asks if you want to update the object you just created in Access. Select Yes.

5. (Optional) After Access embeds the object in a control on the form, you can modify the control. For example, you can resize and reshape it.

The object is saved as part of the form. For example, if the object was created in Windows Paintbrush, all the information about the image is stored within the Access form or report itself; that is, you won't have a separate .pcx file. To edit the image, open the form or report in design view and double-click the image. Windows will launch the application that created the image, allow you to edit the object, and then return you to Access where the new version of the object can be stored.

To Add and Link an Unbound Object to a Form or Report

A linked object is saved as a separate file in the application that created it. When you use a linked object, Access does not save the object within the database—the object is maintained as a file outside Access. Using a linked file rather than an embedded file allows you to create a logo or other graphic object and share it in several Windows applications. When you modify the image in Paintbrush, for example, all applications that have links to the object will automatically use the new version of the graphic file.

With these instructions, you start in the application that created the object, copy the object to the Clipboard, and paste the object into an unbound control on a form or report. The object is stored in a separate file and is not part of Access.

The following instructions assume the object you want to link to your form or report has already been created. If not, first create the object and save it as a separate file.

1. Open the application used to create the object, such as Windows Paintbrush. If the object can be used by more than one application, such as a standard graphics file in Windows Paintbrush format, you can use any application that supports (opens) the object's file format.

2. Open the file containing the object you want to link to your form or report.

3. Copy the object to the Clipboard. In most Windows applications, you must select the object and then select Edit ➤ Copy from the application's main menu.

4. Switch to Microsoft Access.

5. Select the form or report you want to modify and open it in design view.

6. Select Edit ➤ Paste Special from the main menu. Access displays the Paste Special dialog box. Select the Paste Link radio button.

7. Check the Display as Icon check box to display the object as an icon.

8. Select OK.

9. Access adds an unbound object frame to the form or report. You can now move, resize, and modify the object.

To Prevent an Object on a Form or Report from Being Edited

If you have an embedded or linked object on a form and want to temporarily or permanently stop the embedded or linked object from being changed, perform the following steps. These instructions are useful for graphic objects, but are not used for text objects, such as word processing documents or spreadsheets, because converting text-based objects to pictures does not make sense.

1. Open the object in design view.

2. Select Edit from the main menu. From the pull-down menu, select the menu option that reflects the type of object you have (for example: *Microsoft Graph Object*).

3. Select Convert.

Note that this procedure does not delete the object from the form or report—it only breaks the link to prevent editing. To delete the object, delete it as you would any other control—select it in design view and then press Delete or select Edit ➤ Cut from the main menu.

Embedding Objects in Fields

If you have a field in your table that is an OLE Object data type, these instructions show you how to embed an object into the field. Each record can contain a different object.

If you are using a form to update an OLE Object field, these instructions assume that you have added a bound object frame to the form.

To Embed an Object in a Record

Follow these instructions to embed an OLE object in a field in an Access table.

1. Open a form for the table with the OLE field in form view. If you are working with a query or datasheet, be sure you are in datasheet view, not design view.

2. Move to the record that is to contain the OLE object.

3. Select the field (in a datasheet) or the bound object frame (in a form) that will store the object.

4. Select Insert ➤ Object from the main menu. Access displays the Insert Object dialog box and asks for the type of OLE object you want. Only objects listed in this box can be embedded in the field.

5. Select the object and select OK. Windows opens the source application.

6. Create the object you want to embed, or open an existing object using the source application's File ➤ Open menu commands. When you are done creating or editing the object, select File ➤ Exit and Return or File ➤ Update from the source application's main menu.

7. Select Yes if the source application asks if you want to update the object.

When you display the record and double-click the object, Windows automatically opens the source application, displays the object in that application, and allows you to edit the object.

To Embed an Existing File in a Record

These instructions allow you to embed an OLE object in a field in an Access table:

1. Open a form in form view. If you are working with a query or datasheet, be sure you are in datasheet view, not design view.

2. Move to the record that is to contain the OLE object.

3. Select the field (in a datasheet) or the bound object frame (in a form) that will store the object.

4. Select Insert ➤ Object from the main menu. Access displays the Insert Object dialog box and asks for the type of OLE object you want. Only objects listed in this box can be embedded in the field.

5. Select the type of object and then select the Create from File button.

6. Enter the filename or click Browse to locate it. Then select OK.

If you are in form view, Access displays the object. If you are in datasheet view, Access shows the type of object in the cell.

To Link an Object in a Record

These instructions let you link an existing object (saved in a disk file) in an OLE object field of an Access table. They assume the object you want to link to the field has already been created. If not, create the object and save it as a separate file.

1. Open the application used to create the object, for example Windows Paintbrush. If the object can be used by more than one application, such as a standard graphics file in Windows Paintbrush format, you can use any application that supports (opens) the object's file format.

2. Open the file containing the object you want to link to your field.

3. Copy the object to the Clipboard. In most Windows applications, you must select the object and then select Edit ➤ Copy from the application's main menu.

4. Switch to Microsoft Access.

5. Open a form in form view or datasheet view, or open a table or query in datasheet view. The form, query, or table must contain the table that contains the OLE object field you want linked to the source you saved in step 3.

6. Move to the record that you want to modify.

7. Select the OLE object field in the form or datasheet by clicking it or by pressing Tab until the field is selected.

8. Select Edit ➤ Paste Special from the main menu. Access displays the Paste Special dialog box. Select OK. Click Paste Link and select OK.

In form view, Access displays the object. In datasheet view, Access displays the type of object you have linked.

To Make an OLE Object Uneditable

If you want to break the link so that the contents of an OLE object can no longer be edited or changed, follow these instructions. These instructions are useful for graphic objects but are not used for sound or text objects, such as word processing documents or spreadsheets, because converting text-based objects to pictures does not make sense and does not work for sound objects.

Note that this procedure does not delete the object from the field—it only breaks the link to prevent editing. To delete the contents of the field (that is, to remove the object from the field), delete it as you would any other field value—select the field and then press Delete or select Edit ➤ Cut from the main menu.

1. Open a form in form view. If you are working with a query or datasheet, be sure you are in datasheet view, not design view.

2. Select Edit from the main menu. From the pull-down menu, select the menu option that reflects the type of object you have (for example: *Microsoft Graph Object*).

3. Select Convert.

Encrypt or Decrypt a Database

When you encrypt a database, Access compacts the database and makes it difficult, if not impossible, for a user with a file-browsing utility to view the contents of the database. Encryption does not restrict database access.

To Encrypt or Decrypt a Database

To encrypt an unencrypted database or decrypt an encrypted database:

1. Select Tools ➤ Security ➤ Encrypt/ Decrypt Database from the main menu.

2. Select the database you want to encrypt or decrypt and then select OK. Access examines the database and decides which operation (encrypt or decrypt) you want.

3. Enter the name of the new, encrypted (or decrypted) database in the Encrypt As dialog box, or enter the current database name to replace the existing database with an encrypted version, in the Encrypt Database As (or Decrypt Database As) field.

Export a Table or Query

Exporting a table or query allows you to use Access data in another application.

To Export a Table or Query

To create a copy of an Access table in another file format:

1. Close the table or query. If you are working in a multiuser environment, all users must close the table or query.

2. Open the database window by pressing F11 and select the table or query you want to export.

3. Select File ➤ Export from the main menu or click the Export button on the toolbar.

4. Select the type of file format you want to use from the Save as Type text box.

5. In the File Name box, enter a name for the new file the export process will create.

6. Click Save.

7. Access may ask you for further options or may start a wizard, depending on the type of file format you are using. For example, if you are exporting to a text field, Access starts the Export Text Wizard. Complete whatever steps are necessary for the type of file you chose in step 4.

Expression Builder

Access provides a special window for creating expressions. To build an expression, click the Builder button (the one containing an ellipsis ...) following the text box for your expression. For example, to build an expression for a validation rule in the table design window, click the Builder button following the Validation Rule text box. Then create an expression by entering it directly or by selecting values from the three areas below. For example, to build the expression = "WA":

1. Select the Region field in the design grid, and then click the ellipsis box following the Validation Rule.

2. Click the equal (=) sign; or select Operators from the first column, be sure All is selected in the second column, and double-click the = in the third column.

3. Enter the value (**WA** or **"WA"**) in the expression area at the top of the window. Access will insert the quotation marks if it properly parses the expression.

4. Select OK. The expression is copied to the Validation Rule but is not checked for syntax. To verify that the syntax of your expression is correct, click the ellipsis box. If the expression is valid, the Expression Builder is displayed. Otherwise, Access displays an error message, in which case you can edit the syntax or erase it completely and begin again.

To display more variables and fields, click the Tables, Queries, Forms, Reports, or Functions options to expand the options for these items. Click Common Expressions to insert special fields, such as page number or current date and time.

Expression Functions

The following functions can be used in a calculation (*n* is any number or numeric expression).

Abs *(n)*   Absolute value of a number; e.g., Abs (-5) = 5.

Atn *(n)*   Arctangent of *n* expressed in radians.

Cos *(n)*   Cosine of *n*, where *n* is measured in radians.

Exp (number)   *e* raised to a power, where *e* is the base of natural logarithms.

Fix *(n)*   The integer part of *n*, a number or numeric expression; e.g., Fix (2.4) returns 2. When *n* is negative, Fix returns the next *larger* integer; e.g., Fix (-5.6) returns -5. Compare with Int (*n*).

Int *(n)*   The integer part of *n*, a number or numeric expression; e.g., Int (2.7) returns 2. When *n* is negative, Int returns the next *smaller* integer; e.g., Int (-5.6) returns -6. Compare with Fix (*n*).

Log *(n)*   The natural logarithm of *n*.

Rnd *(n)*   A pseudo-random number. If *n* is less than 0, Rnd (*n*) returns the same value after every call. If *n* is zero, Rnd (*n*) returns the last generated number. If *n* is greater than 0 or omitted, Rnd returns the next pseudo-randomly generated number.

Sgn *(n)*   The sign of *n*. Sgn returns 1 if *n* is greater than 0; it returns 0 when *n* is 0; and -1 when *n* is negative.

Sin *(n)*   The sine of *n*, where *n* is measured in radians.

Sqrt *(n)*   The square root of *n*, returned as a number of data type double.

Sum *([FieldName])*   The sum of all values in *FieldName* of a dynaset.

Tan *(n)*   Tangent of *n*, where *n* is measured in radians.

Arithmetic Operators

Access uses the following arithmetic operators:

Operator	What It Performs
&	Concatenates two text strings; e.g., [City] & " " & [State] would return a single text field consisting of the value in the City field, a space, and the value in the State field.
+	Adds two numbers or numeric expressions; e.g., [Sub Total] + [Tax Amount].
-	Subtracts two numbers or numeric expressions (e.g., [Stock On Hand] - [Amt Ordered]) or reverses the sign of a field (e.g., -[Price]).
*	Multiplies two numbers or numeric expressions; e.g., [Sub Total] * [Tax Rate].
/	Divides two numbers or numeric expressions; e.g., [Sales Amt] / [Total Sales].
\	Divides two numbers or numeric expressions and returns an integer or long value.
mod	Divides two numbers or numeric expressions and returns the remainder only.
^	Raises a number to a power; e.g., 10^2 equals 10 to the second power, the result of 10^2 is 100.

Logical Operators

Logical operators can be used on either Boolean (Yes/No) data or numeric data. When they are used with numeric data, they perform bitwise logical operations.

Operator	What It Performs
and	Logical conjunction of two expressions (Both expressions must be true for the expression as a whole to be true.)
eqv	Logical equivalence of two expressions
imp	Logical implication of two expressions
not	Logical opposite of an expression (If the expression preceding "not" is false, the expression as a whole is true.)
or	Logical disjunction of two expressions (If either expression is true, the complete expression is true.)
xor	Logical "exclusive or" of two expressions

See the following lists for further exposition of these logical operators.

AND Operator

Expression1	Expression2	Result
true	true	true
true	false	false
true	null	null
false	true	false
false	null	false
null	true	null
null	null	null

EQV Operator

Expression1	Expression2	Result
true	true	true
true	false	false
true	null	null
false	true	false
false	false	true
false	null	null
null	true	null
null	false	null
null	null	null

IMP Operator

Expression1	Expression2	Result
true	true	true
true	false	false
true	null	null
false	true	false
false	false	true
false	null	true
null	true	true
null	false	null
null	null	null

NOT Operator

Expression1	Result
true	false
false	true
null	null

OR Operator

Expression1	Expression2	Result
true	true	true
true	false	true
true	null	true

OR Operator (continued)

Expression1	Expression2	Result
false	true	true
false	false	false
false	null	null
null	true	true
null	false	null
null	null	null

XOR Operator

Expression1	Expression2	Result
true	true	false
true	false	true
true	null	null
false	true	true
false	false	false
false	null	null
null	true	null
null	false	null
null	null	null

Expressions in Queries

When specifying a criterion in a query window, use an expression to limit the records Access finds or displays. Expressions need an object name or value and an operator.

Operator	Meaning	Example Criteria
=	Equals	= "New Jersey"
<	Less than	< 100
<=	Less than or equal to	<= 100
>	Greater than	> #7/1/99#
>=	Greater than or equal to	>= 21
<>	Not equal to	<> "Seattle"

IN Operator

The In operator is used to specify a set of values a field value must match. For example, to specify in a query that the State field contain WA, ID, or CA, the criteria in the QBE grid should be **In("WA", "ID", "CA")**.

The In operator lets you specify several OR conditions on a single line. The preceding example is equivalent to saying the State field must contain WA or ID or CA.

To *exclude* records that match the values in the list, use the NOT operator. For example, to exclude records from the three states, the criteria in the QBE grid of a query should be **Not In("WA", "ID", "CA")**.

LIKE Operator

The Like operator is used to compare a Text or Date/Time field with a string expression. The Like operator uses a pattern that contains wildcard operators (listed below). For example, the expression [Last Name] Like "B*" matches all last names that begin with the letter B and contain zero or more characters following the B. In a query, the expression Like "B*" is entered in the Criteria row for the Last Name field.

The pattern can contain any of the following wildcard characters:

*	Zero or more characters; examples: the pattern "C*" matches fields containing "Cash" and "credit" but not "money"; 1/*/99 matches all dates in January 1999.
?	A single character; examples: the pattern "B?T" matches fields containing "bat" and "bit" but not "brat"; 1/1?/99 matches all dates from 1/10/99 through 1/19/99.
#	A single number (0 through 9); e.g., "##" matches "01" and "99" but not "A1."
[charlist]	Matches any character in the charlist (e.g., [a-z] matches only letters); characters must be in ascending order: a–z, then A–Z, then 0–9.
[!charlist]	Matches any character *not* in the charlist (e.g., [!a-z] matches strings that do not contain letters).

Expressions

Expressions are used to specify criteria in queries, perform updates in an action query (to multiply a field by 110 percent, for example), and in reports.

Expressions consist of fields in a table called identifiers (for example, Price or Quantity), literals (the value 1000 or "Seattle"), functions (such as Average or Sum), operators (such as * for multiplication), and constants (such as 1.05 and Yes).

Literals are typically text strings that can vary. Constants are values (text, numeric, data, etc.) that remain stable or are rarely changed, such as a tax rate, discount rate, or fiscal year begin date.

Expressions can be used:

- To compute the value of a calculated field; expressions are stored in the Control Source property of a control on a form or report.

- In validation expressions, to compare the value of a field entry with a calculated value; expressions are used in the Validation Rule property of such controls.

- To compute the default value of a control; expressions are used in the DefaultValue property of such controls.

- In queries and filters, to select subsets of records based on a value calculated using other fields or to update fields in the same record (in action queries).

The field reference used in expressions has several parts. You surround the name of the form, report, field, control, and property with square brackets. For example, in an expression you must refer to the field Price as [Price], as in =[Price] * [Quantity].

Separator characters are also used to isolate the names of objects. The exclamation point (!) is used to separate the names of forms, reports, controls, and fields, such as Forms!MyForm.

The dot (.) typically separates a property from the rest of the identifier and is used to separate a method when using Visual Basic code. Access may also require you to use the words *Forms*, *Reports*, or *Screen* when you refer to a field on a form, report, or screen that is not active. This qualifier is necessary to avoid confusion. For example: Forms!Myform.Visible

When you create an expression:

- Enclose object names (the names of fields, tables, queries, forms, reports, and controls) in square brackets; for example, [First Name]

- Put number signs (#) around dates; for example, #7/1/99#

- Put double-quotation marks (") around text; for example, "New Jersey"

To Use an Expression—Examples

To refer to the field named Price on the Inventory form when the Inventory form is not currently the active form, use the identifier Forms![Inventory]![Price] in a calculation. To refer to the default value of the same field when the Inventory form is active, use the identifier [Price].[DefaultValue] in a calculation.

F

Fields

You can work with fields in a table that is displayed in design view.

To Add Fields to a Table

To add fields to an existing Access table:

1. Enter the name of the field (up to 64 characters, including spaces and special characters, but not including periods, exclamation points, and square brackets) in the first blank field in the Field Name column.

2. Select the type of data to be stored in the field. In the Data Type column, enter the type name, or click the down-pointing arrow key and select from the list.

3. Enter a description for the field. The description allows you to explain the purpose of the field or give information about the source of the data. The description is for reference only and is not used within Access when performing tasks or operations.

4. Enter field properties in the area below the field names. Click any field property or press F6 to jump between areas.

To Add Fields in Datasheet View

To add fields to an existing table from the datasheet view:

1. Switch to datasheet view.

2. Select a column where you want to insert the field. Access will insert the field in the table definition in this relative position.

3. Select Insert ➢ Column.

4. Enter data in the column. Access will examine the data and automatically assign a field type, and an index if appropriate. You can change these properties, as well as the field's new name, using the table's design view.

To Use Field Properties

Field properties determine how data is saved and displayed; these properties are different for each data type (text, date, number, and so on). Field properties are set in the lower half of the window used to design a table.

Enter the property value on the corresponding line in the Field Properties window.

The following field properties are available:

FieldSize   Determines the length of a text field or the type of number to be stored; see below.

Format   Determines how data is displayed—Access has predefined formats and you can create your own custom formats.

DecimalPlaces   Determines the number of digits to the right of the decimal in numeric fields.

Input Mask   Determines the pattern that data must conform to when entered in a field or displayed on a form or report.

Caption   Determines the field label used by default in forms and reports.

DefaultValue   Determines the value to be saved in the field of a new record if no entry is made in the field.

ValidationRule   Determines the formula or rule that must be satisfied before the value will be saved in the field.

ValidationText   Determines the text that is displayed on the screen if the validation rule fails.

Required   Specifies whether the field must contain a value.

Indexed   Determines whether the field is used as an index field. Indexes speed up searching and sorting.

To Set Field Size

The FieldSize property is set in table design view. It determines the amount of space reserved for fields with a Numeric or Text data type.

For text fields, enter the maximum number of characters the field can contain. The largest text field size is 255 characters.

For numbers, the FieldSize property determines the length of a number, and thus its minimum and maximum values. Valid settings for a Number data type are listed from smallest to largest.

Byte   Uses 1 byte. Can contain whole numbers from 0 to 255.

Integer   Uses 2 bytes. Can contain whole numbers from -32,768 to 32,767.

Long Integer   Uses 4 bytes. Can contain whole numbers from -2,147,483,648 to 2,147,483,647.

Single   Uses 4 bytes. Can contain numbers (including fractional parts), from -3.402823E38 to 3.402823E38. (E38 represents 10 to the 38th power.) Numbers are accurate to 6 decimal digits.

Double   Uses 8 bytes. Can contain numbers (including fractional parts) from -1.79769313486232E308 to 1.79769313486232E308. Numbers are accurate to 10 decimal digits.

To Insert Fields in a Table

To insert a field in a table, select the row (move the insertion point to the row or click the mouse in the row) below the place you want to place the new field. Select Edit ➤ Insert Row. The field already in this row and all fields in rows underneath are shifted down one row.

To Delete Fields from a Table

To delete a field in a table, select the row (move the insertion point to the row or click in the row) and select Edit ➤ Delete Row.

To delete multiple rows, place the pointer in the row of the first Field Name you want to remove. The pointer changes to a horizontal arrow. Drag down to the last row you want to delete. Each row appears highlighted. Press Delete or select Edit ➤ Delete Row.

To delete all rows, select Edit ➤ Select All from the main menu. Press Delete or select Edit ➤ Delete Row.

To Move Fields in a Table

Move the pointer to the row containing the field you want to move. When the pointer changes to a horizontal, solid arrow, click the mouse. The current record pointer (in the leftmost column) changes to a left-pointing triangle and the row is highlighted. Drag the triangle to the new row and release the mouse button.

To Change Field Types

To change the data type of a field:

1. Open a table in design view.

2. Select the Data Type of the field you want to change.

3. Select the new data type. (You cannot select an Auto increment data type.)

4. Select File ➤ Save from the main menu.

When converting from a larger field size to a smaller one, Access truncates the value. For example, if you convert from a memo to a text field of 40 characters, only the first 40 characters in the memo field will be converted. If you convert from a larger numeric field to a smaller one, Access will make the conversion unless the value will not fit in the new field, in which case no conversion is made.

When you convert from text to numeric, Access interprets the separator characters (period and comma) to determine the numeric value. When you convert from a numeric or date field to a text field, Access displays the number using the General number or date format.

If Access cannot convert a value from the old data type to the new data type, it leaves the new value blank. Access warns you and allows you to stop the conversion.

If the field whose data type you have changed is an index field or primary key for a table and if Access cannot convert a value or the converted value is not unique in the table, Access deletes the entire record. Access warns you and allows you to stop this from happening.

Filters

Filters allow you to set criteria and display the results on a form. Unlike queries, you cannot save a filter's settings for reuse. Filters display all records at once, unlike a Find, which displays records one at a time.

As with queries, the Access table still contains all the records it had before you applied the filter. Additionally, you can modify the records displayed in a filter, just as you can in a query.

To Filter Data Using a Form

You can create a new filter by entering the filter conditions in the form itself without opening the Filter/Query window.

MASTER'S REFERENCE

1. Select Records ➤ Filter ➤ Filter by Form from datasheet view. Access switches to the Filter by Form mode.

2. Click the field where you want to select values.

3. Enter the value or use the down-arrow button to display a list of values throughout the database.

4. Select the first value to enter multiple values and then click the Or tab at the bottom of the screen. Enter the next value and repeat this step for each value in the field you want to select.

5. Click the Apply Filter button in the toolbar or select Filter ➤ Apply Filter/Sort from the main menu.

To remove the filter, click the Apply Filter button again. (This time the pop-up help says Remove Filter.) Or select Records ➤ Remove Filter/Sort from the main menu.

To Create or Modify a Filter

To find a subset of records in the table, set a filter as follows:

1. Open a table in form view or datasheet view.

2. Select Records ➤ Filter ➤ Advanced Filter/Sort from the main menu. Access displays the Filter window.

3. Enter the field name, or drag the field name from the table window at the top of the Filter window to the Field row in the grid at the bottom of the Filter window.

4. Enter the criteria and sort order.

5. Click the Apply Filter button in the toolbar, or select Filter ➤ Apply Filter/Sort from the main menu.

6. Click the Remove Filter button in the toolbar to remove the filter, or select Records ➤ Remove Filter/Sort from the main menu. You can reapply the filter by repeating step 4.

To Remove a Filter

To remove the filter and view all records, click the Remove Filter button or select Records ➤ Remove Filter/Sort from the main menu.

To Save a Filter as a Query

Once your filter works as you desire, you can convert the filter into a query for subsequent execution. Open the Filter Design window by choosing Records ➤ Filter ➤ Advanced Filter/Sort from the main menu. Select File ➤ Save as Query from the main menu and enter the name of the query.

To Use Existing Queries as Filters

If you want to apply a filter that is like a query you have already created for the table you are working with, you can use that query as a filter. This method allows you to temporarily apply the criteria specified in a query.

1. Display the Filter window.

2. Select File ➤ Load from Query.

3. Select the query from the list and select OK.

4. Click the Apply Filter button in the toolbar, or select Filter ➤ Apply Filter/Sort from the main menu.

Filter by Input

You can quickly filter a table on a single field with Filter For. In datasheet view or form view, right-click the field you want to use for the filter. Enter a value in the box after Filter For and press Enter.

Finding Data

To find a specific record or specific value in a single field or all fields of a table or dynaset, use the Access Find feature.

To Find a Value in a Record

1. Display your table in form or datasheet view. (If you are in design view, switch to form view or datasheet view.)

2. Select the column or field you want to search, if you are searching for a value in a single field.

3. Click the Find button in the toolbar. (It looks like a pair of binoculars.) Press Ctrl+F, or select Edit ➤ Find from the main menu.

4. Type the string you want to find in the Find What box. You can use wildcards in this search string.

5. Select where you want to look for the value in the Match box. Select Start of Field (The field must begin with the search string.), Any Part of Field (The string can appear anywhere within the field.), or Match Whole Field. (The string must match the entire contents of a field.)

6. Use the Look In setting to select whether you want Access to search the currently selected field (This is the fastest option, especially if the field is an index.) or all fields in a table or dynaset.

7. Click the More button to see other Find options.

8. Check the Match Case box if you want the search to match upper- and lowercase letters.

9. Check the Search Fields as Formatted box if you want to search for data in exactly the same format as the search string. This option searches data as it is formatted in the table.

10. Check the Find Next button to find the first occurrence of the search string. To find the next occurrence of the search string, check the Find Next button again.

To Find and Replace a Value

To find a text value within a database and replace it with another:

1. Display the form or datasheet in form or datasheet view. (If you are in design view, switch to form view or datasheet view.)

2. Select the column or field you want to search if you are searching for a value in a single field.

3. Select Edit ➤ Replace from the main menu or press Ctrl+H.

4. Type the string you want to find in the Find What box. You can use wildcards in this search string.

5. Enter the replacement string in the Replace With box.

6. Use the Look In setting to select whether you want Access to search the selected field (This is the fastest option, especially if the field is an index.) or all fields in a table or dynaset.

7. Check the Match Case box if you want the search to match upper- and lowercase letters. (Click the More button to show this option and the ones listed below, if they are not visible.)

8. Select Find Next (to find but not replace the value), Replace (to find and replace the next occurrence), or Replace All (to replace all matching values in the table or dynaset).

Finding Duplicate Records

Access provides a Find Duplicates Query Wizard to create a query that finds records that contain the same values in fields you select (such as a field containing a telephone number).

To create a query that finds duplicates:

1. Open the database window by pressing F11.

2. Select the Query tab. Click New.

3. Select Find Duplicates Query Wizard from the New Query dialog box and select OK.

4. Select Tables, Queries, or Both to list the appropriate data source. Select the table or query you want to check, and then select Next.

5. Select the field(s) in the Available Fields list to check for duplicate values. Highlight the field(s) and click the > button.

6. Click the Next button. If you did not select all fields from the table or query in step 5, select the fields in addition to the fields selected in step 5 that you want to appear in the datasheet; then click the > button.

7. Select Next.

8. Enter the name of the query and select the next step you want to take; then select the Finish button.

Access displays a datasheet containing the duplicate records.

Finding Unmatched Records

Access provides a Find Unmatched Query Wizard to create a query that finds records that have a record in one table but no matching records in a related table.

To create an Unmatched Records query:

1. Open the database window by pressing F11.

2. Select the Query button.

3. Select Find Unmatched Query Wizard from the New Query dialog box and select OK.

4. Select Tables, Queries, or Both to list the appropriate data source. Select the table or query you want to appear in the resulting datasheet (the one that you suspect has unmatched records); then select Next.

5. Select the table or query that contains the related records.

6. Highlight the field in each table that you want the query to match. Click the double-headed arrow in the center of the dialog box. Click the Next button.

7. Select the fields you want to appear in the datasheet and click the > button. Select Next.

8. Enter the name of the query and select the next step you want to take; then select the Finish button. Access displays a datasheet containing the unmatched records.

Fonts

Access supports TrueType and PostScript fonts. Fonts add variety to text in forms, reports, and datasheets.

To Change the Font of Text in a Form, Data Access Page, or Report

To change the font used to display text in a form, page, or report:

1. Open the form, page, or report in design view.

2. Select the text object whose font you want to change.

3. Click the font box in the toolbar and select the font name.

4. Click the font size box and select the font size.

5. Select the special effects you want (bold, italic, or underline).

To Change the Font of Text in a Datasheet View

To select a different font for all text displayed in a datasheet view:

1. Open a datasheet.

2. Select Format ➤ Font from the main menu.

3. Select the font, style, and size; check any effects that you want. A sample of your selection is displayed in the window.

4. Select OK.

The text in all columns of the datasheet is changed to the selected font. Access also adjusts row height to accommodate larger fonts.

Formats

Formats control the display of a field. For example, a date format specifies whether the date is displayed as 01/02/99 or as 02 JAN 99.

You can set the format of a field using the Format Property. Access has predefined formats for dates and numbers (including currency). The standard format properties include default values for the DecimalPlaces property (DecimalPlaces is set to Auto). You can override the number of digits to the right of the decimal point by entering a value in the DecimalPlaces property.

Standard Number and Currency Formats

Currency   Uses thousands separator, sets DecimalPlaces property to 2 by default, and displays negative numbers between parentheses in red.

Fixed   Displays at least one decimal (so zero always shows as 0); DecimalPlaces property is set to 2 by default.

General   Displays value as entered.

Percent   Displays value as a percent after multiplying value by 100; then appends the percent sign (%), and sets DecimalPlaces property to 2 by default.

Scientific   Uses scientific notation (for example, 1.23E100).

Standard   Uses thousands separator, sets DecimalPlaces property to 2.

Standard Date Formats

Select one of the following formats for the Format property of a Date and Time field. July 4, 1999, 1:23 P.M. appears as follows:

Format Name	Displayed As
General date	7/4/99; 01:23PM
Short date	7/4/99
Medium date	04-Jul-99
Long date	Varies according to setting in Windows' Control Panel. For example: Friday, July 4, 1999
Short time	13:23
Medium time	01:23 PM
Long time	1:23:00 PM

Custom Numeric and Currency Formats

You can create your own format string using the characters shown below. A format string can specify four formats:

- When the number is positive
- When the number is negative
- When the number is zero
- When the number is null

For example, a format string for a numeric field called Price might look like this:

```
#,##0;(#,##0);"Free";"Price Not Set"
```

If the value is positive, it will be shown with commas as necessary. If the value is negative, it will be displayed in parentheses and with commas as needed. If the value is 0, Access displays the text string *Free*. If the value is null (that is, a value has not been entered for the field), Access displays the text string *Price Not Set*.

The following characters are used in custom numeric formats:

Character	Purpose
.	Decimal separator (actual character used is set in Windows' Control Panel).
,	Thousands separator.
0	Placeholder for a digit; 0 if no digit in this position.
#	Placeholder for a digit; space if no digit in this position.
$	Displays the dollar sign.
%	Percent; multiplies value by 100 and appends the percent sign (%).
E- or e-	Scientific notation with minus sign next to E or e if negative exponent. Used in conjunction with other symbols.
E+ or e+	Scientific notation with minus sign next to E or e if negative exponent, and plus sign next to E or e if positive exponent.

Custom Date and Time Formats

You can create your own format string using these characters:

Character	Purpose
:	Separates hours from minutes, minutes from seconds. The actual separator character is defined in the Windows Control Panel.
/	Separates month, day, and year.
AM/PM	12-hour clock, AM or PM in uppercase.

Character	Purpose
am/pm	12-hour clock, am or pm in lowercase.
A/P	12-hour clock, A or P in uppercase.
a/p	12-hour clock, a or p in lowercase.
AMPM	12-hour clock, morning/afternoon text defined in Windows' Control Panel.
d	Day of month (one digit for 1–9, two digits for 10–31).
dd	Day of month (01–09, then 10–31).
ddd	Day of week (three letters: Mon, Tue, Wed).
dddd	Day of week spelled out (Monday, Tuesday, Wednesday).
ddddd	Month/day/year (same as Short Date format); displays according to the international settings in Windows.
Dddddd	Weekday, Month dd, year (same as Long Date format); displays according to the international settings in Windows.
H	Hour (one digit if 0–9, two digits if 10–23).
hh	Hour (two digits, 01–23).
m	Month (one digit if 1–9, two digits if 10–12).
mm	Month (two digits, 01–12).
mmm	Month abbreviation (Jan, Feb, Mar).
mmmm	Month spelled out (January, February, March).
n	Minute (one digit if 0–9, two digits if 10–59).
nn	Minute (two digits, 00–59).

Character	Purpose
q	Quarter of the year in which date occurs (1 through 4).
s	Second (one digit if 0–9, two digits if 10–59).
ss	Seconds (two digits, 00–59).
ttttt	Long time format (for example, 11:02:03 AM).
w	Day of week (1–7; 1 is Sunday).
ww	Week of the year (1–52).
y	Day number (1–366).
yy	Year (two digits, 00–99).
yyyy	Year (four digits, 0100–9999).

Forms

Forms are screens that can display information and let you edit data in a layout you specify. Forms can consist of a single screen or part of a screen or can span several screens. To simplify your work, you can create forms that look like your current data-entry form.

To Create a Form

To create a new form:

1. Move to the database window by pressing F11.

2. Click the Forms button and click New. At the bottom of the dialog box, Access asks you for the name of the table or query to use for the form. (Instead of clicking New, you can double-click Create Form in Design View or Create Form by Using Wizard to bypass the New dialog box and jump right to the design window or the Form Wizard.)

3. Type the name of the table or query; or click the down-pointing arrow to display the list of available tables and queries and select one.

4. Click the Blank Form button to set up the form yourself. Click the Form Wizards button to have Access lead you through the basic form-design steps.

Forms and Form Wizards

Form wizards simplify the creation of a form from scratch. Form wizards allow you to create columnar reports (with fields displayed vertically, one record per page), tabular reports (with fields displayed horizontally so that many records can be displayed on a page), graphs, and form/subform combinations. They also set the fonts, create headers with the current date and footers with the page number, and can add 3-D effects for text boxes and labels.

Forms created by a Form wizard can be modified or used as they are.

To Create a Form with Form Wizards

1. Move to the database window by pressing F11.

2. Click the Forms button.

3. Double-click Create Form by Using Wizard.

4. Respond to the Form Wizard when it asks which tables and fields you want to include on the form. Select a table. Then highlight the field you want at the beginning of the form and click the > button. The field name is removed from the Available Fields list and added to the Field Order on Form list. In a similar fashion include all the fields you want on the form. Select the Next> button.

5. Respond to the Form Wizard when it asks what layout of form you want. A single-column form lists one record per screen, with fields placed vertically, one above another. A tabular form looks like a spreadsheet: fields are laid out horizontally. Select the form layout you want and select Next.

6. Select the style of the form. When you select a format, the Form Wizard displays a sample in the magnifying glass at the left of the Form Wizard window. Select the Next> button.

7. Enter the name for the form name. This name will appear in the database window list when you select Forms. Select the Finish button. The Form Wizard launches the form and fills the form with the first record in the table.

In addition to the fields you selected, the Form Wizard includes a report title and a horizontal line separating the title from the data. It also fills in a background color on the form.

To Save a Form

To save a form for future use, select File ➤ Save or press Ctrl+S.

To Save a Form Using a Different Name

To keep a copy of a modified form separate from the original form you edited, select File ➤ Save As. Leave As set to form; then enter the new form name, and select OK.

To Copy an Existing Form

To copy an existing form to another file:

1. In the database window, highlight the form you want to copy.

2. Select File ➤ Save As, enter the new form name, and click OK.

To Delete an Existing Form

To delete an existing form from a database:

1. In the database window, highlight the form you want to delete.

2. Press Delete. Access asks you to confirm your request. You can also delete the form by selecting Edit ➢ Cut, but Access does not ask you to confirm your request with this technique.

Select Edit ➢ Undo Cut or Undo Delete from the main menu to undelete a form deleted by mistake. You can only undelete the most recently deleted object.

To Change the Format of a Form

You can use the Access AutoFormat tool to create a new look for a form. In design view, click the AutoFormat button in the toolbar or select Format ➢ AutoFormat from the main menu. Select the "look" of the form that you want from the predefined list, and click Options to apply only font, color, and/or border properties. Select OK to apply the format.

You can create your own AutoFormat layout by clicking the Customize button and choosing the appropriate option. Access lets you create a new format based on your current form, update an existing format with properties from your current form, or delete the selected format.

To Change the Size of a Form or Form Section

The default size of a form or form section may not suit your purpose. Here is how to change the size of a form or form section.

To Change the Height of a Form Section

To increase or decrease the height of a section of a form:

1. Open the form in design view.

2. Move the pointer to the top or bottom border of the section you want to change. The cursor turns into an up-and-down solid arrow with a solid line through it.

3. Click and drag up or down until the section is the size you want.

Similarly, change the width by moving the mouse to the left or right border and dragging the double-headed arrow so the section is the size you desire.

To Change the Size of the Form Display

You can change the size of the form view automatically so that Access can display complete records (or as much of a single record as possible).

With the form in form view, select Window ➢ Size to Fit Form from the main menu.

The behavior of Size to Fit Form depends on the Default View property of the form. When the Default View is set to Continuous Forms, if the window shows more than one record at a time, the last record appears either in its entirety or not at all. If the form displays only one record, the window expands to show as much of the record as possible.

When the Default View property is set to Single Form, Access shrinks the window if a record does not occupy the entire screen and expands the window to show as much of a record as possible when the entire record cannot be displayed at once.

To Attach a Menu to a Form

You can add a custom menu bar to any form. This gives your end user control over specific functions and allows you to execute macros when the user selects a menu option.

1. Create a custom menu using the Customize dialog box.

2. Open in design mode the form that uses this menu.

3. Set the form's Menu Bar property on the Other tab of the Properties sheet to the name of the menu (the name you gave the menu in step 1).

The menu appears when you view the form in form view.

To Set Form Properties

Like controls on a form, a form can have its own set of properties. To set or change the properties:

1. Open the form in design view.

2. Click anywhere in the form not occupied by a control, or select Edit ≻ Form from the main menu.

3. Select View ≻ Properties from the main menu, or right-click and choose Properties.

4. Edit the form properties; then click outside the Form Properties sheet to save your changes or close the Properties sheet.

To Use a Different Table or Query for a Form

If you have designed a form and want to use a different table or query for the form:

1. Open the form in design view.

2. Use Edit ≻ Form to select the form.

3. Open the Properties sheet by selecting the Properties button or selecting View ≻ Properties from the main menu.

4. Enter the new table or query you want to use from the cell to the right of the Record Source property on the Data tab. (Alternatively, select the table or query from the list.)

Subforms

Subforms are forms that are included in other forms. They are generally used to represent the many side of a one-to-many relationship.

A subform is simply a form that is smaller than full-screen size. As with any form, a subform is attached to a table or set of tables. A form inserted into another form is called a subform, but technically remains a separate, modifiable entity.

To Insert a Subform in a Form   To place a subform in a form:

1. Display the form that will include the subform in design view. This is called the main form.

2. Display the database window by pressing F11.

3. Click the Form button and highlight the name of the form to be used as the subform.

4. Drag the subform onto the main form.

When a subform is included on a form, you can edit it directly. With the main form in design view, double-click the subform and Access displays a separate editing window for the form. Save the changes (select File ≻ Save from the main menu) and close the subform. The changes to the subform are reflected in the main form.

Printing a Form

Access allows you to print your data using the layout of your form.

To Preview a Form   To see how the form displayed on your screen will look when printed, open the form in design view, form view, or datasheet view. Select File ≻ Print Preview.

You can also preview a form from the database window. Select the Form button, highlighting the form name, and select File ➤ Print Preview. Access displays a sample of the printout.

From within Print Preview, you can select any of these buttons:

View　Returns you to the datasheet, form, or design view.

Print　Sends the form to the printer.

Zoom　Enlarges the print preview area.

One Page　Shows a single page.

Two Pages　Shows two adjacent pages.

Multiple Pages　Shows multiple pages.

Zoom　Changes size of print preview area by preset ratio.

Close　Returns you to the form or datasheet.

Office Links　Merges or publishes with Word, analyzes with Excel.

Database Window　Returns you to the database window.

New Object　Creates a new object.

Microsoft Access Help　Opens the Office Assistant.

To Print a Form　To create a printout of a form:

1. Select File ➤ Page Setup and set the default printer, page size, orientation, and margins. Click OK.

2. Select File ➤ Print from the main menu or press Ctrl+P.

3. Set the print options (for example, which pages to print), and select OK.

Managing Data with Forms

You can edit data by modifying records in form view or datasheet view.

To Modify Data in a Form　To change values in a record displayed in form view, click the field with the mouse or press Tab until the text in the field to be modified is displayed in reverse video. You can also move to a field by selecting it from the Field drop-down list box on the toolbar.

If you change your mind or make a mistake and do *not* want to update the field, press Esc or click the Undo button in the toolbar (the second button from the right). To accept the new value, press Enter, Tab, Shift+Tab, or other navigation keys, or click another field.

If you have made an error within the record and want to return to the original value for all fields in the record, select Edit ➤ Undo Current Record from the main menu. You must select this option *before* moving to another record.

To Enter a New Record

Option 1:

1. Select Edit ➤ Go To ➤ New Record from the main menu.

2. Enter the data in the appropriate fields. Use Tab to move to the next field and Shift+Tab to move to the previous field. Pressing Tab after the last field on a form moves you to another record.

3. Press the Page Down key to add another record, or press Tab when you are in the last field.

4. Select Edit ➤ Go To ➤ First to view all records.

Option 2:

1. Select Records ➤ Data Entry from the main menu or press Ctrl++.

2. Enter the data in the appropriate fields. Use Tab to move to the next field. Use Shift+Tab to move to the previous field. Pressing Tab after the last field on a form moves you to another record.

3. Press the Page Down key to add another record, or press Tab when you are in the last field.

4. Select Records ➤ Remove Filter/Sort to view all records.

To Delete a Record　If the table from which you want to delete records is not related to another table, you can delete records easily. If the table *is* related to another table (as in a one-to-many relationship), you must delete all records from the many side of the relationship before deleting records from the one side.

1. Display the record that you want to delete. You can use the Find feature to find it, write a query to include the record in a dynaset, use the Page Up or Page Down keys to locate it, or select the record number and enter the number in the Record box at the bottom of the screen. You can also use the menus: Select Edit ➣ Go To and then the record you want (for example First, Last, etc.).

2. Select Edit ➣ Select Record from the main menu, or click the record selector that runs along the left side of the form.

3. Do one of the following to delete the record:

   • Select Edit ➣ Cut

   • Select Edit ➣ Delete Record

   • Press Ctrl+X

   • Press the Delete key

4. Respond to the "confirm delete" message. Select Yes to delete the record or Cancel to keep it.

Moving around a Form　You can move between records using the buttons on the bottom of the form. To view a specific record, enter its record number to the right of Record in the button area and press Enter.

If a form is longer than one page, you can press Page Down to move down one screen. When Access reaches the end of the form (or if the form is only one screen in length), press Page Down to move to the next record.

To move up when viewing a multiscreen form, press Page Up. When Access reaches the top of the form (or if the form is only one screen in length), press the Page Up key to move to the previous record.

G

Graphics

You can use graphics to add variety to a form or report or to add images such as logos to other business documents (data-entry forms, employment applications, and so on).

To Add a Graphic Image to a Form or Report

You can easily add or modify graphic images on a form or report. You can add a bound field to a form or report to display a picture whose contents are stored in a field in a table; the field must have a data type of OLE Object. Unbound fields display the same image on each form or page of a report, which is useful for displaying company logos.

To Resize a Graphic Object

1. Click the object's control.

2. Point at any of the black dots that surround the control. When the pointer changes to a two-headed arrow, drag the dot to resize the object.

To Resize a Graphic Object's Frame

To expand or contract the object frame to exactly match the image it contains:

1. Click the control.

2. Move the pointer over any of the black boxes that surround the image so that the pointer changes to a two-headed arrow; then double-click.

To Adjust the Proportion of a Graphic Object

If a picture's dimensions do not match the dimensions of the control on the form or report, you can adjust the object's scale in several ways.

1. Open the form or report in design view.

2. Select the graphic object.

3. Click the Properties button in the toolbar, or select View ➤ Properties from the main menu, or right-click and select Properties.

4. Click the Format tab and enter one of these values in the Size Mode property:

   • Select Clip to display the graphic without any changes to the scale. If the picture does not completely fit, Access displays as much of the image as it can. Clip is the default property.

   • Select Size Text to change the dimension of the object to fit within the frame. Access changes the aspect ratio (proportions) to accommodate the graphic.

   • Select Zoom to keep the same aspect ratio (proportions) but display the entire image. This setting may result in white space on one side of the image.

Graphs

With graphs, you can quickly display numeric data in a form that emphasizes proportions, trends, and relationships. Access includes Microsoft Graph to handle the graphing and charting tasks.

To Create a Graph with Data in Access

A graph can be based on information in an Access table or query or on data outside Access (for example, data in a spreadsheet). The following directions work with data in Access.

1. Open the form or report in design view.

2. Select Insert ➤ Chart.

3. Move the pointer to the form. Click the upper-left corner of the control and drag to the bottom-right corner; then release the mouse button.

Access displays the Graph Wizard, which leads you through the basic steps of creating a chart. The Graph Wizard asks which table or query to use as a source, which field should be graphed, as well as the title and type of graph. When the Graph Wizard is finished, a graph appears on your form.

To Create a Graph Using Data outside Access

You can include a graph using data from another file, including a spreadsheet. To create a chart, add an unbound object frame to the form or report:

1. Open the form or report in design view.

2. Click the unbound object frame in the toolbox.

3. Move the pointer to the form. Click the upper-left corner of the control and drag to the bottom-right corner; then release the mouse button.

4. Select Microsoft Graph as the object type you want to embed. The Graph application opens.

5. Use Graph to create the chart you want.

6. Select File ➤ Exit and Return.

To Change Access Graphs

To change the style, type, title, legend, and other characteristics of a chart or graph:

1. Open the form containing the graph in form view, the report in report view, or either object in design view.

2. Double-click the graph object. Access goes into chart editing mode. You'll see two windows. One contains the datasheet containing the values to be graphed. The other window shows the chart as it is currently defined.

3. Click anywhere within the chart, and then use these techniques:

   • **To change the title, legends, axes, or data labels**, select Insert from the main menu and the appropriate option from the pull-down menu.

   • **To change patterns displayed in the chart** (such as the pattern in a pie slice), click the data series and then select Format ➢ Selected Data Series from the main menu, or double-click the series directly.

   • **To annotate a chart**, click the Drawing button to display the Drawing toolbar and then select the desired tool (arrow, line, etc.).

To Change the Chart Type

To change the type of chart:

1. Double-click the graphic object.

2. Select Chart ➢ Chart Type from the main menu.

3. Select the type of chart you want (2-D or 3-D), click the type of bar you want from the grid shown in the center of the Chart Type dialog box, and click OK to return to the Microsoft Graph window.

4. Select Chart ➢ Options to change additional chart options. Make your selections and then click OK.

5. Click off the chart object to exit chart editing mode.

Grids

In design view, Access provides grids to help you align and resize controls.

To display a grid for a form or report, select View ➢ Grid from the main menu.

To change the number of points in a grid, open the Property window for the form. Set the GridX and GridY properties in the Format tab to larger numbers to increase the number of grid points.

Gridlines

Access displays datasheets and queries with or without gridlines between columns and rows. To display or hide gridlines, select Format ➢ Cells.

Grouping Data

To specify subtotals in queries, you can use the Group By field to specify breaks in the sort order. Group By also summarizes records in the field specified as Group By. For example, a query can return one record summarizing all data for a state by specifying Group By in the Total row of a query for the State field.

To Summarize and Group Data by Field Values

To include a grouping for data and summarize data when the value in the group field changes:

1. Open a query in design view.

2. Enter the field name in the Field row, or drag the name from the table windows at the top of the form to the Field row.

3. Select View ➢ Totals from the main menu if the Total line is not displayed in the QBE grid.

4. Select Group By in the Total line of the field.

To Set the Interval of a Group

When you create a group report, you can specify the range of values included in each group as follows:

1. Open the report in design view.

2. Click the Sorting and Grouping icon in the toolbar or select View ➢ Sorting and Grouping from the main menu to open the Sorting and Grouping window.

3. Select the field you want to group on. In the Group Properties window, enter the type of group you want in the cell to the right of Group On.

4. Enter the range of values to be included in a group in the cell to the right of Group Interval. For example, if the field has a numeric data type and the Group On value is set to Each Value, enter **100** in the Group Interval cell. Access will group your records in 100s (0–99, 100–199, and so on).

5. Close the Sorting and Grouping window.

Headers and Footers

Headers and footers are special sections on forms and reports usually used to hold information such as a title, the current date and time, and page numbers. In addition, a report footer is

often used for report totals or record counts. (Data access pages also have headers, but they are used to hold data rather than titles.)

Report Headers and Footers

A *report header* is printed or displayed only at the beginning of the report. A *report footer* is printed or displayed only at the end of the report.

To Add or Remove a Report Header or Footer

To add or delete a report header or a report footer:

1. Open the report in design view.

2. Select View ➢ Report Header/Footer to toggle the header or footer band on or off.

Access puts a checkmark next to the menu option when the report header and footer are added to the report.

Form Headers and Footers

Form headers and footers are similar to report headers and footers but apply to forms only. To add or delete a form header or a form footer:

1. Open the form in design view.

2. Select View ➢ Form Header/Footer to toggle the header or footer band on or off.

Access puts a checkmark next to the menu option when the form header and footer are used in a form.

Page Headers and Footers

A *page header* appears at the top of every page. Page headers are useful for column headings. A *page footer* appears at the bottom of every page. Page footers are useful for displaying page numbers.

To Add or Remove a Page Header or Footer

To add or delete a page header or footer:

1. Open the report in design view.

2. Select View ➤ Page Header/Footer to toggle the header or footer band on or off.

Access puts a checkmark next to the menu option when the page header or footer is added to the report.

Group Headers and Footers

A *group header* is displayed at the beginning of a new group of data (such as when the value of a field changes). A *group footer* is displayed at the end of a group of data and is used most often to display subtotals (the total of the group).

To Add or Remove a Group Header or Group Footer

To add or remove a group header or footer, you must have at least one group defined for the report.

1. Open the report in design view.

2. Select the Sorting and Grouping button on the toolbar or select View ➤ Sorting and Grouping from the main menu. You must have at least one field defined on the first Sorting and Grouping line.

3. Select a field name or enter an expression in the Field/Expression column. Select a sort order in the Sort Order box.

4. Set the Group Header property to Yes to add a group header to the report. Similarly, set the Group Footer property to Yes to add a group footer. (No is the default property value for the Group Header and Group Footer properties.)

Group headers can also be used to display part of a group value. For example, if an accounting code is made up of two four-character codes, separated by a hyphen (such as A100-2000), you can create group breaks every time the first four characters of the code change.

To Print Part of a Group Value in the Group Header

1. Open the report in design view.

2. Select the Sorting and Grouping button on the toolbar or select View ➤ Sorting and Grouping from the main menu.

3. Set the Field/Expression column to the field name or expression that contains the values you want to group the report by. (In the accounting example, the field might be Account Code.)

4. Set the Group Header property to Yes by typing **Yes** in the cell to the right of Group Header.

5. Set the Group Footer property to No by typing **No** in the cell to the right of Group Footer.

6. Set the Group On property to Prefix Characters by clicking the down-pointing arrow and selecting the option.

7. Set the Group Interval property to the number of characters to use in the group header value. (In the accounting example above, the property value should be set to 4.) Close the Sorting and Grouping window.

8. Select the text box button from the toolbox. (If the toolbox is not displayed, select View ➤ Toolbox from the main menu.)

9. Add a text box to the group header. Select a text box from the toolbox and drag it into the Group Header section.

10. Select the Properties button in the toolbar or select View ➤ Properties from the main menu.

11. Enter an expression to define the characters to be printed in the cell to the right of Control Source in the Data tab. (In the accounting example, you would enter `=Left([Account Code],4)` in the Control Source cell.)

You can use group headers to separate the first character of a group, such as for a heading in an employee telephone directory. The first group header could display *A*, after which all the employees with a last name beginning with *A* would be listed. The next group header could display *B*, followed by all employees with last names beginning with *B*, and so on.

To print part of a group value in the group header (for example, for headings in a telephone directory):

1. Open the report in design view.

2. Select the Sorting and Grouping button on the toolbar or select View ➤ Sorting and Grouping from the main menu.

3. Set the Field/Expression column of the first line to the field name or expression that contains the values you want to group the report by. (For example, you might use the Last Name field.)

4. Set the Group Header property to Yes.

5. Set the Group Footer property to No.

6. Set the Group On property to Prefix Characters.

7. Set the Group Interval property to the number of characters to use in the group header value. (In the telephone directory example above, set the property value to 1.)

8. Set the Field/Expression column of the *second* line to the field name or expression that contains the values you want to sort the report by. Select the same field selected in step 3.

9. Set the Group Header property to No.

10. Set the Group Footer property to No.

11. Set the Group On property to Each Value.

12. Set the Group Interval property to 1. Close the Sorting and Grouping window.

13. Select the text box button from the toolbox. (If the toolbox is not displayed, select View ➤ Toolbox from the main menu.)

14. Add a text box to the group header.

15. Select the Properties button in the toolbar or select View ➤ Properties from the main menu.

16. Enter an expression to define the characters to be printed in the Control Source box. (Using the Last Name example, enter `=Left([Last Name],1)` in the Control Source box.)

Help

Access offers both a traditional Help system where you can search for information and the Office Assistant.

You can bring up the Office Assistant or the Help system by pressing F1 at any time. If you are in the middle of a procedure, Access may display context-sensitive help based on the task it thinks you are trying to accomplish.

You can also press Shift+F1. The pointer changes to a question mark, which you click on the item you want help about.

To Get Help

To open the Office Assistant:

1. Click the Office Assistant button in the toolbar. Access displays the Office Assistant.

2. Enter your request in the text box, using either a key word or a phrase.

3. Click Search or press Enter, and then select the topic that most closely matches your request.

After you select a topic, Access will open the Microsoft Access Help window. Click the Show button to open another pane in the window with tabs for Contents, Answer Wizard, and Index.

Hyperlinks

Hyperlinks are used to jump to information in a database, in an Office document, or on the Internet. You can enter hyperlink addresses to a record in a table that has a hyperlink field, or you can place a hyperlink in a form or report.

To Enter a Hyperlink Address in a Hyperlink Field

There are a couple of ways to enter an address in a hyperlink field. You can enter a valid hyperlink address yourself or you can get help from the Insert Hyperlink dialog box:

1. Open the table with the hyperlink field in datasheet view or form view.

2. Tab to the hyperlink field. (Don't click the field if it already has an address entered—you'll jump to the address.)

3. Click Insert Hyperlink on the toolbar.

4. Complete the Insert Hyperlink dialog box and click OK.

To Add a Hyperlink to a Form or Report

You can add a hyperlink to a form or report:

1. Open the form or report in design view.

2. Click the Insert Hyperlink toolbar button.

3. Complete the dialog box and click OK. Access will place the new hyperlink in the upper-left corner of the design window.

4. Drag the hyperlink to wherever it should be.

I

Import a Database File

When you import data from another format (Excel, HTML, or text, for example), you copy it to an Access table and save it in Access's own format. You work with a *copy* of the file in Access, *not* with the original file.

Importing data is different than linking data. When you link a database from another format, Access reads data from the original database. No copy is made, and the original database is not converted to Access's own format.

To Import a Database

To use the data stored in another database:

1. Open the database window by pressing F11.

2. Select File ➤ Get External Data ➤ Import from the main menu.

3. Select the file and format of the file you want to import in the Import dialog box, and then select Import. If a wizard starts, follow it through to completion.

Index

When designing a table, you can set an index by selecting a field and assigning the Indexed Property. Memo, Yes/No, and OLE object fields cannot be used as indexes.

Indexes are created or removed when you save the table's design. New indexes can be added to existing tables, and existing indexes can be removed in the Table Design window.

Indexes are automatically updated when records are added, changed, or deleted.

The Indexed property for a table's primary key is set to Yes (No Duplicates) by default if the key is a single field.

To Create a Single-Field Index

To create an index on a single field:

1. Open a table in design view.

2. Select the field to be indexed.

3. Press F6 to move to the General tab of the Field Properties window. Press ↓ until you are in the cell following Indexed. Alternatively, click in the Indexed property cell.

4. Enter one of the following in the cell:

   No   No index is used.

   Yes (Duplicates OK)   Two records can contain the same value in this field.

   Yes (No Duplicates)   No two records can contain the same value in this field.

To change the index from ascending to descending:

1. Click the Indexes button in the toolbar or select View ➢ Indexes.

2. Select Ascending or Descending in the Sort Order column.

To Delete a Single-Field Index

To remove an index created from a single field:

1. Open a table in design view.

2. Select the field from which to remove the index.

3. Press F6 to move to the General tab of the Field Properties window. Press ↓ until you are in the cell following Indexed. Alternatively, click in the Indexed property cell.

4. Enter **No** in the property cell.

To Create a Multifield Index

You can index a table on more than one field (city, state, and zip code, for example). Up to five multifield indexes can be defined for a table.

To create a multifield index:

1. Open a table in design view.

2. Click the Indexes button in the toolbar to display the Indexes window.

3. Enter the name of the index in the Index Name field.

4. Enter the first field to index on in the Field Name.

5. Select the sort order (ascending or descending).

6. Leave the Index Name field blank in the next line; then enter the name of the next field to index in the Field Name column. Select the sort order (ascending or descending). Repeat until all fields are included.

The index will be created when you save the table design or move to datasheet view.

To Delete a Multifield Index

To remove an index created from more than one field:

1. Open a table in design view.

2. Click the Indexes button in the toolbar to display the Indexes window.

3. Click the button to the left of the index row so that the entire row is highlighted.

4. Press Delete.

5. Repeat steps 3 and 4 for all rows of the index.

To view all indexes, click the Indexes button in the toolbar or select View ➤ Indexes. You can change the index name, field name, sort order, and index properties from the Indexes dialog box.

Input Mask

An *input mask* is a predefined format (pattern) that data must conform to when entered in a field. For example, the date edit mask 0#/0#/00 specifies that up to two digits are entered for the month, one or two for the day, and two for the year. The field appears as __/__/__ to the user; the slashes and underscores are added by Access. Input masks are available for text and date/time fields only.

In contrast, a format string is used to *display* data, but is not used for data entry. A format string and edit mask can be defined for the same field.

An input mask can be specified for a field in table design view. Since Input Mask is a field property, you can also specify an input mask for a field on a form or in a query.

You can create an edit mask manually by entering it in the Input Mask text box of the Properties window. To create an input mask using Access's Input Mask Wizard:

1. Click in the Input Mask text box.

2. Click the Build Button (which contains three dots) following the text box for Input Mask. Access starts the Input Mask Wizard.

3. Select the input mask name you want from those listed in the Input Mask Name list. Access displays the edit mask for the field in the Try It box. To test the behavior of your selection, click in the Try It box and enter a value.

4. Answer the remaining questions, selecting Next to continue to the next question or Back to return to a previous selection.

5. Click Create to create the edit mask.

Edit Mask Format

An edit mask consists of three parts: the mask itself, an option for storing edit mask characters in the data itself, and the character used to display a space. The three parts are separated by semicolons.

The first part is the mask itself, such as 0#/0#/00. The characters used and the characters they permit during data entry are shown here.

0   Digits 0–9 only, plus and minus signs (+ and –) are not allowed; entry is required

Digit or space; blanks are converted to spaces, plus and minus signs allowed; entry is optional

9	Digit or space, plus and minus signs are not allowed; entry is not required
L	Letter A–Z; entry required
?	Letter A–Z; entry not required
A	Letter or digit; entry required
a	Letter or digit; entry not required
&	Any character or a space; entry required
C	Any character or a space; entry not required
. , : ; – /	These characters specify the decimal placeholder and separator for thousand, date, and time
<	All characters that follow will be changed to lowercase
>	All characters that follow will be converted to uppercase
!	Fill field from right to left (normal fill is left to right)
\	Character following the backslash is displayed as the ASCII character (\A is displayed as A)

The next part is either 0 or 1. If 0, Access stores the mask characters (/, for example) in the table when it stores the data. If 1 or blank, only the characters entered by the user (the digits in the date, in this example) are stored.

The third part of the mask specifies which character is used to display a space. You can use any ASCII character; use " " to display a blank.

A final input mask is permitted: if the Input Mask property is set to Password, Access uses a password text box where typed characters are displayed as asterisks but stored as the characters entered.

J

Joining Tables

To use more than one table in a query, you can *join* two or more tables. Joins permit you to establish one-to-one, one-to-many, and many-to-many relationships between tables.

- In a one-to-one relationship, a record in Table A has no more than one matching record in Table B. For example, suppose you join an Employee table and a Spouse table. An employee record in the Employee table can have no more than one record in the Spouse table (and in fact may have no matching records in the Spouse table).

- In a one-to-many relationship, a record in Table A has zero or more related records in Table B. For example, a record in the Employee table may have many (or no) matching records in a Dependents table.

- In a many-to-many relationship, a record in Table A has zero or more matching records in Table B, and a record in Table B can be related to more than one record in Table A. For example, if a husband and wife who have a child both work for the same company, each will have matching records to a record in the Child table. The child's record will have two relationships back to the Employee table (one for the father, one for the mother).

When you join two or more tables, Access follows the relationship between the tables in order to report all the relationships. For example, suppose your Employee table (which contains an Employee ID and the employee's name) is related to a Benefits table, and an employee can enroll in a health plan, a life insurance plan, and a retirement plan.

You can join the employee record to an Employee ID field in the Benefits table. When you query the database, Access first looks at the primary table, finds the unique value, and then tries to find the same value in the matching field of the related table. When you define a query, you can specify the employee's name from the Employee table and select fields from the Benefits table.

When you run the query, Access can list the employee's name and information about the health plan in the first datasheet row, the employee's name and information about the life insurance plan in the next datasheet row, and the employee's name and information about the retirement plan in the third datasheet row. Because you have a join, Access knows how to find the related information.

When you join two or more tables, you specify the common field between the two tables. The field must have the same data type in both tables.

A table can be related to a primary table and be the primary table in another join. For example, you can join an Employee table to the Benefits table by using an Employee ID number in both tables. The Benefits table can be related to the table that contains the terms and conditions of the benefits stored in the Description table if both tables contain a Benefits Plan Code. Thus the Benefits table is both a primary table (to the Description table) and a related table (to the Employee table).

Types of Joins

Three types of joins occur between a primary table and a related table:

Equi-join or inner join   Access looks at the primary table, finds the equivalent value in the related table, and reports only those records in the primary table that have matching records in the related table.

Outer join   Access reports on all records in the primary table, whether or not they have matching records in the related table. In addition, Access can display all records in the related table that do not have matching records in the primary table, a condition that should not exist if referential integrity has been turned on.

Self-join   Access looks up a field value in the key value of the *same* table.

To Join Two or More Tables

You can join tables in one of two ways.

- Define the join for use throughout all objects in the database. When you use the two tables, their relationship is automatically shown in a query.

- Define the join on an ad-hoc basis. When you use the two tables you must explicitly define the connection, which is valid only for the current query.

To Create a Universal Join

To create a join between two tables that is known throughout Access:

1. Open the database window by pressing F11.

2. Select Tools ➤ Relationships. Access displays the Show Table dialog box.

3. Choose all tables and/or queries you want to use in your relationship by clicking the table or query name and pressing the Add button. When you are done, click the Close button. Access displays the Relationship window. Your primary table is the one containing the one side in a one-to-one or one-to-many relationship.

4. Drag the related field from the primary table to the related table. Right-click the relationship.

5. Click Join Type to specify the type of relationship. Choose *1* for one-to-one, *2* for one-to-many, or *3* for many-to-one.

6. Select OK.

The Enforce Referential Integrity check box in the Relationships window controls how you delete records. With *referential integrity* on, you cannot delete a record in the primary table if a related record in the related table exists.

To enable referential integrity, click the Enforce Referential Integrity box so that an *X* appears in the box. When you select Create, Access displays the Relationships window.

To Delete a Universal Join

To remove a join known throughout Access:

1. Open the database window by pressing F11.

2. Select Tools ➢ Relationships. Access displays the Relationships window.

3. Click the relationship you want to delete.

4. Press Delete.

5. Select OK.

To Create an Ad Hoc Inner Join within a Query

Using this method, you can join two or more tables while designing a query. These instructions assume that you are working with an existing query in which all necessary tables have been added (though not joined). To add all tables to a query, specify each table when you create a new query, or select Query ➢ Show Table from the main menu in a query's design view.

1. Open a query in design view.

2. Select the field in the primary table you want to relate to a field in the related table.

Select the field by clicking it or highlighting it using ↑ or ↓.

3. Ensure that the field in the related table is displayed in the related table's window. If it is not, use the scroll bars or ↑ and ↓ until the field name appears.

4. Click and drag the field name from the primary table to the corresponding field name in the related table. The pointer becomes a No symbol (a circle with a slash across it). As you move the mouse, the pointer changes into a rectangular box. Drop the box on the field name in the related table.

Access displays a line between the two fields. If the field name moves out of the window, Access displays a line to the window's title bar.

To Delete a Join in a Query

To remove a join between two tables in a query:

1. Open the form in design view.

2. Click the line joining the two tables (the join line becomes bold when you click in the right place) and press Delete. Access removes the line between the tables.

If the join was created in the query, the join is deleted. If the tables are related in a universal join, Access disables (removes) the join for the current query only, but does not remove the universal join itself.

Outer Joins

In an outer join, Access queries display all records in the primary table whether or not they have related records in the related table.

Access supports two types of outer joins:

- In a *left outer join*, all records in the primary table are included in the query, along with all records from the *related* table that have matching values.

- In a *right outer join*, all records in the related table are included in the query, along with all records from the primary table that have matching records.

If you select a right outer join, you can look for all records that do not have a matching record in the primary table. The absence of a matching record denotes a break in the referential integrity if that feature has been enabled.

To Create an Outer Join

To create an outer join between two tables:

1. Create an inner join. See "To Create an Ad Hoc Inner Join within a Query," above.

2. Double-click the line connecting the two tables. Access opens the Join Properties dialog box.

3. Select option 2 in the dialog box to create a left outer join. Select option 3 to create a right outer join.

4. Select OK.

Self-Joins

Self-joins are useful in applications that use hierarchical information within the table itself. For example, in a parts table in a manufacturing application, suppose each part is a subassembly of another part. If each record contains a part's number, description, and subassembly part number, you can join the table to itself to list the part's name and subassembly part's name on the same line. In such a case, you can tell Access to find the description using the subassembly part number by looking for that number in the same table.

To Create a Self-Join

To create a self-join (a join of a table to itself):

1. Open the query in design view.

2. Select Query ➤ Show Table and add another copy of the table if the query does not display two windows for the table you want self-joined at the top of the query window. Access displays the table name followed by _1 in the second field list window.

3. Join the field from the first field list window to the key field name in the second field list window for the table by dragging the field name from the first window to the second.

To Change Inner and Outer Joins

To modify an inner or outer join:

1. Open the query in design view.

2. Double-click the line connecting the two tables. Access opens the Join Properties dialog box.

3. Select option 1 in the dialog box to change an outer join to an inner join. Select option 2 to change an inner join or a right outer join to a left outer join. Select option 3 to change an inner join or a left outer join to a right outer join.

4. Select OK.

To View the Existing Joins in a Database

To display a graphical representation of the existing joins in a database:

1. Open the database window (press F11).

2. Select Tools ➤ Relationships, or click the Relationships button on the toolbar.

K

Keyboard Shortcuts

Some of the Access keyboard shortcuts are as follows:

←   Moves one character to the left.

→   Moves one character to the right.

Alt+Backspace   Undoes typing.

Backspace   Deletes selection or next character to the left.

Ctrl+' or Ctrl+"   Inserts value from the previous record.

Ctrl+:   Inserts current time.

Ctrl+←   Moves one word to the left.

Ctrl+-   Deletes the current record.

Ctrl++   Adds a new record.

Ctrl+→   Moves one word to the right.

Ctrl+;   Inserts current date.

Ctrl+Alt+Spacebar   Inserts a default value.

Ctrl+C   Copies selection to the Clipboard.

Ctrl+End   Moves to the end of a field in a multiline field.

Ctrl+Enter   Inserts a new line in a field, label, or zoom box.

Ctrl+Home   Moves to the beginning of a field in a multiline field.

Ctrl+Spacebar   Selects the current column.

Ctrl+V   Pastes the contents of the Clipboard.

Ctrl+X   Cuts selection and places it on the Clipboard.

Ctrl+Z   Undoes typing.

End   Moves to the end of a line.

Delete   Deletes selection or next character to the right.

Esc   Undoes changes.

F1   Opens help.

F2   Switches between editing mode and navigation mode.

F4   Opens a combo box.

F5   Moves to the Record Number box (bottom of a window) in datasheet view; goes to page number in Print Preview mode.

F6   Moves between the upper and lower parts of a window; moves to the next section of a form.

F9   Recalculates fields.

Home   Moves to the beginning of a line.

Shift+Enter   Saves changes to current record.

Shift+F2   Opens a zoom box.

Shift+F4   Finds the next occurrence of a string when Find or Replace dialog box is not displayed.

Shift+F6   Moves to the previous section of a form.

Shift+F9   Requeries the tables in a query.

Shift+Spacebar   Selects the current record.

To Assign a Macro to a Key

You can create your own keyboard shortcuts by assigning a macro to a key or key combination:

1. Create a new macro or display a macro in design view.

2. Select the Macro Names button on the toolbar if the Macro Name column is not displayed. Access displays the Macro Name column in the grid.

3. Enter the key or key combination you want to use to execute the macro in the Macro Name column. See the list of valid key names that follows.

4. Enter the action you want to take when the key or key combination is pressed. To display a list of options, click the down-pointing arrow key (or press Alt+↓), highlight the option, and press Enter. If you want to perform more than one action, enter the next action in the next row of the grid, leaving the Macro Names column blank.

5. Save the macro by selecting File ➤ Save from the main menu with the name Autokeys.

The following key names are valid:

^A, ^1	Ctrl plus any letter or number
{F1}, {F2}, etc.	Any function key
^{F1}, ^{F2}, etc.	Ctrl plus any function key
+{F1}, +{F2}, etc.	Shift plus any function key
{INSERT}	Insert (Ins) key
^{INSERT}	Ctrl+Ins
+{INSERT}	Shift+Ins
{DELETE}	Delete (Del) key
^{DELETE} or ^{DEL}	Ctrl+Del
+{DELETE} or +{DEL}	Shift+Del

L

Labels

Labels are used either as headings or captions on forms and reports or to describe the contents or purpose of a text box. Labels display descriptive text and are automatically created when you add a bound control to a form or report.

You can also add text to a label that is not attached to a field in the table, as for report or form headings.

To Add a Label to a Form, Page, or Report

To add a text label to a form, page, or report:

1. Open the form or report in design view.

2. Select View ➤ Toolbox from the main menu.

3. Click the Label tool button (the button with the large A on it).

4. Click in the upper-left corner of the area in which you want to place the label on the form or report. Drag to the bottom-right corner of the label's desired location and release the mouse button. Access displays a flashing vertical bar inside the label.

5. Type the text for the label. Click outside the label when you are finished.

To Attach a Label to a Control

To attach a text label to an existing control:

1. Select the Label tool from the toolbox.

2. Move the pointer to the area on the form where you want the label, click, and drag to size the label.

3. Press Enter or click the label. Access puts black boxes at the corners of the label.

4. Select Edit ➤ Cut from the main menu or press Ctrl+X.

5. Select the control to which you want to attach the label.

6. Select Edit ➣ Paste from the main menu or press Ctrl+V. Access attaches the label below the control you selected in step 2.

To Change the Appearance of a Label

Labels are one of the controls Access provides in design view. Since a label is a control, you can change a label just as you would any other control on a form or report. For example, click the Font/Fore Color or Back Color button or open the Properties window and choose the Format tab to select background and foreground colors and 3-D effects. You can also resize or move labels.

To Change the Text in a Label

You can change the text within a label in two ways:

1. Click directly on the label. When the vertical bar (the *I-beam*) appears, make the changes you want and click outside the label to save the new text.

2. Display the Property window. (Click the Properties button in the toolbar, or select View ➣ Properties from the main menu.)

3. Press Tab or ↓ until you have moved to the cell to the right of Caption.

4. Enter the new label text.

5. Click anywhere outside the label or press Tab, Shift+Tab, ↑, or ↓ to move to another cell.

To Delete a Label

Click the label and then press Delete.

To Disconnect a Label from a Field

Select the label and then press Delete.

Layering Access Objects

Access allows you to build new objects on top of existing ones. For example, you can define a query and then build a second query on top of the first one by further refining the criteria. Changes made to the first query are automatically used when you run the second. Thus, you have layered one query upon another.

Use layered objects when the primary object is complex and modifying it could cause errors.

Similarly, you can build a report on top of a query, a form on top of a table, and so on, by using the New Object button in the toolbar.

To add a new layer to an existing Access object:

1. Move to the base object (a table or query, for example) that will serve as the primary object. You can be in any view (not only design view).

2. Select the type of object you want to layer on top of the primary object by selecting your choice from the New Object button in the toolbar. Access opens a new window (New Query, New Form, or New Report) and automatically fills in the Select a Table/Query box.

3. Create the new query, form, or report as you would from the database window.

Lines

You can add lines to forms and reports to draw attention to groups of controls or to provide visual breaks on a page.

To Draw a Line on a Form, Page, or Report

To add a line to a form or report:

1. Open the form, page, or report in design view.

2. Select View ➤ Toolbox.

3. Select the line tool. Click the form or report at the beginning point of the line, drag to the endpoint, and release the mouse button.

You can modify the control using the same procedures as you use with any other control. For example, you can delete a line by clicking it to select it and then pressing Delete. You can also move and stretch or shorten lines.

Link a Database File

If you *link* a database from dBASE, FoxPro, or an ODBC database, you instruct Access to read data from the original database. No copy is made, and the original database is not converted to Access's own format.

When you *import* data from another format (dBASE, Excel, or text, for example), you copy it to Access and save it in Access's own format. You work with a *copy* of the file in Access, *not* the original file.

To link a table, select File ➤ Get External Data ➤ Link Tables. Then follow the directions for importing a database.

List Boxes

List boxes resemble combo boxes—both are used to select values. However, you can add a new value with a combo box.

M

Macros

A macro is a set of instructions that allows you to quickly execute instructions within Access. Macros can also be assigned to command buttons so that clicking a button on a form executes a series of instructions.

A macro group is a set of individual macros that have been entered in a single macro window. Though each macro can be run independently, macro groups typically consist of macros that are related in some way (for example, macros that work on the same table or the same form).

You create and edit macros using the macro's design view, a window that contains a grid similar to that in design view for a table or query.

To Create a Macro

To create a new macro:

1. Open the database window by pressing F11.

2. Select the Macros button.

3. Select New. Access opens the Macro Window. The I-beam is in the Action column.

4. Click the down-pointing arrow at the end of the field in the Action column or press Alt+↓ to display the action options. Select the action you want.

5. Press Tab to move to the Comments column. Enter a description that explains what action the step takes.

6. The Action Arguments section of the screen displays a set of properties and

conditions depending on the action selected in step 5. As you move between the arguments, Access displays explanatory text that suggests what should be entered.

7. Move to the next row in the macro grid at the top of the Macro window to enter another action and go to step 4.

8. Select File ➤ Save from the main menu and enter the name of the macro in the Macro Name box to save the macro.

Many action arguments and conditions in a macro refer to a control on a form or report. When you need to enter such an argument, enter the argument as Forms!*formname*!*control-name* or as Reports!*reportname*!*controlname*, where Forms! and Reports! are reserved words and must be used. An exclamation point must be used between the form or report name and the control name.

To Use Drag-and-Drop to Define Macro Actions

You can add an action to a macro quickly by using drag-and-drop. When you use drag-and-drop, Access sets the action arguments at the bottom of the grid for you automatically.

1. Open the Macro in the design mode.

2. Open the database window by pressing F11.

3. Select Window ➤ Tile Horizontally (or Vertically) from the main menu if you cannot see both the Macro grid and the database window.

4. Select the object from the database window you want to open or run. For example, to have the macro open a table, select the Table button in the database window. Then select the table you want the macro to open by clicking it and holding down the mouse button.

5. Drag the table name to the Action column of the row you are defining in the Macro grid, and then release the mouse button.

6. Access adds the appropriate action to the Action cell and fills in the action argument with the name of the object you dragged. For example, if you selected the Customers table in step 5, Access displays OpenTable in the action cell. Access also changes the values in the Action Arguments at the bottom of the Macro window; the Table Name changes to Customers, the view changes to datasheet, and the mode changes to edit.

To Add an Action to a Macro

To add an action to the end of a macro:

1. Select the first empty row at the end of the macro.

2. Click the down-pointing arrow at the end of the field in the Action column or press Alt+↓ to display the action options. Select the action you want.

3. Press Tab to move to the Comments column. Enter a description that explains what action the step takes.

4. The Action Arguments section of the screen displays a set of properties and conditions depending on the action selected in step 2. As you move between the arguments, Access displays explanatory text that suggests what should be entered.

To insert an action into the middle of a macro:

1. Select the row where you want to insert the action.

2. Click in the square to the left of the row. Access displays a solid left arrow and highlights the row.

3. Press Insert or select Insert ➤ Row from the main menu. Access inserts a blank row. The row originally at this location, and all subsequent rows, are shifted down one row.

4. Click the down-pointing arrow at the end of the field in the Action column or press Alt+↓ to display the action options. Select the action you want.

5. Press Tab to move to the Comments column.

6. Enter a description that explains what action the step takes. The Action Arguments section of the screen displays a set of properties and conditions depending on the action selected in step 4. As you move between the arguments, Access displays explanatory text that suggests what should be entered.

7. Enter the values for these arguments as appropriate for the action you want to perform.

To Delete an Action in a Macro

To remove an action from an existing macro:

1. Select the row containing the action you want to delete.

2. Click in the square to the left of the row. Access displays a solid left arrow and highlights the row.

3. Press Delete or select Edit ➤ Delete Row from the main menu. Access deletes the row and moves all subsequent rows in the grid up one row.

To Move an Action in a Macro

To move an action in a macro to another location within the macro:

1. Select the row containing the action you want to move.

2. Click in the square to the left of the row. Access displays a solid left arrow and highlights the row.

3. Click the left arrow and drag the selected row to the new row position in the Macro grid where you want the action to take place. The pointer changes to an arrow with a box attached at the bottom as you drag.

4. Release the mouse button. The action at the location, and all actions underneath, are shifted down one row.

To Edit a Macro

To modify an existing macro:

1. Open the database window by pressing F11.

2. Select the Macro button. Access displays a list of macros and macro groups.

3. Select the macro you want to edit.

4. Select Design. Access opens the Macro window.

5. In the grid, make the changes you need by adding or modifying actions, comments, or action arguments.

6. Select File ➤ Save from the main menu to save the macro. Select File ➤ Save As and enter the new macro name to save the macro under a new name.

To Copy a Macro

To make a copy of a macro or macro group:

1. Open the database window by pressing F11.

2. Select the Macro button.

3. Select the name of the macro you want to copy.

4. Press Ctrl+C or select Edit ➤ Copy from the main menu.

5. Select Edit ➤ Paste. Enter the name of the macro copy in the Macro Name field of the Paste As dialog box, and then select OK.

To Delete a Macro or Macro Group

To delete a single macro or a macro group:

1. Open the database window by pressing F11.

2. Select the Macro button.

3. Select the name of the macro you want to delete.

4. Press Delete, or select Edit ➤ Delete from the main menu.

5. Access asks you to confirm your request. Click OK to delete the macro or Cancel to return to the database window.

To Delete a Macro in a Macro Group

To delete a macro contained in a macro group:

1. Open the database window by pressing F11.

2. Select the Macro button.

3. Select the name of the macro group, and then select Design.

4. Select the row that contains the macro by clicking the box to the left of the Macro Name column. Access displays the row in reverse video. If the macro you want to delete is longer than one row, select the first row and drag the mouse down so that all rows are selected.

5. Press Delete, or select Edit ➤ Delete from the main menu. Access asks you to confirm your request.

6. Click OK to delete the macro or Cancel to return to the database window.

To Run an Entire Macro

You can run a macro from the database window or from the macro's design view.

To Run a Macro from the Database Window You can start a macro from the database window. To run the macro:

1. Open the database window by pressing F11.

2. Select the macro button.

3. Select the macro you want to run. If you choose to run a macro group, enter the macro group name, a period, and the macro name (e.g., *macrogroup*.opencustomers). Otherwise, Access runs the first macro defined in the macro group.

4. Double-click the macro name or click the Run button.

To Run a Macro from the Macro's Design View You can run a macro from design view. Select the macro you want to run or select the macro within a macro that you want to run. Either click the Run button in the toolbar (the button with a large exclamation point) or select Run ➤ Run from the main menu.

To Run a Macro from Other Locations within Access You can run a macro when you are working with forms, reports, and designs of other Access objects:

1. Select Tools ➤ Macro ➤ Run Macro from the main menu. (If you are editing a macro, use Tools ➤ Run Macro.) Access displays the Run Macro box.

2. Select the name of the macro you want to run.

3. If you choose to run a macro group, enter the macro group name, a period, and the macro name (e.g., *macrogroup*.opencustomers). Otherwise, Access runs the macro defined in the macro group.

4. Select OK.

To Single Step through a Macro

To run a macro one step at a time from the macro's design view:

1. Click the Single Step button in the toolbar, or select Run ➤ Single Step from the main menu.

2. Click the Run button in the toolbar (the button with a large exclamation point). Alternatively, select Run ➤ Run from the main menu.

3. Access displays the Macro Single Step dialog box, which displays the macro name, the action it is performing, and the arguments for the action.

4. Select Step to execute the next action. Select Continue to execute the next and all subsequent actions without single stepping through each action. Select Halt to stop the macro and remove the Macro Single Step window.

To Create a Macro Group

A macro group consists of one or more macros saved in a single macro file. To create a macro group:

1. Create a new macro by following steps 1 through 7 of "To Create a Macro" (above) but do not save the macro.

2. Click the Macro Names button. Access adds a column named Macro Name to the grid.

3. Type the name of the macro in the Macro Name column of the first row (the row that contains the macro's first action). This column is also used to assign a shortcut key or key combination to a macro.

4. Move to the next blank row and create another macro if you want to add another macro to the macro group. Enter a name

for the macro in the Macro Name column of the row that contains the macro's first action. Repeat this step until all macros have been added. (You can modify a macro group and add, change, or delete individual macros within a macro group later.)

5. Save the macro group by selecting File ➤ Save from the main menu. Enter the name of the macro group in the Macro Name box. This step saves the macro group as a single macro object (the individual macros are *not* saved separately and are not listed separately in the Macro list in the database window).

To Debug a Macro

To find a problem in a macro, single step through the execution of the macro. When the macro encounters a problem, an Action Failed dialog box appears and displays the action that caused the error. Press the Halt key to stop the macro, and then correct the macro action that triggered the error.

To Set Macro Conditions

If you need to execute a macro only if a condition is true (for example, if a numeric value in a field is over a maximum value), you can specify a macro condition.

A condition is similar to a criterion used in a query grid. A condition, such as Taxable = Yes, evaluates to true or false. If the condition evaluates to true, the action in the macro is taken. If the condition evaluates to false, Access does not perform the action.

1. Click the Conditions button in the toolbar, or select View ➤ Conditions from the main menu. Access displays a new column called Condition on the grid.

2. Enter the condition you want to evaluate. If the condition involves a field on the current form (the form the macro is working on), you need only specify the field name. If the condition involves a control (field) on a different form, enter the control name in the condition as Forms!*formname*!*controlname*.

3. Enter an ellipsis (three dots) in the second (and succeeding) cells in the Condition column if you want two or more actions to be taken when a condition evaluates to true.

To Assign a Macro to a Control on a Form

To assign a macro to a control on a form so Access will execute the macro when Access events occur, such as when you push a button or when a field becomes current (the cursor enters a field):

1. Display the form in design view.

2. Select the control.

3. In the Event tab of the Properties window, enter the macro name in one of the properties listed in the table below. If the macro is part of a macro group, enter the group name, a period, and the macro name in the OnPush property.

Property	When Macro Runs
AfterUpdate	After data in control is saved
BeforeUpdate	Before data in control is saved
OnDblClick	When the user double-clicks the control
OnEnter	Before moving to this control (such as with Tab)
OnExit	Before the user leaves the control
OnClick	When the user clicks the control (if the control is a button)

To Assign Macros to Buttons

You can assign a macro to a button on a form. When you click the button in form view, Access will execute the actions defined in the macro.

1. Display the form in design view.

2. Select View ➤ Properties from the main menu, or click the Properties button in the toolbar. Select the Event tab.

3. Enter the macro name in one of the properties listed in the table below. If the macro is part of a macro group, enter the macro group name, a period, and the macro name in the OnPush property cell.

Property	When Macro Runs
AfterUpdate	After saving the current record
BeforeUpdate	Before saving the current record
OnClose	Before closing the form
OnCurrent	Before displaying a record (either the first record if the form is being opened, or a different record if the form is already opened)
OnDelete	Before deleting the current record
OnInsert	Before inserting a new record
OnOpen	Before opening the form

To Use the Macro Builder

The Macro Builder is used to create a macro within an event property of a report, section, or control.

To use the Macro Builder:

1. Open the form or report in design view.

2. Open the Properties window if it is not displayed.

3. Select the Event tab. The properties, such as MouseClick and OnDelete, appear.

4. Select the event property corresponding to the macro you want to build, and click the ellipses following the property line.

5. Select Macro Builder from the Choose Builder dialog box to build a new macro, and then enter the macro's name. If you are editing an existing macro, Access immediately displays the macro window.

6. Create (or edit) the macro.

Mailing Data

Access supports mailing the contents of a datasheet, form, report, or module using Microsoft Mail or Windows for Workgroups Mail.

To send data from your database as a mail message:

1. Display the record(s) you want to send in a form or report, or select the data from a datasheet.

2. Select File ➢ Send To ➢ Mail Recipient (as Attachment).

3. In the Send dialog box, select the output format.

4. Windows opens the standard New Message form. Complete the form as directed in your Mail users guide.

Mailing Labels

Mailing labels can be used to create address labels for letters or any other type of label you need (such as labels for the cover of a report).

To Create Mailing Labels

In Access, mailing labels are a special type of report. To create mailing labels:

1. Open the database window by pressing F11.

2. Select the Report button.

3. Select New. Access displays the New Report dialog box.

4. Select the Label Wizard. Select the table or query that contains the fields you want on the mailing label. Click the down-pointing arrow key or press Alt+↓ and then select the table or query name. Click OK.

5. Select the label size and then select Next.

6. Select the font to use and then select Next.

7. Select from the Available Fields list the field to appear on the first line of the report. Click the > button.

8. Press Enter to begin a new line.

9. Highlight the field and press Delete to remove characters or a field from the Prototype label list.

10. Repeat steps 7 through 9 as many times as needed to build your label.

11. Click the Next> button when the label is complete. The Mailing Label Wizard asks you which field you want to sort on. With mailing labels you may wish to sort on the zip or postal code.

12. Select the field from the Available Fields list and press the > button; the field is moved to the Sort order list. To remove a field from the Sort Order list, click the < button. To select all fields, click the >> button. To remove all fields from the sort order list, click the << button.

13. Select the Next> button.

14. Enter a label form name. Choose See the Labels as They Will Look when Printed to preview your work or choose Modify the Label Design to enter design mode. Click Finish.

N

Named AutoCorrect

This new feature of Access 2000 can be used to automatically fix errors that occur when you change the names of fields. To turn this feature on:

1. Choose Tools ➤ Options from the Access menu.

2. Click the General tab.

3. Under Name AutoCorrect, check the box for Track Name AutoCorrect Info.

4. Check Perform Name AutoCorrect.

5. If you want to keep a record of the changes that are made, check Log Name AutoCorrect Changes.

6. Click OK.

Null

A field has a null value if no entry has been made in the field. For example, if you skip a numeric field during data entry, it contains a value of null rather than 0.

You can use the null value in queries and conditions in macros to check if a field has data in it. For example, in the Conditions cell of a query, you can use the expression Is Null to include or exclude records in which the field contains no data.

O

One-to-Many Relationships

In a one-to-many relationship between tables, a table is related to another table through a common field. For example, a customer table can be related to an orders table if both tables contain a field in which the customer number is stored. In a one-to-many relationship, the one side (the customer table) is related to one or more records on the many side (the orders table). In fact, the table on the one side may have no records in the many table. Thus a customer record may have no orders.

One-to-many relationships are created by joining tables.

One-to-One Relationships

In a one-to-one relationship between tables, a record in a table has *only one* related record in another table. A one-to-one relationship is established by joining tables.

Option Groups

An option group is a set of buttons, check boxes, or toggle buttons of which only one can be "on" or "true". Each object in an option group has its own OptionValue property. The OptionValue is returned by Access when you select the object in the group. For example, in a group of three buttons, selecting the first button could return 1, selecting the second button could return 2, and so on.

You create option groups by first creating a group frame, which is bound to a field or set to an expression. An option group can also be unbound.

To Create an Option Group

To combine a set of controls into an option group:

1. Open the form in design view.

2. Select the option group tool from the toolbox.

3. Do one of the following:

   • **To create an option group bound to a field**, select the field from the Field window and drag the field name to the form. This step sets the ControlSource property of the option group to the field name. The field type should be Yes/No, Integer, or Long Integer for best results.

   • **To create an unbound option group**, click the form where you want the option group to appear. You must manually set the expression within the ControlSource property for the option group.

4. Select the type of control you want to use within the option group: choose the check box, option button, or toggle button from the toolbox.

5. Click inside the option group at the position of the upper-left corner where you want the first control to appear. The group control changes to reverse video as soon as the pointer moves into it. Access places the first control in the option group. Repeat this step until you have the number of controls you need in the option group.

6. Set the OptionValue property for each control within the group.

Outer Join

When tables are joined together in an outer join, Access queries display all records in the primary or related table whether or not they have related records in the table on the other side of the relationship.

P

Page Breaks

A page break can be used to start a new screen for a multiscreen form. A page break can also be used to enforce a page break at a selected point on a form when you print a report.

To Create a Multiscreen Form

You can use page breaks to instruct Access to break a long form into several pages. When you use the form in data entry mode, press Page Down and Page Up to move between screens.

To create a form that spans more than one screen:

1. Open the form in design view.

2. Open the toolbox if it is not displayed: press View ➤ Toolbox from the main menu.

3. Select the Page Break tool. Click at the point on the form where you want the new screen to begin. Access displays a short dashed horizontal line at the left side of the form where the page break occurs.

To Create a Page Break in a Report

The page break control in the toolbox forces Access to begin a new page at a specified location. To add a page break to a report form:

1. Open the report in design view.

2. Open the toolbox if it is not displayed: press View ➤ Toolbox from the main menu.

3. Select the Page Break tool. Click at the location on the report where you want the new screen to begin, in a detail section, or in the header or footer section of a control break. Access displays a short dashed horizontal line at the left side of the report where the page break occurs.

Page Numbers

You can add a page number to a report by adding a text box with an expression that contains a variation of the Page function as follows:

1. Begin in the database window by pressing F11.

2. Select the Report button.

3. Select Design.

4. Open the toolbox by selecting View ➤ Toolbox. If the Page Footer section is large enough to contain the page number field, go to step 6.

5. Expand the Page Footer section: move the pointer to the bottom portion of the footer so that it changes to a double-pointed arrow. Drag the pointer down to expand the size of the footer.

6. Click the text box button in the toolbox. Move the pointer to the Page Footer section.

7. Click in the upper-left corner of the area in which you want the text box to appear, and then drag to the lower-right corner of the

text box. Release the mouse button and then drag the box or resize it if you wish.

8. Click inside the text box. Enter **=Page** and click anywhere outside the box. This step will display the number 1 in the text box area of the report on page 1, the number 2 on page 2, and so on.

9. Click outside the text box.

You can make page numbers more explicit. Use any of the following expressions instead of =Page in step 8 above:

Expression	What the Report Will Print
="Page " & Page	Page 1, Page 2, etc.
="-" & Page & "-"	-1-, -2-, etc.
="Page " & Format(Page, "000")	Page 001, Page 002, etc.
="Page " & Page "of " & Pages	Page 1 of 20, Page 2 of 20, etc.

Alternatively, you can enter the page expression in the Properties window. If the Properties window is not open, click the Properties button in the toolbar or select View ➤ Properties from the main menu. Select the text box control in which you want to place the page expression. In the Control Source property, enter the expression you want. Always be sure to begin the expression with an equal sign (=).

Pages

Page is another way to refer to data access page. For information on pages, see "Data Access Pages" earlier in this reference.

Parameter Queries

A parameter query allows you to run a query repeatedly but change a value that's used for record selection criteria each time you run it. A parameter query prompts you for the criteria you want to use when you run the query. Parameter queries eliminate the need to create queries that are identical except for a value in the criteria.

To Create a Parameter Query

To create a query that prompts you for a criteria value:

1. Create a Select query (the standard type of query).

2. Type [**in the criteria row of the QBE grid, type the text prompt you want to display when you run the query, and then type**].

3. If you want to specify the data type for the parameter, select Query ➢ Parameters from the main menu. Access displays the Query Parameters dialog box.

4. Enter the identical prompt text into the Parameter box as you entered in step 2. Do not include the square brackets.

5. Select the data type of the field you will be entering in the Data Type box when Access displays the prompt. Select OK.

6. Run the query. Access displays an Enter Parameter Value dialog box containing your prompt and provides an area for you to enter the value. When you have entered the criterion value, click OK.

Passwords

In the workgroup environment, Access allows you to add, change, or delete passwords. If a user forgets a password, a member of the Admin group must clear the password.

To Add a Password

To add a password for a user:

1. Log on using the username for which you want to add the password.

2. Open a database.

3. Select Tools ➢ Security ➢ User and Group Accounts.

4. Select the Change Logon Password tab.

5. Enter the new password in the New Password text box and enter it exactly the same way in the Verify text box.

6. Press OK. If the passwords don't match, Access asks you to reenter the password in the Verify box.

To Change a Password

1. Log on using the username for which you want to add the password.

2. Open a database.

3. Select Tools ➢ Security ➢ User and Group Accounts.

4. Select the Change Logon Password tab.

5. Enter the existing password in the Old Password Box.

6. Enter the new password in the New Password text box and enter it exactly the same way in the Verify text box.

7. Click OK. If the passwords don't match, Access will ask you to reenter the password in the Verify box.

To Clear a User Password

To clear an existing user password:

1. Log on using the username for which you want to add the password.

2. Open a database.

3. Select Tools ➤ Security ➤ User and Group Accounts.

4. Select the username and then select Clear Password.

5. Click OK.

To Log On to Access Using a Password

If you have established security with Access, Access displays a Logon screen when you start the program.

To log on to a secure Access system:

1. Enter your username in the Name box.

2. Enter your password in the Password box. If you do not have a password assigned, leave the box blank—do *not* enter spaces.

3. Click OK.

Permissions

Permissions determine which users and groups can have read and write authority to a database object. You need to specify three parts to Access to determine permission:

- The object for which permission will be granted

- The user and group name that will be affected by the permission

- The type of permission you are granting

To Assign Permissions to Users and Groups

To assign permission to a user or group:

1. Open the database window by pressing F11.

2. Select Tool ➤ Security ➤ User and Group Permissions from the main menu. Access displays the Permissions dialog box.

3. Select the Object Type and Object Name. Enter the Type directly or select it from the pull-down list.

4. Select either the Users button or the Groups button under the User/Group Name option. Select the User or Group you want to grant permission to for this object.

5. Select the type of permissions to grant to the user or group for the specified object. If an *X* appears in the permission option check box, the permission is granted; if the option's check box is empty, permission is not granted. Select any of the following permission options:

   - **Open/Run** allows the user or group to perform the query.

   - **Read Design** allows the user or group to view but not change the object.

   - **Modify Design** allows the user or group to modify the object.

   - **Administer** allows the user or group to perform administration duties, such as assigning passwords to table/query access.

   - **Execute** allows the user or group to run a form or report object and generate data, or execute a macro object.

   - **Read Data** allows the user or group to view data in a table or query and allows the user or group to run an action query (action queries update database tables).

- **Update Data** allows the user or group to view and modify data in a table or query.

- **Insert Data** allows the user to view and add records.

- **Delete Data** allows the user or group to view and delete data.

6. Select OK to add the permissions.

To Change Permissions to Users and Groups

To change a permission already assigned to a user or group:

1. Open the database window by pressing F11.

2. Select Tool ➤ Security ➤ User and Group Permissions from the main menu. Access displays the Permissions dialog box.

3. Select the Object Type and Object Name on the right side of the Permissions page. Enter the Type directly or select it from the pull-down list.

4. Select either the Users button or the Groups button under the User/Group Name list. Select the User or Group you want to grant permission to for this object. Access displays the permissions that already exist for the object and user/group combination.

5. Select the type of permissions you want to grant to the user or group for the specified object. If an *X* appears in the permission option check box, the permission is granted; if the option's check box is empty, permission is not granted. The permission options are listed in "To Assign Permissions to Users and Groups" above.

6. Select Apply to change the permissions.

Primary Key

A primary key is a field or group of fields that identifies a record in a table. No two records in a table can have the same primary key.

While a primary key is not required, they may be used as indexes to a table; primary keys significantly speed up Access when it searches for values in a table.

To Set the Primary Key

To create the primary key in a table:

1. Open a table in design view.

2. Click in the box to the left of the field name of the row containing the field you want to use as the primary key. Access will display the row in reverse video. To select more than one field, hold down Ctrl while you select each row.

3. Select the Primary Key button from the toolbar (the button that shows a key) or select Edit ➤ Primary Key from the main menu. Access displays a key symbol to the left of the field name.

If you do not specify a key when you save a table's design, Access asks if you want it to create a primary key for you. If you select Yes, Access adds a field to your table and defines it with an AutoNumber data type. Fields with an AutoNumber data type are numbered beginning with the value 1 and automatically incremented by Access when you add new records. You cannot change the value in a field with an AutoNumber data type.

When you define a relationship between two tables, Access first looks at the primary key for each table and suggests that this field be used to join the two tables. Therefore, if the table will be used in relationships with other tables, select the common field (the field used to join the two tables) as the primary key.

To Change the Primary Key

To change the primary key in a table:

1. Open a table in design view.

2. Click in the box to the left of the field name of the row containing the field you want to use as the primary key. Access will display the row in reverse video. To select more than one field, hold down Ctrl while you select each row.

3. Select the Primary Key button from the toolbar (the button that shows a key) or select Edit ➤ Primary Key from the main menu. Access displays a key symbol to the left of the field name and removes the key symbol from fields (rows) that are no longer part of the primary key.

Printing

Access provides an easy way to print all the data you have worked with, whether in form, report, or datasheet view. You cannot, however, print an object from within design view.

To Print an Object

To print data in a form, data access page, report, or datasheet:

1. Select File ➤ Print from the main menu, or press Ctrl+P.

2. Access asks you to specify the print range and number of copies and may ask you to select the print quality, depending on the printer you are using. Select the settings you want.

3. To select the printer, page orientation, paper size, or margins, select Setup, select the settings, and select OK.

4. Select OK to print the object, or select Cancel to return to the object's view without printing it.

Access prints your object and shows its progress in a window in the middle of your screen.

To Preview the Printing of an Object

To look at the layout of a printed object before the object is actually printed:

1. Select File ➤ Print Preview from the main menu, or click the Print Preview button. This button shows a magnifying glass over a sheet of paper.

2. Select one of the following:

   • Select Print to print the object. This is the equivalent of selecting File ➤ Print from the main menu.

   • Select Zoom to display the preview screen in a larger font. Select Zoom again to return to full-screen view.

   • Select one, two, or multiple page views.

   • Select Close to return to the object without printing.

Projects

Projects are new to Access 2000. They are like databases (.mdb files) but they work with data that's stored outside the project file on an SQL Server. Projects are stored in .adp files.

The database window for a project is somewhat different from the window you see for an Access database. Instead of buttons for Tables, Queries, Forms, Reports, Pages, Macros, and Modules, you'll see buttons for Tables, Views, Database Diagrams, Stored Procedures, Forms, Reports, Pages, Macros, and Modules.

When you create a project, you can use existing tables on an SQL Server or create a project for tables that you will create later.

Creating a New Project for Existing Database Tables

To create a new project for tables that already exist in an SQL Server database:

1. Choose File ➤ New from the Access menu.

2. In the New dialog box, double-click Project (Existing Database).

3. In the File New Database window, choose a folder and enter a filename for the new project. Then click Create.

4. In the Data Link Properties window, enter all the information that's needed to access the database for the tables the project will access.

5. Click OK.

Creating a Project for New Tables

To create a project for tables in a database that hasn't been created yet:

1. Choose File ➤ New from the Access menu.

2. In the New dialog box, double-click Project (New Database).

3. In the File New Database window, choose a folder and enter a filename for the new project. Then click Create.

4. The Microsoft SQL Server Database Wizard will start. Follow the instructions to create a new database that will hold the tables for the new project.

Properties

Properties dictate the behavior or specify the features and characteristics of a form or report or the controls on these objects on a form. For example, controls have a default value property, a color property, and a height property.

Properties can be set by using design tools (such as the Palette window) or by entering or selecting the property value directly in a cell in the Properties window.

To Set a Property

To set a property for an Access object:

1. Open a form, data access page, or report in design view.

2. Select the object whose property or properties you want to change. To set the properties of more than one object at a time on a form or report, select all objects. To do so, select the first object and then press and hold the Shift key as you select the remaining objects. To select the entire form or report, select Edit ➤ Select Form or Edit ➤ Select Report.

3. Select the Properties button on the toolbar, or select View ➤ Properties from the main menu, or click the right mouse button.

4. Select the tab representing the type of property you want to change, or select All Properties to list all available properties.

5. Click in the cell to the right of the property you want to change, or press ↓ or Tab until you reach this cell. If you go too far, press ↑ or Shift+Tab to go back.

6. Do one of the following:

- **If the property values are limited**, Access displays a down-pointing arrow at the right side of the cell. Click this arrow or press Alt+↓ to display the valid options; then select the option you want. Some properties are selected using a wizard or a special dialog box. The text boxes for these properties (such as Color, Input Mask, and Validation Rule) are followed by a Builder Button (which contains three dots). Click the button to open the dialog box that controls the property's value. Go to step 7.

- **If the property value is not restricted**, enter the value of the property in the cell.

7. Click in another property cell or anywhere outside the property box to make the property value permanent.

Copying Properties

You can copy the formatting of one object to another using the Format Painter, a feature found in other Microsoft Office Applications.

To copy the format properties (fonts, color, etc.) from one object to another:

1. Select the object that has the properties you want to copy.

2. Click the Format Painter icon in the toolbar.

3. Click the object to which you want to apply the properties.

To copy the format to several controls:

1. Select the object that has the properties you want to copy.

2. Double-click the Format Painter icon.

3. Click each object to which you want to apply the properties.

4. Press Esc.

Q

Queries

The Find feature in Access searches for values within a field, searching and displaying one record at a time.

Queries are used to find more than one record. In addition, queries let you specify the fields you want to see in the datasheet, as well as the order of the fields. You can also sort records and specify criteria to limit which records are displayed.

Records can be displayed in datasheet view, the spreadsheet-like layout used in other areas of Access. As with other grids, you can move columns, change the width of columns or height of rows, and insert columns. You can also update field values in a query for any table on either side of a join.

To run a query, you must tell Access two things:

- Which fields you want to display.

- Which field contains the values you want to look for or limit the search to; for example, you might want to see only records that contain Canada in the Country field.

When you execute a query, Access finds the records you requested and displays them. This set of records is called a dynaset—a set of records that is created dynamically. The dynaset is simply a subset of the records from the complete table. Unlike other database programs that create a subset for display only, Access lets you add, edit, or delete records from the datasheet view of the dynaset.

With the records in datasheet view, you can:

- Change the query by clicking the Design button or selecting View ➢ Design View from the main menu.

- Find a particular value within any of the columns by clicking the Find button (the button with the binoculars), or selecting Edit ➤ Find from the main menu, or pressing Ctrl+F.

- Change the layout of the datasheet: change the font, column order, column width, and so on.

- Save your changes in design view for future use by selecting File ➤ Save As and entering a *new* query name.

In fact, you can even create a new data entry form to display the records in a custom layout by clicking the New Object button on the toolbar and selecting Form.

To Create a New Query

To design a new query:

1. Open the database window by pressing F11.

2. Select the Query button.

3. Select the New Query button, select New Query, and click OK.

4. Use ↑ and ↓ to highlight the table you want to use, and then press Enter or click Add. You can select the table directly by double-clicking the table or query the new query is based on. Click the Both option to see both tables and queries.

5. Repeat step 4 for each table that contains information you will use in your query. Select Close when you have selected all the tables.

Access displays the Select Query window. Notice that at the top of the window Access displays a window listing all fields in a table; Access displays a window for each table you selected in steps 4 and 5. Key fields are displayed in boldface.

If you have not selected a relationship between the tables, Access will look for matching field names between tables and automatically create a join. At the bottom of the Select Query window is another grid, called the query by example grid, or QBE grid for short, which will hold the criteria.

6. Specify the name of the first field you want to see in the resulting datasheet in the first column of the QBE grid. The insertion point is blinking in the first cell of the first column of the QBE grid, which is where the field name must be placed. You can select the field in one of two ways:

   - Click the down-pointing arrow in the cell or press Alt+↓, highlight the field, and press Enter.

   - Click in the table field list window at the top of the window. Select the field name and drag the field name to the first Field cell in the QBE grid. When the pointer points to the Field cell, it changes into a rectangle, indicating that Access is ready to drop the field name into the cell.

7. Repeat step 6 for each field you want to display. Alternatively, if you want to display all fields from a table, you can use one of two shortcuts:

   - Select the first field listed in the table's field list; the field is noted by an asterisk (*). Drag the asterisk to the QBE grid. The * is shorthand for displaying all fields in the datasheet. If you want to enter criteria for any of the fields, you must use an additional column and specify the field. To suppress the field's display a second time (the field is displayed as part of the * designator), click in the Show row so that an *X* does not appear.

- Double-click the field list window's title; then click and drag to the first available row in the QBE grid. Access fills in each field from the table into a separate column in the QBE grid. To enter criteria, select the field's column and enter the criteria in the Criteria row.

8. Press Tab or click in the Field cell of the second column. Repeat steps 6 and 7 until all fields you want to display are included in the QBE grid.

9. Use the Criteria cell of the column corresponding to this field to enter criteria for any of the fields already selected. Otherwise, add the field to a new column in the QBE grid.

10. Enter the criteria. In the Criteria row, enter the expression Access should use to evaluate whether it should include or exclude a record.

11. Run the query.

To Create a New Query with the Query Wizard

To create a new query by answering a series of questions:

1. Open the database window by pressing F11.

2. Select the Query tab.

3. Select the New Query button.

4. Select the wizard appropriate to the type of query you want to perform: Simple Query Wizard, Crosstab Query Wizard, Find Duplicates Query Wizard, or Find Unmatched Query Wizard.

5. Answer the wizard's questions as appropriate.

To Modify a Query Using SQL

You can modify a query created using QBE (query by example) by modifying the Structured Query Language (SQL) statements the QBE generates. To edit the SQL:

1. Run the query.

2. Click the SQL View button in the toolbar, or select View ➤ SQL View.

3. Make the changes to the SQL.

4. Click the Run button (the button with the exclamation point) to run the modified query.

To Run a Query from Design View

If you have a query defined and open in design view, you can run the query by one of these methods:

- Click the down arrow to the right of the View button in the toolbar, and then select Datasheet View.

- Click the Run button (the button with a large exclamation point).

Access creates the dynaset and displays the records in a datasheet.

To Run the Query from the Database Window

1. Click the Query button.

2. Select the query you want to run.

3. Double-click the query name or select Open.

To stop the execution of a query, press Ctrl+Break.

To Save a Query

To save a query design for future use:

1. Select File ➤ Save.

2. If the query is new and has not been saved, Access asks you to name it. Enter the query name and select OK.

Access saves the layout and the properties (including the format, input mask, and top values) of the query.

To Save a Query Using a Different Name

To keep a copy of a modified query separate from the original query, select File ➤ Save As. Enter the new query name and select OK.

Adding Another Related Table to a Query

To add another table to a query:

1. Display the query in design view. (Click the Design button or select View ➤ Query Design.)

2. Select Query ➤ Show Table from the main menu, or click the Show Table button on the toolbar. The Show Table dialog box is displayed.

3. Select the table you want to add from the Table/Query list. Select Add and then select Close.

4. Because Access already knows about the relationship for these two tables, it displays a line between the related fields. If not, you can create the relationship by highlighting a field in one table and dragging it to the related field in another table.

5. Click the Datasheet or Run button on the toolbar, or select View ➤ Datasheet View from the main menu.

To Use a Query to Summarize Data

You can use a query to group fields and calculate totals, averages, and other standard arithmetic calculations. To use this feature, you must display the Total row in the QBE grid, and then select the type of calculation you want to make (called an *aggregate function*).

Aggregate functions perform calculations on groups (aggregates) of records. Aggregate functions include calculating an average or finding the largest or smallest value in a table or query.

1. Open a select query in design view.

2. If the Total row is not displayed in the QBE grid, click the Total button on the toolbar or select View ➤ Totals from the main menu.

3. Build a select query as usual: Drag the field on which you want to use a calculation to the QBE grid. In the Total row click the down-pointing arrow or press Alt+↓. Select from one of the aggregate functions listed below. Aggregate functions specify the type of calculation you want to make.

4. Run the query.

Access uses the following aggregate functions:

Avg Computes the average value.

Count Counts the number of values.

Expression Evaluates an expression for this field.

First Displays the value in the first record (using the current sort order).

Group By   The default setting; this performs no calculation.

Last   Displays the value in the last record (using the current sort order).

Max   Finds the largest (maximum) value.

Min   Finds the smallest (minimum) value.

StDev   Computes the standard deviation.

Sum   Adds all values.

Var   Computes the variance of all values.

Where   Restricts records in a crosstab. (Where specifies a limiting expression; fields that use the Where value are not displayed.)

To limit which records are included in the records used in an aggregate function before it is executed, use the Where function. If you use an expression in the Field row and the Where option in the Total row, Access evaluates the Where expression for a record to determine if the record should be included in any calculations. Fields that use the Where function are not displayed in a query; the Where function allows you to use additional criteria to limit which records are included in a query.

R

Record Locking

Record locking options are set in the Custom Multiuser Options.

Rectangles

To draw a rectangle on a form or report, follow the directions for drawing lines but select the rectangle tool instead of the line tool.

Referential Integrity

Referential integrity controls how your records are maintained when tables are joined. Referential integrity stops you from deleting a record in the primary table if it has a related record in the related table.

To enable referential integrity:

1. Open the database window by pressing F11.

2. Select Tools ➣ Relationships from the main menu.

3. Right-click the line joining two tables and choose Edit Relationships.

4. Check on the Enforce Referential Integrity box.

Use referential integrity to keep joined tables in sync.

Reports

Reports allow you to present your data in print or send your data to disk for printing by someone else or at another computer. You can create reports to list individual records in sorted order, show records grouped by a field value, or summarize data. For example, you can list all customers alphabetically, print all customers by state, or count the number of customers by country.

As with forms, Access provides a wizard, called the Report Wizard, to simplify creating reports. Access also has a Chart Wizard for graphing data and a Label Wizard for creating reports to print labels.

Reports share many features seen in queries: You can save a report and run it again. You can design a report so that it uses the results of a query rather than all records in a table. If you need to report on a subset of records from a table, a query is an efficient screening mechanism that improves the performance of the report feature of Access. This speeds up creating reports because queries are more efficient at selecting records than are reports.

To Create a Single-Column Report

To create a report in which all selected fields are displayed in a column:

1. Open the database window by pressing F11.

2. Select the Reports button.

3. Select the New button. Then choose the Design View to work from scratch; AutoReport: Columnar or AutoReport: Tabular for a quick report; or Report Wizard for more control with only a few questions to answer. You can also choose the Chart Wizard or the Label Wizard in this dialog box.

4. Access needs to know which table or query you want to work with. Click the down-pointing arrow key to display the list of available tables and queries, or press Alt+↓. Use ↑ and ↓ and highlight the table or query and then press Enter. Click OK.

5. You can select the table or query directly by double-clicking the table or query name in the list box.

   Alternatively, enter the name of the table or query in the Choose a Table box.

6. If you pick the Report Wizard option, Access will ask a series of questions.

7. The Report Wizard asks which fields you want to include on the form. Highlight the first field you want included on the report. This field will appear first in the column on the report. Click the > button. The field name is removed from the Available Fields list and added to the Selected Fields list. Similarly, add the other fields you want on the report. Select the Next> button.

8. The Report Wizard asks you how you want to group the data. Select the first field and click the > button. If you wish to create a subgroup of this field, pick another field and press > again. (Choose the Grouping Options button to select intervals at which groups will occur.) Choose the Next> button to continue.

9. Select the sort order for up to four fields on the report. Click the button to the right of the field name to toggle between ascending and descending sort order. Choose Next > to continue.

10. Access asks you to select the position of fields. A tabular layout places fields across the page; a vertical layout puts one field per line. Choose Next> to continue.

11. Select the Style of the report. You can select any format and then view a sample in the magnifying glass at the left of the Report Wizard window. Select the Next> button.

12. Access asks for the report name. This name will appear in the database window list when you select Reports. Enter the name of the report and then select the Print Preview button. Access launches the report and shows you a sample of the report.

13. Click the Cancel button to exit or Finish to create the report.

To Use Snaking Columns on a Report

If your report contains more data than can fit in a single column, you can use a snaking column to wrap the text into the next column. To set up snaking columns:

1. Create a report and open it in design view.

2. Select File ➢ Print and then choose Setup or File ➢ Page Setup. Access displays a Page Setup dialog box.

3. Select the Columns tab.

4. Enter the number of columns you want in the Number of Columns box. Enter the amount of space you want between records in the Row Spacing box.

5. Enter the amount of space you want between columns in the Column Spacing box.

6. Select the desired option in the Column Layout section.

7. Select OK.

To Save a Report

To save a report design for future use, select File ➢ Save. If you have not saved the report before, Access asks you to name the report. Enter a name and select OK.

To Save a Report Using a Different Name

To keep a copy of a modified report separate from the original report, select File ➢ Save As. Enter the new report name and select OK.

To Copy an Existing Report

To make a copy of an existing report:

1. In the database window, highlight the report and open it in design view.

2. Select File ➢ Save As and enter the new report name.

To Close a Report

When you are done with a report and want to return to the database window, select File ➢ Close. If you have made changes, Access asks if you want to save them. Select Yes to save the changes or No to discard them, and then select Cancel to return to design view.

To Change the Format of a Report

You can use the Access AutoFormat tool to create a new look for a report. In design view, click the AutoFormat button in the toolbar or select Format ➢ AutoFormat from the main menu. Select the "look" of the report that you want from the predefined list, and click Options to apply only font, color, and/or border properties. Select OK to apply the format.

You can create your own AutoFormat layout by clicking the Customize button and choosing the appropriate option. Access lets you create a new format based on your current report, update an existing format with properties from your current report, or delete the selected format.

Report Sections

Reports in Access are *banded reports*—they have separate sections, each of which is identified by a band across the top. Standard reports created by the Report Wizard include a band for the report header, report detail, and a report footer.

By default, the Form Wizard places the =Now( ) function in the Page Header. =Now( ) displays your computer system's current date when the report is run. The Page Footer section created by a Form Wizard contains a single control containing =Page. =Page is translated into a page number when the report is printed.

To View a Report with Data

To run the report and display a sample of the output on the screen before you print it, select

File ➤ Print Preview from the main menu or click the Print Preview button. Access displays the report, complete with data from your table or query. At the top of the preview window are buttons to Print, Zoom, and Close, and set the page display for one, two, or multiple pages.

- **To print the report from the Report Preview view**, select the Print button.

- **To inspect or modify the printer settings**, select the Setup button in the Print dialog box. Access displays a dialog box similar to the Printer Setup dialog box in the Windows Control Panel or the Printer Setup options offered in most Windows applications.

- **To see a full page of the report**, click the Zoom button; click it again to return to the close-up view.

Click Close to return to design view.

To Modify a Report

Working in a report's design view is similar to working with a form in a design view. You can click and drag controls to new locations or change their properties (for example, font and font size). As with forms, controls on a report are any of its elements, such as a picture, a field, or a report title.

S

Select Queries

By default, new queries are Select queries. Select queries select records based on your criteria and display them in a form or datasheet.

Other types of queries include action queries and parameter queries.

Sort Order

When you set the sort order in a query, records in a dynaset are viewed in sorted order. You can sort a field in ascending order (0–9 and A–Z) or descending order (9–0 and Z–A) by choosing Ascending or Descending in the Sort row in the QBE grid.

The datasheet is sorted by the first column in the QBE grid that contains a sort option (this field need not be the first column in the grid). If two records have the same value, Access looks at the next field to the right in the QBE grid that contains a sort option, looking to the columns.

You can remove the sorting option from a field by selecting *(not sorted)* in the Sort cell of the field you no longer want to sort.

To perform a quick sort on data displayed in a table, query, or form:

1. Move the cursor to the field you want to sort on.

2. Click the Sort Ascending button on the toolbar to sort the data from A to Z or click the Sort Descending button to sort the data in the reverse order. Alternatively, select Records ➤ Sort and then select Sort Ascending or Sort Descending.

3. Access sorts the data and displays the records in sorted order.

Spell Check

To check the spelling of text within a text box (on a form) or a text column in a datasheet, select Tools ➤ Spelling or press F7. If the word is not found, you can choose from suggested alternatives or add the word to your custom dictionary.

The spell checker's dictionary is shared with other Microsoft Office applications.

Spreadsheets

Access can import and export data from a table to a spreadsheet that supports Lotus 1-2-3 or Microsoft Excel formats.

To Export a Table to a Spreadsheet

To save a table in a file in spreadsheet format:

1. Open the database window by pressing F11.

2. Select the table you want to export.

3. Select File ➢ Export from the main menu.

4. Enter a name for the new spreadsheet file.

5. Using the Save as Type drop-down list, select the spreadsheet format you want. You can select various versions of Microsoft Excel and Lotus 1-2-3.

6. Click Save.

Access creates a spreadsheet by placing the name of each field in a separate column in the first row of the spreadsheet. Each record is saved as a new row in the spreadsheet.

To Import Data from a Spreadsheet

To import data saved in a spreadsheet into an Access table:

1. Open the database window by pressing F11.

2. Select File ➢ Get External Data ➢ Import from the main menu. Choose the type of spreadsheet you want to import using the Files of Type drop-down list. Then select the file to import.

3. Click Import. Access displays the Import Spreadsheet Wizard dialog box.

4. Answer the questions in the Wizard. Check the First Row Contains Field Names box if you want Access to create field names using the values in the first row of the spreadsheet. If you do not check this box, Access creates its own sequentially numbered field names, which you can modify in the table's design view.

SQL Databases

SQL stands for *Structured Query Language*, a standardized technique for accessing data stored in a database. SQL is useful for transferring data between programs.

To Attach or Import an SQL Database Table

To link or import a file from an SQL database:

1. Be sure a Microsoft Access database is open.

2. Select File ➢ Get External Data ➢ Link Tables from the main menu to link an SQL database file. Select File ➢ Get External Data ➢ Import to import an SQL database file.

3. Select <ODBC Database> as the file type.

4. In the Select Data Source window, select the ODBC data source you want to use.

5. Enter your logon ID and password as used on the SQL database server, if required. Select OK.

6. Select the name of the table you want to link or import from the Objects list.

7. Select Import or Link, depending on which action you want to perform.

To Export an Access Table to an SQL Database Table

To export a table defined in Access to a table in SQL Database format:

1. In the database window, select the table you want to export.

2. Select File ➢ Export. Access displays an Export dialog box.

3. Enter a name for the new SQL database file.

4. Select <ODBC Database> for the Save As type.

5. In the Select Data Source dialog box, double-click the SQL Server data source you want to use. Select OK.

6. Enter your logon ID and password that you use to log on to the SQL database server. Select OK.

7. Access logs on to your SQL database server and exports the Access table to an SQL table. Access displays its progress in a status bar at the bottom of the Access window.

SQL Statements

When you create a query, Access allows you to view the equivalent SQL statements in a special window. You can also modify the SQL statements in this window; your changes will be reflected in the QBE grid when you close the SQL window.

You can also use the SQL statements generated in a query in forms, reports, and macros.

To View SQL Statements in a Query

Once you create a query, you can view the equivalent SQL statements and change them this way:

1. With a query in design view, select View ➢ SQL View from the main menu. Access displays an SQL dialog box and presents the SQL statement.

2. Click the Close box in the SQL window when you are done.

To Use SQL Statements from a Query in a Form, Report, or Macro

You can use an existing query or a new query to establish the conditions (and create the SQL expression) you want to use. The following instructions assume the query exists.

1. With a query in design view, select View ➢ SQL View from the main menu.

2. Access displays an SQL dialog box and presents the SQL statement in the SQL Text box. Make any changes as needed.

3. Select the statement using the mouse or keyboard. Press Ctrl+C to copy the text to the Clipboard or use Edit ➢ Copy from the main menu.

4. Click the Close button of the SQL window.

5. Move to the location where you want to place the SQL statement. For example, you can use the statement in a Record Source property of a form or report. Press Ctrl+V or select Edit ➢ Paste from the main menu. Access inserts the text at the new location.

Subdatasheets

See "Datasheets" earlier in this reference.

T

Tab Control

A tab control is a control you place on a form to create a tabbed object.

Tab Order

By default, Access moves between controls on a form from top to bottom, left to right, when you press Tab.

To Change the Tab Order of a Form

To change the order in which pressing Tab moves to the next control:

1. Open the form in design view.
2. Select View ➤ Tab Order. Access displays the Tab Order dialog box and displays the fields in the current tab order.
3. Select the control you want to move by clicking in the box to the left of the field name and dragging the control to the new location. To move more than one control, select the range of consecutive controls by clicking and dragging over a group and then dragging the group to the new location.
4. Click OK.

To Restore the Tab Order of a Form

To restore the tab order to moving between fields from left to right, top to bottom on a form:

1. Open the form in design view.
2. Select View ➤ Tab Order. Access displays the Tab Order dialog box and displays the fields in the current tab order.
3. Select the Auto Order button.
4. Select OK.

Tables

Tables are the building blocks of Access. They store the data you want to keep. Each table is divided into records; each record contains information about a single item. In turn, records are divided into fields, the individual units that keep the lowest level of detail.

To Create a Table

To create a new table in Access:

1. Open the database window by pressing F11.
2. Select the Table button.
3. Select the New button. Choose design view to create a table manually or Table Wizard for step-by-step instructions. Click OK. If you chose design view, enter the field name in the first column for each field you want to include in the table. Select a Data Type for each field. You can enter a description if you wish; the Description field is optional.
4. Set the properties for each field by using the Field Properties section of the Table window.
5. Set the primary key.
6. Close the database design and save the file as prompted.

To Save a Table

To save a table in Access:

1. Select File ➢ Save from the main menu.

2. If the table is new and has not been saved, Access asks you to name the table. Enter the table name and select OK.

3. If you have not defined a primary key in the table, Access asks if it should create one for you. If you click Yes, Access adds a field of data type Counter as the first field in your table.

To Change a Field Property in a Table

To modify the value of a property for a field:

1. Select any cell in the row containing the field you want to change. Use Tab or Shift+Tab to move to the proper row.

2. Select the field property you want to change. You can select a field property in one of two ways:

- Press F6 to move to the Field Properties window and then use ↑ and ↓ to move to the cell next to the property you want to change.

- Click directly in the cell next to the property you want to change.

3. Choose the General or Lookup tab and then enter the new value for the property.

4. Click anywhere else on the screen to set the property value.

To View a Table's Design

To examine the fields in a table:

1. Open the database window by pressing F11. Click the Tables button. Access displays an alphabetical list of the tables in the current database.

2. Highlight the table you want to view. You can use ↑ and ↓ to move the highlight bar to the table name or click the table name with the mouse.

3. Select the Design button at the top of the window, or double-click the table name.

Access displays the table you selected.

Each field in the table is defined and described on a separate line in the spreadsheet-like view.

The first column in the table is used to name each field; field names can be up to 64 characters long. The next column specifies the field type, which tells Access the kind of information that can be stored in the field. For example, a text field can store letters and numbers. The field length is shown or set in the Field Size property setting in the Field Properties box at the bottom of the window.

You can enter a description in the third column of the upper grid. This information is only to remind you of the purpose or content of the field; the text is not used by Access.

Below the table definition window is a Field Properties window. In this section you specify further details about each field. As you move between fields, the Field Properties change to reflect information about the selected field.

Key fields are unique values you assign to a record. No two records in a database can contain the same value in a key field. Since key fields must be unique and may be tied to other tables in a one-to-many or many-to-many relationship, you cannot change the data type of a key field, and you may not change the value in the key field in any record. Data types can be changed for *nonkey* fields.

To View a Table's Data

In design view, you can modify the fields and their properties in a table. To see the actual *data* in the table, you must change to datasheet view.

In datasheet view, Access displays the information stored within records in a *datasheet*, a grid that resembles a spreadsheet.

To switch to datasheet view and see the datasheet, click the Change View drop-down box and choose Datasheet View. Alternatively, you can select View ➤ Datasheet View from the main menu.

Access displays the datasheet view of the table, listing the contents of each field in a column. Columns are arranged in the same order as they are defined. Each record is displayed on a separate line.

To Print a Table

To print records in a table:

1. Open the table in datasheet view or select the table in the database window.

2. Select File ➤ Print from the main menu.

3. Select the print options, and then select OK.

To print selected records in a table:

1. Open the table in datasheet view.

2. Select the records you want to print:

   - **To select a single record**, click in the box to the left of the row; the row is displayed in reverse video.

   - **To select a range of records**, click the first row and drag the mouse to the last row, or click the first row and then press Shift and select the last row in the range.

   - **To select all records**, choose Edit ➤ Select All Records from the main menu.

3. Select File ➤ Print. Access displays a Print dialog box.

4. Choose Selection in the Print Range section.

5. Select OK.

Templates

When you create a form or report, you can use its characteristics as the basis of new forms or reports. The set of characteristics Access uses, such as the sections used, their height and width, and default fonts, is called a *template*.

You do not need to save a special file in order to create a template; Access reads the characteristics from the form or report you specify as a template using the Form Template procedure. When you design new forms or reports without using the Report Wizard and the Form Template option is set, the characteristics will be automatically applied.

To Set a Form or Report Design as a Template

To tell Access which form or report to use as a template for future forms and reports:

1. Select Tools ➤ Options from the main menu. Access displays the Options dialog box.

2. Click the Forms/Reports tab.

3. Enter the name of the form you want to use as the template for new forms in the cell below Form Template.

4. Enter the name of the report you want to use as the template for new reports in the cell below Report Template.

5. Select OK.

Text Files

Access can import two types of text files: one in which each field is delimited by a character (usually a comma) and fixed-width text files in which each field in a record begins at the same position relative to the beginning of the record.

To Import a Delimited or Fixed-Width Text File

To import the data in a delimited or fixed-width text file and use it in an Access table:

1. Open a database file that will contain the data in the text file.

2. Select File ➤ Get External Data ➤ Import from the main menu.

3. Select Text Files for the file type.

4. Choose the file you want to import. Select the Import button. Access displays the Import Text Wizard and displays the name of the text file you selected in the title of the window. Choose the type of file—Delimited or Fixed Width.

5. Click Next or Finish to complete the Wizard and import the file.

To Export an Access Table to a Text File

Access can export a table to either delimited text or fixed-width text files.

1. Open the database window by pressing F11.

2. Click Tables to highlight the appropriate table. Select File ➤ Export from the main menu.

3. Choose Text Files from the Save as Type field.

4. Enter the new filename and choose the destination folder in the Export Table dialog box.

5. Choose Save. Access starts the Text Export Wizard. Answer the Wizard's questions.

Toolbars

A toolbar is a set of buttons that lets you perform common tasks quickly. The built-in toolbar, which appears under the menu by default, changes depending on the type of object you are working on and the view you are using.

To Change the Location of the Toolbar

You can anchor a toolbar along any edge of the screen or create a floating toolbar that can be moved anywhere on the screen.

To anchor the toolbar, drag it to an edge of the screen until the dotted outline becomes a long horizontal or vertical toolbar and then release the mouse button. To create a floating toolbar, click any area within a toolbar that does not contain a button, such as the gray area around and between buttons. Drag the toolbar wherever you want it to be.

To Customize a Toolbar

To change a toolbar:

1. Select View ➤ Toolbars ➤ Customize.

2. Choose the toolbar you want to change and check it to make it visible:

   - **To add a button**, select the icon category and then drag a button from the Buttons section to the desired location in the toolbar.

- **To remove a button** from the toolbar, click the button and drag it off the toolbar.

3. Select Close to return to the active screen.

To Show or Hide a Toolbar

To display or remove a toolbar from your screen, select View ➢ Toolbars ➢ Customize. Select the toolbar you want to display and then click the box next to the desired toolbar. To remove a toolbar, select a toolbar from the list that has a checkmark in front of it, and click inside the box to remove the checkmark. Select Close to return to the active screen.

Toolbox

Access can display a toolbox when you are in design view of a form or report. The toolbox lets you select the type of control you want to add to a form or report. To specify the tool, click it once, select the field you want bound to the control, and move the pointer to the form or report surface. To display the toolbox, choose View ➢ Toolbox when you are in design view.

U

Undo

If you make a mistake, you can often undo a change.

To Reverse an Action or Undo a Change

To revert to an early entry or undo an action, select Edit from the main menu. In the drop-down menu list, the first option shows what you can undo. For example, if you are typing new text in a control, Access displays the option Undo Typing. Select the option and Access undoes your work. If Access displays Can't Undo in the pull-down menu, it cannot reverse your actions.

Unique Values

To display only unique values in a Select or Crosstab query, open the query in design view, click anywhere outside the QBE grid, and select View ➢ Properties from the main menu. Click in the box to the right of Unique Values. Replace the No with Yes and then close the Properties dialog box.

Unlinking Tables

When you link tables from another database, the attachment, called a *link*, remains in place, even if the table no longer exists.

To Remove a Link to a Table

To delete an existing link to a table:

1. Open the database window by pressing F11.

2. Click the Table button.

3. Highlight the table name or click it with the mouse to select it.

4. Press Delete or select Edit ➢ Delete from the main menu. Access removes the link and the table's name from the table list.

User and Group Accounts

In a workgroup environment, user accounts are assigned to an individual. Users are then assigned to group accounts. Permissions (the details of what a user can read, edit, or update) are granted to groups (and thus to all the users

M A S T E R ' S   R E F E R E N C E

defined in that group) as well as directly to users.

You can administer security only if your user account name is a member of the group called Admin.

To Add a User Account

To create a new user account in a secured system:

1. Open the database window by pressing F11.

2. Select Tools ➢ Security ➢ User and Group Accounts.

3. Click the Users tab and enter the username in the Name box. Usernames are *not* case sensitive, can be up to 20 characters long, and may contain letters, numbers, spaces (although the first character *cannot* be a space), and symbols. A username may not contain any of the following:

    " * ? / \ [ ] < > | + = , ; :

    Characters between ASCII 00 and 31.

4. Select New. Access displays the New User/Group dialog box.

5. Access creates a user account code based on the name entered in the Name box plus the four-digit number entered in the Personal ID Number box. Enter the username or skip the field to accept the name entered in step 3; then select OK.

Be sure to keep a record of the Personal ID Number. You will need it to share information across more than one computer system.

To Delete a User Account

To erase a user account in a secured system:

1. Open the database window by pressing F11.

2. Select Tools ➢ Security ➢ User and Group Accounts.

3. Click the Users tab and enter the username in the Name box, or select a name from the pull-down list.

4. Select Delete.

To Use the Special Admin User

Access can restrict the system to authorized users by means of usernames and passwords. To administer the security system, your username must be part of the Admin user group. To set up the security administration of an Access system:

1. Open the database window by pressing F11.

2. Change the password of the Admin account. When Access is installed, the password for this account is blank.

3. Create a new user account for the system administrator. Add the account to the Admin group, which is created when Access is installed.

4. Exit Microsoft Access and restart the program.

5. Log onto Access using the new username and password set in steps 2 and 3.

6. Delete the Admin user account.

To Create a User Group

User groups establish the security levels, called permissions, for users assigned to the group. A user can be a member of more than one group.

1. Open the database window by pressing F11.

2. Select Tools ➤ Security ➤ User and Group Accounts.

3. Click the Groups tab and enter the group name in the Name box. Group names are *not* case sensitive, can be up to 20 characters long, and may contain letters, numbers, spaces (although the first character *cannot* be a space), and symbols. A group name may not contain any of the following:

   " * ? / \ [ ] < > | + = , ; :

   Characters between ASCII 00 and 31.

4. Select New. Access displays the New User/Group dialog box.

5. Access creates a group account code based on the name entered in the Name box plus the four-digit number entered in the Personal ID Number box. Enter the group name or skip the field to accept the group name entered in step 3. Select OK.

Be sure to note the Personal ID Number (PIN). If you want to give users access to another computer system that runs Access, you must create the same group name, including the PIN, on the other computer system.

To Delete a User Group

To remove a user group from the Access security system:

1. Select Tools ➤ Security ➤ User and Group Accounts.

2. Click the Groups tab and enter the group name you want to delete in the Name box or select the group name from the pull-down list.

3. Select Delete.

To Add a User to a Group

To add an existing username to a user group:

1. Open the database window by pressing F11.

2. Select Tools ➤ Security ➤ User and Group Accounts from the main menu to open the Users dialog box.

3. Enter the username in the Name box, or select a name from the pull-down menu.

4. Select the group you want to add the user to from the Available Groups list.

5. Select Add.

To Remove a User From a Group

To remove a username from a user group:

1. Open the database window by pressing F11.

2. Select Tools ➤ Security ➤ Users from the main menu to display the Users dialog box.

3. Enter the username in the Name box, or select a name from the pull-down menu.

4. Select the group from which the user is to be removed from the Member Of list.

5. Select Remove.

V

Validating Data

Validation rules allow you to specify when data entered in Access is acceptable. Validation rules put limits on a field or form, such as insisting that a control contain data, be greater than a minimum value, or that two or more fields contain data that is not mutually exclusive.

A validation rule is an expression that tests the data in a control or form. Validation text appears in a window during data entry if the value entered in the field or form does not satisfy the validation rule. For example, if the Validation text is set to *Date entered is not valid* for a date field, the message will pop up in a window if an entry in the date field does not pass the validation rule—if the expression in the validation rule property does not evaluate to true.

Access automatically prevents duplicate entries if the field bound to a control is the primary key. You set the primary key by setting the field's Indexed property to Yes (No Duplicates) in a table's design view.

Validation rules established for a field in Table design view are applied throughout the database, even if different validation rules are defined for the field in other places (such as on a datasheet or in a form).

To Add a Validation Rule to a Field

To specify a validation rule and the validation text for a field, no matter where it is used within the database:

1. Open the table in design view.

2. Select the field.

3. Press F6 to move to the Field Properties section.

4. Enter the expression you want evaluated in the cell to the right of the Validation Rule text box.

5. Click the Builder Button (which contains three dots) to the right of the text box to use the Expression Builder.

6. Select the Validation Text text box when you have completed and closed the Validation Rule Builder, and enter the text you want to display automatically if invalid data is entered.

To Add a Validation Rule to a Control

To add a validation rule and validation text to a control:

1. Open the form in design view.

2. Select the control.

3. Open the Property window by clicking the Properties button or by selecting View ➤ Properties from the main menu.

4. Enter the expression you want to evaluate in the cell to the right of Validation Rule. Click the Builder Button (which contains three dots) to the right of the text box to use the Expression Builder.

5. Complete and close the Validation Rule Builder.

6. Enter the text you want displayed automatically by Access, if the data entered in the control does not meet the validation criteria, in the cell to the right of Validation Text.

Sample Validation Rules

The following examples illustrate the kind of expressions you can enter in the Validation Rule property of a control.

= "Seattle"   Value entered must equal Seattle.

Not = "WA"   Value entered must not equal WA.

Is Not Null   A value must be entered in the field.

In ("WA", "OR", "CA")   Value must be WA, OR, or CA.

Not In ("WA", "OR", "CA")   Value cannot be WA, OR, or CA.

Between 1 And 10   Value must be greater than or equal to 1 and less than or equal to 10 (that is, 1, 2, 3, 4, 5, 6, 7, 8, 9, or 10).

Between #7/1/99# And #7/31/99#   Date entered must be between July 1, 1999, and July 31, 1999, inclusive.

>=Date()   Date entered must be on or after the system's current date.

Like "W*"   First letter of value must be a W.

To Validate Forms or Controls with a Macro

To use a macro to validate a form:

1. Open the form in design view.

2. Open the Property window by clicking the Properties button or selecting View ➤ Properties from the main menu.

3. Click the Event tab.

4. Move to the event in the Property window that you want to assign the macro to. Some of the valid events are as follows:

   On Current   This event is executed before displaying another record.

   BeforeUpdate   This event is executed before saving a new record or control, or before saving changed data in a record or control.

   On Delete   This event is executed before deleting the current record.

   On Close   This event is executed before closing the form.

   On Insert   This event is executed before inserting a new record.

5. Enter the macro name in the event's cell. If the macro is part of a macro group, enter the macro group name, a period, then the macro name (e.g., *macrogroup.mymacro*).

W

Wildcards

Wildcards allow you to select records whose fields match a pattern. Wildcards can be used on fields that are of data type Text or Date/Time. The wildcard *?* stands for any one character. * stands for any number of characters.

Wizards

A wizard presents you with a series of questions and then uses your answers to perform a complex task quickly.

You can invoke a wizard in several ways:

- When you create a new table, query, report, data access page, or form, Access presents you with the option of creating the object manually or by use of a wizard.

- When designing forms, data access pages, and reports, press the Control Wizards button in the toolbox (if it's not already depressed) and then click the button for the type of object you want to place (a button, option box, or combo box, for example).

- Select a database or query and then select Merge It from the Office Links button on the toolbar to launch the Mail Merge Wizard for incorporating data from an Access table in a Microsoft Word document.

- Select an object and then click the Builder Button following the Input Mask property for the object to invoke the Input Mask Wizard.

A common technique used in wizards is the selection of elements to include. For example, when creating a new table, the New Table Wizard asks you to select which fields from the sample table you want to include in your new table. When two lists appear side by side, select items using the following techniques:

- To select an item, click the item in the left-hand list and click the right-arrow button to add the item to the right-hand list. You can select multiple items from the left-hand list by either selecting the first item and then pressing and holding the Ctrl key as other items are selected, or selecting the first item from a list and pressing and holding the Shift key as you click the last item in the list.

- To remove an item from a list, select the item from the right-hand list and click the left-arrow button. The item is moved to the left-hand list. You can select multiple items to be moved between lists.

- To move all items from one list to another, press the double right or left arrow button.

Z

Zoom Box

A zoom box provides additional room for you to enter expressions and property values. To open a Zoom box, press Shift+F2. Enter the text in the box and then select OK to enter the value or Cancel to restore the original text.

Zoom Button

The Zoom button on the Printer Preview toolbar switches between full-page view and a close-up view. You cannot set the zoom percentage.

Choose the Zoom control pull-down box to choose between predefined zoom ratios.

GLOSSARY

his glossary contains common terms that you're likely to run into when you work with Access. Here you'll find short definitions, along with references to chapters where you can learn more about the topics.

Also remember that any time you see a word underlined with dots, in any Help screen, clicking on that word will take you to a definition (or to a screen where you can make a more specific selection). See Chapter 1 for more information on using Access's built-in Help.

Action

The basic building block of a macro. An action is a task the macro performs, such as opening a table or sounding a beep. You can assign actions to a macro by dragging and dropping an object from the database window to the macro window's Action column. Or you can click in the Action column and choose an action from the drop-down list (Chapter 21).

Action query

A type of query that takes an action on your data. This category includes Append, Delete, Make Table, and Update queries. Delete and Update queries change existing data; Append and Make Table queries copy existing data. See Chapter 10; see also "Select query."

Append

To add records from one table to the bottom of another table (Chapters 8 and 10).

Application

A program designed to do a specific job. Microsoft Access, Microsoft Word, and Microsoft Excel are all examples of Windows applications. An Access application is a database that's designed to do a specific job, such as manage orders, juggle names and addresses, manage accounts receivable—whatever. You can design switchboards, dialog boxes, and data entry forms to help people who know little about Access use your application (Chapter 3 and Chapters 20–29).

Argument

The part of an action or expression that defines what to operate on. For example, in Sqr(81), Sqr() is a function (square root), and 81 is the argument (the value that Sqr() will operate upon) (Chapters 21 and 26).

Attach

See "Link," which is the new name for the Access 2.*x* Attach feature.

AutoNumber field

A field in a table that automatically numbers each new record entered into a table. AutoNumber fields can be incremental or random (Chapter 6).

Bitmap

A graphic image stored in bitmap (.bmp) format (Chapters 8 and 13).

Bound control

A control on an Access form or report that displays data from the underlying table (Chapter 13).

Bound object frame

A control on an Access form or report that displays an OLE object stored within the underlying table (Chapter 13).

Bound OLE object

An OLE object that's stored in an Access table (Chapters 8 and 13).

Calculated control

A control on a form or report that gets its value by performing some calculation on data in the underlying table (Chapter 13).

Calculated field

A field in a query that computes a value based on data in the table. Access will refresh the value in a calculated field automatically, whenever you change values of fields used in the calculated field. You could, for example, define a query field with the expression [Quantity]*[UnitPrice] to calculate the extended price of an item (Chapter 10).

Case-sensitive

In a case-sensitive search, text must match uppercase and lowercase letters exactly. A non-case-sensitive search, by contrast, matches any combination of uppercase and lowercase text. When you ask Access to find or replace text values in a table, you can search with case-sensitive matching on or off (Chapter 9).

Cell

The intersection of a row and column in a datasheet or grid. Each cell in the datasheet stores a single piece of data (Chapters 6, 8, 9, 10, and 21).

Chart

A graphical representation of data in a form or report. Charts can summarize large amounts of data graphically and make the data easier to understand (Chapter 15).

Check box

A control that shows whether you've selected or cleared an option. A checkmark (✓) appears in the box when you've selected it. Check boxes on forms enable you to assign a Yes or No value to Yes/No fields in a table (Chapter 13). Some Windows dialog boxes also use check boxes to let you turn an option on or off.

Clipboard

A general storage area used by all Windows programs, mainly for copying and moving things from one place to another. For example, selecting an item and then pressing Ctrl+C copies that item to the Clipboard.

Code

Instructions for the computer to follow, expressed in a written language such as Visual Basic. The act of creating programs is sometimes called "writing code" or "coding" (by people who do that sort of thing) (Chapter 26).

Column

The visual presentation of a field in a datasheet, query, or filter window. A relational database stores data in tables that you can display in horizontal rows (records) and vertical columns (fields) (Chapters 2, 8, 9, and 10).

Combo box

A control that works like a combined text box and list box. Combo boxes on forms or datasheets allow you to enter values into fields either by typing in the value or by selecting the value from a drop-down list. Some Windows dialog boxes also use combo boxes to let you choose options (Chapters 6, 9, and 13).

Command bar

Another name for a toolbar, which can include toolbar buttons, menus, and shortcut menus.

Command button

A control that opens a linked form, runs a macro, or calls a Visual Basic function. You simply click a command button on a form to open the linked form or start the macro or function. Command buttons work like the push buttons in many Windows dialog boxes and programs (Chapters 11 and 13).

Comparison operator

An operator that compares two values, such as > (greater than) and < (less than) (Chapters 9 and 10).

Control

An item on a form, data access page, report, or dialog box. Controls typically display data, provide decoration, or let the user make choices. For instance, a command button in a dialog box is a control (Chapter 13).

Control menu

Activated by the tiny icon in the upper-left corner of a window, this standard Windows component lets you close, restore, and otherwise manipulate the window it controls. (For these jobs, however, many people prefer to use the Minimize, Maximize/Restore, and Close controls at the upper-right corner of a window, instead of the Control menu.)

Crosstab

A query that computes summary totals based on values for each row and column. Crosstab queries answer questions such as what are my monthly sales by region, who has ordered each of my products, and how many items of each product did they order? (Chapter 10).

Current Record

The record that currently holds the focus (Chapter 8; see also "Focus").

Data access page

An object that's used to browse data from Access or Internet Explorer 5. Data access pages, also referred to as pages, are stored in their own HTML files instead of in the database (.mdb file) or project (.adp file) they belong to.

Data type

The kind of information that will be stored in a field, such as Text, Number, or Date/Time. You define data types in table design view (Chapter 6).

Database

A collection of all the objects—tables, queries, forms, data access pages, reports, macros, and modules—related to a particular topic or subject (Chapter 2).

Database window

The container window that shows all database objects. This window often appears first when you open a database. Usually, you can display the database window by pressing the F11 key (Chapter 1).

Datasheet view (or datasheet)

The view that lets you see several records in a table or query result at a time, as opposed to form view, which generally shows only one record (Chapter 8).

DBMS

An abbreviation for *database management system*. Popular database management systems include dBASE, Paradox, and of course, Microsoft Access (Chapter 2).

Default

A setting that is assumed, and used, unless you change it. For example, the default margin on a report might be 1 inch.

Delete query

An action query that deletes whatever rows match criteria that you specify. Delete queries provide a fast, automatic way to delete a certain set of records from a table without disturbing other records that don't match the criteria (Chapter 10).

Delimited text file

A text file that contains values separated by commas, tabs, semicolons, or other characters. You can import delimited text files into new or existing Access tables (Chapter 7).

Design view

The view that lets you create an object or change its appearance. Clicking on an object name in the database window and then clicking on the Design button takes you to the design view of that object (Chapters 6, 10, 13, 21, and 26).

Detail section

The part of a form or report that displays records from your table or query. Also called the *detail band* (Chapter 13).

Developer (application developer)

A person who uses Access to create specialized, user-friendly applications for less-sophisticated computer users to work with (Chapters 20–29).

Dialog box

A window that lets you select options or provide more information so that Access can carry out a command. Many dialog boxes include an OK button (that continues the command) and a Cancel button (that cancels the command).

Drop-down list

A control that allows you to choose a value from a list on a data access page.

Duplicate key

A value that already exists in a table's primary key field or in an index field that does not allow duplicates. Access won't allow you to enter duplicate key values into a table (Chapters 6 and 8).

Dynaset

The result of running a query or filter, which shows only the set of records requested (Chapters 9 and 10).

Embed

What you do when you insert an object into a form or report. You can embed objects in these ways:

- Use drag-and-drop techniques (Chapters 4 and 8).
- Use the Insert ➤ Object command (Chapter 8).
- Use Copy and Paste options on the Edit menu (Chapter 8).
- Use Insert ➤ Chart or the Chart Wizard toolbox button to embed a chart in a form or report (Chapter 15).
- Use the PivotTable Wizard to embed a Microsoft Excel PivotTable into a Microsoft Access form (Chapter 15).

Equi-join

See "Inner join."

Event

An action, taken by the user, that Access can recognize. For example, a mouse click is an event (Chapter 20).

Expression

A calculation that results in a single value. An expression can contain any combination of Access operators, object names (identifiers), literal values, and constants. You can use expressions to set properties and action arguments; to set criteria or define calculated fields in queries, forms, and reports; and to set conditions in macros. You also can use expressions in Visual Basic (Chapters 6, 10, 13, 21, and 26).

Field

One column, representing a category of information, in a table. Also refers to a fill-in blank on a form (Chapters 6, 8, and 13).

Field list

A small window or drop-down list that shows all the fields in an underlying table or query. You can display field lists in tables, filters, forms, reports, and queries (Chapters 8, 9, 10, and 13).

Field name

The name that you assign to a field. A field name can have up to 64 characters (including letters, numbers, spaces, and some punctuation characters) and must be unique within the table (Chapter 6).

Field properties

Characteristics of a field in a table, as defined in the table design view (Chapter 6).

Filter

A "mini query" that isolates specific records by filtering out unwanted records (Chapter 9).

Focus

A general term for the insertion point, cursor, highlight, or whatever is indicating where your next action will take place. For example, if you click a person's name and the cursor jumps there, we say that the person's name "has the focus."

Foreign key

When a one-to-many relationship exists between tables, the field that uniquely identifies each record on the "one side" of the relationship is called the *primary key*. The corresponding field in the table on the "many side" of the relationship is called the *foreign key* (Chapter 6).

Form properties

Properties assigned to an entire form, as opposed to a section or control on a form. To change form properties, you open the form in design view, open the property sheet, choose Edit ➤ Select Form, and then choose your properties (Chapter 13).

Form view

A way of viewing data in a table one record at a time, similar to a printed fill-in-the-blank form (Chapters 8, 11, and 13).

Function

A procedure that returns a value. For example, in Sqr(81), Sqr() is the square-root function. (The expression returns 9, or the square root of 81.) For a list of built-in Access functions, search the Help Index for *References, Functions* (Chapter 26).

Group

In a secure network system, you can use groups to identify a collection of user accounts, each with its own group name and personal identification number (PID). Permissions assigned to a group apply to all users in that group (Chapter 19).

In a report, you can sort records and organize them into groups based on field values or ranges of values. You also can display introductory and summary data for each group (Chapter 13).

In a query, you can use groups to categorize data and perform summary calculations (Chapter 10).

HTML

Hypertext Markup Language is used to tag files for publication on the World Wide Web. HTML has codes for referencing graphics and formatting text (Chapter 7).

Hyperlink

Text or a graphic associated with a hyperlink address which, when clicked, jumps to information in the same database, another database, another location on your computer or network, or on the Internet (Chapters 6, 8, and 13).

Hyperlink address

The path to a database object, document, Web page, or other file. A hyperlink address may consist of the name of an object in the open database, a specific address in a file like a spreadsheet, a URL pointing to an Internet or intranet location, or a UNC network path pointing to a file on a local area network.

Hyperlink base

A path name added to the beginning of all relative hyperlink addresses.

I-beam

Another name for *mouse pointer*. The I-beam appears when the mouse pointer is on some text. To position the cursor with your mouse, move the I-beam to where you want the cursor to appear and then click the left mouse button.

Index

A feature that speeds up sorting and searching for data in a table. Access maintains each index in sorted order and keeps it in memory for quick retrieval. Primary key fields and certain other fields are indexed automatically. You can define additional index fields in table design view (Chapter 6).

Inner join

A join that combines records from two tables that have matching values in a common field. Suppose two tables—Customers and Orders—each have a CustomerID field. An inner join of these tables would match customers and the orders they placed. No information would appear about customers who haven't placed orders (Chapter 10).

Insertion point

The blinking vertical bar on the screen that indicates where any characters you type will appear. More generally referred to as the *cursor* or the *focus*.

Join

A query operation that combines some or all records from multiple tables. Access supports three types of joins: *inner join*, *outer join*, and *self-join* (Chapter 10).

Key field

The field in a table that uniquely identifies each record in that table, such as a product code or SKU in a products list (Chapter 6).

Label

A control on a form or report that displays descriptive text, such as a title, caption, or instructions (Chapters 11, 12, and 13).

Link (object)

A connection between a source document and destination document. A link inserts a copy of the object from the source document into the destination document, and the two documents remain connected. Thus, changes to the linked object in the source document are also reflected in the destination document. Links provide a powerful and convenient way to share objects among Windows programs (Chapter 8). You also can link main forms or reports with subforms and subreports so that the data on the subform/subreport is in sync with the corresponding data on the main form/main report (Chapters 11, 12, and 13).

Link (table)

You can link tables from other database programs (Paradox, dBASE, FoxPro, and ODBC), from text files and spreadsheets, or from closed Access databases. The linked tables will appear in your open database window. Depending on the file format, after linking tables, you can add, delete, and change their records, just as if you were using "native" Access tables (Chapter 7).

List box

A control that displays a list of values to choose from. List boxes on forms or datasheets allow you to enter values into fields. Some Windows dialog boxes also use list boxes to allow you to choose options (Chapters 6, 9, and 13).

Lookup field

A field that displays and stores values looked up from a field in another table or another part of a form. You can display a lookup field as a *combo box* or *list box* (Chapters 6 and 13).

Macro

A series of actions that can be executed with a single action (Chapter 21 and Chapters 31-35).

Macro group

A set of macros stored in a macro sheet (Chapter 31).

Make Table query

A query that creates a new table from the results (the dynaset) of a previous query. Make Table queries are a handy way to create copies of tables that you want to edit, print, chart, or cross-tabulate. They're also helpful when you need to export data to a nonrelational program, such as a spreadsheet (Chapter 10).

Many-to-many relationship

A relationship in which many records in one table might refer to many records in another, and vice versa. A classic example is an Orders and Products relationship in which an order can include many products and each product can appear on many orders. Often we set up a third table as a go-between so that we end up with two one-to-many relationships. For instance, if we use an Order Details table as the go-between, Orders would have a one-to-many relationship with Order Details and Order Details would have a one-to-many relationship with Products.

Memo field

A field that can store a large amount of text (Chapter 6).

Modal

Describes a form that keeps the focus until you explicitly close the form. Most dialog boxes are really modal forms (Chapter 23).

Module

An Access object that contains one or more custom procedures, each written in Visual Basic. A global module is one you create. A form or report module is one that Access creates automatically (Chapter 26).

Move handle

A square that appears at the top-left edge of a control when you draw or select it in form design or report design view. You can drag a move handle to move the control (Chapter 13; see also "Sizing handle").

Null

An object that has no value. An empty field (Chapter 8).

Null propagation

The tendency for a blank (as opposed to zero) numeric value to cause any calculations that rely on the calculation to be null (blank) as well.

Object

Any element of a database system. Access recognizes these types of objects:

- Controls and database components, including tables, queries, forms, data access pages, reports, macros, and modules
- Special system objects used in Visual Basic programming
- Linked or embedded objects, such as a chart, drawing, spreadsheet cell, Pivot-Table, and table

ODBC

An acronym for *open database connectivity*, a standard created by Microsoft for allowing a single user to access many different databases (Chapter 7).

Office Assistant

A Help tool opened by clicking the Microsoft Access Help button on the toolbar. With this dialog box, you can type in a few words about whatever you want help with and get a list of related topics to view.

OLE

An acronym for *object linking and embedding* (pronounced "olay"). A technique that allows multiple Windows programs (for example, Access, Excel, and Word) to share objects such as pictures, sounds, or charts (Chapters 8, 13, and 15).

OLE client

A program that can hold an object that was initially created by some other program (the *OLE server*) (Chapter 8).

OLE server

A program that can "serve up" an object to an *OLE client*. For example, Paint can serve up pictures to put in your Access database. Sound Recorder can serve up sounds to put in your database (Chapter 8).

One-to-many relationship

Describes a natural relationship between two types of information where for every single item on one side of the relationship, there may be many items on the other side. For example, any *one* customer might place *many* orders with a particular business (Chapter 6).

One-to-one relationship

Describes a relationship between two tables in which each record in the first table can be associated with exactly one record in the second table (Chapter 6).

Operator

A character (or characters) used to perform an operation or comparison. For example, + is the operator used for addition (Chapters 9 and 10).

Option group

A control on a form that frames a set of check boxes, option buttons, or toggle buttons. You can use option groups to provide a limited set of alternative values to choose from (for example, Cash, Check, or Credit Card). The selected option will store a number in the underlying table field. Therefore, if you select the first button in an option group, Access will store the number 1 in the field; if you select the second button, Access stores 2; and so forth. You can use the stored number to make decisions in a macro or Visual Basic program (Chapter 13).

Page

Page can refer to several different things:

- The portion of the database (.mdb file) in which Access stores record data. Each page may contain more than one record, depending on the size of the records.
- A screen of data in a form or a page in a report (Chapters 11, 12, and 13).
- A shorter way of referring to a data access page (Chapter 14).

Parameter query

A query that asks for specific information before doing its job (Chapter 10).

PivotTable

A special type of Microsoft Excel worksheet that's embedded within an Access form. Like Crosstab queries, PivotTables let you quickly summarize large amounts of data in a tabular format. They're more flexible than Crosstab queries, though, because they let you rearrange rows and columns interactively and filter out unwanted data on the fly (Chapter 15).

Precondition

A condition for an action used to test whether running the action will cause a run-time error (Chapter 32).

Primary key

The field in a table that contains information unique to each record in that table. Your social security number is the primary key on the IRS's database; nobody else has the same social security number as you (Chapter 6).

Project

A collection of Access objects similar to a database (.mdb file) that is used to work with data stored on an SQL Server. Projects are stored in .adp files. They don't include queries, but can include database diagrams, stored procedures, and views (Chapters 1 and 2).

Property

A characteristic of an item. Typical properties include size, color, screen location, whether you can update a control, and whether a control is visible (Chapters 6, 10, and 13).

Property sheet

A window that lets you define the properties (characteristics) of a database, a database object, or its individual controls. To display the property sheet for objects other than the database, choose View ➤ Properties from any menu in which it's available. To display database properties, choose File ➤ Database Properties (Chapters 5, 6, and 13).

Query

An Access tool that lets you ask questions about your data, such as, "How many customers live in New York?" You use filters (Chapter 9) and/or queries (Chapter 10) to structure such questions.

Query by example (QBE)

The query technique used by Access and many other modern database management systems. With QBE, you create an *example* of the fields to show, calculations to perform, and sort order to use (Chapters 9 and 10).

QBE grid

The part of the query design window in which you enter the field names and other example elements to construct the query (Chapters 9 and 10).

Read-only

A property of a field, record, or database that allows you to view data but not change it.

Record

A collection of related data (fields) that comprise a single item (row) in an Access table (Chapter 2).

Referential integrity

A set of rules that prevents you from inadvertently deleting, adding, or changing data in one table if that change would cause problems in another table (Chapter 6).

Report

A formatted display of Access data that you can print or preview on the screen (Chapters 12 and 13).

Report properties

Properties assigned to an entire report, as opposed to a section or control on a report. To change report properties, you open the report in design view, open the property sheet, choose Edit ➣ Select Report, and then choose your properties (Chapter 13).

Row

The visual presentation of a record in a datasheet, query, or filter window. A relational database stores data in tables, which you can display in horizontal rows (records) and vertical columns (fields) (Chapters 2, 8, 9, and 10).

Row selector

A small box or bar that you can click to select an entire row when you design a table or macro (Chapters 6 and 8).

ScreenTip

A short description that appears beneath a toolbar or toolbox button if you rest the mouse pointer on the button for a couple of seconds without clicking. To turn Screen-Tips on and off, choose View ➣ Toolbars ➣ Customize, click the Options tab, and then either select (check) or deselect (clear) Show ScreenTips on Toolbars (Chapter 16).

Section

Part of a form or report, such as the header, footer, or detail section (Chapter 13).

Select query

A query that asks a question about your data and returns a *dynaset* (result) without changing the data. See Chapter 10; see also "Dynaset" and "Action query."

Self-join

A table that's joined to itself in a query. For example, if a part consists of other parts, you could identify the "parts of a part" using a self-join on a Parts table (Chapter 10).

Sizing handle

A tiny square that appears around a control when you draw or select it in form design or report design view. To resize the control, drag one of its sizing handles vertically, horizontally, or diagonally (depending on which handle you choose) (Chapter 13; see also "Move handle").

Sort

To put data into some meaningful order, such as alphabetical (A–Z) or numeric (smallest to largest) (Chapter 9).

SQL

An acronym for *structured query language*—a standardized language for asking questions about data in a database. In Access you set up questions by designing queries. Access converts your query to an SQL statement before it answers your question (Chapter 10).

Status bar

The bar along the bottom of the screen that displays the current status of things. To hide or display the Access status bar for a specific database, choose Tools ➢ Startup and then either select (check) or deselect (clear) Display Status Bar. To control the default status bar setting for all Access databases, choose Tools ➢ Options ➢ View and then either select or deselect Status Bar (Chapters 1 and 16).

String

A computer buzzword for a chunk of text. For example, "Hello there" is a string (as opposed to 123.45, which is a number).

Subform

A form that's inside another form or report. You can use subforms to combine (or *link*) data from multiple related tables onto a form (Chapters 11 and 13).

Subreport

A report that's inside another report. You can use subreports to combine (or *link*) data from multiple related tables onto a report (Chapters 12 and 13).

Tab control

A control on a form that has multiple tabbed pages, like the ones seen in Access dialog boxes.

Table

The Access object that holds the data you want to manage (Chapters 2 and 6).

Text box

A control in a form or report that lets you view or enter text (Chapter 13).

Title bar

The bar across the top of a window that describes what's in the window.

Toggle

A menu command or setting that can have only one of two possible values: On or Off (or Yes or No).

Toolbar

A bar or box that offers buttons as shortcuts to specific features. To turn the default Access toolbars on or off, choose Tools ➤ Startup and then select (check) or deselect (clear) Allow Built-In Toolbars. You also can turn individual toolbars on and off by right-clicking on any visible toolbar or by choosing View ➤ Toolbars and selecting or deselecting the toolbars you want to show or hide (Chapters 1, 15, and 24).

Toolbox

A toolbar in the form design, page design, and report design windows that lets you place controls on your design. You can hide or display the toolbox in those windows by choosing View ➤ Toolbox (Chapter 13).

Unbound control

A control on a form or report that isn't tied to the underlying table (Chapter 13).

Unbound object frame

The container for an object that's displayed on a form or report, but isn't tied to the underlying table (Chapters 13 and 14).

Update query

An action query that lets you change data in all or selected records in a table (Chapter 10).

UNC

A standard format, also called *Uniform Naming Convention*, for referring to path locations on a local area network file server.

URL

An address called a *Uniform Resource Locator* that refers to an object, document, page, or even a newsgroup on the Internet or on an intranet. It may also refer to an e-mail address.

User

The person who uses an application.

Validation rule

A rule that defines whether data will be accepted into a table or form. You can define validation rules in the table design window's field properties (Chapter 6) or in the form design property sheet (Chapter 13). Forms automatically inherit rules defined in the table design. Validation rules defined in a form are active only when using the form to enter and edit data. Those validation rules are used in addition to any validation rules defined in the table structure.

Value

The contents of a field or control. For example, if you type *Smith* into the Last Name field in a table, "Smith" is the value of Last Name in that particular record. If you say "X=10," then X has a value of 10.

View

View can have two meanings:

- A way of looking at an object. In Access, you often can pick a view from the database window, the View menu, or a toolbar button. When the focus is on an expression, you can zoom in by pressing Shift+F2.
- A selected group of records from an SQL Server.

Visual Basic (VB)

The programming language that comes with Microsoft Access to give knowledgeable programmers more control over the custom applications they develop (Chapters 26–28).

WHERE clause

An SQL statement that isolates specific records in a table. WHERE clauses are created automatically when you design a query. Not to be confused with bear claws or Santa Claus (Chapter 10).

Wizard

A tool that asks you questions and creates an object according to your answers. For example, you can use wizards to create databases, tables, queries, forms, and reports with just a few mouse clicks. Wizards are available throughout Microsoft Access, Microsoft Office, and Windows 95/98 (Chapters 3, 6, and 10–15).

Zoom

An expanded text box that lets you enter expressions or text more conveniently. You can press Shift+F2 to open a zoom box in property sheets and in the grid in various Access windows (Chapter 10).

You can zoom in Print Preview to change the magnification of the report page, ranging from a close-up view to a full-page view (Chapters 9 and 12).

Finally, OLE and picture objects have a Size Mode (or Picture Size Mode) property, called Zoom, that grows or shrinks the object to fit its frame but keeps the proportions the same (Chapters 8 and 13).

INDEX

Note to the Reader: Throughout this index **boldfaced** page numbers indicate primary discussions of a topic. *Italicized* page numbers indicate illustrations.

Symbols

& (ampersands)
  for access keys, 977
  for concatenation, 1246
  in criteria, 333, 379, 381
  in input masks, 1271
  for underlined text, 743–744
* (asterisks)
  in combo box searches, 1042
  in criteria, 333
  for multiplication, 1246
  in QBE grids, **364**
  in record searches, 306
@ (at signs) for messages, 876, 885, 948
` (backquote characters) in names, 689–690, 1151
\ (backslashes)
  in criteria, 333
  for division, 1246
  in input masks, 1271
^ (carets)
  in criteria, 333
  for exponentiation, 1246
: (colons)
  in input masks, 1271
  in time formats, 1256
  in Visual Basic, 871, 882
, (commas)
  in input masks, 1271
  in number formats, 1256
  in running macros, 966
  in text files, 218, *218*, 222, *223*
$ (dollar signs) in number formats, 1256
" (double quotation marks)
  in delimited text files, 218, *218*, 222, *223*
  in editing tables, 266

  in queries, 84, 340
  in record searches, 306
  for running macros, 966
  for strings, 942, 1082
  for zero length fields, 160
... (ellipses) for macro conditions, 983
= (equal signs)
  for calculated controls, 529
  for conditions in macros, 760–761
  in criteria, 331–332, 1247
  in Immediate pane, 1012
  in search expressions, 1039
  in Visual Basic, 866
! (exclamation points)
  in input masks, 1271
  in macro references, 767, 769
  for queries, 395
  in record searches, 306
> (greater than signs)
  in criteria, 331–332, 1247
  in input masks, 1271
< (less than signs)
  in criteria, 331–332, 1247
  in input masks, 1271
- (minus signs)
  in criteria, 333
  in editing tables, 266
  in input masks, 1271
  in record searches, 306
  for subtraction, 1246
<> (not equal to operator), 332
(number signs)
  in hyperlink addresses, 276
  in input masks, 1270
  in number formats, 1256
  in record searches, 306

V

ABOUT THE CD

The CD-ROM for this book contains:

Fulfill 2000   The world's easiest order-entry system. Prints invoices and receipts and keeps track of customers. Illustrates fancy new techniques, such as autofilling City, State, and Area Code from the Zip Code entry!

Check Writer 2000   *Database Creations* provides a complete Check Writer program. Prints checks, manages accounts, and simplifies reconciliation of bank statements.

USPS TrueType Fonts   *TAZ Information Services* provides shareware TrueType fonts that can print POSTNET and PLANET bar codes on labels and envelopes.

Sample Access Databases   The Order Entry database, NorthwindMacros, and some other databases used as examples for this book.

SQL Server 7 Eval Edition   Microsoft SQL Server 7 Evaluation Edition, a program you can experiment with to learn more about SQL Server databases.

...and more!